Tolley's Property Taxation

Tolley's
Property Taxation

2017–18

Members of the LexisNexis Group worldwide

United Kingdom	RELX (UK) Limited trading as LexisNexis, 1–3 Strand, London WC2N 5JR
Australia	Reed International Books Australia Pty Ltd trading as LexisNexis, Chatswood, New South Wales
Austria	LexisNexis Verlag ARD Orac GmbH & Co KG, Vienna
Benelux	LexisNexis Benelux, Amsterdam
Canada	LexisNexis Canada, Markham, Ontario
China	LexisNexis China, Beijing and Shanghai
France	LexisNexis SA, Paris
Germany	LexisNexis GmbH, Dusseldorf
Hong Kong	LexisNexis Hong Kong, Hong Kong
India	LexisNexis India, New Delhi
Italy	Giuffrè Editore, Milan
Japan	LexisNexis Japan, Tokyo
Malaysia	Malayan Law Journal Sdn Bhd, Kuala Lumpur
New Zealand	LexisNexis New Zealand Ltd, Wellington
Singapore	LexisNexis Singapore, Singapore
South Africa	LexisNexis Butterworths, Durban
USA	LexisNexis, Dayton, Ohio

© RELX (UK) Ltd 2017

Published by LexisNexis
This is a Tolley title

ISBN for this volume: 9780754553847

Printed and bound in Great Britain by Hobbs the Printers Ltd, Totton, Hampshire

Visit LexisNexis at www.lexisnexis.co.uk

About this book

This book is now in its eleventh edition and aims to be a comprehensive source of analysis and explanation of UK property taxation comprised within a single volume. With an extensive contributor list of leading property tax specialists it provides reliable coverage of taxes on property, including CGT, SDLT, VAT and IHT, managing to answer virtually all property tax problems.

Detailed chapters cover everything from REITs and other fund vehicles, to capital allowances and rental investments. This edition has been updated to reflect developments in all property taxes since the 2016–17 edition was published and includes covers all legislation, HMRC's published guidance and other relevant sources of information including the provisions of Finance Act 2017 and the September 2017 Finance Bill and commentary on recent case decisions.

Note that, at the time of writing, the Finance (No 2) Act 2017 had not completed its passage through Parliament. The provisions included in the Act and described in this edition are therefore subject to any changes made during the Parliamentary process.

We would like to thank all the contributors for updating their own chapters again for this edition.

List of Contributors

Contributors

Peter Beckett

Peter is a partner in KPMG's real estate tax advisory practice and has worked exclusively with real estate businesses for over 15 years. He has significant experience in real estate funds having advised on the set-up and implementation of several UK, pan-European and global funds. He has provided tax structuring advice for a large number of property joint ventures and has also advised on the flotation of several AIM-listed and FTSE-listed real estate vehicles. He has significant experience working with UK-REITs.

Irfan Butt, B.Com, FCA, CTA

Irfan Butt is a Tax Director in the London Real Estate team at PricewaterhouseCoopers LLP. He has represented the firm on the HM Treasury & HM Revenue & Customs Islamic Finance Working Group for the alternative finance arrangements legislation and more recently on the changes to the alternative finance investment bonds legislation. Irfan advises both Shariah compliant and conventional real estate investors and fund managers on structuring aspects of UK and pan-European real estate transactions and products.

Patrick Cannon, LLB BCL CTA (Fellow) Barrister

Patrick Cannon qualified originally as a solicitor, but was called to the Bar in 2003 and practices in Tax Chambers, 15 Old Square, Lincoln's Inn. He is also author of *Tolley's Stamp Taxes*, *Stamp Duty Tax Cases* and *Tolley's Disclosure of Tax and VAT Avoidance schemes* and various other publications which can be viewed online free at www.patrickcannon.net.

Satwaki Chanda

Satwaki Chanda is a tax lawyer with a First Class degree in Mathematics. His experience covers a variety of matters, including corporate transactional work, advising entrepreneurs and SMEs, investment funds and real estate planning.

Called to the Bar in 1992, he originally specialised in commercial litigation, but switched to tax in 1998 when he joined a Big Four accountancy practice. He has also worked for City law firms, but is now a freelance author, writing for the educational website: Tax Notes (taxnotes.co.uk), which contains articles on UK taxation, with a particular emphasis on business and property taxes.

Satwaki is currently the editor of *Sumption: Capital Gains Tax*.

Robin Dabydeen

Robin advises on direct and indirect tax issues on a broad range of business matters, principally relating to corporate transactions (with a focus on private equity backed deals and on corporate restructures, together with a proficiency in personal taxation planning relating to investors and management) and on real estate matters. Robin also has considerable experience in advising on the formation and running of investment fund structures (UK and offshore) and fund management arrangements. In addition, Robin has developed an expertise in the design and implementation of tax-efficient real estate structures.

Chris Erwood, CTA ATT TEP

As a longstanding member of the Institute of Taxation (CIOT) and Society of Trusts and Estates (STEP) Chris is a highly qualified tax practitioner with 30+ years practical experience gained from a balanced background with HMRC, Big 4 accountancy and FTSE 100 Industry. In addition to running her own company tax practice, Chris operating in her specialist field of IHT, Estate and trust taxation for the HNWI, acts as a consultant to Davies Mayers Barnett and to the professional helpline provider, TaxAction Ltd. She has written a number of books on her specialist subject, is a popular circuit lecturer to the professional/client audience, a regular contributor to technical journals and expert consultant to the South West professional forum. Chris is a member of: STEP editorial Board, STEP Education committee, STEP Diploma tutorial/ examination panel, joint author of STEP Diploma Taxation manual, STEP West of England Branch committee and is a Quality Assurance Manager on the CIOT exam programme.

Simon Hart

Simon Hart is a Senior Manager at KPMG. He works within KPMG's Investment Management tax practice advising both funds and investment managers on a wide range of tax matters. His clients include traditional and alternative asset managers, as well as sovereign wealth and pension funds. Before joining KPMG he graduated in Government and Economics at the London School of Economics. He is member of the ICAEW.

Louise Hemmingsley

Louise Hemmingsley has been practising VAT for the last 22 years and currently works for LexisNexis as a VAT writer. Louise has worked for the top 4 firms of accountants and in industry for companies such as Siemens and Nortel Networks as their in-house VAT manager.

Geraint Jones

Geraint Jones is a tax partner and Head of Private Clients in the London office of chartered accountants BKL. He has extensive experience advising on property matters, with specialisms in the taxation of non-residents, non-domiciled persons and overseas investors. He has lectured widely and has been extensively quoted in the press. Geraint has been on the Citywealth Leaders

List since 2009 and is also a member of the Society of Trust and Estate Practitioners (STEP).

Richard Jones

Richard Jones is a manager in KPMG's North property tax team, based in their Manchester office. He advises a wide range of clients in the property sector, including investors, developers, house buildings and retail occupiers.

Rachel Kelly

Rachel Kelly is a Senior Policy Officer at the British Property Federation. Her role involves developing industry responses on finance, tax and regulatory issues which impact the real estate sector. Rachel previously worked for PwC in the Investment Management tax team, and has a degree in Economics and Geography from the University of Exeter.

Zigurds G Kronbergs, BSc ARCS MA ACA FCCA

Zigurds G Kronbergs is a tax author of over 30 years' standing. He is a member of both the Institute of Chartered Accountants in England and Wales and the Association of Chartered Certified Accountants and is a dual Latvian-British citizen. Zigurds specialises in UK, Latvian and European tax. He is the European Tax Coordinator for Moore Stephens Europe and, under the name 'Writing Matters', offers writing, editing and translation services. He is the Latvia author for the International Bureau of Fiscal Documentation's Guide to European Taxation, and also contributes significantly to the UK material. He is based in Suffolk and can be contacted on 01284 811752 or 0747 867 6106 and at zigurds@zigurdskronbergs.co.uk.

Melissa Malins

Melissa Malins is a UK tax manager at Diageo Plc. She is involved in compliance, project work and business partnering. Previously Melissa was a Tax Manager in the property team at BDO where she specialised in capital allowances. She has presented on the subject at ACCA conferences and various seminars.

Rory Mullan, MA (Cantab) Barrister

Rory Mullan is a barrister and Chartered Tax Advisor. He was called to the Bar in 2000 and practises from Tax Chambers, 15 Old Square, Lincoln's Inn where he advises individuals, trusts and companies on a wide range of taxation matters. He also represents taxpayers in disputes before the Tax Tribunals and Courts. He has written extensively on tax related matters and is author of *The Interaction of EU Treaty Freedoms and the UK Tax Code*.

Julian Palmer

Julian Palmer is an associate director of CLT International (CLTI), a division of Wilmington plc. He sits on the Law Society's Tax Technical Sub-Committees for Income Tax, Capital Taxes and HMRC powers. He regularly lectures for CLTI and is author of the Foundation STEP manual and teaching materials, a contributor to Atkin's Court Forms and Consultant Editor to Halsbury's Laws of England.

Dominic Rayner, BSc (Hons) Mathematics, ATT, CTA

Dominic Rayner is a Senior Tax Manager at KPMG LLP. He advises on the tax aspects of property joint ventures and complex property transactions, especially those involving leases. He is also a specialist adviser on the taxation of PFI projects.

Matthew Roach

Matthew Roach is a Tax Director at KPMG LLP who specialises in advising international investment management and property companies. He advises on all aspects of tax for property investors, occupiers and managers. He specialises in real estate and investment management fund structures, listings of property companies, M & A transactions and restructurings. His client base includes a number of traditional and alternative investment managers and real estate funds throughout the UK and Europe, and has also worked extensively on international funds that have invested in the Asia Pacific region, the Americas and emerging markets.

Kathryn Sewell

Kathryn Sewell is a specialist in Deloitte's Energy and Resources indirect tax group and has been with Deloitte for over nine years advising on VAT and environmental taxes. This includes advising on climate change levy, aggregates levy and landfill tax both in respect of new infrastructure projects and day-to-day transactions.

Helen Thompson, ACA

Helen Thompson is a Partner in Deloitte's indirect tax practice, specialising in environmental taxes and VAT, and leads Deloitte's Environmental Taxes group. She also chaired the Chartered Institute of Taxation's Environmental Taxes Working Group from 2007–2010. Helen has extensive experience in advising businesses on their environmental tax obligations and liabilities and has provided specialist environmental due diligence services in relation to major acquisitions.

Simon Tivey, FIRRV

Simon leads the rating consultancy 'Simon Tivey Rating' and was previously the Head of Rating at PwC for 25 years. He advises large corporate clients and high net worth individuals on their liability to local government property taxes. Prior to that Simon held senior revenues positions in Local Government. Simon has appeared in many leading Lands Tribunal and Valuation Tribunal cases which have provided more clarity on whether empty rates are due on speculative property developments and on end of life buildings.

Adrian Wills

Adrian Wills is a senior manager in KPMG's North property tax team, based in their Manchester office. He has significant experience of advising businesses both in the private and public sector regarding their property tax issues.

Abbreviations and References

Abbreviations

ABA	Agricultural Building Allowance
ATED	Annual Tax on Enveloped Dwellings
BATR	Business Asset Taper Relief
BPR	Business Property Relief
CAA	Capital Allowances Act 2001
CGT	Capital Gains Tax
CT	Corporation Tax
CTM	Corporation Tax Manual (published by HMRC)
CTSA	Corporation Tax Self Assessment
EC	European Community
ECJ	European Court of Justice
EIS	Enterprise Investment Scheme
ESC	Extra-Statutory Concession
FA	Finance Act
FRS	Financial Reporting Standard
FSMA	Financial Services Management Act 2000
GAAP	Generally Accepted Accounting Principles
GAAR	General Anti-Abuse Regulations
HMRC	Her Majesty's Revenue and Customs
IAS	International Accounting Standards
IBA	Industrial Building Allowance
ICAEW	Institute of Chartered Accountants in England and Wales
ICTA	Income and Corporation Taxes Act 1988
IHT	Inheritance Tax
IHTA	Inheritance Tax Act 1984

IPDI	Immediate Post Death Interest
ITA	Income Tax Act 2007
ITEPA	Income Tax (Earnings and Pensions) Act 2003
ITTOIA	Income Tax (Trading and Other Income) Act 2005
LGFA	Local Government Finance Act
LLP	Limited Liability Partnership
NIC	National Insurance Contribution
OECD	Organisation for Economic Co-operation and Development
PAYE	Pay As You Earn
QCB	Qualifying Corporate Bond
REIT	Real Estate Investment Trust
s	Section
Sch	Schedule
SD	Stamp Duty
SDLT	Stamp Duty Land Tax
SI	Statutory Instrument
SIPP	Self-Invested Personal Pension
SP	Statement of Practice
SSAP	Statement of Standard Accounting Practice
SSAS	Small Self Administered Scheme
TCGA	Taxation of Chargeable Gains Act 1992
TIOPA	Taxation (International and Other Provisions) Act 2010
TOGC	Transfer of a Going Concern
UITF	Urgent Issues Task Force
VAT	Value Added Tax
VATA	Value Added Tax Act 1994
VCT	Venture Capital Trust

References (*denotes current series)

AC	*Law Reports, Appeal Cases, (Incorporated Council of Law Reporting for England and Wales, 3 Stone Buildings, Lincoln's Inn, London WC2A 3XN)
All ER	*All England Law Reports, LexisNexis Butterworths, 35 Chancery Lane, London WC2A 1EL)
App Cas	Law Reports, Appeal Cases
ATC	Annotated Tax Cases, (Gee & Co (Publishers) Ltd, 7 Swallow Place, London W1R 8AB)
BTC	*British Tax Cases
CB	Common Bench Reports
Ch	*Law Reports, Chancery Division
Ch App	Law Reports, Chancery Appeals
KB	Law Reports, King's Bench Division
LR	Law Reports (followed by Court abbreviation)
SC	*Court of Session Cases (Scotland)
Sc LR	Scottish Law Reporter
SLT	Scots Law Times Reports
Sp C	Special Commissioners
STC	*Simon's Tax Cases, (LexisNexis Butterworths, as above)
TC	*Official Tax Cases, (The Stationery Office, 123 Kingsway, London WC2B 6PQ)

Contents

Contents

Chapter 8   Development, redevelopment, refurbishment and maintenance

Richard Jones and Adrian Wills, KPMG LLP

Chapter 9   Capital expenditure—allowances

Melissa Malins, Tax Manager

Contents

Contents

**Chapter 23   From farmland to shops: a case study in the tax issues
facing the parties involved in a property development**

Dominic Rayner, KPMG LLP

Chapter 24   Scottish land and buildings transaction tax

Patrick Cannon, Barrister

Chapter 1

Introduction

[1.1] The taxation of UK property in all its forms is possibly the most varied and challenging area of the UK tax system and it is now impossible for any one adviser to know all the rules and regulations relating to the taxation of property. The subject-matter encompasses a wide variety of taxes from VAT to capital allowances which bear little, if anything, in common other than that they apply to a greater or lesser degree to interests and dealings in UK land. One also has to contend with a wide range of different taxpayers who are involved in UK property from individuals to funds and this presents its own challenges.

Constant change is inherent in the subject matter and keeping up to speed across the range of applicable taxes is truly a challenge. In no particular order this edition includes discussion and analysis of the following developments:

*   2017 has seen a major change in rateable value appeals with the introduction of the controversial Check Challenge Appeal (CCA) system, which it is said will slow down access to appeals (**CHAPTER 19**);
*   details of the new £1000 allowance for property income (**CHAPTER 6**);
*   the proposed substantial shareholding exemption ('SSE') changes and the new rules on the appropriation of trading stock (**CHAPTER 2**);
*   VAT developments including details of the revised legislation regarding the disclosure of indirect tax avoidance schemes coming into effect from 1 January 2018 and UK cases including *Taylor Wimpey* and *J3 Building Solutions Ltd* (**CHAPTER 15**);
*   the introduction of corporate interest restriction rules for UK-REITs (**CHAPTER 3**); and
*   updates on loss carry-forward restrictions and the interest cap (**CHAPTER 10**).

The reader, whether a busy tax practitioner or a professional student, will find a wealth of detailed information in the following chapters. Few if any will have the time to read whole chapters let alone read from cover to cover and most, if not all, will dip into it for answers or confirmation of a pre-existing notion of what the position is in relation to a particular issue. That is no matter for however this book is used by the reader it will be the main or one of the main works regularly consulted by those advising on property taxation.

Chapter 2

Investment versus trading

by
Rachel Kelly,
British Property Federation

with assistance from Kirsten Prichard Jones and Penny Van den Brande,
Macfarlanes LLP

Introduction

[2.1] This chapter deals mainly with transactions in property assets which are directly held by the taxpayer, rather than indirect investment in property via the range of vehicles that are available and discussed elsewhere in this book – see **CHAPTERS 3 AND 4** on REITs and other funds and similar structures. The determination of a property transaction as either investment or trading is fundamental to the taxpayer as it will affect its tax treatment and hence the tax liability arising. The status of a property asset can therefore be of significant interest to the owner of a property who is considering selling it, as well as for example, to the purchaser of shares in a company that owns a property asset (where the purchaser will want to assess potential future tax liabilities within the company). Broadly, we can view property owners as:

- normal trading businesses, who occupy their own premises for the purposes of their own particular trade;
- property investors, who primarily own (but may also develop) their property in order to generate rental income; or
- property traders who acquire or build property to make a profit from reselling it.

Following a review of the UK tax system in 2014, the Office for Tax Simplification (OTS) reported its view that the distinction between trading and investment is often far from obvious and outdated. It recommended the distinction be removed and replaced with an 'overall business approach'. In its response, the Government stated it would consider this recommendation but has not yet taken further action. In November 2016, the OTS issued a progress report and call for evidence in which it again asked for views on whether the distinction between trading and investment companies is still relevant. The OTS is currently analysing feedback received and, in its Annual Report dated 26 June 2017, the OTS confirmed they were due to report on this in Summer 2017.

Owner-occupier traders

[2.2] Persons who occupy their own property for the purposes of carrying on a trading activity, such as a clothing manufacturer or supermarket chain, are generally referred to in property circles as 'owner-occupiers'. Generally, where proceeds arise from the sale of such properties, they are treated as investment profits rather than trading profits. There are tax rules which relate specifically to owner-occupiers and these are considered in CHAPTER 14.

Property development

[2.3] Persons who are involved in property development (ie acquiring land and property and developing it) may act, in doing so, either as property investors or as property dealers. There is a wide spectrum of activities that can fall within the description of property development, ranging from the acquisition of property that requires some degree of refurbishment in order to become income producing to the acquisition of land for the purposes of constructing a new building. Unfortunately, the fact that property development is, on its own, not a reliable indicator that an activity is trading or investment is sometimes overlooked, including by HMRC.

Investment or trading activity?

[2.4] In the context of the property industry where individual asset values can be very substantial, the question of whether a taxpayer is undertaking an investment or trading activity with respect to an asset is obviously an important one. It is possible, though relatively unusual, for a taxpayer to be both a property investor and a property dealer – but it is only possible to be one or the other with respect to any particular property transaction. Although conceptually the distinction between a trading activity and investment is relatively easy to grasp, applying the legal definitions gives rise to difficulties in practice. The tax legislation defines 'trade' rather unhelpfully by stating that '"trade" includes any venture in the nature of trade' (ITA 2007, s 989). It is ultimately the courts that have had to apply definitions such as this in the context of specific factual scenarios, determining, in the process, where the often blurred line between trading and investment activity lies. Many of the cases have been in the area of land and property.

Why is the distinction important?

[2.5] There are significant differences between the tax treatment of the proceeds of sale of the stock of a trade and the proceeds of sale of an investment asset (particularly for individual traders/investors). Differences, which have varied from time to time over the years, include the availability for offset of losses, the availability of tax deductions, tax exemptions and the rates of tax applicable.

Some key differences for certain types of investor deriving money directly from property are illustrated in the table below. The treatment of other kinds of taxpayers is beyond the scope of this chapter, but the distinction between investment and trading remains important.

Taxpayer status	Investment	Trading
UK Individuals	Disposal proceeds are taxed under the capital gains tax rules at a rate of, currently, 10% or 20% (unless this is a disposal of residential property in which case disposal proceeds are taxed under capital gains tax rules at a rate of, currently, 18% or 28%). An annual exemption and various reliefs, including an 'entrepreneurs' relief' (offering a reduced rate for lifetime gains of, for disposals on or after 6 April 2011, up to £10m) are also available (see **CHAPTER 14**).	All profits (both sale proceeds and rental receipts) are chargeable to income tax at the taxpayer's marginal rate.
	Rental income is subject to income tax at the taxpayer's marginal rate, potentially as high as 45% for the tax year 2016/17.	
Overseas Individuals	UK domestic law does not impose UK capital gains tax on the capital appreciation of non-residential UK property arising to a person neither tax resident nor ordinarily resident in the UK. Since 6 April 2015, overseas individuals disposing of UK residential property are subject to capital gains tax (on the capital appreciation after 6 April 2015) at 18% or 28% – see **CHAPTER 14**.	An overseas individual will generally be treated as carrying on a trade in the UK through a branch or agency, so all profits (both sale proceeds and rental receipts) are subject to UK tax as above. An overseas individual deriving profits from trading in and developing UK land on or after 5 July 2016 will be subject to UK income tax on those profits, irrespective of whether the individual is trading through a UK permanent establishment. See **2.21** below and **CHAPTER 13**.
	Rental income is subject to tax at the basic or higher rate, deduction at source may apply under the non-resident landlords scheme (ITA 2007, s 971(1), (2) – see **CHAPTER 5**).	

Taxpayer status	Investment	Trading
UK Corporates	While all profits are chargeable to corporation tax at the applicable rate (which does not differentiate between investment and trading profits), there are still significant differences as regards relief for different kinds of expenditure, the use of losses and the scope for deferring tax charges. The availability of the substantial shareholding exemption ('**SSE**') (TCGA 1992, Sch 7AC) for certain share sales can in some circumstances favour a trading analysis (see below regarding proposed changes) and the operation of the offshore funds tax rules is in certain cases more favourable to funds investing in unlisted companies (Offshore Funds (Tax) Regulations 2009, reg 31A (SI 2009/3001)).	
Overseas Corporates	UK domestic law does not generally impose UK capital gains tax on the capital appreciation of UK property for corporates that are not tax resident in the UK. However, since 6 April 2015, closely held overseas companies disposing of residential property are subject to capital gains tax (on the gains after 6 April 2015) at 20% – see **CHAPTER 14**.	Prior to July 2016, an overseas corporate would generally be treated as carrying on a trade in the UK through a permanent establishment, so all profits (both sale proceeds and rental receipts) were subject to UK tax as above (although the company may have received credit under an applicable double tax treaty against UK tax on those profits for foreign tax paid). An overseas corporate deriving profits from trading in and developing UK land on or after 5 July 2016 will be subject to UK corporation tax on those profits, irrespective of whether the corporate has a UK permanent establishment. Various double tax treaties were amended in 2016 so that overseas corporates are no longer able to claim the benefit of treaty relief if there is no permanent establishment (as more narrowly defined in the relevant double tax treaties) in the UK (this applies to Jersey, Guernsey and the Isle of Man). See **2.21** below and **CHAPTER 13**.

Taxpayer status	Investment	Trading
	Net rental income is subject to tax at the basic rate (currently 20%). This is deducted at source under the non-resident landlords scheme, unless HMRC approve the non-resident landlord to receive income gross and pay tax through self-assessment.	

Proposed SSE changes

[2.6] The Government announced changes at the Autumn Statement 2016 which are intended to relax certain of the SSE conditions. Provided that the draft legislation is passed unchanged in the next Finance Act, the key changes will:

(1)   remove the requirement that the investing company (ie the seller) is trading or is a member of a trading group;

(2)   relax the requirement for the company being sold to be trading after the disposal (unless the disposal is to a connected party);

(3)   introduce a new relief for 'qualifying institutional investors' ('QI'). Assuming this relief is available, the disposing company should be able to benefit from the SSE where neither it, nor the company being disposed of, satisfies the trading test. This will bring the sale of certain property investment companies within the scope of the SSE. On the disposal of shares in a property investment company the whole gain will be exempt provided that at least 80% of shares are held by QIIs. Where between 25% and 80% of the shares are held by QIIs, a proportion of the gain will be exempt, reflecting the proportion held by QIIs. 'QIIs' for these purposes are registered pension schemes, companies carrying on life assurance business, sovereign wealth funds, charities, investment trusts and certain widely marketed investment schemes; and

(4)   relax the requirement for the seller to hold a 10% stake in the company being sold, where at least 25% of the company is held by QIIs, and the seller is both a QII and has paid at least £20 million for their shares.

Trading income

[2.7] Trading income encompasses both income from a trade and income from a profession or vocation (income tax is charged on 'the profits of a trade, profession or vocation' – ITTOIA 2005, s 5). There are many cases in which the boundaries of what constitutes a trade have been explored. An important framework was established by the 1955 Royal Commission on the Taxation of Profits and Income, which identified (in paragraph 116 of its Final Report; 1955 HMSO Cmd. 9474) six 'badges of trade' which have since guided the courts:

(1) the subject matter of the transaction;
(2) the length of period of ownership;
(3) the frequency or number of similar transactions;
(4) supplementary work on assets sold;
(5) reasons for the sale; and
(6) motive when acquiring assets.

Detailed guidance on the badges of trade and their application to transactions in land is provided in HMRC's published internal guidance (see paragraphs 20000 and 60000 of the Business Income Manual, at www.hmrc.gov .uk/manuals/bimmanual/Index.htm). It is worth bearing in mind that HMRC's guidance proposes a slightly different set of criteria to the ones above, although these cover broadly similar considerations.

There are a range of different types of activity that a typical property company, owner-occupier or individual may undertake and a range of differing facts and circumstances that can make the determination of the tax treatment of such transactions very difficult. This can be illustrated by considering the hypothetical scenario below.

Example

(1) Company A buys a plot of land and after two years, obtains planning permission to build an office block. After the office block is completed Company A then sells the property for an overall profit to Company B.
On the face of it, Company A's activity has the characteristics of a trading activity because the objective facts and circumstances suggest an intention on the part of Company A to acquire the land, modify it and then sell it for a profit (in the same way that a manufacturer might acquire raw materials, apply a manufacturing process to them and then sell the end product for a profit). At this stage, we cannot determine the nature of Company B's activity.

(2) Company B buys the office block from Company A and rents it out to Company C, which occupies it for the purposes of its own trade.
Company B's activities seem to display the characteristics of an investment activity, in that they display an apparent intention to acquire the property for the primary purpose of earning rental income (in the same way that someone may acquire shares or income producing bonds to earn an income return from the assets).

(3) After 3 years, Company C buys the property from its landlord (Company B), and undertakes significant refurbishment of the property. Shortly afterwards, Company C is taken over by Company D, which decides to relocate Company C's offices elsewhere; Company C sells the property for a significant profit.
Company C's activities display mixed characteristics. When it acquired the property that it had been occupying as a tenant of Company B, it looked as though it was doing so for the purpose of gaining control of an asset which was important for the long term benefit of its business (to carry out its trading activities). It is likely that the asset would then be held on the balance sheet of Company C as a fixed capital asset, which would suggest that a subsequent disposal would be likely to be treated as a disposal of an investment. However, the fact that the property was subject to significant refurbishment and sold shortly afterwards for a profit displays trading characteristics.

Some of the analysis above might seem quite straightforward, but suppose we were informed of the following additional facts.

Company A is a property investment company that usually develops property and holds it for 20 years. The land on which it built this particular property happened to form an essential part of a proposed new head office development for Big Plc, with the result that Company A's plans changed when it received an offer from Company B which was too good to refuse.

Company B is a developer and trader that won the contract to build the Big Plc head office development on a large plot of land (a small but essential part of which it acquired from Company A). Government intervention over planning permission then put the plans for Big Plc on hold, so Company B's plans changed and it decided to rent out the property acquired from Company A to a self-storage company (Company C) for a period of time. After significant delays, Big Plc abandoned its plans for the new head office and Company C then decided to take advantage of favourable market conditions and buy the property for its own headquarters from Company B. Shortly after, Company D acquired Company C and relocated Company C's head office elsewhere. In the meantime, the planning issues were resolved and the property was able to be sold for a large profit.

The above example helps to illustrate how the facts and circumstances surrounding the acquisition and subsequent events can affect the analysis of a transaction as having the characteristics of trading or investment. It is therefore difficult to make any generalisations or to take 'short cuts' in determining whether a particular transaction is trading or investment in nature; each situation must be judged on its own merits.

HMRC's Business Income Manual acknowledges that the question of whether a trade exists is primarily a question of fact and states that:

'The overall conclusion from case law is that:

- trade cannot be precisely defined, but
- certain characteristics can be identified which are normally those of trade, and
- other characteristics can be found which preclude a profit from being that of a trade.' (BIM2005)

The taxpayer's motive and intention will be relevant but are not necessarily a subjective matter: in most cases, motive and intention are likely to be inferred, on an objective basis, from the surrounding facts and circumstances (including the actual behaviour of the taxpayer). Only where an unequivocal conclusion cannot be reached in that way, because the facts are ambiguous, is an investigation into the subjective purpose of the taxpayer likely to be needed (see, in that connection, *Iswera v Inland Revenue Commissioners (Ceylon)* [1965] 1 WLR 663 and *Clavis Liberty Fund 1 LP v Revenue and Customs Commissioners* [2016] UKFTT 253 (TC)).

The motive for acquisition of the property/evidence for motive

[2.8] As outlined above, the main factor in determining the tax treatment of a property transaction is the taxpayer's underlying motive for acquiring the property (assessed so far as possible by reference to objective factors). In *Simmons v IRC* (1980) 53 TC 461, Lord Wilberforce said at p 491:

'Trading requires an intention to trade: normally the question to be asked is whether this intention existed at the time of the acquisition of the asset.'

That is not always clear and in practice the ability to agree a particular tax treatment depends on the ability of the taxpayer to evidence the motive for the acquisition. Whilst larger property companies tend to be better at evidencing intentions at the time of acquisition through board minutes, business plans, etc, it is rarely done in practice by individual taxpayers and family companies who do not hold regular board meetings. In reality, because of the generally preferential tax treatment afforded (under current law – the position has changed from time to time) to investment disposals – particularly by UK individuals who can benefit from the 10% or 20% capital gains tax rate (18% or 28% in the case of residential property) and an annual exemption – it is rare that HMRC would overturn a transaction presented as a trading transaction. The requirement to provide evidence therefore normally focuses on the evidence to support an investment intention. Examples of types of evidence to support an investment intention include:

- board minutes declaring the intention to seek out investments;
- business plans and financial models evidencing that the decision to acquire was made (and any loan finance was sought) on the basis of rental yields and long-term cash flow analysis;
- the company's objects clause – as evidence of a company's investment objective; and
- advertising for tenants.

If the company's objects clause makes it clear that the company is an investment company with no power to trade, the onus will effectively be on HMRC to demonstrate that the transaction was in fact a trading transaction carried out in breach of the directors' powers. In the absence of evidence to substantiate the motive for an acquisition, HMRC will look at the other badges of trade. In *Tempest Estates Ltd v Walmsley* (1976) 51 TC 305, land was acquired in 1946 by a company whose prime purpose of incorporation was to avoid estate duty. The company's objects (although giving the company authorisation to deal in land) did not indicate a specific trading or investment motive for the acquisition of the land. The bulk of the land was held for a period of 17 years and produced rental income during that time. Nevertheless, when the land was sold the court ruled the transaction to have been an adventure in the nature of a trade. In reaching that decision, the court noted that the company was authorised to deal in land and that the company's directors must at all times have been well aware that the land was likely to increase in value. The court had no hesitation in referring to letters written in 1959 in order to draw inferences as to the directors' intentions in 1946.

In *Rand v Alberni Land Co Ltd* (1920) 7 TC 629, a company was formed in 1904 with the primary object of acquiring, managing and developing with a view to ultimate sale, certain lands in British Columbia which were held in trust for various persons. Although the company formed had a clear trading purpose, it was held that the sales were realisations of investments, as the purpose of the company was to realise the full capital value of the respective interests in the land under the trust. The motives of the major shareholder in the taxpayer were also a significant factor in another important case on the distinction between trading and investment (*Simmons v IRC* (1980) 53 TC 461).

Change of intention

[2.9] As indicated above, it can be very important to recognise changes of taxpayer intention with regard to a property. An example might involve the demolition of a warehouse previously held as a capital asset and the construction for sale of residential flats. The concept of a change in intention was articulated by Megarry J in *Taylor v Good* (1974) 49 TC 277 at p 287E:

> 'Even if the house was purchased with no thought of trading, I do not see why an intention to trade could not be formed later. What is bought or otherwise acquired (for example, under a will) with no thought of trading cannot thereby acquire an immunity so that, however filled with the desire and intention of trading the owner may later become, it can never be said that any transaction by him with the property constitutes trading. For the taxpayer a non-trading inception may be a valuable asset: but it is no palladium. The proposition that an initial intention not to trade may be displaced by a subsequent intention, in the course of the ownership of the property in question is, I think, sufficiently established . . . '

On the basis that it is clearly demonstrable that there is a change of intention from investment to trading then the consequence will be an appropriation of the capital asset to trading stock and a deemed disposal for chargeable gains purposes (albeit the taxpayer may elect to defer the charge to tax until sale of the trading stock; TCGA 1992, s 161). The determination of the date of the change will have implications both for the valuation of the land and the expenditure that is allowable as a trade expense. For appropriations from trading stock, see **8.12** below.

Method of finance

[2.10] Borrowing on a short-term basis to fund the acquisition of a property is generally indicative of an intention to dispose of the property rather than to retain for long-term investment. However, a developer may of course raise short-term finance to fund the development with a view to replacing this with long-term finance secured on the completed development. Even a straightforward investment purchase may be initially funded by short term (or 'bridge') financing, which would not, in the absence of other evidence suggestive of a trading intention, prevent such a transaction from being accepted as investment (*Wisdom v Chamberlain (Inspector of Taxes)* [1969] 1 All ER 332, [1969] 1 WLR 275, CA. See also *Stayton v Revenue and Customs Comrs* [2016] UKFTT 345 (TC) and *Schechter and Schechter v HMRC* [2017] UKFTT 189 (TC)).

Whether the property is income producing

[2.11] Where a property produces no income during the taxpayer's period of ownership it is indicative of a lack of investment intention. A property which produces rental income insufficient to cover expenses would be viewed in a similar way. However, many types of asset, such as works of art and the subject matter of speculative financial transactions, are generally considered not to be trading assets even though they produce little or no income and the benefit to the holder comes as an enhancement in the capital value of the asset. Furthermore, there are of course other reasons why a property may not produce income before disposal – for example if it is owner-occupied, or it is bought with an intention to develop with a view to earning income post-development, but circumstances force a disposal prior to the property producing rental income.

The rental income capabilities of an asset also relate to the analysis of the taxpayer's motive discussed above. In the years leading up to 2007, many individuals and companies in the UK benefited from a rising global property market and made significant gains on the acquisition and eventual sale of residential and commercial properties. The generally held view is that such acquisitions are 'investments' and any gains are taxed accordingly. However, even where the appreciation in property values clearly relates to the income producing capabilities of these assets (as is generally the case with UK commercial property, for example), it could be argued that one of the primary motivations for acquiring these assets is the appreciation in value of the property rather than the rental income produced during the period of property ownership (this is particularly true in the case of the UK residential sector in recent times). The same comparison could be drawn in the context of the ownership of shares in a period of rapidly rising stock market values (in this case, such transactions by individuals will be treated as an investment transaction even though, under general principles discussed below, a case could be made for a trading motive (see *Lewis Emanuel & Son Ltd v White* (1965) 42 TC 369) and *Akhtar Ali* (TC04816)).

In *IRC v Reinhold* (1953) 34 TC 389, the taxpayer bought four houses and sold them two years later after instructing his agent to sell as soon as the opportunity arose. The properties had produced insufficient rent to generate a profit and the taxpayer had ten years earlier bought and sold a hotel for a profit. Although this transaction appeared to show many of the signs of trading, it was nevertheless found to be an investment. Lord Keith stated (at 397) in relation to the taxpayer's expectation of realising a profit on sale:

> 'This is the expectation of most, if not all, people who make investments. Heritable property is a not uncommon subject of investment and generally has the feature, expected of investments, of yielding an income from rents . . . the intention to resell at some date at a profit is not per se sufficient in this case to attract tax . . . '

In *Marson v Morton* (1986) 59 TC 381, Browne Wilkinson V-C stated:

> ' . . . in my judgment in 1986 it is not any longer self-evident that unless land is producing income it cannot be an investment. The legal principle of course cannot change with the passage of time: but life does. Since the arrival of inflation and high rates of tax on income new approaches to investment have emerged, putting the emphasis in investment on the making of capital profit at the expense of income yield . . . the mere fact that land is not income producing should not be decisive or even virtually decisive on the question of whether it was bought as an investment.'

On the other hand, in *Parkin v Cattell* (1971) 48 TC 462, the taxpayer purchased buildings with controlled tenants in occupation, held them for a number of years and sold them when they became vacant. The transactions were held to be trading, the course of dealing indicating that the prime motive for the purchases was to obtain profit on resale rather than to benefit from the rental stream they provided.

That decision could be relevant for companies considering conversion to UK Real Estate Investment Trust (UK-REIT) status and holding significant numbers of low income producing properties, because trading properties are excluded from the tax exempt business of a UK-REIT (see **2.18** below). The low income yield/high capital yield characteristic of UK residential property in general has been one of the factors why residential REITs have been slow to develop in the UK. Rental yields on UK residential property are generally low, with capital values being more a function of the dominant residential owner-occupier market than of rental levels. For that reason, and particularly in the context of properties subject to controlled rents, residential property companies find it necessary to access the capital uplift in the value of their properties by regularly selling properties. An appropriate level of such portfolio 'churn' allows the rental income yield to be topped up with the benefit of capital appreciation, providing a commercial total return to shareholders. Under the existing tax legislation, there is a risk that such sales may be treated as trading and hence incapable of forming part of the tax exempt business of a UK-REIT.

It may nevertheless be possible to substantiate an investment intention for a portfolio of residential properties, assuming other circumstances (particularly the period for which the properties are held) do not indicate trading.

Period of ownership

[2.12] Although a long period of ownership is undoubtedly indicative of an investment intention, there is no clear cut off point as to how long a property needs to be held to constitute investment, and even holding an income producing property for many years is not necessarily conclusive proof that it was held throughout as an investment (see for example *Orchard Parks Ltd (in liq) v Pogson* (1964) 42 TC 442). The general rule of thumb in relation to real property is that holding property for more than five years suggests investment, while a period of ownership of less than three years is indicative of trading.

Other factors are likely to be particularly influential where property is held for between three and five years. Interestingly, the three-year hold rule of thumb is used in the legislation relating to UK-REITs; CTA 2010, Part 12, s 556 confirms that sale proceeds following a development will be treated as arising to a UK-REIT's (taxable) residual business if the cost of development exceeds 30% of the fair value of the property at entry into the UK-REIT regime or acquisition, whichever is later, and the UK-REIT disposes of the property within three years of completion of the development. This rule operates to take the sale proceeds out of the UK-REIT's tax-exempt business, but it does not, in itself, mean the disposal is automatically treated as a trading transaction (so the principles set out in this chapter will still apply to determine whether the disposal is trading or capital in nature).

Reason for the disposal

[2.13] Although this is not as important as the reason for acquisition of the property, it can be an important factor in rebutting the presumption that a short period of ownership indicates a trading intention. For example, a disposal in order to raise finance for an alternative, better yielding investment, or a forced and unexpected need to raise cash or to reduce bank borrowings can be reasons for realising an investment that do not imply a trading motive. The key element, in such cases, is likely to be that an unanticipated event or circumstance has intervened to provoke a change of plan (manifested in an early disposal). In *Tebrau (Johore) Rubber Syndicate v Farmer* (1910) 5 TC 658, a company was formed to acquire land for development as a rubber plantation. It bought two estates but found that it had inadequate finance to develop them. It therefore sold the land to another company in return for shares. It was held that there was no evidence that the land had been bought for resale and that the profit was therefore capital, based on the fact that the land had been acquired as an investment. In addition, in *Terrace Hill (Berkeley) Ltd v HMRC* [2015] UKFTT 75 (TC), an SPV acquired a development of an office property. It was intended that the property would be held for rental income. However, during the development period, in part following the departure of American firms from London following 9/11, the rental market declined. The rental income was disappointing and the calibre of tenant lower than expected so the property was sold. It was held that the evidence that the land had been acquired as an investment was credible and the disappointing letting experience was a more than adequate reason to justify the change of intention and the property was rightly treated as an investment. Those decisions illustrate that the subsequent frustration of the initial investment intention cannot change the nature of the transaction.

HMRC accept this, as can be seen in their guidance on the Taxation of Transactions in UK Land legislation (see Chapter 13). In the guidance (BIM60560), they give examples of investors acquiring property with the intention to hold long term and realise rental income, but being forced by unforeseen circumstances (for example a liquidity event) to dispose of the property after only 18 months or two years. HMRC confirm that the unforeseen circumstances forcing an early sale should not affect the investment status of such transactions.

Expertise of the owner

[2.14] A taxpayer's expertise in property can be an influential factor. For example, HMRC have generally taken the view that builders and estate agents are prima facie likely to be involved in property trading rather than investment (as HMRC argued in *Harvey v Caulcott (Inspector of Taxes)* (1952) 33 TC 159). Even the generation of rental income over a number of years is not conclusive when the investor is a builder. In *Oliver v Farnsworth* (1956) 37 TC 51, a house let for 24 years until its sale in 1953 was held to be part of a builder's trading profits and there are various other cases illustrating this point (*Spiers & Son v Ogden* (1932) 17 TC 117, *Sharpless v Rees* (1941) 23 TC 361, *Hobson (James) & Sons Ltd v Newall (Inspector of Taxes)* (1957) 37 TC 609).

On the other hand, there are examples of cases where builders and estate agents have argued successfully for an investment motive (see *Harvey v Caulcott* above).

'Tainting'

[2.15] In some cases, a taxpayer purchasing a large portfolio with, as a general matter, an investment intention, will be able to identify certain properties which he knows he will want to sell relatively quickly (in the context, perhaps, of rebalancing the portfolio to his own specific requirements). In such circumstances, it may be worth considering acquiring those properties that are likely to be sold on quickly in a separate trading company, to mitigate the risk that HMRC, seeing trading activity early on, might conclude that the entire portfolio was acquired with a trading intention and should be taxed accordingly, particularly where the hold period for the investment properties is – perhaps due to unforeseen events – relatively short. While it is not impossible for a single business to carry on both trading and investment transactions, persuading HMRC of that fact can be difficult (see, for example, *Harvey v Caulcott*, at **2.14** above). Holding the investment properties in an investment company, and the properties earmarked for early disposal in a trading company, should minimise the risk of trading activity tainting the character of the rest of the portfolio.

Supplementary work on assets sold

[2.16] An application for planning consent prior to a sale may be indicative of a trading transaction, particularly if the property is held for only a short period. The acquisition and resale of land for which planning permission had been obtained was held to amount to trading in *Cooke v Haddock I*, ChD (1960) 39 TC 64, *Turner v Last I*, ChD (1965) 42 TC 517 and *Pilkington v Randall*, (1966) 42 TC 662, 45 ATC 32, CA. The same question was considered in the previously mentioned case of *Marson v Morton*, where a taxpayer purchased land with the intention of holding it as an investment for at least two years. In order to increase the value of the land, the taxpayer applied for planning permission. That was regarded by HMRC, applying the badges of trade, as involving the making of modifications to the asset to render it more saleable. However, the court held that, as the original intention was the purchase of an investment, no trade was in fact being carried on. Similarly, the facts in *Taylor v Good*, CA (1974) 49 TC 277 (in which a house bought as a residence was found unsuitable and resold to a developer after planning permission had been obtained) were found not to amount to an adventure in the nature of a trade.

Accounting treatment

[2.17] The presentation of the asset and the transaction in the owner's accounts will also be persuasive. Assets held as investments are presented in the accounts as fixed assets whereas properties held for trading purposes are generally held as trading stock. The accounting treatment is not regarded as the overriding factor, but in the case of an asset correctly held as trading stock in the company accounts, a disposal is likely to be treated as a trading transaction even if other evidence suggests otherwise (see *Granville Building Co v Oxby* (1954) 35 TC 245).

This particular criterion may well be tested more fully over the next few years as the introduction of 'new' UK GAAP (FRS 101 and FRS 102) in 2015 makes itself felt. These changes in accounting standards will force property owners to reconsider whether assets that they hold constitute inventory or fixed assets and on some occasions the conclusion may trigger a reclassification for accounting purposes. Whilst that should not automatically change the tax treatment of gains from an eventual disposal, it could be a deciding factor in some marginal cases.

Real Estate Investment Trusts (UK-REITs)

[2.18] The distinction between investment and trading transactions in property is particularly important in the context of UK REITs, for a number of reasons:

- The regime provides for a tax exemption for the profits of a 'property rental business' (CTA 2010, s 518). Property transactions that are trading in nature do not benefit from that tax exemption even if they are carried out by a UK-REIT, and accordingly continue to be taxed at the prevailing corporation tax rate (19% since 1 April 2017) as part of the UK-REIT's 'residual' business.
- Assets which are held as trading stock do not form part of the tax exempt business, so rental income arising from them is taxed at the prevailing corporation tax rate (CTA 2010, s 604).
- The 'balance of business' tests (CTA 2010, s 531) must be passed by companies and groups which want to enter the regime. These tests look at the assets and income forming part of the (potentially tax exempt) property rental business as a proportion of their total assets and income. In applying these tests, trading assets and income (including rent) arising from trading assets fall on the residual, rather than tax exempt, side of that line.

Generally speaking, in the past, UK-resident companies and HMRC have taken a reasonably flexible approach to the distinction between trade profits under ITTOIA 2005, Part 2 and CTA 2009, Part 3 and property rental business profits under ITTOIA 2005, Part 3 and CTA 2009, Part 4 on the basis that the difference in tax treatment between the two is often not great. In recent years, the property industry has seen growth in a broader range of services being offered by landlords to tenants, including serviced offices and facilities management. It has not been unusual for many such services to be regarded as sufficiently closely connected with the leasing of land to give rise to property rental business profits. Under the UK-REIT rules, the distinction can be rather more significant owing to the tax exemption conferred by the regime on the property rental business profits.

As mentioned at **2.11** above, the distinction is generally felt to pose particular challenges in the context of residential investment, where it is common for the business model to rely on a certain amount of portfolio 'churn' to top up a modest income yield to an acceptable total return for investors. Problems can also arise in relation to shared ownership structures that are popular in the social and affordable housing space, as the increase in an individual's ownership interest in a shared ownership property ('staircasing') can result in trading treatment for the landlord.

UK-REITs are more fully discussed and explained in CHAPTER 3.

Diverted Profits Tax (DPT)

[2.19] The distinction between trading and investment is of further relevance for offshore companies since the introduction of the DPT from 1 April 2015.

DPT can apply to trading profits (as opposed to investment returns) and arises in two circumstances:

- a UK tax resident company or a UK permanent establishment ('PE') enter into arrangements with a related person that lack economic substance, and lower the UK company's or UK PE's taxable profits; or
- a person carries on an activity in the UK as part of its trade, which involves the supply of goods, services or property, but avoids creating a UK PE.

The legislation and HMRC guidance are clear that the DPT can apply to real estate. However, a trading activity will still be required for the tax to apply.

Taxation of capital gains as income

[2.20] Certain property transactions involving the realisation of a gain of a capital nature from the disposal of a property situated in the UK could have historically given rise to a charge to income tax under ITA 2007, Part 13, Chapter 3 or to corporation tax on income under CTA 2010, Part 18. This legislation was replaced from 5 July 2016 by new anti-avoidance legislation, described at **2.21** below. However, it could still apply to, and be used as a basis to challenge, historic property transactions.

Very broadly, the rule sought to target the dressing up of an income profit as capital and could be engaged where a gain was obtained directly or indirectly in circumstances where:

- land, or property deriving its value from land (eg shares in a company which owns land) was acquired with the sole or main object of realising a gain from disposing of all or part of the land; or
- land was held as trading stock; or
- land was developed with the sole or main object of realising a gain from disposing of all or part of the land when developed.

The rule could apply even if the gain was obtained by a person other than the person acquiring, holding or developing the land: it could also be in point if the gain was obtained by a person connected with such a person, or by another person who was a party to, or concerned in, an arrangement or scheme relating to the land which enabled a gain to be realised indirectly or through a series of transactions. See further CHAPTER 13.

Profits from trading in and developing UK land

[2.21] While the basic principles used to identify trading or investment activity, as set out above, remain in place, a new suite of anti-avoidance rules to tax trading profits derived from land in the UK were brought in from 5 July 2016 which could give rise to a charge to income tax under ITA 2007, Part 9A or to corporation tax on income under CTA 2010, Part 8ZB. The rationale for their introduction appears to be twofold. First, the Government indicated an intention to target property developers who set themselves up offshore without a UK permanent establishment, and with the benefit of double tax treaties, in order to keep profits from their developments outside the scope of UK tax. Second, the new rules seek to address perceived shortcomings in existing legislation, described at **2.20** above.

To address these issues and to create a 'level playing field' for UK and non-UK property traders/developers, the legislation applies equally to resident and non-resident businesses, and does not depend on the existence of a permanent establishment in the UK. Broadly, the rules apply to profits on disposals of land not otherwise subject to UK corporation or income tax, where the land was acquired with the intention of realising a profit from development or disposal. Where the rules apply profits from disposals of UK land, and property deriving its value from UK land, are treated as trading profits for UK tax purposes.

The new rules apply to disposals made on or after 5 July 2016, replacing and extending the rules described at **2.20**. The anti-avoidance provisions apply from the date the rules were announced, 16 March 2016.

The new rules have two important differences from the old provisions. First, the definition of land is no longer limited to a direct sale of land or a disposal of control over the land. It is extended to include the disposal of any interest (ie not just a controlling interest) in an asset deriving at least 50% of its value from the land (CTA 2010, s 356OD and BIM60580). Second, whereas the old rules applied where the relevant person had a 'sole or main object' of realising a gain, the new rules apply where 'the main purpose or one of the main purposes, of acquiring the land was to realise a profit or gain from disposing of the land'.

The second of these changes has caused concern in the market, by potentially widening the net significantly as to which transactions could be caught. Arguably 'one of the main purposes' of an acquisition or property by an investor will be to realise a gain on future disposals (this is in the nature of any investment). However, HMRC guidance makes it clear that the rules are not targeted at genuine investors. The guidance makes a distinction between someone who acquires property with the intention of benefitting from capital growth (as well as rental income) over time, and someone who acquires with the intention of profiting from development and/or sale: 'The legislation requires that a main purpose of the arrangement is to obtain a gain from disposing of the property. This condition will not be met in the case of straightforward long-term investment, where the economic benefit arising to the owner is the result of market movement from holding that asset rather than transactions that are in the nature of trading' (BIM60560). HMRC also gives several examples in its guidance at BIM60560. These examples clarify that, where the intention behind the acquisition of property is to hold as a long-term investment, such transactions should not be pulled within the scope of the new rules, even where an investor is forced by unforeseen circumstances to sell early.

Although arguably the legislation is broad enough to apply to investors, it is helpful that HMRC do not regard the legislation as applying to investors and has said these rules do not change the tests that determine whether a transaction is investment or trading: 'These rules do not alter the treatment of or recharacterise investment activities, except where they are part of such a wider trading activity.' (BIM60555).

The rules are summarised below and set out in more detail at CHAPTER 13.

Disposals of land

[2.22] Profits or gains (which includes a loss – CTA 2010, s 356OF) from disposals of any UK land are treated as profits of a trade if any one of the following conditions is met:

- the main purpose, or one of the main purposes, of acquiring the land was to realise a profit or gain from disposing of the land;
- the main purpose, or one of the main purposes, of acquiring any property deriving its value from the land was to realise a profit or gain from disposing of the land when developed;
- the land is held as trading stock;
- in a case where the land has been developed, the main purpose, or one of the main purposes of developing the land was to realise a profit or gain from disposing of the land when developed.

Disposals of property deriving its value from land

[2.23] Profits or gains from a disposal of any property which (at the time of the disposal) derives at least 50% of its value from land in the UK will be treated as profits of a trade where, broadly, the person making the profit or gain has been concerned in an arrangement involving UK land, where the main purpose, or one of the main purposes, of that arrangement is to: (i) deal in or develop that land; and (ii) realise a profit or gain from disposal of property deriving the whole or part of its value from that land.

Anti-avoidance

[2.24] The rules include anti-avoidance provisions, which can be summarised, broadly, as follows:

- a targeted anti-avoidance rule that seeks to counteract any tax advantage arising from arrangements where the main purpose, or one of the main purposes, is to avoid a UK tax charge under the new rules; and
- anti-fragmentation rules intended to catch arrangements where profits are moved to related entities outside the main charge, for example, an offshore property holding company paying an associated offshore development company a fee based on the profits from the relevant disposal.

Chapter 3

Real Estate Investment Trusts

by
Peter Beckett,
KPMG LLP

Introduction

Background

[3.1] A real estate investment trust is essentially a collective investment vehicle that allows investment in real estate in such a way that the tax impact for the investor is similar to that which would arise from a direct investment in real estate. The UK real estate investment trust ('UK-REIT') regime was introduced on 1 January 2007. At the time of writing, there are currently over 60 groups within the UK-REIT regime. The UK-REIT regime currently represents the majority of the main market listed real estate sector (by value). UK-REITs hold investments predominantly in office, retail and industrial property although a small number are invested in other sectors such as healthcare, self-storage, residential and student housing.

A detailed description of the regime is set out below. However, in overview, a UK-REIT is a listed company (not a trust) which carries on a property rental business. The company is not liable to corporation tax on qualifying property rental income or qualifying capital gains. The company is, however, required to distribute broadly 90% of its rental profits each year. These dividends are often termed Property Income Distributions (or 'PIDs') although this is not a term that is used in the legislation. They are generally paid under deduction of basic rate income tax and are taxable in the hands of the shareholder as property income rather than a normal dividend. This achieves the aim of moving the incidence of tax from the company to the investor. Companies wishing to enter the regime are required to meet a number of conditions at the point of entry into the regime. These conditions must then continue to be met each year in order to remain within the regime.

In order to encourage the creation of more UK-REITs, the Government introduced several changes to the regime in Finance Act 2012. These changes removed a number of barriers to entry of the regime that previously existed. In particular, the entry charge was abolished and the listing requirement was relaxed slightly to include shares admitted to trading on alternative platforms such as AIM. The introduction of a diverse ownership rule for institutional investors was also introduced to encourage the creation of new 'institutionally owned' UK-REITS.

Legislation and guidance

[3.2] The main legislative provisions are at CTA 2010, ss 518–609. HMRC have also released detailed guidance notes as part of their manuals. These are available from HMRC's website (www.hmrc.gov.uk/manuals/greitmanual/index.htm) and are referenced numerically with the prefix 'GREIT'.

The legislation allows for either a single-entity REIT or a Group REIT. The majority of UK-REITs are Group REITs. Broadly, a Group REIT comprises a principal company, all of its 75% (effective 51%) subsidiaries, interests in tax transparent entities and corporate joint ventures for which a joint venture election has been made. The rules below are those which apply following the changes introduced in Finance Act 2012. Companies or groups that entered the regime prior to the introduction of these changes will have been subject to different conditions on entry.

Conditions of the regime

[3.3] The principal company must meet a number of conditions to make a valid election to become a UK-REIT and to avoid loss of REIT status subsequently. These conditions relate to the organisation of the company, its property rental business and its distribution policy.

Organisation conditions

[3.4] The legislation (CTA 2010, s 528) sets out six conditions relating to the principal company.

Condition A

[3.5] The principal company must be resident in the UK. It cannot also be resident in another jurisdiction under the laws of that jurisdiction. For these purposes, a tax treaty may be considered to be part of the law of another jurisdiction although this should be checked in relation to local law. This means that a company, which is dual resident under domestic law but UK resident under a treaty tie-breaker clause, will meet this condition.

Condition B

[3.6] The company may not be an Open Ended Investment Company (OEIC). The meaning of OEIC is not limited to the Taxes Act definition but also includes any vehicle with variable capital set up within or outside the UK.

Condition C

[3.7] The ordinary shares of the principal company must be either listed or admitted to trading on a 'recognised stock exchange' (as defined at CTA 2010, s 1137). A list of recognised stock exchanges is included on the HMRC website (www.hmrc.gov.uk/fid/rse.htm). Companies whose shares are not listed but are admitted to trading on a recognised exchange (such as those companies quoted on AIM) must also be traded (CTA 2010, s 528A). The term 'traded' is not defined but a company should in principle qualify in this respect where its shareholders at the beginning of an accounting period do not match those at the end of that accounting period.

The listing condition is relaxed slightly for a newly-formed UK-REIT during its first three years (see **3.27** below).

Condition D

[3.8] The principal company must not be a close company. A close company is defined in existing tax legislation (CTA 2010, ss 439–454). However, the definition is amended for the purposes of the UK-REIT regime as follows:

- The exemptions in CTA 2010, ss 444 and 447(1)(a) do not apply to a UK-REIT.
- A UK-REIT will not be treated as a close company only as a result of having a participator who is an institutional investor. Institutional investor is defined (CTA 2010, s 528(4A)) for these purposes to include:
  - an authorised unit trust
  - an OEIC;
  - a limited partnership;
  - a pension scheme;
  - an insurance company;
  - a sovereign immune body;
  - a charity;
  - a registered social landlord;
  - a UK-REIT; and
  - a non-UK resident equivalent of a UK-REIT.

The inclusion of UK-REITs and their overseas equivalents in the above list is effective from 1 April 2014 (SI 2014/518).

The close company condition is relaxed for a newly-formed UK-REIT during its first three years (see **3.27** below).

Condition E

[3.9] The principal company may only issue one class of ordinary shares. The only other class of shares it may issue is non-voting restricted fixed rate preference shares. The non-voting restricted (fixed rate) preference shares may also be convertible into ordinary shares.

Condition F

[3.10] The principal company may not be party to a loan relationship which is either on non-commercial terms, provides a return of interest which is linked to the results of the UK-REIT or provides for repayment of capital on non-commercial terms.

Property conditions

[3.11] There are certain minimum requirements which a UK-REIT must meet in respect of its property rental business (CTA 2010, s 529). These conditions need to be met by a Group REIT on a consolidated basis. In order to become a REIT, a group must meet these conditions throughout the accounting period; therefore, it must carry on a qualifying property rental business prior to the first day of becoming a REIT. The two property conditions are as follows:

Condition A

[3.12] The property rental business of the group should include at least three properties. This requirement must be met throughout each accounting period. A property is defined in the legislation at CTA 2010, s 529(4)(a) as 'an estate, interest or right by the exploitation of which the business is conducted'. Therefore, a property for these purposes includes a leasehold interest.

[3.13] CTA 2010, s 529(4)(b) provides the following definition of a single 'property':

> 'A property is a single property if it is designed, fitted or equipped for the purpose of being rented, and it is rented or available for rent, as a commercial or residential unit (separate from any other commercial or residential unit).'

This means that a shopping centre, for example, should be viewed as multiple properties if the UK-REIT lets each shop unit separately. Similarly, a property that is leased to three separate, unconnected parties will satisfy this requirement.

Condition B

[3.14] No one property should represent more than 40% of the total gross value of all the properties in the property rental business throughout the accounting period. Properties should be valued in accordance with international accounting standards using a fair value method where there is a choice.

Balance of business conditions

[3.15] There are two balance of business conditions (CTA 2010, s 531) that must be met by any company (or group) that wants to become (or remain) a UK-REIT. Meeting the conditions will demonstrate that a sufficient quantum of its business is property investment. A Group REIT must meet the tests on a consolidated basis and it is not necessary for each company individually in the group to meet the business conditions.

Condition A

[3.16] At least 75% of the profits of the UK-REIT should be derived from its worldwide property rental business. For these purposes, 'profits' are calculated under international accounting standards, excluding:

- tax;
- realised or unrealised gains or losses on the disposal of property;
- changes in the fair value of certain hedging derivative contracts; and
- items which are outside of the ordinary course of the company's business. (CTA 2010, s 531(4)).

Condition B

[3.17] At least 75% of the total value of assets of the group should comprise assets involved in the worldwide property rental business of the UK-REIT, shareholdings in other UK-REITs and/or cash as measured at the beginning of each accounting period.

As in the property conditions, the value of assets is the gross value measured using international accounting standards using fair value where there is a choice of methodology. An asset 'involved' in the worldwide property rental business is one which would be shown as an asset if separate accounts were to be produced for the property rental business. In most cases, assets will qualify to the extent of their use in a property business.

Other assets employed by the REIT such as cars and plant and machinery will not be included within this definition and will be treated as assets of the residual business.

Distribution condition

[3.18] A UK-REIT must distribute, by way of a dividend, 90% of the profits of its property rental business (excluding profits arising on the disposal of properties) and 100% of PIDs received from other UK-REITs by the filing date of the company's tax return which is normally 12 months after the end of the company's accounting period (CTA 2010, s 530). For these purposes, profits are calculated as follows (CTA 2010, s 599):

- Rental profits which are normally taxable as profits of a UK property business or as profits of an overseas property business carried on by a UK entity.
- Less amounts normally available as a deduction against UK property business profits including capital allowances and other expenses. The UK-REIT is not allowed to 'disclaim' capital allowances but must offset the maximum amount of allowances available in each period.
- Plus debits or credits on loan relationships that relate to the tax-exempt business. In practice, a UK-REIT will need to allocate payments made by the company, or each individual company within a Group REIT, by reference to whether the loan relationship relates to the tax-exempt or non tax-exempt business of that company on a just and reasonable basis.
- Plus debits or credits on derivative contracts which are acquired as a hedge of risk in relation to an asset of the tax-exempt business. Whether or not a derivative can be treated as a hedge of risk will depend on whether the acquisition motive can be adequately demonstrated. Designation in the accounts as a hedge is conclusive proof. Debits or credits on a derivative hedging a liability of the tax-exempt business, such as debt financing a property acquisition, are not included within the calculation.

Where a UK-REIT is prevented by UK corporate law from paying a distribution (for example, because it has insufficient distributable reserves), the requirement to pay a dividend is relaxed. HMRC have the power to prescribe which foreign enactments can be treated as creating a relaxation of the distribution condition but no regulations on this point have been provided to date (CTA 2010, ss 530(3), (5)).

This condition must be met by the principal company of the group on behalf of the group as a whole. Subsidiaries of the principal company will continue to make normal distributions as and when they are able to, and have no requirement to distribute profits to their immediate shareholders.

Legislation was introduced in Finance (No 3) Act 2010 to allow a UK-REIT to offer investors a stock dividend as an alternative to or in combination with a cash dividend when meeting the requirement to distribute 90% of the profits of its property rental business. This change applies to distributions made on or after 16 December 2010. This will provide UK-REITs with more flexibility to retain cash for reinvestment into the business. Where a stock dividend has been issued, it may be necessary to use the market value rule (under ITTOIA, s 412). If the application of this rule causes the distribution requirement not to be met, the UK-REIT has an additional six months in which to make a further distribution in order to meet the 90% test.

Breach of conditions

[3.19] Where a UK-REIT breaches certain of the conditions described above, it will result in the UK-REIT's removal from the regime with effect from the end of the accounting period prior to the breach. However, the legislation allows a UK-REIT to breach a number of the conditions of the regime without losing its REIT status, provided the breach is 'minor or inadvertent'.

These 'minor breach' rules are generally relatively straightforward with reference to individual REIT conditions. However, CTA 2010, s 577 provides that a multiple number of minor breaches of separate REIT conditions could result in REIT status being revoked. The multiple breach rules are quite complicated and REITs will need to take particular care where minor breaches have occurred in previous periods.

Conditions which must be met at all times

[3.20] A breach of certain conditions of the regime will always result in removal from the regime with effect from the end of the previous accounting period. The conditions are:

- UK residence condition;
- requirement that the company is not an OEIC;
- requirement that the company does not issue shares other than one class of ordinary share capital and non-voting fixed rate preference shares;
- requirement that the company is not a party to results-linked or non-commercial debt.

These conditions are all 'organisation conditions' which relate to the UK-REIT or the principal company of a Group REIT.

The UK-REIT has an obligation to inform HMRC of a breach of any of the organisation conditions as soon as possible.

Potential 'minor breach' conditions

[3.21] The following conditions can be breached in limited circumstances without causing a UK-REIT to be removed from the regime. Note however that multiple minor breaches of the conditions can result in a loss of REIT status. CTA 2010, ss 561–569 and ss 574–578 indicate that breaches will be dealt with in the following way:

Listing condition

[3.22] A special provision applies where the listing condition (organisation condition C) is breached during the take-over of one UK-REIT by another. At some point during this process, the target UK-REIT will de-list. The provisions therefore ensure that the target UK-REIT does not lose its REIT status in these circumstances.

Where a UK-REIT breaches the listing condition in any other circumstance, it is deemed to have lost its REIT status with effect from the end of the previous accounting period.

Where the listing condition is breached, the UK-REIT must inform HMRC as soon as possible.

Close company condition

[3.23] The same latitude is provided on a breach of the close company condition (organisation condition D) during the takeover of one UK-REIT by another as that provided in respect of the listing condition ie, the breach will not result in a loss of REIT status.

There is also latitude provided in respect of the close company condition where the breach is caused by someone other than the company. This would include the shareholders. Therefore, if, for example, the UK-REIT becomes close because of a share transaction between two shareholders, the UK-REIT will not lose its status. In these circumstances, the breach must be rectified by the end of the following accounting period.

In practice, therefore, it will normally be desirable for the directors of a UK-REIT to be provided with the powers to monitor holdings of shares and to be able to force a sale of shares to ensure that the close company condition can be managed. This may require provisions within the UK-REIT's articles of association.

The UK-REIT must inform HMRC of a breach of the close company condition as soon as possible.

Property conditions

[3.24] CTA 2010, s 575, which deals with breaches of the property owner-ship conditions, indicates that a breach of the '40% value rule' in condition B will only count as a breach on its own merits if it does not arise as a consequence of breaching the 'three property rule' in condition A. Otherwise, in the case of a breach of either condition, one single breach can subsist until the end of the accounting period following the one in which the breach begins to occur. However, if a breach continues over three accounting periods, the

UK-REIT will lose its status. Subject to this, the UK-REIT may only suffer two 'single' breaches in any ten-year period before losing its status.

Balance of business conditions

[3.25] Where there is a breach of balance of business conditions, CTA 2010, s 568 provides that REIT status will not be lost provided the relevant ratio for either assets or income does not fall below 50% in each case. However, if there are three consecutive accounting periods in which either 75% limit is breached, REIT status will be lost (CTA 2010, s 576(1)). Interestingly remaining below 75% but above 50% for two consecutive periods counts as only one 'minor breach' (CTA 2010, s 576(5)). There is a further override provision limiting the number of times that the UK-REIT can breach the tests to two of each of Conditions A and B in any ten-year period (CTA 2010, s 576(2)). For these purposes, a breach of the asset test will count separately from a breach of the profit test.

Distribution condition

[3.26] A single breach of the distribution condition should not result in a UK-REIT losing its status. However, the regulations provide that, if the minimum distribution is not met, a tax charge will be levied on the UK-REIT (CTA 2010, s 564). The tax charge is assessed under miscellaneous income (CTA 2009, s 979) as if income had arisen to the non tax-exempt (residual) part of the principal company of a Group REIT.

The deemed income equals:

$$P - D$$

Where P is 90% of the profits of the property rental business (ie the amount that should have been distributed) and D is the gross amount of profits distributed on or before the normal corporation tax filing date of the company as required by the distribution condition. The deemed income is then charged to tax at the mainstream corporation tax rate (currently 20%).

A relaxation is provided in circumstances where a UK-REIT has calculated and paid the 90% distribution within the relevant time limit based on a self-assessment return which is under an enquiry by HMRC and the taxable profits of the property rental business are ultimately agreed at a higher amount than that shown in the return (CTA 2010, s 530A). No tax charge will be levied on the UK-REIT provided it pays a 'catch up dividend' within three months of the return becoming final. For a Group REIT, this will mean in practice that the principal company will need to pay the dividend following the finalisation of the return of any member of the group. For large groups, this may involve a considerable degree of monitoring of the status of tax returns. This relaxation does not apply to PID income received by a UK-REIT in respect of its shareholdings in other UK-REITs.

A breach of the distribution condition can however lead to loss of REIT status where the UK-REIT has breached other conditions (such as the balance of business conditions) on multiple occasions in the previous ten-year period. This will broadly apply where the UK-REIT has incurred four previous separate minor breaches of various conditions.

Newly elected UK-REITs

[**3.27**] In order to make it easier for newly established companies and groups to be formed as UK-REITs, some conditions are relaxed in certain circumstances.

Broadly, for a company whose shares are not listed but are admitted to trading on a qualifying exchange, the requirement for the shares to be traded does not apply during the first three years after it joins the regime.

In addition, the close company condition (organisation condition D) does not apply for a UK-REIT during its first three years.

Summary

[**3.28**] The table below illustrates the implication of a single breach of any one of the REIT conditions.

Condition Breached	Implication
Listing	Exit from regime unless taken over by another UK-REIT
Close Company	Exit from regime unless taken over by another UK-REIT
Three properties	Exit from regime unless resolved by following accounting period
40% single property value	Exit from regime unless resolved by following accounting period
Distribution	Tax charge
75% asset test	Potential exit from regime if ratio drops below 50%
75% profit test	Potential exit from regime if ratio drops below 50%

As mentioned above, there are complex rules that will affect a company which has multiple breaches of one or more of the various conditions. These rules are beyond the scope of this chapter.

Entry into the regime

Notice

[**3.29**] A company that wishes to join the REIT regime must provide a written notice to HMRC at any time before the beginning of the accounting period in which the company wishes to become a UK-REIT or wishes to become the principal company of a Group REIT. At the time this notice is provided, the principal company needs to meet the following organisation conditions:

- it must be UK resident (Condition A – see **3.5** above);
- it is not an OEIC (Condition B – see **3.6** above).

The notice should specify the date from which the company or group wishes to enter into the regime. The notice must also be accompanied by a statement that the company or principal company reasonably expects that organisation conditions A, B, C, E and F (see **3.4** above) will be satisfied for its first accounting period as a UK-REIT.

If the conditions are met, the regime will apply to the company or group from the first day of the accounting period specified in the notice (and not on the day the notice is given).

Where relevant, a group seeking to enter the regime should consider whether it wishes to make elections to bring one or more of its joint venture companies within the regime (see **3.79** below).

Tax effects of entry

[3.30] When a group enters the REIT regime, there are a number of effects for tax purposes:

- The tax accounting period of all group companies is treated as ceasing and a new accounting period begins. Accordingly, if entry into the regime occurs part way through a company's existing accounting period, this will lead to a number of short tax accounting periods.
- The property rental business of each group company is treated as ceasing and a new property rental business begins. This means that any losses which are directly attributable to that business are trapped and cannot be carried forward to offset profits of the property rental business of the UK-REIT. In practice, this should principally affect UK property business losses and overseas property business losses. Note, however, that this deemed cessation does not apply to the non-exempt activities carried on by companies in the group, although the accounting period of each group member will cease.
- Once the group becomes a REIT, the principal company of the group will be required to submit a tax return for its taxable activity and a computation covering the tax-exempt activities of the entire group. In addition, group companies carrying on taxable activities will need to continue to submit tax returns.
- Capital allowances are deemed to transfer to the new business at tax written down value. It is not possible to change this by making an election to choose a different transfer value under any provisions of the Capital Allowances Act.
- The assets which are 'involved' in the property rental business are deemed to be sold and reacquired at market value on entry. For these purposes, an asset is 'involved' in the property rental business if it is an 'estate, interest or right by the exploitation of which the business is conducted'. Essentially, this will include all properties which are let for rent and the profits of which are taxable as a UK property business or an overseas property business. This includes properties held in joint ventures, unit trusts and partnerships. Any gain or loss accruing on this deemed disposal is not charged to tax.

Entry charge

[3.31] For companies or groups which joined the REIT regime prior to 17 July 2012 an entry charge applied. The entry charge was based on 2% of the gross value of the company or group's qualifying investment properties.

The entry charge was abolished by Finance Act 2012 for all companies or groups which join the regime on or after 17 July 2012.

Acquisitions and disposals near the date of entry

[3.32] An acquisition of property before the date of entry will be included as a qualifying asset at the date of entry provided that:

- the contract date is before the date of entry (for unconditional contracts); or
- the date that all conditions are satisfied occurs before the date of entry (for conditional contracts).

Likewise, a disposal of property before the date of entry will be excluded as a qualifying asset at the date of entry provided that:

- the contract date is before the date of entry (for unconditional contracts); or
- the date that all conditions are satisfied occurs before the date of entry (for conditional contracts).

Treatment of tax losses

[3.33] As mentioned above, the property rental business of each group company is deemed to cease on entry to the regime and a new property rental business begins. The principal effect of this is that losses attaching to those businesses (with the exception of capital losses) are forfeited. These will include UK property business losses and losses of the overseas property business.

Furthermore, losses arising from the first accounting period of the tax-exempt business cannot be carried back to reduce profits earned in accounting periods before a company joined the regime.

Unlike losses relating to a company's tax-exempt business, losses incurred in non tax-exempt activities are not forfeited on joining the REIT regime, and hence can be carried forward and carried back under normal rules.

Capital losses arising from pre-entry activities (including losses from the disposal of assets that would have been utilised for the company's tax-exempt business had they not been disposed of) may be carried forward and used to reduce chargeable gains arising from a post-entry disposal.

The restriction on the use of carried forward corporation tax losses that applies from 1 April 2017 does not apply to a UK-REIT's property rental business (see **3.46** below).

Ownership test and interest cover test

[3.34] There are two further important tests within the REIT regime which are the ownership test and the interest cover test. A breach of these tests will not result in removal from the regime but may result in a tax charge.

Ownership test

[3.35] The ownership test (CTA 2010, ss 551–554) is designed broadly to prevent corporate shareholders from holding 10% or more of the shares in a UK-REIT. Where the test is not met, the UK-REIT (or the principal company of a Group-REIT) may suffer a tax charge. The tax charge applies when a distribution is paid by the UK-REIT to a so-called 'Holder of Excessive Rights', being a company or entity that is treated as a body corporate which:

(a)   is beneficially entitled (directly or indirectly) to 10% or more of the dividends paid by the principal company; or

(b)   is beneficially entitled (directly or indirectly) to 10% or more of the principal company's share capital; or

(c)   controls (directly or indirectly) 10% or more of the voting rights in the principal company.

The reason for the imposition of the charge is to prevent loss of tax to the UK Exchequer through non-resident investors in a UK-REIT making a claim for repayment of tax deducted at source from a property income distribution (see **3.54** below) under the provisions of a tax treaty. In many of the UK's tax treaties, the claim for repayment of tax is increased where a corporate investor holds 10% or more of a company's shares, potentially enabling them to claim repayment of the whole of the income tax deduction from the distribution. Under that scenario profits derived from a UK-REIT's ring fenced business could completely escape taxation in the UK. Although the purpose of the test is to prevent loss of tax in respect of dividends paid to non-resident corporate shareholders, it applies equally to dividends paid to resident corporate shareholders.

If a UK-REIT makes a distribution to a Holder of Excessive Rights, the UK-REIT must provide HMRC with the following information:

• name and address of the person to whom the distribution was made;
• amount of the distribution;
• details regarding the shareholder's interest in the UK-REIT including the percentage interest owned by the shareholder in the UK-REIT's total issued share capital, ordinary share capital, or any other share capital;
• details of the transaction that gave rise to the distribution; and
• what the UK-REIT has done, if anything, to avoid the distribution from having been made (CTA 2010, s 554(2)(b)).

In practice, HMRC may allow groups to fragment their holdings between a number of group companies to ensure that no company breaches the 10% threshold.

Reasonable steps

[3.36] The UK-REIT may avoid a tax charge if it has taken 'reasonable steps' to prevent a distribution from being made to a Holder of Excessive Rights. HMRC have issued guidance (GREIT02125–GREIT02150) on actions that they consider would constitute reasonable steps. These include making changes to the Articles of Association of the UK-REIT company to restrict the creation of a substantial shareholding, or ensuring that any Holder of

Excessive Rights enters into a dividend strip. In this case, the Holder of Excessive Rights would sell their dividend rights to one or more third parties such that neither the Holder of Excessive Rights nor the third parties are beneficially entitled to 10% or more of the UK-REIT dividends.

Assessed tax charge

[3.37] Where a UK-REIT pays a dividend to a Holder of Excessive Rights without having taken reasonable steps to prevent paying the distribution, the principal company will suffer a tax charge (CTA 2010, s 551). The principal company will be treated as having received income, the amount determined by a formula set out below. Tax on the deemed income will be assessed under miscellaneous income (CTA 2010, s 552).

The formula for determining the amount of deemed income is:

$$\left(DO \times SO \times \frac{BRT}{MCT} \right) + \left(DP \times SP \times \frac{BRT}{MCT} \right)$$

where:

DO = the total exempt profits distributed by the ring fenced business with respect to its ordinary shares

SO = the lesser of the percentage of rights in respect of (a) the ordinary shares of the principal company held by the Holder of Excessive Rights or (b) held by the recipient of the distribution

DP = the total exempt profits distributed by the principal company with respect to its preference shares

SP = the lesser percentage of rights in respect of (a) the preference shares held by the Holder of Excessive Rights or (b) held by the recipient of the distribution

BRT = the basic rate of tax in force at the time of distribution

MCT = the corporate rate of tax which applies to the non-ring fenced business.

Example 1

A corporate shareholder owns 20% of the UK-REIT's ordinary share capital and voting rights and 35% of the UK-REIT's preference shares. The shareholder is therefore a Holder of Excessive Rights. The profits of the UK-REIT's tax-exempt property rental business are £1,000,000 during the year and it distributed £900,000 of which the distribution on its preference shares was £60,000. The basic rate of tax is 20%. The corporate tax rate is 20%. At the time of making its distribution, the UK-REIT had not taken any reasonable steps to prevent paying a distribution to the Holder of Excessive Rights.

Upon the UK-REIT's dividend distribution to the 'Holder of Excessive Rights' the principal company of the UK-REIT is deemed to receive income of £189,000 determined as follows:

$$(£840{,}000 \times 20\% \times {}^{20}/_{20}) + (£60{,}000 \times 35\% \times {}^{20}/_{20}) = £189{,}000$$

The UK-REIT would report the income of £189,000 as miscellaneous income for the accounting period in which the distribution was made. Consequently, the tax charge suffered by the UK-REIT (at the normal corporate tax rate of 20%) would be £37,800. This equates to the total amount of distribution received by the Holder of Excessive Rights (£189,000) multiplied by 20%.

It is important to note the following features:

* The tax charge is suffered by the principal company of a Group REIT and therefore all shareholders are indirectly penalised for the shareholder's breach.
* The tax calculation is made by reference to the entire amount of the Holder of Excessive Rights' shareholding rather than simply the amount of the shareholding which exceeds the 10% limit.
* Although the aim of this provision is to prevent loss of tax to the UK Exchequer where treaty claims have been made by non-UK resident corporate investors, the charge will be levied in relation to an excess shareholding held by any corporate investor, whatever their residence status and whether or not the shareholder is within the charge to UK tax.

Interest cover test

[3.38] A UK-REIT will suffer a tax charge if the quantum of its financing costs causes an interest cover ratio to fall below 1.25:1. Some industry commentators have expressed the view that a test of this nature is unnecessary as global REIT markets have generally developed with relatively low levels of gearing. However, the UK Government have not felt comfortable about letting the market decide.

In addition, HMRC identified a potential loss of tax to the UK Exchequer in the event of high levels of interest payments. In particular, were there to be a payment of interest to an unconnected party where a tax deduction for the interest would not be affected by transfer pricing legislation, this would reduce the profits of the tax-exempt business as calculated on a tax basis for the purpose of the distribution test and thereby reduce the distributions payable under deduction of income tax. A further complication could have existed as a result of the relaxation of the distribution condition in circumstances where a UK-REIT is legally prevented from making a distribution. In this case, a UK-REIT could have avoided payment of a distribution even where a large amount of interest is paid on a loan from a connected party where transfer pricing legislation would restrict tax deductions. To the extent that this would have created a restriction of distributable reserves such that no distribution needs to be paid, income payable to the Exchequer would have been reduced.

The interest cover ratio is defined as:

$$\frac{\text{Property Profits}}{\text{Financing Costs}}$$

For a single company REIT, the profit number is the figure calculated under tax principles before the offset of capital allowances and tax deductible financing costs. For a Group REIT, property profits are defined as being the UK profits of the Group REIT's property rental business for the accounting period as set out in the financial statement (G(Tax-exempt)) before deduction of capital allowances and financing costs. This is discussed further at **3.90** below. Tax-exempt rental profits will be those derived from qualifying let property held by UK resident members of the group and UK property owned by non UK resident members of the group. Where the profit number is nil or negative, the interest cover test does not apply.

Financing costs for single entity REITs are broadly as follows:

- interest payable on borrowing taken out for the purposes of the property rental business;
- amortisation of discounts relating to borrowing taken out for the purposes of the property rental business;
- amortisation of premiums relating to borrowing taken out for the purposes of the property rental business;
- amounts in relation to hedging risks of borrowing taken out for the purposes of the property rental business;
- financing expense implicit in payments under a finance lease; and
- alternative finance return (as defined in CTA 2009, ss 511–513).

The calculation of finance costs for a Group REIT is broadly similar but excludes internal financing transactions. This is discussed in more detail at **3.91**.

For accounting periods prior to 17 July 2012, the definition included any costs arising from a financing transaction. In practice, this was a very wide ranging and unclear category of expenditure. Amounts in relation to hedging were not included prior to 1 April 2014 (SI 2014/518).

If a UK-REIT fails to meet the interest cover test, a tax charge is assessed on the principal company of the Group REIT as miscellaneous income for the accounting period in which the breach occurs and may not be offset by any other losses, deficits, expenses, or allowances (CTA 2010, s 543).

For accounting periods beginning on or after 17 July 2012, the tax charge is restricted so that the amount of miscellaneous income subject to corporation tax does not exceed 20% of the UK-REIT's property profits.

The example below illustrates how a tax charge is calculated where a group fails to meet the interest cover test. Under Example A, the interest cover ratio exceeds 1.25 and therefore no tax charge is levied on the UK-REIT. In Example B, the group has incurred financing costs exactly equal to that permitted under the ratio, so again it does not suffer a tax charge. In Example C, the group's financing costs are such that the ratio is less than 1.25. In this case, the principal company will suffer a tax charge. The amount of tax is based on the excess financing costs, which in this example are 100 (900 less 800, the amount which exactly results in a ratio of 1.25). The excess financing costs are then multiplied by the prevailing corporate tax rate (currently 20%). As described above, the aim of this test is to prevent loss to the Exchequer through high interest costs reducing the required level of distributions and thereby reducing the income tax payable.

Example 2

	A	B	C
Profits (after deducting financing costs)	300	200	100
Financing Costs	700	800	900
Profits	1000	1000	1000
Interest cover ratio	1.43:1	1.25:1	1.11:1
Tax Charge	0	0	20

Where a UK-REIT is in severe financial difficulties and fails the interest cover test because of circumstances that have arisen unexpectedly, HMRC has the power to waive the tax charge (CTA 2010, s 543(7)). This let-out applies where the UK-REIT can show it could not reasonably have taken action to avoid the failure.

Operation of the regime

[3.39] As previously described, the aim of the regime is to provide a vehicle which is tax-exempt in respect of the profits of its qualifying property business. Tax on those profits is effectively assessed on the shareholders of the UK-REIT who receive obligatory distributions out of the tax-exempt profits. This section describes how that aim is achieved.

Ring-fenced business and tax exemptions

[3.40] The legislation works by creating a 'ring fence' around that part of the UK-REIT's business which qualifies for tax exemptions. For a single company REIT, the tax-exempt business is deemed to be held in a separate company from the non-tax exempt business. The two separate companies are referred to as C (tax-exempt) and C (residual) respectively.

This treatment is carried through in the context of a Group REIT. Each company within the group may have its own ring fenced company to the extent that it carries on a qualifying UK property rental business. The ring fenced and non-ring fenced businesses of these companies then form deemed groups, G (property rental business) and G (residual). These concepts are explored further at **3.72** onwards.

The foundation of the tax-exempt ring fence of a UK-REIT is the 'property rental business'. This is defined by reference to commonly used tax concepts in the UK such as UK property business and overseas property business. All businesses where profits derived fall to be taxed in this way will therefore automatically fall within the tax-exempt ring fence of a UK-REIT unless the income or type of business is specifically excluded under CTA 2010, ss 604–605 (see **3.43** below).

Property business

[3.41] The property rental business comprises profits that are normally taxable under a property business as defined by CTA 2009, s 205. A property business covers annual profits arising from a business carried on for the exploitation, as a source of rents or other receipts, of any estate, interest or rights in or over land in the UK.

Rental income arising from tied premises that is taxed as a trading receipt under CTA 2009, s 42 may be treated as part of the property rental business (CTA 2010, s 519(2)) in relation to accounting periods ending on or after 22 April 2009. This change was introduced in order to make it easier for certain groups (such as tenanted pub groups) to enter the REIT regime. Certain types of activities are specifically excluded from the scope of the property business. These include:

- Profits arising from the occupation of land. This will include property dealing and the operation of types of trade where there is a substantial provision of services and the activity is taxable as trading income. For example, profits of a company which both owns and manages a hotel will generally be taxable as trading income and this business will therefore not be a qualifying property rental business for REIT purposes.
- Farming and market gardening taxable as trading income under CTA 2009, s 36.
- Profits or rent from mines, quarries and other concerns taxable as trading income.
- Rent in respect of electric-line wayleaves taxable as trading income under CTA 2009, s 277.

PID income received by a UK-REIT in respect of its shareholdings in other UK-REITs will be treated as tax-exempt profits derived from a separate property rental business.

Overseas property business

[3.42] The tax-exempt property rental business also includes income from the exploitation of property which is not situated in the UK and is not trading income and which is derived by a UK resident member of the group. The rules that are applied to determine whether income falls within this category are the same as the property business rules applicable for land located in the UK. In general, losses arising from an overseas property business can only be offset against future profits of the same business. However, for REIT purposes, this restriction is removed and losses are available for offset against all profits of the property rental business, whether the land is situated in the UK or overseas.

Excluded items

[3.43] CTA 2010, ss 604–605 refer to various classes of business and types of income which would normally be taxed as a property business or as the profits of an overseas property business but are nonetheless excluded from being a qualifying property rental business of a UK-REIT. HMRC have the power to make regulations to add or delete items from the list.

The items included in CTA 2010, ss 604–605 are as follows:

- Incidental letting of property held in connection with a trade in property.
- Letting of owner occupied property. Owner occupied property is defined as property which falls in accordance with generally accepted accounting practice to be described as owner occupied.
- Letting of property held for administrative purposes in carrying on the property rental business of the UK-REIT but which is temporarily surplus to those requirements. This relates to space let which is comparatively small compared to the whole space held for administrative purposes and the letting is for a term of not more than three years.
- The provision of services by the UK-REIT in connection with property located outside the UK if income from that service provision would not be taxable under a property business if the property were located in the UK.
- Entering into structured finance arrangements to which CTA 2010, s 770(2) or ITA 2007, s 809BZM(2) applies. In essence, the relevant arrangements will include sales of rental streams which are accounted for as loans.
- Income from caravan sites where material trading activities are carried on as well as the letting of pitches.
- Rents from electric-line wayleaves, siting of gas or oil pipelines, mobile telephone masts or other electronic communication equipment or wind turbines.
- Income from a limited liability partnership in a winding up.

Loan relationship and derivative contracts

[3.44] Debits and credits arising from loan relationships, embedded derivative contracts and certain hedging relationships will also be included within the ring fence provided they have been entered into for the purposes of the tax exempt business. Interest income arising on cash deposits will not be tax exempt, even where the cash represents the proceeds of sale of a qualifying investment property.

Corporate interest restriction rules

[3.45] Corporate interest restriction rules are expected to be introduced in a Finance Bill in late 2017 and will take effect from 1 April 2017. Although a UK-REIT benefits from a corporation tax exemption in respect of its property rental business, it is still required to apply the corporate interest restriction rules to that business when calculating its notional taxable profit. Where an interest disallowance is required under the rules it will increase the amount of notional taxable profit thereby increasing the distribution requirement. In addition, a UK-REIT is required to apply the corporate interest restriction rules to its residual taxable business. An interest disallowance to the residual business will result in an increased corporation tax liability.

There are however special provisions that apply to determine how a UK-REIT should allocate the interest disallowance between its tax-exempt property rental business and its taxable residual business. Under the rules, a UK-REIT is required to calculate the combined total interest disallowance for its entire business (both its property rental business and its residual business). The UK-REIT can then choose to allocate some or all of the total amount to the property rental business or the residual business subject to the following restriction: the allocated interest disallowance to the property rental business must be limited to ensure that the company does not fail its distribution requirement. This could arise where the amount of restricted interest allocated to the property rental business causes the UK-REIT to have insufficient distributable reserves. In general, the distribution requirement is relaxed where a UK-REIT is prevented from paying a distribution because it has insufficient reserves (see **3.18** above). However, HMRC do not want a UK-REIT to be able to rely on this relaxation where the lack of reserves is caused by an allocation of interest disallowance.

In practice, a UK-REIT may prefer to allocate more of the interest disallowance to the residual business in order to avoid having to pay an increased PID. However, this will need to be balanced with the requirement to pay additional corporation tax in the residual business.

Where the amount of the interest disallowance allocated to the residual business exceeds the net tax interest expense of the residual business, it is necessary to bring into account in the accounting period amounts of matching tax interest expense and income equal to the amount of the excess. This ensures that the residual business has sufficient amounts to absorb any disallowed interest not allocated to the property rental business.

Corporation tax loss reform rules

[3.46] The corporation tax loss reform rules which restrict the use of carried forward corporation tax losses, applicable from 1 April 2017, do not apply to a UK-REIT when it calculates the profits of its tax-exempt property rental business.

Capital gains considerations

[3.47] CTA 2010, s 535 provides that a gain which accrues to a UK-REIT on the disposal of an asset which was used wholly and exclusively for the purposes of the tax exempt business is not a chargeable gain. In practice, this will confer exemption on properties which are used wholly in the property rental business. It does not, however, provide exemption for the following disposals:

- shares in companies (regardless of whether they own qualifying rental properties);

- properties which are let but sold as trading stock;
- properties which fall to be treated under the three-year development rule (see **3.50**); or
- properties of the non-exempt business (eg owner occupied property).

These disposals will still be chargeable to tax in the normal way.

Where the disposal of property out of the ring-fenced business amounts to a trade or adventure in the nature of trade, the sale will not be within the ring-fence, but will instead be taxed as trading income as part of the non-tax exempt business. For the purposes of the disposal, the property is treated as though it had never been within the ring fence and the company can reclaim any entry charge attributable to the property.

Although not specified in the REIT legislation one assumes that a property used within the rental business as an investment property would still be capable of being appropriated to trading stock within the same company. In such a situation we would expect the property rental business to recognise a tax exempt disposal at market value, which becomes the base cost of the trading property within the residual business of the company.

Property not wholly and exclusively used for the tax-exempt business

[3.48] Special rules apply where a property is sold that has not been used exclusively in the property rental business. If the periods where the property was used wholly or partly in the non-property rental business amount in aggregate to less than one year, this use is ignored and the whole gain accruing on disposal of the property is exempt.

Where the property has been used wholly or partly in the non-property rental business for periods which in aggregate amount to more than one year, the gain should be apportioned taking into account both the length of time of the alternative use and the extent of this use. Only that portion which reflects the percentage of use in the property rental business is then exempt.

A disposal of part of a property that qualifies for the tax exempt business will not be subject to capital gains tax, regardless of whether the remaining part qualifies or not.

Transfers within a UK-REIT

[3.49] Movement of assets from the non-exempt business to the exempt business will be considered as a deemed sale and reacquisition at market value, and will be chargeable to tax at the standard corporation tax rate. TCGA 1992, s 171 will not apply in this scenario.

A Group REIT will consist of two capital gains groups: one made up of all of the tax-exempt businesses within the Group REIT, and the other made up of all of the non-exempt businesses (CTA 2010, s 601). Consequently, transfers from the non-exempt business across the ring-fence cannot be made under TCGA 1992, s 171(1), as the two businesses are not members of the same capital gains group.

Movement of assets in the reverse direction will, however, be exempt from tax, and the value of the property will be uplifted to its market value at the date of transfer.

Development rule

[3.50] Profits arising on the sale of 'developed property' will be treated as non-qualifying income if the property is sold within three years of the completion of the development. A property will be considered a 'developed property' for these purposes where the cost of development exceeds 30% of the fair value of the property. The value of the property is determined at the time of entry into the REIT regime or at the time the property was acquired, whichever is later, in accordance with international accounting standards (CTA 2010, s 556(3)). HMRC have confirmed that 'costs' generally include all advisors' fees etc associated with the development.

Where a UK-REIT disposes of a developed property to a person other than another member of the same group, any previous deemed acquisition by the UK-REIT and corresponding uplift in basis allowed at that time is disregarded. On sale, the property is treated as having been disposed of by the non-ring fenced business (CTA 2010, s 556(2)). The sale may be on trading account or on capital account according to the normal rules. If the UK-REIT disposes of a 'developed property' outside of three years from the time of completion, the disposal may be within the ring fenced business provided it is not categorised as a trading transaction according to the normal rules.

HMRC have confirmed in guidance that the development rule will not apply in respect of a property development that was fully completed prior to REIT conversion.

Example 3

Assume a group elects into the REIT regime and owns an investment property that is valued at £10m with a tax basis of £6m. As a result of the entry into the regime, the asset is deemed to be sold by the pre-entry company and reacquired by the UK-REIT at market value, being £10m in this example. Further assume the UK-REIT subsequently develops the property and incurs £4.5m of development costs, in which case the development costs will be 45% of the property value, exceeding the 30% threshold.

Scenario 1

If the UK-REIT retains the developed property and continues to maintain the asset as an investment property, there is no impact on the property-holding company as the asset will not have been transferred across the ring fence.

Tax basis prior to entry	£6m
Tax basis immediately after entry	£10m
Tax basis after development	£14.5m

Scenario 2

If the UK-REIT disposes of the asset to a person other than another member of the same group within three years of development, it will be deemed a taxable transaction either on trading account or capital account according to the normal rules. In this case, the deemed sale and reacquisition at the time of entry into the REIT regime and the corresponding uplift in tax basis to market value is disregarded (CTA 2010, s 556(2)). The non-ring fenced business of the property-holding company is treated as having disposed of the asset.

Tax basis prior to entry	£6m
Tax basis immediately after entry	£10m
Tax basis after development	£10.5m (£6m + £4.5m)

Where a group member disposes of a developed property and that company paid the 2% entry charge in respect of the property, a credit may be taken against the tax due upon the sale of the developed property. The credit is determined by the ratio of:

$$\frac{\text{Asset Market Value} \times \text{Tax Paid}}{\text{Market Value}}$$

The 'asset market value' is the value of the asset at the time of entry into the regime (in the example above, £10m). The 'aggregate market value' is the value of all assets at the time of entry for which the 2% entry charge was paid. The 'tax paid' is the total amount of tax that was paid on entry (CTA 2010, s 556(4)).

Capital allowances

[3.51] In calculating the profit of the tax-exempt business, it is necessary to deduct any capital allowances to which the UK-REIT is entitled. A UK-REIT is obliged to take into account the maximum allowances available to it. It is not possible to disclaim any of the allowances. The effect of the capital allowances is to reduce the amount of dividends which the UK-REIT or principal company of the Group REIT needs to distribute each year.

When a company joins the REIT regime, assets are transferred across the ring-fence at their tax written down value at the date of entry into the regime. Similarly, when a company leaves the REIT regime or when it transfers an asset across the ring-fence assets are transferred at their tax written down value for capital allowance purposes. No section 198 elections are possible for these transfers. When a UK-REIT either acquires an asset or sells an asset to a third party, it can however enter into a section 198 election in the normal way.

A UK-REIT may claim for land remediation relief, which provides a deduction of 100%, plus an additional deduction of 50%, for qualifying expenditure incurred in bringing long-term derelict land back into use. Alternatively, a UK-REIT may claim a tax credit equivalent to 16% of the qualifying land remediation expenditure where a loss has been made in respect of its property rental business.

A UK-REIT may also claim 100% first-year capital allowances for expenditure on specific energy-saving plant and machinery (Enhanced Capital Allowances, or 'ECAs'). HMRC have confirmed that it is not possible for a UK-REIT to claim a tax credit in respect of ECAs on the basis that the property rental business is not within the charge to corporation tax.

Distributions

[3.52] Distributions from a UK-REIT or the principal company of a Group REIT have a different treatment from those paid by other UK companies. This is principally due to the fact that the profits being distributed will not have been taxed in the UK-REIT and, therefore, the income needs to be taxed in the hands of the REIT shareholder. In addition, the UK-REIT is required to withhold taxation at source on some distributions.

Distributions paid out of tax exempt income are generally referred to as Property Income Distributions (PIDs). Distributions out of non-exempt profits will be treated as normal dividends. The UK-REIT or principal company of a Group REIT is responsible for collecting and paying all withholding taxes, and informing shareholders what type of dividends are being paid.

Distribution requirement

[3.53] UK-REITs must distribute at least 90% of their tax-exempt income profits and 100% of their PIDs received from other UK-REITs within 12 months of the accounting period end as a dividend. Therefore, a UK-REIT will have to calculate its tax exempt profits (after capital allowances and interest), in advance of the payment deadline to provide sufficient time for this requirement to be met. There is no obligation to distribute profits arising from tax exempt gains.

Where the amount of the PID paid by a UK-REIT is insufficient to meet the distribution requirement, because of changes to the tax returns resulting from an HMRC enquiry, the UK-REIT has a period of three months in which to make an additional distribution out of tax exempt profits without incurring a penalty tax charge. The need to pay a dividend precludes the ability of a UK-REIT to satisfy the distribution requirement by way of a share buy-back. The three-month extension applies only to a shortfall in respect of the 90% distribution requirement; it does not apply where a UK-REIT has failed to meet the 100% distribution requirement in respect of PIDs received from other UK-REITs.

Where the distribution requirement is not met the UK-REIT will suffer a tax charge based on the shortfall of the distribution against the requirement.

Profits for each period are apportioned between six 'pots' for the purposes of determining which distributions are made. Details of these pots are shown below:

POT	PID or Normal dividend	Profits
Pot A	PID	PIDs received from investments in other UK-REITs
Pot B	PID	Tax-exempt rental income profits (90% distribution requirement)
Pot C	Normal	Non-exempt income (trading etc), tax accounting reconciliation differences (eg capital allowances) and pre-conversion undistributed income profits.

POT	PID or Normal dividend	Profits
Pot D	PID	Additional 10% tax-exempt rental income profits
Pot E	PID	Tax exempt gains
Pot F	Normal	Other profits including chargeable gains and tax accounting reconciliation differences on tax exempt gains and pre-conversion undistributed gains.

Property income distributions

[3.54] When a UK-REIT pays a PID, it must withhold income tax from the distribution at the basic rate (currently 20%) (SI 2006/2867, reg 3). The tax credit normally associated with a dividend from a UK company is not available in respect of PIDs.

The UK-REIT or principal company of a Group REIT must submit a return to HMRC for each period in which it makes a PID (SI 2006/2867, reg 4). The return periods are 31 March, 30 June, 30 September, and 31 December each year. The return is due within 14 days after the end of the return period. The UK-REIT must also provide to the shareholder a statement indicating the gross amount of the PID, the amount of tax deducted, and the net distribution being paid to the shareholder.

Certain shareholders will however be entitled to receive PIDs from the UK-REIT without any deduction of income tax (SI 2006/2867, reg 7). Among others, these include:

- a UK tax resident company;
- a non-UK tax resident company that carries on a business through a permanent establishment and is required to bring into account a payment of a relevant distribution in computing its chargeable profits;
- a local authority;
- a charity within the meaning of ICTA 1988, s 506(1);
- the scheme administrator of a registered pension scheme;
- a health service body;
- a public office or department of the Crown;
- the account manager of an ISA account;
- the plan manager of a PEP.

It is normal practice for UK-REITs to determine which shareholders are entitled to receive PIDs without the deduction of basic rate tax. UK-REITs will normally be entitled to obtain the relevant information directly from shareholders in order to ascertain which shareholders qualify for gross dividends.

To qualify as a PID, the dividend can be paid in cash or share capital.

Normal dividends

[3.55] Where a UK-REIT pays a dividend out of either Pot C or Pot F, the treatment of the distribution will be the same as a normal corporate dividend.

Attribution of distributions

[3.56] Dividends must be attributed according to a specific set of rules. A UK-REIT is required to distribute firstly 100% of its PID income received from other UK-REITs. Secondly, it must distribute at least 90% of its rental income profits (CTA 2010, s 550(2)). Once these distribution requirements have been met, by payments out of Pots A and B, a UK-REIT must broadly allocate any further dividend either against Pots C–F in that order or against Pots D–F in that order. In other words, the UK-REIT has flexibility in how much to allocate to Pot C, thereby providing some choice over the apportionment of dividends between PID and normal dividend.

The following example illustrates the attribution rules.

Example 4

	Accounts £	CA's £	Indexation £	Profits as calculated for tax purposes £
PID income from other UK-REITs	100			100
Rental income profit after interest	1,090	(90)		1,000
Tax-exempt gains	200		(20)	180
Trading income	150			150
Gain on sale of HQ building	50			50
Distributable reserves	1,590			
Dividend	(1,250)			
Taken to reserves	340			

The distributable reserves will be apportioned to each of the six 'pots' as shown in the table below.

Scenario 1 in the table below shows the allocation for a UK-REIT that wishes to pay maximum PID possible. In this scenario reserves in Pot C, Pot E and Pot F will be carried forward.

Scenario 2 in the table below shows the allocation for a UK-REIT that wishes to pay minimum PID possible. In this scenario reserves in Pot D, Pot E and Pot F will be carried forward.

	Rental income (incl PID income)	Tax exempt gains	Trading	Other Gains	Total	Scenario 1	Scenario 2
Pot A	100				100	100	100
Pot B	900				900	900	900
Pot C	90		150		240	0	240
Pot D	100				100	100	10
Pot E		180			180	150	
Pot F		20		50	70		
	1,190	200	150	50	1,590	1,250	1,250

Taxation of shareholders

Property income distributions

[3.57] For a UK individual shareholder, a PID will be taxed as income arising from a property business, rather than as a normal UK dividend. The UK-REIT will have already withheld tax at the basic rate before making such a distribution. Accordingly, a UK individual shareholder will owe additional tax only to the extent that their individual rate exceeds the basic rate, or will receive a repayment of tax to the extent that the individual's total income does not exceed their income tax personal allowance.

For a UK corporate shareholder a PID will be taxed as income arising from a property business (CTA 2010, s 548(5)). No withholding tax will have been withheld by the UK-REIT. Accordingly the dividend will be fully taxable in the UK corporate's hands at its relevant rate of corporation tax.

The property business tax treatment will also apply to companies that are partners in a partnership which holds shares in the UK-REIT.

The tax treatment described above will not apply to UK shareholders who are subject to tax on trading income in relation to receipts of dividends from UK companies, such as financial traders and Lloyd's members. A PID will be a trading receipt in their hands to the extent the shares of the UK-REIT are part of their trade.

PIDs payable to non-resident corporate shareholders that carry on a trade in the UK through a permanent establishment are chargeable to tax as profits of a property business where the UK-REIT shares are held by or held for the purposes of the trade.

PIDs payable to other non-resident shareholders are chargeable to income tax, which is collected by deduction at source. The provisions of the non-resident landlord scheme will not apply to these PIDs. Where a non-resident shareholder resides in a country with which the UK has a double tax treaty, the income tax from the PID may be repayable by making the appropriate claim. As discussed at **3.35** above, the regime seeks to prevent corporate shareholders from holding 10% or more of the UK-REIT's shares. Accordingly, the tax that a non-resident shareholder would suffer after making a claim under any of the UK's double tax treaties would likely be maximum 15%.

Normal dividends

[3.58] As discussed above, dividends paid out of a UK-REIT's non-tax exempt business will be treated in the hands of the shareholder as a normal dividend. No withholding will be made by the UK-REIT on the distribution and shareholders will report receipt of the distribution as franked investment income. The normal one-ninth tax credit available on a dividend from a UK resident company (up until April 2016) will attach to a distribution from the UK-REIT's non-tax exempt business.

Manufactured dividends

[3.59] The current rules for manufactured dividends on UK shares will apply equally to dividends paid by a UK-REIT. Broadly, the manufactured dividend received will be treated as property income and will be subject to the deduction of basic rate income tax. The rules are set out in ITA 2007, s 918.

Dividend stripping

[3.60] The standard rules in relation to dividend stripping still apply to a UK-REIT and where this arises a UK-REIT is obliged to withhold tax on a payment of a stripped dividend, regardless of the nature of the recipient. A repayment of the tax withheld can be claimed by the recipient if applicable. The vendor of the strip of a PID will be subject to the normal rules under CTA 2010, ss 752–757.

Shareholder returns on distributions

[3.61] In general, shareholders investing in a UK-REIT would expect a higher return on their investment as a result of the UK-REIT's requirement to distribute at least 90% of the profits derived from its ring fenced business. Additionally, because of the tax exempt status the UK-REIT enjoys with respect to the majority of its income, it should generally have more funds available to distribute to shareholders. It is worth examining, however, the potential impact of the regime on various types of shareholders.

UK corporate shareholder

[3.62] For a UK corporate investing in a UK-REIT, it will generally be tax neutral as compared with investing in any other UK corporate entity (see Table 1 below) assuming there is a full available distribution of profits and assuming taxable and accounting profits are identical. The only difference is the level at which tax is levied. Normally, tax would be paid by the UK corporate before its distribution to shareholders and then the investing UK entity would not owe any additional tax upon receipt of the dividend. Under the REIT regime, the UK corporate will receive its distribution gross, without any deduction of income tax, but will pay the tax due on the ring fenced profits itself as property business profits distinct from other property business profits that it may receive. Therefore, the shareholder will not be able to offset property business losses against PID receipts.

Table 1 – UK Corporate Shareholder – 2017/18

	Non-REIT	UK-REIT
Taxable profits (ring fenced)	100	100
Tax	(19)	0
Distribution (maximum)	80	100
Shareholder tax	0	(19)
Net distribution	81	81

UK tax-exempt shareholder

[3.63] There is a distinct advantage for tax-exempt entities when investing in a UK-REIT. As illustrated in Table 2 below, a tax-exempt entity investing in a UK-REIT would receive its distribution of the UK-REIT ring fenced profits without any deduction of income tax. Where the tax-exempt entity invests in a normal UK corporate, the corporate is subject to tax regardless of the tax-exempt entity's investment, thereby reducing the available return.

Table 2 – UK Tax-Exempt Shareholder – 2017/18

	Non-REIT	UK-REIT
Taxable profits (ring fenced)	100	100
Tax	(19)	0
Distribution (maximum)	81	100
Shareholder tax	0	0
Net distribution	81	100

UK individual shareholder

[3.64] UK higher rate and additional rate individual shareholders are likely to pay less tax in respect of distributions on REIT investments. However, this assumes that because of the UK-REIT's tax exempt status, it should be able to distribute more cash to its shareholders.

Table 3 – UK Higher Rate Individual Shareholder (40%) – 2017/18

	Non-REIT	UK-REIT
Taxable profits (ring fenced)	100	100
Tax	(19)	0
Distribution (maximum)	81	100
Shareholder tax	(26)	(40)

	Non-REIT	UK-REIT
Net distribution	55	60

Table 4 – UK Additional Rate Individual Shareholder (45%) – 2017/18

	Non-REIT	UK-REIT
Taxable profits (ring fenced)	100	100
Tax	(19)	0
Distribution (maximum)	81	100
Shareholder tax	(31)	(45)
Net distribution	50	55

Overseas shareholder (non-treaty jurisdiction)

[3.65] Overseas shareholders should generally be in broadly the same position investing in UK-REITs as compared with investing in other UK non-REIT companies (see Table 5 below). If the shareholder is located in a country with which the UK has a tax treaty, it is possible that the shareholder can reclaim tax withheld to reduce the tax suffered to only 15% (or possibly less in some cases) which could increase the net distribution in the example below from 80 to 85. Ultimately, however, the overall tax benefit to the overseas shareholder will depend on the tax treatment of the dividend in their home country.

Table 5 – Overseas Shareholder (Non-Treaty Jurisdiction) – 2017/18

	Non-REIT	UK-REIT
Taxable profits (ring fenced)	100	100
Tax	(19)	0
Distribution (maximum)	81	100
Shareholder tax	0	(20)
Net distribution	81	80

Exit from the regime

Ways of leaving the regime

[3.66] There are three ways in which a company or group may leave the regime as set out below.

Voluntary exit

[3.67] A UK-REIT or Group REIT may voluntarily elect out of the REIT regime by providing a notice to HMRC (CTA 2010, s 571). The notice must be made by the UK-REIT or the principal company of a Group REIT, and specify the date on which the regime will cease to apply. The date specified must be after the date HMRC receives the notice.

Where a company ceases to operate within the REIT regime by reason of giving notice to HMRC and the regime has applied to the company for less than ten years, tax will be assessed on a different basis for any disposal of an asset that takes place within two years of the date of cessation (CTA 2010, s 581). The tax charge will be determined without accounting for the basis adjustments of any deemed disposals on entry or exit from the regime, or on movements out of the tax-exempt business (CTA 2010, s 581(6)). There will also be no refund of any entry charge attributable to the asset.

HMRC notice

[3.68] HMRC may provide written notice to a UK-REIT indicating that it is terminating its REIT status (CTA 2010, s 572). There are certain conditions under which HMRC may provide such notice to a company, as follows:

- if the UK-REIT has relied on the minor or inadvertent breach conditions in excess of the allowed number of breaches (see **3.19** above);
- if the UK-REIT has been given two notices from HMRC indicating cancellation of a tax advantage obtained by the UK-REIT within a ten-year period (see **3.84** below); or
- if HMRC believes that a breach of the property conditions or balance of business tests, or an attempt to obtain a tax advantage, is so serious that the REIT regime should no longer apply to the company; or
- if a newly formed UK-REIT fails to meet the close company condition (organisation condition D) after the expiry of its first three years (CTA 2010, s 573A – see **3.27** above); or
- if a newly formed AIM listed REIT does not meet the share trading requirement after the expiry of its first three years (CTA 2010, s 573B – see **3.27** above).

Any notice from HMRC to the UK-REIT must state the reason for issuance of the notice. Where a UK-REIT receives a notice from HMRC, the REIT regime will be deemed to have ceased applying from a date before the notice is given. A right of appeal is provided for a UK-REIT that receives a notice. The appeal must be filed with HMRC in writing within 30 days of the termination notice having been given to the UK-REIT.

Where a company ceases to operate within the REIT regime by reason of having received notice from HMRC and the regime applied to the company for less than ten years, HMRC may alter the date of cessation that would normally apply to the company and remove tax exemption from the property rental business. Additionally, HMRC may modify the tax effect resulting from any application of the REIT legislation. A company may appeal should HMRC make an adjustment under this provision.

Automatic exit

[3.69] A UK-REIT will suffer automatic termination of its REIT status if the UK-REIT or principal company of a Group REIT fails to satisfy any of the following company conditions in an accounting period (CTA 2010, s 578):

- UK tax resident company and not resident in another jurisdiction for tax purposes;

- it is not an OEIC;
- it has only one class of ordinary shares and the only other class of shares it has is non-voting fixed rate preference shares; or
- it must not borrow money on terms that effectively entitle the lender to a share of the profits of the UK-REIT.

Where a company suffers an automatic termination of its REIT status, the regime will cease to apply to the company from the end of the previous accounting period. Accordingly, if for example, a company with a 31 December year end suffers an automatic termination in September 2012, its REIT status will be deemed to have ended on 31 December 2011. A company is required to notify HMRC 'as soon as is reasonably practicable' if it has breached one of the conditions listed above.

Where a company ceases to operate within the REIT regime by reason of having suffered an automatic termination and the regime applied to the company for less than ten years, HMRC may alter the date of cessation that would normally apply to the company and remove tax exemption from the property rental business. Additionally, HMRC may modify the tax effect resulting from any application of the REIT legislation. A company may appeal should HMRC make an adjustment under this clause.

A group member will also automatically leave the REIT regime if it is no longer a 75% subsidiary of the principal company. The same exit rules apply in this situation in respect of that group member only. HMRC have confirmed that in the case of a takeover, it should be possible for the relevant company to end its accounting period immediately before the takeover, in order to mitigate the tax costs of exiting the regime. In addition, loss of REIT status may be avoided if the demerger provisions apply or if a joint venture election is made. See also **3.86–3.87** below in relation to the disposal of a company.

Tax effects of exit

[3.70] When a UK-REIT or a Group REIT exits the REIT regime, the tax consequences mirror many of the effects of entry described in **3.30** above relating to the tax effects of a company or group entering the regime.

- The tax-exempt property business of the company is treated as ceasing (CTA 2010, s 579(3)). However, this deemed cessation does not apply to the other activities carried out by the company.
- A tax accounting period of the company is treated as ceasing and a new accounting period begins.
- The qualifying properties which are 'involved' in the property rental business are deemed to be sold and reacquired at market value on entry. Any gain accruing on this deemed disposal is not charged to tax, as the disposing company would still be within the regime at the time of disposal. However, if any of these properties are sold within two years of the date of exit, this deemed sale and reacquisition is ignored. In addition, the deemed sale and reacquisition at market value that occurred when the company entered into the UK-REIT regime (see **3.30**) is also ignored. Accordingly, the tax basis of a property sold within two years of exit from the regime is its historic tax basis prior to entering the

regime. If the property has been the subject of an intra-group transfer in the six years prior to exiting the regime, the rebasing to market value that occurs under the degrouping rules is still valid and is not impacted by the two-year disposal rule.

- Capital allowances are deemed to transfer to the new business at tax written down value. It is not possible to change this by making an election to choose a different transfer value under CAA 2001, s 198 or 199.
- There is no exit charge on leaving the regime. However, as described above in **3.67**, there may be additional tax arising on disposals of assets that take place within two years of the date of cessation.
- Where a single company UK-REIT voluntarily elects to leave the REIT regime within ten years of joining the regime, the two-year disposal rule as described in **3.67** will apply. This rule does not however apply where a single company UK-REIT leaves the regime either by way of HMRC notice or by automatic exit.
- Where a company which is a member of a group REIT leaves the group REIT, the two-year disposal rule also applies to the company leaving the regime. In this case it is regardless of how the company exits the regime.

Treatment of tax losses

[3.71] As the tax-exempt business is deemed to cease on exit from the regime, losses relating to the ring-fenced business, including capital losses, cannot be carried forward. Furthermore, losses arising from the first accounting period after a company's exit from the regime cannot be carried back to reduce profits earned in accounting periods before the company left the regime.

Losses relating to non-tax exempt activities are not affected by a company's exit from the regime, and can be carried forward and carried back under normal rules.

Capital losses relating to assets outside the ring fence can be carried forward after exiting the regime. Likewise, capital losses relating to rental property disposed of before the company's entry into the regime can also be carried forward after exiting the regime. However, as mentioned above, capital losses incurred in the tax-exempt business within the REIT regime cannot be carried forward.

Application of the regime to groups of companies

[3.72] The Group REIT regime applies broadly to groups as defined for chargeable gains tax purposes. The Group REIT includes all 75% owned subsidiaries which are also 51% effective subsidiaries (CTA 2010, s 606(1)). A subsidiary will not be included in the group if it is an insurance company, an insurance subsidiary, or an OEIC (CTA 2010, 606(2)). Additionally, a subsidiary may not be a member of more than one group unless it is an elected corporate joint venture. If a circumstance arises where a company would be a member of more than one group, the rules for capital gains tax groups (see CHAPTER 14) will apply to determine the grouping (CTA 2010, s 606(3)).

Conditions

[3.73] The organisation conditions must be met by the parent company of the REIT group. The other conditions and tests (property conditions, distribution test, balance of business tests, interest cover test, etc) must be met on a consolidated group basis. The REIT's proportionate interest in the assets and profits of an at least 75% owned subsidiary will be included in the REIT tests. However, where the Group REIT owns less than 75% of the subsidiary, the Group REIT's interest in the entity will be considered part of the non-ring fenced business, regardless of the business carried on by the subsidiary. There is an exception to this rule in the case of corporate joint ventures (see **3.79** below).

Financial statements

[3.74] Group REITs have an obligation to provide HMRC with some specific financial statements (CTA 2010, s 527(2)(e)). The company must provide three statements: one statement for the members with respect to their worldwide property rental business (G (Property Rental Business)), one for the members with respect to their UK property rental business (G (Tax Exempt)), and one for the members with respect to their worldwide non-ring fenced business (G (Residual)). The financial statements must be filed with the principal company's tax return for the relevant accounting period (SI 2006/2865, reg 13). The purpose of the statements is to provide HMRC with enough information so that they can determine if the Group REIT has satisfied the balance of business and distribution tests for the accounting period.

The financial statements for the worldwide ring fenced and non-ring fenced businesses are required for the purpose of ensuring that the group REIT has satisfied the balance of business tests and the interest cover test (see **3.38**). Each financial statement should be calculated in accordance with international accounting standards ('IAS') and must specify the respective group's income, expenses, profits, and assets (CTA 2010, s 533(1)). Profits should be calculated before tax and exclude any gains or losses, regardless of whether they are realised or unrealised. Assets should be valued at the beginning of the accounting period using fair value and disregarding any liabilities secured against the property. The Group REIT must also submit a reconciliation between the ring fenced and non-ring fenced financial statements and the audited financial statements of the group for the accounting period (SI 2006/2865, reg 5(4)).

The financial statement for the group's UK property rental business is required for the purpose of determining whether the Group REIT has satisfied the 90% distribution requirement with respect to the profits of its property rental business. Profits for the purposes of this statement are as calculated for tax (CTA 2010, s 533(2)). Profits are measured based on income and exclude any realised or unrealised gains. Intercompany payments are not ignored in preparation of this financial statement, but because it is based on taxable profits, dividends between UK members are not included. There is no requirement to provide a balance sheet with respect to the UK property rental business. Further details on the Group REIT's financial statements are given in **3.90** below.

Non-resident group members

[3.75] A Group REIT is not prohibited from holding property investments through non UK resident group companies. However, if it does, special provisions apply depending on whether the property is located in the UK or overseas.

UK property

[3.76] Rental profits derived from UK property held by a non-resident group member are exempt from corporation tax. This is achieved by treating the profits from UK property as chargeable to corporation tax but falling within the tax exemption conferred by the regime (CTA 2010, s 520). The non-resident company is also not subject to income tax that might otherwise be payable under the Non-Resident Landlord Scheme.

If tax is also suffered overseas on the rental profits, double tax relief will not be available as a credit against UK tax because no UK tax will be suffered. Therefore, the only mechanism to obtain relief for the tax suffered is to claim a deduction for the tax as an expense under ICTA 1988, s 811. The effect of this is to reduce the profits of the exempt business calculated using tax principles and therefore reduce the pool of profits which must be distributed as a PID under deduction of basic rate income tax rather than as a normal dividend.

Where a non-UK resident company holding UK property pays a dividend to a UK resident member of the Group REIT this will be exempt from corporation tax, assuming it meets the conditions within CTA 2009, Part 9A.

Overseas property

[3.77] The special exemptions conferred on rental profits from UK property do not affect the treatment of overseas property held. Therefore, if a non-resident member of a Group REIT owns a property located overseas, the taxation of profits from that property will follow the same principles as if the Group were not in the REIT regime. Tax may be payable overseas on rental profits. Dividends paid out of these profits to a UK resident member of the group should be exempt from corporation tax assuming the conditions within CTA 2009, Part 9A are met.

Indirect ownership of property

[3.78] A UK-REIT may hold property indirectly through a number of vehicles such as a corporate joint venture company, unit trust or partnership. The nature of the vehicle will determine the treatment for the purposes of the various REIT tests.

Corporate joint ventures

[3.79] Where a UK-REIT holds property through a corporate entity that does not qualify as a group member (for example where it holds less than 75% of the ordinary share capital) the shareholding will form part of the non-ring fenced business of the REIT unless the entity qualifies as a corporate joint venture and is elected into the regime. A UK-REIT can elect a single joint venture company or a joint venture group into the REIT regime. The rules for each are set out in different parts of the legislation but are broadly the same. There are seven conditions that must be satisfied in order for a joint venture company or group to be eligible for election into the REIT regime. The seven conditions are as follows:

(1)   the UK-REIT is carrying on the joint venture with another person;
(2)   the corporate joint venture (or at least one of the members of the joint venture group) is carrying on a property rental business;
(3)   the joint venture is a company or a joint venture group;
(4)   the UK-REIT (or its member with the corporate joint venture interest) is beneficially entitled to 40% or more of the profits available for distribution;
(5)   the UK-REIT (or its member with the corporate joint venture interest) is beneficially entitled to 40% or more of the assets available to equity holders in the event of a winding up;
(6)   the corporate joint venture's property rental business does not involve owner-occupied property; and
(7)   the corporate joint venture would satisfy the REIT balance of business tests if the legislation referred to a corporate joint venture company.

Once the UK-REIT elects to treat the corporate joint venture as a member of the REIT, the election will apply unless or until the UK-REIT fails either the fourth or fifth condition listed above. The company must give notice to HMRC specifying a date from which it is electing to include the corporate joint venture. The election must be made prior to the date specified in the notice for which the UK-REIT wants to include the corporate joint venture. The notice must specify the company for which it is electing and the accounting period for which the election will apply. The election is a joint election made by the joint venture company and the principal REIT company. The effect of the election is to bring the UK-REIT's share of the underlying assets and income of the corporate joint venture into its tax exempt business for the purposes of the Balance of Business tests.

The relevant legislation requires the exempt profits to be calculated by reference to the profits after tax rather than profits before tax. This means that in practice the percentage of profits exempted from tax is slightly higher than the UK-REIT's effective interest in the corporate joint venture. The UK-REIT will want to make sure that its corporate joint venture shareholders agreement is drafted appropriately to take this into account and to ensure that all of the tax savings within the corporate joint venture are not shared with its joint venture partner.

Non-elected corporate joint ventures

[3.80] Non-elected corporate joint ventures are treated as 'opaque' for REIT purposes. Therefore, the activities of the entity will be fully taxable. The UK-REIT joint venturer will treat the income of the joint venture as falling outside the tax exempt ring fence. For the purposes of the Balance of Business asset test the value of the shares in the non-elected corporate joint venture will be treated as a 'bad asset'. For the purposes of the Balance of Business income test, any movement in the fair value of the shares together with any dividends received from the non-elected corporate joint venture will be treated as 'bad income'.

Offshore unit trusts

[3.81] An analysis of the UK tax treatment of offshore unit trusts is outside the scope of this chapter but some general comments can be made. Certain offshore unit trusts may be treated as transparent for the purposes of UK tax on income depending on the terms of the Trust Deed and interpretation of local law. These are colloquially known as 'Baker Trusts'. However, UK tax legislation treats these trusts as opaque for capital gains tax purposes.

If a UK member of a Group REIT is a unit holder in a 'Baker' trust which owns UK property, the rental income arising from the property will be taxed as property business profits in the hands of the unit holder and will therefore fall to be treated as part of the tax exempt property rental business of the member.

A sale or full or partial redemption of units in the unit trust will also be taxable because of the capital gains tax opacity of the trust.

See **3.99** below for comments on how these investments are treated for the balance of business tests.

Onshore unit trusts

[3.82] Distributions from UK authorised or unauthorised unit trusts will be taxable in the residual (non-property rental business) part of the member of the Group REIT which holds the units.

A sale or full or partial redemption of units in the unit trust will also be taxable because of the capital gains tax opacity of the trust.

See **3.99** below for comments on how these investments are treated for the balance of business tests.

Partnerships

[3.83] An English limited partnership will be treated as tax transparent for UK tax purposes and the treatment of income and assets will therefore be the same as for an offshore 'Baker' trust. If the partnership is constituted under foreign law, it may be treated as transparent for UK income tax purposes depending on the analysis of the principles of foreign law. A list of foreign partnerships which HMRC view as transparent is given in Tax Bulletin 50.

See **3.99** below for comments on how investments in partnerships are treated for the balance of business tests.

Anti-avoidance

Cancellation of tax advantage

[3.84] Where HMRC believes that the UK-REIT has tried to obtain a tax advantage, it may issue a notice specifying the advantage and indicating how HMRC will counteract the advantage obtained (CTA 2010, s 545(1)). In order to cancel a tax advantage obtained by the UK-REIT, HMRC can issue an assessment against the company, cancel a right of repayment, require the company to return a repayment already made, recompute the tax liability due based on the cancellation of the advantage, as well as impose an additional tax charge equal to the amount of the tax advantage (CTA 2010, s 545(2)–(4)). A UK-REIT will not be deemed to have obtained a tax advantage simply by having elected into the REIT regime, unless entering the regime has as its sole or main purpose the creation, inflation or application of a loss, deduction or expense (CTA 2010, s 545(6)).

HMRC has the power to terminate REIT status if the UK-REIT has received two or more notices specifying a tax advantage in any ten-year period (CTA 2010, s 573).

Prescribed arrangements

[3.85] HMRC have issued regulations (SI 2009/3315), which prevent groups in certain circumstances from restructuring their activities to enable them to meet the UK-REIT conditions and tests. Broadly, the regulations will apply where a UK-REIT (or a member of a Group REIT) enters into 'prescribed arrangements' with a counterparty which leads to an adjustment of the UK-REIT's income, expenses, assets or liabilities. In these circumstances the counterparty may be treated as a member of the Group REIT. This would have the effect of cancelling any advantage that would otherwise have been obtained where the counterparty is a degrouped entity. 'Prescribed arrangements' are defined as arrangements which have the purpose or one of the main purposes of allowing a UK-REIT to meet one or more of the property conditions, balance of business conditions or distribution condition, when without the arrangements those conditions would not be satisfied.

In particular, these regulations seek to prevent occupier groups, such as managed pub groups, from using companies limited by guarantee to degroup their operating activities so that the operating profits are not fully taken into account for the purposes of the Balance of Business test.

Acquisition and disposal of companies

[3.86] The regime includes provisions in relation to a company leaving or joining an existing Group REIT. These are in addition to the special provisions which apply when one UK-REIT takes over another UK-REIT (see **3.22** and **3.23** above).

Acquisition or disposal of a UK resident company

[3.87] At the point at which a company joins a Group REIT (ie when it becomes a '75% subsidiary' of the principal company under the definition in CTA 2010, s 606 and ICTA 1988, s 838), all the provisions that apply to a company when it joins the regime will also apply to the acquired company (see **3.30** above). This means that a new accounting period starts for tax purposes and there is a deemed sale and reacquisition of rental properties at market value. The impact of this is that there is a rebasing of the property within the company. There is no requirement to provide a written notice to HMRC in respect of a company joining an existing Group REIT since it is deemed to be covered by the group's original election which applies to the principal company of the group and all of its qualifying subsidiaries during each and every accounting period.

Where a company which is a member of a Group REIT ceases to be a 75% subsidiary, it leaves the regime. Therefore, an accounting period ends, and there is a deemed sale and reacquisition of rental properties at market value (CTA 2010, s 536(1)–(5)). As mentioned at **3.70**, the two-year disposal rule will also apply to a company which is a member of a group REIT when it leaves the regime.

In the case of a demerger of a subsidiary which subsequently elects to become a UK-REIT in its own right or joins another Group REIT, then the above exit charges will not arise provided a new election is made on or before the date of demerger and the relevant conditions are met within six months of the demerger (CTA 2010, s 559).

Acquisition or disposal of a non-resident company

[3.88] The results of a UK property rental business carried on by a non-resident company will be included within the Group REIT's ring-fenced tax exempt business. There is no requirement for the company to register under the Non-Resident Landlord scheme.

A disposal of a non-resident company will have no impact for the purposes of the REIT regime and normal provisions will apply.

Compliance issues

Tax returns

[3.89] HMRC has the power to give a notice (FA 1998, Sch 18, para 3) to a company requiring that it submits a return of information:

- relevant to the tax liability of the company, or
- otherwise relevant to the application of the Corporation Tax Acts to the company, as may reasonably be required by the notice.

The REIT legislation treats the tax-exempt and non tax-exempt parts of the UK-REIT as separate businesses and each member of a group REIT as separate companies (CTA 2010, s 541). This fiction applies to the tax return filing obligation such that each member of the group may be required to submit two tax returns.

It is understood that in practice HMRC may accept that no return is required from Group REITs in respect of the group's property rental business, and indeed computations of these profits should be included with the return for the principal company. This is purely on a discretionary basis however, and each REIT should consult with their Inspector of Taxes.

Financial statements

[3.90] As discussed in 3.74 above a Group REIT is required to submit three 'financial statements' to HMRC at the same time as the tax return of the principal company of the group (CTA 2010, s 532(2)). The requirement for the content of these statements is set out in the primary legislation. The financial statements need to be submitted in respect of each accounting period which applies for tax purposes. This may be different from the period of account applicable for accounting purposes. The three statements are as follows.

G (property rental business)

[3.91] A statement for the worldwide property rental business of the group REIT prepared using IAS accounting principles showing:

(a) Income.
(b) Expenses. From this category, financing costs should be separately identified as follows:
  – The statement should show all financing costs which are ultimately applied for the financing of the property rental business even if this is not the business of the company paying the costs to an external finance provider but are the costs of another member of the group.
  – Financing costs payable by one member of the group to another should be eliminated.
  – Costs used to fund the UK property rental business should be shown separately from those used to fund the remainder of the worldwide business activities. For these purposes, the UK business will include all rental properties owned directly by UK resident members of the group or indirectly through tax transparent entities as well as UK located rental property owned by non UK resident members of the group. The reason for this separation is that it is the financing costs of the UK business which are used in determining the interest cover ratio (see 3.38 above).
(c) Profits before tax excluding realised and unrealised gains or losses on property. It would seem reasonable to interpret this as the profits and losses on disposal of investment property rather than trading property as exclusion of profits from trading disposals of property would be nonsensical.

(d)   Gross assets at the beginning of the accounting period valued using a fair value method where there is a choice.

G (residual)

[3.92] A statement prepared under the same principles as above for the residual (non property rental) business with the exception that a split of interest payable between the UK business and the non-UK business is not required.

G (tax-exempt)

[3.93] A statement prepared for the UK property rental business specifying the profits of the property rental business of each member of the Group REIT. Capital allowances and financing costs should be separately identified in this statement. If the principal company of the Group REIT does not own a 100% interest in the entity, only the percentage of profits equivalent to the principal company's beneficial entitlement to profits should be shown in the statement.

In addition, a reconciliation needs to be provided between the accounting based 'financial statements' prepared as set out at **3.91** and **3.92** and the audited financial statements for the relevant accounting period.

Rules for preparation

[3.94] In preparing the accounting based financial statements set out at **3.90** above, the regulations provide some additional rules as to how the results of various entities should be brought in.

Members of the Group REIT

[3.95] As set out in **3.72** above, the core Group REIT includes the principal company and its '75% subsidiaries'. The results of these entities are automatically included in the financial statements on a line by line basis. If the principal company does not have a 100% beneficial entitlement to profits of that entity, that proportion which is not owned by the Group REIT should be excluded.

Entities that are not members of the Group REIT

[3.96] Where a member of the Group REIT holds an interest in an entity which is not itself a member, and does not fall within one of the categories at **3.97–3.99** below, the interest in the entity should be valued as an investment asset of the non-property rental business (ie included within the statement at **3.92** above) under generally accepted accounting principles. Income should be included on the same basis. In practice, this is likely to mean that income from these entities will be recorded in the financial statements of the residual business as and when distributions are paid from the entity to a member of the Group REIT. In addition, movements in the fair value of these entities will need to be recorded.

Joint ventures

[3.97] If an election is made in respect of a joint venture company (see **3.79** above), that joint venture is treated as if it were a member of the Group REIT. The results of the joint venture are therefore included in the financial statements on a line by line basis to the extent that it is beneficially owned by the principal company of the Group REIT.

OEICs

[3.98] An OEIC is treated in the same way as a member of the Group REIT only if the beneficial interest of the principal company of the Group REIT is more than 20%. Otherwise, it is treated as a non-member of the group following **3.94** above.

Other non-corporate entities

[3.99] Unit trusts and partnerships are treated in the same way as an OEIC. The results of the entity are included as if it were a member of the Group REIT only if the principal company of the Group REIT owns more than a 20% beneficial interest. Otherwise, it is treated as a non-member as in **3.96** above.

Distributions

Reserves

[3.100] At the end of each accounting period, the principal company must submit a reconciliation showing how distributions made in the period have been attributed between the six profit pots (see **3.53** above). This is likely to involve a calculation of the level of distributable reserves for the profit pots to ensure that the UK-REIT satisfies the distribution requirements of the regime.

Quarterly returns

[3.101] The UK-REIT or principal company of a Group REIT is required to submit a quarterly return (CT61(Z)) to show the amount of PID paid in that quarter and the amount of tax deducted from the payments.

Application of self-assessment

[3.102] The normal corporation tax self-assessment rules will govern the preparation and submission of the UK-REIT's tax returns. By submitting a return on the basis that REIT status is available to the company, an officer of the company will effectively be confirming that all the relevant conditions for this status have been met. HMRC will then have the normal enquiry powers in relation to the basis on which the return has been prepared and will be able to enquire into the rationale for this belief if required. A UK-REIT will therefore need to retain sufficient additional information to be able to respond to these queries if they arise.

Chapter 4

Other fund vehicles

by
Matthew Roach and Simon Hart,
KPMG LLP

Investment structures – choosing the right one

Why invest collectively?

[4.1] Collective investment in property remains a popular asset class despite a period of low inflows to property funds after the 2008 financial crisis. There are some fears that in the wake of the result of the UK referendum on membership of the EU that the property market would suffer and it will become a less attractive asset class. Early indicators in the first few weeks following the referendum were negative, with large property funds becoming mainstream news as a result of having to suspend redemptions. However, in the months since, the UK economy has been more settled and resilient than expected and property funds have been able to allow redemptions, and carry on business as usual.

Through investing collectively rather than independently, investors are able to share the risks and rewards of property ownership. By pooling their funds, investors can get access to a larger, more diverse portfolio of assets, and have these professionally managed. Investors are able to reduce risk by spreading their investments more widely, thereby reducing the effect that any one investment can have on the overall performance of the portfolio.

Collective investment, particularly in the case of individual retail investors, provides investors an opportunity to invest in high value properties that they might otherwise not have been able to afford. It also brings together investors and parties with different skills. For example, a property developer brings development expertise whilst institutional investors (such as banks or pension funds) can provide both a source of finance as well as financial expertise.

The last decade has seen increasing pan-European ownership of property through collective investment funds, with an increasing array of vehicles being used. In addition, certain retail funds now exist which allow small investors to invest in landmark property and realise their investment on demand, providing liquidity not usually associated with investment in property. The suitability of such structures was recently challenged however when certain funds suffered negative publicity as a result of suspending redemptions after the Brexit vote. The publicised asymmetry between asset class and investment vehicle, may result in investors being more cautious when assessing prospective investments and property collective investment vehicles.

Collective investment vehicles

[4.2] There are several different vehicles available to property investors seeking to invest collectively. In the UK the main vehicles used are authorised investment funds, unauthorised unit trusts, limited partnerships and to some extent, limited liability partnerships. Additionally the UK has recently launched the Authorised Contractual Scheme regime, which may also be suitable for collective property investment. UK real estate investment trusts (UK-REITs) are outside the scope of this chapter and covered in detail in CHAPTER 3.

This chapter focuses on the tax attributes of these UK collective investment vehicles and, where appropriate, highlights some of the general commercial characteristics of each. The list of vehicles discussed in this chapter is not exhaustive. As the property market is subject to rapid change, new vehicles and structures are constantly being introduced to meet the demands of the market. In particular, this chapter does not cover multi-tiered offshore structures as the complexity and variations in this field are beyond the scope of this chapter.

What attributes may affect choice of vehicle?

[4.3] The various collective investment vehicles each have specific characteristics and attributes that will appeal to different investors depending upon the nature of their business or their investment or risk profile. These attributes include:

- *Whether the vehicle is open to the public or restricted to institutional investors:* Investments in vehicles such as authorised investment funds can usually be made by the public at large, whereas investment through a partnership is restricted by the terms of the partnership agreement.
- *Whether the vehicle has a pre-determined life versus an ongoing life and whether the vehicle provides investors with a readily accessible means of exit, such as through secondary markets.*
- *Whether the investment vehicle is sufficiently flexible to accommodate specific investor requirements:* For example, a partnership agreement can be specifically tailored to meet individual partners' requirements, such as specifying the partners' respective profit shares. In general, partnerships and other collective investment contractual arrangements usually allow the most flexibility in accommodating a number of investors in a fund (eg allocating profits, minimising capital duties and allowing investors to enter and exit the fund as required). In contrast, a shareholder in a company has more limited input into the structure of the vehicle or how its profits are distributed.
- *The level of administrative and regulatory requirements:* Regulated entities such as authorised investment funds potentially provide more security and less risk but carry with them additional compliance and administrative obligations. Unregulated vehicles can provide more flexibility but may also carry greater risk.

- *Whether the entity is subject to tax, or whether it is transparent for tax purposes:* Vehicles such as partnerships are transparent for tax purposes, which makes them particularly attractive for low tax or tax exempt investors such as Registered Pension Schemes.
- *Whether the vehicle is familiar to investors:* The willingness or otherwise of investors to invest in new or novel structures will have an impact upon the choice of investment vehicle. Vehicles such as companies are well known and understood by investors, whereas limited liability partnerships and Authorised Contractual Schemes are still comparatively new in the context of property investment.
- *The stamp duty or stamp duty land tax (SDLT) aspects of the vehicle:* The stamp duty consequences of seeding a fund and changes in unit-holdings may have a significant impact on which type of vehicle is preferable. A detailed analysis of stamp duty and SDLT is outside the scope of this chapter and covered in detail in CHAPTER 16.

Companies versus funds

[4.4] A specific comparison may be made between a company (with which most investors are familiar) and various potential fund vehicles to help investors assess their suitability as property investment vehicles. The general attributes of companies versus other fund vehicles can be summarised as follows:

Advantages

[4.5] Advantages are:

- Companies are commercially well understood and familiar.
- Shares are usually easily transferable, although it is possible to place restrictions on transferability.
- The affairs of the company are regulated by its memorandum and articles, which provide a level of security and certainty in relation to its governance and administration.

Potential disadvantages

[4.6] Potential disadvantages are:

- Companies generally do not have special exemptions from tax (like some fund vehicles) nor are they tax transparent. As such, there is potentially tax at company level. Investors could therefore effectively suffer two levels of tax. For example, in relation to disposals of property, there could be a tax charge on capital gains at company level and when the investor sells their shares.
- The lack of tax transparency is unattractive for low tax or tax exempt investors, as the profits from the property investment are taxed at the company level before being distributed to investors. Certain investors could achieve a higher post-tax return had they held the property directly or invested through a tax transparent vehicle such as a partnership.

- There may be factors which prevent the payment of dividends in a particular year (for example, a lack of sufficient distributable profits).
- A UK company has to file financial statements and information on its shareholders with Companies House.
- Companies are close-ended vehicles and generally a purchaser must be found in order for shares to be sold.
- Stamp duty may be payable on the purchase of UK company shares.

Types of fund vehicles

Authorised investment funds

[4.7] Authorised investment funds (AIFs) are collective investment schemes authorised by the Financial Services Authority (FCA). In this chapter, when referring to AIF we refer to open-ended investment companies (OEICs) and authorised unit trusts (AUTs). It is now also possible for authorised funds to be established as an authorised contractual scheme, encompassing co-ownership arrangements and authorised limited partnerships. These vehicles have been analysed separately from AIFs.

The taxation of AIFs is predominantly dealt with by the Authorised Investment Funds (Tax) Regulations 2006 (SI 2006/964).

Advantages of AIFs

[4.8] Advantages are:

- AIFs are exempt from corporation tax on capital gains.
- AIFs, with appropriate regulatory status, can be marketed to the general public.
- Units in an AUT or shares in an OEIC are redeemable and are dealt in directly by the manager (or authorised corporate director in the case of an OEIC) who will ensure the AUT or OEIC creates or redeems units/shares as appropriate.
- The affairs of AUTs and OEICs are regulated by specific instruments (the trust deed in the case of an AUT and the instrument of incorporation in the case of an OEIC) which provide a level of security and certainty in relation to governance and administration.
- As regulated vehicles, AIFs must comply with FCA regulation governing the safe keeping of assets.
- From 1 April 2014, there should be no Stamp Duty Reserve Tax payable on the surrender of fund units.

Potential disadvantages

[4.9] Potential disadvantages are:

- For UK property ownership, AIFs may be viewed as less familiar and not as well understood compared to ordinary companies.
- Regulatory costs are potentially high.

- Rental profits are subject to corporation tax (currently at the basic rate of income tax of 20%) in an AIF which means that tax-exempt investors effectively suffer tax they would not have incurred had they invested directly in the properties held by the AIF.
- Open-ended vehicles may not be suitable for long-term property investments and it may be necessary to hold cash or other liquid investments to meet redemption requests.
- The amount of leverage is limited in regulated vehicles.

Property authorised investment funds

[4.10] The PAIF regime is a special tax regime designed to facilitate investment by OEICs in real property (and certain companies that invest in property) and is broadly similar to the UK-REIT regime (see **CHAPTER 3**).

Historically, AIFs have not been a particularly attractive vehicle for real estate investment because the rental profits are liable to corporation tax at the level of the AIF which made them unattractive to tax-exempt investors. It was therefore apparent that a more effective tax regime was required to encourage the development of 'onshore' open-ended property funds.

PAIFs were therefore introduced in April 2008. Essentially, the PAIF rules are an elective tax regime for OEICs. The aim of the regime is to move the point of taxation from the fund to its investors. Further details of the PAIF regime are provided in **4.39** below.

Unauthorised unit trusts

[4.11] An unauthorised unit trust (UUT) is any UK resident unit trust that has not been authorised by the FCA. These vehicles can access a wider range of investments than AUTs, but cannot be marketed to the general public.

Advantages

[4.12] Advantages are:

- UUTs have no costly regulation.
- UUTs can access a wider range of investments than authorised unit trusts.
- UUTs are a useful vehicle for property investment as some pension funds may have restrictions preventing them from either investing directly in certain asset classes or indirectly through certain vehicles such as limited partnerships.
- Units can be transferred.

Potential disadvantages

[4.13] Potential disadvantages are:

- The general exemption from tax on capital gains that applies to AUTs does not necessarily apply to UUTs. A UUT is exempt from capital gains tax only if all its investors are themselves exempt from capital gains tax (for reasons other than residence), and it has registered as an exempt UUT (or 'EUUT'). If a UUT does not meet the conditions to be a EUUT

it becomes a non-exempt UUT (or 'NEUUT'), which is subject to corporation tax, and therefore inefficient. Accordingly, UUTs are usually only invested in by tax-exempt investors such as UK Registered Pension Schemes and charities.
- UUTs cannot be marketed to the public.

In addition to bringing UUTs with taxable unitholders within the scope of corporation tax, Finance Act 2013 also introduced other significant changes to the taxation of UUTs, including removing the requirement to withhold tax from distributions to exempt investors in UUTs. Broadly this means that it is likely that in future the only UUTs that will be established will be EUUTs. These changes are outlined in **4.64**.

Partnership structures

Advantages

[4.14] Advantages are:
- Partnerships offer flexibility to investors in that the partnership agreement can be tailored to meet the individual partners' requirements, such as specifying the partners' respective profit shares.
- Partnerships can benefit from less regulation and cost than AIFs and companies.
- Partnerships are fiscally transparent. This makes them attractive investment vehicles for tax-exempt investors as no tax is suffered at the level of the partnership.

Potential disadvantages

[4.15] Potential disadvantages are:
- Whilst it is possible to transfer partnership interests, there is generally not a readily available public market. Consequently, transfers usually take place by way of a private sale or placing.
- Tax transparent vehicles may not be attractive for certain types of investors (such as pension schemes) from a tax perspective where the underlying property portfolio includes development or other trading strategies. In addition, Registered Pension Schemes are not exempt from tax in respect of income and capital gains derived from property investment LLPs.

Authorised contractual schemes

[4.16] After a period of consultation the tax and regulatory rules for two new types of authorised vehicle were finalised and contractual schemes for collective investment (also commonly referred to as tax transparent funds or TTFs) were introduced with effect from 1 July 2013. These new vehicles are the authorised co-ownership scheme (CoACS) and the authorised partnership scheme.

The CoACS is a fund that is transparent for income and opaque for capital gains (such that units in a CoACS will be treated as assets). These are similar to existing Irish Common Contractual Funds or Luxembourg Fonds Commun de Placement (FCPs). The partnership scheme will be an authorised limited partnership and as such the advantages and disadvantages of this vehicle are as per **4.14** and **4.15** above (albeit with the additional advantages and disadvantages which follow from being an authorised vehicle). The advantages and disadvantages that follow are therefore focused on the CoACS.

Advantages

[4.17] Advantages are:

• There is no tax at fund level or Stamp Duty Reserve Tax on the surrender of units.

• The co-ownership scheme is opaque for capital gains and as such UK capital gains tax only arises, where applicable, on the disposal of units and not on the disposal of property.

• A change in ownership of CoACS units does not give rise to an SDLT charge.

• There is a seeding relief which may apply to allow the initial transfer of properties into a CoACS without any SDLT charge. See **4.92** for further details.

• Sophisticated investors are familiar with similar Irish and Luxembourg vehicles.

• A wide range of investors can invest collectively without tax disadvantages.

Potential disadvantages

[4.18] Potential disadvantages are:

• Tax transparent vehicles may not be attractive from a tax perspective for certain types of investors (such as pension schemes) where the underlying property portfolio includes development or other trading strategies.

• As with AIFs, leverage may be restricted and it is necessary to hold a proportion of liquid assets to meet redemption liabilities.

Other types of fund vehicles

[4.19] A discussion of overseas fund vehicles is outside the scope of this chapter which is intended to cover UK vehicles. However, it is becoming increasingly common to invest in property in the UK and the rest of Europe through non-UK investment structures (such as offshore REITs, Jersey Property Unit Trusts and FCPs) which are briefly discussed below.

Offshore REIT vehicles

[4.20] Real Estate Investment Trusts (REITs) are common to many jurisdictions with developed property markets, particularly the United States, France, the Netherlands, Germany and Australia. Generally, they are closed-ended companies or trusts that hold, manage and maintain real estate for investment purposes by leasing the properties to tenants. They usually have a broad investor base and are often, but not always, traded on a public stock exchange.

It is possible that some offshore REIT-type vehicles may fall to be treated as transparent for UK tax purposes.

The UK also has a REIT regime which is considered in detail in **CHAPTER 3**.

Jersey Property Unit Trusts

[4.21] Jersey Property Unit Trusts ('JPUTs') are another example of a vehicle commonly used for collective property investment. These are Jersey resident unit trusts, which are typically Baker trusts (ie transparent for income but opaque for capital gains) for UK tax purposes. Historically JPUTs were used as a vehicle to hold UK property as there was a seeding relief from SDLT. This was abolished in 2006. Nonetheless JPUTs have become commercially familiar and have many advantages due to both the flexible Jersey regime and UK tax treatment. While a similar UK vehicle does now exist in the CoACS, JPUTs will continue to be a popular vehicle on the basis of a more flexible investment universe and ability to leverage. Guernsey Property Unit Trusts are very similar in nature to JPUTs and are also used to invest in UK property.

Luxembourg FCP (Fonds Commun de Placement)

[4.22] A Luxembourg FCP is an example of a popular non-UK tax transparent vehicle which has widely been used in the marketplace to hold property across Europe. An FCP is an unincorporated, contractual collective investment vehicle, similar to the unit trust in the UK. However, an FCP has no legal personality.

A Luxembourg FCP must have a minimum capital of €1,250,000. There is no legal requirement to maintain accounting reserves and, accordingly, it is usually possible to make dividend distributions up to any amount provided that the minimum capital requirement is met. Under Luxembourg law the management company of an open-ended FCP is obliged to purchase units from its investors when they wish to liquidate their investments (the price at which units are repurchased depends on the net asset value of the fund). If the FCP is closed-ended, an investor is not permitted to request redemption of their units during the life of the fund. An FCP must be regulated by the Luxembourg CSSF (Commission de Surveillance du Secteur Financier).

Whilst an FCP is not subject to Luxembourg tax in respect of its income or realised capital gains, it is assessed to an annual subscription tax on the value of its net assets. The rate of the subscription tax is generally 0.05%; this rate can be reduced to 0.01% or exempted in certain circumstances. The management company is fully subject to corporate income tax. Under Luxembourg domestic legislation, no withholding tax liability arises in relation to distributions paid by an FCP to an investor.

The benefit of an FCP is that it is an increasingly familiar, very flexible and well-regulated vehicle which can be used for pan-European property investment without adding an additional tier of taxation. In 2007 Luxembourg introduced the Specialised Investment Fund regulations which have enabled FCPs to be established under a new simplified, less regulated regime.

Finance Act 2009 introduced TCGA 1992, s 103A which could require an FCP to be treated as a company for UK capital gains tax purposes, and for the investment held in an FCP to be treated as shares in a company (this does not affect the fiscally transparent treatment of the FCP for income purposes). This change made it more attractive for UK investors to invest in FCPs, as it removes the capital gains tax charge for UK investors that previously existed when the FCP disposed of its assets. UK investors are now only subject to capital gains tax on disposal of their units in the FCP.

Summary

[4.23] Investors are becoming more familiar with overseas vehicles such as foreign REITs, JPUTs and FCPs. These vehicles are therefore increasingly being used as collective investment vehicles for pan-European property investment (including UK property) in competition with traditional UK fund vehicles.

The following sections explore the tax treatment of typical UK fund vehicles including AIFs (OEICs and AUTs), PAIFs, UUTs, Limited Partnerships, Limited Liability Partnerships and Co-Ownership Schemes.

Authorised investment funds

[4.24] The taxation of AIFs is largely dealt with by the Authorised Investment Funds (Tax) Regulations 2006 (SI 2006/964).

AIFs as defined for this chapter encompasses both AUTs and OEICs. AUTs and OEICs are two types of collective investment scheme that can be authorised by the FCA under the Financial Services and Markets Act 2000 (FSMA 2000). It is now also possible for authorised funds to be established as an authorised contractual scheme, encompassing co-ownership arrangements and authorised limited partnerships. These vehicles have been analysed separately from AUTs and OEICs.

Although there are structural and legal differences between AUTs and OEICs (AUTs are trusts whereas OEICs are a special form of company), both entities are subject to the same corporation tax rules. OEICs are the more recent legal form for AIFs being introduced in 1997. However, OEICs are now the more dominant form of AIF with approximately 75% of the approximate 3,000 UK AIFs taking the form of OEICs and approximately 65% of funds under the management of AIFs being managed by OEICs.

Regulation by the FCA is the most fundamental aspect to the establishment and operation of UK AUTs and OEICs and for the corporate entities that operate and manage them. The principal regulations which govern AUTs and OEICs are in the FCA's Collective Investment Scheme sourcebook (COLL sourcebook). However, the FCA's regulatory principles and substantial other aspects of the FCA Handbook of regulation and guidance apply to the management and operation of AIFs including elements such as the marketing and distribution of AIFs.

The rest of this chapter will refer to AIFs collectively and what follows, unless expressly stated, can be taken to apply equally to AUTs and OEICs. The text uses certain terms that are applicable to AUTs such as unit or unitholder; the equivalent terms for OEICs are summarised below.

Definition	AUT	OEIC
Investor's interest in the AIF	Unit	Share
Investor	Unitholder	Shareholder
Entity responsible for management of the AIF's assets	Authorised Fund Manager (AFM)	Authorised Corporate Director (ACD)
Entity responsible for holding assets and certain oversight of the AFM/ACD in accordance with the regulations	Trustee	Depositary
Constitutional documents of the fund	Trust deed, scheme particulars	Instrument of incorporation, prospectus

What Is an AIF?

[4.25] An AIF is a collective investment scheme regulated by the FCA. The purpose of an AIF is to allow investors to pool their investments to obtain, amongst other things, the professional management of a diversified portfolio of assets.

An AUT operates under general trust law, which requires a trust to account for trust income and trust capital separately. In a trust, the 'beneficiaries' of a unit trust are the unitholders who share in the income and capital of the trust on the basis of the number of units held.

An OEIC is an investment company with variable capital (ICVC) issued in the form of shares. An OEIC is a company established under the Open-Ended Investment Companies Regulations 2001 (the OEIC Regulations). An OEIC is not governed by or subject to the Companies Act. The OEIC Regulations are made under FSMA 2000, s 262.

The accounts of AIFs are required by regulation to be prepared in accordance with the Statement of Recommended Practice – Financial Statements of Authorised Funds (the AF SORP), the latest edition of which was published in May 2014 by the Investment Association (IA), with additional guidance provided in December 2015. The AF SORP requires the presentation of a Statement of Total Return which includes both the returns on income (revenue returns) and the returns on capital (capital returns).

An AIF is constituted by its trust deed. The trustee must be a firm authorised and regulated by the FCA with the permitted business of being the Trustee or Depository of an AIF. There are a limited number of such authorised firms which are typically a bank or subsidiary of a bank. The trustee is responsible for safeguarding the AIF's assets and has specific duties established by the Regulations of oversight of the AFM and which correlate to the protection of the interests of unitholders. An AFM has the primary regulatory responsibility for the AIF and carries out the day-to-day management of the AIF; the AIF will usually appoint one or more investment managers to manage the portfolio and will often use third party administrators to operate the AIF (however, responsibility remains with the AFM).

The trust deed of an AIF will include provisions concerning:

(a)   its investment objectives;
(b)   the manager's permitted initial periodic and exit charges;
(c)   other charges;
(d)   the scope of investment and borrowing powers,

and will reference to regulations, in particular those in the COLL sourcebook.

AIFs are 'open-ended' (ie they can expand and contract the units in issue in accordance with demand from investors to purchase or redeem units). The number of units of an AIF in issue can increase or decrease each dealing day (typically each working day but may be less frequent for some AIFs). The value of an AIF therefore increases or decreases throughout an accounting period not only as a result of changes in the values of the assets held by the AIF but also as a result of movements in the number of units in issue. If units are created (or sold) and the value of the AIF's investments remains constant, the size or value of the AIF will increase correspondingly, if investors redeem their units, the AIF will contract in size.

The open-ended nature of AIFs can present challenges for managers wanting to operate property AIFs. The manager of an AIF must ensure that the fund maintains appropriate liquidity consistent with the expectations of investors regarding unit dealing as established by both provisions in the fund's prospectus and marketing literature. The COLL sourcebook provides for both Limited Redemption (COLL 6.2.19) and Deferred Redemption (COLL 6.2.21). These rules, together with related guidance, result in AIFs that invest in real property being able to limit redemptions to at least once every six months and to make it clear that the fund has provisions enabling the manager to defer redemptions in times of high redemption levels. While historically a high proportion of the assets of a property AIF had to be held in liquid investments (such as cash, property shares and securities) to meet potential redemptions of units, the COLL Rules can enable a Property AIF to invest in real property (a less liquid asset class than shares in property vehicles) while continuing to meet the reasonable expectations of investors. Property is not an eligible asset for UCITS funds, therefore Property AIFs are either Non-UCITS Retail Schemes (NURS) or Qualified Investor Schemes (QIS) authorised by the FCA. This enables the FCA to provide Rules for Limited Redemption and Deferred Redemption that are not permitted under the UCITS Directive for UCITS funds. The FCA will still expect the manager of a property AIF investing in real property to meet the expectations of investors as set out in FCA perimeter guidance (PERG 9.8) regarding the realisation of their investment.

Types of AIF

[4.26] COLL allows an AIF to be one of three types:

•   a UCITS scheme;
•   a non-UCITS retail scheme (NURS); or
•   a qualified investor scheme (QIS).

A UCITS scheme has to comply with the necessary conditions in order to enjoy the rights available under the UCITS Directive (UCITS stands for Undertaking for Collective Investment in Transferable Securities). The UCITS Directive allows investment funds to be marketed to retail investors across the EU. UCITS funds authorised in one member state can, subject to notification to the competent authority of another member state by the competent authority of the UCITS home member state, be marketed in other member states. The UCITS Directive sets out many conditions that a fund must comply with. These are intended to protect the interests of retail investors and cover matters such as permitted investments, gearing levels, the frequency of pricing and dealing points, segregation of assets from the manager, and the independent custody of assets and certain oversight of the UCITS Manager by the Depository. The latest Directive, UCITS V made various supplementary amendments, and not wholesale change to UCITS IV, which inter alia, allowed for the cross-border management of UCITS funds as well as master/feeder arrangements.

The UCITS name suggests that the Directive only allows funds to invest in 'transferable securities'. However, the eligible UCITS assets have been widened from transferable securities to include cash deposits, derivatives for investment and hedging as well as investment in other funds (but not direct investment in real estate). A number of industry bodies are currently lobbying as part of consultations for UCITS VI for direct property holdings to be eligible investments for UCITS funds but whether this will be included remains uncertain.

A NURS can be marketed to the general public (although not automatically cross border). The FCA has made the NURS subject to many of the same regulations as a UCITS fund with some incremental features. Accordingly, a NURS is able to hold a wider range of investments including real property and alternative funds. Property AIFs and Funds of Alternative Investment Funds that are marketed to the general public will be regulated as a NURS. It should be noted that under the Alternative Investment Fund Managers Directive it may become possible for a NURS to be marketed cross border in the EU.

A QIS can only be promoted to professional investors on the same terms as unregulated collective investment schemes. The FCA's Regulations applicable to a QIS are greatly relaxed compared to a UCITS scheme or NURS.

Gearing

[4.27] An important consideration for AIFs is the level of gearing or leverage of the investment portfolio that is permitted. A UCITS scheme and a NURS are limited to borrowing not more than 10% of the value of the scheme property (in the case of a UCITS scheme, this borrowing must be temporary (not more than three months) but in the case of a NURS it could be permanent). The intention of permitting borrowing by a UCITS scheme or NURS is not intended to support leveraging of the investment portfolio but to provide or enhance liquidity when required for unit dealing and to support the efficient management of the portfolio. Since the development of UCITS III it has been possible to use derivatives and, while there must be global cover for derivative exposures at all times, the use of derivatives may provide an alternative mechanism to leverage investment returns.

By contrast a QIS is allowed to borrow up to 100% of the value of the scheme property. However, the manager of the QIS must take reasonable care to ensure that its borrowings do not exceed the value of its assets.

Umbrella AIFs

[4.28] AIFs can be set up either as a single entity fund or as an 'umbrella fund' which is an entity with a number of separate sub-funds. While either structure is possible for both AUTs and OEICs, for historic reasons AUTs tend to be constituted as single trusts whereas OEICs are most commonly set up as an umbrella company.

An umbrella AIF is established as an entity with a common trust deed (AUT) or instrument of incorporation (OEIC), with a number of sub-funds. In all material respects, including tax, each sub-fund is treated as a separate AIF; it will have its own investment mandate, issue its own units, incur its own expenses, file its own corporation tax return etc. The one exception is that HMRC will typically only view the umbrella AIF as being able to register for VAT, rather than separately registering each sub-fund.

Some consequences of being an umbrella fund are:

- all of the funds of an umbrella must be authorised as the same type of fund (eg a UCITS scheme, NURS or QIS). There can be no mixing of fund types;
- since December 2011 the UK has established rules that require, in all new umbrella OEICs, the sub-funds to be operated and managed on a 'Protected Cells' basis. The Protected Cell structure requires all the sub-funds (or 'cells') to operate under the 'principle of limited recourse' – this means that the assets of one sub-fund cannot be used to meet the liabilities of one or more other sub-funds of the umbrella. The introduction of the Protected Cell Regime is intended to eliminate the risk of contagion between sub-funds; and
- the umbrella entity has one accounting reference date. Therefore, the financial statements of all the sub-funds must be prepared to the same accounting reference date.

Units in AIFs

[4.29] Investments are valued, typically on a daily basis, to determine the price of the units. As AIFs are open-ended, their units can be bought or redeemed at request (subject to specific constraints in the scheme particulars/prospectus) resulting in the creation and cancellation of units. Therefore, demand for the units does not influence the value of units with their value closely correlating to the net asset value of the fund divided by the number of units in issue. The result is that AIF units do not trade at a discount (or premium) to net asset value (as can arise in closed-ended funds such as UK investment trust companies).

Units can be priced on either a single or dual pricing basis. An AIF that is single priced has one price for its units whether the investor is buying or selling (this single price may be adjusted to manage risk of dilution arising from the creation or cancellation of units). A dual priced AIF has separate offer and bid prices for sale and redemption and these are supported by different creation or cancellation prices depending on whether the fund is expanding (unit creation) or contracting (unit cancellation).

AIFs can issue different classes of unit. The 'property' of an AIF must be managed as a whole on behalf of all unitholders. This means that classes of units cannot have different rights to participate in the capital, revenue or distributions of the AIF. However, the different unit classes can provide for different features between unit classes as follows:

- distributable income to be distributed periodically to investors (income units), or to be periodically declared but not paid and instead credited to the retained capital account of the fund (accumulation units);
- the price of units and the distributions made by different unit classes to be denominated in different currencies (currency class units);
- different charging structures for each unit class (eg different levels of annual management fees for different investors (for example, institutional versus retail) based on differential features such as minimum investment limits);
- gross and net unit classes. These are unit classes that provide for distributable income to be distributed or accumulated either gross or net of income tax deductions. Before April 2017, net share classes only applied to 'bond AIFs' paying interest distributions (see **4.35** below) and PAIFs. From April 2017, interest distributions can now be paid to all investors gross, and therefore net share classes only apply to distributions of property income from PAIFs. Gross unit classes are only available to investors entitled to receive income distributions gross without deduction of UK income tax (eg corporates, Registered Pension Schemes and certain other tax exempt investors such as charities); and
- currency class hedging. Hedging instruments can be used to mitigate currency exchange rate risks for the unitholders in that particular unit class.

While many unit class specific features are allowed (as described above), it is not possible to create an AIF with a 'split capital' structure where certain components of the total investment return are allocated to one class and other components are allocated to another class. Split capital structures are used in some closed-ended listed investment vehicles such as investment trusts.

Distributions

[4.30] UK AIFs are required to distribute all of their revenue net of expenses and taxation on an annual basis. While certain specified expenses can be charged against capital in determining the distribution amount, the capital returns and capital of the fund cannot be distributed by a UK AIF. The term distribution also applies to the amount declared in respect of accumulation unitholders where the relevant amount is accumulated into the value of the AIF through the issue of additional units. The date on which revenue is distributed (or accumulated) must not be more than four months after the accounting date. An AIF may make interim distributions of revenue.

Taxation of AIFs

[4.31] The majority of legislation concerning the taxation of AIFs is contained in CTA 2010, ss 612–619 and the Authorised Investment Funds (Tax) Regulations 2006 (SI 2006/964).

AIFs are taxed as investment companies (subject to certain specific rules) and investors are treated as shareholders. An AIF is exempt from tax on capital gains (TCGA 1992, s 100). Tax on capital gains only applies at the investor level when an investor disposes of their interest in the AIF.

If an AIF is more than 60% invested in 'qualifying investments' (broadly interest bearing assets) it is typically referred to as a 'bond AIF' (although no such term features in tax legislation).

Corporation tax calculation

[4.32] An AIF is liable to corporation tax on its taxable income less its allowable management expenses and any interest payable. AIFs pay corporation tax at the basic rate of income tax, currently 20%.

AIFs that invest in real estate will be subject to tax on their net rental profits in accordance with normal taxation principles. An AIF is entitled to claim capital allowances in relation to its property rental business. AIFs, constituted as OEICs, that invest predominantly in real estate may be eligible to elect into the PAIF tax regime (see **4.39** below).

To the extent that any profits, gains or losses attributable to creditor loan relationships or derivative contracts of an AIF are properly accounted for as capital in accordance with the SORP, they are exempt from UK corporation tax. This maintains the corporation tax exemption for the capital profits of AIFs (as noted above, AIFs are exempt from corporation tax on capital gains).

Under regulations effective from 1 September 2009, AIFs may elect into the tax-elected funds ('TEF') regime. To enter that regime, an AIF must meet a number of criteria. One of these is a requirement that the TEF cannot have a property business. Therefore, a TEF cannot be used as a property investment vehicle and the TEF rules have not been considered further in this chapter.

The FINROF (funds investing in non-reporting offshore funds) tax regime that applies to certain AIFs from 6 March 2010 is unlikely to be of direct relevance to AIFs that predominantly invest in property (but could be of relevance to an AIF that holds substantial investments in offshore open-ended property funds that have not applied to enter the UK's reporting offshore fund regime). The FINROF rules are not considered further in this chapter.

Distributions

[4.33] An AIF must distribute all its net income on an annual basis (interim distributions are permitted). Issuing additional units in respect of accumulation units is treated as a distribution. A distribution is treated as a dividend in the hands of investors, subject to the application of the corporate streaming rules (these rules impact AIF investors that are subject to UK corporation tax).

HMRC issued a consultation document in June 2013 which proposed to repeal the corporate streaming rules, but it was subsequently decided for these rules to be retained. Nonetheless, this remains an area which HMRC may consider amending again in the future.

However, a 'bond AIF' (see **4.31**) can elect to pay an interest distribution and a PAIF pays distributions that have three 'streams' (see **4.42** below). An interest distribution is an allowable debit for the purposes of the loan relationship rules subject to certain restrictions that may limit the quantum of the distribution that can be deducted for tax purposes. Nonetheless, a bond AIF paying an interest distribution is unlikely to have any taxable profits.

Any income taxable under the property rental business rules cannot be included in the distribution accounts of an AIF as available for payment as an interest distribution even if the AIF is more than 60% invested in interest yielding assets. Consequently, bond AIFs that wish to maintain their ability to pay interest distributions must exercise caution regarding investing in real estate, UK REITs and PAIFs (property income distributions paid by UK REITs and PAIFs are also taxed as the profits of a UK property business).

Taxation of investors subject to income tax

Dividend distributions

[4.34] Dividend distributions are treated in the same manner as any other UK company dividend. This means that dividends not falling within the dividends allowance of £5,000 (available only to basic and higher rate taxpayers) will be subject to tax at 7.5%, 32.5%, and 38.1%, for basic, higher, and additional rate individuals respectively. The annual dividend allowance is scheduled to reduce to £2,000 from April 2018.

Interest distributions

[4.35] Prior to April 2017, interest distributions were generally paid net after the deduction of income tax at the basic rate (at 20%) – however, individuals who invested in an AIF through an ISA were entitled to receive interest distributions without deduction of basic rate income tax. The AIF was responsible for deducting and paying the income tax withheld to HMRC.

The unitholder was treated as receiving yearly interest after the deduction of tax at the basic rate. The income tax withheld would satisfy the tax liability of basic rate taxpayers. Higher and additional rate taxpayers would have a further income tax liability. If the unitholder's total income tax liability was less than the tax deducted, they were entitled to a repayment of the excess.

The requirement to withhold tax on interest distributions was removed with effect from 6 April 2017. This follows the introduction of the personal savings allowance (or 'PSA') from April 2016, which exempts the first £1,000 of a basic rate taxpayer's savings income, and the first £500 for a higher rate taxpayer. As a result, 'bond AIFs' and PAIFs are no longer required to withholding tax on interest distributions, and therefore net share classes (with the exception of property income from a PAIF) can be priced gross of tax.

Taxation of investors subject to corporation tax

Dividend distributions

[4.36] There are special rules that apply to unitholders within the charge to UK corporation tax that receive a dividend distribution from an AIF – the corporate streaming rules. The unitholder may have to treat part of the dividend distribution as taxable unfranked income. The unfranked part of the distribution is treated as an annual payment received after deduction of income tax at the basic rate and the gross amount is liable to corporation tax. Credit can be taken for the income tax deemed to have been deducted from the payment (it is also possible to secure a 'repayment' of this deemed income tax credit).

However, rules applicable from 22 June 2010 may require all or part of the tax deemed to have been deducted from the distribution to be treated as foreign tax if the AIF has reduced its corporation tax liability by claiming credit relief for overseas tax. The deemed foreign tax must be treated in the same manner as any other overseas tax and, consequently, it would not be possible to seek a reclaim of that tax from HMRC. If any tax deemed to have been deducted from the distribution falls to be treated as foreign tax, a proportionate part of the distribution is treated as overseas income rather than as annual payment received after deduction of basic rate income tax.

The remaining franked component of the dividend distribution is treated by the corporate recipient in the same manner as other dividends from UK companies.

The split of the dividend between franked and unfranked income is largely determined by the nature of the underlying income received by the AIF and is required to be disclosed by the AIF on the dividend voucher sent to unitholders. It is likely that a significant proportion of any dividend paid by a property invested AIF (that is not a PAIF) would be treated as unfranked income in the hands of a UK tax resident company as rental profits are charged to a corporation tax in an AIF.

Interest distributions

[4.37] Interest distributions payable to investors that are subject to corporation tax will be paid without deduction of basic rate income tax.

For corporation tax purposes any investment in a bond AIF is treated as a loan relationship asset of the UK corporate investor with any fair value movements attributable to that holding subject to corporation tax (a holding in a bond AIF must be fair valued for tax purposes). The loan relationship debits and credits to be brought into account each year will therefore include both the distributions recognised by the corporate investor and the movement in the market value of the investment in the bond AIF.

Tax-exempt investors

[4.38] Tax-exempt investors in AIFs could include, amongst others, Registered Pension Schemes, charities and ISA investors.

In general, the tax treatment for tax exempt investors is straightforward in that no tax liability is suffered on dividend or interest distributions. However, a tax inefficiency arises for tax exempt investors when they receive dividends paid out of the property rental profits of an AIF that is not a PAIF.

The inefficiency arises because the AIF may pay corporation tax in respect of its property rental profits. However, the tax-exempt investors cannot reclaim the corporation tax paid at fund level. Therefore, any corporation tax paid by the AIF represents a real cost to a tax-exempt investor (and a cost that they would not have suffered if the underlying properties had been invested in directly).

It is for this reason that alternative tax-transparent property investment vehicles such as Guernsey and Jersey property unit trusts or limited partnerships have often been preferred by tax-exempt investors who wish to invest in real estate. The PAIF regime was introduced to remove this tax inefficiency and to facilitate the development of UK domiciled open-ended property funds and potentially encourage property investment and funds back to the UK (see **4.39** below).

Property authorised investment funds

[4.39] The introduction of the UK Property Authorised Investment Fund (PAIF) tax regime was a welcome addition to the UK funds landscape in 2008. The PAIF tax regime was introduced to provide a tax-efficient open-ended vehicle suitable for a range of investors and had long been demanded by the industry. The PAIF regime was initially introduced from 6 April 2008 with regulations provided by way of statutory instrument inserting regulations into SI 2006/964. Since the introduction of the initial regulations there have been further (relatively minor) changes introduced by way of further statutory instruments which amend and add to the relevant sections within SI 2006/964. The core PAIF rules have in substance changed very little since their introduction.

The PAIF tax regime is designed to move tax from the level of the fund to the level of the investor, meaning investors should not suffer any tax leakage over and above the rates at which they should pay compared to holding assets directly.

After a slow introduction to the regime with limited PAIF conversions, the last few years have seen a significant number of the UK's largest open-ended property funds elect into the PAIF regime, and now the majority of UK open ended property funds targeted to retail investors have elected into the PAIF regime.

Whilst the PAIF regime provides attractive tax benefits, there is still a number of limiting factors which managers need to consider before moving to the PAIF regime. These include:

- As OEICs are open ended, investors in the fund must be able to redeem their shares in the PAIF on demand (subject to any dealing conditions in the prospectus) at or close to the net asset value. This can present new challenges for traditional real estate managers who may be more accustomed to the closed-ended nature of many institutional funds. It also requires managers to determine how much (if any) dilution levy should apply and what proportion of the portfolio should be held in more liquid assets to facilitate redemptions. Immediately following the Brexit referendum the uncertain investment climate led to a number of PAIFs imposing liquidity restrictions on investors who sought to redeem their investments, and again led to industry questions about the suitability of open-ended property funds marketed to retail investors. However these restrictions were removed by most PAIFs by early 2017.

- The PAIF regime does not allow corporate investors to hold more than 10% of a PAIF. Whilst a carve-out is available which allows a corporate investor to structure a holding of greater than 10% through a UK AUT feeder, this creates an additional layer of complexity and also increases the costs of running such a fund. Prior to 1 August 2012 this also created capital gains tax concerns for investors switching between the PAIF and the AUT feeder. However an amendment to the legislation now allows for capital gains tax free transfers (where certain conditions are met) between a dedicated PAIF feeder and the PAIF, which should result in greater flexibility in managing this condition.

Why use a PAIF?

[4.40] The industry had long called for a UK open-ended property vehicle that would be attractive for both institutional and retail investors. Exempt institutional investors, such as pension schemes or charities, found existing UK authorised property funds to be unattractive as they suffer tax at the basic rate on rental income (at fund level) which would otherwise not be suffered if the income had been received directly. While other vehicles exist to eliminate this tax leakage for institutional investors, such as JPUTs, Guernsey Property Unit Trusts or UUTs, these are not generally suitable for retail investors.

The PAIF is suitable for retail, institutional, taxable and tax-exempt investors as it moves the point of taxation away from the fund and to investors, such that no irrecoverable tax arises at the level of the fund. This means that the overall effective tax applied to income and gains derived from investing in property rental businesses for all kinds of investors (taxable and tax-exempt) will be broadly the same as if they had owned the property or REIT shares directly.

The PAIF regime is therefore potentially attractive to large retail fund providers who have to date been limited in their ability to attract UK pension fund investment in retail funds due to the tax suffered.

Further, the vehicle could be used by life companies to restructure and open up their portfolios to outside investors.

What is a PAIF?

[4.41] A PAIF is an AIF whose investment portfolio is comprised predominantly of real property, shares in UK REITs or overseas entities that are 'equivalent' to UK REITS. To become a PAIF, the AIF must be an OEIC (the regime is not available to AUTs). Therefore, an AUT wishing to join the regime must first convert to an OEIC. SDLT relief is available in respect of property that is transferred in connection with the conversion of an AUT to an OEIC for the purposes of entering the PAIF regime.

To enter the PAIF regime, the manager of the OEIC (or the proposed manager in the case of a prospective OEIC), must give advance notice in writing to HMRC that it wants the PAIF rules to apply to the fund. The manager of an existing OEIC will specify in that notice the accounting period from the beginning of which the PAIF rules will apply to the OEIC – the notice to enter the regime must be given at least 28 days before the beginning of that period. The prospective manager of a future OEIC is required to specify that the PAIF rules will apply to that OEIC from the date the OEIC is incorporated and authorised – the notice to enter the regime must be given at least 42 days before the expected date of incorporation and authorisation.

Certain documentation must accompany a notice to enter the PAIF regime:

- a statement by the manager (or proposed manager) that the conditions listed below are reasonably expected to be complied with throughout the specified or first accounting period;
- the instrument (or proposed instrument) of incorporation;
- the prospectus; and
- a copy of the application to the FCA for agreement to changes in the instrument of incorporation and prospectus (in the case of a future OEIC, a copy of the application to the FCA for approval of the company as an OEIC must be submitted).

Once the PAIF regime applies to an OEIC, it remains in the regime indefinitely unless certain events occur (see below).

The following conditions must be satisfied by the OEIC once it has secured entry to the PAIF regime:

- **Property investment business condition**
  The PAIF must carry on a property investment business (PIB). The fund's prospectus and instrument of incorporation must state that its investment objectives are to carry on a PIB and to manage cash raised from investors for investment in the PIB.
  A PIB must be a continuing business that consists of one or more of the following activities:
  - property rental business (this can comprise or include an overseas property business). The definition of property rental business can include the property rental business of an 'intermediate holding vehicle' provided that vehicle only conducts an overseas property business and certain other conditions are complied with. Holding UK property via an 'intermediate holding vehicle' does not qualify as a property rental business and is not permitted by Clause 5.6.18 of the FSA's Collective Investment Schemes Sourcebook (COLL). The purpose of the 'intermediate holding vehicle' regulation is to facilitate investment in overseas property located in jurisdictions where the PAIF would be prevented from holding property directly;

- owning shares in UK REITs;
- owning shares or units in foreign entities that are equivalent to UK REITs. HMRC has published a list of certain foreign entities that are considered to be equivalent (eg a German G-REIT, a Belgian SICAFI) and other entities that may 'sometimes meet the criteria' (eg an Australian listed property trust).

The PIB condition must be met throughout an accounting period.

- **Genuine diversity of ownership condition**

The instrument of incorporation of the PAIF and its prospectus must specify that its shares will be widely available, specify the intended categories of investors and specify that the PAIF manager will market and make available PAIF shares sufficiently widely to reach the intended categories of investor in a manner that is appropriate to attract those investors. It is not the case that PAIFs must be available to the public at large – it is permissible to market a PAIF to a particular category of investor.

The PAIF must not seek to restrict investment in itself to a limited number of specific persons or specific groups of connected persons and nor can it seek to deter a reasonable investor within the specified intended categories of investor.

There are also provisions covering the situation where a PAIF is invested in by an AUT feeder fund. Provided the PAIF and AUT have the same manager, the genuine diversity of ownership condition can be satisfied by reference to the trust deed and prospectus of the AUT and the intended investors in the AUT.

The aim of this condition is to prevent the PAIF legislation being manipulated by a small group of people or a larger connected group so as to obtain a tax advantage. HMRC guidance indicates that it does not consider that this condition would be breached if a PAIF is initially seeded by a single corporate investor (for example, a life insurer) as an indirect investor via a single feeder fund so that the corporate owner-ship condition is not breached. However, the PAIF must then be available to and marketed to suitable investors.

It is possible to seek clearance from HMRC that the PAIF meets this condition.

The genuine diversity of ownership condition must be met throughout an accounting period.

- **Corporate ownership condition**

The PAIF must prohibit any corporate investor from holding a 10% or more beneficial entitlement to the net asset value of the fund and must take reasonable steps to ensure compliance with this condition (for example, regularly reviewing the shareholder register and issuing warnings to corporate investors approaching the 10% threshold). If the 10% threshold is exceeded by a corporate investor, the PAIF must take immediate steps to ensure the relevant holding is reduced below 10% of the net asset value of the fund.

This condition relates to preserving the taxing rights of the UK in respect of rental income derived from UK real estate where overseas investors are concerned.

The instrument of incorporation and prospectus of the PAIF must include provisions requiring an undertaking from corporate investors not to acquire 10% or more of the share capital and to reduce its holding below 10% on becoming aware that it has subsequently breached that threshold. There are also provisions requiring certificates from corporate investors regarding the beneficial ownership of the shares they hold.

However, it is possible for a corporate investor to achieve an indirect interest of 10% or more in a PAIF by investing in a 'feeder' fund that does not take the form of a corporate provided the feeder fund is the beneficial owner of the shares in the PAIF, rather than the company that invests in the feeder fund. The feeder fund could take the form of a unit trust scheme. The PAIF legislation provides that a UK AUT invested in a PAIF will be treated as the beneficial owner of the PAIF investment. Therefore, a corporate holding 10% or more of the issued units of a UK AUT feeder fund would not be treated as holding a 10% or greater beneficial entitlement to the net asset value of the PAIF.

Regulations that came into effect from 1 August 2012 are designed to facilitate the conversion of existing UK AUTs to PAIFs by providing that investors in the converting fund can exchange their units for units in a new AUT which will act as a 'dedicated feeder fund' for the PAIF without suffering a tax charge on any capital gain that would otherwise arise on the disposal of units in the converting fund (a dedicated feeder fund must hold at least 85% of its assets in the PAIF). The same regulations also enable the converting fund to meet the corporate ownership condition during the period that the restructuring is implemented. The regulations also permit an investor to exchange units in a dedicated feeder fund for shares in a PAIF (and vice versa) without suffering a tax charge on any capital gain that would otherwise arise on the disposal of units in the dedicated feeder fund (or shares in the PAIF). The corporate ownership condition must be met throughout an accounting period.

- **Loan creditor condition**
  The terms of any loans made to the PAIF must not be dependent on its results or the value of its assets. The interest payable on the loan must not exceed a reasonable commercial return on the amount loaned to the PAIF. Furthermore, the amount payable by the PAIF on repayment of the loan must not exceed the amount originally borrowed or be reasonably comparable with the amounts generally payable on the redemption of securities listed on a recognised stock exchange.
  The loan creditor condition must be met throughout an accounting period.

- **Balance of business condition**
  At least 60% of the PAIF's net income should be derived from the PIB and at least 60% of the value of the PAIF's assets held at the end of an accounting period must be assets involved in the PIB. Both percentages are reduced to 40% for the first accounting period of newly launched PAIFs. For the purposes of the asset test, the assets must be valued in accordance with accounting standards. If those standards permit a choice between fair value and a cost basis, fair value must be used.

There is no entry charge for AIFs that elect into the regime.

Upon entry into the regime, any existing rental business is treated as ceasing for corporation tax purposes (any losses attributable to a former property rental business cannot be utilised against the PAIF's PIB income). The fund is also treated for tax purposes as having sold and immediately reacquired its PIB assets. However, the deemed disposal does not give rise to chargeable gains or generate any balancing allowances or charges for capital allowances purposes (the assets are transferred at their tax written down value). A new tax accounting period and distribution period commence on entry to the PAIF regime.

Distributions

[4.42] A PAIF is required to distribute all of its net income (as with all AIFs, an issue of additional shares in respect of accumulation shares is treated as a distribution for these purposes). Distributions made by a PAIF are required to be split into three streams: property income distributions (PIDs), interest distributions and dividend distributions. Therefore, investors may receive up to three types of distribution each year. The relative complexity involved in streaming distributions into three components is generally considered to have contributed to the relatively few PAIFs launched since the introduction of the regime.

The PAIF is generally required to deduct basic rate income tax when paying a PID unless the investor is within the charge to UK corporation tax. UK Registered Pension Schemes, charities, and ISA holders and certain other categories of investors are also able to receive gross PIDs and interest distributions from a PAIF. From 6 April 2017, the requirement to withhold income tax has been removed from PAIF interest distributions. The rate of tax deducted from the distribution, where necessary, is as follows:

Type of distribution	Tax deducted, where necessary
PID	Basic rate income tax
Interest distribution	Basic rate income tax (before 6 April 2017). Nil after 6 April 2017.
Dividend distribution	Nil

The PAIF must provide investors with a written statement showing the gross PID, the income tax deducted thereon and the actual amount paid (or provide a written statement enabling the investor to calculate those details).

The PAIF must deliver a return to HMRC for each return period (generally the quarters ending 31 March, 30 June, 30 September and 31 December) in which a PID is paid within 14 days beginning with the day immediately following the end of the return period. Any income tax withheld from the PID must be paid to HMRC within the same time-frame for delivering the return. The return must show the amount of any PID paid in the return period and the income tax due to HMRC in respect of that distribution.

PAIFs versus REITs

[4.43] The key difference between a PAIF and a UK-REIT is that a PAIF is an open-ended vehicle (a UK-REIT is closed-ended in nature). Furthermore, a PAIF is not listed but is subject to FCA regulation. The shares of a UK-REIT are listed but its activities are not the subject of direct supervision by the FCA.

A PAIF can hold shares in a UK-REIT and income from UK-REITs is treated as part of the PAIF's PIB (provided the income is paid in respect of the property rental business carried on by the UK-REIT – UK-REITs can pay both property income distributions and ordinary company dividends). Therefore, a PAIF could be used as a fund of funds investment vehicle to invest in UK-REITs (and/or overseas equivalents to UK-REITS).

The PIB carried on by a PAIF must represent at least 60% of its total business (see the income and asset requirements outlined in the balance of business condition in **4.41** above). That percentage threshold is increased to 75% for a UK-REIT.

A PAIF can pay three types of distribution whereas a UK-REIT can only pay two distribution types.

Taxation of PAIFs

[4.44] The PAIF's income must be separated into two categories: that which is derived from the PIB (the tax-exempt business) and the income that is derived from other activities, the residual business (two distributions can be paid in respect of the residual business).

PAIFs are exempt from corporation tax on capital gains and capital profits attributable to creditor loan relationships and derivative contracts (as is the case for all AIFs).

PAIFs are legal persons for SDLT and pay SDLT on the purchase of UK real estate according to the normal rules. As from Royal Assent of Finance Act 2016 (15 September 2016) there is an SDLT seeding relief potentially applicable to transfers of property portfolios into PAIFs in return for the issue of PAIF shares. The SDLT seeding relief will work in the same manner as the CoACS SDLT seeding relief (see **4.92**).

Tax-exempt business

[4.45] The PAIF is exempt from UK corporation tax on income derived from the PIB. The PIB income retains its identity as it passes from the PAIF to its investors. The PID received by investors is taxed in the same manner as if they owned the PIB assets directly; this effectively moves the point of taxation on the property rental profits from the PAIF to its investors. This overcomes the significant tax inefficiency associated with the broader AIF regime, namely that tax-exempt investors effectively suffer 20% corporation tax on property rental profits at the level of the AIF with no means of recouping that tax paid by the AIF. The taxation of the investors is covered in **4.48** below.

The income of the tax-exempt business is 'ring-fenced' from any other businesses of the PAIF. The tax-exempt part of the business is treated as a separate business from the residual business. This prevents any losses generated in the tax-exempt business being offset against the income of the residual business and vice versa.

The income of the ring-fenced tax-exempt business is generally calculated using the tax rules that apply in respect of a property rental business subject to only a few exceptions:

- notional capital allowances are automatically deducted in arriving at the distributable income of the tax-exempt business (it is not possible to disclaim available capital allowances in computing the PAIF income that must be distributed as a PID);
- while the profits of a property business are generally computed without taking account of any credits or debits attributable to loan relationships and derivative contracts, this rule is disapplied in computing the net income of the tax-exempt business in so far as a loan relationship or a hedging derivative contract relates to that business. The general rule is also disapplied in the case of an embedded derivative if the host contract was entered into for the purposes of the tax-exempt business.

Income and expenditure that is partly attributable to both the tax-exempt and residual businesses should be apportioned reasonably.

Residual business

[4.46] The net income from the residual business of the PAIF is within the charge to corporation tax at the rate applicable to OEICs (currently 20%). The income of the residual business is any income of the PAIF other than income referable to the tax-exempt business. However, the residual business obtains a tax deduction in respect of the income that is distributed to the shareholders as an interest distribution. The amount able to be deducted as an interest distribution is the net income of the PAIF after deducting both the tax-exempt income of the PIB and any other amounts that are allowable for corporation tax purposes (including any exempt dividend income). The tax deductibility of the interest distribution should result in the PAIF having no corporation tax liability.

The dividend distribution component of the total distribution is calculated as the balance of the PAIF's net income after deducting both the PID and the interest distribution.

A PAIF must provide additional information when filing its corporation tax return – a calculation of the net income of the tax-exempt business and the residual business and a reconciliation between its net income and the total income shown in the distribution accounts as attributed to the three different types of distribution.

Potential tax charges on PAIFs

[4.47] If a PAIF makes a distribution to a holder of excessive rights (a company that is beneficially entitled to 10% or more of the net asset value of the PAIF), a tax charge is imposed on the PAIF if it did not take reasonable steps to avoid the possibility of paying such a distribution. The quantum of the charge is determined by the amount of PID income distributed to such a holder. A PAIF must also provide certain information to HMRC on becoming aware it has made a distribution to a holder of excessive rights, including:

- the name and address of the holder(s);
- the percentage of the net asset value of the PAIF held by the holder(s);
- the steps that the PAIF took to prevent the acquisition of an excessive holding; and
- the steps taken (or being taken) to ensure there is no longer a holding of excessive rights.

A PAIF that is a QIS can also suffer a tax charge if broadly the ratio of the net income of its tax-exempt business to the financing costs attributable to that business falls below a certain level. These rules are designed to reduce the scope for extracting the profits of the tax-exempt business as interest instead of PIDs and do not apply to non-QIS PAIFs as they are subject to FCA rules limiting the level of their borrowings.

If a PAIF attempts to obtain a tax advantage for itself or another person, HMRC can issue a notice to the PAIF specifying that advantage and seek to counteract the advantage via:

- an assessment;
- the cancellation of a right of repayment;
- a requirement to return a repayment already made; or
- the computation (or recomputation) of profits or gains, or liability to tax, on a basis specified by HMRC.

In addition to the above remedies, HMRC can also assess the PAIF to an additional amount of income tax that is considered equivalent to the value of the tax advantage.

Taxation of investors

[4.48] Investors are taxed on distributions from a PAIF at their normal rates of taxation. If a PAIF distribution has been paid net of basic rate income tax, the tax withheld can be offset against the investors' tax liability. The manner in which an investor taxes a PAIF distribution will vary depending on the type of PAIF distribution received. The comments below assume that the PAIF shares are held as an investment (and not, for example, held on trading account by a financial trader).

Investors subject to corporation tax

Property income distributions

[4.49] PIDs are charged to corporation tax as profits of a property rental business (unlike most company distributions which are exempt from tax in the hands of most UK corporate recipients). A PID is treated as profits of a separate business from any other property business that the company may have – therefore, losses on another rental business cannot be offset against the PID.

A PID will generally be paid without deduction of income tax to persons within the charge to UK corporation tax.

Interest distributions

[4.50] Interest distributions are treated as payments of interest arising from a loan relationship and are paid without deduction of income tax from April 2017. Therefore, the distribution will be treated as a non-trade loan relationship credit.

Dividend distributions

[4.51] Dividend distributions are treated in the same manner as any other dividend from a UK company (ie they are exempt from corporation tax). Unlike dividends distributions from AIFs that are not PAIFs, there is no requirement to 'stream' dividend distributions from PAIFs (the corporate streaming rules outlined in **4.36** do not apply).

Disposal of shares

[4.52] The normal rules relating to corporation tax on chargeable gains apply to a disposal of shares in a PAIF. If the long-term fund of a life assurance company holds shares in a PAIF, that investment is treated in the same way as holdings in AIFs that are not PAIFs.

Investors subject to income tax (including tax-exempt investors)

[4.53] Basic rate taxpayers will have no further tax to pay on the distributions they receive from a PAIF. Any income tax liability relating to the PID is fully satisfied by the basic rate income tax deducted at source by the PAIF.

Higher or additional rate taxpayers will have a further liability to income tax in respect of the PID which will be computed in their self-assessment tax return.

PAIF investors that are not liable to tax, either because they are tax-exempt investors (such as Registered Pension Schemes, charities or ISA holders), or as a result of not having income in excess of their tax-free personal allowance, can claim a repayment of any income tax deducted from the distribution (the tax credit attaching to the dividend distribution is, however, not repayable). However, as noted above, certain categories of investor are entitled to be paid PAIF distributions gross without deduction of basic rate income tax.

Property income distributions

[4.54] PIDs are normally charged to income tax as profits of a UK property business and the PID will normally be paid net of basic rate income tax. A PID is treated as profits of a separate business from any other property business that the investor may have – therefore, losses on another rental business cannot be offset against the PID.

The amount chargeable to income tax is the gross PID (the cash received plus the income tax shown as deducted from the PID). Despite the treatment of a PID as the profits of a UK property business, it is not declared on the supplementary property pages of an income tax return. Instead, it should be included in the 'other income' section of the main income tax return. Consequently, PAIF investors do not need to obtain and complete the supplementary property pages unless they have other sources of property income.

For non-UK tax resident investors, the non-resident landlord scheme does not apply to the PID even though the PID is treated as income from UK property (this is because the PID is paid under deduction of basic rate income tax).

Interest distributions

[4.55] Until 6 April 2017, interest distributions paid by a PAIF were normally paid net of basic rate income tax and the investor is treated as having received a payment of yearly interest. The requirement to withhold income tax on PAIF interest distribution was removed from 6 April 2017.

PAIF interest distributions fall within the new personal savings allowance (see **4.35**).

Dividend distributions

[4.56] The receipt of a dividend distribution from a PAIF is treated in the same manner as any other UK company dividend. See **4.34**.

Disposal of shares

[4.57] A disposal of shares in a PAIF is treated in the same manner as a disposal of any other capital gains tax asset.

Overseas investors

[4.58] If the investor is resident in a territory which has a double tax treaty with the UK, they may be able to make a treaty claim for repayment of some or all of the UK income tax withheld depending on the provisions of the relevant treaty and the circumstances of the recipient.

As the total distribution will have three components, determined by the quantum of the different types of income in the PAIF, the withholding tax suffered on the total distribution will vary depending on the split of the total distribution between the three distribution types. Therefore, any potential treaty claims would have to be made in respect of each distribution type.

Breaches and leaving the PAIF regime

[4.59] Any breaches of the conditions outlined in **4.41** must be notified to HMRC as soon as reasonably practical together with certain specified information. HMRC can also request information from the PAIF manager if it believes that either a condition has not been complied with or a breach has not been rectified.

The consequences of breaching the conditions of the PAIF regime are as follows.

• Genuine diversity of ownership condition

If a PAIF breaches this condition, certain information must be provided to HMRC within 28 days, including the proposed steps that will be implemented to rectify the breach and the date by which it is proposed the breach will be rectified (that date must be the earliest date that is reasonably achievable). HMRC can issue a termination notice if it is considered that the proposed steps will not rectify the breach or will not do so by the earliest reasonable date. A termination notice results in the OEIC being forced to leave the PAIF regime.

Three different breaches of this condition in three different accounting periods within a period of ten years can result in HMRC serving a termination notice on the fund.

- **Corporate ownership condition**
  Three breaches of this condition in a period of ten years beginning with the first day of the accounting period in which the first breach occurs can result in HMRC serving a termination notice but only if the fund has not taken reasonable steps to prevent the breaches.
- **Loan creditor condition**
  An inadvertent breach of this condition which is rectified within 28 days of it being discovered will not result in the fund being forced to leave the PAIF regime. However, an intentional or negligent breach of this condition can result in the issue of a termination notice as can various multiple breaches of this condition within a period of ten years.
- **Balance of business condition**
  If either of the 40% threshold requirements are not complied with, the fund will cease to be a PAIF. If either of the 60% threshold requirements are not complied with, the fund can remain within the PAIF regime provided both percentages are not below 50% (if either threshold is below 50%, HMRC can issue a termination notice). However, if the balance of business condition is breached in three different accounting periods within a period of broadly ten years, this can result in HMRC serving a termination notice on the fund.

Multiple breaches involving more than one of the above conditions can result in the fund being required to leave the PAIF regime. This would generally require five breaches in a period of ten years beginning with the first day of the accounting period in which the first breach occurs.

HMRC can also serve a termination notice on a PAIF if there is an intentional or negligent breach of a condition outlined in **4.41** or if the PAIF has attempted to obtain a tax advantage (for example, creating or inflating a loss, deduction or expense).

A termination notice must state the reason it has been issued and results in the fund ceasing to be a PAIF at the end of the accounting period before the accounting period during which the event occurs that causes the notice to be served. The OEIC can appeal against the issue of a termination notice.

An OEIC will also leave the PAIF regime if any of the following circumstances occur.

- The fund gives written notice to HMRC that it wants to exit the regime. That notice must specify the date that the fund will cease to be a PAIF (the date must be after the date the notice is given to HMRC).

- The fund ceases to be authorised by the FCA, ceases to be an OEIC or ceases to carry on a PIB. The fund ceases to be a PAIF at the end of the date on which the cessation event occurs.
- The fund is party to a merger or takeover which results in it ceasing to meet one or more of the conditions detailed in **4.41**. The fund ceases to be a PAIF at the end of the date of the merger or takeover.

The consequences of leaving the PAIF regime are as follows.

- The PIB is treated for corporation tax purposes as ceasing immediately before the fund leaves the regime. A new accounting period of the fund will commence.
- Upon exit, the PIB assets are treated as having been sold and immediately reacquired. The deemed disposal does not give rise to chargeable gains or generate any balancing allowances or charges for capital allowances purposes.

Unauthorised unit trusts

[4.60] An unauthorised unit trust (UUT) is defined in ITA 2007, s 989 (CTA 2010, s 1140 for corporation tax purposes) as any unit trust scheme which is neither an authorised unit trust nor an umbrella scheme. There is no such vehicle as an 'unauthorised OEIC'; OEICs can only be formed upon authorisation from the FCA.

UUTs are an attractive vehicle for tax-exempt investors to obtain exposure to UK property and are often used by UK pension schemes for that purpose. However, the restricted range of investors that can participate in a tax efficient UUT has resulted in a number of UUTs migrating to Jersey where a similar result can be achieved for both UK tax-exempt investors and a much wider class of investors.

UUTs have also historically been used for property development activity by pension funds. Income derived from investments or deposits held for the purposes of a registered pension scheme is exempt from income tax. However income from a trading activity undertaken by a registered pension scheme is not investment income and so does not qualify for this tax exemption and will be taxed at penal rates. Therefore UUTs have been used to undertake development activities and block any trading income from flowing through to the pension funds. These arrangements should be unaffected by the amendments made to the taxation of UUTs outlined below, provided all the investors are exempt.

The creation of a unit trust scheme is usually a deliberate act by a fund manager for the purpose of managing investments for a fee. There is a trust deed and the parties are generally aware of the structure and applicable tax regime. In practice, it is possible that a fund sponsor or property manager could bring investors together to co-invest without being aware of the potential legal and tax consequences. If a collective investment scheme is created and the property is held on trust for the investors, this could amount to a unit trust scheme and implications will result. This tends to happen most often with property co-investment and, unless all the investors are exempt from capital gains tax, can give rise to a tax inefficient vehicle with capital gains tax charged within the fund and when investors sell their units.

Taxation of UUTs

[4.61] The taxation rules for UUTs are contained within SI 2013/2819. This was introduced under powers contained within Finance Act 2013 and significantly changed the taxation of UUTs from the old rules, which were based on standard trust tax principles.

Exempt or non-exempt

[4.62] The taxation of a UUT depends on whether it is an exempt UUT ('EUUT') or a non-exempt UUT ('NEUUT'). To be a EUUT certain conditions must be met and an application must be made to HMRC. UUTs that do not meet the conditions or do not apply to HMRC for exempt status are NEUUTs.

NEUUTs are subject to corporation tax with no specific exemptions. Distributions of NEUUTs are treated as dividends. Accordingly, the remainder of this section focuses on EUUTs.

EUUTs should generally not have a tax liability or a requirement to withhold income tax, as further explained below.

Conditions and application procedure for EUUTs

[4.63] In order to be eligible to qualify as a EUUT, a UUT must:

- have UK resident trustees;
- only have eligible investors who are exempt from capital gains tax or corporation tax other than by reason of residence (albeit a UUT manager can hold units pending disposal); and
- be approved under the Regulations.

A EUUT will not be regarded as failing the eligible investors test if there is an ineligible investor in circumstances where, the manager or trustees could not reasonably have been aware an investor became ineligible and once they discovered this, the ineligible investor disposes of its units within 28 days of this time. However, this may not be relied upon more than twice in any period of ten years.

Certain types of fund vehicles (such as Irish Common Contractual Funds) are often used to pool UK pension scheme investors. If those UK pension scheme investors were to invest in a UUT directly, they would be eligible investors. However, it is important to note that whilst vehicles such as an Irish CCF may be transparent for UK income tax purposes, they are opaque for UK capital gains tax purposes and thus exempt from UK capital gains tax purposes due to their non-UK residence. As a result, care needs to be taken when determining an investor's eligibility as vehicles such as Irish CCFs may not be considered to be eligible investors in a UUT by HMRC.

To become approved the managers of a UUT must make an application to HMRC. This must contain the following:

- a statement specifying the first day of the period of account for which approval is sought;
- a copy of the UUT's deed;
- a copy of the UUT's most recent prospectus;
- a statement specifying the arrangements that will be in place to ensure that all investors are eligible investors;
- a statement noting whether equalisation arrangements will be operated.

HMRC must generally respond to an application within 28 days.

Tax treatment of EUUTs

[4.64] EUUTs are exempt from capital gains tax.

Income of EUUTs is however within the charge to income tax (with various dis-applications). However, in practice, there should not normally be any income tax liability because EUUTs are treated as making a (deductible) distribution of their post-tax income to the unitholders in proportion to their rights annually. There is no requirement for income tax to be withheld from this deemed distribution (unlike the previous regime applicable to UUTs).

There are possible exemptions from deemed payments being deductible, applying ITA 2007, s 450 to the deemed payment and where income is attributable to a non-eligible unitholder (but the EUUT still qualifies as such because of the application of the exemption described above).

Therefore, if operated correctly, a UUT is a tax efficient vehicle for tax-exempt investors to hold property. In effect, tax-exempt investors generally suffer no tax on an investment in a EUUT and, therefore, achieve the same position had they invested directly.

It is also worth noting the following:

- Investors are taxable on the amount of the deemed distribution arising each period.
- The accounts of a EUUT need to be prepared in accordance with the IA SORP and be audited.
- The existing 'white list' provisions that are available for other types of investment funds are also available to EUUTs to provide certainty that defined financial transactions should not be characterised as trading transactions for tax purposes.
- EUUTs are also allowed to compute notional income from offshore non-reporting funds in the same manner as AIFs.
- EUUTs must provide a statement to unitholders showing the amount of income treated as received under the regulations.
- There are certain restrictions for AIFs investing in EUUTs, including preventing the AIF from paying interest distributions to investors and subjecting the AIF to the full rate of UK corporation tax, rather than the basic rate of 20%.

Comparison of OEICs, AUTs, PAIFs, UUTs, CoACSs and non-resident companies

[4.65] The following table provides a comparison of the tax position of OEICs, AUTs, PAIFs, UUTs, CoACSs and a non-UK resident company holding UK property.

	OEIC	AUT	PAIF	EUUT	CoACSs	Company (non-resident)
Type of entity	Special type of company formed under FSMA	Trust but treated as a company for tax purposes	OEIC (special type of company formed under FSMA)	Trust arrangement, income flows to trustees on behalf of unitholders	Contractual arrangement	Company not tax resident in the UK
Basis of taxation	Chargeable to corporation tax but with special rules	Chargeable to corporation tax but with special rules	Chargeable to corporation tax on non-PIB profits (but unlikely to pay corporation tax due to tax deduction for interest distribution)	Notionally chargeable to income tax on rental profits	Transparent for income tax (therefore rental profits taxed according to status of unitholder). Exempt from gains.	Chargeable to income tax on UK rental profits
Property rental profits	Taxed at basic rate of income tax (20% for 2015/2016)	Taxed at basic rate of income tax (20% for 2015/2016)	Exempt from corporation tax —	Taxed at basic rate of income tax (20% for 2015/2016)	Depends on the status of the unitholder —	Taxed at basic rate of income tax (20% for 2015/2016)
Deductions	Allowable expenses of property rental business, capital allowances, management expenses, loan relationship debits	Allowable expenses of property rental business, capital allowances, management expenses, loan relationship debits	Capital allowances (notionally deducted in the computation of the PID), management expenses, loan relationship debits (including interest distribution)	Expenses incurred wholly and exclusively for the purposes of the property rental business and deemed distributions each period	Expenses incurred wholly and exclusively for the purposes of the property rental business. Capital allowances may be available.	Expenses incurred wholly and exclusively for the purposes of the property rental business

	OEIC	AUT	PAIF	EUUT	CoACSs	Company (non-resident)
Gains	Not taxable	Not taxable	Not taxable	Not taxable	Not taxable	Outside scope of UK capital gains tax if not UK resident and not carrying on a trade in the UK through a permanent establishment (but see comments below regarding certain disposals of UK residential property).

From April 2013 the scope of UK capital gains tax was extended to charge gains arising on the disposal of UK residential property valued at greater than £2m, which has been progressively reduced to £500,000 by 2016, by certain non-natural persons (including non-resident companies and collective investment schemes), unless certain exemptions apply. The table above does not include the capital gains issues in respect of UK residential property valued at greater than £500,000. Additionally, the table does not include details of the CGT charge extended to non-resident individuals on UK residential property as this is outside the scope of this chapter.

Limited partnerships

Introduction

[4.66] For tax purposes, a partnership is effectively 'tax transparent' so that its profits are taxed directly in the hands of each partner. This can be of benefit to investors as it means that they only need to consider their own tax status and profile when evaluating a potential investment with no need to consider additional taxation at the entity level. For example, if a tax-exempt Registered Pension Scheme invests in a partnership, any investment return attributable to that Scheme should be exempt with no tax suffered at the level of the partnership. This will be discussed in detail below.

Partnerships are also very flexible vehicles in that the partnership agreement can be drafted to meet the different needs of the different investors. A summary of the relative merits of partnerships is included at **4.82**.

Features of a limited partnership

[4.67] Reference must be made to general UK law for the definition of a partnership. 'Partnership' is defined by the Partnership Act 1890 (PA 1890) as 'the relation which subsists between persons carrying on a business in common with a view of profit'. Partnerships do not constitute companies or associations incorporated under the Companies Acts. Partnerships (except limited liability partnerships) are not separate legal entities in England and Wales and are generally treated as tax transparent (a Scottish partnership has legal personality but is still treated as fiscally transparent to preserve equality in the tax treatment of all UK partnerships). A new class of English limited partnership – the private fund limited partnership (PFLP) was introduced from 6 April 2017. The changes introduced a 'white list' of activities of limited partners which will not affect their limited liability status. However, the PFLP regime does not alter the existing position that English limited partnerships do not have legal personality.

The taxable profits and losses of the partnership are generally computed at the level of the partnership but any tax liability on the partnership profits rests with the actual partners.

A partnership with one or more limited partners can be formed under the Limited Partnerships Act 1907 (LPA 1907). Broadly, the liability of such a partner is limited to the amount of the agreed capital contribution of that partner (or no capital in the case of a PFLP). The capital contribution could take the form of property contributed to the partnership.

The PFLP regime does not alter the tax attributes of the LPA 1907 regime, and therefore the tax comments below apply equally to both regimes.

Partners

[4.68] Limited partners, who may be either individuals or companies or both, cannot participate in the management of the business beyond the provision of advice (see above comments in **4.67** regarding the 'white list' of LP activities). The business is managed and bound by one or more 'general' partners whose liability is not limited and who are responsible for all debts and obligations of the partnership (LPA 1907, s 4(2)). At least one general partner is required and the general partner will usually be a limited company.

If both individuals and companies are partners in the same partnership, the taxable profits of the partnership will have to be computed using both income tax and corporation tax rules. The profits computed under income tax principles will be used to ascertain the taxable profits attributable to a partner who is an individual while the profits calculated using corporation tax rules will be used to determine the taxable profits attributable to a corporate partner.

There is no limit on the number of partners in a general or limited partnership.

Limited partnerships as unit trusts

[4.69] A limited partnership could be considered a unit trust scheme under FSMA 2000 and can become authorised as a partnership authorised contractual scheme. However, the Capital Gains Tax (Definition of Unit Trust Scheme) Regulations 1988 (SI 1988/266) states that a limited partnership shall not be treated as a unit trust scheme for capital gains tax purposes.

Registration and compliance

[4.70] The partnership and the amount of capital contributed by the limited partners must be registered with the Registrar of Companies (LPA 1907, s 8). Any changes in the partners, their capital contributions and the partnership business must be notified within seven days to the Registrar (LPA 1907, s 9). In practice, flexibility can be achieved through the contribution of a small amount of capital with further contributions taking the form of a loan or advance. Under the PFLP regime, limited partners are not required to contribute any capital to the partnership.

Under the self-assessment regime, the partnership must complete a partnership tax return (albeit no assessment of tax is made on the partnership itself). The partners must include their share of the taxable profits of the partnership (determined in accordance with the profit sharing provisions in the partnership agreement) in their own tax returns. If a UK tax resident company is a partner in a partnership that holds UK property, it will include its share of the rental profits derived from its investment in the partnership in its corporation tax return using the information contained in the partnership tax return (corporation tax returns must be submitted within one year of the end of the tax accounting period).

If a non-UK tax resident company or an individual is a partner in a partnership that holds UK property, they will be subject to the income tax regime. Under the self-assessment tax regime, income tax returns must be submitted by the first 31 January following the end of the tax year (5 April). However, the filing deadline for paper returns is the first 31 October following the end of the tax year.

Tax treatment for a partnership owning UK property

[4.71] The taxable profits attributable to the property investment business carried on by the partnership are computed and then split between the partners in accordance with the provisions of the partnership agreement. If any partner is subject to income tax (eg a UK tax resident individual), the profits or losses of the property business carried on by the partnership are calculated as if the partnership were a UK resident individual (ITTOIA 2005, s 849(2)). Each partner is then assessed as if his share of that taxable profit or loss were derived from a property business carried on by that partner alone (ITTOIA 2005, s 852).

If any partner is a UK resident company or an overseas company that holds their interests as part of a UK permanent establishment, the taxable profits and losses generated by the property investment business are calculated using corporation tax rules and then split amongst the partners in accordance with the profit-sharing arrangements of the partnership (CTA 2009, ss 1259–1261). Any profits allocated to a UK tax resident company will be subject to corporation tax as if the property business was directly carried on by the company (CTA 2009, ss 1262, 1265). The share of the taxable profit or loss must be allocated to the accounting periods of the corporate partner in which that profit or loss arose (it is possible that the tax accounting period of a corporate partner may not coincide with the period that the partnership prepares accounts for).

If a partnership carrying on a UK property business holds a number of investment properties, the rental profits from which are taxable under the property rental business rules, it is treated as a single business. Consequently, rental losses arising on one property can be set against rental profits arising on another property.

Relief

Interest

[4.72] Expenses incurred 'wholly and exclusively' for the purposes of a property rental business carried on by a partnership are generally deductible against rental income subject to some specific rules (ITTOIA 2005, ss 34 and 272). This provides tax relief for interest paid by a partnership on a loan that represents a partnership liability. The loan relationship rules would apply in respect of such interest when computing the profits of a partnership that has corporate partners.

Interest payable on a loan which an individual has borrowed to purchase a share in a partnership which carries on a property rental business, will be treated as a deductible expense for that individual in computing their income tax liability provided they are not a limited partner in a limited partnership formed under the LPA 1907 or a member of an investment LLP (ITA 2007, ss 398–399). From 6 April 2017 the amount of interest deductions available to individuals investing in UK residential property will be gradually reduced such that relief will only be available at the basic rate of income tax from 2020.

Capital gains tax

[4.73] Due to the fiscally transparent nature of a partnership, each partner is generally regarded as owning a fractional share of the partnership capital gains tax assets (including investment properties) according to their interest in the partnership, rather than owning an interest in the partnership itself. The fractional interest of a partner in the capital gains tax assets of the partnership will usually be set out in the partnership agreement. Tax on capital gains arising on the disposal of partnership assets is assessed directly on the partners, not the partnership (TCGA 1992, s 59). In practice, these principles can be complex to apply. HMRC has provided additional guidance in Statement of Practice D12 (SP D12), first published in January 1975 and last revised in September 2015.

Certain key events and their capital gains impact are summarised below.

A change in profit sharing ratios

[4.74] Paragraph 4 of SP D12 covers the situations where there is a change in profit-sharing ratios upon partner joining or leaving the partnership and where the ratios are altered even though no partner joins or leaves the partnership (eg a reallocation of partnership shares caused by a revision to the partnership agreement). A change in profit sharing ratios is treated as a disposal of the partnership assets (including any investment property held by the partnership) for a partner who reduces or surrenders his share and as an acquisition of such assets for a partner who acquires a share or increases his share.

No consideration and no revaluation in the accounts

[4.75] Provided there is no direct payment of consideration outside the framework of the partnership accounts and there has been no revaluation of the partnership assets in those accounts, the consideration for the disposal will be treated as equal to the appropriate fraction of the capital gains tax base cost. Consequently there will be neither a gain nor a loss at that point (SP D12, para 4). However, see the comments below regarding transfers between connected partners and transactions not conducted on arm's-length terms.

A partner whose partnership share reduces will carry forward a smaller proportion of base cost to set against proceeds arising on a subsequent disposal of that asset and a partner whose partnership share increases will carry forward a larger proportion of base cost. For example, if X and Y previously owned 50% each of a partnership investment property purchased for £100,000 and X gives 20% to Y so that X now has 30% and Y now has 70%, X will be treated as having disposed of 20% of the property and Y as having acquired that 20%. The total tax base cost of the investment property of £100,000 remains the same but is split between X and Y according to the new ratio 30:70.

	X's share	Y's share	Total base cost
Old share	50%	50%	£100k
Old base cost	£50k	£50k	£100k
New share	30%	70%	£100k
New base cost	£30k	£70k	£100k

The reduction to the tax base cost available to a partner whose profit sharing ratio reduces in the circumstances outlined in para 4 of SP D12, could result in the ultimate taxable gain accruing to that partner on an actual disposal of partnership assets differing from their economic gain. Amounts payable to the partners on the termination of a partnership may be adjusted to compensate any partners whose liability to tax on chargeable gains has arisen (or increased) due to the reduction of their allowable base cost to the extent of any tax benefit that has accrued to the partners whose profit shares have increased. Any such adjustments debited to the partners whose tax base costs are deemed to have increased on a change in profit-sharing ratios may be able to be treated as adjustments to the payments out of partnership capital upon termination rather than as consideration for the disposal of either part of any partner's share in the partnership assets or any other non-partnership asset (section 3.2 of the *British Venture Capital Association guidelines 1987*). In Finance (No 2) Act 2015, legislation was introduced with the effect that base cost shifts are not effective for carried interest partnerships.

However, the nil gain/nil loss treatment referred to above will not apply if the partners concerned are connected (other than by the fact that they are partners in the partnership) or the transaction is not otherwise conducted on an arm's-length basis. In these circumstances, the transfer of the share in the partnership assets may be treated as having occurred at the market value of what has been transferred – this results in the transfer being treated in the same manner as payments made outside the framework of the partnership accounts (see **4.77**).

It should also be noted that Finance Act 2014 and 2015 introduced various changes to the taxation of partnerships (see **4.90**), including anti-avoidance rules concerned with the disposal of income streams and assets using partnerships. These could also apply where transactions are not at arm's length or in substance amount to a disposal.

The property has been revalued in the accounts

[4.76] If an asset (eg investment property) held by the partnership has been revalued in the partnership accounts (with the revaluation surplus shared amongst the capital or current accounts of the partners in accordance with their fractional share of the increased value), and there is a subsequent alteration in the profit sharing ratios, a partner whose ratio reduces is regarded as disposing of a fractional share of the asset in question – the upward revaluation of the asset would not in itself generate any tax liability. The fraction disposed of is the difference between the old and the new share of the partner in that asset and the disposal is deemed to be for consideration equal to that fraction of the increased value at the revaluation. The partner whose ratio correspondingly increases will have his base cost increased by the quantum of the deemed consideration. If in the example above, the property had been revalued in the partnership accounts at £150,000, X would be regarded as disposing of his 20% share for £30,000 (20% of £150,000) at the point at which the profit sharing ratios changed. Y would be treated as acquiring the increased share in that asset for £30,000 (ie the same amount). A capital gain of £10,000 (£30,000 less 20% of the original base cost) would accrue to X. X's remaining base cost would be £30,000 (30% of the original base cost) and Y's new base cost would be £80,000 (50% of the original base cost plus 20% of the revalued base cost).

	X's share	Y's share	Total
Old share	50%	50%	
Old base cost	£50k	£50k	£100k
Revaluation	£75k	£75k	£150k
New share	30%	70%	
Consideration	£30k (20% × £150k)	£30k (20% × £150k)	

	X's share	Y's share	Total
Base cost of disposed share	(£20k) (20% × £100k)	NA	
Chargeable gain	£10k (£30 – £20k)	NA	
New base cost	£30k (30% × £100k)	£80k ((50% × £100k) + (20% × £150k))	£110k

This treatment could result in a partner incurring a capital gains tax liability without having received any funds from the partnership to pay the tax.

The same principles outlined above would apply if the asset had been subject to a downward revaluation and there was a subsequent alteration in the profit-sharing ratios of the partners.

Capital gains tax liabilities arising in the scenario where partnership assets have been revalued and profit-sharing ratios are subsequently altered are reasonably common in partnerships that invest in property. If there is a management fee performance incentive established in the form of a share in the partnership profits with hurdles dependent on investment performance, each subsequent change in profit-sharing ratios will be treated as giving rise to a disposal of partnership assets by the partners whose profit shares reduce. Therefore, if the investment properties have been the subject of an upward revaluation prior to the investment performance hurdles being satisfied, capital gains tax liabilities may ensue if and when those hurdles are satisfied.

Payment is made outside of the accounts

[4.77] If on a change in partnership sharing ratios, a payment is made directly between the partners outside the framework of the partnership accounts, that payment is added to the consideration (if any) that is deemed to arise in the situations outlined in both **4.75** and **4.76** above. Such payments could be made in respect of goodwill that is not reflected in the balance sheet of the partnership – in that scenario, the partner receiving the payment may have no tax base cost to set against the taxable receipt. The partner who makes the payment will only be able to deduct that payment for tax purposes on a subsequent disposal of his share in the partnership asset(s).

Other profit share issues

[4.78] The investment management fee payable by a limited partnership to the general partner may be structured as a 'priority profit share' instead of a fee. This is where the amount payable to the general partner is funded out of the profits of the partnership with any profits being paid to the general partner in priority to any profits being allocated to the limited partners.

Contribution of assets to a partnership

[4.79] HMRC's approach to the situation where a partner contributes an asset such as an investment property to the partnership by means of a capital contribution was clarified in Revenue & Customs Brief 03/08 and is now also clarified in the September 2015 update of SP D12.

The Brief (and now SP D12) confirm that where an asset is transferred to a partnership by means of a capital contribution, HMRC considers that the correct application of the capital gains tax legislation is that the partner in question has made a part disposal of the asset equal to the fractional share that passes to the other partners. HMRC indicated that the approach previously adopted by some inspectors (that the contribution was made on a no gain/no loss basis as a result of an erroneous application of para 4 of SP D12) was incorrect but stated that they would consider themselves bound by statements made by inspectors in individual cases prior to the issue of that Brief. The transfer of an asset to a partnership is now dealt with in HMRC's capital gains manual (CG 27900).

Capital allowances

[4.80] Capital allowances on qualifying assets may be shared among the partners in accordance with the profit-sharing arrangements of the partnership (CTA 2009, s 1262(1); ITTOIA 2005, s 850(1)). Provided at least one partner remains a continuous member of the partnership, any change in the identity of the partners (eg a partner joining or leaving), will not constitute a disposal of the qualifying assets for capital allowances purposes. Therefore, capital allowances can continue to be claimed as if the present partners had at all times been carrying out the qualifying activity such as a property investment business (CAA 2001, s 263).

Although open to interpretation, the general view is that capital allowances should be included in the computation of the taxable profit or loss of the partnership. This means that any decisions regarding capital allowances (such as a CAA 2001, s 198 election or whether capital allowances should be disclaimed) are determined collectively by the partners prior to the split of the total taxable profit or loss of the partnership amongst the individual partners in accordance with the profit-sharing arrangements.

Distributions from partnerships

[4.81] Distributions received by a partner from a partnership are ignored for tax purposes because partnerships are tax transparent. Partners are assessed directly on the profits allocated to them in accordance with the provisions of the partnership agreement, irrespective of the timing of the distribution of those profits by the partnership.

Advantages/disadvantages

[4.82] A key advantage of limited partnerships as fund vehicles is their transparency for tax purposes. This makes them attractive to investors who are not subject to UK tax, such as Registered Pension Schemes. However, conversely this may be a disadvantage where there is trading activity. Furthermore, there is no taxation on distributions from a partnership which facilitates the efficient repatriation of cash: each partner's share of the taxable profit or loss is calculated separately with the payment of partnership distributions having no bearing on that calculation.

Additionally foreign jurisdictions widely recognise limited partnerships as transparent vehicles such that any applicable domestic exemptions and double taxation treaties should apply with reference to each limited partner's entitlement. This may be beneficial for investors such as Registered Pension Schemes who in many jurisdictions enjoy beneficial treatment.

Limited partnerships can also offer a degree of simplicity and familiarity not found with certain other fund vehicles. There is also considerable flexibility in drafting the terms of partnership agreements. Incentives can also be provided to the general partner of a limited partnership regarding the management of the investments by linking its investment management fee to performance.

However, partners reducing their partnership sharing ratios could face a tax charge in certain circumstances where no cash is received from the partnership to fund this charge (see **4.76** above). This can be exacerbated in the case of limited partnerships used as property investment vehicles as (a) a revaluation of the partnership assets may be more common and (b) the manager may be entitled to a share in the partnership profits that is determined by reference to the performance of the partnership (certain 'carried interest' arrangements may result in a disposal of partnership interests by the other partners).

Furthermore, partnership interests are not as readily marketable or transferable as shares in a company (partnerships cannot be listed on a UK stock exchange with the exception of the Specialist Funds Market). Whilst private transactions can take place, there is no established and readily available secondary market; often the initial partners are institutions who invest for the long term and there may be pre-emption rights for the incumbent partners.

SDLT is payable on the sale of a partnership interest where the partnership invests in real estate – a sale of such a partnership interest is treated as a disposal of a fraction of the underlying real estate. The rate of SDLT levied on transfers of real estate is usually higher than that applying on a sale of shares. (This is discussed further in **CHAPTER 16** on Stamp duty land tax.)

Limited liability partnerships

Legislative background

[4.83] Limited liability partnerships (LLPs) were introduced by the Limited Liability Partnership Act 2000 (LLPA 2000) as a new body corporate under general law. An LLP has legal personality separate from its members. The liability of its members is limited to the level of their capital contribution unless they are negligent in relation to work carried out for a client. LLPs are subject to some aspects of company law but are generally treated as partnerships for tax purposes. Unlike the limited partners of a limited partnership formed under the LPA 1907, the members of an LLP can participate in the day-to-day management of its business. The aim of the LLP regime is to combine the corporate benefits of limited liability with the tax benefits and commercial flexibility of a partnership.

Features

[4.84] The rights and duties of the members of an LLP are determined by the terms of the LLP agreement. Every member of an LLP is an agent of the LLP and binds the LLP when acting with the authority to do so.

Two specific types of LLP are referred to in tax legislation (ITA 2007, s 399(6), s 1004) other than those that carry on a trade, profession or business:

(1)   Investment LLP – an LLP whose business consists wholly or mainly in the making of investments and the principal part of whose income is derived from investments (ITA 2007, s 399(6)).

(2)   Property investment LLP – an LLP whose business consists wholly or mainly in the making of investments in land and the principal part of whose income is derived from investments in land (ITA 2007, s 1004).

Whether an LLP is an investment LLP or a property investment LLP is determined for each period of account of the LLP.

LLPs tend to be used by professional bodies and property investment LLPs are not common in practice.

Registration/compliance

[4.85] LLPs must be registered with at least two members. Where a person becomes a member of an LLP or ceases to be a member of an LLP, the LLP must give notice of this to the Registrar of Companies within 14 days. An LLP must file an annual return and accounts with Companies House and an audit may be required.

Tax treatment

[4.86] Although an LLP is regarded as a body corporate under general law, an LLP is generally treated as a partnership for direct tax purposes. Consequently, an LLP constitutes a fiscally transparent entity. Therefore, provided an LLP carries on a trade, profession or business (including a property investment business) with a view to profit, each member will be assessed to tax on their share of the LLP's taxable profits or chargeable gains as if they were members of a partnership governed by the PA 1890 (CTA 2009, s 1273(1); ITTOIA 2005, s 863(1)).

The detailed treatment of the taxation of partnerships is discussed under the previous section on limited partnerships.

Some pension scheme tax exemptions are disapplied if the pension scheme invests in a property investment LLP (eg Registered Pension Schemes are not exempt from tax in respect of income and capital gains derived from a property investment LLP). The normal tax exemptions that apply in respect of the pension business of a life insurance company or the tax-exempt business of a friendly society are also disapplied in the context of an investment in a property investment LLP.

If an LLP does not carry on a trade, profession or business with a view to profit or is in liquidation or being wound up by a court order, the LLP is generally treated as a body corporate for tax purposes and will be chargeable to corporation tax on its taxable profits and gains.

Relief

Interest relief

[4.87] Tax relief for interest paid by an LLP is broadly the same as for a limited partnership. However, no tax relief is available for interest paid by an individual member of an LLP on a loan taken out for the purposes of investing in an investment LLP (ITA 2007, s 399).

Capital gains

[4.88] The capital gains tax treatment of LLPs is broadly the same as for partnerships given LLPs are generally treated as fiscally transparent. Provided an LLP carries on a trade or business with a view to profit, the capital gains tax assets held by the LLP are treated as held by its members and any tax due on the disposal of those assets is assessed and charged on the LLP members. SP D12 (covered in detail above) extends to LLPs that carry on a trade or business with a view to profit.

However, on liquidation, the LLP is treated as a company for capital gains tax purposes and gains will be computed by reference to the date on which the LLP's assets were first acquired by the LLP and their cost at that date. The LLP ceases to be transparent for capital gains tax purposes so that the capital gains realised by an LLP in the liquidation period will be treated in the same manner for tax purposes as those of any other corporate body. Furthermore, the members of the LLP will be taxed on any gain (or given relief for any loss) that arises on the disposal of their capital interest in the LLP – the allowable base cost of each LLP member is determined according to their historical capital contributions as if the LLP had never been transparent.

If the affairs of an LLP are wound up in an orderly way, without the appointment of a liquidator, the transparency of the LLP is preserved during the period the LLP disposes of its assets provided the winding up is not for reasons connected with tax avoidance and the winding up period is not unreasonably prolonged.

A temporary cessation in the carrying on of a trade or business does not affect the transparency of the LLP for capital gains tax purposes (Tax Bulletin 50).

Advantages and disadvantages

[4.89] Like limited partnerships, LLPs are commercially flexible (the LLP members have flexibility in the drafting of the LLP agreement), are generally transparent for tax purposes and also limit the liability of their members.

As a body corporate, LLPs have the additional advantage of being able to create fixed and floating charges in the same manner as a company.

However, publicly available accounts are required to be lodged with the Companies House which may be commercially unattractive. There are also a number of other Companies House formalities that must be complied with (for example, registering changes in the identity of the LLP members).

As noted above, a disadvantage of property investment LLPs is that Registered Pension Schemes are not exempt from tax in respect of income and capital gains derived from such LLPs (unlike limited partnerships). The normal tax exemptions that apply in respect of the pension business of a life insurance company or the tax-exempt business of a friendly society are also disapplied in respect of property investment LLP investments. Therefore, relatively few LLPs are used to invest in property and limited partnerships are used instead.

Finance Act 2014 changes to partnership taxation

[4.90] Finance Act 2014 introduced some wide-ranging measures which alter the taxation of partnerships. In brief, the major changes were concerned with:

(i)   'salaried' members – which broadly aims to tax those LLP members which are in substance employees as employees rather than self-employed;

(ii)   'mixed' member partnerships – which broadly aims to prevent tax motivated partnership allocations to non-individuals; and

(iii)   loss allocation and disposal anti-avoidance measures – which broadly aim to prevent the use of partnerships to manipulate losses or in substance dispose of income streams or assets.

While these changes are expected to have significant effects on trading partnerships (including property managers structured as LLPs), there should be little to no impact on property investment partnerships as a result of (i) and (iii) above, and a relatively low impact as a result of (ii).

The impact as a result of (i) should be minimal as this change only applies to LLPs, and the impact of (iii) should likewise be minimal as this generally requires a tax-avoidance motive.

The mixed member rules could have some effect as these could, in certain circumstances, cause profits to be reallocated (for tax purposes) from (say) a corporate GP to an individual LP. This would be the case where there is a tax benefit as a result of the allocation to the GP (eg paying corporation tax rather than income tax), the individual LP has the power to enjoy by any means in the future the allocation to the GP (eg by virtue of being shareholder), and the allocation to the GP is attributable to the LP's power to enjoy. Accordingly, those impacted most by this change will likely be property fund managers that have interests in a partnership as both an LP and because of a shareholding in the GP. However, it is unlikely to affect external investors.

Authorised contractual schemes

[4.91] From 1 July 2013 contractual schemes for collective investment (also commonly referred to as tax transparent funds or TTFs) were introduced. This introduced two new vehicles, being the authorised co-ownership scheme (CoACS) and the authorised partnership scheme. At the date of writing there are several umbrella CoACSs established that hold property.

The partnership scheme is an authorised limited partnership and the tax features are as discussed under limited partnerships in **4.66** to **4.82**.

The CoACS is a UK tax transparent fund, similar to a Luxembourg FCP and an Irish Common Contractual Fund. While this vehicle was introduced mainly to compete with the Luxembourg and Ireland vehicles in the traditional investment management sector it could be a vehicle suitable for collective property investment.

Tax treatment

[4.92] The CoACS is transparent for income and opaque for capital gains (such that units in a CoACS are treated as assets). Income is therefore taxed according to the status of the unitholder on an arising basis, and the disposal of a unit is potentially chargeable to capital gains tax.

CoACSs are not subject to Schedule 19 SDRT on surrenders of units, and pursuant to legislation included in Finance Act 2016 CoACSs are opaque for SDLT purposes. This means there is no SDLT on the issue or surrender of CoACS units, and the scheme operator is responsible for paying SDLT.

As from Royal Assent of Finance Act 2016 (15 September 2016), a seeding relief potentially applies, meaning that property can be transferred into a CoACS without an SDLT charge. Per the HMRC policy paper, the key features of the SDLT seeding relief are:

- a defined seeding period of 18 months within which seeding transactions are eligible for relief, providing that the fund has not yet been opened to investors and the sole consideration for a transfer is units in the fund acquiring the property portfolio;
- a 'portfolio test' limiting the application of the relief to transactions where a minimum value of properties are transferred in order to eliminate the risk of enveloping;
- a mechanism to recover SDLT that had been relieved where a fund ceases to qualify as a CoACS, or the portfolio test is not met at any time within three years of the end of the seeding period; and
- a mechanism to recover some or all of the SDLT relieved where some or all units received in consideration of the initial seeding are disposed of within three years of the end of the seeding period and where a seeded property is occupied by a person connected with the fund.

These changes should mean that the CoACS can become a viable vehicle for investing in real estate without concerns or disadvantages associated with the SDLT treatment of the vehicle.

The PAIF SDLT seeding relief will operate in the same manner.

Previously, there has been some uncertainty as to the treatment of a CoACS for capital allowances purposes. This is because it was unclear whether allowances should be calculated at the level of the CoACS (similar to a partnership or the pragmatic approach that JPUTs have adopted) or whether each unitholder themselves should claim allowances. At the time of writing in summer 2017, draft regulations have been introduced which will allow a CoACS to make an election to calculate capital allowances at the level of the CoACS which should remove this uncertainty.

VAT registration

[4.93] VAT registration will be required when the income (or sale proceeds, as the case may be) derived by a property fund is subject to VAT and exceeds the current VAT registration limits (see **15.1** below and subsequent paragraphs on the VAT rules applicable to UK property interests etc). Voluntary VAT registration may sometimes be beneficial where the registration threshold is not exceeded, in order to facilitate a recovery of VAT incurred on the acquisition or development/redevelopment of property interests or to ensure that a transfer is treated as a transfer of a going concern and, as such, disregarded for VAT purposes (see **15.121** below).

It is the 'taxable person' who should be registered for VAT. However, in the context of a property fund, it is not always clear who the taxable person is and, therefore, who should register for VAT and opt to tax (if applicable). HMRC have often had to take a practical approach to VAT registration in individual cases and there has been a degree of uncertainty as to how joint owners of property interests should be registered. Some of the more general issues are considered below. However, paragraphs **15.194–15.200** below should be consulted for further detail. In all cases, it is useful to provide a full explanation to HMRC in a covering letter as to how the property is held with details of all parties concerned.

For investment funds, the VAT registration requirements will depend on the structure of the fund. For a trust vehicle, where legal and beneficial ownership is split, it is in principle the beneficial owner who should register for VAT and make any option to tax (see **15.196** below). If there is more than one beneficial owner, they will be treated by HMRC as a partnership for VAT purposes. This has no legal significance but is merely a means to register the vehicle for VAT (see **15.194** below). However, in practice, where there are a large number of beneficial owners (which may be the case for an AUT), HMRC generally consider that it is the legal owner who should register and opt to tax (see **15.196** below). For an AUT, that would generally result in the trustee registering for VAT.

For limited partnerships under the Limited Partnerships Act 1907, it is the general partner who is treated as carrying on the business of the partnership for VAT purposes. Therefore, the general partner should register for VAT and exercise any option to tax (see **15.195** below).

Limited liability partnerships are treated in the same manner as companies.

More details on the VAT rules that apply to partnerships are set out in CHAPTER 15.

Chapter 5

Overseas investors

by
Geraint Jones
BKL

Introduction and scope of UK taxation

[5.1] Entities of all types are able to own, occupy and invest in property in the UK and it is common for individuals and entities based overseas to do so. This chapter contrasts the position for overseas investors with that for UK investors and also covers additional matters which specifically arise for overseas investors.

Income and capital gains from property are charged to UK tax according to the following rules.

Companies

Charging provisions

[5.2] Charging provisions are as follows:

(a) A UK resident company is chargeable to:
   (i) Corporation tax (at 19% for 2017/18) on all of its profits. The term profit includes all sources of income and capital gains, other than those gains that are specifically charged to capital gains tax (CTA 2009, ss 2–5(1); TCGA 1992, ss 1 and 8). The rate of corporation tax will further reduce to 17% from 2020.
   (ii) Capital gains tax (at 28%) for gains realised on the disposal of high value residential properties that fall within the annual tax on enveloped dwellings (ATED) regime; see **5.28** (TCGA 1992, ss 1, 2B).
(b) A non-UK resident company is chargeable to:
   (i) UK corporation tax (at 19% for 2017/18) on income or capital gains from UK property if it operates in the UK through a permanent establishment (PE) situated in the UK (CTA 2009, s 5(2) and (3); TCGA 1992, ss 10 and 10B). In addition (for disposals on or after 5 July 2016) non-resident companies that deal in or develop land in the UK are liable to corporation tax on the profits of that trade. See **5.26** and **CHAPTER 13**. The change to the corporation tax rate to17% will also apply as above.

A PE is defined by CTA 2010, s 1141 as:

- a fixed place of business through which the company wholly or partly carries on its business; or
- an agent acting on behalf of the company which has, and habitually exercises, authority to do business on the company's behalf.

A fixed place of business specifically includes the following:

- place of management;
- branch;
- office;
- factory;
- workshop; and
- building site or construction or installation project.

(ii) Capital gains tax (at 28%) for gains realised on the disposal of high value residential properties that fall within the annual tax on enveloped dwellings (ATED) regime; see **5.28** (TCGA 1992, ss 1, 2B). The capital gains on non-residential UK property arising to non-UK resident companies without a UK PE are generally outside the scope of UK taxation subject to specific anti-avoidance provisions discussed later in this chapter. However, a significant reform has extended capital gains tax (at 20%) to non-residents owning UK residential property from April 2015. See **5.29** for further details.

(iii) UK income tax (if it does not have a PE in the UK) at the basic rate of 20% on income arising from a trade of dealing in or developing UK land or any other income arising within the UK which is not chargeable to corporation tax. Companies are not liable to higher rates of income tax (ITA 2007, s 11). However, in order to comply with the BEPS action plan and in particular the implementation of the new restrictions on interest relief within the UK (see **5.13** and **5.16**) it is proposed that in future, overseas companies will pay corporation tax on such income.

Both UK and overseas investors may also potentially be liable to the annual tax on enveloped dwellings ('ATED'). The ATED is based on a banding system on residential property that is 'enveloped', which is to say that its ownership is via a corporate 'wrapper' or 'envelope' and its value is more than £500k for chargeable periods beginning on or after 1 April 2016 (FA 2013, s 94 and FA 2014, ss 109, 110). Further detail is set out at **5.28**.

Summary

[5.3] A company that is carrying on a UK trade in property, or in dealing in or developing UK land (including buildings and structures), rather than holding property in the UK for investment purposes will automatically be assessed to corporation tax on its profits regardless of the company's tax residence (see below). The distinction between holding of property for investment purposes and conducting a property trade is determined by the intentions of the entity upon acquisition. The potential tax benefit is therefore that capital gains on the disposal of the property will not be subject to UK taxation, unless the trade involves either dealing in or developing UK land, or it is within the ATED regime (for more details see **5.28**), and is not within the extension of the capital gains regime to non-residents owning UK residential property from April 2015. Broadly speaking therefore the benefit is expected to endure for non-residents holding commercial property for investment purposes and in other limited circumstances. The tax benefits from maintaining an investment status and a non-UK tax resident status therefore remain potentially large and so the distinction between investment and trading in commercial property is often the subject of scrutiny by the tax authorities.

A note on company residence

[5.4] A company incorporated in the UK is regarded for the purposes of the Taxes Acts as resident there, irrespective of any rule of law giving it a different place of residence (CTA 2009, s 14).

There is no statutory definition of residence for companies incorporated outside the UK. The courts have determined that such a company will be a UK tax resident if it is centrally managed and controlled in the UK. See *De Beers Consolidated Mines v Howe* (1906) 5 TC 198, HL. See also: *Calcutta Jute Mills Co Ltd v Nicholson* (1876) 1 TC 83 (Ex D); *New Zealand Shipping Co Ltd v Thew* (1922) 8 TC 208, HL.

Determining the place of central management and control is a question of fact. However, HMRC will look to factors such as whether in fact the directors themselves exercise management and control, and if so where that central management and control is exercised. The place of directors' meetings will usually be of significance, if they are the means through which central management and control is exercised and, most importantly, where strategic and policy decisions are made. See *Laerstate BV v HM Revenue & Customs Comrs* [2009] UKFTT 209 TC and *Development Securities (No 9) Ltd and others* [2017] UKFTT 565 (TC).

However, a company that is considered UK tax resident under the above tests may also be deemed to be resident in another jurisdiction under its corresponding rules of tax residency. In such circumstances, the relevant double taxation agreement between the two countries (see **5.12**) may award residency to one of the two territories (typically by reference to where the 'effective management' of the company resides). Should an otherwise dual resident company be considered non-UK resident under the terms of the applicable treaty, then for domestic UK purposes, the company is also considered to be non-UK tax resident (CTA 2009, s 18).

European companies (SEs)

[5.5] The tax residence of an SE (a European Company formed pursuant to Council Regulation (EC) No 2157/2001) is determined by the place of its registered office. If an SE transfers its registered office to the UK on or after 1 April 2005 in accordance with Council Regulation (EC) 2157/2001, Art 8, it is regarded as resident in the UK for tax purposes upon registration in the UK. If a different place of residence is given by any rule of law, that place is not taken into account for tax purposes. Where this rule applies, the SE is not treated as ceasing to be UK-resident by reason only of the subsequent transfer from the UK of its registered office (CTA 2009, ss 16 and 17). This provision is subject to CTA 2009, s 18 which deals with companies treated as non-UK resident under double taxation arrangements.

Value Added Tax

[5.6] Unlike other taxes, Value Added Tax (VAT) is chargeable on grants or licences relating to immoveable property (i.e. land and buildings) by reference to where the property is located, and not where the investor is resident. Thus, any property situated within the UK is potentially within the scope of UK VAT. For VAT purposes, the UK includes the Isle of Man but excludes the Channel Islands. For full details on the VAT liability of land-related supplies in the UK see CHAPTER 15.

Individuals

Charging provisions

[5.7] An overseas investor who is domiciled outside the UK may still become UK resident by virtue of their presence in the UK. As such, this section contrasts the position for UK residents with non-UK residents.

(a)   Residence was previously determined by a person's physical presence in the UK during the tax year, intention and case law. It is now determined by Statutory Residence Test (SRT) (see **5.8** below).

(b)   Ordinary residence was more habitual than residence and was looked at for a period of several years as opposed to just one year. The concept of ordinary residence was abolished with the introduction of the SRT from 6 April 2013. Although it is argued that there is now more clarity, the impact is largely unchanged in terms of taxing income and gains as described in the table below.

(c)   Domicile is a different concept from residence and ordinary residence since it relates to an individual's 'homeland'. It is also more than just nationality. A person acquires their domicile at birth and under UK law, legitimate children acquire their father's domicile and illegitimate children, their mother's. It is possible to change one's domicile but this is beyond the scope of this text. The concept of domicile continues to exist following the introduction of the SRT. With effect from 6 April 2017, individuals resident in the UK for more than 15 of the last 20 years are deemed domiciled in the UK for all tax purposes. In addition, individuals who are born in the UK with a UK domicile of origin to UK-domiciled parents can no longer claim non-domicile status whilst they are resident in the UK.

The following table broadly summarises the impact of the various factors on the scope of UK taxation for an individual's income.

	Income subject to UK taxation
UK resident and UK domiciled	Worldwide income
Non-resident	UK source income
UK resident but not domiciled and has been resident in the UK for more than seven of the past nine years:	
Foreign income and gains are less than £2k.	UK source income and income remitted from overseas
Foreign income and gains are £2k or greater and an election has been made to be assessable on the remittance basis and the annual £30k charge for those who have been resident for more than seven of the past nine years (or £60k for those who have been resident for more than 12 of the past 14 years).	UK source income and income remitted from overseas
Foreign income and gains are £2k or greater and the election to be assessable on the remittance basis has not been made.	Worldwide income
UK resident but not domiciled and has been resident in the UK for seven of the past nine years or less and a remittance basis election has been made.	UK source income and income remitted from overseas

The following table summarises the impact of the various factors on the scope of UK taxation for an individual's capital disposals, subject to the exceptions noted below:

	Disposals subject to UK taxation
UK resident and UK domiciled	Worldwide assets
UK resident but not domiciled and a claim is made to be assessed on the remittance basis on the same basis as above	UK assets and gains remitted from overseas
UK resident but not domiciled and a claim is not made to be assessed on the remittance basis	Worldwide assets
Not resident	Outside the scope, except for disposals of UK residential property

Individuals who are resident (or ordinarily resident prior to 6 April 2013) in the UK for a given tax year are liable to capital gains tax (CGT) in relation to all disposals of chargeable assets which occur in that year, no matter where in the world the assets are situated (TCGA 1992, s 2). If they arrive in or depart from the UK during a tax year, that year could be a split year and they will only be chargeable to CGT on any gains accruing in the UK part of the year, but may be subject to the temporary non-residents charge in (b) below if they subsequently return to the UK. The CGT charge could result in double taxation in relation to disposals of assets which are also subject to tax in other territories. In these circumstances double taxation relief may be available under the relevant tax treaty.

Individuals who are not resident (nor ordinarily resident prior to 6 April 2013) in the UK are not liable to CGT except on the disposal of UK residential property since 5 April 2015, even in relation to assets situated in the UK. There are, however, two main exceptions to the above rules:

(a)   An individual who is not resident in the UK but who carries on a trade in the UK through a branch or agency is chargeable to CGT in relation to disposals of business assets situated in the UK (TCGA 1992, s 10).

(b)   Individuals who acquire assets before temporarily leaving the UK and then dispose of those assets whilst abroad remain chargeable to CGT in relation to these disposals if they resume UK residence within five years. Gains arising in the year of departure are taxed in that year. Later gains are taxed in the year in which residence resumes (TCGA 1992, s 10A).

Consideration should also be given to whether the income tax charge on profits and gains from dealing in or developing UK land applies. (See **5.26** and **CHAPTER 13**.)

Statutory Residence Test ('SRT')

[5.8] The SRT is divided into three 'tests' that potentially apply to determine an individual's residence status for a tax year. The tests need to be considered in order, and every year. If any test reaches a conclusion on the residence status, there is no need to consider the subsequent tests. This process is shown in the table below and a brief overview of the tests follows.

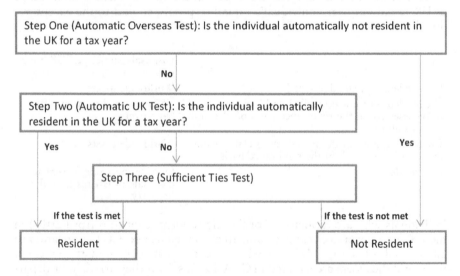

Automatic Overseas Test

An individual would be conclusively non-UK resident in a tax year if the individual meets any of the following conditions:

- was resident in the UK in any of the prior three UK tax years, and spends no more than 15 days in the UK in a given tax year; or
- has not been resident in the UK in any of the prior three UK tax years and spends no more than 45 days in the UK in a tax year; or
- works full time overseas (provided certain conditions are met).

Automatic UK Residence Test

An individual is conclusively UK resident if none of the above applies, and the individual:

• spends 183 days or more in the UK; or
• has their only home or all homes in the UK; or
• works full time in the UK for a relevant period (provided certain conditions are met).

If an individual is not treated as UK resident by the Automatic Residence Test, they will need to consider the Sufficient Ties Test. This area is complex and reference should be made to FA 2013, Sch 45 and HMRC guidance RDR3.

Sufficient Ties Test

Where residence has not been determined under the Step One or Step Two tests above, then it will be determined by a final Step test which looks at a combination of days spent in the UK and 'connection factors' to the UK, or 'ties'.

The more 'connection factors' an individual has with the UK in any one year, the fewer days he or she can spend in the UK in that year without becoming resident. The individual first identifies how many connection factors he or she has with the UK and then can determine the maximum number of days he or she can spend in the UK in the year concerned without becoming resident. The areas covered by the Sufficient Ties Test includes family, accommodation, work, number of days spent in the UK and whether the number of days spent in the UK is more than any other country. These tests contain a number of broad definitions, the discussion of which is beyond the scope of this text.

Summary

[5.9] Simply owning property in the UK does not in itself constitute residence in the UK for tax purposes. This is advantageous as it will often mean that only income sourced directly from those properties will be taxable on a non-resident in the UK (unless the property is high value residential property owned via a corporate wrapper or envelope – see **5.28** or the capital gains tax charge for non-residents owning UK residential property from April 2015 applies – see **5.29**). However, it is very important for effective tax compliance and planning purposes to ensure that the residency position is certain as it is likely to be the subject of HMRC scrutiny.

Income tax rates

[5.10] The applicable rate of income tax for individuals is determined by cumulative income bands. There is a Basic rate, a Higher rate and an Additional rate. The rates for 2017/18 are 20%, 40% and 45% respectively.

As with a UK resident individual, an individual who is a national of a European Economic Area (EEA) state is entitled to a personal allowance which will offset against their UK taxable income, unless they are claiming the remittance basis. Certain other double taxation treaties also confer the right to a personal allowance.

UK resident individuals who claim the remittance basis in respect of overseas income or gains are not entitled to the income tax personal allowance or the annual capital gains tax exemption.

Capital gains tax rates

[5.11] Capital gains are charged to tax at four rates for gains accruing on or after 6 April 2016, dependent on the level of taxable income and the type of gain. Gains accruing on residential property not covered by the principle private residence exemption (and those on certain profit-related returns payable to investment managers) are charged to tax at 18% or 28%, dependent on the income level. Other gains are charged at 10% or 20%.

An annual exemption (£11,300 for 2017/18) is available for all individuals to set against their total assessable capital gains for the tax year unless a remittance basis claim has been made.

Treaties

[5.12] Many overseas countries will tax their residents on their worldwide income (which may include the rental income from UK property). Since this income will also be subject to taxation in the UK, each country will have their own double taxation rules which may provide relief against tax suffered in the UK. The relevant double taxation treaty will determine which country has the primary taxing rights for specific income.

Where a treaty operates between the UK and an overseas country the primary taxing rights will usually be with the country in which the property is situated.

Almost all of the treaties the UK has with other territories treat income from 'immovable property' in line with the OECD model. That is to say that the UK will retain the right to tax rental income derived from property situated in the UK. None of the UK treaties grant an exemption from income tax on rental income derived from UK property.

The OECD model treaty defines 'immovable property' as being that which is defined by the laws of the country in which the property is situated. This removes any doubt as to what this may include. The model treaty also provides an explanation of what income will be taxed and this is defined as 'income derived from the direct use, letting, or use in any other form of that property'. Clearly, it is important to review the actual treaty in place when reviewing the tax position if such a treaty exists.

The majority of treaties state that non-UK companies are liable to UK corporation tax only if they trade through a PE in the UK, though the charge arising on profits and gains from dealing in or developing UK land may now apply (see **5.26** and **CHAPTER 13**). The definition of PE is defined in the treaty and may differ from the UK definition of a PE. For example, the OECD model definition is very similar to the definition provided by the UK legislation, but only regards a building site, construction or installation project as being a PE if it lasts for more than 12 months (see **5.2** above).

Most, but not all, UK treaties state that land is taxable in the country in which it is situated, therefore a non-resident may not be liable to taxation at all on the disposal of a UK property because the UK does not impose tax on capital gains made by non-UK residents, unless they fall within the ATED regime (see **5.28** below) or the extension to the capital gains regime to non-residents owning UK residential property from April 2015 — see **5.29**. However, the charge arising on profits and gains from dealing in or developing UK land may apply (see **5.26** and **CHAPTER 13**). Clearly, the relevant treaty should be checked in each case, as in some cases the overseas territory may have taxing rights, though as a result of the new rules for taxing dealers in, and developers of, UK land, it is HMRC's intention to update treaties to provide for the UK's taxing rights over land situated in the UK, and those with Jersey, Guernsey and the Isle of Man have already been amended.

Base Erosion and Profit Shifting (BEPS)

[5.13] The OECD's Action Plan on Addressing Base Erosion and Profit Shifting (BEPS) is aimed at Government concern about the potential for multinational companies to reduce their tax liabilities through shifting of income to no- or low-tax countries. A number of Action Plans have been identified.

Action 6 of the BEPS Action Plan identified treaty abuse, and in particular treaty shopping, as one of the most important sources of BEPS concerns. Whilst tax treaties are intended to prevent double taxation by dividing taxing rights between countries, these can sometimes be exploited by the use of artificial or contrived transactions. The OECD has been examining the most effective way of preventing treaty abuse and has published a final report which provides both a minimum treaty standard to be adopted by all countries participating in BEPS, and specific treaty rules which address treaty shopping and other treaty abuses. It also includes changes to the OECD Model Tax Convention which clarify that tax treaties are not intended to create opportunities for non-taxation or reduced taxation through tax evasion or avoidance, and identify the tax policy considerations that countries should consider before deciding to enter into a tax treaty with another country.

Discussions drafts have been issued for the treaty entitlement of non-collective investment vehicles (non-CIV) funds and the treaty residence of pension funds. Developments in this area should be kept under close review to enable consideration of any impending changes to obtaining tax treaty benefits.

The report on Action 15 concluded that a multilateral instrument to modify bilateral tax treaties to implement the tax treaty-related BEPS measures was desirable and such an instrument should be available for signature by 31 December 2016.

Action 4 of the BEPS Action Plan seeks to review the position adopted with respect to the deductibility of interest. The final report's recommended approach ensures that an entity's net interest deductions are directly linked to its level of economic activity, based on taxable earnings before deducting net interest expense, depreciation and amortisation (EBITDA). The options are:

(a)   a fixed-ratio rule based on a benchmark net interest/EBITDA ratio. Possible ratios are between 10% and 30%;

(b)   a group ratio rule which allows an entity to deduct more interest expense in certain circumstances based on the position of its worldwide group; and

(c)   targeted rules to address specific risks.

If a country chooses not to introduce the group ratio rule, it must apply the fixed-ratio rule to multinational and domestic groups without improper discrimination. This is an area that should continue to be closely monitored as a restriction based on EBITDA could have a significant impact on the tax position of entities in the Real Estate industry.

Details of the UK implementation of these rules are set out in **5.19** below.

Value Added Tax

[5.14] The VAT rules applicable to individuals are the same as for companies, although any income accruing to individuals from property in the UK is only within the scope of UK VAT if it is received in the course or furtherance of business, as opposed to in a private capacity. This will include, for instance individuals pursuing a property investment or development business in the UK. See **CHAPTER 15** for a full discussion of the VAT rules.

General tax issues arising for overseas investors in UK property

[5.15] The tax liabilities applicable when acquiring, holding and disposing of UK property are in many respects the same regardless of residence considerations. However, in certain cases there is a specific distinction for those investing from overseas as set out below.

Computation of rental income assessment

[5.16] Rental income earned from holding UK property is taxable in the UK as 'property income' (see **CHAPTER 6** for full details on rents from property). The profits are calculated as profits of a property business for taxpayers subject to corporation tax (CTA 2009, s 209) or income tax (ITTOIA 2005, s 268). Both property business income and property income are herein referred to as 'rental business' or 'profits of the rental business'.

The profits of the rental business for both payers of income tax and corporation tax are computed broadly in the same manner, with the main differences being the rules for giving relief for interest and losses. Both are computed using the same principles as for trading profits (CTA 2009, s 210(2) and ITTOIA 2005, s 272(2)). Expenses are deductible from the rental income if they are incurred 'wholly and exclusively' for the purposes of the rental business (CTA 2009, s 210(2) and ITTOIA 2005, s 272(2)). Examples of expenses which could fall into this category are advertising and marketing costs, council taxes and rates, rent payable on a head lease, service charges and utilities.

Capital allowances may be available in respect of fixtures and fittings within the property (see **CHAPTER 9** for full details on capital allowances). A distinction to the allowances available to overseas investors arises where plant and machinery is leased by a person who is not resident in the UK and does not use the plant and machinery exclusively for earning profits chargeable to tax (CAA 2001, s 105). To the extent that the lease was finalised prior to April 2006, in these circumstances the plant and machinery should be allocated to a separate pool and is subject to writing down allowances at 8% on a reducing balance basis with effect from April 2012 (CAA 2001, ss 107, 109).

Tax relief for costs incurred incidental to the acquisition of the property, such as legal fees, are only relievable against capital gains on a subsequent disposal, where applicable.

Income that does not relate to the rental business will not be subject to UK tax where there is no UK trading through a branch or agency. Equally, expenses not relating to the UK rental business will not be deductible for tax in the UK.

Financing costs and interest expenses are also allowable deductions in the computation of the profits of the rental business where they are incurred in relation to the property (CTA 2009, ss 210, 54 and ITTOIA 2005, ss 272(2), 34). The incidental costs incurred when obtaining loan finance are also eligible for tax relief against the taxable profits of rental activity where the interest on the loan is deductible in calculating the rental profits (ITTOIA 2005, ss 272(2), 58). A restriction on finance cost relief for individuals has been phased in from 2017/18, with the result that relief will be limited to only a basic rate deduction from their income tax liability from 2020/21. (See **CHAPTERS 6** and **10** for full details on the restrictions for financing costs.) The effect of the legislation on non-resident companies subject to income tax is currently unclear.

For a UK resident company, the loan relationship rules apply to interest income and interest expenses and the World Wide Debt Cap (WWDC rules) or new BEPS compliant interest restriction rules (see below) may also apply to non-UK companies (resident in the UK or carrying on a trade of dealing in or developing UK land or any other trade in the UK through a PE). In contrast, in the case of a non-resident without a UK PE who are currently subject to income tax, only interest and expenses that are incidental to the rental business will be tax deductible. As previously referred to, it is proposed that all non-resident companies who have taxable income in the UK will be subject to corporation tax. This will accordingly ensure that they are potentially within the ambit of the interest restriction rules.

Where more than one property is owned, by an individual or by one entity, all UK properties will constitute a single property business for taxation purposes (CTA 2009, ss 205, 1270(2) and ITTOIA 2005, s 264). Therefore the profits and losses from the individual properties are amalgamated to determine the assessable profits of the rental business for a tax year.

Rental losses

Income tax

[5.17] Where a taxpayer is subject to income tax (broadly a non-UK resident company without a UK PE and all individuals) and they incur losses in the rental business, the loss will be carried forward to the following year of assessment for relief against future profits of the rental business (ITA 2007, s 118(2) and (3)). Where there are no profits, or insufficient profits, to use the entire loss in the following year then the unutilised element of the loss will be carried forward indefinitely for use against profits of the rental business of a future period (ITA 2007, s 119). The use of brought forward rental business losses is mandatory and the taxpayer cannot choose the amount of set off; the utilisation will be at the earliest available opportunity. Where the loss brought forward is lower than assessable profits for the year, the entire loss must be utilised in that year. Certain losses relating to capital allowance claims are available for relief against other income.

Corporation tax

[5.18] By comparison, UK resident companies who are subject to corporation tax on their property business assessment, and incur property business losses may have more flexibility in utilising losses. Property business losses can be utilised in the first instance against the company's total profits for the period in which the loss arises (CTA 2010, s 62(3)).

To the extent that the property business loss cannot be offset against the company's total profits of the current year then, if the company continues to carry on a property business in the succeeding accounting period, the loss will be carried forward to that period and treated as a property business loss of that period (CTA 2010, s 62(4) and (5)).

Where the company does not continue to carry on a property business but it is a company with investment business in the UK, then any loss which cannot be used under CTA 2010, s 62 shall be carried forward to the succeeding accounting period and be treated as if it were management expenses deductible for that period under CTA 2009, ss 1219, 1221, 1223 (CTA 2010, s 63). In addition, current year property business losses may be surrendered to other group companies by way of group relief.

Please note that F(No 2)A 2017 proposes significant changes to loss relief for companies within the scope of corporation tax. The main reforms (subject to finalisation) are the following:

- Carried forward losses arising after 1 April 2017 of whatever description (aside from capital losses) will be usable against profits from different sources of income and the profits of other group companies.
- However, there will also be a restriction on the use of losses carried forward so that companies cannot reduce their profits arising on or after 1 April 2017 by more than 50%. This restriction will apply to a company's (or group's) profits above £5 million and it should be noted that brought forward losses arising at any time will be subject to this restriction.

Financing

[5.19] Overseas investors in UK property will, in line with usual commercial practice, often seek to finance the purchase of the property using loan finance which is often a cheaper source of finance than equity. This may have a beneficial tax impact compared with equity as the offset of loan interest against rental income will reduce the assessable amount of profits of the rental business and thus the final tax liability.

There is now a restriction on the allowable interest expense deduction (as outlined in **5.16**) in relation to the amount of the borrowing where the funds are borrowed on arm's length terms from an unconnected third party. However, where the funds are borrowed from a connected party, or from a third party but are guaranteed by a related party, the interest deduction is subject to the UK transfer pricing provisions (TIOPA 2010, Part 4). This is to prevent a potential advantage being exploited by investors who finance the purchase of properties with loans from related companies, and charge high rates of interest on the loan or borrow more than would have been possible in an arm's length situation.

TIOPA 2010, Part 7 sets out the legislation with respect to the World Wide Debt Cap (WWDC) to restrict UK tax deductions for finance expenses by reference to external finance expenses of the global group. A full analysis is beyond the scope of this text but a summary is set out below.

The WWDC does not apply to taxpayers subject to income tax (broadly a non-UK resident company without a UK PE and all individuals) but does apply to UK companies (resident in the UK, or carrying on a trade of dealing in or developing UK land or any other trade in the UK through a PE) that are part of a large worldwide group where that group fails the gateway test.

The group is deemed to be large, if at any time any member of the group falls within the definition provided in the Annex to European Commission Recommendation 2003/361/EC of 6 May 2003, subject to certain amendments (TIOPA 2010, s 344).

The gateway test is failed if the net debt of all UK companies in the group exceeds 75% of the gross debt of the worldwide group.

The legislation applies to periods of account of the worldwide group that start on or after 1 January 2010. This is a complex area of tax and for further insight, reference should be made to *Tolley's Corporation Tax 2017–18*.

New interest restriction rules

[5.20] As above at **5.19** relief for excessive interest can currently be denied under the UK's transfer pricing regime or the worldwide debt cap rules for corporation tax. September 2017 Finance Bill proposes that the latter is to be replaced by a new restriction which is expected to take effect retrospectively from 1 April 2017. This is so as to implement:

- Going forward, companies or groups operating in the UK will be required to calculate their interest expenses in the UK, including all associated finance costs except for loan impairment expenses (the 'interest').

- Restrictions on tax relief will arise where the Interest in the UK of the company/group exceeds the interest capacity as set out below, subject to always being able to offset a *de minimis* amount of £2 million per annum.

- Where the Interest is greater than £2 million, the company/group will be required to calculate its taxable profits in the UK before interest, capital allowances and allowable amortisation of intangible assets (the 'UK EBITDA'). Interest relief will then be restricted to 30% of the UK EBITDA.

An alternative method of calculation of the amount of deductible interest is available:

> companies/groups can elect to calculate a 'group ratio' percentage based on the worldwide group's consolidated accounts (based on IFRS consolidation rules). This is equal to the net group interest expenses divided by the group's earnings before interest, tax depreciation and amortisation. (The 'worldwide EBITDA'.).

Under this group ratio rule, interest can instead be deducted in the UK group up to the group ratio as applied to the UK EBITDA, even where that is higher than the amount given by the fixed ratio rule. The group ratio percentage to be used is 100% (ie, interest up to the full amount of UK EBITDA is available) where the group is loss making or where the group ratio percentage would otherwise be greater than 100%.

The amount of relief calculated is though subject to an overarching limit in that the group cannot deduct more interest in the UK than the global net group interest expense. In other words, interest cannot be pushed into the UK under this modified debt cap rule.

Excess tax interest that cannot be deducted under these provisions can be carried forward indefinitely and added to the interest cost in future periods, ie potentially it may be relieved in years were the interest burden is less.

Furthermore, spare interest relief capacity that is unused in a given period can also be carried forward up to five years. There is no provision for carry back.

Transfer pricing

[5.21] TIOPA 2010, Part 4 provides that where a company transacts with connected parties and a UK tax advantage is gained by way of the transaction not being on an arm's length basis, an adjustment to the tax calculation will be required to increase the tax liability to a position that would reflect the taxable result that would be expected in a normal commercial situation. The rules apply to overseas companies paying income tax as well as to UK companies paying corporation tax.

Further, where a loan is obtained from a third party but it has been guaranteed by an associate then the value attributable to the guarantee also needs to be considered under the provisions of TIOPA 2010, Part 4.

As well as adjusting interest rates, these provisions enable HMRC to treat loan interest as disallowable on the basis that in a third party lending situation a capital contribution would be expected to be injected by way of security against the loan. In practice, this can be an area of much contention with HMRC. It is therefore important to document clearly the rationale and basis for charges.

It is often difficult to obtain comparative public data to support the arm's length rate due to many investors being private individuals, private companies and private funds. Further, due to the relatively secure nature of the underlying asset, ie the property, banks are often willing to lend a higher loan to value amount than other industries. It is therefore, important to maintain documentation where possible to support the arm's length rate applied.

There are no restrictions on the residence of the lender when determining the available tax deduction although if the lender is non-UK resident then there may be a withholding tax requirement on interest (see **5.23** below).

Management expenses

[5.22] Other areas caught by the transfer pricing legislation may include the charging of management expenses in respect of time spent in relation to the management of the UK property where these amounts are not at an arm's length. Again where these are deemed to be excessive, HMRC may determine that a proportion of the expenses should be disallowed for tax purposes. In practice, this can be an area of much contention with HMRC due to a lack of public information. It is therefore important to document clearly the rationale and basis for charges.

For the purposes of TIOPA 2010, Part 4, a connected person is as defined by CTA 2010, s 1122 and applies both to transactions within the UK and between UK and non-UK resident parties.

Withholding tax on interest

[5.23] Withholding tax at 20% may be deductible where interest is paid from a UK source to an overseas recipient. A double tax treaty will often reduce the rate of withholding tax significantly. Similarly for payments between the UK and other EU member states, withholding taxes on interest are automatically reduced to 0% under the EU Parent-Subsidiary Directive subject to certain anti-avoidance provisions.

UK source interest is not defined in the legislation but is based on the decision in the case of *Westminster Bank Executor and Trustee Co (Channel Islands) Ltd v National Bank of Greece SA (1970) 46 TC 472*. In their manuals (SAIM9090), HMRC state that the most important factor in deciding whether or not interest has a UK source is the residence of the debtor and the location of his/her assets. Other factors taken into account are:

- the place of performance of the contract and the method of payment;
- the competent jurisdiction for legal action and the proper law of contract;
- the residence of the guarantor and the location of the security for the debt.

An overseas recipient is any person whose usual place of abode is outside of the UK.

It is necessary to look at the facts on a case by case basis and review any available treaty protection.

The withholding tax requirements only apply to 'annual interest', defined as interest on loans capable of exceeding one year, although the loan itself does not actually have to exceed one year (ITA 2007, s 874). An exception to the withholding tax requirements is where the interest is payable on an advance from a bank and at the time the interest is paid, the recipient bank is within the charge to corporation tax for that particular interest source (ITA 2007, s 879). After a consultation, HMRC announced in October 2012 that it would not take forward a proposal to abolish the concept of annual interest. As a result there will continue to be no withholding tax requirement in connection with interest on short loans but changes were introduced in FA 2013 for compensation payments, speciality debt and interest in kind which may need to be considered depending on the specific circumstances.

Taxation of property dealing profits

[5.24] It is HMRC's view that the use of an overseas company may be to avoid UK taxation on property income, and therefore various anti-avoidance provisions have existed to minimise the cost to the Exchequer of offshore planning. Finance Act 2016 brought more clarity and introduced provisions to charge non-residents to tax on the profits of dealing in or developing UK land. (See **5.26** and **CHAPTER 13**.)

Trading v investment

[5.25] As mentioned earlier in this chapter, even before the introduction of the FA 2016 rules on dealing in or developing UK land, trading transactions involving property in the UK will generally give rise to a UK tax liability. This may have been the case even if just one property was purchased and re-sold though HMRC may have difficulty in enforcing the liability as the non-resident has no UK assets, and it may be difficult to obtain agreement that an overseas jurisdiction will enforce the payment of tax on behalf of the UK. However, where the non-resident company is resident in an EU member state, EU Council Directive 77/799 has direct effect which covers mutual assistance by the competent authorities of member states. Broadly, this provision allows for both the spontaneous exchange of information as well as permitting requests for information and co-operation between member states to effect a correct assessment of taxes on income and capital and, subject to certain limitations, this may assist a member state in assessing and recovering tax.

The determination of whether a UK trade is being carried out is dependent on a number of factors supported by case law. In *Maclaine & Co v Eccott* (1926) 10 TC 481 it was determined that the trade is conducted where the contracts of sale are concluded rather than the location of the properties involved. However, subsequent case law has indicated that in certain situations a trade may be carried on in the UK despite contracts being signed abroad. This decision was reached in *Firestone Tyres and Rubber Co v Lewellin* (1957) 37 TC 111 because the trading operations were taking place in the UK. A detailed analysis of the so called 'badges of trade' is outside the scope of this chapter.

It is necessary for the taxpayer to review each potential transaction and clearly document the intent of the transaction at the outset. Recent case law (*Terrace Hill (Berkley) Ltd v Revenue and Customs Comrs* [2015] UKFTT 75 (TC)) also outlines the importance of oral evidence and credible witness testimony in the event of HMRC challenge.

Dealing in or developing UK land

[5.26] Finance Act 2016 introduced rules designed to tax offshore property developers on their UK profits arising from a trade which involves either dealing in or developing UK land (including buildings and structures) and they apply to disposals on or after 5 July 2016 unless the gain is attributable to a period of ownership before the intention to develop the land, or it is covered by the principal private residence exemption (CTA 2010, Part 8ZB and ITA 2007, Part 9A). Full details of the charge can be found in **CHAPTER 13**.

As a result of the FA 2016 changes the previous 'Transactions in land' anti-avoidance rules in CTA 2010, Part 18 and ITA 2007, Part 13, s 752 et seq were repealed.

Transfer of assets abroad

[5.27] ITA 2007, Part 13, s 714 et seq exists to prevent the avoidance of income tax by UK resident individuals who transfer assets to non-UK entities and by UK resident individuals who may benefit from such assets. If the provisions apply, income of the non-UK entity may be taxed as income of the UK resident individual transferor or UK resident beneficiary who receives the benefit from the non-UK entity. These provisions should only apply in the event of a UK tax avoidance motive.

Annual tax on enveloped dwellings ('ATED') and related chargeable gains

Scope

[5.28] The annual tax on enveloped dwellings ('ATED') applies specifically to high value UK residential property which is owned, completely or partly by a company, a partnership (where one or more of the partners is a company), or a collective investment vehicle such as a unit trust or collective investment scheme, with effect from 1 April 2013 (FA 2013, s 94).

'Dwellings' are deemed not to include hotels, guesthouses, hospitals, student halls of residence, boarding schools, care homes and prisons – so these fall outside the ATED regime. However, a dwelling for ATED purposes may be part of a larger mixed use property and includes the garden and grounds (FA 2013, s 115).

It should be noted that the tax liability applicable under the ATED regime is the same regardless of residence status but note that it does not apply to an individual's ownership of residential property.

Both UK and overseas investors may potentially also be liable to ATED-related chargeable gains.

See **CHAPTER 22** for full commentary.

Non-resident capital gains tax ('NRCGT')

Introduction

Scope

[5.29] From 6 April 2015, non-UK residents are subject to capital gains tax on the disposal of UK residential property (TCGA 1992, s 14B). Only the proportion of the gain relating to the period after 5 April 2015 is subject to NRCGT, however, see **5.31**. The primary objective in widening the CGT regime to include non-UK residents disposing of UK residential property was to address the imbalance which existed between the treatment of UK residents and non-residents. The Government has tried to minimise the impact on institutional investors who support the development and supply of UK housing.

Broadly speaking the following non-resident persons are subject to NRCGT:

- individuals;
- personal representatives;
- companies that are closely held. A company is closely held if it is under the control of five or fewer participants and none of those participants are themselves diversely held (TCGA 1992, Sch C1); and
- funds (eg in the form of Unit Trusts which are not authorised and Open Ended Investment Companies that fail the widely marketed test (TCGA 1992, Sch C1)).

The following main categories are not subject to NRCGT:

- if already chargeable to corporation tax or income tax on the disposal on the basis of a trade in the UK;
- exempt entities such as Charities, Registered Pension Schemes and companies carrying on life assurance business in accordance with FA 2012, s 56; and
- potentially exempt entities such as diversely held companies (being a company which is not closely held), eg institutional investors, an authorised Unit Trust, Open Ended Investment Companies that are widely marketed.

Requirements

[5.30] The NRCGT rules apply essentially to UK dwellings and this has a broadly similar but not completely identical definition to that found in the Stamp Duty Land Tax and ATED provisions (TCGA 1992, Sch B1, para 4). Note specifically that NRCGT applies to disposals of UK residential property that is let on a commercial basis as part of a property rental business (which is excluded from the scope of ATED and ATED related CGT).

Overview of the calculation of the NRCGT gain or loss

[5.31] The normal rules apply for the purposes of calculating a gain or loss but note that only the gain arising after 5 April 2015 is chargeable and this is arrived at as follows.

The 'default' position in the absence of an election is that the NRCGT gain will be calculated as the proportion of the total gain that arose from 6 April 2015 by reference to a re-based value as at 5 April 2015.

The legislation makes alternative methods of calculation available:

- The taxpayer may elect to adopt either of the following methods of calculation as an alternative:
  - a straight-line time apportionment of the total gain;
  - a retrospective computation incorporating the full gain or loss arising since acquisition of the property (beneficial to the taxpayer where the period of ownership prior to 5 April 2015 gives rise to a loss).

The rate of NRCGT is as follows:

Individuals	18% or 28% depending on taxable UK income and chargeable gains for the tax year (after annual exempt amount £11,300 for 2017/18 and reliefs e.g. Principal Private Residence).
Companies	19% post-indexation relief to relieve the gain attributed to inflation from 6 April 2015.
Trustee(s)	28% (after half the individual exemption £5,650 for 2016/17 exemption).

Losses are ring-fenced and cannot be used against ATED-related gains (TCGA 1992, ss 2(7B)).

Where a property within the scope of ATED is disposed of (e.g. a property which is owned, completely or partly by a company), the gain that has accrued from 5 April 2013 is subject to ATED-related CGT, currently at the rate of 28%. Where capital gains chargeable from 5 April 2015 and 2016 are liable to both ATED CGT and NRCGT then ATED CGT will take precedence.

Notification requirement

[5.32] A non-resident person must report the disposal of a UK residential property within 30 days of the disposal on a NRCGT return along with a self-assessment of the CGT due, with payment being made no later than 30 days following the completion of the sale, or if the non-resident already files tax returns within the self-assessment regime, the non-resident may pay NRCGT as part of the normal end of year tax payment. Reporting the disposal of UK residential property is required irrespective of whether a gain or a loss is made on the disposal although a person is not required to deliver an NRCGT return, but may choose to do so, where the disposal is a no gain/no loss disposal, or where no chargeable gain accrues on the grant of an arm's length lease to an unconnected person for no premium.

The Government's expectation is that most non-residents are subject to capital gains in their country of residence and NRCGT merely alters the balance of the taxing rights in the UK's favour.

Diverted Profits Tax

Introduction

[5.33] Finance Act 2015 introduced a new UK Diverted Profits Tax ('DPT') with effect from 1 April 2015 to combat the use of contrived arrangements by multi-national companies with business activities in the UK. These new rules apply where arrangements are designed to divert profits from the UK by either avoiding the creation of a UK permanent establishment ('PE') or as a result of being party to transactions lacking economic substance.

Land and buildings have been expressly brought within the scope of DPT since this legislation applies to supplies of services, goods or other property. This legislation is complex and is open to different interpretations. Where the various conditions are met, there appear to be only limited scope exemptions.

Overview

[5.34] The DPT is designed to discourage taxpayers from structuring their business and in such a way that:

- gives rise to a 'tax mismatch' which results in an overall reduction in the tax to pay in the UK (with a corresponding increase in the foreign tax to pay) using arrangements or entities which lack economic substance; or
- intentionally avoids the creation of a UK PE.

The two applicable arms of the legislation have come to be known as 'transactions lacking economic substance' and 'avoided UK PE' respectively. Diverted profits which fall within the scope of either of these two arms of the new legislation will be subject to a tax charge of 25%. Note that the DPT tax rate is higher than the main rate of UK corporation tax, being 20%.

While DPT is not technically self-assessed, companies are required to notify HMRC within three months of the end of an accounting period in which they are potentially within the charge thereby requiring internal review and calculations to be performed to determine if the taxpayer is impacted. For the first accounting period in which the DPT is in force (ie accounting periods ending on or before 31 March 2016) companies have six months from the end of the accounting period to notify HMRC. The criteria for notifying HMRC is intentionally more broadly drafted than the criteria for DPT to apply, which results in companies having a requirement to notify HMRC despite considering that no DPT charge will actually arise.

Exceptions

[5.35] There are of course certain exceptions:

- small and medium enterprises as defined by TIOPA 2010, s 172 (broadly those with fewer than 250 employees and either turnover or balance sheet total less than EUR 50m and EUR 43m respectively) are outside the scope of the new legislation;
- in respect of the 'avoided UK PE' arm, where sales or relevant expenses are below £10m and £1m respectively the DPT should not apply;
- subject to satisfying the conditions, certain loan relationships (broadly intra-group financing) may be exempted from the application of DPT in respect of 'transactions lacking economic substance'.

Summary/application to non-resident UK property owners

[5.36] The legislation is widely drawn and ascertaining whether it will apply can be an onerous and expensive process, with potentially minimal certainty ultimately achieved. Taxpayers may be required to carry out detailed analyses of their entire supply chains to determine whether there is an artificial 'tax mismatch' (a condition of DPT's application) that would not exist in the hypothetical world where a tax charge does not affect commercial decisions.

The current lack of industry, case law and practical experience results in uncertainty in the application of the DPT legislation to non-resident UK property owning structures. Given the penal rate of DPT (namely 25%, see above) and the reducing UK corporation tax rate (currently 20% reducing to 19% in 2017 and 17% in 2020), it is possible that all but the most passive of non-resident UK property owners will be, at some level, incentivised to carry out activities on-shore (and be subject to UK corporation tax).

Inheritance tax on non-domiciled individuals holding UK residential property

[5.37] The Government has announced that a Finance (No 2) Act 2017 will be introduced to Parliament in Autumn 2017 such that a new inheritance tax (IHT) charge will be introduced in respect of UK residential property held indirectly by non-UK domiciled individuals (eg via a non-UK company or held in an excluded property trust). The relevant legislation was removed from the 2017 Finance Act prior to the general election. Therefore, even where such property is held by say, an offshore company, it will still be subject to IHT on a 'relevant event', for example, the death of the individual.

The Government intend that the IHT charge will be based as far as possible on other definitions of residential property which currently exist within tax legislation used for the NRCGT definition in TCGA 1992, Sch B1 (see 5.29).

Collection of tax from non-resident landlords

Scope

[5.38] It is often more difficult in practice for HMRC to collect the tax payable by non-residents on rents received and so overseas investors in receipt of rental income derived from UK properties are subject to special provisions under ITA 2007, s 971 – the non-resident landlord scheme (NRL). Though the regulations use the term 'overseas investors', they are actually aimed at a wider group than suggested and also catch persons whose usual place of abode is outside the UK.

Individuals have a usual place of abode outside of the UK if they usually live outside of the UK. Temporary stays outside of the UK for six months or less can be ignored for the purposes of the non-resident landlord scheme.

Companies are normally regarded as having a usual place of abode overseas if their main office or place of business is outside of the UK and they are incorporated outside of the UK. However, if the company is regarded as UK resident for tax purposes then it is not caught by the NRL scheme even if it is incorporated outside of the UK.

The UK branch of a non-resident company is not caught by the NRL scheme provided it is within the charge to UK corporation tax.

Requirements

[5.39] The legislation requires that the tenant or letting agent, where there is one, deducts basic rate income tax (20% for 2017/18) from rental payments at source which are due to a non-resident landlord. The deduction at source is applied to the gross rents payable excluding VAT and net of allowable expenses paid by the agent or tenant. The provisions also extend to any person to whom a notice is issued by HMRC (SI 1995/2902).

The tenant or letting agent is obliged to pay over to HMRC the tax deducted each quarter within 30 days of the end of the quarter to which it relates. They must also make an annual return to HMRC by 5 July following the tax year and must provide the landlord with an annual certificate by the same date.

The landlord receives a tax credit for the tax deducted at source through the self-assessment tax return, and where the tax deducted exceeds the actual tax liability for the period then a repayment of the excess is available.

Exceptions

[5.40] The Regulations do provide certain exceptions to the above which are summarised as follows:

(a)   Regulation 3(5) provides that where no notice has been issued, no income tax shall be deducted where the annual rental stream payable to a non-resident is less than £5,200 (£100 per week). Where the property is owned for less than one year this figure is reduced proportionately. It is worth considering that often rental income is calculated by reference to a 53-week year, and so care should be taken that the rental income for the year does not exceed £5,200 in total.

(b)   The non-resident can elect to receive rental income gross under the non-resident landlord scheme. The application is made under reg 17, and is made using HMRC forms NRL 1, NRL 2 or NRL 3 as appropriate which are available on their website.

The form requires the non-resident to provide various details to assist HMRC to identify both the non-resident and the prescribed persons that make payments to the non-resident.

The applicant will have to be able to make a statement of one of the following:

• they have complied with all obligations imposed on them under CTA 2009, CTA 2010, TIOPA 2010, ITA 2007, ICTA 1988 and TMA 1970 prior to application; or
• the applicant has not had any such requirement; or
• the applicant does not expect to be liable to pay any amount by way of UK income tax for the year in which the income is paid, and will notify the board if he does become liable.

The applicant must also confirm that he will fully comply with all obligations imposed on him under the Act and inform the board if his usual place of abode ceases to be outside the UK.

If granted, the ability to receive rents gross will apply from the date of notice. The landlord will still be required to file a UK tax return and by making the election the non-resident undertakes to operate self-assessment in respect of the rental income, and comply with their UK tax duties. Applications are dealt with by the HMRC Charities, Savings and International 1 unless the land-lord's tax affairs are dealt with by HMRC Public Departments 1, and HMRC reserve the right to revoke this election if any of the regulations are broken.

Summary

[5.41] This ability to apply to make payments gross can be of great importance to businesses, as cash flow is improved and capital allowances and deductible expenditure can be considered in relation to the tax calculations. This also reduces the administrative burden as landlords would not need to make repayment claims for the excessive tax that has been deducted at source.

Value Added Tax

[5.42] Prior to 1 December 2012, registration for VAT was required where the taxable income deriving from an overseas investor's/developer's UK property exceeded the VAT registration threshold relevant at that time. Finance Act 2012 legislated for this registration threshold to be reduced to zero for businesses established outside the UK with effect from 1 December 2012. An overseas taxpayer can register direct from its overseas residence/office or through an agent in the UK. However, HMRC may require non-established persons to appoint a UK-established (from 15 September 2016) tax representative if the business is established in a country outside the EU that has not agreed to mutual assistance provisions with the UK. Registration for VAT at an early stage is normally a requirement if purchasing another party's business as a transfer of a going concern (see CHAPTER 15 for further discussion on VAT registration), or is desirable in other cases where substantial amounts of VAT may be incurred in the early stages of investment, eg on the purchase price or subsequent development or refurbishment works. This will facilitate early VAT recovery and benefit cash flow.

Anti-avoidance – attributed gains

[5.43] A number of anti-avoidance provisions exist where an overseas company would fall into the definition of a close company in the UK (CTA 2010, s 439).

A close company is a UK tax resident company that is controlled by five or fewer participators or has participators who are directors (CTA 2010, s 439(2)). Control is broadly defined as having greater than 50% of ordinary share capital or voting power or distributable income, or in the instance of a winding up, the rights to more than 50% of the company's assets.

The principal provision is that UK resident shareholders can be taxed on capital gains realised by the non-UK company. The gain is apportioned between the shareholders in proportion to their interests (TCGA 1992, s 13). Note that if such a gain is chargeable and falls within the NRCGT or ATED regime, the NRCGT or ATED charge takes priority. An exemption from the attributed gain applies for shareholders who hold 25% or less of the company's shares. There are exemptions to exclude gains from genuine business activity overseas from the scope of the charge.

Chapter 6

Property investments—rents

by
Zigurds Kronbergs
Tax Writer

Introduction

[6.1] This chapter discusses some of the key considerations for the property investor to consider in order to identify an efficient tax strategy. It provides an update of various key developments affecting property-business owners and their overall context for UK corporation tax and income tax liabilities.

Much of what follows is potentially affected by the measures originally introduced in the March 2017 Finance Bill, omitted from the Finance Act 2017, and now reintroduced in the September 2017 Finance Bill. At the time of going to press, this was entering Committee Stage. Given the current political situation, while this chapter is written on the basis that those provisions will be enacted without significant amendment, the usual warning that legislation may nevertheless be subject to amendment as it proceeds through its parliamentary stages is even more noteworthy.

The taxation system surrounding the taxation of rents arising in the UK is possibly one of the most complex in the world, providing both opportunities and pitfalls for the unwary. This chapter reviews the current regime for taxing the property income of individuals and companies. The chapter is divided into six sections:

(1) An overview of the current tax regimes for individuals and companies.
(2) Rental computations: tax deductions and reliefs including loan interest.
(3) Matters relevant to particular types of property business and receipts.
(4) Particular types of ownership.
(5) Overseas issues.
(6) Anti-avoidance provisions affecting a property business.

Overview

[6.2] There are two distinct legal bases of taxation for owners of rental income, dependent upon whether the profits are chargeable to income tax (which applies, broadly speaking, to landlords who are individuals, trustees, partnerships of individuals, or trustees or non-resident companies without a UK permanent establishment to which the rents are attributable) or to corporation tax (which applies to landlords who are UK-resident companies or other bodies corporate, corporate members of partnerships or non-resident companies with a permanent establishment in the United Kingdom to which the rents are attributable). The computation of profits, but not losses, is broadly similar for both types of owner, including the computation and recognition of profits and allowable deductions. The legislation remains separate, falling under CTA 2009, Part 4 (formerly Schedule A) and CTA 2010, Part 4, for companies etc and under ITTOIA 2005, Part 3 for individuals.

Historically, the charge to income tax and corporation tax used a schedular system. Income from land was taxed under Schedule A or Schedule D. The schedular system was abolished under the Tax Law Rewrite process, and the concept of a property business introduced.

For income tax purposes from 2005–06 onwards, income from property is taxed under ITTOIA 2005, the provisions dealing with losses are within ITA 2007 (applying from 2007–08 onwards).

For companies with accounting periods ending after 31 March 2009, on the other hand, income from property is taxed under CTA 2009, Part 4, with the provisions for dealing with losses being found in CTA 2010, Part 4, Chapter 4 for accounting periods ending after 31 March 2010.

Profit computations under income tax

[6.3] If the legislative provisions in the September 2017 Finance Bill (as cl 16 and Sch 2) are enacted without significant amendment, most computations for the tax year 2017–18 and beyond of the profits of a property business subject to income tax will be carried out on a cash basis, unless the taxpayer opts for the new basis not to apply.

The material below first looks at the rules that apply to 2016–17 and prior tax years, before discussing the prospective new regime.

Accruals (or GAAP basis) for years 2016–17 and previous

[6.4] The income tax rules span 12 Chapters of Part 3 of ITTOIA 2005, to catch every possible type of property business.

The charge to income tax on rental profits (that is, the profits of a property business) is imposed upon individuals, trustees and non-UK resident companies carrying on investment activities in the UK by ITTOIA 2005, s 268.

As the regime is based upon the computation of rental profits as if a trade were being carried on, ITTOIA 2005 draws heavily upon legislation that previously underpinned the old Schedule A rules. The descriptions used in the legislation are found at ITTOIA 2005, Part 3, Ch 2 (ss 263–267). In particular, ITTOIA 2005, s 264 defines an individual's (actually, a person's) 'UK property business' as being every business that the person carries on for generating income from land in the United Kingdom and every transaction that the person enters into for that purpose otherwise than in the course of such a business. The identical definition, mutatis mutandis, as respects a company is found at CTA 2009, s 205.

Following the abolition of Schedule A for income tax purposes from 6 April 2005, ITTOIA 2005, ss 263–265 prescribe a tax upon all such businesses and transactions as a single property business. The property business will be either a 'UK property business' (s 264), or an 'overseas property business' (s 265), depending upon where the property or properties is or are located.

Income tax is charged on the 'full amount of profits arising in the tax year', with the exception of foreign income accruing to an individual who is not domiciled in the United Kingdom for which the remittance basis is available (ITTOIA 2005, s 270). The person liable is the recipient of the income or person entitled to it (ITTOIA 2005, s 271); a person cannot confuse the legal capacity in which rental income is received. For example, a trustee or trustee in bankruptcy could not amalgamate a property business operated in the trustee's capacity as an individual with that of the trust.

The computational bases of profit are prescribed at ITTOIA 2005, s 272 ff; profits must be calculated in the same way as for the profits of a trade, with certain prescribed exceptions. The rules mutually adopted are detailed at ITTOIA 2005, s 272(2). The permissive rules are given express priority by ITTOIA 2005, s 274, meaning that they take precedence over prohibitive rules in determining amounts to be brought into or exempt from the charge to tax.

The main features of the current rules include:

- the computation of the profits and losses of a property business along trading principles, thus the arising basis applies to the recognition of income and expenses;
- tax and payments on account of tax due are made on 31 January under the self-assessment system;
- a requirement to notify HMRC of the commencement of a property business – penalties are levied for late notification and late filing;
- the system applies to furnished and unfurnished lettings, rent-a-room, furnished holiday lets (FHLs) and all other ancillary receipts connected to or forming the property business;
- activities regarded as a trade, such as keeping a hotel or guest-house, need not adopt a fiscal year-end basis period; they are kept separate from an individual's property business activities;
- occasional letting activities by traders and professional partnerships may be included within their computation of trading profits and do not need to be separated;
- rents from foreign property are foreign income, potentially benefiting from the remittance basis if claimed by non-UK domiciled individuals. Income and losses from foreign property are ring-fenced; and
- certain activities are specifically excluded from the regime, including incidental receipts by traders (see ITTOIA 2005, s 273).

Interest and penalties are levied in most circumstances upon late and/or incorrect returns of property profits. All returns (including third-party returns) are liable to the usual HMRC Enquiry rules.

The new rules from 2017–18 onwards

Introduction

[6.5] Under the proposed new cash basis rules, for the purposes of income tax, from the tax year 2017–18 onwards, the profits of a property business must be computed on the cash basis (ITTOIA 2005, s 271C) unless one of five conditions (Conditions A to E) applies.

Those five conditions (listed in ITTOIA 2005, s 271A) are as follows:

- Condition A: the business is carried on at any time in the tax year concerned by a company, a limited-liability partnership, a partnership in which at least one partner is not an individual, or trustees;
- Condition B: the receipts of the business, measured by the cash basis, exceed £150,000 in the tax year (the ceiling is reduced pro rata if the business is not carried on for the whole of the tax year);
- Condition C: the business consists of or includes a property business that is carried on jointly with a spouse or civil partner, the share of each party in the joint business is 50% by default (as they have made no declaration to the contrary) and the other party does not use the cash basis;
- Condition D: the taxpayer claims a business-premises renovation allowance (see **6.39**) and there is an event in the tax year that would give rise to a balancing adjustment;
- Condition E: the taxpayer elects not to apply the cash basis.

In other words, the cash basis will apply to the majority of property businesses carried on by an individual alone or jointly with the individual's spouse or civil partner, or by a partnership of individuals, unless they opt for it not to apply. On the other hand, substantial property businesses, property businesses carried on with a corporate partner and property businesses with special circumstances (to which Condition C or D apply) will continue to use the GAAP or accruals basis, with no option to apply the cash basis.

Where any of Conditions A to E does apply, the profits of the business are to be calculated in accordance with GAAP (ITTOIA 2005, s 271A(1)). This means, in effect, continuation of the current regime, under which profits are computed on an accruals basis.

The accruals basis

[6.6] Where in 2017–18 and subsequent years, taxpayers are obliged, or opt to, use the GAAP or accruals basis, the rules applicable to all property businesses prior to 2017–18 (see **6.4**) will continue to apply, with some minor legislative tweaks.

Thus, it is to be made explicit that ITTOIA 2005, s 272, which prescribes which trade-computation rules also apply to property businesses, refers only to GAAP computations (ITTOIA 2005, ss 271E(2)(a); 272 (as prospectively amended)). It is now prospective ITTOIA 2005, s 271E(1) that provides that 'the profits of a property business are calculated in the same way as the profits of a trade'.

The cash basis

[6.7] Those computations that must be carried out under the cash basis are to face a new but similar set of rules. Prospective ITTOIA 2005, s 272ZA contains a table of trade-computation provisions that are to apply to property businesses. This is largely the same as the Table for the GAAP basis under ITTOIA 2005, s 272, but omits:

Section 33	[restrictions on] capital expenditure (inapplicable to the cash basis and replaced by prospective ITTOIA 2005, s 307B);
Section 35	[restrictions on] bad and doubtful debts (onerous under the cash basis);
Section 43	employee benefits: unpaid contributions when profits calculated before end of nine-month period (inapplicable under the cash basis);
Sections 48–50B	car hire (inapplicable under the cash basis);
Section 94A	costs of setting up an SAYE option scheme or CSOP scheme;
Section 94AA	deductions in relation to salaried members of limited-liability partnerships (cash basis does not apply);
Sections 148A–148J	special rules for long funding leases (inapplicable to the cash basis);
Section 155	levies and repayments under FISMA 2000; and
Sections 188–191	unremittable amounts (onerous under the cash basis)

The table includes ITTOIA 2005, ss 106C–106E (amounts not reflecting commercial transactions), which apply to the cash basis only, and are hence missing from the s 272 table.

Also excluded are ITTOIA 2005, ss 291–294 (deductions for certain expenses incurred by tenants under taxed leases) (prospective ITTOIA 2005, s 276A).

The cash basis rules introduce new sections (prospective ITTOIA 2005, ss 307A–307F) providing for the treatment of capital expenditure, capital receipts and deductions for loans.

As a rule for the cash basis generally, taxpayers may not claim capital allowances (except in respect of cars). However, hitherto, they have generally been entitled to receive a full deduction in the relevant basis period for capital expenditure that would have qualified for plant and machinery allowances, except in respect of integral features (existing CAA 2001, s 33A). That section, even in the version substituted by the new rules, is not to apply to the cash basis computation for property businesses; it is to be replaced by ITTOIA 2005, s 307B, which contains a list of non-deductible capital expenditure. For full details, see **6.34**.

ITTOIA 2005, ss 307C, 307D provide an additional restriction on deductions for the cost of loans where the 'total loan amount for the tax year' exceeds the aggregate value of the properties measured on the last day of the tax year. See further **6.30**.

As a corollary for the deductions for certain types of capital expenditure under the cash basis, capital receipts must generally be taken into account when computing profits under the cash basis (ITTOIA 2005, ss 96A, 96B).

ITTOIA 2005, ss 307E–307F provide for the treatment of capital receipts and deemed capital receipts of a property business under the cash basis. These provisions cover two separate cases.

In Case 1, disposal proceeds or capital refunds are received in a cash basis year in respect of assets for the capital expenditure on which a deduction has been made under the cash basis or (where GAAP applied at the time) a capital allowance has been claimed and a deduction has been allowed under ITTOIA 2005, s 58 or 59 for the incidental costs of loan finance or under the relief for replacement domestic assets (see **6.46**).

In Case 2, disposal proceeds or capital refunds are received in a GAAP year following a tax year which was a cash basis year and they relate to an asset for the capital expenditure on which either (1) a deduction has been allowed under the cash basis but would not have been allowed under the GAAP basis or (2) a deduction has been allowed under ITTOIA 2005, s 58 or 59 for the incidental costs of loan finance or under the relief for replacement domestic assets (see **6.46**) in a tax year before that in which the taxpayer last entered the cash basis.

In both cases, the capital receipt is to be brought into account as a cash basis receipt, unless it has already been brought into account under another head or the disposal value is to be brought into account under CAA 2001.

Prospective ITTOIA 2005, s 307F provides for deemed capital receipts to arise if an asset ceases to be used for the purposes of the property business without being disposed of or there is a 'material increase' in the proportion of non-business use of the asset.

Profit computations under corporation tax

[6.8] The charge to corporation tax on rental profits is levied under the provisions of Part 4 of CTA 2009.

The rules for companies span ten Chapters of Part 4.

The main features of the current rules are:

- taxable income is calculated on the same principles as for income tax, using generally accepted accounting principles (GAAP);
- relief for interest paid follows the loan-relationship rules in Part 5 of CTA 2009; interest is not an expense in the corporation tax computation;
- interest cap rules are introduced for companies within a worldwide group with effect from 1 April 2017;
- specific rules for management expenses, group relief and other losses;
- investment companies may deduct the costs of management expenses following the rules in CTA 2009, s 1219;
- capital allowances are deducted and balancing charges added to taxable profits. It is not possible to carry back surplus capital allowances;
- profits from furnished accommodation and furnished holiday lettings (FHLs) are within the scope of corporation tax (CTA 2009, Part 4, Ch 6);

- tax is due nine months after the company's accounting year-end and an annual corporation tax return must be filed 12 months after that year end;
- loss relief for losses brought forward is capped for very large losses with effect from 1 April 2017;
- there are potential income and corporation tax charges upon accommodation occupied by, or transferred to, directors or employees upon advantageous terms; and
- non-UK resident companies investing in UK property may, subject to certain requirements, register for a special scheme, the Non-Resident Landlord scheme, the principal advantage of which is payment of income tax on rental profits at the basic rate of income tax.

CTA 2009, Part 4, Ch 2 (ss 203–208) introduces the concept of a 'property business', a term which is relevant for income from both UK and overseas land. All the income from a company's UK land interests is treated as a single business under CTA 2009, s 205 (which includes the letting of furniture – CTA 2009, s 248).

A similar rule applies to bring together all income arising to companies liable to UK corporation tax from foreign properties into a single 'overseas property business' (CTA 2009, s 206).

Companies coming into or leaving the charge to income tax

[6.9] Companies can be within the charge to income tax on the profits of a UK property business if they are themselves non-resident companies (CTA 2009, s 3). However, should a change in the location of its management and control establish UK residence, a previously non-resident company will cease to be subject to income tax and will instead be subject to corporation tax on the profits of its (new) UK property business. Coming within the charge to corporation tax will represent the commencement of a UK property business. The migration will have the result that the company ceases to be within the charge to income tax and permanently ceases to carry on its UK property business chargeable to income tax (ITTOIA 2005, s 362).

Self-assessment

[6.10] Almost all returns of property income will fall within the self-assessment system. The 31 January filing deadline for income tax businesses is well known and from April 2011, limited companies have a similar obligation to file and pay self-assessment taxes online.

Penalties for late or incorrect property business returns

[6.11] Penalties are imposed for both incorrect and late returns of rental income and/or expenses contained in a self-assessment return. There are also similar tax-related penalties for VAT and PAYE misdemeanours. Landlords are no exception.

Penalties are imposed on a sliding scale of erroneous actions under the following headings:

Mistakes after reasonable care was taken	0%
Failure to take reasonable care	up to 30%
Deliberate understatement of profits	20%–70%
Deliberate understatement & concealment	30–100%

Clearly there is huge scope for negotiation. The amount of penalty is significantly reduced if full cooperation is given to HMRC, including free access to relevant records such as the lettings books and receipts for key items of expenditure.

However, the averages vary wildly depending upon the Inspector's viewpoint and the above 'average' baseline of 30% is in line with the HMRC approach to evasion before April 2009. The high-end penalties are far more draconian than the 'old' pre-2009 regime and an obvious deterrent.

The late filing and late payment penalty models are broadly similar. These are designed to encourage filing and payment by the correct dates by introducing an escalating series of penalties depending upon the number of failures within a set penalty period. Further penalties will arise if there is a prolonged delay in filing returns or paying the tax due.

The penalties include a right of appeal against penalty decisions if the taxpayer has a reasonable excuse for the lateness. Late payment penalties may also be avoided where taxpayers have agreed a time-to-pay arrangement with HMRC.

Scope of a property business

[6.12] The meaning of 'generating income from land' includes 'exploiting an estate, interest or right in or over land as a source of rents or other receipts'. This is given further breadth by ITTOIA 2005, s 266(3)(b) and CTA 2009, s 207(3)(b) to include 'payments in respect of the exercise of any other right over land'. Payments in respect of licences and annual payments issuing out of land are also expressly included within the scope of other receipts. It can be seen that the concept of a property business is extremely broad and no narrower than the old Schedule A rules.

Certain activities are specifically excluded from being within a property business, including the generation of income from farming and market gardening in the UK, receipts related to tied premises, certain receipts in connection with the operation of caravan sites where a trade is carried on, rents from surplus business accommodation and payments for wayleaves. Receipts from mines and quarries etc, called 'section 12(4) concerns' (where income tax is concerned) or 'section 39(4) concerns' (where corporation tax is concerned) are also excluded as being carried on for the purpose of generating income from land (ITTOIA 2005, s 267; CTA 2009, s 208).

Rental computations

Accruals (GAAP) basis: income tax

[6.13] The rules described below (**6.13–6.15**) do not apply to cash basis computations.

ITTOIA 2005, s 270 prescribes that income tax is payable on the 'full amount of profits arising in the tax year'. Where rental streams are consistent and broadly similar moneys are received each month, simple time apportionment by reference to the number of days aligns the tax liability reasonably accurately (ITTOIA 2005, s 275(1)–(3)). Where this is not attained, perhaps because receipts are irregular, then a calculation by reference to the actual date of receipt rather than time apportionment is acceptable/appropriate (ITTOIA 2005, s 275(4)). This was demonstrated in *Marshall Hus & Partners Ltd v Bolton (Inspector of Taxes)* [1981] STC 18, 55 TC 539, where the company apportioned each accounting period by reference to the actual deals contracted over a period of six years. The arising basis would not apply for any year when the remittance basis is claimed for foreign income (ITTOIA 2005, Part 8).

Apportionment: income tax

[6.14] The concept of profits arising in the tax year is worthy of a little more thought, and sight of the lease agreements relevant to the property business is a prerequisite of preparing accurate tax computations. Most leases provide for rental payments in advance, meaning the correct recognition of income apportions moneys received in the year to 5 April for the use of the property after 5 April and includes moneys received in the year prior to 6 April for the use of the property in that tax year.

Example 1

Theresa owns a block of flats and the tenants are charged an annual rent on 1 January, with a rent review on 31 December. Theresa uplifts her rents at each review, but some of the tenants are elderly ladies and pay very late, if at all. Two of the ladies do not pay Theresa the increase due on 1 January 2018.

Theresa's self-assessment for 2017–18 is as follows:

Rents due	1 January 2017	£600,000
Rents due	1 January 2018	£630,000

The rent due on 1 January 2017 is for the use of the property from then to 31 December 2017. As part of the rent due falls into the previous tax year, 2016–17, the 95 days to 5 April 2017 are apportioned to 2016–17 and excluded from the computation. The balance is taxed in 2017–18, ie $270/365 \times £600,000$. Under the same principle, part of the rent due on 1 January 2018 falls into this year, viz $95/365$ of £630,000.

The self-assessment for 2017–18 is £607,808, based upon rental profits of:

(270/365 × 600,000) plus (95/365 × 630,000).

Theresa could consider a bad-debt claim for the rent uncollected, but it is unlikely this would be deductible in the tax year 2017–18, as the time period may be too short for HMRC to regard the non-payment as irrecoverable at 5 April 2018, particularly if legal action against the elderly ladies has not begun or is not contemplated.

Ordinary expenses follow the same apportionment rule. One-off exceptional expenses require more detailed consideration.

Example 2

Suppose Theresa notices a large hole in the roof one unhappy day; she obtains several estimates and a budget of £25,000 is eventually agreed with Racket Roofing on 28 February 2018. Mr Racket did not give a time when works would begin but required £15,000 as a deposit for materials and initial works immediately and the balance of £10,000 by two further stage payments on 28 April 2018 and 28 May 2018. Mr Racket did not give a firm timescale for completion of the works. Clearly Theresa has quantified to the best of her ability the specific cost of the work. She has also contracted to pay for the repair in the tax year 2017–18, although the stage payments and completion of the works are not expected to occur until 2018–19. As the rules for a property business follow ordinary accounting principles, it would be prudent for the provision of the expense to be recognised in 2017–18 and a deduction claimed. The expenses of a property business are considered further below.

Basis period: income tax

[6.15] Under the GAAP basis, the basis period for a property business chargeable to income tax is the year to 5 April. It is not necessary to adopt a fiscal accounting year-end, but for practical reasons, most property businesses do so. If a non-fiscal year-end is chosen, it may be necessary to file and amend self-assessment tax returns based upon an apportionment of two years' accounts and to estimate certain figures if accounts are not finalised. For example, suppose Phillip runs a successful furnished-letting business but decides to adopt a 31 January year-end to cope with the Christmas season. The entry on his 2017–18 tax return, to be filed by 31 January 2019, would comprise 301/365 of the accounts to 31 January 2018 and an estimate of the anticipated profits, ie 64/365, of the accounts to 31 January 2019. If Phillip wished to file his tax return promptly he would have to estimate his profits to 31 January 2019.

There are two exceptions to the fiscal year-end basis period. The letting of surplus accommodation by a trader or professional partnership may be included as a receipt in the mainstream accounts adopting the usual accounting period year-end.

Where the property business is actually a trade, the accounting year-end may be adopted.

Under the cash basis, the tax year is of necessity the basis period.

Example 3

> Phillip has developed his furnished letting business into a guest-house; he notices trade picks up significantly over the summer season. A 30 April year-end is chosen, as tax payments on the summer trade can then be delayed, as they will not fall due until the 31 January in the year after that in which the accounting period ends.

The new £1,000 property allowance

[6.16] With the intention of providing simplicity and certainty for taxpayers with small amounts of income from property rents, a new £1,000 allowance for property income is introduced with effect from 2017–18. Individuals with property income of no more than £1,000 are exempt from income tax on that income and will not have to declare it in their tax returns. Individuals with property income greater than £1,000 receive partial relief if they opt to pay tax on the difference between their rental income and the allowance and not deduct their property expenses.

In what follows, it is assumed that the measures now contained in cl 17 and Sch 3 of the September 2017 Finance Bill will be enacted without material amendment.

The allowance is applicable against an individual's 'relevant property income' from a 'relevant property business' (ITTOIA 2005, s 783B(1)). A 'relevant property business' is any property business (whether a UK or an overseas property business) except one all the receipts of which are rent-a-room receipts (see **6.51**) or the notional separate business that is regarded as carried on by persons receiving distributions of property income from an authorised investment fund or from a REIT (ITTOIA 2005, s 783BA). 'Relevant property income' consists of the individual's 'relievable receipts' from his or her relevant property business(es) (ITTOIA 2005, s 783BC). 'Relievable receipts' are all receipts that would be brought into account in computing the individual's property-business profits, excluding rent-a-room receipts and balancing charges from an excluded source of receipts (ITTOIA 2005, s 783BB).

Excluded from using the allowance are individuals:

- who are carrying on a property business in partnership;
- who claim the tax reduction under ITTOIA 2005, s 274A in lieu of the non-deductible element of mortgage interest (see **6.30**);
- who qualify for rent-a-room relief whose receipts under the scheme do not exceed the £7,500 limit but have made an election to disapply the full relief and individuals whose receipts under the scheme do exceed the £7,500 limit and have not elected for the alternative method of computing profits (see **6.51**);
- whose property income includes payments direct or indirect payments from an employer or from the employer of a person connected to the individual or from a partnership in which that individual is, or is connected to, a partner or from a close company in which the individual is a participator or an associate of a participator.

Where a qualifying individual's relevant property income does not exceed £1,000, the income is not charged to tax (subject to an election to the contrary, for which see below) (ITTOIA 2005, s 783B(3)) nor are any expenses associated with that income recognised (ITTOIA 2005, s 783BF).

However, the individual may elect not to receive full relief. Any such election must be made within one year of the normal self-assessment filing date for the tax year concerned (ITTOIA 2005, s 783BJ). The profits or losses of the property business would then be computed on the normal basis, setting expenses against income. Opting not to claim the allowance would be beneficial if there is a loss in that tax year which the individual can set off against other income.

Where the qualifying individual's relevant property income does exceed the £1,000 allowance, the individual may receive partial relief, subject to making an election for an alternative calculation of profits (ITTOIA 2005, s 783B(4)). The election for partial relief must be made within one year of the normal self-assessment filing date for the tax year concerned (ITTOIA 2005, s 783BK). The first such elections, for the tax year 2017–18, must thus be made no later than 31 January 2020.

Under the election, the profits charged to income tax are computed by deducting the £1,000 allowance from the relievable receipts but no expenses are brought into account (ITTOIA 2005, s 783BH). If the individual has more than one relevant property business, the individual may allocate the allowance between the relevant businesses as he or she sees fit, but not so as to create a loss in any one business (ITTOIA 2005, s 783BI).

Loss relief

Income tax losses of a property business

[6.17] The starting point is the long-enshrined principle that losses from rented properties are not regarded as trading losses. The principle frequently appears before Tax Tribunals (see most recently *Azam (P) v Revenue & Customs Comrs* [2011] UKFTT 18 (TC)). The legislation has stood the test of time and is worthy of a brief review (for further details see **CHAPTER 21**).

The provisions governing income tax losses for a property business are contained in ITA 2007, Part 4. Broadly, the computation rules mirror those for the calculation of profits and losses of a trade. There are three mechanisms for loss relief:

- Carry-forward against future years' property-business profits. There are separate 'pools' for FHL losses (see below).
- Upon a claim, a deduction from general income where there is either a 'capital allowances connection' that can be established or there exists a 'relevant agricultural connection'. This enables the loss to be relieved against general income for the year of loss or the subsequent year.
- A deduction from general income or treatment as a capital loss for certain post-cessation payments and events in connection with a UK property business.

A 'capital allowances connection' exists where, in calculating the loss, there is an excess of capital allowances over balancing charges (ITA 2007, s 123(2)).

There are complexities arising from the involvement of AIA (Annual Investment Allowance). The meaning of 'agricultural connection' is broader and relates to agricultural expenses attributable to land in dedicated agricultural use (ITA 2007, s 123(4), (5)).

Where profits are computed under the cash basis, no 'sideways' relief against general income is to be available under the proposed new application of the cash basis to the profits of a property business (prospective ITA 2007, s 127BA).

Corporation tax losses of a property business

[6.18] A loss incurred in a UK property business may be set off in the current accounting period (against total profits) or in a future accounting period against profits of the UK property business (CTA 2010, s 62). If the measures now incorporated in the September 2017 Finance Bill as s 18 and Sch 4, are enacted unchanged, relief by carry-forward will no longer be automatic and will be subject to the making of a claim. However, where there would otherwise be sufficient profits to absorb the loss entirely, the company will be able to choose to set off part only of the loss brought forward if it so wishes. The new rules are to apply in relation to accounting periods and notional accounting periods beginning after 31 March 2017. Periods straddling 1 April 2017 will be divided into two notional periods, one ending on 31 March and the other beginning on 1 April.

If the UK property business is discontinued, the loss may still be carried forward as a management expense provided the company has investment business (CTA 2010, s 63). The same new rules concerning the making of a claim and the availability of partial set-off are also envisaged for this relief. The availability of such a loss against an eventual gain is extremely useful.

Losses from a UK property business are also available for surrender to other group companies as part of a group relief claim in the accounting period of the loss (CTA 2010, ss 99(1)(e), 102). Under the measures referred to earlier, 'carried-forward losses' (strictly speaking, brought-forward losses), including the losses of a UK property business, are to be available for group relief in relation to accounting periods and notional accounting periods beginning after 31 March 2017 (CTA 2010, s 188BB(1)(a)(v)), subject to conditions set out in CTA 2010, Part 5A.

The carried-forward losses of a UK property business available under ITTOIA 2005, s 62(3) for set-off against the total profits of the company form part of the deductions subject to restriction under the new restrictions on the overall deductibility of carried-forward losses. These will only affect companies that have more than a maximum of £5 million (allocable among companies in a group) of profits against which the loss may be set.

As regards losses of an overseas property business, these may only be relieved by carry-forward against profits of the overseas property business in subsequent periods. These rules will be unaffected by the new loss set-off rules described in the preceding paragraphs.

For corporate FHL losses, there have been substantive changes where foreign properties are involved, for which see below at **6.47**.

Choice of structure

[6.19] There is sometimes a perception that corporate ownership of a property portfolio secures valuable tax advantages. Perhaps it does for some, certainly in terms of commercial risk-management, but the decision can be marginal. Although there have been successive reductions in the mainstream corporation tax rates, reduced to 19% for the years starting 1 April 2017, 2018 and 2019, and to 17% for the year starting 1 April 2020, making limited companies a popular ownership structure for property portfolios, this advantage has to be balanced against the countervailing series of measures implemented in the Finance Act 2013, Finance Act 2014 and both 2015 Finance Acts placing additional tax burdens on corporately held property and property held by other 'non-natural' persons. For property companies that are part of a worldwide group, the new restrictions on interest deductibility will also need to be kept in mind.

The existing measures enacted in 2013–15 include:

• a 15% SDLT rate upon certain purchases of residential property costing more than £500,000 (effective from 20 March 2014);
• an annual charge (ATED) on residential dwellings ranging from £3,500 per annum for properties worth more than £500,000 and less than £1 million (from 1 April 2016); and £7,000 per annum for properties worth more than £1 million and not more than £2 million (from 1 April 2015); and £218,200 for properties worth more than £20 million) (see CHAPTER 22);
• CGT on gains from the sale of residential property that is subject to the annual charge ('ATED-related gains', effective from April 2013); and
• from 6 April 2015, individuals, trustees, and certain companies who are not resident in the UK and sell a UK residential property need to notify HMRC of the transaction since CGT will be imposed on any capital gain ('NRCGT gain') that relates to the period after 5 April 2015.

Exceptions to the SDLT levy are possible, especially for property developers with a two-year trading history (for further details, see CHAPTER 16).

If the measures contained in prospective TIOPA 2010, Part 10 are enacted as published in the September 2017 Finance Bill as s 20 and Sch 5, for a company that is part of a worldwide group, that part of net interest expense in excess of £2 million (measured on a group-wide basis) may, broadly, be set off to the extent only that it does not exceed 30% of 'tax-EBITDA' (earnings before interest, tax, depreciation and amortisation).

A full discussion of the measures is beyond the scope of this chapter, but for residential property portfolios, the measures present a significant 'challenge' to the use of UK or offshore corporate or partnership vehicles. In particular the following scenarios will require re-evaluation.

• UK/non-UK company holding UK property.
• Non-UK trust holding UK property.
• UK/non-UK partnerships with a corporate partner holding UK property.
• UK/non-UK collective investment scheme holding UK property.

Before these new measures, the abolition of taper relief from April 2008 had popularised the choice of a company as a suitable ownership structure. This was because many unincorporated landlords perceived a lower capital gains tax exposure through corporate ownership, compensating for the perceived disadvantages following the removal of taper relief.

The alternative of a limited liability partnership (LLP) continues to be a popular choice of ownership structure. For the residential-property landlord, this is nevertheless also targeted by the 'non-natural person' amendments.

Commencement and cessation

[6.20] A property business cannot begin until the first property is let. This should be evident from a contract to exploit the ownership of the land or building concerned and where as a result of that contract some sort of receipt arises. It is possible for the same individual to carry on a property business in a different capacity and for the new property business to be distinguished from an extension or continuity of an existing one.

Example 4

Jeremy has run an established lettings business for a number of years. He is appointed as a trustee of his late sister's estate, part of which includes a similar-scale property business. Jeremy cannot merge the two businesses, as they are carried out in separate legal capacities and are therefore two separate businesses.

There are special rules for expenditure incurred before the property business commences. For the purposes of income tax, they are found in ITTOIA 2005, s 57 and for the purposes of corporation tax they are found in CTA 2009, ss 61 and 330. Relief is given for qualifying expenditure incurred up to seven years prior to the date of commencement and is treated as incurred upon the first day the business begins. Relief must not have been claimed elsewhere. Capital expenditure is outside the scheme, nor are capital allowances any longer available.

Once the business has commenced, expenses on subsequent properties need no special rules to obtain a deduction, as they are part of the ongoing property business and recognisable as they arise.

The date that a property business ceases may be less apparent. There is a school of thought that labels a property business as a friend for life if even one property is retained. The landlord may decide one day to retire and wind down the business, not replacing departing tenants and putting his more valuable properties up for sale. The process may be time-consuming and one or two properties may be kept on to provide a retirement nest-egg. The business has simply scaled down, it has not ceased. Cessation occurs when the entire portfolio has been disposed of, or used for another purpose. Departing tenants would not have been replaced for a substantial period.

If a business lies dormant, but is revived some time afterward, the interval period is important in deciding whether the old business has continued (with any brought-forward losses in fact) or a new business has begun. In practice, a three-year period (although often less) is regarded by HMRC as evidence of cessation of the old business, particularly if entirely new properties are let.

Example 5

> Diane plans extensive round-the-world holidays and does not know exactly when or indeed if she will return to the UK. She has a small portfolio of residential properties and places it in the management of a local agent with instructions that tenants need not be replaced once their leases expire. She will decide after a year whether she wishes to actually sell the properties as they become empty, depending upon market conditions. Diane has such a good time that she does in fact sell all but one of the properties but returns to the UK after five years, eager to begin again. She acquires several new properties from the proceeds of the first portfolio and lets them. She has ceased her old business at the time that the penultimate property was sold rather than on the date of her departure. She has commenced a new business when the retained property is first let again. Any losses upon cessation of the old business will have expired upon cessation and are not transferable to a new business.

There are special rules to tax post-cessation receipts excluded from the final years of the property business. These are provided by ITTOIA 2005, ss 349–356 for the purposes of income tax and by CTA 2009, ss 280–286 for corporation tax.

For individuals carrying on a property business chargeable to income tax, in the absence of post-cessation receipts to absorb them, post-cessation expenses may form the basis of sideways loss relief against general income. For the purposes of income tax, claims for relief must be made no later than the first anniversary of the normal self-assessment filing date for the tax year for which the relief is to apply (ITA 2007, s 125), ie no later than 31 January 2020 for relief relating to the tax year 2017–18. There is no such possibility for corporation tax.

Example 6

> Jeremy winds up his personal rental portfolio and ceases the business on 31 December 2017. He had some outstanding litigation against a bad payer, which has now failed as the tenant is untraceable. The tenant had been due to pay Jeremy £5,000 on 1 September 2016, which falls in the tax year that ends on 5 April 2017. Jeremy has until 31 January 2019 to claim relief for the bad debt as a post-cessation expense and may make a claim for sideways relief for the tax year 2016–17 (ITA 2007, s 125).

Prior to the abolition of taper relief in April 2008, there was a fairly generous regime available to commercial landlords upon cessation and sale of the rental asset. It provided for business-asset taper relief upon gains realised prior to that date where premises were let to traders. The provisions increased in their generosity from 1998 to allow full taper relief after 2002 for commercial landlords. For residential landlords, business-asset taper relief might exempt up to 40% of a gain with further relief for indexation for assets acquired prior to 1998.

This regime was replaced by a flat rate 18% or 28% charge upon gains from property sales sheltered to a limited (and potentially contentious) extent by entrepreneurs' relief, the detailed conditions for which are contained in TCGA 1992, ss 169H–169S and, from 6 April 2016, investors' relief (for disposals of holdings in unlisted trading companies). At face value, the second-home owner with a 'small' gain reduces his tax bill by more than 50% in the new regime. But the commercial landlord is in a much trickier position. The coincidental landlord letting commercial premises perhaps as part of his overall trade may still secure the relief depending upon degree and the ability to demonstrate that the asset concerned has no 'investment' characteristics. It should be noted that, whereas the rates of capital gains tax have been cut to 10% and 20% from 6 April 2016 for most types of capital gain, the rates for gains from residential property are set at 20% and 28%.

The most common scenario might be one where the business proprietor or business partners retain their business premises privately and let them to their personal company or partnership. Formerly, full business-asset taper relief would usually work very favourably. From 6 April 2008, TCGA 1992, s 169P presents some problems. In particular, there is a rent restriction in operation in associated disposal scenarios, such as where the business is sold in conjunction with the land asset concerned. The rent restriction operates to limit any entrepreneurs' relief claimed by reference to the extent to which the rent charged was less than the open-market rent. Where the rent charged to the business was the full market rent, therefore, entrepreneurs' relief is not available at all.

The new investors' relief (TCGA 1992, ss 169VA–169VY, introduced by FA 2016, s 87 and Sch 14) is of little help here. First, the lower rate of capital gains tax (10%) that it offers applies only to gains from the disposal of shares or of an interest in shares in unlisted companies for which the investor has subscribed. Second, even if the property were held in a corporate envelope, the company must be a trading company or the holding company of a trading group. Third, the investor may not be an officer or employee of the company, unless he or she is an 'unremunerated director' and neither that person nor a connected person had previously been connected with the company or involved in the carrying-on of all or part of its trade.

Deductions

Income tax: 2016–17 and previous years

[6.21] The profits of a property business are calculated in the same way as profits of a trade (ITTOIA 2005, s 272), but the legislation limits which of the rules regarding the calculation of trading income are to apply to a property business to those specifically listed in ITTOIA 2005, s 272(2). This means, inter alia, that receipts must be recognised in accordance with generally accepted accounting practice (ITTOIA 2005, s 25). Moreover, ITTOIA 2005, s 274 provides that 'relevant permissive rules' take precedence over 'relevant prohibitive rules'.

'Relevant permissive rules' are those provisions in the property-business rules (ITTOIA 2005, Part 3, ie ITTOIA 2005, ss 260–364), excluding ITTOIA 2005, ss 291–294 (tenants' expenses), which allow a deduction in calculating the profits of a property business. 'Relevant prohibitive rules' are those provisions of ITTOIA 2005, Part 3, as applied by ITTOIA 2005, s 272, but excluding ITTOIA 2005, ss 36 (unpaid remuneration), 38 (employee-benefit contributions remaining to be made), 48 (car rental restriction), 55 (crime-related payments) and 272A (restriction on loan finance), to the extent that they may prohibit or restrict the amount of the deduction. These excluded prohibitive rules have precedence nothwithstanding the presumption in favour of permission. However, the precedence of permission over prohibition is in every case overruled if there is any taint of tax avoidance (ITTOIA 2005, s 272(1A)).

There are two primary considerations to obtain a deduction for expenses in the rental computation under the GAAP basis. Expenses must be incurred 'wholly and exclusively' for business purposes; this is the foundation stone of the old Schedule D, Case I rules and is enshrined anew in ITTOIA 2005, s 34(1). Secondly, expenditure must not be of a capital (durable) nature (ITTOIA 2005, s 33).

The concept of 'wholly and exclusively' is most easily understood within its full legal context, namely no deduction is allowed for 'an expense not incurred wholly and exclusively for the purpose of the trade' (for which read property business). HMRC interpret this as meaning that expenditure is disallowed where there is no easily identifiable proportion of an expense that relates to the business.

Example 7

Vince takes his family on a summer holiday to Devon where he has just purchased a holiday cottage that he intends to rent out. One day, Vince will fund his retirement from its income, but for the time being he is going to let the cottage to long-term tenants and has made arrangements to show people around during the family holiday. Vince keeps his travel receipts as he thinks he may be able to set them against tax. HMRC's view would be that the expenses are not 'wholly and exclusively' incurred in the property business (relieved as pre-trading expenditure); they are not the sole purpose of the expenditure and are not deductible as the business element is indistinguishable from the private element.

Where a distinction is easily drawn, such as where dual-purpose expenditure upon utility bills or repair costs is incurred, an apportionment of the expense is deductible, although strictly the 'wholly and exclusively' rule is not met. Vince needed to pay for gas, electricity and water during the family holiday, and, luckily, prospective tenants visited each day, so there was some definable business use of the cottage. As a clear apportionment of the utility bills can be made, a portion of the costs can be introduced on the first day of the business and deducted in computing the first year's profits. Vince was happy about this and the cottage was tenanted soon afterwards on a long-term basis. At the end of each letting, Vince used the cottage for a fortnight for family holidays at Easter and during the summer every year. Vince would be able to distinguish business and private use of the cottage and pro rata repair costs, obtaining a deduction of 337/365 for any revenue expenditure.

Income tax 2017–18 and subsequent years: accruals (GAAP) basis

[6.22] Where profits are calculated under the GAAP basis, the rules are to be essentially unchanged going forward.

The profits of a property business continue to be calculated in the same way as profits of a trade (ITTOIA 2005, s 271E(1)), but the legislation limits which of the rules regarding the calculation of trading income are to apply to a property business to those specifically listed in ITTOIA 2005, s 272(2). This means, inter alia, that receipts and expenses must be recognised in accordance with generally accepted accounting practice (ITTOIA 2005, s 271B). It also continues to be the case that ITTOIA 2005, s 274 (as amended) provides that rules permitting deductions take precedence over rules prohibiting a deduction.

Income tax 2017–18 and subsequent years: cash basis

[6.23] Under the cash basis, receipts of the business are brought into account when they are received and expenses of the business are brought into account when they are paid (ITTOIA 2005, s 271D(2)), subject to any adjustment authorised or required by law in calculating profits for income tax purposes generally (ITTOIA 2005, s 271D(3)). The profits of a property business are calculated in the same way as profits of a trade (ITTOIA 2005, s 271E(1)), but the legislation limits which of the rules regarding the calculation of trading income are to apply to a property business to those specifically listed in ITTOIA 2005, s 272ZA(1). This means, inter alia, that receipts must be recognised in accordance with generally accepted accounting practice (ITTOIA 2005, s 271B). Moreover, ITTOIA 2005, s 274 (as amended) continues to provide that 'relevant permissive rules' take precedence over 'relevant prohibitive rules'.

'Relevant permissive rules' are those provisions in the property-business rules (ITTOIA 2005, Part 3, ie ITTOIA 2005, ss 260–364), excluding ITTOIA 2005, ss 291–294 (tenants' expenses), which allow a deduction in calculating the profits of a property business. 'Relevant prohibitive rules' are those provisions of ITTOIA 2005, Part 3, as applied by ITTOIA 2005, s 272A, but excluding ITTOIA 2005, ss 38 (employee-benefit contributions remaining to be made) and 55 (crime-related payments), to the extent that they may prohibit or restrict the amount of the deduction. These excluded prohibitive rules, together with ITTOIA 2005, ss 272A (restriction on loan finance) and prospective 307D (deduction for costs of loans) have precedence notwithstanding the presumption in favour of permission. However, the precedence of permission over prohibition is in every case overruled if there is any taint of tax avoidance (ITTOIA 2005, s 272(1A)).

Under the proposed new cash basis rules for property businesses, the prohibition on capital expenditure is contained in ITTOIA 2005, s 307B. Instead of a general prohibition, the section specifies what particular expenditure of a capital nature is not to be deductible.

The prohibition is to extend to expenditure on:

(1)   the acquisition or disposal of a business or part of a business;
(2)   education or training;
(3)   the provision, alteration or disposal of land, except where incurred on the provision of a fixture attached to land other than ordinary residential property other than expenditure incurred on the provision of a building, walls, floors, ceilings, doors, gates, shutters, windows or stairs, a waste-disposal system, a sewerage or drainage system or a shaft or similar structure for housing a lift, hoist, escalator or moving walkway;
(4)   the provision, alteration or disposal of an asset for use in ordinary residential property (but excluding expenditure on the replacement of domestic items, for which see **6.46**);
(5)   the provision, alteration or disposal of an asset that is not a depreciating asset, any asset not acquired or created for use on a continuing basis in the property business, a car, a 'non-qualifying intangible asset' or a financial asset.

A depreciating asset is an asset that is reasonably expected to have a useful life of less than 20 years or one whose value will have declined by 90% or more within 20 years. A non-qualifying intangible asset is an intangible asset that must cease to exist within 20 years of the date on which the capital expenditure is incurred.

These provisions, which are replicated for trades on the cash basis, are designed to simplify the rules. One may question whether it is simpler to understand a provision with 20 subsections (new ITTOIA 2005, s 307B) or one with just two sections (the existing ITTOIA 2005, s 33A).

Be that as it may, given this long list of exclusions, what deductions may a taxpayer with a property business under the cash basis still make in respect of capital expenditure? These deductions would include:

•   Expenditure on most forms of free-standing plant or machinery (excluding cars) except on those for use in a dwelling other than one that is part of an FHL business; and
•   Expenditure on a fixture other than where it is connected with the exclusions listed in (3) above.

Cars are excluded as cash basis businesses may still claim capital allowances for cars.

Corporation tax

[6.24] The profits of a property business are calculated in the same way as profits of a trade (CTA 2009, s 210), but the legislation limits which of the rules regarding the calculation of trading income are to apply to a property business to those specifically listed in CTA 2009, s 210(2). This means, inter alia, that receipts must be recognised in accordance with generally accepted accounting practice (CTA 2009, s 46). Moreover, CTA 2009, s 214 provides that 'relevant permissive rules' take precedence over 'relevant prohibitive rules'.

'Relevant permissive rules' are those provisions in the property-business rules (CTA 2009, Part 4, ie CTA 2009, ss 202–291, excluding CTA 2009, ss 231–234 (tenants' expenses), which allow a deduction in calculating the profits of a property business. 'Relevant prohibitive rules' are those provisions of CTA 2009, Part 4 or CTA 2009, Part 20, Chapter 1 (general restrictions on deductions), but excluding CTA 2009, ss 56 (car rental restriction), 1288 (remuneration unpaid after nine months), 1290 (employee-benefit contributions remaining unpaid after nine months) and 1304 (crime-related payments), to the extent that they may prohibit or defer or restrict the amount of the deduction. These excluded prohibitive rules that have precedence nothwithstanding the presumption in favour of permission. However, the precedence of permission over prohibition is in every case overruled if there is any taint of tax avoidance (CTA 2009, s 214(1A)).

As for income tax, there are two primary considerations to obtain a deduction for expenses in the rental computation under the GAAP basis. Expenses must be incurred 'wholly and exclusively' for business purposes; this is the foundation stone of the old Sch D, Case I rules and is enshrined anew in CTA 2009, s 54(1). Secondly, expenditure must not be of a capital (durable) nature (CTA 2009, s 53).

The concept of 'wholly and exclusively' is most easily understood within its full legal context, namely no deduction is allowed for 'an expense not incurred wholly and exclusively for the purpose of the trade' (for which read property business). HMRC interpret this as meaning that expenditure is disallowed where there is no easily identifiable proportion of an expense that relates to the business.

Deductions generally

[6.25] The more common types of allowable expenses most likely to be met in a property business are as follows:

(1) Advertising.
    Advertising to find a tenant is usually allowable as a revenue expense. Advertising in connection with a property sale or purchase is capital expenditure and is to be specifically excluded under the cash basis.
(2) Bad debts.
    In practice, bad debts are deductible in the year in which the debt becomes bad or doubtful, which will probably be a substantial amount of time after the rent became due. Evidence of legal action is usually sufficient to permit a deduction. Landlords can often insure against this event and any recovery proceedings must be fully brought into the tax computation. For income tax, the legislation is derived from ITTOIA 2005, s 35. In the circumstances where a managing agent misappropriated rents, HMRC might take a humane approach. However, there is

case law to the contrary, which found the amounts misappropriated as inadmissible (*Pyne v Stallard-Penoyre* (1964) 42 TC 183). For companies, the loan-relationship rules prescribe special consideration of debts written off or considered bad between connected parties.

If a rent is waived for a private reason, there is no legal basis upon which to allow relief on the money due and the expected amount is taxable in full. If rent is waived because a tenant cannot pay and the landlord agrees to this, the waiver probably amounts to a revision of the terms of the lease and prevents the landlord from taking recovery action for it. The waiver is therefore effective in revising the terms of the lease and rent due. The gross income to be included in the property business as a taxable receipt is accordingly reduced at the time the amendment becomes effective.

No deduction may be made in respect of a provision for bad debts under the cash basis, as the essence of that basis is that income is only recognised when it is received.

(3)   Cavity wall insulation.

The Landlord's Energy Saving Allowance, which developed the cavity-wall and loft insulation allowances introduced in April 2004 to provide 'green relief' for landlords, was available for expenditure incurred before 1 or 6 April 2015. Its terms are explained briefly at **6.40** below.

(4)   Common parts.

Expenditure on common parts usually arises from the provision of cleaning or maintenance services or the payment of utility bills and is usually always an allowable deduction with any restriction appropriate to the landlord's occupation if he resides in the building. Expenditure upon common parts may create additions to the capital allowance pool by the addition of, for example, central heating or air-conditioning systems (see **CHAPTER 9** for a fuller explanation of capital allowances). Enhanced security systems and fire-precaution works are usually deductible as revenue. However, some expenditure on common parts may enhance the let building or provide an asset of an enduring nature and so be capital in nature. For example, suppose Basil decides to repair the worn-out car park and at the same time create a tennis court from the same asphalt contractor. He may deduct the cost of the repairs, but the recreational facilities are capital.

(5)   Entertaining.

The definition of business entertainment within a property business is no different from ordinary trading rules (ITTOIA 2005, ss 45–47, 272; CTA 2009, ss 1298–1300). An exception is made for the provision of free meals to all employees, provided this is not incidental to the entertainment of others. The cost of entertaining, for example, a potential tenant or useful letting agent would not be deductible. The cost of providing communal meals to tenants or a Christmas party would not be deductible unless a separate charge were levied and included in the property-business receipts.

(6)   Incidental costs of finance.
      Incidental costs of loan finance are expressly permitted by statute in respect of income taxpayers (ITTOIA 2005, ss 58, 59, 272); the definitions extend to guarantee fees and commissions. For corporation tax, these matters are dealt with in the loan-relationship rules.

(7)   Insurance.

(8)   Interest (see further **6.29** and **6.30** below).

(9)   Legal and professional costs.
      Legal and professional costs upon purchase or amendment to the title of a property used in the property business are capital. Legal costs related to improvements may in some circumstances be allowable, where, for example, they relate to health and safety, fire or security works. Otherwise fees arising from property improvements would normally be capital, but it is necessary to consider the nature of the intrinsic work being carried out.
      Fees arising from planning consents or negotiations under the Town and Country Planning Acts would relate to the use of the land or property and be regarded as capital on first principles.
      Allowable legal and professional fees are sometimes distinguishable by the fact that they cover a short and recurrent period, for example, normal accountancy expenses incurred in preparing property-business accounts and annual subscriptions to landlord associations. Costs related to fair rent and rent arbitrations or the cost of evicting an unsatisfactory tenant in order to re-let the property are revenue despite the fact there is some protection of the asset. This is restricted to actual professional costs and would not permit a provision for any 'lost' rent or diminution of rent payable following an adverse rent arbitration.
      Under the cash basis, deductions for capital expenditure in connection with the provision, alteration or disposal of land are to be specifically excluded, and provisions are not recognised.

(10) Premiums paid.

(11) Rates and council tax.
      Where property overhead costs are not passed on to the tenant, a deduction is due both under the accruals (GAAP) basis and the cash basis. This includes council tax and water-services payments, ground rent and ground annuals, electricity and gas charges. A principal feature of council tax is that it is charged upon the occupants of the building with joint and several liability for spouses and civil partners. There is therefore a requirement for the lease agreement to reflect the fact if the bearer of the liability is to be the landlord in order for the landlord to receive a deduction.

(12) Rent collection.

(13) Repairs.

(14) Salaries and wages.
      Salaries and wages are fully deductible for staff engaged in the property business. There is a real danger of PAYE visits regarding cleaners and casual assistants as the PAYE system applies fully to employees in a property business, including annual returns and P11D forms. Redundancy payments and the cost of pension contributions are deductible. The rules regarding late payment of remuneration (ITTOIA 2005,

ss 36, 274(1); CTA 2009, ss 214(1)(b)(ii), 1288), ie that remuneration unpaid more than nine months after the end of the period of account is not deductible until paid apply. This rule is unnecessary under the cash basis. Payments made by the landlord to himself are not deductible. Payments to a spouse and relatives are subject to the usual cynicism by HMRC and must be proportionate to the work carried out and the experience or qualifications of the employees concerned.

(15)   Travelling expenses.
       This includes the expenses of overseas landlords travelling to and from the UK to service rental properties.

Owner occupation

[6.26] There are two further points of note where there is owner occupation. Where a part of the home is set aside for use as an office, it may qualify for a pro rata deduction of running costs if that use is clearly defined and receipted.

Exceptionally high repair costs may be restricted pro rata to the period of ownership of a property if it is only let for a relatively short period during that time.

Example 8

Theresa paid for roof repairs on her home, which was partly let to a lodger for a two-year period. Mr Racket charged Theresa £18,000. She was reasonably happy as she had lived there for ten years and knew the roof would one day need attention. The inspector asked to see the home survey carried out when the house was purchased, Theresa found this and it highlighted the need for repair. The expenditure was apportioned as 8/10 disallowable, reflecting the fact that only in two of the ten years did Theresa carry on a property business. There was a further restriction for Theresa's private use of the unlet part of the home.

Repairs

[6.27] Where the following features are present, HMRC are inclined to argue that repair costs are capital:

*   The price paid was substantially reduced to reflect the dilapidated state of the property. This would not apply where the price is slightly lower to reflect normal wear and tear; the subsequent costs of repainting are ordinary repairs.
*   The tenant makes an agreement to reinstate the property to a good state of repair. The tenant subsequently sub-lets the property and his refurbishment costs will be capital.
*   A property cannot be unoccupied because it is in a poor state of repair. The subsequent restoration works will be largely capital in nature.

Additionally, HMRC take the view that a repair relates merely to the individual component parts of a particular asset. They believe that almost any entirety is capable of being dissected into pieces, each of which is capable of repair (see HMRC *Property Income Manual*, para PIM2020). The first part of the interpretation has some basis but the second often does not. The analysis is derived from Buckley LJ, when he considered the necessity to identify the 'entirety' that is being repaired in the case of *Lurcott v Wakeley and Wheeler* [1911] 1 KB 905. The 'doctrine of entirety' grew up around the issue it has stood the test of time. It is helpful to look at part of his findings.

> 'Repair is restoration by renewal or replacement of subsidiary parts of the whole. Renewal as distinguished from repair is reconstruction of the entirety not necessarily the whole, but substantially the whole (subject of the claim) . . . the test is whether the act to be done is one which in substance is the renewal or replacement of defective parts or the renewal or replacement of substantially the whole.'

Example 9

> Mr Johnson has never really like the pathway to his hotel. Several of the bricks are cracked or discoloured, so he decides to replace it completely with a shingled forecourt enhanced by ambient lighting, waterfalls and features. Had Mr Johnson replaced the loose or discoloured bricks, this would have been a repair, as the bricks were removable and capable of being replaced one by one. Further, the replacement project has the hallmarks of capital expenditure as it is a durable thing and goes far beyond a mere repair.

Repairs might be considered restorative where they include painting and decorating and masonry works, timber and damp treatments; replacement of broken windows including the additional cost of double glazing; repairs to roof and drainage goods. There is a requirement to use similar materials as far as possible and any significant improvements attained by redecoration that go beyond simple upkeep would be disallowed as capital. This follows *Conn v Robins Bros Ltd* (1966) 43 TC 266. HMRC's opinion of what constitutes qualifying expenditure upon repairs was updated in Tax Bulletin 59, July 2002, now reproduced at the foot of para PIM2020.

Repairs may embrace the replacement of defective parts of a building, and there is a fine line between restoring the asset if an alteration of the building is attained by the works. An improvement takes on its ordinary meaning and an alteration means 'a reconstruction of the property'. In this way where a kitchen is replaced but it is necessary to install new upgraded units and flooring, there is no 'alteration' if much the same kitchen as the old one reappears, so the expenditure is not capital but revenue. By contrast, if the kitchen refurbishment results in the creation of a new dining area, or the addition of new doorways, there would be an alteration and a restriction for capital expenditure would be necessary.

Some improvements may be modest and so treated as revenue; they may not even be visible to the naked eye. For example, if lead pipes are replaced by copper pipes, there is clearly an enhancement to the property of an enduring nature; however, partly because it is now impossible to purchase or have tradesmen work with lead piping and the upgrade is marginal, it would be unreasonable to view the expenditure as capital. On a significant scale, where perhaps a hotelier installs upgraded piping or electrical systems capable of providing greater pressure or enhanced efficiency and achieving significant cost savings or upbeat reviews and publicity, then there may be the danger that the improvement is more ostensible and an alteration has been achieved. In practice, the distinction is one of degree and what may be permissible as repairs to residential premises may not be permissible for commercial premises and HMRC could take a seemingly harsh approach to the latter.

Repairs arising from the past or anticipated to arise in the future receive distinct tax treatment. The inherent cost of repairs passes out to capital where a rundown property is acquired for letting if the state of disrepair is discounted in the purchase price and the property is all but unusable. This would contrast with a property acquired where the price is reduced marginally to allow for normal wear and tear, when expenditure on repairs would be deductible.

Example 10

> Nicola acquires two investment properties next door to each other. Number 1 has had a sitting tenant in residence for 50 years who has just died, whereas Number 2 has been empty for six months and requires minor redecoration works. Nicola pays £200,000 for Number 1 and £250,000 for Number 2. Estimates are obtained for the refurbishment works and these are £28,000 for Number 1 and £5,000 for Number 2. The allowable repair expenditure would be restricted to £5,000 for the whole property business; there is no deduction for the past repair works that have not been carried out and are reflected in the purchase price.

Specific provisions for anticipated future repairs are deductible, except under the cash basis. This is incurred once there is a commitment to a programme of expenditure, usually by way of written contracts. In the above example of Theresa and Racket, Theresa had incurred the expenditure in the year prior to 5 April and although Racket could not provide a completion date, a contract clearly existed and provided the basis for the deduction. A general repair provision is not allowable under normal accounting principles, under either basis: Theresa could not obtain a deduction for the years when she stared at the sky through the hole in the roof as she had made no commitment to repair it.

The end result of expenditure on alterations is often an improvement rather than a restoration of the asset concerned. This point was highlighted in *Conn v Robins Bros Ltd* (1966) 43 TC 266. The business premises were archaic and in an advanced stage of decay and HMRC contended there had been intrinsic alterations to the property preventing a tax deduction on the grounds that at least some of the expenditure was capital. However, it was demonstrated that there was a structural necessity to incur alterations in order to repair the famous chimney stack, walls and flooring. Buckley J said:

> 'But the fact that there were alterations in the structural details of the building does not seem to me to be a good ground for proceeding upon the basis that the work produced something new. On the contrary, I think it is implicit in the Commissioners' finding that the result of this work was not to produce something new but to repair something which had previously existed. Upon that basis it seems to me that there is no ground for regarding this expenditure as a capital expenditure.'

Furthermore:

> 'If the work had not been carried out it would have been impossible to carry on the business. The work was incurred to allow the company to continue to earn profits by putting its existing asset into a proper state of repair.'

The *Robins Bros Ltd* case is an authority for the use of modern materials and building techniques which produces prima facie alterations but does not convert revenue expenditure into capital.

Capital expenditure on the alteration of land or buildings is to be non-deductible under the cash basis.

There is, of course, a separate regime for capital allowances, which is explained in outline at **6.33** below and in more detail in **CHAPTER 9**. There are two points relevant to repairs of plant or machinery in the capital allowance pool. The fact that expenditure on an asset receives capital allowances does not prohibit a deduction for the costs of bona fide repairs against rental income. If grants are received for repairs to these assets, this must be reflected in the capital allowance pool.

Grants received for building works must be included in the income of the property business, unless it was appropriate to make a separate adjustment in the capital allowance computation. Net insurance recoveries for damage to buildings are included in the receipts of the property business. This can be accounted for by claiming a deduction when the expenditure was incurred and bringing in the recovery upon receipt.

Dilapidations

[6.28] Where a tenant makes a dilapidation payment to the landlord at the end of the lease, the receipt is effectively in respect of depreciation or damage to the landlord's property. It would therefore appear to be a part-disposal of part of the landlord's property and liable to capital gains tax following the rules in TCGA 1992, s 22. In practice, HMRC may look at what the landlord actually does with the property afterwards and if it is re-let or retained for letting in the immediate future, regard the payment as income as if it were compensation for loss of earnings. It is included in the income receipts of the property business. This practice follows a Privy Council case, *Raja's Commercial College v Gian Singh & Co Ltd* [1977] AC 312, [1976] 2 All ER 801, PC, which demonstrated that amounts received as dilapidations by the college were taxable as income receipts 'because they plug a hole in the landlord's income as opposed to the landlord's capital':

> 'Held, dismissing the appeal, that, where damages were received by a trader as compensation for loss of trading receipts, the compensation was to be treated for income tax purposes in the same way as the trading receipts would have been treated had they been received as profits in any year instead of compensation and that there was no logical reason why the treatment of damages for income tax purposes should depend on whether the recipient was a trader or an investor; accordingly, the damages which were awarded in place of lost income fell to be treated as income.'

Interest

General rules

[6.29] Interest is allowable on loans used to buy, repair or improve land or property used in the property business. Improvements and repairs may include alterations to the building. For the purposes of income tax, the principal requirement to obtain a deduction is the 'wholly and exclusively' rule (as discussed above). The deduction is made in the same way (but see below) as all other allowable expenses and calculated on the accruals basis. Special rules apply to loan costs under the cash basis, for which see **6.31**.

Upon a strict interpretation of the 'wholly and exclusively' requirement, interest paid on personal-account overdrafts is not deductible. HMRC usually take a permissive approach and allow a deduction based upon an apportionment of the interest paid between private drawings or funds used to purchase other non-rental investments and the loan capital used in the property business.

Where equity is swapped between personal and 'business' assets, the position is a little more complex. Suppose Basil wished to purchase a yacht and obtain some tax relief on loan interest paid. He spots that one of his more valuable rental properties has relatively high equity and decides to draw a further mortgage upon it and apply the funds towards the yacht purchase. Is the interest on the loan deductible for the letting business? At first sight, on a strict reading of the law, namely ITTOIA 2005, s 34(1), one might say that the interest is wholly disallowable, as the loan has not been obtained 'for the purpose' of the property business.

However, this is to confuse the purpose for which the funds made available by the loan are used with the function of the loan itself. The proprietor of a business is entitled to withdraw capital from that business and to replace the capital withdrawn with a loan. As the author of HMRC's *Business Income Manual* puts it, in para BIM45700:

> 'A proprietor of a business may withdraw the profits of the business and the capital [he has] introduced to the business, even though substitute funding then has to be provided by interest-bearing loans. The interest payable on the loans is an allowable deduction. This is on the basis that the purpose of the additional borrowing is to provide working capital for the business.'

The fact that once withdrawn, the funds are used to purchase a private asset is irrelevant, in just the same way that the tax system does not look at drawings used to finance day-to-day living expenses. This reasoning is based on general principles. The example often cited in the literature is that of a taxpayer borrowing against a let property to repay the mortgage on his or her own home.

The one, important, caveat is that the funds withdrawn from the business must not cause the capital account to become overdrawn. That is to say, the deductibility of the interest on the loan will be restricted or denied altogether if the amount withdrawn causes the proprietor's cumulative withdrawals to exceed the aggregate of the capital originally invested and the profits of the business. Put another way, as is widely held in commentary, as long as the amount borrowed against business assets does not exceed the taxpayer's equity in those assets, the whole of the interest on the loan will be prima facie deductible.

As is the case with tax, however, things are rarely that simple. The mere fact that the capital account is overdrawn does not necessarily mean that the overdraft is financing private expenditure. Nor, contrariwise, does a capital account that remains in credit necessarily mean that all the loan interest will be deductible. One has to look at the balance sheet (or 'the statement of financial position' in IFRS parlance) of the business to see what is being funded. If the loan is funding business losses or providing working capital, there will not be a disallowance. By the same token, even if the capital account remains in credit, the loan could be partly or wholly funding private expenditure. Particular care must be taken in this context with property revaluations. This is illustrated by Example 3 in para BIM45690, where 'Ms A', the taxpayer, borrows on the back of a property revaluation and then withdraws a large amount of the loan. Her capital account remains nominally in credit, but if one strips away the increased value of the property from the capital account, it is clearly overdrawn. As the HMRC author reminds us,

> 'Her capital account is not overdrawn. But the relevant question is what business items have been funded by the loan? . . . The revaluation profit . . . is a non-cash item that cannot fund drawings. She has withdrawn more than the total of the profits earned by the business and the capital she invested in the business.'

A good review of the principles comes in the Special Commissioners' decision in *Silk v Fletcher* [2000] SpC 201 (SPC 202), which is also summarised in para BIM45725, where the Special Commissioner states 'Accordingly, even if S's capital account was not overdrawn, it did not follow that all the interest was deductible.'

Where a property is used partly privately or is unavailable for substantial periods of time, interest must be restricted pro rata on a fair and reasonable basis to reflect the period or quotient that the property is unavailable for arm's length letting. This would not include periods where the landlord is actively repairing the property to re-let it or whilst the property is empty and he is advertising to find a new tenant. Were he to occupy the property himself, or let it at a non-commercial rate, during a period of repairs or whilst seeking a tenant, interest would be regarded primarily as for a private and unallowable purpose. This follows the rules discussed above in respect of the concept of expenditure incurred 'wholly and exclusively' for the purposes of a business.

Incidental costs associated with the provision of loan finance are allowable under the provisions of ITTOIA 2005, s 58 (as explicitly applied by ITTOIA 2005, s 272 and by ITTOIA 2005, s 272ZA for the cash basis in 2017–18 and subsequently), which covers the main administration fees etc usually incurred in arranging loans and mortgages. Of course, there is a prerequisite that the property is to be used in the property business. For the purposes of corporation tax, it will be recalled, the loan-relationships rules in CTA 2009, Part 5 apply, and the proposed new corporate interest restriction may also apply.

'Cash back' offers and variations on that theme have encouraged budding property entrepreneurs into the housing market. Any initial reduction in the first few years' payments do not attract special tax relief, ie interest is deductible as paid rather than attracting any further notional relief on the discount. HMRC have historically stated they will not charge 'cash-back' receipts to capital gains tax or as part of the income receipts of the property business.

Example 11

Ignoring for the moment the new rules for deduction of finance costs operative from 6 April 2017, suppose Ruth purchases an investment property on a buy-to-let mortgage and the first two years' interest payments are £20,000. Under the terms of her mortgage offer there is a discount reducing the interest payments to £17,500 over the two-year period. Ruth receives £1,000 as cash-back when the loan is drawn down. The deductible interest over the two-year period is £17,500 accountable on the accruals basis or as paid under the cash basis. There is no tax liability arising on the cash-back but if Ruth had claimed arrangement fees as part of the incidental costs of arranging finance, she may find the deduction restricted by the cash-back offer if it is written in terms of the reimbursement of specific fees.

Swap contracts are commonly used in rental-finance arrangements. HMRC have stated that they are happy for non-corporates, ie individuals, trustees and partnerships, to include profits or losses on swap contracts used specifically to hedge interest payments as receipts or deductions in a property business (originally in Tax Bulletin 66, August 2003, extracts from which now appear in HMRC *Property Income Manual*, para PIM2140). The accounts must recognise the full economic profit on the swap over the life of the contract and some consistency is required between risk recognition and payments under the contract concerned. With regard to lump sums payable on termination of a contract, HMRC take a 'consistency' approach and regard them as almost exclusively income receipts taxable as miscellaneous income if not as receipts of the property business:

'. . . in general, all cash flows made or exchanged under or in connection with a swap will be income whether they take the form of periodic payments or are rolled up into a lump sum payable at any point.'

HMRC's approach to the tax treatment of borrowings levered with financial futures and options is explained at Statement of Practice SP3/02. Under specific circumstances non-corporate swaps may be regarded as receipts of a trade or business depending on their significance.

Interest on a partner's capital account is a notional accounting concept and is not deductible as an expense of the property business.

Phase out of marginal relief for dwelling-related loans

[6.30] As from 6 April 2017, in an effort to damp down the buy-to-let market, a phase-out of marginal-rate relief against income tax for the finance costs of residential properties begins to take effect, with a view to limiting relief to the basic rate on the entire finance costs from 6 April 2020.

This is to be achieved by phasing out the deduction for the costs of a 'dwelling-related loan', meaning so much of a loan taken out for the purposes of a property business as is justly and reasonably attributable to that part of the business that is aimed at generating income from a dwelling-house or part of a dwelling-house or from estates, interests or rights in or over a dwelling-house or part. This includes anything done to construct or adapt a dwelling-house or part that is to be used for generating income, but excludes any part of the business consisting of the commercial letting of furnished holiday accommodation. The costs of a dwelling-related loan include interest, a return economically equivalent to interest for the recipient and the incidental costs of obtaining the loan (ITTOIA 2005, s 272B, inserted by F(No 2)A 2015, s 24).

The withdrawal of the straight-forward deduction will be staged as follows:

- in 2017–18, the deduction from property income (as is currently allowed) is restricted to 75% of finance costs;
- in 2018–19, the deduction from property income (as is currently allowed) will be restricted to 50% of finance costs;
- in 2019–20, the deduction from property income (as is currently allowed) will be restricted to 25% of finance costs; and
- from 2020–21 the deduction as currently allowed will be withdrawn altogether.

In addition to, and from 2020-21 wholly instead of, the decreasing deduction for interest, there is a new, limited, reduction of tax deduction, calculated as follows. Where an amount (A) has been disallowed under ITTOIA 2005, s 272A in calculating the profits of a property business, any individual liable to income tax on all or some proportion of those profits has a 'current-year [relievable] amount' of N% of A, where N is the proportion of the profits to which the individual is entitled. The full relievable amount in any tax year is the sum of (a) the 'current-year amount'; (b) the 'current-year estate amount' (only where the individual has an interest in a deceased person's estate containing a property business); and (c) the 'brought-forward amount' (un-used relievable amounts from previous years). The 'actual amount' ('AA') on which relief may be given is then normally the lower of (a) the relievable amount and (b) the sum of (1) the smaller of the 'adjusted profits' of the property business of the year (the profits after any deduction under ITA 2007, s 118 for losses brought forward) and the share of the adjusted profits on which the individual is liable to income tax other than as estate income and (2) so much of the relievable amount as consists of current-year estate income. This amount is referred to as L. In most cases, L = AA. However, if the individual has more than one property business and the total (S) of the Ls for each property business is greater than the individual's adjusted total income (ATI) for the year, the actual amount, AA, for any one property business (and therefore relievable amount) is given by (ATI/S) x L. The amount of the reduction in respect of a relievable amount is AA x BR, where BR is the basic rate of income tax. An individual's ATI is the net income of the year (Step 2 in the calculation in ITA 2007, s 23), reduced by savings income and dividend income and personal allowances deducted at Step 3 in the calculation in ITA 2007, s 23 (ITTOIA 2005, s 274AA, inserted by FA 2016, s 26(1)).

In the simple case, where an individual carries on a property business alone, the new relief works as shown in Example 12.

Example 12

Suppose Arlene has two properties that she lets out. In all three years 2016–17, 2017–18 and 2018–19, interest payments on the mortgages that she took out to finance the purchase amount to £4,600. In 2016–17, the profits of Arlene's property business (before deduction of interest) are £8,750, in 2017–18 they are £9,975 and in 2018–19, they are £9,000. There are no losses brought forward from earlier years in any of the three tax years. Arlene's marginal rate of tax is 40%. Suppose the basic rate of tax remains 20% in 2017–18 and 2018–19.

In 2016–17, Arlene may deduct the whole of the £4,600 interest against the profits of the business, reducing them to a taxable amount of £4,150, thereby reducing her tax bill by £4,600 x 40% = £1,840.

In 2017–18, Arlene's deduction against profits is limited to £4,600 x 75% = £3,450. She is also entitled to a tax reduction as follows:

Amount disallowed (A) = £1,150. Arlene's share of the taxable profits (N) = 100%. Relievable amount (N% x A) = £1,150. BR = 20%.

In this simple case, AA = L.

L is the lower of:

(1)   the sum of the relievable amount (£1,150) + any unrelieved amount brought forward = £1,150; and
(2)   adjusted profits of the property business = £9,975.

L therefore = £1,150.

Amount of reduction = AA x BR = £1,150 x 20% = £230.

Total tax saving = £3,450 x 40% = £1,380 + £230 = £1,610.

In 2018–19, Arlene's deduction against profits is limited to £4,600 x 50% = £2,300. She is also entitled to a tax reduction as follows:

Amount disallowed (A) = £2,300. Arlene's share of the taxable profits (N) = 100%. Relievable amount (N% x A) = £2,300. BR = 20%.

In this simple case, AA = L.

L is the lower of:

(1)   the sum of the relievable amount (£2,300) + any unrelieved amount brought forward = £2,300; and
(2)   adjusted profits of the property business = £9,000.

L therefore = £2,300.

Amount of reduction = AA x BR = £2,300 x 20% = £460.

Total tax saving = £2,300 x 40% = £920 + £460 = £1,380.

There is a corresponding deduction given under ITTOIA 2005, s 274B, 274C (substituted by FA 2016, s 26(1)) for trustees in respect of accumulated or discretionary income. It similarly provides that where an amount (A) has been disallowed under new ITTOIA 2005, s 272A in calculating the profits of a property business, trustees liable to income tax on all or some proportion of those profits are to receive a 'relievable amount' of N% of A, where N is the proportion of the profits represented by accumulated or discretionary income. The actual amount of the relief is then given by BR × L, where BR is the basic rate of income tax and L is the lower of (a) the sum of relievable amount for the year and any unused relief brought forward from an earlier year and the adjusted profits or the share of the adjusted profits by reference to any deduction under ITA 2007, s 118. Similarly, there is provision for carry-forward where L is less than the relievable amount.

Indirect investment in a property business is also caught by the new rules. Under ITA 2007, s 399A, inserted by F(No 2)A 2015, s 24(7), there is the same progressive withdrawal of the direct deduction in relation to the relief obtainable under ITA 2007, ss 383 and 398 for interest on a loan to invest in a partnership, where the partnership carries on a UK or overseas property business wholly or partly carried on for the purpose of generating income from dwelling-houses, again excluding furnished holiday accommodation. The withdrawal of the deduction applies to so much of the interest as may justly and reasonably be referable to that part of the property business. ITA 2007, s 399B, also inserted by F(No 2)A 2015, s 24(7), provides the alternative relief to the lost deduction, which is simply the basic rate of tax times the amount of interest that has been disallowed by ITA 2007, s 399A.

These restrictions do not apply to furnished holiday lettings (for which see **6.47** below).

Interest paid abroad is deductible to the same extent but there are special rules requiring the deduction of basic rate tax (ITA 2007, s 874). There should be no issue on deductibility where the parties are at arm's length. A non-resident is defined as an entity 'whose usual place of abode is outside the UK'.

Where a double taxation agreement exists between the UK and the country of residence of the lender, the lender may apply to receive the interest gross or with a reduced rate of withholding tax. Applications should be made to LBS DT Treaty Team, Barkley House, Castle Meadow Road, Nottingham NG2 1BA, who will review the double taxation agreement concerned and provide the lender with authorisation in accordance with the appropriate Treaty.

Where the letting business is such that it constitutes a trade, and is not a property business as such, there are two caveats to be entered as respects losses arising from interest payments. Before a claim for sideways loss relief under ITA 2007, ss 64–70 can be successful, the trade must be commercial (ITA 2007, s 66). This was considered in *Brown v Richardson* [1997] STC (SCD) 233, where the claim failed primarily because the proprietor knew there could never have been a profit due to the high level of borrowings. In a similar but distinct case, a landlord borrowed £276,000 to purchase three holiday cottages in Cornwall costing £343,000. Large loss relief claims arising primarily from interest payments were challenged by HMRC on the grounds of commerciality, later to be successful in *Brown v Richardson*. The Special Commissioners allowed the taxpayer's appeal as the claim to loss relief was a specific test rather than a subjective one (see now ITA 2007, s 74). This opinion was formed as the taxpayer explained in the stated grounds for his appeal against the first General Commissioners' decision that he fully antici-pated a fall in interest rates and could demonstrate that the portfolio would be profitable within three years (*Walls v Livesey (Inspector of Taxes)* [1995] STC (SCD) 12, SCD).

Cash basis: further restriction on loan costs

[6.31] Under the cash basis, as it is to apply beginning with 2017–18, there is a further restriction on loan costs, additional to that provided under ITTOIA 2005, ss 272A, 272B, 274A–274C, for which see **6.29**.

This extra restriction applies where the aggregate of 'business amounts' of loans a deduction for the costs of which (including interest) would otherwise be allowed for a tax year ('L') exceeds the values of all the properties involved in the property business at the end of the tax year ('V'). As can be appreciated, this new provision obliquely addresses the question of the allowability of loan interest where the loan is used to finance drawings etc (just discussed earlier under **6.29**).

The 'business amount' of a loan is the proportion of the loan that the amount of loan costs that the wholly and exclusively rule (ITTOIA 2005, s 34, as applied by ITTOIA 2005, s 272ZA) would allow to be deducted bears to the total loan costs. The values of the properties are their market values at the time that they were first brought into the business (not their current market values, thereby excluding any subsequent capitalised increase in value), plus any capital expenditure incurred on them that has not been brought into account in computing the profits of the business.

Loan costs are interest and any incidental costs of obtaining finance by means of the loan.

Where L does exceed V, the amount that may be deducted for loan costs is V/L times the unrestricted deduction.

This rule is applied first, before considering any restriction under the marginal-rate relief withdrawal. The amount of interest that is subject to restriction under those rules is therefore the amount as already restricted under this rule.

Example 13

Michelle computes the profits of her property business under the cash basis. At 5 April 2018, she has a loan of £150,000 secured on her single buy-to-let property, which she acquired for £125,000 a few years previously, but is now valued at £200,000. She has incurred £10,000 of improvement expenditure. In the tax year 2017–18, she paid interest of £4,000 on the loan. Incidental costs were negligible. The loan wholly funds working capital and all of the interest is in principle deductible, subject to the new phase-out of marginal-rate relief.

L is therefore £150,000 and V is £125,000 + £10,000 = £135,000.

As L > V, the deductible loan costs, before the phase-out rules, are:

£4,000 x (£135,000/£150,000) = £3,600

Corporation tax rules

[6.32] There is a separate regime for calculating relief for corporation tax purposes. Under the familiar loan-relationship rules, now found in CTA 2009, Part 5, interest paid is not an expense in the rental computation of the trade or business (as it is for income tax) but is a debit to be brought into account in calculating the company's profit or loss from its 'loan relationships'. The loan-relationship rules extend to include other debits in respect of borrowings, such as bad debts and finance costs and to credits such as loan waivers.

For accounting periods beginning after 31 March 2017, UK companies that are part of a worldwide group are to be subject to a restriction on the deductibility of net interest expense. Under the measures as published in the September 2017 Finance Bill, the first £2 million of net interest expense may be deducted in full, subject to existing rules, but the deduction in respect of any excess is to be limited to no more than 30% of 'tax-EBITDA', ie earnings before interest, tax, depreciation and amortisation.

For non-UK resident companies such as those within the Non-Resident Landlord Scheme, who are liable to income tax on the property business, CTA 2009, Part 5 does not prohibit a deduction for interest paid.

Capital allowances

Accruals (GAAP) basis

[6.33] Relief for capital expenditure is specifically prohibited as a deduction in computing the profits of the property business under the accruals basis (ITTOIA 2005, s 33, as applied by ITTOIA 2005, s 272). Under the cash basis, as it is to apply in 2017–18 and future years, the general prohibition is replaced by specific prohibitions (prospective ITTOIA 2005, s 307B). As regards capital allowances under the cash basis, see **6.34**. Further, the Capital Allowances Act 2001 prevents capital allowances from being available for plant and machinery used or installed in 'dwelling-houses' (CAA 2001, s 35).

There is no statutory definition of a 'dwelling-house'; the question has therefore come before the tax courts on a number of occasions. From this we know that the term has been given its full and ordinary interpretation to include:

- houses in multiple occupation (HMOs);
- student accommodation;
- residential property let commercially;
- any property that forms a dwelling for day-to-day use, excluding an office, factory or commercial premises.

(HMRC Brief 45/2010)

Instead of capital allowances, the law traditionally permitted a 10% 'wear and tear allowance' (see **6.46** below). With effect from 2016–17, this has been replaced by a relief for the replacement of domestic items provided for use in a dwelling-house. It should be noted that there are also various 'green' capital allowances offering relief for specific types of expenditure.

The mechanics of each allowance are discussed in more detail at CHAPTER 9.

There are three fundamental issues to consider before a valid capital allowance claim may be filed by any entity:

- Is the expenditure actually capital?
- Am I eligible to make a claim/Did I pay for, or incur the expenditure?
- What types of allowance are available or optimal?

1. *Capital or revenue?* The first question has been argued before the courts on a regular basis for as long as the Act and its preceding enactment have been in existence. A variety of tax cases have been heard; perhaps the most relevant test is to consider the 'enduring benefit' of the expenditure in establishing its capital nature.

The second question now concerns former ownership and the past tax history of any fixtures in the building and any plant or machinery etc within it.

2. Carrying on a trade or business is normally, but not always, a prerequisite for claiming a capital allowance. Thus, plant and machinery allowances may be claimed for 'special leasing' (ie leasing otherwise than in the course of a trade or other qualifying activity) and by employees and office holders who incur capital expenditure on assets that are necessarily provided for use in the employment or office. Each code has its own particular rules, but for the purposes of plant and machinery provided for the purposes of property letting, the landlord must be carrying on a 'qualifying activity'. Those pertinent to letting are (CAA 2001, s 15(1)):

- an ordinary UK property business;
- an ordinary overseas property business;
- a section 12(4) concern: mines; transport undertakings etc;
- a UK furnished holiday-lettings business;
- an EEA furnished holiday-lettings business; or
- managing the investments of a company with investment business;

3. *Which allowance?*

The current tax regime has left almost every landlord being able to access something.

For the commercial landlord, the most common allowances are or have been the following:

- plant and machinery allowances (short-life, long-life or regular);
- the annual investment allowance for plant and machinery;
- integral features allowances within the plant and machinery code;
- energy-saving enhanced plant and machinery allowances;
- landlord's energy-saving allowance (ended April 2015);
- flat-conversion allowances (withdrawn from April 2013);
- business-premises renovation allowances (withdrawn from April 2017);

- sea walls.

An overview of the mainstream allowances follows in **6.35**. The legacy and miscellaneous allowances are then outlined for completeness.

Capital allowances under the cash basis

[6.34] Under the cash basis for property businesses as it is due to apply beginning with 2017–18, the rule relating to capital allowances is contained in CAA 2001, s 1A, which is to apply equally to the cash basis for trades, professions and vocations also.

The general rule is that cash basis taxpayers may neither claim capital allowances (including the annual investment allowance) nor be liable to balancing charges, nor have to take disposal values into account, with two exceptions. The first concerns cars and the second concerns assets in relation to which capital allowances had been claimed (strictly, on which qualifying expenditure has been incurred) before the taxpayer entered the cash basis.

The single type of asset capital expenditure on which qualifies for a capital allowance is a car, as defined for capital allowance purposes under CAA 2001, s 268A. Allowances may be made, disposal values must be taken into account and balancing charges may be incurred accordingly (CAA 2001, s 1A(4), (5)).

The second exception is made where qualifying expenditure was incurred on an asset at a time when the accruals (GAAP) basis applied to the property business and before the cash basis begins to be applied to the business for a tax year by virtue of ITTOIA 2005, s 271D whereas the accruals basis applied in the previous tax year, and no deduction would be allowed for the expenditure in a cash basis year if it were paid in such a year. In that case, a disposal value must be brought into account when a disposal event occurs and a balancing charge may apply as a result.

It should be noted that 'qualifying expenditure' may have been incurred in respect of any category of capital allowance, not merely plant and machinery.

The material in **6.35–6.40** does not apply to businesses under the cash basis.

Plant and Machinery Allowances

[6.35] There is no statutory definition of plant and machinery. Many interpretations have been tested in case law. CAA 2001, ss 21 and 22 provide lists of exclusions under the headings of buildings, structures and land. A debate upon what constitutes plant or machinery is beyond the scope of this chapter, but it should be noted that case law is based upon the very precise circumstances of the business concerned and the exact use to which the equipment is put.

For example, *Yarmouth v France CA* (1887) 19 QBD 647 demonstrates that a *horse* qualified as plant for the purpose of plant and machinery capital allowances and the decision was upheld in various other cases, including one heard in the House of Lords. Yet the Earl of Derby case found a *stallion* did not, as he did not 'diminish in value by reason of wear and tear' and fell outside the objective of a depreciation allowance (*Derby (Earl) v Aylmer*

(Surveyor of Taxes) [1915] 3 KB 374, 6 TC 665). This is logical and highlights the danger of a 'ready-made' approach to what expenditure may qualify as plant.

For most plant and machinery, the expenditure is pooled so that writing-down allowances at 18% are calculated on the balance of the pool (after adding acquisitions and deducting sale proceeds) at the end of the period. The basis period for capital allowances is the accounting year, usually the year to 5 April for a property business, unless the activities amount to a trade.

However, long-life assets, which are those having an estimated useful life of at least 25 years, must be placed in a separate pool (the 'special-rate pool'), for which writing-down allowances are limited to 8%. It is quite feasible that lifts and radiators, for example, may be regarded as long-life assets. Certain assets are specifically excluded from the category of long-life assets. These include cars and fixtures in a dwelling-house, hotel, office, retail shop or showroom. Expenditure on certain other assets must also be allocated to the special-rate pool. Such assets include thermal insulation, integral features (see **6.36** below) and cars (other than 'main-rate' cars).

Yet other assets may qualify by election as 'short-life assets'. The idea is to accelerate the availability of capital allowances in respect of assets (eg computers) that have a short useful life. Each asset in respect of which short-life treatment is chosen is placed into a separate pool of its own, although allowances are still calculated at no more than 18%. If the asset is not completely written off or disposed of within eight years, it must revert to the appropriate other class pool. In addition to writing-down allowances, a 100% first-year allowance is available for certain limited types of expenditure (eg on energy-saving plant and machinery, cars with low carbon dioxide emissions, environmentally beneficial plant and machinery and plant and machinery for use in designated assisted areas).

Assets with an element of private use must be allocated to special single-asset pools of their own.

Capital allowances, including balancing allowances and charges arising from balancing adjustments, in a property business are determined in the same way as for a trade.

The capital element of hire-purchase charges to purchase plant and machinery may be included in the expenditure forming a claim for capital allowances. Interest payments receive relief as normal revenue business expenses, restricted for any private use in accordance with the 'wholly and exclusively' rule (as discussed above).

Integral features allowances

[6.36] The introduction of allowances for integral features in buildings was a practical solution for both property entrepreneurs and tax inspectors in agreeing initial capital allowance claims for new commercial buildings. CAA 2001, s 21 expressly prohibits expenditure on non-fixtures, ie certain integral features, because they were deemed to be part of the building, preventing tax relief for initial or replacement expenditure. This disallowance was reinforced by the arguments in *IRC v Scottish and Newcastle Breweries Ltd* [1982] 2 All ER 230, [1982] 1 WLR 322, HL, which made life extremely difficult for the entrepreneur. However, from April 2008, plant and machinery allowances may be claimed in respect of expenditure on categories listed as integral features, namely:

- electrical systems (including a lighting system);
- cold water systems;
- space or water heating systems;
- ventilation and similar systems, including floors and ceilings comprised within;
- lifts, escalators and moving walkways;
- external solar shading.

Expenditure on integral features is allocated to the special rate pool, on which writing-down allowances of 8% are calculated (see **6.35** above).

Annual Investment Allowance

[6.37] The Annual Investment Allowance (AIA) for expenditure on plant and machinery allows immediate write-off of up to £200,000 (from 1 January 2016). Since the introduction of AIA in 2009, the maximum amount has been as high as £500,000 and as low as £25,000. Because of the frequent changes in the amount of the allowance, persons claiming the AIA will almost invariably encounter straddling-period rules (the latest of which covers periods straddling 1 January 2016), the effect of which is to deter front or end-loading to take advantage of a higher maximum at the beginning or end of the period. One hopes that the promise that the latest change will be the last as long as the AIA remains available will be respected.

The AIA scheme can complement other capital allowances schemes, as above. There are no restrictions on the business/company's size, number of employees or assets.

There are, however, restrictions to claims made by grouped companies or groups under common control, where substantial financial or commercial interdependence subsists. The allowance is not available in a year in which the trade is permanently discontinued, and there is specific avoidance legislation preventing a double allowance, such as with FYA (CAA 2001, s 52A).

Legacy allowances

Business premises renovation allowance (BPRA)

[6.38] All three 'regeneration reliefs' are now closed to new expenditure. The one that was most recently still available is the business-premises renovation allowance, the last date for qualifying expenditure on which was 1 or 6 April 2017.

Introduced in FA 2005, business premises renovation allowance (BPRA) was available to individuals and companies incurring capital expenditure to bring disused business premises back into use. The allowance was geographically restricted to certain disadvantaged areas in Great Britain and Northern

Ireland. It took effect on 11 April 2007 under the Assisted Areas Order 2007 (SI 2007/107). The relief was subject to the EU rules governing State Aid, including an overall project cap of €20 million. The legislation relating to BPRA is found in CAA 2001, Part 3A and the Business Premises Renovation Allowances Regulations 2007 (SI 2007/945).

The allowance was available for persons incurring qualifying expenditure in respect of a qualifying building who also had the 'relevant interest' in that building (CAA 2001, s 360A). The 'relevant interest' is generally the interest in the qualifying building which the person who incurred the qualifying expenditure had at the time that person incurred it (CAA 2001, s 360E). The allowance was thus available to both landlords and tenants.

Qualifying expenditure was expenditure incurred on building works, architectural or design services, surveying or engineering services, planning applications, or statutory fees or statutory permissions in connection with:

(a)   the conversion of a 'qualifying building' into 'qualifying business premises';
(b)   the renovation of a 'qualifying building' that was or would be 'qualifying business premises'; or
(c)   repairs to a qualifying building incidental to its conversion or renovation.

Certain types of expenditure were excluded, such as the acquisition of land, the provision of plant or machinery other than integral features (see **6.36** above), public-address systems and kitchen and catering facilities (CAA 2001, s 360B). The receipt of State Aid or a grant or subsidy prevented any claim to, or required the recovery of, any BPRA (CAA 2001, s 360L).

A 'qualifying building' was a building or structure (or part thereof) situated in a disadvantaged area (designated as such by HM Treasury) when the work was begun and which had been unused for at least the preceding year after having been used for the purposes of a trade, profession or vocation or as an office or offices, and not used as a dwelling or part of a dwelling (CAA 2001, s 360C). Thus, expenditure on commercial buildings, such as offices and shops, attracted the allowance, in respect of which no capital allowances would otherwise have been available under CAA 2001.

'Qualifying business premises' were qualifying buildings used, or available and suitable for letting for use, for the purposes of a trade, profession or vocation or as an office or offices, and not used as a dwelling or part of a dwelling (CAA 2001, s 360D). In order to comply with State Aid rules, an eclectic mixture of trades were excluded from the relief, eg the primary agricultural-products sector, including milk producers, fisheries and aquaculture, the coal and steel industry, transport and shipbuilding (SI 2007/945, reg 4(2)). The relief was introduced in tandem with the phasing out of ABA and IBA, presumably with the objective of safeguarding investment in industrial buildings in deprived areas.

The first allowance available was a 100% initial allowance in the chargeable period in which the expenditure was incurred. The person entitled to the allowance was able to claim a reduced amount instead of the full amount

(CAA 2001, s 360G). However, no allowance was available if the qualifying building did not constitute qualifying business premises when first used by the person holding the relevant interest or at the first time the premises were suitable for letting for a qualifying use. The allowance was recouped if the relevant interest was sold before that time (CAA 2001, s 360H).

Where the initial allowance was not claimed in full or at all, a writing-down allowance of 25% of the qualifying expenditure was available at the end of any chargeable period when the person concerned was entitled to the relevant interest, had not granted a long lease of the qualifying building out of that interest in return for a capital sum, and the qualifying building constituted qualifying business premises. The claimant was entitled to claim a reduced amount, but in either case the amount of the allowance could not exceed the residue of expenditure (the tax written-down value or the balance of expenditure in respect of which allowances had yet to be claimed (CAA 2001, ss 360I, 360J)). BPRA writing-down allowances will therefore remain available for a number of years.

Balancing adjustments, in the form of a balancing allowance or balancing charge, are made when a 'balancing event' occurs (CAA 2001, s 360M(1)). A balancing event can be any one of six occasions (eg a sale of the relevant interest, the cessation of use of the qualifying building as qualifying business premises and also the grant of a long lease of the qualifying building out of the relevant interest in return for a capital sum) (CAA 2001, s 360N).

No balancing adjustment is made if the balancing event occurs more than five years after the premises are first used or suitable for letting for a qualifying use (CAA 2001, s 360M(3)). Balancing adjustments are made only once, on the first occurrence of a balancing event (CAA 2001, s 360M(5)).

Flat-Conversion Allowances (withdrawn from April 2013)

[6.39] The first of the three regeneration reliefs that was introduced followed the recommendations and report by Lord Rogers upon the regeneration of urban areas, set up by the Government's Urban Task Force, was the flat-conversion allowance. This was a capital allowance designed to encourage investment in disused dwellings above shops and offices (CAA 2001, Part 4A).

An allowance of up to 100% was given on the conversion of part of a qualifying building into a qualifying flat; the renovation of a flat in a qualifying building if the flat was or was to be a qualifying flat; or on repairs to a qualifying building incidental to either of the above. A qualifying building was a building of no more than five storeys, the ground floor of which had to be authorised for business use and the upper stories had to have been intended originally as dwellings. The building had to have been constructed before 1 January 1980. A qualifying flat had to be in a qualifying building, suitable for short-term letting as a low-cost dwelling, and have no more than four rooms, access to which did not involve going through the business premises. The scheme was based on the industrial-buildings code, but there were some exceptions:

• flat-conversion allowances (withdrawn for expenditure incurred after 31 March or 5 April 2013) were not transferable to a subsequent purchaser of the interest in the flat;

- no balancing charges or allowances were made provided that the flat was held for seven years following completion;
- the allowance was not available to 'high-value' flats or flats constructed above buildings built after 1980.

Flat-conversion allowances went to the person that held the relevant interest. There were ways around the possibility that relief might be clawed back, principally by not making amendments to the lease within seven years of the claim.

Landlord's Energy-Saving Allowance

[6.40] The third extinct regeneration relief is the landlord's energy-saving allowance, strictly speaking, the deduction for expenditure on energy-saving items (ITTOIA 2005, ss 312–314, Energy-Saving Items (Income Tax) Regulations 2007 (SI 2007/3278); CTA 2009, ss 251–253, Energy-Saving Items (Corporation Tax) Regulations 2008 (SI 2008/1520)). The deduction was available in respect of capital expenditure wholly and exclusively incurred for the purposes of a property business involving dwelling-houses and which was ineligible for allowances under CAA 2001. Expenditure was eligible for this allowance if incurred after 5 April 2004 (after 7 July 2008 for corporation tax) and before 1 April or 6 April 2015 on the cost of the following in unfurnished residential property that was let or available for letting:

- loft insulation or cavity-wall insulation;
- solid-wall insulation (from 6 April 2005);
- draught proofing and hot-water system insulation (from 6 April 2006); and
- floor insulation works (from 6 April 2007).

The allowance was restricted to £1,500 per dwelling-house. The deduction was not available for the 'rent-a-room' scheme and properties let as furnished holiday lettings.

Miscellaneous capital allowances

Sea walls

[6.41] This review of property-business capital allowances cannot be concluded without some thought to landlords reading this book in contemplation of a sea view. Happily, expenditure on making or extending a sea wall qualifies for a special scheme of 'capital allowances', which permits costs to be written off on a straight-line basis over a 21-year period, for the purposes of both income tax and corporation tax (ITTOIA 2005, s 315; CTA 2009, s 254). This is a deduction; it is not a capital allowance as such. No deduction is available if the expenditure has received a capital allowance. The deduction extends to expenditure providing protection against tidal, but not inland, rivers.

The deduction is also to be available under the cash basis, in the year in which the qualifying expenditure is paid and in the next 20 years (prospective ITTOIA 2005, s 315(7)).

Example 14

> Eileen constructs a sea wall; the works cost £21,000. She is entitled to claim a deduction of £1,000 for each year for the next 21 years, provided the land bound by the wall continues to be used in the property business, ie Eileen does not move or retire. Were Eileen to sell the land and a property business to continue, the new proprietor may enjoy any remaining allowance.

Overseas aspects

Overseas property business

[6.42] A person who derives income from foreign real property is said to have a single 'overseas property business' in respect of:

(a)   every business the person carries on for generating income from land outside the United Kingdom; and

(b)   every transaction that the person enters into for that purpose (ie for generating income from such land) otherwise than in the course of such a business.

(ITTOIA 2005, s 265; CTA 2009, s 206).

With regard to income tax, the profits of an overseas property business are charged to UK income tax only if the person carrying on the business is a UK resident (ITTOIA 2005, ss 268, 269(2)). This is simply common sense, in order to exclude persons having no connection to the United Kingdom from a potential charge to UK tax. There is no need for an equivalent provision for corporation tax, as that tax applies only to companies and other bodies corporate resident in the United Kingdom or trading in the United Kingdom through a permanent establishment. An exception is made for persons carrying on a trade of developing or dealing in UK land, but that is not of concern in this chapter.

As with a UK property business, the rules for calculating the profits of an overseas property business are the rules applicable to trading income specified in ITTOIA 2005, s 272 or CTA 2009, s 210. From 2017–18, equally, the cash basis may apply in exactly the same circumstances as for a UK property business. An interesting proviso is that when encountering foreign land law, the rules are to be interpreted so as to give the closest possible result to that produced by applying those rules to a UK property business (ITTOIA 2005, s 363; CTA 2009, s 290); this may be relevant to, for example, the application of lease premium rules to foreign property.

For the purposes of income tax, losses may be carried forward or used in restricted ways for sideways loss relief, but with carry-forward relief under ITA 2007, s 118, profits and losses are ring-fenced, prohibiting the set-off of losses from a UK property business against the profits of an overseas property business and vice versa. As with a UK property business, sideways relief is available to the extent that the loss from the overseas property business has a capital allowances connection (see **6.17** above), except under the cash basis, in which there is no sideways relief.

The rules to be introduced, with effect from 1 April 2017, relaxing the application of carried-forward losses but restricting the set-off of very large losses against total profits (see **6.18**) are not to apply to the losses of an overseas property business.

For the purposes of corporation tax, there is also no sideways relief, and losses from an overseas property business must be carried forward and set off against future profits from that business (CTA 2010, s 66). However, losses from a UK property business are not ring-fenced in this way, and may be set off against the company's total profits (including profits from an overseas property business) of the same accounting period or carried forward for set-off against total profits of subsequent periods (CTA 2010, s 62), with the proviso that the business is carried on commercially or as a statutory function (CTA 2010, s 64).

This ring-fencing complicates matters when it comes to claiming relief for foreign tax, which the UK landlord is very likely to have suffered on the rental income in the country of source. Relief for foreign tax by way of credit must follow the 'source by source' rule (TIOPA 2010, ss 42, 44), requiring separate tax computations for each property. The rule for allocating losses is to do so in the way most favourable to the taxpayer. This normally means setting them first against profits that have suffered the lowest rates of tax, so as to give the taxpayer the maximum possible relief.

For the purposes of income tax, occasional rental receipts from a foreign property arising in a foreign trade must be treated as trading receipts, under the priority rule of ITTOIA 2005, s 261, reversing the provisions of ITTOIA 2005, s 4(1) where rental income from a UK property that may arise from a trade is to be treated as property income.

Example 15

Andrea has a successful property development business in Tuscany; she occasionally lets finished apartments in low season whilst they are awaiting sale. She must include the rental receipts within the trading account of the property development business, and not treat them as receipts of an overseas property business.

Overseas landlords

[6.43] Rents received by persons whose 'usual place of abode is outside the United Kingdom' (this is not quite the same thing as being non-resident) from UK property are in principle liable to deduction of income tax at source (ITA 2007, s 971) but may benefit from special treatment under the Non-Resident Landlords Scheme, a system introduced in tandem with self-assessment in 1996–97. The legislative background is found in ITA 2007, ss 971, 972 and the Taxation of Income from Land (Non-Residents) Regulations 1995 (SI 1995/2902).

The scheme is available to non-UK resident:

- individuals, whose usual place of abode is outside the UK;
- trusts managed and controlled outside the UK, provided all the trustees have their usual place of abode outside the United Kingdom;
- companies managed and controlled outside the UK.

Overseas landlords investing in UK property have two alternatives for paying income tax on the rental profits of the business. The agent or, if one is not acting, the tenant, will be instructed by HMRC to deduct basic rate income tax at source. There is a rough and ready deduction for some but not all of the expenses that are likely to have arisen. The tax is accountable to HMRC on a quarterly basis. HMRC are vigorous in pursuing letting agents and visiting properties in multiple residential or business occupation to police the scheme. Alternatively, and usually preferably, the landlord may register as an overseas landlord under the Scheme, not have income tax deducted from rents and account for the rental profits on a fiscal basis under the self-assessment system once an application for registration has been approved by HMRC's Specialist Personal Tax (SPT) – Personal Tax International (PTI) in Bootle.

Having had an application approved, the individual, trust or company files returns under the self-assessment system. The full range of deductions that apply to ordinary UK property businesses conducted by UK residents is available. Payment of tax at the basic rate of income tax on the profits of the UK property business is due on 31 January next following the tax year. NRL schemes are regularly reviewed for compliance, and the facility can be withdrawn at any time, particularly for a failure to deliver punctual or accurate returns of income.

The deduction of tax at source may not be a desirable way to organise the tax liability of a rental portfolio. Where rents are to be paid under deduction of tax, HMRC expect tenants or agents to make quarterly payments (by 31 March, 30 June, 30 September and 31 December) of income tax irrespective of whether tax has been paid over to the UK agent in that quarter. Neither are HMRC averse to turning up on the doorstep of non- or late-paying tenants for overdue quarterly payments. The only excuse for non-payment where a UK agent is not involved with the letting is where rents are less than £5,200 pa. HMRC show little hesitation in instituting bankruptcy proceedings in recovery actions against overseas landlords in cases where tenants default knowingly or unwittingly on the deduction of tax at source. As the property is obviously UK-situs, HMRC have little practical difficulty in enforcing a charge and a landlord based overseas may be unaware of the situation.

If a non-UK resident company actually becomes UK-resident, the property business is treated as permanently ceasing and a new property business begins. The profits become liable to corporation tax and the previous income tax charge ceases at that date. Non-resident companies investing in the UK but not carrying on a trade must prepare accounts and tax computations under the income tax rules.

In practice, the compliance of overseas landlords is monitored quite keenly by HMRC. Property agents with overseas landlords on their books are obliged to register as agents with Specialist Personal Tax (SPT) – Personal Tax International (PTI) irrespective of whether they are deducting tax at source. There are detailed quarterly and annual agent returns and agents' offices are particular favourites for compliance visits.

Much of the local project work carried out by HMRC has property returns as its origin and the newly introduced Statutory Deposit Scheme will make it even easier for tax inspectors to differentiate between prospective landlords advertising in local papers or on the books of multiple agents from those asking and achieving good rents.

Particular types of property business

Buy-to-let landlords

[6.44] There is no special regime for the 'buy-to-let' entrepreneur and the income arising and expenses allowable fall within the ordinary property business regime. They are assessable to either income or corporation tax, depending upon the type of ownership structure. The perception that there is a particular tax regime is not correct, and no special capital allowances are possible for dwelling-houses held by the buy-to-let investor. However, landlords must bear in mind the new rules restricting tax relief for interest payments, the prospective cash basis rules and the higher SDLT (LBTT in Scotland) charge on the acquisition of additional residential properties.

The landlord will wish to obtain relief for interest payments and agent fees as well as renovation costs and improvements to let properties. Again, these will fall within the ordinary revenue/capital rules permitting deductions for revenue expenditure but not for capital expenditure, as outlined above. It should be noted that, as discussed above, income tax relief for interest costs is ultimately to be wholly limited to the basic rate of income tax (see **6.29** above).

There are one or two particular tax issues that may be relevant here:

- Whether or not a 'trade' exists, permitting access to important loss and capital gains tax reliefs. The standard HMRC approach is dissective; there is, in their opinion, simply an investment activity and the issue of scale, gearing and risk are not significant enough to change the substance of the property business and convert it into a trade. In particular, the approach is demonstrable as recently as in *Rashid v Garcia (Status Inspector)* [2003] STC (SCD) 36.
- The choice of a suitable tax 'structure'. There are no particular differences to the ordinary approach for income and capital gains tax planning. 'Married-couple partnerships' also follow the ordinary rules, deeming a 50/50 ownership unless there is clear and factual evidence of different shares.

Particular types of receipts

Surplus business accommodation

[6.45] Occasionally, businesses and professional partnerships let accommodation which is temporarily surplus to requirements. Rents so received may be included within the ordinary accounts and need not adopt a fiscal year-end (ITTOIA 2005, s 21). There is a requirement for the receipts to be comparatively small and have been acquired or used in the trade in the last three years. The term 'temporarily let' has been taken to mean three years in total. The legislation originates from a Revenue Decision which applied this treatment by concession (RD 9). It is helpful to recall that where a trade or profession winds down 'trading activities' any dilution of income afterwards or investment activities carried on after the mainstream trade has ceased may actually rule out eligibility for entrepreneurs' relief if the asset is not in substance a 'relevant business asset' as described in TCGA 1992, s 169L. A benchmark of 20% is often used.

There can be difficulties with entrepreneurs' relief where rental income is involved (TCGA 1992, s 169L(4)(b)). For the business proprietor, cum coincidental landlord, envisaging entrepreneurs' relief to be available upon gains arising from the sale of business premises let at any time, there can be a problem where assets have been held as investments. There is an important distinction between an asset held for investment and one that is opportunistically rented, but still fundamentally in use as part of the trade. The difference might be demonstrable from:

- the length of the sublease for the surplus accommodation;
- the fact that the let unit is not the majority of the asset but merely an incidental part of it;
- the fact that the tenant's presence might actually be beneficial to the landlord's trade or business.

HMRC would probably look at these factors with the length of lease as their first consideration, and it would be important in any argument securing entrepreneurs' relief that this is reasonably short.

What about the business owner who decides, or is forced in a flat market, to let his business premises after his trade ceases whilst awaiting a buyer? Thought needs to be given to TCGA 1992, s 169I(2)(b) and (4) to ensure that:

- the asset sale is achieved within three years of the cessation;
- the trade is carried on at the time of cessation from the premises now let.

As the relief has evolved, and certainly in the current economic climate, HMRC have been encouraged to adopt a more relaxed approach to this aspect of entrepreneurs' relief.

Furnished lettings

[6.46] Furnished lettings require specific legislation as part of the receipts relate to the use of land and part to the hire of furniture. There is no requirement to apportion the tax computations between their component parts as the furnished-lettings receipts are all part of the property business. Any sum payable for the use of furniture is brought into account as a receipt of the property business and a deduction is allowed for revenue expenditure incurred in connection with providing furniture (ITTOIA 2005, s 308; CTA 2009, s 248). The prospective cash basis rules are also to apply with effect from 2017–18.

As regards capital expenditure under the accruals basis, CAA 2001, s 35(2) specifically excludes claims for capital allowances for expenditure on plant and machinery let in dwelling-houses. By way of compensation, a 10% wear-and-tear allowance was introduced by concession in 1975–76 and given statutory effect for the purposes of income tax from the tax year 2011–12 as ITTOIA 2005, ss 308A–308C and for the purposes of corporation tax for accounting periods after 31 March 2011 as CTA 2009, ss 248A–248C. These statutory rules have now themselves been replaced by a new deduction for the replacement of domestic items, with effect from 6 April 2016 for the purposes of income tax and from 1 April 2016 for the purposes of corporation tax.

Under the old rules, a deduction could be claimed of 10% of the gross rent plus any premium due less property overheads such as on utilities and council tax and any other expenses normally borne by the tenant, termed the 'relevant rental amount'. The deduction had to be the subject of an election, which once made was irrevocable. It replaced, and could not be claimed in addition to, the deduction for providing furniture under ITTOIA 2005, s 308 or CTA 2009, s 248 and the deduction for the replacement or alteration of trade tools under ITTOIA 2005, s 68 or CTA 2009, s 68 (as applied by ITTOIA 2005, s 272 and CTA 2009, s 210, respectively). The deduction could, however, be claimed in addition to the cost of replacing or renewing fixtures in the let building such as bathroom and kitchen fittings or central heating goods for which a deduction as revenue expenditure should have been available.

The election could not be made in respect of furniture in furnished holiday-lettings property (see **6.47** below).

As an alternative to making the election, the actual cost of replacement furniture including electrical goods could be claimed under the extra-statutory 'renewals basis', which was withdrawn in respect of expenditure incurred after 5 April 2013 (income tax) or after 31 March 2013 (corporation tax). It was not possible to swap between the alternative claims in each year. The cost of initial furniture was not deductible under the renewals basis.

The wear-and-tear deduction was intended to compensate the landlord for depreciation on movable items that the landlord actually supplied for use and that usually a tenant might provide himself. Examples are white goods, crockery, kitchen utensils, televisions, curtains and floor coverings.

The new relief for the replacement of domestic items, which replaces the wear-and-tear allowance, is available for expenditure incurred after 31 March 2016 (in the case of corporation tax) or after 5 April 2016 (in the case of income tax). The relief takes the form of a deduction in computing the profits of the property business.

Four conditions have to be met for the relief to be available:

(1)   The person claiming the deduction must be carrying on a property business involving a dwelling-house.

(2)   That person must incur capital expenditure on a new domestic item to replace an old domestic item that was provided for use in the dwelling-house solely for the use of the tenant (lessee).

(3)   The expenditure is incurred wholly and exclusively for the purposes of the property business but is not otherwise deductible by virtue of being capital expenditure under either the accruals basis or the cash basis.

(4)   The expenditure does not qualify for capital allowances.

If these conditions are satisfied, a deduction may be made equal in amount to the cost of the replacement item, but only where it is the same or substantially the same as the old item it is replacing. Where it is not the same or substantially the same (eg where it represents an improvement), the deduction is limited to what the cost of the same or substantially the same new item would have been. 'Domestic item' means an item for domestic use, such as (but not limited to) furniture, furnishings, household appliances and kitchenware, but excludes fixtures (ITTOIA 2005, s 311A; CTA 2009, s 250A, both inserted by FA 2016, s 73).

The new deduction, just like the old deduction, is not available for a furnished holiday-lettings business.

The wear-and-tear deduction was withdrawn for the purposes of income tax with effect from the tax year 2016–17. For the purposes of corporation tax, it was withdrawn with effect for accounting periods beginning after 31 March 2016, but accounting periods straddling 1 April 2016 are divided into two, so that the wear-and-tear deduction still applies in respect of the deemed accounting period ending on 31 March 2016 (FA 2016, s 74). The deduction under ITTOIA 2005, s 68 and CTA 2009, s 68 for the replacement or alteration of trade tools was also withdrawn, in respect of expenditure incurred after 31 March 2016 (in the case of corporation tax) or after 5 April 2016 (in the case of income tax) (FA 2016, s 72).

Furnished holiday lettings

[6.47] A furnished-lettings business is not a trading activity, even where a high number of residential units are owned and serviced by the landlord. The pivotal test is the extent to which income is derived from the landlord's investment in the land as opposed to the provision of services to the tenant. Simple cleaning of communal areas and provision of a TV area or recreational facilities are not a hallmark of trade. If the economic return is principally from the appreciation in value of the let property, that is clearly not a trading receipt. If these services extend to cleaning the tenant's own room and bed-making and laundry provisions, HMRC would usually accept that a trade is being carried out. This enables various capital and income reliefs, perhaps the most important of which are full loss relief and entrepreneurs' relief.

This attitude grew from the failure to establish that trading activities existed in two cases, both of which were lost by the taxpayer: *Gittos v Barclay (Inspector of Taxes)* [1982] STC 390, 55 TC 633 and, more famously, *Griffith (Inspector of Taxes) v Jackson* [1983] STC 184, 56 TC 583. However, the dividing line between servicing an investment and carrying on a trade is a fine one. Following its success in *Gittos* and *Jackson*, the Government of the day introduced a scheme to preserve investment in furnished holiday-lettings and protect to some extent the interests of thousands of seaside landladies with small guest-houses dependent then upon retirement relief and rollover reliefs on significant capital gains built up in the business.

This resulted in the introduction of the 'furnished holiday-lettings' (FHL) scheme in FA 1984, under which the commercial letting of furnished holiday accommodation was treated for certain purposes as if it were a trade. However, this privileged treatment came to an end on 6 April 2012.

Prior to 6 April 2012, the commercial letting of furnished holiday accommodation in the UK had attracted valuable income tax and capital gains tax reliefs. This is because the activity was taxed as if it were a trade for most important purposes rather than an investment activity. From this unusual position, a number of valuable reliefs flowed, enabling potential claims by either companies or individuals for:

- full trade loss relief;
- capital allowances;
- the former landlord's energy-saving allowance (see **6.40** above);
- certain capital gains reliefs (including business-asset rollover relief, entrepreneurs' relief, relief for gifts of business assets, relief for loans to traders and exemptions for disposals of shares by companies with a substantial shareholding); and
- relevant UK earnings for individuals when calculating the maximum relief due for pension contributions.

The Finance Act 2011, however, saw substantial changes in the tax benefits from FHL portfolios, with effect from 6 April 2012. The two most important changes were the restriction of loss relief and the extension of the favourable treatment to FHL businesses involving property in EEA states outside the United Kingdom.

Whilst the loss relief restrictions were a blow to the industry, the extension of the EEA loss reliefs was no doubt welcome to the UK-based landlord letting foreign properties. It is not yet known if the EEA reliefs will continue after the United Kingdom has withdrawn from the European Union.

In effect, proprietors of properties let as furnished holiday accommodation are no longer regarded as carrying on a trade for certain tax purposes. Instead, landlords of FHL properties are regarded as carrying on either a UK property business or overseas property business consisting of or including the commercial letting of furnished holiday accommodation in the United Kingdom and/or in one or more EEA states. To put it in other words, the FHL business is either the entire property business or a subset of a wider property business. Profits from the FHL business are separated where necessary from any other parts of the property business by a precise or, if preferred, 'just and reasonable' apportionment.

Where this is the case, whereas most of the reliefs listed above have been specifically preserved, the availability of loss relief has been restricted.

The changes also saw a tightening of the conditions that need to be met in order for the letting to be regarded as commercial and qualify for the reliefs in the first place. It is worth stating the rules, as they now apply, in full.

The activity must be one of the commercial letting of furnished holiday accommodation. To be commercial, the letting must be carried on on a commercial basis with a view to realising profits. Accommodation is furnished accommodation if it provides for the use of furniture together with the use of the property. For the accommodation to be regarded as holiday accommodation, it must meet three conditions: the availability condition, the letting condition and the pattern-of-occupation condition. The availability condition is met if the accommodation is available for commercial letting as holiday accommodation for at least 210 days. The letting condition is met if the accommodation is commercially let as holiday accommodation to members of the public for at least 105 days. However, letting to the same occupant for a continuous period of more than 31 days ('longer-term occupation'), abnormal circumstances excepted, is not regarded as letting of holiday accommodation. The pattern-of-occupation condition is met if no more than 155 days is taken up by periods of longer-term occupation (ITTOIA 2005, ss 323, 325; CTA 2009, ss 265, 267). The period over which these days are measured is, for the purposes of income tax, normally a tax year. However, if the property was not let previously, the tests are applied over the first 12 months of letting; if the letting stops during the tax year, the tests are applied over the last 12 months of letting (ITTOIA 2005, s 324). For the purposes of corporation tax, the period is normally the 12 months ending with the last day of the accounting period. If the property was not let previously, the tests are applied over the first 12 months of letting; if the letting stops during the accounting period, the tests are applied over the last 12 months of letting (CTA 2009, s 266).

One difficulty in fulfilling these requirements is dual use of the accommodation to provide longer-term accommodation off-season. A claim could then fail on one or more of the conditions mentioned earlier.

In practice the appointment of a specialist agent to manage the property is helpful in demonstrating the availability requirement. For example, HMRC offices dealing with holiday properties in Devon and Cornwall have been known to ask for evidence that accommodation is available to the general public, and placing the property on the books of a dedicated agent may go some way toward this.

Problems may also arise where the portfolio is backed by sizeable loan finance, particularly in the case of holiday accommodation also used by the proprietor. It is always key to show a viable (commercially justifiable) profit-to-loan repayment ratio, otherwise the primary commerciality requirement cannot be met as sufficient profits would never be made. Readers might allude to *Brown v Richardson* [1997] STC (SCD) 233, a case lost by the hapless taxpayer who, in addition to his high-debt ratio had the added misfortune that the inspector obtained his loan application, which referred to the purchase of a 'holiday home'. Tax Bulletin, 31 October 1997 specifically referred to business plans to demonstrate commercial motives for purchase.

Income tax rules

[6.48] Reliefs that have been specifically preserved are the following:

(a)   for the purposes of capital gains tax, the commercial letting of FHL accommodation is treated as if it were a trade for the purposes of rollover relief under TCGA 1992, ss 152–157 on replacement of business assets, gift relief under TCGA 1992, s 165, entrepreneurs' relief under TCGA 1992, s 169S(1) and trade loans relief under TCGA 1992, s 253 (TCGA 1992, ss 241, 241A);

(b)   the availability of plant and machinery capital allowances under CAA 2001, Part 2, for which both a 'UK furnished holiday-lettings business' and an 'EEA furnished holiday-lettings business' is a qualifying activity. However, the rule in CAA 2001, s 35 disqualifying allowances for plant and machinery for use in a dwelling-house remains in force;

(c)   income chargeable to tax immediately derived from a UK FHL business or an EEA FHL business counts as an individual's relevant UK earnings for pension contributions under FA 2004, s 189(2)(ba), (bb).

(ITTOIA 2005, ss 322, 322A.)

The former landlord's energy-saving allowance under ITTOIA 2005, s 312 was not available (ITTOIA 2005, s 313(3)).

Whereas, for the purposes of income tax, ITA 2007, s 127 provides for the carrying-on of a UK FHL business to be treated as a single trade chargeable to income tax, full sideways relief and terminal-loss relief is denied. Instead, losses of a UK FHL business are available only for set-off against future UK FHL profits. Similarly, the carrying-on of an EEA FHL business is treated under ITA 2007, s 127ZA as a single trade chargeable to income tax (regardless of whether the properties are in just one or in two or more EEA states), full sideways relief and terminal-loss relief is denied. Instead, losses of an EEA FHL business are available only for set-off against future EEA FHL profits. There is no cross set-off between UK and EEA profits and losses.

However, as with a property business generally, where and to the extent that a loss in a property business arises from a capital allowances connection, sideways relief is possible (see **6.17** above), except under the cash basis.

Where a landlord has both a UK and an EEA FHL business, or a UK or overseas property business distinct from an FHL business, he must keep separate records and make separate computations (ITTOIA 2005, ss 327–328B). This will be particularly important, it should go without saying, if the UK business is subject to the cash basis.

Corporation tax rules

[6.49] The restrictions and reliefs are broadly similar for corporation tax. The reliefs that have been specifically preserved are the following:

(a)   for the purposes of corporation tax on chargeable gains, the commercial letting of FHL accommodation is treated as if it were a trade for the purposes of rollover relief under TCGA 1992, ss 152–157 on replacement of business assets, gift relief under TCGA 1992, s 165, entrepreneurs' relief under TCGA 1992, s 169S(1); trade loans relief under TCGA 1992, s 253 and relief under TCGA 1992, Sch 7AC on the disposal of substantial shareholdings (TCGA 1992, ss 241, 241A); and

(b)   the availability of plant and machinery capital allowances under CAA 2001, Part 2, for which both a 'UK furnished holiday-lettings business' and an 'EEA furnished holiday-lettings business' is a qualifying activity. However, the rule in CAA 2001, s 35 disqualifying allowances for plant and machinery for use in a dwelling-house remains in force.

(CTA 2009, ss 241, 241A).

The former landlord's energy-saving allowance under CTA 2009, s 251 was not available (CTA 2009, s 252(3)).

Whereas, for the purposes of corporation tax, CTA 2010, s 65 provides for the carrying-on of a UK FHL business to be treated as a single trade chargeable to corporation tax, relief against total profits is denied. Instead, losses of a UK FHL business are available only for set-off against future UK FHL profits.

Similarly, the carrying-on of an EEA FHL business is treated under CTA 2010, s 67A as a single trade chargeable to corporation tax (regardless of whether the properties are in just one or in two or more EEA states), relief against total profits is again denied. Instead, losses of an EEA FHL business are available only for set-off against future EEA FHL profits. There is no cross set-off between UK and EEA profits and losses.

Under the proposed new rules restricting the overall deductibility of carried-forward losses (CTA 2010, Part 7ZA), so much of a carried-forward UK or EEA FHL loss as is set off against FHL profits of a subsequent period is to be ignored when computing the restriction.

Where a corporate landlord has both a UK and an EEA FHL business, or a UK or overseas property business distinct from an FHL business, it must keep separate records and make separate computations (CTA 2009, ss 269, 269A).

Averaging basis

[6.50] If more than one property is in use for an FHL business, averaging elections may be useful to pool the lettings of other properties where one would not meet the letting condition, as above. Any election must be made by the first anniversary of the normal self-assessment filing date for the tax year concerned (ITTOIA 2005, s 326). An election for the tax year 2017–18 must therefore be made no later than 31 January 2020. The averaging election is also available for corporation tax (under CTA 2009, s 268), the time limit for which is two years from the end of the accounting period concerned.

Primarily originally intended as a means of softening the blow occasioned by the lengthening of the minimum letting period from 70 days to 105 days, which became effective from 2012–13, there is another election available for underused properties. Once a property has qualified as an FHL property, the landlord may elect for it to continue to qualify as such for the next tax year or next two tax years (or accounting periods in the case of corporation tax) even if it fails the letting condition (and only the letting condition) in that first year or period or in both. The election may not be made in respect of the second year or period if it has not already been made in respect of the first. There must, however, be a genuine intention to meet the letting condition and this election is not available if the averaging election has been made (ITTOIA 2005, s 326A; CTA 2009, s 268A).

Rent-a-room scheme

[6.51] The 'Rent-A-Room' scheme was introduced in 1992–93 as a special relief to landlords who let part of their home (for which the legislation is now found in ITTOIA 2005, Part 7, Ch 1 (ss 784–802)). For the avoidance of doubt, HMRC confirmed that the relief did not extend to the use of the home as an office (Tax Bulletin, 12 August 1994, now reproduced in HMRC's *Property Income Manual*, para PIM 4002). HMRC rely upon first principles in defining 'residence' as opposed to a work facility and in particular, cite the guidance in *Pepper v Hart* as illustrative of their point of view.

The scheme works in a relatively straightforward way to exempt from income tax gross receipts of £7,500 per annum from lettings to lodgers in a landlord's own home. Before 2016–17, the limit had remained static at £4,500 for many years.

In order to claim the relief, the individual must have 'rent-a-room receipts'. These arise to the individual in return for the use of furnished accommodation in a 'residence' in the United Kingdom or in respect of goods and services such as meals, laundry and cleaning supplied in connection with the use of the accommodation; what is more, were it not for the relief, the receipts would have to be taxable as trading income, income of a property business or as 'miscellaneous income' (income not otherwise brought into charge to tax, or the old Schedule D, Case VI sweeping-up charge). During some or all of the period concerned, the residence must be that individual's only or main residence. The period in question depends on whether the letting would otherwise be part of a trade or constitute a property business. In the case of a trade, the reference period is the basis period for the tax year. In the case of a property business, the reference period is the tax year, but if the letting begins or ends during the tax year, it is the period beginning on the later of the start of the tax year and the commencement of the letting and ending on the earlier of the end of the letting and the end of the tax year (ITTOIA 2005, ss 785, 786). A 'residence' can be a building or part of a building occupied or intended to be occupied as a separate residence, but it may also be a caravan or houseboat (ITTOIA 2005, s 787).

The full limit of £7,500 applies only if the individual meets the 'exclusive-receipts condition'. This condition is met if, in respect of each residence from which the individual derives rent-a-room receipts, no receipts accrue to any other person for the use of the residential accommodation or associated goods and services at any time in the reference period referred to in the preceding paragraph or the 12 months beginning or ending at the same time as the reference period begins or ends when the residence concerned is at the same time the individual's only or main residence (ITTOIA 2005, s 790). If the exclusive-receipts condition is not met, the relief limit is £3,750 (ITTOIA 2005, s 789(3)). The simplest example of this would be where the residence is jointly owned, say by a married couple, and the letting is carried out in both their names. However, it is important to note that the relief is only ever halved, no matter how many other persons are deriving rents. So, for example, if three sisters – Olga, Masha and Irina – all lived together in the same house as their only residence, and each let a room to a lodger, all three would have a limit of £3,750 if all the other conditions were satisfied.

The scheme requires the actual physical residence of the taxpayer. Moving abroad or moving into job-related accommodation would mean the taxpayer now had a different only or main residence, so the rental receipts no longer qualified for rent-a-room relief once the reference period during which the move occurs comes to an end. Remember, it is not necessary for the residence to be the taxpayer's only or main residence throughout the reference period, merely for some part of it during which the letting was carried on. If, however, the taxpayer simply moves home and continues with a lodger in the new home, then the rents from the old home (up to the end of the reference period for the tax year, even if the lodger remains in occupation and has the whole home at his or her disposal) and the new home (from the date the letting there commences or when the taxpayer takes up residence, if later, until the end of the tax year) are combined and the relief and the relief limit is applied to the total gross furnished letting receipts for the tax year concerned (ITTOIA 2005, s 788).

How the relief is given depends both on how the rents would otherwise be treated for tax purposes, and on whether qualifying rents are no more than, or exceed, the relief limit. If the limit is not exceeded and the receipts would otherwise be the income of a trade (where, for example, the landlord is running a guest-house or bed-and-breakfast business), the relief is given by treating the profits (or losses) of the trade as nil (ITTOIA 2005, s 792). If, on the other hand, the receipts would otherwise be treated as income of a property business, those receipts and any expenses associated with them are left out of account in calculating the profits of the property business (ITTOIA 2005, s 793). The third possibility is that the rents would otherwise be chargeable to tax under ITTOIA 2005, Part 5, Ch 8 (the sweeping-up provisions). This would be the case where, for example, the lodger had merely a licence to occupy or some other agreement. Where this is so, the relief is given by treating the rents from each such agreement net of any expenses associated with them as nil. Note that in all these cases, expenses cannot first be set off against the rents. Rent-a-room relief is given in respect of gross rents.

There is nothing to prevent a claim for rent-a-room relief in respect of a long-term lodger that the landlord has in a house otherwise run as a guest-house or in which the landlord carries on a bed-and-breakfast business, as long as the house is also the landlord's only or main residence, and the other conditions are met.

If an individual's gross rent-a-room receipts exceed £7,500 in the tax year, or whatever other exemption limit applies, the individual has two choices. Unless the individual opts (under ITTOIA 2005, s 800) for the so-called 'alternative basis' to apply, the entire amount will be taxed as either income of a trade, income from a property business or income not otherwise chargeable to tax ('miscellaneous income'), but expenses and capital allowances (if any) may be claimed in the normal way. If the landlord chooses the alternative basis, however, the effect is to bring into charge as income of a trade, property business or as miscellaneous income only the excess over the exemption limit. Where some of the receipts are taxable as, say, income of a trade and others as income of a property business, the exemption limit is reduced pro rata. There is no deduction for expenses or capital allowances if the alternative basis is chosen.

Example 16

> Tim has a house in Cumbria, with two spare bedrooms, which he lets out to students. In 2017–18, he receives £10,500 in rent, with expenses of £3,200. He claims rent-a-room relief and opts for the alternative basis of calculation. The rents are taxable as income of a property business. Since Tim is entitled to the full £7,500 exemption limit, the profits of his property business for 2017–18 are taken as £10,500 – £7,500 = £3,000. Had Tim not opted for the alternative basis, his taxable profit would have been £10,500 – £3,200 = £7,300.

If expenses are significant and in the event of a loss, the alternative basis is clearly not beneficial.

If a taxpayer 'does nothing', the normal basis of taxation (income less expenses) will apply. If an election under ITTOIA 2005, s 800 is to be made, it must be made in writing (making the appropriate entry in the individual's tax return suffices), specifying the tax year in which it is first to apply, no later than the first anniversary of the normal self-assessment filing date for the tax year concerned. Hence an election for the alternative basis to apply from 2017–18 must be made no later than 31 January 2020. Once made, the election remains in force unless the taxpayer gives written notice in the same way to withdraw it. The same time limits apply. Withdrawing the election does not prevent a further election in a future year.

HMRC have power to extend the time limit in exceptional circumstances.

It is also possible for a landlord to opt out of the rent-a-room scheme in any year, even when receipts fall within the exemption limit, eg when a loss is incurred or anticipated. The same time limits apply as for the alternative-basis election.

Brought-forward losses are not extinguished if a landlord wishes to join the scheme, instead they are carried forward or are available for set-off against any years when a surplus above the scheme limit is made, which is the only occasion when losses can be used in combination with the rent-a-room scheme. A useful outline of these rules can be found in HMRC's *Property Income Manual* at para PIM4040.

Property income distributions

[6.52] Real Estate Investment Trusts (REIT) were launched in the UK on 1 January 2007. They introduced a new concept of property ownership following a nine-year consultation period with the property profession. REIT companies are collective investment vehicles and provide entrepreneurs with an opportunity to invest in real estate as shareholders. The benefits of the regime to the provider are the opportunity to operate a property portfolio without the burden of tax upon income and gains, provided certain requirements are met. As one of the principal requirements is a distribution of at least 90% of profits to shareholders, the investment is an easily accessible one with potentially lucrative returns, comparing well to direct property ownership. Detailed information on the regime is contained in **CHAPTER 3**.

Tipping rights

[6.53] Tipping usually gives something of a finality to the use of land. It will not be used again in a trade or be easily reclassified for development. Once a site has been filled, it is the point of no return and each act of tipping and payments to do so are therefore capital in nature.

Tipping rights have become incredibly expensive since the late 1960s. Tipping sites last for up to 20 years and rights to acquire them reflect both the longevity of the asset and their high value. They are capital transactions as a lasting benefit is obtained. In *Rolfe (Inspector of Taxes) v Wimpey Waste Management Ltd* [1989] STC 454, 62 TC 399, CA, the rights were only for a short period but were still regarded as intrinsically capital in nature.

Wayleaves

[6.54] Wayleaves are rights over land usually arising from the siting of utility apparatus such as electric, telephone or telegraphic equipment. The apparatus may run under the land, for example apparatus using underground conduits or pipework (ITTOIA 2005, s 22(5), (6)).

A distinction needs to be made between rents for 'electric-line wayleaves' and rents for other wayleaves. 'Electric-line wayleaves' are 'easements, servitudes or rights' in or over UK land enjoyed in connection with an electric, telegraph or telephone wire or cable, including poles or pylons supporting those wires or cables and apparatus used in connection with the wires or cables (eg a transformer) (ITTOIA 2005, s 345).

The default position is for rents receivable for 'electric-line wayleaves' to be taxable under ITTOIA 2005, Part 3, Ch 9 as property income distinct from a property business (formerly a Schedule D, Case VI receipt) (ITTOIA 2005, s 344). If, however, the person receiving or entitled to the rent is carrying on a property business on some or all of the land to which the wayleave relates, and receipts (other than the wayleave rents) from that land are brought into account in the property business, then the wayleave rents are also included in the profits of the property business (ITTOIA 2005, s 346(1), (2)). This is also the default position for wayleaves that are not UK electric-line wayleaves.

Where the person receiving or entitled to the wayleave rents carries on a trade on some or all of the land to which the wayleave relates, and has no other receipts or expenses in respect of any of the land to be brought into account as receipts or expenses of a property business, the person may opt for the income and expenses to be brought into the computation of the trade (profession or vocation) in preference to their being treated as receipts of a property business or under ITTOIA 2005, Part 3, Ch 9 (ITTOIA 2005, s 22(2), (3)).

Not all receipts connected to wayleaves et al are income receipts. For example, payments for disturbance and compensation for the return of land to its ordinary state are capital receipts. A lump-sum payment for the granting of wayleave rights over a long period or in perpetuity may be a capital receipt but much will depend upon whether there has actually been a part-disposal. The decisions in *Davis (Inspector of Taxes) v Powell* [1977] 1 All ER 471, [1977]

1 WLR 258, and *Drummond (Inspector of Taxes) v Austin Brown* [1985] Ch 52, [1984] 2 All ER 699, CA refer. These receipts may not necessarily be received by the landlord; they may be paid to tenants with agricultural tenancies or business concerns with long leases over certain land.

Wayleaves upon foreign property are caught by ITTOIA 2005, s 22(1), which extends the legislation to include receipts from overseas property.

Service charges

[6.55] A service charge is an ordinary revenue receipt of a property business, although the landlord's right to it may create tax and legal issues arising from its expression in the lease. There are usually four ways of capturing a service charge in a lease. By far the most straightforward for the landlord is the creation of a separate management company to receive the charge and administer the fund. The four ways are:

(1)   The lease may simply require that the tenant pays a service charge as additional rent upon specific dates.

(2)   The lease provides for a service charge to be paid to the landlord and a separate payment to a trustee into a reserve fund.

(3)   The lease refers to the payment of a covenant to the landlord to reimburse him for the service charge, part of which will be a separate reserve fund.

(4)   The lease requires a separate payment to a management company.

Where a lease simply requires an additional service charge to the landlord, the effect on the rental computation is straightforward. As an exception, if the landlord is required under the terms of the lease to set aside a reserve fund, he must do so out of his own money and any interest or gains arising on the fund are assessable as his personal income or as income of a deemed trust rather than being included in the property-business receipts.

The separation of payments into a reserve fund managed by a trustee might invoke the settlement legislation and both landlords and tenants may find themselves unwitting participants in a discretionary or more usually interest-in-possession trust. In practice, HMRC do not seek to regard payments of service charges by tenants under a lease as settlements although the strict position would not rule this out. In particular the accumulation of large trust funds could be liable for ten-year charges in the normal way and exit charges upon the payment out of funds for maintenance costs. It may be prudent in these circumstances for recourse against the tenant for potential IHT liabilities if pursued.

In practice, HMRC are happy to accept the inclusion of covenanted payments as mainstream rental receipts. Previously there were potential restrictions with loss reliefs as the strict position was that they were Schedule D Case I or Case VI receipts under the old Schedule A rules.

Flat management companies

[6.56] Given the above complexities and the fact that it is prudent for landlords to make separate arrangements to manage the maintenance of large rental portfolios, flat management companies have grown up as a popular way to administer service charges. The usual arrangement is for each tenant to hold a share in the company that administers the management of the building. The arrangement is common in larger-scale residential properties.

Sometimes, flat management companies will be beyond the scope of tax, where they do not generate surplus income and the tax position will be as per other incorporated organisations and small liabilities will be regarded as 'dormant' for corporation tax purposes.

The requirement to notify HMRC of a trade applies as usual and the £100 penalty for not filing will no longer be reduced to zero when no tax is payable.

The trade is the provision of services and the profit is the reserve fund. But HMRC were happy to flex the rules for mutual concerns meaning there is usually no tax charge upon the profits of the trade. Readers requiring more information upon surpluses arising within a mutual trading arrangement are directed to the very old but still useful, albeit contrary, cases of *Cornish Mutual Assurance Co v IRC* [1926] AC 281, 12 TC 841, HL and *Styles v New York Life Assurance Company* (1889) 2 TC 460, HL.

The practical position is that there are a number of factors that may prevent the mutual rules from applying correctly. If a tenant does not subscribe for a share, there can be no mutuality. If the management company also manages a block of annexed garages partly let privately, there are two trades. Rather than take a dissective approach, HMRC changed the emphasis away from the mutuality of the company or arrangement to say that provided the receipts were paid away by way of maintenance and repair costs over the course of five years, they were happy not to tax the activities of the management company (Tax Bulletin 37, October 1998, now referenced in HMRC *Property Income Manual*, para PIM1070).

The introduction of the new Schedule A rules in 1998 (now rewritten for the purposes of corporation tax as the rules for a property business in CTA 2009, Part 4) emphasised the necessity for consistency with the trading-income rules and correct accounting principles. From 1 April 1998 receipts from residential service charges from owner-controlled flat management companies fall outside the scope of a property business as under LTA 1987, s 42 these are usually received by the landlord in his capacity as trustee. It was not correct to include as income within the property business receipts to which the landlord was not beneficially entitled. Accordingly, service charge funds and sinking funds are capital receipts in the landlord's hands and, for example, interest arising on service charges deposited in a bank account are taxed at the rate applicable to trusts. LTA 1987, s 42 has an implied power to accumulate (Tax Bulletin 37, October 1988; but see also Tax Bulletin Issue 48 for trustees who consider they are outside the scope of LTA 1987, s 42, for which now see HMRC *Property Income Manual*, para PIM1070).

For LTA 1987, s 42 to apply, the lease must express the payment to the landlord as a service charge in substance or effect. The amount must be variable according to the costs or anticipated costs of maintenance. The definition of service charge for the purposes of LTA 1987, s 42 is found in LTA 1985, s 18 and if a lease simply referred to use of parts of the rent payable for repairs and maintenance for which the landlord was responsible it would be outside the scope of LTA 1987, s 42. The practical effect of s 42 may place the landlord in an invidious position. Section 42 establishes the existence of a trust but it does not say what type of trust has been created. In the absence of this, the landlord may become in effect the settlor, which is an indirect and potentially dangerous route to the provisions of ITTOIA 2005, s 624, under which the income of the trust in which the settlor retains an interest becomes taxable on the settlor. The logical alternative is that the tenant is the settlor of the trust and again this may be undesirable.

Rents received by flat management companies are outside the scope of LTA 1987, s 42.

The provisions do not apply to registered social landlords (RSL) or their tenants. Certain other exempt bodies are defined at LTA 1987, s 58.

HMRC struggled with this difficult position and with the remedial measures contained in Tax Bulletin 48 for trustees who considered they were outside the scope of LTA 1987, s 42 and in applying it. In practice, the industry has created its own solution.

Perhaps partly as a result of the confusion, the commonhold association has become a popular way to get around the problems of LTA 1987, s 42. A commonhold association is a company limited by guarantee. It is taxed in the same way as a flat management company. It is regulated by Part 1 of the Commonhold and Leasehold Reform Act 2002 (and the associated regulations, SI 2004/1829). The commonhold association is formed of unit holders who are the only members. They own and manage the common parts and give effect to the commonhold association.

Whereas LTA 1987, s 42 does not apply to registered social landlords and other exempt landlords, the terms under which sinking funds and/or service charge funds are held by exempt landlords may still create a trust. This requires consideration of the application of TB 37.

Lease premiums

[6.57] Lease premiums are sums paid by incoming tenants as a consideration for granting the lease. This may be followed by a reduction in the rent paid and taxed on the landlord. Without special rules, which are contained in ITTOIA 2005, Part 3, Ch 4 (income tax) or CTA 2009, Part 4, Ch 4 (corporation tax), lease premiums and similar receipts might be converted to capital and avoid income tax. The legislation catches other types of similar transactions upon short leases in addition to simple premiums (ITTOIA 2005, ss 278–283; CTA 2009, ss 218–223). An alternative tax charge known as the 'additional calculation rules' is available (ITTOIA 2005, ss 287–289; CTA 2009, ss 227–229).

The scenarios caught by the lease premium rules include:

• amounts treated as lease premiums when work is required or improvements are carried out;
• sums payable instead of rent;

- sums payable for the surrender of a lease;
- sums payable for the variation or waiver of terms of a lease;
- assignments for profit or leases granted at undervalue.

Further provisions (ITTOIA 2005, ss 284–286; CTA 2009, ss 224–226) catch sales with the right to re-conveyance attached or leaseback.

The lease premium rules apply to leases of 50 years or less (short leases) (ITTOIA 2005, s 276(6); CTA 2009, s 216(6)). Entities already carrying on a property business are charged to income tax or corporation tax upon the amount of the premium. A new property business begins upon the day of receipt, if receipts had not existed before or where a third party is the recipient (see, eg ITTOIA 2005, s 277(2), (3) (income tax); CTA 2009, s 217(2), (3) (corporation tax)).

The taxable receipt is derived from a formula by reference to the number of whole years of the life of the lease other than the first, $[P \times (50-Y)/50]$, where P is the premium and Y is the number of whole years other than the first of the duration of the lease (ITTOIA 2005, s 277(4), to be read with s 277(5) for circumstances in which this may be reduced; CTA 2009, ss 217(4), (5)).

Tenant improvements (ie obligations placed on the tenant to carry out improvement work) are sometimes agreed at the inception of a new lease. They may create an increase in the value of the landlord's property which might otherwise escape tax. Where this is attained by virtue of an obligation derived from the lease, it is regarded as an income receipt of the landlord and treated as if it were a premium (ITTOIA 2005, s 278(1)–(3); CTA 2009, s 218(1)–(3)). This deemed premium is taxed in addition to any real premium due under ITTOIA 2005, s 277 or CTA 2009, s 217. The extent to which an obligation adds value may be contentious; the obligation to provide a new shop front written into the lease may not add any value at all. The upgrading of a car park to the rear may add a considerable premium, depending upon the location of the premises. HMRC usually quantify additional premiums created in this way by reference to their District Valuation Office.

Sums payable for waivers or variations to a lease are brought within the property business as income receipts by a similar premium calculator as above, by reference to the number of whole years the waiver or variation has effect after the first year (ITTOIA 2005, s 281(4); CTA 2009, s 221(4)). The concept of a waiver is broad and includes more than a simple abandonment of a lease term. In *Banning v Wright* [1972] 2 All ER 987, 48 TC 421 the House of Lords held that the word 'waiver' applied to a payment to the landlord as part of a settlement of a breach of the terms of the lease.

Similar rules apply to the assignment at a profit of short-term leases originally granted at an undervalue. A lease is regarded as granted at an undervalue if the terms under which it was granted are such that the landlord could have required the payment of an additional sum by way of a premium or additional premium. The additional sum that could have been charged is the undervalue. A profit is made on an assignment of a lease where the consideration for the assignment exceeds any premium for which it was granted. If the assignment in question is not the first assignment of the lease, the profit is taken to be the excess of the consideration for the present assignment over the consideration for the immediately previous assignment (ITTOIA 2005, s 283; CTA 2009, s 223).

Assignments of such leases may be made by persons other than the original tenant; they are treated as creating a new property business and the assignor is deemed to receive income at the time the consideration for the assignment becomes payable (ITTOIA 2005, s 282(1); CTA 2009, s 222(1)). This may form a new UK property business if the land is UK situs or a new overseas property business if situated outside the UK. The sum is taxable by reference to the premium formula on the profit on the assignment, where the smaller of (a) the profit on the assignment and (b) the excess of the undervalue over the total profits made on previous assignments (if any) takes the place of the premium in the standard formula.

Where additional sums are payable by a tenant in lieu of the whole or part of the rent due under the terms of a lease or agreement of 50 years or less, they are charged as income in the same way as a premium using the standard formula above, substituting the additional sum for the premium (ITTOIA 2005, s 279; CTA 2009, s 219).

Similar rules apply to sums payable for the surrender of short leases. The taxable receipt, ie the sum payable as compensation for the surrender, is charged using the standard formula, substituting the sum payable for the premium. Where the person entitled to the receipt is a third party, a new property business begins and the income is taxed upon the recipient when the sum becomes payable (ITTOIA 2005, s 280; CTA 2009, s 220).

Sales with a right to reconveyance attract income tax charges upon the amount (if any) by which the price at which the estate or interest in the land is sold exceeds the price at which it is to be reconveyed and (a) the earliest date at which the reconveyance could take place is within 50 years of the sale and (b) the person to whom the reconveyance is to be made is the seller or a person connected with the seller. The definition of 'connected person' is taken from ITA 2007, s 993 (income tax) or CTA 2010, s 1122 (ITTOIA 2005, Sch 4; CTA 2009, Sch 4).

The amount chargeable to tax is given by the standard formula, substituting the excess of the sale price over the reconveyance price (ITTOIA 2005, s 284; CTA 2009, s 224).

Sales reserving the right for the seller or a connected person to receive a lease directly or indirectly out of the estate or interest sold within 50 years of the sale at the earliest attract a charge to tax on the excess (if any) of the sale price over the total of any premium for the lease and the value at the date of sale of the right to receive a conveyance of the reversion immediately after the lease begins to run.

The amount brought into the property business of the seller is calculated using the standard formula, substituting the excess for the premium. The 'additional calculation rules' are not available to reduce the charge (ITTOIA 2005, s 285; CTA 2009 s 225).

During economic recessions and sometimes where a new development requires a fillip, landlords offer rent-free periods or capital payments to attract new or particular types of tenants. These payments are called 'reverse premiums' and the connection to the landlord's interest or right over the land can easily be drawn. The tax position of a reverse premium depends upon the type of tenant to whom it is made. Where the payment is to a trader or prospective trader, the receipt is taxable in his hands as revenue (ITTOIA 2005, s 101; CTA 2009, s 98). In other circumstances, the receipt is regarded as in connection with a property business whether in the UK or overseas (ITTOIA 2005, ss 101, 311; CTA 2009, ss 98, 250). Care is required where the parties are not at arm's length, when the entire payment is caught in the transaction entered into (ITTOIA 2005, s 311(4), (5); CTA 2009, s 250(4), (5)). Otherwise, it is usual for payments to be received over a number of years and they may be accordingly recognised.

Contributions towards a tenant's fit-out costs require careful drafting as to who will actually have the entitlement to capital allowances in the building. It is important that any agreement addresses this issue, as valuable allowances may otherwise be lost.

Apportionments on the sale of land

[6.58] When property is sold, statute provides that there is some consistency in the tax computations of the vendor and purchaser (ITTOIA 2005, s 320; CTA 2009, s 259). The legislation applies to all property-business receipts, no matter how wide their scope and for the purposes of both income tax and corporation tax.

The legislation does not apply to apportionments of income and expenses on transfer of a property other than by sale, for example on death or bankruptcy or by way of gift or exchange. The income would pass out of the ITTOIA 2005, s 320 provision upon death or bankruptcy, meaning that a disposal by a personal representative or trustee in bankruptcy does not imply an apportionment upon a subsequent purchaser.

Compensation

[6.59] In certain circumstances, compensatory payments arising where a landlord has given notice to a tenant under the Landlord and Tenant Act 1954 will usually be tax-free in the hands of the tenant. The wording of the notice is important since if the tenant has sought to surrender the lease, any payments will often be taxable.

The tax-free status of such compensatory payments arose following *Drummond (Inspector of Taxes) v Austin Brown* [1985] Ch 52, [1984] 2 All ER 699, CA. The bona fide nature of the payment arises from a right incorporated in legislation rather than an asset disposal. That builds upon the earlier agricultural compensation case of *Davis (Inspector of Taxes) v Powell* [1977] 1 All ER 471, [1977] 1 WLR 258.

There is no exemption if there is no genuine 'notice to quit' served by the landlord. Therefore, an ad hoc capital receipt for the surrender of an expiring lease is taxable in the hands of the tenant unless the requisite documents demonstrate that the payment is compensatory, for loss of a right, in nature.

Compulsory purchase will invoke special capital gains tax rules, including the opportunity to roll over an arising gain against future land purchases, or for small part disposals to be disregarded entirely. Care is required as the rules provide for a strict apportionment of the compensation payment into its component parts, potentially triggering income tax charges. Professional valuations of the land component are essential (instead of important).

Income excluded from a property business

[6.60] The receipts from certain activities ('concerns') are not taxable as receipts of a property business; they are taxed instead as if they were profits of a trade, although the common source of profits is land (ITTOIA 2005, s 12; CTA 2009, s 39). These activities are referred to as 's 12(4) concerns' (income tax) or 'section 39(4) concerns' and the common ones concern the operation of:

• mines and quarries (including gravel pits, sand pits and brickfields);
• ironworks, gasworks, waterworks, canals, docks;
• rights of fishing;
• rights of tolls, bridges, ferries, markets and fairs;
• railways; and
• concerns that are similar to any of the above.

Although ostensibly a mixed bag, perhaps these concerns share their business scale and commitment to specialist plant and equipment and so trade categorisation in common. Rents received as part of the deemed trade of any of the above concerns are included in the trade computation and do not form a separate property business (ITTOIA 2005, s 335; CTA 2009, s 270). If this is not evident, the words 'as if the concern were a trade' in ITTOIA 2005, s 12(1) or CTA 2009, s 39(1) are relevant and important deferrals or exemptions may not be available. Within this context, the cases of *Harris (Surveyor of Taxes) v Edinburgh Corpn* (1907) 5 TC 271, (1907) SC 1233 and *Ystradyfodwg and Pontypridd Main Sewerage Board v Bensted* [1907] AC 264, 5 LGR 865, HL, might be useful.

The former special reliefs for mineral royalties, under which half were taxable as income and half as capital gains was abolished with effect from 1 or 6 April (the former date for the purposes of corporation tax and the latter for the purposes of income tax) 2013.

Hotels and guest-houses are taxed as trades under ITTOIA 2005, Part 2 or CTA 2009, Part 3, as the case may be. Proprietors can claim important pension, holdover, entrepreneurs' and investors' reliefs against profits and gains arising.

Rents, including premiums, from tied premises and any receipts and expenditure are taxed as income from a trade (ITTOIA 2005, s 19; CTA 2009, s 42).

Receipts from the letting of caravan sites where the operator provides services to the site tenants and 'material activities' may be included within the receipts of the trade at the trader's option (ITTOIA 2005, s 20; CTA 2009, s 43).

Particular types of ownership

Married couples and civil partnerships

[6.61] ITA 2007, s 836 et seq provide the statutory basis for spouses and civil partners living together as being entitled to equal shares in jointly owned property. Yet this is frequently not an accurate conclusion. It is possible to apportion taxable income in different shares by making a declaration under ITA 2007, s 837 to reflect the true beneficial interest.

It is not possible to make alternative appropriations other than those which reflect the facts. These provisions do not apply where spouses or civil partners are mutual members of a trading activity or a partnership. In that instance, the allocation of profits or losses would be in accordance with the partnership deed or agreement.

Life interest trusts

[6.62] Where a life interest trust exists, it will usually be the trustee who is carrying on the property business and who will be liable for the tax on the profits. However, there are certain features of a settlement that may originate a tax charge upon the life tenant as he will be the person regarded as carrying on the business. Those features are where particular laws apply to the settlement that should be reasonably apparent:

- the trustees have delegated their executive powers to the life tenant as the beneficiary under s 9 of the Trusts of Land and Appointment of Trustees Act 1996; or where
- the trustees have delegated their executive powers to the life tenant under the provisions of s 29(1) of the Law of Property Act 1925; or where
- land is held in a settlement governed by the Settled Land Act 1925.

Property investment LLPs

[6.63] Partnerships, whether general, limited or limited liability remain popular choices for property structures. Not only is the potential available for commercial protection but also the ability to access personal loss reliefs, although these have been capped at the greater of (a) £50,000 and (b) 25% of the taxpayer's adjusted total income since 2013–14 (ITA 2007, s 24A) (see further below). Where a corporate partner is utilised, income streams can be taxed at the main corporation tax rate (currently 19% and set to fall to 17% from the financial year 2020), as opposed to a maximum of 54% (including 9% national insurance contributions in the case of a trade) in the hands of pure individuals. Indeed, until recently, a corporate partner might have enjoyed exemption from the scope of UK capital gains if properly non-resident and outside the scope of the attributive legislation in TCGA 1992, s 13. Now, however, high-value UK residential property held through a non-resident corporate vehicle is liable to ATED (the annual tax on enveloped dwellings) under FA 2013, Part 3 since 1 April 2013 and capital gains from such property are liable to capital gains tax under TCGA 1992, ss 2B–2F since 6 April 2013.

Furthermore, all disposals of an interest in UK residential property by a non-resident (individual or company) are potentially liable to capital gains tax under TCGA 1992, s 14B where they realise a so-called NRCGT (non-resident capital gains tax) gain since 6 April 2015. In both cases, broadly speaking, only the post-6 April 2013 or the post-6 April 2015 element of the gain is within the charge. Complex provisions exist where the two charges to tax would interact. These charges significantly reduce the advantage of using structures involving bodies corporate.

Limited liability partnerships (LLPs) are a partnership/corporate hybrid which are transparent for the purposes of income tax and capital gains tax as regards their members who have subscribed capital. They are a popular alternative to a corporate investment structure in property portfolios. The principal reasons are the lower tax cost of distributions and 'liquidation'. The commercial protection afforded by a company is as easily attainable by the members of an LLP and losses can be utilised more effectively by the individual members. Special provisions restrict the losses available to 'sleeping partners' who work for less than 10 hours per week. There is a fuller discussion on LLPs in CHAPTER 4.

Although the potential tax savings are attractive, property investment LLPs face an assortment of difficulties. First, restrictions on interest relief for partnership members was specifically aimed at preventing the 'distortion' of a creating 'see-through' companies with the end result of creating tradable interests. Under these provisions, interest relief in respect of loans to purchase an interest in a partnership is denied where the partnership is an 'investment LLP' (ITA 2007, s 399(2)(b)).

Second, the loss relief rules in ITA 2007, s 104 restrict the sideways loss relief available to limited partners carrying on a trade to, broadly, the amount of capital they have contributed to the partnership. The same restriction applies to members of a limited liability partnership carrying on a trade, whether or not they are limited partners (ITA 2007, ss 107–108). Further, on top of all these restrictions, there is an overall cap under ITA 2007, s 103C of £25,000 on the total of sideways relief and capital gains relief that can be claimed in any one tax year by an individual who is either a 'non-active' partner or a limited partner.

Where the partnership carries on a property business rather than a trade, loss reliefs are already circumscribed as described in 6.19. These losses, where incurred by an individual, together with sideways trade losses and many other forms of loss relief, are subject since 6 April 2013 to a cap on the total of all affected losses that can be deducted in any one tax year to the greater of £50,000 and 25% of the individual's adjusted total income (ITA 2007, s 24A). The affected reliefs are:

(a)   trade loss relief against general income (under ITA 2007, s 64);

(b)   early trade losses relief (under ITA 2007, s 72);

(c)   post-cessation relief (under ITA 2007, s 96);

(d)   property loss relief against general income (under ITA 2007, s 120);

(e)   post-cessation property relief (under ITA 2007, s 125);

(f)   employment loss relief against general income (under ITA 2007, s 128);

(g)   share loss relief (under ITA 2007, Part 4, Ch 6);

(h)   relief for interest payments (under ITA 2007, Part 8, Ch 1);

(i)   the deduction for liabilities relating to a former employment (under ITEPA 2003, s 555);

(j)   relief for losses on strips of government securities (under ITTOIA 2005, s 446); and

(k)   relief for losses by persons other than trustees on listed securities held since 26 March 2003 (under ITTOIA 2005, s 454(4)).

Property dealers, builders and property developers

[6.64] A significant number of property development businesses may consider during periods of a depressed property market letting all or part of their property stock if only on a short-term basis. Appropriations of investment properties to or from trading stock can pose both difficulties and opportunities for proprietors of property businesses, whether incorporated or unincorporated. There are two primary considerations requiring thought in these circumstances. The difficulties are posed by the new anti-avoidance legislation on dealing in or developing UK land under ITA 2007, Part 9A (income tax), introduced by FA 2016, s 79(1) or CTA 2010, Part 8ZB (corporation tax), introduced by FA 2016, s 77(1). These new provisions replace the previous legislation, rewritten in ITA 2007, Part 13, Ch 3 (income tax) and CTA 2010, Part 18 (corporation tax).

The authority is provided to HMRC in *Coates v Arndale Properties Ltd* (1984) 59 TC 516.

The problem a potential property investor faces by reclassifying property held as trading stock as investment property is provided by TCGA 1992, s 161, which produces an immediate deemed disposal at market value at the time of reclassification. This produces a tax charge probably not accompanied by cash funds. If the cash flow is available to meet the charge, this may provide a valuable planning tool. Provided there is a bona fide reclassification, a property that is underperforming realises a trading loss that is capable of being set against profits in the year of appropriation or being group-relieved.

A greater difficulty is posed for the property developer who intends to construct a property that will be retained for investment. The classification of the property is crucial as frequently property increases in value markedly as the development stages progress. If the property is regarded as trading stock then a sale or an appropriation after development will produce a large profit, which will be taxed as income. If the property has been appropriated in the early stages, little intrinsic value will have been imputed and the tax charge will be much lower. This would be a good opportunity at a time of property 'recession'. However, one would have to have primary regard to the objectives of the investor in acquiring an investment in an underdeveloped state, as clearly the property would not be fit for the purpose of letting and HMRC may argue that the investment company has diversified into development activities. So, whilst this would provide a useful advantage on paper, the reality is that there would be only very exceptional circumstances where this would be a commercial course of action.

In practice, it is not unknown for exceptional circumstances to arise. They do so on a daily basis and it is not in the least uncommon for development trades and investment activities or their assets to be transferred between associated entities, such as upon retirement or after commercial disagreements. A further complication is that the new legislation does not provide for a clearance procedure, which was available under the previous code.

HMRC treat appropriations with some cynicism, not least as they are often between connected persons. As a matter of routine, there would be requests to see:

- board minutes and formal resolutions documenting the classification of the property; and
- reconciliations of balance sheet entries detailing the reclassification from trading stock to fixed assets.

This authority is taken from *Oliver v Farnsworth (Inspector of Taxes)* (1956) 37 TC 51, 35 ATC 410 and *Speck v Morton* (1972) 48 TC 476.

Finally, within a group of property-dealing and investment companies, TCGA 1992, s 161(3) provides a useful opportunity to convert a capital loss within the group into a trading loss where a dealing company acquires an investment property for marketing and sale, ie as part of its trading stock. Upon transfer, the dealing company may compute the cost as either:

- market value; or
- market value as reduced by any gain or '*as reduced by any loss*' (s 161(3)).

Provided the motive test is passed and the transaction is evidenced as not for fiscal reasons, the loss may then be set off by the group in the usual way. This is not a straightforward matter; *Coates v Arndale Properties Ltd* has stood the test of time and brought this type of transaction to public notice. Intending transferees must clearly minute their course of action and ensure that any third-party sale is conducted through the development company post-acquisition.

The HMRC approach to examining the accounts of builders, property developers and investors has been to use the avoidance provisions contained within the previous code (ITA 2007, Part 13, Ch 3 or CTA 2010, Part 18) almost as a starting point.

HMRC's Business Income Manual, para BIM51505, appears to encourage the avoidance critique. It states: 'where the profits are not trade profits, liability to tax may in certain circumstances arise under the stand-alone charge on land transactions. Where appropriate in a contentious case, alternative assessments should be made in respect of trade profits and the land transactions charge.'

It is not yet clear how HMRC will be approaching the new legislation.

It is possible that the ATED legislation may give property development companies greater appeal, as they provide a key exemption from the annual charge where a successful track record is evident. Rental investment of up to 20% of the company's income or balance sheet, may be integrated into the development trade, without compromising the development status of the trade.

Anti-avoidance

[6.65] HMRC's list of DOTAS avoidance schemes continues to grow slowly but surely, but at the time of writing, there are no features on property-based arrangements. HMRC have adequate recourse to anti-avoidance provisions in examining the accounts of property businesses. Readers may be fairly familiar with some of the more popular themes of the previous anti-avoidance code concerning artificial transactions in land by companies and/or individuals (former ITA 2007, Part 13, Ch 3 and former CTA 2010, Part 18 (already referred to)).

Property-tax avoidance cases feature regularly in law reports and the breadth of the 'motive tests' inherent in the legislation possibly explain why. But robust defences are possible in responding to any HMRC threat to regard property profits as trading rather than capital receipts and some of the following arguments illustrate the point.

An exemplary case might be *IRC v John Lewis Properties plc* [2002] EWCA Civ 1869, [2003] Ch 513, [2003] 2 WLR 1196. This remains of interest to the property sector to this day, with key citations in almost every case that has at its heart the intrinsic characteristics of land purchases and investments, and so their correct tax treatment. This most helpful case evaluated the reality of property transactions involving rents and their commercial motive. The dicta referred to no less than 27 property tax cases affecting rental streams in the judgments and skeleton arguments. The facts are that John Lewis Properties (JLP) owned various freehold or long leasehold interests in five properties and entered into an agreement to assign the right to receive rents over a five-year period. In return, a lump sum was paid to the company, which was calculated on the basis of rents receivable. The company regarded the receipt as capital and attached rollover relief claims in respect of refurbishing existing stores and opening new ones. HMRC regarded the receipt as income and sent a large demand for corporation tax negating the rollover claims. Upon appeal, the company was successful at the Special Commissioners who concurred there had been a part-disposal of the properties concerned. HMRC appealed to the Court of Appeal, which looked at the substance of the transaction, noting the increase in the profits of JLP after the date of assignment and ruled against HMRC by a 2-1 majority, refusing leave to appeal to the House of Lords. The case demonstrates, inter alia, the importance of commercially driven decisions as opposed to avoidance-based transactions in land, or concentration upon the legal consequences of the assignment. It notes during its course the contrast between the facts of Rabobank's payment to JLP as compared to the circumstances of *McGuckian, Ramsay* or *Furniss*.

> 'the question of whether the money was received as capital or income depends on what the expenditure is calculated to effect from a practical and business point of view rather than the juristic classification of the legal rights'.
>
> Dyson LJ.

However, the reader should note the legislative changes (the 'rent-factoring' provisions) in FA 2000 that swiftly followed this decision were subsequently replaced by FA 2006 and are now found in CTA 2010, Part 16, Ch 2.

Overseas companies, or more likely their shareholder directors, might once have regarded the UK as a tax haven for offshore property investors. Even before the ATED and NRCGT legislation was enacted in 2013 and 2015, respectively, there were several caveats to bear in mind.

First, there was the appetite HMRC had for regarding multiple property purchases as forming a trading activity, rendering the sale of properties as trading rather than capital receipts. A second danger was posed by TCGA 1992, s 13, which attributes gains made by a closely held non-resident company to its UK-resident 25% participators. It provides that if the non-resident company would be a close company if it were UK-resident:

- UK-resident participators with an interest (alone or with connected persons) of 25% or more may be taxed on their share of any capital gains;
- irrespective of whether any money has or will be received; and
- irrespective of any losses available in the overseas company.

The legislation on transfers of assets abroad should also be considered. Corollary arrangements involving the transfer of foreign properties between UK and non-UK trusts brought Lord Wilberforce's opinion on what was then ICTA 1988, s 739 into everyday tax vocabulary (see *Vestey v IRC (No 2)* [1980] AC 1148, [1979] 3 All ER 976, HL). Although the taxpayers won in that case, the legislation was amended and may now be found in ITA 2007, Part 13, Ch 2.

HMRC has had related success in the courts in 2009 (*Burns v Revenue & Customs Comrs* [2009] STC (SCD) 165). The reader might find the case helpful to get into the mindset of the approach to the transfer-of-assets-abroad legislation; that is, the issue of what is a commercially motivated land-based transaction involving the transfer of ownership and property-income streams abroad. The taxpayer lost badly and the defences available under what are now ITA 2007, ss 736–742 failed. There was pronounced to be tax avoidance in hand rather than tax mitigation and assessments upon property business profits of £160,000 pa were upheld.

It therefore seems appropriate to go about any tax planning with the following anti-avoidance based objectives in mind:

- Where a non-resident company or trust is used, that the relevant local tax treaty provisions are durable and appropriate.
- Where there is a relocation out of the UK that policy decisions and policy makers are indeed located in the desired jurisdiction.
- Any foreign structure is free of potential attributions under TCGA 1992, s 13 or ITA 2007, Part 9A or CTA 2010, Part 8ZB.
- Any trust-type vehicle is compliant with the changes to the offshore fund rules, which target gains made by UK investors, construing them as income. See TIOPA 2010, s 354 and SI 2009/3001.
- The desired purpose of debt or share ownership is not open to dissemination and would be robust if queried by HMRC.

All this, of course, will not protect interests in UK residential property held through foreign corporate vehicles from the annual charge to ATED on property worth £500,000 or more of capital gains from disposals of such properties ('ATED-related gains') from a charge to capital gains tax at 28% on the element of the gain accruing since 6 April 2013, although there are exemptions for, eg property developers. Nor will non-resident persons, legal or natural, normally avoid a charge to capital gains tax at 28% on the element of the gain ('NRCGT gain') accruing since 6 April 2015 on the disposal of UK property interests.

For ATED and NRCGT gains, see CHAPTERS 22 and 5 (respectively).

Sale and leaseback of land and other issues

[6.66] CTA 2010, Part 19 counters certain avoidance devices based on arrangements for the sale and leaseback of land or any interest in land. CTA 2010, Part 19, Ch 1 limits the deduction for rent payable to a commercial rent, and CTA 2010, Part 19, Chapter 2 deals with the situation where a lessee incurs additional rental liability for a comparatively short period in return for the payment of a lump sum.

There are several ways to avoid tax or circulate tax payments within trust arrangements. Here HMRC like to take the settlement-provisions route and the reader might consult ITTOIA 2005, ss 619(1) and 623 regarding the examination of trust deeds and schedules where there are large trust property-business losses at stake. These provisions are applied to prevent settlors of life-interest trusts from, in particular, setting off personal property losses against deemed trust income or vice versa.

As outlined above, appropriations and transactions between related property-dealing and investment companies are subject to close scrutiny. The area has provided two tax cases which have stood the test of time, and demonstrate the HMRC attitude toward potential avoidance issues. This was highlighted in the decisions in *Coates v Arndale Properties Ltd* (1984) 59 TC 516 and *New Angel Court Ltd v Adam* TL 3696, where it was noted that the transaction in question, the intra-group purchase of nine properties and correlating loss claim under TCGA 1992, s 161(3), was ineffective as '[t]here was no purpose other than tax for the transfer'.

But that is not to deny a commercially driven transaction might succeed. But the frequency with which HMRC are prepared to take these types of transactions all the way to the Supreme Court should be noted and the area generally is one where the prospective property entrepreneur may expect to be challenged.

It may be observed, as ever, from the above, that the taxation of property businesses in the UK is no less complex than when this chapter was first written.

Chapter 7

Premiums

by
Dominic Rayner,
KPMG LLP

Foreword

[7.1] Latinists should note that the initial research on this chapter concerned the correct English plural of 'premium'. In *Modern English Usage* (1965), Fowler insists on 'premiums'. He lists 'premia' as a word to avoid alongside 'asyla', 'alba' and 'musea'.

Introduction

[7.2] Mention premiums and short leases, and students swotting for their tax exams will immediately quote the formula (dating from 1963) for calculating the landlord's tax liability. But short lease premiums are relatively rare in the commercial property sector. More common is to see a prospective tenant of office or retail space demanding a large upfront sweetener from the landlord, to make the ongoing rental obligation more palatable.

The recent recessionary period has strengthened the bargaining position of those retailers and other property occupiers who are still able to fulfil their lease obligations. This means that landlords are frequently having to accept shorter lease terms and tenant break options as well as granting rent-free periods at inception. Few tenants can access the cash to pay a large lease surrender payment, but there are many sublettings, assignments and lease variations as occupiers seek to manage their exposure to rental liabilities. Landlords generally continue to be unwilling to negotiate lease surrenders from tenants, but some have had to suffer tenants using insolvency procedures to exit or renegotiate leases, including CVA.

To avoid confusion in a chapter headed 'premiums' which covers sums being paid from landlord to tenant and vice versa at the start and end of a lease, the following should clarify the nomenclature.

Premium	A sum paid by a tenant to a landlord for the grant of a new lease
Reverse premium	A sum paid by a landlord to a tenant to enter into a new lease
Surrender payment	A sum paid by a tenant to a landlord to accept surrender of a lease

Reverse surrender payment	A sum paid by a landlord to a tenant in return for surrender of the lease

The tax positions of payer and recipient are explained for each of these four transactions, and the tax treatment of payments for variations and assignments of leases is also set out. It is often important with transactions in leases to look at how both parties are affected, as there may be an adverse tax mismatch (eg payment taxable on recipient but not deductible for payer). This tax leakage is not helpful to the parties trying to negotiate the amount to be paid for the transaction, so needs to be borne in mind, and minimised where possible; there are often two ways of achieving a similar outcome, and one may be more tax-efficient than the other.

The corporation tax rules pertaining to lease premiums are mostly set out in the consolidated and re-written CTA 2009, and cover the tax treatment of such transactions for companies. Despite continual colloquial references to it, Schedule A is no longer the heading under which companies' income from rent, deemed lease premiums, etc is taxed. Corporation tax is now chargeable on the profits of a UK property business (CTA 2009, s 209). The corporation tax rules for lease premiums are effectively duplicated in the tax legislation for individuals and other persons subject to income tax, in ITTOIA 2005. The two sets of rules give rise to the same outcome in most material cases, so only need to be learnt once. Those people who long for the familiarity of the old-style legislation (pre-modernisation and pre-simplification) will be glad to know that the applicable capital gains rules are still those of TCGA 1992.

If it is not explicitly stated otherwise, it is assumed that all property interests referred to in this chapter are held as fixed assets in the UK GAAP accounts of the companies or other persons involved, and that all disposals are capital gains disposals. In practice this is not always the case, as explained in, for example, **CHAPTER 13** at para **13.5** ff dealing with CTA 2010, s 815 (and ITA 2007, s 752).

This chapter does not cover the new Scottish Land and Buildings Transaction Tax (LBTT), which was introduced on 1 April 2015. It is assumed that all property transactions referred to are in the UK but not in Scotland. For details on LBTT, see **CHAPTER 24**.

Length of lease

[7.3] Before looking at the tax effect of paying for or granting a new lease at a premium, it is first necessary to know how long the tax legislation deems that lease to be. The tax position on grant or surrender of a ten-year lease could be substantially different from that on grant or surrender of a 40-year lease.

Stamp duty land tax

[7.4] For stamp duty land tax (SDLT) purposes it is simple to calculate the length of a lease. If a lease is stated to be for a term of 25 years, the SDLT on its grant will be calculated as though it is a 25-year lease, irrespective of the potential for a tenant to break the lease early or extend the lease by renewal (FA 2003, Sch 17A, para 2).

VAT

[7.5] For VAT purposes, the answer is the same – a lease purporting to be of a certain length will be treated as though it is of that length. The fact that there could be an extension or early termination is not relevant. See **7.9** below for the liability of premiums.

Income tax, capital gains tax and corporation tax

[7.6] The position for corporation tax, capital gains tax and income tax is less simple.

The term of a lease (ie its length or duration) is defined for corporation tax purposes by CTA 2009, s 243, for capital gains tax purposes by TCGA 1992, Sch 8, para 8 and for income tax purposes by ITTOIA 2005, s 303. Fortunately, all three sets of rules are very similar and should result in the same answer for most leases. The rules determine the effective duration of a lease by establishing the best estimate of the period for which the lease is likely to continue.

Under normal circumstances, the length of a lease is equal to the term expressed in the lease itself. However, in the following situations, the lease may be treated for tax purposes as being longer or shorter than that.

- If the lease contains terms which make it likely that it will terminate earlier than the expiry date.
  The lease will be treated as one that terminates at the earliest date which it is unlikely to last beyond. (The income tax and corporation tax rules say that this provision will not bite if the premium for the lease was 'substantially greater' than it would have been for a lease of this shorter duration.) See **7.13** for a new exception to this general rule.
  The capital gains rules specify the example of an increase in rent combined with the tenant having the right to terminate the lease. If, in those circumstances, it is unlikely that the lease will endure beyond the date of the tenant's option to terminate, then it will be deemed to be a lease ending on that date.
- If the lease provides the tenant (or a connected person) with an option to extend the lease beyond a given date, or if the tenant (or a connected person) is entitled to the grant of a further lease for the same premises. In determining the length of the lease, for income tax and corporation tax purposes 'account may be taken' of the possible later termination date resulting from the extension or further lease.
  For capital gains purposes, the maximum extension available to the tenant must be added to establish the length of the lease (limited by any right of the landlord to determine the lease during this time).
- For capital gains purposes only, if the terms of the lease provide for it to be terminated by the landlord at any point, the lease is to be treated as ending at the earliest point at which the landlord could terminate it.

Example 1

Albarn lets a property to Coxon for ten years at a premium of £20,000, with rent of £5,000 a year for the first five years, and £30,000 a year for the remainder. Coxon has an option to terminate the lease after five years.

Although this lease would be treated as a ten-year lease for SDLT and VAT purposes, it would almost certainly be treated as a five-year lease for capital gains tax purposes. This is because it seems likely at the date of grant that Coxon will terminate the lease after five years rather than endure the rent increase. For the same reason, the lease would probably be treated as a five-year lease for income tax purposes as well – assuming that the £20,000 premium paid for the lease is not substantially greater than it would have been for a lease expiring after five years. If it was, the lease would be deemed to have a term of ten years for income tax purposes.

Example 2

Polly grants a lease to Jean for 15 years at a premium of £25,000 and rent of £5,000 each year. Jean is given an option in the lease to extend the term for another 15 years for no premium but annual rent of £3,000.

This lease would be treated as a 15-year lease for SDLT and VAT purposes, but would be treated as a 30-year lease for capital gains purposes. It would probably be treated as a 30-year lease for income tax purposes because at the time of grant it would seem likely that Jean would exercise the option to extend the lease.

For income tax and corporation tax purposes, these rules on establishing the length of a lease should be applied:

• By taking into consideration the facts known or ascertainable at the time the lease was granted (or at the time when the terms of the lease were varied or waived).
• Under the assumption that all parties concerned act as if they were at arm's length, even if they are connected.
• There is a further rule that certain 'benefits', if conferred to secure a tax advantage, may be excluded when determining whether a lease is unlikely to continue beyond a certain date. ('Benefits' do not include vacant procession, beneficial occupation of the premises, the right to receive rent at a reasonable commercial rate in respect of the premises or payments made which would not be expected to be made by parties acting at arm's length if no other benefits had been conferred – CTA 2009, s 244; ITTOIA 2005, s 304.)

Grant of new lease for a premium

[7.7] Taxpayers should beware of transactions involving lease premiums. The recipient of a premium could find himself having taxable income when he expected to receive a capital payment which he could shelter. In fact, care should be taken with all transactions involving leases because, in certain circumstances, they can be deemed to involve the receipt of a lease premium, even when no new lease is granted.

Lease premiums – SDLT

[7.8] For non-residential property, SDLT will be paid on the grant of the lease at 2% on any part of the premium above £150,000 but below £250,000, and at 5% on any part of the premium above £250,000 (and if VAT is applicable to the premium, the SDLT will be chargeable on the VAT-inclusive amount). In addition, SDLT will be payable at 1% of the net present value of all the rents payable under the lease (excluding the first £150,000), and at 2% on any part of that net present value which exceeds £5m. SDLT rates, tables and details of the rental calculations are shown in detail at CHAPTER 16 at paras **16.22** and **16.31**.

For residential property, a lease premium paid by an individual is subject to the same progressive rates of SDLT as apply to purchases of freehold land (see **16.22**). The rate of SDLT on a lease premium is now 12% on any part of a lease premium above £1.5m, if the lease is of residential property. For buy-to-let residential property or additional homes, there is an additional SDLT charge of 3% (see **16.22**).

If a company (or other non-natural entity) pays a premium of over £0.5m for a lease of residential property, then there is a 15% SDLT charge over the whole of the premium. There are many exceptions to this, including for buy-to-let landlord companies and property development companies – for more details see **16.22**.

Lease premiums – VAT

[7.9] The VAT treatment of a lease premium depends chiefly on whether the property is residential or non-residential property.

Residential property

[7.10] A lease premium will be zero-rated where all of the following three conditions are satisfied.

(1)   The premium must represent consideration for the first grant of a 'major interest' in the property (in England, Wales and Northern Ireland, this requires a lease term of more than 21 years, in Scotland of at least 20 years).

(2)   The lease must be for a property designed as one or more 'dwellings', or intended to be used solely for a 'relevant residential purpose' or for a 'relevant charitable purpose' (see CHAPTER 15 para **15.155** ff for definitions of these terms).

(3)   The landlord must be the person who constructed the building/part of the building (either the actual developer or the person who commissioned the construction work) or the person who converted the building/part of the building from non-residential use into dwellings or for use solely for a relevant residential purpose (VATA 1994, s 96, Sch 8, Group 5, Item 1).

Zero-rating also applies where the building has been only partly constructed/converted and the above three tests are met. HMRC accept the former as being where a building is clearly under construction, which is typically taken to mean it has progressed beyond the foundation stage (often known as 'the golden brick'); and the latter as being where a real and meaningful start on the conversion has been made, ie more than just securing or maintaining the existing structure (HMRC Notice 708, paras 4.7.4, 5.7.3).

Zero-rating also applies to any building which is more than ten years old and has not been lived in during the ten years immediately preceding the moment when the 'person constructing' grants the first major interest in the renovated building, for use as a dwelling or for a relevant residential purpose (VATA 1994, s 96, Sch 8 Group 5; HMRC Notice 708, paras 5.3.2–5.3.4).

In all other cases, the premium for a lease of residential property will be consideration for a supply that is exempt for VAT purposes (VATA 1994, Sch 9, Group 1, Item 1).

HMRC accept that supplies between members of a VAT group can be ignored for the purposes of determining whether the first grant has been made. However, the company making the grant must be the person who has constructed/converted in order for the grant to be zero-rated – a member of the same VAT group would not be sufficient.

The fact that a building may have been used for short-term letting in between construction and sale does not preclude the first grant of a major interest being zero-rated. In recognition of the fact that recent market conditions have led to property developers having to rent unsold dwellings for a period, HMRC have published guidance on the recovery of input tax in these circumstances (VAT Information Sheet 07/08).

Non-residential property

[7.11] A premium for the grant of a lease of non-residential property will be consideration for an exempt supply, unless the landlord has opted to tax. If an option to tax has been exercised, the premium will be standard-rated. It should be noted that an option to tax cannot apply to residential buildings.

For detailed discussion of the option to tax see **CHAPTER 15** at paras **15.64–15.120** ff.

Exceptions are premiums for grants of leases and other interests in land (other than the freehold) which are always standard-rated, such as car parking facilities.

Buildings intended to be used for a 'relevant charitable purpose', such as a village hall, are dealt with under the residential heading.

Example 3

Red Baron Property Developments Limited commissions the construction of a shop in England with two flats above. It grants a ten-year lease of the shop to Biggles Limited, a 20-year lease of flat 1 to Algie, and a 30-year lease of flat 2 to Ginger.

The VAT treatment of the premiums paid for the leases will be as follows:

Leaseholder	No option to tax made	Option to tax made
Biggles Limited	Exempt	Standard-rated
Algie	Exempt	Exempt
Ginger	Zero-rated	Zero-rated

Corporation tax, capital gains tax and income tax – general rules

[7.12] In the absence of special rules, a lease premium would be treated as a capital payment by the tenant and a capital receipt by the landlord. The grant of a lease would be considered a wholly capital transaction for tax purposes. To prevent the multitude of tax planning opportunities this would leave, a premium for the grant of a lease of 50 years or less is deemed to be part income, not entirely capital. The non-capital element is taxed as income of a UK property business, so the rule effectively deems a lease premium to be a partial prepayment of rent. The shorter the lease, the more a premium is treated as income in the hands of the recipient, so that a premium for a one-year lease is all deemed rental income. Conceptually, this makes sense, as a premium for a five-year lease feels much more like a (possibly disguised) payment of rent than a premium paid for a 40-year lease.

For income tax and corporation tax purposes, the grant of a lease for a premium requires two calculations – one for the deemed rental income, the other for the capital gain or loss arising.

If a new lease, granted for a premium, has a term (see **7.3** above) of more than 50 years, there will be no deemed rental income and only a capital gains calculation to do. If a new lease, granted for a premium, has a term of less than two years, there will be no capital gains calculation and the whole of the receipt will be taxable as rental income.

Where a lease granted for a premium has a term of between two years and 50 years, the short lease premium formula comes into play. The way the formula works, the lease premium is assumed to be taxable as rental income, but for each complete year of the lease except the first, 2% of the premium is excluded from the amount taxed as rent (CTA 2009, s 217; ITTOIA 2005, s 277). This calculation can be seen in action in the two examples below.

Example 4A

On 1 May 1991 Boz Limited grants a 30-year lease to Spy Limited for a premium of £20,000 and annual rent of £5,000. Boz Limited has capital gains base cost in the property of £30,000. After the lease is granted, the interest Boz Limited retains is valued at £180,000.

Boz Limited has rental income of:

£20,000 – (2% × (30 – 1) × £20,000) = £8,400

The remainder of the receipt is capital gains disposal proceeds and the part disposal formula must be used. The basis of this, and the A/(A+B) formula used in the calculation of base cost for part disposals, are described at **CHAPTER 14** para 14.27 ff. The novel point where short lease premiums are concerned is that the 'A' which is the numerator of the fraction should exclude the amount of the premium assessable as rental income.

For short leases, the formula is often written a/(A+B) where the numerator 'a' is the amount taxable as capital gains proceeds (ie the premium excluding the deemed rental income), 'A' is the whole amount of the premium received, and 'B' is the value of the reversion (the interest retained by the recipient which is subject to, and has the benefit of the income from, the new lease).

Example 4A (continued)

The capital gain assessable on Boz Limited is:

	£
Proceeds £20,000 – £8,400	11,600
Base cost: $£30,000 \times \dfrac{11,600}{20,000+180,000}$	(1,740)
Gain before indexation allowance, etc	9,860

Example 5A

On 1 May 2001 Hogarth Limited grants a 20-year lease to Gilray Limited at a premium of £70,000 and annual rent of £5,000. After the lease is granted, the interest retained by Hogarth Limited is valued at £130,000. Hogarth Limited has base cost in the land of £500,000.

Hogarth Limited has rental income of:

£70,000 – (2% × (20 – 1) × £70,000) = £43,400

The remainder of the receipt is taxed as capital gains disposal proceeds, calculated as follows:

		£
Proceeds £70,000 – £43,400		26,600
Base cost:	$£500,000 \times \dfrac{26,600}{70,000 + 130,000}$	(66,500)
Capital loss		(39,900)

Income tax/corporation tax relief for payer of premium for short lease

[7.13] A certain symmetry can be found in the way that a tenant paying a premium on grant of a short lease is able to obtain relief for part of that premium. In one way this is unusual – a lease premium is clearly capital in nature, but remember that the short lease premium rules (CTA 2009, s 217; ITTOIA 2005, s 277) operate to tax part of the lease premium as income on the landlord. A corresponding deduction is available to the tenant, although the symmetry does not extend to the timing of the tax relief for the tenant. The landlord is taxed upfront on the appropriate percentage of the premium as rental income. The tenant is able to claim a deduction for the amount being assessed on the landlord as rent, but the deduction has to be spread evenly over the term of the lease. (No deduction is available to the tenant for the capital gains element of the premium.) The deduction is given to a corporation taxpayer by CTA 2009, s 63 if the tenant is trading from the property, or by CTA 2009, s 232 if the tenant has taken the lease for the purposes of a property rental business. If the tenant is an income taxpayer the deduction is given by ITTOIA 2005, s 61 or by ITTOIA 2005, s 292.

Examples 4A and 5A (continued)

In Example 4A above, Spy Limited would be entitled to short lease premium relief of £8,400/30 = £280 each year.

In Example 5A above, Gilray Limited would be entitled to annual short lease premium relief of £43,400/20 = £2,170.

For leases granted after 1 April 2013, the tenant is unable to claim a deduction for the amount assessed on the landlord as rent if the lease has a term longer than 50 years but is treated as being a short lease for corporation tax purposes. A long lease would be treated as a short lease for tax purposes if it was unlikely to endure beyond a date less than 50 years from commencement (see **7.6** above). The new legislation giving effect to this rule is in CTA 2009, s 232(4A), (4B) for companies with a property business and s 63(5A) for trading companies. The equivalent income tax rules are in ITTOIA 2005, s 292(4A), (4B) and s 61(5A).

Example 6

The Solzhenitzyn Trust is a UK public sector body exempt from corporation tax, income tax and capital gains tax. It grants a lease for 100 years to Denisovich Limited. The lease has a break clause after 10 years at the option of the tenant. The lease document contains an obligation on the part of the tenant Denisovich Limited to construct a new cancer hospital on the demised land. Applying CTA 2009, s 243 the lease is only 10 years in duration for tax purposes. Applying CTA 2009, s 218 (see 7.16 below) the value by which the landlord's estate is enhanced by the construction works is a deemed lease premium assessable on the landlord (but because of the Trust's exemptions, no tax is payable). Denisovich Limited would still be entitled to the short lease premium relief under CTA 2009, s 232 were it not for s 232(4A) and (4B) – the relief is denied because the lease has a term longer than 50 years and, for the purposes of establishing entitlement to short lease premium relief, the break clause must be ignored.

Continuity of short lease premium relief

[7.14] On assignment of a lease from the original tenant to another person, it is common for the short lease premium relief to be forgotten. Whether the person acquiring the lease pays the original tenant for the assignment of the lease, or whether the assignor makes a payment on assignment, the right to claim the short lease premium relief passes to the new tenant under the existing lease – despite the fact that the new tenant did not pay the premium. CTA 2009, s 63(3)(b) is clear that the person who occupies the land and is entitled to 'the taxed lease' is the person who can claim the short lease premium relief for the period for which he is so entitled. A 'taxed lease' as defined by CTA 2009, s 227(4) is the lease on the grant of which the landlord was originally taxed on an actual or deemed lease premium.

Short lease granted out of a short lease

[7.15] When a short lease is granted by a landlord to a tenant for a premium, the landlord will have some UK property income and a capital gains receipt. If the tenant subsequently grants a sublease out of that short leasehold interest, also for a premium, the tenant is then treated as itself having a mixed receipt of deemed rental income and capital gains proceeds. The calculation of the taxable premium received by the tenant from the subtenant is complicated by the fact that a premium was paid by the tenant on the headlease. Without a special rule for this scenario, the tenant would have the usual calculation of deemed rental income on receipt of the premium for the sublease, and continue to claim the short lease premium relief each year in respect of its headlease. Instead, the legislation entitles the tenant to set any unrelieved short lease premium relief that it has in relation to the headlease against the deemed rental element of the premium on the sublease – to the extent that the lease terms overlap (CTA 2009, s 228; ITTOIA 2005, s 288).

The landlord is unaffected by his tenant granting a sublease.

The premium received by the tenant on grant of the sublease, to the extent that it is taxable as rent, reduces short lease premium relief being claimed by the tenant in relation to the headlease before it actually gives rise to a chargeable amount. Any excess short lease premium relief can continue to be claimed by the tenant. The simplified legislation on this matter in CTA 2009, ss 227–233 goes to some length in stating this result. Cursory inspection of the formulae and definitions will be inadequate for non-logicians.

The capital gains element of the premium received by the tenant for the sublease is taxable as capital gains disposal proceeds. The capital gains element of the premium paid on the headlease can be set against it as eligible capital gains base cost, although that base cost must be reduced in accordance with the 'wasting' formula in TCGA 1992, Sch 8 (see **CHAPTER 14** at para **14.22** for a fuller explanation of the rules for wasting assets). For leases the wasting assets rules are complemented by a formula which ensures that the base cost does not waste in a straight-line manner. Rather, the table in TCGA 1992, Sch 8, para 1 wastes the base cost of a lease according to a curvilinear formula. For example, after five years of a 40-year lease, 96% of the premium remains as eligible capital gains base cost. After 35 years of that lease, only 28% of the base cost is left.

The following examples show the way the formulae work for calculating the income tax or corporation tax position for a short lease granted out of a short lease, and the way the capital gains part disposal and lease wasting rules are applied.

Example 4B

Following on from Example 4A above, the tenant Spy Limited grants a sublease to May Limited for ten years on 1 May 2005 for a premium of £40,000.

The deemed rental income is:

	£
Premium received	40,000
Less: allowable reduction	
2% × (10 − 1) × 40,000	(7,200)
	32,800
Less: deemed rental element of premium for headlease	
£8,400 × 10/30	(2,800)
Amount of premium taxable as rental income	30,000

The short lease premium relief that May Limited can claim is £32,800 spread over ten years, ie £3,280 per year.

The short lease premium relief that Spy Limited can claim during the term of the ten-year lease to May Limited is nil – the relief has all been utilised in sheltering part of the deemed rental income arising on the premium from May Limited. When the sublease expires in 2015, Spy Limited will again be able to claim its £280 of short lease premium relief annually until its headlease expires in 2021.

Spy Limited makes a capital gain on the grant of the sublease, calculated as follows.

	£
Premium received	40,000
Less: Allowable base cost:	
$£20,000 \times \dfrac{64.116 - 31.95}{87.330}$ (W1)	(7,539)
Capital gain (ignoring indexation)	32,461
Less: amount assessed as rental income	(30,000)
Taxable gain before any reliefs	2,461

W1 (figures from table in TCGA 1992, Sch 8)

Occasion	Years	%
Grant of headlease	30	87.330
Grant of sublease	16	64.116
Expiry of sublease	6	31.195

Note that the amount of the premium assessable as rental income is the final figure deducted in arriving at the gain. It can only reduce a gain; it cannot create or enhance a loss (TCGA 1992, Sch 8, para 5).

Example 5B

Following on from Example 5A above, the tenant Gilray Limited grants a sublease to Bell Limited for ten years for a premium of £10,000 on 1 May 2005.

The deemed rental income assessable on Gilray Limited is:

	£
Premium received	10,000
Less: allowable reduction	
2% × (10 – 1) × £10,000	(1,800)
	8,200
Less: deemed rental element of premium for headlease	
£43,400 × 10/20	(21,700)
Amount of short lease premium relief remaining	13,500

The short lease premium relief that Bell Limited can claim is £8,200 spread over ten years, ie £820 each year.

The short lease premium relief that Gilray Limited can claim is £1,350 each year for the ten-year term of the sublease. This is equal to the annual deduction for £2,170 that would have been due, less the deemed rental income calculated on the grant of the sublease (£8,200 spread over the ten years of the sublease). Once the ten-year sublease has ended, the annual short lease premium relief Gilray Limited can claim will revert to £2,170 for the remainder of the term of the headlease. (Note that if Gilray Limited had not paid a premium for its headlease, the £8,200 would all have been taxed in the year the sublease was granted.)

Gilray Limited makes a capital loss on the grant of the sublease to Bell Limited, calculated as follows.

	£
Premium received	10,000
Less: Allowable base cost:	
$£70,000 \times \dfrac{64.116 - 31.195}{72.770}$(W1)	(31,668)
Capital loss	(21,668)
Adjust for: remaining short lease premium relief	13,500
Allowable capital loss	(8,168)

W1 (figures from table in TCGA 1992, Sch 8)

Occasion	Years	%
Grant of headlease	20	72.770
Grant of sublease	16	64.116
Expiry of sublease	6	31.195

Note that the excess short lease premium relief remaining, after the deemed rental income on the sublease premium is sheltered, is adjusted for in the calculation of the allowable capital loss (TCGA 1992, Sch 8, para 6). This can only reduce the loss; it cannot create or enhance a capital gain.

Deemed lease premiums

[7.16] In addition to the straightforward situation where a landlord is treated as having taxable rental income derived from a premium paid for a short lease, there are seven other circumstances in which a landlord can find himself with deemed rental income:

(1) Where the terms of a lease of 50 years or less require the tenant to carry out works to the property.
The increase in the value of the landlord's estate is the amount of the deemed premium for the short lease. (Note that works which would be treated as repairs if incurred by the landlord do not trigger this provision.)

Example 7

> Consider these circumstances: Cuillin Limited wants a 20-year lease over a new office building, not yet built. The landlord, Torridon Limited, could build the new offices, and then lease them to Cuillin Limited for 20 years in return for a premium. Torridon Limited would be taxed on 62% of the premium immediately; only 38% would be taxed as a capital gains receipt. This is poor tax planning for Torridon Limited as no base cost can be set against the deemed rental element of the premium, and any capital loss arising cannot be set against the taxable rental income.
>
> If instead Torridon Limited and Cuillin Limited agreed that a smaller premium would be paid for the bare land and the tenant Cuillin Limited agreed to build a new office on the land, the economics would seem to be broadly the same, but Torridon Limited would have paid less tax. To correct this, CTA 2009, s 218 treats the value by which Torridon's land is to be enhanced by Cuillin's construction works as a lease premium received by Torridon Limited, additional to any actual premium payable by the tenant for the lease. (ITTOIA 2005, s 278 achieves the same result for income tax purposes.)

Note that there is no SDLT on the value of construction works carried out by a tenant on the land he has leased (FA 2003, Sch 4, para 10) provided the works are carried out after the 'effective date' of the lease (see CHAPTER 16 para **16.4** ff).

(2)   Where the terms of a lease of 50 years or less require the tenant to pay the landlord a sum instead of part of the rent for some year or years of the lease.

   The amount payable instead of the rent is treated as a lease premium for a lease deemed to be of length equal to the period for which the rent is reduced (CTA 2009, s 219; ITTOIA 2005, s 279). The amount not taxable as rental income will be taxable as capital gains proceeds (TCGA 1992, Sch 8, para 3(2)).

(3)   For a lease of 50 years or less, where the terms subject to which it is granted provide for the tenant to make a payment to the landlord in the event of surrendering the lease (CTA 2009, s 220; ITTOIA 2005, s 280).

   The amount payable on surrender is a deemed lease premium in the year the sum is paid (see **7.30** below). The lease for the purposes of this calculation is its length at commencement. The amount not taxable as rental income will be taxable as capital gains proceeds (TCGA 1992, Sch 8, para 3(2)).

(4)   Where a sum is payable by the tenant for variation of a term of the lease, or where the tenant makes a payment for the waiver of a term of the lease (CTA 2009, s 221; ITTOIA 2005, s 281).

   The amount paid is treated as a premium for a lease with length equal to the period for which the variation has effect (see **7.55** below for an example of this.) The amount not taxable as rental income will be taxable as capital gains disposal proceeds (TCGA 1992, Sch 8, para 3(3)).

(5) Where a lease is assigned for a profit having previously been granted at an undervalue (CTA 2009, s 222; ITTOIA 2005, s 282). This is an anti-avoidance provision, preventing someone escaping a tax charge on a lease premium through the use of artificial transactions.

The lower of the profit on assignment and the undervalue at which the lease was granted is treated for income tax and corporation tax purposes as a premium for a lease whose length is its length at commencement. This provision is made more complicated if there are multiple assignments of the lease.

(6) Where land is sold with the right to buy it back later for a lower price (CTA 2009, s 224; ITTOIA 2005, s 284). This rule prevents the avoidance in the following example.

Example 8

Lawson Limited is a landlord which leases its property to Capaldi Limited. The lease has 100 years unexpired. The annual rent is £250,000. MacKay Limited has £2m to invest and requires a fixed income stream. It offers Lawson Limited a £2m premium for an overriding ten-year lease of the property, such that he would become the immediate landlord of Capaldi Limited for ten years. If Lawson Limited accepted, it would have a large premium for a short lease, most of which would be taxable as income. Instead it offers to sell the freehold of the property to MacKay Limited for £10m (a capital gains transaction) and buy it back ten years later for £8m.

CTA 2009, s 224 would catch this transaction (or ITTOIA 2005, s 284 for income tax purposes) and impose a tax charge on the landlord in the period when the land is sold. There is a deemed short lease premium equal to the amount by which the sum received for sale of the land exceeds the repurchase price. The length of the deemed lease is equal to the period between sale of the land and the earliest date it could be bought back. In this case, Lawson Limited would be treated as though in receipt of a £2m premium for a ten-year lease.

(7) Another anti-avoidance provision: where land is sold with the promise of the grant of a lease back to the seller (unless the lease back is granted within a month). The legislation is in CTA 2009, s 225 and ITTOIA 2005, s 285.

There are other conditions for the application of this rule: the land must be sold for more than the premium (if any) for the leaseback; the land must also be sold for more than the value of the right to buy back the land immediately after the lease is granted. This provision is to prevent tax avoidance through artificial transactions, such as the following example.

Example 9

Jules owns freehold land. Butch would like to lease the land for 20 years and is prepared to pay a premium. Instead Jules proposes that the land be sold to Butch for £5m, but with Jules having the right to take a 100-year leaseback of the property starting in 20 years' time for a premium of £4m. There is no right to repurchase the freehold reversion after the grant of the 100-year lease, but if there were it would be valued at £100,000. ITTOIA 2005, s 285 would catch this transaction and impose taxable rental income on Jules – who would be treated as though in receipt of a £900,000 premium for a 20-year lease.

Short lease premium relief is available for deemed lease premiums, just as it is for an actual lease premium. The relief needs to be spread over an appropriate period, and the conditions of CTA 2009, s 63 or 232 (or ITTOIA 2005, s 61 or 292) must be fulfilled, in particular those of entitlement to the lease and occupation of the land during the relevant period. If the lease has a term longer than 50 years but is treated as 'short' for tax purposes, the tenant will be unable to claim short lease premium relief for leases granted after 1 April 2013 (CTA 2009, s 232(4A), (4B); ITTOIA 2005, s 292 (4A), (4B)). See Example 6 at **7.13** above.

Grant of new lease for a premium – capital allowances

[7.17] The grant of a lease for a premium is generally of no consequence for capital allowances purposes.

Owners of enterprise zone property should note that the grant of a lease for a premium can give rise to a clawback (though not a balancing allowance) if the lease is granted within seven years of the first use of the building (FA 2008, Sch 27, para 31). See **CHAPTER 9** para **9.51** for more details.

Example 10

Hannibal Limited incurred £8m of enterprise zone qualifying expenditure on a vehicle workshop in 2009. 100% initial allowances were claimed in that year so the residue of expenditure is nil. Since 2009, Hannibal Limited has seen the market value of its freehold land increase to £11m. A sale of the freehold to Murdoch Limited in 2014 would give rise to a balancing charge of £8m, ie the whole of the allowances claimed. Similarly, the grant by Hannibal Limited of a lease to Murdoch Limited for a premium of £11m would give rise to a balancing charge assessable on Hannibal Limited.

A balancing charge can only arise on the sale of the relevant interest (or the grant of a long lease for a premium out of that relevant interest) within seven years of first use of the building (FA 2008, Sch 27, para 31).

The entitlement to capital allowances on fixtures which are qualifying plant and machinery requires the taxpayer to hold an interest in the land to which the assets are fixed (see **CHAPTER 9**). The grant out of that interest of a lesser interest (say, a sublease), even for a premium, does not represent a disposal for capital allowances purposes.

When taking possession of land under a new lease, a tenant also generally takes possession of all fixtures attached to the land, some of which may qualify as plant and machinery (see **CHAPTER 9** para **9.98** ff for more details). If a lease is granted for a premium over land incorporating some qualifying fixtures, it is possible for the two parties involved to make a joint election that the transaction should be treated as a disposal by the landlord and an acquisition by the tenant for capital allowances purposes. If the plant and machinery election is made (CAA 2001, s 183) then there would be a reduction in the plant and machinery pool of the lessor and an equivalent addition to the pool of the lessee. If no election is made, there is generally no disposal and no acquisition.

Where a tenant disposes of a lease which is the relevant interest in an enterprise zone building, either to the landlord or to another party, whether for consideration or not, the disposal represents the sale of the relevant interest and a balancing adjustment will arise (if the assignment of the lease is within seven years of first use of the building).

There would also be a disposal for the purposes of calculating capital allowances on fixed plant and machinery where a lease is assigned or surrendered. This is unlikely to give rise to a balancing event unless the disposal marks the cessation of business. A just and reasonable proportion of the consideration paid (if any) for the assignment or surrender of a lease should be treated as the disposal value for the qualifying plant and machinery. If no consideration is paid for the assignment or surrender, or if payment is made by the assignor or by the surrendering tenant, the assignee cannot claim any allowances as it has incurred no capital expenditure.

An election under CAA 2001, s 198 jointly made by both parties (assuming consideration has been paid) can be made to fix the proportion of any payment which is deemed to have been paid for qualifying fixtures.

Landlord is a developer, not an investor

[7.18] There will be no capital gain if it is a property developer who is in the role of landlord when a lease is granted – his disposal will be on trading account and the capital gains rules do not apply. Instead the property developer's calculation of trading profits will be based on the accounting profit realised from the transaction. However, the rules on short lease premiums still apply and so there would be a taxable premium if the lease was for 50 years or less. To avoid double counting, CTA 2009, s 136 rides to the rescue and excludes from the developer's trading income any amount assessed as rental income under CTA 2009, s 217 et seq (ITTOIA 2005, s 158 does the same job for an income taxpayer with property income assessed under ITTOIA 2005, s 277 et seq). This means the tenant can still claim relief for the rental element of the short lease premium paid under CTA 2009, s 63 or s 232 (or under ITTOIA 2005 s 61 or s 291 as appropriate if an income taxpayer). The landlord/developer has broadly the same result as if it had sold freehold land, though there are some differences:

- When a developer grants a lease for a premium and retains a reversionary interest, there may not be any rent payable under the lease. Whether there is or not, the value of the reversion retained by the developer will lead to an appropriate proportion of the developer's cost being excluded from its cost of sales.
- It is common to have a trading loss once the amount taxable as rental income is excluded. The normal rules on relief for trading losses apply to this.

Example 11

Cale Limited has a property development trade. In 2013 Cale Limited grants Reed Limited a 26-year lease over a studio for a premium of £10m. No rent is payable. The land cost Cale Limited £1m and construction cost was £6m. The reversion (ie the interest retained by Cale Limited) is valued at £1.6m.

The accounts show a profit of £4m as follows:

Turnover	£10m	
Cost of sales:		
Cost of land plus construction		£7m
Less: cost attributable to reversionary interest retained		(£1m)
	(£6m)	
	£4m	

The amount taxable as rental income is:

£10m × 2% × (50 − (26 − 1)) = £5m

The result for the property development trade (by application of CTA 2009, s 136 or ITTOIA 2005, s 158) is:

£4m − £5m = a loss of £1m.

The £1m trading loss can be set against the rental profits in 2013 or carried forward against future profits of the same trade if there are other reliefs available in 2013.

It is not clear from the legislation, but HMRC practice is that the s 136 (or s 158) relief should not be available before the lease premium is taxed, whatever the timing of the recognition of the income in the developer's accounts or the date of grant of the leases.

Lease inducements – reverse premiums, etc

[7.19] A reverse premium is generally a cash payment made from landlord to tenant at the start of a lease. The most common scenarios in which a reverse premium is paid are:

- an out-of-town retail park signs up an anchor tenant, one who will inspire others to sign leases of adjacent retail space, to benefit from the anchor's footfall;
- a speculative development on a former industrial site or in a disadvantaged area – to attract tenants at a reasonable level of rent a landlord will probably have to pay them an inducement, to get them to commit to leases of the property.

Anchor tenants

[7.20] 'Anchor tenant' is a term with different meanings in different contexts. The term is commonly understood to mean a company with a strong rental covenant signed up by a landlord wishing to let space in a large property to multiple tenants. Once an anchor tenant is in place, the landlord hopes others will follow. The anchor tenant is often given preferential terms, or is paid a large sum when entering into the lease. The definition for VAT purposes of an anchor tenant is especially relevant. The question is whether the tenant is providing more to a landlord than a firm promise of future rental payments and some good publicity. Whether anything else is being provided can affect the VAT treatment of a payment made to the 'anchor tenant' in question.

Stamp duty land tax

[7.21] There is no SDLT to be paid on a reverse premium because the person acquiring the chargeable interest is the tenant (FA 2003, s 43(3)(a)) and the tenant is not paying any consideration (FA 2003, Sch 17A, para 18).

VAT

[7.22] For reverse premiums, the VAT rules are the same for residential and non-residential property. In most cases, a reverse premium payment from the landlord to the tenant will be outside the scope of VAT.

Where tenants enter into obligations of the sort that are normal for tenants, the reverse premium does not represent a supply for VAT purposes (VAT Notice 742, para 10.1). This effectively means that reverse premium payments have the same VAT effect as rent-free periods.

There will only be a supply where the payment of a reverse premium by the landlord is linked to a benefit provided by the tenant outside normal lease terms. HMRC give three examples (Business Brief 12/05):

(1)   Where the tenant carries out building works to improve the property by undertaking necessary repairs or upgrading, beyond the usual repairing obligations or the tenant's fit-out of the property.
(2)   Where the tenant carries out fitting-out or refurbishment works which were the landlord's responsibility.
(3)   Where the tenant acts as an 'anchor tenant'.

In order to be an anchor tenant, HMRC suggest that the tenant must have agreed to act as such, allowing the landlord the right to use their tenancy to market the property. The mere mentioning of the tenant in the marketing material for the property is not sufficient.

A more detailed discussion on the VAT implications of reverse premiums can be found in CHAPTER 15, para **15.187** ff.

Corporation tax and income tax

[7.23] For corporation tax purposes, the receipt of a payment in return for entering into a lease is taxable, unless it is exempt for one of the reasons stated below. CTA 2009, s 98 (or ITTOIA 2005, s 99 for an income taxpayer) taxes as income any receipt from a landlord (or connected person) or anyone acting on the landlord's instructions. If the tenant is a trading company, the receipt will be taxable as trading income; if the tenant is a property investor, the receipt will be taxable as rental income (CTA 2009, s 250).

If the landlord and tenant are connected, a reverse premium received will be taxed in the period of receipt. Otherwise, it will be taxed in line with its recognition as income in the accounts of the recipient company. The accounting treatment of such a receipt is governed by UITF28, if accounts are being prepared under 'old' UK GAAP. This recommends spreading the receipt over the period for which (it is assumed that) the tenant is paying an increased level of rent – above the level that would have been negotiated between the parties had the reverse premium not been on offer. Typically this will mean spreading the profit and loss account benefit of the reverse premium over the period of the lease up to the first rent review – often at the fifth anniversary of the grant of the lease. If the relevant accounting rules are satisfied, and the lease has no rent review dates and contains no unusual provisions, a reverse premium could potentially be spread over the whole term of a lease. If a company's accounts are being prepared under International Accounting Standards or under 'new' UK GAAP (FRS102), a reverse premium would generally be recognised as income over the full term of the lease, and the tax treatment would be expected to follow this accounting treatment. Companies converting to FRS102 accounts or to IFRS accounts will need to take into account the impact of these different rules on the timing of income recognition.

Non-standard reverse premiums

[7.24] A straightforward payment of cash to a new tenant to induce them to take a lease of a building is taxable as income under the rules set out in **7.23** above. CTA 2009, s 96(2) specifically refers to the receipt of a 'payment or other benefit' as the trigger for a tax charge. HMRC recognise that some lease inducements that could be construed as reverse premiums do not fall within the scope of those words, and can be treated as tax-free.

For example, HMRC have stated that a payment made from landlord to tenant to complete the construction of an unfinished building is not taxable as a reverse premium, notwithstanding that the relevant expenditure will not qualify for capital allowances (HMRC Business Income Manual, 41085). If an addition to the building enhances the value of the landlord's reversion, and would generally be taken into account when setting the market rent at a rent review, then it is probably part of the construction of the building, not part of the fit-out. If work on the building fails those tests, it is probably part of the fit-out and a payment to fund it would be within para 1(a) of the reverse premium rules for the recipient. Contributions to a tenant's fit-out expenditure are dealt with further at **7.25** below.

The benefit to a tenant of a rent-free period is not treated as a taxable reverse premium (HMRC Business Income Manual, 41075, 41080); see Example 12 below. Essentially, only if cash is paid by the landlord to the tenant, or if the landlord assumes or satisfies a liability of the tenant, will the reverse premium rules bite. In particular, if a tenant moves premises, and the new landlord pays a debt the tenant owes to the old landlord, or agrees to pay the tenant's rent for the remainder of the old lease, that would represent a taxable reverse premium on grant of the new lease. On the other hand, if a landlord agrees to replace a lease which a tenant finds onerous (eg because the rent is proving too expensive) with a new lease with lighter obligations (eg lower rent) the benefit to the tenant of that arrangement will not be treated as a taxable reverse premium, however it is accounted for.

Note that a payment by an existing tenant to a company or individual to get them to accept an assignment of an existing lease does not fall within the definition of a reverse premium – see **7.41** ff below.

Capital allowances

[7.25] A lease inducement escapes being taxed as a reverse premium if it is taken into account in calculating the tenant's entitlement to capital allowances (CTA 2009, s 97(1)). To fall within this, the payment must be structured as a contribution by a landlord to the tenant's cost of fitting out the property.

Example 12

Ukridge Limited is a landlord of a large shopping centre. It would like to secure Threepwood Limited as a tenant at a rent of £100,000 per annum. Threepwood Limited requires an inducement of £150,000 before signing up to the lease. The lease is duly signed, with Ukridge Limited being required to make a £150,000 payment on the day of commencement. This is taxable as a reverse premium on Threepwood Limited under CTA 2009, s 96 however it uses the receipt. In its 'old' UK GAAP accounts and its tax computations it will be spread evenly over the period of the lease up to the first rent review. Threepwood Limited spends £80,000 of the receipt on fitting out the store but this does not change the tax treatment of the receipt.

As a well-known department store, the presence of Threepwood Limited will attract other tenants to the centre. Threepwood Limited agrees that Ukridge Limited may market the remaining units on this basis. In this case, Threepwood Limited appears to be acting as an 'anchor tenant' and the £150,000 inducement payment will be subject to VAT. Ukridge Limited is likely to have opted to tax, so should be able to recover this VAT. If the contract is silent on VAT, the inducement payment will be deemed to be VAT-inclusive, and Threepwood Limited will have to account to HMRC for £25,000 of the receipt, without being able to pass the cost on to Ukridge Limited.

Pirbright Limited agrees to take a 20-year lease of the adjoining unit at a fixed annual rent of £175,000. Pirbright Limited negotiates a £200,000 sweetener from Ukridge Limited, stated in the agreement for lease to be a contribution to Pirbright's costs of fitting out the new premises. Pirbright Limited spends £300,000 on fit-out works, of which 75% is agreed to qualify for capital allowances. £150,000 of the £200,000 contribution reduces the capital allowances that Pirbright Limited can claim (CTA 2009, s 97(1)). The remaining £50,000 is treated as a reverse premium, taxable over the term of the 20-year lease, following the treatment in

Pirbright's accounts prepared under FRS102 ('new' UK GAAP). Ukridge Limited is entitled to capital allowances on £150,000 under the contribution allowances rules (CAA 2001, s 538).

Pirbright Limited is not an anchor tenant so the VAT treatment of the payment will depend on whether the cost of its fit-out is a cost that a landlord would normally be expected to incur. If this is the case, the payment will be VATable. Otherwise, the payment will be outside the scope of VAT.

Psmith Limited wishes to take a 20-year lease of a unit in the shopping centre. It negotiates a rent-free period of 18 months and a rent of £120,000 per annum, being reviewed to market rent after ten years. A rent-free period is not treated as a taxable reverse premium for corporation tax purposes. Psmith Limited prepares IFRS accounts (rather than UK GAAP) so will spread the effective value of the rent-free period (£180,000) in its accounts across the whole 20-year term of the lease, ie each year's accounts will contain an expense for rent payable of £111,000. This represents an acceleration of the tenant's tax relief for the rent. The landlord should have the opposite position, so he will face the problem of initially paying tax on rent not yet received – though this is probably preferable to paying a reverse premium which is not deductible at all against rental profits.

Provided nothing tangible is given in return the rent-free period need not be treated as a barter and no supply has been made for VAT purposes.

Payer of reverse premium

[7.26] A landlord, who is a property investor, does not obtain a deduction from rental profits for the payment of a reverse premium. This is because it is regarded as a capital payment – being expenditure on (enhancing the value of) an identifiable asset, namely the landlord's own interest in the land. The landlord may well be able to obtain a deduction for the reverse premium paid in the event of a disposal of his interest in the property. In the capital gains calculation, the landlord may deduct his acquisition cost of the property and also any enhancement expenditure on that asset. The payment of a reverse premium should represent eligible enhancement expenditure (TCGA 1992, s 38(1)(b)) so long as the tenant remains in occupation of the property under the terms of that lease.

Payer of reverse premium is developer, not investor

[7.27] The tax treatment of a property developer (taxable as a trader, not a property investor) paying a reverse premium is different. A property developer will generally be seeking to sell his property to a property investor. Whatever the stage of development when the investor commits to purchasing it, the investor would certainly prefer the property to be tenanted, or to have tenants-in-waiting who have committed to signing leases when the property is complete. Securing tenants for the property enables or eases the developer's sale of the property. Consequently, the payment of a reverse premium is wholly and exclusively for the purposes of his trade, and so deductible from trading profits in line with his accounts.

Construction Industry Scheme (CIS)

[7.28] Reverse premiums are specifically excluded from the CIS regime (Income Tax (Construction Industry Scheme) Regulations 2005, SI 2005/2045). If the payment falls within the definition of reverse premium in CTA 2009, s 96, or within the exclusion of s 97(1), the CIS need not be operated on it (reg 20).

Lease surrender (payment from tenant to landlord)

[7.29] There are a number of ways that a lease can come to an end. The most common ones are:

- expiry, usually by effluxion of time;
- merger, where the tenant acquires the landlord's interest (freehold or lease as appropriate) or the immediate landlord acquires the lease from the tenant;
- surrender, where the tenant gives up the lease to its immediate landlord.

A lease surrender payment is conventionally paid from the tenant to the landlord so that the tenant can be released from the burdensome rental liability that the lease has become. If a landlord wants a tenant out of a property and is prepared to pay the tenant to surrender its lease, that is described as a 'reverse surrender' payment (see **7.34** ff below).

If a tenant finds a lease onerous – perhaps the rent is too expensive after a market value rent review – or if the leased property is simply surplus to requirements, the tenant may be prepared to pay a large sum to the landlord for the landlord to accept a surrender of the lease.

Income tax, capital gains tax and corporation tax

[7.30] Whether the tenant is a company or business trading from the premises, or is itself a landlord with tenants, it will obtain no tax relief for the payment to the landlord. The payment of a sum to release a person from a continuing annual obligation has long been regarded as capital (*Mallett v Staveley Coal & Iron Co Limited* (1928) 13 TC 772, CA and other cases) – disallowable in the calculation of trading profits or rental profits. Further, the payment would not be an eligible deduction in the calculation of a capital gain – the payment does not represent acquisition cost, expenditure on enhancement or an incidental cost of disposal, and so does not fit within any of the three legs of TCGA 1992, s 38.

Although the tenant obtains no tax deduction for the payment, the landlord will be taxable on the receipt.

If the original lease contained provision for payments to be made by the tenant on early surrender, the receipt would be taxable on the landlord as a deemed lease premium (CTA 2009, s 220; ITTOIA 2005, s 280) on a lease having the same length it did at commencement. So if the lease was initially for 100 years, the payment on surrender would all be taxable on the landlord as a capital gain. If the lease was for 40 years when granted and contained provision for a payment to the landlord in the event of surrender, 22% of the payment would be treated as taxable as rental income and the remainder as capital gains disposal proceeds (TCGA 1992, Sch 8, paras 3, 5).

If the terms subject to which the lease was granted contain no provision as to payment of a sum to the landlord in the event of early surrender, the short lease premium rules will not apply and instead all of the receipt will be taxable under the capital gains legislation. It will be treated as a 'capital sum derived from an asset' (TCGA 1992, s 22), namely the landlord's own interest in the land. The landlord can set off some of his base cost against the receipt.

The landlord will be treated as having a part disposal, with his interest in land being valued after the tenant's exit, meaning that application of the A/(A+B) – or a/(A+B) – formula results in a partial set off of base cost against the receipt.

This adverse tax mismatch (landlord gets taxed, tenant has no tax relief) is unfortunate for the parties to the transaction. The problem is exacerbated if soon afterwards the landlord makes a payment of a reverse premium to a new tenant of the same property, to induce the new tenant to take up a new lease. The landlord obtains no deduction from his rental profits for the payment of a reverse premium (see **7.32** below), whereas the new tenant will be taxed on it under CTA 2009, s 96 (see Example 19A at **7.57** below). This double adverse tax mismatch is not uncommon, and the tax leakage does not ease the negotiations of the parties involved in the transactions.

There may be alternative ways for a tenant to structure their exit from a lease.

(1)   For example, if the tenant is liable for dilapidations to the property during the tenancy, a payment to the landlord in lieu of doing the repairs would generally be deductible for the tenant. The liability to make good dilapidations (tax deductible) is often forgotten in the negotiation of a payment to get the landlord to accept a surrender of the lease (not deductible) and ensuring that the tenant has no ongoing liability to the landlord (including any liability for dilapidations).

(2)   Instead of surrendering the lease to the landlord, the tenant could sublet the property, if it has landlord's consent to do so, and if a willing subtenant can be found. Often this will be more tax-efficient – and the tax relief should accrue at the start of the sublease, while the economic loss is deferred over its term. (A loss arising on the sublease of surplus premises is a deductible expense, following the decision in *IRC v Falkirk Iron Co Limited* (1933) 17 TC 625, CS.)

Example 13

Morrissey Limited leases premises from Gedge Limited under a 30-year lease granted in 2003 at an annual rent of £25,000. Morrissey's business has suffered lately and it is struggling to remain profitable in such expensive premises. Gedge Limited has refused to accept a lease surrender. Marr & Co have indicated that they would be prepared to sublease the property for 20 years at £20,000 per annum. In 2013 Morrissey Limited grants the sublease to Marr & Co and continues to trade from other (cheaper) premises. Morrissey Limited can foresee a rental loss of £5,000 per annum on the lease from Gedge Limited for the remaining 20 years of the headlease. Under FRS12 (also under FRS102 if adopting 'new' UK GAAP) Morrissey Limited is obliged to provide for the whole of this loss in its accounts as soon as the liability arises. It should be deductible against the profits of its trade in the year the sublease is granted.

(3)   Another possibility is that a tenant wishing to exit a lease could assign it directly to a new tenant prepared to take on the rental obligation. The landlord may give permission for this if the lease does not already include a right for the tenant to assign. For the new tenant, the receipt from the old tenant should be tax-free – it is not caught by the short lease premium rules, it is not rent, it does not fall within the definition of a reverse premium in CTA 2009, s 96 and for the capital gains rules it is not a capital sum derived from an asset because the new tenant had no relevant asset. The tax-free status of the receipt might mean the outgoing tenant can negotiate the payment of a lower amount, and so share in the tax-efficiency.

(4)   A tenant wishing to exit a lease could seek the landlord's agreement to a variation to the lease, perhaps along the lines of that in Example 17. This could result in early termination becoming possible in a more tax-efficient manner.

Stamp duty land tax

[7.31] If a payment is made by the tenant to get the landlord to accept the surrender there will be no SDLT on the transaction. This is because the person making the payment is not acquiring a chargeable interest in land. The acquirer is the landlord, who is paying no consideration for it.

VAT

Residential property

[7.32] A lease surrender payment is treated as consideration for an exempt supply by the landlord to the tenant.

Non-residential property

[7.33] A lease surrender payment is treated as consideration for a supply by the landlord to the tenant. This will be exempt, unless the landlord has opted to tax its interest in the property, in which case it will be standard-rated (VATA 1994, Sch 9, Group 1, Note 1A).

In both cases, however, a payment from the tenant at the end of the lease may not relate to a lease surrender. A tenant may be required under the lease to return the property in a certain state. To avoid these costs, the tenant may instead make a compensatory payment to the landlord for failing to carry out this term of the lease. HMRC consider such a 'dilapidations payment' to be outside the scope of VAT. (HMRC Notice 742, para 10.12)

An alternative to surrendering the lease would be for the tenant to sublet the property. For residential property, any premium paid by the subtenant under this sublease would be exempt (as the tenant would not have 'person constructing/converting' status). For non-residential property, any premium paid by the subtenant would be exempt, subject to the tenant's option to tax.

Reverse surrender of lease (payment from landlord to tenant)

[7.34] It is not uncommon for a landlord to want a tenant out of a property. The landlord may wish to sell the property with vacant possession, or there might be an opportunity to redevelop an old industrial site for housing. Until the recent recessions, landlords of commercial property were sometimes keen to be rid of longer-term tenants on fixed rents agreed long ago. It can be worthwhile for the landlord to pay such a tenant to get them to surrender their lease. Then the landlord can install a new tenant at a higher annual rent, which means higher income for the landlord, increased capital value of the property and so enhanced capacity to borrow against it. It also means that the higher rent payable by the new tenant can be put forward as evidence when the landlord is in negotiations with the tenant next door over the market value rent review due under the terms of their lease.

Income tax, capital gains tax and corporation tax

[7.35] For the tenant, an amount received in return for surrender of the lease is a capital sum received for the disposal of a fixed asset – a capital gains receipt for tax purposes. The tenant may deduct eligible capital gains base cost from the amount received. This would include the capital gains element of any premium paid for the lease, appropriately wasted according to the table in TCGA 1992, Sch 8. It would also include any enhancement expenditure fulfilling the criteria of TCGA 1992, s 38(1)(b). Any short lease premium relief not claimed because the lease has terminated early is extinguished and is left unclaimed.

One complication with this calculation for the tenant is that if the lease is a wasting asset (50 years or less unexpired at the time of surrender) there may need to be two separate calculations – one covering assets eligible for capital allowances, one covering ineligible assets. Relevant legislation is in TCGA 1992, s 47 and TCGA 1992, Sch 8, para 1(6). The calculation can become quite complicated. For a corporation taxpayer, this rule can mean that indexation allowance would be restricted even though there is a gain over all.

The rules in TCGA 1992, s 47 apply only where the asset being sold is itself a wasting asset, eg a short lease. They do not apply to a disposal of freehold land or to the grant or assignment of a lease of more than 50 years.

Note also that only enhancement expenditure still reflected in the state of the property at the time of disposal is eligible to be set off against the capital receipt.

Example 14

Gordon Limited paid a £1.4m premium to Thurston Limited, owner of a new building, for a 60-year lease in 1993, with rent of £60,000 per annum. In 1997 Gordon Limited paid £20,000 for new signage. In 2005 Gordon Limited paid £1.1m to re-fit the building – this also involved a corporate re-branding, including the replacement of all signage. 50% of the re-fit expenditure qualified for capital allowances. (Tax written down value of these assets in 2013 is £100,000.) In 2009 Gordon Limited paid £200,000 to extend the car park. Throughout, Gordon Limited has traded as a nightclub. Thurston Limited now wishes to convert the building into offices and in 2013 offers Gordon Limited £5m to surrender the lease.

Because the lease is a wasting asset at the time of its disposal in 2013, the calculation needs to be done in two parts, one for the assets qualifying for capital allowances and the other for the non-qualifying assets. Although the agreement states that £1m is payable for 'fixtures', the two parties have jointly signed an election under CAA 2001, s 198 stating that £550,000 of the £5m proceeds is deemed to be for the assets qualifying for capital allowances (which leaves £4,450,000 as the proceeds for the ineligible assets). Note that the £20,000 paid for new signage in 1997 is not eligible capital gains base cost, as it is expenditure on an enhancement which was no longer reflected in the state of the building at the time of disposal. Since the entity surrendering the lease is a company, indexation allowance is available on the disposal, but as can be seen below, the amount available is affected by the way the wasting asset rules split the calculation in two.

	£
Qualifying assets	
Proceeds (limited to cost)	550,000
Less: Cost of re-fit	(550,000)
Unindexed gain	—
Indexation allowance (restricted)	—
Capital gain on qualifying assets	—
Non-qualifying assets	
Proceeds (total less amount attributed to qualifying assets)	4,450,000
Less: Lease premium £1,400,000	
Less: $£1.4m \times \dfrac{100-95.457}{100}$	(1,336,398)
Re-fit (ineligible part) £550,000	
Less: $£550,000 \times \dfrac{99.289-95.457}{99.289}$	(528,773)
Car park £200,000	
Less: $£200,000 \times \dfrac{97.595-95.457}{97.595}$	(195,619)

Unindexed gain

Indexation allowance on the three elements of base cost (calculations not shown separately)	(1,493,296)
Gain after indexation allowance	895,914

It can be seen from the example above that if the capital allowances element of the expenditure was included along with the remainder, there would be more indexation allowance available. Indexation is restricted for the element qualifying for allowances, because indexation may not create a loss, only reduce a gain, and that rule applies for each part of the calculation. The qualifying assets also have lower deemed proceeds than their share of the sale price (because of the restriction to cost of the capital allowances disposal value, and the s 198 election). The calculation seems involved, but this example is no more complex than a simple real-life scenario.

Note that the s 198 apportionment should be used as the proceeds for the capital allowances qualifying part of the capital gain calculation, even though it could be much higher or lower than the value of the qualifying assets at the time of their sale. TCGA 1992, s 47(2)(d) says that an apportionment made for capital allowances purposes should be used for the qualifying part of the capital gain; an election under s 198 seems to result in just such an apportionment.

Position of landlord making surrender payment

[7.36] The landlord making the payment to the tenant for surrender will generally be treated as making a capital payment. This will not be deductible from the profits of the landlord's property rental business because it involves the acquisition of a capital asset, namely the tenant's lease, and enhancement of the landlord's own interest in the land.

The landlord may be able to add the payment made for surrender to their capital gains base cost in preparation for a future disposal. This will depend on the reason for wanting the tenant out of the property. For example, if a landlord could sell a tenanted property for £5m but could sell the same property with vacant possession for £10m, it is worthwhile for the landlord to pay, say, £3m to get the tenant to surrender the lease. In that case, the payment of £3m would be eligible enhancement expenditure for the purposes of TCGA 1992, s 38(1)(b). HMRC confirm in their Capital Gains Manual, 71262 that a payment by the landlord to procure surrender is eligible base cost so long as the result is reflected in the property at the time of disposal. HMRC say that if a new lease is granted to a new tenant on similar terms to the old lease, the landlord would not have enhanced the value of the property in paying for the lease surrender, and the payment would not be eligible capital gains base cost.

Stamp duty land tax

[7.37] If a 'reverse surrender' payment is made by the landlord to the tenant, the landlord will be deemed by FA 2003, s 43(3)(b) to have acquired the tenant's interest. SDLT will be charged on the amount paid by the landlord.

VAT

Residential property

[7.38] The 'reverse surrender' payment is treated as consideration for a supply by the tenant to the landlord, which would be exempt. In practice, most residential tenants are individuals and as such the surrender of a lease is unlikely to be seen as undertaken in the course of business.

Non-residential property

[7.39] The payment is treated as consideration for a supply from the tenant to the landlord. This will be an exempt supply by the tenant, unless the tenant has opted to tax its interest in the property (*Lubbock Fine & Co v Customs and Excise Comrs*, C-63/92 [1994] QB 571, [1994] 3 All ER 705, ECJ). This could give rise to an irrecoverable VAT cost to the landlord if the landlord has not opted to tax its interest in the building, and does not intend to.

Note that if the landlord does decide to opt to tax in order to recover VAT on such a supply, in spite of having made prior exempt supplies, the landlord should not require prior permission to opt to tax from HMRC, provided certain conditions are fulfilled. The conditions for this 'Automatic Permission Condition' were changed with effect from 1 May 2009. (HMRC Notice 742A, para 5.2, Condition 3, as amended by VAT Information Sheet 06/09).

Lease surrender – capital allowances

[7.40] The surrender of a lease involves the tenant in a disposal of his interest for capital allowances purposes.

If there is a payment from landlord to tenant for the surrender (a reverse surrender payment), there is a disposal value to be calculated, either by making a just and reasonable apportionment of the amount paid, or by the parties entering into a joint election under CAA 2001, s 198.

If there is no payment, or if the surrender payment is from tenant to landlord, there is a disposal value of nil, and the landlord is not entitled to claim any allowances on fixtures added to the building by the tenant, because the landlord will not have incurred any capital expenditure on them.

Lease assignments

[7.41] A lease assignment is distinct from the grant of a new lease or the termination of a lease in that it provides for the continuation of an interest in land rather than its creation or termination. Similarly, the rights and obligations provided for in the lease continue to exist, though on assignment of a lease they become vested in a new tenant.

Payment from new tenant to old tenant – VAT

[7.42] A payment from a new tenant to the old tenant for the assignment of a lease is treated as an exempt supply, subject to the assignor opting to tax (if the property is non-residential).

If the assignment is part of a wider transaction for the disposal of a business (or the property is already sublet, so that the assignment represents the sale of a property letting business), it may be possible that the assignment could be treated as part of the 'transfer of a going concern' (see CHAPTER 15 para **15.121** for full details of the implications of transferring a property business).

Where the rights and obligations of a lease are assigned, but this does not include the assignment of a right of occupation (a 'virtual assignment'), this is not a supply of an interest in land for VAT purposes, and the payments are consideration for standard-rated supplies (*Abbey National plc v Customs and Excise Comrs* [2006] EWCA Civ 886, [2006] STC 1961, [2006] NLJR 1100). For a fuller discussion on this see CHAPTER 15, para **15.11** ff.

Payment from new tenant to old tenant – stamp duty land tax

[7.43] The person acquiring the lease will have to pay SDLT at the appropriate rate on this transaction – 5% on the part of the consideration (VAT-inclusive if applicable) exceeding £250,000.

If the assignment is of a lease over residential property, the acquirer will have to pay SDLT at the same progressive rates as if it was a freehold purchase (see CHAPTER 16 at **16.22**). The rate of SDLT for any part of the consideration over £1.5m is now 12%. If the assignee is a company or other non-natural person, and the consideration is in excess of £0.5m, then the rate of SDLT is 15% on the whole consideration. There are exceptions to this for buy-to-let landlord companies, property development companies and some other taxpayers (see **16.22**). There is a 3% SDLT surcharge for purchases of buy-to-let properties and additional homes (see **16.22**).There is no SDLT to pay on the rents due under the lease as a result of the lease assignment – SDLT on rents is only payable on the grant of a new lease. There is an exception to this – where the transaction is the assignment of a lease, and there was no SDLT on its grant because of, for example, SDLT group relief (FA 2003, Sch 7). To stop avoidance of SDLT on the grant of a lease, the first non-exempt assignment is subject to SDLT as though it was the grant of the lease, if SDLT group relief was claimed on the actual grant (FA 2003, Sch 17A, para 11).

Payment from new tenant to old tenant – corporation tax, income tax and capital gains tax

[7.44] Upon assignment, someone who has occupied property under a lease will have a capital gains disposal of his interest in the property when it is assigned to a new tenant. There is no deemed rental income to calculate on the disposal because the assignment is not the grant of a new lease. Eligible base cost to set against the capital gains proceeds includes any premium paid on grant of the lease and subsequent enhancement expenditure (though base cost must be wasted in accordance with the table in TCGA 1992, Sch 8).

If the person making the payment intends to occupy the property for the purposes of a trade, or to sublet it for the purposes of a property rental business, he will obtain no deduction against his profits for the lease assignment payment. He will have eligible capital gains base cost in the event of a future disposal of the property.

If the person making the payment is a property developer, who is acquiring the lease with a view to redeveloping the site, or selling it at a profit, the payment will form part of his cost of sales and will be deductible against his trading profits.

Payment from old tenant to new tenant – VAT

[7.45] A payment from a tenant to a new prospective tenant to accept the assignment of a lease is standard-rated. The payment is consideration for a standard-rated supply of services from the new tenant to the old (*C&E Comrs v Cantor Fitzgerald International (C-108/99)*, CJEC 2001). For a fuller discussion of this see **CHAPTER 15**, para **15.11** ff.

Payment from old tenant to new tenant – stamp duty land tax

[7.46] There is no SDLT on this transaction as the person acquiring the chargeable interest in land is receiving rather than paying chargeable consideration (FA 2003, Sch 17A, para 18).

Payment from old tenant to new tenant – corporation tax, income tax and capital gains tax

[7.47] There is no corporation tax deduction for the person making the payment. The old tenant does have a capital gains disposal with nil proceeds, but the payment to the new tenant is not eligible for a deduction in the capital gains calculation. This is because it is not expenditure on the enhancement of the old tenant's lease and is not an incidental cost of disposal.

There is generally no tax liability for the recipient of the payment (the assignee) because:

- the payment is not a reverse premium – it is not paid in connection with the grant of a new lease and it is not paid by the landlord;
- it is not a capital sum derived from an asset, because the new tenant has no relevant asset until he receives the payment.

HMRC generally accept that a receipt in these circumstances is tax-free, unless the new tenant is providing some other service or giving up a right.

Example 15

Sherwin rents a shop from Shacklock under a lease with 8 years unexpired. Sherwin wishes to relocate his business to larger premises, but Shacklock is unwilling to take the risk of finding a new tenant for his property. Sherwin offers Conan an assignment of the lease; but Conan cannot afford to take on the full rental obligation. Sherwin offers Conan £100,000 if Conan will accept assignment of the lease. Conan agrees and the transaction proceeds.

Neither Sherwin nor Shacklock has any SDLT liability as neither party has paid consideration for the acquisition of a chargeable interest in land.

For corporation tax purposes, the £100,000 is not a deductible expense for Sherwin, neither in computing trading profits nor as part of the base cost (or incidental cost of disposal) in calculating Sherwin's capital loss on the assignment.

Conan's £100,000 receipt is not a reverse premium (as it does not relate to the grant of a new lease); it is not proceeds on the disposal of any capital gains asset; and Conan had no chargeable asset from which he could have derived a capital sum (TCGA 1992, s 22). Consequently, Conan's receipt escapes being taxed.

Lease variations

[7.48] It is common for leases to be varied – to permit something previously prohibited such as assignment or subletting, or to deal with changing circumstances, eg a large building being built next door. Lease variations become more relevant from a tax perspective when significant payments are made by one party to get the other to accept the changes. Usually it will be the tenant paying for the lease to be varied, and some prohibition removed.

If either the term (ie the length) of the lease is varied, or the premises demised under the lease are altered, that can be, in law, a deemed surrender of the old lease and grant of a new lease. This is potentially troublesome from a tax point of view and is usually best avoided. For example, if the term needs to be altered, the lease could instead be varied to insert a break clause, or a reversionary lease could be granted which would effectively extend the lease.

Landlord pays for variation – stamp duty land tax

[7.49] FA 2003, s 43(3)(d) states that the variation of a lease in the landlord's favour will only lead to an SDLT charge where the term of the lease is reduced or the variation is treated (for SDLT purposes) by FA 2003 as the grant of a new lease. In particular, there will be an SDLT charge where a lease is varied during its first five years such that the rent is increased (FA 2003, Sch 17A, para 13).

Although it would be the landlord making the variation payment to the tenant, to agree an increase in the tenant's rent, it is the tenant who must pay the SDLT, because FA 2003 treats this as the grant of a new lease for rent equal to the amount of the increase.

Where a lease is varied such that the term of the lease is shortened, that is deemed by FA 2003, Sch 17A, para 15A to be an acquisition of a chargeable interest in land by the landlord. If the landlord makes a payment to the tenant to achieve such a variation, the landlord must pay SDLT on that amount.

Example 16

Jack rents an ageing office building from Meg under a lease with 20 years unexpired. Meg offers to pay Jack £1m so that Jack can re-fit the building. In return Jack agrees to an increase in rent of £75,000 per annum.

Meg's payment is not a deductible expense of her property business, though it may be additional base cost in the property.

Jack's receipt is taxable as a capital sum derived from his lease. He may have some base cost to set against the receipt. Jack can be thought of as disposing of his right to continue in occupation of the property at the current (lower) level of rent, with proceeds of that disposal equal to the amount received from Meg.

Landlord pays for variation – VAT

[7.50] The payment is for a supply in relation to land from the tenant to the landlord. The payment should be treated in the same way as a payment for the surrender of a lease – exempt unless (in the case of non-residential property) the tenant has opted to tax, in which case it will be standard rated. For a fuller discussion on the VAT issues see CHAPTER 15, para 15.185 ff.

Landlord pays for variation – corporation tax, capital gains tax and income tax

[7.51] A tenant who receives a lease variation payment would be treated as in receipt of a capital sum derived from an asset (TCGA 1992, s 22), namely his lease. The tenant would be entitled to deduct part of his base cost against the receipt. The part disposal rules will apply, and the A/(A+B) formula should be used. If the lease is for 50 years or less, the wasting asset rules will apply and the base cost that can be set off will have to be reduced by the percentages in the table in TCGA 1992, Sch 8.

The landlord paying for the lease variation would not obtain a tax deduction against rental profits for such a payment, but would probably be able to add it to the base cost of the property in the event of a disposal in future: it is likely that the landlord will be enhancing the value of his property if he is paying to vary the terms of the lease.

Tenant pays for variation – VAT

Residential property

[7.52] A payment from the tenant to vary any of the terms of a lease will be an exempt supply by the landlord. A potential exception is where the variation is so fundamental that it constitutes the surrender of the existing lease and the grant of a new lease (HMRC Notice 742 para 10.5). If this new grant represented the first grant of a major interest by the person constructing/

converting the building, it would be zero-rated, otherwise it would be exempt (see **7.9** above). For a fuller discussion on the VAT issues see CHAPTER 15, para **15.185** ff.

Non-residential property

[7.53] A payment from the tenant to vary any of the terms of a lease will be an exempt supply by the landlord, unless the landlord has opted to tax, in which case the supply will be standard-rated.

Tenant pays for variation – stamp duty land tax

[7.54] FA 2003, Sch 17A, para 15A states that where a payment is made by a tenant to reduce the amount of rent chargeable under his lease, that is treated as 'an acquisition of a chargeable interest [in land] by the lessee', ie the tenant must pay SDLT on the payment made to reduce the amount of rent. The same goes for any other lease variation paid for by the tenant (sub-para 1A), other than reduction in the term of the lease.

Tenant pays for variation – corporation tax, capital gains tax and income tax

[7.55] A sum paid by a tenant to vary its lease is treated as capital for tax purposes (*Tucker v Granada Motorway Services Limited* (1979) 53 TC 92, HL). It is expenditure the purpose of which is the improvement or enhancement of a fixed capital asset of the business – the lease.

Although the variation payment is capital in tax case law, it can have an income element: the sum paid to the landlord for the variation is potentially a deemed lease premium, taxable on the landlord in whole or in part as rental income. If the lease has 50 or fewer years unexpired, CTA 2009, s 221 (or ITTOIA 2005, s 281 for an income taxpayer) deems a payment for commutation or reduction of any rent or waiver of any restriction to be a premium for a lease. The deemed length of the lease for the purpose of this calculation is equal to the period of time over which the lease variation or waiver has effect (subject to the rule on effective duration of the lease in CTA 2009, s 243 or ITTOIA 2005, s 303). The element of the lease variation payment not assessable on the landlord as deemed rent will be treated as capital gains proceeds (TCGA 1992, Sch 8, para 3(3)).

Example 17

Calder granted Beattie a 60-year lease of a warehouse in 1991 at a rent of £500,000 per annum. In June 2013, Beattie pays Calder £3m in order for Calder to accept the variation of the lease as follows: a break clause at the option of the tenant to be inserted into the lease, exercisable in June 2017. Calder's lawyers advise that this is a variation of the lease, not a surrender and re-grant.

SDLT payable by the tenant on the £3m variation payment of £2,000 plus 5% of £2.75m (the consideration above the £250,000 threshold, giving an SDLT cost of £139,500).

ITTOIA 2005, s 281 would deem the payment for variation of the lease to be a premium for a lease of four years, as the circumstances make it likely that the lease will not last beyond 2017 (ITTOIA 2005, s 303). Calder will be deemed to have a receipt of rental income equal to 94% of £3m = £2.82m and capital gains proceeds of the remainder, £0.18m.

Beattie will be able to claim a deduction for the part of the lease variation payment assessable on Calder as rental income. The deduction will accrue evenly over the remaining effective duration of the lease, ie £2.82m spread over 4 years – £705,000 per year.

Note that CTA 2009, s 232(4A) is not relevant in this example – although Rule 1 of CTA 2009, s 243 applied in determining the length of the lease for tax purposes, Calder would still have had a (smaller) 'taxable receipt' if Rule 1 had not applied.

Rent factoring

[7.56] Payments similar to premiums can sometimes be made without acquiring any interest in land at all. Consider this example.

Example 18

Bloomer Limited leases a sports centre to Finney on a 50-year lease for £5m per annum. Bloomer Limited owns the freehold and wishes to develop the site further but needs funds. Bloomer Limited seeks funds from Lawton Bank plc, and it is agreed that they will advance £35m in return for the right to the next ten years' rent. The bank is paying a £35m 'premium' upfront for ten annual payments of £5m – in economic terms, a substantial part of the interest that Bloomer Limited holds in the property. (An alternative way of describing the commercial transaction is that the bank is lending £35m over ten years and total interest on the debt over ten years will be £15m.) If there were no legislation covering this transaction, Bloomer Limited might be able to shelter £35m of capital gains disposal proceeds (eg with base cost and capital losses brought forward); then over ten years Bloomer Limited could exclude rents of £50m from its tax computations, because they are being paid from Finney to the bank. (If the initial transaction is viewed as a loan, this is equivalent to obtaining a tax deduction not only for interest paid to the lender, but also on the repayments of principal). CTA 2010, s 759 may apply to this transaction: if Bloomer's accounts show the £35m as a loan rather than proceeds of a fixed asset sale, then it may be a 'finance arrangement'. In that case s 759 states that the £35m receipt will be treated as a loan to Bloomer Limited. There would be an allowable deduction only for the interest element of Bloomer's deemed payments to the bank – not for the full amount of the rent assigned to the bank.

Note that FA 2003, s 48 (1)(b) can deem such an assignment of a right to rents to be a chargeable land transaction in certain circumstances, meaning the transaction could give rise to an SDLT liability.

Under TCGA 1992, s 263E Bloomer Limited would be treated as having made no capital gains disposal on entering into the finance arrangement.

The legislation on rent factoring and 'finance arrangements' applies to individuals, partnerships and companies. It applies wherever a payment is received which is recorded in the recipient's accounts as giving rise to a financial obligation and where the 'borrower' makes a disposal of an asset for the benefit of the 'lender'. The legislation for income taxpayers is at ITA 2007, s 809BZA et seq.

Transactions in leases and tax mismatches

[7.57] The following show examples of transactions in leases and tax mismatches.

Example 19A

Absolute Limited, leases a non-residential property from Malaprop Limited under a 30-year lease. Absolute Limited is facing financial difficulties and would like to downsize – the £1m annual rent is becoming onerous. Absolute Limited and Malaprop Limited agree that in return for a payment of £3m, Malaprop Limited will accept a surrender of the lease, which has 20 years unexpired, from Absolute Limited. Immediately after this lease is surrendered, Malaprop Limited grants a new lease to Brinsley Limited at £1m per annum for 25 years, but with upward-only market rent reviews every five years. Brinsley Limited negotiates a reverse premium of £3m as its price for entering into the lease.

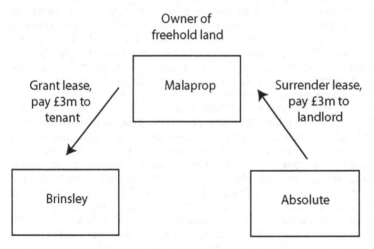

£3m surrender payment

- The full £3m receipt is taxable on Malaprop Limited as a capital gains receipt (some base cost will be deductible but not much because Malaprop Limited has retained its full interest and it is not devalued).
- There is no tax deduction for Absolute Limited, paying a capital sum to escape an onerous obligation.

- There is net tax leakage of 19% of £3m = £570,000 (reduced in the short term by 19% of the base cost that Malaprop Limited can set off, though Malaprop Limited will have a lower base cost in the event of a future disposal).

£3m reverse premium

- The full £3m receipt is taxable on Brinsley Limited as income, spread over five years.
- No deduction is available for Malaprop Limited (though base cost may be enhanced).
- There is net tax leakage of 19% of £3m = £570,000 (unless or until Malaprop Limited sells the freehold).

No SDLT is payable on the £3m payments for either transaction, because neither payment is made by the person acquiring the chargeable interest in land. SDLT will be payable on the rental element of the lease taken out by Brinsley Limited (£278,130 on a 25-year lease with annual rent of £1m).

The corporation tax position is that there are two adverse tax mismatches, and overall there is short-term tax leakage of up to £1.14m (depending on the amount of base cost that can be set against the receipt by Malaprop Limited).

Contrast Example 19A with the following transactions which achieve a similar commercial outcome.

Example 19B

Absolute Limited leases a property from Malaprop Limited, details the same as above. Absolute Limited agrees that it will assign the lease directly to Brinsley Limited. Absolute Limited will have to pay £2.7m to get Brinsley Limited to accept an assignment of the lease. Subsequent to this, Brinsley Limited agrees with Malaprop Limited to accept a variation to the lease that upward-only five-yearly rent reviews will be added to the lease. The benefit to the landlord of the lease variation is valued at £200,000. No payment will be made for this, but in return Malaprop Limited will grant a five-year lease to Brinsley Limited commencing in 20 years' time (a reversionary lease) with rent equal to the market rent at that time (or £1m per annum if higher).

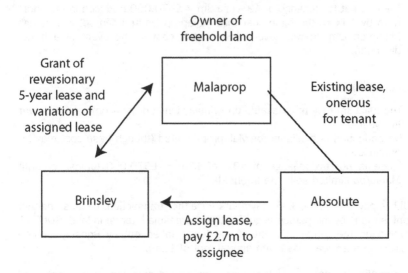

Absolute Limited obtains no tax deduction for the £2.7m payment paid on assignment, but Brinsley Limited receives it tax-free (which is why Absolute Limited was able to negotiate a lower payment). No SDLT is payable on this transaction, and net tax leakage here is nil.

The lease variation inserting the rent review clauses is valued (to the benefit of the landlord) at £200,000. No SDLT is payable on this variation because the lease is more than five years old.

For corporation tax purposes, no reverse premium will be deemed to have been paid on the grant of the reversionary lease because no monetary or similar consideration was paid. HMRC take the view (Business Income Manual, 41075) that the 'payment or other benefit' required for the provisions of CTA 2009, s 96 to bite has to include the payment of money or the forgiveness of debt or the assumption of a liability.

SDLT will only be charged on the rent payable on the five-year reversionary lease, based on an estimate of the market value rent in 20 years' time.

By cutting out the transactions involving the £3m payments to and from the landlord, the same commercial result is achieved, but the benefits of structuring the transaction in the alternative way are:

- the amount of SDLT payable is lower,
- the amount of corporation tax payable by Malaprop Limited and Brinsley Limited is nil instead of up to £1.2m.
- Absolute Limited has managed to exit its lease by paying £300,000 less than the £3m that Malaprop Limited would have accepted.

The economic result of this transaction will be taxed, so it is not felt that the new General Anti-Abuse Rule (GAAR, FA 2013, Part 5) would be applied to alter the tax results of the commercial transactions described in this Example.

Chapter 8

Development, redevelopment, refurbishment and maintenance

by
Richard Jones and Adrian Wills,
KPMG LLP

Introduction

[8.1] This chapter will cover the tax issues concerning commercial developers (whether they are property traders or investors) and trading companies who undertake refurbishment of their properties for the purposes of their business. It will not cover the related VAT issues in detail as these are dealt with comprehensively in **CHAPTER 15** (VAT) but the relevant issues will be highlighted in this chapter and cross-referenced to **CHAPTER 15**.

Investing v dealing

[8.2] Property transactions are often divided into three categories – investment, dealing and development. However, in tax terms, the concept of development is not a separate category. The activity of development is simply a means to an end.

The question of whether a developer is investing or dealing in land will determine how they are taxed. As discussed in **CHAPTER 2**, there is little statutory guidance and a body of case law has established some general principles to help decide the question. The key factor will be the motive of the developer in acquiring the property. If the intention is to develop property in order to generate rental income, the property will be treated for tax purposes as being held by the developer as an investment. If the intention is to develop property in order to sell it on completion of the building, the property will form part of the developer's trading stock which is held for resale, such that the developer will be treated for tax purposes as carrying on a trade.

Circumstances may arise where the developer has more than one motive on the acquisition of a property. It is not possible for an asset to be both trading stock and an investment asset for tax purposes at the same time, or to possess an indeterminate status. Where there is more than one motive, the dominant motive will normally determine whether a property is held as an investment or as trading stock. Alternatively, the property may be split into two parts with each part treated separately. For example, a developer may wish to build an office block to hold on completion of the development as an investment, but be aware that the local council are unlikely to grant planning permission unless the development incorporates a number of residential flats. The developer will then undertake the development in the knowledge that he will dispose of the flats. In this scenario the asset is effectively split into two elements, the office block (which will be held as an investment asset) being separated from the flats. The sale of the flats is likely to be treated as trading transaction (see the decision of the *Privy Council in Iswera v IRC (Ceylon)* [1965] 1 WLR 663, where a taxpayer who built a private residence was required to acquire a larger site than she needed, and who therefore sold the surplus land, was taxed on the sale of the surplus land as a trading transaction, and not as an acquisition incidental to the acquisition of an investment).

Where land is treated for tax purposes as being held for investment, the developer will be taxed on any profit made from a disposal of the land as a capital gain. Where land is treated for tax purposes as being held for resale, the developer will be taxed on any profit made from a disposal of the land as income.

There are also circumstances where the taxpayer's motive is to realise a profit in connection with a development but which does not amount to a trade or an adventure in the nature of a trade. In such circumstances, HMRC may still seek to tax the profit as income under Income Tax Act 2007 (ITA 2007) (Part 9A for income tax purposes) and Corporation Tax Act 2010 (CTA 2010) (Part 8ZB for corporation tax purposes). HMRC state that 'this legislation should always be understood in the context that it is taxing only what are, in substance, trading profits' (BIM 60555). It is discussed in detail in **CHAPTER 13**.

The distinction between investing and dealing in land has become of more importance for developers who are individuals. Individuals who are subject to capital gains tax on the disposal of a particular development will now be taxed at a rate of up to 20% for non-residential properties and 28% for residential properties rather than at their highest income tax rate for dealing in land (which in most cases is likely to be 45% for 2017/18). The distinction between investing and dealing can also affect a shareholder's eligibility for Entrepreneurs' Relief on any future sale of the business.

For corporation tax purposes, the rate of tax is the same regardless of whether the development profit is characterised as a chargeable gain arising from the disposal of an investment or as trading income arising from dealing in land. Where the profit is characterised as a chargeable gain, an indexation allowance will be available to reduce the taxable gain.

Property development by non-residents

[8.3] The distinction between investing and dealing in land is particularly important for non-UK tax residents who carry out a development or redevelopment in the UK. Finance Act 2016 introduced rules to ensure that non-resident companies developing and dealing in UK land will, whether residential or not, be subject to tax in the UK, regardless of whether they have a UK permanent establishment. These rules, together with changes to a number of double tax treaties aim to ensure that many offshore developers and dealers in UK land will be subject to UK income or corporation tax. The charge applies to disposals that occur on or after 5 July 2016, but anti-avoidance rules exist to tax disposals on or after 16 March 2016. Where a non-UK tax resident acquires UK non-residential property with the intention of holding it as an investment following the completion of any development, it will not be taxable on any capital gain which is realised from a disposal of the completed development. Capital gains realised on the disposal of UK residential property is generally likely to be subject to UK tax.

Recent Finance Acts have introduced additional rules affecting the taxation of residential properties which can affect non-residents.

FA 2013 introduced the annual tax on enveloped dwellings ('ATED'), which applies to certain resident property with a value in excess of a threshold owned by 'non-natural' persons. This threshold is currently £500,000.

In parallel to this, a tax on capital gains was introduced for properties subject to the ATED under the 'ATED related CGT charge' with effect for disposals on or after 6 April 2013.

Finance Act 2015 (FA 2015) introduced the non-resident capital gains tax charge (NRCGT), which expands the scope of capital gains on residential property to certain non-UK tax residents, not just those covered by the ATED. The charge applies to gains made by individuals, trustees and closely held non-resident companies and funds. Companies and funds which are not closely held are not caught by the charge. It only applies to appreciation in value from April 2015. The charge applies to 'property used or suitable for use as a dwelling or in the process of being constructed or adapted for use as such', and unlike the ATED, applies to residential property used for letting purposes. However, there are exclusions for certain types of property for communal use such as boarding schools, nursing homes and certain types of student accommodation.

A diverted profits tax ('DPT') was introduced from 1 April 2015 as part of FA 2015. The charge is levied on companies involved with transactions which lack economic substance, or which avoid the creation of a UK permanent establishment. HMRC guidance has confirmed DPT will apply to real estate transactions and therefore is something overseas property investors should consider.

These changes are considered further at **CHAPTER 5**.

Computation of property trading profits

[8.4] The tax liability of investors in property in respect of rental income and premium receipts has been discussed in **CHAPTER 6** and **CHAPTER 7**. This section concentrates on the position of a developer who carries on a trade, such that any profit made on a sale of the development will be taxed as trading income.

Recognition of income

[8.5] For tax purposes, accounts prepared according to generally accepted accounting practice are the starting point to assess the developer's taxable profits (see CTA 2009, s 46 for corporation tax and ITTOIA 2005, s 25 for income tax).

In contrast to the position for recognising capital gains, where the normal date of disposal is at the time a contract is entered into or, if the contract is conditional, the time when the conditions are satisfied (see Taxation of Chargeable Gains Act 1992 (TCGA 1992), s 28), there is no specific rule for determining when properties should be treated as being acquired or disposed of in assessing the taxable business profits of a developer carrying on a trade. The taxing point will follow the timing of the profit recognition through the accounts.

International accounting standards

[8.6] Detailed commentary, on when and how the general revenue recognition guidance should be applied in the construction of real estate, has been published by the International Financial Reporting Interpretations Committee (IFRIC) of the IASB in IFRIC Interpretation 15 *Agreements for the Construction of Real Estate*.

IFRIC 15 addresses whether an agreement for the construction of real estate should be recognised under IAS 11 or IAS 18. The scope of IFRIC 15 also deals with agreements where the construction of real estate is only one component of the agreement (such as an agreement which also includes the sale of land or the provision of property management services).

The background to the publication of IFRIC 15 is the divergence in practice between developers in applying the relevant accounting standards for the construction of real estate and the associated revenue recognition.

Entities that undertake the construction of real estate, directly or through subcontractors, may enter into agreements with one or more buyers before construction is complete. These agreements can take on various forms depending on their underlying substance. A contract meets the IAS definition of a construction contract if the buyer is able to specify the major structural elements of the design of the real estate before construction begins and/or major structural changes once construction is in progress, regardless of whether or not this ability is exercised.

Revenue is recognised by reference to the stage of completion as construction progresses. By contrast, if construction could take place independently of the agreement and buyers have only a limited ability to influence the design of the real estate (eg to select a design from a range of options specified by the entity, or to specify only minor variations to the basic design), the agreement will be accounted for under IAS 18 as an agreement for the sale of goods. In simple transactions revenue will be recognised on contractual completion when the buyers obtain possession.

In summary, IFRIC 15 requires revenue arising from agreements for the construction of real estate to be recognised by reference to the stage of completion of the contract in the following cases:

- the agreement meets the definition of a construction contract in accordance with IAS 11;
- the agreement is only for the provision of services in accordance with IAS 18, eg the entity is not required to supply construction materials; and
- the agreement is for the sale of goods, but the revenue recognition criteria are met *continuously* as construction progresses.

In all other cases, revenue is recognised when all of the revenue recognition criteria of IAS 18.14, described below, are satisfied:

- the entity has transferred to the buyer the significant risks and rewards of ownership;
- the entity retains neither continuing managerial involvement to the degree usually associated with ownership or effective control over the goods sold;
- the amount of revenue can be measured reliably;
- it is probable that the economic benefits associated with the transaction will flow to the entity; and
- the costs incurred or to be incurred in respect of the transaction can be measured reliably.

In applying the percentage of completion method to agreements within the scope of IAS 18, the requirements of IAS 11 in respect of the recognition of revenue and related expenses apply.

Although not part of the interpretation, the Information Note to IFRIC 15 contains two helpful flowcharts and three illustrative examples to assist with determining which accounting standard to apply.

The commentary above refers to current accounting standards and practice. In May 2014 the International Accounting Standards Board (IASB) published IFRS 15 *Revenue from Contracts with Customers*. This will replace both IAS 18 *Revenue* and IAS 11 *Construction Contracts*, and also result in the withdrawal of IFRIC 15 *Agreements for Construction of Real Estate*. IFRS 15 requires the recognition of revenue based on the satisfaction of performance obligations. Performance obligations may be satisfied at a point in time (eg from the sale of a good) or over time (eg the rendering of services or some construction arrangements).

IFRS 15 is effective, subject to EU endorsement, for annual periods beginning on or after 1 January 2018. IFRS 15 introduces comprehensive guidance on identifying significant components of construction transactions. In most cases, revenue in respect of a 'traditional' over time construction contract may be recognised at a similar time and quantum under both standards. This will depend on the method that entities historically used to measure the progress towards completion and whether that changes under IFRS 15.

For a point in time sale, an entity recognises revenue when it satisfies a performance obligation by transferring a good or service. Under IFRS 15 a good or service is transferred when the customer obtains control of it. This may result in some entities recognising revenue later than may have been the case under IAS 18.

UK GAAP

[8.7] The FRC has published FRS 100 *Application of Financial Reporting Requirements*, FRS 101 *Reduced Disclosure Framework*, FRS 102 *The Financial Reporting Standard applicable in the UK and Republic of Ireland* and FRS 105 *The Financial Reporting Standard applicable to the Micro-entities Regime*. These new standards are effective for accounting periods beginning on or after 1 January 2015.

FRS 101 applies many of the recognition and measurement requirements of IFRS but provides some exemptions from the disclosure requirements of IFRS.

FRS 102 is intended to be a simplification of the general principles of IFRS. Chapter 23 applies to revenue from the sale of goods, rendering of services and construction contracts.

The basic principle is that revenue is measured at the fair value of consideration received or receivable. Revenue associated with the rendering of services is recognised based on the percentage of completion of the transaction when the amount of revenue, costs and stage of completion can be measured reliably and it is probable that the benefits of the transaction will be received by the entity. If the outcome of a construction contract can be measured reliably (ie the stage of completion, future costs and collectability of billings can be estimated reliably), revenue is recognised according to the stage of completion. If the outcome of a construction contract cannot be estimated reliably revenue is recognised only to the extent of contract costs incurred, when it is probable that those amounts will be recoverable.

Revenue from the sale of goods is recognised when the significant risks and rewards of ownership are transferred, continuing managerial involvement is not indicative of control or ownership, the amount of revenue and the related costs can be measured reliably and it is probable that the benefits of the transaction will be received by the entity. No specific guidance is given in respect to the sale of property. However, in most cases the risks and rewards of ownership pass when legal title or possession transfers to the buyer which is likely to be following legal completion of the sale and actual receipt of the cash proceeds. There may be cases when recognising revenue at the date of exchange of unconditional contracts may be appropriate. This potentially has the risk that, if the sale is not completed, for example where it turns out the developer has a defective title to the land in question or the purchaser is unable to raise the necessary funds, a reversal of the relevant accounting entries would be required. It may therefore be more prudent in such instances to wait until the sale of the property has been completed before recognising revenue.

The main difference between UK GAAP and IFRS is that IFRIC 15 provides more detailed guidance on the accounting for the construction of real estate. These arrangements are accounted for under either IAS 11 or IAS 18, primarily depending on when control of the constructed asset passes to the customer. IFRIC 15 introduces the concept of continuous transfer. The continuous transfer method is not included in FRS 102.

Whilst IFRS is generally more prescriptive than FRS 102, we would expect that in the significant majority of cases, transactions involving real estate would be recognised at the same time and same quantum under both standards.

Deduction of expenditure

General principle

[8.8] The scope of allowable deductions in calculating trading profits is very broad, and therefore most expenditure attributable to development is likely to meet the 'wholly and exclusively' test of deductibility for tax purposes.

Trading stock

[8.9] While respectful of changes in accounting terminology, land or properties owned by a property trader at the end of an accounting period represent its stock in trade and work in progress. These properties will be accounted for as current assets in the financial statements. Building costs which have been incurred in respect of completed buildings will form part of the cost of that trading stock in the accounts. If building costs relate to buildings still under construction, they will be accounted for as part of the cost of work in progress. No tax relief will be available for such expenditure until these costs are expensed in the profit and loss account (typically when the relevant property is sold).

Where a property trader capitalises interest in its accounts, by adding the interest to the cost of its trading stock (as opposed to charging it through its profit and loss account as an overhead), tax relief will only be available for the interest when it is charged to the profit and loss account. Where interest on a loan is not related to a specific development, but is an overhead of the business and expensed accordingly (on the basis that the loan is to be used as working capital to meet general expenses of the business), tax relief will be available on an accruals basis. In both cases, the usual suite of rules affecting the deductibility of interest payable would (for example, transfer pricing and the corporate interest restrictions) need to be considered.

Rights and interests retained in trading stock

[8.10] It may be the case that following a sale of property, the developer will continue to retain an interest in the property. For example, a developer could build a block of flats, and then sell off each flat by way of a lease for 99 years at a premium and low ground rent. The developer will have made a part disposal of the property that he holds as trading stock. The freehold interest retained (ie the reversionary interest), which will entitle the holder to the ground rent, will continue to be treated as stock in the developer's accounts, on the assumption that the developer has no plans to retain this interest as an investment asset, and valued as stock at the lower of its cost or net realisable value (see the House of Lords decision in *Hughes v Utting & Co Ltd* (1940) 23 TC 174). Any profit realised on a subsequent sale of the freehold interest subject to the lease will be treated as a trading receipt.

In order to determine the cost of the reversionary interest, the amount relating to the part disposed of and the value of the stock retained will follow their treatment in the taxpayer's financial accounts, provided these are prepared in accordance with generally accepted accountancy practice. The method stated by HMRC that should be used at BIM 51540 (which would seem likely to be comparable to the value followed in the financial statements) for calculating the cost of the reversion is to adopt the formula used by the Special Commissioners in *John Emery & Sons v IRC* (1936) 20 TC 213 (and approved by the High Court in *Heather v Redfern & Sons* (1944) 26 TC 119) as follows:

Cost of reversion

$$= \text{Expenditure on property} \times \frac{\text{MV of reversion}}{\text{MV of reversion} + \text{Premium received}}$$

Example 1

Suppose that a plot of land is acquired for £50,000 and 10 flats are erected at a total construction cost of £900,000. The expenses of purchase and sale, and the provision of services, amount to £50,000. The total expenditure on the property is therefore £1,000,000. The flats are each sold at a premium of £150,000 and a ground rent of £300 per annum (the capitalised value of the ground rent being £3,000, using a multiple of 10 for illustrative purposes). The total premiums received are therefore £1,500,000 and the capitalised value of the reversionary interest in all 10 flats is £30,000:

$$\text{Cost of reversion} = £1,000,000 \times \frac{£30,000}{(£30,000 + £1,500,000)}$$

ie £19,608.

The cost attributable to the leases disposed of is therefore £1,000,000 less £19,608 ie £980,392.

Appropriations to trading stock

[8.11] There may be circumstances when an asset has not been acquired as trading stock, but is subsequently appropriated by the taxpayer for the purposes of his trade as trading stock (whether or not at the commencement of that trade). This is a complex area of case law where decisions have turned by reference to specific fact patterns. The taxpayer will be treated as having sold the asset for its market value at the time of the appropriation so that a chargeable gain or allowable loss will arise (see TCGA 1992, s 161(1)). An election can be made by the taxpayer to defer any gain by rolling it into the trading stock cost of the asset (see TCGA 1992, s 161(3) and s 161(3ZB) (if an ATED asset) (see **CHAPTER 22**)). The effect of the election is to avoid a 'dry' tax charge on any capital gain at the time of the appropriation, and instead tax the gain under the income or corporation tax rules on any subsequent sale.

Example 2A

A company acquires a building for £8,000,000 with the intention of letting it, so as to hold the property as an investment. Within a comparatively short period of time, a decision is taken to develop and sell the property. The board of directors consider that the property is no longer held as an investment, and so they decide to appropriate the property to trading stock. At this point, the market value of the building is £10,000,000. The tax consequences are as follows:

Chargeable gain under TCGA 1992, s 161(1)	£
Market value of building at date of appropriation	10,000,000
Cost (assuming nil indexation)	(8,000,000)
Chargeable gain	2,000,000
Effect of election under s 161(3) TCGA 1992	
Market value of building at date of appropriation	10,000,000
Deduct chargeable gain	(2,000,000)
Revised value of building for tax purposes	8,000,000

It is also possible to make the election where a property is transferred intra-group from a company which held it as an investment to a company which will hold it as trading stock (see TCGA 1992, s 173(1)). The transferee company will be deemed to have acquired the asset other than as trading stock and then for the purposes of TCGA 1992, s 161(1), to have immediately appropriated it for the purposes of its trade to trading stock, so that the transferee company could then make an election under TCGA 1992, s 161(3) or s 161(3ZB).

Prior to 8 March 2017, where an asset is standing at a loss, the appropriation rules can have the effect of converting what would otherwise be a capital loss into a more useful trading loss. For example, the trading loss can be surrendered by way of group relief. The trading loss will be realised on disposal of the stock item. However, FA 2017 introduced changes which will only permit this election to be made where the appropriation into trading stock would give rise to a chargeable gain and not an allowable loss. These rules took effect for appropriations which took place on or after 8 March 2017.

Example 2B

The facts are as stated in Example 2A except that this time the market value of the building is £8,000,000 and its original cost is £10,000,000.

Capital loss under TCGA 1992, s 161(1)	£
Market value of building at date of appropriation	8,000,000
Cost	(10,000,000)
Capital loss	2,000,000
Effect of election under s 161(3) TCGA 1992	
Market value of building at date of appropriation	8,000,000
Add capital loss	2,000,000
Revised value of building for tax purposes	10,000,000

There must be a genuine appropriation to trading stock, otherwise the courts will deny the tax benefit by not applying the appropriation rules (see for example the House of Lords decisions in *Coates v Arndale Properties Ltd* (1984) 59 TC 516, and *Reed v Nova Securities Ltd* (1985) 59 TC 516). However, where there is a genuine appropriation to trading stock, an election made under TCGA 1992, s 161 will not be held to be invalid simply because a fiscal advantage is obtained (see the Court of Appeal decision in *New Angel Court Ltd v Adam* (2004) 76 TC 9).

Appropriations from trading stock

[8.12] If a property which was acquired as trading stock is developed and subsequently let, there may be an appropriation from trading stock if the property is not subsequently sold. This would seem to require a positive decision or to be inferred from a course of action (see the leading decision of the House of Lords in *Simmons v IRC* [1980] STC 350); as with appropriations to trading stock, this is a complex area of case law. At the date of any such appropriation, the deemed consideration is the amount brought into the accounts of the trade for tax purposes, under TCGA 1992, s 161(2). This deemed consideration will be the market value of the asset, under the principle established in the House of Lords decision of *Sharkey v Wernher* (1955) 36 TC 275, and as put into statute by CTA 2009, s 157.

Further detailed provisions that clarify the scope of the market value rule are at CTA 2009, ss 156–161.

Separate rules relating to the valuation of trading stock on cessation of trade exist (see ITTOIA 2005, s 173 for income tax purposes and CTA 2009, s 162 for corporation tax purposes).

Where a property is transferred intra-group from a dealing company to an investment company, the transferor will be treated as though it had appropriated the property from trading stock, so that a trading gain or loss will arise (see TCGA 1992, s 173(2)). The property will then be treated as transferred to the investment company as a nil gain/nil loss disposal for capital gains purposes under TCGA 1992, s 171.

In contrast to the position where there is an appropriation to trading stock (where any capital gain can be rolled over into the trading stock cost of the property going forward), there is no equivalent rollover relief where a property is appropriated from trading stock. Any profit which arises at the date of appropriation cannot be rolled over into the capital gains base cost of the property. Presumably the relief is given only on an appropriation to trading stock as the expectation would be that the property will be sold within the normal course of the trade, ie within a relatively short period following the date of appropriation, as compared to a property which is transferred from trading stock to be held as an investment.

Where a property is likely to be retained after development, and is currently held as trading stock, consideration should be given to making an appropriation from trading stock before the development commences. This will normally minimise any trading profit as the value of the property is likely to be substantially less at the start of the development in comparison to its value at the completion of a development. If the property is not transferred to an investment company within the group (ie it is to be held as an investment property in the same company that acquired it as trading stock), steps such as a board minute to record the decision to appropriate from trading stock, showing the asset as a fixed asset in the financial statements, or altering the objects clause in the company's memorandum of association would support an argument for appropriation.

Purchase price left outstanding

[8.13] Where the developer (on sale of a property) agrees to leave part of the purchase price outstanding at the time of sale (for example because of an agreement that the amount outstanding should be treated as a loan until the property is sold on), the developer will still be immediately taxable on the whole amount of the purchase price. These facts arose in the decision in *Lock v Jones* (1941) 23 TC 749, where a builder agreed to sell a property to a company in which he was a shareholder, for a profit of £12,500. The profit of £12,500 was to be treated as a loan to the company which would not be repaid until the property was sold. The company was unable to realise a profitable resale and therefore held onto the property. The builder was held to be immediately taxable on the profit of £12,500.

If the actual value of the outstanding purchase price is less than the nominal face value of that debt, the developer can bring the actual value into account as its trading receipt.

Where the developer produces financial statements prepared in accordance with generally accepted accounting principles, the amount brought into account in those financial statements should be accepted by HMRC as the taxable amount.

Particular problems of development

Interest

Tax deductibility of corporate interest

[8.14] The tax legislation covering tax deductions for interest expense is complex and it is relevant to consider the total position in each period to establish if interest is tax deductible. Noted below are key areas that should be considered for property related borrowings but other areas such as transfer pricing legislation should also be considered prior to claiming tax relief.

Relief for interest is covered in more detail in **CHAPTER 10**.

Corporate interest restrictions

[8.15] Finance Act 2017 introduced legislation to restrict the tax deductibility of interest to adopt the recommendations of Action 4 of the OECD's BEPS project. The rules took effect from 1 April 2017 and apply to net UK interest deductions above £2m per annum. Broadly, the rules restrict the tax deductibility of interest to 30% of EBITDA but introduced substantial complexity. The rules only apply for corporation tax purposes, therefore non-resident companies subject to income tax under the non-resident landlord scheme are not affected. HMRC are however consulting on bringing non-resident landlords within the scope of corporate tax with the implication that the corporate interest restrictions will also apply to such taxpayers.

Rolled-up interest

[8.16] The lender may agree that interest payable under a development agreement can be rolled up, so that it is not payable until the development is completed or sold. As deficits on loan relationships cannot be carried back to be offset against capital gains, historically this has led to difficulties for an investment company where the interest was subject to the late interest rules applicable to connected parties at CTA 2009 Part 5 Chapter 8 and was not therefore deductible on an accruals basis. For example, if the disposal of a property was deemed to take place on the exchange of contracts, but the rolled up interest would be expected to be paid out of the completion monies, and the delay between the two dates was significant, this could lead to the capital gain arising before tax deductions were available for the interest. Previously it was preferable from a tax perspective to ensure that the dates of exchange and completion arose in the same accounting period, unless the taxpayer had sufficient income to offset the interest arising in the later period.

Changes to the scope of the late paid interest legislation were introduced by FA 2015. These rules have been repealed where the loans are issued to companies which are treated as connected companies for the purposes of the UK loan relationship legislation and for certain joint venture arrangements. The impact of the change is that from 1 January 2016, the rules have been amended to bring the tax treatment in line with the accounting treatment so that interest is now relieved on an accruals basis for new loans entered into on or after 3 December 2014 (subject to consideration of other potentially relevant legislation, eg transfer pricing). Loans in existence before 3 December 2014 will become deductible on an accruals basis for amounts accruing from 1 January 2016 (unless there has been a substantial modification of the debt prior to this point or a change in the lender, in which case the accruals basis will apply from the later of 3 December 2014 and the date on which the change is made).

Note that the late paid interest legislation will however continue to apply in other circumstances (eg where a loan is made to a close company by a participator (eg an individual shareholder) and therefore it should be determined on a case-by-case basis whether the legislation could apply to a financing transaction by reference to a detailed consideration of the arrangements.

Interest to be treated as a distribution

[8.17] Where the lender under the terms of a loan agreement is entitled to participate in the profits made in respect of a property development, the interest could be treated as a distribution under CTA 2010, s 1000 para F unless the recipient is within the charge to corporation tax and the rate of interest does not exceed a reasonable commercial return (see CTA 2010, s 1032). This can therefore represent a problem where a company that is a developer borrows from an overseas lender. Such interest will not be deductible for corporation tax purposes.

Capitalised interest

[8.18] A UK property investment company (within the charge to corporation tax) will, in general, obtain relief for interest costs under the loan relationship rules as the costs pass through its profit and loss account. Such a company can also claim a tax deduction where, under generally accepted accountancy practice, interest costs are capitalised as part of the fixed cost of the asset (see CTA 2009, s 320). If that asset is then depreciated no tax relief is available as the amount is charged to the profit and loss account. By contrast, a non-UK resident investor in UK property is subject to income tax under the non-resident landlord regime and it is therefore likely that tax relief for interest costs which are capitalised in the balance sheet will not be available until the property is sold, to the extent to which that sale is subject to UK tax. The interest costs debited to the profit and loss account in the tax year of sale would only be available to shelter rental income for that period and potentially on any chargeable gain in the case of a sale within the scope of NRCGT. It may therefore be preferable for a non-UK investor to ensure that, if appropriate, the generally accepted accountancy practice which applies to its investment vehicle permits interest costs during the development phase to be debited to the income statement rather than capitalised in the balance sheet. Where the non-UK investment vehicle is not required to file accounts locally, it may be feasible for that vehicle to apply the principles of UK generally accepted accountancy practice when submitting its UK income tax returns, in order to claim tax relief for interest costs.

Note separately that the accounting treatment may differ depending on whether IFRS or FRS 102 has been adopted. IAS 23 requires capitalisation of interest on qualifying assets such that there is no choice, however, FRS 102 gives an option to capitalise.

Interest and anti-fragmentation

[8.19] The expansion of the transitions in UK land rules includes provisions that where interest is paid to a connected party based on sharing development profits, an amount can be taxable on the payer of interest (see CTA 2010, s 356OH for corporation tax and ITA 2007, s 517 for income tax). Further commentary on this matter can be found at CHAPTER 13.

Capital allowances

[8.20] Where a trading company holds a property as trading stock, it will not be entitled to claim capital allowances. Under Capital Allowances Act 2001, s 4(2), (CAA 2001) any expenditure which is deductible in computing trading profits is excluded from the definition of 'capital expenditure'. A tenant may be entitled to claim capital allowances on fixtures within a property where he pays a premium in connection with the letting of property that is held as trading stock by its landlord, providing the fixtures have not been used for the purpose of a qualifying activity prior to the granting of the lease (CAA 2001, s 184). The qualifying expenditure on which the tenant can claim capital allowances will be calculated by a just and reasonable apportionment of the premium (in whole or in part) paid between the building and its fixtures (CAA 2001, s 562).

Capital allowances are covered in more detail in **CHAPTER 9.**

Site assembly

[8.21] Site assembly (ie where for example the developer will purchase a number of adjacent sites from different vendors in order to amalgamate and sell as a single enlarged site) can potentially crystallise significant tax liabilities, even though there may be no cash payments passing between the relevant parties. For example, if company A exchanges site X for site Y from company B, both parties will have made a disposal. How the disposal will be characterised will be dependent on whether the relevant site is being held by company A or company B for the purposes of a trade or as an investment based on general principles previously discussed. The exchange will also represent a disposal for SDLT purposes. The exchange of sites will also constitute a transaction for VAT purposes and both parties will need to understand their respective VAT implications, for example whether either or both parties have exercised an option to tax.

Another problem will be where company A promises not only to exchange site X for site Y, but also to erect a building on site X for the benefit of company B. How the agreement between the parties is worded will determine the acquisition cost of site Y for company A. If the agreement simply states that company A will incur the cost of erecting a building on site X, then the value of site Y will be the value of site X plus the cost of erecting the building. If the agreement stipulates that A will provide a completed building on site X, then it could be argued that the value of site Y is the value of site X plus the value of the completed building, and not simply its cost thus increasing the potential tax charges.

If site X has been acquired by company A in order to swap it for site Y, then its swap with company B for site Y and the agreement to erect a building on site X are likely to constitute a trading transaction, with the profit being equal to the difference (if any) between the value of site Y and the expenditure incurred by company A. If company A already held site X, then the tax treatment on its exchange will depend on whether site X has been held as trading stock or as an investment. If site X has been held as an investment, consideration should be given as to whether company A has appropriated it to trading stock prior to any exchange. These types of arrangements also require careful consideration from a VAT perspective to ensure, for example, that A does not incur irrecoverable VAT on the costs of constructing a building on site X when it is exchanged for site Y.

Obtaining vacant possession

[8.22] Having purchased land for the purposes of an intended development, the developer may have to make a payment to a sitting tenant to obtain vacant possession. For a property trader, the payment to a tenant on the surrender of his lease will be allowable as an expense in work in progress or as a trading stock cost, so that it is deductible when the cost is amortised in the income statement, typically when the property is sold. If a landlord makes a payment to a tenant to obtain vacant possession, this is a supply for VAT purposes by the tenant to the landlord. If the tenant has exercised an Option to Tax then VAT may be due in respect of the payment and landlords will need to determine whether the payment they make is inclusive or exclusive of any VAT that may be chargeable.

For a property investor, the expense will only be allowable if it satisfies the test of being enhancement expenditure under TCGA 1992, s 38(1)(b). The requirement that the expenditure is reflected in the state or nature of the land at the time of its disposal may mean that a deduction cannot be obtained where the land is sold after a time when the tenant's lease would otherwise have expired. Suppose for example that the developer makes a payment to a tenant to secure vacant possession of his freehold land at a time when the tenant's lease has five years left to run. If the building is sold ten years after the date of the payment, the payment will not be reflected in the nature of the freehold interest in the land held by the developer, since the lease would have expired in any event. However, if the exit of the tenant increases the value of the landlord's property – for example, if it enables the landlord to put a new lease in place with a more lucrative tenant, and that lease is running at the time of the disposal – then there is an argument that the exit payment is reflected in the nature of the asset on disposal thus meeting the requirement at TCGA 1992, s 38(1)(b).

The tenant may not want to move out, and instead of receiving a cash payment, may insist on being provided with suitable alternative accommodation. In this case, providing the above conditions are met, the value of the alternative accommodation should still constitute enhancement expenditure, on the basis that the cost was incurred to increase the value of the building being developed (see for example *Chaney v Watkis* (1986) 58 TC 707).

Purchasing a company to acquire the target property

[8.23] It is often the case that where land is held by a company and the controlling shareholders are individuals, the shareholders would prefer to sell the company rather than the company sell the land, in order to obtain the benefit of being taxed once as a capital gain (or, if non-resident, potentially as trading income following the FA 2016 changes referred to at **8.3** above). Otherwise, if the land is sold by the company, the company will pay tax on any profit in the absence of any available losses. If the company then distributes the after tax profits by way of a dividend to the shareholders, the shareholders will be subject to tax on the dividend. Alternatively, if the company had no other assets and was subsequently liquidated after the land disposal, the shareholders would be subject to tax on any capital distribution as if they had made a disposal of their shares.

Where a developer has to acquire the shares in a company in order to obtain the land, rather than the land directly, the price paid by the developer may reflect any Stamp Duty Land Tax savings and any latent gain in respect of any future disposal of the land. How much the price can be discounted by any latent gain will be a matter for negotiation between the parties, and may depend on the surrounding commercial factors, such as how eager the developer is to acquire the land, the tax profile of the vendors, and how soon the developer may wish to dispose of the development. After acquisition of the company, the developer may transfer the land intra-group to a company which is carrying out the development. The treatment of this intra-group transfer will depend on how the land is held in the target company and the intentions of the purchaser on acquisition (ie to develop land and sell or to hold as an investment).

As noted at **8.2**, CTA 2010, Part 8ZB (ITA 2007, Part 9A) contains certain anti-avoidance provisions that can apply where a tax benefit from transactions in land or property (such as shares) deriving its value from the land is obtained. The provisions target the avoidance of corporation tax on income (or income tax) on what are in essence trading transactions where the profit is realised in a capital or non-taxable form. It can apply to gains of a capital nature where land (or property deriving its value therefrom) is acquired or developed with the main purpose, or one of the main purposes, of realising a profit or gain from the land. If the anti-avoidance rules are in point, the gain will be chargeable to tax as income rather than capital.

De-grouping charges

[8.24] Where a company leaves a group as a result of a disposal of shares by a group company, any degrouping charge arising on the disposal will often be made by way of an adjustment to the consideration taken into account for calculating the gain or loss on the disposal of shares of the transferee company. Any exemption or relief that applies to the share disposal, such as the Substantial Shareholdings Exemption, can apply to exempt the notional gain.

Cost of obtaining planning consents

[8.25] The costs of successfully obtaining planning consent will form part of the costs of the development. The costs of unsuccessfully applying for planning consent, or of obtaining planning consent which is abandoned, should be deductible as trading expenses in a property dealing company, but obtaining a deduction in an investment company will be more problematic. In order to obtain a deduction the developer would need to show the costs were wholly and exclusively incurred for the purposes of enhancing the value of the land and were reflected in the state or nature of the property at the time of its disposal, as set out at TCGA 1992, s 38(1)(b). It may be possible to argue that where the costs incurred on an unsuccessful preliminary application (such as work in preparing detailed plans and on site investigation) have defrayed the costs on a later application which is successful, then those costs should be allowed as a deduction, as they have contributed to the obtaining of planning consent, which is then reflected in the state of the completed development. In order to support such a claim, it may be necessary to demonstrate that the costs incurred on the aborted application actually led (even if indirectly) to an increase in the value of the land.

The Community Infrastructure Levy and s 106 planning agreements

[8.26] The Community Infrastructure Levy Regulations 2010 came into force with effect from 6 April 2010. The Regulations empower local authorities in England and Wales to charge a Community Infrastructure Levy ('CIL') on most types of new development in their area in order to support the provision of local infrastructure.

Developers who incur CIL wholly and exclusively for the purposes of their development trade (but not in relation to a fixed capital asset of the trade) should be able to claim tax relief for the payment of the CIL. However, where the development in respect of which the CIL is paid is treated as a fixed capital asset, CIL may not be an allowable cost in computing a chargeable gain for corporation tax or capital gains tax purposes.

A landowner may be required to carry out works on land which is owned by the local authority, and a property developer should be able to claim such costs as part of its cost of stock in trade. In the case of a property investor, on a strict interpretation of the test in TCGA 1992, s 38(1)(b), it could be argued that the cost of the relevant works is not reflected in the state or nature of the retained development, as the expenditure has not been directly incurred on the retained development. However, where the costs of the relevant land and related works are incurred as a condition of obtaining planning permission, HMRC may not in practice contest a tax deduction for such costs.

Pre-lets

[8.27] A developer may hold property as trading stock and wish to let part of that property prior to selling it. For example, a housebuilder could be building a number of units on a development, and may wish to let some of the completed units before the whole development is completed and sold. Any rental income which arises from letting part of the property will be taxed as the profits of a property business and not as trading income. Any revenue expenses of the letting of the trading stock should be deducted from the rental income. Any net profit will be taxed as property income. Importantly, any excess of letting expenditure of the trading stock over rental income can be treated as a trading expense instead of being carried forward as a loss of the property business (see PIM 4300). This will ensure that the excess expenditure will be allowable as a deduction against any trading profit arising from the eventual disposal of the trading stock. Currently, if the excess expenditure was instead treated as a loss of the property business, the taxpayer could end up on the disposal of the development with a tax loss that could not be utilised against his trading profits. This distinction between losses generated after April 2017. A future Finance Act in 2017 is expected to introduce these rules. Corporation tax loss relief is covered in more detail in **CHAPTER 6**.

If a developer rents properties before he completes his intention to sell them then he will be making VAT-exempt supplies before the intended zero-rated sales. The making of VAT-exempt supplies could impact upon a developer's entitlement to reclaim VAT incurred on development costs (including VAT on any land purchases) and HMRC VAT Information Sheet 7/08 provides guidance on how developers can calculate whether they may have to repay some of the VAT they had previously claimed in full.

VAT

[8.28] VAT is considered in detail in **CHAPTER 15**. Some particular points in relation to VAT and development are noted below but a key issue for property developers will be the recovery of VAT in relation to expenditure incurred during the development phase (input VAT). Entitlement to reclaim input VAT will depend on whether the supplies made from/of the completed development are a taxable supply for VAT purposes. A taxable supply is one which is not exempt.

The default VAT position for transactions involving property (eg a sale or lease) is that they are exempt from VAT with the consequence that there is no VAT recovery entitlement in respect of VAT charged to the developer on associated expenditure such as professional fees and building costs. Irrecoverable VAT therefore becomes an additional cost to the developer.

Landlords and developers of commercial property can elect to charge VAT (opt to tax) on supplies that would otherwise be exempt, thus allowing recovery of related input VAT. For further details concerning the option to tax please refer to **CHAPTER 15**, para **15.64** ff.

Whether a developer wishes to opt to tax a commercial building can depend on whether the occupier can recover VAT in full. The levels of rent chargeable by a landlord may to some extent be determined by the VAT position of the tenant. If a tenant cannot recover VAT in full then the irrecoverable VAT element forms part of the 'rent cost' to the tenant. Sectors that cannot recover VAT in full include the finance, insurance, health and charity sectors.

Some supplies by developers are mandatorily taxable, rather than exempt. The sale of the freehold interest in new commercial buildings, ie those completed within the period of three years prior to the date of the first supply and which are not dwellings or intended for relevant residential or relevant charitable use, will be standard-rated (at 20%).

The first grant of a major interest by a person constructing a building designed as a dwelling, or otherwise intended to be used solely for relevant residential or relevant charitable use, will be treated as zero-rated. Zero-rating will permit the developer to recover input VAT on associated expenditure without having to charge VAT. Further details in connection with the zero-rating of residential etc buildings by a developer can be found in **CHAPTER 15**, para **15.134** ff.

Building work is generally standard-rated. A contractor can zero-rate his services where the building work is new construction work relating to dwellings, or in some circumstances, to a building intended solely for relevant residential or relevant charitable use. Certain services such as those of an architect or surveyor cannot be zero-rated unless they form part of a zero-rated design and build contract. Building work in connection with the conversion, renovation or alteration of residential buildings may be subject to the reduced rate of VAT of 5% in certain circumstances. For further details on the treatment of VAT in connection with building work, please refer to CHAPTER 15, para **15.220** ff.

In order to maximise VAT recovery, it will be important for the developer to register for VAT at the earliest opportunity. A property developer who is not registered for VAT but who intends to make a taxable supply on the completion of a building should apply for VAT registration as soon as they intend to incur input tax in relation to expenditure on the development. A developer can also choose to make monthly VAT returns rather than the usual quarterly VAT returns, which will speed up VAT recovery and improve cash flow during the development phase.

Refurbishment

[8.29] The distinction between expenditure that is revenue for tax purposes (and thus eligible for immediate tax relief), and capital expenditure (where tax relief may be limited), is a complex area of tax law with a large volume of decided cases. The following is very much an overview of this difficult area; a fuller consideration of this subject area is beyond the scope of this volume.

Property traders

[8.30] If refurbishment work is carried out by a dealer or developer who holds a building as trading stock, the expenditure will normally be treated as revenue expenditure which is added to the cost of the building as stock in trade and deductible when the costs are expensed to the income statement – typically when the building is sold. There may be expenditure which constitutes repairs, where for example part of the building is pre-let prior to sale, but the costs of establishing the split may not be justified where the building is to be sold within a relatively short timeframe.

Property investors

[8.31] Where a building is held as an investment, the expenses of any refurbishment work will be treated as either capital or revenue. If the expenses are capital, they will normally be treated as enhancement expenditure for capital gains purposes, provided that they meet the test at TCGA 1992, s 38(1)(b) as referred to above. In addition, capital allowances will be available for certain kinds of capital expenses, such as the cost of plant and machinery within buildings (for example lifts). Allowances may also be due on demolition costs, provided that they meet the conditions at CAA 2001, s 26. The expenditure therefore has to be broken down into three elements – repairs, qualifying expenditure on plant and machinery, and other improvement work.

It will be necessary to closely examine the costs involved in order to determine which category the costs should fall into.

Some capital expenditure (eg on certain fixtures and fittings) will qualify for capital allowances and will also be treated as enhancement expenditure for capital gains purposes enabling the taxpayer to effectively claim double tax relief. However, where capital allowances have previously been claimed, the enhancement expenditure will only be available to reduce a potential capital gain and will not be able to create or increase a capital loss (as is also the case with indexation allowance).

For residential properties, where the property is furnished, capital allowances cannot be claimed on furniture, furnishings or fixtures within the property. The taxpayer can instead claim a deduction for the 'net cost' of replacing a particular item (the original cost of the item cannot be claimed). The amount of deduction is the cost of the new replacement item, limited to the cost of an equivalent item if it represents an improvement to the old item (beyond the reasonable modern equivalent), plus the incidental costs of disposing of the old item and acquiring the replacement item, less any amounts received on the disposal of the old item.

Prior to 1 April 2016 for corporation tax (6 April 2016 for income tax) a wear and tear allowance of 10% of net rentals was available.

Trading companies that are owner occupiers

[8.32] Trading concerns that are neither property traders nor property investors will often acquire properties with a view to refurbishing them for the purposes of their trade, for example hotel groups, utility companies and retail chains. The properties which they acquire will normally be treated as fixed assets of the business. These companies will often incur significant ongoing refurbishment costs for the purposes of their business. Given the amount of expenditure involved, the extent to which such companies can claim a tax deduction for these costs, and the timing of any relief given, will be an important consideration in determining their tax exposure.

Capital or revenue

[8.33] Refurbishment costs will be treated as capital if they constitute improvements or the replacement of a whole asset. If the expenditure is treated as capital, and it is reflected in the state or nature of the building at the time of its disposal, it will be allowable as a cost in the computation of any capital gain or loss arising from the disposal.

Repairs or improvement

[8.34] Refurbishment costs will be treated as revenue if they constitute repairs or the like for like replacement of part of an asset. A provision for repairs to premises that the taxpayer expects to undertake in the future will only be deductible if the provision is for revenue expenditure and is made in accordance with FRS 12. Under FRS 12 provisions should be made in the financial statements when:

- the business is under a present legal or constructive obligation;
- the obligation is as a result of a past event;
- it is probable that there will be a 'transfer of economic benefits' arising from the obligation; and
- a reliable estimate of the amount of the provision can be made.

Similar accounting principles applied to previous UK GAAP. Care should be taken in accounting for dilapidation provisions. Provisions should only be recognised when damage that requires repair has been made, not before or in anticipation of damage. Hence, building a provision up on a straight line basis over the life of a lease is not an acceptable policy unless it reflects consistent damage being made. In many cases, the event resulting in the provision occurs at the start of the lease eg the installation of partitions which will need removing.

If the carrying out of improvements means that repairs need not be undertaken, the notional figure of what the repairs might have cost will not be treated as revenue expenditure. In *Lawrie v IRC* (1952) 34 TC 20, a manufacturing firm replaced an existing building by one that was 20% larger. The roof of the old building was in a substantial state of disrepair, and the firm claimed that five-sixths of the cost of the new roof should be treated as expenditure on repairs and allowed as a revenue deduction. The Court of Session upheld the decision of the Commissioners that the expenditure on the building was capital and the cost of the roof was an inseparable part of this, and therefore no deduction could be allowed for the notional cost of repairs, which was obviated by the work done.

The two leading cases on the dividing line between repairs and improvements are *Law Shipping Co Ltd v IRC* (1923) 12 TC 621 and *Odeon Associated Theatres Ltd v Jones* (1972) 48 TC 257 which represent the opposite sides of this division. In the *Law Shipping* case, a company purchased a second-hand ship before it was about to start a voyage. It turned out not to be seaworthy, and when the ship reached port it was not allowed to leave until extensive work had been carried out. The company had in effect bought a dilapidated ship and the works were held to be improvements. When the works were completed, the company had something different to that which it had originally purchased. In *Odeon v Associated Theatres*, a company acquired a number of cinemas during and immediately after the war. Repairs and redecoration which would normally have been carried out on a regular basis had not been carried out due to wartime restrictions. As the state of disrepair had not affected the price paid for the cinemas, and they were operational prior to the repairs being carried out, the cost of the repairs was held to be revenue and not improvements. These principles have been considered in a more modern context in the contrasting decisions of the cases *Auckland Gas Co Ltd v IRC* [2000] STC 527 and *Transco plc v Dyall (Inspector of Taxes)* [2002] STC (SCD) 199.

Alterations

[8.35] Alterations will usually be regarded as capital, but this will not always be the case. For example, in *Conn (Inspector of Taxes) v Robins Bros Ltd*

(1966) 43 TC 266, 45 ATC 59 a company carried on its business in premises which were over 400 years old. It replaced a slate roof, strengthened the floor and replaced the shop front eliminating a bow front. The High Court upheld the decision of the General Commissioners that the expenditure was on essential repairs and was therefore an allowable deduction. Repairs to a building of this age, and new building techniques, may have required structural alterations but these were not necessarily capital as a result. HMRC summarise this principle by saying that if an asset has 'simply been repaired so as to do the same job that it was doing before' then the cost will be revenue (BIM 35455).

Reinstatement of property

[8.36] Repairs to reinstate a property are normally deductible as revenue expenditure. The fact that a taxpayer may have bought the property a short time prior to carrying out the repairs does not mean that the repairs will be treated as capital expenditure. However, HMRC may regard a change of ownership as meaning that the expenditure should be treated as capital expenditure, where one or more additional factors are present. The following are examples of such factors:

- A property is acquired which was not in a fit state for use in the taxpayer's business until the repairs had been carried out or could not be let without repairs being made shortly after acquisition.
- The dilapidated state of the property meant that the price paid for the property was substantially reduced. A deduction will not be denied where the purchase price simply reflects the reduced value of the asset due to normal wear and tear (for example, where the property is acquired in-between normal exterior painting cycles). This will remain the case even where the taxpayer makes the repairs shortly after acquiring the property.
- The taxpayer agrees to reinstate the property to a good state of repair. For example, a tenant may be granted a lease of a property for 15 years which is in a poor state of repair and agree to refurbish it. The tenant's expenditure will be capital but under the short lease premium rules (see CHAPTER 7), some tax relief may be available.

Costs of maintenance – leased premises

[8.37] Where a taxpayer is granted a lease of a property in good repair, the expenses of maintaining the property will normally be deductible. This will normally include a payment made to the landlord at the end of their lease on account of dilapidations (ie overdue repairs) which the tenant was required to make but has not done so.

A landlord may have an insurance policy which covers the cost of some repairs. HMRC will normally only allow as a deduction the excess of the costs of the repairs over the proceeds received under the insurance policy. HMRC will allow the approach taken in the accounts of deducting the costs of the repairs when the expense is incurred and crediting the insurance proceeds as an income receipt when they are received.

A tenant's payment of rent will be treated as including a payment to defray the cost of work of maintenance of, or repairs to, the demised premises, not being work required by the lease to be carried out by the tenant. Where a tenant is required to make a contribution towards the work, the landlord is taxable in full, but equally the cost of repairs will be allowable in full. However, it may not be appropriate to simply net off the tenant's contribution against the cost of the repairs, as the repairs may be incurred in a later accounting period.

Dilapidations

[8.38] Where a tenant makes a payment at the end of a lease to make good dilapidations, the direct tax treatment for the landlord will depend on what he in fact does with the property as follows:

- Where the landlord disposes of the property or occupies it himself, the payment by the tenant is likely to be treated as a capital receipt (and therefore possibly a chargeable gain) as compensation for the tenant being in breach of the terms of the lease, ie of the covenant to keep the property in a good state of repair.
- Where the landlord does not expend the payment from the tenant in making good the dilapidations, the payment is likely to be compensation for the lower rent the property can now command, and therefore be treated as a receipt of the rental business.
- Where the landlord uses the payment to make good the dilapidations, he will not be taxed on the receipt of the payment so long as he in fact carries out the repairs (and assuming the property will continue to be let). The landlord will not obtain a deduction for the amount of the payment as the cost of the repairs has been met by the tenant and not by the landlord. Should the receipt and expenditure be accounted for in different taxable periods a timing mismatch is likely to arise. If the cost of the repairs exceeds the payment received from the tenant, the landlord will obtain a deduction for the amount of the excess. If the payment exceeds the cost of repairs, the excess payment will be treated in accordance with the first two bullet points above.

Where property is to be refurbished prior to it being let, and certain works are required by the tenant, it may be more tax efficient to allow the tenant to carry out the works himself, and allow the tenant a rent free period and/or an inducement payment to cover the costs (although the impact of the reverse premium rules would need to be considered – see **CHAPTER 7**, para **7.19** ff). If the tenant is carrying on a trade and shows a trading loss in the accounting period in which the cost of the works is incurred, it may be able to use that trading loss quicker than the landlord, for example by carrying back that loss to offset profits of an earlier period. Losses arising from a property rental business by contrast cannot be carried back to an earlier period.

VAT on refurbishment

[8.39] A developer carrying out the refurbishment of a building will generally not be able to claim input tax unless it is a commercial property and he exercises the option to tax. In most cases it will therefore make sense for the developer to consider opting to tax any commercial building prior to undertaking a major refurbishment, particularly if the potential purchaser or tenant will be able to recover VAT charged on the lease/sale.

Refurbishment does not equate to construction for VAT purposes, therefore the refurbishment of relevant residential and relevant charitable buildings will not be zero-rated. The subsequent disposal of the refurbished building by way of sale or grant of a long lease will be an exempt supply for VAT, unless such sale or lease is the first grant of a major interest by the person who originally constructed the building. Consequently, a VAT cost is likely to arise on the refurbishment of residential property.

The zero-rating relief for construction works in connection with the approved alteration of a 'protected building' was withdrawn from 1 October 2012. However, if a 'protected building' is substantially reconstructed (as defined) the first grant of a major interest in it by the developer can be zero-rated such that most of the related VAT costs can be recovered as input VAT. For further details, please refer to **CHAPTER 15**, paras **15.177** and **15.225**.

There are also additional VAT rules that might benefit any projects that convert existing buildings into dwellings etc, for example by way of the reduced rate (currently 5%) for the works and the ability to recover the VAT in certain circumstances. For further details see **CHAPTER 15**, paras **15.224** and **15.243** ff.

Deferred revenue expenditure

[8.40] Deferred revenue expenditure means expenditure which is allowable 'revenue' expenditure for tax purposes but which has been accounted for by posting the expense somewhere on the balance sheet rather than writing it off immediately to the income statement as it is incurred. The expenditure is then usually written off to the income statement over a period of time, by being charged as an expense or depreciated. Deferred revenue expenditure covers both amounts which are sometimes shown in current assets as well as amounts sometimes booked as part of a fixed capital asset.

It is HMRC's view (see BIM 42215) that expenditure which is revenue in terms of tax law, but which is deferred, ie capitalised in the balance sheet in accordance with correct accounting practice, can only be relieved for tax purposes as and when it is recognised in the income statement in accordance with generally accepted accounting practice. This means that relief will not be given on an earlier paid or incurred basis.

For some taxpayers, such as property investment companies, expenditure which has been deferred may only be released to the income statement on disposal of the property. Investment properties under generally accepted accountancy practice are included in the balance sheet at their market value or, assuming the fair value method is adopted, at their fair value. In both cases depreciation is not charged. Provided that the property retains its value, the capitalised revenue expenditure will not be released to the income statement until the property is eventually disposed of. In these circumstances there may be an argument that a tax deduction is due when the expenditure is capitalised, or alternatively, that it should be allowed as a deduction in the periods in which it would have been released to the income statement had it been required to be depreciated. However, HMRC may not agree to any such approach.

If the view of HMRC is followed, then it will represent a significant cash flow disadvantage for those companies with substantial fixed assets (such as hotels, utility groups and retailers), who may find that tax relief for property refurbishment expenditure or major periodic repairs/enhancements will be spread. Taxpayers in this situation should consider developing a strategy to ensure they can maximise their tax relief and some taxpayers may wish to reorganise their activities with a view to accelerating tax relief for such items of expenditure.

Reviewing the accounting treatment

[8.41] For properties which are not held as investment properties, major periodic expenditure on assets will be added to fixed assets in the balance sheet and then depreciated, in accordance with generally accepted accountancy practice.

Considering the depreciation policy

[8.42] For expenditure which is deferred, consideration should be given to when the expenditure will be depreciated or amortised in accordance with generally accepted accountancy practice. For accounts purposes, where an asset is made up of two or more separate components with substantially different useful economic lives, each component should be depreciated over its individual life. Where an item of capitalised expenditure includes both 'capital' and 'revenue' elements for tax purposes, it is open to the taxpayer to determine how much of any depreciation of that expenditure relates to each element. HMRC have acknowledged that any reasonable method of identifying the revenue element will be accepted, provided it is consistently applied, and excludes amounts for which relief has already been given. Accordingly, for tax purposes, it would seem open to a taxpayer to allocate the depreciation charge firstly to the revenue element and secondly to the capital element, provided that a careful record is kept of the amounts and the policy is applied consistently from year to year.

Remediation of contaminated and derelict land

[8.43] Land remediation relief provides a corporation tax incentive to businesses acquiring contaminated or derelict land and which then incur costs to eradicate or mitigate the contamination or dereliction. The aim of the incentive is to encourage developers and investors to participate in the regeneration of urban sites and buildings. Provided the relevant conditions are satisfied, a company carrying on a UK property business or trade is entitled to land remediation relief for revenue or capital expenditure.

For property developers/dealers, the relief in respect of the qualifying land remediation expenditure will not be available until the costs have been expensed to the income statement, typically when the relevant land is sold, as the expenditure included in trading stock in the balance sheet will then be debited to the income statement.

A corporation tax deduction can be claimed where qualifying expenditure is incurred on staffing costs or materials employed directly in the relevant land remediation. Relief can also be claimed for expenditure on sub-contractor costs, but where the company and the sub-contractor are connected, certain conditions have to be met. Where a corporation tax loss is generated by the claim, a tax credit may be reclaimed from HMRC.

A corporation tax deduction can also be claimed for qualifying capital expenditure where an election is notified to HMRC within two years of the accounting period within which the capital expenditure is incurred. Land remediation relief is covered in more detail in **CHAPTER 9**.

Chapter 9

Capital expenditure —allowances

by
Melissa Malins,
Tax Manager

Introduction

[9.1] Capital allowances save tax. That is their function. The benefits can range from a means of temporarily improving cash flow through to a permanent tax saving. It all depends upon a number of factors arising, not only from the tax legislation but also from the taxpayer's short and long term goals and objectives. The first deductions in respect of capital expenditure were introduced in 1878, but the basis for the current system of capital allowances began with ICTA 1945 and the basic approach, ie they reduce an individual's or organisation's income or profits for tax purposes, remains the same although the complexity of the legislation, and its interpretation, does tend to put a few hurdles in the way.

Following an overhaul of the capital allowance regime in 2007, in more recent years the main provisions of the regime have remained constant.

The scope of items that can qualify for capital allowances in property and property related work is wide, anything from amusement park rides to windmills, and from poultry houses to public address systems. In many cases the difference between expenditure being eligible for allowances and being ineligible may hinge upon the operational use of the assets in question – the phrase function versus setting will often be heard in connection with capital allowance claims. This, if the term can be used in conjunction with taxation, is the fun and the frustration, a term perhaps more commonly used, of attempting to interpret the legislation to maximise the potential tax relief on capital expenditure.

Recent announcements with regards to changes on the use of brought forward corporate tax losses together with the introduction of greater restrictions on interest deductibility (likely to be limited to 30% of EBITDA as a result of BEPS), is likely to mean capital allowance claims will become even more pertinent when considering tax mitigation.

In regard to property transactions, capital allowances have a part to play in all stages of a property's life cycle:

- build – direct capital expenditure incurred in building new or extending existing premises, fitting out, or refurbishing existing premises;

- buy – the acquisition of an interest in property, which can cover freehold purchases, long leaseholds, or any other form of property acquisition;
- maintain – capital allowances continue to play a major part in an ongoing business as property, be it owner occupied or of an investment type which will require improvements and ongoing capital expenditure. Eligibility for tax allowances will require constant monitoring; and
- sell – the disposal of an interest in property.

Each situation has a potential commercial impact on one or both of the parties on a short or long term basis, which is why capital allowances should never be viewed in isolation but as part of the wider tax and business strategy. When considering the treatment of expenditure for tax purposes it is also important to think about the accounting treatment of certain items. If expenditure is not considered to enhance value then in order to get the optimal tax treatment it needs to be written off to the profit and loss account. This will obviously need to be considered in conjunction with shareholder requirements and the bottom line.

Capital allowances are claimable against 'qualifying expenditure' incurred by a taxpayer, generally the person or company with the appropriate interest in the land that allows a claim to be made, subject to claims made by previous owners and certain requirements being fulfilled. There continues to be much debate over big names paying little or no corporation tax due to diversion of profits out of the UK. Capital allowances are a recognised and relatively safe way of reducing taxable profits and should be taken advantage of.

There are some basic questions to be asked in deciding whether or not it is possible or, just as importantly, worthwhile to make a capital allowances claim. Many of the questions are applicable at every stage of a property's life cycle, while some are only relevant at the build/buy stage or at the disposal stage:

Building stage

(1) Why is the property being built? – Is it to run a business from, so owner occupied? Is it for investment purposes – if so for what type of tenants? Is it for trading purposes?

The purpose of the property build will determine whether expenditure may be eligible for capital allowances. A property trading business will not attract capital allowances as the property will be held as stock in the Balance Sheet. Equally to the extent that property for an investment business consists of residential property capital allowances will not be available.

(2) Is the expenditure capital?

(3) What type of allowance is available and what are they worth to me?

Buy stage

Instead of building property, at the start of a business venture a taxpayer may instead purchase second-hand property. In this case many of the questions are the same as for new builds but the history of the property may significantly impact eligibility for capital allowances. Issues to consider at this stage include:

(1)   Why is the property being acquired? As above, what is the purpose of the acquisition? What will the property be used for?
(2)   Is the expenditure capital?
(3)   Am I eligible to claim allowances?
(4)   What types of allowance or allowances are available and what are they worth to me?
(5)   What is the status of the seller? Has he/she provided all of the necessary details to maximise capital allowance eligibility going forwards?
(6)   Where applicable, is it preferable to purchase property or the vehicle holding the property and also should each portfolio be held in separate vehicles to facilitate future sale?

Holding stage

(1)   Am I incurring capital expenditure or revenue expenditure?
(2)   Can I maximise my claims by purchasing environmentally friendly assets?

Sell stage

(1)   Shall I dispose of individual property or the vehicle which may be holding the property?
(2)   What elections do I need to enter into with the purchaser to ensure that I don't lose out on capital allowances?

This chapter aims to provide readily accessible responses to these questions at the level of detail needed to allow preliminary assessments to be made and action to be considered. It is not, and cannot be, a substitute for an in depth analysis of the legislation in CAA 2001 and subsequent Finance Act amendments, or the related Special Commissioner's decisions or case law. It is, hopefully, a working guide to help negotiate the capital allowance maze of around 14 different types of allowances, more than 100 cases which contribute to the principles, and HMRC views and practices in dealing with claims.

It cannot, however, be emphasised enough that with regard to property, when it comes to tax matters a detailed understanding of the specific project in question, the tax position of all parties involved, and the legislation, is essential if the maximum benefit is to be achieved. In tax, and particularly capital allowances claims, the devil really is in the detail. This is more than amply evidenced in the decisions made by the courts on what is, and what is not, eligible for allowances. So the starting point in determining if capital allowances are available is to establish if the expenditure is capital in nature.

Is it capital?

[9.2] Guidance on what constitutes capital expenditure was given in *Atherton v British Insulated and Helsby Cables Ltd* (1925) 10 TC 155, which, although neither a property nor a capital allowances case, is generally accepted as an appropriate definition. Viscount Cave, in the House of Lords, said:

> ' . . . when an expenditure is made, not only once and for all, but with a view to bringing into existence, an asset or an advantage for the enduring benefit of the trade

. . . there is good reason (in the absence of special circumstances leading to an opposite conclusion) for treating such expenditure as properly attributable not to revenue but to capital.'

And while the above forms the general guideline the good Viscount Cave demonstrates true legal wisdom by leaving an escape clause with his parenthesis.

In the capital allowances case of *Hinton v Maden & Ireland* (1959) 38 TC 391, which centred on whether a shoemaker's knives and lasts with a life expectancy of between one and five years were plant, Lord Jenkins, referring to *Yarmouth v France* (1887) 19 QBD 647 and the requirement for durability, ie enduring benefit for an item to be plant and therefore capital expenditure, said:

'The intention, no doubt, is to keep and use [the knives] for so long as they are serviceable and I cannot regard the circumstance that they wear out in a relatively short time as investing them with so transitory a character as to take them out of the category of plant to which they would otherwise belong . . . '

While each case is dependent upon its individual merits HMRC will usually accept that if an asset has a working life of more than two years it is capital expenditure.

Expenditure that is not capital expenditure, ie that which is classified as revenue expenditure, cannot qualify for capital allowances. Any expenditure that is taken as a trading deduction, eg where a developer constructs a new building with a view to selling it on completion, is not capital expenditure and cannot, therefore, qualify for capital allowances. If, however, the developer became an investor, ie he transferred his development to capital account, it would be possible to claim capital allowances on the costs incurred.

The capital/revenue divide is not, however, always straightforward. As pointed out by Lord Upjohn in *Strick v Regent Oil Co Ltd* (1965) 43 TC 1:

'no part of our law of taxation presents such almost insoluble conundrums as the decision whether a receipt or outgoing is capital or income for tax purposes'

An alternative, and in many cases more accurate, view was given by Sir Wilfred Greene MR almost thirty years earlier in *IRC v British Salmson Aero Engines* (1938) 22 TC 29 when he opined:

'it is almost as true to say that the spin of a coin would decide the matter almost as satisfactorily as an attempt to find reasons'

The key issue is that, from a purely tax viewpoint, many, if not most, taxpayers would prefer to account for expenditure as revenue because the expenditure is fully tax deductible in the year of expenditure, as opposed to the majority of capital allowances regimes which spread the benefit over a number of years. The revenue treatment gives a better return on investment but stakeholders in the business might not appreciate the effect on the annual profit and loss account. This is an area where the potentially different strategies and objectives of small or private businesses can be at odds with those of larger and public corporations. In addition, HMRC have a vested interest in ensuring that capital costs do not end up as revenue as that could erode the tax base.

The major problem area in property on the capital/revenue divide is with regard to repairs, maintenance and renewals and how the costs of such items are categorised into revenue expenditure or capital expenditure. There are a number of cases on the topic but the two generally used for guidance are *Law Shipping Co Ltd v IRC* (1923) 12 TC 621 and *Odeon Associated Theatres Ltd v Jones* (1971) 48 TC 257.

In *Law Shipping* a ship was purchased and repairs carried out. The repairs were claimed as a revenue deduction but the court held that the ship could not have been used in the trade until the repairs has been carried out, so the expenditure was part of the costs of acquiring the ship and, therefore, capital in nature. In the *Odeon* case, however, while it was known at the time of purchase that the repairs were necessary, as was the situation in *Law Shipping*, the need for the repairs did not impinge on the use of the premises nor was it reflected in any reduction to the purchase price. It was, therefore, held that the expenditure was revenue in nature.

A side issue arising from these judgments is that repairs to reinstate worn or dilapidated assets can still be revenue items even if ownership changes before repairs are carried out. A typical example of this type of expenditure would be cyclical maintenance such as, say, external redecoration with any related repair works arising.

Repair and maintenance is generally understood to cover restoring an asset, or more precisely, part of an asset, to its original state so that it performs its original task in a manner similar to that originally intended. The definition of the asset, or 'entirety' is critical in determining which side of the capital/revenue line expenditure may fall, especially as a range of items may quite easily fall to either side dependent upon the specific circumstances. And those that fall on the capital side may qualify under a range of capital allowances regimes, or may be totally ineligible for allowances.

The leading cases on 'entirety' are *O'Grady v Bullcroft Main Collieries Ltd* (1932) 17 TC 93 and *Jones & Co (Devonvale) Ltd v IRC* (1951) 32 TC 513 and they demonstrate the potential difficulties surrounding the concept of the 'entirety'.

In *O'Grady* the colliery chimney became unsafe and needed to be replaced. It was a separate structure from the other buildings and was only connected to the furnace by the flues. The company claimed the costs of building a replacement chimney as revenue expenditure but the Commissioners decided it to be capital because the chimney was held to be a separate entity and therefore the new chimney an 'entirety'. In the appeal by the company against the Commissioners decision, Rowlatt J said:

> 'Of course, every repair is a replacement. You repair a roof by putting on new slates instead of old ones, which you throw away. There is no doubt about that. But the critical matter is . . . what is the entirety? The slate is not the entirety of the roof. You are repairing the roof by putting in new slates. What is the entirety? If you replace in entirety, it is having a new one and it is not repairing an old one. I think that it is very largely a question of degree, but it seems to me the Commissioners have taken the only possible view here.'

In *Samuel Jones*, where the chimney in a paper processing plant became unsafe, a new chimney was constructed near to the existing and connected to the factory by the flues. The Commissioners, guided by *O'Grady*, found that the cost of demolition was revenue and the cost of the new chimney was capital expenditure. In the Court of Session, however, the Lord President (Cooper) took the view that the factory was the entirety and that the chimney was physically, commercially and functionally an inseparable part of it. As the chimney was regarded as being part of the 'entirety' of the factory and not as an asset in itself, the demolition and rebuilding costs were held to be revenue expenditure.

Notwithstanding the 'entirety' aspect which was the key focus of the court's decision there was a significant difference between the works undertaken in each case. In *O'Grady* it was acknowledged that the new chimney was functionally a significant improvement on the existing one, ie it was taller, of greater diameter, and constructed of engineering brick as opposed to the original built in common brick. In *Samuel Jones*, however, it was agreed that 'there was no appreciable improvement' in the new chimney as it was a modern like for like replacement.

In *Philips v Whieldon Sanitary Potteries Ltd* (1952) 33 TC 213, Donovan J reviewed *O'Grady* and *Samuel Jones* and attempted to clarify the position of 'premises' and 'entirety':

> 'the premises . . . may sometimes be the whole of the trader's business and may sometimes be a specific building forming part of these premises. Thus if a factory window were blown out and had to be repaired, it would obviously be wrong to argue that as the entirety of the window had been restored it was not a repair to the premises. In such a case the "premises" would be the entire factory, in relation to which the window would be a repair and nothing else. But if, for example, a retort house in a gasworks was destroyed and had to be rebuilt, one would hardly call that a repair to a gasworks. The size of the retort house would compel one to regard that as the premises; and since it had been replaced in full it could not be said to have been repaired. These examples illustrate what I think is the truth, that there is no one line of approach to the problem that is exclusively correct. In some cases it will be the right to regard the premises as the entire factory, and in others as some part of the factory. Whichever alternative is the right one to adopt will depend upon the facts of the particular case.'

In the more recent case of *Transco v Dyall (Inspector of Taxes)* [2002] STC (SCD) 199, [2002] STI 767 it was held that the whole of a gas distribution network was the 'entirety' and works carried out on it were, therefore, revenue. HMRC did not appeal the case but instead appear to rely on a New Zealand Case, *Auckland Gas Co Ltd v IRC* (2000) 73 TC 266, to support their capital v revenue viewpoint. The case was heard before the Privy Council, where Lord Nicholls said:

> ' . . . the desire to solve a maintenance problem is not inconsistent with carrying out work of a capital nature . . . '

Those who have attempted to use foreign cases to support or justify claims will be aware that HMRC are keen to point out that only UK cases set a precedent. In this instance, however, HMRC felt that, while Privy Council cases are not binding in the UK, the fact that the Privy Council included senior Law Lords who specifically referred to UK tax cases would give no reason to expect that a decision in a UK case would be any different. It will be interesting to note how HMRC react to future capital allowances claims, or others, where a similar situation arises which does not agree with HMRC understanding or interpretation.

Going forward, the possibility of EU law (in the short term, depending on the UK's exit procedures) impacting on interpretations should not be discounted.

Where the 'repair or maintenance' expenditure leads to a significant improvement in the asset, or part of the asset, it is in all probability capital expenditure. This, however, must be balanced with the case of *Conn v Robins Bros Ltd* (1966) 43 TC 266 where the replacement of an ancient oak floor with a concrete floor, which to all intents and purposes was an improvement and should therefore have been regarded as capital, was in fact accepted as a revenue deduction because it was the 'nearest modern equivalent' of construction within the 400 year old premises from which Robins Bros operated.

Refurbishment projects bring a mix of revenue deductions and capital expenditure, some of which is eligible for capital allowances and some ineligible. They are particularly tricky with regard to establishing the revenue/capital divide and then the sub division of the capital expenditure into capital and eligible and capital and ineligible, especially when the 'entirety' concept is considered.

Example 1

Richard refurbishes a newly acquired office block that has passed its last planned maintenance cycle and is in need of a range of repair and maintenance works. He wants to upgrade the facilities and introduce air conditioning. This involves removing the existing suspended ceiling system, which could be considered in need of repair or replacement in any event, to allow for the installation of the new air conditioning and replacing the ceilings with a new modern equivalent.

The air conditioning will qualify for plant and machinery allowances under the integral features allowances category, but what of the ceiling replacement:

- is it a capital cost ancillary to the eligible plant and machinery installation of air conditioning and therefore also eligible for plant and machinery allowances; or
- is it a revenue item as a replacement of part of the 'entirety' constituted by the office block?

This is but one example of the potential difficulties encountered in (a) deciding what to allocate where in any project, and (b) establishing a case to support the decision in response to any HMRC challenges.

The accounting treatment adopted by the claimant is usually accepted as supporting the choice made regarding allocation but in this, and other potentially contentious capital allowances issues, it is not necessarily definitive, and HMRC will usually look closely at such situations and actively challenge items categorised as revenue expenditure if it is felt that, notwithstanding the proposed accounting treatment, it appears under their guidelines to be capital in nature.

Am I eligible to claim allowances?

[9.3] It may be stating the obvious but only those within the charge to tax can claim capital allowances. That does not mean that non-taxpayers are unaffected by capital allowances. The impact and influence of non-taxpayers is dealt with under the sections on Acquisition and Disposal later in the chapter, but the claims process starts with a taxpayer.

In order to claim allowances the claimant must have incurred expenditure and or have a 'relevant interest' in the property or asset. Individual allowances regimes have their own nuances in this area and the specific variances from the general rule are dealt with as each of the regimes is considered in detail.

The general rule is that a person carrying on a 'qualifying activity' who incurs 'qualifying expenditure' which results in that person owning the plant and machinery as a result of incurring the expenditure is eligible to claim capital allowances.

A 'qualifying activity' as listed in CAA 2001, s 15(1) is:

(a)   a trade;
(b)   an ordinary UK property business;
(c)   a UK furnished holiday lettings business;
(d)   an ordinary overseas property business;
(e)   an EEA furnished holiday lettings business;
(f)   a profession or vocation;
(g)   a concern listed in ITTOIA 2005, s 12(4) or CTA 2009, s 39(4) (mines, transport undertakings etc);
(h)   managing the investments of a company with investment business;
(i)   special leasing of plant or machinery; and
(j)   an employment or office.

There are a number of exclusions and limitations, and with regard to property the main ones relate to plant and machinery in dwelling houses. Allowances for furnished holiday lettings used to be restricted to UK property but from 2011 are available on an EEA wide basis, and there is the prospect of retrospective claims in this area as part of bringing UK legislation into line with EU law (again with our impending exit from the EU, these rules will need to be monitored closely).

Up to April 2016, instead of capital allowances, a wear and tear allowance (broadly a deduction of 10% of rent minus rates) used to be available to property investors who let UK furnished residential accommodation. From April 2016 this allowance has been abolished and has been replaced by the replacement relief. Under the replacement relief landlords of residential properties (be they unfurnished, part furnished or fully furnished) will be able to claim tax relief, in full, for the replacement costs of furniture, furnishings, appliances and kitchen ware – beds, sofas, cupboards, carpets, white goods, televisions etc. It is only the replacement costs that are tax deductible, however, so not the initial expenditure to purchase the item for the first time. In addition the replacement asset must be substantially the same as the original one to qualify for full relief. Otherwise relief is limited to the cost that would have been incurred to replace the original item. The legislation for the replacement relief is contained within FA 2016, s 73.

'Qualifying expenditure' is generally more straightforward than the qualifying activity and covers capital expenditure on the provision of plant or machinery wholly or partly for the purposes of the qualifying activity carried on by the person incurring the expenditure. 'Qualifying expenditure' incurred in advance of a qualifying activity commencing is treated as if it was incurred on the first day that the qualifying activity commences.

In addition, there are other requirements that come in to play in determining eligibility with regard to holding a relevant interest in the property. This is generally covered by the fact that the ownership of the asset, and therefore the right to claim, passes to the person incurring the expenditure on the asset. There is, however, a range of anti-avoidance measures in place to ensure that assets are not claimed under more than one allowances regime at a time, or by more than one person at a time. This is partially reflected in the more detailed requirements regarding relevant interests that are covered in the subsequent sections on each allowance.

Capital allowances are not an automatic tax relief. They must be claimed. There is no requirement to make a claim on potentially eligible capital expenditure, and until one is included in a tax computation the legislation does not apply. Once they are claimed, however, it is possible to 'disclaim', or defer using them. In the majority of cases taxpayers want to use the capital allowances claimed as quickly as possible to gain the maximum cash advantage, but there may be occasions where other available allowances or forms of tax relief, which might not be transferable or might be time limited, may be utilised before capital allowances. Claiming allowances just to increase a trading loss carried forward may not be in the best interests of a taxpayer, especially if there are non-trade profits to shelter in a future year. In this instance a higher capital allowance pool would be preferable. In most cases it is possible to disclaim capital allowances and claim the amounts disclaimed in later years. There are exceptions and these are covered in the detailed review of individual allowances regimes. An alternative strategy, where there is no immediate or short term need for allowances, is not to make a claim in the first place and to wait until allowances are needed before claiming. And as claims can be made at any time while the claimant still owns the asset this is not a problem provided that fully detailed and appropriate records of the expenditure incurred are retained and available to prove the claim. In practice this is not always the case and can lead to difficulties in securing the full amount of allowances potentially available.

In regard to claims made for allowances on fixtures in the purchase of second-hand buildings, FA 2012 introduced changes which could limit or even eliminate a purchaser's ability to claim allowances on any purchases from April 2012. HMRC's hope is that capital allowances in such situations will, eventually, be dealt with as an integral part of the property sale process (and thus also limit the risks that allowances are claimed more than once on the same expenditure). This does happen at present in many cases with parties to a transaction agreeing capital allowances elections, but the changes to the legislation now mean that unless purchasers actively pursue the issue they may not be entitled to claim any allowances. At its simplest, where a vendor has claimed capital allowances and if the purchaser and vendor have not agreed a figure for capital allowances or referred the claim to a tax tribunal within two years of the transaction, the purchaser, and any subsequent purchaser, will be unable to claim allowances on the fixtures covered by the transaction. The changes are now fully operational (since April 2014), having been partially introduced in April 2012. The added complexities, introduced in April 2014, have put an additional burden on to the vendor in a transaction. In order to protect the position for future owners of the property the vendor is obliged to 'pool' or collate the expenditure on assets qualifying for capital allowances even in the event that the vendor hasn't made a claim itself (see **9.100**).

Claims are usually made in the tax return:

- by 31 January following the fiscal year end for individuals via their return of income for income tax purposes; and
- within 12 months of their period end for companies in their annual return of profits (FA 1998, Sch 18, para 79).

It should be noted that pre-trading expenditure may be claimed.

The taxpayer may withdraw or amend the claim at any point up to two years after the end of the relevant accounting period or the date when the assessment for that period becomes final, whichever is later.

In the past revised claims could be notified by letter giving all of the relevant detail and reasons for the amendment together with the amount of the change to the tax position, and HMRC limited such amendments to a six year limit. Under the self-assessment regime, however, the time limit is removed and revisions to claims require an amended return of profits (FA 1998, Sch 18, para 81).

Revisions to claims usually arise for two main reasons:

- the detail of the claim and the identification of the costs of the assets claimed is unclear; or
- the basis of the claim, in terms of the legislation, is regarded as wrong.

It is, therefore, essential that any claim is well founded in the legislation and appropriately supported with an identifiable and auditable trail to the costs claimed.

In some cases, where the amount involved is significant to the taxpayer's figures for the year, or contains potentially contentious items, it may be helpful to agree with HMRC to submit the claim in advance of the tax return to try and secure certainty prior to the actual submission. This can be particularly helpful where apportionment calculations are involved and other parties, eg the Valuation Office Agency, may be involved.

Once submitted, HMRC may challenge a claim within 12 months from the submission date or, if later, two years from the end of the accounting period in which the claim is made.

What types of allowances are available?

[9.4] In terms of claiming allowances there are four mechanisms:

- writing down allowances (WDAs) – the most common method of allowing tax relief when it is available on capital expenditure; the relief is spread over a number of years following the capital investment, either on a straight line basis or on a reducing balance basis dependent upon the specific circumstances;
- first year allowances (FYAs) – where the rate of allowances is specially increased to allow a greater proportion of the costs of investments to qualify for tax relief against the business's profits in the year that the expenditure is incurred;
- initial allowances (IA) – a term used in past legislation and generally superseded by FYAs; and
- balancing allowances (BA) – an amount falling due to a claimant on the occasion of a disposal event where the allowances due to the claimant are greater than those already utilised, in which case the balancing amount is added to the claimant's capital allowances pool.

Where a taxpayer requires to pay back allowances, for whatever reasons, there are balancing charges (BC) – the reverse of a balancing allowance, ie where the claimant has taken more allowances than are available following the disposal event the difference between the two amounts is deducted from the claimant's capital allowances pool (if there is no pool available a monetary amount may be substituted in lieu).

The most straightforward, and usually greatest, tax advantages from capital allowances in property projects tend to be secured on works involving direct expenditure, ie building, fitting out, or refurbishing. The focus of this section is in identifying the range of allowances that may be available on property and property related projects, and identifying the extent of what may be claimed together with any exclusions or limitations that may be imposed. The key is to know what is available and then to consider how best to take advantage of the different allowances regimes in play. To this end each of the allowances regimes is analysed in terms of what is available and what is allowable, together with the consequences and opportunities arising from acquiring or disposing of an interest in property.

In descending order of benefit to taxpayers, allowances available in the tax year 2016–17 and allowances which have been withdrawn are as follows:

- 150% first year allowances:
  - Land Remediation Relief (covering contaminated land and bringing long-term derelict land back into productive use) (previously proposed to be withdrawn from 2012 but retained following consultation);
- 100% first year allowances:
  - Annual Investment Allowance (AIA) to a maximum of £200,000 (from January 2016 onwards) (previously £500,000/£250,000/£25,000/£100,000/£50,000);
  - Enterprise Zones: First Year Allowances for Designated Areas (EZFYA) (the original EZA scheme ceased from April 2011);
  - Research and Development Allowances (RDA);
  - Energy Saving Plant Enhanced Capital Allowances (ECA);

- Landlord's Energy Saving Allowance (LESA) (a temporary measure until 2015);
- Business Premises Renovation Allowances (BPRA) (due to end in March 2017);
- 18% reducing balance basis (the main pool) (previously 20%):
  — Plant and Machinery Allowances: Fixtures (P&M/PMA);
- 8% reducing balance basis (the special rate pool) (previously 10%):
  - Integral Features Allowance (IFA);
  - Insulation to existing buildings;
  - Plant and Machinery Long Life Assets (LOLA);

An amendment from 2009-2010 of particular interest to smaller businesses was the introduction of the new small pools clause (CAA 2001, s 56A) that changed the situation in regard to tracking and calculating allowances due each year. When the amount left in the pool, either the main pool or the special rate pool, is £1,000 or less it may be written off in its entirety. This appears to be a small but helpful measure in terms of compliance generally, and the fact that it is not compulsory to claim the whole amount means that small businesses will be able to adopt the most beneficial approach to their individual circumstances. The measure does not apply to single asset pools.

What is the comparative benefit of each of these allowances?

[9.5] The changes to the legislation over recent years also included changes to the depreciation rates claimable against the various categories of allowances. On the assumption that the full amount of allowances can be utilised the following table summarises the cumulative tax savings potentially available over the first five years, and at the end of ten years.

	Cumulative tax saving %					
Allowances	*Year 1*	*Year 2*	*Year 3*	*Year 4*	*Year 5*	*Year 10*
150% FYA	150					
100% FYA	100					
18% reducing balance	18.0	34.4	45.9	55.1	62.5	82.3
8% reducing balance	8.0	15.3	22.1	28.3	34.1	56.5

Given the announcement in Budget 2016, and now contained within Finance Act 2016, of the further drop in corporation tax rates to 19% in 2017 and now 17% in 2020 it cannot be ruled out that the new look of Conservative Government may look to reduce the rates of capital allowances to help fund the drop in the main rate. This would chime with the stated objectives of preferring to reduce corporation tax rates as a key instrument of policy. Whether the net effect is advantageous to businesses is a matter of conjecture. It may, however, be another step towards a longer term goal of equalising all capital allowances in property, and perhaps beyond, at some form of standard rate, either straight line or reducing balance, to simplify the system.

Expenditure incurred

[9.6] The date that expenditure is incurred, or is deemed to be incurred, is the common starting point for all capital allowances claims. It is the date on which the obligation to pay becomes unconditional (CA11800 superseding HMRC Tax Bulletin 9, November 1993).

If a buyer is legally required to pay for goods on delivery the obligation to pay becomes unconditional when the goods are delivered. This applies even if goods are sold with a 'Romalpa', (ie reservation of title), clause because the vendor has fulfilled his part of the bargain which makes the obligation to pay unconditional.

HMRC refer to 'milestone' contracts and payments under those contracts. This is a catch-all terminology to cover assorted situations where items of plant, eg manufacturing process machinery, are manufactured over a pro-longed period and payments are geared towards completion of set or identifiable phases such as completion of a significant part or delivery of an element to the premises. An example would be, say 10% on completion of design, 60% on completion of manufacture, 15% on installation on site, and 15% on completion of commissioning of the new plant. Property is, however, somewhat different and while percentage payments may be agreed in certain circumstances the majority of new build projects are paid for on the basis of a monthly certificate issued by the architect or engineer stating the value of the works undertaken. HMRC consider that the obligation to pay condition is effective from the date of any such certificate.

Claims are made for the expenditure incurred during an accounting period. Some payments, however, made beyond the end of the accounting period may be included in capital allowances expenditure for the period if the obligation to pay becomes unconditional within one month of the end of the accounting period. This means that work carried out within the period but not certified until up to one month beyond the period end would be eligible for inclusion in the capital allowances claim (CAA 2001, s 5(4)).

If an agreement requires any consideration to be paid at a date that is four months or more after the obligation to pay becomes unconditional, the consideration is treated as occurring on the later date. If, as part of such an agreement, there is a requirement to make a part payment within the four month period the payments should be split, with the payment made within the four months regarded as being incurred when the obligation to pay became unconditional and the balance being regarded as being incurred on the date when payment was required to be made (CAA 2001, s 5(5)).

If an obligation to pay becomes unconditional on a date earlier than that which accords with normal commercial practice and the sole or main benefit which might be expected to arise is to advance expenditure to a period earlier than would otherwise have been the case the expenditure will be treated as incurred 'on or before which it is required to be paid' (CAA 2001, s 5(6)). This simple, if somewhat inelegantly phrased, anti-avoidance measure just means that tinkering with the obligation to pay conditions so as to be able to claim in a period earlier than would normally be the case will not work.

Most construction contracts include 'retention' clauses that can vary but are usually in a range of up to 5% of the expenditure incurred, dependent upon the specific circumstances of the works being undertaken. The objective of the retention clause is to allow a period during which any defects or remedial works may be identified and rectified. Retention money is only considered unconditional, and therefore claimable, when the condition giving rise to the retention is satisfied.

The general rules about the date that expenditure is incurred do not apply where expenditure is incurred before a trade begins or a building or structure is bought unused. In these cases the expenditure is regarded as occurring on the first day of trading or the date when the purchase price becomes payable, respectively. It should, however, be noted that claims for plant and machinery allowances may be made during the progress of a project if there is an ongoing qualifying activity, eg while IBAs may not be claimed before the building is brought into use it is possible to claim the plant and machinery element during the construction period if the claimant has other qualifying activities.

Land remediation relief (contaminated and derelict land)

General

[9.7] Contaminated land relief makes 150% first year allowances available to any company incurring approved expenditure from 11 May 2001 (FA 2001, Sch 22). It is not available to individuals, partnerships or trusts, although a company that is a member of a partnership may be able to claim its share of the partnership's qualifying land remediation expenditure. Unlike capital allowance land remediation relief is available to property investors and developers alike.

Introduced as part of a package of measures to help regeneration of mainly brownfield sites it actually has a coverage much wider than the title suggests. It can include removing anything that might be 'harmful' to the environment, which opens up a range of possibilities in maximising the tax relief available.

This is an interesting situation in that what is, by any standards, capital expenditure is classified as revenue for the purposes of the legislation.

As a measure of the government's commitment to review the effectiveness of this legislation a consultation document on tax incentives for brownfield land was issued in March 2007 and proposals came forward in December 2007 indicating that land remediation relief would be extended to a number of new items such as the removal of foundations or obsolete services from land designated as long term derelict land, ie land derelict since 31 March 1998. There were also indications that the costs of removal of Japanese knotweed and treatment, either on or off site, would be eligible for relief.

FA 2009 brought these items within the scope of expenditure incurred from 1 April 2009 (Note: the legislation refers to 'the removal of Japanese knotweed' and not to its treatment. Hopefully this is just a drafting oversight and it may reflect the movement away from landfill options to more sophisticated forms of remediation.)

What qualifies in principle?

[9.8] Land in the UK that has been acquired for the purposes of a trade or a property business.

Land is regarded as being 'contaminated' if 'substances' in or under the land are causing harm, or there is the possibility of them causing:

* harm to the health of living organisms;
* interference with the ecological systems of which any organisms form part;
* offence to the senses of human beings;
* damage to property; or
* the pollution of controlled waters, or the possibility of their pollution through the entry of any poisonous, noxious, polluting or solid waste matter.

'Substances' are any natural or artificial substance, whether in solid or liquid form or in the form of a gas or vapour. A substance is matter having uniform properties (eg asbestos is a substance but life forms are not regarded as substances).

'Controlled waters' generally means within territorial waters, ie the three-mile limit. Specifically it encompasses:

* for England and Wales, the Water Resources Act 1991, Part III;
* for Scotland, the Control of Pollution Act 1974, s 30A;
* for Northern Ireland, the Water (Northern Ireland) Order 1999, art 2(2) covering waterways and underground strata.

Notwithstanding personal sensitivities, the costs involved in moving human remains in burial sites are not considered to fall within the scope of this legislation. Where, however, there is a need to move remains to allow development to proceed, and it is judged that there may be some form of health risk involved in the process then the extra over costs of protection against such risk will be allowable as qualifying land remediation expenditure.

Naturally occurring contaminants do not qualify for relief but the new legislation allows for the treatment of radon, arsenic, and Japanese knotweed. The 'polluter pays' principle prevents an owner from making claims on contamination arising during his ownership. The exception to this rule, however, is that if a site was clear of Japanese knotweed at the time of purchase but has since become contaminated through natural means then a claim may be made.

Until November 2008 HMRC had resisted claims that Japanese knotweed was eligible under the 'harm' test but in a Technical Note they then accepted that it was eligible and that they would settle any outstanding claims or claims for in-date years. This included costs of removal of Japanese knotweed to landfill. The new legislation excludes landfill as a treatment and it is considered an inappropriate method of remediation.

Generally 'Derelict Land' is land as defined under the English National Land Use Database (NLUD) and the Scottish Vacant & Derelict Land Survey (SVDLS) but this is not definitive as there are no similar lists for Wales or Northern Ireland.

The items that now qualify for relief are the removal of:

- post-tensioned concrete heavyweight construction;
- foundations of buildings or other structures or machinery bases;
- reinforced concrete pilecaps;
- reinforced concrete basements; or
- underground pipes or other apparatus for the supply of electricity, gas, water or telecommunication services or for drainage or sewerage.

Both the date from which land is deemed derelict and the items allowable across the remediation reliefs can be changed by secondary legislation, ie the apparently ever increasing use of Statutory Instruments to change legislation rather than take them through scrutiny or debate in parliament.

What costs qualify?

[9.9] Qualifying expenditure covers steps, operations or works undertaken in:

- preventing or minimising;
- remedying or mitigating

the effects of any harm, or pollution of controlled waters, by reason of which the land is polluted, or restoring the land or water to its former state.

This includes any necessary preparatory works to determine if the site is polluted and any action necessary. These costs are only recoverable if the company actually carries out remedial activities. If, after investigation, the site is found not to be contaminated, or if it is contaminated and the company does not proceed with the remediation works, these costs are not allowable under this legislation.

All costs incurred through using subcontractors to effect land remediation works should be eligible.

Where, however, connected parties are involved, eg the sub-contractor is connected to the claimant, the whole of the costs will only be claimable if the subcontractor has treated the payments as income in the course of his trade, ie revenue expenditure as opposed to capital expenditure, and it has not been the subject of any subsidy.

In addition to the usually expected range of costs that may be claimed, eg specialist asbestos removal contractors or any other specialists required to execute remediation works, there is provision for the costs of employees directly involved in remediation to be claimed. There is a sliding scale as follows:

80% or more of time spent on remediation	100% recovery
20%–80% spent on remediation	a pro-rated allowance
20% or less time spent on remediation	nil recovery

The amount that can be recovered covers all emoluments, pension contributions and Class 1 National Insurance contributions.

Administrative and secretarial costs appear not to be allowed, but given the nature of certain types of remediation works and the requirement for appropriate health and safety aspects, the exact definition of what constitutes administration or secretarial work leaves this a slightly grey area.

What does not qualify?

[9.10] There are six main factors that prevent a claim:

(1) the expenditure has already received a tax deduction in an earlier period;
(2) a capital allowance has been made in respect of the expenditure;
(3) the land is contaminated because of the actions, or inaction, of the claimant or a connected person;
(4) the expenditure would have been incurred irrespective of the contamination;
(5) the expenditure is subsidised;
(6) the land is a nuclear site in terms of the Nuclear Installations Act 1965 and the licensee's responsibility has not yet ended.

A potentially difficult area is where it appears that the purchase price of the land or property has been discounted to take cognisance of the fact that there is contamination and this may be regarded as a 'subsidy'. This is a somewhat specious viewpoint and interprets the word 'subsidy' in the legislation in a perverse way. The whole point of the legislation was to lessen the risk element so that development would take place. Given that many contaminated land sites actually have negative values the term 'subsidy' should be viewed in its normally accepted definition, ie a grant towards the cost of an asset.

A 'subsidy' could, however, arise if the vendor agrees to pay for part of the remediation works. In this case the vendor's contribution would have to be deducted from any claim.

As with most tax allowances there are anti-avoidance provisions to prevent a company entering into any arrangement (which includes any scheme, agreement or understanding whether or not legally enforceable) which has as its sole or main objective obtaining a deduction or credit which would not otherwise have been allowed or entitled, or would have been smaller but for the arrangement entered into (FA 2001, Sch 22, para 29).

How does it operate?

[9.11] Contaminated land relief claims must be made in the relevant tax return and can only be amended by amending the return (FA 2001, Sch 23, para 4).

It can be given by way of a deduction against profits of a trade or Schedule A business, of an amount equal to 150% of the costs incurred in the year in which the remediation works are undertaken.

Within two years of the end of the accounting period in which the expenditure is incurred the company needs to elect to treat the land remediation expenditure as a deduction in computing its Schedule D Case I or Schedule A tax computation. If the expenditure is incurred in advance of the commencement of the trade the expenditure will be deemed to have been incurred on the first day of trading. (A pro forma election is contained in **APPENDIX 1** to this chapter at 2.3.)

If a loss situation occurs the company may surrender the loss and claim a land remediation tax credit of 16% (or whatever percentage is applied at the time). A loss arising, however, must be reduced by any set off in the current year and no account should be taken of losses brought forward or carried back.

In broad terms, if immediate cash flow is not the key driver it may be more beneficial to forego the tax credit and utilise the allowances against future profits.

Example 2
Claiming 100% relief in the year of expenditure

Princess Charlotte Ltd is carrying on a trade and incurs land remediation expenditure of £100,000 in an accounting period. This is an allowable deduction in computing his Case I loss for corporation tax purposes. Because of contaminated land allowances it can claim an additional 50% in allowances, ie £50,000, in respect of the expenditure. Its total deduction against profits is therefore £150,000.

After taking other expenses into account, however, the company has an overall trading loss of £160,000 in the accounting period. It has other income of £20,000 in the period. It can make a claim to surrender the full amount of its qualifying land remediation loss in exchange for a payment of land remediation tax credit, as follows:

(a)	150% of qualifying land remediation expenditure	£150,000 (£100,000 × 150%)
(b)	The unrelieved trading loss in the period	£140,000 (£160,000 – £20,000)
(c)	Qualifying land remediation loss is the lesser of the two amounts	£140,000

The tax credit payable is £140,000 × 16% ie £22,400 and the trading loss carried forward to the next period is £20,000, ie £160,000 less £140,000.

Example 3
Claiming partial relief

George Ltd has a trading loss of £200,000 of which £150,000 is qualifying land remediation loss. It claims a payable tax credit of £16,000.

The amount of tax credit claimed, ie £16,000 equates to a qualifying land remediation loss of £100,000, ie £16,000 ÷ 16 × 100 = £100,000.

The carry forward loss is, accordingly, £100,000, ie the original trading loss of £100,000 less the £100,000 qualifying land remediation loss surrendered.

Disposal

[9.12] It should be noted that on disposal of an asset it is only the actual cost of any remediation works which is allowable as part of the base cost for CGT purposes, ie the additional 50% uplift in allowances is disallowed (TCGA 1992, s 39).

Annual investment allowance

General

[9.13] Annual investment allowance (AIA) is a 100% first year allowance available, from January 2016 onwards, for the first £200,000 of expenditure on plant and machinery per annum (decreased from £500,000 in the previous year and previously £250,000, £25,000, £100,000 and £50,000). George Osborne announced in his Summer Budget 2015 that the allowance would be set at £200,000 from 1 January 2016 and it would remain at this level going forward. This is a welcome announcement given it was previously stated that it would revert to £25,000 in 2016. It is also good news that this will hopefully now be the end of the continual yo-yoing of the allowance. Changing rates each year has been leading to complicated calculations where accounting periods span the changes. The AIA is available to individuals, partnerships of individuals and companies. It replaces the 40% and 50% first year allowances previously available to SMEs but it is not restricted by the turnover, assets, or employee numbers of the claimant and as such is available to all businesses, subject to certain qualifications. It does not replace any of the existing 100% FYA schemes and anti-avoidance provisions prevent any double relief being claimed. There are anti-avoidance provisions to disallow property loss relief against general income to the extent that the loss is attributable to the AIA. They apply to losses arising as a result of relevant tax avoidance arrangements entered into on or after 24 March 2010. The loss will be attributable to the AIA before anything else, including any other capital allowances.

Now that we are probably focusing on 31 December 2016 and later year ends, the calculation of the available allowance has become more straightforward. Previously, where a business had an accounting period that spanned the changes to the AIA amount it needed to consider two separate time periods.

Example 4

Corbyn Ltd, incurred £450,000 of expenditure on items to assist in an election campaign (items qualifying for capital allowances) in its year ended 30 November 2016. The expenditure was incurred as follows:

December 2015: £50,000

April 2016: £400,000

To determine its AIA Corbyn Ltd needs to split its period into two parts: 1 December 2015 to 31 December 2015 (when £500,000 was the available AIA); and 1 January 2016 to 30 November 2016 (when £200,000 is available for the AIA).

Pro-rating the amounts leads to Corbyn Ltd being able to claim the AIA on the following level of expenditure:

1 December 2015 to 31 December 2015: 1/12 x £500,000 = £41,667

1 January 2016 to 30 November: 11/12 x £200,000 = £183,333

So a total AIA of £225,000

Corbyn Ltd should, of course, first allocate, the AIA as far as possible to expenditure in the special rate pool, notably long life assets or integral features.

What qualifies in principle?

[9.14] Expenditure incurred on qualifying plant and machinery after 1 April 2008 for corporation taxpayers and 6 April 2008 for income taxpayers qualifies for the AIA (CAA 2001, s 38A). The level of the AIA has changed over the years to its current (and hopefully now permanent), amount of £200,000.

One of the key aspects of AIA is that it may be claimed against any of the plant and machinery categories on which expenditure has been incurred; ie in addition to the main plant and machinery items available on a 18% per annum reducing balance basis it may also be claimed on integral features or long life assets which are both available on a 8% per annum reducing balance basis. If expenditure on qualifying assets exceeds £500,000/£250,000 the balance above the limit is allocated to the appropriate plant and machinery pool, ie 18% per annum reducing balance for the general plant and machinery pool and 8% per annum reducing balance for the 'special rate' plant and machinery pool. It should be noted that AIA is also available on leased assets unlike the previous FYAs for SMEs.

While the objective of the allowances is to be available to all there are some restrictions where groups of companies or elements of common control are involved (CAA 2001, ss 51C–51J).

The main restriction is where companies are legally and economically inter-dependent. In such a situation there will be one AIA for the group. Where a singleton company is controlled by a person or persons but they do not control any 'related' company each company will be entitled to an AIA. Similarly, with unincorporated businesses, provided the same person(s) do not control a 'related' business each entity will be entitled to its AIA.

Where one or more unincorporated businesses or companies are controlled by the same person(s) and, in the tax or financial year and at the end of the chargeable period, they share the same premises or more than 50% of turnover is within the same NACE classification (EU equivalent of UK standard industrial classification of economic activity) then only one AIA is available. It should, however, be noted that eligibility for AIA is treated separately for unincorporated businesses and companies so the foregoing example does not apply where there is a combination of an unincorporated business and a company.

What does not qualify?

[9.15] Expenditure incurred in the chargeable period in which the qualifying activity is permanently discontinued is ineligible, as is expenditure on a ring fence trade chargeable under ICTA 1988, s 501A.

AIA is also unavailable where the qualifying plant is 'provided for other uses' (CAA 2001, ss 13, 13A) and where it is gifted (CAA 2001, s 14).

There is also a somewhat convoluted restriction with regard to expenditure where the provision of plant or machinery is connected with a change in the nature or conduct of the trade or business carried on by someone other than the person incurring the expenditure, and where the main purpose or one of the main purposes is to enable a person to obtain an allowance to which they would not otherwise have been entitled.

How does it operate?

[9.16] Claims are made in the normal manner for capital allowances with pro-rated adjustments to the maximum level of claim where chargeable periods are greater or less than a year.

Double relief, ie claiming an AIA and an FYA, is prohibited by CAA 2001, s 52A and the usual restriction on artificial arrangements is included.

The AIA is a 'use it or lose it relief'. If it is not used in the year it cannot be carried forward.

To make the most of the relief the AIA should be allocated first to the special rate pool.

Enterprise zones: first-year allowances for designated areas (EZAFYA)

General

[9.17] Enterprise zones were first established in FA 1980 as a means of encouraging investment in development to help create employment in depressed areas of the country. Over the period 46 areas of 'special need' were designated as enterprise zones; see *Tolley's Capital Allowances 2017–18* and 100% first-year allowances were available for new build industrial and commercial buildings. The allowance covered the total building cost including, by exception, the plant and machinery within the building and was available to the person who incurred, or was deemed to have incurred, expenditure on construction of the building. It did not cover acquisition costs.

Enterprise zone allowances were withdrawn, with industrial building allowances, from April 2011.

The new allowances regime flows from the Government's decision, announced in the 2011 Budget, to create new enterprise zones with simplified planning and business rates discounts. There are currently 46 enterprise zones in England but another two are expected before the end of 2017 (see enterprise zones.communities.gov.uk/enterprise-zones-list/).

On enterprise zones where enhanced capital allowances are available (assisted areas), businesses now have up to eight years from the launch of the enterprise zone to make their investment.

What qualifies in principle?

[9.18] Unlike the previous EZA regime which covered the total costs involved, ie building and plant and machinery, the new allowance is only available on expenditure incurred on items designated as plant and machinery.

In addition, the premises must be within a 'designated area' within the enterprise zone and not all enterprise zones contain designated areas. The requirement for a 'designated area' and the following criteria that must be met in order for the expenditure to qualify are mechanisms to avoid the relief falling foul of EU rules and regulations on the provision of state aid.

In order to qualify the expenditure must be incurred

- by a company (unincorporated businesses and partnerships of companies are ineligible);
- by a UK-resident company which is liable to corporation tax, and that carries on a trade or a mining, transport or similar undertaking per ITTOIA 2005, s 12(4) or CTA 2009, s 39(4);
- for an investment purpose rather than operating aid, ie expenditure in setting up a new business, expanding an existing business, or on a fundamental change to a product or production process of, or of service provided by, a business carried on by the company;
- on new and unused plant and machinery;
- within a period of eight years from the launch of the EZ.

Designated area boundaries are quite strictly drawn so despite the title of the zone, eg Telford, it does not necessarily mean the whole area in the title is eligible for allowances. It is necessary to check the exact area eligible and the actual perimeter of the area, so in these terms it is not dissimilar to the old EZ regime. There are currently only eight zones in assisted areas that qualify for the relief.

It should be noted that 'designated areas' are made by Treasury Order, which in this instance can be retrospective. This means that expenditure incurred from 1 April 2012 can still be claimed even if the 'designated area' status is not granted until after the Finance Bill is passed. In addition there is also a provision that the areas cannot be reduced in size or revoked retrospectively, which gives an added level of confidence in finalising the taxation aspects of possible investment options.

What costs qualify?

[9.19] Expenditure on new and unused plant and machinery incurred by a company on the provision of plant and machinery for use primarily in an area which is a designated assisted area at the time.

There is an upper limit on the amount that can be claimed on any one project of €125 million.

What does not qualify?

[9.20] The restrictions on claiming this allowance focus on the entity or sector involved. If the company incurring the expenditure is, or forms part of, an 'undertaking' that is engaged in the

- fishery and aquaculture sectors (Council Regulation (EC) No 104/2000);
- coal, steel, shipbuilding or synthetic fibres sectors;
- management of waste of other 'undertakings';
- primary production of agricultural products;
- on-farm activities necessary for preparing an animal or plant product for first sale;
- first sale of agricultural products by a primary producer to wholesalers, retailers or processors where the sale does not take place on separate premises reserved for that purpose,

then it cannot make a claim under this regime.

There are further restrictions in regard to firms 'in difficulty' or 'subject to an outstanding recovery order'. These relate to specific European Commission regulations. The first in regard to State Aid for Rescuing and Restructuring Firms in Difficulty (EC 2004/C 244/02) and the second where the EC has declared the aid package illegal.

For clarification, the legislation, while allowing expenditure in the air transport and road freight sectors, specifically excludes the allowances from applying to of means of transport and transport equipment.

The usual anti-avoidance provisions apply and if other forms of allowances or state aid are available claimants need to consider which is the most beneficial to claim.

It should be noted that the new plant and machinery should be in place for five years.

How does it operate?

[9.21] EZAs are claimed in the same way as other capital allowances.

The taxpayer may claim 100% allowances in the year the expenditure is incurred or choose to limit the claim to any amount up to the 100%. If an amount less than the full 100% is claimed, for whatever reason, the balance falls to be claimed as a writing down allowance of 18% or 8% per annum depending upon the classification of the assets to plant and machinery or integral features.

Research and development allowance (RDA)

General

[9.22] RDA is a 100% first year allowance on capital expenditure incurred by a person carrying on a trade in connection with research and development related to that trade, or by someone on his behalf, or, having incurred the expenditure he sets up a trade connected with the research and development (CAA 2001, s 439).

RDAs were known as Scientific Research Allowances until FA 2000 when the name, but not the scope, changed.

What qualifies in principle?

[9.23] The definition is detailed in ITA 2007, s 1006 but for practical property purposes it can be summarised as:

(a)   research and development which may lead to or facilitate an extension of that trade; and

(b)   research and development of a medical nature which has a special relation to the welfare of workers employed in that trade.

What costs qualify?

[9.24] Expenditure on research and development is primarily expenditure incurred for carrying on research and development but, from a property perspective; it also includes expenditure incurred in providing facilities for carrying out research and development.

As with, the now abolished, IBA, even if the whole of the property involved is not in use for the qualifying purpose, so long as the non qualifying element is not more than 25% of the total cost it may be included in the claim. If the cost of the non qualifying element is more than 25% then it is ineligible for RDA and the RDA claim will be reduced accordingly. It may be that there are other allowances available on the costs that are ineligible for RDA but that is a matter of detail dependent upon the exact use of the property.

Example 5

Bill's Research Ltd buys an office block to use for qualifying research purposes. It has a flat incorporated within the building. They pay £1,000,000 for the building excluding the land element. The cost attributable to the flat, on an apportioned basis, is £200,000, ie 20%. As this is less than the 25% cut off point the whole of the £1,000,000 qualifies for RDAs.

Ben's Research Ltd buys a similar office block to use for qualifying research purposes and it has a large penthouse flat as part of the building. Of the £1,000,000 purchase price the cost attributable to the flat, similarly apportioned, is £300,000. As this is more than the 25% limit of £250,000, Ben's Research only secure RDAs on £700,000, ie the total expenditure less the ineligible amount.

What does not qualify?

[9.25] No allowances are available for the acquisition of land or interests in land. Neither are RDAs available where an asset eg a building, is acquired for another purpose and then used for research and development, although costs incurred in any necessary conversion works could possibly be claimed as RDAs, or alternatively through any other appropriate allowances regimes, eg P&M etc.

It should be noted that professions or vocations are unable to claim RDA. It is only available to those carrying on a trade.

How does it operate?

[9.26] RDA is claimed in the same way as other capital allowances, ie on the corporation tax return for companies and on the income tax return for individuals and partnerships.

There is no requirement to claim the full 100% allowance but if it is not claimed and only a reduced amount, say 50%, is claimed then the balance cannot be claimed later (CAA 2001, s 441(3)). This is a significant difference from other first year allowance regimes where any amounts unclaimed in the first year can usually be claimed at a later date.

Disposal

[9.27] A disposal event occurs if there is a cessation of ownership of the qualifying asset or if it is demolished or destroyed while still owned by the claimant. A change of use away from an approved research and development use is not regarded as a disposal event within the legislation.

If a disposal event arises there is a balancing charge if the disposal value is greater than the amount of any unclaimed RDA. The charge is the lesser of the amount by which the disposal value exceeds any unclaimed RDA, or the RDA claim actually made.

Example 6

Little Weed Research Ltd build a laboratory for £2,000,000 for a qualifying activity but do not claim 100% allowances and instead only claim 75%, ie £1,500,000. This leaves unclaimed allowances of £500,000 which Little Weed cannot claim in the future because writing down allowances are not available under the RDA legislation (CAA 2001, s 441(1)).

Two years later Little Weed sells the laboratory to Bill's Research Ltd for £2,500,000. The RDA claim made of £1,500,000 is less than the amount by which the disposal value £2,500,000 exceeds the unclaimed RDA of £500,000 (£2,500,000 – £500,000 = £2,000,000) and so the balancing charge is £1,500,000, ie the RDA claim made.

The disposal value is determined by the disposal event.

Disposal event	Disposal value
Sale of asset at not less than market value	Net proceeds
Demolition or destruction of asset	Net amount received for the remains together with any insurance money or other capital compensation
Any other event	Market value

Acquisition

[9.28] Where a building or structure is purchased and it falls within the definition of eligibility for RDAs the cost needs to be apportioned between eligible buildings or structures and ineligible land in accordance with CAA 2001, Ch 5 (Apportionment). (The subject of apportionment is dealt with in detail under the general plant and machinery heading later in this chapter.)

Energy saving equipment and environmentally friendly equipment: enhanced capital allowance (ECA)

General

[9.29] 100% first year allowance on the costs of energy saving or environmentally friendly plant or equipment is available to any taxpayer with a relevant interest, and also, for energy saving plant, to an 'energy services provider' being a person carrying on a qualifying activity consisting wholly or mainly in the provision of energy management services (CAA 2001, s 45A).

The allowance is available for expenditure incurred from 1 April 2001 for energy saving plant and machinery.

As part of the government's drive towards greater energy efficiency FA 2001 introduced legislation with a view to encouraging investment in energy saving plant and machinery by increasing the allowances from the standard plant and machinery basis of 25% per annum reducing balance basis (now 18%) to 100% first year allowances. And in FA 2003 the same principle was extended to what was termed environmentally beneficial plant which currently covers water efficient investments. It is likely that further technologies will be added in years to come as part of the government's overall drive to reduce carbon emissions and to reduce energy use so this could be a growing area which should be monitored for new opportunities each year.

In an innovative move to encourage investment in environmentally friendly expenditure from those who cannot offset capital allowances against profits the government has introduced a payable tax credit for companies with losses arising from capital expenditure on certain approved 'green technologies'. The scheme was initially referred to at consultation stage as Payable Enhanced Capital Allowances but appears in the legislation under Sch 25 as First year tax credits.

It must be remembered, however, that most if not all of the items that qualify under the ECA legislation would already have qualified under CA 2001 for plant and machinery allowances, eg taxpayers who got excited about being able to claim energy efficient lighting soon discovered that the lighting only qualified in the limited number of situations where it already qualified as plant and machinery. From FA 2008, however, the introduction of integral features allowances (IFA) and the extension of the definition of qualifying plant to cover electrical installations including lighting systems meant that it is possible to claim energy efficient lighting in its entirety.

The actual benefit of this legislation, from a purely tax perspective, is at best a quicker use of the allowances for those who have the capacity to utilise them. Taking a wider commercial viewpoint, however, there are four factors to be considered with regard to acting on the ECA legislation and making a claim. These are:

- the initial capital cost of approved energy saving assets against the capital cost of assets performing a similar function which are not approved;
- the tax relief differential between 100% first year allowances and an 8% or 18% reducing balance basis;
- the costs of compliance, ie researching, deciding and recording the relevant information to justify the claim;
- the forecast savings to energy bills resulting from the use of the energy saving assets.

From the foregoing it can be seen that the decision to make a claim under this legislation requires input from beyond accounting and tax personnel. It must be considered at the design stage of any new project and will require expert advice from the structural engineer.

What qualifies in principle – energy saving plant and machinery

[9.30] Expenditure incurred, or contracts entered into, for energy saving or environmentally friendly plant and machinery as specified by Treasury Order(s) applicable at the time the expenditure was incurred or the contract entered into.

The item must be included in the Energy Technology List ('ETL') at the time the expenditure is incurred. If it has been removed from the list or added at a later date it will not qualify. For more detail, see:

www.gov.uk/government/publications/energy-technology-list-etl-information-for-purchasers.

To search for a specific product see:

https://etl.beis.gov.uk/engetl/fox/live/ETL_PUBLIC_PRODUCT_SEARCH.

The original energy saving technologies and items specified as eligible came into effect for expenditure incurred from 1 April 2001. Subsequent amendments and additions are identified in the following list with their effective dates alongside.

Plant and machinery or integral features are considered energy-saving if:

(a)   it falls within a technology class specified;

(b)   it meets the energy-saving criteria set out in that list;

(c)   it falls within one of the classes of:

    (i)   air-to-air energy recovery (from 26 August 2004):

        –   plate heat exchangers (or recuperators);

        –   rotating heat exchangers (including thermal and desicant heat wheels);

        –   run around coils;

        –   heat pipe heat exchangers;

    (ii)   automatic monitoring and targeting (from 5 August 2003) (but portable equipment must be of a type within one of the two above lists, and a component based fixed system within the class 'automatic monitoring and targeting equipment' in the Energy Technology list):

        –   portable AMT equipment;

        –   component based AMT equipment;

    (iii)   boiler equipment:

        –   automatic boiler blowdown control equipment;

        –   biomass boilers and room heaters;

        –   burners with controls;

        –   combustion trim controls (withdrawn from 2 August 2012);

        –   condensate pumping equipment;

        –   condensing economisers;

        –   flue gas economisers;

        –   gas-fired condensing water heaters;

        –   heat recovery from condensate and boiler blowdown;

        –   hot water boilers;

        –   localised rapid steam generators;

        –   optimising controls for wet heating systems;

        –   retrofit burner control systems;

        –   sequence controls (withdrawn from 2 August 2012);

        –   steam boilers;

    (iv)   combined heat and power (CHP);

    (v)   compressed air equipment (from 5 August 2002):

        –   energy saving controls for desicant air dryers (withdrawn from 2 August 2012);

        –   flow controllers (from 11 August 2008);

        –   master controllers (from 11 August 2008);

        –   refrigerated air dryers with energy saving controls;

    (vi)   compact heat exchangers (from 26 August 2004) (removed 8 October 2010);

    (vii)   heating, ventilation and air conditioning (HVAC) equipment:

        –   heating ventilation and air conditioning (HVAC) zone controls (from 26 August 2004);

        –   close control air conditioning equipment (from August 2009);

    (viii) heat pumps for space heating (from 5 August 2002):

- air source: air to water heat pumps;
- air source: gas engine driven split and multi-split (including variable refrigerant flow) heat pumps;
- air source: packaged heat pumps;
- air source: split and multi-split (including variable refrigerant flow) heat pumps;
- ground source: brine to air heat pumps (withdrawn August 2009);
- ground source: brine to water heat pumps;
- water source: packaged heat pumps;
- water source: split and multi-split (including variable refrigerant flow) heat pumps;
- heat pump dehumidifiers (from 11 August 2008);
- heat pump driven air curtains (from 2 August 2012);

(ix) lighting:
- high efficiency lighting units;
- lighting controls;
- white emitting diode lighting units for amenity, accent and display lighting (LED) (from 11 August 2008);

(x) motors and drives:
- integrated motor drive units;
- permanent magnet synchronous motors;
- single speed ac induction motors;
- variable speed drives;
- switched reluctance drives;

(xi) pipework insulation;
- refrigeration pipework;
- chilled water pipework;
- non-domestic heating and hot water services (excluding insulation within individual buildings);
- process pipework;

(xii) refrigeration equipment (from 5 August 2002):
- absorption & other heat driven cooling & heating equipment;
- air cooled condensing units;
- automatic air purgers;
- automated permanent refrigerant leak detection systems;
- cellar cooling equipment;
- commercial service cabinets;
- curtains, blinds, sliding doors and covers for refrigerated display cabinets;
- evaporative condensers;
- forced air pre-coolers;
- refrigeration compressors;
- refrigeration system controls;
- refrigerated display cabinets;

(xiii) solar thermal systems (from 5 August 2002) (provided that the system or the solar collector included in it is of a type included in the Energy Technology Products list) (see (f) below);

(xiv) thermal screens (withdrawn 7 September 2006);

        (xv)   uninterruptable power supplies (from August 2009):
           –   static uninterruptable power supply units or packages;
           –   rotary uninterruptable power supply units or packages;
        (xvi) warm air and radiant heater;
        (xvii) waste heat to electricity conversion equipment;
        (xviii) high speed hand air dryers (from October 2011).

(d)   it is of a type that is specified in, and has not been removed from the Energy Technology Products list;

(e)   Budget 2012 introduced a restriction on claiming the 100% allowances where feed-in tariffs (FITs) or renewable heat incentive tariffs (RHIs) are paid in respect of electricity or heat generated (or gas or fuel produced). The allowances cannot be claimed on the plant generating the power if such payments are made. This took effect from April 2012 generally and took effect from April 2014 for CHP schemes (the exact dates dependent upon whether corporation tax or income tax applies). Going forward a choice will be available as to whether to take the allowance or the feed in tariff but it will not be possible to benefit from both.

(f)   Budget 2012 also classified expenditure incurred on solar panels from April 2012 as special rate expenditure, ie 8% per annum writing down allowance.

The approved technology categories are updated annually by Treasury Order (usually in July) as part of the budget cycle. Updated new categories, sub-categories, and amendments to existing qualifying criteria are then added to the Energy Technology List (ETL). It should be noted that where amendments are made expenditure is only qualifying from the date of the amendment. Updates or revisions to criteria are only identified through the ETL and it is prudent to check each year for changes to the criteria within each technology heading or sub-heading. There are times when it may be questionable if the end benefit is worth the effort required to secure the additional allowance and this may well be why the uptake of this allowance has not been as high as predicted over recent years.

The ETL incorporates all the technologies and products that may qualify for ECAs. To see if a particular product qualifies refer to:

https://etl.beis.gov.uk/engetl/fox/live/ETL_PUBLIC_PRODUCT_SEARCH.

While the DECC covers the technologies related to energy savings it is the Department for Environment Food and Rural Affairs (DEFRA) that deals with water efficient technologies.

It lists all of the approved technologies and the specific items of plant that qualify for ECAs by technology, by manufacturer, and by manufacturer's product reference. This is provided to allow taxpayers to provide the supporting information necessary to justify ECA claims.

The way that the system works is that manufacturers apply to have their products listed within the appropriate technology lists or sub headings and provide information to DEFRA demonstrating how the products meet the energy saving criteria; if successful, the products are added to the various lists and incorporated in the website. The product lists are updated on a monthly basis and only qualify for allowances once approved. The current approved products list runs to 964 pages and has over 20,000 products listed.

Energy efficient lighting and pipework insulation, however, are not recorded in this manner. For these technologies it is only the manufacturers who can provide eligible products in these areas that are listed. It is, therefore, incumbent upon the claimant to ensure that any products used are from a range of the manufacturer's products that actually comply with the ECA legislation.

Gas refuelling stations

[9.31] In addition to the generally eligible items listed ECAs are also available on plant and machinery in gas refuelling stations which covers any premises, or parts of premises where vehicles are refuelled with natural gas or hydrogen (CAA 2001, s 45E). The items allowable for the enhanced allowances include storage tanks, compressor, pumps, controls and meters, and any equipment for dispensing the gas or hydrogen to the fuel tank of a vehicle. While this is not of significant importance at present (there are only two makes of car currently on the market which utilise this technology and less than 15 actual gas refuelling stations in the UK at present), the potential future growth of such stations as part of the means of reducing the carbon footprint of the UK may lead to it being a very useful allowance. A number of commercial haulage operators and transport companies are converting their vehicles or are seriously looking at the overall benefits to be obtained from conversion. When combined with the continuing development of duel fuel cars by a range of manufacturers this does suggest that this is a growing area. Expenditure incurred from 17 April 2002 qualifies for the enhanced allowances, and there is the usual range of unsurprising anti-avoidance measures linked to it (CAA 2001, s 46). FA 2008 changes the terminology from 'natural gas' to 'biogas' and defines biogas as produced from the anaerobic conversion of organic matter and used for propelling vehicles. The changes apply to expenditure incurred from 1 April 2008 and the scheme which was originally due to expire on 31 March 2008 has been extended to 31 March 2013.

What costs qualify?

[9.32] Expenditure incurred on the provision of approved assets covered by the Energy Technology Products list published on the ECA website www.eca .gov.uk.

Expenditure on the provision of many items of plant that are purchased as part of the services installations within a building contain a mix of items, some that are approved under the energy saving scheme and some that are not. In order to help with the principles of the energy saving scheme the Treasury has devised a system whereby the parts of a larger entity that meet the relevant energy saving criteria can qualify even if the entity itself does not meet the ECA criteria. The detail of the amounts available in such situations is dealt with under Treasury Orders which specify the maximum amounts available for ECA for each item of plant so designated, eg optimising controllers for heating systems should be claimed on the actual costs incurred or a maximum amount of £3,000 plus £300 for each zone controlled. There are other examples where the allowable element is based upon a percentage of the cost of the entity but all of the information necessary to make such claims is contained within the ECA website. It includes an easy to use ready reckoner tool which, on a simple menu based approach, allows claimants to work through the relevant technologies and items to establish how much of their expenditure should be eligible for ECA.

In recognising that, in the drive to encourage energy saving, new methods of working with regard to managing energy in properties were evolving it became apparent that the general rule with regard to being eligible to claim allowances, ie having a relevant interest in the land, could be seen to be limiting the potential opportunities. The concept of the 'energy services provider', who did not have a traditional relevant interest but could still claim allowances, was born.

An 'energy service agreement' is an agreement between an 'energy service provider' and another party, who may or may not be a taxpayer. This allows the 'energy services provider' to be able to claim allowances where the other party is not a taxpayer and is therefore unable to claim allowances in any event.

The agreement covers the design of plant or machinery, or of a system or systems incorporating plant or machinery, procurement and installation, operation, and maintenance of the entity or entities. And, that payment is linked, wholly or partly, to either energy savings or increased energy efficiency resulting from the provision or operation of the plant and machinery by the energy services provider.

In order to qualify for ECA compliance with the following is required (CAA 2001, s 180A):

(a)   an 'energy service agreement' is entered into;
(b)   the 'energy services provider' incurs capital expenditure under the agreement on the provision of plant and machinery;
(c)   the plant or machinery becomes a fixture;
(d)   at the time the plant and machinery becomes a fixture its client has an interest in the land but the 'energy services provider' does not;
(e)   the plant or machinery is not provided for leasing and is not provided in a dwelling house;
(f)   the operation of the plant and machinery is carried out wholly or substantially by the 'energy services provider' (or a person connected with him);
(g)   the energy service provider and the client are not connected persons;
(h)   the client and the 'energy service provider' elect that CAA 2001, s 180 should apply.

What does not qualify?

[9.33] Second hand plant or plant that falls within the Long Life Asset ('LLA' – see also **9.103** ff) definition, ie having an estimated useful economic life of 25 years or more, does not qualify.

Leased energy saving plant is ineligible unless covered by an 'energy saving agreement'.

Railway assets are also excluded. Apart from the obvious rolling stock, the term 'railway asset' covers anything which is, or is to be, comprised in any railway station, railway track or light maintenance depot and is provided wholly and exclusively for the purposes of a railway business. This means that expenditure incurred on any property used in such a manner will not qualify under the ECA legislation. If, however, the 'wholly and exclusively' condition is absent it would appear that the LOLA legislation may take effect. HMRC accept that the 'wholly or mainly' condition is met if at least 75% of the building is used for one of the exempt purposes.

If, at any point, an energy efficiency certificate, environmental certificate for a technology, or specific plant item is revoked it not only ceases to be available as a claims item but any past claims made must be adjusted. The taxpayer has three months from discovering that a technology or item has been revoked to make the necessary amendments. This was thought to be specifically aimed at specialised or 'one off' designs such as Combined Heat and Power (CHP) installations where what is actually constructed is at variance with what was accepted as complying with the legislation to the extent that what is actually constructed does not meet the proposed energy saving criteria.

In practice, however, it is somewhat worrying that the reason given on the ECA website for the withdrawal of the three technologies so far removed from the lists (Multiple Speed Motors and Thermal Screens from the energy list and Electronic Drain Taps from the environmentally friendly list) is that ECA intervention has been 'successful' ie it has assisted the market penetration of these new technologies. If this rationale is to be applied across the board for new technologies as they are added to the list it means added uncertainty and an increased compliance burden for taxpayers. The initial decision tree as to whether or not to utilise plant and machinery from the lists is complex enough without the added uncertainty of having to revise tax computations just because the product's market share has increased. How this approach encourages the use of energy saving plant, much of which may be more expensive than other less environmentally friendly alternatives, is unclear.

How does it operate?

[9.34] ECA is claimed in the same way as other capital allowances ie on the corporation tax return for companies and on the income tax return for individuals and partnerships.

There are, however, certain additional requirements before some claims can be made.

Automatic Monitoring and Tracking systems (AMT) need a certificate of energy efficiency before a claim can be made for them. Businesses can choose any AMT components provided they meet the Energy Technology Criteria list and they must then complete an application form giving details of the installation and the site address and submit it to the Carbon Trust. DEFRA will issue certificates in response to such applications and the company can use this as entitlement to claim the ECA.

Combined Heat and Power (CHP) installations tend to be large scale and custom designed. They, therefore, need to be certified as 'Good quality CHP' and have a certificate of energy efficiency issued confirming that the scheme meets the requirements of the Energy Technology Criteria list. The certificate is issued by DEFRA based upon the proposed design or on the completed installation. A prudent taxpayer would wish to ensure that the certificate was in place before embarking on the scheme.

The Energy Technology Criteria list sets out the required energy saving standards for lighting and pipework insulation, rather than attempting to list every possible product that might qualify under these headings. It falls, therefore, to anyone making a claim for such items to ensure that they can demonstrate that the relevant standards have been met. This can be achieved by seeking confirmation from the manufacturer or from the contractor installing the plant or equipment that it meets the standard.

Disposal

[9.35] If an energy services provider assigns his rights under an energy services agreement for a building, or item of plant, the assignee is regarded as being an energy services provider who has incurred expenditure on the plant and machinery for the price paid to the existing energy services provider.

If an energy services provider receives a capital payment from the client in the energy services agreement to discharge his obligations under the contract the client is regarded as having purchased the plant for that amount.

Acquisition

[9.36] If a purchaser pays a capital sum for a building which has an energy services agreement in place and pays a capital sum to the energy services provider then the purchaser is regarded as the owner of the plant and machinery as it is a fixture. The purchaser will not be entitled to 100% ECA because the plant is second hand but may be able to claim plant and machinery allowances on the plant and machinery under a just apportionment of the total purchase price paid for the building.

What qualifies in principle – environmentally beneficial plant and machinery

[9.37] This is almost identical to the energy saving legislation, but with Water Technologies substituted for Energy Technologies. It applies to expenditure incurred from 1 April 2003 and the list, in alphabetical order, is as follows:

(1)   cleaning in place equipment (from 22 September 2005):
  –   monitoring and control equipment;
  –   spray devices;
(2)   efficient showers (from 22 September 2005):
  –   aerated showerheads;
  –   auto shut off showers (electromagnetic systems/mechanical and pneumatic push systems);

- electromagnetic systems;
- mechanical and pneumatic push systems;
- flow regulators;
- low flow showerheads;
- thermostatic controlled showers;
(3) efficient taps (electronic drain taps withdrawn 7 September 2006):
- automatic shut-off taps;
- electronic taps;
- low-flow screw down taps/lever taps;
- spray taps;
(4) efficient toilets:
- low flush toilets;
- retrofit WC flushing devices;
- urinal controls;
(5) efficient washing machines (for large scale fabric washing) (7 September 2006):
- efficient commercial washing machines;
- efficient industrial washing machines (efficient continuous batch washers (CBWs) or washer tunnels/efficient washer extractors);
(6) flow controllers:
- control devices;
- flow limiting devices;
(7) leakage detection equipment:
- data loggers;
- pressure reducing valve controllers;
- remote reading and leak warning devices;
(8) meters and monitoring equipment:
- flow meters;
- water management software;
(9) rainwater harvesting equipment (from 26 August 2004):
- monitoring and control equipment;
- rainwater filtration equipment;
- rainwater storage vessels;
- water level and consumption indicators;
- mains back up control units;
(10) small scale slurry and sludge dewatering equipment (7 September 2006):
- belt press equipment;
- centrifuge equipment;
- filter press equipment;
(11) vehicle wash reclaim units (16 August 2007):
- partial or full reclaim units;
(12) water management equipment for mechanical seals (formerly 'waste management for mechanical seals' (16 August 2007));
- seal water recycling units;
- internal flow regulators;
- monitoring and control units;
(13) water efficient industrial cleaning equipment (formerly 'efficient wash water reclaim units' (16 August 2007)).
- scrubber driers (walk behind machines);

- scrubber driers (ride on machines);
- steam cleaners.

(14) water reuse;
- efficient membrane filtration systems;
- efficient wastewater recovery and reuse systems (R & R).

(15) grey water recovery and reuse system (from 7 August 2013).

In addition, subsections are being added within the main technologies headings as more products are developed that meet the overall criteria. The approved technologies list, adding or removing technologies or amending the criteria for inclusion, is updated annually and enacted by Statutory Instrument.

To search for specific products refer to:

www.gov.uk/government/uploads/system/uploads/attachment_data/file/53527 4/water-technology-product-list-2016.pdf.

There is provision for allowances on parts of installations where the whole asset does not qualify, as there is in the energy saving part of this regime, and the detail can be found on the website www.eca-water.gov.uk.

Again, as in the energy section, a certificate of environmental benefit can be issued for unique or specially designed installations that seek to minimise water use or improve water quality. It applies specifically to water reuse systems, where the two sub technologies need an appropriate certificate of environmental benefit from DEFRA before a 100% first year allowance will be allowed.

Generally, all other requirements and restrictions are similar to the energy-saving plant although the exception is that there is no provision under this part of the legislation to allow for similar arrangements to that of 'energy service providers' under the energy saving rules.

First-year tax credits

General

[9.38] As part of the drive to encourage investment in green technologies, companies within the charge to corporation tax that make a loss through investing in qualifying energy saving or environmentally beneficial plant and machinery may be able to a claim a first year tax credit. The amount claimable will be 19% of the loss surrendered subject to being capped at an amount equal to the total of the company's PAYE and National Insurance Contributions for the period in which the loss is surrendered, or £250,000, whichever is the higher amount. The £250,000 tax credit equates to an actual loss of around £1.3 million.

The legislation, introduced under FA 2008, Sch 8, is perhaps slightly more complex than it need be, but any provision dealing with potential loss making situations presents particular difficulties and needs to tread a fine line between encouragement and the potential for abuse. In this instance, however, it will be interesting to see the extent to which the tax credits are taken up over the next few years.

What qualifies in principle?

[9.39] Only expenditure incurred under CAA 2001, s 45A (energy-saving plant or machinery), or CAA 2001, s 45H (environmentally beneficial plant or machinery) for the purposes of a qualifying activity, the profits of which are chargeable to corporation tax, may qualify to be included in the tax credit calculation.

Losses from a trade, an ordinary property business, an overseas property business, a furnished holiday lettings business, or from managing the investments of a company with an investment business may all qualify but the key factor is that it only applies to companies within the charge to corporation tax.

What costs qualify?

[9.40] Losses incurred carrying on a qualifying activity and costs incurred from 1 April 2008 to 31 March 2018 on items of plant and machinery on the ECA technology and product lists.

What does not qualify?

[9.41] Expenditure incurred by companies that at any time during the chargeable period are entitled to make claims under co-operative housing or self-build societies regulations (ICTA 1988, ss 488, 489) is ineligible, as is expenditure by charitable companies or scientific research organisations (ICTA 1988, ss 505 and 508).

Losses that could be off-set against other taxable profits in the same period or surrendered as group relief are not eligible to be used to claim first year tax credits. The full range of ineligible losses is detailed in CAA 2001, s 262A, Sch A1, Part 1, para 10 et seq.

Additional VAT liabilities that qualify for first year allowances under CAA 2001, s 236 are not claimable under this clause.

How does it operate?

[9.42] The claim is made as part of the return or amended return as necessary. The detail with the claim must provide appropriate information to identify the plant and confirm that it qualifies as ECA qualifying plant or machinery (ie description and manufacturer's reference, the amount of the expenditure, and the date incurred). If the plant or machinery is of a type that requires Defra certification (eg a combined heat and power plant (CHP)) the appropriate certification must be part of the claim documentation.

Payment of tax credits is not income of the company for tax purposes.

It should be noted that there are assorted provisions on restrictions on losses carried forward.

Generally there will be no payment of tax credits if the company's return is under enquiry, there are outstanding corporation tax liabilities, or there are outstanding PAYE or Class 1 NICs liabilities outstanding for the periods ending in the chargeable period. HMRC do, however, have discretion to make a provisional payment in whole or in part pending resolution of outstanding matters. There are also provisions that allow HMRC to decide that no payments will be made.

A company may be able to claim R&D tax credits along with first-year tax credits. There is no upper limit in these tax credit regimes and the first-year tax credit upper limit is not reduced when R&D tax credits are claimed. A loss, however, may only be surrendered once.

Disposal

[9.43] There is a clawback of the credit if the item(s) on which the original claim was made is disposed of within four years. The four year period is measured from the date the initial expenditure is incurred through to the end of the chargeable period for which the tax credit was paid. So, in practice this could actually be near enough a five-year period dependent upon the specific circumstances.

Landlord's energy saving allowance (LESA)

(For expenditure incurred prior to April 2015)

[9.44] In addition to the capital allowances available under CAA 2001 for energy saving expenditure it should be noted that there are other deductions available for approved energy saving expenditure. The Landlord's Energy Saving Allowance (LESA) was initially introduced in 2004 as a tax deduction for non corporate landlords (ITTOIA 2005, s 312) who installed approved energy-saving items to rented residential property. FA 2007 proposed to extend this to corporate landlords who let residential property but it was subject to state aid approval by the European Commission. Approval was granted and expenditure incurred by corporate landlords from 7 July 2008 is claimable (SI 2008/1520). The allowance provides a tax deduction in computing rental income up to a maximum of £1,500 per property for expenditure incurred until 5 April 2015. Previously the allowance was per 'building' but FA 2007 widened the definition so that, for example, the maximum allowance is available for each flat within a building.

The term 'relevant expenditure' means expenditure incurred in acquiring and installing an energy-saving item in a dwelling house, or in so far as it is for the benefit of a dwelling house, expenditure incurred in acquiring and installing an energy saving item in a building containing that dwelling house.

The items against which this allowance may be claimed were previously identified as follows:

- the installation of cavity wall insulation and loft insulation, from 6 April 2004 (SI 2004/2664);
- solid wall insulation between, from 7 April 2005 (SI 2005/1114);
- draught proofing and insulation for hot water systems, from 6 April 2006 (SI 2006/912);

- floor insulation, from 6 April 2007 (SI 2007/831).

The new nomenclature from SI 2008/1520 for the purposes of ICTA 1988, s 31ZA(5) is as follows:

(a)   hot water system insulation;
(b)   draught proofing;
(c)   cavity wall insulation;
(d)   solid wall insulation;
(e)   floor insulation; and
(f)   loft insulation.

No deduction is available if the energy saving item is installed during the course of construction, or if the person incurring the expenditure does not have an interest in the property. Neither is there a deduction if the property is furnished holiday accommodation or let under the rent-a-room scheme.

For new property investment businesses the deduction is available for expenditure incurred up to six months before the business commenced providing that it was not incurred before 6 April 2004 (ITTOIA 2005, s 313(5) and Sch 2, para 73), or the operative date for the subsequent additions to the list.

Where only part of the expenditure would qualify for relief the tax deduction is calculated using a just and reasonable apportionment.

Business premises renovation allowance (BPRA)

General

[9.45] With effect from 31 March 2017 for corporate tax payers or 5 April for individuals, BPRA was withdrawn. Previously, this relief allowed for a 100% allowance in the year of expenditure on bringing empty and redundant business properties in 'disadvantaged areas' back into use. This measure was introduced in FA 2005, s 92, Sch 6 and as CAA 2001, Parts 1–3A and came into effect for expenditure incurred from 11 April 2007 following state aid approval from the EC.

The stated intention was that the regime would run for a five-year period and, as with similar legislation aimed at encouraging economic development, any projects which had commenced before the legislation became operative would not qualify for the allowance.

This measure is 'part of the government's holistic approach to regeneration'. The headline legislation, in common with the Flat Conversion Allowances, may entice potential developers to look at the possibilities but, in the vast majority of cases, it was thought that it would be unlikely to make a significant impact on regeneration. Even the Regulatory Impact Assessment carried out admitted that 'it is a relatively modest measure, so its direct impact on regeneration could also be modest'. And the RIA was carried out before restrictions on availability in certain industries were added. Notwithstanding these caveats it has proved to be an exceedingly worthwhile allowance in the right circumstances.

Budget 2011 extended the period of availability from its original end date of 2012 through to 2017. It was also limited to projects not exceeding €20 million in order to avoid falling foul of EU regulations on State Aid.

What qualified in principle?

[9.46] The qualifying tests were that it must:

(a)   be situated in one of the (2000) designated disadvantaged areas when the renovation or work begins (defined as areas specified as development areas by the Assisted Areas Order 2007 (SI 2007/107) and all of Northern Ireland);

(b)   have been unused throughout for a period of one year immediately prior to work commencing;

(c)   on last use, have been in use for the purposes of a trade, profession or vocation, or an office whether or not for the purposes of a trade, profession or vocation;

(d)   on last use, not have been a dwelling or part of a dwelling; and

(e)   where part of a building or structure, on that date had not been last occupied and used in common with any other part of the building or structure other than a part as respects which the condition in (b) is met, or which had last been used as a dwelling.

Put simply, only premises or parts of premises that were unoccupied for a year qualify, and premises used as dwellings do not qualify.

The qualifying areas can be found using the HMRC website which has a postcode check tool to assist would be claimants (www.hmrc.gov.uk).

What costs qualified?

[9.47] In Budget 2014 it was announced that from April 2014 the criteria for qualifying expenditure was to be tightened. Relief was then only available for the actual costs of construction and building work, and for certain specified activities such as architectural and surveying services.

The legislation also provided that additional associated but unspecified activities (such as project management services) qualified for relief, limited to 5% of the actual costs as newly specified.

What did not qualify?

[9.48] Expenditure incurred on or in connection with the following was ineligible for the allowance:

(a)   acquisition of land or rights over land;

(b)   extension to a qualifying building (except to the extent required for the purposes of getting to or from qualifying business premises);

(c)   development of land adjoining or adjacent to a qualifying building;

(d)   provision of plant or machinery, other than that which is or becomes a fixture under CAA 2001;

(e) any premises that are refurbished by, or used by, businesses engaged in:
  (i) fisheries and aquaculture;
  (ii) shipbuilding;
  (iii) the coal industry;
  (iv) the steel industry;
  (v) synthetic fibres;
  (vi) primary production of certain agricultural products;
  (vii) the manufacture of products which imitate or substitute for milk or milk products.

The amount of any allowance will be reduced by the amount of any grant received towards the cost of the works. Where a grant is repaid an equivalent amount of allowance will be made.

How did it operate?

[9.49] BPRA was claimed in the same way as other capital allowances, ie on the corporation tax return for companies and on the income tax return for individuals and partnerships.

The taxpayer must have had an appropriate 'relevant interest', usually a freehold or a lease, in the property or the part of the property being developed when expenditure is being incurred in order to claim against the qualifying expenditure.

It is also possible for the taxpayer to claim the allowances if he secures a relevant interest as a result of the renovation or conversion (CAA 2001, s 360).

Disposal/acquisition

[9.50] There were no balancing charges or allowances provided that there was no disposal event within five years of the premises being brought back into use, and there were no transfer of allowances to a subsequent purchaser (previously seven years but the announcement of the reduction was made in Budget 2014 and is effective from April 2014).

The possible disposal events were:

(a) the sale of the relevant interest;
(b) the grant of a long lease in consideration of a capital sum;
(c) if the relevant interest is a lease, its coming to an end other than by the holder acquiring the headlease;
(d) the demolition or destruction of the flat;
(e) the premises ceasing to be qualifying (without being demolished or destroyed) (CAA 2001, s 393N).

Where more than one balancing event took place the balancing adjustment is made on the first of them.

Balancing event	Proceeds from event
Transfer of relevant interest	Net proceeds of sale if the relevant interest is sold
	Market value if the transfer is other than by way of sale
Grant of a long lease out of the relevant interest for a capital sum	The capital sum paid for the grant, or, if less than the commercial premium, the commercial premium
The coming to an end of a lease where a person entitled to the lease and a person entitled to any superior interest are connected persons	Market value of the relevant interest at the time of the event
Death of the person who incurred the qualifying expenditure	Residue of qualifying expenditure immediately before
Demolition or destruction of the flat	Net amount received plus any insurance or compensation receipts

Plant and machinery allowances (P&M)

General

[9.51] 100% allowances granted at a rate of 18% per annum on a reducing balance basis for expenditure on qualifying plant and machinery or fixtures, or at a rate of 8% per annum reducing balance for expenditure on qualifying integral features.

Until FA 2008 plant and machinery was a single category with allowances available on a 25% per annum reducing balance basis. FA 2008 introduced a new sub-category of plant and machinery, integral features (IFAs), and also introduced separate depreciation rates for each. This section focuses on plant and machinery generally and is followed by a section on integral features.

Plant and machinery allowances are important because in a great number of properties they may be the only tax relief available. They are also important because the amount of tax that may be saved can be quite significant. The following table shows the normal distribution of P&M allowances, including integral features, available in typical capital projects as a percentage of the total construction expenditure incurred.

	%
Office buildings	15–40
Hotels and leisure centres	25–60
Shopping centres	5–20
Retail units and warehouses	1–10
Industrial complexes	5–40
PFI projects, schools, hospitals etc	20–55
Fitting out premises	40–95
Refurbishment projects	30–95

In past years, in industrial buildings or hotels where there was a mix of allowances, ie plant and machinery and industrial buildings allowances, it was possible to secure almost the entire capital expenditure as allowances under one regime or the other, and it was really about the timing of allowances in terms of the split between the different depreciation rates available.

The ending of industrial buildings allowances, however, puts all buildings on an equal footing in that plant and machinery allowances, and its sub-sets, are the only option available and the focus for maximising tax relief.

Where an IBA pool or HBA pool was large at the time the allowances ceased to be available (April 2011) it may be worth revisiting the expenditure to see if any of it could have qualified as plant. Where this is the case it may be possible to claim on the remaining WDV.

In addition, the introduction of the new integral features category affects overall tax relief because of the lower and differential depreciation rates now applicable. Studies indicate that the integral features/plant and machinery ratio could approximate to an 80/20 split. In the example of an office showing total allowances of 40% this would mean 32% of the expenditure would qualify as integral features at 8% per annum reducing balance and 8% would qualify as plant and machinery at 18% reducing balance. The actual split between the categories, however, will be dependent upon a detailed analysis of the specifics of individual projects based upon the specification of the works being undertaken and the impact of any operational requirements reflected in the works being undertaken.

The refurbishment figures in the table above include revenue deductions for elements of refurbishment projects that involve repair and maintenance expenditure.

It is wrong to suggest that there is a set target for the amount of qualifying plant and machinery or fixtures within any specific building or building type because most commercial or industrial buildings are unique in either their detailed form of construction or use, so results outside the above ranges are possible and can still be correct. Where a claim is outside the range indicated it should be re-examined to ensure that a correct assessment has been made, ie neither an under claim which would lead to paying too much tax nor an over claim which could lead to penalties. Under self-assessment the taxpayer is responsible for any errors made in submissions so it is essential to ensure that sufficient and appropriate detail is available to support any claims made.

The range is also influenced by what is, and what is not, included within the construction cost eg in an office development the works being undertaken might be a fully fitted out building or it might only be a developer's shell and core specification and this will be reflected in the outcome, eg 35% of a fully fitted building might be the equivalent of a 20% claim on a shell and core development and a 75% or so claim by the person fitting out the offices. The following demonstrates the possibilities.

Example 7

> Richard builds an office block to a shell and core specification for £10m and claims 20% in allowances, ie £2m. Richard then lets it in a shell and core condition to Charles who spends £4m on fitting it out to his operational requirements and claims 75% in allowances, ie £3m.
>
> If Charles, however, was not a taxpayer or did not wish to incur the fitting out costs it could make commercial sense for Richard to take the office block to a fully fitted out stage, ie spend the whole £14m and make the claim £6m, ie 36%.

Between the two situations outlined in the example there is a range of other potential scenarios that can all have an impact on the overall commercial decisions made in regard to the proposed investment. These could include contributions to expenditure, incentive payments, and subsidies and the possible impact of these measures is examined in more detail later in the chapter.

Quoting percentages for claims, other than in the broadest terms, is not to be encouraged without appropriate knowledge of the detail involved. It is not unusual for claimants, or colleagues, to opine to the practitioner that a better result may be achievable based upon percentages quoted in articles in the technical press, or even revered text books. The actual outcome of any claim is dependent upon the specific detail of the property under review and the quality of the supporting information.

Recent years have seen HMRC consider replacing capital allowances with some form of depreciation allowances as used, for example, in New Zealand where just about every item conceivable in business use has a defined useful life for tax purposes. But it was not to be, at least for the present, and the current state of play with regard to capital allowances is that there are items definitely excluded from being claimed, items which may be eligible in certain situations, and a large grey area in between which could fall into either classification.

This, in part, explains why until recently capital allowances claims were usually so contentious and in the top two most frequently queried items in tax returns. Recent research suggests that they are now causing less contention but the reasons are not totally clear. It may be that, with self-assessment, claimants have moved to presenting more detailed and robustly researched claims that HMRC can fully understand and accept, or it may be that taxpayers have tired of the, at times, long and wearisome struggle to secure claims and have opted for simpler and less challenging claims. It is probably a mixture of the two.

The balance of this section highlights the reasons behind such apparent anomalies and delves deeper into what may qualify, what may not, and how to recognise the differences and to act accordingly.

What qualifies in principle?

[9.52] The worthy and helpful *Tax Law Rewrite*, of which Capital Allowances Act 2001 is a product, was not intended to change existing case law but to clarify the legislation, which it has done, in part. It has, however, been somewhat limited by the fact that there is no statutory definition of plant and machinery, which leads to a somewhat strangulated approach in attempting to define what is not and what may be eligible for plant and machinery allowances, ie the Act lists what is excluded from being part of a plant and machinery claim for buildings or structures, and then lists expenditure unaffected by the exclusions. To the untrained eye it could appear that some aspects of expenditure occur in both lists, which they do.

The key point is that there are multiple Special Commissioners', High Court and House of Lords decisions that, through appropriate interpretation, can justify a staggeringly wide range of items to be considered as plant and machinery, eg from aerials to zoo cages. It depends upon who uses it and for what purpose. One of the best examples is a painting hanging on a wall. In an office it would not qualify for allowances but in a public house, hotel or restaurant it could.

The basis of the current system of capital allowances and plant and machinery allowances stems from 1945, but prior to that there were a number of disputes about plant and machinery under various taxation regimes and these form the roots of many of the accepted decisions on what may or may not be plant or machinery.

Machinery has always been less contentious than plant because it is generally accepted that machinery has moving parts and is thus readily identifiable and not subject to dispute. HMRC have generally tended to regard a machine as something which applies mechanical power (Tax Bulletin 13, October 1994). Whether this is still the case when many aspects of what would be regarded as traditional machinery, with moving mechanical parts, is now run with microchips and electronic processors is open to debate, but to date HMRC have accepted that technological change has not altered the purpose or output of machines or machinery.

Plant, on the other hand, has been contentious for a long time, and a case involving a dead horse and an injured workman give us the best guidance on what is, and what is not likely to be 'plant'. In 1887 in the case of *Yarmouth v France* (1887) 19 QBD 647, CA Lindley LJ said:

'There is no definition of plant in the Act; but in its ordinary sense, it includes whatever apparatus is used by a business man for carrying on his business, not his stock-in trade, which he buys or makes for sale; but all goods and chattels, fixed or moveable, live or dead, which he keeps for permanent employment in his business.'

On that basis, and given the workman's trade, a live horse was plant and a dead one meant that the workman was entitled to compensation for the loss of his 'plant'.

Over the years since then there have been a number of cases in the courts trying to refine this view, both before the introduction of the modern system of capital allowances in 1945 and since. Many of the cases since 1878 have been involved with property and property related matters because property disputes generally tend to be about significant sums of money.

In 1944 in the case of *J Lyons & Co Ltd v Attorney-General ChD* [1944] 1 All ER 477 a new concept was introduced by Uthwatt J, the 'setting' test:

'In the present case, the question at issue may, I think, be put thus: Are the lamps and fitments properly to be regarded as part of the setting in which the business is carried on or as part of the apparatus used for carrying on the business? In this case the lamps and their fitments are owned by a caterer and used in the premises exclusively devoted to catering purposes. But the presence of lamps in this building is not dictated by the nature of the particular trade there carried on, or by the fact that it is for trade purposes that the building is used. Lamps are required to enable the building to be used where natural light is insufficient. The actual lamps themselves, so far as the evidence goes, present no special feature either in construction, purpose or position and, being supplied with electricity from public suppliers, they form no part of an electric lighting plant in or to the hereditament.

In my opinion these lamps are not, in the circumstances, properly described as "plant", but are part of the general setting in which the business is carried on. They would not, I think, in any catalogue of this trader's assets, fall under the heading "machinery and plant".'

This view, that if it is merely setting, then it is not plant translated into a definition that plant was 'apparatus with which the trade was carried on'.

In *Benson (Inspector of Taxes) v The Yard Arm Club* [1979] STC 266, 53 TC 67 the claimants operated a restaurant on the *Hispaniola*, a ship moored on the Thames at Victoria Embankment in London and claimed the entire 'ship' as plant under the capital allowances legislation. Templeman LJ rejected the claim:

'I can see no difference between a restaurant in the Thames and a fish and chip shop in Bethnal Green.'

This was further expanded by Shaw LJ who said:

'A characteristic of plant appears . . . to be that it is an adjunct to the carrying on of the business and not the essential site or core of the business itself.'

This produced the 'functional' test, ie whether the asset functions as apparatus used in carrying on the activities of the business, in which case it is plant, or if it was merely the premises in which the business activity is carried out it is not plant.

This definition was expanded further in the cases of *Wimpy International v Warland; Associated Restaurants Ltd v Warland* (1988) 61 TC 51, [1989] STC 273, CA which involved claims for refurbishing restaurants in the Wimpy and Pizzaland chains, both taxpayers being part of the same group (for clarification this is Wimpy, the hamburger people and not Wimpey the housebuilder and contractor). Hoffmann J (as he was then, now Lord Hoffmann QC) posed three questions:

- Is the item stock in trade? – If so it cannot be plant.
- Is it used for carrying on the business? – The equivalent of the functional test in *Benson*. The asset must be more than being used in the business, it must be used for carrying on the business.
- Is the item the business premises or part of the premises? – The premises test; if the answer is 'yes' then it cannot be plant.

He expanded the premises test question in order to differentiate items that, while they may appear to be part of the premises, could still be eligible as plant. He asked:

(1)   Does the item appear visually to retain a separate identity?
(2)   With what degree of permanence has it been attached to the building?
(3)   To what extent is the structure complete without it?
(4)   To what extent is it intended to be permanent or alternatively is it likely to be replaced within a short period?

These are questions of fact and degree and not regarded, even by HMRC, as absolute hurdles that must each be surmounted.

In general the following are the three main tests that are used to determine eligibility of items for allowances:

* the functional test;
* the business use test;
* the premises test.

There is a fourth which is regarded by many as the same as the premises test but which can, in fact, lead to slightly different conclusions:

* the completeness test.

There are, however, many instances where the tests can and do overlap. The following summaries show where specific tests and combinations of the tests have been approved by the courts.

The functional test

[9.53] One of the key cases is *IRC v Barclay Curle* (1969) 45 TC 221, HL where a dry dock was held to be plant. The claimant carried on a trade of shipbuilding and repairing on the Clyde and built a new dry dock. It claimed the total costs of construction including excavations, concrete works, dock gates, and the systems associated with emptying and filling the dock. While the Crown argued that the basin element, ie the structure, was merely 'setting' in which operations were carried out Lord Reid viewed the operation as a two stage process. The first was to isolate the ship from the water and the second was to inspect it and carry out repairs. On that basis the second stage could well be 'setting' but the first stage was most definitely not, as it performed a function in the trade, ie moving the ship in and out of the dock. He said:

'The whole dock is, I think, the means by which, or plant with which, the operation is performed. . . . I do not say that every structure which fulfills the function of plant must be regarded as plant, but I think one would have to find some good reason for excluding such a structure. And I do not think that mere size is sufficient.'

The fact that the dry dock might also be a structure did not prevent it from being regarded as an item of plant.

Similarly, in *Cooke v Beach Station Caravans Ltd* (1974) 49 TC 514, ChD, where a caravan park operator built two heated swimming pools to attract customers to the park and claimed them in their entirety. HMRC felt that while certain elements of the installations such as heating and filtration systems qualified as plant and machinery, others, such as the costs of excavation and construction of the pools and surrounds, did not. On appeal Megarry J, however, supported the Special Commissioners' viewpoint that all of the expenditure incurred qualified as plant and machinery. In addition to accepting that the pools were self-contained units and the fact that the purpose was to attract customers he added that they performed an active function in the running of the business and that the pools were 'part of the means whereby the trade is carried on, and not merely the place at which it is carried on'.

Another case that is interesting and the more so given current legislation and interpretation is *Schofield v R&H Hall Ltd* (1974) 49 TC 538 [1975] STC 353, CA(NI) where the taxpayer built grain silos to hold grain in a position where it could be easily discharged into lorries rather than continue the previous process of bagging the grain on board ship and transferring it to lorries on the dock side. They were held to be plant as they were part of the apparatus to transfer the grain from ship to lorry, ie they had a functional role in the business. If they had been primarily for a storage purpose they may well have been found to be 'setting' and rejected as plant and machinery, but possibly claimed as industrial buildings allowances.

Under the current legislation it is possible that HMRC would accept the silos as plant without the authority of *Schofield* and attempt to have them classified as Long Life Assets (LOLAs), ie having a life expectancy of 25 years or more and therefore subject to the reduced depreciation rate of 8% per annum reducing balance.

In *B & E Security Systems Ltd v HMRC* [2010] UKFTT 146 (TC), construction works for a control room for security surveillance was deemed to qualify for capital allowances by the First-tier Tribunal on the grounds that the works were incidental to the installation of plant. It is rare for an entire building (a control centre) to qualify as plant as it is usually the individual items within such a structure which attract capital allowances.

Pushing the boundaries, especially with the current legislation, it is interesting to look at the Australian case of *Wangaratta Woollen Mills v Federal Commissioner of Taxation* (1969) 1/9 CLR 1, which has been quoted in the House of Lords. A dye house was held to be almost entirely an item of plant. One of the key design features was that some of the external walling acted as part of the ventilation system, ie the design was such that a cavity was created between an external skin and an internal skin to create a duct for the circulation of air as part of the ventilation system. CAA 2001, ss 21–23 would suggest that such a claim would be unlikely to succeed in the UK but there may be extenuating circumstances where a claim could be mounted.

As a side note it is worth remembering that although HMRC do not consider themselves bound by decisions in foreign jurisdictions they are not averse to using such decisions to defend positions that they advance, even where a UK case is counter to the foreign case as illustrated by the *Auckland Gas* and *Transco v Dyall* cases highlighted earlier under **9.2**.

The business use test

[9.54] In *Jarrold v John Good & Sons Ltd* (1962) 40 TC 681, CA the dispute was over some movable partitions in John Good's offices. Pearson LJ summarised matters:

' . . . the shortest question in this case is whether the partitioning is part of the premises in which the business is carried on, or part of the plant with which it is carried on . . . '

and Pennicuik J added:

' . . . the setting in which a business is carried on, and the apparatus used for carrying on a business, are not always necessarily mutually exclusive . . . '

The court upheld the Commissioners' decision that the partitions qualified as plant because they formed a particular function in John Good's business, ie they allowed different departments to be segregated from each other regardless of how they expanded or contracted. This judgment confirmed that the same asset could be regarded as plant in one business but not in a different business, ie the nature of trade being undertaken was a critical element in deciding whether or not an item was plant.

In current practical terms merely using a demountable or relocatable partitioning system in a project is insufficient to secure them as being eligible for plant and machinery allowances. There needs to be evidence that the reasoning to use them is linked to the needs of the business and its operating practices if such a claim is to be accepted by HMRC.

A similar outcome was reached in *Leeds Permanent Building Society v Proctor* (1982) 56 TC 293, ChD where a claim was made for a range of decorative screens which were used for purposes including decorative window displays to attract customers and providing privacy for those inside the branch. The screens were capable of being demounted but, in practice, were not as they were incapable of reuse without considerable alteration for any business other than the Leeds Permanent Building Society, and in some cases they were only of use in a specific branch, and when the Society vacated any branches the screens were removed. HMRC's view was that the screens were part of the 'setting' and therefore ineligible as plant. The High Court held that the screens were plant, and HMRC now take the view that there are certain situations where an item which was not part of the premises but part of the setting can also qualify as plant.

The importance of this test was magnified in *IRC v Scottish & Newcastle Breweries Ltd* (1982) 55 TC 252 [1982] STC 296, HL where Scottish & Newcastle, carrying on trade as a hotelier, fitted out and refurbished a range of licensed leisure and hotel premises. The claims included lighting, decorative assets and sundry other items intended, as part of the company's overall objectives, to create an atmosphere to attract customers to its establishments. It was accepted that part of the company's trade was to create an 'ambience' and allowances were given for a range of items used to create this. Lord Cameron, in the Court of Session, felt that 'setting' and 'plant' could overlap and said:

' . . . the question of what is properly to be regarded as "plant" can only be answered in the context of the particular industry concerned and, possibly, in the light also of the particular circumstances of the individual taxpayer's own trade . . . '

In the light of these comments it is worth considering the potential for claims under CAA 2001, s 23 LIST C, 14. Decorative assets provided for the enjoyment of the public in hotel, restaurant or similar trades. The question arises on how wide can 'similar trades' be interpreted. Especially as retailers and financial institutions adapt their business models and marketing efforts to meet current trends eg bank branches that co-exist with coffee shops within the same demise.

Which leads to the retail sector and its influence on the business use test. There are two cases which are trendsetters, one reported and one which has come, anonymously, into the public domain via revisions to HMRC guidance notes on capital allowances.

The public one is *Cole Brothers v Philips* (1982) 55 TC 188, [1982] STC 307, HL where Cole Brothers, a company in the John Lewis group, claimed capital allowances on the fitting out of the John Lewis store at Brent Cross in London. As part of the claim they included the entire electrical installation. HMRC rejected the submission and adopted a piecemeal approach and suggested the following:

- wiring to heating and ventilating equipment; clocks; fire alarms; smoke alarms; and burglar alarms;
- wiring to lifts and escalators;
- trunking for the telephone system;
- emergency lighting system;
- stand-by systems;
- public address and staff location systems;
- wiring to cash registers; TV workshop; and electrical department;
- additional sockets for the television sales area;
- the fitments for the display of fittings in the lighting department.

HMRC rejected the balance of the electrical works that included transformers, switchgear, and the lighting and wiring installations, some of which were specially designed for the store. The Commissioners decided that 'the multiplicity of elements in the Brent Cross installation, and the differing purposes which they serve' precluded them from considering the entity approach. As the case progressed from the Commissioners to the Court of Appeal the transformers and switchgear were, however, allowed but the lighting and wiring was not. In the House of Lords the point was made by Lord Wilberforce that:

> 'As regards the main electrical system, there is no finding that it was in any way special to the taxpayer company's business, or anything more than the standard equipment of a commercial business.'

Lord Hailsham, however, said that his decision was made 'not without some wavering from time to time' because he saw no problem in accepting the electrical installation as an entity in principle, but as the Commissioners had made their decision as they were entitled to do on the facts before them he rejected the company's appeal. (He also made the observation that had he been a Commissioner he may have found for the company.) This is yet another example of the importance of the need for fully detailed, well supported and soundly built claims from the outset.

The unreported case, where the claimant won the entire electrical installation, resulted in an HMRC guidance note (CA 21180) on to how to deal with claims where an entire installation was claimed as a plant item. In order to qualify the installation has to comply with all of the following:

- it is specifically designed and built as a whole, that is it is a fully integrated entity; and
- it is designed and adapted to meet the particular requirements of the trade; and
- the end user items of the electrical installation function as apparatus in the trader's business; and
- the electrical installation is essential for the functioning of the business.

The same approach is advocated for any complete entity or system that is claimed as plant, eg electrical, water, sewerage or gas installations.

If the installation failed any of the tests the approach to identifying which parts qualify for allowances is to be carried out on a piecemeal basis and giving allowances only on items that are already recognised as being eligible for plant and machinery allowances.

With the introduction of integral features in FA 2008 and the listing of 'an electrical system including a lighting system' as a qualifying integral features item the foregoing notes on electrical systems may appear to be redundant. This is not necessarily the case as it may be possible to claim certain items as plant and machinery at 18% reducing balance where they may be regarded as outwith 'an electrical system' or are related to the specific operational requirements of the occupier. As this is new and as yet untested legislation in terms of a definition of 'an electrical system' there may be some interesting results to be had by deconstructing past lines of reasoning and re-building them in a different format in terms of integral features or plant and machinery.

The premises test

[9.55] The basis of the premises test flows through a number of cases, ie is the item the premises or part of the premises, and if so it is not plant. As made clear by the detailed questions posed by Lord Hoffman this is not necessarily an easy question to answer and has given rise to a number of cases where entire buildings or structures have been claimed. In *Benson v Yard Arm Club* (1979) 53 TC 76, [1979] STC 266, CA Templeman LJ said:

' . . . if, and only if land, premises or structures in addition to their primary purpose perform the function of plant in that they are the means by which a trading operation is carried out . . . the land, premises or structures are treated as plant'

and he followed that by confirming that premises only become plant if they function as plant.

Cases since then that have attempted to claim the entire building or structure have included a car wash, *Attwood v Anduff Car Wash Ltd* (1996) 69 TC 575, [1997] STC 1167, CA, an all weather race track, *Shove v Lingfield Park 1991 Ltd* [2004] EWCA Civ 391, (2004) 76 TC 363, [2004] STC 805, CA, and artificial football pitches in *IRC v Anchor International Ltd* (2004) 77 TC 38, [2005] STC 411, CS, where only the synthetic top layer of the pitches was allowed as plant and the excavations and filling below the top layer were regarded as ineligible as they constituted the alteration of the land for the purpose only of installing the plant.

The completeness test

[9.56] This could be considered as an alternative way of asking one of Hoffmann J's questions in *Wimpy* on an item that might be considered to be plant: ie to what extent is the structure complete without it? It is, however, a slightly more nuanced approach in terms of what might qualify and is necessary to combat any attempted limited interpretation of responses to Hoffmann J's question.

A building or structure may well be complete for a range of uses using Hoffmann J's question, but if it is not complete for the specific uses or operational requirements of the occupier or proposed occupier then there may be a range of items that could be reasonably claimed as plant, or plant related costs, eg an office block may be complete in the generally accepted sense of the term and available for use, but it would not be if the intended user required, for example, a special level of lighting illumination beyond that installed. There is a range of user, or trader, specific items that could be regarded as 'plant' that could fall outside of the simple interpretation of Hoffmann's scope and this is supported in *Cole Brothers Ltd v Philips* (1982) 55 TC 188, [1982] STC 307, HL, where Vinelott J referred back to *Lyons* case where Uthwatt J drew a distinction between lighting which was added to a building which was otherwise complete to be used for its intended purpose and lighting which was needed to make a building complete for its intended purpose. Lighting which was added to an otherwise complete building might be plant; lighting which was needed to make a building complete for its intended purpose was not plant, eg if there was insufficient natural light for a building to be usable electric lighting added would not be plant.

Also in *Cole Brothers* Oliver LJ opined:

> 'A building may be incomplete without some form of electrical installation but if the occupier installs a system specially adapted for the particular purpose for which he intends to use the building the fact that the building would be incomplete if the electrical system were to be removed does not prevent the electrical system being plant.'

And while the new integral features allowance allows entire electrical systems to be claimed as integral features on an 8% reducing balance basis the potential for classification of certain elements as plant and machinery on the 18% reducing balance basis should not be overlooked.

Notwithstanding the test options, CAA 2001, s 23 attempts to clarify what may or may not be plant and machinery by way of listing general and specific building elements

Buildings

[9.57] The legislation states that expenditure on the provision of plant or machinery does not include expenditure on the provision of a building. It then expands the definition to cover any asset that is incorporated within the building or any asset, which, although not incorporated in the building (whether because the asset is moveable or for any other reason) is in the building and is of a kind normally incorporated in a building. To ensure an understanding of the meaning, CAA 2001, s 21(3) specifically excludes the following from qualifying as P&M.

List A: assets treated as buildings (ie assets ineligible for P&M allowances)

[9.58] Assets treated as buildings are as follows:

(1)   walls, floors, ceilings, doors, gates, shutters, windows and stairs;
(2)   mains services, and systems for water, electricity and gas;
(3)   waste disposal systems;
(4)   sewerage and drainage systems;
(5)   shafts or other structures in which lifts, hoists, escalators and moving walkways are installed;
(6)   fire safety systems.

While this appears to reduce somewhat the scope of potential claims, help is at hand. CAA 2001, s 21(3) is subject to s 23, and List C, which outlines items that may be claimed as P&M.

List C: expenditure unaffected by ss 21 and 22 (ie potentially qualifying P&M expenditure)

[9.59] Expenditure unaffected by ss 21 and 22 is as follows:

(1)   machinery (including devices for providing motive power) not within any items on this list;
(2)   gas and sewerage systems provided mainly (entire item removed from this list and now classified as Integral Features under FA 2008):
    (a)   to meet the particular requirement of the qualifying activity; or
    (b)   to serve particular plant or machinery used for the purposes of the qualifying activity;
(3)   space or water heating systems; powered systems of ventilation; air cooling or air purification; and any floor or ceiling comprised in such systems [entire item removed from this list and now classified as Integral Features under FA 2008];
(4)   manufacturing or processing equipment; storage equipment (including cold rooms); display equipment; and counters, checkouts and similar equipment;
(5)   cookers, washing machines, dishwashers, refrigerators and similar equipment; washbasins, sinks, baths, showers, sanitary ware and similar equipment; furniture and furnishings;
(6)   hoists [lifts, escalators and moving walkways removed from this list and now classified as Integral Features under FA 2008];
(7)   sound insulation provided mainly to meet the particular requirements of the qualifying trade;
(8)   computer, telecommunication and surveillance systems (including their wiring or other links);

(9)   refrigeration or cooling equipment;

(10)   fire alarm systems; sprinkler and other equipment for extinguishing or containing fires;

(11)   burglar alarm systems;

(12)   strong rooms in bank or building society premises; safes;

(13)   partition walls, where moveable and intended to be moved in the course of a qualifying activity;

(14)   decorative assets provided for the enjoyment of the public in hotel, restaurant or similar trades;

(15)   advertising hoardings; signs, displays and similar assets;

(16)   swimming pools (including diving boards, slides and structures on which such boards or slides are mounted);

(17)   any glasshouse constructed so that the required environment (namely, air, heat, light, irrigation and temperature) for the growing of plants is provided automatically by means of devices forming an integral part of its structure;

(18)   cold stores;

(19)   caravans provided mainly for holiday lettings;

(20)   buildings provided for testing aircraft engines run within buildings;

(21)   moveable buildings intended to be moved in the course of the qualifying activity;

(22)   the alteration of land for the purpose only of installing plant or machinery;

(23)   the provision of dry docks;

(24)   the provision of any jetty or similar structure provided mainly to carry plant or machinery;

(25)   the provision of pipelines or underground ducts or tunnels with a primary purpose of carrying utility conduits;

(26)   the provision of towers to support floodlights;

(27)   the provision of:
   (a)   any reservoir incorporated into a water treatment works; or
   (b)   any service reservoir of treated water for supply within any housing estate or other particular locality;

(28)   the provision of:
   (a)   silos provided for temporary storage;
   (b)   storage tanks;

(29)   the provision of slurry pits or silage clamps;

(30)   the provision of fish tanks or fish ponds;

(31)   the provision of rails, sleepers and ballast for a railway or tramway;

(32)   the provision of structures and other assets for providing the setting for any ride at an amusement park or exhibition;

(33)   the provision of fixed zoo cages.

But having given with one hand, items 1 to 16 on the list are qualified under CAA 2001, s 23(4) in that any asset whose principal purpose is to insulate or enclose the interior of a building or to provide any interior wall, floor or ceiling which (in each case) is intended to remain permanently in place, will not be eligible for P&M allowances.

Structures

[9.60] As with buildings the legislation excludes plant and machinery from being claimed on structures and any works involving the alteration of land. A structure is held to be a fixed structure of any kind that is not a building.

List B: excluded structures and other assets (ie assets ineligible for P&M allowances)

[9.61] Excluded structures and other assets are as follows:

(1)   a tunnel, bridge, viaduct, aqueduct, embankment or cutting;
(2)   a way, hard standing (such as a pavement), road, railway, tramway, a park for vehicles or containers, or an airstrip or runway;
(3)   an inland navigation, including a canal or basis or navigable river;
(4)   a dam, reservoir or barrage, including any sluices, gates, generators and other equipment associated with the dam, reservoir or barrage;
(5)   a dock, harbour, wharf, pier, marina or jetty or any other structure in or at which vessels may be kept, or merchandise or passengers may be shipped or unshipped;
(6)   a dike, sea wall, weir or drainage ditch;
(7)   any structure not within items 1 to 6 other than:
   (a)   a structure (but not a building) within Chapter 2 of Part 3 (meaning of 'industrial building') (note: this section is withdrawn as the Chapter and Part are deleted as part of the phasing out of industrial buildings allowances);
   (b)   a structure in use for the purposes of an undertaking for the extraction, production, processing or distribution of gas; and
   (c)   a structure in use for the purposes of a trade which consists in the provision of telecommunication, television or radio services.

Further expenditure unaffected by ss 21 and 22 (ie additional potential P&M expenditure)

[9.62] In addition to the possible claims to be made under List C there are eight other areas where claims may be available in relation to property. They are:

• building alterations connected with the installation of plant or machinery, s 25;
• demolition costs, s 26;
• thermal insulation of buildings, ss 28, 68;
• safety at designated sports grounds, s 30 (to be abolished after 2012 subject to consultation);
• safety at regulated stands at sports grounds, s 31 (to be abolished after 2012 subject to consultation);
• safety at sports grounds, s 32 (to be abolished after 2012 subject to consultation);
• personal security, s 33;
• software and rights to software, s 71.

Integral features allowances (IFA)

General

[9.63] The IFA category, introduced in FA 2008, expanded the range of items that may be claimed as plant and machinery allowances but also gave a significantly reduced depreciation rate, for both the limited range of newly allowed items and a significantly larger range of existing allowable items.

Having established that an item of plant or machinery qualifies it needs to be classified as either plant and machinery and entered in the main pool at an 18% reducing balance or as an integral feature and put in the special rate pool at 8% reducing balance.

It should be noted that the Annual Investment Allowance (AIA) can be used on any item that qualifies for IFA. It should also be noted that no IFA item can be categorised as a Short Life Asset (SLA).

What qualifies in principle?

[9.64] From the tax year commencing 2008 the assets defined as 'integral features' are:

- an electrical system (including a lighting system);
- a cold water system;
- a space or water heating system, a powered system of ventilation, air cooling or purification, and any floor or ceiling comprised in such a system;
- a lift, an escalator or moving walkway;
- external solar shading.

Expenditure on the provision of items on the list in a building or structure used for the purpose of the taxpayer's qualifying activity is eligible for IFA.

How does it operate?

[9.65] The legislation applies from 1 April 2008 for corporation tax purposes and from 6 April 2008 for income tax.

For projects with expenditure spanning the change in legislation it requires expenditure incurred up to the relevant date to be analysed and claimed under the old legislation and expenditure post the relevant date to be analysed under the new legislation. It also impacts on situations where sampling or pro-forma approaches are used as these will no longer reflect the detail of the legislation.

When it comes to replacing an item classified as an integral feature there are restrictions on claiming like for like replacement as a revenue deduction. If more than 50% of the cost of replacement (at the time the expenditure was incurred) is incurred in any 12-month period the costs are treated as capital and are eligible to be claimed as integral features. Similarly, if less than 50% is incurred in one period and an amount in the following period takes the expenditure above the 50% mark it too is treated as an integral feature.

The special rate pool

[9.66] Special rate expenditure is detailed in FA 2008 Chapter 10A and refers to expenditure incurred after the relevant date ie 1 or 6 April 2008 on:

(a)   thermal insulation under s 28;

(b)   integral features under s 33A;

(c)   long-life assets; and

(d)   long-life assets where expenditure was incurred before the relevant date but allocated to a pool on or after the relevant date.

The writing down allowance is 8% per annum reducing balance basis and the specific details applicable to each of the categories is dealt with in their sections within this chapter.

Disposals

[9.67] Disposals generally are similar to existing legislation, ie a just apportionment, and the anti-avoidance clause provides that where the disposal value brought in by the vendor, for avoidance purposes, is less than the notional tax written down value then the notional tax written down value will be used in the vendor's computations. The purchaser is unaffected as the purchaser's claim can only be based upon the actual price paid.

The widening of the range of items claimable presents an opportunity for purchasers to carry out a just apportionment of the purchase price on the first acquisition after 1 or 6 April 2008, and to claim for items that were not previously allowable, ie entire cold water systems and entire electrical installations. In such a situation a CAA 2001, s 198 election cannot be used because the items would not have been claimed as they were ineligible under the previous legislation.

In sales between connected persons (CAA 2001, s 575), however, this course of action is not an option because any of the integral features items that did not qualify under the previous legislation are ineligible in such a situation, ie if it was not qualifying expenditure when the vendor acquired the asset then it will not be qualifying expenditure in the purchaser's hands.

Generally when a disposal takes place there will be a need to redefine the existing plant and machinery into plant and machinery and integral features categories and allocate them to the main pool or the special rate pool, ie 18% reducing balance or 8% reducing balance. In what appears to be either a concession or a means of reducing the administrative burden it is possible for the vendor and purchaser in an intra-group transfer to keep expenditure in the main pool. This applies to 'a pre-commencement integral feature' which is defined as:

(a)   qualifying expenditure was incurred on it before the relevant date and it has been allocated to the seller's main pool, or

(b)   qualifying expenditure was incurred on or after the relevant date and allocated to the seller's main pool because of a previous election under IFA,

and the integral feature 'is treated as having been sold by the seller to the buyer at a price which gives rise to neither a balancing allowance not a balancing charge', ie tax written down value (TWDV). In the buyer's hands the expenditure on the integral feature would go into the main pool, if actually allocated to a pool. For this to take effect it is necessary for both parties to make an election to HMRC within two years of date of the sale.

After costs have been allocated to the two pools, ie the main pool and the special rate pool, it will be necessary to have sufficient records in place to provide appropriate information on the claims and balances to allow for future elections to be agreed when a disposal takes place. This has not always been the case in the past.

What costs qualify?

[9.68] Expenditure incurred on the provision of machinery or plant is eligible for plant and machinery allowances.

The extent of the term 'provision' was highlighted by Lord Reid in *Barclay Curle* when he said:

> ' . . . if the cost of the provision of plant can be more than the cost of the plant itself, I do not see how expenditure that must be incurred before the plant can be provided can be too remote . . . '

This is generally regarded as all the usual or normal costs incurred in the design, procurement and installation of an eligible item. HMRC, however, like to restrict the element of 'provision' and use the case of *Ben-Odeco Ltd v Powlson* (1978) 52 TC 459, HL as the basis of identifying costs that may be regarded as too remote to be on the 'provision' of plant or machinery.

Ben-Odeco Ltd borrowed to finance the construction of an oil rig and claimed the commitment fees and the interest attached to the loan as part of the cost of the rig and therefore eligible for capital allowances. The House of Lords rejected the claim as the costs were not on the provision of the rig but were the costs of obtaining finance to acquire the rig, ie they were too remote to be considered as part of the 'provision' of the plant. Lord Wilberforce held that the fees:

> 'were expenditure on the provision of money to be used on the provision of plant, but were not on the provision of plant and so not within [CAA 2001, s 11(4)].'

It is not unknown for HMRC to attempt to interpret Lord Reid narrowly and Lord Wilberforce widely.

List C (see **9.59**), identifies the 33 general and specific headings for items that may qualify for allowances. There are, in addition, two further general areas where costs incidental to plant and machinery and fixtures expenditure are eligible. They are:

- building alterations connected with the installation of plant or machinery, CAA 2001, s 25;
- demolition costs, CAA 2001, s 26.

Demolition costs related to the removal of existing plant or in removal and replacement of existing plant or machinery qualify for allowances.

Building alterations qualify where they are 'incidental to the installation of plant or machinery'. Lord Reid, in *Barclay Curle* said:

' . . . the exigencies of the trade require than when new machinery or plant is installed in existing buildings more shall be done than mere installation in order to ensure that the new machinery or plant may serve its proper purpose . . . '

And, probably, the most comprehensive example of works 'incidental' to the installation of new plant in an existing building is the installation of a new lift.

Example 8

The process will involve some, if not all, of the following – removal of existing ceiling and floor finishes; diversion and alterations to air conditioning systems, cutting of holes on floors; construction of new lift shafts, installation of the lift which may also include demolition and rebuilding of external walls in order to bring the lift into the building, making good finishes around the new lift shafts, replacing floor and ceiling finishes, and construction of a lift pit and or motor room. The actual cost of the lift, while not an insignificant amount, can be significantly increased when the works 'incidental' to its installation are added to the cost.

Careful attention should be paid to the potential for costs 'incidental' to the installation of plant and machinery as they can have a significant effect on the amount claimed for tax relief.

Statutory eligible expenditure

[9.69] Notwithstanding the general rules and cases determining what is, and what is not, plant or machinery there are a certain property related items that would not normally qualify for plant and machinery allowances but which are eligible under this heading. They are:

- thermal insulation;
- fire safety (withdrawn under FA 2008);
- safety at sports grounds (withdrawn from April 2012);
- personal security assets.

Thermal insulation of buildings

[9.70] Originally introduced under CAA 2001, s 28, to allow expenditure incurred in adding thermal insulation to an existing industrial building (as defined in CAA 2001, ss 271(1), 274) to be claimed as plant and machinery it was extended and clarified by FA 2008 to cover any building other than a dwelling and to include adding insulation against heat loss. It has also been included in the special rate pool which means that the depreciation rate is now on a 10% reducing balance basis. The expenditure can be claimed by a trader, or a landlord, provided that the trader is in occupation of the premises, or the premises are let by the landlord. Expenditure incurred from 1 April 2001 for corporation tax purposes and 6 April 2001 for income tax purposes is eligible.

In one of the many apparent quirks of the legislation, or injustices, dependent upon how the legislation is viewed, incorporating the insulation in a new build project, and before it is occupied or let, automatically disallows it from being claimed as plant and machinery.

The general principle is that expenditure incurred to prevent loss of heat from an existing building should qualify. It is not required to be the sole reason for the expenditure but it must be one of the reasons. This means that expenditure allowable can include items such as roof lining insulation products, draught excluders, cavity wall insulation, and even double glazing where it meets the general principles.

Disposal/acquisition

[9.71] If a disposal event occurs a disposal value of nil is used as the intention of the legislation is that the allowance is only available to the person incurring the expenditure (CAA 2001, s 63(5)).

Personal security assets

[9.72] Under CAA 2001, s 33 individuals or a partnership of individuals carrying on a trade, profession or vocation and incurring expenditure to meet a special threat arising wholly or mainly from their trade profession or vocation will be eligible for allowances.

A security asset is one that improves personal security and can include:

(a)   alarm systems;
(b)   bullet resistant windows in houses;
(c)   floodlighting and similar facilities;
(d)   reinforced doors and windows;
(e)   perimeter walls and fences.

If there are other uses for the asset but they are incidental to its main security use, or if the asset improves the security of the individual's family or household as well as the individual the allowances are still due in full.

Where, however, the asset has more than one use the allowances should be apportioned.

Disposal/acquisition

The disposal value is nil.

End of qualifying plant

[9.73] A final note on what can qualify, which although not directly property, could well link in with certain property and property related activities. Guard dogs, horses in a riding school or animals in a circus may qualify as plant which suggests that their housing may also qualify. Which takes us full circle, or near enough, to *Yarmouth v France* (1887) 19 QBD 647, 57 LJQB 7 where we started.

What does not qualify?

[9.74] There are a number of items that have been held, over the years, by the courts not to be plant or machinery. In addition to the knowledge that there is little point in claiming such items without being prepared for battle (in this David and Goliath struggle between the individual taxpayer and HMRC it should be pointed out that, based upon the results of court decisions, Goliath tends to win in the majority of cases), there is also guidance to be found in some of the judgments as to aspects that might have swayed the decision from rejection to approval. Furthermore, understanding how and why certain items have been rejected should help in formulating future claims in, or bordering on, these issues. Items rejected include:

- A prefabricated laboratory and gymnasium provided in a school (*St John's School (Mountford & Knibbs) v Ward CA* (1975) 49 TC 524, CA), rejected because it was a building providing shelter to the users. HMRC accepted that gymnasium equipment (and presumably laboratory equipment) would qualify but not the building.
- The canopy over a service area of a petrol retailer (*Dixon v Fitch's Garage Ltd* (1975) 50 TC 509, ChD), rejected, despite the fact that sales had increased since the introduction of the canopy, on the basis that petrol could be sold without a canopy. The Irish case of *O'Culachain v McMullin Bros H/C(I)* (1991) 1 IR 363, however, while based on similar circumstances produced a different result: the canopy was accepted as plant on the grounds that it had a function in the trade being carried out:

    ' . . . the provision of an attractive setting for the sale of . . . products, the advertisement and promotion of those products, the creation of an overall impression of efficiency and financial solidarity in relation to the business of selling petrol and the attraction of customers to stop and purchase those products . . . '

    The use of signage, advertising, and general branding has developed over the past 30 years and there may be sufficient ground to claim substantial elements of, if not the total, cost of such canopies.
- The stand at a football ground (*Brown v Burnley Football & Athletic Club Ltd* (1980) 53 TC 691, ChD), rejected by Vinelott J on the grounds that the stand was 'the setting or place where, rather than the means by which, the trade is carried on', but the Irish case of *Roscommon Racecourse (O'Grady v Roscommon Race Committee* (1992) 4I IR 425) found to the contrary and allowed the stand at the racecourse.
- An inflatable cover for a tennis court (*Thomas v Reynolds* (1987) 59 TC 502, ChD), rejected; however, the judge pointed out that he may well have come to a different conclusion had evidence that the claimant produced to the court been accepted (as it had not already been raised before the General Commissioners the judge could not accept it – a salutary lesson about the need for thorough claims preparation and presentation).

- Shop fronts (*Wimpy International Ltd v Warland CA* (1989) 61 TC 51, CA), rejected as plant and machinery on initial installation but allowed as a revenue deduction on replacement.

- Quarantine kennels (*Carr v Sayer* [1992] STC 396, ChD), fixed kennels regarded as a permanent structure were rejected but movable kennels were accepted by HMRC.

- Lighting affixed to storage platforms in a warehouse (*Hunt v Henry Quick Ltd* (1992) 65 TC 108, [1992] STC 633, ChD, and *King v Bridisco Ltd* (1992) 65 TC 108, [1992] STC 633, ChD), rejected on the grounds that lighting generally does not qualify for plant and machinery allowances. This illustrates a slight contradiction in that the mezzanine floor, which was the main element of the plant and machinery claim, was accepted, but the lighting, which was only necessary because of the installation of the floor, ie 'the plant' was rejected. It could have been 'incidental' to the plant installation and therefore eligible. (Since the introduction of Integral Features Allowances (IFAs) the lighting would now qualify under this category.)

- False ceilings used in concealing pipework, wiring etc and partly supporting services used within buildings (*Benson v Yard Arm Club and Wimpy*) rejected on the basis that they merely provided a covering and had no functional element in the trade. Ceilings are, however, eligible where they are part of the services installation, ie a plenum, or where they perform a function in the trade, eg decorative features in the hotel, restaurant or similar trades.

- Putting greens at a golf course (*Family Golf Centres Ltd v Thorne* [1998] STC (SCD) 106) rejected on the basis that the greens were not plant but part of the premises where the company carried on its trade.

- Plant and machinery in student accommodation has been the subject of a major HMRC rethink. In response to the changes in student accommodation from traditional halls of residence to apartment block buildings HMRC, in Brief 66/08, updated its view of what was and what was not eligible for allowances. Plant and machinery in 'dwellings' is generally ineligible for allowances and HMRC's view was that student bedrooms were 'dwellings' but that communal areas within flats, ie kitchens and living rooms were not 'dwellings' and therefore only they could be subject to capital allowances claims for fitting out etc. In addition areas to which the residents had no access would also qualify for allowances. In Revenue & Customs Brief 45/10, however, HMRC confirmed its revised view that kitchens and lounges were part of a 'dwelling' as these areas are needed 'to provide the facilities for day to day private domestic existence', and therefore claims could not be made for these areas. The new guidance would only be applied to capital expenditure from 22 October 2010. The whole area of definition of 'dwellings' is a difficult one and subject to different interpretations in different circumstances and ownerships, eg an hotel company operating accommodation may be eligible to claim plant on machinery on individual bedrooms whereas an individual or property company may not. In terms of interpretations HMRC appears to adopt whichever interpretations best suits its purposes (see CHAPTER 15, para 15.156).

A more complex area is where claims have been rejected in part. These tend to be where entireties are claimed, ie the building is claimed to act as one item of plant as with the dry dock in *Barclay Curle*:

- An underground electricity substation (*Bradley v London Electricity plc* (1996) 70 TC 155 [1996] STC 1054, ChD), rejected as it was claimed as a single entity and the court held that it was merely a building holding plant and machinery. The plant and machinery and the concrete plinths supporting the plant and machinery were allowed.
- A building housing a car wash (*Attwood v Anduff CarWash Ltd* (1997) 69 TC 575, [1997] STC 1167, CA), rejected along similar lines to *London Electricity*, ie even a structure whose only purpose is to house plant is nevertheless only the premises in which the business is carried on.
- A planteria was rejected (*Gray v Seymours Garden Centres (Horticulture)* (1995) 67 TC 401, [1995] STC 706, CA) because although the glasshouse in question had elements of plant in the manner of its ventilation it was basically a building in which the business was carried on.
- An artificial all weather race track (*Shove v Lingfield Park 1991 Ltd* [2004] EWCA Civ 391, (2004) 76 TC 363, [2004] STC 805, CA), rejected on the basis that it functioned as part of the premises of the racecourse, ie the effect of the all weather track was to enlarge the area of the racecourse space available to function as premises on which more frequent horse racing could take place, and its identity was not regarded as separate from the grass racecourse or other parts of the premises on which Lingfield's trade was conducted.
- Five-a-side football pitches (*IRC v Anchor International Ltd* (2004) 77 TC 38, [2005] STC 411, CS) were rejected but the synthetic football playing surface was accepted as plant and machinery on the basis that 'equipment does not cease to be plant merely because it also discharges an additional function, such as providing the place in which the business is carried out'.
- Kitchen tiles (*JD Wetherspoon Plc v Revenue and Customs Comrs* (2007) SpC 657) fixed to walls to provide wipe clean surfaces to meet health and safety workplace provisions claimed as being building alterations incidental to the installation of plant were rejected, despite claims that the kitchen equipment could not be used unless the health and safety provisions were met, on the basis that they did not have 'sufficient nexus with the installation of equipment such as cookers to be incidental thereof'. (The subsequent appeal in 2009 confirmed this decision but made further points on what was eligible and what was ineligible in works of alteration and these points are covered under para **9.88** below.)

How does it operate?

[9.75] P&M allowances are claimed in the same way as other capital allowances, ie on the corporation tax return for companies and on the income tax return for individuals and partnerships.

Depreciation of fixed assets charged in the accounts is not allowed as a deduction in computing taxable profits so capital allowances may be claimed.

The two main plant and machinery allowances are first year allowances (FYA) and writing down allowances (WDA).

FYA is only due in certain defined situations (already covered above at **9.4** and in paras **9.17** EZA, **9.22** RDA, and **9.29** ECA). Any unrelieved FYAs are treated as WDAs.

Most plant and machinery is taken as WDAs and entered into a pool. Pools can cover a single asset or a class of assets dependent upon the specific factors pertaining to the situation, eg the main pool tends to include all expenditure that is not required to be kept and identified in separate pools. Separate pools are required for short life assets and assets used partly for purposes other than the qualifying activity.

From 2008 there are two plant and machinery pools, the main pool for plant and machinery and the newly introduced special rate pool.

The main pool WDAs is on an 18% per annum reducing balance basis.

The special rate pool is found under Special Rate Expenditure in the new FA 2008 Chapter 10A and refers to expenditure incurred after the relevant date ie 1 or 6 April 2008 on:

(a)   thermal insulation under s 28;
(b)   integral features under s 33A;
(c)   long-life assets; and
(d)   long life assets where expenditure was incurred before the relevant date but allocated to a pool on or after the relevant date.

The writing down allowance is on an 8% per annum reducing balance basis.

Short life assets

[9.76] Short Life Assets (SLAs) were introduced as a class in 1986 in an attempt to align the allowable depreciation of certain assets with their actual working lives, eg where heavy use or rapid obsolescence is a factor. It allows the taxpayer to write off the asset over its life but the asset must be scrapped or sold at the end of its life. It is probably most commonly used for groups of small items, mainly chattels as opposed to machinery or plant or fixtures, as groups of assets or 'classes' may be bundled together. It can, however, be adopted in any situation where it is not excluded provided the detailed procedures are followed and SLA elections and computations are correctly made (CAA 2001, Pt 2 Ch 9, ss 83–89). There are the usual anti-avoidance measures regarding connected persons and assets ineligible for SLA treatment include machinery or plant which is:

•   let otherwise than in the course of a qualifying activity;
•   used only partly for the purposes of a qualifying trade;
•   subject to a partial depreciation subsidy;
•   received by way of gift or originally provided for another purpose;

- leased after 26 July 1989 except where used for short term leasing;
- leased outside the UK which only qualifies for a 10% WDA;
- an integral feature;
- a long life asset.

The key benefit is given at the time of disposal. Assets which are separately pooled as short life assets may create balancing allowances which would otherwise just reduce the value of the main plant and machinery pool and not lead to an immediate tax deduction. If, however, the asset is not scrapped but sold on, it may create a balancing charge if the asset is categorised as an SLA and consequently it may not be advantageous to elect for the SLA treatment.

Budget 2011 extended the period for Short Life Asset treatment from four years to eight years to give it a wider scope in terms of items that could be included within the category, ie more plant and machinery or fixtures (excluding integral features). It also means that any remaining balance of qualifying expenditure will not now transfer to the main pool until eight years after the chargeable period in which the expenditure was incurred. It does not, however, address the main problem of SLAs in regard to the election process and the need to keep records of the individual SLA pools that are required for each item or class of item, and the need to make separate annual writing down allowance calculations and separate balancing adjustment calculations when an item is disposed of with the new eight-year cut-off point.

As with most tax decisions it is a twofold process. Firstly, crunch the numbers, to identify the potential upsides and downsides, and then make an educated guess on the likely position of the business in the years to come. (A pro forma election is contained in **APPENDIX 1** to this chapter at 2.2.)

Fixtures

General

[9.77] Fixtures are assets that are installed or otherwise fixed to a building or land so as to become part of the building or land in law, as opposed to chattels that are tangible moveable objects.

They are important because when buildings are bought, sold or leased, there is a potential tax implication, eg when an office block is bought or sold 10% to 20% of the purchase price may be eligible for plant and machinery allowances as fixtures.

The introduction of IFAs impacts on the potential benefits available when buying property from April 2008 on two fronts. First, the IFA extends the range of items that may be claimed under the fixtures legislation. Secondly, the inclusion of the IFA in the special rate pool, currently at 8% reducing balance reduces the NPV of any allowances. What is yet to be determined is the overall result of the changes in real benefit terms. This will tend to be sector project and client specific and a clearer picture should emerge in the coming year(s).

The introduction of the IFA category also presents further opportunities when acquiring a second hand property. Items which may not have been eligible for capital allowances when acquired by the seller and therefore not included in the joint s 198 election, eg general lighting, should now fall into the integral features category and represent qualifying expenditure for the buyer. It is therefore very important to, wherever possible, obtain a breakdown of the assets included in the election together with the total assets purchased so that any additional qualifying expenditure can be clearly identified. Capital allowances on IFA's are the exception to the new 'pooling' requirement where the vendor incurred such expenditure prior to 2009. General lighting would not have been a qualifying expense for a previous owner and so there would be no requirement for such expenditure to be identified prior to sale (see **9.100** for more details of the pooling requirement).

What qualifies in principle?

[9.78] Before 1985 when a tenant installed plant and machinery into premises and that plant and machinery became part of the building no one could claim capital allowances. The tenant was ineligible because, even though he had incurred the expenditure, the plant or machinery did not 'belong' to him because it had become a 'landlord's fixture', and the landlord was ineligible because he had not incurred the expenditure on the plant and machinery. This meant that a tenant who refurbished premises and installed air conditioning or a lift was ineligible to claim tax relief on his expenditure while a landlord incurring similar expenditure would have been eligible. This anomaly was resolved in the case of *Stokes v Costain Property Investments* (1984) 57 TC 688, CA and through FA 1985 which supported the decision by allowing tenants to claim allowances for 'landlord's fixtures' installed:

> ' . . . expenditure incurred on the provision of machinery or plant which is so installed or otherwise fixed in or to a building or any other description of land as to become, in law, part of that building or land . . . '

The legislation applied for expenditure incurred from 11 July 1984 and specified that where any dispute arose as to whether or not an item had become, in law, part of a building or land and it has a material effect on the tax liabilities of two or more parties then the question may be determined by the Special Commissioners as if it were an appeal.

Where machinery or plant is treated as belonging to one person no other person can claim allowances on the plant and machinery at the same time unless that person has made a contribution to it, in which case there can be an apportionment of the allowances to the relevant parties.

Furthermore where a lessee takes an assignment of a lease and pays a capital sum that wholly or partly represents expenditure on fixed plant, the lessee can claim capital allowances on that element of the payment in respect of the plant (CAA 2001, s 181). The lessee is not able to make a claim if anyone else has an interest in the property and has claimed allowances as a result.

A lessee can also claim allowances where a capital sum is paid on the grant of a lease and the sum wholly or partly relates to expenditure in respect of a fixed plant. However, if the lessor would otherwise have been entitled to the allowances, both the lessee and the lessor must make an election within two years of the commencement of the lease for the lessee to be available to claim (CAA 2001, s 183) (a proforma election is included in Appendix 1).

What costs qualify?

[9.79] Expenditure incurred by a person with the relevant interest qualifies for allowances and the eligible costs follow the same principles as P&M.

Items generally eligible for allowances

[9.80] A list showing the potential range of items that may qualify for allowances is included at APPENDIX 2 to this chapter, Capital Allowances Checklist. As with all lists, however, it needs to be treated with caution. The previous sections highlight some of the intricacies of determining if an item qualifies or not, and, while some items such as a heating installation should qualify in all situations the fact that some items may qualify in one situation but not another can lead to erroneous over claiming with its potential consequences, or even missed opportunities to claim allowances.

The legislative guidance on what may or may not qualify is summarised under **9.57–9.62** and **9.69–9.75**, but interpreting this against actual physical construction work and related documentation can be fraught with problems. The following summarises what are most likely to be the major contentious issues arising in capital allowances claims. They cover a range of issues where the case law is either unclear or may be misunderstood, or where there may be practical problems in establishing definitive costs of items.

Professional fees

[9.81] For capital allowances purposes the obvious and practical approach in dealing with architects', surveyors', engineers' and other professional fees incurred on construction projects is to apportion them between qualifying costs and non-qualifying costs. HMRC, however, believed that the principles in *Ben-Odeco* (see **9.68**) could and should be applied to professional fees. HMRC official reasoning runs as follows:

> 'Where professional fees are paid in connection with a building project that includes the provision of plant or machinery, only the part, if any, which relates to services can properly be regarded as on the provision of plant and machinery can be qualifying expenditure for plant and machinery allowances. In determining how much of a combined fee relates to such services, the services to which the fee relates will need to be analysed. It is not appropriate simply to apportion the fee by reference to the building costs of the plant and machinery and of other assets as that will commonly overstate the extent to which services relate to the provision of the plant and machinery.

> You should adopt the same approach to preliminaries. These are indirect costs incurred over the duration of a project, which will often include demolition works and site preparation, as well as the construction of a building. Items like site management, insurance, general purpose labour, temporary accommodation and security are preliminaries.' (CA20070)

As professional fees can be anything between 5 and 20% of the costs of a capital project, dependent upon the size and scope, this is a very important area because it can lead to a significant diminution in a capital allowances claim if not addressed.

Professional fees tend to be agreed as either a percentage of the expenditure incurred or as a lump sum. Professional firms do not, as a rule, analyse their fees on the basis of what might or might not be plant and machinery. The assumption that they have the ability to do so with any accuracy in the first place is misguided. So the prospect of analysing fees appears to place an unnecessary burden upon the taxpayer both in attempting to achieve it and probably facing a bill from the professional team to prepare it.

HMRC were reluctant to apply a pro-rated amount in the absence of any directly proven linkage between the professional fees and the expenditure on plant. The following example demonstrates the concept of direct linkage.

Example 9

> Sarah intends to build a factory with air conditioning for a total cost of £1,000,000 and Lynne, her architect proposes a 10% fee, ie £100,000.
>
> As the project gets underway on site Sarah decides to omit the air conditioning which costs £200,000 and reduces her capital spend to £800,000.
>
> Lynne submits her fee note on completion of the project as 10% of £800,000 ie £80,000.
>
> Once the factory is in operation, however, Sarah realises that she actually needs air conditioning but it will now cost £300,000 to install. She instructs Lynne to proceed and Lynne will fee her 10% ie £30,000 for her work on this part of the project.

Empirical studies by the Royal Institution of Chartered Surveyors and other professional bodies in the construction and engineering industries have confirmed this linkage.

Furthermore, given the complexity of modern buildings and the inter-relationships between the design and procurement teams it is a fact of life that each member of the professional team is involved in areas beyond that which what the layman may be aware, eg installing a lift involves not only the architect from an overall design and planning aspect but also the structural engineer, services engineer, the electrical engineer, the quantity surveyor, and possibly specialist acoustic and other engineers dependent upon the specific circumstances. Attempting to apportion their time, effort and cost other than by way of pro-rating costs is an almost impossible and costly exercise whose accuracy would be open to question.

This view has now been endorsed by the various *JD Wetherspoon* hearings between 2007 and January 2012 (see **9.82** below) and HMRC should now accept pro-rating of professional fees without too many challenges.

Preliminaries

[9.82] Contractors' preliminaries are the common services and facilities provided by the main or managing contractor on a building project. They cover items such as site management, temporary site facilities, site power, security, scaffolding and safety, and all the necessary common services that, if devolved to individual sub-contractors would lead to duplication and significant additional cost. An example is the provision of tower crane on a site. The crane lifts materials to various parts of the site to allow work to progress. It distributes plant and machinery items and items that are not plant and machinery. Similarly, the welfare facilities, if not provided by the main or management contractor, would need to be provided by the individual plant and machinery contractors and the costs of these facilities would be absorbed in their contract price.

HMRC held the same view on preliminaries as they do on professional fees and were reluctant to accept a pro-rated basis of apportionment. This was unfortunate because, despite HMRC reservations, it is an equitable way to apportion professional fees and contractors' overheads and preliminaries (and the Valuation Office Agency used to accept this as an equitable solution before it was deleted, without explanation, from their guidance notes in the early 1990s).

Dependent upon the form of procurement adopted in arranging a capital project, and the form of contract used, the preliminaries element of a project may account for between 7% and 50% of the construction cost, eg while the preliminaries in a traditionally tendered building project may be 7% to 20%, those on a management contract may be 30% to 50% because the basis of pricing and tendering is different.

A final point worth noting on the subject of fees and preliminaries is in the Australian case of *BP (Kwinana) Ltd v Federal Commissioner for Taxation (1961)* where Justice Kitto, a man quoted in a number of House of Lords cases with approval, stated:

'Where a taxpayer spreads an item of indirect cost over several parts of the construction which has included both plant and other things, and does so in proportion to the direct cost of each, it is, in my opinion, irrelevant to criticise his method.

Accuracy in such matters is often unattainable. But that is not to say the "cost", in the relevant sense, cannot be determined, or that an apportionment of indirect costs is necessarily wrong because it involves some degree of arbitrariness. That the claim is justified in principle seems to me to be clear.'

And that appears to be a reasoned response to any attempt to impose a somewhat selective interpretation of the principle in *Ben-Odeco*.

In the case of *JD Wetherspoon Plc v Revenue and Customs Comrs* (2007) SpC 657, the Commissioners stated:

'We do not consider that it can have been the intention of parliament that if a taxpayer is to be entitled to include preliminaries in capital expenditure claimed it should be necessary to enter into a detailed assessment in order to allocate the preliminaries' (para 111).

They confirmed the principle that insofar as items claimed as preliminaries can be properly attributed to or apportioned to a measured item they are part of the cost of that item.

They finally concluded that while the allocation of preliminaries should be as accurate as reasonably possible the extent of any allocation or attribution other than a global apportionment should be reasonable and proportionate to the amount of money involved and the work necessary for a detailed exercise.

The comments applied equally to professional fees.

The case was appealed and in their decision in December 2009 (TC00312) their view was that a global apportionment basis was reasonable. They went on to state:

'This, of course, is not a conclusion that global apportionment of preliminaries is legitimate in all cases. HMRC are clearly entitled to investigate the figures in any case to see whether a more specific breakdown is reasonable and proportionate. However in our judgement a global apportionment which accords with commercial practice will normally be appropriate.'

And this point was reinforced when the case came before the Upper Tribunal (FTC/05 & 83/2010 [2012] UKUT 42 (TCC)) in January 2012 where the decision to pro-rate was agreed 'unhesitatingly' and the Commissioner's decision in their general approach to preliminaries was described as 'plainly correct'. This should now, hopefully, remove this from the contentious items list.

Building alterations connected with the installation of plant and machinery

[9.83] Where there is refurbishment or upgrading of premises this can be a significant cost element. The installation of a lift in an existing building, per the example at **9.68**, gave a summary of the physical operations necessary for that operation, and therefore 'connected' with the installation of plant and machinery. In terms of making a capital allowances claim, however, actually establishing the costs involved can be significantly more problematic. Tendering and procurement procedures in the construction industry are not, as some believe, undertaken with tax legislation as the main focus. The documentation is prepared to enable contractors to price the work based upon their interpretation of how the works will be carried out. In practical terms, and assuming that a traditionally tendered bill of quantities is used as the pricing basis, this means that the costs relating to the lift example could be in eight to ten different trade packages and, dependent upon the scope of the project and detailed descriptions used, may not be separately or readily identified as relating solely to the lift works. This means that in many cases establishing the costs associated with alterations connected with the installation of plant and machinery may require an element of approximation, but provided there is a sound basis of assessment it should prove acceptable to HMRC.

In *JD Wetherspoon v Revenue and Customs Comrs* (2007) SpC 657 a claim was made for ceramic kitchen tiles on the walls of a newly created kitchen. The basis of the claim was that health and safety legislation required wipe clean surfaces before kitchen operations would be allowed and the expenditure was incidental to the installation of plant ie cookers etc. While accepting that the cookers were plant, the Commissioners rejected the claim on the basis that the tiling 'did not have a sufficient nexus with the installation of equipment such as cookers to be incidental thereto for section 66' (CAA 2001, s 25). This may be viewed as a limitation on what may be claimed under this heading but it appears to accord with long-standing HMRC practice and procedure.

In contrast the Commissioners did allow toilet doors and cubicles as they did have sufficient nexus with the toilet installation. And in their 2009 decision they accepted that toilet lighting had been specifically designed to serve a trade specific function, ie creating an appropriate ambience, and therefore qualified as plant and machinery. They also accepted special floor finishes in the area of disabled toilets to assist with wheelchair usage, and the costs of creating or altering floors to accept plant and machinery being installed within existing premises. While these are specifically leisure and hospitality related functions the principles may be extended to other areas.

In January 2012, however, when the *Wetherspoon* saga came to an end (see **9.82** above) the decisions previously given in regard to alterations were upheld. One point that was raised was in regard to the concrete blockwork toilet partitions where the Tribunal expressed the view that had HMRC appealed the previous decision to allow them the Tribunal would have upheld the appeal.

Builders work in connection with services (BWIC)

[9.84] This refers to the works carried out in connection with the 'services' installations in a building and applies to new build projects as well as fit outs and refurbishments. The services installations comprise the gas, electrical and mechanical installations and encompass heating and ventilating, plumbing, fire protection, lifts, security and any specialist installations lifts, and similar installations. The type of work executed under this heading includes items such as cutting holes or chases for pipework or wiring runs, firestopping openings created for services pipework, and similar general builders' work necessary to accommodate the services installations. It may be priced on an individual item basis which can allow specific items to be identified and claimed but is more commonly priced as a percentage of the services installations involved. Given HMRC views on pro-rating generally the allocation of the cost between that applicable to the qualifying expenditure and the non qualifying can be problematic.

Suspended ceilings

[9.85] Suspended ceilings do not generally qualify for allowances unless they form a 'plenum ceiling', ie they are part of the air conditioning system where the ceiling void acts as the return air duct for the air conditioning system. The usual layout for an air conditioning system is that there are two sets of ducts within the ceiling void ie a supply delivering the fresh air and a return air duct drawing the air away from the area serviced to be treated. Where a 'plenum' system is designed the return air duct is omitted and the ceiling void acts as the duct and thus qualifies as part of the air conditioning installation. Under the current legislation it would now qualify as Integral Feature (IFA).

Suspended ceilings may also qualify where they form a feature in a hotel, restaurant, or similar situation. Suspended ceilings that are there solely for aesthetic reasons in, eg covering pipework or electrical wiring, do not qualify.

Raised floors

[9.86] Floors are specifically excluded from being claimed. Raised floors, however, may qualify in certain circumstances, eg where they form a 'plenum floor' similar to a 'plenum ceiling' but the floor acts as the duct. Similarly, where there is a gas dousing system of fire protection and the raised floor acts to draw the gas away once the fire has been extinguished a raised floor will qualify. As a plenum floor and part of an air conditioning system the floor would qualify as an Integral Feature, but as part of a fire protection system it may qualify as Plant & Machinery.

HMRC are against allowing raised floors generally based upon the decision in *Wimpy* but there may be instances where a case may be made dependent upon the reasoning for installation and use to be made of them, eg installing them in a building which did not have them previously to accommodate specific operational requirements.

Electrical installations

[9.87] Notwithstanding, or perhaps because of, the case law on them, electrical installations tended to be the most contentious element in any claim. Disputes usually focused on two aspects of electrical installations, ie lighting and power.

Light fittings did not generally qualify for capital allowances. They may, however, have qualified in whole or in part if they were part of the 'plenum' in an air conditioning system, ie return air light fittings as part of a plenum ceiling. They may also have qualified, dependent upon their use, in hotel, restaurants or similar trades (see **9.88**). They may also have qualified where there was a specific need for special lighting, eg enhanced levels of lighting for specific operations within a property.

Power to identified plant and machinery or fixtures was eligible for capital allowances, eg dedicated power supplies to items ranging from lift installations to hand dryers. General fixed power such as wall sockets in premises was not eligible. The main area of dispute, however, was usually in regard to the power supply where HMRC may have felt that the cost of transformers and switchgear should have been split between eligible and ineligible for allowances reflecting the split between the eligible and ineligible costs of the whole installation. This was their starting position when *Cole Brothers v Philips* HL (1982) 55 TC 188, [1982] STC 307, HL went before the Commissioners. By the time the case reached the House of Lords, however, HMRC had stepped back from this position. Oliver LJ said:

> 'We were, however, told that the Crown, in agreeing the amount to be allowed for the transformers, had included in it the cost of ancillary switchgear – and indeed it seems only logical.'

In a case where only part of the electrical installation qualified for allowances the full amount of the transformers and switchgear still qualified.

The designation of 'an electrical system (including a lighting system)' as an integral feature under the IFA category in FA 2008, thus allowing the entire electrical system to qualify for allowances, should remove a large element of dispute. Indeed the fact that light fittings now qualify without question means that there may be an increased take up of energy efficient fittings that will qualify for 100% ECA first year allowances.

There still remains, however, an element of uncertainty over the exact definition of 'an electrical system' and the potential split between the 18% and 8% pools, eg fire alarm systems, while electrically operated, are not necessarily part of the electrical system as defined.

Ambience

[9.88] In 'hotel, restaurant and similar trades' decorative assets for the enjoyment of the public are eligible for capital allowances (CAA 2001, s 23(4) List C, Item 14). Through case law this has translated into items creating an 'ambience' to attract custom. Hence bric-a-brac, or features built into a public house or hotel, to create a specific atmosphere may be eligible capital spend when it comes to claiming allowances. How far the creation of an 'ambience' can be extended is, in many ways, dependent upon the trading concept envisaged and the designer's creativity. From a capital allowances viewpoint it potentially offers some interesting aspects to claims.

As the term 'similar trades' has not been tested before the courts it is possible that any premises within the hotel or leisure sectors could adopt a similar approach. And when considering the basics of the court decisions with regard to 'ambience' and applying them to the changing face of commerce it may even be possible that a case could be made for 'ambience' in a number of retailing situations where certain expenditure may be otherwise ineligible for allowances.

An interesting example may be found in the increasing joint use of premises where elements may be eligible in one aspect of the operation but not another, eg financial services institutions and coffee bars sharing retailing space.

The *JD Wetherspoon* case re-appears here where decorative wood panelling was claimed and rejected by the Commissioners. Their rationale was that having accepted the wood panelling as an example of embellishment 'it did not qualify as plant because it would be more appropriately described as having become part of the premises than as having a retained separate identity'.

Wetherspoon's appeal against this decision, the January 2012 decision referred to above, was rejected on the grounds that the panelling had not only become 'part of the premises', notwithstanding the method of fixing, but was also an 'unexceptional component'. And for the same reasons the decorative cornicing, architraves and balustrading were also rejected. This probably means that HMRC will adopt a more restrictive approach to such claims and that taxpayers will have to provide appropriate detail to demonstrate why items do not fail this new 'unexceptional' test.

Prefabricated units

[9.89] There have been various attempts over the years to improve construction efficiency through manufacturing elements of buildings off site and bringing them to site already completed or partially completed to be erected on site. Precast concrete floors and wall panelling are the most obvious examples although there are a range of systems that allow whole buildings to be prefabricated and erected on prepared foundations. It can be particularly cost effective from an operational viewpoint where one design is to be used in multiple new build locations, eg a restaurant or hotel chain. From a capital allowances viewpoint it can present problems in identifying and establishing the costs of the plant and machinery or fixtures elements within the overall cost as tendered pricing systems rarely, if ever, provide sufficient detail to fully analyse the costs to the level of detail envisaged by the legislation, or HMRC in terms of proof. The practical solution is to ensure that there is some form of cost breakdown provided that can align in some form to either the Standard Form of Cost Analysis published by the Building Cost Information Service of the RICS or to the generally accepted capital allowances headings. In the absence of a cost breakdown, however, it is possible to synthesize costs to arrive at a notional analysis.

Prefabrication can take many forms. At a simple level it can be the use of prefabricated 'pod' units, most frequently toilets or even complete bathroom units for hotels for example, where a self-contained unit is placed in position and merely 'plugged' in to the drainage and electrical systems, which suggests that it is item of plant in itself and therefore wholly eligible for allowances. The possible counter is that elements of the 'pod', eg the walls or floors are ineligible because walls and floors are specifically excluded by the legislation. There may be grounds for arguing either case but, as in most capital allowances hearings, the decision is dependent upon the particular facts of the case in point.

Revenue/capital split

[9.90] The revenue/capital split was considered in detail in **9.2** but it is flagged up again because it does represent one of the most contentious and ongoing areas of potential friction in claims where refurbishment or maintenance and repair works of premises is carried out. The revenue element of a refurbishment project can quite easily be anywhere between 5 and 30%, or more, of the expenditure incurred dependent upon the works being undertaken. And in a maintenance programme it can be 100%. As there can be disputes about whether or not repair and maintenance is an improvement and therefore potentially ineligible it is helpful, wherever possible, to separate repair and maintenance works from works of a general refurbishment nature. In many cases this is neither a cost effective solution nor a practical one from an administrative viewpoint but it can avoid lengthy, and costly, debate on the issue.

Disability Discrimination Act 1995

[9.91] The Disability Discrimination Act 1995 (DDA) requires building occupiers who provide goods, facilities and services to members of the public to take reasonable steps to remove physical barriers to access. Notwithstanding the general guidelines this has to be dealt with on an individual building and businesses basis but HMRC has published guidance on its approach (*Disability Discrimination Act – new access requirements-tax guidance*) to help clarify the situation. It is helpful but, with a few minor exceptions, all of the items covered would be claimable as alterations to a building or revenue items in any event:

(a)   moveable ramps;
(b)   new sanitary ware installed in existing buildings and the costs 'incidental' to installation;
(c)   signage;
(d)   new handrails;
(e)   special anti-glare lighting, or lighting installed in sales areas or their equivalent (where specifically required for the purposes of that trade);
(f)   specialist door handles;
(g)   evacuation chairs.

The plant and machinery eligible items highlighted include lifts and hoists, and where installed in existing buildings the 'incidental' costs.

HMRC will also accept a range of minor works in existing buildings to comply as revenue deductions. DDA specific items include items such as warning signs or transparencies on glass doors; using coloured or fluorescent strips to improve visual recognition; painting car park spaces; replacing handrails or repositioning them for improved access; and re-hanging doors to open outwards for better access, eg toilet cubicles or changing room cubicles; and possibly replacing doors too.

Other revenue items, which are mostly of a minor nature, would include cutting back protruding or overhanging objects: replacing cracked or uneven paving flags; repairs to floors to level the surfaces; and car park resurfacing (provided there is no element of improvement – even when exhibiting a spirit of public generosity: the Treasury knows not to be too profligate).

How does it operate?

[9.92] P&M allowances for fixtures are claimed in the same way as other capital allowances, ie on the corporation tax return for companies and on the income tax return for individuals and partnerships.

In order to make a claim the taxpayer must have some form of interest in the land. Under the fixtures legislation an interest in land is defined as:

(a)   the fee simple estate in the land or an agreement to acquire it;
(b)   in Scotland, the estate or interest of the proprietor of the dominium utile (or, in the case of property other than feudal property, of the owner) and any agreement to acquire that estate or interest;

(c)   any leasehold interest in, or in Scotland lease of, the land (whether a headlease, sublease or underlease) and any agreement to acquire such an estate, or in Scotland, lease;

(d)   an easement or servitude or any agreement to acquire an easement or servitude;

(e)   a licence to occupy land.

Where any right is assigned or conveyed by way of security the person having that right is regarded as retaining the interest in the land.

This issue is crucial, especially where there are complex deal structures such as in some PFI projects where holding the 'wrong' interest can lead to any allowances due falling to an entity that cannot utilise allowances, or utilise the amounts due in a commercially sound manner.

There are two key cases that flag up the problems that can arise and how the right to allowances may be lost. They are *Melluish v BMI (No 3) Ltd* [1995] STC 964, 68 TC 1 and *J C Decaux Ltd v Francis* [1996] STC (SCD) 281, SCD.

In *Barclays* the case concerned the leasing of a disparate range of items of plant and machinery, from central heating to cremators, to a local authority. This was a complex case involving some 201 separate transactions where Barclays claimed ownership of the fixtures and the capital allowances on them in housing and in operational council buildings such as offices, leisure centres and crematoria. The court held that an election could be made under the equipment leasing rules to give the lessor the allowances even where the lessee, the local authority in this case, was a non-taxpayer. The Finance Act the following year amended the legislation to prevent this situation arising on any expenditure incurred from 23 July 1996. CAA 2001, s 178 gives the conditions for an equipment lessee to have a 'qualifying activity' and specifically excludes equipment leases of plant and machinery for use in a dwelling house.

Decaux carried on a trade of leasing automated public conveniences to local authorities. It also supplied bus shelters and other advertising units which were not leased to the local authorities but were provided on the basis that *Decaux* could use them for advertising purposes. All of the items were fixed to the ground with electrical and plumbing services to the toilets. All allowances were refused (under s 11) because the assets, being fixed to the land no longer belonged to *Decaux*, and (under s 176) because they did not have an interest in the land when they incurred the expenditure. It was insufficient that the incurring of the expenditure brought into being an interest in the land. It was held that the right to enter in order to maintain the assets was a mere contractual right which fell short of 'a licence to occupy'.

This case was important because it also covered the distinction between chattels and fixtures, and laid down principles enacted under CAA 2001, s 179.

Following the *Decaux* case FA 1997, Sch 16 directed that where affixation to the land is merely incidental, allowances are available on leased fixtures irrespective of whether the lessee is carrying on a trade but, for this to apply, the following conditions must be met;

(a)   the plant is fixed to land and not a building;

(b)   the equipment lessee has an interest in that land at the time he takes possession of the plant;

(c)   the plant may be severed from the land (and will belong to the lessor) at the end of the lease;

(d)   the plant is of a type that may be re-used following such severance;

(e)   the lease is accounted for as an operating lease (see **9.109**).

If, for whatever reason, any fixture might be deemed to belong to two or more parties it is the one with the highest interest who would be entitled to the allowances.

Disposal

[9.93] A disposal event occurs when a claimant:

(a)   ceases to own the asset;

(b)   loses possession of the plant and machinery, and it is reasonable to assume that the loss is permanent;

(c)   abandons plant and machinery that has been in use for mineral exploration or access at the site where it was in use;

(d)   loses the use of the plant and machinery through its destruction, dismantling, or otherwise;

(e)   begins to use the plant wholly or partly for purposes other than the qualifying activity;

(f)   permanently discontinues the qualifying activity;

The disposal value that is required to be brought into account by the claimant is dictated by the event.

CAA 2001, s 61: disposal events and disposal values; plant and machinery

Table – disposal values: general

[9.94]

Disposal event	Disposal value
1. Sale of the plant or machinery, except where item 2 applies.	The net proceeds of the sale, together with:
	(a) any insurance money received in respect of the plant or machinery as a result of an event affecting the price obtainable on the sale, and
	(b) any other compensation of any description so received, so far as it consists of capital sums.
2. Sale of the plant or machinery where:	The market value of the plant or machinery at the time of sale.
(a) the sale is at less than market value;	
(b) there is no charge to tax under Schedule E;	

Disposal event	Disposal value
(c) the condition in subs (4) is met by the buyer.	
3. Demolition or destruction of the plant or machinery	The net amount received for the remains of the plant or machinery, together with: (a) any insurance money received in respect of the demolition or destruction; and (b) any other compensation of any description so received, so far as it consists of capital sums.
4. Permanent loss of the plant or machinery otherwise than as a result of its demolition or destruction	Any insurance money received in respect of the loss and, so far as it consists of capital sums, any other compensation of any description so received.
5. Abandonment of the plant or machinery which has been in use for mineral exploration and access at the site where it was in use for that purpose.	Any insurance money received in respect of the abandonment and, so far as it consists of capital sums, any other compensation of any description so received.
6. Permanent discontinuance of the qualifying activity followed by the occurrence of an event within any of the items 1 to 5.	The disposal value for the item in question.
7. Any event not falling within any of items 1 to 6.	The market value of the plant or machinery at the time of the event

Nil disposal values

[9.95] If the expenditure was recorded under the categories in CAA 2001, s 27(2), ie:

- thermal insulation of industrial buildings;
- fire safety;
- safety at designated sports grounds;
- safety at regulated sports ground
- safety at other sports ground;
- personal security,

the disposal value to be brought in is nil.

If a person undertaking a 'qualifying activity', ie a trade, an ordinary Schedule A business, a furnished lettings business, an overseas property business, or a profession or vocation makes a gift of plant or machinery to:

- a charity within the meaning of ICTA 1988, s 506 (charities: qualifying and non-qualifying expenditure);
- a body listed in ICTA 1988, s 507(1) (various heritage bodies and museums); or
- a designated educational establishment within the meaning of ICTA 1988, s 84 (gifts to educational establishments),

the disposal value is nil.

If a person disposes of plant and machinery as a gift where there is a charge to tax under Schedule E, the disposal value is nil.

CAA 2001, s 196: disposal values in relation to fixtures: general

Table – disposal values: fixtures

[9.96]

Disposal event	Disposal value
1. Cessation of ownership of the fixture under s 188 because of a sale of the qualifying interest except where item 2 applies.	The part of the sale price that falls to be treated for the purposes of this Part as expenditure incurred by the purchaser on the provision of the fixture, or would fall to be so treated if the purchaser were entitled to an allowance.
2. Cessation of ownership of the fixture because of a sale of the qualifying interest where the sale is at less than the market value, and the condition in sub-s (2) is met by the purchaser.	The part of the price that would be treated for the purposes of the Part as expenditure by the purchaser on the provision of the fixture if the qualifying interest were sold at market value, that sale took place immediately before the event which causes the former owner to be treated as ceasing to be the owner of the fixture, and that event were disregarded in determining that market value
3. Cessation of ownership of the fixture under s 188 where neither item I not item 2 applies, but the qualifying interest continues in existence after that time or would so continue but for its becoming merged in another interest.	The disposal value given for item 2.
4. Cessation of ownership of the fixture under s 188 because of the expiry of the qualifying interest.	If the person receives a capital sum, by way of compensation or otherwise, by reference to the fixture, the amount of the capital sum. In any other case, nil.
5. Cessation of the ownership of the fixture under s 190 because the lessee has become the owner under s 183	The part of the capital sum given by the lessee referred to in s 183 that falls to be treated for the purposes of this Part as the lessee's expenditure on the provision of the fixture.
6. Cessation of ownership of the fixture under s 191 (severance)	The market value of the fixture at the time of the severance.
7. Cessation of ownership of the fixture because s 192(2)(a) (assignment of rights) applies.	The consideration given by the assignee for the assignment.
8. Cessation of ownership of the fixture because s 192(2)(b) (discharge of equipment lessee's obligations) applies on the payment of a capital sum.	The capital sum paid to discharge the financial obligations of the equipment lessee.
9. Permanent discontinuance of the qualifying activity followed by the sale of the qualifying interest	The part of the sale price that falls to be treated as expenditure incurred by the purchaser on the provision of the fixture, or would fall to be so treated if the purchaser were entitled to an allowance.

Disposal event	Disposal value
10. Permanent discontinuance of the qualifying activity followed by the demolition or destruction of the fixture.	The net amount received for the remains of the fixture, together with any insurance money received in respect of the demolition or destruction, and any other compensation of any description so received, so far as it consists of capital sums.
11. Permanent discontinuance of the qualifying activity followed by the permanent loss of the fixture otherwise than as a result of its demolition or destruction.	Any insurance money received in respect of the loss and, so far as it consists of capital sums, any other compensation of any description so received.
12. The fixture begins to be used wholly or partly for purposes other than those of the qualifying activity.	The part of the price that would fall to be treated for the purposes of this Part as expenditure incurred by the purchaser on the provision of the fixture if the qualifying interest were sold at market value.

Disposal value limits

[9.97] Generally the disposal amount cannot exceed the amount claimed by the person disposing of the plant and machinery. This is not the case, however, where the person disposing of the plant and machinery has acquired it as a result of a transaction or series of transactions with connected parties.

This is best shown in a property sale situation.

Example 10

Martin Ltd builds an office block for £10m and claims £4m in plant and machinery allowances. If he sells to Chris Ltd, a connected person, after one year for £11m they could agree a s 198 election amount of £1, ie Martin Ltd having utilised the first year's £1m retains the £3m balance of allowances less the amount of the s 198 election.

If Chris Ltd sells the building to Robert Ltd for £11m and agrees and signs a s 198 election for £1 the matter ends there and Robert Ltd has allowances of £1.

If, however, Robert Ltd does not sign the election the allowances will be arrived at by a 'just apportionment' of the purchase price. Which means that Robert Ltd may be entitled to allowance of up to £4m, dependent upon the outcome of the 'just apportionment' calculation.

Finance Act 2012 introduces a range of measures which take effect from April 2012 as a means of tightening up the disposal process in relation to capital allowances. These measures, which primarily affect purchasers, are covered in the relevant acquisition scenarios below.

Acquisition

Purchase of a property via a company ie buying the shares as opposed to buying the building

[9.98] Where a property is acquired via the acquisition of a company the purchaser walks into the shoes of the existing company and proceeds as if any claims were being made as direct expenditure by that company.

Purchase of a new building, or a used building where there has been no previous capital allowances claim

[9.99] On the purchase of a new building from a trader, the claimant has an unrestricted claim for capital allowances using a 'just and reasonable apportionment' basis, CAA 2001, s 562(3). The actual costs incurred by the vendor are regarded by the legislation as irrelevant as the apportionment is based solely upon the price paid for the interest in the property.

Unrestricted claims can provide significant amounts in tax relief. The following table shows the potential amount of P&M allowances available in a typical transaction as a percentage of the total paid for the property.

The introduction of the new Integral Features Allowance (IFA) as a sub-set of P&M means that the actual year-on-year tax benefits are somewhat more complex to calculate because of the differential depreciation rates currently available on the categories. While there is a reduction to the overall benefit using a net present value calculation of the benefits this may well be set off with the future tax savings if taxation rates rise in the coming years.

Office buildings	10%	25%
Hotels and leisure centres	10%	35%
Shopping centres	5%	20%
Retail units and warehouses	1%	10%
Industrial complexes	2%	20%
PFI projects, schools, hospitals etc	10%	30%

The diminution from the amounts claimed as compared with projects where construction expenditure is directly incurred arises from the use of the apportionment basis of arriving at the amount due. This is a specialist area which requires a mix of taxation knowledge, construction costing techniques, and property valuation experience. There are variants on the actual basis used for the apportionment calculation but the generally accepted Valuation Office Agency formula is:

$$\text{£Purchase Price} \times \frac{\text{£Plant and Machinery}}{\text{£Land Value} + \text{£Build Cost}} = \text{Capital Allowances}$$

The land value is the assessed land value of the bare site. The build cost is the estimated cost to construct the building including the plant and machinery and fixtures. And the plant and machinery cost is the assessed cost of the P&M.

The only fact in this calculation is the purchase price. All of the other elements are subjective assessments as to what assets may be eligible for allowances and what values may be placed against them. This is an area where specialist property and construction cost advice is essential on two counts. Firstly in ensuring that all costs and items may be identified, and secondly, because HMRC tend to use the Valuation Office Agency to review and assess apportionments it is helpful to have appropriately experienced personnel to provide matching technical expertise to defend challenges to the claim.

Evidence of the subjectivity of the process may be gleaned from anyone who has had a quotation to carry out any capital project, be it a simple home improvement through to a new factory – the prices quoted can vary by a significant margin, and it is the same with apportionment calculations. The pricing of a building project can vary greatly dependent upon the detailed specification, the actual method of construction adopted, and the timeframe within which it is to be delivered. Usually the key determining factor in the calculation is the land value as this can influence the outcome quite dramatically. The return from two identical office blocks that cost the same to build and contain the same plant and machinery can vary by as much as 20% dependent upon the location and land value.

Dependent upon market conditions at the time of sale it is possible for the land value assessments and build cost estimates to exceed the purchase price. This is probably most frequently encountered when a property is the subject of a distress sale but, as the basis of the calculation is a 'just apportionment' of the price paid, no matter whether it is a low price or a high price the overall outcome will be same, ie an apportionment of the purchase price paid into qualifying and non-qualifying expenditure. The actual effect, however, is that the amount of allowances usually drops in absolute terms and as a percentage of the purchase price.

In any apportionment calculation carried out following FA 2008 it will be necessary to split the capital allowances figure into plant and machinery (PMA) and integral features (IFA) so that the amounts may be entered in the two new pools ie the main pool for PMA and the special rate pool for IFA. Notwithstanding the reductions to depreciation rates claim totals should be larger because the IFA legislation extends the range of items that can be claimed. (Details of the IFA legislation are at para **9.63**.)

Purchase of an existing building where there has been a previous capital allowances claim

[9.100] Since April 2014 legislation has significantly tightened the scope for capital allowance claims where second hand buildings are purchased and there have been capital allowance claims by previous vendors.

Whilst a CAA 2001, s 198 election, a joint election made between vendor and purchaser to set the disposal and acquisition value for qualifying fixtures, (a pro-forma election draft is shown in APPENDIX 1 to this chapter at **1.1**) used to be the preferred method for agreeing capital allowance qualifying expenditure when properties exchanged hands, since April 2012 it has become the only route (subject to going down the tribunal path). There is no longer the option for a just and reasonable apportionment. This part of the legislation (contained within CAA 2001, s 187A) is referred to as the 'fixed value requirement'.

In practice, it is highly unlikely that purchasers would want to go to the expense of a tax tribunal unless there were significant amounts in dispute so the real effect of the change is that vendors and purchasers will need to agree an election within two years of the transaction taking place or the purchaser, and any subsequent purchaser, will be unable to claim any allowances on the fixtures in the transaction. This reverses the previous position where the potential advantage lay with the purchaser in avoiding agreeing an election and hoping that a 'just apportionment' would deliver a better result than any amount offered by the seller at the time of the transaction.

In subsequent sales the amount of allowances available to a purchaser will be restricted to the 'fixed value' amount.

A s 198 election is not, however, mandatory. If the vendor does not require a disposal value to be brought in, no election is possible. With the removal of a just and reasonable approach to fixtures in a property sale the election is expected to be the default position.

Elections do, in any event, help vendors by giving them certainty on their tax position but the whole process is dependent upon the tax position of the parties, eg a vendor who has a large pool of allowances that he is unlikely to need may be more amenable to parting with the full amount of his capital allowances claim than someone who has nothing left in his pool and may be facing a tax charge if he concedes more than the tax written down value of his claim.

Elections are irrevocable. HMRC will not accept elections involving non-resident purchasers who are not within the UK tax net.

Example 11

Andrew owns an office block which he built for £10m and claimed £3m in P&M in 2004. Having claimed allowances in 2004 of £0.75m, ie 25% of the £3m claim, he has £2.25m of allowances left in his pool. He expects that in the coming years he will be able to fully utilise the allowances in his pool. In 2005 he sells the block to Euan for £11m and stipulates that, as part of sale conditions, the s 198 election figure for plant and machinery to be transferred to Euan is £1. Euan agrees and they both sign the election within the two year period and submit it to HMRC. Andrew keeps all of the allowances less the amount of the election, £1, and going forward Euan can only pass on £1 in P&M allowances for the office as it now stands should he sell it on. Should, however, Euan carry out any capital works he will be able to claim capital allowances on his expenditure and these would become available as part of the negotiations on any subsequent sale or transfer of interest in the property.

April 2014 marked the full introduction of CAA 2001, s 187A.

The second part of the legislation, which became effective from April 2014, is that a purchaser will only be eligible to claim allowances if the vendor has brought the costs and a disposal value into his tax computations. This is referred to as 'the pooling requirement'. In practice what this means is that if the vendor has not made a claim for capital allowances (no obligation to actually claim the allowance but just to identify the qualifying expenditure) there will be no allowances for the purchaser to receive. It is not uncommon for owners not to make claims if they have no need for capital allowances, eg they have losses or other tax reliefs which made the claiming of capital allowances unnecessary, but for transactions from April 2014 if there has been no claim then the allowances are lost to all parties. Allowances that are able to be passed on to a purchaser are almost always worth something in a transaction so a failure by a potential vendor to have claimed allowances could impact on the sales price. The exception to this rule is the purchase of integral features which may have been incurred by the vendor before they came into existence. For example general lighting incurred in 2007 by the previous owner will not need to be pooled as it was not a qualifying asset then. This does not preclude the new owner from claiming allowances on the lighting going forward. As the years progress in the new regime, however, it will become increasingly unlikely that significant value will be able to be apportioned to such items.

The third part of the legislation covers situations where there has been a previous claim but the current vendor has been unable to claim allowances and or no election has been signed, eg ownership by a non-taxpayer, or circumstances where a joint election was not possible because of the form of disposal. In this situation the purchaser needs to receive a written statement from the vendor confirming that no election was executed within the two-year time limit, and that neither was an application made to a Tribunal within the two year limit. The purchaser also needs a written statement from the previous capital allowances claimant confirming the amount that was brought in as the disposal value when the property was sold to the non-taxpayer. This is known as the 'disposal value statement' and without it the purchaser will be unable to claim allowances. As there is no compulsion on past claimants to provide such information to a prospective purchaser this could well be a difficult area. This means that even non-tax payers who cannot claim capital allowances eg pension funds, still need to be mindful of the capital allowance position when they purchase properties so that they can preserve the value of allowances for future purchasers.

Acquiring a long lease for a premium

[9.101] If acquiring a long lease from a lessor who is entitled to allowances and paying a lump sum which includes a payment for fixtures the lessee and lessor can jointly elect that the fixtures are treated as belonging to lessee (CAA 2001, s 199). The election needs to be made and submitted to HMRC within two years of the date on which the lease takes effect (CAA 2001, s 193). If the election is not agreed within the two-year period the lessor keeps the allowances and the lessee loses any entitlement. This option is not open to connected persons. (A pro forma election is contained in APPENDIX 1 at 1.2.)

In a similar situation where the lessor is not entitled to allowances, eg a non-taxpayer, pension fund etc, or the lessor has not claimed allowances, the lessee is treated as being the owner of the fixture (CAA 2001, s 194). This means that there is no need for an election but the lessee will need to carry out a 'just and reasonable apportionment' of the amount paid for the fixtures as detailed above for unrestricted claims.

The changes outlined above in **9.94** flow through, where relevant, to lease situations.

Integral features

[9.102] Since the introduction of integral features, s 198 elections now need to differentiate between integral features and non-integral features to be valid (unless of course the fixtures did not qualify as integral features as they were purchased prior to April 2008).

Plant and machinery long life assets (LLAs)

General

[9.103] From April 2012 LLA's have attracted allowances of 8% per annum on a reducing balance basis and are included in the special rate pool. Originally introduced as 6% per annum reducing balance basis on expenditure on long life assets incurred from 26 November 1996. It did not apply to contracts let before 26 November 1996 and where the expenditure was incurred before the end of 2000.

What qualifies in principle?

[9.104] Long life asset expenditure is expenditure on plant or machinery which, if new, can reasonably be expected to have a useful economic life of at least 25 years, or, if not new, could reasonably have been expected when new to have a useful economic life of at least 25 years. The useful economic life ends when the asset ceases to be used by any person as a fixed asset of a business.

The definition matches that in FRS15 except that the LLA legislation looks at its use as an asset in any business and not just the use in the particular business it comes under when new. If, however, the asset is likely to be scrapped at the end of its use in that particular business it should not be regarded as a LLA.

Similarly, if there is no second hand market for the asset HMRC will generally follow the depreciation policy adopted by the claimant.

The 25 year test should be applied to the asset as a whole and not to its constituent parts.

The tests as to the reasonableness of the expected economic life can be listed as follows:

- the accounting treatment of the asset – if the asset is to be depreciated over a period of less than 25 years this could be a sign that it is not a LLA. HMRC, however, may not be content that the accounting treatment reflects the actual potential economic life and may look for other aspects;
- technical obsolescence – what appears to be state of the art today is quickly superseded by newer and more efficient technologies;
- commercial obsolescence – most premises are refurbished in a 15 to 20-year cycle;
- physical deterioration – there are not that many items in properties qualifying for P&M allowances that are likely to last beyond 25 years eg a boiler in a PFI hospital that runs 24 hours a day for 365 days a year is more likely to be replaced within 25 years than an intermittently used building.

The expenditure must exceed £100,000 per annum for the legislation to apply, otherwise it will be treated as ordinary plant and machinery. There are anti-avoidance provisions to ensure that artificial arrangements or related party transactions are not used to circumvent the £100,000 annual limit.

In a property context the following types of property may expect to be challenged as containing long life assets:

- industrial properties;
- PFI projects, schools hospitals, prisons, etc;
- any property that does not fall within those excluded, eg greenhouses.

Notwithstanding the foregoing, HMRC, in Tax Bulletin 57, recognise that two identical assets could have different lives dependent upon their use, and consequently each asset must be dealt with on its own facts.

What costs qualify?

[9.105] The basis of costs for long life assets is the same as for plant and machinery generally.

What does not qualify?

[9.106] Items that might be classified as LLAs must already qualify for capital allowances. The purpose of the LLA regime is to diminish the writing down allowance available so, in a reverse to the normal position with regard to exclusions from qualification, in this instance the more restrictions to qualification as a LLA the better for the taxpayer.

In a property context an asset cannot be a LLA if it is plant and machinery which is a fixture in, or is provided for use in, a building used wholly or mainly as, or for purposes ancillary to the purposes of, a dwelling house, retail shop, showroom, hotel or office.

Similarly expenditure on the provision of railway assets for use wholly and exclusively in a railway business incurred before 1 January 2011 cannot be classified as a LLA. The term 'railway asset' covers anything which is, or is to be, comprised in any railway station, railway track or light maintenance depot and is provided wholly and exclusively for the purposes of a railway business.

HMRC accept that the 'wholly or mainly' condition is met if at least 75% of the building is used for one of the exempt purposes.

There is also an expenditure limit in that companies, individuals, and partnerships of individuals who spend less than £100,000 per annum are excluded from the long life assets regime. The amount is reduced or increased if the chargeable period is less or more than 12 months.

The exclusion does not apply to expenditure incurred on the provision of plant or machinery for leasing; on the provision of a share in plant or machinery; or expenditure which qualifies for allowances under CAA 2001, s 538, contributions.

In a peripheral property context HMRC agreed with the National Farmers Union that sophisticated greenhouses, ie a minority, which qualify as machinery and plant and where expenditure was incurred before 31 December 2005, would not be subjected to the LLA regime.

On a specific item basis, an asset which is part of a larger entity cannot be classified as a long life asset if the entity is excluded from the legislation, or if the entity is within the legislation the entity is not a long life asset. This opens up the 'entity', or 'entirety' concept touched on previously in **9.2** Is it capital?, in **9.51–9.75** Plant and Machinery, and **9.77–9.90** Fixtures sections such as *Brown v Burnley Football and Athletic Co Ltd* (1980) 53 TC 357, ChD, *O'Grady v Bullcroft Main Collieries Ltd* (1932) 17 TC 93, and *Samuel Jones & Co (Devonvale) Ltd v IRC* (1951) 32 TC 513. If it can be shown that the asset under question is part of a larger 'entity' or 'entirety' it will not be a long life asset.

How does it operate?

[9.107] LLAs are claimed in the same way as other capital allowances, ie on the corporation tax return for companies and on the income tax return for individuals and partnerships.

FA 2008 introduced the new 'special rate pool' with a now 8% reducing balance rate for LLAs and IFAs. Previously the assets were kept in a separate long life asset pool but expenditure incurred from 1 or 6 April 2008 must be put in the new pool.

Overseas leased long life assets that would qualify for WDAs of 10% are added to the LLA pool and while previously qualifying for allowances at 6% reducing balance will now qualify at 8%.

As the concept of LLAs is relatively new as compared with, say, fixtures, it has been difficult to reach any consensus on what items should fall within the LLA legislation. Given the significant impact that they could have on tax relief, combined with the uncertainty on definition, HMRC actively sought out industry groups in an attempt to bring some certainty to this area. To date HMRC has reach agreements on long life assets with industry groups covering the airline, greenhouse, printing and water supply industries.

Disposal/acquisition

[9.108] Second hand long life assets remain long life assets and go into the long life asset pool of the new owner.

Leasing and capital allowances

General

[9.109] The FA 2006, Ch 9 (Miscellaneous provisions), introduced legislation which changed the rules on leases of plant and machinery. A new concept known as 'a long funding lease' was introduced with the intention that the lessee would be eligible for capital allowances instead of the lessor where such a lease is in operation (CAA 2001, s 34A).

It is unlikely that the normal range of plant and machinery leased with offices or other commercial or industrial premises will fall within the long funding lease definitions at present because the legislation excludes 'background plant and machinery' (CAA 2001, s 70R), ie the usual range of services and the like to be found in most let buildings, from the long funding lease conditions. A further exclusion is plant and machinery that is not regarded as 'background plant and machinery' provided it does not exceed 10% of the value of the background plant and machinery, and does not exceed 5% of the value of the property (CAA 2001, s 70U).

This means that anything that is not within the two excluded categories may fall within the long funding legislation eg anything considered a chattel. In property generally this may not be a large amount but in the licensed leisure and hospitality sectors, and in some manufacturing or process industries there could be an impact and it may make commercial sense to buy rather than lease, or to develop alternative arrangements.

CAA 2001, s 70T allows the list of 'background plant and machinery' to be updated by Treasury Order and SI 2007/303 (28 February 2007) provides details of the current listing.

Contributions, inducements, grants and subsidies

Grants

[9.110] Grants should generally be deducted from expenditure qualifying for capital allowances. This was decided in *Cyril Lord Carpets Ltd v Schofield* (1966) 42 TC 637, NI CA where the company incurred expenditure on plant and machinery and subsequently received grants from the Northern Ireland Government. The court dismissed the company's appeal and held that the expenditure had been 'met' by the grants either directly or indirectly (within the meaning of what is now CAA 2001, s 532).

European Community (EC) grants are deducted from expenditure that qualifies for capital allowances.

There are four exceptions to the rule, ie where the grant money is not deducted from the amounts claimed for capital allowances. They are:

- a grant under the Industrial Development (Northern Ireland) Order 1982, Pt III, being a grant not exceeding 45% of the expenditure incurred and made under an agreement up until 31 March 2003;
- insurance and compensation for assets destroyed, demolished or put out of use;
- contributions received from persons who are not entitled to tax relief, ie they cannot claim capital allowances on it or deduct it in calculating profits, a deduction in calculating profits and who are not public bodies;
- grants from the Football Trust paid out of the proceeds of Spot the Ball competitions (letter from HMRC to the Football League 21 January 1991).

A public body is generally defined as the Crown or any government or public or local authority. But in *McKinney v Hagans Caravans (Manufacturing) Ltd* (1997) 69 TC 526, CA NI the term 'public body' (previously referred to as a public authority) was held to include an international fund established to promote economic and social advancement in Northern Ireland. With this, somewhat wider view, a public body could be an organisation which includes some, but not necessarily all, of the following; a constitution which derives from some public source; performance of a public service; public control and accountability; absence of private profit; public funding.

Where a grant is repaid, either voluntarily or compulsorily, it may be possible to make a capital allowances claim on the amount but only if the grant was made by the Crown, government or any other public body, or, the repaid grant is taxable in the hands of the person who made the grant as a balancing adjustment or revenue receipt (ESC B49).

Contributions

[9.111] A person making a capital contribution to an asset can claim capital allowances if the recipient would have been treated as incurring the expenditure and would have been able to claim the allowances, or if the recipient is a public body.

If the contributor and the recipient are connected persons no claim is allowed.

Contributions follow the allowances granted to the asset and should be kept in a separate pool. In most cases there is no need to bring in a disposal value if a disposal event arises with regard to the asset on which the contribution was made. If, however, the contributor transfers the relevant activity then the claim would cease.

Property investors, however, will be required to bring in a disposal amount if, having contributed to fixtures, the property is sold. A s 198 election could be used to cover this situation and an appropriate figure negotiated ie between £1 and the original amount of the claim but with separate pools required for plant and machinery and integral features there should be a figure and/or details entered for each pool.

The relationship between the tenant, or potential tenant, receiving a contribution to fitting out expenditure and the landlord making the contribution can be complex. The objective on both sides is to do the best commercial deal possible but the starting point of each is somewhat different.

The following examples highlight the possible issues and possible route to resolution.

Example 12

Gordon hopes to lease premises from landlord Tony. Gordon intends spending £6m in fitting out his new office and he expects to secure plant and machinery allowances on 75% of his expenditure, ie his claim will be £4.5m. His landlord, Tony, has agreed to make a £1m contribution to the fitting out. Ideally, Gordon wants the contribution to be made in connection with items and assets that fall within the £1.5m of his ineligible expenditure eg general building works or items specifically excluded from being plant and machinery by the legislation. The landlord, however, would prefer that it be identified as a contribution towards the costs of items qualifying for plant and machinery allowances. This would give the landlord a £1m claim and reduce the tenant's claim to £3.5m, while in the tenant's preferred scenario the landlord would have no claim and the tenant would secure the full £4.5m.

Assuming that they wish to proceed with the deal they must negotiate some form of agreement on the split. Ignoring it does not solve the problem. In the absence of any detail on this issue in the contribution documentation a pro-rated apportionment of the total claim to the total expenditure may be used ie each party claims the same percentage of eligible costs on their expenditure. In this case while the total claim remains the same ie £4.5m, the claim split would be 75% qualifying and 25% ineligible for each of the parties, so the figures would be:

Tenant £5m expenditure   £3.75m qualifying/£1.25m ineligible
Landlord £1m expenditure   £0.75m qualifying/£0.25m ineligible

And while this may appear to be an equitable solution it may not be the optimum result for both parties when other accounting and commercial issues are considered.

The above example assumes that both parties are taxpayers who can utilise the allowances, and who wish to use them. If, however, one of the parties is a non-taxpayer, or is a taxpayer who has ample tax capacity for current and foreseeable future needs, then the dynamic changes and a wider commercial viewpoint can be taken of the value of the allowances to the respective parties.

Another aspect arising from the same issue is whether the tenant actually wishes, or can actually afford, to carry out the fitting out. In this situation there may be an agreement for the landlord to carry out the works and adjust the rental level accordingly, possibly building in an element of the additional tax savings being achieved by the landlord.

Inducements

[9.112] There are three basic forms of inducements, excluding contributions already covered, that landlords can offer potential tenants, and a number of variants dependent upon the specific circumstance. The three are:

- a rent-free period;
- a reduced rent;
- a reverse premium.

There are a range of issues outwith the tax advantages in determining the best outcome for the parties but from a strictly tax perspective the possible outcomes for each of the options is as follows.

Other tax treatment arising from inducements (and contributions) is addressed in **CHAPTER 7** on premiums at paragraphs **7.19** ff.

Rent-free period

[9.113] A rent-free period is simple and straightforward. It allows the tenant to fit out the premises without paying rental and the landlord only delays collecting rental income. If both are taxpayers there are no significant tax implications. Although the tenant may make some saving under UTIF 28 where, using the accruals concept, the rental 'saving' is spread over the period to the next rent review or the end of the lease whichever is the shorter. It should, however, be noted that from 1 January, 2005 accounts made up using International Accounting Standards require any incentives to be spread over the term of the lease under SIC15 ie there is no option to utilise a shorter period as in UTIF28.

Reduced rental for a limited period

[9.114] A midway solution. The tenant pays rental and claims it as a deduction and the landlord secures some income. Again the implications of UTIF 28 and SIC15 will have an impact but this could be factored in to the commercial deal struck on either the reduced rental level or the period of the reduced rental.

A reverse premium

[9.115] This usually means that the landlord pays the tenant a lump sum. Since 9 March 1999 a reverse premium from a landlord (or his nominee, or person acting under the direction of the landlord, or connected to the landlord) is now taxable in the tenant's hands as Schedule D Case I or II trading receipts with the tax charge following the accounting treatment, ie spread over the period of the lease or the next rent review date, whichever is the shorter. Payments by an outgoing tenant to an incoming tenant do not fall within this part of the legislation.

Payment of a reverse premium may make sense for a developer who intends to sell on the building immediately after completion because he would be able to add it to his costs and deduct the lump sum in calculating his profit. As the developer would not be eligible for capital allowances this is a sensible option to be considered.

Relationship with other taxes

Capital gains tax

[9.116] CGT is the term generally used as shorthand for both capital gains tax on individuals and corporation tax on gains for companies.

There are three elements that need to be in play for a CGT event to occur. There must be a chargeable person, a chargeable disposal of a chargeable asset, and a chargeable gain.

The timing of the disposal is the date of the contract, or if under a conditional contract the date when the condition is met. This is a different definition from that used in calculating capital allowances

Claiming capital allowances does not affect the base cost for CGT calculations. As always, there is an exception to the rule and it is with regard to land remediation relief where, in certain circumstances, there may be a CGT liability (see TCAP24.17/18).

The base cost, ie the cost for tax deduction purposes, for a property being disposed of comprises the following elements:

(a)   the amount or value of the consideration given wholly and exclusively for the acquisition of the asset, or for the provision of the asset;

(b)   costs incidental to the acquisition of the asset such as fees, commission or remuneration paid for the professional services of any surveyor, valuer, auctioneer, accountant, agent or legal adviser; costs of transfer or conveyance (including stamp duty), and advertising costs;

(c)   the amount of any expenditure wholly and exclusively incurred on the asset for the purpose of enhancing its value;

(d)   expenditure incurred on establishing, preserving or defending title to, or a right over, the asset (TCGA 1992, s 38).

The fact that expenditure has attracted capital allowances does not prohibit deduction of that expenditure in a CGT computation. Special rules, however, apply where the result would be a loss (TCGA 1992, s 41). In the computation of a capital loss, there is excluded from the sums allowable as a deduction any expenditure to the extent that capital allowances have been made in respect of it (CG15410). The allowances referred to comprise not only first year or writing down allowances, but also any balancing allowance or charge brought about as a result of the disposal itself (TCGA 1992, s 41(6)).

VAT

[9.117] As an initial guide the relationship between VAT and capital allowances is quite simple and is dependent upon the status of the taxpayer. If the taxpayer is:

(a)   a taxable person who makes only taxable supplies, he will exclude the VAT element from his capital allowances claims;

(b)   a partly exempt person (see **CHAPTER 15**, para **15.288**), he will be able to allocate the irrecoverable VAT element as appropriate;

(c)   not a taxable person for VAT purposes, he can claim all of the VAT relating to the capital allowances assets.

The taxpayer can only claim VAT in relation to capital allowances where there is an element of irrecoverable VAT involved. If a taxpayer makes supplies that are exempt from VAT he is unable to reclaim any input VAT costs.

If any irrecoverable VAT has been charged on any assets qualifying for capital allowances that VAT will form part of the qualifying cost and should be added to the appropriate capital allowances claim.

Where a property is acquired second-hand and the price is apportioned to identify the plant and machinery element of the purchase price applicable to fixtures, the irrecoverable VAT incurred by the vendor should also be apportioned.

A more sophisticated relationship between capital allowances and VAT is found in the Capital Goods Scheme (see **CHAPTER 15**, para **15.288**) which applies to capital expenditure on the following goods and works:

(a)   computers and items of computer equipment worth £50,000 or more;
(b)   land and buildings (or parts of buildings) and from 3 July 1997 civil engineering work worth £250,000 or more;
(c)   a building (or part of a building) in which the owner's interest (or right over or licence to occupy) is taxed under the rules relating to the change of use of a residential or charitable building where the value taxed under those rules is £250,000 or more;
(d)   a building (or part of a building) to which the developer's self-supply was £250,000 or more;
(e)   a building not falling within (c) or (d) which was constructed by the owner and first brought into use by him after 31 March 1990 if the value of all taxable supplies of goods or services made to him after that date in connection with the construction are £250,000 or more;
(f)   a building which the owner alters (including constructing an extension or annex) where an additional floor area of 10% or more is created and the value of all taxable supplies or goods or services made to him after the date in connection with the alteration are £250,000 or more;
(g)   a civil engineering work constructed by the owner and first brought into use by him from 3 July 1997 if the aggregate value of taxable supplies to the owner after the date relating to the land or in connection with the construction of the work is £250,000 or more; and
(h)   a building which the owner refurbishes or fits out where the value of capital expenditure on the taxable supplies of services and goods affixed to the building made to the owner in connection with the refurbishment from 3 July 1997 is £250,000 or more.

A partly exempt taxpayer's VAT recovery can, and tends to, vary from year to year. Prior to the capital goods scheme a partly exempt taxpayer undertaking a capital project could end up paying more, or less, tax, dependent upon the year the project was undertaken. For obvious, but distinctly opposite, reasons, neither the taxpayer nor HMRC were happy with this situation and the Capital Goods Scheme came into being.

The scheme is aimed at spreading the amount recovered under the scheme over five years for the computing element and ten years for the land and buildings element ie the deductible portion of the VAT on land and buildings is allowed at 10% per annum on a straight line basis, but is re-calculated each year to take account of the business's overall change in its VAT recovery portion.

The VAT capital goods scheme is discussed more fully in CHAPTER 15 at 15.288 ff.

Stamp duty land tax (SDLT)

[9.118] SDLT, which was introduced from 1 December 2003, has made stamp duty a more significant cost element for commercial property purchasers, and one more difficult to circumvent. The detail of SDLT is dealt with in CHAPTER 16 but in relation to capital allowances it is essential, as it is where any form of sophisticated tax planning or structuring is involved, to ensure that the appropriate 'qualifying interest' is with a party who can actually utilise the allowances.

Private finance initiative projects

PFI/PPP

[9.119] The traditional PFI project, if the word traditional is appropriate for a ten year history, took capital allowances very seriously and built them in to the bidding models. Prudent caution was probably the watchword as making low assumptions could contribute to losing the bid and overestimating the amount of allowances potentially available could impair the projected operational performance.

Plant and machinery allowances are available in schools, hospitals, prisons and virtually any PFI project, as fixtures under the same principles of eligibility as for any other capital project, although it might be difficult to justify the costs of creating an 'ambience' in prisons. The majority of any eligible expenditure is usually P&M and, in a number of cases, perhaps some LLAs. PFI road projects would generally qualify as highway undertakings and attract IBAs with perhaps some elements capable of being claimed as P&M, eg signage, control systems and the like.

The changes introduced by FA 2008, ie the reductions in depreciation rates, the introduction of integral features, and the abolition of IBAs will have an impact on both operators and clients for existing and future PFI projects. On existing projects, dependent upon the specific terms of the agreements, it may lead to increased charges to accommodate the losses incurred through the changes. On future projects it may lead to adjustments to potential payment mechanisms to accommodate the effects of the current changes.

The changes to allowances regimes ie changes to the rates of WDA and the abolition of IBA will have an impact not only on the pricing of future PFI contracts but also potentially on the payment mechanisms of a range of existing projects dependent upon the detailed terms and conditions agreed.

The potential key problem area and differentiation in PFI projects, as with any sophisticated structure, is to ensure that the allowances end up with someone who can use them. There have been instances where allowances became trapped in entities that would be unlikely to be able to use them for 20 years or so, if at all.

A more recent development in some areas, spurred on by the prospect of securing relief for the balance of expenditure that did not attract tax relief, is the composite trade approach which allows all of the construction expenditure to be written off on the profit and loss account, or against income receivable. This wipes out the need for capital allowances and produces a much more tax efficient result.

The majority of PFI projects appear to be undertaken by Special Purpose Vehicles (SPVs), and for an SPV to qualify for composite trade status it has to demonstrate that it actually operates a composite trade. The requirements are that it has a trade of providing design and construction services as well as ancillary support services. It must not have a leasehold interest in the land but only some form of subordinate right of access, eg a licence, to provide its services or exploit those rights as a source of rent. The usual method of complying with this requirement is for the public sector body to retain land ownership and be the occupier of the premises but, dependent upon the specific circumstances pertaining, there may be variants on this approach.

Notwithstanding all of the foregoing, as PFI clients become more sophisticated and a commonality of knowledge and approach is built up by them there is a greater pressure on PFI bidders to share the benefits arising from the composite trade approach, eg since February 2003 the Department of Health (DoH) has stipulated that composite trade status is the preferred option for NHS schemes and bidders. And any decision by a Health Trust not to follow this route must be referred to the DoH Private Finance Unit. The DoH also expect that the full benefit of the tax saving will be passed on the Trusts through reduced unitary charges.

For a variety of reasons it is unlikely that all PFI bidders will go along the composite trade route. And those that do will be subjected to strict scrutiny by HMRC to ensure that they are complying with the legislative requirements. There are potential difficulties with accounting for a PFI trade, especially if FRS 5 is applicable and the property might not be reflected on the SPV's balance sheet ie the asset may be 'off balance sheet'. This is potentially problematic because the criteria that determine whether the property is a fixed asset for accounting purposes are different from those which determine if it is capital for tax purposes.

Appendix 1

Pro formas

1.0 Required within two years of the date of the transaction, or the date that a lease takes effect

    1.1 Section 198 Election: Apportionment of consideration in the acquisition of a fixture

    1.2 Section 183 Election: Grant of a new lease or other qualifying interest in land

2.0 Required within two years of the end of the accounting period in which the transaction takes place

    2.1 Section 83 Election: Short life asset election

    2.2 FA 2002 Schedule 22 Election: Capital expenditure on land remediation

1.1 Section 198 Election: Apportionment of consideration in the acquisition of a fixture

HM Revenue and Customs

Capital Allowances Election

Under the provisions of CAA 2001, s 198, we elect that the amount agreed by both parties as the disposal value attributable to fixtures in connection with the sale and purchase of (description of property) on (date of transaction) for (amount of consideration) will be (agreed amount of allowances to be transferred, which cannot be greater than the vendor's original claim or claims for the property).

The attached schedules list the fixtures covered by this agreement ie Schedule A: Plant and Machinery, Schedule B Integral Features.

. . . .	. . . .	. . . .
Vendor	Date	Tax reference
. . . .	. . . .	. . . .
Purchaser	Date	Tax reference

(The election should be sent to both parties' Inspectors of Taxes.)

1.2 Section 183 Election: Grant of a new lease or other qualifying interest in land

HM Revenue and Customs

Capital Allowances Election

Under the provisions of CAA 2001, s 183, we elect that the fixtures at the premises (details of demised premises) listed in the attached schedules are treated as belonging to (the lessee) for capital allowances purposes and that the sum paid be regarded as qualifying expenditure in respect of those assets (Schedule A Plant and Machinery, Schedule B Integral Features).

On (date of lease) a lease for (number of) years was granted by (lessor) to (lessee) for (details of the premises) for consideration of (£ capital sum agreed).

. . . .

Lessor   Date

. . . .

Lessee   Date

2.1 Section 83 Election: Short life asset election

HM Revenue and Customs

Short Life Asset Election

Under the provision s of CAA 2001, s 83, we elect to treat the following items of machinery or plant acquired in the accounting period ended . . . . as short life assets

Asset   Date of expenditure   Expenditure

. . . .

Secretary

. . . .

Date

2.2 FA 2002 Schedule 22 Election: Capital expenditure on land remediation

HM Revenue and Customs

Land Remediation Deduction

Under FA 2001, Sch 22, we elect for capital expenditure incurred on land remediation to be deducted in computing profits on the trade.

Details of the timing, the work executed, and the costs incurred are provided on the attached schedule.

. . . .
Company secretary

. . . .
Date

Appendix 2

Capital allowances checklist

The following is a list of items that have been included in capital allowances claims with regard to property as either plant and machinery, integral features, industrial, or hotel buildings allowances, and accepted by HMRC as eligible for capital allowances.

Some of the items are generally accepted but with others it is entirely dependent upon the specific circumstances in which they were utilised for the purposes of the businesses involved.

Integral Features

- an electrical system (including a lighting system)
- a cold water system
- a space or water heating system, and any floor or ceiling comprised in such a system
- a powered system of ventilation, and any floor or ceiling comprised in such a system
- air cooling or air purification, and any floor or ceiling comprised in such a system
- a lift, escalator or moving walkway
- external solar shading

Plant and Machinery

- advertising signs and signage
- aerials
- aircraft engine testing buildings
- alterations to buildings ancillary to the installation of plant or machinery
- amusement park rides
- aquaria
- automatic barriers and gates
- architect's fees, in part or in total
- baths
- beehives
- bicycle holders
- boilers
- burglar alarms
- bus shelters used for advertising purposes
- cable TV systems
- canopies
- canteen fittings and equipment
- caravans and caravan sites

- carpets
- car park lighting
- car wash apparatus
- catwalks
- ceilings, decorative, dependent upon the circumstances
- cleaning cradles
- cold rooms
- compressors
- containers
- counters
- checkouts
- décor
- demolition costs when removing existing plant or machinery or in creating access for new plant and machinery
- display equipment
- dry risers and wet risers
- electricity sub-stations
- energy-saving investments
- fences
- fire safety expenditure
- fish tanks and ponds
- fixtures
- floodlights
- flooring
- furniture and furnishings
- gas installations
- grain silos
- greenhouses
- insulation
- mezzanine floors
- milking parlours
- mirrors
- murals
- paintings and pictures
- partitions, moveable
- plant rooms
- poultry houses
- professional fees
- public address systems
- railways
- reservoirs
- roads
- runways
- safes
- strongrooms
- safety at sports grounds
- sanitaryware
- seating
- screens
- security systems

- sewerage systems
- shelving
- shop fronts
- showers
- shutters
- smoke detectors
- silage clamps
- sound insulation
- stairs
- storage equipment
- swimming pools
- telecommunication systems
- temporary buildings
- waste disposal systems
- water supplies and tanks
- water towers
- windmills
- zoo cages

Chapter 10

Relief for interest payable

by
Satwaki Chanda,
Barrister

Overview

[10.1] Many acquisitions of property involve a loan or funding of some sort arranged by the purchaser whether the property is being acquired as an investment or for development. In most cases it will be crucial that the purchaser obtains any available tax deduction for his funding costs, including interest payable. In order for a tax deduction to be available various conditions have to be satisfied and it should not be assumed that a tax deduction will be given automatically. The conditions to be satisfied depend upon which tax is relevant.

UK resident companies and non-UK resident companies trading in the UK through a branch or agency are within the charge to corporation tax. Since 2016, so are certain non-UK resident companies dealing in UK situated property. For corporation tax purposes, an interest deduction is available according to the loan relationship rules in CTA 2009, Part 5.

Any person who is outside the scope of corporation tax is charged under the income tax provisions. As well as individuals and trustees, this currently includes non-resident companies investing in UK land. For income tax purposes an interest deduction can be given either as a trading expense or as an expense of a UK or overseas property business. However, individuals and trustees are subject to restrictions on interest relief in calculating the profits of a rental business, for both UK and overseas property. These restrictions do not apply to non-resident corporate landlords.

There are proposals to bring non-UK corporate landlords into the corporation tax net instead of charging them under the income tax rules. As a result, non-resident companies would be subject to the same restrictions on interest relief that apply to UK companies under the loan relationship rules and other corporate provisions (see Consultation Paper '*Non-resident companies chargeable to income tax and non-resident capital gains tax*' published 20 March 2017 at tinyurl.com/ljplstw).

Corporation tax

[10.2] For corporation tax purposes, interest paid by a company is treated as a debit in its 'loan relationship' which means in effect that it is offset against any interest received (which is a credit in its loan relationships) and any resulting deficit (or surplus) is brought into account for tax purposes. Relief is normally available on an accruals basis although there are exceptions mentioned below. Other related expenses such as funding costs and bad debts are also treated as debits in the company's loan relationships.

A company has a 'loan relationship' wherever:

(a) the company stands in the position of a creditor or debtor as respects any money debt (CTA 2009, s 302(1)(a)); and

(b) the debt arises from a transaction for the lending of money (CTA 2009, s 302(1)(b)).

For these purposes 'money' includes sterling and foreign currency. Almost any loan will give rise to a loan relationship. However, an unpaid or deferred purchase price is not strictly regarded as a loan relationship although it can become one if an instrument is issued representing security or the rights of the creditor for the debt (CTA 2009, s 303(3)). Interest on unpaid or deferred purchase consideration is, however, relieved as if it had arisen in a loan relationship (CTA 2009, s 479(1)). A loan will not be a loan relationship to the extent that it arises from rights conferred by shares in a company. This means that most types of shares are not loan relationships (CTA 2009, s 303(4)).

Trading and non-trading loan relationships are treated separately. A trading loan relationship is one to which a company is a party for the purposes of a trade carried on by it (such as property dealing or developing, but not investment) (CTA 2009, s 297). Interest and other debits on trading loan relationships are treated as trading expenses in computing the trading profits (CTA 2009, s 297(3)).

On the other hand, interest and other debits on non-trading loan relationships are set-off against credits arising from non-trading loan relationships (CTA 2009, ss 300 and 458(1)). Any resulting net surplus of credits is taxed under CTA 2009, s 299(1). Any resulting surplus of debits is called a non-trading deficit on the company's loan relationships and the basic rule is that the non-trading deficit must be carried forward and set off against profits for the accounting period after the deficit period.

For deficits arising in accounting periods before 1 April 2017 (pre-1 April 2017 deficits), carry-forward relief is only available against non-trading profits (CTA 2009, s 457(1)). However, for deficits arising for accounting periods beginning on or after 1 April 2017 (post-1 April 2017 deficits), carry-forward relief is available against a company's total profits (CTA 2009, ss 463G, 463I inserted by September 2017 Finance Bill). The following rules apply to carry forward relief (CTA 2009, ss 457–458, 463G–463I amended by/inserted by September 2017 Finance Bill):

(a) the relief must be claimed, except in the case where the full amount of a pre-1 April 2017 deficit is being carried forward, in which case the relief is automatic. Claims must be made within two years of the end of the accounting period that follows the period in which the deficit arose;

(b)   if there are insufficient profits to relieve the entire amount of the deficit, the balance may be carried forward to subsequent accounting periods, or relieved in accordance with the alternative reliefs available (see below);

(c)   there is no requirement to utilise the whole amount of the deficit. The company can make a partial claim, with the balance carried forward to future accounting periods, or for set-off under any of the alternative reliefs available;

(d)   a post-1 April 2017 deficit cannot be set against total profits if the company is a company with an investment business that has become small or negligible. In these circumstances, carry-forward relief is only available to set off against non-trading profits;

(e)   post-1 April 2017 deficits may be carried forward to be set against future non-trading profits of another group member (carry-forward group relief). The company must however, have income producing assets at the end of the relevant surrender period (CTA 2010, ss 188BB–188BD, 188BF inserted by September 2017 Finance Bill). Furthermore, carry forward group relief does not apply if the company is a company with investment business and that business has become small or negligible (CTA 2009 s 463G, CTA 2010 s 188B(1)(a)(i) inserted by September 2017 Finance Bill). A claim for carry forward group relief may be made at any time up to the first anniversary of the filing date of the return (FA 1998, Sch 18, para 74);

(f)   from 1 April 2017, the ability to carry forward a non-trading deficit is subject to the corporate loss restrictions which apply where the company's profits exceed £5 million. In these circumstances, the total amount of losses from various sources that can be carried forward cannot exceed £5 million plus 50% of profits in excess of that figure. For these purposes, 'losses' is not limited to non-trading loan relationship deficits, but includes (amongst other things) property losses, management expenses, non-trading deficits on intangible assets and trading losses. If the company is a member of a group, the £5 million figure may be split and allocated between group members (CTA 2009, Part 7ZA inserted by September 2017 Finance Bill).

As an alternative to carry-forward relief, the company may make a claim to treat all or part of the non-trading deficit as follows:

(a)   set against the company's profits of the same period (CTA 2009, ss 459(1)(a), 463B(1)(a) inserted by September 2017 Finance Bill);

(b)   carried back for set-off against profits and gains of non-trading loan relationships in the previous 12 months (CTA 2009, ss 459(1)(b), 463B(1)(b));

(c)   surrendered as group relief in the deficit period (CTA 2010, ss 99(1) and 100).

Any claim to relieve the deficit against the current or previous year must be made within two years of the end of the accounting period in which the deficit arises (or the following period in the case of a carry-forward claim) (CTA 2009, ss 460, 463C inserted by September 2017 Finance Bill). Claims for group relief may be made at any time up to the first anniversary of the filing date of the return (FA 1998, Sch 18, para 74).

Computation

[10.3] The rules for computing debits and credits are the same for all loan relationships whether or not they are trading or non-trading relationships. The debits and credits are such sums which when taken together fairly represent for the accounting period in question:

(a)   all profits and losses of the company which arise to it from its loan relationships and related transactions (excluding interest or expenses);

(b)   all interests under those relationships; and

(c)   all expenses incurred by the company under or for the purposes of those relationships and transactions.

(CTA 2009, s 307(3).)

The computation includes exchange gains and losses arising from loan relationships (CTA 2009, s 328). Only amounts that are recognised in accordance with generally accepted accounting practice are to be brought into account (CTA 2009, ss 309 and 313).

The expenses referred to in (c) above are those incurred directly:

(1)   in bringing any of the loan relationships into existence;

(2)   in entering into or giving effect to any of the related transactions;

(3)   in making payments under any of those relationships or as a result of any of those transactions; or

(4)   in taking steps to ensure the receipt of payments under any of those relationships or in accordance with any of those transactions.

(CTA 2009, s 307(4).)

CTA 2009, Part 5, Chapter 8, deals with the position where there is late interest in relation to a loan relationship where there is a connection between the parties, namely: where the parties are connected (CTA 2009, s 374); where the creditor is a participator in a close company (CTA 2009, s 375); where one of the parties has a major interest in the other (CTA 2009, s 377); and where the loan is made by trustees of an occupational pension scheme (CTA 2009, s 378). In those circumstances if interest is paid more than 12 months after the end of the accounting period in which it accrues and the lender has not brought the corresponding credits representing the full element into account, then a debit is not available for the interest until it is paid (CTA 2009, s 373). With effect for debtor relationships entered into after 3 December 2014 the rules in CTA 2009, s 374 (parties are connected) and CTA 2009, s 377 (one of the parties has a major interest in the other) have been repealed by FA 2015, s 25.

Where the loan transaction is not at arm's length the debits and credits to be brought into account are to be determined on the basis that the transaction was entered into on the terms on which it would have been entered into between independent persons except for:

(a)   amounts which fall to be adjusted under TIOPA 2010, Part 4 or fall within that part without being adjusted (provision not at arm's length) (CTA 2009, s 447, though note the insertion of CTA 2009, s 447(4A) with effect from 1 April 2016 which means that after that date the application of s 447 is limited where the loan is matched. As a result, the amount of exchange gain or loss excluded by the section cannot exceed the exchange gain or loss arising on the unmatched element of the loan. This change was intended to ensure that s 447 does not exclude any exchange gain or loss arising on the matched element of the loan);

(b)   the rights under a loan relationship were acquired at less than market value (CTA 2009, s 444(4));

(c)   where the lender and borrower are members of the same group of companies for capital gains purposes under TCGA 1992, s 170 (CTA 2009, ss 335(2), 335(6) and 444(5)).

If a loan relationship is for an 'unallowable purpose' the debits attributable (on a just and reasonable apportionment) to the unallowable purpose are not to be brought into account. A loan relationship has an unallowable purpose if its purposes include a purpose which is not amongst the business or other commercial purposes of the company. Any activities in respect of which the company is not within the charge to corporation tax is not a business or commercial purpose of the company. An example given by HMRC is that of borrowing by a golf club to fund a new club house where because of mutual trading the income from members of the club is not taxable so that the loan interest would need to be apportioned to prevent a deduction for that part attributable to the mutual trading.

Restrictions on finance costs

[**10.4**] Prior to 1 April 2017, the debt cap rules operated to restrict the deduction of a company's finance costs where the company's, or (if the company is part of a group) the group's, UK net debt exceeded 75% of the group's worldwide gross debt. These rules applied if the company's net debt was at least £3 million.

From 1 April 2017, the debt cap rules are replaced by new rules whereby interest expenses are restricted to 30% of the company or group's earnings before interest, tax, depreciation and amortisation. These restrictions only apply where the group's net interest expense is at least £2 million (TIOPA 2010, Part 10, introduced by September 2017 Finance Bill). However, these restrictions do not apply to interest expenses incurred by a company engaged in property investment, provided that the following conditions are satisfied (TIOPA 2010, ss 432–439, inserted by September 2017 Finance Bill):

(a)   the properties involved must be let on short leases to tenants that are unrelated to the company. For these purposes, a short lease is one with an effective duration of 50 years or less under the rules relating to leases set out in CTA 2009, Part 4;

(b)   all, or all but an insignificant proportion of the company's income and assets must derive from the letting of property or ancillary activities;

(c)   the properties must be recognised as assets on the company's or group balance sheet;

(d)   the lender's recourse in relation to the loan must only be to the income, assets or shares of the company or of another company qualifying under the public infrastructure exemption. This means that guarantees by third parties are forbidden. However, guarantees provided before 1 April 2017 are disregarded, as are non-financial guarantees by related parties such as guarantees relating to the performance of services; and

(e)   the company is 'fully taxed' in the UK, whereby every activity carried on by the company is within the charge to corporation tax, and it has not made any claim for double taxation relief.

The company or group must make an election to ensure that the exemption applies. If an election is made, no restriction on interest deductions will apply where the creditor is unrelated. The election must be made before the start of the relevant accounting period, although elections for any period beginning before 1 March 2018 can be made retrospectively. An election can be made on a group basis.

Income tax

General

[10.5] For the purpose of computing the taxable profits of a property business for income tax purposes, interest payable is revenue expenditure, as opposed to capital, whatever the nature of the loan (ITTOIA 2005, ss 29, 272). Whether or not it is deductible in computing those profits depends on general principles, in particular the 'wholly and exclusively' rule, ie interest incurred wholly and exclusively for the purposes of a property business is an allowable deduction from the profits of that business.

Computing the profits of a property business

[10.6] The profits (or losses) of a property business are computed for income tax purposes in the same way as those of a trade. The specific trading income provisions of ITTOIA 2005 which apply to property business are, however, limited to those listed at ITTOIA 2005, s 272(2) (note that the list changed slightly with effect for trading transactions made on or after 16 March 2016 so that amounts within ITTOIA 2005, s 28A – bringing into account money's worth arising in the course of a trade – are included and items under ITTOIA 2005, s 68 – alteration and replacement of trade tools – are omitted: see FA 2016, ss 71, 72) and these include the fundamental rules that profits or losses be computed in accordance with generally accepted accounting practice (GAAP), that capital receipts and expenditure be excluded and that, subject to any specific rule to the contrary, expenditure is not deductible unless incurred wholly and exclusively for the purposes of the business. Interest payable is therefore allowable if it is brought into account as a debit in calculating the profits of a property business under generally accepted accounting practice and is incurred wholly and exclusively for the purposes of the business.

The basis period rules for trades do not apply to property businesses. Although property income is computed similarly to trading income, it retains its nature as investment income as opposed to earned income and does not count as relevant earnings for pension contribution purposes (subject to the rules for furnished holiday lettings).

In practice, a cash basis may be used instead of a full earnings basis (as required by GAAP) where gross annual receipts do not exceed £15,000, provided that it is used consistently and gives a reasonable overall result not substantially different from that produced on an earnings basis (see HMRC Property Income Manual PIM1101, the section entitled 'use of cash basis').

Profits or losses on contracts taken out to hedge interest payments deductible in computing profits or losses of the property business will normally be taxed or relieved as receipts or deductions of that business. Such profits or losses would generally be computed on an accruals basis in accordance with normal accountancy practice.

Where, exceptionally, a period of account of a property business does not coincide with a tax year, profits must be apportioned to tax years. This must normally be done by reference to the number of days in the periods concerned, but the taxpayer may choose any other method, eg months and part-months, if it is reasonable to do so and so long as the chosen method is applied consistently (ITTOIA 2005, s 275, Sch 2, para 62).

Residential property after 6 April 2017

[10.7] Finance Act 2015, made significant changes to the position on computation of profits in relation to let residential property from 6 April 2017. It added ss 272A and 272B to ITTOIA 2005, which effectively restrict the deduction of finance costs related to the let residential property. The rules apply to property businesses carried on by an individual or a partnership, but do not apply to companies unless the company acts in a fiduciary or representative capacity (ITTOIA 2005, s 272A(5)).

The new provisions restrict the deduction of costs when calculating the profits of each residential property on a sliding scale for the first three years after the introduction of the provisions so that in 2017/18 the deduction for finance costs will be restricted to 75%, in 2018/19 to 50%, for 2019/20 to 25% and thereafter to 0%.

The rules in ss 272A and 272B restrict the deduction for income tax purposes, and s 274A gives a reduction for the calculation of income tax liability for individuals (and individual partners in partnerships) by reference to the amount of finance costs that have been disallowed. The amount of relief will be calculated under s 274A(3) using the following formula: BR × L, where BR is the basic rate of income tax and L is the lower of:

(i)   the amount of costs of a 'dwelling-related loan' (defined earlier in s 272B(2)) that would have been deductible in calculating the profits of a property business for the tax year but for the new s 272A, plus any amount brought forward from previous years; and

(ii) the profits of the property business for the year after the deduction of any losses brought forward under ITA 2007, s 118, or the percentage of the adjusted profits of the property business on which the individual is liable to income tax if that is lower.

Section 274A, however, goes on to restrict the total relief across all of an individual's property businesses to the individual's total adjusted income for the year, if that is lower than the relief calculated under s 274A.

While ITTOIA 2005, ss 274A and 274B were only introduced by FA 2015, they have been completely replaced by FA 2016, s 26. The replacement sections are intended to clarify that the basic rate tax reduction is available to beneficiaries of deceased persons' estates and ensure that the basic rate tax reduction applies and is calculated as intended.

Similar rules apply to interest on a loan within ITA 2007, s 398 that has been used to invest in a partnership that has used the proceeds of the loan to generate income from a residential property business under ITA 2007, ss 399A and 399B.

Withholding tax and loan situs rules

General

[10.8] ITA 2007, s 874 sets out the basic duty to deduct tax from certain payments of interest. This provision became effective for income tax purposes for the tax year 2007/08 commencing on 6 April 2007 and for corporation tax purposes for accounting periods ending after 5 April 2007. For previous tax years and accounting periods the relevant provision was ICTA 1988, s 349.

Duty to deduct

[10.9] The duty to deduct tax applies if a payment of yearly interest arising in the UK is made:

(a)   by a company;
(b)   by a local authority;
(c)   by or on behalf of a partnership of which a company is a member; or
(d)   by any person to another person whose usual place of abode is outside the UK.

(ITA 2007, s 874(1).)

In practice, the main situation in which tax must be deducted is where interest is paid by a person (individual, company or trustee) to another person whose usual place of abode is outside the UK.

The person by or through whom the payment is made must, on making the payment, deduct from it a sum representing income tax at the basic rate in force for the tax year in which it is made (ITA 2007, s 874(2)). The basic rate is currently 20%.

The duty to deduct applies to yearly interest arising in the UK. Various exceptions from the duty to deduct are made by ITA 2007, s 874(3) and (4) and include interest paid by building societies, interest paid by a bank in the ordinary course of its business and interest paid by a company to another company beneficially entitled to the interest that is either resident in the UK or if not so resident, is carrying on a trade there through a permanent establishment and the payment is brought into account in calculating its chargeable profits. A further notable exception is that contained in ITTOIA 2005, ss 757–767 for the payment of interest by a company to an associated company in another EU member state and/or the terms of EU Interest and Royalties Directive 2003/49/EC.

Yearly interest

[**10.10**] The term 'yearly interest' is not defined in the ITA 2007 but the courts have frequently considered its meaning. Non-yearly or 'short' interest does not give rise to a duty to deduct and is interest arising in respect of obligations which are not intended to exist for a full year. In the context of property transactions, interest on delayed completion moneys will normally be 'short' interest although opinions differ on this point (see for example *Corinthian Securities v Cato* (1969) 46 TC 93, *Minsham Properties Ltd v Price (Inspector of Taxes)* [1990] STC 718 and *Macarthur (Inspector of Taxes) v Greycoat Estates Mayfair Ltd* [1996] STC 1). The distinction between yearly interest and short interest will not always be clear. Initially, the distinction will usually depend upon the intention of the parties as to the duration of the loan. However, if a loan facility intended to last for less than a year (giving rise to short interest) is extended to a year or more (even if rolled-over into another 'short' loan of less than a year), the interest arising may be re-characterised as yearly interest and a duty to deduct would arise.

In *IRC v Hay* (1924) 8 TC 636, Lord Anderson held that the authorities established the following propositions regarding yearly interest:

(a)   the loan must not be a short loan;
(b)   the loan must have a measure of permanence;
(c)   the loan must not be repayable on demand (but see *Corinthian Securities v Cato* above); and
(d)   the loan must have a tract of time.

UK Source

[**10.11**] The requirement that the interest must be 'interest arising in the United Kingdom' means that the interest must have a UK source. This is apparent from ITA 2007, s 884 which excludes 'relevant foreign income' from the duty to deduct in ITA 2007, s 874. 'Relevant foreign income' is defined as income arising from a source outside the UK by ITTOIA 2005, s 830(1) (by way of ITA 2007, s 989). The 'source' for this purpose normally means where the source of the obligation is situate. In law, an obligation is normally situate in the place where the primary obligation to pay is performed. In *Kwok Chi Leung Karl v Commissioner of Estate Duty* [1988] STC 728 a promissory note was issued by a company incorporated in Liberia but resident in Hong Kong and the note was payable at Monrovia. Because the primary obligation to pay was expressed to be performed in Monrovia, the debt was held to be situated there rather than Hong Kong. HMRC's basic approach to ascertaining the source of interest is set out in its Savings and Investment Manual SAIM9090 as follows:

'Whether or not interest has a UK source depends on all the facts and on exactly how the transactions are carried out. HMRC consider the most important of factor in deciding whether or not interest has a UK source to be

• the residence of the debtor and the location of his/her assets.

Other factors to take into account are

• the place of performance of the contract and the method of payment;
• the competent jurisdiction for legal action and the proper law of contract;
• the residence of the guarantor and the location of the security for the debt.

This list of factors is derived from the leading case on the source of interest, *Westminster Bank Executor and Trustee Co (Channel Islands) Ltd v National Bank of Greece SA* (1969) 46 TC 472.

HMRC consider the residence of the debtor to be most important because this, along with the location of the debtor's assets, will influence where the creditor will sue for payment of the interest and repayment of the loan. "Residence" in these circumstances is not the same as tax residence. Residence of the debtor is residence for the purposes of jurisdiction.'

There are additional requirements to consider for companies. These are set out in the Savings and Investments Manual, SAIM 9095. This says:

'Interest paid by companies

In deciding whether or not interest has a UK source, in addition to the factors described in SAIM9090, there are other matters to be taken into account for companies.

Companies and branches

Where the debtor is a company it may of course have more than one residence – for example it may be registered in a US state but managed and controlled from the UK. Jurisdiction in relation to a corporation will in general depend on where the corporation does business (except where the EU Regulation or the 1968 Convention apply – see SAIM9090). So for these purposes it will be resident where it carries on business. If a debtor company has a number of places of residence/business then to decide the location of the debt you have to look at the terms of the loan agreement. The loan agreement should say where the interest and loan are payable, which (if the company is also resident in that place) will determine whether or not the interest has a UK source.

When it comes to considering loans made to a branch of a UK company the source of the interest is overseas if all the following factors apply:

• an overseas branch of a UK resident company has entered into a loan agreement overseas;
• the loan is for the business of the overseas branch;
• the overseas branch pays the interest from its income;
• the loan agreement obligations are enforceable in the jurisdiction in which the branch is situated.

Conversely, where a branch of a non-UK resident company enters into a loan agreement in the UK for the business of its UK branch and the UK branch pays the interest then the interest is regarded as having a UK source.

Companies within the EU

Under both the EU Regulation and 1968 Convention, domicile is the main ground of jurisdiction and will, at first sight, determine the rules for the recoverability of debts. EU Regulation 44/2001 provides for a definition of domicile for corporations so that the company is domiciled where it has its statutory seat (in the UK its registered office), central administration or its principal place of business. However, it is important to note that a corporation is not domiciled in a country for these purposes merely because it does business there. If an EU based company carries on business in a country in which it is not domiciled you have to consider the terms of the loan agreement to determine the situation of the debt. For example, if a company which has its principal place of business in the UK also carries on business in another Member state, where the interest and loan are payable in that other Member state and that member state's courts have jurisdiction then the interest will be non-UK source.

For branches of EU companies the position is as described above for branches generally.'

'Usual place of abode'

[10.12] In relation to the payment of interest to a person 'whose usual place of abode is outside the United Kingdom', the concept of 'abode' is different from 'residence' for tax purposes. HMRC treat a person's abode as being as follows:

(a)   an individual's place of abode is outside the UK if he or she usually lives abroad, unless that arrangement is temporary;

(b)   a company whose main place of business is outside the UK will usually have its usual place of abode abroad unless it is resident in the UK. A non-UK resident company, that has a permanent establishment in the UK within the charge to corporation tax does not have a usual place of abode abroad; and

(c)   trustees, including personal representatives, have a usual place of abode abroad if each trustee, considered as an individual or a company as the case may be, has a usual place of abode there. If one trustee does not have his usual place of abode abroad, then the trust does not have its usual place of abode abroad (see HMRC's Savings and Investments Manual SAIM 9080).

For the purposes of (b) above, the payment of interest to a UK resident company whose business is abroad or to the UK permanent establishment of a non-UK resident company within the charge to corporation tax (and not exempted by the terms of a double taxation agreement) can normally be made without deduction of tax.

Thin capitalisation and transfer pricing

[10.13] Thin capitalisation is an aspect of transfer pricing and is a term used to describe a situation in which a borrower has borrowed money in excess of what it could normally borrow at arm's length leading to increased interest payments which are claimed as a deduction for corporation tax or income tax purposes. An associated issue is whether the rate of interest charged on the borrowing is an arm's length rate. UK taxable profits could relatively easily be artificially reduced by the use of excessive borrowing and/or interest rates. Accordingly, anti-avoidance provisions exist for both corporation tax and income tax to deny a tax deduction for interest payments that are regarded as excessive. These provisions need to be considered when structuring loans in relation to property acquisition and development. The provisions apply regardless of whether the interest is 'short' or yearly interest and to discounts where these are used in place of interest, ie the repayment of a higher principal than was originally borrowed. These provisions are contained in TIOPA 2010, Part 4 (considered below). There are also other provisions which may apply for example to treat excessive payments of interest by a company as a distribution for corporation tax purposes (and thus not deductible) under CTA 2010, s 1000), and interest paid in excess of a reasonable commercial rate for certain types of loan under ITA 2007, Part 8, Chapter 1.

TIOPA, Part 4

[10.14] TIOPA 2010, Part 4 is to be construed with the aim of securing consistency between the effect given to the basic rules and the principles of the OECD model tax convention and transfer pricing guidelines, as revised by the report, Aligning Transfer Pricing Outcomes with Value Creation, Actions 8–10 – 2015 Final Reports, published by the OECD on 5 October 2015 (TIOPA 2010, s 164). In the context of TIOPA, the transfer pricing guidelines means the version of the Transfer Pricing Guidelines for Multinational Enterprises and Tax Administrations approved by the Organisation for Economic Co-operation and Development (OECD) on 22 July 2010 or such other document approved and published by the OECD in place of that (or a later) version or in place of those Guidelines as is designated for the time being by order made by the Treasury, including, in either case, such material published by the OECD as part of (or by way of update or supplement to) the version or other document concerned as may be so designated (FA 2011, s 58).

In addition to the basic rules discussed below, FA 2016, s 66 and Sch 10 introduce complicated provisions to deal with the issue of 'hybrid mismatches'. They introduce new rules to counteract tax avoidance through hybrid and other mismatch arrangements which result in a deduction for various payments where there is no corresponding inclusion in ordinary income, or in double deductions from ordinary income. The new hybrid mismatch rules effectively replace the existing anti-arbitrage rules in Part 6 of TIOPA 2010. A discussion of the rules is beyond the scope of this title.

The basic rule

[**10.15**] TIOPA 2010, Part 4 applies where provision (the 'actual provision') has been made or imposed as between two persons (the 'affected persons') by means of a transaction or series of transactions, and at the time the provision was made or imposed ('Condition B') or at the time of the making or imposition of the actual provision or within the period of six months beginning with the day on which the actual provision was made ('Condition A') either:

(a)   one of the affected persons was directly or indirectly participating in the management, control or capital of the other; or

(b)   there was a person or persons who was or were directly or indirectly participating in the management, control or capital of each of the affected persons.

(TIOPA 2010, ss 147 and 148.)

If the actual provision differs from the provisions which would have been made at arm's length as between independent enterprises (or if no provision would have been so made) and confers a 'potential advantage' (see below) in relation to UK taxation on one of the affected persons or (whether or not the same advantage) on each of them, the profits and losses (and certain items treated as losses) of the potentially advantaged person, or of each of them, are computed for tax purposes as if the arm's length provision had been made or imposed (or, as the case may be, no provision made) instead of the actual provision (TIOPA 2010, s 147). FA 2011 makes significant changes to the provisions for group relief in CTA 2010 by inserting a new Part 21B. Where CTA 2010, Part 21B applies, the transfer pricing rules in TIOPA 2010, Part 4 will be of no effect (CTA 2010, s 938N). See also HMRC International Manual INTM503060. There are exceptions to the rule that the arm's length provisions will be used, and these are set out in TIOPA 2010, ss 147(7), 165, 166, 213 and 214.

'Transactions' etc

[**10.16**] A 'transaction' for these purposes includes arrangements, understandings and mutual practices (whether or not legally enforceable) (TIOPA 2010, s 150(1)), and a 'series' of transactions includes a number of transactions entered into (whether or not one after the other) in pursuance of, or in relation to, the same arrangement (TIOPA 2010, s 150(2)). A series of transactions is not prevented from being regarded as the means by which provision has been made or imposed between two persons by reason only that:

(a)   there is no transaction in the series to which both the persons are party;

(b)   that the parties to any arrangement in pursuance of which the transactions in the series are entered into do not include one or both of those persons; and

(c)   that there is one or more transactions in the series to which neither of those persons is a party.

(TIOPA 2010, ss 150(3) and (4).)

'Participation in management' etc

[10.17] The meaning of 'indirectly participating' is now exceedingly complex, and there are different sections dealing with each meaning. In addition to applying for the purposes of TIOPA 2010, s 148(2) and (3) (fulfilling Conditions A and B), each provision may also apply for other purposes of TIOPA (which are not relevant here).

A person is for these purposes treated as directly participating in the management, control or capital of another person at a particular time if and only if (but subject to the provisions below on persons acting together in relation to finance arrangements), at that time, the other person is a body corporate or partnership which that person controls (within CTA 2010, s 1124) (TIOPA 2010, s 157). Similarly indirect participation requires that the person (the 'potential participant') either would be taken to be participating directly if certain rights and powers (see TIOPA 2010, ss 159, 160(6) and 163), including future rights and powers, were attributed to him, or is one of a number of 'major participants' in the other person's enterprise.

The provisions are as follows:

(a)   indirect participation by a potential direct participant (TIOPA 2010, s 159);

(b)   indirect participation by one of several major participants (ie where the terms of the 40% test are met (TIOPA 2010, s 160));

(c)   indirect participation for the purposes of financing cases in relation to s 148(2)(a) and s 148(3)(a) (TIOPA 2010, s 161); and

(d)   indirect participation for the purposes of financing cases in relation to s 148(2)(b) and s 148(3)(b) (TIOPA 2010, s 162).

A potential direct participant ('P') is taken to be participating in the management, control or capital of another person ('A') at a particular time if P would be directly participating if any of the following rights were attributed to P (to the extent not already attributed to P under TIOPA 2010, s 157):

(i)   rights and powers P is entitled to acquire at a future date;

(ii)   rights and powers which P will become entitled to acquire at a future date;

(iii)   rights and powers of another if they may be exercised on behalf of P, under the direction of P or for the benefit of P;

(iv)   rights and powers of people with whom P is connected (within the meaning in TIOPA 2010, s 163); and

(v)   rights and powers which would be attributed by subsection (2) to a person with whom P is connected were it being decided under that subsection whether that connected person is indirectly participating in the management, control or capital of A.

A person is a 'major participant' in another person's enterprise when the other person is a body corporate or partnership, and he is one of two persons who control (as above) the other person, each of whom has at least 40% of the holdings, etc giving that control (again after attribution of certain rights and powers as above) (TIOPA 2010, s 160(3)).

A person ('A') is a 'major participant' in another person's enterprise when the other person is a body corporate or firm, and the 40% test is met in the case of two people who taken together control the body corporate or firm and A is one of them (TIOPA 2010, s 160(4)). In relation to the 40% test the rights to be taken into account when determining control include all those set out in TIOPA 2010, s 159(2) (TIOPA 2010, s 160(5)).

Persons acting together in relation to financing arrangements

[10.18] In relation to financing cases there are two different sets of circumstances (one set which apply for the purposes of limb (a) of Condition A and B, and one set which apply for limb (b)). Financing arrangements are arrangements made for providing or guaranteeing, or otherwise in connection with, any debt, capital or other form of finance.

For the purposes of TIOPA 2010, s 161 (limb (a) of Conditions A and B at **10.15** above), a person (P) is treated as indirectly participating in the management etc of another (A) at the time of making or imposition of the actual provision if:

(a)   the actual provision relates, to any extent, to financing arrangements for A;

(b)   A is a body corporate or firm;

(c)   P and other persons acted together in relation to the financing arrangements; and

(d)   P would be taken to have control of A if, at any 'relevant time', there were attributed to P the rights and powers of the persons mentioned in (c) above (see **10.17** above). The rights and powers of any person (and not just P) are to be taken to include those that would be attributed to that person by s 159(2) were it being decided under s 159(2) whether that person is indirectly participating in the management, control or capital of A (TIOPA 2010, s 161(5)).

'Relevant time' means a time when P and the other persons were acting together in relation to the financing arrangements, or a time in the period of six months beginning with the day on which they ceased so to act (TIOPA 2010, s 161(4)). On this basis, transfer pricing adjustments may be triggered by events occurring up to six months before the necessary relationship exists between the parties.

It is immaterial whether the persons acting together did so at the time the actual provision is made or imposed or did so at some earlier time (TIOPA 2010, s 161(3)).

'Financing arrangements' are defined in TIOPA 2010, s 161(6) as arrangements made for providing or guaranteeing, or otherwise in connection with, any debt, capital or other form of finance.

TIOPA 2010, s 162 sets out further cases where the transfer pricing rules will apply. A person ('Q') is also treated as indirectly participating in the management, control or capital of affected persons (as defined in TIOPA 2010, s 147(1), see **10.15** above) if:

(i)   the actual provision (as defined in TIOPA 2010, s 147(1), see **10.15** above) relates, to any extent, to financing arrangements for one of the affected persons ('B');

(ii)   B is a body corporate or firm;

(iii)   Q and other persons acted together in relation to the financing arrangements; and

(iv)   Q would be taken to have control of both B and the other affected person if, at any relevant time, there were attributed to Q the rights and powers of each of the other persons mentioned in paragraph (c).

'Financing arrangements' and 'relevant time' have the same meaning as in TIOPA 2010, s 161. It is also immaterial whether Q and the other persons acting together in relation to the financing arrangements did so at the time of the making or imposition of the actual provision or at some earlier time (TIOPA 2010, s 162(3)) and the rights and powers of any person (and not just Q) are to be taken to include those that would be attributed to that person by s 159(2) were it being decided under s 159(2) whether that person is indirectly participating in the management, control or capital of A.

For more details on the financing arrangements rules, see the HMRC website (at www.gov.uk/guidance/transfer-pricing-transactions-between-connected-co mpanies) (TIOPA 2010, Part 4).

Thin capitalisation

[10.19] Previously excessive payments of interest by thinly capitalised companies were treated as distributions. Post-FA 2004, interest attributable to the excessive part of debt finance between connected companies is disallowed under the transfer pricing legislation. The main features of the old regime otherwise remain (see below) and the general transfer pricing provisions apply. In particular, the provisions for compensating adjustments apply, including for guarantors of third party loans, and exemption from deduction at source under ITA 2007, s 874 can be claimed. There are separate provisions relating to securitisation financing arrangements in TIOPA 2010, ss 199–203.

Provision in relation to securities

[10.20] The transfer pricing rules apply to a provision which differs from an arm's length provision where both of the affected parties are companies and one issues a security to the other in circumstances where there is a special relationship (there is a special relationship where the participation condition in TIOPA 2010, s 148 is met). In considering whether the 'actual provision' is at arm's length, account is to be taken of all factors including whether, in the absence of a 'special relationship' (and whether or not it is the business of the lending company to make loans generally):

(a)   the loan would have been provided at all in the absence of that relationship;

(b)   the amount would have been advanced; and

(c)   the rate of interest or other terms of the loan would have been agreed.

(TIOPA 2010, ss 152(2) and (3).)

A 'security' includes securities not creating or evidencing a charge on assets (TIOPA 2010, s 154(6)). A 'special relationship' in this case means any relationship where the issuing company and lending company are connected under the circumstances set out at **10.15** and **10.18** above.

In considering whether the provision is made at arm's length, no account is to be taken of (or of any inference capable of being drawn from) any 'guarantee' provided by a company with which the issuing company has a 'participatory relationship', when determining:

(i) the appropriate level or extent of the issuing company's overall indebtedness;

(ii) whether it would be expected that the issuing company and a particular person would have become parties to a transaction involving the issuing of securities by the issuing company or the making of a loan, or a loan of a particular amount to the issuing company; and

(iii) the rate of interest and other terms expected in such a transaction.

(TIOPA 2010, s 152(6).)

A company ('A') has a 'participatory relationship' with another ('B') in this case where one of them is directly or indirectly participating in the management, control or capital of the other, or the same person or persons is or are directly or indirectly participating in the management, control or capital of each of them (TIOPA 2010, s 154(5)).

A reference to a 'guarantee' in this context includes a reference to any surety and a reference to any other relationship, arrangements, connection or understanding (whether formal or informal), such that the person making the loan to the issuing company has a reasonable expectation that the in the event of a default, the person will be paid by, or out of the assets of one or more companies (TIOPA 2010, s 154(4)).

Clarification is provided by HMRC of their view on the thin capitalisation rules in HMRC International Manual at INTM570000 ff. Under the heading of 'guarantee' at paragraph INTM539000, it is explained that actual assets or liabilities such as shares in subsidiaries and intra group loans are not to be disregarded when assessing the borrowing capacity of a company but that they should be taken into account to the same extent that they would be by any unconnected lender. This effectively means that all assets and liabilities in direct or indirect subsidiaries should be taken into account. It goes on to explain that the repeal of the UK grouping rule in calculating an individual company's debt capacity does not in practice affect the UK sub-group as a whole because of the provisions for loan guarantees and in particular the compensating adjustment for guarantors.

Guarantees etc

[10.21] Similar provisions apply under TIOPA 2010, s 153 where the actual provision is made or imposed by means of a series of transactions which include the issue of a 'security' by one of the affected persons and the provision of a 'guarantee' by the other affected person (whether or not the issuing company and lending company are so connected) (TIOPA 2010, s 153(1)). The effect of the provisions is that the interest attributable to the excessive part of such a loan is disallowed as if the loan was received from the connected party.

In considering whether the provision is at arm's length, account is to be taken of all factors including whether, in the absence of a 'special relationship' (and whether or not it is the business of the guarantor to make guarantees generally – TIOPA 2010, s 153(4)):

(i)   the guarantee would have been provided at all;
(ii)   the particular amount would have been guaranteed; and
(iii)   the consideration for the guarantee or other terms would have been agreed.

No account is to be taken of any guarantee (or inference drawn from a guarantee) provided by a company with which the issuing company has a 'participatory relationship', when determining any of (i) to (iii) above (TIOPA 2010, s 153(2) and (6)).

Potential advantage

[10.22] The actual provision confers a 'potential advantage' on a person in relation to UK taxation where the effect of making or imposing the actual provision, instead of the arm's length provision, would be one or both of 'Effect A' and 'Effect B'. Effect A is that a smaller amount (which may be nil) would be taken for tax purposes to be the amount of the person's profits for any chargeable period. Effect B is that a larger amount (or, if there would not otherwise have been losses, any amount of more than nil) would be taken for tax purposes to be the amount for any chargeable period of any losses of the person (TIOPA 2010, s 155).

In determining the chargeable profits or allowable losses for this purpose there is to be left out of account any income of that person which is disregarded income within the meaning given by ITA 2007 s 813 (limits on liability to income tax of non-UK residents) or disregarded company income within the meaning given by ITA 2007, s 816. In addition, TIOPA 2010, Part 7 and provisions relating to excessive interest being treated as a distribution (found in CTA 2010, s 1000) are to be disregarded when making the calculation for the purposes of determining if Effect A and/or Effect B have occurred (TIOPA 2010, s 155(5) and (6)).

For accounting periods that commenced *on or after 1 April 2004* the transfer pricing provisions apply to transactions between UK-resident taxpayers as they do to cross-border transactions (FA 2004, ss 30(2), 37).

Exemption for dormant companies

[10.23] The transfer pricing provisions do not apply, when calculating the profits or losses for any chargeable period, to companies which are dormant through the 'pre-qualifying period' and apart from s 147, the company has continued to be dormant at all times since the end of the pre-qualifying period. The pre-qualifying period is:

(a)   if there is an accounting period of the company that ends on 31 March 2004, that accounting period; and
(b)   if there is no such accounting period, the period of three months ending with that date.

For these purposes, 'dormant' has the same meaning as in Companies Act 2006, s 1169 (TIOPA 2010, s 165).

Exemption for small and medium-sized enterprises

[10.24] The transfer pricing provisions do not apply, when calculating the profits or losses for any chargeable period, to a company which is a small or medium-sized enterprise (TIOPA 2010, s 167). Such companies are as defined in the Annex to the Commission Recommendation 2003/361/EC of 6 May 2003 with the modifications set out in TIOPA 2010, s 172(4) to (7). Broadly, a small enterprise is defined as a business with less than 50 employees and either turnover or assets of less than €10m and a small or medium-sized enterprise as a business with less than 250 employees and either turnover of less than €50m or assets of less than €43m. Associated enterprises are taken into account in determining whether a company is a small or medium-sized enterprise (see particularly, Articles 2 and 3 of the Annex to the Commission Recommendation).

Exceptions

[10.25] The exemption will not apply to small or medium sized enterprises where they are within the TIOPA 2010, s 167 exemptions:

(a)   the enterprise elects for the exemption not to apply, such election being irrevocable (TIOPA 2010, s 167(2)); or

(b)   at the time the actual provision was made or imposed, the other affected person or a 'party to a relevant transaction' is resident and liable to tax in a 'non-qualifying territory' (whether or not also resident in a 'qualifying territory') (TIOPA 2010, s 167(3)).

In addition, it will not apply to any provision made or imposed by a medium-sized enterprise if HMRC give that person a notice requiring the person to calculate the profits and losses of that chargeable period in accordance with s 147(3) or (5) in the case of that provision (TIOPA 2010, s 168).

As regards (b) above, where the actual provision is or was imposed by means of a series of transactions, a 'party to a relevant transaction' is defined by TIOPA 2010, s 167(4) as a person who, if the actual provision is or was imposed by means of a series of transactions, is or was a party to one or more of those transactions.

A 'non-qualifying territory' is a territory which is not a qualifying territory. A 'qualifying territory' is the UK or any territory in relation to which 'Condition A' or 'Condition B' is met (TIOPA 2010, s 173(1)). Condition A is that:

(i)   double taxation arrangements have been made in relation to the territory;

(ii)   the arrangements include a non-discrimination provision; and

(iii)   the territory is not designated as a non-qualifying territory for the purposes of this subsection in regulations made by the Treasury.

(TIOPA 2010, s 173(2)).

Non-discrimination provision is explained at TIOPA 2010, s 173(4) as being a provision to the effect that nationals of a state which is a party to those arrangements (a 'contracting state') are not to be subject in any other contracting state to any taxation or any requirement connected with taxation which is other or more burdensome than the taxation and connected requirements to which nationals of that other state in the same circumstances (in particular with respect to residence) are or may be subjected (TIOPA 2010, s 173(4)).

Transfer pricing notices issued to small and medium-sized companies

[10.26] Where a transfer pricing notice (which may only be given following a notice of enquiry) is issued to a medium-sized enterprise in accordance with TIOPA 2010, s 168, it may be given in relation to any provision specified, or of a description specified, in the notice or every provision in relation to which one or other of the assumptions in s 147(3) and (5) would, apart from s 166(1), be required to be made when calculating the person's profits and losses for tax purposes (TIOPA 2010, s 169).

The recipient of a notice may appeal in writing to the officer of HMRC identified for the purpose in the transfer notice (TIOPA 2010, s 169(4)), within 30 days from the date the notice is given but only on the grounds that the company is a small rather than a medium-sized enterprise (TIOPA, s 170(1)).

The company receiving the notice may amend the company tax return to which the notice related at any time within 90 days of the date the notice was given, or if an appeal is made, the day on which the appeal is finally determined or abandoned. HMRC may issue a closure notice once the 90 days have elapsed, or if earlier, once the tax return has been amended for the purpose of complying with the notice (TIOPA 2010, s 171).

Where a medium-sized company is not excepted from exemption, there is no need for the company's tax return to take account of the transfer pricing rules. However, this does not prevent the company's tax return from becoming incorrect if a transfer pricing notice is issued and the return is not amended within the period of 90 days as noted above.

In relation to small-sized companies s 167A provides for transfer pricing notices to be issued. A notice may be given where provision has been made or imposed as between the person and any other person by means of a transaction or series of transactions, the basic pre-condition in s 147 is met in respect of the provision, and the transaction, or one or more of the series of transactions, is taken into account in calculating, for the purposes of Part 8A of CTA 2010 (profits arising from the exploitation of patents etc), the relevant IP profits of a trade or a person who is or was a party to the transaction or transactions.

Appeal against a transfer pricing notice issued under s 167A is made under TIOPA 2010, s 170.

Elimination of double counting

[10.27] Where a potential advantage is conferred on only one of the affected persons (the 'advantaged person'), and the other person (the 'disadvantaged person') is within the charge to corporation tax (or income tax) in respect of profits arising from the relevant activities then (except as below) the disadvantaged person may claim application of the arm's length provision rather than the actual provision (overriding any applicable time limits for the necessary adjustments) (TIOPA 2010, s 174). Such a claim may only be made if the arm's length provision has similarly been applied in the case of the advantaged person (in his return or following a determination) and the computations in the case of each of them on that basis must be consistent (TIOPA 2010, s 176).

A TIOPA, s 174 claim may not be made if:

(a)   the participation condition (see s 148) would not be satisfied but for ss 161 or 162 (see **10.20** above);

(b)   the actual provision is provision in relation to a security issued by one of the affected persons ('the issuer'); and

(c)   a guarantee is provided in relation to the security by a person with whom the issuer has a participatory relationship.

The definition of 'participatory relationship' for these purposes is set out in TIOPA 2010, s 175(2). 'A' has a participatory relationship with 'B' where one of A and B is directly or indirectly participating in the management, control or capital of the other, or the same person or persons is or are directly or indirectly participating in the management, control or capital of each of A and B (TIOPA 2010, s 175).

Section 174 is now also subject to TIOPA 2010, s 174A. This was introduced by FA 2014, s 75 and prevents the disadvantaged person making a claim in certain circumstances where they are within the charge to income tax. The circumstances in which s 175A applies are the following:

(i)   the disadvantaged person is a person (other than a company) within the charge to income tax in respect of profits arising from the relevant activities; and

(ii)   the advantaged person is a company.

Claims: time limits

[10.28] The claim must be made within two years of the making of the return or the giving of the notice taking account of the determination, as the case may be, and a claim based on a return which is subsequently the subject of such a notice may be amended within two years of the giving of the notice (TIOPA 2010, s 177(1)–(3)). (These time limits may be extended in certain cases where HMRC fails to give proper notice to disadvantaged persons under TIOPA 2010, s 186(3)).

Thin capitalisation

[10.29] Where the thin capitalisation provisions above apply, a compensating adjustment may be claimed (and the claim may be amended) by the disadvantaged person or by the advantaged person on behalf of the disadvantaged person under TIOPA 2010, s 182. Such a claim (a 's 182 claim') may be made before or after the arm's length provision has been applied (in the return or following a determination, but is taken to be made on behalf of the disadvantaged person where made by the advantaged person) but the claim must be consistent with that computation. If the claim is not consistent with the computation, it is treated as if it were amended to make it consistent, allowing for any required adjustments to be made. In making a s 182 claim before the transfer pricing provision is applied, the lending company is not treated as chargeable on so much of the interest subject to the transfer pricing adjustment (see **10.31**) and thus, the condition for deducting tax at source is not met. The borrowing company may thus pay interest to a non-resident lender without deduction of tax at source.) Claims must be made or amended before the expiry of the time limits noted at **10.28** above and the provisions of TMA 1970, Sch 1A (claims made outside a return) apply for this purpose (TIOPA 2010, ss 180–184 and FA 1998, Sch 18, para 59).

Thin capitalisation: guarantees

[10.30] Under certain circumstances things done by the issuing company will be attributed to the guarantor company under TIOPA 2010, ss 192–194. These rules will apply where:

(a)   one of the affected persons ('the issuing company') is a company that has liabilities under a security issued by it;

(b)   those liabilities are to any extent the subject of a guarantee provided by a company ('the guarantor company');

(c)   in calculating the profits and losses of the issuing company for tax purposes, the amounts to be deducted in respect of interest or other amounts payable under the security are required to be reduced (whether or not to nil) under s 147(3) or (5).

The amounts to be deducted are reduced by virtue of TIOPA 2010, s 153.

TIOPA 2010, ss 192–194 provide for a transfer pricing adjustment to disallow interest follows from the provisions of a guarantee, the guarantor company can claim a compensation adjustment as if it was the borrower (the 'issuing company') and had paid the interest subject to the disallowance under these rules.

Amounts are brought into account in computing the guarantor company's profits and losses accordingly. Where there is more than one guarantor, the total amount claimed by way of a compensating adjustment must not exceed the amount of interest disallowed. A claim can also be made by the issuing company on behalf of the guarantor company or companies. Where a claim is made by a guarantor and the lending company subsequently makes a claim for a compensating adjustment in respect of the same loan, the claim made by the lending company must be reduced to the extent of the claim made by the guarantor company. A claim made by the guarantor company will not be allowed where the lending company has earlier made a compensating adjustment claim for the full amount of the interest disallowed. The provisions above relating to claims and time limits apply equally to claims made by a guarantor company or by the issuing company on behalf of the guarantor company (TIOPA 2010, ss 192–194).

The tax treatment where actual interest exceeds arm's length interest

[10.31] Where Conditions A–D in TIOPA 2010, s 187 are met, then the interest (to the extent which it exceeds the arm's length interest) paid under the actual provision is subject to certain special treatments. Condition A is that interest is paid by any person under the actual provision. Condition B is that the profits and losses are to be calculated as if the arm's length provision had applied (under TIOPA 2010, s 147(3) or (5)). Condition C is that the amount ('ALINT') of interest that would have been payable under the arm's length provision is less than the amount of interest paid under the actual provision, or that there would not have been any interest payable under the arm's length provision (so that ALINT is nil). Condition D is that the person receiving the interest paid under the actual provision makes a claim (either under TIOPA 2010, s 174 or s 182) (TIOPA 2010, s 187(2)–(5)).

The effect of this is that the interest paid under the actual provision (to the extent which it exceeds ALINT):

(a)   is not to be regarded as chargeable under ITTOIA 2005, Part 4, Chapter 2 (interest on savings and investment income);

(b)   is not subject to the provisions of ITA 2007, Part 15 (deduction of income tax at source); and

(c)   is not required to be brought into account under CTA 2009, Part 5 (loan relationships) as a non-trading credit.

(TIOPA 2010, s 187).

Finance Act 2014 introduced provisions to prevent s 187 treatment of interest in circumstances where TIOPA 2010, s 174 is prevented from applying by s 174A. TIOPA 2010, s 187A applies where Conditions A to C in s 187 are met in circumstances where s 174A prevents a claim under s 174. Where these circumstances are present, interest paid under the actual provision, so far as it exceeds ALINT is treated as a qualifying distribution for income tax purposes.

Foreign taxation

[10.32] Where a claim for a compensating adjustment is made, Assumptions A and B are made, as respects any foreign tax credit which has been or may be given to the disadvantaged person. Assumption A is that the foreign tax paid or payable by the disadvantaged person does not include any amount of foreign tax which would not be or have become payable were it to be assumed for the purposes of that tax that the arm's length provision had been made or imposed instead of the actual provision. Assumption B is that the amount of the disadvantaged person's relevant profits in respect of which the disadvantaged person is given credit for foreign tax does not include the amount (if any) by which the disadvantaged person's relevant profits are treated as reduced in accordance with s 174(1) (TIOPA 2010, s 188).

Where the application of the arm's length provision in a computation following such a claim involved a reduction in the amount of any income, and that income also falls to be treated as reduced under TIOPA 2010, s 112 by an amount of foreign tax (where credit relief is not available), the former reduction is treated as made before the latter, and the deductible foreign tax excludes that paid on so much of the income as is represented by the amount of the former reduction (TIOPA 2010, s 189).

Any adjustment to double tax relief as above may be made by setting the amount of the adjustment against any relief or repayment to which the disadvantaged person is entitled in pursuance of his claim under s 174 and nothing in the Tax Acts limiting the time within which any assessment is to be or may be made or amended prevents that adjustment from being so made (TIOPA 2010, s 189(3)).

Balancing payments

[10.33] Where certain qualifying conditions are met, there is provision for balancing payments to be made between the advantaged and disadvantaged person (TIOPA 2010, s 196). The qualifying conditions are:

(a)   Condition A is that only one of the affected persons ('the advantaged person') is a person on whom a potential advantage in relation to United Kingdom taxation is conferred by the actual provision;

(b)   Condition B is that the other affected person ('the disadvantaged person') is within the charge to income tax or corporation tax in respect of profits arising from the relevant activities;

(c)   Condition C is that one or more balancing payments are made to the advantaged person by the disadvantaged person; and

(d)   Condition D is that the sole or main reason for making that payment or those payments is that (by virtue of s 147(3) or (5)) the profits and losses of the advantaged person are to be calculated as if the arm's length provision, rather than the actual provision, applied.

(TIOPA 2010, s 195).

Where each of those conditions is met, and to the extent that such balancing payments do not in aggregate exceed the amount of the available compensating adjustment, the balancing payment is not to be taken into account in calculating profits or losses of either of the affected persons for the purposes of income tax or corporation tax and is not to be treated as a distribution for the purposes of corporation tax. The 'available compensating adjustment' is the difference between the profits and losses of the disadvantaged company computed on the basis of the actual provision and computed for the purposes of making the compensating adjustment above (taking profits as positive amounts and losses as negative amounts) (TIOPA 2010, s 196).

Balancing payments made by guarantors: thin capitalisation

[10.34] There are similar rules where there is a guarantor company (TIOPA 2010, ss 197–198). The conditions for these rules to apply are:

(a)   Condition A is that one of the affected persons ('the issuing company') is a company that has liabilities under a security issued by it;

(b)   Condition B is that those liabilities are to any extent the subject of a guarantee provided by a company ('the guarantor company');

(c)   Condition C is that, in calculating the profits and losses of the issuing company for tax purposes, the amounts to be deducted in respect of interest or other amounts payable under the security are required to be reduced (whether or not to nil) under s 147(3) or (5);

(d)   Condition D is that that reduction is required because of s 153;

(e)   Condition E is that one or more balancing payments are made by the guarantor company to the issuing company; and

(f)   Condition F is that TIOPA 2010, s 147(3) or 147(5) applies because of TIOPA 2010, s 153 or TIOPA 2010, ss 192–194 apply (see **10.30** above).

The consequence of these conditions being fulfilled is that, to the extent that the total amount of those payments does not exceed the total amount of the reductions within s 197(4) (the amounts to be deducted in respect of interest or other amounts payable under the security), the payments shall not be taken into account for corporation tax purposes when computing profits or losses of the guarantor company (or companies) or of the issuing company, or be regarded as distributions (TIOPA 2010, s 198).

Election to pay tax instead of balancing payment: thin capitalisation

[10.35] Special provisions apply where the actual provision subject to a claim for a 'compensating adjustment' above, is a provision in relation to a security (the 'relevant security') (see **10.29** and **10.30**). In that case, instead of making a balancing payment as above, the disadvantaged company may elect to assume responsibility for the additional tax liability in relation to any accounting period of the advantaged company where the additional liability results from the transfer pricing adjustment in relation to the relevant security (ie a disallowance of interest or other amounts). The tax liability in this case would not be treated as a liability of and recoverable from the advantaged company but would be treated as a corporation tax liability of the disadvantaged company. The disadvantaged company may only make such an election where the following conditions are met:

(a)   both of the affected persons are companies;

(b)   that only one of the affected persons ('the advantaged person') is a person on whom a potential advantage in relation to United Kingdom taxation is conferred by the actual provision;

(c)   the other affected person ('the disadvantaged person') is within the charge to income tax or corporation tax in respect of profits arising from the relevant activities;

(d)   the actual provision is provision in relation to a security; and

(e)   the 'capital market condition' is met.

(TIOPA 2010, s 199).

The capital market condition is that the actual provision forms part of a capital market arrangement (as defined in Insolvency Act 1986, s 72B(1)). The capital market arrangement involves the issue of a capital market investment (as defined in Insolvency Act 1986, s 72B(1), Sch 2A, paras 1–3). The securities that represent the capital market investment are issued wholly or mainly to independent persons and the total value of the capital market investments made under the capital market arrangement is at least £50 million (TIOPA 2010, s 204).

The election, which is irrevocable, must be made in the disadvantaged company's tax return (whether by amendment or otherwise) for the chargeable period in which the relevant security is issued and has effect for that period and all subsequent chargeable periods (ie the lifetime of the loan). For this purpose, securities issued in a chargeable period beginning before 1 April 2004 are treated as though issued in a chargeable period beginning on that date (TIOPA 2010, s 203). HMRC may refuse to accept such an election but only after a notice of enquiry has been issued to the disadvantaged company in respect of the tax return containing the election (TIOPA 2010, s 203).

The above provisions relating to an election to pay tax instead of a balancing payment apply equally, with necessary modifications, in cases where a transfer pricing is made in respect of third party loans subject to a guarantee provided by a connected company (see above). The modified provisions are found at TIOPA 2010, ss 201 and 202. Those sections will apply where:

- only one of the affected persons ('the advantaged person') is a person on whom a potential advantage in relation to United Kingdom taxation is conferred by the actual provision;
- that the other affected person ('the disadvantaged person') is within the charge to income tax or corporation tax in respect of profits arising from the relevant activities (see s 216);
- that the actual provision is made or imposed by means of a series of transactions which include: (a) the issuing of a security ('the relevant security') by one of the affected persons ('the issuing company'), and (b) the provision of a guarantee by the other affected person; and
- the capital market condition is met (see s 204). The capital market condition is found in TIOPA 2010, s 204.

For the purposes of s 199(6) or s 201(6), the capital market condition is met if—

(a) the actual provision forms part of a capital market arrangement,
(b) the capital market arrangement involves the issue of a capital market investment,
(c) the securities that represent the capital market investment are issued wholly or mainly to independent persons, and
(d) the total value of the capital market investments made under the capital market arrangement is at least £50 million.

Pre-transaction guidance

[10.36] Revenue Policy International, 100 Parliament Street, London SW1A 2BQ may be approached for pre-transaction guidance on the likely tax treatment in particular cases when financial arrangements are in the process of being put in place.

Advance pricing agreements

[10.37] A taxpayer ('A') may apply to HMRC for an agreement, on a prospective basis, on the resolution of complex transfer pricing issues relating to any one or more of the following matters which fall, or might fall, to be determined:

(a)   If A is not a company, the attribution of income to a branch or agency through which A has been carrying on a trade in the United Kingdom or is proposing to carry on a trade in the United Kingdom.

(b)   If A is a company, the attribution of income to a permanent establishment through which A has been carrying on a trade in the United Kingdom or is proposing to carry on a trade in the United Kingdom.

(c)   The attribution of income to any permanent establishment of A (wherever situated) through which he has been carrying on, or is proposing to carry on, any business.

(d)   The extent to which income which has arisen or which may arise to A is to be taken for any purpose to be income arising outside the UK.

(e)   The treatment for tax purposes of any provision operating between A and any 'associate' of his.

(f)   The treatment for tax purposes of a provision made or imposed between a 'ring fence trade' carried on by A and any other activities so carried on.

(TIOPA 2010, s 218(2)).

Persons are 'associates' for this purpose if (as above in relation to TIOPA, Part 4) one directly or indirectly participates, at the time of the making or imposition of the provision, in the management, control or capital of the other, or the same person or persons so participate in the management, control or capital of each of them (TIOPA 2010, s 219).

The application must set out

(i)   that it is an application to the Commissioners;

(ii)   that it is an application for the clarification by agreement of the effect in A's case of provisions by reference to which questions relating to any one or more of the matters mentioned in s 218(2) are to be, or might be, determined;

(iii) A's understanding of what would in A's case be the effect, in the absence of any agreement, of the provisions in relation to which clarification is sought,

(iv)   the respects in which it appears to A that clarification is required in relation to those provisions; and

(v)   how A proposes that matters should be clarified in a manner consistent with that understanding.

(TIOPA 2010, s 223).

Where HMRC and the taxpayer have entered into such an agreement (an 'advance pricing agreement' or 'APA') in relation to a chargeable period, then (except as below) any questions relating to those matters are, to the extent provided for in the APA, to be determined in accordance with the APA rather than by reference to the legislative provisions which would otherwise have applied (TIOPA 2010, s 220). However, where the relevant matter falls within (d) or (e) above and not within (a), (b) or (c) above, the only legislative provisions which can be displaced are those contained in TIOPA 2010, Part 4 (TIOPA 2010, s 220(5)). Where an APA relating to a chargeable period beginning or ending before the date of the APA provides for the manner in which consequent adjustments are to be made, those adjustments are to be made in the manner provided for by the APA (TIOPA 2010, s 206).

An APA does not, however, have effect in relation to the determination of any question which relates to:

(i)   a time after that from which an officer of HMRC has revoked the APA in accordance with its terms; or

(ii)   a time after or in relation to which any provision of the APA has not been complied with, where the APA was conditional upon compliance with that provision; or

(iii) any matter as respects which any other essential conditions have not been, or are no longer, satisfied.

(TIOPA 2010, s 221).

It is for HMRC to ensure that the APA is modified so as to be consistent with any double taxation arrangements (TIOPA 2010, s 229).

Where the APA makes provision for its modification or revocation by HMRC, this may take effect from such time (including a time before the modification or revocation) as HMRC may determine (TIOPA 2010, s 225(2)).

Any party to an APA must provide HMRC with all such reports and other information as he may be required to provide under the APA or by virtue of any request made by an officer of HMRC in accordance with its terms (TIOPA 2010, s 228).

An APA is deemed never to have been made where, before it was made, the taxpayer fraudulently or negligently provided HMRC with false or misleading information in relation to the application for the APA or in connection with its preparation, and HMRC notifies the taxpayer that the APA is nullified by reason of the misrepresentation. A penalty not exceeding £10,000 may apply for so giving such false or misleading information (TIOPA 2010, ss 226 and 227).

Where an APA has effect in relation to any provision between the taxpayer and another person, then in applying the 'double counting' rules (see **10.27**) of TIOPA 2010, Part 4 to the other person, the arrangements set out in the APA similarly applying in determining any question as to:

(A)   whether the taxpayer is a person on whom a potential advantage in relation to UK taxation is conferred by the actual provision; or

(B)   what constitutes the arm's length provision in relation to the actual provision.

This is subject to any APA made between HMRC and the other person. The notice requirements of TIOPA 2010, s 185 are correspondingly amended (TIOPA 2010, s 222).

Example

On 1 July 2014, B Ltd is granted a loan of £5m at 6% interest per annum from an unassociated bank. The loan is guaranteed by B Ltd's parent company, G plc. Both companies draw up accounts for the year ended 30 June and neither company qualifies as a small or medium-sized enterprise for transfer pricing purposes. Following an enquiry into B Ltd's return for the accounting period ending 30 June 2015, HMRC successfully maintain that, in the absence of the guarantee from G plc, the bank would not have advanced more than £1m to B Ltd. Accordingly, an adjustment is made to increase B Ltd's profits for the period by £240,000 in disallowing the interest on £4m of the loan.

G plc could make a claim (or B Ltd could claim on its behalf) of a corresponding adjustment before or after the transfer pricing adjustment is made in B Ltd's return, or following the determination (but within the required time limit), so that it is treated as having paid the interest subject to the disallowance. Accordingly, provided the interest in G plc's case would not be subject to a transfer pricing adjustment, G plc could claim a deduction for £240,000 in respect of the interest paid by B Ltd.

G plc can make a balancing payment of up to £240,000 to B Ltd without it being treated as a distribution or charge on income or otherwise taken into account for tax purposes. Alternatively, where the conditions (a) and (b) in **10.35** above are met, G plc can elect to pay the tax liability in respect of the interest disallowed, of £72,000 (at 30%). In that case, B Ltd would not have to pay the tax liability arising in respect of the transfer pricing adjustment.

Chapter 11

Agricultural land

by
Julian Palmer

Introduction

[11.1] The availability or otherwise of the special tax treatment relating to agricultural land is dependent upon whether the occupant of the land is farming. Diversification from farming risks losing valuable concessions and it is necessary for the practitioner to have a clear understanding of the activities operating on the land, by whom and the form of the business structure.

Income tax

Meaning of 'farming'

[11.2] For income tax purposes 'farming' means the occupation of land wholly or mainly for the purposes of husbandry, which includes (for example) hop growing and the breeding and rearing of horses and grazing of horses in connection with those activities, but excludes market gardening, being occupation of land as a garden or nursery for the purpose of growing produce for sale (ITA 2007, s 996(1), (2)). It is to be noted that the legislation is only indicative as to what 'husbandry' might include; an intensive enterprise such as rearing poultry is not farming.

Farming is treated for income tax purposes as the carrying on of a trade or part of a trade (where the land is managed on a commercial basis with a view to the realisation of profits) (ITTOIA 2005, s 9(1)). All farming carried on by a person is treated as one trade (ITTOIA 2005, s 9(2)). As such if John Bull owns Green Farm in Herefordshire and White Farm in East Anglia he will be treated as operating one trade with aggregation of profits and losses. All farming carried on by a farmer is treated as one trade, unless being part of another trade. Farming carried on by a farmer will be treated separately from trade carried on by his partners (ITTOIA 2005, s 859(1)). Thus if John Bull owns Green and White Farms, but owns Black Farm in partnership with John Arbuthnot, John Bull will be treated as carrying on one trade in Green and White Farms and another trade with Arbuthnot.

A person who moves from one farm to another without an interval, or gives up a portion of his land, or takes over additional land (whether or not he or she succeeds to the trade of his predecessor on that land) is chargeable on the basis of a continuing trade notwithstanding the change (see *Bispham v Eardiston Farming Co (1919) Ltd* (1962) 40 TC 322). Where there is an interval between the discontinuance at one farm and commencement at another, the farming should be treated as discontinued and a new trade as having commenced only where the facts support the conclusion that there was a permanent discontinuance of the original trade (HMRC Business Income Manual, BIM55115).

The occupation of land by a farmer is generally recognisable. HMRC's view is that occupation is not synonymous with ownership or legal possession; the farmer must be in occupation of the land (BIM55055). In certain cases this is not clear-cut. There has in the past been a tendency to commingle farm income with other categories of income. The HMRC Business Income Manual is quite clear into which category income should be allocated.

Short term grazing lets (less than 365 days)

[11.3] The agreement is a licence over the land for a period of, usually, 364 days without a right of renewal. Under such an arrangement the owner is treated as remaining in occupation of the land and is regarded as occupying it wholly or mainly for the purposes of husbandry, whereas the grazier will not be treated as farming unless he occupies other land and the grazing is an integral part of that farming in which case the grazing profits may be included in the computation of farming profits (HMRC Business Income Manual, BIM55065).

Farm land let for 365 days or more

[11.4] Under such circumstances the landlord will not be treated as being in occupation and as such the rents would not constitute farming profits even where he or she is at the same time farming on other land (*Bennion v Roper* [1970] 46 TC 613).

Contract farming

[11.5] Contract farming is an arrangement whereby a contractor carries out operations of husbandry as agent for the landowner. In contract farming cases the landowner is likely to be the occupier of the land and therefore farming. The contractor is not farming and is chargeable under ITTOIA 2005, Pt 2.

Share farming

[11.6] Share farming should be contrasted to contract farming. Under the contract farming arrangement the contractor acts as agent for the landowner, whereas under a share farming arrangement the two parties jointly farm the same land. The agreement will not amount to a partnership provided that each party has their own business, albeit that the two businesses are very closely linked (see specifically HMRC Business Income Manual, BIM55080 on what HMRC would not generally regard as being share farming). Ordinarily the landowner provides the farm land, buildings, fixed equipment and machinery, whereas the share farmer provides labour, field and mobile machinery, with both parties sharing such costs as seed, fertilisers etc. If the arrangement is genuine then the agreement between them will result in them both being accepted as farming. They will have concurrent rights to the land and both are contributing to an undertaking of husbandry (HMRC Business Income Manual, BIM55070, 55075 and see also 55080–55085 and 55640).

Intensive livestock breeding

[11.7] Diversification into intensive breeding of livestock or fish does not amount to farming (see *Lean & Dickson v Ball* (1925) 10 TC 341, *Jones v Nuttall* (1926) 10 TC 346, and *Peter Reid v IRC* (1947) 28 TC 451), since the animals are separated from the land and fed entirely on purchased feed. On the other hand, profits resulting from diversification into, for example, free range poultry, will be aggregated with other farm income.

Orchards

[11.8] The initial expenditure incurred by a fruit farmer on the planting, staking etc of a new orchard is disallowable as representing capital expenditure (see *IRC v Pilcher* (1949) 31 TC 314). After the trees have been planted, all subsequent expenditure on cultivation and production is allowable in full as a revenue charge (see *Vallambrosa Rubber Co Ltd v Farmer* (1910) 5 TC 529).

Following *Pilcher* the expenditure incurred by a fruit farmer on grubbing up an old orchard is capital in nature. However, where there is a subsequent planting of new fruit trees, both the grubbing and replanting expenditure is normally allowable as a revenue deduction on a 'renewals' basis, subject to certain conditions.

(1) Since grubbing and indeed planting expenditure is initially capital in nature, a deduction cannot be claimed on the renewals basis until the old trees have been grubbed *and* the replacement fruit trees have been planted.

(2) Renewals treatment cannot be claimed to the extent that the replanted area exceeds the grubbed area.

(3) The allowance should be calculated by reference to the area grubbed and replanted. For example, if ten hectares were grubbed up and only three hectares planted, the renewals allowance would include 30% of the grubbing costs plus 100% of the planting costs. Not only is this a practical approach but it also recognises that the agronomy of fruit production has changed and facilitates a full deduction even where tree planting density has increased.

(4) The planting must take place within a reasonable time of the grubbing (and vice versa) of the old orchard. It is not possible to be definitive about what is a reasonable time since it will vary from case to case depending on the facts but we would expect replanting to take place as

soon as is practical taking into account agricultural advice and all the circumstances of the farm. HMRC will accept up to two years as reasonable but that is not to rule out longer periods where it is justified on the facts.

(5)   Where the replanting takes place on different land and predates the old orchard being grubbed up, HMRC will still consider a renewals basis claim where the farmer or grower can show a clear replacement link at planting and the old orchard is grubbed within two years of the new one being planted. Again, as in 4 above, a period longer than two years is not ruled out where it is justified on the facts. HMRC need to be satisfied in the circumstances of each case that what has occurred is replacement and not expansion.

(6)   Where a grant or subsidy is receivable, the renewals allowance must be reduced by this amount.

(7)   Whether or not an orchard has been replaced will ultimately be a question of fact but renewals should be taken to include:

(a)   replacement trees planted in a different field on another part of the farm; and

(b)   where the fruit type has changed (say apples to plums).

If a farmer/grower wishes to use the renewals basis, then the onus is on them to make the claim and have the documentation available to support such. These records will need to identify the physical areas grubbed and replanted, when the work was done and the direct costs associated with each (HMRC Business Income Manual, BIM55275).

Short rotation coppice

[11.9] The above ground harvesting of a perennial crop of densely planted trees at intervals of less than ten years is treated as farming (FA 1995, s 154). BIM55120 sets out the tax treatment for this 'crop': costs following the planting of the cuttings together with the costs of restoring drainage will be allowed as a revenue cost, whereas the costs of planting the cuttings and reinstatement once the cycle of harvesting the coppice is over will be regarded as capital expenses.

Sale of turf

[11.10] Receipts from sales of turf should be treated as part of the farming receipts, or as receipts arising from a right over land (that is the right to take turf from the land) assessable as UK property income (ITTOIA 2005, s 264 and see HMRC Business Income Manual, BIM55200 and PIM1050, sub-head (c) and *Lowe v JW Ashmore Ltd* (1970) 46 TC 597).

Averaging profits for farmers

[11.11] Where farming, market gardening or intensive rearing of livestock or fish on a commercial basis for the production of food for human consumption is undertaken by an individual (but not a limited company) an averaging claim may be made in relation to two consecutive tax years in which he has been carrying on that qualifying trade if the relevant profits of the tax years are less than 75% of the relevant profits of the other year or the relevant profits of one (or both) of the tax years are nil (see ITTOIA, 2005, Pt 2, Ch 16). If an averaging claim is made, the amount taken to be the taxpayer's profits of each of the tax years is averaged.

The Finance Act 2016 has introduced five-year averaging. From 6 April 2016, farmers have the choice to average their profits over two or five years. Clearly, those who have been farming for less than five years have only the two-year option. ITTOIA 2005, s 222A(2) introduces a volatility test, which may be met in one of two ways:

(a)   by comparing the latest year's profits with the average of the previous four and determining that the latest year's profits are less than 75% of the average of the previous four; or

(b)   by determining that relevant profits of one or more (but not all) of the five tax years to which the claim relates are nil.

Finance Act 2016, s 19(5) has removed the marginal relief (where the profits are between 70% and 75%) once found in ITTOIA 2005, s 223(4), so that from 6 April 2016 full two-year averaging relief will only be available whether the profits of one year are 75% or less of the profits of the other year (ITTOIA 2005, s 223).

The effect of the adjustment, subject to certain exceptions (see ITTOIA 2005, ss, 224(3), 225(2) and TMA 1970, Sch 1B, para 3), is to treat the profits to be the relevant profits of the tax years to which the claim relates for all income tax purposes

Capital allowances

[11.12] With agricultural buildings allowance (ABA) phased out since 2011, the farmer must now turn to claiming capital allowances on expenditure in the same manner as other businesses holding commercial property for investments. With buildings constructed for intensive sectors, such as intensive pig and hen houses and cattle courts having shorter lives than other farm buildings it is essential that farmers and practitioners review the availability of:

*   enhanced capital allowances on certain energy efficient plant and machinery at a rate of 100%;

*   annual investment allowance – (AIA) set at a permanent level of £200,000 from 1 January 2016. The AIA applies to both the main rate (18%) and the special rate (8%) (see **CHAPTER 9** at **9.14**);

*   the excess above the AIA figure will benefit from plant and machinery writing down allowances at either 18% or 8% depending upon pool allocation.

There is no capital allowance given for the construction of or structural alterations to the fabric of the building.

Capital gains tax

[11.13] Since farming is treated as a trade for the purposes of income tax it follows that farming is a trade for capital gains tax purposes provided the farming activities are conducted on a commercial basis with a view to the realisation of profits. The assets of the business, whether trading as a sole trader or in partnership will, subject to the qualifying criteria (see CGT **CHAPTER 14** at **14.46**), benefit from entrepreneur relief on the disposal (TCGA 1992, Sch A1, para 22(1)), the land and the buildings will separately benefit from roll over relief, and on the gift of agricultural land holdover relief will be available. The disposal of land let subject to a farm business tenancy will be subject to the 18%/28% rates (for 2015/16) or 10%/20% rates (for 2016/17) as applicable. BN50 introduced an extension to the holdover provisions to include agricultural property located in the European Economic Area (EEA) even where someone other than the donor farms the land.

The recent decision of *Allen v HMRC* [2016] UKFTT 342 is a reminder that provided the landowner takes an active participation in the husbandry of the land he will be regarded as trading; this despite granting grazing rights to a third party for part of the year and therefore CGT reliefs (and most probably APR on a charge to IHT) are available to the taxpayer. In this case, the claim was for (now abolished) business asset taper relief, but the decision provides scope to claim entrepreneur's relief and rollover relief on similar facts.

Inheritance tax

Agricultural property relief

[11.14] From the point of view of the practitioner there is an important distinction between agricultural relief and business relief, discussed at **17.33**. Agricultural relief is available in respect of the categories of property enumerated in IHTA 1984, s 115 (see below) and in many instances there need be no connection between the ownership of the asset and the carrying on of the activity upon which relief is based. That is in sharp contrast to the treatment of land and interests in land for the purposes of business property relief, where the connection between the ownership of the land or interest and the running of a business is close.

In relation to bare land it must be shown either that the land was occupied by the transferor for the purposes of agriculture throughout the two years preceding the transfer; or that it was owned by the transferor for seven years prior to the transfer and was throughout that period occupied (by him or another) for agricultural purposes: see IHTA 1984, s 117.

Doubt persists as to what is a sufficient agricultural purpose. To take an extreme example, *Dixon v IRC (SpC 297)* [2002] SWTI 43, tells us that a rural cottage enjoying a reasonable sized garden that was intermittently used for purposes recognisable by any devotee of The Good Life did not constitute agricultural property.

A more common situation, in relation to marginal land, is specifically covered by IHTA 1984, s 142C so that land within a habitat scheme is regarded as agricultural land. Land that was formerly farmed but which is now largely left fallow because its owner relies upon the Single Farm Payment for his only income from the land is probably still treated as occupied for the purposes of agriculture.

IHTA 1984, s 115(4) provides that the use of land as a stud farm is agricultural use. This includes the breeding and rearing of horses and grazing them in connection with those activities. The loose boxes and other buildings used in connection with the stud farm are treated as farm buildings.

Farming need not be profitable. Many agricultural communities will appreciate that. There are few cases directly in point, and HMRC have in the manual at BIM55725 put forward the argument that stud farming must be viable to qualify for the relief, but actually that assertion is without direct authority in the statute. This again is an example of the distinction between agricultural property relief and business property relief. Business property relief (see IHTA 1984, s 103(3)) is not available in respect of a business that is 'carried on otherwise than for gain'.

Agricultural property relief (APR) was restricted to agricultural property located in the UK, the Channel Islands or the Isle of Man. From 22 April 2009 land within the EEA will qualify. Accordingly, any tax due or paid after 23 April 2003 will qualify for a refund.

Following the Court of Appeal decision in *Starke v IRC* [1995] STC 689 a tripartite division of the definition of 'agricultural property' has been adopted by subsequent Special Commission decisions.

Agricultural property means (IHTA 1984, s 115(2)):

Limb 1	agricultural land or pasture
Limb 2 . . . and also includes . . .	woodland and any building used in connection with the intensive rearing of livestock or fish if the woodland or building is occupied with agricultural land or pasture and the occupation is ancillary to that of the agricultural land or pasture
Limb 3 . . . and also includes . . .	such cottages, farm buildings and farmhouses, together with the land occupied with them, as are of a character appropriate to the property

In *Starke* the executors argued that the definition of 'agricultural land' should take into account the enlarged definition of 'land' in the Interpretation Act 1978, which would have included 'buildings and other structures'. The argument fails as the default definition in the 1978 Act can only apply where there is no contrary intention. The definition of 'agricultural land' is intended to restrict the meaning.

There is no definition of 'agriculture' within the IHTA 1984. 'Agriculture' is defined in the Agricultural Tenancies Act 1995, s 38(1) as including 'horticulture, fruit growing, seed growing, dairy farming and livestock breeding and keeping, the use of land as grazing land, meadow land, osier land, market gardens and nursery grounds, and the use of land for woodlands where that use is ancillary to the farming of land for other agricultural purposes'.

Here are a number of cases which have important ramifications for the practitioner are considered in detail; the first considers the second limb (*Williams (PR of Williams Dec'd) v HMRC* [2005] STC (SCD) 782), the others the third limb (*Lloyds TSB (PRs of Antrobus Dec'd) v Twiddy DET/47/2004, Lloyds TSB Private Banking plc v Twiddy EWLands DET_47_2004* and *Arnander, Lloyd and Villiers (Executors of McKenna) v Revenue and Customs Comrs* [2006] STC (SCD) 800), *Golding and Middleton v HMRC* [2011] UKFTT 351, *Hanson (as trustee of William Hanson 1957 Settlement) v HMRC* [2012] UKFTT 95 (TC), [2012] SFTD 705 and *HMRC v Joseph Nicholas Hanson (as Trustee of the William Hanson 1957 Settlement)* [2013] UKUT 0224 (TCC).

Limb 2 – limited APR for intensive livestock breeders

[11.15] There are two requirements to qualify under this limb:

- the woodland or buildings must be *occupied with* agricultural land or pasture; and
- that occupation is *ancillary* to that of the agricultural land or pasture.

The issue of *occupation* was considered in the House of Lords ratings case of *Farmer v Buxted Poultry Ltd* [1993] 1 All ER 117 in which it was held that for one building to be 'occupied together with' another building or land, both must serve a common purpose, be under common occupation and management and form a single unit.

The facts of *Williams* were that the deceased farmed the land (see diagram below) until 2000, when she let the 'blue land' to Summers Poultry Limited (SPL) under a farm business tenancy.

Blue land:	three broiler houses (2 × 100' × 60' and 1 × 245' × 60'), 80,000 bird capacity	Green land:	let to neighbour to graze horses – 0.32 acres	Red land:	Dwelling house and gardens occupied by deceased – 0.51 acres
	Dutch barn used for storage of materials and equipment used in the broiler houses and other part of the blue land	Orange land:	occupied by a neighbour to graze stock. HMRC agreed the land qualified for 100% APR – 3.99 acres		
	Bio-security margin				
	Small orchard in the corner which produced cider apples				
	2.59 acres				

The issue before the Special Commissioner was whether the blue land and the buildings attracted APR. The following points may be drawn from Mr Hellier's decision:

(1)   The tenant was in occupation of the blue land to the exclusion of the landlord, since SPL had physical occupation, had the power to exclude other persons and controlled the use of the land.

(2)   The only land occupied with the buildings was the blue land. Any other land in occupation of SPL either as freeholder or tenant could have been taken into account provided there was contiguity and/or propinquity.

(3)   For the buildings to be *ancillary* to the land occupied with them the buildings (or woodland) must be used:

> 'for purposes which either serve or assist the purposes for which the other land is occupied, or which form an "add-on" or a smaller (subsidiary or subordinate) part of the overall agricultural purposes for which the other land is also occupied . . . In the determination of whether or not woodland or buildings are occupied for a purpose which forms a subsidiary or subordinate part of the purpose for which the land is occupied, the extent of the physical activities undertaken and in some circumstances the turnover generated by those activities would be relevant, but . . . rarely would the area occupied be a significant factor.'

Accordingly, it was held that:

• the buildings themselves did not qualify as being agricultural property under limb 2 since they did not serve the purposes of occupation of any of the blue land including the land on which they were built;

• the remainder of the blue land (ie excluding the 30,000 sq ft of concrete and earthen floors) was used for agricultural purposes since it served the occupation of the broiler houses and qualified for APR under limb 1;

• likewise, but to a limited extent, so did the growing of cider apples;

• although not part of the land for the purposes of limb 2, the Dutch barn was of an appropriate character of the property and was a farm building under limb 3;

• the poultry houses amounted to farm buildings and would also fall within limb 3 if of a character appropriate to the property. Taking the whole of the agricultural land (6.8 acres), the fact that the poultry houses occupied approximately 10% of the area, that they dominated the blue land and impacted on the view from the orange land it was held that they failed limb 3.

• The only parts that qualified for APR under IHTA 1984, s 116 were the orange land of 3.99 acres and that part of the blue land which remains after having excised the broiler houses.

The general advice (which would apply equally to intensive pig breeding) for the intensive poultry farmer is that:

• the poultry houses will not benefit from agricultural property relief;

• the land that surrounds the poultry houses will benefit from agricultural property relief;

• any building ancillary to the farming operation is likely to qualify as it is ancillary to the farming operation carried on at the unit; and

- the poultry farmer who occupies the property (rather than lets the land) would ordinarily claim BPR; and
- in either case, any 'farmhouse' will not benefit from APR since the 'character appropriateness' (limb 3) will not be satisfied.

Farmhouses

[11.16] There is no hard and fast rule as to what constitutes a farmhouse, but in assessing the property it has been suggested that it should be considered through the eyes of the rural equivalent of the reasonable man on the Clapham Omnibus. In the cases of *Dixon v IRC Sp C 297* and *Lloyds TSB (as personal representatives of Rosemary Antrobus deceased) v IRC SpC 336* the Special Commissioner followed (with approval) McCutcheon's position:

> 'The present position is that the "character test" is considered against three main tests:
>
> 1. the elephant test:
>   although you cannot describe a farmhouse which satisfies the character test you will know it when you see it!
> 2. man on the (rural) Clapham Omnibus:
>   would the educated rural layman regard the property as a house with land or a farm?
> 3. Historical dimension:
>   how long has the house in question been associated with the agricultural property and is there a history of agricultural production?' (McCutcheon BD (Ed) McCutcheon on Inheritance Tax (London, Sweet & Maxwell 2005, para 14–131)

In *Antrobus*, Crookhill Priory was held to be a farmhouse and of a character appropriate to qualify for APR. However, the Revenue issued a Notice of Determination in mid-February 2004 by contending that the agricultural value was £425,932.50 against the agreed market value of £608,475. The Lands Tribunal decision was handed down in October 2005 reported as *Lloyds TSB Private Banking (Antrobus' Personal Representative) v Twiddy DET/47/2004: Antrobus II.*

The agricultural value of any agricultural property is taken to be the value which would be the value of the property if the property were subject to a perpetual covenant prohibiting its use otherwise than as agricultural property (IHTA 1984, s 115(3)). No evidence was brought before the Tribunal of any property sold on the open market subject to the s 115(3) covenant. The Valuation Office Agency has a history of challenging the availability of APR on farmhouses on the grounds that s 115(3) is equivalent to the standard planning occupancy condition (AOC) (the AOC in a planning permission provides that 'the occupation of the dwelling shall be limited to a person solely or mainly working, or last working, in the locality in agriculture or in forestry, or a widow or widower of such a person and to any resident dependents' DoE Circular 11/95 para 45) and it is observed by de Souza that:

> 'the element of disallowance generally requested started off at 15 per cent in 1993, but rose to 25 per cent in May 1994. By the end of 2000, initial demands from district valuers tended to be in the 30 to 33 per cent range and *Buccleuch*-style lotting were also being raised.' ([2006] PCB Mar/Apr p 53)

In *Antrobus II* HMRC succeeded in its claim for a 30% disallowance based not on the hypothetical covenant but on the value that a property would ordinarily be reduced by if encumbered by an AOC. In the view of the Tribunal:

'. . . it is the person who lives in the farmhouse in order to farm the land comprised in the farm and who farms the land on a day to day basis. It is likely, although it may not necessarily always be the case, that his principal occupation will consist of farming the land comprised in the farm. We do not think that a house occupied with a farm is a farmhouse simply because the person living there is in overall control of the agricultural business conducted on the land; and in particular we think that the lifestyle farmer, the person whose bid for the land is treated by the appellant as establishing the agricultural value of the land, is not the farmer for the purpose of the provisions.'

The conclusion is flawed, in the opinion of the author, on a number of accounts:

• The AOC does not require there to be a nexus between the farmhouse and the agricultural holding which is envisaged in the Valuation Office Agency Inheritance Tax Manual. In *Rosser v IRC* [2003] STC (SCD) 331 it was held that the farmhouse was 'a dwelling for the farmer from which the farm is managed'. Given that PPG7 Appendix E states that a development under an AOC is permitted even where it is self-contained and has no direct relationship with the rest of the unit, this seems far removed from the character appropriate conditions in *Antrobus I*.

• The Tribunal entertained the suggestion that the extension of the AOC to retired persons latterly in agriculture may have some relevance to retired farmers and widows. This illustrates a clear misunderstanding of s 115 (limb 3) since it was held in that upon the retirement of the farmer the farmhouse ceased to be of a character appropriate to the property.

• There is no earlier case which holds that where a farmer winds down his farming operations (but does not retire) through the use of contractors, taking on a partner or employing a manager he loses the status of the farmhouse.

Even if the Tribunal were correct in its interpretation, the correct valuation should not be to deduct an arbitrary percentage from the value that a lifestyle farmer is prepared to pay for the property, but instead to value the property on the basis of what a working farmer would have bid for the property.

The issue of what constitutes a farmhouse has been further considered in *Arnander, Lloyd and Villiers (Executors of McKenna) v Special Commissioners of HM Revenue and Customs* [2006] STC (SCD) 800. Dr Brice re-visited her decision in *Antrobus I* and also the Northern Ireland decision of *Higginsons Executors v IRC* [2002] STC (SCD) 483 (decided around the same time as Dr Brice gave her judgment in *Antrobus I*) and came to the conclusion that the house was not a farmhouse and also not occupied for the purposes of agriculture during the period of two years ending with the date of transfer.

The *McKenna* case centred around the Rosteague Estate which comprised 188 acres, 52 acres of foreshore, 10 acres of woodland, 110 acres of farmland, and main house, lodge, stable flat, cottage and gardens of 6 acres. Rosteague House was an 8,000 sq ft Elizabethan Manor House. The house sold for £3m following the death of Lady McKenna. Mr McKenna died on 29 January 2003, aged 91. He had suffered from ill health for the preceding six years. His wife, Lady McKenna died aged 92 on 16 June 2003 at a nursing home. As a result of a new farmhouse being built in 1908 and the occupants taking up an agricultural tenancy of the land, it was accepted that the house became disassociated with farming operations from that point onwards. However, in 1984 the tenants surrendered their tenancy and Mr McKenna entered into a series of contract farming arrangements under a number of different agreements. The McKennas had very little in the way of contractual obligations. From 1995 an agent, who had purchased a property on the estate, took the decisions on behalf of the McKennas as they became more infirm. The question was very much whether the house was one from which the farming operations were conducted. Dr Brice concluded, that:

'if the farmer of the land is the person who farms it on a day-to-day basis rather than the person who is in over all control of the agricultural business conducted on the land then Mr McKenna was not the farmer. The purpose of the occupation of Rosteague House was not to undertake the day-to-day farming activities.'

Can it now be said that all contract farming arrangements will result in APR being lost on the farmhouse? Probably not: the agreements granted the majority, if not all, control to the contractor (including entering into machinery agreement, claiming subsidies in his own name etc) in return for a fixed remuneration. In the opinion of the author, these agreements were an attempt to rent the land by another means and get round the decision in *Starke*.

McKenna is significant in one area and that relates to the likelihood of HMRC challenging cases where the inherent value of the estate is mainly attributed to the large house, the value of which is disproportionate to the agricultural profitability from contract farming. Thus, in *McKenna* the house constituted 65% of the value of the entire estate and yet the particulars of sale made no mention of the fact that it was apparently a farmhouse.

Subsequently, the Upper Tier has had the opportunity to consider the decision in *Atkinson v Revenue and Customs Comrs* (TC00042) [2010] UKFTT 108 (TC), [2010] SWTI 2123. In this particular case the deceased acquired Abbotsons Farm in 1957 and over the years entered into a number of farming partnerships of some 195 acres, the farmhouse and a bungalow known as Croftlands culminating in 1996 with the deceased entering into a written partnership with his daughter-in-law and grandson. On entering into the 1996 partnership the tenancy of the farm (protected under the Agricultural Holding Act and granted to a prior partnership of the deceased, son and daughter-in-law) was assigned to the 1996 partnership.

In 2002 the deceased became ill and following a spell in hospital entered into a care home where he stayed until his death in October 2006. HMRC argued that the deceased could not be realistically regarded as having been in occupation of the bungalow and still less that the bungalow was occupied for the purpose of agriculture. The Executors were able to show that throughout the period of the partnership the entire holding was occupied for the purposes of the partnership's farming activities: in the case of the bungalow despite the deceased's occupation at the nursing home, the bungalow contained the deceased's possessions and on occasion he visited the bungalow. Additionally he continued to participate in partnership matters. The First-tier Tribunal decided that the deceased's occupation was occupation for the purposed of agriculture 'in the relevant sense because the bungalow was still used to accommodate the diminishing needs of the senior partner'. The Upper Tribunal did not agree and said that there had to be some objective connection between the occupation of the bungalow and the relevant agricultural activities. Accordingly, there still needed to be some relevant connection between the use of the bungalow and the activities of the rest of the farm. As such, once Mr Atkinson moved to a care home (without a reasonable prospect of returning to the bungalow) the connection with use of the property for agricultural purposes was lost and so, since not occupied for the purposes of agriculture, APR was lost.

The question as to whether a farmhouse with very little agricultural land had the appropriate character and corresponding agricultural property relief was considered in *Golding and Middleton v HMRC* [2011] UKFTT 351. The case before the First-tier Tribunal was to determine whether the farmhouse was of a character appropriate for use with the adjoining 16.29 acres, growing vegetables mainly for his own consumption and selling eggs at the farm gate from a limited flock of 70 hens. Mr Dennis Golding (the deceased) lived an impoverished lifestyle, with no electricity in any of the bedrooms, a spartan kitchen, apples stored in another room, the roof was partly covered with a tarpaulin and in need of serious repair. Nevertheless, the Tribunal took the view that in a very limited way Mr Golding was still working on the farm when he died.

The appellants could only show very limited income from the farm, but the Tribunal accepted that farming is very much a vocational activity (particularly with age) and that the lack of substantial profits was not detrimental to a decision that the farmhouse was of an appropriate character.

The case highlights a number of interesting aspects:

- the Tribunal accepted that with age there came a reduction in farming activity and commensurate profits;
- the taxpayer should show that the deceased worked to the best of his abilities up to the date of his death;
- any claim should be supported by filed and accepted accounts whether showing losses or modest profits;
- the diminution of profits, or a meagre income, is no bar to the farmhouse, rundown or dilapidated as it may be, carrying the character appropriate badge; and
- HMRC's assertion that the character appropriateness test is one of function only is misguided and that following *Rosser* the better view is to look at the principles in the round and look at the broad picture: the question is one of fact and degree and any factor could be relevant.

This question of little agricultural land associated with a farmhouse has been further considered in *Hanson (as trustee of William Hanson 1957 Settlement) v HMRC* [2012] UKFTT 95 (TC), [2012] SFTD 705. In this case, before the First-tier Tribunal, the deceased died owning a life interest in a farmhouse and a half share interest in 36 acres which were farmed by the deceased's brother.

During his lifetime the deceased, along with his brother, had farmed around 800 acres. The land was partitioned in 1991 between the deceased and his brother. Thereafter the deceased farmed his holding in partnership with his two sons before splitting the holding between his two sons (Joseph taking about 128 acres of agricultural land and Andrew taking some land with development potential), selling about 100 acres and retaining the said 36 acres.

The dispute surrounding the farmhouse, which at the date of death was occupied by Joseph and his family and from which at all times the farming operations had been run, was whether or not the farmhouse was agricultural property within the meaning of IHTA 1984, s 115(2).

The tribunal held that s 115(2) was to be literally interpreted, that the definition is self-contained in the section and so inferences from other areas of the Act (eg as argued by HMRC referring to s 116(1)) are not to be applied, and considered that 'the meaning discernible from the words of the definition in section 115(2) IHTA is that cottages, farm buildings and farmhouses in the third limb of the definition must be of a character appropriate to agricultural land or pasture (including woodland and any building within the second limb of the definition) in the same occupation, but that it is not required that the cottages, farm buildings and farmhouses should be in the same ownership as the agricultural land or pasture (as expanded by the second limb of the definition).' As such the relief sought by the Appellant was granted.

The significance of the case is that there need be common occupation not common ownership and common occupation. Taking the scenario of father owning a five-bedroom farmhouse with, say, 260 acres of land and son (with family) owning a two-bedroom house, say, within the village or close to the farm, it appears, following the decision in *Hanson* that:

— father could give the land to son;
— father could vacate the farmhouse for his son's house;
— son (with family) could occupy the farmhouse; and
— because of common occupation of the farmhouse and the farmland (but not common ownership) APR under s 115(2) is available on father's death.

The Upper Tier (*HMRC v Joseph Nicholas Hanson (as Trustee of the William Hanson 1957 Settlement)* [2013] UKUT 0224 (TCC)) approved the First-tier decision affirming the position that the nexus between farmhouse and agricultural land or pasture was common occupation and not occupation and ownership. Provided that there is a functional connection between farmhouse and the farmland then the taxpayer will have gone a long way in establishing a nexus between limb 1 and limb 3 by which the 'character appropriate' test is to be assessed [para 63]. The Tribunal took the view that, 'A single farming unit is likely (at least it is not easy to envisage a case where this is not so) to be in a single occupation. And that is why occupation can be a reliable touchstone for identifying "the property" referred to in limb 3' [para 62]. In theory there may be cases where common occupation may not necessarily establish a sufficient nexus, but in such situations it is difficult to see how the taxpayer could, in such remote circumstances, demonstrate that the 'character appropriateness' test had been fulfilled. The Tribunal could not think of an example and neither can the writer.

Business property relief

[11.17] Business property relief (BPR) is addressed in more detail in **CHAPTER 17**, but in brief, BPR is available on relevant business property. BPR at 100% is available on property falling within one of the following three categories:

- a business or an interest in a business (ie sole proprietorship or a partnership share); or
- a shareholding in an unlisted company (including AIM);
- any other securities in an unlisted company provided that the transferor has a controlling interest.

BPR at 50% is available if the relevant business property is

- a controlling shareholding in a listed company (ie 50% + 1 share); or
- land, buildings, machinery or plant used immediately before the transfer and used wholly or mainly for the purposes of a partnership of which he was a member or a company in which he had a controlling shareholding,

provided the partnership interest or company shares are themselves relevant business property, ie trading activities.

No relief is available in a number of circumstances including investment business or companies, dealing in, amongst others, land or buildings.

There are numerous cases where HMRC have argued that BPR is not available where farmers have diversified into letting property formerly used for agricultural purposes or that caravan parks are investment properties since the owner lets land or caravans rather than supply services of which only the accommodation is part. As a matter of practice, HMRC have a tendency not to look at the whole of an estate, but compartmentalise it into buildings or land that qualify for APR, buildings or land qualifying for BPR and then parts that have no reliefs available. Alternatively, HMRC deny the claim for BPR all together leaving the personal representative to challenge the decision. And so it was in the case on the death of the Fourth Earl of Balfour (*Brander (representative of James (dec'd), Fourth Earl of Balfour v Revenue and Customs Comrs* [2009] UKFTT 101 (TC), [2009] SFTD 374). The estate in question was the Whittingehame Estate, East Lothian comprising:

(1) 1900 acres of thereabout;
(2) two in-hand farm;
(3) three let farms;
(4) woodland;
(5) let sporting rights;
(6) two sets of let commercial buildings; and
(7) 26 let houses and cottages.

Lord Balfour had the Scottish equivalent of a life interest in the Estate until 2002 and thereafter a freehold interest until his death in June 2003. The question arose to what extent BPR was available. On first blush, and following HMRC's general approach of dividing property one might say that much of the estate's income was derived from property investment (items 3, 5, 6 and 7) and therefore did not qualify for BPR. The Tribunal found that the Estate was a traditional Scottish landed estate, the work force was not rigidly divided so that each member worked exclusively on one activity all the time, and that Lord Balfour, whether as life tenant, subsequent partner, and ultimately freeholder managed the estate with his secretary involved in all administrative aspects. Looking at the management of the Estate as a whole and the type of occupant taking up leases and the holistic approach taken by Lord Balfour the Tribunal found no difficulty in rejecting the argument that the business carried on at the Estate (at any time after 1999 – it being unnecessary to consider the position before then) was wholly or mainly making or holding investments.

What is notable about this case is:

- the liberal approach (in following the *Farmer* principles), taken by the Tribunal in looking at this most traditional of Scottish estates and finding that although perhaps as much as 50% of the estate was let, the active management, the considered letting and the like by Lord Balfour was indicative of an enterprise of more than simply investment in land; and
- the fact that in the latter stages of his life Lord Balfour acceded management to his factor/land agent. Nonetheless, they reported to Lord Balfour and he maintained overall management of the Estate. By not so passing the entire responsibilities to his land agents BPR was available. This position can be contrasted with the *McKenna* case above, where the hands off approach resulted in the loss of APR.

The Upper Tax Tribunal has subsequently dismissed HMRC's appeal, permitted on a point of law.

Chapter 12

Woodlands

by
Julian Palmer

Introduction

[12.1] Successive governments have recognised the value of woodlands, with the current government's vision being for a great variety of well-managed woodlands which will include woodlands for timber production to strengthen local economies, for economic regeneration to re-clothe industrial dereliction, for access and recreation and for biodiversity to enhance the environment.

Income tax

[12.2] The commercial occupation of woodlands in the UK is not a trade or part of a trade for any income tax (under ITTOIA 2005, Pt 5, Ch 8) purposes if the woodlands are managed on a commercial basis with a view to the realisation of profits (ITTOIA 2005, s 11; cf ss 267, 768). Similarly, the commercial occupation of land being prepared for forestry purposes will not amount to the carrying on of a trade or part of a trade (ITTOIA 2005, s 10). It follows that the planting and maintenance of the woodland is not a deduction for income tax purposes and equally losses arising from occupation are not trading losses.

What amounts to woodland was considered in *Jaggers (t/a Shide Trees) v Ellis* [1997] STC 1417 in which Lightman J held that the terms 'woodland' and 'forestry' were not words of art, but were words in common usage and to be treated as synonymous. The case centred around whether the cultivation of Christmas trees benefited from woodland exemption. Expert evidence showed that commercial forestry (for timber) was planted at five to six feet intervals, whereas the Christmas trees were planed at three feet intervals with the taxpayer pruning the lead shoot and side branches to produce a bushy pattern unlike that which would be adopted for timber production. Lightman J held that 'woodlands' connoted a wood, a sizeable area of land to a significant extent covered by growing trees of some maturity, height and size. Whilst there was no mathematical or scientific formula for deciding the area of land, the density of the trees etc, it could not be assumed that land covered with any trees constituted woodland and a good rule of thumb was whether the wood was capable of being used as timber. Whether the trees on a particular area of land are such as to entitle it to be regarded as woodland is very much a matter of impression and personal judgment for the viewer. He may find it as difficult (if not impossible) to give his definition of woodlands as he would of an elephant, but he will know when he has had the pleasurable experience of seeing either.

HMRC regard the production of Christmas trees by a farmer as falling within his farm profits, whilst a specialist 'Christmas tree farm' is regarded as falling within the definition of 'market gardening' (ITA 2007, s 996(5): 'the occupation of land as a garden or nursery for the purpose of growing produce for sale') and as such taxed as a trade under ITTOIA 2005, s 9. However, where Christmas trees are derived from the top of felled trees from commercial woodlands or thinning from land being prepared for forestry, then the profits will be covered by the woodlands exemption (HMRC Business Income Manual, BIM55210).

Short rotation coppice, defined as 'a perennial crop of tree species planted at high density, the stems of which are harvested above ground level at intervals of less than 10 years' (ITA 2007, s 996(6)) falls outside of the woodlands exemption and, since 29 November 1994, has been treated as farming rather than forestry (see HMRC Business Income Manual, BIM55120).

As a general rule where a grant under the Woodland Grant Scheme has been made by the Forestry Commission in respect of land, it is likely that the woodlands exemption would apply, although 'it will always be a question to be decided on all of the facts of the case concerned' (HMRC Business Income Manual, BIM55210). The Woodland Grant Scheme and Farm Woodland Premium have been closed and replaced in England by a suite of grants (the English Woodland Grant Scheme), in Wales by the Glastir Woodland Creation Grant (for landowners with more than 0.25 hectares of land identified by the Forestry Commission and conservation bodies in Wales as suitable for new planting) and presently there are no new woodland grants available through the Scottish Forestry Commission (instead there are eight grants which may be sought under the Rural Development Programme 2014–2020), but it would seem that in the majority of cases the woodland would be operated on a commercial footing and not merely for public amenity space or conservation and so benefit from woodlands exemption.

The owner of commercial woodland that lets the land does not benefit from the woodland exemption but is instead taxed under ITTOIA 2005, Pt 3.

Activities (such as converting timber to finished product) which go beyond the mere commercial occupation of woodlands will not attract the woodland exemption but be treated as a separate trade and be taxed under ITTOIA 2005, Pt 2.

Capital gains tax

[12.3] As with income tax, generous provisions apply to the disposal (see TCGA 1992, ss 21–34 for the general meaning of disposal) of woodland under the capital gains tax regime.

Consideration for the disposal of trees (woodland does not include short rotation coppicing: FA 1995, s 154) (including saleable underwood) standing, felled or cut on woodlands managed by the occupier on a commercial basis with a view to the realisation of profits are excluded from the computation of the gain provided that the person making the disposal is the occupier (TCGA 1992, s 250(1)). A capital sum received under an insurance policy in respect of the destruction of or damage or injury to trees (or saleable underwood) by fire or other hazard is also excluded from the computation of the gain. This overrides the general rule in TCGA 1992, s 22(1) concerning sums received under insurance policies (HMRC Capital Gains Manual, CG73201).

Where the underlying land is disposed of, the values attributed to the trees (or saleable underwood) at the time of acquisition or disposal are excluded from the computation of the gain (TCGA 1992, s 250(4), (5)).

The exemptions under TCGA 1992, s 250(1) and (2) apply in respect of timber from commercial woodlands. Any sums received in respect of felled trees from other woodlands are within the charge to CGT. However, each tree is treated as a single chattel and a chargeable gain could therefore only arise in the unlikely event of the single tree being sold for more than £6,000 (more than £3,000 before 6 April 1989). The provisions of s 262(4) regarding 'sets' do not apply to trees (HMRC Capital Gains Manual, CG73220).

Trees growing on woodland may be disposed of by the owner granting to another person the right to enter the woodland and fell the trees. If the trees are growing on a commercial woodland, the exemption in s 250(1) will apply. If the trees are not growing on a commercial woodland, the capital gains tax consequences depend on the precise nature of the right which is granted. If the person to whom the right is granted is not entitled to benefit from the future growth of the trees, that is if he must fell the trees within a short time, the owner of the woodland is treated as disposing of the trees as individual chattels. If the person to whom the right is granted is entitled to benefit from the future growth of the trees, that is if he is granted the right to fell trees over a long period, then the owner is treated as having made a part-disposal of his land (HMRC Capital Gains Manual, CG73221).

For the purposes of TCGA 1992, s 165, the term 'trade' is given the same meaning as in the Income Taxes Act. Accordingly, holdover relief is available on the gift of woodland managed on a commercial basis. BN50 has extended this relief to woodland within the European Economic Area (EEA) from 22 April 2009. Rollover relief (TCGA 1992, ss 152–157) applies in relation to the occupation of woodlands where the woodlands are managed by the occupier on a commercial basis. It is, however, doubtful that gains on trading assets can be rolled into woodland. The Capital Gains Manual at CG60500 states that 'Roll-over relief is available where the old *and* the new assets are used in certain specific activities which are not trades', which appears to preclude the opportunity to roll gains either from deemed trades to trades or vice versa.

Whilst woodlands themselves may not attract entrepreneur relief, shares in a company operating a commercial woodland would benefit from the 10% rate. The tax advantages available under enterprise investment schemes, venture capital trusts, corporate venturing and enterprise management incentives are unavailable to companies commercially occupying woodland.

Inheritance tax

Woodland relief on death

[12.4] IHTA 1984, Pt V, Ch III accords a special deferral relief in respect of chargeable transfers arising from trees or underwood (but not the land) on death within the UK and EEA which do not benefit from a prior claim of APR or BPR.

It is important to note that whilst HMRC and the practitioner may refer to the relief as 'woodlands relief' no part of Pt V, Ch III uses the word 'woodlands' save for the Chapter heading. Whilst the interpretation of headings and side notes has moved on since *R v Hare* [1934] 1 KB 354 in which it was said that:

> 'Headings of sections and marginal notes form no part of a statute. They are not voted on or passed by Parliament, but are inserted after the Bill has become law. Headnotes cannot control the plain meaning of the words of the enactment, though they may, in some case, be looked at in the light of preambles if there is any ambiguity in the meaning of the sections on which they can throw light.' (per Avory J at 355–356)

nevertheless headings amount to no more than guidance as to the particular section and provide no more than the context for interpretation of the words of the Chapter – see *R v Montila* [2004] 1 WLR 3141. As was noted at **12.2** in *Jaggers* Lightman J limited the definition of woodland to a wood applied to timber production. The relief available for inheritance tax extends to 'trees or underwood' (IHTA 1984, ss 125 and 126). Underwood is defined as 'small trees, shrubs etc., growing beneath higher timber trees – a quantity, kind or particular area of this undergrowth' (*New Shorter Oxford English Dictionary*, 5th ed, 2003). Any issues relating to whether woodland benefits from relief is referred to the Valuation Office Agency by HMRC to assess whether the woodland benefits first from agricultural property relief (HMRC Inheritance Tax manual, IHTM04373). The VOA Inheritance Manual (Section 10 Part 1: Relief for Non-Agricultural Woodlands) provides meanings to words which are purportedly within the relevant section of the IHTA 1984. For instance within the manual (at 10.3) 'Woodland' as referred to in s 125(1) is any land on which trees or underwood are growing. Woodlands may therefore include wooded parkland, strips of land with trees lining roads, tree belts etc, but for relief any woodlands must not be agricultural property as defined in s 115(2) whilst at 10.4, 'The term "timber" in the remainder of the section refers to "trees or underwood"'. Neither the word 'woodland' nor 'timber' appear in IHTA 1984, s 125; however, such insight is useful in maintaining an argument that the case of *Jaggers* has no relevance to IHT and woodlands relief should be extended to any trees and underwood which are not being cultivated for the purposes of timber production or comprise agriculture property.

The value of the trees or underwood growing at the date of death may be left out of the account in determining the value transferred on the death. An election in writing to the Board may be made by the personal representatives or any other person liable for the whole or part of the tax within two years of the death or such longer time as the Board may allow. The effect of the election is to defer the payment of tax to a date when the trees or underwood are disposed of. If there is no disposal then the tax falls due on the subsequent death, unless a further election is made following that death.

Relief is only available:

(1) on the occasion of death; and
(2) the land is situated in the UK or from 22 April 2009 a state within the European Economic Union; and
(3) the land is not agricultural land within the meaning of IHTA 1984, s 115(2); and
(4) the deceased was either beneficially entitled to the land throughout the five years immediately preceding his death, or
(5) the deceased became beneficially entitled to the land otherwise than for a consideration in money or money's worth; and
(6) a person liable for the whole or part of the tax elects in writing to the Board within two years of the death or such longer time as the Board allows.

A person will not be regarded as being beneficially entitled to the land where:

(a) the land is held under a trust (other than one satisfying IHTA 1984, s 49(1)), eg a discretionary trust or relevant property trust; or
(b) the land is subject to a contract of sale; or
(c) the land is an asset of a company in which the deceased held shares (*Short v Treasury Commissioners* [1948] AC 534; *Maccura v Northern Assurance Company* [1925] AC 619); or
(d) the land is a partnership asset since a partner's entitlement is not to a share of a particular asset but the net proceeds of sale (see Partnership Act 1890, ss 39, 44).

The effect of the election is that the value of the trees and underwood (but not the land itself) is left out of the deceased's account. Clearly, the land cannot qualify for agricultural relief, but if the deceased commercially occupied the woodland then the land may qualify for business property relief – see below.

Where the value of the trees or underwood has been left out of the deceased's account, a tax charge will arise when any or all of the trees or underwood are disposed of (whether together with or apart from the land on which they were growing), if the disposal occurs before any part of the value transferred on the death of any other person is attributable to the value of the land on which the trees or underwood grows (IHTA 1984, s 126(1)). No charge will arise in one of three circumstances:

(1) a disposal made by any person to a spouse or civil partner (IHTA 1984, s 126(2)); or
(2) where tax has already been charged and paid in respect of an earlier disposal (IHTA 1984, s 126(3)) arising out of the same death; or
(3) where there has been an intervening death and no election was made on that death to defer the tax again.

A person liable to tax must deliver an account (Form IHT 100 (boxes A6 and F4) and Form IHT405 and IHT 100f: Cessation of conditional exemption and disposal of trees and underwood) within six months of the end of the month in which the disposal occurs. The tax on the net proceeds of sale is due in one sum, whilst tax arising from a chargeable transfer (eg by settlement to a discretionary trust or relevant property trust) may be paid by instalments over ten years at the option of either the transferor or transferee (IHTA 1984, s 229).

The amount of tax to be charged on the disposal of the trees or underwood is determined as being either the net proceeds of sale or, in the case of a gift or sale at an undervalue, the net value of the trees or underwood at the time of disposal in any other case (IHTA 1984, s 127(1)). In calculating the net sale proceeds or net value the following expenses may be deducted provided that they are not allowable for income tax purposes (IHTA 1984, s 130(b)):

(1)   disposal of the trees or underwood; and
(2)   replanting within three years of the disposal (or such longer period as the Board may allow) to replace the trees or underwood disposed of; and
(3)   replanting to replace trees or underwood previously disposed, so far as not allowable on the previous disposal (IHTA 1984, s 130(c)).

The District Valuer is obliged to ignore any allowable expenses as well as any obligation to replant. The net value will be the higher of:

(1)   the value of the trees for sale for felling including any underwood; or
(2)   the value of the standing trees or underwood as part of the transferor's estate.

The disposal may have been together with or apart from the land on which the trees or underwood are growing, but the District Valuer's valuation will always exclude the value of the underlying land.

A valuation on the basis of (2) above will probably only apply when immature woodland or growing timber of high amenity value is involved. When valuing on this basis the District Valuer should not apply the concept of loss to the transferor because the purpose of the valuation is to arrive at the net value of the timber itself (VOA Inheritance Manual Section 10, Part 1, para 10.16).

The sum representing the net proceeds of sale or net value is added to the cumulative total of the deceased's estate (where successive claims have been made the estate to which the net sale proceeds or net value is added to is the last estate for which relief under IHTA 1984 s 125 was claimed). Tax is charged at the rate(s) which would have been charged on the estate at the top marginal rate. Where deferred tax becomes payable and there has been a reduction in the rates by substitution of a new table of rates, the tax is calculated on the rates in force at the date of disposal and not those that would have originally applied on death (IHTA 1984, Sch 2, para 4).

Where the disposal constitutes a chargeable transfer, the value transferred is calculated as if the value of the trees or underwood had been reduced by the tax chargeable under IHTA 1984, s 126.

Agricultural property relief (APR)

[12.5] Where the woodland is occupied with agricultural land or pasture and the occupation is ancillary to that of the agricultural land or pasture a claim for

APR should be made. Examples of such woodland include woodland belts, game coverts, fox coverts, coppices grown for fencing materials on the farm and clumps of amenity trees or spinneys (HMRC Inheritance Tax manual, IHTM24032). The corollary is that amenity parkland or woodland used for the production of commercial timber will not be agricultural property, but benefit from either woodlands relief or business property relief.

A fuller discussion on APR can be found in **CHAPTER 17** at **17.30**.

Business property relief (BPR)

[12.6] If the woodland does not qualify as agricultural property, it may form part of a business in which the deceased had a qualifying business interest.

If the value of the trees and underwood has not been left out of the deceased's estate relief at 50% is available on the subsequent disposal if:

(1)   the value of the trees and underwood would have been taken into account in determining the value of any relevant business property; or

(2)   would have been taken into account if the provisions relating to business property relief had been in force at the date of death.

BPR is calculated not as a reduction in the value of the property, but as an appropriate percentage of the value that might be attributed to the relevant business property (IHTA 1984, s 104(2)). Where there is a disposal of BPR qualifying woodland the value attributed to the transfer of value arising on this transfer is first reduced by the tax chargeable under IHTA 1984, s 126 (IHTA 1984, s 114(2)).

A fuller discussion of BPR can be found in **CHAPTER 17** at paragraph **17.33**.

Value added tax

[12.7] The owner of commercial woodland can register for VAT in either of the following circumstances:

• the woodland is leased or otherwise let to another party who exploits it and the owner is making a taxable supply for VAT purposes of granting the right to fell timber etc (see **CHAPTER 15** at **15.57** for details); or

• the owner fells the timber and extracts underwood which is then sold (or is used by the owner in manufacturing other products).

In the latter case the owner can register for VAT in advance of making taxable supplies of timber etc, on a voluntary basis, in order to facilitate the recovery of VAT incurred on the purchase and cultivation/maintenance of the woodland before any sales take place.

A recent (and rare) case on the application of VAT on woodlands came before First-tier Tribunal (*Will Woodlands (a charity)* [2017] UKFTT 578 (TC)). Will Woodlands, a charity incorporated by guarantee with the aim of 'conserving, restoring and establishing trees, plants and all forms of wildlife in the UK and securing and enhancing public employment of the natural environment of the UK' owned various estates establishing woodlands, with the remainder of the estates mainly being farmed or let for grazing. The charity engaged woodland services and had trees planted to be converted to timber at some future date and sought to recover the VAT on such supplies in full. HMRC contended (a) that these activities were residual to its conservation objectives and that the VAT should not be attributable as taxable activity or should be apportioned; and (b) that the manner of apportionment of the VAT should be on an income basis and not, as previously agreed with the charity, by reference to land use (ie apportioned against the woodland parts of the estates).

On an objective determination, following *Sub One Ltd (t/a Subway) (in Liq) v Revenue and Customs Comrs* [2014] EWCA Civ 773, [2014] STC 2508, [2014] SWTI 2111, the status of the taxpayer as a charity was irrelevant – there was no distinction that could be made between the activities of the charity in relation to the management of the woodlands and that of a commercial operator (save perhaps for the higher conservation standards operated by the charity). The Tribunal found that there was no activity being carried on in the woodland areas which was not part of the woodland and that there were no costs incurred in relation to those areas which are not costs of those operations. The Tribunal favoured the charity following its approval of '*Sveda*' *UAB v Valstybine˙ mokescˇiu̯ inspekcija prie Lietuvos Respublikos finansu̯ ministerijos, third party: Klaipe˙dos apskrities valstybine˙ mokescˇiu̯ inspekcija* C-126/14 [2016] STC 447 in that capital goods were acquired with the intention of carrying out economic activities. Here the charity had trees planted for their economic value in 20–150 years' time as timber.

In terms of the apportionment of VAT, the burden of proof shifted from the taxpayer to HMRC to rebut the method of apportionment adopted for many years in favour of its own methodology. It failed to do so. Since there was no duality of use, the Tribunal considered the charity's method as fair and reasonable.

Chapter 13

Anti-avoidance

by
Robin Dabydeen,
Winckworth Sherwood LLP

Introduction

[13.1] This chapter is in two parts. The first part deals with provisions relating to the entirely new regime (which was under the Finance Act 2016) to corporation tax and income tax which apply to a non-resident that carries on a trade of dealing in or developing UK land and to certain transactions in land which are contained in the Corporation Tax Act 2010 (CTA 2010) for corporation tax purposes and in the Income Tax Act 2007 (ITA 2007) for income tax purposes, and which provisions were replaced entirely by new rules made under Finance Act 2016. The second part of this chapter outlines other anti-avoidance measures at HMRC's disposal which are of general application but which also enable artificial schemes involving land to be discovered by HMRC and attacked.

Other anti-avoidance provisions, for example in relation to VAT, are addressed in the relevant chapters. By way of background, on 16 March 2016 (and at the time of Budget 2016), HMRC issued a technical paper ('Technical Paper') on the subject of the taxation of profits from trading in and developing UK land. According to the Technical Paper, some property developers use offshore structure to avoid UK tax on their profits from trading in property in the UK. The Technical Paper states that legislation (in line with international standards) would be put in place to ensure a level playing field between UK developers and those based in offshore jurisdiction. The Technical Paper then stated that legislation would put in a specific set of rules to tax trading profits derived from UK land, and that these measures would come into effect under the Finance Bill 2016.

The new regime (as discussed in detail below) was introduced with remarkable haste in the Finance Bill 2016 with an effective date in respect of disposals made on or after 5 July 2016. In addition, specific anti-forestalling rules were introduced to counteract any transactions entered into after 15 March 2016 (but these measures will not be considered in this chapter).

On 9 September 2016, HMRC issued draft guidance note, 'Profits from a trade of dealing in developing UK land' ('draft HMRC Guidance') which provides a relatively comprehensive guide of HMRC's views on the intended workings of the new measures. On 28 January 2017, HMRC updated this guidance to its

Business Income Manual (at paragraphs BIM60510 to BIM60900) and which can be found at the following website: www.gov.uk/hmrc-internal-manuals/b usiness-income-manual/bim60510.

In summary (and as discussed in detail below), the new regime represents a fundamental change in the taxation of UK property development projects and (in this author's view) requires further legislative clarification, not least because parts of the new measures are not aligned with other existing anti-avoidance regimes. Whilst it is recognised that some international operators implemented aggressive tax planning structures in respect of UK real estate projects and which therefore justify a significant change in how UK tax is charged on these projects, some aspects of the new rules (notably, the new anti-fragmentation rule) are likely to adversely affect purely commercial arrangements.

It is important to note that the Offshore Property Developers Task Force ('OPDTF'), which was established by HMRC in 2016 to investigate tax avoidance related to offshore developers of UK land, will continue to exist notwithstanding the introduction of the new regime. In particular, this means that the OPDTF may investigate offshore structures which sought to argue that the development in question falls outside of the charge to UK tax, under the pre-Finance Act 2016 rules.

Taxation of transactions in UK land: the Finance Act 2016 rules

Trading in UK land by a non-resident: specific tax charge

[13.2] Under the amended CTA 2009, s 5 (for the purposes of corporation tax) and the amended ITTOIA 2005, s 6 (for the purposes of income tax) a specific charge to UK tax will arise in the event that a non-resident carries on a trade of dealing in or developing UK land – these are entirely new and distinct provisions that now provide for a specific charge to UK tax in respect of trading profits arising from UK land irrespective of the territorial status of that non-resident. For ease of explanation, this chapter will look at the new position under corporation tax rules (though this position will be the same under the income tax rules).

Prior to Finance Act 2016 (FA 2016), a non-resident company which carries on a trade in UK land was only within the charge to UK corporation tax on a territorial basis – notably to the extent that it carried on a trade in the UK through a permanent establishment (PE) situated in the UK, and that profits were attributable to this UK PE. In HMRC's view, this legislative approach allowed some developers to argue that they are able to use offshore structures which operated within the context of these rules. Although in this au-thor's view, it would be difficult in practice to avoid creating a UK PE in respect of a construction project at a UK land site (particularly since the introduction of the General Anti-Avoidance Rules and Diverted Profits Tax rules), there has been much tax planning which relied upon a non-resident company being resident in a jurisdiction which had a double taxation agreement ('DTA') that contains a definition of PE that does not explicitly include a building site (notably, this was ostensibly the case in relation to the UK's DTAs with the Crown dependencies of Jersey, Guernsey and the Isle of Man until these treaties were amended in order to align them with the OECD Model Treaty in March 2016).

Under the new CTA 2009, s 5(2), a non-UK resident company is within the charge to corporation tax (in two circumstances) if:

(a)   it carries on a trade of dealing or developing UK land (as defined in the new CTA 2009, s 5B), or

(b)   it carries on a trade in the UK (other than a trade of dealing in or developing UK land) through a permanent establishment in the UK.

Since the legislative changes made by FA 2016, it is no longer necessary for a non-UK company to have a UK PE in order to be within the charge to corporation tax in each case where that company carries on a trade of dealing in or developing UK land ('UK property trade' for the purposes of this chapter and which meaning is discussed below). Instead under CTA 2009, s 5(2)(a) ('Non-Resident Trading in Land Tax Charge' for the purposes of this chapter) it is merely sufficient that such a non-resident is carrying on such a UK property trade in order for the Non-Resident Trading in Land Tax Charge to bite. This means that it is no longer necessary to prove a UK territorial presence for a non-resident company which carries on a UK property trade (previously because such a non-resident company carries on a UK property trade through a UK PE or because such a company is tax resident in the UK, under the long-established 'central management and control' test). As a consequence of this new focus on the existence of a UK property trade as the determinant factor, a new CTA 2009, s 5(2A) is incorporated and which provides that where a non-resident company which carries on UK property trade then in this case, such a non-resident company is chargeable to corporation tax on all of its profits wherever arising that are profits of the trade.

This new emphasis on the existence of a UK property trade as being the determinant test as to whether a non-resident company is within the charge to corporation tax raises two important tax law considerations – firstly, the crucial 'dealing versus investment' test (as discussed in **CHAPTER 2**), ie whether the land in question is acquired with a view to be developed for a profit on disposal or whether it is acquired for investment purposes (notably, to generate a rental income) as this would determine the existence of a UK property trade. Interestingly, the draft HMRC Guidance (at page 10) focuses on a list of factors which may determine the existence of a UK property trade but does not properly recognise the primary factor of the motive or intention of acquisition (again, as discussed in **CHAPTER 2**). In this author's view, the importance of ensuring that the intention at acquisition of a UK property is properly evidenced at the outset is magnified because of these new rules (including the new and very wide 'transaction in land' anti-avoidance rules, discussed below). Secondly, it may be necessary to consider long-established tax law principles (notably under the 'badges of trade' principles) to determine whether a particular business venture is in the nature of trade. A discussion of these tax principles are outside of the subject-matter of this chapter but, in the author's view, the existence of a UK property trade should be self-evident but nonetheless, these principles remain as a valid test in determining the existence of a trade, particularly in borderline cases.

Otherwise, CTA 2009, s 5(2)(b) preserves the cardinal international law principles of requiring a UK PE (in respect of a non-resident company which carries on a non-property trade in the UK) as a requirement of that non-resident being within the charge to corporation tax.

In summary, the Non-Resident Trading in Land Tax Charge imposes a specific charge to corporation tax on a non-resident company which carries on a UK property trade, and which together with CTA 2009, s 5(2A) applies the specific tax charge to catch all profits of the UK property trade, irrespective that it may not have a UK PE (for example, by virtue of being resident in a jurisdiction with a suitably formulated DTA, which was the fulcrum of many previous planning techniques that sought to remove the charge to UK corporation tax from applying).

Example 1

> Overseas PropCo is not resident in the UK and is resident in a jurisdiction which has a DTA which contains a definition of PE that does not explicitly include a building site. It purchases a block of flats to develop and sell in Manchester. Under CTA 2009, s 5(2A), Overseas PropCo is within the charge to corporation tax, and all profits from the trade of developing UK land will be subject to corporation tax.

The equivalent income tax rules are set out in ITTOIA 2005, s 6(1A).

Specific tax charge: targeted anti-avoidance rule ('TAAR')

[13.3] Under FA 2016, a new CTA 2009, s 5A is incorporated, and which is an anti-avoidance provision that is intended to counter arrangements designed to avoid profits being brought within the charge to corporation tax by virtue of the new Non-Resident Trading in Land Tax Charge. The framing of this TAAR is in line with the usual HMRC approach – it states that the TAAR rule applies if a company has entered into an arrangement the main purposes or one of the main purposes of which is to obtain a relevant tax advantage for the company, which is then defined (under CTA 2009, s 5A(5)) as being a tax advantage in relation to tax chargeable by virtue of the tax charge at CTA 2009, s 5(2A). The TAAR at CTA 2009, s 5A(5) also incorporates other familiar anti-avoidance provisions – for example, the tax advantage is to be counteracted by means of adjustment by way of assessment, the modification of an assessment, amendment or disallowance of a claim, or otherwise whether by HMRC or by the company (CTA 2009, ss 5A(3) and 5A(4)).

Where this TAAR is distinct in its definition of a tax advantage, which is extended to include obtaining tax advantage through exploiting a double taxation agreement, where that advantage is contrary to the objects and purposes of the provisions of the treaty (CTA 2009, s 5A(2)). It is well-established under UK law that the terms of a tax treaty takes precedence over domestic tax law (and the TAAR appears to recognise by virtue of the carve-out for 'legitimate' treaty planning) nonetheless, in this author's view, the existence of these new provisions means that careful consideration is required in cases where there may be a conflict between the provisions of a treaty (which may permit relief from UK tax law) and the Non-Resident Trading in Land Tax Charge.

The equivalent income tax rules are set out in ITTOIA 2005, s 6A(2).

Specific tax charge: meaning of a UK property trade

[13.4] Under FA 2016, a new s 5B sets out the meaning of a UK property trade in relation to non-UK companies. For the purposes of these provisions, the meaning of 'land' is defined to include buildings and structures, any estate, interest or right in or over land and land under the sea or otherwise covered by water (CTA 2009, s 5B(3)).

In essence, a non-resident company is treated as carrying on a UK Property Trade in two circumstances:

(a) if the non-resident company's activities consist of dealing in UK land or developing UK land for the purpose of disposing of it (CTA 2009, s 5B(1)(a) and (2)). Clearly, whether any such activities are caught will usually be determined on a factual basis but again, it is crucial to note that the intention of the non-resident company may be a critical issue, and which should be assessed in accordance with the long-established 'investment versus dealing' legal principles (as discussed in **CHAPTER 2**); or

(b) if the non-resident company's activities are caught by the new anti-avoidance regime governing 'transactions in UK land', as set out in CTA 2010, Part 8ZB (and as discussed below).

Transactions in UK land: anti-avoidance regime

[13.5] As part of the FA 2016 legislative changes which introduced the Non-Resident Trading in Land Tax Charge (as discussed above), the long-standing 'transaction in land' rules in CTA 2010, Part 18 ('pre-FA 2016 Transactions in Land rules' for the purposes of this chapter) were entirely replaced by a new set of anti-avoidance rules, as set out in CTA 2010, Part 8ZB ('FA 2016 Transactions in UK Land Regime' for the purposes of this chapter). In essence, it can be said that the objective of the FA 2016 Transactions in UK Land Regime is to prescribe the treatment of certain transactions which are then deemed to give rise to profits of a UK property trade.

Although some key elements of the pre-FA 2016 Transactions in Land rules have been maintained (with a view of preserving the long-established tax rules which seek to ensure that certain transactions involving UK land and which are structured to give rise to capital gains can be transformed into income profits although the new rules have been extended to catch profits, which is necessary in order to recognise the emphasis on the taxation of a UK property trade), the FA 2016 Transactions in UK Land Regime significantly expands the anti-avoidance rules and covers four areas:

(a)   It sets out certain prescribed transactions covering a disposal of UK land whereby the disposal proceeds are deemed to be profits of a UK property trade. In essence, these rules are derived from the pre-FA 2016 Transactions in Land rules but have also been extended in their ambit.

(b)   It sets out certain property disposal transactions which derive their value from UK land and whereby the disposal proceeds are deemed to be profits of a UK property trade. Again in essence, these rules are derived from the pre-FA 2016 Transactions in Land rules but have also been significantly recalibrated.

(c)   An entirely new 'anti-fragmentation' rule which seeks to prevent profits from being fragmented between associate parties, and which seeks to ensure that those fragmented profits are reconsolidated and charged to UK tax as trading profits of a UK property trade. In the author's view, this is the most radical development under the FA 2016 Transactions in UK Land Regime as it would appear to fiscally invalidate the tax position of associated parties, which may have a valid role in participating in UK real estate development projects. It also raises important legal questions as to whether this new regime is intended to run in tandem with the existing UK and OECD transfer pricing rules, the GAAR rules and the Divided Profits Tax Rules (if this is the case then there are serious legislative inconsistencies) or is intended to be a 'stand-alone' regime which exclusively governs UK property trade transactions (again if this is the case then there are serious legislative inconsistencies which are likely to create great uncertainty in the sector and which will require legislative configuration that provides greater consistency).

(d)   A new TAAR which applies in respect of the FA 2016 Transactions in UK Land Regime.

The new regime does not state the purpose of CTA 2010, Part 8ZB is for preventing the avoidance of corporation tax by companies concerned with land or the development of land, unlike the pre-FA 2016 Transactions in Land rules (at CTA 2010, s 815(1)).

Unlike the pre-FA 2016 Transactions in Land rules, the FA 2016 Transactions in UK Land Regime does not provide for a statutory clearance procedure. Given the breadth of the new rules (and the ambiguities created by some of its provisions) and given too that no statutory clearance procedure is available, it is the author's view that careful consideration is therefore required in cases where a real estate development project may appear to run counter to the new regime.

Again for ease of explanation, this chapter will look at the new regime in respect of the corporation tax rules (though this position will be the same under the income tax rules). The equivalent income tax rules are set out in the new ITA 2007, Part 9A.

The pre-FA 2016 rules

[13.6] In understanding the FA 2016 Transactions in UK Land Regime (in terms of statutory interpretation, particularly in areas where there is ambiguity on the ambit of the new regime), it is also useful to have a broad understanding of the old regime.

The pre-FA 2016 Transactions in Land rules were first introduced in 1969 and were very broadly framed tax rules which sought to re-characterise capital gains into income in relation to certain prescribed transactions involving the disposal of land. In brief terms, the pre-FA 2016 Transactions in Land rules would substitute income treatment instead of a gain of a capital nature, where that gain was obtained from the disposal of UK land and where any of four conditions ('CTA 2009, s 189 conditions') are satisfied. The conditions in CTA 2009, s 819 generally required that the sole or main objective of the transactions in question is to realise a gain from a disposal of the land in question.

Also, although case law (notably, *Page (Inspector of Taxes) v Lowther* [1983] STC 799, 57 TC 199 held that a tax avoidance purpose was not a condition precedent to the application of the old rules, the old rules did state the purpose of the rules were for the preventing of the avoidance of corporation tax by companies concerned with land or the development of land (at CTA 2010, s 815(1)). In contrast, there is no such statement in the FA 2016 Transactions in UK Land Regime, which would immediately suggest that the new regime should immediately apply once the requisite conditions are satisfied.

Where any of the CTA 2009, s 819 conditions are satisfied then the gain realised from the disposal of the UK land in question would be treated as income when the gain is realised and would be charged as miscellaneous income for income tax purposes (for individuals) or for corporation tax purposes (for companies) on the full amount of income treated as arising.

Disposals of UK land: profits treated as trading profits

[13.7] The FA 2016 Transactions in UK Land Regime applies a specific tax charge (at CTA 2010, s 356OC) which brings profits and gains within the meaning of profits of a property trade ('s 356OC deemed trading profits' for the purposes of this chapter) provided that certain conditions (as set out in CTA 2010, s 356OB) are satisfied ('s 356OB conditions' for the purposes of this chapter). Although the s 356OB conditions are broadly similar to CTA 2009, s 819 conditions, there are important legislative differences which are intended to broaden the scope of the long-standing tax re-characterisation charge, notably to catch all profits (and not merely capital gains, as was the case under the pre-FA 2016 Transactions in Land rules) arising from the prescribed transaction. Moreover, references to profits and gains include a loss (CTA 2010, s 356G).

In broad terms, the s 356OB conditions are satisfied where a 'person' realises a profit or gain from a 'disposal' of land in the UK and where any of 'Conditions A to D' are met in relation to the land. Where the s 356OB conditions are satisfied, then the s 356OC will operate and the deemed trading profits will be attributed to the chargeable company in question, which is generally the company which has realised the profit or gain on the disposal of the land in question (CTA 2010, s 356OG).

The key terms of s 356OB are summarised as follows.

Person

[13.8] The meaning of person (as defined in s 356OB(2)) is largely identical to the old rules, and is defined as:

(a)   the person acquiring, holding or developing the land;

(b)   a person who is associated (which meaning is derived from the established 'connected persons' tests at CTA 2010, ss 1122 and 1123) with the person at paragraph (a) at the relevant time. For the purpose of these rules, the 'relevant time' means any time in the period beginning when the activities of the project begins and ending six months after the disposal (s 356OB(8)). A 'project' is then defined to mean all activities carried out for dealing or developing land or for the purposes of Conditions A to D; and

(c)   a person who is a party to or concerned in, an arrangement which (as with the old rules) is very broadly defined to catch any arrangement which is effected in respect of the land and which enables a profit or a gain to be realised by any indirect method or by any series of transactions.

Conditions A to D

[13.9] The conditions also largely reiterate CTA 2009, s 819 conditions, except that the s 356OB conditions import the 'main purpose or one of the main purposes' test (instead of relying upon the 'sole or main objective' test that applied under the old rules). The conditions are as follows.

(1)   Condition A: the main purpose or one of the main purposes of acquiring the land was to realise a profit or gain from disposing of the land.

(2)   Condition B: the main purpose or one of the main purposes of acquiring any property deriving is value from the land was to realise a profit or gain from disposing of the land.

(3)   Condition C: the land is held as trading stock.

(4)   Condition D: (where the land has been developed) the main purpose or one of the main purposes of developing the land was to realise a profit or gain from disposing of the land.

The main purpose or one of the main purposes test

[13.10] As described above, the s 356OB conditions import the 'main purpose or one of the main purposes' test (instead of relying upon the 'sole or main objective' test that applied under the old rules). Although a discussion of the tax law principles related to the 'main purpose' test is not within the remit of this chapter, these principles will be key in determining whether this test is satisfied for the purposes of any transactions which may fall within the relevant provisions of FA 2016 Transactions in UK Land Regime. The 'main purpose' test is well rooted in UK tax legislation, and has been the subject of much case law –Lightman J's judgment in *IRC v Trustees of Sema Group Pension Scheme* [2002] EWCA Civ 1857, [2003] STC 95, 74 TC 593 remains pertinent – notably that the making of a tax saving will not necessarily be one of the main objects of a transaction merely because it is a relevant feature in the decision to proceed. In other words, the non-tax reasons why a transaction is structured in a way which may run foul of the FA 2016 Transactions in UK Land Regime will clearly have a factual bearing for the purposes of the 'main purpose' test.

According to the draft HMRC Guidance, a person may have more than one main purpose in entering into a transaction, and 'a main purpose' is a wider test than requiring something to be 'the main purpose'. The draft HMRC Guidance then goes on to state that it is therefore important to consider the question of trading alongside the main purpose test when considering whether or not this legislation applies, to ensure that what are genuinely non-trading transactions are not brought within its scope. The draft HMRC Guidance then provides the following examples which are highly illustrative of the intended HMRC approach.

Example 2

A non-resident property investor purchases a property with the primary purpose of realising rental income from the land purchased. When the investor purchased the land one of the factors they considered was likely capital appreciation of the land. After letting out the property for seven years they make some repairs and dispose of the land. This is an example of an investment not trading transaction. The main purpose of the transaction is the rental income. Whilst the long-term capital appreciation could be a main purpose, it is clearly not a profit from a disguised trading transaction and would not therefore meet Condition A.

Example 3

A non-resident property investor purchases a property with the intention of developing then selling the property. After developing the property they let it out for six months while they wait for the market to pick up. In this instance a main purpose of acquiring the land was to realise a profit from disposing of the land and Condition A would be met.

Example 4

An individual property investor acquires an old block of flats. They rent the flats out for several years then decide to build new flats on the site. They obtain planning permission for a new development which they complete and sell.

In this example there has been a change of intention and CTA 2010, s 3560L will apply. Only the profit relating to the period after the change of intention should be taxed as a trading profit. The portion relating to the period where there was an investment intention should not be included in the tax calculation.

Disposals of property deriving its value from UK land: profits treated as trading profits

[13.11] Under the pre-FA 2016 Transactions in Land rules, a very broad 'anti-enveloping' rule had existed for many decades. In broad terms, it has been long-established that an anti-enveloping rule is required as it is possible to realise profits from a disposal of properties that derives its value from land rather than the land itself. For this reason, these types of transactions are known as 'enveloping'. The intention of those rules is to ensure that the correct amount of tax is paid where land is disposed of in any form of 'envelope'.

FA 2016 Transactions in UK Land Regime imposes similar anti-enveloping provisions (under CTA 2010, s 356OE) but only applies where (directly or indirectly) more than 50% of the value of the property is disposed, which a welcome development as it brings greater certainty by introducing this threshold test.

In essence, this applies in cases where a profit or gain is realised from a disposal of any property which derives its value from UK land provided that the conditions set out in CTA 2010, s 356OD are satisfied ('section 356OE deemed trading profits' for the purposes of this chapter).

CTA 2010, s 356OD applies to a situation where:

(a)   a person realises a profit or a gain from a disposal of any property (which includes any asset) and which (at the time of disposal) derives at least 50% of its value from UK land,

(b)   where that person is a party to (or is concerned) in an arrangement concerning the land ('project land'), and

(c)   where the arrangement meets a specified condition.

Under CTA 2010, s 356OD(2), the specified condition is that the main purpose or one of the main purposes of the arrangement is to deal in or develop the project land and to realise a profit or gain from the disposal. Under CTA 2010, s 356OR(2), the term 'property deriving its value' is defined (on a non-exhaustive basis) to include any shares, partnership interests or interests in settled property which derives its value directly or indirectly from UK land. It also includes any option, consent or embargo which affects the disposition of land. As such it applies to any asset which derives its value (directly or indirectly) from UK land.

Where the conditions of CTA 2010, s 356OD are satisfied then s 356OE will treat the proportion of the profit or gain attributable to the UK land for corporation tax as the profits of a UK property trade carried on by the chargeable company. Again, this will generally be the company which has realised the profit or gain on the disposal of the land in question (CTA 2010, s 356OG).

The meaning of 'disposal'

[13.12] The pre-FA 2016 Transactions in Land rules did not specifically define the meaning of 'disposal' but did define a disposal of land as including where control of the land is effectively disposed. In contrast, the new rules provide a definition of 'disposal' (at CTA 2010, s 356OQ) – in broad terms, this states that a disposal of land or property deriving its value of land can be through one or more transactions or by any arrangement, and it includes a part disposal. This specific reference to part-disposal (with no legislative measures to limit a disposal to only where there is a change of control, as was the case under the old rules) raises interesting questions as to how far a part-disposal of an asset which derives its value from UK land may trigger s 356OE deemed trading profits. From the Technical Paper, it is clear (at page 13) that the extended meaning of disposal is deliberate in order to potentially widen the scope of the new regime.

In addition to the general meaning given to 'land' (which is the same as CTA 2009, s 5B(3) definition mentioned earlier in this chapter), property deriving its value from land is widely defined under CTA 2010, s 356OR.

The examples provided by the draft HMRC Guidance (and which are set out below) are very helpful as these illustrate HMRC's thinking as to how it intends this rule should operate.

Example 5

Company X owns 100% of Company Y. Company Y purchases a piece of UK land and carries out the development of a block of flats. Company Y has no other substantial assets so over 50% of the company's value relates to the land. The intention of Company X is for Company Y to develop the land and to dispose of their shares in Company Y when the land is developed. When the development is completed Company X sells the shares in Company Y to a third party.

In this example the disposal meets the criteria and the disposal is a disposal of property deriving its value from land. The profits should be treated as trading profits of Company X.

Example 6

A company disposes of their shareholding in a property development company. The shares were purchased with the intention of making a profit from dealing in the land. The shares are worth £10m, £6m of the value relates to a block of flats based in the UK and £4m to a housing development outside the UK. In this instance, and assuming that the acquisition costs of the shares is nil, the block of flats is the relevant UK asset and the relevant amount is £6m. If consideration paid for the shares were £5m, and 60% of that cost related to the UK development, the relevant amount would be £3m (£6m less 60% of £5m).

Example 7

An individual purchases shares in a property development company which is developing a large housing estate. The shares were valued at £10m and the value is derived entirely from UK Land. The individual purchased the shares with the intention of disposing of 40% of their shares after the properties have been developed. They intend to hold on to the remaining 60% for the capital appreciation. In this instance the relevant UK assets are the £4m of shares. The remaining £6m are investment assets, and not subject to the new legislation.

Anti-fragmentation rules

[13.13] The FA 2016 Transactions in UK Land Regime introduces an entirely new and very broad anti-avoidance rule (at CTA 2010, s 356OH) which are aimed at preventing profits arising from the development of UK land or any activities which contribute to a profit or gain from the disposal of UK land) being fragmented between associated parties ('Anti-Fragmentation Rules' for the purposes of this chapter). In the Technical Paper, it appeared that the objective is to counter planning techniques which aim to place those profits outside the charge to corporation tax, for example by moving some or all of the profits to a person not carrying on a trade of dealing in developing land in the UK. However as will be seen, the Anti-Fragmentation Rules are usually broad, and will catch all associated party transactions (other than those with an insignificant value) notwithstanding that those transactions may have bona fide commercial reasons.

The Anti-Fragmentation Rules apply where all of the following conditions are met:

(a)   a company ('C') disposes of UK land,
(b)   any of the Conditions A to D of the s 356OB conditions are satisfied, and
(c)   a person ('R') who is associated with P at a 'relevant time' has made a 'relevant contribution' to any of the following activities: (i) the development of the land or (ii) any other activities directed towards realising a profit or gain from the disposal of the land.

Under the Anti-Fragmentation Rules, C and R will be considered as though they are the same person. In effect, this means that any profit or gain realised by C will be treated as if C and R were one person (CTA 2010, s 356OH(3)). In fiscal terms, this means that any profits accruing to R (by virtue of its relevant contributions) will be attributed to C for the purposes of determining its profits realised from the UK property trade in question. Section 356OI then sets out that any profit or gain arising from the application of the Anti-Fragmentation Rules shall be calculated using the rules for the computation of trading profits (in CTA 2009, Part 3).

Under CTA 2010, s 356OH(7), any 'contribution' made by R to the activities is a 'relevant contribution' unless the profits made as a result of the contribution are insignificant when considered in relation to the size of the 'project'. The definition of a 'contribution' (at CTA 2010, s 356OH(8)) is very wide and is non-exhaustive and includes, for example, professional and other services and a financial contribution (including the assumption of risk). Under CTA 2010, 356OH(10), a 'project' is defined as all activities carried out for the purposes of a UK property trade and other purposes mentioned in Conditions A to D of the s 356OB conditions.

The draft HMRC Guidance explains (at page 27) that a contribution is likely to be significant if it is a 'Low Value Added Service' ('LVAS') and where the payment is no more than 5% of the costs of the project. It then states that a LVAS is a service which is:

- supportive in nature;
- does not require the use of unique and valuable intangibles and does not lead to the creation of such intangibles; and
- does not involve the assumption of control of substantial or significant risk and does not give rise to the creation of significant risk (or value).

In the author's view, the introduction of the Anti-Fragmentation Rules appears to introduce a 'stand-alone' version of the Diverted Profits Tax regime in respect of projects related to UK property trade but which appears to be independent of the Diverted Profits Tax regime, the UK transfer pricing regime and the GAAR rules but without setting a qualitative threshold in the same way that these other regimes have done – for example, the economic substance test, the arm's length test and the reasonableness test respectively. It also does not establish a 'main purpose' test (in contrast with other parts of the new rules). For this reason, the Anti-Fragmentation Rules are likely to impose much uncertainty on the real estate development sector. For example, it is likely to create much doubt on the role of non-UK associated participants who properly provide non-LVAS activities to the project for bona fide commercial reasons.

The examples provided in the draft HMRC Guidance are again illustrative. Indeed, Example 9 may also be illustrative of how bona fide non-UK associated participants who provide non-LVAS activities to the project for bona fide commercial reasons may be affected.

Example 8

Company X carries on a trade of dealing or developing UK land. It receives admin services from a group company and pays a mark-up of 2% on the costs. In this instance, the contribution would be regarded as insignificant and would the anti-fragmentation rules would not apply.

Example 9

Company Y carries on a trade of dealing or developing UK land. A group company (Company Z) designs all of the buildings. Company Y pays Company Z 10% of the profits for the architectural services. In this instance, the contribution would not be regarded as insignificant and the anti-fragmentation rules apply.

Transactions in land: targeted anti-avoidance rule ('TAAR')

[13.14] The FA 2016 Transactions in UK Land Regime introduces a 'TAAR' which applies if the company enters into arrangements where the main purpose or one of the main purposes is to avoid a 'relevant tax advantage', which is defined as a tax advantage in relation to tax chargeable as a result of applying the provisions of Part 8ZB. Again (as discussed above), the key legislative test here will be the main purpose test as measured against the facts of the transaction.

In its Technical Paper, HMRC provides a fascinating example as to the ambit of this TAAR, which provides an insight into HMRC's views – non-resident U acquires shares in Company X, which is free of debt and which holds land. U develops the land – at the end of which the value of the land is 100. U makes a capital contribution of 110 so that less than 50% of the value of the shares in Company X is derived from land. When the shares are sold for 210, the TAAR will negate the tax advantage by recognising an indirect sale for 100. In the author's view, this arrangement is likely to be in breach of the GAAR rules (as discussed below), which again raises questions as to how the various anti-avoidance regimes will operate.

Transactions in land: supplementary provisions

[13.15] Key supplementary provisions include:

Calculations of profits

[13.16] Under CTA 2010, s 356OI the profits or gains which arises from the application of Part 8ZB are to be calculated using the rules for the computation of trading profits in CTA 2009, Part 3, subject to any modifications which may be appropriate.

'Change of intention' exemption

[13.17] Helpfully, there is a limited exemption (which also existed under pre-FA 2016 Rules that applies to certain prescribed situations where some of the gain may be attributable to a period before the intention to develop the land was formed (CTA 2010, s 356OL)). Under this provision, only the profits relating to the period where the intention is to make a gain would fall within Part 8ZB (under either of the s 356OC deemed trading profits provision or the s 356OE deemed trading profits).

Tracing Value Rules

[13.18] In order to determine the extent to which a value of any property or right is derived from any other property or right, there is a rule (at CTA 2010, s 356OM) which states that value may be traced through any number of companies, partnerships or trusts. Under this rule, property should then be attributed to the shareholders, beneficiaries or partners in whatever way is appropriate in the circumstances.

Conclusion: when to watch out

[13.19] By way of conclusion, typical circumstances where the anti-avoidance provisions may apply include:

(1)
- any development project where there are several associated parties providing contributions to the project;
- any arrangements which are undertaken with a view to obtaining a tax advantage under the anti-avoidance rules;
- long-term investor developing land with a view to selling at a profit;

(2) a sale of shares in a land-dealing company;

(3) a sale of shares in a land-investment company, those shares having originally been acquired for resale;

(4) land-trading profits that are treaty protected, but in respect of which a person has presented the opportunity for making the gain to the trader (eg an overseas company in Jersey);

(5) a gift under which a transfer (for example, a transfer by X Ltd to its subsidiary for nothing) may not in reality be a gift (enhanced share value). See also 'gifting' schemes described above;

(6) a gift by Mr X to his overseas trust, which onward sells at a gain, of land acquired for developing;

(7) a gain made on a share sale that is treaty protected but in respect of which HMRC may give a notice for tax to be deducted at source;

(8) a sale to a developer by a charity (ie a long-term investor) which takes an equity slice in the development profit;

(9) a sale of land by an investor following quickly on its acquisition, where there is insufficient evidence to show that he did not intend to obtain a gain from its disposal;

(10) the granting of put and call options so that the land is 'effectively' sold; or

(11) a sale of shares in a company (X Ltd) on terms that there is further share sale consideration payable which is determined by the profits made on disposals of developed property by X Ltd (eg flats are developed by X Ltd after the sale of shares and sold to purchasers).

Other anti-avoidance measures

Introduction

[13.20] This part of the chapter outlines measures whose application is not restricted to land transactions and which are available to HMRC to attack what they consider to be artificial schemes and arrangements designed to avoid tax.

A: General Anti-Abuse Rule

Introduction

[13.21] Under FA 2013, Pt 5 and Sch 43, the General Anti-Abuse Rule (GAAR) became law on 17 July 2013. With the introduction of the GAAR, there is now, for the first time in the UK, a general rule of law that applies to most UK taxes (with the notable exception of VAT) that will seek to counteract any tax advantages arising from tax arrangements that are abusive in their purpose. By introducing this general legal rule, the GAAR represents a significant expansion in HMRC's anti-avoidance.

By way of background, the GAAR was introduced following a detailed but short consultation programme which began with a study group of tax experts (led by Graham Aaronson QC). That study group was instructed by the government in December 2010 to consider whether there should be a general anti-avoidance rule for the UK. In its report of 21 November 2011 (Study Group Report), the study group recommended that a narrowly focused general anti-avoidance rule targeted at abusive tax avoidance schemes should be introduced into the UK tax system. In the 2012 Budget, the Government announced that it accepted the broad recommendations of the Study Group Report.

The GAAR legislation in FA 2013 is largely based upon the principles developed in the Study Group Report but with some material differences. In particular, the GAAR legislation has not adopted the Study Group Report's recommendation that there should be specific legislative exemptions for 'reasonable tax planning' arrangements nor does it provide for any mechanism for statutory clearances.

The GAAR applies to income tax, capital gains tax, inheritance tax, corporation tax, petroleum revenue tax, stamp duty land tax and the annual tax on enveloped dwellings. It is also intended that the GAAR will be extended to cover national insurance contributions (which will require separate legislation). The GAAR will not extend to VAT because of the potentially difficult interactions with the EU doctrine of abuse of law.

The burden of proof falls on HMRC which must show that the tax arrangements in question are abusive.

A unique feature of the GAAR is that its operations will, in effect, be overseen by an independent advisory panel (GAAR Advisory Panel), which will be composed of noted tax practitioners but which will be established by the Commissioners. In particular, the GAAR Advisory Panel is required to approve of any HMRC guidance issued in respect of the GAAR, and is required to deliver opinions on any counteraction notices. In addition, a court or tribunal is required to take into account any opinions of the GAAR Advisory Panel in determining any issue in connection with the GAAR. This aspect of the GAAR has caused some concern as it would appear that the judiciary would be obliged to consider the opinions of an HMRC appointed body but in light of the established constitutional and juridicial principles of statutory interpretation, this aspect should be considered as persuasive authority.

Another unique feature of the GAAR is that its rules are intended to be covered by much detailed guidance (GAAR Guidance). Although the GAAR Guidance will not have legislative effect, the legislation specifically provides that a court or tribunal must take into account any GAAR Guidance in determining any issue in connection with the GAAR. As noted above, it is required that the GAAR Guidance is approved by the GAAR Advisory Panel. Again the same concerns apply here as it requires a court to consider the published views of a government appointed panel but in this author's view, this aspect should be considered as persuasive authority by virtue of the established constitutional and juridicial principles of statutory interpretation.

The GAAR Guidance is stated to have two main objectives. The first object is to give (in layperson's language) a broad summary of what the GAAR is designed to achieve, and how the GAAR is intended to operate so as to achieve this objective. The second objective is to be an aid to the interpretation and application of the GAAR by providing further detailed discussions of its purpose, to consider particular features of the GAAR and, where appropriate, illustrate that discussion by means of examples.

The GAAR Guidance is divided into five parts (Parts A to E). To date, Parts A to D have been approved by the GAAR Advisory Panel.

The GAAR Rules

[13.22] In broad terms, the stated purpose of GAAR is intended to counteract 'tax advantages' which arise from 'tax arrangements' that are 'abusive' (FA 2013, s 206(1)). From a UK tax law viewpoint, many of these terms are immediately recognisable to a practitioner. However, the term, 'abusive', is a new concept to UK direct taxation principles but on a closer analysis, it can be seen that many of its principles appeared to be derived from case law.

In assessing its impact, the GAAR can be broken down into two constituent limbs. In broad terms, the first limb looks to see whether the main purpose of a transaction can be treated as a tax arrangement which is intended to obtain a tax advantage. Under the second limb, the test is then to ascertain whether the tax arrangement in question should be regarded as abusive for the purposes of the GAAR.

The first limb

[13.23] It can be said that the first limb (which incorporates the two very familiar concepts, 'tax arrangements' and 'tax advantage') constitutes the first filter in determining whether the GAAR applies. In particular, FA 2013, s 207(1) states:

> "Arrangements are 'tax arrangements' if, having regard to all of the circumstances, it would be reasonable to conclude that the obtaining of a tax advantage was the main purpose, or one of the main purposes of the arrangements".

'Arrangements' (as defined in FA 2013, s 214) is a long-standing tax definition which includes any agreement, understanding, scheme, transaction or series of transactions (whether or not legally enforceable).

Any arrangements would then be treated as 'tax arrangements' if, having regard to all the circumstances, it would be reasonable to conclude that the obtaining of a tax advantage was the main purpose or one of the main purposes of the arrangements. Again, this is a familiar term which is used in other statutory anti-avoidance provisions (for example, under TCGA 1992, s 137).

The GAAR legislation similarly provides a very broad definition to the meaning of 'tax advantage' (as defined in FA 2013, s 208) – for example, this would include obtaining a relief or increased relief from tax, an avoidance or a reduction of a charge to tax and so on.

In other words, the first limb sets out some familiar hoops to a tax adviser in determining whether 'tax arrangements' are in existence.

According to the HMRC GAAR Guidance, the first limb (which is determined by the 'tax arrangements' test) is widely drawn and deliberately sets a low threshold for initially considering the possible application of the GAAR.

Once a transaction is caught under the first limb, it must then be considered whether it is caught by the second limb. If it is so caught, then the transaction will be subject to the GAAR.

The second limb

[13.24] The novelty of the GAAR lies in the deliberate use of the term, 'abusive', which is then defined by reference to the classic legal test of 'reasonableness' – in particular, a tax arrangement is 'abusive' (as defined in FA 2013, s 207(2)) if, 'they are arrangements the entering into or carrying out of which cannot reasonably be regarded as a reasonable course of action in relation to the relevant tax provisions, having regard to all the circumstances'.

This is commonly referred to as the 'double reasonableness' test. Under the GAAR Guidance, this test (and in particular, its emphasis on 'cannot reasonably be regarded') is the crux of the GAAR test. According to the GAAR Guidance (at paragraph C5.10.1), the test does not ask whether entering into or carrying out the arrangements was a reasonable course of action in relation to the relevant tax provisions. Instead the test asks whether there can be a reasonable held view that entering into or carrying out the tax arrangement in question was a reasonable course of action.

The GAAR legislation then (in FA 2013, s 207(2)(a)–(c)) provides examples of circumstances which should be considered in assessing the second limb. In the GAAR Guidance (at paragraph C5.4), these examples are combined together with the 'double reasonableness' test to formulate a number of key elements which are determinative of the second limb:

- The concept of a reasonable course of action in relation to the relevant tax provisions.
- Comparing the substantive results of the arrangements with the principles on which the relevant tax provisions are based, and with the policy objectives of those provisions.
- Seeing whether there are contrived or abnormal steps.
- Seeing whether the arrangements are intended to exploit any shortcomings in the relevant tax provisions.
- The 'double reasonableness' test – whether the arrangements cannot reasonably be regarded as a reasonable course of action.

It can be seen that these key elements are actually distilled from the case law which have developed under the *Ramsay* principle (as discussed below).

The GAAR legislation (at FA 2013, s 207(4)) then goes on to give three examples of circumstances that might indicate that tax arrangements are abusive. These are:

- The arrangements result in significantly less income, profits or gains being taken into account for tax purposes than the true economic amount.
- The arrangements result in significantly greater deductions or losses being taken into account for tax purposes than the true economic cost or loss.
- The arrangements result in a claim for the repayment or crediting of tax that had been, and is unlikely to be paid.

GAAR Guidance – Examples

[13.25] Part D of the GAAR Guidance sets out a series of examples whose purpose is to illustrate when an arrangement might or might not, applying the double reasonableness test, be treated as abusive in the context of the GAAR. Providing a detailed overview of Part D of the GAAR Guidance is outside of the scope of this chapter.

However, it is worthwhile to consider the breakdown of the categories of examples which is set out in Part D of the GAAR Guidance (at paragraph D of Part 1) as this categorisation is instructive of the thinking of the GAAR Advisory Panel in its approach to arrangements. At present, the examples are categorised as follows:

- Straightforward legislative choice – these arrangements are not abusive.
- Long established practice – these arrangements are not abusive.
- Situations in which the law deliberately sets precise rules or boundaries – these arrangements are not abusive unless artificial steps are introduced.
- Standard tax planning combined with some element of artificiality – whether these arrangements are abusive will depend on level of artificiality.
- Transactions that exploit a shortcoming in legislation the purpose of which is to close down a form of activity – abusive.
- Contrived or abnormal arrangements that produce a tax position that is inconsistent with the legal effect and economic substance of the underlying transaction – abusive.

Part D of the Guidance then goes on to look at specific examples of arrangements.

Other GAAR issues

[13.26] If tax arrangements are found to be abusive then the tax advantage must be counteracted on a 'just and reasonable' basis.

Finance Act 2013 Sch 43 sets out detailed procedural requirements which govern the GAAR, and which are too detailed to be discussed in this chapter. In broad terms, the procedures are designed to ensure that the GAAR is treated as a specific 'stand alone' body of law, with its own rules on administration etc.

In the July 2015 Budget, the Government confirmed that it would proceed with the introduction of a GAAR-related penalty, and that draft legislation for this penalty would be published in the 2015 Autumn Statement, which will also consider ways to further strengthen the GAAR. It is likely that any changes will be implemented in Finance Act 2016.

A codification of the *Ramsay* principle?

[13.27] Many commentators view the proposed 'double reasonableness' test as nebulous and highly subjective. It is, however, the view of this author that this new GAAR test based upon 'reasonableness' arguably represents the best compromise precisely because it avoids an overly prescriptive approach and because it is so rooted in juridical principles. Moreover, whilst there is a clear danger that the GAAR could become misused by HMRC, the legislative background of the GAAR should remain instructive – notably, HMRC (in its consultation) acknowledges that the GAAR should not affect 'the centre ground of tax planning' and is not aimed at introducing a 'broad spectrum' catch-all rule. Seen through the prism of the *Ramsay* principle, it is hoped that the courts will anchor any eventual GAAR legislation to this legislative purpose.

B: The Ramsay principle

[13.28] One weapon in HMRC's armoury used to target artificial transactions which are not shams (as they were in *Hitch v Stone (Inspector of Taxes)* [2001] EWCA Civ 63, [2001] STC 214, [2001] 09 LS Gaz R 40 is the principle of statutory interpretation derived from *W T Ramsay Ltd v IRC* [1982] AC 300, [1981] 1 All ER 865 [1981] STC 174, ('the *Ramsay* principle') and subsequent cases.

Although the *Ramsay* principle has been the subject of much juridical discussion, it is now recognised that the *Ramsay* case did not introduce a new doctrine operating within the special field of revenue principles but brought it within generally applicable principles of statutory interpretation (*Barclays Mercantile Business Finance Ltd v Mawson* [2005] STC 1 at 33). Instead, the essence of the *Ramsay* principle is to give to the statutory provision a purposive construction in order to determine the nature of the transaction in question to which it was intended to apply, and to decide whether the actual transaction (which might involve considering the overall effect of a number of elements intended to operate together) answered to the statutory description (see *Barclays Mercantile Business Finance Ltd* at 32).

The *Ramsay* principle has been considered and applied in numerous cases, including *Furniss (Inspector of Taxes) v Dawson* [1984] AC 474, [1984] 1 All ER 530, which held that a court was entitled to look at the end result of a series of transactions and apply the principles of statutory construction to the relevant tax statute to that end result, and *MacNiven (Inspector of Taxes) v Westmoreland Investments Ltd* [2001] UKHL 6, [2003] 1 AC 311, [2001] 1 All ER 865 which has had a controversial history but which established that when a court is searching for the meaning with which Parliament has used the statutory language in question then the court should have regard to the underlying purpose that the statutory language is seeking to achieve. More recently, the scope and application of the principle have been reconsidered and reformulated by the House of Lords in the cases of *Barclays Mercantile Business Finance Ltd v Mawson* (see above) (where the approach taken by the Special Commissioners in *Campbell v IRC* [2004] STC (SCD) 396 was praised), *IRC v Scottish Provident Institution* [2004] UKHL 52, [2005] 1 All ER 325, [2004] 1 WLR 3172 [2005] STC 14, *Tower MCashback LLP 1 and another v Revenue and Customs Comrs* [2011] UK SC 19, [2011] 3 All ER 171, [2011] STC 1143 and the Court of Appeal in *Mayes v Revenue and Customs Comrs* [2011] EWCA Civ 407, [2011] STC 1269. For recent examples where the taxpayers were unsuccessful, see *MacDonald (Inspector of Taxes) v Dextra Accessories Ltd* [2005] UKHL 47, [2005] 4 All ER 107,[2005] STC 1111 and *Trennery v West (Inspector of Taxes)* [2005] UKHL 5, 149 Sol Jo LB 147, [2005] STC 214.

The decision in *Campbell v IRC* (see above) is helpful in that it explains (in particular at paras 69 to 76) that the *Ramsay* principle has been applied in at least four different contexts, as follows:

(a)   to ascertain whether a series of self-cancelling, preordained transactions, effected solely to generate an allowable loss for CGT purposes, should be respected for the purposes of CGT legislation. The House of Lords held that they were not, even though the transactions were to be respected for the purposes of other statutes: *W T Ramsay Ltd v IRC* (see above) at 181, 190;

(b)   to ascertain the true parties and the true dealing in a transaction. So where the true dealing was between the taxpayer (Mr Dawson) and a particular purchaser, Wood Bastow Holdings Ltd, in that the sale of shares by Mr Dawson to Wood Bastow was a practical certainty, and inserted sale of the shares by Mr Dawson to a wholly owned creature company (Greenjacket Ltd) and a sale of those same shares by Greenjacket to Wood Bastow was ignored and the disposal treated as a disposal of the shares by Mr Dawson to Wood Bastow: *Furniss v Dawson* (see above) at 156 and 166–167. The test adopted by the House of Lords was that the inserted steps had to have an exclusive tax avoidance purpose and the ultimate transaction must be preordained before the inserted steps could be ignored;

(c)   to ascertain the true nature of a receipt in the hands of a taxpayer. So where a taxpayer, entitled to a dividend which has been declared, sells the right to that dividend to a third party for a sum which is funded by the very dividend payment itself, the receipt by the assignee is income, not capital, for the purposes of ICTA 1970, s 478: *IRC v McGuckian* [1994] STC 888, as explained by Lord Hoffmann in *Macniven v Westmoreland* (see above) at paras 51–57 and by Lord Millett in *Collector of Stamp Revenue v Arrowtown Assets* in the Court of Final Appeal of the Hong Kong Special Administrative Region (4 December 2003) '*Arrowtown*' at para 147; and

(d)   to ascertain the true nature of instruments issued solely for tax avoidance purposes. In *Arrowtown*, the question before the Hong Kong Court of Final Appeal was whether shares which carried deferred rights, where there was no right to a winding up and only a right to a dividend if the issuing company made profits greater than the Gross National Product of the United States, constituted 'issued share capital' for the purposes of Hong Kong stamp duty legislation which exempted transactions between companies which had a 90% shareholding relationship from stamp duty. The shares were issued solely to create an artificial relationship between companies in order to obtain the stamp duty relief. The court held that such 'shares' were not 'issued share capital' for stamp duty purposes, despite the fact that the shares were respected as being shares for Hong Kong company law purposes and that fact that the shares carried a valuable right to appoint a director (*Arrowtown* (above) at paras 152–157).

An exhaustive analysis of the application of the *Ramsay* principle is beyond the scope of this chapter but it is mentioned here because it can be invoked to attack transactions involving land (see, for example, *IRC v Bowater Property Developments Ltd* [1988] STC 476, one of four conjoined appeals including *Craven v White*).

An overview of the proposed UK general anti-avoidance rule is set out at **13.21** above. At first sight, it may appear that the *Ramsay* principle of a purposive approach in statutory interpretation will be superseded by this 'umbrella' new UK anti-avoidance rule, although it is likely that the courts will continue to play a central role in determining the parameters of the general anti-avoidance rule.

C: Abusive practice for VAT purposes

[13.29] VAT legislation in the UK (ie VATA 1994) implements a European Directive that has the objective of harmonising VAT systems across the European Union. As such, domestic legal concepts such as the *Ramsay* doctrine do not apply to VAT.

For many years aggressive VAT planning was implemented on the assumption that such arrangements would be tolerated by the Sixth VAT Directive (now the Principal VAT Directive). It was ultimately HMRC that litigated the issue, which led to the judgment of the ECJ in *Halifax and others v Commissioners of Customs & Excise* (Case C-255/02), which was handed down on 21 February 2006.

The facts of *Halifax* are complex, but essentially Halifax wanted to construct a number of call centres and would have been able to recover only 5% of any input tax incurred as a consequence. To mitigate this cost (which was around £7,000,000) it implemented a scheme which on the face of it enabled the input tax on the construction of the call centres to be recovered. HMRC disallowed the input tax claim in question, a decision which became the subject of the appeal.

Whilst stating at paragraph 73 that ' . . . taxpayers may choose to structure their business so as to limit their tax liability', the ECJ made it clear that this freedom is limited in principle and at para 69 of its judgment the ECJ set out a general abuse principle:

'The application of Community legislation cannot be extended to cover abusive practices by economic operators, that is to say transactions carried out not in the context of normal commercial operations, but solely for the purpose of wrongfully obtaining advantages provided for by Community law'.

The ECJ went on at paras 74 and 75 of its judgment to define what is meant by 'abusive practice' in this context and it introduced a two-limb test:

(i)   the transactions concerned result in the accrual of a tax advantage, contrary to the purpose of the Directive; and

(ii)   it must be apparent after taking into account objective factors that the essential aim of the transaction is to obtain a tax advantage.

The concept of an abusive practice has been refined and clarified by the ECJ post-*Halifax* in cases such as *Ministero dell'Economia e delle Finanze v Part Service Srl* (Case C-425/06 [2008] ECR I-897, [2008] STC 3132, ECJ), *The Commissioners for Her Majesty's Revenue & Customs v Weald Leasing Limited* (Case C-103/09) and *The Commissioners for Her Majesty's Revenue & Customs v RBS Deutschland Holdings GmbH* (Case C-277/09).

A detailed analysis of the development of the abusive practice test (with commentary on domestic case law) can be found in **CHAPTER 15** at **15.299** et seq.

D: Disclosure of tax avoidance scheme rules

[13.30] Provisions for the disclosure of tax avoidance schemes (the 'DOTAS' rules) have been introduced to tackle what HMRC and HM Treasury perceive as an unacceptable level of tax planning using artificial devices. The purpose of the provisions is to ensure that HMRC receive detailed information about tax avoidance schemes which take advantage of loopholes in legislation almost as soon as steps are taken to implement schemes, or shortly after schemes are proposed. This enables HMRC and the Treasury to block loopholes in the legislation much sooner than would otherwise have been the case (there can be a delay of up to two years between the implementation of a scheme and the filing of a tax return, which may or may not disclose sufficient details about a scheme to put HMRC on notice), or to challenge the schemes by technical argument and assessment where they do not consider the scheme to be technically sound. Building upon the success of the DOTAS regime and with an increased impetus on clamping down on perceived 'rogue' promoters, a new set of rules aimed at 'high risk promoters' was introduced in Finance Act 2014. In addition, a significant new development in Finance Act 2014 was the introduction of a new regime, the 'Follower and Accelerated Payments' rules which are aimed at counteracting delays in settling tax claims where the tax arrangements in question have failed to succeed in the courts – the most controversial feature of these new rules may require that an accelerated payment of the disputed tax is made prior to when the actual settlement is determined. Both of these new regimes are outlined at **13.43** below.

Since 4 November 2013, the DOTAS regime is extended to cover disclosure obligations in relation to the annual tax on enveloped dwellings ('ATED'). In broad terms, these rules are intended to apply any changes to the relevant holding structure of the property in question, any reduction in its taxable value to £2m or less or any reduction of the taxable value which would cause the property to fall within a lower tax band than it otherwise would if the arrangement was not implemented. There are certain 'safe harbours' which exclude the obligation to make a disclosure – (again in broad terms) these relate to arm's length transactions between unconnected persons and certain intra-group transactions.

From a property tax perspective, the success of the DOTAS rules are perhaps best demonstrated by the blocking legislation which has been introduced in respect of stamp duty land tax schemes, under the regulations which came into force on 6 December 2006 (and then later replaced by permanent retrospective provisions introduced by FA 2007). Although different views abounded about whether some of the marketed schemes would be susceptible to a challenge based on the *Ramsay* principle, the disclosure rules now provided added clout in HMRC's anti-avoidance armoury. According to the *Financial Times* (13 July 2012), HMRC has legislated 60 times to close schemes as a result of the DOTAS rules since its introduction in 2004. In July 2014, the Treasury confirmed that the Government had introduced 42 changes to tax law since 2010 as a consequence of the operation of the DOTAS regime.

The disclosure regimes applied by legislation currently in force in relation to: income tax, corporation tax; CGT; SDLT; IHT and VAT are outlined below. The relevant legislation is found in FA 2004, Pt 7 and the detailed features of the regime are set out in various statutory instruments (the DOTAS Regulations). Detailed guidance is published by LexisNexis in *Simon's Taxes* (Division A7.2) and in relation to VAT in *De Voil Indirect Tax Service* (Division V5.213). The Law Society has also published guidance (see www.l awsociety.org.uk/productsandservices/practicenotes/taxavoidance.page)

A separate disclosure regime exists in relation to National Insurance Contributions but is outside the scope of this chapter.

Updates and prospective changes (2017/18)

[13.31] HMRC issued guidance on the DOTAS regime, 'Guidance to the disclosure of tax avoidance schemes' (with an effective date from 4 November 2013), which was amended in September 2015 to incorporate legislative changes which were made in Finance Act 2014 and Finance Act 2015 (www.hmrc.gov.uk/aiu/dotas-guidance.pdf).

Following consultations in 2014, measures to strengthen the DOTAS regime were included in Finance Act 2015 (s 117 and Sch 17). These changes included increasing the penalty for persons using schemes which do not comply with their reporting requirement, and giving new powers to HMRC to obtain details of users of undisclosed schemes from introducers. The changes also enable HMRC to publish information about schemes and promoters that it receives under the DOTAS rules.

On 16 July 2015, HMRC introduced additional regulations which extend the standardised tax products and loss scheme hallmarks, and to introduce a new financial products hallmark. By way of brief background, these proposed amendments were introduced because of HMRC's previously expressed concern (as set out in its July 2014 consultation) that the DOTAS regime does not catch a sufficient number of transactions.

On 17 August 2016, HMRC launched a consultation on strengthening tax avoidance sanctions. Following this consultation, draft legislation was introduced (under Finance Bill 2017) which will apply sanctions to persons that enabled the use of defeated tax avoidance schemes but these new provisions were not enacted due to the general election. However, it is anticipated that these new provisions will be enacted at the earliest opportunity.

Outline of FA 2004, Part 7: disclosure of tax avoidance schemes

[13.32] For income tax, corporation tax, CGT and SDLT the main DOTAS rules are contained in FA 2004, Pt 7. (Note that FA 2004, s 318(1) defines 'tax' for these purposes as including petroleum revenue tax, inheritance tax or stamp duty reserve tax, so there is scope under FA 2004, Pt 7 for the enactment of further regulations requiring the disclosure of schemes involving these taxes.) They are supplemented by regulations contained in secondary legislation and by detailed guidance (as updated) published by HMRC. With an effective date from 4 November 2013, HMRC issued new guidance on the DOTAS regime, 'Guidance to the disclosure of tax avoidance schemes' (http://www.hmrc.gov.uk/aiu/dotas-guidance.pdf). Since 1 August 2006, the requirement to disclose applies to a wider range of transactions than when the requirement was first introduced in 2004 and some of the regulations and guidance that came into force in previous years has been superseded.

The disclosure provisions contained in FA 2004, Pt 7 are expressed in terms of 'promoters' of 'notifiable arrangements' and 'notifiable proposals'. FA 2004, s 306(1) defines 'notifiable arrangements' as any arrangements which:

(a)   fall within any description prescribed by the Treasury by regulations;
(b)   enable, or might be expected to enable, any person to obtain an advantage in relation to any tax that is so prescribed in relation to arrangements of that description; and
(c)   are such that the main benefit, or one of the main benefits, that might be expected to arise from the arrangements is the obtaining of that advantage. 'Advantage' is defined at FA 2004, s 318(1).

Whether a particular scheme was notifiable was considered in *Comrs of Revenue and Customs v Mercury Tax* [2009] STC (SCD) 743, which contains some useful guidance on the application of the provisions.

A 'notifiable proposal' is defined as a proposal for arrangements that, if entered into, would be notifiable arrangements (whether they relate to a particular person or to any person who may seek to take advantage of them) (FA 2004, s 306(2)).

Who makes the disclosure?

[13.33] Where a disclosure is required, FA 2004, s 308, as amended by FA 2008, provides that it must generally be made by 'a person who is a promoter in relation to a notifiable proposal' who will send 'prescribed information' to HMRC within 'the prescribed period' (currently five days) after the 'relevant date', ie within five days of the earliest of: (a) the date on which the promoter first makes a firm approach to another person in relation to a notifiable proposal; (b) the date on which the promoter makes the notifiable proposal available for implementation, or (c) the date on which the promoter first becomes aware of any transaction forming part of notifiable arrangement. The so-called 'co-promoter' rule originally relieved promoters of the requirement to make a disclosure to HMRC where there is more than one promoter in relation to the scheme. This has been amended by FA 2008 to the effect that a co-promoter will now only be relieved of the duty to notify the proposal or arrangements to HMRC if he holds the information disclosed to HMRC and either the person who has made the disclosure has notified HMRC of the identity and address of the co-promoter, or the co-promoter holds the reference number allocated by HMRC to the scheme under FA 2004, s 311 (called an 'SRN', see below).

The person making the disclosure may not be the promoter. The client may need to make the disclosure where:

(a) the promoter is based outside the UK (FA 2004, s 309), in which case disclosure must be made within five days of the client entering into the first transaction implementing the scheme; or

(b) there is no promoter (FA 2004, s 310), in which case disclosure must be made within 30 days from the day after the day on which the person enters into the first transaction forming part of the notifiable arrangements; or

(c) there is no promoter because the promoter is a lawyer and legal professional privilege applies (see below), in which case disclosure must be made within five days (or 30 days in relation to SDLT schemes) from the day after the day on which the person enters into the first transaction forming part of the notifiable arrangements.

Under FA 2004, s 312B, there is an additional requirement for the user of a tax avoidance scheme to provide information to the promoter that will enable HMRC to identify that client. The details of the information that the client must provide and the timing by which it must be provided are set out in regulations (the Tax Avoidance Schemes (Information)(Amendment) Regulations 2013 (SI 2013/2592)). In broad terms, these regulations require that within ten days of first entering into the arrangements or within ten days of receiving a reference number for the relevant arrangements from HMRC (whichever is the later), the user must provide the promoter with the user's unique taxpayer number or national insurance number. Failure to comply with this requirement will make the user liable to a penalty not exceeding £5,000.

In addition, under FA 2004, s 313ZB, HMRC is given powers to require the promoter of a tax avoidance scheme to provide further information about parties to the scheme in cases where it suspects the reported clients are not the only parties to the scheme. The details of the information that the client must provide and the timing by which it must be provided are set out in regulations (the Tax Avoidance Schemes (Information)(Amendment) Regulations 2013 (SI 2013/2592)). In broad terms, these regulations require that the promoter must provide HMRC with the other parties' names and addresses and details of how they may be involved in schemes, within ten days of receipt of the written notice from HMRC. Failure by the promoter to provide the required information will make the promoter liable to a penalty not exceeding £5,000.

Who is a promoter?

[13.34] FA 2010 amended the definition of a promoter with effect from 1 January 2011 to include persons who market fully designed schemes in order to solicit clients to whom they will sell the schemes. As in practice, promoters often market schemes through introducers (ie person whose role it is to introduce potential clients to the promoter), the definition now incorporated 'introducers'. Accordingly, a person is a 'promoter':

(a)   in relation to a notifiable proposal if, in the course of a 'relevant business' the person ('P') is to any extent responsible for the design of the proposed arrangements, makes a firm approach to another person ('C') in relation to the notifiable proposal with a view to P making the notifiable proposal available for implementation by C or any other person, or makes the notifiable proposal available for implementation by other persons (FA 2004, s 307(1)(a));

(b)   in relation to a notifiable arrangements if, he is a promoter of a notifiable proposal that is implemented by those arrangements or if, in the course of a 'relevant business', he is to any extent responsible for the design, organisation or management of those arrangements (FA 2004, s 307(1)(b)).

Amending provisions inserted by FA 2010 define 'introducer'. A person is an introducer in relation to a notifiable proposal if the person makes a 'marketing contact' with another person in relation to the notifiable proposal (new FA 2004, s 307(1A)). The amending sub-section introduced more robust tests ie 'firm approach' and 'marketing contact' which are defined in FA 2004, ss 4A–4C.

For the purposes of both notifiable proposals and notifiable arrangements, 'relevant business' is defined as any trade, profession or business that involves the provision to other persons of services relating to taxation or is carried on by a bank or by a securities house as defined, with special provisions to cater for groups of companies (FA 2004, s 307(2)–(4)).

Note that, by way of exception to the general definition, FA 2004, s 307(5) provides that no person is to be treated as a promoter or introducer by reason of anything done in 'prescribed circumstances'. At the time of writing, the Tax Avoidance Schemes (Promoters and Prescribed Circumstances) Regulations 2004 (SI 2004/1865) (as amended by the Tax Avoidance Schemes (Promoters, Prescribed Circumstances and Information) (Amendment) Regulations 2004 (SI 2004/2613)). One important exception for lawyers is contained in reg 6 (introduced by amendment) provide that a person is not to be treated as a promoter in relation to a notifiable proposal or notifiable arrangements where his involvement with the proposal or arrangements is such that he is not required to provide the information prescribed by virtue of the application of legal professional privilege. In such a case, the duty to disclose shifts back to the client.

Because it may not always be certain when a scheme is notifiable until, for example, an order is made to make the scheme notifiable under FA 2004, s 306A (see below), the reference to a 'promoter' or 'introducer' includes a reference to a person who would be a promoter or introducer were the scheme to be notifiable (FA 2004, s 307(6)).

What information must be disclosed under FA 2004, s 308?

[13.35] The 'prescribed information' which must be disclosed is defined as sufficient information as might reasonably be expected to enable an officer of the Board of HMRC to comprehend the manner in which the proposal is or the arrangements are intended to operate, including the promoter's name and address, details of the provisions by virtue of which the proposal is or the arrangements are notifiable, a summary of the proposal or arrangements and the name (if any) by which it is or they are known, information explaining each element of the proposed arrangements (including the way in which they are structured) from which the tax advantage expected to be obtained arises, and the statutory provisions, relating to any of the prescribed taxes, on which the tax advantage is based (see SI 2012/1836, reg 4). But nothing in FA 2004, Pt 7 requires any person to disclose any 'privileged information' ie information with respect to which a claim to legal professional privilege (or, in Scotland, to confidentiality of communications) could be maintained (FA 2004, s 314).

The scope of the 'legal professional privilege' exemption in this context has been the subject of much debate. It applies to communications passing between a legal adviser and his client with the purpose of providing legal advice, ie advising the client about the law, but may also, in the relevant legal context, include advice on what should prudently and sensibly be done (see *Three Rivers District Council and others v Governor and Company of the Bank of England (No 5)* [2004] UKHL 48, [2005] 1 AC 610, [2005] 4 All ER 948). Note that in a different context at the time of writing the scope of 'legal professional privilege' and whether it extends to advice given by accountants has been tested in judicial review proceedings in the High Court and has been held not to apply, though that decision is under appeal (see *R (on the application of Prudential plc and Prudential (Gibraltar) Limited v Special Comr of Income Tax* [2009] EWHC 2494 (Admin), [2010] 1 All ER 1113, [2010] 3 WLR 1042). Provided that privilege has not been waived, the exemption from disclosure also applies to privileged communications in a client's or a promoter's possession, though it is not clear whether this is a view shared by HMRC (see Guidance at paras 3.5 and 3.6).

Additional requirements to provide information

On 12 August 2013, HMRC published a consultation of tax avoidance schemes ('Raising the stake on tax avoidance') which, amongst other things, seeks to extend the list of prescribed information that promoters and users of tax avoidance schemes must currently provide to HMRC under the DOTAS rules.

As a consequence of this consultation, new powers were granted to HMRC under FA 2014, s 284 (which inserted FA 2004, s 310A) to obtain further specified information or documents where a person has already provided prescribed information (in compliance with FA 2004, ss 308–310). Under these new powers, a person has ten days in which to comply with the request by HMRC (or such further period as HMRC may allow). In cases where a person fails to comply with such a request then HMRC may apply to the tribunal for an order of performance. In addition, failure to provide the requested information or documents will make the person liable to a penalty not exceeding £600 per day.

Information about clients

[13.36] Section 313ZA applies to a client who has implemented a scheme and to a promoter who is subject to the 'reference number information requirement' ie he has notified (or ought to have notified) clients of the SRN allocated to the scheme by HMRC (see below). Under FA 2004, s 313ZA(3) promoters are required to provide prescribed information about clients and to do so within a prescribed period after the 'relevant period' prescribed by regulations. It is understood that the prescribed information is intended to be the names and addresses of clients; the 'relevant period' will be each calendar quarter, and that the 'prescribed period' will be 14 days (so promoters will be required to provide to HMRC lists of clients who have implemented a scheme and have been issued with a SRN in each calendar quarter, and to do so within 14 days of the end of the quarter, unless HMRC have given notice under FA 2004, s 312(6) that promoters are no longer required to provide clients with SRN information).

Information from introducers

[13.37] Section 313C provides that HMRC may require a person whom they suspect is an introducer of a notifiable scheme to provide prescribed information about any other person who has provided him with information about a scheme. The requirement must be by written notice. The other person who has provided the introducer with information about the scheme is likely to be the promoter of the scheme, but in some circumstances may be a further intermediary.

It remains to be seen how these provisions will be implemented.

Consequences of failure to comply with the disclosure regime

[13.38] When disclosed to HMRC, HMRC may allocate and, if it does so, must issue the person making the disclosure and any other co-promoter whose identity and address has been notified to HMRC with an 8-digit scheme reference number for the disclosed scheme (FA 2004, s 311). These are known as SRNs.

The promoter must provide the SRN to each client that uses the scheme within 30 days of the later of either the date on which he becomes aware of any transaction forming part of the arrangements and involving the client, or the date when the SRN is notified to the promoter (FA 2004, s 312). Duties are also imposed on clients of promoters of notifiable schemes to pass SRNs to other likely parties to the scheme who might reasonably be expected to gain a tax advantage from it (FA 2004, s 312A). Failure to comply with these duties can also give rise to penalties under TMA 1970, s 98C(1).

Where parties to notifiable arrangements have been provided with an SRN, this and information relating to the time when the tax advantage is either obtained or is expected to be obtained must be included in their tax returns or disclosure forms (FA 2004, s 313).

Failure to make a disclosure gives rise to penalties. Initial penalties are determined by the First-tier Tax Tribunal, and there is a right of appeal against their imposition (TMA 1970, s 100C). Under TMA 1970, s 118(2), a person who has a reasonable excuse for failure to comply with any of the requirements is deemed not to have defaulted and as a consequence is not liable to a penalty. If the reasonable excuse ceases, the person must then comply without unreasonable delay.

The provisions imposing penalties have been amended by FA 2010. Under the amended provisions, which took effect from 1 January 2011, there is now a £600 penalty for each day during the 'initial period' for a failure to comply with any of the requirements set out in s 98C(2)(a)–(c), and a fixed penalty of £5,000 for any other case. The 'initial period' (defined in TMA 1970, s 2ZA) is the period of non-compliance beginning on the day after the deadline for complying, and ending when the penalty is determined, or when the person complies if earlier.

In determining the level of penalty for failure to disclose a scheme, the Tribunal is required to take account of all relevant matters, including the need for the penalty to be an adequate deterrent, having regard in particular to:

- in the case of a promoter's failure to make a disclosure within the prescribed period, to the fees received or likely to have been received in connection with the scheme; and
- in the case of a taxpayer's failure to make a disclosure within the prescribed period, to the tax advantage obtained or sought from the scheme (TMA 1970, s 2ZB).

Where the daily penalty determined under subsection (1)(a)(i) appears inappropriately low, TMA 1970, s 2ZC provides that the Tribunal may increase the penalty to an amount not exceeding £1 million.

HMRC may apply for orders under FA 2004, s 306A (see below) where they have evidence to satisfy the tests in that section but cannot prove that a scheme is notifiable and therefore cannot prove that the time limit for notifying is to be calculated from the relevant dates in FA 2004, s 308(2). If non-compliance continues after an order is made, HMRC may seek a penalty, but in the absence of further evidence, the Tribunal will only be able to determine a penalty on the basis that the duty arose from the s 306A order itself, and that the time limit for compliance, and the 'relevant day' for the purposes of determining the 'initial period', are to be calculated from the date of the order. If evidence subsequently comes to light, eg from a belated notification, TMA 1970, s 2ZD allows HMRC to apply to the Tribunal for the daily penalty to be backdated accordingly. From 1 January 2011, where an order has been made under either FA 2004, s 306A or s 314A and there is a failure to comply, the daily penalty increased to £5,000.

New and amended provisions increase the Treasury and HMRC's vires to make changes to the penalty amounts.

HMRC powers to tackle non-compliance

[13.39] Where HMRC suspect non-compliance with the obligations imposed by the disclosure regime, they may enquire into the reasons a promoter has failed to notify a scheme (FA 2004, s 313A); obtain an order from the First-tier Tax Tribunal requiring the (would be) promoter to supply specified information in support of his views that a scheme is not notifiable (FA 2004, s 313B); obtain an order from the First-tier Tax Tribunal that a scheme is, or is to be treated as notifiable (FA 2004, ss 306A and 314A) and also call for specified information where it appears that a disclosure is not complete (FA 2004, s 308A).

Where these powers have been used by HMRC, penalties for non-compliance are increased.

Income tax, corporation tax, IHT and CGT: the 'hallmarks'

[13.40] For income tax, corporation tax and CGT, arrangements that must be disclosed to HMRC have the following 'hallmarks' defined in the Tax Avoidance Schemes (Prescribed Descriptions of Arrangements) Regulations 2006 (SI 2006/1543) (as amended) which came into force on 1 August 2006. These are:

(a) wishing to keep the arrangements confidential from another promoter;
(b) wishing to keep the arrangements confidential from another HMRC promoter;
(c) arrangements for which a premium fee could reasonably be obtained;
(d) arrangements that include off market terms (nb repealed with effect from 1 January 2011);
(e) arrangements that are standardised tax products;
(f) arrangements that are loss schemes;
(g) certain leasing arrangements; and
(h) certain pension schemes.

For inheritance tax purposes the hallmarks are set out in the Inheritance Tax Avoidance Schemes (Prescribed Descriptions of Arrangements) Regulations 2011 (SI 2011/170):

•   if as a result of any element of the arrangements property becomes relevant property; and
•   where a main benefit of the arrangements is that an advantage is obtained in relation to a relevant property entry charge.

Following a consultation in July 2012 ('Lifting the Lid on Tax Avoidance Schemes'), the DOTAS rules were expanded from 4 November 2013 with an objective to improve the information available to HMRC and to tighten the 'confidentiality hallmark' tests. In particular, the amendments to the confidentiality hallmark are intended to trigger the test if 'it might be reasonably expected that a promoter or user (instead of a specific promoter or user) would wish to keep the way in which any element of the arrangements (including the way in which arrangements are structured) that secures, or might secure, the tax advantage confidential from HMRC'. HMRC felt that this amendment was required to put beyond doubt that the confidentiality hallmark tests are intended to apply to any scheme that HMRC would be likely to take action to counter if HMRC knew about it (as it previously appeared that some promoters took the view that the relevant confidentiality hallmark test did not apply if other promoters were already selling the same scheme).

Detailed guidance about when the hallmarks set out above apply is contained in the Guidance published by HMRC on their website, and is not repeated here.

Stamp duty land tax and DOTAS

[13.41] Provisions for the disclosure of schemes where an SDLT advantage might be expected to be the main benefit are contained in the Stamp Duty Land Tax Avoidance Schemes (Prescribed Description of Arrangements) Regulations 2005 (SI 2005/1868), which came into force on 1 August 2005, as amended by the Stamp Duty Land Tax Avoidance Schemes (Prescribed Descriptions of Arrangements) (Amendment) Regulations 2010 (SI 2010/407). In July 2012, HMRC published two sets of regulations which amend the relevant SDLT DOTAS regulations. In broad terms, the amending regulations remove the financial thresholds for disclosure, update the list of excluded arrangements and require notification of certain sub-sale type transactions. Since then, the other significant developments are the extension of the disclosure requirements which were introduced in Finance Act 2013 (and outlined above at **13.37**). The Finance Act 2014 amendments (as discussed at **13.35** above) also apply to the SDLT DOTAS rules.

VAT and DOTAS

[13.42] A detailed analysis of the VAT disclosure regime in relation to property matters is provided in CHAPTER 15 at **15.302**.

Recent developments/consultations

Spotlights

[13.43] On HMRC's website is an on-line publication called 'Spotlights' (http://www.hmrc.gov.uk/avoidance/spotlights.htm); its purpose is to make tax advisers and taxpayers aware of the risks of using specified avoidance schemes and schemes that incorporate 'generic avoidance devices' that are likely to invite a challenge from HMRC. In Spotlights HMRC list what they consider to be indicators of tax planning that taxpayers should be wary of, such as 'it seems very complex given what you want to do', 'taxation of income is delayed or tax deductions accelerated' and 'there is a requirement to take out insurance against the failure of the tax planning'. From a property tax perspective, the most relevant spotlights relate to VAT and SDLT.

Other developments

[13.44] As a consequence of an August 2013 consultation ('Raising the stake on tax avoidance'), a new anti-avoidance regime, the 'Follower Notices and Accelerated Payments' rules (under FA 2014, Part 4), was introduced on 17 July 2014 (and which are outside of the scope of this chapter). In broad terms, this new regime is aimed at taxpayers who have participated in an avoidance scheme which has failed because of a successful challenge by

HMRC against another taxpayer. Accordingly where the tax planning in question has failed, HMRC now has very broad powers to expedite the settlement of disputed tax claims against other participants, which include a right to obtain an accelerated payment of the tax prior to the final settlement of the claim.

Although the 'Follower Notices and Accelerated Payments' rules represent a separate regime from the DOTAS regime, it is instructive that HMRC can require accelerated payment of the disputed tax if the tax arrangements in question relate to arrangements which fall within the DOTAS regime or are subject to a counteraction notice that has been issued under the GAAR (and where at least two members of the GAAR Advisory Panel have opined that entering into the tax arrangements was not a reasonable course of action).

Also as a consequence of the 12 August 2013 consultation, a new regime which relates to 'high-risk' promoters was introduced on 17 July 2014 (under FA 2014, Part 5), which again represents a separate set of rules from the DOTAS regime but which seeks to build upon the success of the DOTAS regime (and is outside of the scope of this chapter).

In broad terms, this new regime targets certain promoters of tax avoidance schemes ('high risk promoters') where these promoters have failed to comply with their duties under the DOTAS regime. Under this new regime, a high risk promoter is identified by reference to a 'threshold' condition which targets specified behaviours. Once a high-risk promoter is identified, the rules then provide for a 'conduct' notice to be applied to such a promoter. If a high-risk promoter fails to comply with a conduct notice then HMRC (with the approval of the tribunal) may issue a 'monitoring' notice to that promoter. The rules provide that HMRC may publish details of high-risk promoters who are subject to a monitoring notice. Moreover, information requirements will apply to monitored promoters, as well as intermediaries and clients of monitored promoters.

In the Autumn Statement 2014, the Government announced that it would introduce a new tax, the Diverted Profits Tax ('DPT') to counter the use of aggressive tax-planning techniques used by multi-national enterprises to divert profits from the UK. The DPT legislation was included in Part 3 of Finance Act 2015, and applies from 1 April 2015. The DPT regime is beyond the scope of this chapter but, in brief terms, the DPT applies in two prescribed circumstances – firstly, where a company with an existing UK taxable presence is a party to arrangements involving transactions or entitles that lack economic substance and, secondly, in cases where foreign companies make substantial sales in the UK while avoiding the creation of a UK permanent establishment; such arrangements are often combined with other arrangements that allow the foreign company to transfer profits to tax haven jurisdictions. If any of the conditions of these prescribed DPT scenarios are satisfied then a tax charge of 25% of the diverted profits will arise, as assessed by HMRC.

It is highly instructive that HMRC's interim guidance on the DPT (https://www.gov.uk/government/uploads/system/uploads/attachment_data/file/422184/Diverted_Profits_Tax.pdf) includes two examples of specific real estate scenarios in which the DPT would apply.

Under the first example (at page 15 of the Interim Guidance), a UK resident company makes rental payments for property used by it in the course of a trade to a connected UK company that owns the freehold. The freehold is subsequently transferred to an affiliate in a tax haven, and the rental payments are increased, on the alleged grounds that with the change of ownership, the group is taking the opportunity to review the rental payments and move them to current market rates. If the relevant conditions of the applicable DPT rules are satisfied then the DPT charge will apply.

Under the second example (at page 46 of the Interim Guidance), the scenario here, in very broad terms, looks at UK property development project, which avoids using a UK permanent establishment by ensuring that the development is carried out by a company based in a low-tax territory but all of the work (including all critical decisions) is taken by a UK management team. In the author's view, although the features of this example do not precisely match widely used planning structures which (again, in broad terms) seek to rely upon certain double tax treaties which do not treat UK development property as giving rise to a UK permanent establishment, it should be considered that these types of structures are likely to be caught by the DPT rules.

The Criminal Finances Act 2017 introduced two new corporate criminal offences in respect of the facilitation of tax evasion of UK tax and of non-UK tax. If a relevant body is successfully prosecuted, it will face an unlimited fine and possible ancillary sanctions. In essence, this new legislation (which is outside of the scope of this chapter) is derived from established principles under the Bribery Act 2010.

Chapter 14

Capital gains tax

by
Rory Mullan,
Barrister

Introduction

[14.1] The charge to capital gains tax as it applies to land and related property requires consideration of a number of issues, some of which are of specific relevance to real property, while others are of a more general application. This chapter begins with a basic outline of the charge followed by a more detailed consideration of some of the issues which arise in the context of property transactions. Where a detailed consideration of the capital gains tax consequences of a particular transaction is necessary, the reader should refer to a more specialised work on capital gains tax and to the relevant legislation.

Rates of capital gains tax

[14.2] Significant alterations to the charge to capital gains tax were introduced by FA 2008. One element of these changes resulted in a simplification of the manner in which the charge to capital gains tax is calculated. A single flat rate of 18% was briefly introduced in place of the various different rates (linked to the marginal rate of income tax) which previously applied. Further, a number of reliefs which were previously available were abolished, including taper relief (which was replaced by a rather more limited entrepreneurs' relief) and indexation relief.

As with all such changes, there were winners and losers. Those who held assets qualifying for business asset taper relief, and those who held assets for a significant period of time were adversely affected by the loss of reliefs. In contrast, those holding investment properties will have benefitted from the reduction in the rate of tax.

The simplification (and benefits) offered by these changes has been diluted by further alterations in the F(No 2)A 2010 which introduced a new top rate of capital gains tax at 28% which applied to gains accruing on or after 23 June 2010.

FA 2016 lowered the rates for capital gains tax from April 2016 for certain assets. The rate is reduced to 10% rising to 20% where the individual is subject to the income tax higher rate or the dividend upper rate.

Those lower rates do not apply uniformly. FA 2016 also introduced different rates for 'upper rate gains'. 'Upper rate gains' includes residential property gains, NRCGT gains, and gains accruing under TCGA 1992, s 103KA(2) (carried interest). These gains are charged at the rate of either 18% or 28% depending on the level of the unused basic rate band (TCGA 1992, s 4BA).

The rate of capital gains tax accruing to trustees and personal representatives is 28% in respect of upper rate gains and 20% for other gains (TCGA 1992, s 4(3) and (4)).

Further, if the amount chargeable to capital gains tax (that is the amount of chargeable gains after the annual exempt amount) exceeds the unused basic rate band, the rate on the amount of that excess will be 20% (TCGA 1992, s 4(5)) subject to TCGA 1992, s 4BA.

The reliefs which applied prior to the introduction of the flat 18% rate have not been reintroduced with the addition of a higher rate of charge to capital gains tax. An entrepreneurs' relief was, however, brought in with these changes. That relief has become more important as its scope has been successively expanded. A 10% rate is now available to the extent that gains do not exceed £10 million (TCGA 1992, s 169N(4) and FA 2011, s 9) as compared with £1 million when the relief was introduced. FA 2016 introduced an additional relief, investors' relief, which applies a 10% rate to the disposal of qualifying shares in an unlisted trading company held by individuals (TCGA 1992, ss 169VA–169VR).

The highest rate of capital gains tax remains significantly lower than the highest rate of income tax (at 45%) so the distinction between income and capital can be very relevant. Persons buying and selling land at a profit will need to be wary of the risk that they might be trading or that their activities fall within the scope of ITA 2007, Pt 13, Ch 3, Transactions in Land.

A special rate of 20% applies to companies which are subject to the charge to capital gains tax on non-residents (TCGA 1992, s 4(3B)).

Upper rate gains

[14.3] The concept of 'upper rate gains' was introduced in FA 2016. They consist of residential property gains, NRCGT gains (discussed below at **14.51** ff, and gains accruing under TCGA 1992, s 103KA(2) or (3) (TCGA 1992, s 4BB)). They include both UK and non-UK residential property interests.

The meaning of disposal of a UK residential property interest is defined in TCGA 1992, Sch B1 and is discussed below at **14.54**.

The meaning of disposal of non-UK residential property interests is provided by TCGA 1992, Sch BA1. It includes land that has at any time in the relevant ownership period consisted of or included a dwelling, an interest in non-UK land that subsists for the benefit of land that has at any time in the relevant ownership period consisted of or included a dwelling, or an interest in non-UK land that subsists under a contract for an off-plan purchase. The meaning of dwelling is similar, but not identical to the meaning of dwelling for the purposes of TCGA 1992, Sch B1 discussed below at **14.57** (TCGA 1992, Sch BA1, para 4).

TCGA 1992, Sch 4ZZC makes provision for the computation of gains or losses on disposals of residential property interests which are not non-resident CGT disposals. The calculation is complex and made worse by the fact that different rules will apply depending on whether the disposal of the relevant property interest is also a relevant high value disposal (TCGA 1992, Sch 4ZZC).

Scope of the charge to capital gains tax

[14.4] The starting point for the charge to capital gains tax is that it is a tax on chargeable gains accruing to a person on the disposal of assets (TCGA 1992, s 1(1)). The width of this basic proposition becomes apparent when it is noted that every gain, no matter where arising or to whom it arises, will be a chargeable gain unless otherwise expressly provided (TCGA 1992, s 15(2)). The narrower scope of the tax can only be appreciated by a more detailed consideration of a number of subsidiary issues related to this basic proposition. Firstly, it must be asked, who is within the charge to capital gains tax? Secondly, what assets give rise to a chargeable gain? And thirdly, when does a disposal occur? If the answers to these questions lead to a conclusion that a chargeable gain does arise, then it becomes necessary to determine how the charge to tax on the chargeable gain is to be calculated and if, or to what extent, any relief can be claimed. These issues are each considered briefly below.

Persons outside the charge to capital gains tax

[14.5] Not every person who realises a chargeable gain on a disposal will be subject to a charge to capital gains tax. The main categories of persons who may fall outside the charge, a class which has been reduced in recent years with the extension of the charge to certain companies and non-UK residents, is as follows.

Companies

[14.6] Companies, which include any bodies corporate or unincorporated associations (but not partnerships) (TCGA 1992, s 288) are (subject to two noticeable exceptions) not chargeable to capital gains tax in respect of gains accruing to them (CTA 2009, s 4). They are, however, liable to corporation tax in respect of chargeable gains and the provisions on capital gains tax contained in TCGA 1992 are intended to apply with like effect for the purposes of the charge to corporation tax on chargeable gains (TCGA 1992, s 8(5)).

In this chapter, where reference is made to individuals and capital gains tax the same principles will, in general, apply in respect of charge to corporation tax on chargeable gains.

There are, however, notable reliefs specifically relating to the charge to corporation tax on capital gains which have no equivalent in relation to the charge to capital gains tax on individuals (for example the group relief provisions in TCGA 1992, Pt VI, Ch 1). Similarly, however, there are reliefs which are available to individuals on the charge to capital gains tax but will not apply for the purposes of the charge to corporation tax on capital gains (for example the entrepreneurs' relief provisions in TCGA 1992, ss 169H ff).

There are also a number of specific areas where gains on assets held by companies may be calculated and charged in a different manner to that which applies for individuals (see for example CTA 2009, Part 8 which applies to gains and losses of a company from intangible fixed assets).

ATED-related gains

[14.7] A notable exception to the exclusion of companies from the charge to capital gains relates to gains which are 'ATED-related gains' (TCGA 1992, s 1(2A) and CTA 2009, s 2(2A)). Very broadly the charge covers disposals by companies of dwellings with a value of more than £2 million (£1 million from 6 April 2015 and £500,000 from 6 April 2016) which have for a single day or more been subject to the annual tax on enveloped dwellings (ATED) charge (TCGA 1992, ss 2B–2F).

ATED and the charge to capital gains tax on ATED-related gains are dealt with in **CHAPTER 22**. (See also **CHAPTER 5** at **5.28**.)

Another related exception whereby companies can be liable to capital gains tax concerns the charge on non-residents disposing of UK residential property introduced by FA 2015 with effect from 6 April 2015. In such circumstances the rate of charge will be 20% rather than 28%.

Non-resident persons

[14.8] Although the general rule is that persons who do not meet the residence condition, that is to say persons or deemed persons who are not resident in the UK, will not be subject to capital gains tax in respect of chargeable gains accruing on the disposals of assets (TCGA 1992, s 2), there are a number of important exceptions to this. The latest exceptions concern disposals of residential property situated in the UK, where liability will arise regardless of residence, and liability for ATED-related gains.

Ordinary residence

[14.9] As a result of changes introduced by FA 2013 ordinary residence is no longer relevant for tax purposes. Prior to such changes ordinary residence in the UK would also bring a person within the charge to capital gains tax and, more generally, the charge to capital gains tax applied if a person was either resident or ordinarily resident.

As such for periods prior to 2013/14 references to residence should be read as references to residence or ordinary residence (FA 2013, Sch 46, Part 3). From 2013/14 residence, which is now subject to a statutory definition (FA 2013, Sch 45), is the only relevant criterion. It is accordingly potentially possible from 5 April 2013 for a person to be ordinarily resident in the UK but outside the scope of the charge to capital gains tax (assuming that such person is not resident in the UK).

Temporary non-residents

[14.10] Where an individual is temporarily non-resident (which occurs when that individual ceases to be resident in the UK, having been resident in the UK in four out of the seven years of assessment immediately preceding the last year in which he was so resident (FA 2013, Sch 45, para 110)) then if he returns to the UK before five further years of assessment have elapsed he will be subject to capital gains tax in respect of all of the gains and losses which would have accrued to him if he had been UK resident throughout that period. Those gains are treated as accruing to him on the year of return. This treatment will not apply to gains or losses arising from assets acquired while the individual was non-UK resident or to gains which were brought into account for the purposes of the UK charge to capital gains tax (TCGA 1992, ss 10A and 10AA).

The rules on the charge on temporary non-residents have been rewritten by FA 2013, with the legislation introduced in that Act (TCGA 1992, ss 10A and 10AA) only applying where the year of departure is in 2013/14 or after (FA 2013, Sch 45, para 158).

Split year treatment

[14.11] If a year of assessment is a split year as regards an individual and the gain accrues in the overseas part of that year the gain is not chargeable to capital gains tax, notwithstanding that the individual is UK resident (TCGA 1992, s 2(1B)).

The provisions concerning split years are contained in FA 2013, Sch 45, Part 3. A detailed consideration is beyond the scope of this work, but broadly a split year occurs where during a year of assessment a UK resident person: goes to work overseas in a tax year; is a partner of a person working overseas; ceases to have a home in the UK; starts to have a home in the UK; starts to have a home only in the UK; starts full-time work in the UK; ceases full time work overseas; or is a partner of a person ceasing work overseas.

Non-resident persons with a branch or agency in the UK

[14.12] A person who is not resident in the UK will be chargeable to capital gains tax on certain disposals if he is carrying on a trade, profession or vocation in the UK through a branch or agency (TCGA 1992, s 10). This charge applies to disposals of assets situated in the UK and used for the trade or for the branch or agency. A similar provision applies for the purposes of the charge to corporation tax on chargeable gains in relation to companies carrying on a trade through a permanent establishment (TCGA 1992, s 10B).

Gains of non-resident companies

[14.13] The chargeable gains accruing to a company which is not resident in the UK and which would be a close company if it were so resident are treated as accruing to participators in that company who are UK resident. The gains are attributed in proportion to the participator's interest as a participator in the company (TCGA 1992, s 13(1)–(3)).

The provision has been subject to significant amendments taking effect from 5 April 2012 (although introduced in FA 2013, s 62). These changes extend the defences to the application of the charge in an attempt (which is likely to have been unsuccessful) to make the measure compliant with EU law.

The charge does not apply where the relevant participator and persons connected would be apportioned less than one-quarter of the gain (this was previously one-tenth) where the gain accrued on the disposal of an asset used for the purposes of a trade carried on outside the UK (which is now expressly stated to include provision of furnished holiday letting). New exemptions also apply where the asset was used for 'economically significant activities' which is stated to be commercial activities carried on with staff, premises and equipment commensurate with the size and nature of those activities. FA 2013 also introduced a motive defence where it can be shown that neither the disposal nor the acquisition of the asset formed part of arrangements for the avoidance of capital gains tax or corporation tax (which would seem to permit arrangements for the avoidance of other taxes, for example SDLT) (TCGA 1992, s 13(4), (5) and s 13A).

Where the charge does apply relief is available in respect of tax paid on distributions made by the company within three years of the gains arising (TCGA 1992, s 13(5A), (5B)). Relief is also available in respect of any gain on a disposal of an interest in the company (TCGA 1992, s 13(7)).

Gains of non-resident trusts

[14.14] Gains accruing to the trustees of a non-resident trust will be attributed to the settlor of that trust if he has an interest in it, he has a UK domicile and he is resident in the UK (TCGA 1992, s 86, Sch 5). That charge may, however, be in breach of the settlor's EU law rights and accordingly unenforceable as against that settlor.

Where the gains of a non-resident settlement are not attributed to the settlor in a year of assessment, they are treated as trust gains remaining in the settlement. These will subsequently be treated as chargeable gains of any beneficiary receiving a capital payment from the trustees (TCGA 1992, ss 87–87B). A detailed analysis of the extent of these provisions is beyond the scope of this work.

Non-resident companies holding residential property

[14.15] The charge on ATED-related gains (considered in **CHAPTER 22** and **CHAPTER 5**) applies to non-resident companies (TCGA 1992, ss 2(7A) and 2B). Indeed it was initially conceived to apply only to non-resident companies with the extension to all companies prompted by concerns to ensure that the provisions did not operate in favour of UK companies who would otherwise be paying the lower rate of corporation tax on gains.

There is now a related charge which will also apply where non-residents dispose of residential property. That charge is imposed at a lower rate of 20%, although where a gain falls under both regimes, ATED-related gains (taxed at 28%) will take priority.

Non-resident persons holding residential property

[14.16] FA 2015 introduced a charge to capital gains tax which applies to non-residents on the disposal of residential property situated in the UK (TCGA

1992, s 14D). This is considered further at **14.51** below. Where a gain would be subject to both this charge and the charge on ATED-related gains, the latter will apply in priority.

Non-domiciled persons

[14.17] Persons who are resident but are not domiciled (or deemed to be so domiciled) in the UK will not be subject to capital gains tax in respect of chargeable gains accruing on assets situated outside the UK provided that they claim and qualify for the remittance basis in that year (see ITA 2007, ss 809B ff). If, however, amounts are remitted to the UK in respect of those chargeable gains (as to which see ITA 2007, Pt 14, Ch A1), then such amounts are treated as gains accruing when they are remitted to the UK (TCGA 1992, s 12).

It is to be noted that a remittance basis previously applied in relation to income tax for persons not ordinarily resident in the UK. That was never the case for capital gains tax which only permitted a remittance basis for persons not domiciled in the UK. The abolition of ordinary residence for tax purposes has accordingly aligned the remittance basis for the two taxes.

This is an area which has seen very significant alteration as a result of changes introduced in FA 2008, Sch 7, a full discussion of which is beyond the scope of this work.

Trustees of settlor interested trusts

[14.18] Until 6 April 2008, trustees of a settlement were not chargeable to capital gains tax in respect of chargeable gains accruing to them in a year of assessment in which a settlor had, or was treated as having, an interest in the settlement by virtue of TCGA 1992, s 77. That section has now been repealed (FA 2008, Sch 2, para 5), so that trustees of UK resident trusts will always be liable for gains accruing to them.

A significant consequence of this change is that losses accruing to a settlor can no longer be set off against trust gains (which would have been treated as accruing to the settlor).

Settlors of non-resident trusts continue to be liable to capital gains tax on gains of the trustees (TCGA 1992, s 86, Sch 5). As noted, there is a question as to whether these provisions are compliant with EU law.

What assets give rise to a chargeable gain?

[14.19] All forms of property are to be treated as assets for the purposes of capital gains tax. This applies whether such assets are situated in the UK or not (TCGA 1992, s 21). TCGA 1992, s 275 gives the rules as to where assets are treated as situated for the purposes of capital gains tax. Rights or interests (otherwise than by way of security) in or over immovable property are treated as situated in the same place as that immovable property.

Expressly included within the definition of assets is incorporeal property, and in particular options and debts, currency other than sterling and any property which is created by a person disposing of it or which otherwise comes to be owned without having been acquired. Property in this context bears the meaning of that which is capable of being owned, in the normal legal sense. It includes a right of action (*Procter v Zim Properties Ltd* [1985] STC 90 although see Extra Statutory Concession D33). It is in general irrelevant that rights cannot be turned to account by transfer or assignment, they will still be an asset for capital gains tax purposes (*O'Brien (Inspector of Taxes) v Benson's Hosiery (Holdings) Ltd* [1980] AC 562, [1979] 3 All ER 652[1979] STC 735).

A somewhat surprisingly exception to this wide definition was adopted by the Upper Tribunal in *Hardy v HMRC* [2016] UKUT 332 (TCC). It held that the contractual rights under a contract to buy land are not assets for the purposes of capital gains tax (para 40). Although the decision was given in the context of losses, logically it follows that there is no charge on a gain accruing on the assignment of a right to purchase land, because that assignment is not the disposal of an asset.

Unascertainable consideration as a separate asset

[14.20] A right to unascertained future consideration on a disposal of an asset (*Marren (Inspector of Taxes) v Ingles* [1980] 3 All ER 95, [1980] 1 WLR 983 [1980] STC 500) is a separate asset for capital gains tax purposes. This is of relevance where entrepreneurs' relief is available on the disposal of the primary asset since it will not be available on the secondary asset (the right to the unascertained consideration). Where taper relief was relevant, it was often sensible to ensure that the consideration was ascertained but conditional so that there would be a single disposal of the primary asset and that conditional consideration would be brought into account. To the extent that it contributed to the chargeable gain, taper relief would have been available in respect of it.

Since the abolition of taper relief, such an approach is no longer appropriate, and it is likely to be preferable to draft any agreement so as to defer any tax on the secondary asset.

Example 1

A purchases Blackacre in 2003 for £100,000. He uses it for the purposes of his trade for more than a year until his business ceases. He sells it for £150,000, with a further £100,000 to be paid if planning permission is granted in the next year. Planning permission is granted 10 months later.

Since the deferred consideration is ascertainable, TCGA 1992, s 48 applies and it is taken into account in determining A's gain on the disposal of Blackacre. A's chargeable gain is accordingly £150,000.

On the basis that the disposal qualifies for entrepreneurs' relief, a 10% rate applies giving a charge of £15,000.

If the entrepreneurs' relief is not available on the disposal capital gains tax would be paid on a gain of £150,000. At a rate of 20% this would give a charge of £30,000.

B purchases Whiteacre in 2003 for £100,000. He also uses it for the purposes of his trade for more than a year until the business ceases and he sells it for £150,000, with a further unascertainable sum to be paid if planning permission is granted in the next year. The value of the right to that unascertainable sum is £50,000. Planning permission is granted 10 months later and B is paid an additional £100,000.

B's chargeable gain on the disposal of Whiteacre, taking into account the value of the unascertainable deferred consideration is £100,000.

The application of entrepreneurs' relief means that B pays capital gains tax on a gain of £100,000 at a rate of 10%. This would give a charge of £10,000.

If entrepreneurs' relief is not available capital gains tax would be paid on a gain of £100,000 at a rate of 20%. This would give a charge of £20,000.

When, however, the planning permission is granted and A receives a further £100,000 he is taken to have disposed of his right to the unascertainable deferred consideration.

This is a separate asset from Whiteacre which has never been used in the business and does not qualify for entrepreneurs' relief. As such, B is required to pay capital gains tax on an additional gain of £50,000.

The tax on the additional gain of £50,000 will be (at a rate of 20%) £10,000, giving a total of £20,000 where entrepreneurs' relief is available and £30,000 where it is not.

Where entrepreneurs' relief is available, it can be seen that in this example the use of deferred ascertained consideration can result in a tax saving of £5,000 because the deferred element qualifies for the relief.

Where the relief is not available, the same amount of tax is ultimately payable in both examples. The difference, however, would be that the tax on the gain from the secondary asset would only have to be paid when that gain was realised. In the context where entrepreneurs' relief is not available, having an unascertained consideration offers both a timing and a cash flow advantage.

While it can be seen that, since taper relief is no longer available, it is preferable to have an unascertained consideration, so that any charge on the conditional right is deferred until the condition was satisfied, it may still be advantageous to arrange matters so that there is a fixed deferred consideration where entrepreneurs' relief is available.

Milk quotas

[14.21] A similar issue which arises from time to time relates to whether one asset derives from another or whether it is a separate asset disposed of in its own right. This can be important in determining the allowable cost of acquisition of the asset as in the former case there will be a part disposal of the original asset.

Although it is connected with land farmed by a milk producer, HMRC consider that a milk quota is a separate asset from the land to which it is attached (*Cottle v Coldicott (Inspector of Taxes)* [1995] STC (SCD) 239). This has the consequence that an apportionment is necessary when land is bought together with a milk quota.

Wasting assets

[14.22] Wasting assets are generally assets with a predictable useful life which does not exceed 50 years (TCGA 1992, s 44). However, freehold land will never be a wasting asset, regardless of its nature or the buildings or works on it. Plant and machinery is always regarded as having a predictable life of less than 50 years but a life interest in settled property will only be a wasting asset when the life expectancy of the life tenant is 50 years or less.

The disposal of a wasting asset which is tangible movable property will not give rise to a chargeable gain or an allowable loss unless, throughout its ownership, the asset has been used and used solely for the purposes of a trade, profession or vocation and capital allowances were or could have been claimed on acquisition or enhancement expenditure (TCGA 1992, s 45). Where it has been used in this way for part of the period of its ownership, an apportionment will be made.

Where a chargeable gain or an allowable loss will accrue on disposal, then in calculating the allowable expenditure the difference between the acquisition cost and the residual or scrap value, if any, which the asset will have at the end of its predictable life (ascertained at the time of acquisition) is written off at a uniform rate over that predictable life of the asset. A similar treatment applies to any enhancement expenditure (TCGA 1992, s 46).

Where, however, the wasting asset in question is a lease of land, then the restriction on the allowable expenditure does not take place on a straight line basis (TCGA 1992, Sch 8, para 1). This is discussed in detail at para **14.149** below.

The restrictions on allowable expenditure do not apply where, throughout its ownership, the asset has been used and used solely for the purposes of a trade, profession or vocation and capital allowances were or could have been claimed on acquisition or enhancement expenditure (TCGA 1992, s 47, Sch 8, para 1(6)). Where it has been used in this way for part of the period of its ownership, an apportionment will be made.

When does a disposal occur?

[14.23] Although a person may hold an asset which has increased in value, that increase in value will not give rise to a charge to capital gains tax until the person has disposed of the asset, or is treated as having disposed of the asset. Although the term 'disposal' is not defined in the TCGA 1992, it is established that it is given its normal meaning, albeit normal in a special sense to refer to a legal concept. In the context of land, this will generally require a disposal of the entire beneficial interest, so that although a contract may give a purchaser beneficial rights in the property that will not amount to a disposal (see *Underwood v Revenue and Customs Commissioners* [2008] EWCA Civ 1423, [2009] STC 239 at [40] and [41]).

There are a number of further situations where a disposal is treated as occurring, although it might be that as a matter of ordinary language, one has not occurred.

Time of disposal

[14.24] The time at which a disposal and acquisition take place under an unconditional contract will be the time when that contract is made. It will not be the time when the asset is conveyed or transferred if that is later (TCGA 1992, s 28(1)). Where the contract is conditional, the time at which the disposal and acquisition is made is the time when the condition is satisfied. Similarly, where there is an option, the time of disposal and acquisition will be when the option is exercised (TCGA 1992, s 28(2)). It is to be noted that the operation of this provision is limited to determining the time of the disposal. It does not operate to determine the parties to the disposal, who may change between contract and completion (see *Jerome v Kelly (Inspector of Taxes)* [2004] UKHL 25, [2004] 2 All ER 835, [2004] 1 WLR 1409).

This provision is sometimes utilised to retain the benefits of a relief which is being withdrawn (for example business asset taper relief which applied to disposals made before 6 April 2008). Generally the taxpayer would enter into an unconditional contract with a related company or trustees at a time when the relief is available, with the intention of the company or trustees selling the benefit of the contract (or completing and selling the asset) to an unrelated third party at a later date. Since the disposal would be treated as taking place at the time when the contract was made the relief should be available (see *Burt v Revenue and Customs Commissioners* [2008] STC (SCD) 814, SpC 684 where similar issues arose in the context of retirement relief).

Obviously, since the contract is required to be unconditional, the disponor is bound to enter into it, and there can be no provision whereby he can unilaterally escape its consequences. Nevertheless, where the contract becomes undesirable to both parties it is open to them to agree to rescind it, which would have the consequence that no disposal would take place. On a similar point, however, where it is sought to complete the contract, it will be necessary to ensure that a disposal is actually made under the contract (see *Underwood v Revenue and Customs Commissioners* [2009] STC 239 where it was held that there was no actual disposal under the contract in question).

Changes in beneficial ownership

[14.25] In determining whether a disposal has occurred for the purposes of capital gains tax, the principal concern is with changes in beneficial ownership. In this respect, nominees and bare trustees are ignored (TCGA 1992, s 60).

Where property is placed in settlement, there is a disposal of the entire property which becomes settled property, regardless of any right or interest retained by the settlor. There will be no further disposal on a change of the terms of the settlement or on a change of trustees (although see *Jasmine Trustees Ltd v Wells* [2007] EWHC 38 (Ch), [2008] Ch 194, [2007] STC 660 as to what is required to effect a change of trustees for capital gains tax purposes). There will, however, be a deemed disposal of settled property followed by its immediate reacquisition for a consideration equal to its market value by the trustees when any person becomes absolutely entitled, as against the trustees to that settled property (TCGA 1992, s 71(1)). This will include the situation where property is transferred to a separate settlement (as to which see *Roome v Edwards* [1982] AC 279, [1981] STC 96 and *Bond (Inspector of Taxes) v Pickford* [1983] STC 517).

Assets destroyed or of negligible value

[14.26] Where an asset is destroyed it is treated as having been disposed of for capital gains tax purposes (TCGA 1992, s 24(1)). Moreover, where an asset becomes of negligible value (which HMRC take to mean worth next to nothing (CGT Manual 13125)) without having been destroyed, its owner can make a claim so that it is treated as if he had sold, and immediately reacquired, the asset for a consideration of an amount equal to the value specified in the claim (TCGA 1992, s 24(2)).

For these purposes a building can be taken to be an asset separate from the land on which it is situated, although the deemed disposal will be treated as relating to the site on which the building was situated (TCGA 1992, s 29(3)).

Part disposal

[14.27] The term 'disposal' is expressly widened to include what is termed a 'part disposal' of an asset (TCGA 1992, s 21(2)). Generally, a part disposal will have occurred where the disponor retains some right, interest or part of an asset. A part disposal can occur where an interest or right in or over an asset is created, for example on the grant of a lease out of a freehold interest. It can also occur where the interest or right subsisted before the disposal, for example on the sale of a piece of land out of a larger plot.

Where a part disposal does occur, special rules apply to determine the allowable deduction in calculating the gain (TCGA 1992, s 42). Any expenditure which cannot be said to be wholly attributable to the part disposed of (or to the part undisposed of) is apportioned to the part disposed by reference to the following fraction:

$$\frac{A}{A+B}$$

A is the amount or value of the consideration for the part disposed of and B is the market value of the undisposed property.

Example 2

Blackacre and Whiteacre are acquired together as a single asset for £100,000. Blackacre is subsequently sold for £75,000. The market value of Whiteacre at that time is taken to be £50,000.

The allowable expenditure apportioned to Blackacre is £60,000 (100,000 x (75,000/(50,000 + 75,000))) giving a chargeable gain of £15,000. The allowable expenditure on a future sale of Whiteacre will be £40,000.

Where there is a part disposal of land, HMRC provide that an alternative basis can be adopted (Statement of Practice D1 Part disposals of land) under which any fair and reasonable method of apportioning part of the total cost to it will be accepted. The cost of the part disposed of is then deducted from the total cost of the land (or the balance of total cost) to determine the cost of the remainder of the land for future disposals. This avoids the necessity of obtaining a market valuation of the part retained.

Example 3

As above Blackacre and Whiteacre are acquired together as a single asset for £100,000. Blackacre is subsequently sold for £75,000. On the basis that Whiteacre is half the area of Blackacre and all other factors being equal, then rather than obtaining a separate valuation for Whiteacre, the cost might be apportioned as to £66,000 to Blackacre and as to £34,000 to Whiteacre.

If the disposal is a '*small part disposal*' then different rules may apply. A small part disposal is one where the consideration received (or deemed to be received) for the land disposed of does not exceed one-fifth of the market value of the entire holding before the disposal (TCGA 1992, s 242). A claim can be made so that there is deemed to be no disposal, but the allowable expenditure for the remaining part is reduced by the amount of the consideration received.

This does not apply to transfers between spouses or within groups of companies which are on a no gain/no loss basis or to a disposal out of a lease for less than 50 years. It also does not apply if the consideration received exceeds £20,000, or if the consideration for that disposal, taken with all other disposals of land in the same year, exceeds £20,000.

Example 4

Blackacre and Whiteacre are acquired together as a single asset for £100,000. Blackacre is subsequently sold for £20,000 and the properties have not decreased in value.

The taxpayer can make a claim so that no disposal is treated as occurring on the sale of Blackacre. The allowable expenditure on a subsequent sale of Whiteacre will be £80,000.

Further rules apply in respect of both part disposals out of leases and part disposals to an authority under compulsory powers. Both of these situations are considered in more detail below.

Capital sums derived from assets

[**14.28**] There will be deemed to be a disposal of assets by a person where a capital sum is derived from them, even in circumstances where the person paying such capital sum does not acquire an asset (TCGA 1992, s 22). Examples of such capital sums include capital sums received as compensation for or under a policy of insurance for any kind of damage or injury to assets, capital sums received in return for forfeiture or surrender of rights, and capital sums received for use of assets.

Statutory compensation paid by a landlord on the termination of a lease will not be chargeable to capital gains tax, as it is derived from a statutory right, and not as compensation (*Drummond (Inspector of Taxes) v Austin Brown* [1985] Ch 52, [1984] STC 321).

A number of exceptions and concessions to the application of this rule apply. Firstly, a claim can be made so that there is no disposal to the extent that compensation or insurance money is used (or all but a small amount of it is used) to restore the damaged asset (TCGA 1992, s 23). Roll-over relief is available on similar principles under this section where the asset is replaced within a year (or such longer period as the inspector allows) and where the asset destroyed is a building and the capital sum is paid to construct or acquire a new building on other land, such hold-over relief can be claimed (TCGA 1992, s 23(4)–(7)). HMRC regard 5% of the capital sum, or £3,000 as being a small amount for the purposes of this relief (RI 164, February 1997, Capital gains tax: meaning of 'small' in TCGA 1992 ss 23, 116, 122, 133, 243).

No acquisition or disposal is taken to occur where capital sums are derived from an asset in circumstances where that asset or a right or interest in it is transferred by way of security (TCGA 1992, s 26).

Extra statutory concession D33 (Capital gains tax on compensation and damages) provides that where a capital sum is derived from a right of action, HMRC will permit the taxpayer to treat that capital sum as deriving from the underlying asset in relation to which the right of action arose, and to claim any relief or exemption available in respect of that underlying asset. Where there is no underlying asset, the concession states that any gain will be exempt from capital gains tax. This is consistent with TCGA 1992, s 51(2) which provides that sums obtained by way of compensation or damages for any wrong or injury suffered by an individual in his person or in his profession or vocation are not chargeable gains. Further concessionary treatment applies to payments made in recognition of, and in recompense for, the past loss or deprivation of overseas property in circumstances where no form of legal redress was then available to the owner (ESC D50 Treatment of compensation).

Value shifting

[14.29] If the owner of land (or of any other type of property) becomes a lessee of that land or other property (for example on a sale and leaseback) and there is a subsequent adjustment of the rights and liabilities under the lease which is generally favourable to the lessor then there is deemed to be a disposal by the lessee of an interest in the land or other property (TCGA 1992, s 29(4)).

Similarly, where an asset is subject to a right or restriction of any type, there is deemed to be a disposal of that right or restriction if it is extinguished or abrogated (whether in whole or in part) by the person entitled to enforce it (TCGA 1992, s 29(5)).

Options

[**14.30**] The grant of an option is the disposal of an asset (namely the option). This is expressly stated to include both the situation in which the grantor binds himself to sell property he does not own and never has occasion to own because the option is abandoned and also the situation where the grantor binds himself to buy property but does not acquire that property because the option is abandoned (TCGA 1992, s 144). The grant of an option will not be a part disposal (see *Strange v Openshaw* [1983] STC 416).

Where the option is exercised, the grant of the option and the transaction entered into on exercise of the option are treated as a single transaction. The exercise of the option does not give rise to a disposal. Similarly, the abandonment of an option will not give rise to a disposal unless it is either a quoted option to subscribe for shares in a company, a traded option a financial option, or an option to acquire assets to be used for the purpose of a trade.

Example 5

In January 2006 and for a consideration of £10,000 A acquires from B an option to purchase Blackacre on the payment of a further £100,000. This is a disposal by B on which he makes a chargeable gain of £10,000.

In January 2007 A exercises the option. The earlier disposal of the option is disregarded and B is now treated as making a single disposal of Blackacre at this time.

The provisions deeming an acquisition or disposal to be for a consideration equal to the market value of an asset are disapplied in respect of certain options (TCGA 1992, ss 144ZA–144ZD). For a more detailed consideration of these provisions the reader should refer to a specialist capital gains tax text.

Mortgages and charges

[**14.31**] The conveyance or transfer by way of security of an asset or of an interest or right in or over it (including a retransfer on redemption of the security) does not give rise to any acquisition or disposal of the asset (TCGA 1992, s 26(1)).

Dealings with an asset to enforce a security are treated as done as nominee for the person entitled to the asset subject to the security, charge or incumbrance (TCGA 1992, s 26(2)).

An asset is deemed to be acquired and disposed of free of any security subsisting at the that time, and where an asset is acquired subject to any security, the full amount of any liability assumed by the person acquiring the asset forms part of the consideration for the acquisition and disposal in addition to any other consideration (TCGA 1992, s 26(3)).

Migration

[**14.32**] Where trustees of a settlement cease to be resident in the UK, they are deemed to have disposed of the settled property (subject to certain limited exceptions) and reacquired it at its market value at that time (TCGA 1992, s 80). No such deemed disposal applies where individuals become non-resident although, as discussed above, a temporary non-resident may become liable in respect of gains arising while he was non-resident.

This charge on migration is almost certainly contrary to EU law and as such, unenforceable (see C-371/10: *National Grid Indus BV v Inspecteur van de Belastingdienst Rijnmond* [2012] STC 114, ECJ). A reference to the CJEU has now been made on this issue by the First-tier Tribunal (C-646/15: *Trustees of the P Panayi Accumulation & Maintenance Settlements v Revenue and Customs Comrs* (OJ 2016 C-48/22)).

Partition

[14.33] Where a partition of joint interests in land (for example, a single holding of land held jointly is partitioned to two holdings of land held individually) takes place in a manner such that the values of the interests of the parties in the whole precisely reflect the values of the individual interests after the partition, the partition will not have given rise to a disposal for capital gains tax purposes (see *Jenkins (Inspector of Taxes) v Brown* [1989] 1 WLR 1163, [1989] STC 577).

By concession (ESC D26 Relief for exchanges of joint interests) HMRC allow a roll-over relief, similar to that arising on compulsory purchase (discussed below) where there is an exchange of joint interests in land resulting in joint owners becoming sole owners. Relief will not be allowed under the concession where the new holding would qualify for principal private residence relief unless such relief would be available on the disposal of the joint interest in any event.

The concession will also apply to a parallel exchange of interests in milk or potato quota associated with land subject to a partition.

How is the chargeable gain calculated?

[14.34] The two primary questions which arise when one seeks to calculate a chargeable gain are what the disposal proceeds were, and what sums are allowable as a deduction in calculating the gain (allowable expenditure).

Disposal proceeds

[14.35] The basic position is that the consideration actually payable for the acquisition of an asset will be the proceeds taken into account in calculating the gain. That sum need not necessarily be paid to the person making the disposal, but must be part of the consideration for that disposal (see *Revenue and Customs Comrs v Collins* [2009] EWHC 284 (Ch), [2009] STC 1077, 79 TC 524).

There are, however, a number of exceptions and qualifications to this basic proposition.

Sums taken into account as income tax

[14.36] As discussed below at para **14.152**, sums which are charged to income tax or are taken into account in computing profits or losses are excluded from the consideration for the disposal of assets (TCGA 1992, s 37(1)). However, sums which are allowable as a deduction for income tax will not be allowable as a deduction in calculating capital gains (TCGA 1992, s 39).

Deemed market value consideration

[14.37] Where an asset is disposed of otherwise than by way of a bargain made at arms' length (most particularly when the asset is gifted) or where an asset is disposed of for a consideration which cannot be valued or for a consideration which is provided in the form of services, then the asset is treated as having been disposed of for a consideration equal to its market value (TCGA 1992, s 17(1)). This treatment will also apply where the acquisition and disposal are between connected persons (TCGA 1992, s 18).

Assets disposed in a series of transactions

[14.38] Where, within a period of six years, two or more transactions are made to persons connected with the disponor additional issues arise. In particular, a consideration which is greater than the market value of the assets disposed of (when taken individually) may be treated as having been received by the disponor. This will be because the market value of the assets when taken together is greater than the market values of the assets taken individually. The disposal consideration will be deemed to be the appropriate portion of that greater market value of all the assets taken together (see TCGA 1992, ss 19, 20).

Deferred consideration

[14.39] The consideration taken into account on a disposal includes (in the first instance) sums which the disponor obtains the right to receive, even where that right is postponed or contingent, without regard being had to any risk that all or any part of that consideration will prove to be irrecoverable. An adjustment will be made if consideration which was brought into account without having been paid subsequently proves to be irrecoverable on a claim being made to that effect (TCGA 1992, s 48).

Where that deferred consideration is unascertainable at the time of disposal, then the market value of the right to receive the unascertained consideration is brought into account, and the right to that unascertained consideration is a separate asset ((*Marren (Inspector of Taxes) v Ingles* [1980] 3 All ER 95, [1980] STC 500), as discussed above).

Contingent liabilities

[14.40] In computing a gain, no allowance is made for any liability remaining with, or assumed by, the person making the disposal if that liability is contingent on a default by an assignee of a lease in respect of liabilities assumed by him. Similarly no allowance is made where the contingent liability relates to a covenant for quiet enjoyment or other obligation, warranty or representation which is assumed by the vendor or lessor (TCGA 1992, s 49(1)).

If, however, the liability is subsequently enforced, a claim can be made for an adjustment to be made in respect of the gain (TCGA 1992, s 49(2)).

This can raise questions as to what amounts to a contingent liability.

A contingent liability is a liability which depends for its existence upon an event which may or may not happen (*Winter v IRC* [1963] AC 235, [1961] 3 All ER 855). It has been held to include sums payable under a settlement of litigation concerning a representation made in the course of a sale of shares (*Ben Nevis v HMRC* [2012] UKFTT 377(TC)). The term is widely construed and does not depend upon an event which may or may not happen at the time of disposal, further the connection between the liability and the consideration received is not to be drawn too narrowly (*Revenue and Customs Comrs v Sir Alexander Fraser Morrison* [2015] STC 659).

Allowable expenditure

[14.41] The rules deeming a market value consideration to have been received on a disposal will also apply to deem a market value consideration to have been paid on the acquisition of an asset. This value will be allowed as a deduction in calculating any gain.

Where the deemed market value rules did not apply on acquisition, then the amount allowable as a deduction in calculating the chargeable gain will be, in the first place, those amounts given by way of consideration, in money or money's worth, which were paid wholly and exclusively for the acquisition of the asset. Added to this will be those incidental costs which were incurred in the acquisition or provision of the asset. These will include (see TCGA 1992, s 38(1)(a), (2)):

(1)   fees, commission or remuneration paid for the professional services of any surveyor, valuer, auctioneer, accountant, agent or legal adviser;
(2)   the costs of any transfer or conveyance (including stamp duty and stamp duty land tax);
(3)   the costs of advertising to find a buyer or seller; and
(4)   the costs reasonably incurred in making any valuation or apportionment required for the purposes of the computation of the gain (including expenses reasonably incurred in ascertaining market value where so required).

In addition to these amounts, all of those amounts which were wholly and exclusively incurred on the asset for the purpose of enhancing its value will be allowable as a deduction. This will only apply where the expenditure is reflected in the state or nature of the asset at the time of the disposal (TCGA 1992, s 38(1)(b)). This leaves a question as to expenditure which merely increases the value of an asset (*F D Fenston Will Trusts v HMRC* [2007] UKSPC SP00589) or merely maintains its upkeep (*Raha v Revenue & Customs* [2010] SWTI 2591).

The 'state or nature' of an asset is to be determined by reference to the rights and obligations which the asset confers or imposes upon its owner. Expenditure which has no effect upon those rights will not be relevant expenditure. Thus expenditure to relieve a taxpayer of a purely personal obligation to sell shares to a third party was not allowable expenditure (see *Blackwell v Revenue and Customs Comrs* [2017] EWCA Civ 232, [2017] 4 All ER 188, [2017] STC 1159). It is an open question, however, whether that analysis will apply in the same way to land, in circumstances where a contract concerning that land may not be purely personal.

Also allowable will be those amounts expended for the purpose of establishing, preserving or defending title to, or to a right over, the asset in question (TCGA 1992, s 38(1)(b)).

The final category of allowable expenditure will be the incidental costs of making the disposal (TCGA 1992, s 38(1)(c)).

These amounts of allowable expenditure will be restricted where there is a part disposal (as explained above) (see TCGA 1992, s 42).

Forfeited deposits

[14.42] Expenditure incurred by way of a deposit for a purchase of land is not allowable expenditure if the sale does not subsequently go through and the deposit is forfeited. This is primarily on the basis that the rights acquired under the contract are not regarded as assets for capital gains tax purposes, but also because the deposit with a view to acquiring the contractual property and not the contractual rights. That has been held to be expenditure with a dual purpose (see *Hardy v HMRC* [2016] UKUT 332 (TCC)).

31 March 1982 rebasing

[14.43] In computing the gain or loss accruing on the disposal of an asset held on 31 March 1982 there is deemed to have been a sale and reacquisition of that asset at its market value on 31 March 1982 (TCGA 1992, s 35(1), (2)).

Before 6 April 2008, this treatment was not automatic, but only applied if it reduced the gain or loss. While that will continue to be the case for corporation tax purposes (TCGA 1992, s 35(2A)), the deemed disposal is now automatic for capital gains tax purposes (FA 2008, Sch 2, paras 57ff).

Indexation allowance

[14.44] Before 6 April 2008 relief was available where on the disposal of an asset there was an unindexed gain. The relief took the form of an indexation allowance (by reference to the retail prices index) which was allowed to reduce or to extinguish that unindexed gain (TCGA 1992, s 53). It could not however create a loss. This relief, which was only available for capital gains tax purposes in respect of periods of ownership up to 31 March 1998 has now been removed for capital gains tax purposes entirely (FA 2008, Sch 2, paras 77 ff).

The relief will, however, continue to be relevant for corporation tax purposes, and also for capital gains tax purposes where there has been a no gain/no loss disposal before 6 April 2008 (TCGA 1992, s 56(2)).

The indexation allowance is determined by aggregating the indexed rises in each item of allowable expenditure. It is calculated by multiplying each amount of allowable expenditure by a figure expressed as a decimal and determined by the formula:

$$\frac{(RD - RI)}{RI}$$

RD is the retail prices index for the month of disposal (although not later than April 1988 for capital gains tax purposes) and RI is the retail prices index for March 1982 or the month in which the expenditure was incurred, whichever is the later.

Taper relief

[14.45] In calculating a chargeable gain for capital gains tax (but not corporation tax) purposes before 6 April 2008, that gain was reduced by applying taper relief to it. The extent to which a chargeable gain was eligible for taper relief was determined by reference to two factors: the number of whole years during which the asset was held; and whether at any given time the asset was a business asset or a non-business asset (see TCGA 1992, s 2A now repealed). Business in this context generally meant trade, and did not include property rental (see *Jones & Southam v Revenue and Customs Comrs* (TC00256) [2009] UKFTT 312 (TC), [2010] SWTI 295).

This relief has been abolished (FA 2008, Sch 2, paras 23 ff) in respect of disposals on or after 6 April 2008. There is no transitional relief.

Entrepreneurs' relief

[14.46] The abolition of taper relief together with the introduction of a flat 18% rate of capital gains tax was of benefit to persons disposing of non-business assets where, as a result of the introduction of the 18% flat rate, they were almost certain to enjoy a lower rate of tax, regardless of how long they had held a particular asset. For those who had owned assets qualifying as business assets, the increase from a maximum effective rate of 10% (after only two years ownership) was likely to be more keenly felt. It was to meet the objections of such persons that an 'entrepreneurs' relief' was introduced in TCGA 1992, ss 169H–169S by FA 2008, Sch 3. When capital gains tax was increased to 28%, entrepreneurs' relief was increased to cover £5 million of gains to meet the further objections which followed (F(No 2)A 2010, Sch 1). That has now been further increased to cover £10 million of gains in relation to disposals after 6 April 2011 (FA 2011, s 9).

The relief is available in respect of certain disposals by individuals, trustees and partners, although it must be claimed on or before the first anniversary of 31 January following the year in which the disposal is made (TCGA 1992, s 169M).

Broadly, in relation to individuals, the relief applies on:

(1)   the disposal of the whole or part of a business owned by an individual (for these purposes each partner in a partnership is deemed to own the business (TCGA 1992, s 169I(8)) for the period of one year before the date of the disposal (as to which see **14.24** above) (TCGA 1992, s 169I(2)(a) and (3));

(2)   the disposal of the assets of a business where the business has ceased where the individual owned the business for a year before such cessation and the disposal takes place within three years of such cessation (TCGA 1992, s 169I(2)(b) and (4));

(3)   the disposal of shares in a trading company or holding company of a trading group by an individual who is an officer or employee of the company and holds 5% of the ordinary share capital and voting rights (TCGA 1992, s 169I(2)(c) and (6) and 169S(3)). The meaning of ordinary share capital was considered in *McQuillan v HMRC* [2016] UKFTT 305 and *Alan Castledine v HMRC* [2016] UKFTT 145 (TC). These cases demonstrate that the issue can be difficult, and that particular regard to the facts will be necessary in marginal cases; and

(4)   the disposal of shares within three years of it ceasing to be a trading company where the conditions at 3 were satisfied for the year before it ceased to be a trading company (TCGA 1992, s 169I(2)(c) and (7)).

A similar relief applies to disposal by trustees where the assets in question were held by the trustees on interest in possession trusts for the benefit of an individual who carries on the business or is an employee of the trading company and has a 5% interest in the trading company (TCGA 1992, s 169J). Further relief is given under TCGA 1992, s 169K where an individual sells his interest in a partnership or a company the assets of which have been used for the purpose of the business and such sale is part of the individual's withdrawal from that business.

Although the above allows one to establish that relief is available in principle, it remains necessary to consider other limitations. Entrepreneurs' relief only applies to the disposal of a business to the extent of gains arising from assets, including goodwill, used for the purposes of that business which are not shares, securities or investments (TCGA 1992, s 169L). Relief for goodwill is, however, excluded on a disposal to a related party save where the related party is a company and certain ownership conditions are met (TCGA 1992, s 169LA).

The relief applies to gains on relevant business assets after setting off any losses incurred on the disposal of relevant business assets. Those gains are charged at a rate of 10%. The relief is limited to the extent that the aggregate of such gains (after set off) in a person's lifetime does not exceed £10m (TCGA 1992, s 169N). That limit only applies for gains made after 6 April 2011 (FA 2011, s 9). The limit was £5m for gains made between 24 June 2010 and 6 April 2011, £2m for gains made between 6 April 2010 and 23 June 2010 (FA 2010, s 4) and £1m for gains made before that.

In calculating the amount of relief available to an individual or trustees, the gains of individuals are aggregated with gains accruing to trustees where the individual has the relevant interest in possession to enable the trustees to qualify for the relief (TCGA 1992, s 169N). Where an individual is a basic rate taxpayer, the gains subject to entrepreneurs' relief are treated as the lowest part of his chargeable gains (TCGA 1992, s 4(5)).

Where entrepreneurs' relief is available, gains of up to £10m will be chargeable at a rate of 10%. The limit of £10m applies to gains qualifying for relief in a person's lifetime. On current figures the maximum value of the relief for a given individual will be £1.8m (ie the difference between a 10% charge on a gain of £10m and a 28% charge on a gain of £10m). This is a substantial increase in the value of the relief which until 6 April 2010 offered a maximum tax saving of £80,000. As such, entrepreneurs' relief has become significantly more valuable and planning to obtain it more worthwhile.

Assets of a business or part of a business

[14.47] An issue which arises in the context of entrepreneurs' relief, particularly in the context of the sale of land which is used in a business is the distinction which is sometimes drawn between assets of the business (where relief is not available unless the business ceases) and part of the business (where relief is available) (TCGA 1992, s 169I(2)).

That distinction was widely applied in the context of retirement relief (see for example *McGregor (Inspector of Taxes) v Adcock* [1977] 3 All ER 65, [1977] STC 206; *Atkinson v Dancer* [1988] STC 758, 61 TC 598; *Pepper (Inspector of Taxes) v Daffurn* [1993] STC 466, 66 TC 68; *Jarmin (Inspector of Taxes) v Rawlings* [1994] STC 1005, 67 TC 130; *Wase (Inspector of Taxes) v Bourke* [1996] STC 18, 68 TC 109; *Barrett (Inspector of Taxes) v Powell* [1998] STC 283, 70 TC 432; *Purves v Harrison* 73 TC 390). Those cases show that the issue is generally one of fact and that regard will be had to all of the circumstances in determining whether it can genuinely be said that there has been a sale of part of the business, including the nature and extent of the activities after the sale.

Gilbert t/a United Foods v HMRC [2011] UKFTT 705 (TC) was an example of the issue arising in the context of entrepreneurs' relief. The business involved sales representation selling food on commission for a number of suppliers. The taxpayer sold part of a customer database and goodwill to one of the suppliers (reducing the customer base substantially) and HMRC argued that scaling down of business was not a sale of part of the business. In contrast the Tribunal considered that the proper test was whether what was sold was a viable section of the business, suggesting the approach of considering what would be the case if the transferee was an empty shell until the transfer. Could the activities of the transferee using only the assets and liabilities transferred be capable of constituting a trade or business?

Gilbert was not, however, cited in *Russell v HMRC* [2012] UKFTT 623 (TC) which involved the sale of farmland and in which the Tribunal relied entirely on the approach in the earlier retirement relief cases and concluded that the sale of farmland was merely a sale of assets used in the business.

It is of course to be noted that these issues do not arise if the sale of assets is in connection with the cessation of the business, the assets were used in that business when it ceased and the sale is within three years of the cessation of the business (TCGA s 169I(2)(b) and (4)).

Losses

[14.48] Generally the amount of a loss accruing on a disposal of an asset shall be computed in the same way as the amount of a gain accruing on a disposal (TCGA 1992, s 16(1)). This has the consequence that where it is provided that a gain is not to be chargeable, any corresponding loss will not be allowable (TCGA 1992, s 16(2)).

Allowable losses from a year of assessment can be deducted from any capital gains arising in that year of assessment (TCGA 1992, s 2(2)). Where different rates of capital gains tax apply, they can be deducted from capital gains in the most beneficial manner (TCGA 1992, s 4B). Where losses are not allowed as a deduction in a year of assessment, they will be allowed as a deduction in a later year of assessment, but cannot (except where the disponor has died) be used in respect of gains arising in an earlier year of assessment (TCGA 1992, ss 2(3), 62).

Anti-avoidance provisions in TCGA 1992, s 16A are intended to disallow losses which accrue as a result of arrangements intended to confer a tax advantage. Other provisions restrict the extent to which losses are available to non-UK domiciled individuals claiming the remittance basis (TCGA 1992, ss 16ZA–16ZD).

Annual exempt amount and rates of capital gains tax

[14.49] An individual is not chargeable to capital gains tax except to the extent that his taxable amount (that is chargeable gains after losses and relevant reliefs) exceeds the annual exempt amount (£11,300 for 2017/18). That does not, however, apply to non-UK domiciled individuals claiming the remittance basis (TCGA 1992, s 3).

As from 6 April 2008 a flat rate of 18% was introduced for capital gains tax purposes to replace the marginal rates of tax which applied in earlier years. As noted at **14.2** above this simplification has been short lived.

From April 2016, the capital gains tax rates are as follows:

- 10% basic rate and 20% higher rate;
- 18% and 28% for upper rate gains;
- 20% for trustees or for personal representatives (excluding residential property);
- 28% for trustees or personal representatives on upper rate gains;
- 10% for gains which qualify for entrepreneurs' relief;
- 28% for ATED-related gains; and
- 20% for companies paying non-resident CGT on the disposal of UK residential property.

Gains which are not chargeable gains or are eligible for relief

[14.50] There are three broad categories of relief from capital gains tax. These categories do not relate to the assets disposed of nor to the persons making the disposals, rather they relate to the manner in which relief is given. In certain cases, a claim will be needed in order that the favourable treatment applies, in other cases it will apply automatically, regardless of any claim.

Firstly, provisions may expressly provide that gains shall not be chargeable gains. In this case, the gain will never come into the charge to tax. Gains falling within this category, whether on the making of a suitable claim or otherwise, include the following:

(1)   the gain on the disposal of tangible movable property which is a wasting asset (TCGA 1992, s 45(1) and see above at para **14.22**);

(2)   winnings from betting, including pool betting, or lotteries or games with prizes (TCGA 1992, s 51);

(3)   any gain on a disposal of assets by personal representatives to legatees (TCGA 1992, s 62(3));

(4)   the gain on the deemed disposal and reacquisition of assets by trustees of certain interest in possession trusts brought to an end by the death of the life tenant (TCGA 1992, ss 72, 73);

(5)   gains on disposals of certain interests under a settlement (TCGA 1992, s 76);

(6)   gains accruing to an authorised unit trust, investment trust, venture capital trust or court investment fund (TCGA 1992, s 100);

(7)   gains accruing in the disposal of gilt edged securities and qualifying corporate bonds (TCGA 1992, s 115);

(8)   gains accruing on the disposal of government non-marketable securities (TCGA 1992, s 121);

(9)   gains on the disposal of certain shares qualifying for relief under the business expansion scheme, seed enterprise investment scheme and enterprise investment scheme or venture capital trust regimes (TCGA 1992, ss 150, 150A, 150E, 151A);

(10)   gains accruing on the disposal of an interest in a dwelling house which is an individual's main residence (TCGA 1992, s 223 and see below at para **14.54**);

(11)   gains accruing on disposals of various rights to and under certain superannuation funds, annuities and annual payments (TCGA 1992, s 237);

(12)   gains accruing to the original creditor on the disposal of a debt that is not a debt on a security (TCGA 1992, s 251);

(13)   gains accruing to a charity which are applicable and applied for charitable purposes (TCGA 1992, s 256);

(14)   the gain on the disposal of a chattel where the consideration does not exceed £6,000 (TCGA 1992, s 262);

(15)   gains accruing on the disposal of a passenger vehicle (TCGA 1992, s 263);

(16)   gains accruing on the disposal of a decoration awarded for valour or gallant conduct which was acquired otherwise than for consideration in money or money's worth (TCGA 1992, s 268);

(17)   gains accruing on the disposal of currency acquired by an individual for his personal expenditure outside the UK (TCGA 1992, s 269); and

(18)   gains accruing on the disposal of certain stock transferred in pursuance of any Act of Parliament or belonging to the Crown (TCGA 1992, s 271).

Secondly, legislation may provide that a given disposal is to be treated as if it gives rise to neither a gain nor a loss. In this case, although the person disposing of the property avoids a charge to capital gains tax, the person acquiring the property is likely to have a larger charge to tax in the future than would be the case if he was treated as acquiring it at its market value.

Transfers which are expressly treated as being for a consideration of such amount as gives rise to neither a gain not a loss on the making, where such is necessary, of a suitable claim include the following:

(1)   transfers between spouses and civil partners (TCGA 1992, s 58);
(2)   property reverting to settlor on the death of a life tenant (TCGA 1992, s 73(1));
(3)   schemes of reconstruction involving the transfer of a business (TCGA 1992, ss 139–140A);
(4)   a disposal of a qualifying asset of a business in relation to a transfer of the business on which disincorporation relief has been claimed (TCGA 1992, s 162B);
(5)   transfers between companies subject to group relief (TCGA 1992, s 171);
(6)   disposals of assets on the amalgamation of business societies (TCGA 1992, s 215);
(7)   disposals of assets on the incorporation of a friendly society (TCGA 1992, s 217A);
(8)   disposals of land between the Housing Corporation, the Secretary of State or Scottish Homes and housing associations (TCGA 1992, ss 218–220);
(9)   transfers of value to employee trusts which are exempt for inheritance tax (TCGA 1992, s 239);
(10)   certain gifts to charity (TCGA 1992, s 257);
(11)   works of art etc disposed of subject to a relevant undertaking (TCGA 1992, s 258);
(12)   certain gifts of land to housing associations (TCGA 1992, s 259);
(13)   disposals of land by local constituency associations of political parties following a reorganisation of constituencies (TCGA 1992, s 264); and
(14)   disposals pursuant to an agreement for the sharing of transmission facilities (TCGA 1992, s 267).

Reliefs which can operate in a similar manner to the above reliefs, but may operate differently where there is a disposal at an undervalue, include the following:

(1)   hold-over relief on gifts of business assets (TCGA 1992, s 165); and
(2)   hold-over relief in relation to gifts on which inheritance tax is chargeable (TCGA 1992, s 260).

These are considered in more detail at paras **14.103–14.120** below.

The third broad category of relief is where a gain is treated as not arising on the disposal of an asset, but that gain is only deferred and will accrue to the disponor of that original asset on the disposal of a different asset. This is generally referred to as roll-over relief. Examples include

(1)   roll-over relief where compensation moneys paid after the destruction of an asset are used to purchase a replacement (TCGA 1992, s 23(4)) (see above at **14.28**);

(2) roll-over relief on the replacement of business assets (TCGA 1992, s 152);

(3) roll-over relief on the transfer of a business to a company (TCGA 1992, s 162);

(4) roll-over relief on certain employee share ownership trusts (TCGA 1992, s 229); and

(5) roll-over relief on compulsory acquisition (TCGA 1992, s 247).

A further means by which the charge to capital gains tax is expressly excluded on a disposal is where assets are deemed to have been acquired at market value without a corresponding disposal having taken place. The most significant such provision is where, on death, personal representatives are deemed to acquire the assets of the deceased for a consideration equal to their market value on the date of death, but those assets are not deemed to have been disposed of by the deceased (TCGA 1992, s 62(1)).

A final important area to consider is that of double taxation relief. This may be available under the provisions of the Taxation (International and Other Provisions) Act 2010 or under a relevant double taxation convention. A detailed consideration is beyond the scope of this work.

Disposals of UK residential property by non-UK residents

[14.51] FA 2015 has introduced the concept of a *non-resident CGT disposal* (see TCGA 1992, s 14B). The gain accruing on such a disposal is referred to as a NRCGT gain (TCGA 1992, s 57B and Sch 4ZZB). A NRCGT gain gives rise to a liability to UK capital gains tax on non-UK residents disposing of residential property situated in the UK (TCGA 1992, s 14D). This applies equally to individuals, trustees, personal representatives and companies. As an exception to the general rule that capital gains tax is chargeable only on UK residents this is a noteworthy and significant extension to the legislative scheme, singling out the UK residential property sector for particular consideration.

Relief in relation to deemed disposals

[14.52] The UK capital gains tax legislation includes a number of charges on deemed disposals where property would cease to be within the charge to capital gains tax by reason of the owner of such property ceasing to be UK resident. A corollary of the extension of the charge to certain non-UK residents is that the charge on such a deemed disposal is no longer justifiable on the basis that the asset is outside the scope of the charge to UK capital gains tax. This has been recognised in the legislation with the result that where the property in question would be within the charge to tax on non-resident CGT disposals such deemed disposals are to be treated, in the absence of an election to the contrary, on a no gain/no loss basis.

This applies to deemed disposal of assets held by a branch or permanent establishment under TCGA 1992, s 25 (TCGA 1992, s 25ZA), the deemed disposal by emigrating trustees (TCGA 1992, ss 80 and 80A), the deemed disposal by the recipient of property on which hold-over relief has been claimed (TCGA 1992, ss 168 and 168A) and the deemed disposal on a company becoming non-resident (TCGA 1992, ss 185 and 187B).

When is there a non-resident CGT disposal

[14.53] The concept of a non-resident CGT disposal is central to the NRCGT charge. Although the definition is itself in relatively wide terms it is currently limited by references to disposals of UK residential property.

For a non-resident CGT disposal, there must be a disposal of (i) a UK residential property interest by (ii) a person who is not UK resident in the tax year of the disposal. This will include an individual who makes the disposal during the overseas part of a split year.

The concept applies to individuals, trusts, personal representatives and companies. Disposals from branches or permanent establishments which would otherwise be chargeable under TCGA 1992, ss 10A and 10B are, however, excluded (TCGA 1992, s 14B(5)).

Disposal of a UK residential property interest

[14.54] There will be a disposal of a UK residential property interest if there is a disposal of an interest in UK land and either (i) the land has consisted of or included a dwelling at any time during the *relevant ownership period* or (ii) the interest subsists for the benefit of land which has consisted of or included a dwelling during the *relevant ownership period* or (iii) the interest subsists under a contract for an off plan purchase (TCGA 1992, Sch B1, para 1(1)–(3)).

It is relevant to note that the requirement under (i) and (ii) need only be met at any time during the relevant ownership period. Nevertheless, periods during which the interest in question is not a dwelling will be relevant in computing the NRCGT gain.

Interest in UK land

[14.55] The definition of *interest in UK land* is in almost identical terms to the definition of chargeable interest for SDLT purposes (FA 2003, s 48 and TCGA 1992, Sch B1, para 2).

It includes any estate, interest, right or power in or over land in the UK and the benefit of any right affecting such, save to the extent that the interest is an excluded interest. Excluded interests are (i) security interests (rights securing the payment of a sum of money) (ii) licences to use or occupy the property and (iii) in England, Wales and Northern Ireland a tenancy at will or a manor. The only difference with the SDLT exclusions is that neither an advowson nor a franchise is an excluded interest.

Express provision is also made to include the grant of an option binding the grantor to sell an interest in UK land within the scope of *interest in UK* land in circumstances where it would not otherwise be so regarded. This would not, however, seem to include an option which could be discharged in some way other than by selling an interest in UK land (contrast FA 2003, s 46(2)).

Relevant ownership period

[14.56] The *relevant ownership period* is the period beginning with the later of the date of the first acquisition of any part of the interest being disposed of and 6 April 2015 and ending with the day before the disposal (TCGA 1992, Sch B1, para 1(4)).

Dwelling

[14.57] Confusingly, the legislation provides a definition of *dwelling* which is different to those definitions of that term which apply for SDLT purposes (both the definition of residential property in FA 2003, s 116 and of dwelling in FA 2003, Sch 4A, para 7) and ATED (FA 2013, s 112).

The NRCGT definition of *dwelling* includes the familiar definition of dwelling as building or part of a building which is used or suitable for use as a dwelling or one which is being constructed or adapted for such use. It also includes land intended to be occupied as part of the dwelling (TCGA 1992, Sch B1, para 4(1), (2) and (11)).

A building ceases to be a dwelling when it is demolished to ground level or to ground level subject only to a façade retained as a condition of planning consent (TCGA 1992, Sch B1, para 7). Planning permission as a requirement was confirmed in *J3 Building Solutions v HMRC* [2016] UKFTT 318 (TC).

There are, however, a number of relevant and important exclusions from this definition not all of which apply in other statutory definitions (TCGA 1992, Sch B1, para 4(3)–(9)). These are:

(a)   residential accommodation for school pupils;

(b)   residential accommodation for members of the armed forces;

(c)   a home or other institution providing residential accommodation for children;

(d)   a home or other institution providing residential accommodation with personal care for persons in need of personal care by reason of old age, disability, past or present dependence on alcohol or drugs or past or present mental disorder;

(e)   a hospital or hospice;

(f)   a prison or similar establishment;

(g)   a hotel or inn or similar establishment;

(h)   any other institution that is the sole or main residence of its residents;

(i)   buildings occupied by students and managed or controlled by their educational establishment within Housing Act 2004, Sch 14; and

(j)   purpose built student accommodation of at least 15 bedrooms which is occupied for at least 165 days a year.

Temporary unsuitability as a dwelling

[14.58] Temporary unsuitability of a property for use as a dwelling will not in general cause that property to cease to be treated as a dwelling (TCGA 1992, Sch B1, para 4(10)). This is subject to two exceptions where the unsuitability is caused by accidental damage and where it is caused by works undertaken in accordance with planning permission.

Where the temporary unsuitability is caused by damage which was accidental or beyond the control of the disponor (not being damage caused in the course of making alterations) and the unsuitability lasted for at least 90 consecutive days ending at or before the end of the relevant ownership period, the property will not be treated as a dwelling during the period of unsuitability of use and works to restore the property will be disregarded in determining whether it is a dwelling (TCGA 1992, Sch B1, para 6).

There is also provision (TCGA 1992, Sch B1, para 8) that where a dwelling is wholly or partly demolished so that it ceases to be suitable as a dwelling it will be treated as unsuitable for use as a dwelling (and therefore not a dwelling) during any period when works were not in progress or the building was not used as a dwelling in connection with that work provided that the result of the works is that the building has ceased to exist or become suitable for use otherwise than as a dwelling; that planning permission has been obtained as necessary; and that conditions of such permission have been complied with. If those conditions are not met, the works are taken not to have affected the building's suitability as a dwelling, although they may be met by retrospective planning permission (TCGA 1992, Sch B1, para 9).

Contract for off-plan purchase

[14.59] A contract for off-plan purchase is a contract for the acquisition of land consisting of or including a building to be constructed or adapted for use as a dwelling (TCGA 1992, Sch B1, para 1(6)).

A contract for an off-plan purchase is treated as being a dwelling at all times in computing the NRCGT gain (TCGA 1992, Sch 4ZZB, para 10).

Computing the NRCGT gain

[14.60] A non-resident CGT disposal gives rise to a charge to tax on the amount of the chargeable NRCGT gain accruing to that person in the tax year of disposal less any unused losses accruing to the person on disposals of UK residential property interests in that and previous tax years (TCGA 1992, s 14D).

Losses which do not relate to UK residential property cannot be set against NRCGT gains (TCGA 1992, ss 2(7B) and 14D(4)). In contrast, however, allowable NRCGT losses which have been carried forward or accrue in a split year will be available to set against other gains of the taxpayer (TCGA 1992, ss 2(2A) and (2B)).

As with other losses, relief can only be given once in respect of NRCGT losses which also cannot be carried back except on death (TCGA 1992, ss 62 and 14E).

The calculation of the NRCGT gain is complicated by provisions which seek to exclude gains accruing before 5 April 2015 from charge as well as periods during which the interest disposed of was not a dwelling. Moreover, different rules will apply where a disposal is a *relevant high value disposal* that is to say a disposal by a person within the charge to ATED (see TCGA 1992, s 2C and TCGA 1992, Sch 4ZZB, Part 4).

Computation rules where no relevant high value disposal

Interest acquired before 5 April 2015

[14.61] Where the disposal is not a relevant high value disposal or does not comprise a relevant high value disposal the NRCGT gain is computed by firstly determining the post-April 2015 gain. This is the gain which would have accrued to the disponor on the assumption that the property was acquired at its market value on 5 April 2015. That gain is then reduced by reference to the number of days since 5 April 2015 in which the interest disposed of was wholly or partly a dwelling as a proportion of the entire number of days in that period. Where there are a number of dwellings, this may require a just and reasonable apportionment (TCGA 1992, Sch 4ZZB, para 6). The deemed acquisition on 5 April 2015 is disregarded for purposes of determining whether the asset is a wasting asset (TCGA 1992, Sch 4ZZB, para 24).

An off-plan contract is treated as being a dwelling throughout its period of ownership (TCGA 1992, Sch 4ZZB, para 10).

Interest acquired after 5 April 2015

[14.62] Where the interest is acquired after 5 April 2015 or a suitable election is made the entire gain falls within the scope of charge reduced as per the post-5 April 2015 gain above, that is to say by reference to the proportionate period of ownership in which the interest was a dwelling with just and reasonable apportionment for mixed use of multiple dwellings (TCGA 1992, Sch 4ZZB, para 9).

Election between alternative methods of computation for persons who have held land on 5 April 2015

[14.63] As an alternative to the use of the actual market value of the property on 5 April 2015 a taxpayer may elect for the post-April 2015 gain to be determined either (i) on a straight-line time apportionment basis or by a retrospective basis of computation (TCGA 1992, Sch 4ZZB, para 2). An election will be irrevocable and must be made on a tax return or a NRCGT return (TCGA 1992, Sch 4ZZB, para 3).

If a straight-line time apportionment election is made the post-April 2015 gain is determined as the fraction of the total gain by reference to which the period of post-April 2015 ownership bears to the total period of ownership (TCGA 1992, Sch 4ZZB, para 8).

An election for retrospective basis of computation has the effect that the NRCGT gain is calculated by reference to the entire gain with no adjustment for pre-5 April 2015 periods of ownership. A similar election for ATED-related gains will be binding for these purposes (TCGA 1992, Sch 4ZZB, para 9).

Computation in cases involving a relevant high value disposal

[14.64] The disposal of an interest in a dwelling by a non-UK resident company is potentially subject to the charge to capital gains tax on ATED-related gains and also subject to the charge on non-resident CGT disposals. Where this is the case the disposal will involve a *relevant high value disposal* and different rules will apply to calculate the gain.

ATED applies to dwellings (as defined in FA 2013, s 112) held by a company, a partnership of which a company is a member and a collective investment scheme where the value of the interest in the dwelling exceeds the *threshold amount* (FA 2013, s 97). Disposals by individuals, trustees and personal representatives are not within the scope of ATED and are excluded persons insofar as a gain accrues to them on a disposal of partnership assets of property held for the purposes of a relevant collective investment scheme (TCGA 1992, s 2B).

For a full discussion as to the scope of ATED see **CHAPTER 22**.

ATED-related chargeable gains are charged at a rate of 28%. In contrast NRCGT gains which accrue to a company are charged at 20% (TCGA 1992, s 4). Where both are in point, the legislation gives priority to the ATED-related chargeable gains. It does this by calculating the NRCGT gain by reference to the proportion of the relevant ownership period in which the interest in question was a dwelling but excluding those days which are ATED chargeable days.

Relevant high value disposal

[14.65] Where the interest disposed of is within the scope of ATED and the consideration for the disposal exceeds the *threshold amount* (£2 million for 2014/15 reducing to £500,000 for 2016/17) the disposal will involve a relevant high value disposal (see TCGA 1992, ss 2C and 2D).

Restriction on elections

[14.66] Where there is a relevant high value disposal, it is not possible to elect for a straight-line time apportionment (TCGA 1992, Sch 4ZZB, para 2(2)). It is, however, possible to elect for the retrospective basis of computation, that is to say, for no rebasing. Such an election made under TCGA 1992, Sch 4ZZA for purposes of ATED-related chargeable gains will be binding in determining the NRCGT gain (TCGA 1992, Sch 4ZZB, para 2(5)).

Calculating the NRCGT gain

[14.67] The methodology for calculating the NRCGT gain is essentially the same as for disposals where there is no relevant high value disposal, save that the gain is reduced not only by reference to those days of ownership in the relevant period during which the property was not a dwelling, but also by reference to those days of ownership in the relevant period during which the property was not within the charge to ATED (TCGA 1992, Sch 4ZZB, paras 12(5) and 13–15). In this way, the NRCGT gain excludes ATED-related chargeable gains (which take priority).

Companies

[14.68] In addition to a lower rate of 20% applying to companies, provision is also made for the inclusion of indexation relief in relation to the calculations (TCGA 1992, Sch 4ZZB, para 22). There is also significant provision for group relief to apply in relation to non-resident capital gains accruing to companies.

Group relief

[14.69] Qualifying members of a group of companies (all of which are required to be non-resident) may make a pooling election, forming a NRCGT group, as a result of which assets within the charge to non-resident CGT can be transferred among that NRCGT group without any charge to tax. Disposals out of the group will be liable to capital gains tax with the members being liable on a joint several basis (TCGA 1992, ss 188A–188K).

Exemption for eligible persons

[14.70] The charge on NRCGT gains will not apply to certain eligible non-resident persons upon their making a claim (TCGA 1992, s 14F). This is, however, subject to restrictions intended to prevent the exploitation of the exemption for tax avoidance purposes.

Eligible persons

[14.71] The categories of eligible persons are (i) diversely held companies (ii) unit trust schemes and open-ended investment companies meeting specified conditions and (iii) companies carrying on life assurance business.

Diversely-held companies

[14.72] A diversely held company is a company which is not a *closely-held company* as defined in TCGA 1992, Sch C1.

The definition of closely held is similar but not identical to the definition of close company in CTA 2010, Chapter 2, Part 9. Importantly it includes companies which are not resident in the UK. There are, however, other differences: for example a company under the control of participators who are directors would be a close company (if UK resident) but would not necessarily be a closely held company.

Very broadly a closely-held company is one which is either under the control of five or fewer participators (as defined for corporation tax purposes: CTA 2010, s 454) or in relation to which five or fewer participators (or companies owned by them) are entitled to acquire the greater part of the assets on a notional winding up (disregarding rights of loan creditors) (TCGA 1992, Sch C1, paras 2–4).

A company will not be closely held where it only satisfies the conditions by reason of a diversely held company being one of the five or fewer participators (TCGA 1992, Sch C1, para 5(2)). A similar exclusion applies where the treatment as a closely-held company depends upon loan creditor participators who are diversely held companies or qualified institutional investors. Qualified institutional investors include widely marketed schemes (see TCGA 1992, para 5(4)(a) and s 14F(5)), qualifying pension schemes, companies carrying on life insurance businesses and sovereign funds (TCGA 1992, Sch C1, para 5(3)–(5)).

Interests held by qualified institutional investors (and collective investment schemes) are also treated as held by more than five participators for purposes of determining whether a company is closely held (TCGA 1992, Sch C1, para 6).

Schemes

[14.73] A scheme, being a unit trust scheme or an open-ended investment company incorporated by virtue of regulations under FSMA 2000, s 262 (or its equivalent under foreign law) will also qualify if it is a *widely marketed scheme* either on its own account or having regard to the documentation of investors under the same management which are open ended investment companies or authorised unit trusts.

A *widely marketed scheme* is one which meets conditions which broadly relate to information as to the intended categories of investor, require that units are made widely available in a way which is sufficient to reach the intended categories of investor and prohibits provisions which would limit or deter investors (TCGA 1992, Sch C1, para 11).

Companies carrying on life assurance business

[14.74] A company carrying on a life assurance business within FA 2012, s 56 will be an eligible person if the interest in UK land, which is the subject of the disposal, is held to provide benefits to policyholders in the course of the company's business.

Anti-avoidance

[14.75] Provision is included to prevent the application of the closely held companies rules through use of cell companies or divided companies. These are loosely defined as companies in relation to which some or all of the assets are available to meet particular liabilities and in relation to which some or all of the members and creditors have right primarily in relation to particular assets. The question of whether a company is closely held is addressed by reference to the cell or division of the company realising the gain (TCGA 1992, s 14G).

There is also a motive test exclusion where arrangements are entered into with the main purpose of avoiding non-resident CGT which would otherwise arise as a result of an exemption not being available. In such circumstances the arrangements are to be disregarded (TCGA 1992, s 14H).

Relief on disposal of principal private residence

[14.76] The most significant relief from capital gains tax on disposals of interests in land is undoubtedly that which applies to the gain accruing on the disposal of a dwelling-house which has been the only or main residence of a relevant individual.

Although the application of this relief is in many aspects relatively straight-forward, it has come under increasing scrutiny from HMRC in recent years leading to numerous appeals to the Tax Tribunal.

In addition, Finance Act 2014 has introduced a number of changes which have made the relief less generous than had previously been the case. In particular, periods in which a person is deemed to occupy a property as his only or main residence have been reduced from 36 months to 18 months for disposals after 6 April 2014 (FA 2014, s 58).

In addition, the introduction of the charge to tax on non-residents in relation to dwellings in the UK has led to added complications. In particular, a concern that non-residents would always elect for the treatment of their UK residence as their main residence for the purposes of the relief (their non-UK residences falling outside the scope of the charge to capital gains tax in any event) has led to the introduction of new rules concerning disposals of residences by non-UK residents.

Nature of the relief

[14.77] Where the relief applies, no part of any gain is a chargeable gain. This is, however, subject to possible reduction in the level of relief where a dwelling-house has not been the individual's only or main residence through-out the period of ownership. The meaning of 'residence' and 'period of ownership' are considered below.

Apportionments of consideration will be made where a person disposes of a dwelling-house only part of which is his only or main residence (TCGA 1992, s 222(10)). Such an apportionment operates by relieving part of the gain from charge, not by removing the asset or any part of it from charge. As such, where another relief is in point, its applicability is determined by reference to the asset and gain as a whole (*Jeffries v Revenue and Customs Comrs* [2009] UKFTT 291 (TC), [2010] SFTD 189, [2010] SWTI 234).

In this chapter, the person referred to as the relevant individual will be the person residing in the property in order for relief to apply. As discussed below, however, the gain may not necessarily accrue to that person. The relief is available on gains accruing to individuals, trustees and personal representatives.

The relief is never available on a disposal by a company.

Property qualifying for the relief

An interest

[14.78] The relief extends to any interest in the property, whether it is a leasehold or freehold interest, whether it is a legal or equitable interest, and whether ownership is of the entire interest or of an undivided share as a tenant in common or a joint tenant. Shares in a company holding a dwelling-house will not give an interest in that dwelling-house.

Dwelling-house

[14.79] An interest in a dwelling-house or part of a dwelling-house which is, or has at any time in the relevant period of ownership been the only or main residence of a relevant individual (a qualifying dwelling) will qualify for the relief (TCGA 1992, s 222(1)(a)).

There is no statutory definition of dwelling for these purposes (in contrast to the position for NRCGT gains). The term dwelling-house will include a flat as well as a house. It is also likely to include a garage which comes with the flat or house. It will not include a partly built building which is as yet uninhabitable (*Makins v Elson (H M Inspector of Taxes)* [1977] STC 46).

HMRC accept that a group of flats may be a single dwelling house if they are all occupied by the relevant individual and his or her family, they are within the same block and they are contiguous (Capital Gains Manual 64305). Where a group of flats are occupied by a single family, but are not contiguous, it will be difficult to show that they are a single dwelling (*Honour (Inspector of Taxes) v Norris* [1992] STC 304, 64 TC 599). Further where a dwelling house has a fully self-contained flat with its own access attached to it, that flat will not automatically be regarded as part of the qualifying dwelling.

A dwelling-house can include another person's dwelling house if use of the latter is for the purpose of serving the former as a residence (*Batey (Inspector of Taxes) v Wakefield* [1982] 1 All ER 61, [1981] STC 521). This is a question of fact and degree, although no building can form part of a dwelling-house which includes a main house unless that building is appurtenant to, and within the curtilage of, the main house (*Lewis (H M Inspector of Taxes) v Rook* [1992] STC 171). In *Richie v HMRC* [2017] UKFTT 449 (TC), the First-tier Tribunal qualified the approach in *Lady Rook* to the effect that the correct test is to consider whether a building in dispute was within the curtilage of, and appurtenant to, the 'main house' in circumstances where there is not an obvious 'main house' (paras 195–198).

A houseboat may qualify as a dwelling house (Hansard 21 March 1985) as can a caravan (*Makins v Elson (H M Inspector of Taxes)* [1977] STC 46). Mobility and connection to services will be relevant concerns in this regard (see Capital Gains Manual 64325 and *Moore v Thompson* [1986] STC 170). In particular, a caravan which has been rendered immobile and is connected to mains water and electricity is much more likely to be regarded as a dwelling-house. The importance of this issue is likely to relate to the availability of relief in respect of the land used with the caravan or houseboat than it is in relation to relief on the caravan or houseboat itself.

Land used with the dwelling-house

[14.80] Land which is used for occupation and enjoyment of a qualifying dwelling as its garden or grounds and is of an area of up to 0.5 of a hectare, or such larger area as is required for the reasonable enjoyment of the dwelling house, will also qualify for the relief (TCGA 1992, s 222(1)(b), (2), (3)).

Whether land is occupied and enjoyed as garden or grounds will be a question of fact. The fact of registration under a single title will be irrelevant. Garden and grounds will be given their normal meaning. In this respect, grounds have been taken to be an area of enclosed land surrounding a large house or other building while a garden has been held to require some degree of cultivation (*Fountain v HMRC* [2015] UKFTT 419 (TC)).

Occupation means possession of the land while enjoyment is taken to mean possession without contested claims from third parties (see RI 119, August 1995, Capital gains tax: private residence relief-garden or grounds). Neither requires residence or use.

The test of whether land is occupied and enjoyed with the qualifying dwelling as its garden or grounds is to be determined as at the date of disposal (*Varty (Inspector of Taxes) v Lynes* [1976] STC 508). This can have the anomalous consequence that a garden sold at the same time as, or before, the sale of a qualifying dwelling to which it is attached will qualify for relief, but a garden sold after that qualifying dwelling will not qualify for relief. This is because it is not, at that time, occupied *with that* residence.

HMRC have stated that they will not take this point 'where the taxpayer ceased to occupy the house before he sold it' unless the garden has development value (See *Tolley's Yellow Tax Handbook*, Press Releases, June 1976, CCAB). In any event, it is doubtful that the decision in *Varty (Inspector of Taxes) v Lynes* applies to deny relief where the taxpayer has simply ceased to reside in a dwelling (see Capital Gains Manual 64377).

HMRC generally accepts that land surrounding and in the same ownership as a qualifying dwelling is the grounds of that qualifying dwelling, unless that land is used for some inconsistent purpose. This will include land which has traditionally been part of the grounds of the residence. If land is used for agriculture, commercial woodlands, trade or business or has been fenced off from the residence to be sold for development HMRC consider that it will not qualify for relief. Further, if land is separated from the qualifying dwelling by other land which is not in the same ownership as the residence, it will usually not be part of the garden or grounds, although HMRC accept that there can be exceptions to this. (See RI 119, August 1995, Capital gains tax: private residence relief-garden or grounds).

In respect of this latter point, it was held by the Special Commissioners in *Wakeling v Pearce* [1995] STC (SCD) 96 that a parcel of land separated from a qualifying dwelling was on the facts of that case subject to the relief.

As regards the question of when a larger area is required for the reasonable enjoyment of the dwelling-house, it has been held that this is a question of what is objectively required, ie necessary, at a house in order to enjoy it as a residence. This is not the same thing as what an individual taxpayer may subjectively wish to do (see *Longson v Baker (Inspector of Taxes)* [2001] STC 6).

Land not used with the dwelling-house

[14.81] Where part of the land occupied with a qualifying dwelling is used for its occupation and enjoyment as garden or grounds and part of the land so occupied is not (the non-qualifying land), then so much of that non-qualifying land as is most suitable for occupation and enjoyment with the qualifying dwelling, up to an area of 0.5 of a hectare, will still qualify for relief (TCGA 1992, s 222(4)).

In order for this to apply then (i) the land in question must be occupied with the qualifying dwelling and (ii) part of it must be occupied and enjoyed with the residence as its gardens or grounds.

Limitations on non-UK residents

[14.82] A dwelling-house will be deemed not to be occupied as a residence by a person at any time in his or her period of ownership which falls within a tax year or partial tax year during which neither the person disposing of the residence nor his or her spouse or civil partner was resident in the UK unless that person (or his or her spouse or civil partner) spends at least 90 days (or the equivalent proportion of a partial tax year) in a *qualifying house*. For these purposes a *qualifying house* is one in which the disponor, his spouse or civil partner has an interest in and which is in the UK (TCGA 1992, ss 222A–222C).

Residence for these purposes is determined by reference to liability to tax in another territory by reason of domicile or residence, or by reference to the application of the statutory residence test (FA 2013, Sch 45, Part 1) as if references to the UK were to the overseas territory (TCGA 1992, s 222B(6)–(9)).

Second homes

[14.83] A relevant individual may have an interest in two or more residences in a given period. Relief is, however, only available in respect of one residence. The default position is that this will be the 'main residence', although in determining which residence is the main residence of a relevant individual, no regard is had to any property in which that individual resides if he does not own an interest in it (for example by reason of residing there under licence).

A residence will be treated as a main residence if an election is made by giving notice to HMRC within two years from the date when the relevant individual first had two such residences (TCGA 1992, s 222(5)). A notice of election may be varied at any time by a further notice to HMRC. That further notice will only be effective in relation to the period of two years preceding the date on which it was given (TCGA 1992, s 222(5)). An exception to this concerns non-resident CGT disposals qualifying for the relief: for so long as a property subject to an election has not been disposed of, the election may be varied by the person making a non-resident CGT disposal at the time of filing an NRCGT return (TCGA 1992, s 222A). The original election will, however, continue to have effect subject to such variation (TCGA 1992, s 222(6A)).

The question of which of two residences is the main residence is a question of fact and degree (*Harrison v HMRC* [2015] UKFTT 539 (TC) at para 41). If, however, there is a notice, it will apply to treat a residence as a main residence (even if it is not) and will conclusively operate to do so (*Ellis v Revenue and Customs Comrs* [2013] UKFTT 775 (TC), [2013] SFTD 144 [2013] SWTI 1251). An election will not, however, be effective unless it can be shown that the property to which the notice relates is in fact a residence (see *Harte v Revenue and Customs Comrs* (TC01951) [2012] UKFTT 258 (TC), [2012] SWTI 2219).

If the relevant individual is living with his spouse, and they have two residences the notice to HMRC must be given by both of them (TCGA 1992, s 222(6)). If the qualifying dwelling is owned by trustees, the election must be made by the trustees and the relevant individual jointly (TCGA 1992, s 225(1)(b)).

A change in the combination of residences will give rise to a new two-year period (see *Griffin (Inspector of Taxes) v Craig-Harvey* [1994] STC 54). Accordingly, where the period for making an election has expired, it may be possible to resurrect it by entering into a short term lease of a new residence – although actual residence (as to which see below) will be necessary.

In order to enable the relevant individual to elect that one of two dwelling houses is his main residence, he must first establish that the dwelling house which he elects to treat as his only or main residence is in fact a residence (*Moore v Thompson (H M Inspector of Taxes)* [1986] STC 170).

By concession (ESC D21 Private residence exemption: late claims in dual residence cases) where the interest of an individual in one of his residences has no more than a negligible capital value on the open market (for example a weekly rented flat) then this two-year time limit will be extended if the individual was unaware that a nomination could be made. The nomination may be made within a reasonable time of the individual becoming aware of the possibility of making a nomination, and it will be regarded as effective from the date on which the individual first had more than one residence.

If a relevant person has more than one residence and a notice electing for one of them to be treated as his main residence has not been made, then the question of which is in fact his main residence will be determined as a matter of fact and degree.

This is not determined solely by reference to the way in which he divides his time between the two (*Frost (Inspector of Taxes) v Feltham* [1981] 1 WLR 452, [1981] STC 115 (a case on mortgage interest relief)).

HMRC consider that the following factors are of relevance in determining this issue (Capital Gains Manual 64545):

(1)   If the individual is married or in a civil partnership, where does the family spend its time?

(2)   If the individual has children, where do they go to school?

(3) At which residence is the individual registered to vote?
(4) Where is the individual's place of work?
(5) How is each residence furnished?
(6) Which address is used for correspondence?
    (a) Banks and Building Societies
    (b) Credit cards
    (c) HMRC
(7) Where is the individual registered with a doctor/dentist?
(8) At which address is the individual's car registered and insured?
(9) Which address is the main residence for council tax?

It is clear that the question will be one of fact and degree, and that it is best avoided by means of a suitable election (*Harrison v HMRC* [2015] UKFTT 539 (TC)).

Right to future profits

[14.84] Relief is given in respect of future profits received under certain agreements where an individual has disposed of an interest in his main residence and the disposal is a consequence of a change to the situation of his or a co-owners place of work and that change was required by the employer of the individual or the co-owner (TCGA 1992, s 225C).

For the relief to apply the agreement must include a term entitling the individual to a share of the profit made by the purchaser; the purchaser's disposal of the dwelling-house must be within three years; and the agreement must be made with the employer or a person operating under an agreement with the employer. The share of the profit received is treated as a gain attributable to the initial disposal.

This provision applies from 6 April 2009. Before that a concession (ESC D37 Private residence exemption: relocation arrangements) gave a similar treatment.

Meaning of residence

[14.85] Whether a dwelling-house is also a residence is a question of fact albeit one which can be difficult to determine. The term 'residence' is given its ordinary meaning and considerations as to the meaning of the term in other contexts have been taken to be relevant. As such, statements as to residence being 'one's settled or usual abode' (*Levene v IRC* 13 TC 486 at 505) or 'a place where a man is based or where he continues to live, the place where he sleeps or shelters and has his home' (*Ricketts v Registration Officer for the City of Cambridge* [1970] 2 QB 463, [1970] 3 All ER 7, CA) have been used to indicate its meaning in the context of the relief.

Although there have been suggestions that residence must have a degree of permanence it has been made clear in several cases that there is no minimum period which is required in order for a dwelling house to qualify as a residence (*Moore v Thompson* [1986] STC 170). Indeed, a taxpayer was successful in establishing residence even though he only occupied a property for two months (*Dutton-Forshaw v HMRC* [2015] UKFTT 478 (TC)). Even occasional and short residence in a dwelling can cause it to be a residence. The difference between residence in a property and mere occupation is one of fact and degree. A Tribunal must consider the quality as well as the length of the occupation (*Regan v HMRC* [2012] UKFTT 570 (TC)). Generally it will be necessary to show some degree of continuity or some expectation of continuity to turn mere occupation into residence (*Kothari v HMRC* [2016] UKFTT 127 (TC)). In this respect, a distinction may be drawn between temporary accommodation and a settled abode (*Goodwin v Curtis* [1998] STC 475).

On this point, the reason for the purchase and occupation of the dwelling can be decisive. In *Morgan v HMRC* [2013] UKFTT 181 (TC) a property was purchased with the intention of providing a matrimonial home for the taxpayer and his fiancée. It was occupied for a short period before the engagement was broken off frustrating the purpose of the purchase and the taxpayer moved out. The Tribunal considered that the taxpayer need only show 'that at the time when he moved into the property, it was his intention to make it his permanent residence, even if he changed his mind about it the following day' (para 26) so that the relief was available. Such an emphasis on the taxpayers intent can, however, be equally relevant in showing that a property is not a residence. If a property is on the market it is likely to be regarded as a temporary home as there is no expectation of continuity of occupation (*Bradley v HMRC* [2013] UKFTT 131 (TC)).

The onus of proof is on the taxpayer to show that a property has been his residence, which means his home or the place where he lives. Mere occupation may not be enough having regard to all of the background facts, particularly if the quality of that occupation by the taxpayer is such that it is properly to be regarded as being occupied with a view to renovation rather than with a view of making the property his residence (*Moore v HMRC* [2010] UKFTT 445 (TC) and *Springthorpe v HMRC* [2010] UKFTT 582 (TC)). The availability of objective documentary evidence such as notifications of changes of address to third parties will be relevant to refute suggestions that occupation lacks the requisite degree of permanence (*Favell v HMRC* [2010] UKFTT 360 (TC)). Although not a pre-requisite, such evidence has been said to be relevant in demonstrating a person's connection to a property to the 'wider world' and accordingly adding to the overall picture (*Llewellyn v HMRC* [2013] UKFTT 323 (TC) at para 49).

Deemed residence

Periods of absence

[14.86] The qualifying dwelling will always be treated as if it were the relevant individual's only or main residence in the last 18 months of ownership of a qualifying dwelling. This period of deemed residence has been reduced from 36 months by FA 2014, s 58 but does not apply in respect of disposals by certain disabled persons and long-term residents of care homes and their spouses (TCGA 1992, s 225E).

In addition, the following are treated as periods during which the qualifying dwelling was the relevant individual's only or main residence if, both before and after the period, the qualifying dwelling was the individual's only or main residence (TCGA 1992, s 223(3)):

(1)   any period or periods of absence of up to three years,

(2)   any period of absence throughout which the individual worked in an employment outside the UK, and

(3)   any period or periods of absence of up to four years during which the individual could not reside in the qualifying dwelling because of the situation of his place of work or because his employer reasonably required him to reside elsewhere.

As regards deemed residence for absence by reason of employment within 2 and 3, HMRC will by concession apply such deemed residence to a spouse living with such an employee (ESC D3 Private residence exemption: periods of absence). These will also, by concession, apply where an individual does not by reason of his employment resume residence in the qualifying dwelling (ESC D4 Private residence exemption: periods of absence).

For non-resident CGT, disposals periods of residence before 6 April 2015 will be disregarded for these purposes unless an election is made specifying the date in which the dwelling-house was a residence. Where such an election is made, periods before 5 April 2015 are included in determining whether periods of absence are up to three years (TCGA 1992, s 223A).

Work-related residences

[14.87] Where a relevant individual resides in job-related living accommodation and intends in due course to occupy the qualifying dwelling as his only or main residence, he is treated as occupying the qualifying dwelling as a residence (TCGA 1992, s 222(8)).

For these purposes, job-related living accommodation is either:

(1)   living accommodation which is provided because such provision is necessary, customary or part of special security arrangements and is because of the employment of the relevant individual, his spouse or civil partner (TCGA 1992, s 222(8A)(a)); or

(2)   living accommodation which the relevant individual, his spouse or civil partner is required to live in under the terms of an arm's length contract where that contract also requires him to carry on a trade, profession or vocation on premises or other land provided by another person (TCGA 1992, s 222(8A)(b)).

This does not include accommodation provided by a company to one of its directors (or to the director of an associated company) unless that director has no material interest in the company and either the employment is as a full-time working director or the company is neither a trading company nor an investment company, or the company is a charitable company (TCGA 1992, s 222(8B)). Equally it does not include living accommodation provided by a company in which the relevant individual, his spouse or civil partner has a material interest or accommodation provided by a person with whom the relevant individual, his spouse or civil partner carries on a trade or business in partnership (TCGA 1992, s 222(8C)).

Divorce or separation

[14.88] Relief is given under TCGA 1992, s 225B where a partner to a marriage or civil partnership ceases to occupy the matrimonial home on separation or divorce and subsequently disposes of his or her interest to his spouse or civil partner. The relief applies to disposals after 6 April 2009. Before that, a concession (ESC D6: Private residence exemption: separated couples) applied in a similar manner.

For the relief to apply the disposal must be either under an order of the Court or made as part of an agreement in connection with the dissolution or annulment of the marriage or civil partnership, a judicial separation or separation in other circumstances such that the separation is likely to be permanent (TCGA 1992, s 225B(2)). Further, the property must have continued to be the only or main residence of the spouse or civil partner since the disponor ceased to reside there (TGCA 1992, s 225B(3)) and he must not have given notice that another property is his main residence (TGCA 1992, s 225B(4)).

Delay in taking up residence

[14.89] Where an individual either builds a house for use as his only or main residence, or renovates an existing house for such use, there may be a period of ownership (while building work or renovation is taking place) during which he is not occupying the property. By concession (ESC D49 Private residence relief: short delay by owner-occupier in taking up residence) the period before the individual uses the house as his only or main residence in these circumstances is treated (provided it does not exceed one year) as a period in which he does so use it. If there are good reasons outside the individual's control for the period exceeding one year it can be extended up to two years.

If the house is not used as an only or main residence within the period allowed, no relief will is given for the period before it is so used.

Relief under this concession does not affect any relief due on another qualifying dwelling in respect of the same period.

Off-plan purchase

[14.90] Where an individual purchases off-plan, it will be impossible for him to occupy the property immediately upon his contracting to purchase it. In *Higgins v HMRC* [2017] UKFTT 236 (TC), HMRC argued that this period before occupation was possible and had to be taken into account in calculating principal private residence relief by TCGA 1992, s 28. This unmeritorious argument was rejected by the First-tier Tribunal which held that period of ownership for the purposes of s 222 begins on the date when ownership has been physically and legally completed.

Disposal to spouse

[14.91] Where a spouse or a civil partner disposes of his or her interest in the qualifying dwelling to his partner (including on death), then that partner's period of ownership is taken to include the period of ownership of the spouse or civil partner making the disposal. If, however, the qualifying dwelling was not the only or main residence of both throughout the period of ownership of the disposing spouse or civil partner, it will be deemed to be the only or main residence of both for those periods in which it was the only or main residence of the disposing civil partner (TCGA 1992, s 222(7)(a), (b)).

Disabled persons and persons in care homes

[14.92] Where a disposal is made by a person who is a disabled person or long-term resident of a care home, or the spouse of such a person and the property disposed of is the only dwelling owned by such a person some relief is granted by treating the period of deemed residence as the last 36 months rather than the last 18 months (TCGA 1992, s 225E).

Persons qualifying for the relief

Individuals

[14.93] Where the relevant individual, that is the person residing in the qualifying dwelling, also owns an interest in the qualifying dwelling, then the relief will be available on a disposal of his interest in the qualifying dwelling (TCGA 1992, s 222).

Spouse or civil partner

[14.94] Where an individual is living with his spouse or civil partner the relief is restricted so that they cannot each claim relief on separate residences. Rather, for so long as they are living together a single residence is eligible for relief in relation to both of them. Where they have two residences, so that an election to treat one of them as a main residence affects both the individual and his spouse or civil partner, the notice to HMRC must be given by both (TCGA 1992, s 222(6)).

This treatment only applies for so long as they are both (i) married or in civil partnership and (ii) living together. Relief in respect of different properties will be available for so long as they have separate main residences and are not living together.

As discussed above, by concession a qualifying dwelling may be treated as a divorced or separated partner's main residence in certain circumstances where he is no longer living there.

Trustees of a settlement

[14.95] The relief will also be available on a gain accruing to the trustees of a settlement on a disposal of an interest in a qualifying dwelling where that interest is settled property and during the trustees' period of ownership the qualifying dwelling was the only or main residence of a relevant individual who was entitled to occupy it under the terms of the settlement. This requires a claim on the part of the trustees. Since, however, a claim is required in order that the relief is available, it would seem that an allowable loss will accrue to trustees in circumstances where they suffer a loss and no claim is made. By contrast an allowable loss can never accrue to an individual on a sale of a principal residence (TCGA 1992, s 16(2)).

An interest in a dwelling-house will be settled property if it is held in trust, unless someone is absolutely entitled to that property as against the trustee, that is to say the trustees hold as nominee or on bare trusts (TCGA 1992, ss 60, 68). Where the property is held for persons as tenants in common or joint tenants it will not be settled property (see *Harthan v Mason* [1980] STC 94). Where, however, an undivided share in the property is held on trusts, the remaining undivided share will also be settled property, even where it is held for persons absolutely (see *Crowe v Appleby (Inspector of Taxes)* [1975] 3 All ER 529, [1975] STC 502).

A relevant individual will be entitled to occupy a qualifying dwelling under the terms of a settlement where he has a right to do so under the terms of the settlement and also where the trustees have a discretionary power to permit such occupation (see *Sansom v Peay (Inspector of Taxes)* [1976] 3 All ER 375, [1976] STC 494). By contrast where there is no power to permit occupation and no right to demand a right of occupation, relief will not be available. That will, however, be a matter of construction of the trust instrument in question.

It has been suggested that the combined effect of ss 12 and 22 of the Trusts of Land and Appointment of Trustees Act 1996 is that beneficiaries of a trust holding an undivided interest in land will not be entitled to occupy that land, so that this relief would not be available. It is the author's view that this curiously literal approach to the construction of the relevant provisions is unsustainable, and that even in those circumstances, relief will be available in respect of the undivided share of a qualifying dwelling held by the trustees, and that such relief is available regardless of whether it is held in life interest or discretionary trusts.

HMRC concede that a relevant individual who is a discretionary beneficiary paying rent to the trustees will be entitled to occupy the property under the terms of the settlement for the purposes of the relief (Capital Gains Manual 65407). While this may be correct in many circumstances, care will be required to ensure that relief is available where such arrangements are adopted. In particular, relief is likely to be denied where the person occupying is not a beneficiary of the settlement (see Capital Gains Manual 65407).

Use of a settlement may provide a means of obtaining relief in respect of more than one family residence. In particular, an individual may own one property which is his main residence and on which relief is available. If a second property is held by trustees of a settlement created by that individual, and the trusts of the settlement permit inter alia the children of the individual to reside in it, and they do so reside in it, relief may also be available in respect of that property. HMRC are likely to consider the facts of such an arrangement carefully (Capital Gains Manual 65407).

Personal representatives

[14.96] Relief is available in respect of a gain accruing to the personal representatives of a deceased person on the disposal of a qualifying dwelling. The relief is only available if both immediately before and immediately after the death of the deceased person, the qualifying dwelling was the only or main residence of one or more relevant individuals and those relevant individuals were between them, entitled (either as legatees of the estate of the deceased or life tenants of a trust so entitled) to 75% or more of the net proceeds of disposal of the deceased's interest in the qualifying dwelling. The personal representatives must make a claim for such relief (TCGA 1992, s 225A).

Difficulties with the application of this relief might be avoided by assenting the interest in the property to the legatee or legatees before any sale takes place. Care should, however, be taken to ensure that the qualifying dwelling is the legatee's residence for at least some period of actual as opposed to deemed ownership (see TCGA 1992, s 62).

Any notice to treat the residence as a main residence is to be a joint notice by the personal representatives and the relevant individual or individuals.

Period of ownership

[14.97] The 'period of ownership' in relation to a dwelling-house will be taken to begin from the first acquisition on which allowable expenditure is incurred. Different periods do not apply in relation to different interests in the dwelling-house (TCGA 1992, s 222(7)).

Where a spouse or a civil partner disposes of his or her interest in the qualifying dwelling to his partner (including on death), then that partner's period of ownership is taken to include the period of ownership of the spouse or civil partner making the disposal. If, however, the qualifying dwelling was not the only or main residence of both throughout the period of ownership of the disposing spouse or civil partner, it will be deemed to be the only or main residence of both for those periods in which it was the only or main residence of the disposing civil partner (TCGA 1992, s 222(7)(a), (b)).

A period of ownership does not include any period before 31 March 1982 (TCGA 1992, s 223(7)).

In relation to NRCGT gains, the period of ownership is treated as beginning on 6 April 2015, unless an election for retrospective treatment has been made (TCGA 1992, s 223(7A) and Sch 4ZZB, para 9).

Reduction of relief

[14.98] If the qualifying dwelling has been a relevant individual's only or main residence throughout the disponor's period of ownership (or throughout that period except for all or any part of the last 18 months (36 months if the disposal is before 5 April 2014)) then no part of any gain accruing on the disposal of the disponor's interest will be a chargeable gain (TCGA 1992, s 223(1)).

Periods of non-residence

[14.99] Where the qualifying dwelling has not been the only or main residence of a relevant individual throughout the period of ownership, then relief applies to only a fraction of the gain. That fraction is the length of the part or parts of the period of ownership during which the dwelling-house was or was deemed to be the individual's only or main residence (including in any event the last 18 months (36 months if the disposal is before 5 April 2014 or relief under TCGA 1992, s 225E 'Disposals by disabled persons or persons in care homes etc' applies) of the period of ownership) divided by the total length of the period of ownership (TCGA 1992, s 223(2)).

Lettings

[14.100] Where relief would be reduced because the qualifying dwelling or any part of it is or has at any time in the period of ownership been wholly or partly let by him as residential accommodation then relief may be available to reduce the chargeable gain. In particular, the part of the gain which would be a chargeable gain by reason of the letting will be a chargeable gain only to the extent to which it exceeds the lesser of either:

(1)   the part of the gain which is not otherwise a chargeable gain; and
(2)   £40,000 (see TCGA 1992, s 223(4)).

This is not restricted to lettings where persons making their homes in the premises which are let but includes accommodation provided to paying guests staying there overnight or on holiday (Owen v Elliott [1990] STC 469).

Part of qualifying dwelling used for trade or business

[14.101] An apportionment will be made where part of a qualifying dwelling is used exclusively for the purpose of a trade, business, profession or vocation. Relief will not be available in relation to that part of the apportioned gain relating to that use (TCGA 1992, s 224(1)). Further adjustments will be made where during the period of ownership the part of the dwelling used for the purposes of a trade changes (TCGA 1992, s 224(2)).

As from 9 December 2009 where a property was occupied by another person under an adult placement scheme that occupation is to be disregarded and does not amount to the use of the dwelling-house for the purposes of a trade, business profession or vocation (TCGA 1992, s 225D).

Qualifying dwelling acquired for purpose of realising a gain

[14.102] Relief is not available if the acquisition of an interest in the qualifying dwelling 'was made wholly or partly for the purpose of realising a gain from the disposal of it'. Similarly it is not available in relation to any gain which is attributable to any expenditure which was incurred wholly or partly for the purpose of realising a gain from the disposal (see TCGA 1992, s 224(3)).

If a qualifying dwelling is acquired to provide a home then it is unlikely to have been acquired to realise a gain from it. The fact that there may be a hope or even an expectation of profiting from the property is not enough (see *Jones v Wilcock* [1996] STC (SCD) 389).

Hold-over relief claimed

[14.103] If the gain which would accrue on a disposal (absent any relief) would be reduced directly or indirectly as a result of a claim for hold-over relief under TCGA 1992, s 260 having been made on one or more earlier disposals, then relief under TCGA 1992, s 223 will not be available (TCGA 1992, s 226A). This applies by removing relief from the entire gain, and not merely the held-over gain.

This restriction applies to disposals made on or after 10 December 2003 regardless of the date of any earlier disposal on which hold-over relief was claimed (see FA 2004, Sch 22, para 7(3)). Where however, the original disposal (on which hold-over relief was claimed) was before 10 December 2003 transitional provisions apply so that any period after 10 December 2003 is treated as a period of non-residence (see FA 2004, Sch 22, para 8).

Where this transitional relief is in issue, it is likely to be advisable to maximise it by making a disposal of the qualifying dwelling, perhaps by transfer to a settlement (or a separate settlement where the property in question is already settled). On any subsequent disposal of the property from the settlement, the allowable expenditure will not fall to be reduced, so full relief should be available. Where the qualifying dwelling is held by an individual such an approach will require careful consideration of the inheritance tax consequences.

There is an exception to this treatment in relation to maintenance funds for historic buildings (TCGA 1992, s 226B)).

Hold-over reliefs

[14.104] Two separate provisions of the TCGA 1992 enable a claim to hold-over relief to be made on the disposal of certain assets. These provisions apply firstly in respect of gifts of business assets (TCGA 1992, s 165) (business asset hold-over relief) and secondly on gifts on which inheritance tax is chargeable (TCGA 1992, s 260) (IHT hold-over relief). The circumstances in which these reliefs are available is considered in more detail below.

Where both reliefs are in principle available, then only IHT hold-over relief will apply (TCGA 1992, s 165(3)(d)).

Conditions for availability of the relief

Persons eligible

[14.105] In order for hold-over relief to be available there must be both a disposal and an acquisition of an asset.

For IHT hold-over relief the disponor and acquirer must both be either individuals or trustees of a settlement. As such, the relief is not available on a disposal to or by a company (TCGA 1992, s 260(1)). For business asset hold-over relief, the disponor must be either an individual or trustees. There is only a restriction on the type of person the acquirer must be where the asset is shares or securities, in which case the acquirer cannot be a company (TCGA 1992, s 165(1), (3)(ba), Sch 7, para 2). Restrictions in respect of companies will not apply to corporate trustees (see RI 222 Corporate trustees and hold-over relief).

The relief will only apply on a claim being made by both parties, unless the acquirers are the trustees of a settlement, in which case a claim by the disponor of the asset is sufficient (TCGA 1992, ss 260(1), 165(1)(b)).

The relief will only be available if the acquirer is resident in the UK (TCGA 1992, ss 261, 166).

Disposal made otherwise than under a bargain at arm's length

[14.106] In order for hold-over relief under either provision to be available, the disposal must be made otherwise than under a bargain at arm's length (TCGA 1992, ss 260(2), 165(1)(a)). Such a disposal would be deemed to be made for a consideration equal to the market value of the assets disposed of in the absence of the relief (TCGA 1992, s 17). It is noted, however, that it is not necessary that there should be an absolute gift, and a sale at an undervalue will also qualify for relief.

Gifts on which inheritance tax is chargeable

[14.107] Although the heading of TCGA 1992, s 260 is 'Gifts on which inheritance tax is chargeable etc' and this is how the relief has been characterised in this chapter, it is not strictly true that inheritance tax must be chargeable in order for the relief to be available.

The principal circumstance in which IHT hold-over relief is available is a chargeable transfer within the meaning of IHTA 1984 which is not a potentially exempt transfer within IHTA 1984, s 3A (TCGA 1992, s 260(2)(a)). Gifts which would be chargeable but for being within the inheritance tax annual exemption of £3,000 will still qualify for relief.

Since 22 March 2006 the categories of transfers of value which for inheritance tax purposes qualify as potentially exempt transfers have been significantly restricted. A potentially exempt transfer can now be made only on a gift by an individual to another individual and on a gift to a very limited class of trusts, the most significant of which is the disabled persons trust (see IHTA 1984, ss 3A(1A), 89). Accordingly, the substantive trusts of a settlement are no longer likely to be of significant relevance to the question of whether IHT hold-over relief is available. The most important issue relating to the availability of the relief, as discussed below at **14.114**, will be the persons who may benefit under the settlement.

The disposal only needs to be a chargeable transfer for inheritance tax purposes. As such it does not need give rise to a charge to inheritance tax. In particular, a disposal will still qualify for relief even if no charge arises because the value of the transfer of value falls within the relevant individual's inheritance tax nil rate band (IHTA 1984, s 7, Sch 1).

Additionally, it is to be noted that inheritance tax is chargeable only in respect of the reduction in the value of a person's estate, and not on the value of the asset itself (IHTA 1984, s 3). Subject to the discussion below at **14.114**, it will generally be possible to exploit this difference in approach to enable relief to be obtained without a charge to inheritance tax.

The relief is also available on an individual beneficiary becoming absolutely entitled to trust property in circumstances where that trust property had immediately before that occasion been held on either: accumulation and maintenance trusts within IHTA 1984, s 71; trusts for a bereaved minor within IHTA 1984, s 71A; or age 18 to 25 trusts within IHTA 1984, s 71D, and inheritance tax would not otherwise be chargeable on that occasion (TCGA 1992, s 260(2)(d), (da), (db)).

Other circumstances in which this hold-over relief will be available are relatively discrete and of limited importance. These include disposals to political parties qualifying for relief under IHTA 1984, s 24; various disposals to maintenance funds for historic buildings qualifying for relief under either IHTA 1984, s 27 or 57A or Sch 4, para 9, 16 or 17; and disposals qualifying for relief under IHTA 1984, s 30 or 78 by reason of a Treasury designation (TCGA 1992, s 260(2)(b), (c), (e) and (f)).

Business assets

[14.108] Business asset hold-over relief is only available in respect of certain assets (business assets). There are a number of categories of assets which qualify as business assets.

Firstly, an asset will be a business asset in relation to an individual disponor if it is, or is an interest in, an asset used for the purposes of a trade, profession or vocation carried on by either that individual, his personal company or a member of a trading group of which the holding company is the disponor's personal company (TCGA 1992, s 165(2)(a)). It is irrelevant that his company may rent for use of the asset.

Where the disponor is a trustee, the trade, profession or vocation can be carried on by the trustee or a beneficiary with an interest in possession in the settled property disposed of (TCGA 1992, Sch 7, para 2). There is no provision for relief in respect of assets used in the trade of a company owned by trustees.

Secondly, shares will be a business asset for the purposes of the relief if they are unlisted shares in either a trading company or the holding company of a trading group and an individual disponor can exercise at least 5% of the voting rights in that company, or trustee disponors can exercise at least 25% of the voting rights in that company (TCGA 1992, s 165(2)(b), (8), Sch 7, para 2(2)(b)).

A personal company of an individual is a company in respect of which that individual can exercise at least 5% of the voting rights (TCGA 1992, s 165(8)).

The definitions of 'holding company' trading company' and 'trading group' are to be found in TCGA 1992, s 165A.

Extended meaning of trade

[14.109] The term trade is extended to include occupation of woodlands on a commercial basis with a view to the realisation of profits (TCGA 1992, s 165(9)). It will also include commercial letting of furnished holiday accommodation in the UK and in the EEA (TCGA 1992, s 241(3) and s 241A(4)).

Agricultural property

[14.110] Property qualifying for inheritance tax agricultural property relief under IHTA 1984, Pt V, Ch II at the date of disposal will be treated as being used for the purposes of a trade for the purposes of determining whether it is a business asset (TCGA 1992, Sch 7, paras 1, 3).

How hold-over relief operates

[14.111] Where hold-over relief is claimed, it generally operates by reducing the chargeable gain which would otherwise accrue on the disposal to zero. The amount of the consideration which the acquirer is treated as having provided to obtain the asset in question (ie the market value of the asset) will be reduced by the amount of that gain. As such, the gain is deferred until the subsequent disposal of the asset by the acquirer (TCGA 1992, ss 260(3), (4), 165(4), (6)).

This is subject to an exception where there is a sale at an undervalue (so that actual consideration is paid) and the disposal is not one which occurs by reason of a beneficiary becoming absolutely entitled against trustees. Where the actual consideration exceeds the allowable deductions, then the chargeable gain shall only be reduced to the amount by which the actual consideration so exceeds those allowable deductions. Equally, the deemed cost of acquisition is only reduced to the extent that the chargeable gain is reduced (TCGA 1992, ss 260(3), (5), (9), 165(4), (7)).

Where inheritance tax is payable on a disposal, the amount of that inheritance tax (to the extent it does not exceed the chargeable gain) is allowed as a deduction in computing the chargeable gain (TCGA 1992, ss 260(7), 165(10)). Suitable adjustments are to be made if the amount of inheritance tax payable subsequently changes (TCGA 1992, ss 260(8), 165(11)).

HMRC will not generally require a computation of the held-over gain as at the date of disposal where the relief is not restricted. The parties will, however, have to jointly apply for this treatment, make informal estimations of value and certify that they believe the gain to exceed the allowable expenditure. The parties will be bound if they claim on this basis, although HMRC will not (see SP 8/92 Valuation of assets in respect of which capital gains tax gifts hold-over relief is claimed).

Restrictions on the reliefs

Reduction in business asset hold-over relief

[14.112] If a business asset was not used for the purposes of the trade, profession or vocation throughout the period of its ownership by the disponor, the amount of the chargeable gain eligible for hold-over relief is reduced on a time apportionment basis (TCGA 1992, Sch 7, para 5).

Similarly where the asset is a building or structure and, during its ownership (or a substantial part thereof), only part of that building or structure was used for the purposes of a trade, profession or vocation, then a just and reasonable apportionment is made to reduce the part of the chargeable gain qualifying for hold-over relief (TCGA 1992, Sch 7, para 6).

Neither of these restrictions apply to assets deemed to be used for the purposes of a trade by reason of qualifying for agricultural property relief (TCGA 1992, Sch 7, paras 5(2), 6(2)).

Hold-over relief on the disposal of shares which are business assets may also be restricted if the company whose shares are disposed of owns, among its chargeable assets, assets which are not business assets. This applies if the disponor has owned more than 25% of the voting rights of the company in the previous 12 months. An apportionment is made to reduce the part of the chargeable gain qualifying for hold-over relief by reference to the business assets and total chargeable assets held by the company. Further provisions apply where the company in question is a holding company (TCGA 1992, Sch 7, para 7).

Non-resident acquirers

[14.113] Save to the extent that relief is being claimed in respect of NRCGT gains (TCGA 1992, ss 167A and 261ZA) hold-over relief under both sets of provisions will only be available if the person acquiring the asset (the acquirer) is resident in the UK (TCGA 1992, ss 261, 166). Similarly, relief will not be available if the acquirer would not be liable to UK tax on a disposal of the asset by reason of being treated as non-resident under a double taxation convention (TCGA 1992, ss 261(2), 166(2)).

Business asset hold-over relief is not available if the acquirer is a company which is controlled by such a person or persons and he or they are connected with the disponor (TCGA 1992, s 167).

Where the disposal is to trustees of a settlement who are treated for capital gains tax purposes as UK resident (TCGA 1992, s 69) but carry on the general administration of the trust outside the UK, then neither IHT hold-over relief nor business asset hold-over relief will be available if the trustees could subsequently claim double taxation relief on a disposal of the asset in question (TCGA 1992, s 169).

Settlor interested trusts

[14.114] Neither IHT hold-over relief nor business asset hold-over relief will be available on a disposal to trustees of a settlement if the settlor (or a person who has claimed hold-over relief on an earlier disposal of the asset) has an interest in the settlement or may acquire such an interest under an arrangement (TCGA 1992, s 169B).

For these purposes an arrangement is any scheme, agreement or understanding, whether or not legally enforceable (TCGA 1992, s 169G) and a settlor is an individual from whom property in the settlement has originated (TCGA 1992, s 169E).

A person has an interest in a settlement if property is or may be applied for the benefit of that person, his spouse, his civil partner, his dependent child or his dependent step child (TCGA 1992, s 169F). A dependent child is an unmarried child under the age of 18, and the possibility of acquiring a dependent child or stepchild is ignored (TCGA 1992, s 169F(4A), (4B)). This does not preclude a widow of a person benefiting, nor does it preclude arm's length transactions with the settlement (see *Lord Vestey's Executors v IRC* [1949] 1 All ER 1108, 31 TC 1).

There are limited exceptions to this provision relating to maintenance funds for historic buildings and disabled persons trusts (TCGA 1992, s 169D).

Deemed chargeable gains on gilt edged securities or qualifying corporate bonds

[14.115] Hold-over relief does not apply to a gain on gilt edged securities or qualifying corporate bonds which are deemed to be chargeable by reason of TCGA 1992, s 116(10)(b) (TCGA 1992, ss 260(6), 165(3)(c)).

Withdrawal of relief

Emigration of acquirer

[14.116] If either IHT hold-over relief or business asset hold-over relief has been claimed and the acquirer ceases to be resident in the UK, then a chargeable gain equal to the amount of relief claimed will be deemed to have accrued to the acquirer immediately before he became non-resident (TCGA 1992, s 168). There will be a corresponding uplift in the base cost of the asset (TCGA 1992, s 168(10)).

This only applies, however, if the acquirer ceases to be UK resident within six years after the end of the year of assessment in which the relevant disposal was made (TCGA 1992, s 168(4)).

If the acquirer became non-resident for a period of less than three years by reason of an employment performed entirely outside the UK and does not dispose of the asset during that period, this charge will not apply (TCGA 1992, s 168(5)).

Where this provision applies, the acquirer is given a right to recover the tax paid from the disponor (TCGA 1992, s 168(9)).

Settlement becoming settlor interested

[14.117] If either IHT hold-over relief or business asset hold-over relief has been claimed and the settlement subsequently becomes settlor interested then a chargeable gain equal to the amount of relief claimed will be deemed to have accrued to the disponor (TCGA 1992, s 169C). There will be a corresponding uplift in the base cost of the asset (TCGA 1992, s 169C(8)).

This only applies, however, if the settlement becomes settlor interested within six years after the end of the year of assessment in which the relevant disposal was made (TCGA 1992, s 169C(2), (3), (11)).

Interaction with other reliefs

Principal private residence relief

[14.118] As discussed above (see para **14.103**) a claim to IHT hold-over relief can have the effect that principal private residence relief is denied on a later disposal of a qualifying dwelling-house.

Entrepreneurs' relief

[14.119] Entrepreneurs' relief is left out of account in calculating the held-over gain. Where, however, an apportionment restricting relief might be made under TCGA 1992, s 169P it may be worthwhile making a disposal and claiming hold-over relief in order to maximise the available entrepreneurs' relief on a disposal a year later.

Taper relief

[14.120] Taper relief would have been left out of account in calculating the held-over gain.

Indexation allowance

[14.121] Indexation allowance would have been included in calculating the held-over gain.

Uplift on base cost on death

[14.122] Generally, on the death of a person entitled to an interest in possession in settled property to which IHTA 1984, s 49(1) applies there is a deemed disposal of that settled property but no chargeable gain accrues (TCGA 1992, ss 72(1)(b), 73(1)(a)). Where that settled property was previously subject to a claim to hold-over relief, the death of the life tenant in these circumstances will not give rise to a chargeable gain, but there will be no uplift to the extent of the held-over gain (TCGA 1992, s 74).

Roll-over relief on the transfer of business assets

[14.123] TCGA 1992, Pt V (Transfer of business assets, Entrepreneurs' Relief and Investors' Relief) contains provision granting roll-over relief in two important situations, namely the replacement of business assets (TCGA 1992, s 152) and the transfer of a business to a company (TCGA 1992, s 162). These are considered in more detail below. Another important roll-over relief, that which applies following the compulsory purchase of land, is considered in the next section.

Where roll-over relief applies, the gain on the disposal of one asset will be deferred by means of a reduction in the allowable expenditure on another asset which is subsequently acquired. It differs from hold-over relief in that the original disponor (rather than the acquirer) will be ultimately liable in respect of the deferred gain.

Replacement of business assets

[14.124] The roll-over relief on the replacement of business assets only applies on a disposal of qualifying assets (the old assets) by a person carrying on a trade. The consideration for the disposal of the old assets must be used to acquire new qualifying assets (the new assets).

Further, both the old and the new assets must have been and must be used solely for the purposes of the trade of the disponor (or a company of which an individual disponor holds more than 5% of the voting rights) throughout the period of ownership and in this regard, the new assets cannot be acquired with a view to realising a gain on them (TCGA 1992, ss 152(1), (5), 157). There must be a reasonable proximity in time between the acquisition of the new assets and their being taken into use for the purposes of the trade (*Milton v Chivers (Inspector of Taxes)* [1996] STC (SCD) 36).

If an asset is not let or used for any non-trading purpose, but is not used for the purposes of a trade because it is being enhanced (for example, a building is being built on land), then, the relief is available if the enhanced asset is subsequently used for the trade (see ESC D24 Relief for the replacement of business assets: assets not brought immediately into trading use and *Steibelt (Inspector of Taxes) v Paling* [1999] STC 594 where it was noted that this was not a concession, but an interpretation of TCGA 1992, s 152).

Land may not qualify for relief on the basis that it is not taken into use and used solely for the purposes of a trade where, on acquisition of the freehold, vacant possession is not obtained (*Campbell Connelly & Co Ltd v Barnett (Inspector of Taxes)* [1994] STC 50).

The relief will also by concession apply where the same asset is repurchased for purely commercial reasons (ESC D16 Relief for the replacement of business assets: repurchase of the same asset). The gain on a part disposal of an asset cannot, however, be rolled-over to the necessarily earlier acquisition of the main asset (*Watton (Inspector of Taxes) v Tippett* [1997] STC 893).

The new assets must be acquired (or unconditionally contracted for) in the period beginning 12 months before and ending three years after the sale of the old assets (TCGA 1992, s 152(3)). There is provision for making a claim where it is anticipated that new assets will be purchased (TCGA 1992, s 153A). The disponor must not have ceased to be UK resident between the disposal of the old assets and the acquisition of the new assets (TCGA 1992, s 159).

The relief must be claimed. Where it is so claimed, the disponor (but no other person) is treated as having disposed of the old assets for a consideration which is such as to give rise to neither a chargeable gain nor an allowable loss. The consideration for which he acquired the new assets is treated as being reduced. The amount of that reduction is the difference between the actual consideration received for the old assets and the amount which the disponor is treated as having received for those assets. The acquisition cost of the acquirer is unaffected by the claim (TCGA 1992, s 152(1)(a), (b), (2)).

The relief will not apply to the charge in respect of NRCGT gain, unless the new assets are an interest in UK land which is a dwelling (TCGA 1992, s 159A).

Reduction of relief

Building only partly used for a trade

[14.125] Where a person disposes of a building in circumstances where part of that building was not used for the purposes of his trade then the relief will still apply as if the part which was used for the trade, together with any land occupied for purposes ancillary to that trade, was a separate asset. In these circumstances it will be necessary to apportion consideration for the acquisition and disposal of the building or structure and any other land (TCGA 1992, s 152(6)).

Use for non-trade purpose

[14.126] If old assets are not used for the purposes of the trade throughout the period of ownership, then an apportionment is made as if there are two separate assets having regard to the time and extent to which the asset was, and was not, used for the purposes of trade (TCGA 1992, s 152(7)).

Use of part of consideration

[14.127] If only a portion of the consideration received for the old assets is applied in acquiring the new assets then relief is only available to the extent that the amount of the consideration which is not so applied is less than the amount of the gain accruing on the disposal of the old assets (TCGA 1992, s 153).

Acquisition of depreciating assets

[14.128] Where the new asset is a depreciating asset, the consideration for which it is acquired is not reduced. Rather, the relief will operate by deferring the chargeable gain, so that it is deemed not to accrue until the earliest of (i) the disponor disposing of the new asset, (ii) the disponor ceasing to use the new asset for his trade and (iii) ten years from the acquisition of the new asset (TCGA 1992, s 154(1), (2)). A depreciating asset is an asset which is, or will become in ten years, a wasting asset (see para **14.22**).

The gain from the old asset may be rolled-over to a further new asset acquired within the three year period so that the above treatment does not apply (TCGA 1992, s 154(4)–(6)).

Qualifying assets

[14.129] As stated above, only certain classes of assets will qualify for the roll-over relief, regardless of whether they are used wholly for the purposes of a trade.

Buildings and land

[14.130] Generally, any land, building, part of a building or permanent or semi-permanent structure in the nature of a building which is occupied and used solely for the purposes of the trade will be a qualifying asset for the purposes of the relief (TCGA 1992, s 155). This is subject to the exception that land used either in a trade of dealing in or developing land (where any profit on the sale of the land would not be trading profits), or in a trade of providing services to an occupier of land in which the trader has an interest will not be a qualifying asset (TCGA 1992, s 156).

Other assets

[14.131] The other qualifying assets are as follows:

(1)   fixed plant or machinery which does not form part of a building or of a permanent or semi-permanent structure in the nature of a building;
(2)   ships, aircraft and hovercraft;
(3)   satellites, space stations and spacecraft (including launch vehicles);
(4)   goodwill;
(5)   milk quotas and potato quotas;
(6)   ewe and suckler cow premium quotas;
(7)   fish quotas;
(8)   payment entitlements under the single payment scheme of income support for farmers; and
(9)   rights of a member of Lloyd's under a syndicate and any asset which a member of Lloyd's is treated as having acquired by virtue of FA 1999, s 82.

Transfer of a business to a company

[14.132] The roll-over relief on the transfer of a business to a company only applies to the transfer of a business as a going concern by a person who is not a company. The business need only be a going concern at the time of transfer (*Gordon v IRC* [1991] STC 174).

All of the assets of the business other than cash must be transferred wholly or partly in exchange for the issue of shares in a company to the disponor (TCGA 1992, s 162(1)). The relief will apply automatically unless an election to the contrary is made (see TCGA 1992, s 162A).

Although the shares are treated as being acquired for a market value consideration (TCGA 1992, s 17) the allowable expenditure will be reduced by the amount of the rolled-over gain, apportioned to each share by reference to its value (TCGA 1992, s 162(3)).

The rolled over gain will be determined by taking the cumulative total of the chargeable gains less the cumulative total of the allowable losses on the assets disposed of. This is then reduced in the fraction which the allowable expenditure on the shares bears to the value of the value of the consideration received by the disponor.

Example 6

A transfers a business worth £100,000 to B Ltd in exchange for the issue of 40,000 shares. The cumulative gain on the assets of the business is £30,000.

Since the value of the shares will be equal to the value of the assets transferred, the entire gain is rolled over and the shares have a base cost of £70,000.

If the business was transferred in consideration of the issue of 40,000 shares and a loan of £25,000, then the value of the shares would be £75,000. Only £22,500 of the gain would be rolled over (30,000 × (75,000/100,000)). A would pay tax on a gain of £7,500, and the shares would have a base cost of £52,500.

By concession (ESC D32 Transfer of a business to a company) HMRC do not treat the assumption of business liabilities by the company as amounting to consideration received by the disponor.

What amounts to a business for these purposes

[14.133] The business need not be a trade, so the relief will also cover most situations where assets are actively being put to gainful use for the purpose of making a profit. Nevertheless, care should, however, be taken where the property consists of a letting business. In *Ramsay v Revenue and Customs Comrs* [2013] UKUT 0226 (TCC) the Upper Tribunal overturned a decision of the FTT which had held incorrectly that a property consisting of ten flats, five of which were let to tenants did not amount to a business for the purposes of these provisions.

The Upper Tribunal made clear that while passive receipt of rents was unlikely to be regarded as a business for these purposes, relatively extensive activities would be sufficient, as the term 'business' is to be afforded a wide meaning. The Tribunal approved (at paras 64 to 66) the list of factors which were referred to in *Customs and Excise Comrs v Lord Fisher* [1981] 2 All ER 147, [1981] STC 238 although considered that the degree of activity would be relevant:

" . . . in my judgment the word 'business' in the context of s 162 TCGA should be afforded a broad meaning. Regard should be had to the factors referred to in Lord Fisher, which in my view (with the exception of the specific references to taxable supplies, which are relevant to VAT) are of general application to the question whether the circumstances describe a business. Thus, it falls to be considered whether Mrs Ramsay's activities were a 'serious undertaking earnestly pursued' or a 'serious occupation', whether the activity was an occupation or function actively pursued with reasonable or recognisable continuity, whether the activity had a certain amount of substance in terms of turnover, whether the activity was conducted in a regular manner and on sound and recognised business principles, and whether the activities were of a kind which, subject to differences of detail, are commonly made by those who seek to profit by them.

. . .

66. There remains, however, the question of degree. That is relevant to the equation because of the fact that in the context of property investment and letting the same activities are equally capable of describing a passive investment and a property investment or rental business. Although resolution of that issue will be assisted by consideration of the Lord Fisher factors, to those there must be added the degree of activity undertaken. There is nothing in the TCGA which can colour the extent of the activity which for the purpose of s 162 may be regarded as sufficient to constitute a business, and so this must be approached in the context of a broad meaning of that term".

Compulsory purchase of land

[14.134] The acquisition of land under compulsory purchase powers will give rise to a corresponding disposal. Given the involuntary nature of such disposal it is necessary to have some form of relief to reduce the potentially costly consequences of the crystallisation of any gain. It would be particularly harsh if, in addition to being required to dispose of land, a person was not in a position to purchase replacement land of equal value, because a significant proportion of his receipts has been subject to tax. To this end, there are a number of roll-over reliefs which ensure that the charge to tax is deferred where the land is in fact replaced.

Apportionment of consideration

[14.135] Where land is acquired under compulsory purchase powers, it may be appropriate to make an apportionment, so that part of the consideration is apportioned as compensation for loss of goodwill or for disturbance or is apportioned in some other way. Where that is the case, that apportionment is to take place, notwithstanding that any statutory provision might deem the sums received to be paid only for the land and not as compensation for any other loss (TCGA 1992, s 245(1)). (See HMRC Guidance *Goodwill in trade related properties* [2009] SWTI 460 for the latest HMRC views as to how an apportionment is to be made between goodwill and tangible assets.)

Time of disposal

[14.136] The normal rule is that the time at which a disposal and acquisition take place is the time when an unconditional contract is made or when the condition of a conditional contract is satisfied. It is not (if different) the time when land is conveyed or transferred (TCGA 1992, s 28). Under a compulsory purchase, there may not be a contract under which the land is acquired. In this case, the time of disposal will be when the compensation is agreed or otherwise determined (TCGA 1992, s 246). (The fact that there may be an appeal is disregarded in this respect.)

Roll-over relief on compulsory acquisition

Conditions for relief to apply

[14.137] The relief, which must be claimed, applies to a disposal of land. For these purposes land includes any interest in or right over land, messuages, tenements, and hereditaments, houses and buildings of any tenure (TCGA 1992, ss 247(8), 288(1)).

This disposal must be to a person or body of persons who are either acquiring the land compulsorily or who have been (or could be) authorised to acquire it compulsorily for the purposes for which it is acquired. This will also be satisfied if another person or body of persons have been (or could be) authorised to acquire it for the acquirer (TCGA 1992, ss 247(1)(a), 243(5)). This will not apply where the legislation assumes a voluntary acquisition of land by a public authority (see *Ahad v Revenue & Customs Comrs* [2009] UKFTT 353 (TC) [2010] SWTI 627 concerning the powers of the Commission for the New Towns).

HMRC accept that this will, however, include the situation where a tenant exercises a statutory right to acquire a freehold reversion or to extend a lease (see SP 13/93 Compulsory acquisition of freehold or extension of lease by tenant).

The consideration for the disposal (or part of it) must be applied in purchasing new land (TCGA 1992, s 247(1)(c)). For these purposes, consideration will include sums paid for severance of and for injury to adjoining land owned by the disponor (TCGA 1992, s 247(6)).

The new land must be acquired (or unconditionally contracted for) in the period beginning twelve months before and ending three years after the sale of the old land (TCGA 1992, ss 247(5), 152(3)). There is also provision for making a claim where an unconditional contract has not been completed and also where it is anticipated that new land will be purchased (TCGA 1992, ss 247(5), 152(4) and 247A).

Operation of the relief

[14.138] The relief only applies to the disponor. It does not affect the allowable deductions of the acquiring authority (TCGA 1992, s 247(4)).

Where all of the consideration provided for the old land is used to purchase qualifying land, then the disponor is treated as having disposed of the old land for a consideration which is such as to give rise to neither a gain nor a loss. The allowable deductions on the new land will be correspondingly reduced to the extent that this deemed consideration for the old land is less than the actual consideration paid for it (TCGA 1992, s 247(2)).

Where only part of the consideration for the old land is applied in acquiring the new land, then relief is only available to the extent that the amount of the consideration which is not applied is less than the amount of the gain accruing on the disposal of the old land (TCGA 1992, s 247(3)).

Example 7

Blackacre is subject to compulsory purchase for £100,000 giving rise to a chargeable gain of £30,000.

If £70,000 is applied in the purchase of Whiteacre, the entire £30,000 gain will be subject to charge. No relief is available.

If £90,000 is applied in the purchase of Whiteacre, a gain of £10,000 will be subject to charge, as Blackacre will be deemed to have been disposed of for a consideration of £80,000 and Whiteacre will be deemed to be acquired for a consideration of £70,000.

If the entire £100,000 is applied in the purchase of Whiteacre, the entire gain will be relieved. Blackacre will be deemed to have been disposed of for a consideration of £70,000 and Whiteacre will be deemed to be acquired for a consideration of £70,000.

Restrictions on the relief

Advertisement

[14.139] The relief will not be available if the disponor has advertised the land for sale, or has otherwise indicated that he is willing to dispose of the land, whether to the authority or to any others person (TCGA 1992, s 247(1)(b)).

Interest in a dwelling-house

[14.140] New land will not be eligible for the relief if it is an interest in a dwelling-house eligible for principle private residence relief at any time during the period of six years from the date on which it is acquired (TCGA 1992, s 248(1)).

There will be a clawback of the relief if the new land becomes such a dwelling-house within the six-year period (TCGA 1992, s 248(2)).

Depreciating assets

[14.141] Where the new land is a depreciating asset, typically a lease of less than 60 years, the consideration for which it is acquired is not reduced. Rather, the relief will operate by deferring the chargeable gain, so that it is deemed not to accrue until the earliest of the disponor disposing of the new land, or ten years from the acquisition of the new land (TCGA 1992, ss 154(1), (2), 248(3)). A depreciating asset is an asset which is, or will become in ten years, a wasting asset (see para **14.22**). Accordingly, it can be seen that this provision will apply where the new land is a lease with a term of less than 60 years.

The gain from the old land may be rolled-over if different new land which is not a depreciating asset is acquired within the three-year period so that the above treatment does not apply (TCGA 1992, ss 154(4), (6), 248(3)).

Part disposals under compulsory powers

[14.142] Where the compensation or purchase price includes an amount given for the severance of the land from other land which the disponor retains or for that retained land being injuriously affected, there is deemed to be a part disposal of the retained land (TCGA 1992, s 245(2)).

Where there is a part disposal by reason of compulsory purchase and the consideration for the part disposed of is small in relation to the market value of the entire holding before the disposal, a claim can be made so that there is deemed to be no disposal, but the allowable expenditure on the remaining land is reduced to the extent of the consideration received (TCGA 1992, s 243(1), (2)). This can only apply, however, to the extent that there is allowable expenditure to be reduced (TCGA 1992, s 244).

For these purposes, the question of what is small is a question of fact and degree (*O'Rourke v Binks* [1992] STC 703). Nevertheless, HMRC will accept that consideration is small if it is less than 5% of the total value or is less than £3,000 (see RI 164 Capital gains tax: meaning of 'small' in TCGA 1992 ss 23, 116, 122, 133, 243). Other cases will be determined on their merits.

A claim cannot be made under this provision if a claim for roll-over relief is made (TCGA 1992, s 248(4)).

Further, the relief will not apply if the main holding of land is a wasting asset (most relevantly a lease of less than 50 years (see para **14.22**)) (TCGA 1992, s 243(4)). The same restriction on advertising or indicating a willingness to dispose of the land as applies for the roll-over relief apples for the purposes of this relief (TCGA 1992, s 243(1)(b)).

Specific rules applying to leases

[14.143] For the purposes of the capital gains tax legislation a lease of land is expressly defined to include an underlease, sublease or any tenancy or licence, any agreement for such and any corresponding interest applying to land outside the UK (TCGA 1992, Sch 8, para 10(1)). Accordingly, for these purposes it covers a much wider range of interests than the leasehold interest properly so called under the law of property.

Where a gain or loss on the disposal of a lease is subject to capital gains tax, a number of rules specific to leases will apply to calculate that gain or loss. In particular, where the lease has a duration of less than 50 years at the time of disposal ('a short lease') different rules apply to determine the chargeable gain.

Duration of the lease

[14.144] An initial issue relates to the duration of that lease for capital gains tax purposes. Although this will normally be the term of the lease as expressed in the lease itself the two concepts are not synonymous. For capital gains tax purposes (and different rules can apply for different taxes) provisions of the lease or circumstances which are likely to arise can be relevant so that the lease is treated as having a longer or shorter duration than the term expressed (TCGA 1992, Sch 8, para 8). In this respect, the duration of a lease is determined as at the date of grant or disposal by reference to those facts which were known or ascertainable at that time and which are of relevance (TCGA 1992, Sch 8, para 8(6)).

There are three main rules which lead to the duration of the lease for capital gains tax purposes diverging from the default position that the duration of a lease is identified with its agreed term. Firstly, a lease including provision for its determination on notice given by the landlord is taken to expire at the earliest date on which it could be so determined by the landlord (TCGA 1992, Sch 8, para 8(2)).

Secondly where any provision of the lease or any other relevant circumstances make it likely that the lease will cease before the expiration of its term, then the lease is to be treated as having been granted only for that shorter period of time. This is aimed at provisions under which an increase in the rent or some other increase in his obligations are likely to induce a tenant to give notice and thereby determine his lease (TCGA 1992, Sch 8, para 8(3), (4)).

Thirdly, where the terms of the lease enable the tenant to extend the lease beyond a given date, the lease is treated as continuing for as long as it could be extended by the tenant (TCGA 1992, Sch 8, para 8(5)). The terms of the lease must enable such extension. A statutory right to be granted a new lease is not sufficient (*Lewis v Walters (Inspector of Taxes)* [1992] STC 97). Further, this provision will not apply where the landlord can, in any event, determine the lease by notice.

By concession, where the extension of a lease involves its surrender and the grant of a new lease, then if the terms of the new lease relate to the same property and do not differ other than in duration in rent, HMRC will not treat the surrender as a disposal or part disposal of the old lease provided that the transaction is on arm's length terms, is not part of a larger scheme of transactions, and the lessee does not receive a capital sum (see ESC D39 Extension of leases).

Meaning of premium for capital gains tax purposes

[14.145] For capital gains tax purposes the term premium is taken to include any sum (other than rent) paid by a tenant to his landlord, in his capacity as landlord, in consideration for the grant of a lease (see *Clarke (Inspector of Taxes) v United Real (Moorgate) Ltd* [1988] STC 273). It will include sums paid to an intermediate or a superior landlord. Additionally it will be assumed that a sum paid in connection with the granting of a tenancy has been paid by way of premium unless it can be shown that other sufficient consideration has been provided (TCGA 1992, Sch 8, para 10(2)).

No charge to capital gains tax arises in respect of reverse premiums unless it is not chargeable to income tax and the sum received by the tenant derives from an asset held by him. These are considered elsewhere (see **CHAPTER 7** at para **7.19** ff).

Deemed premiums

[14.146] Certain sums are deemed to be payable by way of a premium for a grant of a lease of land including: any sum which becomes payable by a tenant under the terms of the lease in lieu of the whole or part of the rent for any period; any consideration paid by a tenant for the surrender of the lease; and any consideration paid by a tenant (otherwise than by of rent) for the variation or waiver of any of the terms of a lease (TCGA 1992, Sch 8, para 3(2), (3)). These sums are treated as premiums payable under the lease at the time when they are actually paid.

Where a payment is made in lieu of the whole or part of the rent for any period and the terms of the lease did not provide for such a payment, the capital sum is chargeable under general principles as a part disposal by the landlord (see Capital Gains Manual 71372).

Statutory compensation paid by a landlord on the termination of a lease will not be chargeable to capital gains tax as it is paid in consequence of a statutory right (*Drummond (Inspector of Taxes) v Austin Brown* [1985] Ch 52, [1984] STC 321).

The receipt of a deemed premium does not require any recomputation of the gain accruing on the receipt of any earlier premium. Rather, there is deemed to be a further part disposal of the freehold or other asset out of which the lease is granted. If, however, the premium is deemed to have been received for the surrender of a lease the landlord is deemed to dispose of his interest in the lease.

Exclusion of sums chargeable to income tax

[14.147] Sums payable by way of rent will not be treated as part of a premium for the grant of a lease. Additionally, where part of a premium (or a deemed premium) is treated as a receipt of a UK property business by virtue of ITTOIA 2005, ss 277–281, then that part is excluded from the consideration in calculating the gain on the disposal. It will not, however, be left out of account as part of the denominator in determining the allowable expenditure on a part disposal (TCGA 1992, Sch 8, para 5(1) and see Example 8 below).

Further, where a sublease is granted out of a lease, the amount chargeable to income is not taken into account in calculating the gain in the first instance, but is deducted from any gain calculated (as to which see Examples 11 and 12 below).

Where the disposal is the granting of a sublease out of a short lease (which is considered below) the sum which is treated as a receipt of the UK property business will directly reduce any gain accruing on the disposal, although a loss for capital gains tax purposes cannot be created or increased by this exercise (TCGA 1992, Sch 8, para 5(2)).

The provisions of ITTOIA 2005, ss 277–281 charging part of a premium to income tax apply only in respect of which leases have a duration of less than 50 years (short leases). The amount to be treated as income is determined by the formula:

$$P \times \frac{(50 - Y)}{50}$$

where P is the premium or deemed premium and Y is the number of complete periods of 12 months other than the first comprised in the duration of the lease.

It is noted that the income tax provisions only apply to the extent that actual consideration is paid by way of a premium for a lease. Where a lease is deemed to be granted for a market value consideration under TCGA 1992, s 17 then only that amount which is treated as income by reference to the actual consideration will be taken to reduce that deemed premium.

Example 8

A grants a 41-year lease of Blackacre to B for a premium of £10,000. The market value premium for such a lease would be £20,000.

The amount chargeable to income tax is £2,000:

$$10{,}000 \times \left(\frac{(50-40)}{50} \right)$$

The consideration to be taken into account for capital gains tax purposes is £18,000 (20,000 – 2,000).

Grant of a lease for a premium

[14.148] The grant of a lease at a premium is a part disposal out of the interest from which the lease is granted. Unless the lease in question is a sublease granted out of a lease which has a duration of less than 50 years (a short lease), the normal part disposal rules apply. In applying those rules (as to which see above at para **14.27**) the right to any rent or other sums payable under the lease (other than the premium) is treated as part of the undisposed property and is valued as at the time of the part disposal (TCGA 1992, Sch 8, para 2).

Example 8A

Following on from Example 8, assuming the freehold was acquired for £50,000 and the freehold reversion was worth £35,000 when the lease was granted, the allowable expenditure (calculated using the part disposal rules) will be £16,364:

$$\frac{18{,}000}{(20{,}0000+35{,}000)} \times 50{,}000$$

(Note that although the amount of premium chargeable to income tax is left out of account in the numerator of the part disposal calculation, it is included in the denominator.)

The chargeable gain will be £1,636:

$$18,000 - 16,364$$

Leases as wasting assets

[14.149] Leases with a duration of less than 50 years (short leases) will be treated as a wasting asset for capital gains tax purposes. This has the consequence that in calculating the gain or loss on a disposal of a short lease, special rules apply to write off the amount of allowable expenditure. However, unlike the general rule applying to most wasting assets, where allowable expenditure is written off at a uniform rate (TCGA 1992, s 46), there is a curved line restriction on sums of allowable expenditure incurred in respect of short leases (TCGA 1992, Sch 8, para 1). This curved line restriction operates by reducing the allowable expenditure by reference to the duration of the lease at the time of acquisition and/or the time of expenditure on the lease and also by reference to the duration of the lease at the time of disposal of the lease.

The table to TCGA 1992, Sch 8, para 1 gives the percentages of allowable expenditure (the relevant percentage) which are allowable by reference to the duration of the lease at a given time. It is set out below for convenience:

Years left until expiry of lease	Percentage of expenditure allowable	Years left until expiry of lease (continued)	Percentage of expenditure allowable (continued)
50 (or more)	100	25	81.100
49	99.657	24	79.622
48	99.289	23	78.055
47	98.902	22	76.399
46	98.490	21	74.635
45	98.059	20	72.770
44	97.595	19	70.791
43	97.107	18	68.697
42	96.593	17	66.470
41	96.041	16	64.116
40	95.457	15	61.617
39	94.842	14	58.971
38	94.189	13	56.167
37	93.497	12	53.191
36	92.761	11	50.038
35	91.981	10	46.695
34	91.156	9	43.154
33	90.280	8	39.399
32	89.354	7	35.414
31	88.371	6	31.195
30	87.330	5	26.722
29	86.266	4	21.983

Years left until expiry of lease	Percentage of expenditure allowable	Years left until expiry of lease (continued)	Percentage of expenditure allowable (continued)
28	85.053	3	15.959
27	83.816	2	11.629
26	82.496	1	5.983
		0	0

In the first instance, where a lease was acquired with a term of more than 50 years and was subsequently disposed of when that term was less than 50 years, then in calculating any gain, the allowable expenditure will be reduced by the relevant percentage taken from the table by reference to the duration of the lease at the time of disposal.

Example 9

A acquires a 52 year lease of Blackacre in 1999 for £100,000. He disposes of the lease in 2007 when the unexpired term is 44 years for £150,000.

Only 97.595% of the expenditure on acquisition is allowable (see table above), giving rise to a gain of £52,405.

Matters are complicated somewhat where, in the first place, the lease is acquired with a term of less than 50 years and is disposed of before it has determined by effluxion of time. In these circumstances, the allowable expenditure is reduced by reference to the relevant percentages applying by reference to the time remaining on the lease at both acquisition and disposal. The fraction given in the legislation is as follows:

$$\frac{P(1) - P(3)}{P(1)}$$

In this fraction, $P(1)$ is the relevant percentage determined by reference to the duration of the lease at the time of acquisition and $P(3)$ is the relevant percentage determined by reference to the duration of the lease at the time of disposal.

A further fraction which is given relates to enhancement expenditure incurred by the disponor during his ownership of the lease:

$$\frac{P(2) - P(3)}{P(2)}$$

Here $P(2)$ is the relevant percentage determined by reference to the duration of the lease at the time when the enhancement expenditure was incurred and $P(3)$ is once again the relevant percentage determined by reference to the duration of the lease at the time of disposal.

An added complication arises where the duration of the lease is not an exact number of years. In this case the relevant percentage is arrived at by taking the relevant percentage from the Table for the whole number of years remaining on the lease, plus one-twelfth of the difference between that and the percentage for the next higher number of years for each odd month (counting an odd 14 days or more as one month) (TCGA 1992, Sch 8, para 1(6)).

Example 10

A acquires a 47 year lease in Blackacre in 1999 for £100,000. He expends £10,000 on improving Blackacre in 2002 (when the unexpired term is 44 years). He disposes of his lease of Blackacre for £150,000 in 2007 (when the unexpired term is 39 years).

The allowable expenditure on the acquisition cost is reduced by £4,105:

$$\left(£100,000 \times \left(\frac{98.902 - 94.842}{98.902} \right) \right)$$

and the allowable expenditure relating to the enhancement of Blackacre is reduced by £282:

$$£100,000 \times \left(\frac{97.595 - 94.482}{97.595} \right)$$

The gain is therefore £44,387:

$$(150,000 - (100,000 - 4,105) - (10,000 - 282)).$$

An exception to this treatment arises where a lease is acquired subject to a sublease which is otherwise than at a rack-rent. If the value of the lease on the expiry of the sublease is likely to exceed the allowable expenditure on its disposal, then the lease is not to be treated as a wasting asset until the end of the duration of the sublease. Whether this alternative approach applies is determined at the beginning of the period of ownership (TCGA 1992, Sch 8, para 1(2)).

This treatment will also not apply where, during the period of ownership, the property subject to the lease has been used solely for the purposes of a trade, profession or vocation and capital allowances have or could have been claimed in respect of the cost of the lease or any enhancement expenditure related to it. If the land has been used only partly for these purposes an apportionment will take place (TCGA 1992, Sch 8, para 1(6), s 47).

Subleases out of short leases

[**14.150**] Where a sublease is granted for a premium out of a short lease (that is to say a lease which has a duration of less than 50 years) the normal part disposal rules do not apply (TCGA 1992, Sch 8, para 4).

In these circumstances, it is necessary firstly to determine the notional premium (the notional premium) which would be obtainable for the sublease on the assumption that the rent payable under it is the same as that payable under the short lease out of which it is granted. This is a matter of valuation.

Where the actual premium is equal to or greater than that notional premium then the allowable expenditure is reduced by reference to the amount which it would be written off over the period of the sublease (TCGA 1992, Sch 8, para 4(2)(a)). This is calculated using the relevant percentage figures set out in the Table above at para **14.149** and using the following formulae (the first applies to the acquisition costs of the lease and the second to the costs of expenditure relating to the lease):

$$\frac{P(4) - P(5)}{P(1)}$$

or

$$\frac{P(4) - P(5)}{P(2)}$$

As above, $P(1)$ is the relevant percentage determined by reference to the duration of the lease at the time of acquisition of the lease and $P(2)$ is the relevant percentage determined by reference to the duration of the lease at the time enhancement expenditure is incurred on it. In this equation, however, $P(4)$ is the relevant percentage determined by reference to the duration of the lease at the time when the sublease is granted and $P(5)$ is the relevant percentage determined by reference to the duration of the lease at the time when the sublease comes to an end.

In making these calculations, no reduction is made in respect of so much of the premium as is chargeable to income tax under ITTOIA 2005, ss 277–281, although that amount will be reduced from the gain. It cannot, however, create a loss (TCGA 1992, Sch 8, para 5(2)).

Example 11

In 1999 A acquires a 30-year lease of Blackacre for a premium of £100,000. In 2005, he grants B a sublease for a duration of 11 years over the whole of Blackacre in return for a premium of £90,000. The rent payable under the sublease was the same as the rent payable under the original lease.

A's lease has a duration of 24 years when the sublease is granted. It will have a duration of 13 years when the sublease comes to an end.

Income tax on £72,000 is payable on the grant of the sublease.

$$£90,000 \times \frac{(50 - 10)}{50}$$

A's allowable expenditure on the grant of the sublease is £26,858:

$$\left(£100,000 \times \left(\frac{79.622 - 56.167}{87.330} \right) \right)$$

giving rise to a gain of £63,412:

$$90,000 - 63,412$$

As noted, the amount of the premium received which is subject to income tax is £72,000.

Since this is greater than the gain, the gain will be reduced to zero. It will not create a loss.

If the actual premium is less than the notional premium, then the allowable expenditure is further reduced in the fraction which the actual premium bears to the notional premium (TCGA 1992, Sch 8, para 4(2)(b)).

Example 12

If in the example above, the rent payable under the sublease was greater than that under the lease and the notional premium would have been £150,000, then the allowable expenditure is further reduced to £16,114:

$$£26,858 \times \left(\frac{90,000}{150,000} \right)$$

This would give rise to a gain of £73,886:

$$90,000 - 16,114$$

The amount of the premium received which is subject to income tax will once again be £72,000.

As before, this is taken into account in reducing the amount of the gain subject to capital gains tax, in this instance to £1,886:

$$73,886 - 72,000.$$

An additional factor which may need to be taken into account relates to the land over which the sublease is granted. If the sublease is a sublease of part only of the land comprised in the lease, then the allowable expenditure attributable to it is further reduced in the proportion which the value of the land comprised in the sublease bears to the value of that and the other land comprised in the lease (TCGA 1992, Sch 8, para 4(3)).

Interaction with other taxes

[14.151] Although this chapter is concerned primarily with the capital gains tax consequences of a transaction, no tax can be considered in a vacuum. In particular, the application of other taxes may determine whether capital gains tax is relevant at all. The particular application of those taxes are considered in further detail elsewhere in this book. It is, however, important to appreciate how the operation of different rules and different taxes interact with each other.

Income tax

[14.152] The general rule is that any sum which is chargeable to income tax will be left out of account in determining the charge to capital gains tax. Express provision is made in TCGA 1992, s 37 for the situation where a person makes a disposal and any money or money's worth which is paid as consideration on that disposal is either charged to income tax as that person's income or is otherwise taken into account as a receipt in computing the income or profits or gains or losses of that person for the purposes of the Income Tax Acts (see *Drummond v Revenue and Customs Comrs* [2009] EWCA Civ 608, [2009] STC 2206, 79 TC 793, for a consideration of which amounts are taken into account as a receipt for the purposes of the Income Tax Acts).

In these circumstances, the amount subject to income tax is to be excluded from the consideration which is to be taken into account in the computation of the gain for capital gains tax purposes. Further, more specific provisions applying to leases are included in TCGA 1992, Sch 8 para 5 and these were considered above.

There are exceptions to this general rule relating to capital allowances and to the capitalised value of rights to income (TCGA 1992, s 37(2), (3)).

There are also similar restrictions on the taking into account for the purposes of allowable expenditure of certain sums which are or would be allowable as a deduction for income tax purposes (TCGA 1992, s 39).

It can be seen from this that, particularly in relation to transactions in land, it will be a necessary precursor to the consideration of any capital gains tax issues to determine whether a transaction is trading or investment, and whether a receipt is capital or income. Even if a receipt is income, anti-avoidance provisions may apply to treat it as capital. See, for example, the charge to income tax on transactions in land under ITA 2007, Pt 13, Ch 3 (as to which see CHAPTER 2). This can have significant consequences in relation to the amount of tax payable and continues to be of importance where the highest rate of capital gains tax, at 20% (except in certain circumstances), is significantly lower than the highest rate of income tax, at 45%.

Example 13

A, as part of his property trading business, sells Blackacre, realising a gain of £100,000. This is an income receipt subject to income tax on which tax of up to £50,000 would be due.

B sells Whiteacre realising a gain of £100,000. The gain was not an income receipt. The maximum amount of capital gains tax payable would be £20,000 regardless of the length of ownership or use to which Whiteacre was put.

Corporation tax

[14.153] As stated above, with the exception of ATED-related gains companies fall outside the charge to capital gains tax (TCGA 1992, s 1(2)), although there is a charge to corporation tax on capital gains. While broadly similar principles apply in calculating the charge to corporation tax on capital gains, there are specific rules which apply only in relation to capital gains tax arising to companies.

Inheritance tax

[14.154] Where a chargeable transfer of value is made for inheritance tax purposes, any liability to capital gains tax which results from that transfer and *which is borne by the donee* is taken to reduce the value of that chargeable transfer (IHTA 1984, s 165(1)). If, however, that capital gains tax charge is *borne by the donor* it will be left out of account in determining the value of the transfer of value (IHTA 1984, s 164).

Hold-over relief under TCGA 1992, s 260 may be available in respect of a disposal where a transfer of value is a chargeable transfer of value for inheritance tax purposes. This is subject to restrictions on disposals to non-residents and settlor interested trusts (TCGA 1992, ss 169–169C, 261).

Where hold-over relief is available, any inheritance tax paid on the disposal will be taken into account in computing the gain on a subsequent disposal (TCGA 1992, ss 67(1)–(3), 165(10), (11) and 260(6), (7)).

Where a charge to inheritance tax arises on a person's death, then the valuation of any asset forming part of his estate for inheritance tax purposes is to be taken to be the market value of that asset for capital gains tax purposes at the date of death (TCGA 1992, ss 62, 274). Accordingly, although a low valuation may reduce a charge to inheritance tax, it will result in a greater gain for capital gains tax purposes if property is subsequently disposed of.

This provision will not have any application where there was no chargeable transfer of value on death for inheritance tax purposes.

Example 14

On death, A's Will provides that a sum equal to his available nil rate band should pass to his son B with the remainder passing by exempt transfer to his wife C. This has the result that no inheritance tax is payable on A's death.

Although the executors of A may appropriate Whiteacre to A in satisfaction of his legacy, that valuation will not be binding for capital gains tax purposes.

If the remainder passed to D, A's daughter, then inheritance tax would be payable and the valuation of Whiteacre which would apply to determine the charge to inheritance tax would also apply for capital gains tax purposes.

Stamp duty land tax

[14.155] The charge to stamp duty land tax will be one of the expenses which is allowable in calculating a chargeable gain.

Although there is no express provision equating chargeable consideration for stamp duty land tax purposes with allowable deductions for capital gains tax purposes, many similar principles apply in calculating them. This can create a tension when tax planning is involved in a transaction, as a lower chargeable consideration on acquisition (with a lower charge to stamp duty land tax) may result in a higher charge to capital gains tax on disposal (as there will have been a lower base cost). This will, however, only be an issue in a small number of specific circumstances.

Value added tax

[14.156] The treatment of charges to VAT for capital gains tax purposes is set out in Statement of Practice D7 (see also Statement of Practice B1). This provides that if VAT has been suffered on the purchase of an asset, and such VAT can be reclaimed as input tax, then the cost of that asset for capital gains tax purposes will be the cost exclusive of VAT. Where input tax cannot be reclaimed, then the acquisition cost for capital gains tax purposes will be inclusive of the VAT borne. Where an asset is disposed of, any VAT chargeable will be disregarded in computing the capital gain.

Chapter 15

Value added tax

by
Louise Hemmingsley,
LexisNexis

Introduction

[15.1] VAT on property and construction is a significant area of business risk. Large sums are involved, the rules are complex and ever-changing, and HMRC's approach is not always predictable or consistent. VAT is sometimes seen as simply 'washing through' the business, rather than as sticking as a cost. Even where this is true – and often it is not – steps still need to be taken to make it so or to mitigate the effect of any cashflow disadvantage. The issues also need to be addressed early – if an election, notification, indemnity or warranty is needed, it is needed in advance of the transaction in question. Errors, or false assumptions, cannot readily be corrected after the event and could result in the imposition of penalties by HMRC if VAT has been under declared.

This chapter provides an overview of the current main rules. But it cannot do justice to every detailed aspect of the subject and it is not intended to; specialist advice should always be taken. Please note that historical VAT rules can be found in previous editions of *Tolley's Property Taxation*.

Basics of property VAT

[15.2] Property transactions are in principle exempt from VAT, but there are various exceptions and also an 'option to tax', which may be exercised by the VAT registered business who has an interest in the property in question. The option allows the business to charge VAT on the transaction which then enables them to recover any related input VAT incurred.

Exemption applies unless:

- The transaction falls short of the exemption, or perhaps includes other taxable services to which the property element is incidental. In this case, it will be standard-rated unless there is another reason for it not to be. Some points about this are considered in paras **15.4** to **15.18**.
- The transaction is covered by a statutory exception to exemption. The main exceptions cover some freehold new buildings, car parking, hotel and holiday accommodation and various recreational and similar activities. These are generally standard-rated, and are dealt with in paras **15.19** to **15.60**.

- The owner has opted to tax. In this case the transaction is standard-rated unless the option is disapplied. The option to tax is considered in paras **15.64** to **15.120**.
- The transaction is outside the scope of VAT. This might be because:
  - it is non-business;
  - the property is not situated in the UK or Isle of Man (hereafter referred to as the UK) – in this case it may be subject to VAT in another jurisdiction;
  - it is between members of a VAT group;
  - it is a transfer of a going concern (TOGC) (see paras **15.121** to **15.131**); or
  - payment is not consideration for a supply, but is for example compensatory (see paras **15.179** to **15.193**).
- It is zero-rated. This is relevant to dwellings, and certain other residential or charity buildings, where a developer is selling the freehold or granting a long lease. Zero-rating can also apply to grazing rights, the sale *in situ* of a residential caravan or houseboat. Zero-rating overrides exemption and is considered in paras **15.132** to **15.177**.

Property transactions are also sometimes covered by other exemptions: for education; for certain sports facilities; and for sales of assets on which the owner was unable to recover any VAT. These exemptions are looked at in paras **15.61** to **15.63**.

Property costs

[15.3] Building work is generally standard-rated, although some work on dwellings, and other residential or charity properties, is zero-rated (see paras **15.221** to **15.242**) or subject to the reduced rate of 5% (see paras **15.243** to **15.273**). In some cases, businesses should also account for VAT on building work that they carry out for themselves (see para **15.279**). Professional services are generally standard-rated.

Business occupiers can recover VAT to the extent that their activities are taxable. Most can recover VAT in full, but the finance, insurance, health and education sectors, and parts of the public sector, are important exceptions. A fuller list of these 'VAT-averse' occupiers is given in para **15.108**.

Landlords, developers etc can recover VAT where their sales or lettings are taxable, including zero-rated, but not generally otherwise.

Businesses with both taxable and exempt activities need to determine their VAT recovery under the partial exemption rules, considered in paras **15.280** to **15.287**. Their initial VAT recovery may have to be adjusted in the light of later events, notably under the Capital Goods Scheme (CGS) (see paras **15.288** to **15.297**), which involves revisiting the position for a period of up to ten years.

VAT related to non-business activities is normally irrecoverable, but there are special arrangements allowing VAT refunds to local authorities, museums, certain charities and academies (see para **15.287**) and for certain work to dwellings, charity buildings, churches and memorials (see paras **15.274** to **15.278**).

Exemption

[15.4] If a property transaction is to be exempt, it must meet certain criteria and must not fall within one of the exceptions to exemption (exemptions are to be construed strictly). As explained in para **15.2** the exemption can, however, be overridden in various ways, including by an option to tax, by zero-rating or by a TOGC.

The EC Principal VAT Directive

[15.5] The starting point here is Article 135 of the EC Principal VAT Directive 2006/112/EC (the Directive). This provides for exemption under three headings: the leasing or letting of immovable property, the supply of buildings and the supply of land. 'Supply' includes an outright disposal, and other interests in property as defined by the member state.

Article 135(1)(l) exempts 'the leasing or letting of immovable property'. Article 135(2) then requires some specific exclusions from this exemption, as well as allowing member states to apply further exclusions. The specific exclusions, shown in para **15.20**, cover hotel and holiday accommodation, parking facilities, lettings of permanently installed equipment and machinery, and the hire of safes.

So to be exempt under this heading, the transaction:

- must be 'leasing or letting' (paras **15.11** to **15.18**, and in particular para **15.13**);
- must concern immovable property (paras **15.7** to **15.10**); and
- must not be within one of the exclusions.

Article 135(1)(j) exempts 'the supply of a building or parts thereof, and of the land on which it stands'. New buildings are excluded, and should therefore be taxable, but Article 371 allows some member states to retain exemption for the time being.

Finally, Article 135(1)(k) exempts 'the supply of land which has not been built on'. Building land is excluded and should be taxable, but again Article 371 allows some member states, including the UK, to retain exemption for now.

UK law

[15.6] The UK exemption is supposed to be consistent with the Directive. It is drafted in an entirely different way, drawing on (English) land law, but has essentially the same effect and is increasingly interpreted in terms of the Directive. There are, however, a few areas where the UK's position may be questionable.

VATA 1994, Sch 9 Group 1 item 1 exempts:

'The grant of any interest in or right over land or of any licence to occupy land, or, in relation to land in Scotland, any personal right to call for or be granted any such interest or right.'

The law then lists exceptions in the following areas:

- some freehold sales of new or uncompleted buildings or civil engineering works (paras **15.22** to **15.25**);
- parking facilities (paras **15.26** to **15.32**), and similar facilities for aircraft or boats (paras **15.33** to **15.35**);
- hotel, holiday and similar accommodation (paras **15.36** to **15.52**);
- some sports and similar facilities (para **15.53**);
- viewing accommodation at places of entertainment (para **15.55**);
- rights to take game or fish or to remove standing timber (paras **15.56** and **15.57**);
- storage and hairdressing facilities (paras **15.58** and **15.59**);
- rights to acquire any of the above; and
- some leases granted to developers before 1 March 1997 (para **15.21**).

A further exception is in VATA 1994, Sch 10, Part 2 and covers the sale or letting of some residential or charity buildings on which zero-rating has previously been claimed (para **15.170**).

Other exemptions that are sometimes relevant to property are noted in paras **15.61** to **15.63**.

Exemption: land/immovable property

[15.7] In terms of the UK law, 'land' includes areas of water such as lakes, rivers and the seabed. It includes natural features on or under the land, such as trees and minerals. And it includes man-made structures attached to the land, such as buildings and items incorporated into them, walls and oil rigs. The main difficulties are with potentially removable items, and with transactions where the land element is arguably subsidiary.

The Directive takes a slightly different approach, dealing with supplies of land and buildings separately in Article 135, and saying that a 'building' 'shall mean any structure fixed to or in the ground'. More significantly, in scoping the exemption for 'leasing or letting', it refers not to land but to 'immovable property'.

Case law on 'immovable property'

CJEU cases

- In *EC Commission v France* (CJEU Case C-60/96) [1999] STC 480, ECJ, the CJEU held that 'immovable property' did not cover touring caravans, tents, mobile homes and light-framed leisure dwellings that were fixed to the ground. They were 'movable' since they could in fact be easily moved. France was therefore in breach of the Directive by exempting the leasing and letting of such items (paras 15.50 and 15.52).
- In *Maierhofer v Finanzamt Augsburg-Land* (CJEU Case C-315/00) the CJEU held that temporary buildings were 'immovable property'. The buildings could be dismantled and moved, but the process was too labour-intensive for them to be 'movable' in terms of the Directive. The domestic law of the member state was irrelevant, and exemption did not require the lessor to have any interest in the land itself. It was enough for the structure to be 'immovable'.

- In *Fonden Marselisborg Lystbådehavn v Skatteministeriet* (CJEU Case C-428/02) [2006] STC 1467 – a case about the mooring and storage of boats – the CJEU concluded that fenced-off mooring berths, and winter storage sites equipped with a 'cradle', were 'immovable property'. Other aspects of this case are noted in paras **15.13** and **15.27**.

UK cases

- In *Aquarium Entertainments Ltd* (VTD 11845), a company granted a lease on a building in which it had been required to install fire doors, alarms etc. It proceeded to do so, and charged a separate rent for these items. The Tribunal held that there was a separate supply, and that this was taxable – partly because the Directive contemplated taxation for fixed equipment even if the UK had not actually implemented this.
- *University of Kent* (VTD 18625) concerned the hire of portable pre-fabricated units for use as temporary student accommodation. The units had no foundations, apparently resting on legs, and although they were connected to the water and electricity mains their physical attachment to the land was slight. The units could be disconnected and removed in a few hours – far more quickly than those in *Maierhofer* – and the Tribunal concluded that they were not 'immovable property'.
- In *Argents Nurseries Ltd* (VTD 20045), a company owned premises which it let to a subsidiary. It acquired two 'poly tunnels', installed them on the site and charged a separate rent for them. These were large structures, similar to greenhouses, with upright columns concreted into the ground. The Tribunal saw them as the subject of a separate supply from the land. In the light of *Maierhofer*, this was a 'leasing or letting of immovable property'. But the tunnels were 'fixed equipment', so the supply was taxable under the Directive. The Tribunal took no account of the UK's failure to implement this provision (see para **15.8**).
- *Queen Mary, University of London (QM)* (TC01094) entered into a leasing arrangement with a subsidiary of a bank (LPIC), so that LPIC could claim capital allowances on plant and machinery. LPIC leased the property, with the plant and machinery, back to QM. The Tribunal held that the supply was of the plant and machinery, being merely 'dressed up as a lease of the land', and was standard-rated as such.
- In *Sibcas Ltd* ([2017] UKUT 298 (TCC)), the business manufactured and leased movable pre-fabricated accommodation units. Sibcas entered into a contract with a school to provide units that were to be used as temporary classroom accommodation. The issue before the Tribunal was whether the provision of the units could be treated as an exempt supply of immovable land/property. The Upper Tribunal that the units were fixed to the ground using substantial foundations and could not be moved easily. Therefore the supply of the units was exempt from VAT.

Fixed items leased separately

[15.8] One issue here is where an item is fixed to the land, but owned separately from it. The Directive contemplates the letting of this being within the exemption for 'immovable property', but gives specific exclusions for 'permanently installed equipment and machinery' and for safes.

The UK, however, has not implemented these – mandatory – exclusions, apparently in the belief that any separate supply of leasing fixed equipment, or a safe, would not be exempt anyway. The UK does, on the other hand, exempt the letting on site of residential caravans and houseboats (see paras **15.50** and **15.52**). It is not clear that any of this is sustainable in the light of the case law summarised in para **15.7**.

Items sold or leased with the land

[15.9] Sales and lettings of land or buildings often include various 'fixtures and fittings'. These are not generally seen as the subject of a separate supply. So they can be included in an exempt sale or letting, even if on their own they would be taxable.

One question to consider here is whether the purchaser or tenant sees acquiring the item as 'an aim in itself' or merely as 'a means of better enjoying' the property – a distinction derived from the CJEU judgment in *Card Protection Plan*. But in some cases UK law specifically contemplates a single supply being split, with each element being treated accordingly – a point brought out by the CJEU in *Talacre*. Both cases are looked at below.

Selected case law on single and multiple supply

- *Card Protection Plan* (CJEU Case C-349/96) was about a registration and insurance service for credit cards. One question was whether this involved one supply or two. The CJEU laid down what are regarded as the definitive tests on this subject. In particular, it said that:
    - 'a supply which comprises a single service from an economic point of view should not be artificially split';
    - 'the essential features of the transaction must be ascertained in order to determine whether the taxable person is supplying the customer, being a typical customer, with several distinct principal services or with a single service';
    - there is 'a single supply in particular in cases where one or more elements are to be regarded as constituting the principal service, whilst one or more elements are to be regarded, by contrast, as ancillary services which share the tax treatment of the principal service';
    - 'a service must be regarded as ancillary to a principal service if it does not constitute for customers an aim in itself, but a means of better enjoying the principal service supplied'.

Most purchasers and tenants will see the use of an item included in a sale or letting as 'a means of better enjoying' the property, rather than as 'an aim in itself', so that the item is not the subject of a separate supply. The application of CPP was considered in *Colaingrove Ltd* [2015] UKUT 80 (TCC), [2005] STC 1725 which concerned the VAT treatment of the supply of a static caravan with an optional veranda or decking. HMRC considered that where a caravan was supplied with an optional veranda or decking, there were two separate supplies made, and the supply of the veranda/decking was liable to VAT at the standard rate. The taxpayer appealed on the basis that they considered that only a single supply was being made and that the veranda was ancillary to the supply of the caravan and should therefore have the same VAT treatment. The Upper Tribunal agreed with the taxpayer and held that it was a single supply for VAT purposes. HMRC have accepted this decision and this is confirmed in HMRC Revenue & Customs Brief 12/15.

But the law sometimes contemplates a single supply being split:

- *Talacre Beach Caravan Sales Ltd* (CJEU Case C-251/05) concerned the sale of zero-rated caravans. UK law specifically excludes removable contents from the zero-rating, and the CJEU held that this still applied even if there was a single supply of caravan and contents. See also *Cottingham Park Lodges Ltd* (TC05576) regarding the amount allocated to the removable content.

There may also be a separate supply where items are charged for separately – this was the case with equipment in *Aquarium Entertainments* and in *Argents Nurseries*, (para **15.7**), and with cleaning charges in *Tellmer* and *Field Fisher Waterhouse* (para 15.210).

Land as the subsidiary element

[**15.10**] Sometimes the land element is less important than the facilities etc that go with it. The letting of a recording studio might be an example. In this case, there may be a single, normally taxable, supply of the facilities – in terms of *Card Protection Plan*, the land is a means of better enjoying the facilities.

HMRC certainly see this in relation to licences to occupy land – a letting falling short of a lease (see para **15.18**). In their Notice 742, they say that the exemption here does not cover:

'any grant of land clearly incidental to the use of the facilities on it, such as hiring out safes to store valuables, the right to use facilities in a hair dressing salon or granting someone the right to place a free standing or wall mounted vending or gaming machine on your premises'.

The point is less likely to arise with a lease or sale, as opposed to a licence to occupy, since the land element has greater substance. The leasing of a purpose-built facility housing a large piece of built-in scientific equipment might perhaps be taxable on the grounds that the land and building are subsidiary, and this was also the conclusion in relation to capital allowances-driven leasing in *Queen Mary*, noted in para **15.7**.

This was confirmed in *Byrom (t/a Salon 24)* ([2006] EWHC 111 (Ch), [2006] STC 992) which concerned a 'massage parlour' letting rooms by the day to self-employed 'masseuses'. The High Court accepted that the provision of the room was probably the most important element, but did not see the facilities – which included telephone and reception, use of shared areas, card handling and advertising – as ancillary to it, and concluded that there was a single taxable supply.

Exemption: types of transaction

[**15.11**] The exemption covers disposals and lettings, and various other types of property transaction.

Law

[**15.12**] UK law exempts:

'The grant of any interest in or right over land or of any licence to occupy land, or, in relation to Scotland, any personal right to call for or be granted any such interest or right'.

Several points are worth noting about the UK provisions:

* The law says that a 'grant' includes an assignment or surrender. A surrender (in Scotland, a renunciation) is the disposal of a lease etc back to the landlord, such that the lease is normally extinguished. An assignment (in Scotland, an assignation) is any other outright disposal of a lease etc by the tenant.
* The reference to an 'interest in or right over land' is intended to cover legal and equitable interests in terms of (English) land law (para **15.16**). This may not always be correct in terms of the Directive, but member states do have some leeway in scoping the exemption. Scottish personal rights are brought into the exemption in order to create parity of treatment with England.
* A 'licence to occupy' is an occupational right falling short of a lease, and is now interpreted in line with 'leasing or letting' in the Directive.
* It does not generally matter whether the interest etc is paid for by means of a capital sum, rent or some other consideration.

Leasing and letting

[15.13] The reference in the Directive to 'leasing or letting' has been considered by the CJEU on a number of occasions (see below). It has held that the exemption needs to be construed strictly and consistently across the EU, regardless of national land law.

In *Stichting Goed Wonen*, and subsequent cases, the CJEU has held that the leasing or letting of immovable property must:

* relate to immovable property (see para **15.7**);
* confer the right to occupy particular property as if the person were the owner;
* confer a right to exclude anyone else from enjoyment of the right to occupy;
* be for an agreed period; and
* be in return for payment (or, in some versions, for rent).

The Court has, however, since qualified the exclusivity point in *Temco* and *Fonden Marselisborg Lystbådehavn*, and in *Temco* it also decided that an agreed period was not, after all, a criterion in itself, putting a greater emphasis on passivity.

CJEU case law on 'leasing or letting'

* In *Lubbock Fine & Co* (CJEU Case C-63/92) the CJEU held that 'leasing or letting' included 'a change in the contractual relationship' between landlord and tenant – in this case, the surrender of a lease. This now appears incorrect, and the Court has since tried to distance itself from it. The correct answer was perhaps that the transaction was within the alternative exemption for 'the supply of a building'.

- In *European Commission v Ireland* (CJEU Case C-358/97) and *European Commission v United Kingdom* (CJEU Case C-359/97) the CJEU did not see road tolls as leasing or letting since the motorist did not get the use of the road for a defined period. It regarded this as an essential element of letting.
- In *Stichting Goed Wonen* (CJEU Case C-326/99) the Court held that national land law was irrelevant, and that certain property rights were exempt, since they had the same fundamental characteristics as leasing or letting. It saw these as:

    'conferring on the person concerned, for an agreed period and for payment, the right to occupy property as if that person were the owner and to exclude any other person from enjoyment of such a right'.

- The Court took the same approach in two cases about reverse premiums (see para 15.15), *Cantor Fitzgerald International* (CJEU Case C-108/99) and *Mirror Group plc* (CJEU Case C-409/98).
- *Stockholm Lindöpark* (CJEU Case C-150/99) concerned the provision of golfing facilities. The CJEU saw this as consisting of both a passive activity of making the course available and 'commercial' activities such as supervision, management and maintenance. The latter, rather than 'leasing or letting', were likely to be the main element. In any case, use of the course was likely to be restricted as regards the purpose and period of use, and the period of enjoyment was an essential element of a lease.
- *Seeling* (CJEU Case C-269/00) was about a sole proprietor's application of a property to his personal use. This was a supply. A letting would have been exempt, but the CJEU held that this did not apply here – 'leasing or letting' required two parties. The supply was therefore taxable. (For the context of this case, see para 15.181.)
- In *Sinclair Collis Ltd* (CJEU Case C-275/01) the CJEU held that the provision of space for cigarette machines did not amount to the 'leasing or letting of immovable property' since it conveyed only limited rights of possession or control, which were effectively the exclusive right to sell cigarettes on the premises. (On this case, see also para 15.18.)
- In *Temco Europe SA* (CJEU Case C-284/03) a company provided space to associated businesses. They shared the premises and there was no set duration to the arrangement – both factors that had told against exemption in earlier cases. The CJEU nevertheless saw this as 'leasing or letting', being arrangements which:

    'have as their essential object the making available, in a passive manner, of premises or parts of buildings in return for payment linked to the passage of time.'

In trying to justify these apparent inconsistencies, the CJEU explained that:

'while the Court has stressed the importance of the period of letting in those [earlier] judgments, it has done so in order to distinguish a transaction comprising the letting of immovable property, which is usually a relatively passive activity linked simply to the passage of time and not generating any significant added value . . . from other activities which are either industrial or commercial in nature . . . or have as their subject-matter something which is best understood as the provision of a service rather than simply the making available of property.'

and that, effectively, exclusivity could be shared:

'The presence in the contract of such restrictions on the right to occupy the premises let does not prevent that occupation being exclusive as regards all other persons not permitted by law or by the contract to exercise a right over the property.'

- In *Fonden Marselisborg Lystbådehavn* (CJEU Case C-428/02), boat moorings were let for a period, but if a boat owner was going to be absent for more than 24 hours his or her mooring was made available, without reimbursement, to visitors. The Court accepted that this limitation to exclusivity did not preclude 'leasing or letting' – 'since such occasional use does not cause harm to the lessee, it cannot be regarded as altering the relationship between him and the [lessor].' (For other aspects of this case, see paras 15.7 and 15.27.)
- *CO GE P Srl* (CJEU Case C-174/06), concerned a warehouse concession granted by a port authority. The CJEU had little trouble in concluding that this was 'leasing or letting'.
- In *Walderdorff* (CJEU Case C-451/06), the CJEU held that the grant of fishing rights was not 'leasing or letting'. The rights were non-exclusive, and did not convey a right to occupy the waters, but only to fish in them.
- In *RLRE Tellmer Property sro* (CJEU Case C-572/07) the Court concluded that cleaning charges in conjunction with exempt lettings were not themselves within the exemption. (On this, see para 15.210.)
- In *Regie communale autonome du stade Luc Varenne* (CJEU Case C-55/14) the owner of a football pitch allowed it to be used by a football club on a specified number of days per year. Owing to the nature of the club's contractual relationship with the owner the CJEU considered that it amounted to the provision of access to sporting facilities.

Additional payments

[15.14] The exemption only covers payments that actually are consideration for the exempt supply. In some cases, particularly under leases, this is not the case and the payment is actually for something else:

- Additional payments made directly in connection with taking the exempt supply – such as a reimbursement of the vendor's or landlord's legal costs – will be further consideration for that supply.
- The accepted view in the UK is that service charges payable by a tenant are also generally further consideration for the lease, and exempt if this is exempt. But if the tenant can choose whether or not to take the services, it is a separate supply which takes its own, normally standard-rated, liability. The same applies to metered supplies of power, water etc. The CJEU took an apparently different view of service charges in a Czech case, *Tellmer*, but the actual UK implications of this have still to be tested. It should be noted that the judgment in *Tellmer* was qualified by the Order issued by the CJEU in *Purple Parking* (CJEU Case C-117/11) [2012] STC 1680, ECJ. There is more about this, and about service charges generally, in paras **15.211** to **15.219**.
- If the contractual obligation for services is between the tenant and a separate management company, the service charge is consideration for a separate supply. This is normally standard-rated, subject to a concession for residential property (dealt with in para **15.219**). The same applies to service charges levied on freeholders.
- A tenant might make a payment in connection with a variation to the lease, for the removal of a restrictive covenant, or for consent to assign, sub-let, or make alterations. These payments follow the treatment of

the lease and can therefore be exempt, but careful thought is required in some instances as it is not always straightforward. Some lease variations may strictly involve a surrender of the lease and the grant of a new lease – see para **15.185**.

- The same applies if the tenant is simply reimbursing the landlord's costs in connection with a variation, consent etc, although the payment is generally seen as outside the scope of VAT if the tenant is merely exercising rights he already has under the lease. In either case, any VAT on the landlord's costs cannot be recovered by the tenant, even if paid direct by the tenant – if the lease is exempt this will normally mean that the VAT is irrecoverable and that the tenant must reimburse it gross of VAT.
- Some payments are outside the scope of VAT, being for example of a compensatory nature – see para **15.184**.

Reverse premiums

[15.15] Payments are sometimes made in the 'wrong' direction – by vendor to purchaser or by landlord to tenant – usually to encourage the purchaser or tenant to take the property. Sometimes these are simply an adjustment to the purchase price etc, but in other cases they are treated as follows:

- If a landlord pays an inducement, or eg a contribution to fit out works, to an incoming tenant, this does not generally involve a supply at all. If there is a supply, it is because the tenant is seen as doing something more than simply taking a lease, and the treatment will depend on what that is, but it will generally be standard-rated. This follows from the CJEU judgment in *Mirror Group plc* (CJEU Case C-409/98), and there is more about the issue in paras **15.187** to **15.191**.
- If a tenant assigns a lease, and makes a payment to the assignee to take it, it is generally accepted that the assignee is making a supply to the assignor, being the assumption of an onerous obligation. Any such supply is standard-rated in the light of the CJEU judgment in *Cantor Fitzgerald International* (CJEU Case C-108/99). In many cases, however, there may in fact be an argument that there is no supply at all.
- If a tenant surrenders a lease, and makes a payment to the landlord to take it, the landlord is seen as making a supply to the tenant. UK law treats this as exempt, subject to any option to tax exercised by the landlord, and refers to the supply as a 'reverse surrender'. This was introduced in the wake of the CJEU judgment in *Lubbock Fine* (CJEU Case C-63/92) and was supported by the Tribunal in *Central Capital Corporation Ltd* (VTD 13319). Dilapidations payments, however, are generally outside the scope of VAT owing to their compensatory nature (see para **15.184**).
- Payments are sometimes made by vendor to purchaser on a freehold disposal, perhaps because the land requires decontamination. Often this will simply be a discount against the purchase price. Where there is actual payment, case law (para **15.184**) suggests that the position depends on whether the purchaser is taking on what would otherwise be a continuing obligation of the vendor – if so, the purchaser is making a standard-rated supply.

Exemption: interests in and rights over land

[15.16] The UK exemption refers to 'any interest in or right over land'. These concepts are based on English land law. Some equivalent rights in Scotland are not interests in land, but are brought into the exemption as 'personal rights'. This paragraph looks at the scope of these interests and rights, and licences to occupy land are considered in para 15.18.

The UK exemption covers legal, beneficial and equitable interests in land, *profits à prendre*, easements, wayleaves, rights of entry and their Scottish equivalents. In practice, this includes:

- The fee simple, ie the freehold, or:
  - in Scotland, the interest of the owner;
  - in Northern Ireland, the interest under a fee farm grant;
  - a commonhold interest.
- A lease.
- The right to acquire a property, if the acquisition itself would be exempt. This can be conditional, or require further payment as with a call option or right of pre-emption. (But a put option is not an interest in land, and the grant of it is normally standard-rated.)
- The right to the income from a property – but see para 15.17.
- The removal of a restrictive covenant etc.
- Certain rights to remove produce from the land, such as the right to extract minerals or oil or a 'profit of turbary' (turf). These are *profits à prendre*. Other such rights are generally outside the exemption, either because they are specifically excluded from it (game, fish, timber – see paras 15.56 and 15.57) or because exemption is seen as overridden by zero-rating (edible crops, fruit, grazing rights).
- Certain rights such as a right of way or a right of support (eg to lean a shed against a wall), but only where land law recognises these as an easement, wayleave or, in Scotland, a servitude. This means, in particular, that the benefits and obligations must attach to specific, generally neighbouring, land.
- Certain rights to come onto land to perform a specific task, such as the laying of water pipes, recognised by land law as a right of entry.

Rights to income and virtual assignments

[15.17] Sometimes the legal and beneficial ownership of land are separated, with the beneficial owner enjoying any income from it. This involves the legal owner holding the property on trust for the beneficial owner. The beneficial interest is an interest in land in itself, and the disposal of it is within the exemption. It is also the beneficial owner who is generally treated as making any supplies to third parties (see para 15.196).

Other dealings in the right to income from a property are seen differently:

- Where the owner sells a rental stream for a capital sum, HMRC regard the purchaser as making an exempt supply of finance and the owner as making either also an exempt supply of finance to the purchaser or no supply at all. The rental stream itself they continue to see as consideration for supplies by the owner. This seems inconsistent with a direct tax case, *John Lewis Properties plc* ([2001] STC 1118) (see para **6.52**), but does fit with *MBNA Europe Bank Ltd* ([2006] EWHC 2326 (Ch), [2006] 39 LS Gaz R 34), a VAT case about credit card receivables.

• Where there is a 'virtual assignment' of a lease – a disposal of the economic benefits and burdens without the lease itself – and a 'virtual leaseback' such that the owner continues to occupy the property, paying 'rent' to the counterparty, HMRC do not see the 'virtual leaseback' as capable of exemption. Rather, they see a taxable supply of property management etc. Their views were given in Business Brief 16/05. The Court of Appeal agreed in *Abbey National plc* ([2006] EWCA Civ 886, [2006] STC 1961) – the arrangement was not 'leasing or letting' since it conveyed no occupational rights. The case did not directly address the treatment of virtual assignments themselves, and it may be that any supply here can still be exempt as the grant of an interest in land, although various possible rationales for this were eliminated in a non-VAT case, *Clarence House Ltd v National Westminster Bank plc* ([2009] EWCA Civ 1311, [2010] 2 All ER 201, [2010] 1 WLR 1216).

Another aspect of *Abbey National* is considered in para **15.196**.

Exemption: licences to occupy land

[15.18] The UK exemption also covers licences to occupy land. These allow someone to occupy land on terms which fall short of a tenancy, and do not need to be agreed in writing.

HMRC have had considerable difficulty in maintaining a consistent policy in this area, although it is clear that the exemption should only cover (exemptions are to be construed strictly) something that is 'leasing or letting of immovable property' in terms of Article 135(1)(l) of the Directive, so that the CJEU case law in para **15.13** is directly relevant. A definition was also offered by the House of Lords in one of these cases, *Sinclair Collis* ([2001] UKHL 30) – a licence to occupy was:

> 'a licence to go into possession, not necessarily exclusive possession, or to go on to the land and take some degree of control of it. If neither of these features is present, the licence cannot, in my opinion, properly be described as a licence to occupy.'

HMRC has successfully challenged whether pitches at fairs and exhibitions are correctly exempted from VAT as licences to occupy. In *Kati Zombory-Moldovan t/a Craft Carnival* [2016] UKUT 433 (TCC), the taxpayer organised craft and garden fairs and it sold spaces to businesses/individuals at the events in order for them to sell their products to the general public who paid an entrance fee to enter the fair. Craft Carnival accounted for VAT on the entrance fees but not on the spaces provided to stall holders which were treated as exempt supplies of a licence to occupy land. HMRC considered that the supplies made to the stall holders were not exempt supplies and the supply should be treated as a composite supply of taxable services that consisted of the organisation of the craft/garden fair and the provision of an allocated space which enabled the stall holder to trade. However, Craft Carnival was of the opinion that they provided the stall holder with an allocated space at the event which was the exempt lease of immovable property. Craft Carnival also argued that if HMRC was correct that the supply to the stall holder was more than a right to occupy a particular space at the event, the supply was still exempt from VAT as the supply of the space was the predominate supply and all other supplies were incidental to that supply.

The Upper Tribunal held that it would be artificial to split the supply made to the stall holder into more than one supply. The Tribunal went onto state that the stall holders paid a fee to participate in a high quality expertly organised fair and that one element of that composite supply was the provision of an allocated space to sell their products. As a result, Craft Carnival had responsibilities that exceeded the mere provision of a suitably sized pitch and therefore the supplies were not exempt from VAT.

The Tribunal in this case took a similar view to the tribunal in the case of *International Antiques and Collectors Fairs* [2015] UKFTT 354 (TC) where it was held that the stall holders were provided with the provision of services which allowed them to sell goods at an expertly organised and operated antiques and collectors fair which could not be exempt from VAT.

There have also been many other UK decisions in this area. Some of these are noted in para **15.10,** and others are listed in *Tolley's VAT Cases,* but it should be remembered that they are less authoritative than CJEU cases. On a practical level, however, it may be more sensible not to fall foul of HMRC's views than to follow CJEU judgments, but that is a matter to take advice on. HMRC's published guidance is reproduced below.

Licences to occupy land – HMRC's examples

The following examples are taken from HMRC's Notice 742 (May 2012 version).

HMRC see the following as examples of a licence to occupy:

- the provision of a specific area of office accommodation, such as a bay, room or floor, together with the right to use shared areas such as reception, lifts, restaurant, rest rooms, leisure facilities and so on;
- the provision of a serviced office but only where the use of phones, computer systems, photocopiers etc is incidental to the provision of office space;
- granting a concession to operate a shop within a shop, where the concessionaire is granted a defined area from which to sell their goods or services;
- granting space to erect advertising hoardings;
- granting space to place a fixed kiosk on a specified site, such as a newspaper kiosk or flower stand at a railway station;
- hiring out a hall or other accommodation for meetings or parties and so on (but not wedding or party facilities where the supplier does more than supplying accommodation, for example by assisting with entertainment and arranging catering). The use of a kitchen area, lighting and furniture can be included;
- granting a catering concession, where the caterer is granted a licence to occupy a specific kitchen and restaurant area, even if the grant includes use of kitchen or catering equipment;
- granting traders a pitch in a market or at a car boot sale, or
- granting a specific space for the installation of a 'hole in the wall' cash machine (ATM).

HMRC see the following as not being a licence to occupy:

- the rental by a hairdressing salon of chair spaces to individual stylists, unless a clearly demarcated area is provided (such as a floor or whole salon) and no other services;
- the hire of tables in nail bars to self-employed manicurists;
- providing another person with access to office premises to make use of facilities, such as remote sales staff away from home having access to photocopiers and the like at another office;
- allowing the public to tip rubbish on your land;
- storing someone's goods in a warehouse without allocating any specific area for them;
- granting of an ambulatory concession, such as an ice cream van on the sea front or a hamburger van at a football match;
- allowing the public admission to premises or events, such as theatres, historic houses, swimming pools and spectator sports events;
- wedding facilities (including, for example, use of rooms for a ceremony, wedding breakfast and evening party);
- hiring out safes to store valuables, or
- granting someone the right to place a free standing or wall mounted vending or gaming machine on your premises, where the location is not specified in the agreement.

Exceptions to exemption

[15.19] Some types of transaction are specifically excluded (or excepted) from exemption. It should be remembered that exemptions are construed strictly, and that exceptions therefrom should be construed differently as the effect of them is to subject the supply in question to the taxable sphere of VAT.

The Directive

[15.20] Under the Directive:

- The exemption for the supply of buildings excludes new buildings and other new structures fixed to or in the ground (Articles 135(1)(j) and 12).
- The exemption for the supply of land excludes building land (Articles 135(1)(k) and 12), which should therefore be taxable, but a derogation in Article 371 allows the UK not to apply this for the time being. At one time it tried to tax building land through a 'developer's self-supply', but this was abolished in 1997.
- The exemption in Article 135(1)(l) for the 'leasing or letting of immovable property' is subject to exclusions contained in Article 135(2):
  - (a) 'the provision of accommodation, as defined in the laws of the Member States, in the hotel sector or in sectors with a similar function, including the provision of accommodation in holiday camps or on sites developed for use as camping sites';
  - (b) 'the letting of premises and sites for the parking of vehicles';
  - (c) 'the letting of permanently installed equipment and machinery';

(d)   'the hire of safes'.

The UK has implemented (a) and (b). It has taken the view that it does not need to legislate (c) or (d), on the questionable grounds that any separate supply of these would not be exempt anyway – see para **15.8**.

Article 135(2) also allows member states to 'apply further exclusions to the scope of the exemption' for leasing and letting. The UK has done so.

UK law

[15.21] The UK exemption excludes the following, all of which are therefore standard-rated unless, in the particular case, there is some other reason for them not to be:

- Freehold sales of new or uncompleted buildings or civil engineering works (Sch 9, Group 1, item 1, para (a)) (see paras **15.22** to **15.25**). This does not apply to dwellings or to certain buildings for residential or charitable use.
- The provision of facilities for parking vehicles (Sch 9, Group 1, item 1, para (h)) (see paras **15.26** to **15.32**).
- The provision of facilities for storing/housing/mooring aircraft or boats (Sch 9, Group 1, item 1, para (k)) (see paras **15.33** to **15.35**).
- Hotel and similar accommodation, holiday accommodation, camping facilities and temporary siting of caravans (Sch 9, Group 1, item 1, paras (d) to (g)) (see paras **15.36** to **15.52**).
- The provision of facilities for sport or physical recreation (Sch 9, Group 1, item 1, para (m)) (see para **15.53**), subject to some further exemptions (see para **15.54**).
- The right to occupy a box, seat or other accommodation at a sports ground, theatre, concert hall or other place of entertainment (Sch 9, Group 1, item 1, para (l)) (see para **15.55**).
- The right to take game or fish (Sch 9, Group 1, item 1, para (c)) (see para **15.56**).
- The right to remove standing timber (Sch 9, Group 1, item 1, para (j)) (see para **15.57**).
- Call options, pre-emption rights and Scottish personal rights to acquire an interest etc in land which would be taxable under one of the rules above (Sch 9, Group 1, item 1, para (n)).
- Residually, 'developmental tenancies' created by the former developer's self-supply (see para **15.20**) (Sch 9, Group 1, item 1, para (b)). This applies to some leases granted before 1 March 1997.
- Self-storage facilities (Sch 9, Group 1, item 1, para (ka)) (see para **15.58**).
- Hairdressing facilities (Sch 9, Group 1, item 1, para (ma)) (see para **15.59**).

Also, certain sales or lettings of buildings that previously qualified for zero-rating as for 'relevant residential' or 'relevant charitable' use are automatically standard-rated under VATA 1994, Sch 10, Part 2 (see para **15.170**) – this overrides exemption or any other treatment.

Exceptions to exemption: new buildings and civil engineering works

[**15.22**] The freehold sale of new or uncompleted buildings or civil engineering works is standard-rated. This does not apply to dwellings or to some other residential or charity buildings – these will be zero-rated or exempt. These rules are not often applied, since vendors of new commercial buildings will usually have opted to tax anyway, but the rules do override the anti-avoidance provisions for the option (paras **15.113** to **15.120**).

Law

[**15.23**] VATA 1994, Sch 9, Group 1, item 1, para (a) refers to:

'the grant of the fee simple in –

(i)   a building which has not been completed and which is neither designed as a dwelling or number of dwellings nor intended for use solely for a relevant residential purpose or a relevant charitable purpose;

(ii)   a new building which is neither designed as a dwelling or number of dwellings nor intended for use solely for a relevant residential purpose or a relevant charitable purpose after the grant;

(iii)   a civil engineering work which has not been completed;

(iv)   a new civil engineering work;'

Interpretation

[**15.24**] For these purposes:

- 'Fee simple' means the freehold or equivalent, as explained in para **15.16**.
- A building or civil engineering work remains 'new' until three years after 'completion' (VATA 1994, Sch 9 Group 1 Note 4). Under ibid Note 2, 'completion' is:
  - for a building, when an architect issues a certificate of practical completion in relation to it or it is first fully occupied, whichever happens first. It appears that 'occupation' need not involve physical occupation, and that a building is 'occupied' if the owner has let the building to a tenant who could go into occupation.
  - for a civil engineering work, when an engineer issues a certificate of completion in relation to it or it is first fully used, whichever happens first.
- The rules are not confined to developers – they apply to any sale of the freehold while the building is still 'new'.
- HMRC are likely to see the sale of a partly completed building or works as standard-rated if the project has progressed beyond foundation stage, but otherwise as potentially exempt. Following their defeat in *Virtue (t/a Lammermuir Game Services)* (VTD 20259), they accepted in Revenue & Customs Brief 64/07 that the sale of a serviced building plot was a single exempt supply of land, rather than partly standard-rated.

- UK law does not define a building or civil engineering work, but this should probably be considered in terms of the reference in Article 12(2) of the Directive to 'any structure fixed to or in the ground'. HMRC are likely to consider that an extension is not a new building, although the Tribunal in *Capital One Developments Ltd* (VTD 18642) came to a different view.

- If a payment is made some time after title passes, the position is looked at in terms of what was on the site when title passed. So if bare land is sold, but only paid for once a building is under construction, the supply can still be exempt – it is still seen as a supply of bare land. And if a building is completed and sold in 2012, a payment in 2017 is still taxable – what matters is that the building was new in 2012. These points apply even where the tax point only arises on payment (see para **15.204**). Before 9 April 2003, the position was looked at only at the tax point – if a building was completed and sold in 2002, a further payment creating a tax point in 2012 can be exempt because the building is no longer new.

- The tests for whether a building is 'designed as a dwelling or number of dwellings' are the same as for zero-rating, as explained in paras **15.135** to **15.140**. If different parts of the building are in different uses, the sale price should be split, with part treated as standard-rated and part as zero-rated or exempt.

- Similarly, 'relevant residential purpose' and 'relevant charitable purpose' are defined in the same way as in paras **15.155** et seq and **15.161** et seq, although there is no requirement here for the purchaser to certify the intended use. Vendors are advised to obtain clear warranties about this. The 'solely' requirement is discussed in para **15.152**.

Options and pre-emption rights

[15.25] Call options and pre-emption rights are exempt, but only if the main supply would be exempt. So an option to acquire a freehold new commercial building is standard-rated. HMRC see the three-year limit applying in terms of when the option is granted, not when it is exercisable: if a building is completed in 2012, they see an option granted in 2012 as standard-rated, even if it cannot be exercised until 2017 when the building is no longer new.

A 'put option' is standard-rated.

Exceptions to exemption: parking of vehicles

[15.26] VATA 1994, Sch 9, Group 1, item 1, para (h)) implements this by taxing:

'the grant of facilities for parking a vehicle'.

The provision does not offer any further explanation, but various points have emerged from case law.

Vehicles

[15.27] In *Fonden Marselisborg Lystbådehavn* (CJEU Case C-428/02), the CJEU concluded that 'vehicles' covered all means of transport, and specifically boats. (Other aspects of this case are noted in paras **15.7** and **15.13**.) The UK deals with boats and aircraft separately (paras **15.33** to **15.35**), but the Tribunal has generally seen caravans as vehicles and HMRC say that bicycles are also included.

Grant

[15.28] The 'grant of facilities' is taken to include any grant, assignment or surrender of a lease or licence, whether or not to the end user, whether for a premium or rent, and regardless of its length. Excess and penalty charges are generally seen as outside the scope of VAT.

HMRC accept that freehold sales are not included. This may not go far enough. The Tribunal in *Internoms Ltd* (VTD 16527) saw a 120-year lease, granted for a premium, as taxable, but it is not clear that this is correct.

Parking facilities

[15.29] HMRC say that there must be a specific grant (etc) of facilities designed for, or specifically provided for, parking vehicles, and this appears consistent with case law.

* If the premises are designed for parking, they are seen as parking facilities unless the terms of the letting preclude use as such. This covers garages, car parks, taxi ranks etc and spaces in these.
* If the site is not designed for parking, being for example bare land, the presumption is that it is not parking facilities. HMRC see it as parking facilities only if the agreement etc refers to use for parking and that use is not merely incidental to something else, or if it is provided for the construction of a garage or car park.
* HMRC accept that a vehicle left on land or in a building may not necessarily be 'parked'. They do not see the provision of parking as covering the following, which can therefore be exempt:
  - storage provided to motor dealers, vehicle transportation firms, distributors or auctioneers;
  - exhibition space, but see Revenue & Customs Brief 22/12;
  - lettings for, or at, a market, car boot sale or travelling fair or circus, even if the property is used at other times as a car park.

Incidental parking

[15.30] In *Henriksen*, the CJEU held that parking facilities should not be taxed as such if they were 'closely linked to' an exempt letting for some other purpose. So if a house and garage are let together they are both exempt.

HMRC suggest in their Notice 742 that parking should not be taxed as such if it is subsidiary to another letting by the same landlord to the same tenant, provided that it is on, or reasonably near to, the main premises. This includes, say, the provision of communal parking on an industrial estate. The lettings need not be under the same agreement, or on similar terms.

Henriksen also indicated that the parking could be exempt if it was provided in conjunction with an exempt letting by a different landlord, if the parking was part of the same complex as the main property. HMRC have not followed this.

Case law on parking facilities

[15.31] The Tribunal and the Courts have considered a range of issues in this area:

- In *Henriksen* (CJEU Case C-173/88), the CJEU held that lettings of garages for parking were exempt where they were 'closely linked to the [exempt] letting of immovable property for another purpose'. This applied if the landlord and tenant were the same parties or – as in the actual case – if the parking and the main property were part of a single complex.
- The Court of Session in *Trinity Factoring Services Ltd* ([1994] STC 504, CS) held that the letting of lock-up garages was standard-rated where the lessees were permitted to use them for parking, even if they actually used them to store goods.
- In *Internoms Ltd* (VTD 16527), the Tribunal decided that a 120 year lease, for a premium, of two parking spaces was taxable – even though the tenant did not use the spaces, and was thought to have taken them for their development potential, the lease only permitted use for parking.
- In *Venuebest Ltd* ([2003] STC 433), the High Court held that the letting of spare spaces in a car park to a car park operator was taxable.
- *Routledge* (VTD 18395) concerned the letting of 'the Granby Halls Car Park' to a rugby club. The Tribunal accepted that the description was merely intended to identify the land, which had once been a car park, and that this did not make it parking facilities. It was not laid out as a car park, and any use for parking was trivial – it was actually used to give access to the rugby ground. The letting was therefore exempt.
- *Hopcraft* (VTD 18590) was about the provision, in a compound, of storage for caravans. The Tribunal thought that caravans were vehicles, and that the supply was taxable. It suggested that the difference between parking and mere storage was one of availability:

  'vehicles are parked when they are placed in a position where they can readily be recovered by their owners for use at short notice, whereas storage means that they are placed in a position where they can be said to have been put away because they will not be required at short notice'.

  The actual duration of the storage was not a primary consideration. Caravan storage had also been found to be parking facilities in *D H Commercials* (VTD 14115) and in *Newall* (VTD 18074). The provision of a caravan pitch is sometimes exempt (see para 15.51).
- In *Civilscent Ltd* (TC00070), a residential developer argued that parking spaces provided to residents were zero-rated under the provisions discussed in para 15.134 et seq. HMRC successfully contended that they were standard-rated, despite their published position on incidental parking (para 15.30), which might have suggested that the alternative to zero-rating was exemption.

- In *Vehicle Control Services* ([2012] UKUT 129 (TCC)), the Upper Tribunal agreed with the First-tier Tribunal that monies received in relation to parking enforcement could not be damages for the tort of trespass as the operator did not own the land. It was considered that the monies amounted to consideration for the supply of a service by the operator to the land owner. The Court of Appeal took a different view ([2013] EWCA Civ 186) and held that the payments were in the nature of damages and were not consideration for a supply.

Cases concerning local authority parking are noted in para 15.32.

Local authorities

[15.32] The provision of parking by a local authority may be non-business. HMRC accept this for on-street car parking, but not for local authority car parks. This has been tested in protracted litigation by *Isle of Wight Council*. Following a CJEU judgment (CJEU Case C-288/07) the High Court ([2009] EWHC 592 (Ch), [2009] STC 1098) remitted the case back to a Tribunal for a further hearing on factual aspects. The Upper Tribunal ([2014] UKUT 0446 (TCC), [2015] STC 460) agreed with the conclusions drawn by the First-tier Tribunal (TC02320) on remission that standard-rating would prevent a distortion of competition. The matter was referred to the Court of Appeal who issued their ruling in January 2016 confirming that treating the parking as non-business would lead to a distortion of competition so these supplies are liable to VAT.

Public sector tolls are outside the scope of VAT as non-business, as are congestion charges.

Exceptions to exemption: mooring facilities, aircraft etc

[15.33] VATA 1994, Sch 9, Group 1, item 1, para (k)) standard-rates:

'the grant of facilities for housing, or storage of, an aircraft or for mooring, or storage of, a ship, boat or other vessel'.

The law also says that 'mooring' includes anchoring or berthing.

This is intended to supplement the rules for the parking of vehicles, although the CJEU judgment in *Fonden Marselisborg Lystbådehavn* (CJEU Case C-428/02) (see para **15.27**) suggests that this may be unnecessary since 'vehicles' covers all means of transport anyway.

Interpretation

[15.34] As with parking, HMRC accept that the rules do not cover freehold sales, but see them extending to any other interest. Similar points to those in para **15.30**, about incidental parking, also apply here.

HMRC consider that the provision of mooring rights includes cases where the boat owner is simply allocated a stretch of river bank, lays down the mooring and retains title to the ground tackle.

Exceptions

[15.35] There are several cases where these rights are not seen as standard-rated:

- HMRC see mooring rights for houseboats as exempt, apparently on the grounds that they are not 'boats';
- Some of these facilities may be zero-rated if they are provided at a Customs port or airport recognised by HMRC – see HMRC Notice 744C;
- The provision of moorings by a non-profit making body may be exempt as sports facilities (see para **15.54**), if the boat owners can be seen as participating in a sport, such as sailing.

Exceptions to exemption: hotels and holiday accommodation – overview

The Directive

[15.36] Article 135(2)(a) of the Directive excludes from the exemption:

> 'the provision of accommodation, as defined in the laws of the Member States, in the hotel sector or in sectors with a similar function, including the provision of accommodation in holiday camps or on sites developed for use as camping sites'.

Such accommodation is therefore taxable. Although member states have some flexibility over the scope of taxation, the CJEU in *Blasi* (CJEU Case C-346/95, [1998] ECR I-481, [1998] STC 336) observed that the provisions:

> 'should be broadly construed since their purpose was to ensure that the provision of temporary accommodation similar to, and hence in potential conflict with, that in the hotel sector, was subject to tax'.

Member states can, and a number have, apply a reduced rate to hotel and holiday accommodation.

Unlike the UK, the Isle of Man applies the reduced rate of 5% to most hotel and holiday accommodation other than timeshares (Notice 709/3A MAN). This does not extend to the provision of meals, other than breakfast provided under an inclusive tariff. Further details are at www.gov.im/customs.

UK law

[15.37] UK law contains separate provisions taxing:

- hotel and similar accommodation;
- holiday accommodation;
- caravan pitches; and
- camping.

The scope of these is looked at in paras **15.38** to **15.52**.

Exceptions to exemption: hotels etc

Law

[**15.38**] VATA 1994, Sch 9, Group 1, item 1, para (d) taxes:

'the provision in an hotel, inn, boarding house or similar establishment of sleeping accommodation or of accommodation in rooms which are provided in conjunction with sleeping accommodation or for the purpose of a supply of catering'.

It also explains (ibid Note 9) that a 'similar establishment':

'includes premises in which there is provided furnished sleeping accommodation, whether with or without the provision of board or facilities for the preparation of food, which are used by or held out as being suitable for use by visitors or travellers'.

Types of establishment

[**15.39**] In most cases it is clear whether premises are covered by the rules, but there can be difficulties, particularly with what is a 'similar establishment'.

But if a passer-by can simply walk in and obtain accommodation, subject to availability, this is a strong pointer towards the property being within these rules. HMRC take a broad view, as shown below. Case law might indicate a slightly narrower interpretation, suggesting that a 'similar establishment':

- is primarily concerned with providing sleeping accommodation; if the main purpose of the establishment is, for example, to provide welfare or teaching, it is probably not a 'similar establishment';
- does not seek to organise the activities of its occupants;
- is likely to be run for profit; and
- is the sort of establishment that accommodates people for short stays, even if in practice all the occupants are there long-term.

Hotel, inn, boarding house or similar establishment? – HMRC's views

HMRC's Notice 709/3 (June 2013) says that the following are covered by the rules for hotels etc:

'*Hotels, inns and boarding houses*: Commercial establishments providing lodging (furnished sleeping accommodation) and possibly meals and other facilities such as laundry services, communal TV/rest rooms and telephone services for guests and visitors. Your establishment does not have to provide food or other facilities to be regarded as a hotel, inn or boarding house.'

'*Similar establishments*: Establishments with similar characteristics to hotels, inns and boarding houses; and any premises, in which furnished sleeping accommodation is provided, that are used by or held out as being suitable for use by visitors or travellers (but not if such use is only occasional).'

'*Motels, guesthouses, bed and breakfast, private residential clubs, halls of residence and hostels*: These all have the characteristics of establishments similar to and are in competition with hotels, inns and boarding houses. This also includes service flats for use by guests other than as a permanent place of residence. This includes:

motels

guesthouses
bed and breakfast establishments
private residential clubs
hostels, and
serviced flats (other than those for permanent residential use).'

Case law suggests that some of this is – and particularly the reference to halls of residence – is too sweeping.

Hotel, inn, boarding house or similar establishment? – selected case law

Student accommodation

A number of cases have concerned accommodation for students. The provision of such accommodation by a university, school etc, in conjunction with education, is, however, exempt in any case under the education exemption (para 15.63).

- In *McMurray* (VTD 39), the Tribunal decided that a hall of residence was not a 'similar establishment' because of its selectivity over residents, its high degree of control over them and its emphasis on corporate living.
- *Soka Gakkai International UK* (VTD 14175) concerned residential courses about Buddhism. The Tribunal decided that the premises were not a 'similar establishment' because their main purpose was to provide religious teaching.
- In *International Student House* (VTD 14420), a charity provided accommodation for overseas students, together with counselling, welfare and an activities programme. The Tribunal thought that this, together with the lack of a profit motive, meant that the premises were not similar to a hotel, inn or boarding house.
- *Acorn Management Services Ltd* (VTD 17338) concerned accommodation for overseas students. This was a more commercial undertaking than in the other cases, and without the same emphasis on corporate living. The Tribunal decided that the premises were a 'similar establishment' and that the accommodation was taxable.
- In *The Principal & Fellows of Lady Margaret Hall* (TC04181) [2014] UKFTT 1092 (TC), the First-tier Tribunal did not consider that the accommodation in question was taxable as it was not a 'similar establishment' to a hotel. Reasons included the fact that the duration of stays differed, as did the dining arrangements.

Accommodation for patients

- *Macmillan Cancer Trust* (VTD 15603) was about an establishment that was clearly similar to a hotel, and was advertised as such, but which also provided care to people with cancer. The Tribunal thought that the establishment was not used in the same way as a hotel, and that there was a single exempt supply of welfare services, with no separate taxable supply of accommodation.
- A different conclusion was reached in relation to some types of visitor in *St Dunstan's* (VTD 17896), but this was in a different context, and it is not clear that HMRC themselves thought that the Tribunal was correct. Another aspect of this case is noted in para 15.162.

Hostels etc

- Homeless hostels etc have been found to be 'similar establishments' in *Namecourt Ltd* (VTD 1560) and *North East Direct Access Ltd* (VTD 18267).
- In *Dinaro (T/A Fairway Lodge)* (VTD 17148), on the other hand, such a hostel was found not to be a 'similar establishment' because of the levels of selectivity over, and supervision of, residents and the attempt to foster a corporate or family atmosphere.
- *Atlas Property London Ltd* (TC03797) [2014] UKFTT 674 (TC) concerned the provision of accommodation for the homeless. HMRC were successful in arguing that the establishment was not similar to a hotel as, for example, the accommodation was not open to the general public and that the services accompanying the accommodation were limited.

Longer-term accommodation

- In *McGrath* ([1992] STC 371, QB), a guesthouse was a similar establishment despite the accommodation being provided on a long-term basis and residents regarding the property as their home.
- But in *Holding* (VTD 19573) accommodation in the appellants' home and in a bungalow in the grounds was not a similar establishment. It was not similar to a hotel in view of the long stays and limited advertising, nor similar to a boarding house in view of the lack of regular catering.

Serviced flats

- In *Mills* (VTD 1686), flats let long-term, with cleaning and laundry services, were found not to be a 'similar establishment'.
- But in *BJ Group* (VTD 18324), flats let mainly for short periods, and with a much higher level of service provision, were a 'similar establishment'.

Wedding venues

- A wedding venue where overnight accommodation was also available was a 'similar establishment' in *Leez Priory* (VTD 18185), as was a country house let mainly for weddings in *Acrylux Ltd* (TC00173). Guidance was also given by the Tribunal in *Drumtochty Castle Limited* (TC02111). The letting of such a venue may well, however, be taxable anyway, even where no accommodation is provided – see *Chewton Glen* in para **15.40**.
- In *Blue Chip Hotels Ltd* (TC05078) [2017] UKUT 204 (TCC), the taxpayer owned a large hotel that had a licensed wedding room for civil ceremonies. The hotel offered wedding packages which included the hire of the room and catering facilities, etc. The wedding room however could only be used for the actual ceremony. The hotel levied separate charges for the use of the wedding room and the supply of other items included in the wedding package. The supply of the wedding room was treated as an exempt supply and the other services as taxable supplies. HMRC concluded that a composite supply was being made that was taxable at the standard rate. The taxpayer appealed. The Tribunal held that the hire of the wedding room should be a separate supply for VAT purposes, even if it was supplied as part of a wedding package. However, it could not be treated as an exempt supply as the provision of licensed premises in which a civil ceremony could be conducted went beyond the passive letting of land. Appeal dismissed. The taxpayer appealed and the Upper Tribunal dismissed its appeal agreeing with

the First-tier Tribunal that the supply of the services by the hotel added significant value, by supervising the room and making a responsible person available to conduct the ceremony, etc and therefore could not be exempt from VAT.

Taxable accommodation

[15.40] Not all accommodation in a hotel etc is standard-rated. The letting of a conference room or retail unit is normally exempt, although many hotels have opted to tax in order to ensure full VAT recovery. The standard-rating only applies to:

- sleeping accommodation;
- accommodation in rooms provided in conjunction with sleeping accommodation – eg in a suite; and
- accommodation in rooms provided for the purpose of a supply of catering.

The third of these items is relevant to room hire for a dinner or function, and clearly applies when the hotel is also providing the catering. HMRC appear to see it also applying when the catering is provided by someone else, but case law is inconsistent on the point. HMRC released Revenue & Customs Brief 2/13 which confirmed a change in policy with regards to room hire where the catering is provided by a third party. HMRC historically considered that the room hire would be exempt from VAT unless the supplier has opted to tax. However if the room has been provided for the purposes of catering then the whole supply, including the value of the third-party catering, will be liable to VAT at the standard rate. Supplies made with effect from 22 January 2013 are liable to VAT. This rule does not apply where the catering is not the purpose of the room hire. So if a conference package includes room hire and a meal, the catering is taxable but the room hire can still be exempt. HMRC also accept that the entire charge can be exempt where only coffee, tea, biscuits etc are provided.

In *Chewton Glen Hotels Ltd* (VTD 20686), however, the Tribunal concluded that room hire for wedding ceremonies was standard-rated even where little or no catering was provided. This was on the basis not of these rules, but on the grounds that the supply was not within the exemption for 'leasing or letting' in the first place.

28-day rule

[15.41] Where an individual stays at a hotel etc for more than 28 days, Sch 6, para 9 provides that a reduced amount of VAT is due for the rest of their stay. If the standard rate of VAT is 20%, the effect is broadly similar to a 4% rate. This includes cases where the supply is, for example, to a local authority, provided the same individual is in occupation throughout. Please note that with effect from 1 April 2015, hotels, inns, boarding houses and similar establishments must treat all breaks in the guest's stay as starting a new period for the purposes of the 28-day rule, unless the guest can return at any time and continue their occupancy of the room, or a similar room, as if they had never vacated it.

Sales and lettings of hotels etc

[15.42] The exception from exemption is for accommodation *in* a hotel etc. It does not apply to the sale or letting of the entire building, and this is treated like any other transaction concerning commercial property. In *Asington Ltd* (VTD 18171), a block of furnished flats was let to a company which provided short-term serviced accommodation in them. The lettings by the company were seen as taxable, but the lettings to it as exempt.

Exceptions to exemption: holiday accommodation

Law

[15.43] VATA 1994, Sch 9, Group 1, item 1, para (e) taxes:

'the grant of any interest in, right over or licence to occupy holiday accommodation'.

It also explains (VATA 1994, Sch 9, Group 1, Note 13) that:

'"Holiday accommodation" includes any accommodation in a building, hut (including a beach hut or chalet), caravan, houseboat or tent which is advertised or held out as holiday accommodation or as suitable for holiday or leisure use, but excludes any accommodation within paragraph (d).'

The reference to para (d) means that accommodation which is potentially taxable both as hotel etc and holiday accommodation is treated as the former.

Note 11(b) adds that para (e) includes:

'any supply made pursuant to a tenancy, lease or licence under which the grantee is or has been permitted to erect and occupy holiday accommodation.'

These rules are essentially relevant to lettings for rent, and their effect is to ensure wide-ranging standard-rating. Service charges are generally standard-rated in the same way as rent, but optional or metered supplies of electricity, gas or water may be zero-rated or taxable at 5% – see paras **15.212** and **15.213**.

As a result of para (n), any payment for a right or option over such accommodation is also standard-rated. But Notes 11(a) and 12 contain further rules about freehold sales of holiday homes, long leases and leases for a premium – these are dealt with in paras **15.45** to **15.46**.

Interpretation

[15.44] Anything within the definition of holiday accommodation is treated as such. This applies even if it is only advertised as holiday accommodation in order to circumvent housing legislation (*Sheppard* (VTD 481)). The occupier does not need to be on holiday, and – as with the reference to beach huts – the accommodation does not need to be sleeping accommodation. Also, 'includes' in Note 13 indicates that this is not an exhaustive definition – there may be other cases that are taxable as holiday accommodation.

In particular, HMRC have a tendency to see accommodation that cannot be occupied throughout the year as holiday accommodation. In Notice 709/3, they say that:

'Holiday accommodation includes, but is not restricted to, any house, flat, chalet, villa, beach hut, tent, caravan or houseboat. Accommodation advertised or held out as suitable for holiday or leisure use is always treated as holiday accommodation. There may be a restriction under which occupation of the property throughout the year is not permitted, but this will not always be the case.'

Location will also be a factor – HMRC may well assume that short residential lets are holiday accommodation if they are in central London, or if they are at a resort in the holiday season.

Conversely, however, HMRC recognise that accommodation may only be holiday accommodation in season, and that off-season lets may be exempt. They say that they will accept this if:

* the letting is for more than 28 days;
* the local holiday trade is seasonal;
* the letting is out-of-season, ie generally in the period October to Easter;
* there is evidence that it is (purely) as residential accommodation.

Exceptions to exemption: holiday accommodation – further rules for buildings

Law

[15.45] There are further provisions, essentially about holiday homes. These are complicated.

VATA 1994, Sch 9, Group 1, Note 11(a) says that para (e) includes (and therefore taxes):

'any grant excluded from item 1 of Group 5 of Schedule 8 by Note (13) in that Group'

VATA 1994, Sch 8, Group 5 zero-rates the grant of a 'major interest' by a person constructing a building designed as a dwelling or number of dwellings, or converting a non-residential building to such a building. These terms are fully explained in para **15.134** et seq, but a major interest is the freehold, or a lease for more than 21 years (in Scotland, for at least 20 years), and for leases only the first payment is zero-rated. Note 13 to that Group takes certain transactions out of zero-rating, and Note 11(a) to Sch 9, Group 1 then makes these standard-rated. Note 13 – and therefore Note 11(a) – covers cases where:

'(i)   the interest granted is such that the grantee is not entitled to reside in the building or part, throughout the year; or

(ii)   residence there throughout the year, or the use of the building or part as the grantee's principal private residence, is prevented by the terms of a covenant, statutory planning consent or similar permission.'

But, importantly, this only applies where the grant would otherwise be zero-rated.

Also, Sch 9, Group 1, Note 12 restricts taxation as holiday accommodation by saying that:

'Paragraph (e) does not include a grant in respect of a building or part which is not a new building of –

(a)   the fee simple, or
(b)   a tenancy, lease or licence to the extent that the grant is made for a consideration in the form of a premium.'

So although ongoing rent of holiday accommodation is always standard-rated, a capital sum, whether for a lease etc or the freehold, is exempt unless the building is 'new', in which case it is standard-rated. As in para **15.24**, 'new' means within three years of the earlier of practical completion or first full occupation.

Interpretation

[15.46] HMRC have had some problems interpreting these rules, and a tendency to confuse Notes 11(a) and 13. They will often regard a restriction on residence as meaning that property is necessarily taxable as holiday accommodation. This is incorrect. Such a restriction might be an indication, but it is only actually a legal test under Note 11(a), in cases where the supply would otherwise be zero-rated.

In a 1994 case, *Ashworth*, the Tribunal accepted this incorrect reading of the law, but concluded that it gave too broad a meaning to holiday accommodation. HMRC therefore announced that they would not see accommodation with restricted occupancy rights as holiday accommodation if:

* the development itself was not a holiday or leisure development; and
* it was not marketed as such; and
* there was no restriction on use as a principal private residence.

So they would not see a restriction on all-year use *alone* as defining a property as holiday accommodation. They cannot, however, be relied upon always to follow this approach.

Ashworth is summarised, with other cases, below.

Rules for holiday homes etc – selected case law

* *Ashworth* (VTD 12924) concerned the ground rent and service charge on a 99 year lease on a marina property, which the tenants used as their sole residence. The lease did not allow them to occupy the property in February. HMRC claimed that this restriction meant that the payments were standard-rated. This was a misreading of the UK law, since the charges were not otherwise zero-rated. The Tribunal nevertheless agreed under UK law, but then went on to hold that the charges were exempt under the Directive. This was also highly questionable, because the Directive allows member states to apply further exclusions to exemption.
* In *Livingstone Homes UK Ltd* (VTD 16649), sale agreements for new houses said that they 'shall be used as holiday dwelling houses only and for no other purpose'. The sales were otherwise zero-rated, but HMRC argued that Note 11(a) applied, saying that this restriction meant the properties could not be used as a principal private residence. The Tribunal disagreed – holiday accommodation and a principal private residence were not mutually exclusive, and the sales were zero-rated.
* A similar issue arose in *Loch Tay Highland Lodges Ltd* (VTD 18785). The planning consent said that the properties 'shall be used solely for holiday accommodation and shall not be occupied as the sole or main residence of

any occupant', and the sale contracts that they 'shall be used and occupied solely as a holiday dwellinghouse and for no other purpose'. Note 11(a) was relevant because the sales were otherwise zero-rated, and applied because the planning consent clearly prohibited use as a principal private residence. But the Tribunal also held that the sale contract precluded occupation throughout the year – a further obstacle to zero-rating – and that *Livingstone* had been wrongly decided.

- Similarly, in *Herling Ltd* (TC00205), a developer's sales of properties were standard-rated because of a planning condition that they 'shall be used for holiday accommodation only and for no other purpose'.
- An attempt to circumvent these rules was successful in *Lower Mill* (see para 15.299).

Timeshares etc

[15.47] The initial price of a timeshare in UK holiday accommodation is exempt, unless the building is less than three years old, in which case it is standard-rated. This is a result of Note 12: Note 11(a) does not apply as the supply would not otherwise be zero-rated. Ongoing charges, such as service charges, are generally standard-rated (but see para **15.209** et seq). In principle, these points apply however the charges are presented, but some further points have emerged from the case law noted below.

Timeshares in hotels etc are likely to be standard-rated under the rules in para **15.38** et seq, regardless of the form of payment or the age of the building.

Timeshares etc – selected case law

- In *Court Barton Property plc* (VTD 1903), the sale of shares that each conveyed a right to a week's holiday accommodation was found to be a supply of holiday accommodation. The Tribunal allocated £1 to the exempt sale of the share itself and saw the balance as taxable.
- In *RCI Europe* (CJEU Case C-37/08), the CJEU concluded that payments to participate in a UK-based timeshare exchange scheme were taxable according to the location of the property, and so outside the scope of UK VAT in relation to non-UK properties.
- And in *Macdonald Resorts Ltd* (CJEU Case C-270/09) the CJEU concluded that the UK sale of 'points' entitling purchasers to use holiday accommodation in the UK or Spain was not taxable as such – VAT was only due as when the points were redeemed, and then in the country where the accommodation was located.
- In *Fortyseven Park Street Limited* (TC05318) the appellant sold fractional interests in a residence located at a London Mayfair Property. The purchaser paid a substantial upfront price, in exchange for the right to occupy a residence at the property for a maximum number of nights each year and to obtain access a range of related benefits, such as the option to exchange stays at the property for stays in other properties, etc during that period. The appellant argued that the purchaser was receiving an exempt licence to occupy but HMRC considered that it was the provision of accommodation in a hotel, inn, boarding house or similar establishment. The First-tier Tribunal

held that the appellant made supplies of a licence to occupy land but that these supplies were taxable as the provision of accommodation in a hotel, inn, boarding house or similar establishment. Appeal dismissed.

Exceptions to exemption: camping, caravans and houseboats

[15.48] Holiday accommodation in a tent, caravan or houseboat is standard-rated as holiday accommodation under the rules in paras **15.43** and **15.44**, but there are further points about each.

Camping

[15.49] VATA 1994, Sch 9, Group 1, para (g) taxes:

'the provision of pitches for tents or of camping facilities'.

This applies whether or not for holiday use.

Caravans

[15.50] Although the letting of a caravan on site is potentially standard-rated as holiday accommodation, HMRC generally see this as applying only if the letting is as holiday accommodation and is on a caravan park advertised or held out as for holiday use. In other cases they accept that the letting can be exempt. Also, the sale or leasing of a residential caravan (more than 7 metres long or more than 2.55 metres wide) is currently zero-rated under VATA 1994, Sch 8 Group 9. Following announcements made as part of the 2012 Budget, from 6 April 2013 revised legislation subjects some caravans to the standard rate and some to the reduced-rate; the availability of the zero-rate will therefore be limited.

Caravan pitches

[15.51] VATA 1994, Sch 9 Group 1 para (f) taxes:

'the provision of seasonal pitches for caravans, and the grant of facilities at caravan parks to persons for whom such pitches are provided'.

Other lettings of caravan pitches are exempt.

Note 14 (the wording of which changed with effect from 1 Match 2012) explains that:

'A seasonal pitch for a caravan is–
(a)   a pitch on a holiday site other than an employee pitch, or
(b)   a non-residential pitch on any other site.'

A new Note 14A was introduced with effect from 1 March 2012 to supplement the newly re-worded Note 14:

'employee pitch' means a pitch occupied by an employee of the site operator as that person's principal place of residence during the period of occupancy;

'holiday site' means a site or part of a site which is operated as a holiday or leisure site;

'non-residential pitch' means a pitch which—

(a)   is provided for less than a year, or

(b)   is provided for a year or more and is subject to an occupation restriction,

and which is not intended to be used as the occupant's principal place of residence during the period of occupancy;

'occupancy restriction' means any covenant, statutory planning consent or similar permission, the terms of which prevent the person to whom the pitch is provided from occupying it by living in a caravan at all times throughout the period for which the pitch is provided.

The off-site storage of caravans has generally been seen as the standard-rated provision of parking facilities – see para **15.26** et seq.

Houseboats

[15.52] Holiday accommodation in a houseboat is standard rated. HMRC accept that other lettings of houseboats, but not of other small moored vessels, are exempt.

But the sale or leasing of a houseboat – defined in terms of being designed or adapted for permanent habitation and not being readily capable of self-propulsion – is zero-rated under VATA 1994, Sch 8 Group 9. For zero-rating to apply to leasing, HMRC expect the lessee to be able to remove the houseboat from its mooring.

HMRC see mooring rights for houseboats as exempt.

Exceptions to exemption: sports facilities

[15.53] VATA 1994, Sch 9, Group 1, para (m) taxes:

'the grant of facilities for playing any sport or participating in any physical recreation'.

Note 16, however, says that this does not apply, so that such facilities can still be exempt:

'where the grant of the facilities is for –

(a)   a continuous period of use exceeding 24 hours; or

(b)   a series of 10 or more periods, whether or not exceeding 24 hours in total, where the following conditions are satisfied –

(i)   each period is in respect of the same activity carried on at the same place;

(ii)   the interval between each period is not less than one day and not more than 14 days;

(iii) consideration is payable by reference to the whole series and is evidenced by written agreement;

(iv)   the grantee has exclusive use of the facilities; and

(v)   the grantee is a school, a club, an association or an organisation representing affiliated clubs or constituent associations.'

The potential impact of *Regie communale autonome du stade Luc Varenne* (see above at para **15.13**) should be considered generally in relation to the above.

HMRC take the view that these rules cover any premises designed or adapted for playing any sport or taking part in any physical recreation, such as swimming pools, football pitches, dance studios and skating rinks, or parts of the premises such as an individual court.

HMRC do not see a general purpose hall as sports facilities if it merely has floor markings eg for badminton, even when it is actually let for playing sport. But they are likely to regard the supply as taxable if equipment, such as racquets and nets, is also provided.

There is some doubt about lettings to intermediaries, who will admit others. The Tribunal in *Queens Park Football Club Ltd* (VTD 2776) held that the letting of Hampden Park to the Scottish FA, for international matches, was a grant of sports facilities and standard-rated. But in *Abbotsley Golf & Squash Club Ltd* (VTD 15042), the letting of golf courses to a golf club was seen as exempt, the only grant of sports facilities being by the club.

HMRC generally take a strict approach to the 'series of lets' rules in Note 16(b), but may also challenge any deliberate attempt to fall foul of them in order to preserve taxation. In *Polo Farm Sports Club* (VTD 20105), the Tribunal disagreed with their view that lettings on consecutive days could be exempt under these rules – the interval between the lettings was the period of hours overnight and not, as HMRC argued, a day, so that condition (ii) was not met and the lettings were taxable.

HMRC give their views on various other points in their Notice 742.

Other exemptions

[15.54] Two other, non-property, exemptions can also be relevant here:

*   Sports facilities provided by a non-profit making body are potentially exempt under Sch 9, Group 10. This was held to include berthing and storage for boat owners in *Swansea Yacht & Sub Aqua Club* (VTD 13938). Further details of the exemption are in HMRC's Notice 701/45.
*   Lettings of sports facilities by the public sector, or by a non-profit making body, for use by students or pupils are likely to be covered by the education exemption – see para **15.63** and HMRC's Notice 701/30.

Exceptions to exemption: other cases

Viewing accommodation

[15.55] VATA 1994, Sch 9, Group 1, para (l) standard-rates:

'the grant of any right to occupy a box, seat or other accommodation at a sports ground, theatre, concert hall or other place of entertainment'

HMRC consider that this applies whether or not a match, performance etc is taking place at the time, although they, and the Tribunal, took a different view in *Southend United FC* (VTD 15109). They do not see it as covering non-viewing accommodation, such as retail space, or the letting of the whole premises.

Game and fish

[15.56] VATA 1994, Sch 9, Group 1, para (c) standard-rates:

> 'the grant of any interest, right or licence consisting of a right to take game or fish unless at the time of the grant the grantor grants to the grantee the fee simple of the land over which the right to take game or fish is exercisable'.

Note 8 adds that:

> 'Where a grant of an interest in, right over or licence to occupy land includes a valuable right to take game or fish, an apportionment shall be made to determine the supply falling outside this Group by virtue of paragraph (c).'

So shooting or fishing rights as such are standard-rated. Freeholds carrying such rights can be wholly exempt, but for leases etc the element relating to the rights is taxable if it is 'valuable'. HMRC consider that rights are valuable if they account for more than 10% of the total value. However, it may be that a transaction concerning the acquisition of sporting rights will comprise the transfer of a going concern such that no supply will take place for VAT purposes.

Rights to acquire sporting rights of this kind are also taxable, although certain *pro indiviso* rights in Scotland are arguably exempt.

The CJEU judgment in *Walderdorff* (CJEU Case C-451/06) (see para **15.13**), however, suggests that fishing rights are standard-rated anyway, and that para (c) is actually superfluous, perhaps along with some of the UK's other exceptions to exemption.

Some arrangements may be non-business and outside the scope of VAT. This was the case in *Fisher*, where family and friends participated in pheasant shoots and contributed to the cost. However, a shoot run along such lines will invariably involve one or more let days per season which would of course amount to a business.

- If the business is operating a still water fishery and it charges customers for a fishing session then the supply of the right to catch fish will be liable to VAT at the standard rate. However if the customer has one of the following options then it may be possible to split the charge between the standard-rated right to catch fish and the zero-rated fish providing they can be treated as 'food' for VAT purposes. The customer has a clear option regarding whether they can return any fish that are caught or take them.
- The customer makes a separate payment for any fish they decide to keep after the session is over.
- The fish that are taken by the customer are of a type that are generally treated as human food.

However the Tribunal held in *Stocks Fly Fishery (A Partnership)* (TC04994) [2016] UKFTT 218 (TC) that the right to catch fish was the predominate supply and that any fish that were taken away by the angler were to be treated as ancillary to the main supply of the right to catch fish. Therefore the whole supply was liable to VAT at the standard rate.

HMRC do not see taxable fishing rights as including the letting of a lake without fish which will be exempt from VAT unless the lessor has opted to tax.

The issue of a rod licence by the National Rivers Authority or similar type of organisation which do not actually grant the recipient with a right to fish are outside the scope of VAT.

Standing timber

[15.57] VATA 1994, Sch 9, Group 1, para (j) standard-rates:

'the grant of any right to fell and remove standing timber'.

This does not apply to a dealing in land that includes valuable timber. The sale of felled timber is generally standard-rated, but in some cases may be taxable at 5% as domestic fuel.

Self-storage

[15.58] With effect from 1 October 2012 FA 2012, Sch 26, para 5 removed 'the grant of facilities for the self-storage of goods' from exemption by inserting a new item 1(ka) to VATA 1994, Sch 9, Group 1. Self-storage is defined in Note 15A to item 1. The definition of self-storage is wide (wider than what one would consider to be self-storage in common parlance), and the potential application of the legislation to seemingly innocent scenarios should therefore be considered carefully, although HMRC are understood to place great weight on the use to which the premises in question are put by the customer as opposed to the general characteristics of the premises. Reference should be made to VAT Information Sheet 10/13.

Hairdressing facilities

[15.59] Item 1(ma) to VATA 1994, Sch 9, Group 1 subjects to the standard-rate of VAT 'the grant of facilities to a person who uses the facilities wholly or mainly to supply hairdressing services'. This is supplemented by Notes 17 and 18.

Change of use following zero-rating

[15.60] Some construction and other work to a 'relevant residential' or 'relevant charitable' building is zero-rated (see para 15.224 et seq). This can also apply to a sale or long lease by a developer of such a property (para 15.151 et seq). Where someone received a zero-rated supply on this basis, in relation to a building completed before 1 March 2011, VATA 1994, Sch 10, Part 2 potentially standard-rates any sale or letting by them for some other use if this happens within ten years of the building being completed. This does not just override exemption, but any other treatment, including as outside the scope. There is more about this in para 15.170.

Other exemptions

[15.61] Three other exemptions are potentially relevant to some property transactions.

Goods on which input tax was irrecoverable

[15.62] VATA 1994, Sch 9, Group 14 exempts supplies of goods where the supplier incurred VAT on the goods and could not recover any of it. This also applies if the supplier acquired the goods on a TOGC (para 15.121 et seq) and the transferor had been in this position.

For property, these rules apply to freeholds, and leases exceeding 21 years (in Scotland, of at least 20 years), if:

- the supply would otherwise be standard-rated, other than under the option to tax;
- the supplier, or their predecessor under a TOGC, incurred VAT on the acquisition or construction etc of the property; and
- that VAT was *wholly* irrecoverable.

The exemption applies extremely rarely, and in most cases the supplier would prefer to opt to tax in order to override it.

Education

[15.63] Some property transactions are covered by the exemption for education in VATA 1994, Sch 9, Group 6.

This is mainly relevant to education providers – the exemption covers closely related goods or services as well the education itself. The provision of residential accommodation for the students or pupils – which might otherwise be taxable under the rules in para 15.38 et seq – is the most common example, but HMRC also see the exemption as covering the provision of student parking.

The exemption also includes supplies to an education provider by a public or non-profit making body, such as a charity letting sports facilities to a school.

Reference should be made to Notice 701/30.

Option to tax

[15.64] The option to tax, or election to waive exemption, allows vendors and landlords to tax what would otherwise be exempt property transactions, and so recover related input tax.

Article 137 of the Directive provides that member states 'may allow taxable persons a right of option for taxation' for exempt property transactions. They 'shall lay down the detailed rules governing exercise of the option' and may restrict its scope.

The UK legislation relating to the option to tax is set out in VATA 1994, Sch 10. The option is a very useful facility, particularly where the purchaser or tenant is fully taxable and can recover the VAT charged on the transaction itself, but exercising an option to tax is not always advantageous and this is considered in paras 15.107 to 15.112.

The main points about the option are as follows:

- The option is unilateral, and personal to the owner – it does not bind anyone else, although there are further points about VAT groups and partnerships, trusts etc – see paras **15.66** to **15.68**.

- There are rules about the physical scope of the option – in particular, it is not possible to opt on only part of a building – see paras **15.69** to **15.72**.

- Supplies of some types of land or building, such as dwellings, cannot be taxed under the option – see paras **15.73** to **15.80**.

- The option can only be exercised from a current date and then needs to be notified to HMRC within 30 days – see paras **15.81** to **15.88**. It should be noted that the time limit for notifying an option to tax is different when it relates to an option to tax that has to be exercised by a buyer in relation to a TOGC – see para **15.128**.

- The option may require HMRC's prior permission if the owner has previously made exempt supplies – see paras **15.89** to **15.92**.

- The option is basically irrevocable, but with some limited exceptions – see para **15.102**.

- Where there is an existing lease when a landlord opts, the rentals will become subject to VAT from a current date and the landlord can usually add VAT to the rent – see para **15.65**.

- An option can sometimes allow recovery of past as well as future input tax – see paras **15.93** to **15.101**.

- There are complex anti-avoidance rules. These may be relevant where an anticipated occupier is not fully taxable, and regardless of whether avoidance is involved – see paras **15.113** to **15.120**.

Implications for existing contracts

[15.65] In principle, opting means that VAT becomes due on all future supplies of the property, including existing leases and other contracts.

The owner can nevertheless opt unilaterally, and need not consult tenants etc unless the lease etc requires this.

As a general rule, any agreed price includes VAT unless the contract says otherwise. But this does not apply here. If VAT becomes due because of an option exercised after an agreement, lease etc was entered into, it can be added to the price, rent, service charge etc unless a provision in the agreement, lease etc specifically says otherwise. For a tenancy or lease, this provision must refer to VAT or to VATA 1994, s 89. Such a provision will not prevent the landlord from exercising an option to tax, but it will have the effect of making the rent payable inclusive of VAT such that the VAT cost will need to be borne by the landlord. Accordingly, the terms of a lease must be considered carefully.

The option applies according to the normal tax point rules in para **15.201** et seq. This means, for example, that rent due before the option takes effect, but only paid afterwards, is taxable under the option.

Option to tax: person opting

[15.66] The option is unilateral and does not require the consent of any purchaser or tenant. It is personal and does not bind anyone else, but there are special rules for VAT groups, and issues with partnerships, trusts etc.

VAT groups

[15.67] The option is exercised by the individual member of a VAT group, but also binds any 'relevant associate'. In practice, this generally means that the option applies to the whole group.

A 'relevant associate' means anyone who:

(i)   was VAT grouped with the person opting to tax when the option first had effect;

(ii)   has been subsequently VAT grouped with them when they had an interest in, right over or licence to occupy the property or any part of it;

(iii)   has been VAT grouped with anyone in (i) or (ii) above when they had an interest in, right over or licence to occupy the property or any part of it;

(iv)   has been VAT grouped with anyone in (iii) above when they had an interest in, right over or licence to occupy the property or any part of it.

This continues to apply to someone who has left the VAT group. But there is an exception to this where they are no longer connected with the person who opted (in the same terms as in para **15.117**), have no continuing interest etc in the property and will make no further supplies arising from a disposal of it.

Partnerships, trusts etc

[15.68] For partnerships, it is the partnership as a whole that is VAT registered and opts to tax. For English limited partnerships, however, it is (usually) the general partner alone. Where there is a split between legal and beneficial ownership, it is the beneficial owner who should opt. If there is more than one, HMRC will expect them to register and opt together as a partnership. There is more about these issues in para **15.194** et seq.

Option to tax: physical scope

[15.69] In general, the owner has a free choice as to what is covered by the option, but there are specific rules for buildings and for options exercised before 1 March 1995.

Buildings

[15.70] It is not possible to opt on only part of a building, or planned building. If the option applies to any part of a building, it applies to the whole building and to any land within the curtilage of the building, such as a yard or forecourt.

Also:

- Buildings linked internally or by a covered walkway are treated as a single building. HMRC consider that the linkage – or planned linkage – must be such as to allow the free movement of people and goods between the buildings. But they do not see buildings as linked merely by a car park, public thoroughfare or something required by law, such as a fire escape.
- A complex is treated as a single building if it consists of a number of units grouped around a fully enclosed concourse, such as an enclosed shopping precinct, that is entered through doors.

Building work may cause an option to spread:

- If an opted building is extended, the option will cover the extension.
- If two existing buildings, one of which is opted, are subsequently linked, the option does not spread from one to the other unless they are merged structurally to form a single building.
- Similarly, if some buildings in an unenclosed complex have been opted, HMRC do not see the option spreading to the others if the complex is subsequently enclosed.
- If an opted building is sub-divided into separate units, the option will apply to all the units.

Demolition and construction

[**15.71**] An option applies to the land and to any building on it, and in principle it survives the construction or demolition of a building. But:

- If the option was exercised on bare land, and a new building is then constructed on it, it is generally possible to exclude the building from the option. There are time limits for this, and the decision must be notified to HMRC on form VAT 1614F.
- If the option was exercised before 1 June 2008, and clearly applied only to a building, HMRC accept that the owner can treat the option as revoked if the building is demolished.

Options exercised before 1 March 1995

[**15.72**] Less flexible rules apply for options exercised before 1 March 1995, although these are often overlooked, including by HMRC:

- 'Parades, precincts and complexes divided into separate units' are treated as single buildings, so that an option on one building in a parade etc applies to all of them.
- An option on agricultural land applies to any other agricultural land unless separated by non-agricultural land (but not merely by a road, railway, river etc) or by land in or over which the owner (and any relevant associate as in para **15.67**) has no interest, right or licence to occupy. Agricultural land includes any building on the land.

Option to tax: exceptions

[15.73] An option exercised on certain types of land or building has no effect. This is relevant to:

- dwellings (see paras **15.74** and **15.75**);
- buildings for a 'relevant residential' purpose (see para **15.76**);
- buildings for a 'relevant charitable' purpose (see para **15.77**);
- land for residential development by a housing association or an individual (see paras **15.78** and **15.79**);
- pitches for residential caravans and moorings for residential houseboats (see para **15.90**); and
- cases covered by the anti-avoidance rules (see paras **15.113** to **15.120**).

The effect of the option is also overridden by zero-rating, by the exemptions for education and for sports facilities referred to in paras **15.63** and **15.54** and by non-supply treatment, such as a TOGC (para **15.121** et seq).

Dwellings: already 'designed as' a dwelling

[15.74] Under VATA 1994, Sch 10, para 5, the option has no effect on a sale or letting of a building or part of a building which is 'designed or adapted, and is intended, for use as a dwelling or number of dwellings'. There are various points here:

- 'Designed or adapted' is defined in terms of Sch 8, Group 5, Note 2 (see para **15.135** et seq) – in particular, this means that the dwelling must be self-contained.
- This provision does not apply – so that the option does have effect – if the property is intended for commercial use, as holiday accommodation or for demolition (even if for residential development). But an intention to use it as a dwelling temporarily, pending a change, will be enough to prevent the option applying.
- The price may need to be split for buildings in mixed use. For pubs that include flats, it is normal for 10% of the total price to be treated as relating to the flat, and HMRC will generally accept this.
- For leases, the position may change during the course of the lease.

Dwellings: conversions and other cases

[15.75] VATA 1994, Sch 10, para 6 says that the option has no effect where a purchaser or tenant 'certifies that the building or part of the building is intended for use as a dwelling or number of dwellings', unless it is intended for some other use in the meantime. These rules are not relevant where para 5 applies, so they mainly concern properties intended for conversion to dwellings.

There is a prescribed form of certificate, Form VAT 1614D. A purchaser or tenant can only issue it if they:

- intend to use the property as a dwelling or dwellings;
- intend to convert the property for use as a dwelling or dwellings; or
- are 'a relevant intermediary'.

A 'relevant intermediary' must intend to dispose of the property to someone else – a specific person – who intends to convert it for use as a dwelling or dwellings, or to another relevant intermediary: in theory, there can be any number of relevant intermediaries through to the person actually carrying out the conversion.

There are further rules about the timing of a certificate:

- It is only effective if it is issued before the supply is made, eg on completion in the case of an outright disposal.
- If the price has been legally fixed, eg on exchange of contracts, the purchaser or tenant can only issue a certificate with the agreement of the vendor or landlord.
- A relevant intermediary can only issue a certificate if it has already received one from its purchaser.

The certificate is still valid, and disapplies the option, if the purchaser or tenant changes his mind before the transaction is completed, although HMRC accept that it can be withdrawn in these cases. The option is also still disapplied if the certificate should never have been issued in the first place, although the person issuing it may then be liable to a penalty.

Other residential buildings

[**15.76**] The option is potentially disapplied on a building, or part building, intended for use 'solely for a relevant residential purpose' (RRP). A nursing home or student accommodation may be examples (see paras **15.155** to **15.160**). The same provisions apply to these buildings as to dwellings, as explained in paras **15.74** and **15.75**. So:

- Under Sch 10, para 5, the option has no effect on a sale or letting of a building or part of a building which is 'designed or adapted, and is intended, for use . . . solely for a relevant residential purpose'. But in this case there is a clear requirement for the purchaser or tenant to inform the vendor or landlord, in advance, of the intended use.
- Under Sch 10, para 6, the option has no effect where a purchaser or tenant 'certifies that the building or part of the building is intended for use . . . solely for a relevant residential purpose'. The certification requirements are the same as for dwellings.

As noted in para **15.152**, HMRC do not interpret 'solely' quite literally, and in this context they are content for it to be taken as meaning at least 95%, if both parties agree.

Charity buildings

[**15.77**] VATA 1994, Sch 10, para 7 says that the option has no effect on a sale or letting to a person where the building or a part of a building is 'intended by the person for use solely for a relevant charitable purpose,' (RCP) 'but not as an office'.

A relevant charitable purpose means use by a charity for non-business activities or as a village hall or similarly (see paras **15.161** to **15.164**). HMRC interpret the reference to 'an office' narrowly. In Notice 742A, they refer only to 'an office for general administration, for example, head office functions of the charity', and in other cases they still see the option as potentially disapplied. And in the same way as at para **15.76**, they are content for 'solely' to be taken as at least 95%, if both parties agree.

Housing associations

[15.78] Under VATA 1994, Sch 10, para 10, the option does not apply to a sale or letting of land to a:

> 'relevant housing association . . . if the association certifies that the land is to be used (after any necessary demolition work) for the construction of a building or buildings intended for use –
>
> (a)   as a dwelling or number of dwellings, or
> (b)   solely for a relevant residential purpose.'

A relevant housing association means (in England) a private registered provider of social housing, (in Wales and Scotland) a registered social landlord or (in Northern Ireland) a registered housing association, and certification must be on certificate VAT 1614G. As with certificates for conversions to dwellings, it needs to be issued before the supply is made, and requires the agreement of the vendor or landlord if the price has already been legally fixed.

'Solely for a relevant residential purpose' has the same meaning as in para **15.152** et seq, although HMRC have not suggested that the 95% interpretation of 'solely' can automatically be used in this context.

Disapplication of the option under this provision can be a real nuisance to vendors. To deal with this, it is not unusual for the vendor to commence construction, prior to sale, of the buildings required by the housing association. The sale is then potentially zero-rated. This is sometimes referred to as a 'golden brick' arrangement (see para **15.143**).

Individuals

[15.79] Under VATA 1994, Sch 10, para 11, the option has no effect on a sale or letting:

> 'made to an individual if –
>
> (a)   the land is to be used for the construction of a building intended for use by the individual as a dwelling, and
> (b)   the construction is not carried out in the course or furtherance of a business carried on by the individual'.

There is no certification requirement, but it is advisable to obtain warranties from the purchaser or tenant.

Residential caravans and houseboats

[15.80] VATA 1994, Sch 10, paras 8 and 9 provide that the option has no effect in relation to:

> 'a pitch for a residential caravan'; or

'facilities for the mooring of a residential houseboat'.

There must be no prohibition in any covenant, planning consent etc on residence throughout the year. There is no certification requirement, but it is advisable to obtain warranties from the purchaser or tenant if there is any doubt about the intended use of the site.

Other points about sites for caravans and houseboats are in paras **15.51** and **15.52.**

Option to tax: making and notifying an option

[15.81] All options to tax must be notified to HMRC, but the decision to exercise an option to tax and notifying it to HMRC are separate acts. It is good practice to record a decision to exercise an option to tax, perhaps in board minutes, but there is no legal requirement to do so, and usually the notification and HMRC's acknowledgment of it provide acceptable evidence for the option. HMRC's permission may, however, be needed where there have been previous exempt supplies of the property, and in this case different arrangements apply – see paras **15.89** to **15.92.**

Time limits

[15.82] The option can take effect from a current date or future date, but not retrospectively. It should be notified to HMRC within 30 days of the decision being taken, but they may accept a late notification. HMRC will generally do so if they are satisfied that the taxpayer really did take a decision to exercise an option to tax at the earlier date and that it can be evidenced. HMRC set out their policy on late notification in Notice 742A and VATLP22430 et seq. They may, however, be open to the criticism that their generosity to a vendor or landlord on this issue may be to the detriment of the purchaser or tenant, as seen in *Marlow Gardner & Cooke* in para **15.86.**

Form of notification

[15.83] HMRC produce a notification form, VAT 1614A, but will accept other formats provided the same information is provided. A different form may be needed if the person has previously made any exempt supplies of the property (see para **15.91**). It is best for the notification to be made by the owner, and signed by a responsible person such as a director. If a professional adviser notifies HMRC, HMRC will expect to see evidence that the owner has authorised them to do so.

There is no requirement to notify tenants, but it is at least courteous to do so.

Where to notify

[15.84] The notification can be sent:

- by post to: Option To Tax National Unit, HM Revenue & Customs, Ground Floor, Portcullis House, 21 India Street, Glasgow, G2 4PZ;
- by fax to 03000 529 807; or

- by email (attaching a signed and scanned form or letter) to optiontotax nationalunit@hmrc.gsi.gov.uk

But:

- if the business is registering for VAT on the strength of the option, the notification should be enclosed with the registration application and sent to the HMRC registration unit;
- overseas businesses registered with HMRC's Non-Established Taxable Persons Unit should notify there;
- larger businesses with an allocated 'client relationship manager' (or CRM) may in practice be able to notify him or her.

Retaining evidence

[15.85] It is important to retain a copy of the notification and of HMRC's acknowledgement of it – this may need to be produced to HMRC, or to a purchaser or tenant. HMRC have no central record, and often no record at all, of options notified before 2003.

Some options made before 1 March 1995 did not need to be notified to HMRC, and in these cases alternative evidence may be needed.

Errors

[15.86] There can also be problems where an option has been notified in error, or where the owner has been charging VAT without notifying an option. Case law demonstrates that the position may be difficult to prove in the absence of evidence, and that the presumption will be that an option has been exercised.

Selected case law on notifying the option

- In *Devoirs Properties Ltd* (VTD 6646), a letter saying 'we wish to charge VAT on our rental invoices' was held to prove that the company had indeed opted.
- In *Fencing Supplies Ltd* (VTD 10451), a company had charged VAT on rent without consciously opting. The Tribunal decided that this nevertheless amounted to opting, and that VAT was therefore also due on the sale of the property. It was helped to this conclusion by the fact that the law at the time would not have required the company to notify the option, but the case is still regularly cited before the Tribunal.
- In *Blythe Limited Partnership* (VTD 16011), solicitors were supposed to notify an option on four properties, but did so on 16. Fortunately there was evidence that this was an error, and the Tribunal accepted this. HMRC commented in Business Brief 17/99, and the case has made them more wary of accepting notifications from professional advisers.
- In *Classic Furniture (Newport) Ltd* (VTD 16977), the Tribunal accepted, surprisingly, that a company had opted merely by recovering VAT to which it was not otherwise entitled.

- In *Rathbone Community Industry* (VTD 18200), HMRC held an old letter from an accountancy firm, notifying an option to tax on behalf of the owner. There was no evidence that the firm had ever acted for the owner, but there was no evidence either that the owner had not opted. The Tribunal could not credit that the firm had sent the letter without good reason, and concluded that the option had in fact been exercised.
- In *Marlow Gardner & Cooke Ltd Directors Pension Scheme*, the purchaser of a property challenged the VAT charged by the vendor. The vendor claimed to have opted, but the evidence for this was weak, and its solicitors had previously offered other, spurious, explanations for VAT being due. 30 days after the sale, the vendor notified HMRC of an option, giving an effective date six years earlier. HMRC accepted this, and so did the Tribunal (VTD 19326) and the High Court ([2006] EWHC 1612 (Ch)). VAT had therefore been properly due. Curiously, in the interval between the disputed events and the Tribunal hearing, HMRC 'clarified' their policy in Business Brief 13/05, in terms suggesting that they should not have accepted the notification.
- In *Grenane Properties Ltd* (TC00494), a company was owned by three individuals, one of whom was also a partner in an accountancy firm. On the evidence, the Tribunal accepted that staff at the firm had acted on their own initiative in notifying an option to tax, that the partner-director had not perused documents before signing them, and that the company had never in fact intended to opt.
- In *Mill House Management UK Ltd* (TC00960), the Tribunal found that HMRC had acted reasonably in rejecting late notifications of options to tax. The company had purported to charge VAT to tenants, but it had not registered for VAT, and there was no evidence that it had consciously opted.
- In *Exeter Estates Limited* (TC02632) the taxpayer opted to tax land by reference to the Land Registry title number only. This was a mistake and it sought to 'clarify' the extent of its original notification to exclude buildings. The Tribunal agreed that this was effective.

Opting on multiple properties

[**15.87**] The option is generally exercised property-by-property. But:

- In some cases an option necessarily covers more than one property, for example because they are linked (see paras **15.69** to **15.72**).
- It is possible to exercise a single option covering a number of properties – for example on an entire trading estate or geographical area, or indeed on the entire UK. Any new acquisition within the area will then automatically be opted. But in this case the permission rules (para **15.89** et seq) need to be considered for all relevant properties together, and it may be difficult or impossible to revoke the option under the rules in para **15.104** or **15.105**.
- It is also possible to have an automatic option on each property acquired, by making a 'real estate election'.

The real estate election

[**15.88**] A person exercising a real estate election, or REE, is in principle treated as having opted on any property where they, or a member of their VAT group, subsequently acquire an interest in it, a right over it or a licence to occupy it, so that there is no need to notify HMRC of an option on the specific property.

The REE does not apply if an option would ordinarily be covered by the permission rules in para **15.89**. Nor does it cover properties where the person already held an interest, right or licence, or properties on which they, or a member of their VAT group, had already opted to tax. In some cases, however, an existing option will cease to apply if the person no longer has an interest in the property or right to any proceeds from it. The person may also be able to exclude new acquisitions from the effect of the REE under the revocation rules in para **15.104**. The REE itself can only be revoked by HMRC.

The legislation is in VATA 1994, Sch 10, paras 21 and 22. Someone exercising a REE must notify HMRC on Form VAT 1614E, normally within 30 days, and needs to provide them with extensive information, both initially and subsequently on request. Whilst a few people have found the REE a useful facility, the information requirements, and the complexity of the rules, have undoubtedly deterred others.

Option to tax: permission to opt

[15.89] If the owner has made exempt supplies of the property, for example by letting it, in the preceding ten years, it can only opt with HMRC's permission. This also applies if it intends to make such supplies before the effective date of the option. This rule is in VATA 1994, Sch 10, para 28 and is intended to stop owners recovering excessive input tax under the option.

In some cases permission is available automatically; in others it must be specifically sought.

Automatic permission

[15.90] In their Notice 742A, HMRC have set out various sets of circumstances where permission to opt is available automatically, and need not be sought. In these cases, the option should be notified in the normal way, as explained in para **15.81** et seq: Form VAT 1614A provides for the person to specify which set of circumstances applies.

Automatic permission is available in most cases where the option is being exercised in relation to a new third party letting, or a sale with vacant possession, and in some other circumstances. The rules concerning the application of the various automatic permission conditions can be extremely complicated and great care is needed when deciding which of them may be relied upon.

Specific permission

[15.91] Where automatic permission is not available (ie none of the automatic permission conditions are available), the person should submit VAT Form 1614H to HMRC. This serves both as the request for permission and the notification of the option itself. The form asks questions about past and future use of the property, about input tax and about any own occupation. The person also needs to specify when they wish the option to take effect – this can be a current date, or any future date.

In considering the request for permission, HMRC's main interest will be in what input tax the owner proposes to recover, and whether this is reasonable in relation to the mix of taxable and exempt supplies. It is rare for permission to be refused outright, and if HMRC are not satisfied their normal approach is to request further information and/or to debate the amount of input tax recovery.

In some cases it may be worth foregoing some input tax for the sake of obtaining permission quickly, or transferring the property into another group company that does not require permission to opt.

Once HMRC give permission, the person is automatically treated as having opted with effect from the date they originally specified, although in some cases they may be able to revoke the option *ab initio* under the 'cooling off' rules in para **15.104**.

Failure to obtain permission

[15.92] If the owner overlooks the need for permission, and simply notifies an option, the option is not valid. VATA 1994, Sch 10, para 30 allows HMRC to dispense with the permission requirement and to treat it as valid, from the original notification date, although they say they will only do so if the error resulted from a minor oversight, or if revenue is at risk.

Option to tax: recovering input tax

[15.93] Exercising an option to tax usually means that all future supplies of the property will be taxable (subject to the rules set out above), and that any future input tax wholly related to the property can be recovered in full. Generally speaking, such input tax cannot be recovered until the option is exercised, but might be recoverable afterwards.

The position depends first of all on whether the owner actually has opted, is intending to opt or has made no decision.

No decision on the option

[15.94] In some cases the owner will be intending to let or sell a property, but will not have decided whether to exercise an option to tax – the decision might depend on the VAT position of the future tenant or purchaser.

In these circumstances, HMRC's general view is that the owner can only intend to make exempt supplies, so that input tax is irrecoverable. In particular, they tend to take this approach where the property is ready for immediate occupation.

They do, however, accept a different answer for developers, at the early stages of a project when it is unclear what, if anything, will be built. In these cases, they will accept that the input tax can be treated as residual, in the same way as a general overhead, and recoverable according to the developer's general partial exemption position (see para **15.280** et seq). This may be helpful if the developer already makes other, taxable, supplies.

The Tribunal agreed with HMRC's position in *Lawson Mardon*, summarised in para **15.100**, but some of the other case law noted there might suggest that residual recovery should apply more broadly.

In some cases it may be possible to recover the VAT later on, as considered in para **15.96** et seq.

If the business is not registered for VAT, it cannot recover VAT at the time anyway, and is subject to stricter time limits on back claims when it does register.

Intending to opt

[15.95] In theory, if the owner has a clear intention to opt and only to make taxable supplies, related input tax ought to be recoverable.

HMRC's views are set out in Notice 742A and in Business Brief 14/04. They relaxed their approach slightly following their defeat in *Beaverbank*, summarised in para **15.96**, but so slightly that the successful appellant itself would not have benefited from the change.

HMRC will accept input tax recovery based on a mere intention to opt only in 'exceptional circumstances'. They expect there to be 'unequivocal documentary evidence' of the intention, probably in more than one document, and are unlikely to be persuaded by purely internal evidence. They are also unlikely to accept an intention to opt where the supplies might be imminent, or if the option requires their permission.

In general, it is therefore more sensible to opt early, with effect from a future date if necessary, than to rely on a mere intention to do so. Once the owner does opt, it may be able to recover earlier VAT, as considered in para **15.96** et seq.

If the business is not registered for VAT, it cannot recover VAT it incurs on a current basis anyway, and HMRC will not be prepared to register it on the basis of just an intention to opt.

After opting – general points

[15.96] Once the owner has opted, it can normally assume that any future supplies will be taxable and that all future input tax will be recoverable (but bear in mind the subject matter of para **15.65** above). It may also be able to recover some past VAT at this point. This depends on whether permission was needed for the option, on any past use of the property and on whether the business was VAT registered when the VAT was incurred.

Past VAT might be recovered under:

- the terms of HMRC's specific permission for the option (para **15.91**);
- a partial exemption annual adjustment (para **15.282**);

- regulation 109 (para **15.286**), on the basis that there has been a change of intention from making exempt supplies to making taxable supplies;
- the CGS (para **15.288** et seq) where there has been previous exempt use of the property;
- if the owner was not VAT registered when the VAT was incurred, either the CGS or, if this does not apply, under reg 111, as noted in para **15.97**.

After opting – no prior use

[**15.97**] If the owner has not used the property at all, opting now should allow recovery of past VAT that has not been recovered already and now relates to intended taxable supplies.

The owner will generally need to make a formal claim for past VAT under reg 109 of the VAT Regulations (SI 1995/2518) (see para **15.286**). This is on the basis that the owner's intentions have changed from making exempt supplies to making taxable supplies. But:

- Any VAT incurred in a VAT return period commencing more than six years before the change of intention will be out of time. HMRC sometimes try, incorrectly, to apply shorter time limits.
- Input tax that does not really become attributable to the future taxable supplies should be excluded. VAT on fees related to an earlier, aborted, project or transaction might be an example. In the light of *Royal & Sun Alliance*, summarised in para **15.100**, HMRC may also expect VAT on rent and other ongoing costs to be excluded, at least if the property was available for occupation when the VAT was incurred. It should be possible to claim for such VAT if the property was being constructed or otherwise prepared for occupation at the time. HMRC's views were given in Business Brief 14/04.
- The *Royal & Sun Alliance* case also suggested that a reg 109 claim requires the owner to have previously intended to make at least some exempt supplies, so that no claim can be made if it had simply not decided whether or not to opt. HMRC indicated in Business Brief 14/04 that they would ignore this.
- There is a further issue if the owner was not VAT registered when the VAT was incurred. For capital expenditure of £250,000 or more, the VAT may be recoverable under the CGS (see para **15.288** et seq). In other cases, it is sometimes possible to claim the VAT under special provisions in reg 111, but this is subject to stricter time limits than reg 109 – four years before registration for goods, and only six months for services. Services here will include any lease of no more than 21 years (in Scotland, of less than 20 years), and any building work (including, generally, the materials element in this). Where the time limits are a problem, it may sometimes be possible to register from an earlier date, but not if this depends on an option to tax that had not been exercised at that time.

After opting – following prior lettings

[**15.98**] If there have been prior exempt lettings, much of the VAT that the owner incurred in the past is likely to relate to those, and to remain irrecoverable if it now exercises an option to tax. But there are several categories of past input tax which it might be able to recover:

- If the lettings have ceased, the owner may be able to make a SI 1995/2518, reg 109 claim, as explained in para **15.97**, for the period the property has been empty.
- VAT may have been incurred during the exempt lettings that actually relates to later use, such as fees connected with a reletting or planned refurbishment. This may be claimable in the same way under reg 109.
- If the owner incurred capital expenditure amounting to £250,000 or more during the exempt lettings, some of the VAT may become recoverable, once the option is exercised, under the CGS (see para **15.288** et seq).

But the position is complicated by the permission rules for the option. If the owner needs HMRC's specific permission to opt (para **15.91**), it will need to agree any recovery of past input tax with them in the process, whilst the automatic permission rules do not always allow for back claims.

If the VAT in question was incurred before the business was registered for VAT, any claim will also be subject to the same points as explained in para **15.97**.

After opting – following prior occupation

[15.99] If the business has occupied the property, it will have dealt with VAT relating to the period of occupation according to whether its supplies were taxable or exempt. If the business was fully taxable, it will have recovered input tax in full anyway. In other cases there may be scope for a back claim in the same way as if there had been prior lettings, but without the complication of the permission rules.

Case law

[15.100] Case law has been influential in shaping the points made in paras **15.93** to **15.99**, but the decisions have not been wholly consistent either with each other or with HMRC's policy.

- *Lawson Mardon Group Pension Scheme* (VTD 10231) concerned a claim for input tax in advance of the option being exercised. The Tribunal held that:

  'An intention to make taxable supplies at some future date if and when an election had been made is insufficient, in my opinion, particularly where, as in this case, no firm decision had been taken to exercise the option for taxation.'

- In *AA Insurance Services Ltd* (VTD 16117), a tenant incurred VAT on a payment to its landlord, for accepting the surrender of the lease. The tenant had opted, but this did not allow the VAT to be recovered because the Tribunal did not think the surrender itself had been a supply – the only payment had been by the tenant. The legislation has since been amended to ensure that the surrender of a lease for no consideration can be a supply, but a similar point arose in *British Eventing*, below.
- In *London & Exmoor Estates Ltd* (VTD 16707), the Tribunal rejected a claim for input tax recovery on the costs of an aborted acquisition by a prospective purchaser who had not opted.

- As noted in para 15.86, the Tribunal in *Classic Furniture (Newport) Ltd* (VTD 16977), accepted that, merely by claiming input tax to which it was not otherwise entitled, a company had opted to tax – the claim was therefore valid.
- *Beaverbank Properties Ltd* (VTD 18099) was another case about the costs of an aborted acquisition where the purchaser had not opted. But the Tribunal accepted that it would have opted, and that the input tax was attributable to intended taxable supplies and recoverable. As noted in para 15.95, HMRC modified their policy slightly in the light of this decision.
- In *Royal & Sun Alliance Insurance Group plc* ([2003] STC 832), a business had vacated a number of surplus properties and sought to dispose of them. It continued to incur VAT on rent and service charges. It had not decided whether to opt, and when it later did so it sought to recover this VAT retrospectively. After protracted litigation, the majority judgment in the House of Lords decided that the earlier VAT had effectively been used up while the properties were vacant. It did not relate to the later taxable supplies under the option, and so remained irrecoverable.

  HMRC commented in Business Brief 14/04, but have ignored two further points in the judgment:

  (i)   the conclusion that a regulation 109 claim cannot be made unless the business previously had an actual intention to make exempt supplies;

  (ii) a hint that the appellant had been entitled to residual input tax recovery when the VAT was incurred.

  There is more about the reg 109 aspects of this case in para 15.286. Following this case, the Tribunal in *Capital One Developments Ltd* (VTD 18642) specifically agreed the point at (ii) – that input tax on property expenditure was residual if the business did not know whether it was going to make taxable or exempt supplies. More significantly, the CJEU judgment in *Fini* (see para 15.281) suggests that the House of Lords was incorrect in its main conclusion.
- In *British Eventing Ltd* (TC00664), the company held an onerous lease, under which it was obliged to carry out substantial works. Had it commissioned these itself, the VAT would only have been partly recoverable. So it sought to opt to tax, to assign the lease to a subsidiary for £10 plus VAT, and against this to recover VAT on a payment of £340,000 to the subsidiary. The subsidiary would then undertake the works. HMRC refused it permission to opt (see para 15.91), but the Tribunal concluded in any case that the assignment was not a supply (see para 15.179), and that the VAT could not be attributed to it. The VAT on the £340,000 was therefore only partly recoverable, in the same way as if it had been incurred on the works.

Exempt letting or disposal

[15.101] In some of the scenarios in paras **15.93** to **15.99**, the business might still make exempt supplies in the property, if the option is disapplied under the rules in paras **15.73** to **15.80** or **15.113** et seq. In this case, the business may need to repay past input tax to HMRC. This might be under:

- a partial exemption annual adjustment (para **15.282**);
- regulation 108 (para **15.286**), on the basis that there has been a change of intention from making taxable supplies to making exempt supplies;

- the CGS (para **15.288** et seq) where there has been previous taxable use of the property.

If the owner has recovered input tax under the option, but has not in fact made taxable supplies under it, an exempt supply will potentially trigger a repayment to HMRC under reg 108. This largely mirrors the position for a claim under reg 109, as described in para **15.97** – the repayment can exclude input tax more than six years old, or that will not relate to the exempt supplies, such as VAT connected with an aborted taxable letting or incurred on ongoing costs such as rent.

If the owner will now make both taxable and exempt supplies in the property, a partial repayment may be required, calculated as an adjustment to the partial exemption position for the period when the VAT was first incurred.

The same should apply if the owner recovered VAT on the strength of an intention to opt, but in this case HMRC might see the original claim as invalid and potentially subject to interest and penalties.

Option to tax: duration and revocation

[15.102] The option continues to apply until it is revoked or it lapses. This can only happen in defined circumstances.

It can happen automatically in some cases where the person:

- fails to notify the option to HMRC (see para **15.81** et seq);
- has had no interest etc in the property for six years (see para **15.103**);
- currently has no interest in the property and exercises a Real Estate Election or 'REE' (see para **15.88**); or
- ceases to be a 'relevant associate' of the person that opted (see para **15.67**).

The person can also choose to revoke an option in some cases:

- where a new building is constructed (see para **15.71**);
- where an existing building is demolished (see para **15.71**);
- within six months after the effective date (see para **15.104**); or
- more than 20 years after the effective date (see para **15.105**).

Option lapsing after six years

[15.103] Under VATA 1994, Sch 10, para 24, an option will lapse automatically in certain cases. Subject to some further provisions where the person is or has been a member of a VAT group, this will apply if the following conditions are met:

- The person opted at least six years ago.
- The person has not held a 'relevant interest' in the property, or in any part of it, for six years. A relevant interest means an interest in, right over or licence to occupy the property, as explained in paras **15.16** and **15.18**.

- The person will make no further supplies in relation to any disposal of such an interest. This condition is intended to deal with cases where, for example, overage payments might arise from an earlier sale of the property.

The option will cease to apply on the day that the conditions are met. If for some reason the person still wants an option to have effect, they can exercise a new one if they wish.

Revocation within six months

[**15.104**] VATA 1994, Sch 10, para 23 allows an option to be revoked in the first six months, subject to specific conditions. Where these are met, this 'cooling off' facility gives a person who has opted a chance to reconsider. This may be useful where it transpires that a prospective tenant or purchaser cannot recover VAT in full. It also allows someone who has exercised a real estate election or 'REE' (para **15.88**) the chance to remove a particular property from the effects of it.

This facility is potentially available where all the following conditions are met:

- Less than six months have elapsed since the effective date of the option.
- No output tax has become chargeable as a result of the option.
- There has been no VAT-free TOGC of the property (see para **15.121** et seq) to or by the person since the effective date of the option.

In this case, the person can seek HMRC's permission to revoke the option, submitting Form VAT 1614C to them within the six-month period. Or, if any one of three further conditions is met, they do not need permission, and can simply notify HMRC of their revocation, again using Form VAT 1614C. These three further conditions (which have the force of law) are given in Notice 742A, but can be summarised as follows:

- Neither the person, nor a relevant associate (para **15.67**), has recovered any VAT purely by virtue of the option.
- Any such input tax will have to be repaid through a partial exemption annual adjustment (para **15.282**) or under reg 108 (para **15.286**).
- Any such input tax has been recovered entirely on one asset subject to the CGS (para **15.288**) and accounts for less than 20% of all the input tax incurred on it.

Revocation is backdated to when the option first took effect, so the result is much the same as if the option had never been exercised.

Revocation after 20 years

[**15.105**] VATA 1994, Sch 10, para 25 provides for revocation of the option after 20 years. The person needs to notify HMRC on Form VAT 1614J, and in some cases needs their permission to revoke. Notice 742A sets out conditions for revocation (see 1 to 5 below). Of these:

- Revocation is available without HMRC's permission if either 1 is met or all of 2 to 5 are met.
- Revocation is not available at all if neither 1 nor 2 is met.

- Otherwise, revocation may be available with HMRC's permission if 2 is met, but the taxpayer needs to explain in seeking permission which of 3 to 5 are not met, and why not.

The conditions are merely summarised here, and readers should refer to Notice 742A for the full text and explanatory notes.

(1) The person has no 'relevant interest' (ie an interest in, right over or licence to occupy the property – see paras **15.16** and **15.18**) in the property, and if they have disposed of such an interest no further supply will or might arise from the disposal (such as an overage payment).

(2) The person held a relevant interest in the property after the option took effect, and more than 20 years ago.

(3) The person is not liable to make CGS (para **15.288**) adjustments in relation to the property or, if they are, the maximum amount that could be repaid to HMRC is £10,000.

(4) The person has not in the last ten years made a supply of a relevant interest in the property that was for less than market value, or that they intend or expect will give rise to a later supply for significantly greater consideration, other than as a result of a normal rent review (overage and 'balloon' payments might be examples).

(5) The person has not received a supply that will to any extent be attributable to any use of the property more than 12 months after revocation. (HMRC have indicated that this refers to pre-payments spanning revocation, and not to general capital expenditure.)

References to the person also include any 'relevant associate' (para **15.67**) connected with them.

Form VAT 1614J should be used to notify HMRC of revocation, or as the case may be to seek their permission. If the person gives incorrect information, their revocation will be invalid unless HMRC decide otherwise.

HMRC have been particularly concerned about the interaction between revocation and the CGS. If revocation would result in CGS repayments of more than £10,000, HMRC are unlikely to agree to it if the person is retaining the property, since in this case the repayments would generally be spread over a period of years (see para **15.293**). But they do not have the same objections where the property is being disposed of, since this accelerates the repayments (para **15.294**). Owners wanting to revoke on a disposal can seek HMRC's advance agreement, conditional on the disposal actually occurring.

Revocation after 20 years: VAT groups

[15.106] The rules in para **15.105** do not allow someone to revoke an option by which they are caught as a 'relevant associate' (see para **15.67**). But broadly similar rules allow them to cease to be treated as a relevant associate, so that the option no longer applies to them.

Option to tax: pros and cons of opting

[15.107] The option allows input tax to be recovered or retained, including through the CGS (para **15.288**) or where there is a 'self-supply' of a previously

RRP/RCP building (para **15.169** et seq). This can be a significant benefit to the owner. But since it must generally last at least 20 years, and impacts on all transactions in the meantime, opting is not a decision to be taken lightly.

If there are existing lettings in place, it may be important to check the terms of leases – some do not allow the landlord to opt, or provide that the rent is VAT-inclusive if he does. Beyond this, there are four main potential disadvantages to opting and these are explained below.

Occupiers

[15.108] Occupiers with exempt or non-business activities will be unable to recover the VAT in full. An option may therefore reduce rents and disposal values, particularly in areas – notably financial districts – with a high concentration of VAT-averse businesses.

Unless ownership is split, the rule that the option applies to whole buildings can exacerbate this problem – the owner cannot opt on one floor of the building without opting on all of it.

VAT-averse sectors

The following sectors etc cannot generally recover VAT in full. Most will have very low levels of recovery, although parts of the financial sector can recover 60% or more of their VAT.

- Insurance
- Finance
- Education (but not local authority schools or academies)
- Central government and government agencies
- Health and welfare (including the NHS)
- Trade Unions and some professional bodies
- Betting, gaming and lotteries
- Burial and cremation
- The Post Office
- Landlords with residential or other exempt lettings
- Charities (certain charities can recover VAT incurred on costs relating to their non-business activities)
- Non-profit making cultural bodies
- Small businesses that are not registered for VAT, or that use a flat rate accounting scheme

Cashflow

[15.109] Even if the VAT charged is recoverable, it can create a substantial cashflow cost, particularly on a sale – it may be several months before the purchaser can recover the VAT. Vendors often need to accommodate this, and sales sometimes fall through because of it.

Administration

[15.110] Opting creates additional accounting and invoicing requirements, and the actual process of opting can be a burden where HMRC's specific permission is required (para **15.91**). Overseas investors may be concerned that opting and registering requires more of a presence and visibility in the UK.

Stamp duty land tax

[15.111] Stamp duty land tax (SDLT) can provide the greatest single objection to opting. It is levied on the VAT-inclusive price or rent, even if the VAT is recoverable. If the standard rate of VAT is 20%, a 4% SDLT liability therefore becomes 4.8%. If purchasers or tenants take account of this in what they are willing to pay, this may outweigh the benefits of opting. There is therefore often a desire on the part of the buyer to seek to argue that its purchase comprises a TOGC to prevent a charge to VAT from arising. However, in practice some buyers prefer the certainty afforded by an increased charge to SDLT as opposed to a contingent liability to pay VAT in the future in the event that the transaction in question turns out not to have comprised a TOGC in the first place.

Managing the conflict

[15.112] Owners have found various ways of managing some of these issues, for example by:

- incurring costs in a separate entity so that VAT can still be recovered pending a decision to opt;
- separating interests in a property so as to opt on just part of a building, or for a limited period;
- sidestepping the permission rules by transferring the property to another entity;
- timing transactions, tax points or VAT return dates in order to mitigate cashflow problems;
- ensuring that an option to tax is disapplied under the anti-avoidance rules in para **15.113** et seq.

Some of these arrangements may, however, need to be disclosed to HMRC under the rules in para **15.302**, and contrived transactions may be particularly open to challenge.

Option to tax: anti-avoidance rules

[15.113] The (extremely complex) anti-avoidance rules are in VATA 1994, Sch 10, paras 12–17. Very broadly, they apply where:

- the property is within the CGS (para **15.288** et seq) or expected to come within it; and
- it is envisaged that the property will be occupied by the vendor/landlord, by someone financing them (referred to as a 'development financier'), or by someone connected with either of these; and
- it is envisaged that that occupation will be in activities that are less than 80% taxable.

The rules seek to counter VAT planning which, typically, converted VAT on a capital cost into VAT on rent, but they apply whether or not VAT planning is involved.

The effect of the rules is that an option to tax has no effect, so that sales and lettings remain exempt.

When to consider the rules

[15.114] The rules should be looked at at the time of the 'grant' – essentially on a sale, or when a new lease, licence etc is granted.

For leases etc, the position does not generally need to be revisited – the rules will continue to apply, or not, throughout the term of the lease, even if the tenant, or the tenant's use of the property, changes. There are two exceptions to this. A new grant is treated as occurring, so that the rules need to be looked at afresh, if:

- having made exempt supplies under the lease etc, the landlord then opts to tax; or
- the identity of the landlord changes, because the previous landlord has disposed of the property, or granted an overriding lease, subject to the existing letting.

The rules do not, in any case, apply to 'grants' made before 26 November 1996, or to grants in pursuance of a written agreement entered into before that date and actually made before 30 November 1999.

Conditions

[15.115] The rules apply if three tests are met at the time of the 'grant'. The three tests outlined below must be considered.

Test One – Capital Goods Scheme

[15.116] his test is contained in VATA 1994, Sch 10, para 13. It considers the position under the CGS.

This test is met if, at the time of the grant, any of the following applies:

- The property is within the CGS in the hands of the grantor.
- The grantor, or a 'development financier' (see para **15.119**), intends or expects that the property will be within the CGS in the hands of:
  (i) the grantor, or
  (ii) anyone to whom the property is to be transferred.
- In some cases, the 'grant' arises as a result of a new landlord making supplies under an existing lease etc, and the property is only not in the CGS in his hands because the CGS adjustment period has expired. This point is in Sch 10, para 13(7) and is slightly obscure. The wording of the legislation suggests that it only applies where the property would still have been in the CGS in the hands of the previous landlord, but HMRC ignore this apparent limitation in Notice 742A.

The CGS is explained in para **15.288** et seq, but broadly a property is in the CGS where the person in question has incurred VAT on expenditure of £250,000 or more in acquiring the property, or in carrying out works to it, in the last nine to ten years. The 'intended or expected' rule might apply if, for example, a refurbishment is planned (there is seemingly no temporal restriction). It will also apply if the transaction at issue is a sale for £250,000 or more – that fact in itself means that the test is met, since the property will come into the CGS in the hands of the purchaser.

The CGS does not, however, apply where the expenditure is incurred purely with a view to sale. This point proved decisive in *Shurgard* (para **15.120**).

Test Two – identity of occupier

[15.117] This test is met if, at the time of the grant, the grantor, or a development financier, intends or expects that the property will be occupied by either of them, or by someone connected with either of them.

In this context:

- A development financier has a wide meaning, and includes a tenant making an advance payment, or a loan during the course of building work. This is looked at in para **15.119**.
- The intention or expectation need not be immediate – the test will, for example, apply if a landlord expects, when granting the lease, to occupy the property at some future date before the CGS adjustment period has expired.
- Occupation need not be of the whole property – for example the test applies to the sale of a property where the vendor's subsidiary occupies one floor. But this is looked at in terms of the area subject to the grant, so a lease on a different floor would not be caught in this way.
- Occupation of a building by a development financier (or someone connected with a development financier) is, however, ignored where it accounts for no more than 10% of the lettable space – of the building as a whole, or of the part in which the grantor has an interest. This exception is in Sch 10 para 15A. It was intended to help deal with problems in multiple occupancy buildings, where the presence of a bank branch could effectively preclude a developer or investor borrowing from that banking group. HMRC's Notice 742A prescribes the method of measurement, where actual measurement is necessary.
- Similarly, occupation by the grantor itself, or by someone connected with it, is ignored if it accounts for no more than 2% of the lettable space. This is also under VATA 1994, Sch 10 para 15A, and was introduced on 1 March 2011.
- The meaning of 'occupation' was at issue in *Newnham College*, summarised in para **15.120**. Following their defeat in this case, HMRC offer the following view in Notice 742A:

  'A person is in occupation of a building or land if they have:
  - a physical presence, and
  - the right to occupy the property as if they are the owner.

  This means they will have actual possession and control of the land, together with the ability to exclude others from the enjoyment of such rights.

  Normally a legal interest in or licence to occupy the land, will have been granted to them. However, occupation could also be by agreement or de facto and it is therefore necessary to take into account the day to day arrangements, particularly where these differ from the contractual terms. An exclusive right of occupation is not a requirement; an agreement might, for example, allow for joint occupation. It is also not necessary for a person to be utilising all of the land for all of the time for them to be considered as occupying it.'

• 'Connection' is considered in the terms of the Corporation Tax Act 2010, s 1122, and includes companies under common control. But for these purposes, and for the option to tax generally, any connection is ignored where it arises only as a result of Government shareholdings. This is intended to deal with potential problems created by Government intervention in the banking sector. A further issue was raised by a direct tax judgment, *Kellogg Brown & Root Holdings (UK) Ltd* ([2010] EWCA Civ 118, [2010] STC 925), which indicated that listed companies might be connected because they happen to have a number of shareholders in common. HMRC do not, however, expect companies to check this point for the purposes of the option to tax, unless perhaps there is a specific reason to do so.

Test Three – use by the occupier

[15.118] This test considers the occupiers identified by Test Two, and their use of the property. The test is met if, at the time of the grant, the grantor, or a development financier, intends or expects that any of those occupiers will not use the property at least 80% for 'eligible purposes'.

Occupation for 'eligible purposes' means occupation:

• by a taxable person (ie someone who is or should be VAT registered) in making taxable supplies, or other business supplies in relation to which they are entitled to recover input tax; or
• by someone who is not a taxable person, but whose supplies are treated as such supplies made by someone else who is a taxable person; or
• by a Government department, agency, NHS Trust etc covered by VATA 1994, s 41; or
• by a local authority or similar body covered by s 33, in the course of non-business activities; or
• by a taxable person solely on account of an ATM.

The position needs to be considered for the whole period when the property will be within the CGS. The option might be disapplied on account of an occupier whose activities are currently 90% taxable, but who is planning to increase its level of exempt activities – but only if the grantor or financier is aware of this initially.

The 80% figure does not appear in the legislation itself, which refers instead to occupation being 'wholly, or substantially wholly' for eligible purposes. 'Substantially wholly' is then defined as at least 80% in text in Notice 742A having the force of law.

'Development financier'

[15.119] The tests in paras **15.116** to **15.118** refer to a 'development financier'. This is defined in VATA 1994, Sch 10, para 14, and means someone who finances the expenditure that puts the property – or is intended or expected to put the property – into the CGS in the grantor's hands. It therefore includes someone financing not only development, but also for example acquisition or refurbishment. This can be by:

- Providing finance for the expenditure by, directly or indirectly:
  - providing funds for meeting the whole or any part of the cost – including by making a loan, providing a guarantee or security for a loan, providing any of the consideration for the issue or acquisition of shares or securities issued wholly or partly to raise the funds or making any other transfer of assets or value which makes the funds available;
  - procuring the provision of such funds by anyone else;
  - providing funds for discharging any or all of the liability that has been or may be incurred by any person for or in connection with the raising of funds to meet the cost; or
  - procuring that any such liability is or will be discharged, in whole or in part, by anyone else.
- Entering into an agreement, arrangement or understanding – whether or not legally enforceable – to do any of the above. This would seem to apply whether or not the finance is actually taken up.

The term is therefore very broad indeed and to a large extent its actual meaning untested. For example, it seems strictly to include a tenant making normal payments of rent, if the landlord uses these to repay borrowing taken out to acquire or develop the property. Because of this, HMRC's views are often more important in practice than the letter of the law. Their approach is narrower than the law, but not overtly concessionary:

- HMRC do not see normal payments of rent or service charges as 'financing'. This was covered in a Commons answer in March 1997, when the rules were being introduced:

  > 'the measure has been drafted so as not to disturb ordinary arms-length commercial leasing arrangements and genuine speculative property development. In these circumstances a tenant simply paying rent is not providing the finance for the landlord's initial purchase or construction of the building.'

- They regard financing the acquisition or development of the property as *directly* financing it. If the developer etc already has the funds, or has secured full funding from elsewhere, HMRC do not appear to see payments by a future tenant as the provision of finance, even if this allows the developer to release funds previously earmarked for the development, or to repay borrowing taken out for the development.
- They treat 'financing' as a one-off event, rather than as ongoing. So they will look at the position only at the point when the person is first committed to providing the finance, and will only see the option as disapplied if it is expected *at the time* that the other conditions for this will be met. They will only revisit the matter if further funding is agreed later on.

The material below says more about HMRC's policy.

HMRC's approach to 'financing' and the anti-avoidance rules

HMRC's internal VAT manual 'Land and property' (VATLP24000) gives the following summary on what does and does not constitute 'financing' (or 'funding'). References to capital items are to the CGS position.

Funding	*Not Funding*
Tenant's contribution to landlord's fitting out costs ie funding something which becomes the landlord's capital item.	Rents and service charges.
Agreement to pay premium entered into before construction completed and paid for, which is then used to finance that construction.	Agreement to pay premium entered into after construction has been completed and paid for.
Transfers of land by tenants to landlords at less than open market value or at nil consideration.	Transfer of land by tenant to landlord at open market value.
	Tenant paying the landlord or third party contractor direct in relation to the tenant's own capital item.
	Bank providing normal commercial finance for development and later quite separately takes a lease of part of the development.
	Incidental or trivial payments.
	Tenant signing up to an agreement to lease and the prospective rental income is used to secure third party funding.

'Development financiers' – examples

In these examples, D is a developer and T is a tenant whose use of the property will be less than 80% taxable. The development cost exceeds £250,000, so that the property is subject to the CGS in D's hands. The examples are intended to illustrate HMRC's approach, rather than necessarily the letter of the law.

- D and T enter into an agreement for lease, under which T will pay a premium for the future lease. HMRC are likely to see T as a development financier – so that D's option is disapplied – if D could not proceed with the development without the premium, or the promise of it, even if D merely uses the prospective premium as security for a loan. But they do not appear to take this view if D has already secured full funding, even if it uses the premium to refinance the development.
- D is responsible for fitting out the building, but does so at T's expense. If T pays a capital sum towards the work, HMRC will see T as a development financier, so that D's option is disapplied. Strictly this applies however small T's payment, but HMRC are likely to ignore incidental payments such as a reimbursement of D's additional professional fees. If T pays by way of additional rent, HMRC will not see this as finance if the payments only start

once T can actually take the lease and go into occupation, but they might do so in other cases. HMRC are likely to take a similar view where the tenant asks for changes to the specification of the building.

- T is responsible for fitting out the building, but asks D to do it. This requires care. HMRC should not see T as a development financier if the arrangements and payments for the work are clearly separate from those for the letting, but in practice it is safer for T to engage the contractor direct, or perhaps an associate company of D's.

- T sells the development site to D, for D to carry out the development and grant a lease back to T. If the sale price is below market value HMRC will see T as a development financier, so that D's option is disapplied. The same applies if T transfers other land to D as a 'gift' or at below a market price.

- T provides plant or labour to D for D to carry out the development. If T does not charge for this, or charges less than a market price, HMRC will see the arrangement as disapplying D's option, unless perhaps it is clearly trivial or incidental.

- T is a member of the same corporate group as the bank financing D's development. This potentially disapplies D's option, even if the arrangements are entirely coincidental. HMRC do not, however, take this view if the bank agrees to provide the finance before there is any intention or expectation that T will take space in the development, unless it subsequently agrees to provide further finance.

Case law

[15.120] The case law in this area has demonstrated a number of points, not least the breadth of HMRC's interpretation.

- In *Winterthur Life UK Ltd* (VTD 15785), the occupiers of a property chose to acquire it through their pension scheme. The Tribunal found that their contributions to the scheme amounted to the provision of finance, so that the trustee's option was disapplied.
  Following this case, HMRC consider that pension fund contributions constitute 'financing' if the pension fund member makes the contribution with the intention or expectation that the money will be spent on a building for the occupation of the fund, the contributing member etc, or subsequently has to approve the expenditure for this.

- In *Brambletye School Trust Ltd* (VTD 17688), a school leased a sports hall to a subsidiary, which ran a sports club. Pupils were members of the club, and – at least supposedly – used the hall in that capacity rather than as pupils. The Tribunal held that, even were this so, the school was occupying the hall since the pupils were supervised by school staff. The option was therefore disapplied on the lease.

- *Newnham College* was a similar case, where the college leased a library building to a subsidiary, which ran the library for use by the college's students and fellows. The library was staffed by college employees, but they were seconded to the subsidiary. The Court of Appeal ([2006] EWCA Civ 285) considered 'occupation' to involve possession or control (compare the quote from *Sinclair Collis* at para 15.18) and decided that the presence of students, fellows and seconded staff was not enough to mean that the college was occupying the building. The college's option to tax was not disapplied.

The House of Lords ([2008] All ER (D) 210 (Apr)) dismissed HMRC's appeal against this by a 3–2 majority. The Lords accepted the Court of Appeal's approach to 'occupation', but differed on whether the College actually was in possession or control. Amongst the majority, Lord Mance saw 'an important distinction between occupation of land and merely using it'. HMRC's views following this case are noted in para **15.117**.

- *Shurgard Storage Centres UK Ltd* (VTD 20797) concerned an attempt to exploit the anti-avoidance rules, so as to remove the effects of an unwanted option to tax. The purchaser of a property, S, intended to occupy it in exempt activities, but the vendor, W, had opted. Prior to the sale, W carried out works, to a value of £300,000, financed by S. The idea was that the property would then be subject to the CGS, with S as a 'development financier'. The Tribunal agreed with HMRC that the work did not bring the property into the CGS, since it had been undertaken purely with a view to sale. W's option was not disapplied, and the sale was taxable.

Transfer of a Going Concern (TOGC)

[15.121] The disposal of a business as a going concern is potentially a non-supply. This also applies to the transfer of a separately operable part of a business. This can be relevant to occupiers – such as a retailer selling a shop – and to investors and others disposing of a property held for letting. Paragraphs **15.122** to **15.130** look at the conditions for this, and para **15.131** at the consequences.

VAT-free treatment as a TOGC is mandatory where it applies. If VAT is charged in error, the purchaser has no legal right to recover it from HMRC, and should look to the vendor to reimburse it as there has been a breach of contract. HMRC's attitude with regards to refunding the VAT will, however, largely depend on whether or not the vendor has accounted to them for the VAT.

TOGC treatment will generally assist VAT cashflow, and prevents SDLT being chargeable on the VAT amount in so far as it relates to property (see above). But it also applies where the transaction would otherwise be exempt or zero-rated.

This can be a difficult area. Vendors need to rely on the purchaser's intentions, and sale agreements need to deal with these adequately and with a number of other points. HMRC's approach is known to be inconsistent across the UK. Consequently, care is therefore needed, particularly when acting on the sale side.

TOGC: general conditions

The Directive

[15.122] Article 19 of the Directive says that:

'In the event of a transfer, whether for consideration or not or as a contribution to a company, of a totality of assets or part thereof, Member States may consider that no supply of goods has taken place and that the person to whom the goods are transferred is to be treated as the successor to the transferor.

Member States may, in cases where the recipient is not wholly liable to tax, take the measures necessary to prevent distortion of competition. They may also adopt any measures needed to prevent tax evasion or avoidance through the use of this Article.'

Article 29 of the Directive gives effect to Article 19 in relation to services.

UK law

[15.123] The UK rules are in Article 5 of the VAT (Special Provisions) Order 1995. Article 5(1) says that, subject to further rules about the option to tax:

'there shall be treated as neither a supply of goods nor a supply of services the following supplies by a person of assets of his business –

(a) their supply to a person to whom he transfers his business as a going concern where –
  (i) the assets are to be used by the transferee in carrying on the same kind of business, whether or not as part of any existing business, as that carried on by the transferor, and
  (ii) in a case where the transferor is a taxable person, the transferee is already, or immediately becomes as a result of the transfer, a taxable person or a person defined as such in section 3(1) of the Manx [VAT] Act;
(b) their supply to a person to whom he transfers part of his business as a going concern where –
  (i) that part is capable of separate operation,
  (ii) the assets are to be used by the transferee in carrying on the same kind of business, whether or not as part of any existing business, as that carried on by the transferor in relation to that part, and
  (iii) in a case where the transferor is a taxable person, the transferee is already, or immediately becomes as a result of the transfer, a taxable person or a person defined as such in section 3(1) of the Manx [VAT] Act.'

The following need to be considered when determining whether the transfer of assets must be treated as a TOGC.

Business assets transferred as part of a going concern

[15.124] There are various points here:

- The TOGC rules do not apply to non-business assets, eg of a sole proprietor or charity. In *Peddars Way Housing Association* (VTD 12663), a local authority's disposal of its housing stock was not a TOGC, in part because its lettings of the properties had been non-business.
- The business probably needs to be trading, or only closed temporarily, although it does not need to be profitable and might be in receivership. In their Notice 700/9, HMRC say that:

  'There must be no significant break in the normal trading pattern before or immediately after the transfer. The "break in trade" needs to be considered in the context of the type of business concerned, this might vary between different types of trade or activity. For example, HMRC do not consider that where a "seasonal" business has closed for the "off-season" as normal at the time of sale, that there has necessarily been a break in trade. In addition, a short period of closure that does not significantly disrupt the existing trading pattern, for example, for redecoration, will not prevent the business from being transferred as a TOGC.'

- HMRC consider that there must be an outright transfer of the assets, and previously considered that the grant of a lease cannot be a TOGC. However, their position has changed as a result of the judgment of the First-tier Tribunal in *Robinson Family Limited* (TC02046). There is more on this below (para **15.125**).
- HMRC consider that the asset must continue to exist after the transfer, and they had historically considered that the surrender of a lease which then merges with the freehold cannot be a TOGC, notwithstanding that the benefit of rental income continued (ie from an underlease which survived beyond the transfer). This has now changed following the issue of Revenue & Customs Brief 27/14 and such a surrender can amount to a TOGC.
- There may be a question over TOGC treatment if the vendor has not yet made any supplies. HMRC's Notice 700/9 says, vaguely, that:

  'If you are registered for VAT but you have not yet made taxable supplies, the transfer of your business might not be the transfer of a "going concern". However, where sufficient preparatory work has been undertaken prior to making taxable supplies there may be a business capable of being transferred as a going concern.'

  This issue has been considered in the cases noted below.

Paragraph **15.130** says more about the transfer of a property letting business.

Case law – TOGC treatment before trading commences

- A sale of growing woodlands was a TOGC in *Hordern* (VTD 8941).
- A sale of development land to another developer was seen as a TOGC in *The Golden Oak Partnership* (VTD 7212). The vendor had undertaken preliminary work including the construction of driveways and provision for electricity, gas and sewerage.
- But in *Gulf Trading and Management Ltd* (VTD 16847), a sale of development land was not a TOGC. In this case the vendor had not started work, and had merely erected fencing and engaged surveyors and architects.
- In *Dartford Borough Council* (VTD 20423), the Council sold land to an investor, with the benefit of an agreement for lease. It had spent over £7m on preparatory work, including to roads, power lines and a watercourse. The Tribunal rejected HMRC's contention that the sale was not a TOGC.
- In *Royal College of Paedeatrics and Child Health* ([2015] UKUT 0038 (TCC)) a conditional agreement for lease was put in place and relied upon to ensure that the sale of the underlying property subject to such agreement comprised a TOGC. HMRC have accepted for some time that an agreement for lease can mean that the sale of the superior interest will comprise a TOGC. However, in this case it was the conditional nature of the agreement for lease and that the buyer was heavily involved in sourcing the 'tenant'. Although the First-tier Tribunal (TC02617) considered the sale comprised a

TOGC, the Upper Tribunal took a different view, and was heavily influenced by the fact that it was the buyer who sourced the 'tenant' which led it to conclude that the 'tenant' was not part of the seller's business at all – the effect being that the seller did not have a business capable of transfer. It is unfortunate that the Upper Tribunal did not embark on a more thorough analysis of the various legal issues given the relative importance of the case.

Same kind of business

[15.125] The rules require that the assets are 'to be used by the transferee in carrying on the same kind of business . . . as that carried on by the transferor'.

This is about the transferee's intentions at the time of the transfer – it is not about what actually happens (although this might be the best evidence of the intentions), nor about what the transferee could have done.

The transferee does not need to intend to carry on the same kind of business for very long. How long probably depends on the intensity and nature of the activity – a week or two might suffice for a retail business; longer for a property letting business (on this, see para **15.130**).

An intention immediately to sell the business, or to close it down, will prevent TOGC treatment. But temporary closure might not – as noted in para **15.124**, HMRC say that 'a short period of closure that does not significantly disrupt the existing trading pattern, for example, for redecoration' is not a problem.

TOGC treatment generally requires both parties to make supplies to third parties. Outsourcing, or vertical integration, might well not be a TOGC. And HMRC do not see the sale of a property to a sitting tenant as a TOGC unless there are other lettings which the tenant will take over and continue.

HMRC see a VAT group as a single entity for these purposes, so that, for example, the letting of a property to another member of a VAT group cannot be a business capable of TOGC treatment.

Various points are illustrated by the case law summarised below.

There are further issues with property transactions where the purchaser is a nominee. These are looked at in para **15.130**.

Case law – same kind of business?

- *Dearwood* ([1986] STC 327, QB) concerned the sale of premises and stock by a company selling reproduction furniture to one selling fitted kitchens and bedrooms. The High Court concluded that this was a TOGC because the purchaser could have carried on the vendor's business. It now appears that this was the wrong test, and that the Court should have looked at what the purchaser intended to do, not what it could have done – this approach was taken by the Tribunal in *Hartley Engineering Ltd* (VTD 12385) and subsequent cases, and has since found support from the CJEU in *Zita Modes*, below.
- In *ICB Ltd* (VTD 1796), the purchase of two quarries was not a TOGC, since the motive was not to carry on a quarrying business but to acquire a convenient source of raw materials for use in an existing business.

- In *Jones* (VTD 6141) the Tribunal found that the sale of nightclub premises which the purchaser was converting to a restaurant was a TOGC because the nightclub remained open for a few days after the sale.
- *Morland & Co plc* (VTD 8869) concerned the sale of 98 tenanted public houses. But the vendor was an investor which had been letting the properties to another brewer, whereas the purchaser was itself a brewer. They were seen as carrying on different kinds of business, so that the sale was not a TOGC.
- *Jeyes Ltd* (VTD 10513) concerned the outsourcing of a manufacturer's bottling plant. The manufacturer continued as the plant's main customer after the sale. The case was actually about the imposition of a penalty, but in finding against HMRC the Tribunal observed that the transaction had probably been a TOGC.
- In *Hallborough Properties Ltd* (VTD 10849), the sale of properties by a developer to an investor was a TOGC. The Tribunal, noting that letting was part of the developer's normal activities, did not see them as engaged in different kinds of business.
- *Kwik Save Group plc* (VTD 12749) concerned the sale of some retail stores by A to B and their immediate onward transfer to B's separately VAT-registered subsidiary C. The transfer from B to C was held not to be a TOGC because B had not carried on the business; this clearly meant that the sale by A to B was not a TOGC either, although this was not at issue in the case. The Tribunal also saw no significance in whether B had actually taken title, or had entered into agreements to purchase and sell and then directed A to sell direct to C.
- An Indian restaurant and an Italian restaurant were found to be the same type of business in *Tahmassebi (t/a Sale Pepe)* (VTD 13177).
- In *International Supplier Auditing Ltd* (VTD 18111), a company had already sold its business and ceased to trade when it sold some remaining assets – cars, office equipment, a trading name etc – to another company. The Tribunal rejected HMRC's argument that this had been a TOGC.
- Similarly in *Buckley (Jewellery) Ltd* (VTD 18178), an insolvent company had already ceased to trade when it sold moulds, brand names and intellectual property. HMRC said that this was a TOGC. The Tribunal disagreed.
- *FMCG Home Services Ltd* (VTD 18377) was another case about outsourcing, in this case of an insurer's activity of collecting premiums. The Tribunal saw the parties as carrying on a different kind of business, so that the transfer of the activity was not a TOGC. (It is understood that HMRC did not resist FMCG's appeal, but nevertheless consider the case to have been correctly decided.)
- *Zita Modes Sarl* (CJEU Case C-497/01) concerned the sale of a Luxembourg clothing business to a perfumery business. The CJEU held that, where a member state had introduced non-supply treatment for TOGCs, this must apply:

  'to any transfer of a business or independent part of an undertaking . . . The transferee must however intend to operate the business or the part of the undertaking transferred and not simply immediately to liquidate the activity concerned and sell the stock, if any.'

  Member states that used non-supply treatment could not restrict it other than as provided for by the Directive, but the significance of this point has been greatly reduced by the subsequent addition of what is now the last sentence of Article 19 (see para **15.122**).
- The hire of plant with and without a driver was seen as the same kind of business in *HCL Equipment Ltd* (VTD 19222).

- *Winterthur Swiss Insurance Company* (VTD 19411) concerned the disposal of parts of an insurance business. The appellant accepted that the parties were not carrying on the same kind of business, but contended that this was not a valid test in the light of *Zita Modes*, above. The Tribunal rejected this, suggesting that it seemed inherent in *Zita Modes* that the parties did carry on the same kind of business.

- In *Morton Hotels Ltd* (VTD 20039), the purchaser of some hotels financed the acquisition by means of an immediate sale and leaseback with a third party, but then continued to operate them in the same way as the vendor. The Tribunal did not see this as preventing TOGC treatment – the legislation required that the assets were to be used in carrying on the same kind of business, not that they were to be used in the same way or that the interest in them be retained in the same form. The Tribunal was not called upon to consider the treatment of the sale and leaseback itself, and the decision carries no suggestion that this was a TOGC.

- In *Robinson Family Limited* (TC02046) a tenant sought to dispose of its interest in land as a property letting business. As the lease in question was granted by the Belfast Harbour Commissioners it was only possible for the current tenant to grant a sub-lease to a third party. It did this, ostensibly with the benefit of on-going negotiations in relation to heads of agreement in relation to an interested tenant. Although, disappointingly, the issue as to whether a lettings business existed in the first place via the heads of agreement was not considered in detail, it was held by the First-tier Tribunal that in substance the grant of the sub-lease amounted to the transfer of a business. HMRC did not appeal this judgment and issued Revenue & Customs Briefs 30/12 and 27/14 (see para 15.130).

VAT registration

[**15.126**] If the vendor is a taxable person – ie VAT registered or required to be registered – the purchaser must already be a taxable person, or must immediately become a taxable person as a result of the transfer. This is often the case, since the purchaser of a going concern must take account of the vendor's turnover from the business (see VATA 1994, s 49(1)(a)), or from the part being transferred, in determining when and whether it must register. But in practice it is clearer, where possible, to rely on the purchaser actually being registered. Whether a purchaser is a taxable person for other reasons is a question of fact.

If a non-resident business is acquiring assets in the UK as part of a TOGC then it should check the VAT registration requirements noted in VATA 1994, Sch 1A. HMRC published guidance on Revenue & Customs Brief 11/16 on their view of the correct VAT treatment of TOGCs involving a non-resident purchaser. A summary of main points mentioned in the Revenue & Customs Brief has been provided below.

It is a condition of treating a transaction as a TOGC that where the seller is a taxable person the buyer must also be, or immediately become as a result of the transfer, a taxable person. It is therefore important for the seller to know the registration status of the buyer so the correct tax treatment can be applied.

The UK has a compulsory VAT registration threshold for persons established in the UK. However, there are different rules for determining whether a non-established person is liable to register for VAT than there are for a person established in the UK. There is no VAT registration threshold for non-established persons, who must register for VAT in the UK either immediately they make any taxable supply there or if they expect to do so in the following 30 days. As there is no registration threshold there is no need for a non-resident purchaser to take into consideration any supplies made by the business before it was transferred (the 'backward look'). The requirement for a non-resident business to register for VAT in the UK is simply determined on whether the supplier has made a supply in the UK or intends to make supplies in the UK within the next 30 days.

In these circumstances the seller may have less certainty over whether the buyer will become a taxable person following the transfer. HMRC gives the following example:

> It may be the intention of a non-established and non-taxable person to immediately suspend the newly acquired business for a period of six weeks while the business premises are refitted. There being no taxable supplies made or expected to be made within a 30-day period following the transfer, the buyer would not be liable to be a taxable person under the terms of the non-established person legislation and the transaction cannot be a TOGC.

Where the parties are aware that a non-established buyer does not intend to make taxable supplies at the point of transfer and does not intend to do so within the 30-day period, the non-established business can voluntarily register for VAT. If the seller is VAT registered then the purchaser must register before the transaction for the TOGC condition to be met. HMRC have stated that in their opinion a voluntary registration must be in place at the time of the transaction in order for the transaction to be treated as a TOGC.

HMRC have also stated in the Brief that if a supply by the seller spans the date of the transfer HMRC will accept that these become supplies made by the buyer immediately following the transfer. HMRC provide the following example:

> Where a tenancy agreement has effect at the time of the transfer the non-established person will have made a supply which, assuming an option to tax is in place, will be taxable and liability to register for VAT follows. In these circumstances it would not matter that a consideration had not at that point been received and was not perhaps expected within 30 days of the transfer. When the consideration becomes payable and the fact that it may be discounted by reference to a rent holiday has no impact.

The rules do not allow for the purchaser to be VAT-registered in another jurisdiction, which is outside of the UK for VAT purposes and the Tribunal in *Winterthur* (also noted in para **15.125**) saw this as valid.

If the vendor is not a taxable person, the status of the purchaser is irrelevant.

Transfer of part of a business

[15.127] If part of a business is being sold, it must be capable of separate operation. This is normally taken to mean that the part being sold must not depend on other business activities of the vendor and purchaser. It is not necessary for either party actually to operate it separately. The sale of one investment property out of a portfolio, or of one shop out of a chain, will normally qualify as capable of separate operation.

TOGC: further conditions – option to tax

[15.128] There are further conditions for TOGC treatment, concerning the option to tax.

These conditions apply if the transaction would, without a TOGC, be standard-rated either because the vendor has opted or because the sale is of a freehold new building or civil engineering work (see para **15.22** et seq). They do not apply if it would only be standard-rated for some other reason, or if it would be exempt because the vendor's option would be disapplied.

Where the conditions do apply, they require the purchaser to have notified HMRC of an option to tax, and to have notified the vendor that, essentially, the option will not be disapplied under the anti-avoidance rules (para **15.113** et seq). Both these steps must be taken before there is a tax point in relation to the sale. This normally means before completion, but if a deposit is paid, other than to a stakeholder, it needs to be done before this happens (see para **15.203**). If the purchaser requires HMRC's specific permission to opt (para **15.91**), they take the view that this must actually have been obtained before any tax point.

If the purchaser fails to meet these conditions, the transfer of the property will not be a TOGC and will be standard-rated.

Notification to the vendor

[15.129] As well as notifying HMRC of the option, the purchaser must notify the vendor that the Value Added Tax (Special Provisions) Order 1995, Article 5, para (2B) (as amended) does not apply to it. This is normally included as a standard clause in the sale agreement and sometimes takes the form of a warranty, an approach that goes further than the requirements of the legislation, but one which results in certainty.

The purchaser cannot give this notification if two conditions are met:

* The first condition concerns the CGS (para **15.288** et seq). It applies if the purchase price exceeds the CGS threshold of £250,000 or if the property is in the CGS in the hands of the vendor.
* The second condition is that the purchaser's supplies of the property 'will, or would fall, to be exempt supplies' under the anti-avoidance rules in para **15.113** et seq. This appears to cover cases where the purchaser's option is disapplied under those rules, or would be were it to opt.

TOGC treatment depends on the notification being given, so there can still be a TOGC if the notification is incorrect. But purchasers must take care that it is correct, and may be committing an offence if they do not.

And although this is intended as an anti-avoidance rule, it can be a problem in normal commercial transactions:

- A common example is where the purchaser is obtaining finance for the acquisition of a property from a bank that is coincidentally a major tenant in it, or a member of whose corporate group is a major tenant. This will normally mean that the purchaser's option will be disapplied under the rules in para **15.113** et seq, at least in relation to the lettings to the bank, so that it cannot give the necessary notification and the purchase cannot be a TOGC. The purchaser will incur VAT, not all of it which – in view of the exempt letting to the bank – will be recoverable.

  This problem does not, however, normally arise where, for example, the bank is merely occupying one unit in a shopping centre: as noted in para **15.117**, occupation by a financier is ignored if it accounts for no more than 10% of the lettable area of a building.

TOGC: property letting – HMRC's approach

[15.130] HMRC's Notice 700/9 gives some examples of TOGCs and non-TOGCs in the context of investors and others disposing of property that is held to let. This is reproduced below.

There are some further points that the examples do not directly deal with:

- HMRC will not see a TOGC if the vendor has only just commenced the business before the sale, or if the purchaser intends immediately to dispose of it rather than continuing it. It is less clear how long the parties need to run the business for. HMRC have repeatedly declined to comment on this, pleading that it depends on the nature of the business. For property letting, it is generally accepted that a three month rental cycle is long enough, although it is likely that a shorter period would actually suffice if some income is derived from the property in the meantime or if the landlord has carried out an act of being a landlord (some comfort may be derived here from *Kwik Save*).

- There might nevertheless be a TOGC where the purchaser intends to resell immediately, but to lease the property straight back and to continue the same business as the vendor. This was the case in *Morton Hotels Ltd* (para **15.125**). It is less clear to what extent HMRC accept this, particularly in the context of property letting.

- In the light of *Kwik Save* (para **15.125**), HMRC do not generally see a TOGC arising in the context of a sub-sale. If A agrees to sell to B, and B agrees to sell to C, there are successive supplies A-B and B-C, rather than a potential TOGC A-C, even if completion is direct from A to C. In Scotland, however, there can be a TOGC from A to C in these cases, because B does not acquire an interest in land, but only a personal right.

- As noted in para **15.125**, HMRC do not see the letting of a property between members of a VAT group as a business capable of TOGC treatment. So there is no TOGC if the only tenant is VAT grouped with either the vendor or the purchaser.

- Where a number of properties are sold together, only some of which are tenanted, the question can arise whether there is a single TOGC or whether each property must be considered separately. In Notice 700/9, HMRC say that:

'The transfer of a number of sites or buildings where some of the sites or buildings are let, or partially let and some are unlet, needs to be considered on a case by case basis. The nature of the sites or building and their use are all factors for consideration. It is important to look at whether the assets can be identified as a single business or an identifiable part of a business. In addition all the [other conditions for a TOGC] would need to be met. For example the sale of a chain of shops or pubs could be a TOGC whereas the sale of a grouping of disparate properties might not.'

- Where property is held on trust, it is usually the beneficiary, rather than the nominee legal owner, who is seen as making the supplies to tenants (see para **15.196**). The TOGC rules do not deal with this adequately where the purchaser is a nominee, since they require it to be the purchaser who carries on the business.

To deal with this, HMRC accept that the vendor, nominee purchaser and beneficiary can agree that the beneficiary will be treated as the transferee for the purposes of the TOGC rules. This only applies where the business being transferred is a property letting business, and where the identity of the beneficial owner is known to the transferor.

HMRC suggest the following form of wording:

'X, Y and Z confirm that they have agreed to adopt the optional practice set out in Customs' Business Brief 10/96 in relation to the purchase of the property pursuant to an agreement dated () between X and Y.

Following the transfer of the property Y will hold the legal title as nominee for Z, the beneficial owner.'

Alternatively the point can simply be written into the sale agreement, provided the beneficiary is a party to this.

The arrangement is optional but not always commercially acceptable. If it is not used, the sale will be treated as a supply to the nominee, and not as a TOGC. The beneficial owner should nevertheless be able to recover the VAT charged (see para **15.196**).

Further details can be found in HMRC's Notice 700/9.

TOGCs of properties held to let – HMRC's views

HMRC's Notice 700/9 contains the following material:

'Examples of when a property business can be transferred as a TOGC

If you:

- own the freehold of a property which you let to a tenant and sell the freehold with the benefit of the existing lease, a business of property rental is transferred to the purchaser. This is a business transferred as a TOGC even if the property is only partly tenanted. Similarly, if you own the lease of a property (which is subject to a sub-lease) and you assign your lease with the benefit of the sub-lease, this is a business transferred as a TOGC.
- own a building where there is a contract to pay rent in the future but where the tenants are enjoying an initial rent free period, even if the building is sold during the rent free period, you are carrying on a business of property rental.
- granted a lease in respect of a building but the tenants are not yet in occupation, you are carrying on a property rental business.

- own a property and have found a tenant but not actually entered into a lease agreement when you transfer the freehold* to a third party (with the benefit of a contractual agreement for a lease** but before the lease has been signed), there is sufficient evidence of intended economic activity for there to be a property rental business capable of being transferred.
- are a property developer selling a site as a package (to a single buyer) which is a mixture of let and unlet, finished or unfinished properties, and the sale of the site would otherwise have been standard rated, then subject to the purchaser opting to tax for the whole site, the whole site can be regarded as a business transferred as a going concern.
- own a number of let freehold* properties, and you sell one of them, the sale of this single let or partly let property can be a TOGC of a property rental business.
- have a partially-let building this is capable of being a property rental business, providing that the letting constitutes economic activity. This may include electricity sub-stations or space for advertising hoardings providing that there is a lease in place.
- purchase the freehold and leasehold of a property from separate sellers without the interests merging and the lease has not been extinguished, providing you continue to exploit the asset by receiving rent from the tenant, then such a transaction can be a TOGC.

Examples where there is not a TOGC

If you:

- are a property developer and have built a building and you allow someone to occupy temporarily (without any right to occupy after any proposed sale) or you are 'actively marketing' it in search of a tenant, there is no property rental business being carried on.
- own the freehold of a property and grant a lease, even a 999-year lease, you are not transferring a business as a going concern. You are creating a new asset (the lease) and selling it while retaining your original asset (the freehold). This is true regardless of the length of the lease. Similarly, if you own a headlease and grant a sub-lease you are not transferring your business as a going concern.***
- sell a property where the lease you granted is surrendered immediately before the sale, your property rental business ceases and so cannot be transferred as a going concern – even if tenants under a sublease remain in occupation. When the lease is brought to an end the property rental business carried on by the former freeholder has ceased and cannot be transferred.****
- sell a property freehold to the existing tenant who leases the whole premises from you, this cannot be a transfer of a going concern because the tenant cannot carry on the same business of property rental. This would remain the case even if the new freeholder vacated the property on acquisition and found a new tenant since when the lease is brought to an end the property rental business carried on by the former freeholder has ceased.
- have granted a lease in respect of a building and the tenant is running a business from the premises. The tenant then sells the assets of his business as a going concern and surrenders his lease to you. You grant the new owner of the business a lease in respect of the building. This is not a transfer by you of a property rental business.'

* As in the first example, the references here to a sale or transfer of the freehold should hold equally good for the assignment of a lease – what HMRC are trying to distinguish between is an outright disposal and the grant of some lesser interest, retaining a reversion.

** HMRC nevertheless argued the opposite in *Dartford Borough Council* (see para 15.124). Regard should also be had to the recent judgment of the Upper Tribunal in *Royal College of Paediatrics and Child Health* [2015] UKUT 38 (TCC), where it was held that an agreement for lease that was conditional on the sale of the property in question taking place could not constitute a business for TOGC purposes (see para 15.124).

*** Although this paragraph still remains in the public notice it has, generally speaking, been superseded by Revenue & Customs Brief 30/12. HMRC now accept that the grant of a lease can amount to a TOGC, but only in circumstances where the reversionary interest retained by the seller has a value of less than 1% of the asset in question prior to its sale.

**** See Revenue & Customs Brief 27/14.

TOGC: consequences

[15.131] Where a transaction is a TOGC:

- It is not a supply for VAT purposes and no VAT can be charged.
- There is a saving if the sale would otherwise be subject to both VAT and stamp duty land tax (SDLT) (see CHAPTER 16). SDLT is assessed on the price including VAT, so that if the VAT rate is 20% it increases a 4% SDLT rate to an effective 4.8%. TOGC treatment avoids this.
- There are no VAT cashflow considerations – this is generally beneficial.
- In HMRC's view, input tax related to a TOGC, eg on fees, is recoverable according to whether the activity transferred is taxable or exempt. This is based on their reading of the CJEU judgment in *Abbey National plc* (CJEU Case C-408/98).
- If the transferor was within the CGS (see para **15.288** et seq), the transferee takes on the transferor's obligations under the scheme and may have to make adjustments based on his original input tax recovery. HMRC take the same view of any adjustments needed under SI 1995/2518, reg 108 or 109 (see para **15.286**), but the legal basis for this is unclear.
- The transferee may need information about the transferor's VAT position. The transferor is obliged to comply with reasonable requests for information, copies of documents or access to records. HMRC can also disclose information to the transferee, or require that records are retained by the transferee rather than the transferor.
- The transferee will generally need to register for VAT, if it is not already registered. As noted in para **15.126**, this will necessarily apply if the transferor was registered or should have been registered, and the transferor's turnover counts as the transferee's in determining whether and when the transferee should register.
- If the whole business is transferred, the transferor will generally need to deregister. The transferee can choose to take on the transferor's VAT number and liabilities. This is rarely advisable and therefore unusual.
- If the transferee is a member of a partly exempt VAT group, it may have to account for VAT on a 'self-supply' of any assets included in the TOGC, the supply of which would be subject to VAT. This requires the VAT group to account for output VAT on the market value of the assets. It treats the same amount as input tax, which it can recover to the same extent as if it had incurred the VAT on the actual acquisition of the asset.

This does not apply if the assets are subject to the CGS, or if HMRC are satisfied that the transferor acquired the assets more than three years earlier. HMRC can also agree to reduce the amount of VAT due if the transferor has not had full input tax recovery on the assets. In Notice 700/9, they say that it can be reduced to nil if the transferor's partial exemption recovery rate, in the partial exemption year (para **15.282**) when the assets were purchased, is equal to or less than the transferee's recovery rate in the year when the assets are acquired.

- Person constructing status (see para **15.134**) is now considered by HMRC to be capable of passing from a vendor to a purchaser in a TOGC (see Revenue & Customs Brief 27/14).

Zero-rating

[15.132] Zero-rating is primarily relevant to housebuilders, who can zero-rate the initial grant of a 'major interest' in the property. A major interest is the freehold or a lease exceeding 21 years (in Scotland, of at least 20 years).

Zero-rating is also relevant, in a similar way, to someone:

- constructing a building for a 'relevant residential' or 'relevant charitable' purpose (RRP/RCP), including the construction of a self-contained RCP annexe;
- converting a non-residential building to a dwelling or RRP building;
- substantially reconstructing a listed dwelling or RRP/RCP building.

These various areas are looked at in paras **15.134** to **15.178**.

In many of these cases, the associated building work can also be zero-rated, or taxed at the reduced rate of 5% (see para **15.220** et seq).

Some other points relevant to buildings of these kinds are considered elsewhere:

- the option to tax does not generally apply to them or, in some cases, to sites for constructing them (para **15.73** et seq);
- the standard-rating for new freeholds does not apply to them (para **15.22** et seq);
- some lettings of dwellings are standard-rated as the provision of holiday accommodation (para **15.43** et seq).

Other cases

[15.133] Zero-rating can also apply to:

- the sale or leasing, including *in situ*, of a residential caravan or houseboat (see paras **15.50** and **15.52**);
- grazing rights, and rights to remove crops or fruit – these are seen as zero-rated supplies of food or animal feeding stuffs (but for fish and game see para **15.56**);
- at least in theory, some transactions contracted for before 21 June 1988, and that would have been zero-rated at that date.

Zero-rating: person constructing a dwelling – overview

[15.134] VATA 1994, Sch 8, Group 5, item 1 zero-rates:

'The first grant by a person –
(a)   constructing a building –
          (i)   designed as a dwelling or number of dwellings . . .

of a major interest in, or in any part of, the building, dwelling or its site.'

These requirements points are considered in paras **15.135** to **15.146**. Further issues concern the extent of the 'site' (para **15.148**), an exception for cases where there are limited occupancy rights (para **15.147**), and the developer's ability to recover input tax (paras **15.149** and **15.150**) – this is specifically blocked for some items incorporated into dwellings.

The supply does not have to be to the end user.

Zero-rating: person constructing a dwelling – 'dwelling'

[15.135] The zero-rating in para **15.134** requires that the building is 'designed as a dwelling or number of dwellings' (eg a block of flats). It does not matter whether it is actually used as such.

VATA 1994, Sch 8, Group 5, Note 2 says that:

'A building is designed as a dwelling or a number of dwellings where in relation to each dwelling the following conditions are satisfied –
(a)   the dwelling consists of self-contained living accommodation;
(b)   there is no provision for direct internal access from the dwelling to any other dwelling or part of a dwelling;
(c)   the separate use, or disposal of the dwelling is not prohibited by the term of any covenant, statutory planning consent or similar provision; and
(d)   statutory planning consent has been granted in respect of that dwelling and its construction or conversion has been carried out in accordance with that consent.'

These points are considered below.

Also, the structure needs actually to be a building. This is more often an issue for RCP projects (see **15.163**) than with dwellings, but in particular houseboats were found not to be dwellings in *Parkinson* (VTD 17257) and *Dunster* (TC00727). They might, however, alternatively qualify for zero-rating under the rules mentioned in para **15.52**.

Self-contained; internal access

[15.136] The 'self-contained' and 'internal access' tests in Note 2(a) and (b) (para **15.135**) suggest that each unit must provide living accommodation behind its own front door, and that access from one unit to another must be via, say, a corridor. The unit probably needs to have all the facilities necessary to daily life, but it is debatable how far this goes. HMRC rejected zero-rating in *Agudas Israel Housing Association* (VTD 18798), where flats for elderly residents had limited cooking facilities, but the Tribunal disagreed:

'In our view, in the twenty-first century, premises with their own front door, en suite bathing facilities and the ability to cook with a microwave cooker and a kettle are self-contained living accommodation. The factor of the limited nature of the cooking facilities is outweighed by the factor of the direct access to the Square from a resident's own front door to which he or she has his or her own key.'

Reference should also be made to Revenue & Customs Brief 2/14.

In *Capital Focus Ltd* (TC05193), the taxpayer purchased a commercial property that it intended to convert into a single residential unit. The business registered for VAT as an intending trader and recovered the VAT charged on the purchase of the property. HMRC allowed the input tax reclaim on the assumption that the sale of the property would be treated as the zero-rated sale of a converted single residential unit (VAT 1994, Sch 8, Group 5, item 1(b)). However, the taxpayer subsequently changed his mind and converted the property into a single residential house that contained multiple occupancy units with some shared facilities. Four of the rooms had en suite facilities and the other six rooms shared two bathrooms. None of the rooms had a wash basin. All residents shared the communal kitchen facilities. Each room had its own key and could be locked by the occupant. HMRC considered that the conversion was in fact an exempt supply and sought to recover the input tax claimed by the business.

The business appealed and the appeal concerned the condition in Note 2(a) and whether the dwelling consisted of self-contained living accommodation. The Tribunal stated that it was not necessary for each of the rooms to be a self-contained dwelling as the house taken as a whole constituted a self-contained dwelling as it contained the basic elements of living. Therefore, the question concerned whether a multiple occupancy dwelling met the requirements in Note 1(b). The Tribunal held that although the zero-rating provisions did not specifically include a property with multiple occupancy in its definition, it did not exclude them either. They considered that the purpose of the legislation was to zero-rate the creation of new dwellings and a multiple occupancy property where people resided in it as a dwelling could be zero-rated under these provisions. Appeal allowed.

Separate use or disposal

[15.137] The Note 2(c) requirement that 'separate use, or disposal of the dwelling is not prohibited' (para **15.135**) raises various issues, and case law in this area is noted below. But, in particular:

- It seems clear that any prohibition needs to be overt. HMRC do not always accept this, and will sometimes ask for a positive statement from the planning authority that separate use and disposal are permitted. But a requirement that the use be 'incidental' or 'ancillary' to that of another property has much the same effect as a prohibition on separate use.
- Zero-rating is not prevented by a prohibition on separate letting (but see the different approach in *Sharples*, below).
- A mere requirement for landlord's consent should not be a problem (but see *Opal Carleton*, below).

- HMRC say that occupancy restrictions as to, for example, the age of residents, or their type of employment, are not a problem. But they have taken a different view where residents have to work in a specific business (see *Wendels,* below). Whilst the Tribunal rejected this, it does appear that a requirement that the property be used in conjunction with adjoining commercial premises can fall foul of Note 2(c). HMRC take the same view of 'independent living' units at care homes, where planning permission prevents separate use from the care home. They commented on this in Revenue & Customs Brief 66/07, also saying that they did not see such units as eligible for zero-rating under any other heading.

Selected case law on 'separate use or disposal'

- In *Sherwin & Green* (VTD 16396), the planning authority seems to have intended to prohibit separate disposal, but the condition it actually imposed prohibited only sub-division. This was not an obstacle to the Note 2(c) test being met.
- *Oldrings Development Kingsclere Ltd* (VTD 17769) concerned a 'studio room' in the grounds of an existing house. The planning authority claimed that separate use was not permitted, but it had not actually imposed a condition to this effect, so that again the Note 2(c) test was met.
- In*Harris* (VTD 18822) the Tribunal held that the tests needed to be considered at the time of construction – the subsequent lifting of a prohibition on separate use made no difference.
- In *Milligan* (VTD 19224), there was a planning condition requiring occupation of the new accommodation to be 'in connection with, and ancillary to' an existing dwelling, and prohibiting occupation as 'an independent dwelling house'. This fell foul of Note 2(c). Similar decisions, involving essentially similar planning conditions, were reached in *Giblin* (VTD 20352) and *Bracegirdle* (VTD 20889).
- In *Nicholson* (VTD 19412), the Tribunal did not see a condition that use be 'incidental' to that of an existing house as a prohibition on separate use or disposal, but the Upper Tribunal disapproved this decision in *Lunn* (below).
- *Cussins* (VTD 20541) concerned a planning requirement that the dwelling be occupied in conjunction with adjoining commercial premises – the Tribunal concluded that Note 2(c) did not merely require the new accommodation to be separate from any other dwelling, and that, by limiting the market for the property, the planning permission was a prohibition on separate disposal, as well as on separate use.
- In *Sharples* (VTD 20775), the Tribunal thought that a prohibition on disposal was still a prohibition, despite an exception for transactions with the appellants' pension scheme. But it also thought that the reference in Note 2(c) was to a disposal of occupancy rights and did not apply where, as here, the only prohibition was on a freehold disposal.
- In *Lunn*, the Tribunal thought that a requirement that use be 'incidental or ancillary' to that of another house did not prohibit separate use, but the Upper Tribunal ([2009] UKUT 244 (TCC)) took a more purposive approach, and rejected this.
- *Opal Carleton Ltd* (TC00635) concerned works to existing student halls of residence. The company argued that these were subject to 5% VAT as a 'changed number of dwellings' (see para 15.243), which required the new accommodation units to meet the same tests as in Note 2. The Tribunal

dismissed this, on the strange grounds that non-student use would have required the consent of the landlord, and discussions with the local authority about parking provision. It also thought that student accommodation could not be dwellings, since the law made separate reference to it (para 15.155). This was confirmed by the Upper Tribunal.

- In *Wendels* (TC00737), the planning authority had given consent for a new dwelling, but limited occupation to someone employed at an adjacent cattery, or their dependent, widow etc. The Tribunal rejected HMRC's contention that this was a prohibition on separate use or disposal. Another aspect of this case is noted in para 15.275. A similar decision was reached in *Phillips* (TC01227).

- In *Sherratt* (TC01180), the construction of a farmhouse, on a farm where there was no existing dwelling, was subject to a planning condition that it could not be disposed of separately from the rest of the farm. It therefore fell foul of Note 2(c).

- In *Stevens* (TC01617) a restriction was in place but the Tribunal decided that a restriction had to be imposed by a planning authority in order for it to be effective. Note that following *Anthony Barkas* [2014] UKUT 558 (TCC) it seems that such a restriction would need to be enforceable.

Planning consent

[**15.138**] Note 2(d) requires, as seen in para **15.135**, that planning consent has been granted in respect of the dwelling and the work carried out in accordance with it. This is usually straightforward, but:

- Permission needs to have been granted for the work at the time it is done. If the permission was actually for an extension, 'retrospective' consent for new construction will not meet the condition (*Watson* (TC00780), *Abbeytrust Homes Ltd* (TC01024)). See also *The Master Wishmakers* (TC05624) and *Cavendish Green Ltd* (TC05356) where the Tribunal held that the supply could not be zero-rated as the necessary planning permission was not in place at the relevant date.

- On the other hand, in *Cottam* (VTD 20036), the test was still met where the planning authority had said that the work did not require consent. The Tribunal held that Note 2(d) did not imply a formal process, and that the planning authority must have meant either that the work was covered by general consent or that, by saying no consent was required, it was actually granting consent.

- It seems debateable whether the wording of the Note actually requires the consent to be as a dwelling. HMRC think that it does, as did the Tribunal in *Davison* (VTD 17130), where the consent had actually been for a double garage, although not in *Oldrings Development Kingsclere Ltd* (VTD 17769), where it had been for a 'studio room'.

- HMRC have come to attach increasing importance to planning use classes, suggesting that (in England) Note 2(d) requires the consent to be for C3 use, whereas some units that are actually dwellings will be within a C2 consent, or will be classed as C4.

Mixed use; common parts

[15.139] If the building is designed partly as a dwelling and partly as something else, perhaps a shop, only the dwelling is zero-rated and the sale price etc needs to be split accordingly.

The zero-rating extends to common parts, such as an entrance area and corridors in a block of flats, although the value of these too may need to be apportioned if the building is not just dwellings. HMRC have sometimes questioned the treatment of more extensive communal areas such as a lounge or laundry, but since Business Brief 11/03 have accepted zero-rating provided such areas were only used by residents and their guests. They are less likely to do so for leisure or gym facilities, although the Business Brief confused matters by suggesting that these would necessarily be used by others.

Business use and 'live/work units'

[15.140] Business use does not prevent zero-rating, since the test is based on design, not on use. But there can be an issue where the dwelling is designed to incorporate a work area, such as an office or workshop. HMRC are likely to see zero-rating as confined to the residential part if the planning consent provides for a specific area or square footage for work use – in this case the price must be apportioned, and the work element will be exempt or standard-rated (as for example with the sale of a new freehold). There is, however, also a danger in these cases that they will say that the residential part cannot be zero-rated either, if there is a prohibition on it being used or disposed of separately from the work area, as in *Cussins* (see para **15.137**).

Zero-rating: person constructing a dwelling – 'person constructing'

[15.141] The zero-rating in para **15.134** requires the grantor to be 'a person constructing' the building. There are two questions here – whether the works amount to construction, and whether the grantor can be seen as undertaking the works.

Construction

[15.142] An entirely new building, freestanding and incorporating nothing from any previous building, will qualify for the zero-rating. In other cases, the scope for zero-rating is limited:

VATA 1994, Sch 8, Group 5, Note 16 says that:

'For the purpose of this Group, the construction of a building does not include–

(a)   the conversion, reconstruction or alteration of an existing building; or

(b)   any enlargement of, or extension to, an existing building except to the extent the enlargement or extension creates an additional dwelling or dwellings; or

(c)   subject to Note (17) below, the construction of an annexe to an existing building.'

Note 17 does not apply to dwellings. Note 18 adds that:

'A building only ceases to be an existing building when:

(a)   demolished completely to ground level; or

(b)   the part remaining above ground level consists of no more than a single facade or where a corner site, a double facade, the retention of which is a condition or requirement of statutory planning consent or similar permission.'

HMRC interpret these rules strictly, but various points are worth highlighting.

*   If the new building is replacing an existing building, there must be a point when there is nothing above ground level. Foundations can be retained, as can the slab of the ground floor.

*   A single retained facade can be any exterior wall and need not face onto the street. A double façade, on the other hand, needs to be on a 'corner site', and in *Samuel* this was held to mean a street corner or some other similar visible location.

*   The retention of a façade must be a planning requirement – HMRC take the view that it must be an explicit requirement, imposed by the planning authority, rather than the developer's own idea – the inference being that an unsuccessful application to demolish the facade must be submitted first. HMRC succeeded on this point in *Pollock and Heath* and in *Hall*, although not in earlier cases nor more recently in *Almond* or *Samuel*.

*   The retention of party walls in a terrace etc is not a problem if they continue to be external walls of the individual dwelling. This can be in addition to the required retention of a facade.

*   Internal linkage to an existing building does not automatically deny zero-rating, but for dwellings it creates a number of potential obstacles:

    –   There may well be problems with the Note 2 requirements about internal access (para **15.136**) or about separate use or disposal (para **15.137**).

    –   An enlargement or extension cannot be zero-rated except 'to the extent' it 'creates an additional dwelling or dwellings'. HMRC take this to mean that the new dwelling or dwellings must be contained entirely in the enlargement or extension. They may well resist zero-rating where, for example, the new dwelling includes what was previously roofspace. The Tribunal rejected this in *Jahansouz*, where the previous roof had been removed first. And previously in *Smith*, on different facts, it had suggested that an apportionment might be appropriate, although HMRC do not accept this.

    –   An annexe to an existing building cannot, in this context, be zero-rated, even if it does create an additional dwelling, but an annexe is likely to fall foul of Note 2 anyway. Annexes are looked at in relation to RRP/RCP buildings in para **15.165** et seq.

*   HMRC accept that a building is 'constructed' where it is dismantled and re-erected on a different site, or where it is bought and assembled in 'kit' format.

Selected case law on 'construction'

These cases were largely about whether the works were zero-rated under the rules in para 15.221 or about the 'DIY' refund scheme (para 15.275), but the points apply equally to the zero-rating of a major interest by a 'person constructing'.

- In *Bugg* (VTD 15123), a bungalow was demolished and replaced in stages. By completion of the project, nothing seems to have remained of the original bungalow, but the project was held not to be 'construction' since there had at all times been something standing above ground level. Similar decisions were reached in *Tinker* (VTD 18033) and in *Gilder* (VTD 18143).

- In *Midgley* (VTD 15379), works to extend a farmhouse revealed that the existing building was unstable and in need of demolition. A single wall was retained, and the rest was demolished to ground level and replaced. The planning authority granted retrospective permission for the 'construction of a replacement dwelling incorporating part of an existing wall'. The Tribunal accepted that the works were zero-rated – only one facade was left and, implicitly at least, this had been a condition of planning consent. The Tribunal took a similar approach in *Naylor* (VTD 17305).

- In *Evans* (VTD 17264), however, the construction of a new dwelling incorporating a single wall of a previous building was standard-rated, since the retention of the wall had not been a requirement of planning consent. Similar decisions were reached over a retained chimney in *McCallion* (VTD 19367) and over a small part of a wall in *Halliwell* (VTD 19735).

- In *Smith* (VTD 17035), a new dwelling was built onto the side of an existing dwelling and incorporating part of the first floor of it. An extension that creates an additional dwelling can be zero-rated, but HMRC argued that this did not apply since the new dwelling was not wholly created out of the extension. The Tribunal decided that zero-rating applied to the part that was in the extension.

- *Gillin* (VTD 19985) concerned works to a 'mobile home' resting on steel legs, rather than on foundations. The result was a stone dwelling with conventional foundations. The Tribunal rejected the contention that this was not work to an existing building.

- In *Pollock and Heath* (VTD 20380), HMRC argued that works involving the retention of a corner facade did not qualify as 'construction', since the appellants had chosen to retain it. The Tribunal agreed, saying that the retention of a façade had to be something imposed by the planners. A similar decision was reached in *Hall* (TC00037), even though the planning department had indicated beforehand that it was likely to refuse consent if the facade was not being retained. But subsequently, in *Almond* (TC00132), the Tribunal took a different view, holding that it was enough that the work had to be in accordance with the plans, which showed the facade being retained.

- In *Clark* (TC00552), two non-adjoining facades were to be retained, so that the work did not qualify. It made no difference that one of them had collapsed during the project and had entirely to be rebuilt – it had still been 'retained' for these purposes.

- In *Jahansouz* (TC00637), a pitched roof was removed, and a new flat constructed under a slightly higher roof. HMRC did not see this as 'construction' because the new flat was partly within the previous roofspace, but the Tribunal rejected this – it was still an extension creating an additional dwelling, under Note 16(b).

- In *Samuel* (TC00872), the planning authority had insisted that they could not give consent for a new building, but only for an extension. In order to comply with this, two small external walls of a previous bungalow were incorporated into a much larger new house. Despite clear evidence that this was at the planners' insistence, HMRC took the same line as in *Hall* and *Almond*, above, saying that their retention had not been an explicit planning condition. The Tribunal rejected this – it was clearly a requirement. But given that there were two retained walls, Note 18(b) also required them to be on a 'corner site'. The Tribunal thought that this meant they had to be on a street corner, or something similar, which these were not.

• In *Jack Wilson* (TC03454) the Tribunal considered that a condition of planning consent (taking the form of the retention of a façade) does not necessarily need to be explicitly set out in the planning permission itself if it is clear that the retention was required by the planning authority.

• In *J3 Building Solutions Ltd* ([2017] UKUT 253 (TCC)), the business had demolished the existing residential coach house and various extensions, with the exception of the walls of the coach house which formed part of the boundary wall of the site. A new dwelling was constructed on the site and it physically touched the retained walls at each end of the wall and on top of the walls. The business considered it was constructing a new zero-rated dwelling and HMRC considered that it was an exempt alteration/extension of an existing building. The Upper Tribunal held that the existing building remained and that it was incorporated into the new structure and this amounted to an alteration so the supply could not be zero-rated.

Role in construction

[15.143] A 'person constructing' needs actually to be involved in the construction. It is not enough merely to own the land on which construction is carried out.

HMRC's Notice 708 says that:

'You are a "person constructing" a building if, in relation to that building, you are, or have at any point in the past:

• acted as a developer – you physically constructed, or commissioned another person to physically construct, the building (in whole or in part) on land that you own or have an interest in; or

• acted as a contractor or sub-contractor – you provided construction services to the developer or another contractor for the construction of the building, sub-contracting work as necessary.'

This can sometimes mean that no-one is capable of granting a zero-rated major interest.

There are some further points here:

• Where legal and beneficial ownership are split, it is the beneficial owner who is treated as making the grant, so it is the beneficial owner who needs to have carried out or commissioned the work.

• If a building is sold during construction, and completed by the purchaser, both parties can be 'a person constructing'. But this will not apply if the sale is at too early, or too late, a stage:

– In HMRC's view, the first owner will need to have taken the work beyond foundation level – there is some support for this in *Stapenhill Developments*, summarised below, and it gives rise to the term 'golden brick' to describe a sale that is deliberately delayed until this stage (see also para **15.78**). HMRC accept in these cases that an earlier payment can still be zero-rated if works have progressed beyond the foundations by the time of the actual sale.

– Conversely, HMRC will not see the purchaser as 'a person constructing' if the sale only happens once the building is complete and ready for occupation.

- There is no time limit on 'person constructing' status – potentially it can last for centuries if the property continues to be owned by the same legal entity, although zero-rating will only apply if there has been no previous grant of a major interest. This general point was confirmed by the Court of Session in *Link Housing Association*.

- Someone with historic 'person constructing' status can therefore grant a zero-rated major interest in order to recover VAT on alterations or other work being done now, but this is not obviously the intention behind the zero-rating, and HMRC are not keen on the point. If the major interest is granted to someone connected to the 'person constructing', any attempt to recover VAT on this basis is likely to require disclosure to HMRC under the rules in para **15.301**.

- 'Person constructing' status attaches to the individual member of a VAT group, not to the group as a whole. The grant of a major interest by another member of the group will therefore not be zero-rated. HMRC will, however, ignore intra-group transactions in considering what is the 'first grant' of a major interest.

- HMRC announced in Revenue and Customs Brief 27/14 that a business acquiring a completed residential or charitable development as part of a transfer of a going concern inherits 'person constructing' status and is capable of making a zero-rated first major interest grant in that building or part of it as long as:

  — a zero-rated grant has not already been made of the completed building or relevant part by a previous owner (HMRC consider that the grant that gives rise to the TOGC should be disregarded);

  — the person acquiring the building as a TOGC would suffer an unfair VAT disadvantage if its first major interest grants were treated as exempt (eg a developer restructures its business. This entails the transfer (as a TOGC) of its entire property portfolio of newly constructed residential/charitable buildings to an associated company, which will make first major interest grants. If these were treated as exempt, the transferee might become liable to repay input tax recovered by the original owner on development costs under the Capital Goods Scheme or partial exemption 'claw back' provisions and would incur input tax restrictions on selling fees that would not be suffered by businesses in similar circumstances – HMRC would consider this to be an unfair disadvantage);

  — that person would not obtain an unfair VAT advantage by being in a position to make zero-rated supplies.

Selected case law on 'person constructing'

- In *Monsell Youell Developments Ltd* (VTD 538), A owned a site, obtained planning permission and constructed roads, sewers and landscaping. Houses were then built by an associated company B, in accordance with A's plans and specifications, and sold by A. The Tribunal did not think A's role was sufficient for it to be 'a person constructing'.
- In *Hulme Educational Foundation* (VTD 625), A let land to B, which sub-let it to C. C constructed buildings, apparently on its own account – A was not a party to the construction contract. The Tribunal held that A was not 'a person constructing', holding that this required that:

  'construction must be physically done by the person concerned or by his servants or agents, or the person must himself directly enter into a contract or arrangement for another to do the physical construction works'.

- *Stapenhill Developments Ltd* (VTD 1593) concerned the sale of a large development site on which the vendor had undertaken some civil engineering work, and had commenced but abandoned the construction of three dwellings. The Tribunal held that it was not 'a person constructing a building', and that for this to apply 'a building must be seen to be under construction on the land'. Similar decisions were reached in *Permacross Ltd* (VTD 13251) and *Cameron New Homes Ltd* (VTD 17309).
- In *Link Housing Association* (CS [1992] STC 718), the Court of Session confirmed that 'person constructing' status was open-ended. A developer had built houses and let them on short tenancies. Their sale some years later was zero-rated.

Zero rating: person constructing a dwelling – first grant of a major interest

[**15.144**] The zero-rating in para **15.134** requires that the sale or lease is 'the first grant . . . of a major interest'.

Major interest

[**15.145**] A major interest is the freehold, or a lease exceeding 21 years (in Scotland, of at least 20 years). It also includes a commonhold interest and, in Northern Ireland, the estate of a person holding land under a fee farm grant.

HMRC accept that an agreement for lease granted for consideration can count as a lease for these purposes, and that a lease with a break clause can be seen as good for the full term.

If a lease is initially too short to qualify, HMRC will sometimes accept that this can be dealt with through a deed of rectification. The Tribunal also accepted this in *Isaac* (VTD 14656).

First grant

[**15.146**] Zero-rating only applies to the first grant – including an assignment or surrender – of a major interest. Any subsequent grant will be exempt.

Zero-rating can still apply if a short, exempt, lease has been granted first, or if a major interest has been granted to another member of a VAT group.

If a zero-rated grant covers only part of the building, this does not prevent zero-rating for a subsequent grant over another part of it. In some cases a grant may be partly zero-rated. An example is given below.

For major interest leases, zero-rating only applies to the premium or, if there is no premium, to the first instalment of rent. Thereafter the lease is exempt. This is intended to confine the developer's VAT recovery to capital expenditure etc incurred in constructing the building and granting the lease. Where the interest in the dwelling is sold in tranches under a shared ownership scheme, only the first tranche is zero-rated.

First grant of a major interest – example

A developer constructs a building consisting of two flats, A and B, granting leases and then selling the building, as follows:

• *99-year lease on flat A.* This is the first grant of a major interest. The premium, or if there is no premium the first payment of rent, is zero-rated. Subsequent rent will be exempt.
• *5-year lease on flat B.* This is not a major interest and is exempt.
• *Freehold sale of the whole building.* This is the first grant of a major interest in flat B and in the common parts, and is zero-rated to that extent. But it is the second grant of a major interest in flat A, and this element is exempt. Alternatively, if the purchaser is VAT registered, the sale may be a TOGC (see para 15.121 et seq).

Exempt transactions will have input tax implications and may also require CGS adjustments – see para 15.296.

Restrictions on residence

[15.147] VATA 1994, Sch 8, Group 5, Note 13 denies zero-rating for a dwelling where:

'(i)   the interest granted is such that the grantee is not entitled to reside in the building or part, throughout the year; or
(ii)   residence there throughout the year, or the use of the building or part as the grantee's principal private residence, is prevented by the terms of a covenant, statutory planning consent or similar permission.'

VATA 1994, Sch 9, Group 1, Note 11(a) then says that, where this applies, the grant is standard-rated. These rules are aimed, not entirely accurately, at holiday homes, and are looked at in paras 15.45 and 15.46.

Extent of the zero-rated grant

[15.148] Zero-rating extends to the 'site' of the building, such as the grounds and garden of a house, or the communal areas around a block of flats. In *Stapenhill Developments Ltd* (VTD 1593) (see also para 15.143), the Tribunal held that:

'the site of a building in the context of the provision means a reasonable plot of land surrounding the building. What is a reasonable plot must depend on the size, nature and situation of the building and the nature of the surrounding land.'

In the light of this, HMRC will not accept zero-rating for very extensive grounds, farmland etc included in a sale or lease.

VATA 1994, Sch 8, Group 5, Note 3 also specifically extends zero-rating to a garage:

'provided that:

(a)   the dwelling and the garage are constructed or converted at the same time; and

(b)   the garage is intended to be occupied with the dwelling or one of the dwellings.'

So an interval between completion of the dwelling and construction of the garage will deny zero-rating (*Chipping Sodbury Town Trust* (VTD 16641)), although this did not apply in *Palmers of Oakham* (TC00959), where it was the garage that was built first.

The zero-rating may not strictly cover other subsidiary buildings, such as workshops or summerhouses, although HMRC do not necessarily take this point.

Parking spaces provided in conjunction with the zero-rated lease of a flat etc should also qualify for zero-rating. But in *Civilscent Ltd* (TC00070), parking spaces made available subsequently were found to be standard-rated, essentially because tenants had had no promise of obtaining one when they took the lease. (As noted in para **15.31**, HMRC's published guidance might, however, have suggested that the parking was exempt, rather than standard-rated.)

Fixtures will be part of the zero-rated grant, but if valuable loose items, such as furniture, are included in the sale HMRC may expect output tax to be accounted for on these.

Zero rating: person constructing a dwelling – input tax recovery

[15.149] A zero-rated grant allows the developer to recover related input tax, but there are several restrictions to this:

•   Under Article 6 of the Value Added Tax (Input Tax) Order 1992 ('the blocking order'), the developer cannot recover input tax on certain items incorporated into the building or site, but which are not regarded as 'building materials'. 'White goods' and carpets are seen as examples, and there is more about the meaning of 'building materials' in para **15.223**. This position was challenged by *Taylor Wimpey* (TW), both under the Directive and on the grounds that many of the relevant items are not actually 'incorporated'. The First-tier Tribunal however dismissed the appeal and held that input tax was not recoverable on white goods. However, interestingly the First-tier Tribunal said that the question regarding whether the builders block was lawful needed to be decided by the CJEU. TW appealed against this decision and the Upper Tribunal dismissed the taxpayers' appeal. The Upper Tribunal held that the input tax blocks introduced by the UK government were not unlawful under EU law and it refused to make reference to the CJEU in respect of this issue. The Upper Tribunal went on to consider what was meant by 'incorporated' and 'ordinarily incorporated by builders in a building of that description'. The Upper Tribunal provided useful guidance in this regard and concluded that the test of incorporation should not be determined by either reference to the English land law definition or by whether the item was part of a single supply of a zero-rated dwelling. The Upper Tribunal held that they did not consider that there should be a prescriptive test, but there must be a material degree of attachment of the item in order for it to be treated as installed or incorporated into a building. The installation must also be designed to make the item more than temporary, such as attachment either to a physical part of the building or to the supply of electricity, gas, drainage, water or ventilation. The Upper Tribunal decision will mean that most of the input tax incurred on the items claimed by TW will not be recoverable as a result of being incorporated in the building or being specifically covered by the blocking orders.

- For leases, only the first payment is zero-rated. Subsequent rents payable under the lease are exempt, and service charges are seen in the same way. The idea is that the developer can recover input tax on construction-related costs, and on professional fees etc related to the zero-rated grant, but not input tax related to the ongoing lettings, such as VAT on maintenance. (The prospect of future exempt supplies ought, strictly, to restrict the initial recovery of VAT as well, but this is not the intention, and HMRC do not take this point in practice.)
- Developers can recover input tax in anticipation of granting a major interest, but will have to repay all or some of it if they actually grant a short exempt lease. This is discussed in para **15.150**.
- If the developer incurs VAT on expenditure of £250,000 or more, the building is likely to be within the CGS. This might require a repayment to HMRC if, for example, the zero-rated grant of a lease is followed within ten years by an exempt sale of the freehold or by an overriding lease. There is more about this in para **15.296**.
- There is a further issue with any VAT incurred before the developer registered for VAT. If the VAT was incurred on capital expenditure of £250,000 or more, it might be recoverable under the CGS (see para **15.288** et seq). In other cases, it is sometimes possible to claim the VAT under special provisions in reg 111, but this is subject to strict time limits, as discussed in para **15.97**. In particular, these mean that VAT on building work that is not in the CGS can only be claimed if it was incurred within six months before registration. The best answer is to register early, and if necessary retrospectively. But HMRC will not generally agree to the backdating of an existing registration.

Short leases

[15.150] Developers that only ever intend to grant short, exempt, leases cannot recover input tax under these rules unless it is 'de minimis' (para **15.282**). Similarly, a developer who originally intends to make a zero-rated supply and then abandons that intention, and decides only to grant short leases, will normally have to repay input tax recovered to date under reg 108 (para **15.286**).

The position is more complicated where a developer retains the intention to make a zero-rated supply, but grants an exempt short lease in the meantime. In this case, the VAT is normally partly repayable to HMRC. The 1992 High Court judgments in *Briararch* and *Curtis Henderson*, noted in para **15.286**, were about this situation, but the issue acquired new importance from 2008 with the downturn in the housing market. HMRC commented in Information Sheet 07/08, setting out suggested methods of calculating the repayment due to them.

An alternative in this situation is to grant a zero-rated major interest to someone else, such as an associated company, and for it to enter into the exempt short lettings. HMRC confirmed in Revenue & Customs Brief 54/08 that they would not challenge this sort of arrangement, provided it was not used to secure recovery of input tax that would not normally be recoverable.

The position will be different if the interim lettings are as holiday accommodation, and taxable under the rules in para **15.43** et seq. This may mean that there are no exempt supplies and that input tax remains fully recoverable.

Zero-rating: person constructing an RRP/RCP building

[**15.151**] These rules apply to certain buildings for a 'relevant residential purpose' (RRP) or a 'relevant charitable purpose' (RCP). These terms are explained in para **15.155** et seq and para **15.161** et seq.

VATA 1994, Sch 8, Group 5, item 1 zero-rates:

'The first grant by a person –

(a)   constructing a building – . . .

       (ii)   intended for use solely for a relevant residential or a relevant charitable purpose . . .

of a major interest in, or in any part of, the building . . . or its site.'

'Person constructing', 'major interest' and 'first grant' have the same meanings as for dwellings, as in paras **15.141** to **15.146**, except that in some circumstances the construction of an RCP annexe can be treated as the construction of a building. This does not apply to RRP annexes. Annexes – both RRP and RCP – are considered in para **15.165** et seq.

Also as for dwellings, zero-rating extends to materials incorporated into the building, and to the 'site' of the building. As in para **15.148**, this means a reasonable plot, although for some RRP/RCP uses this might mean quite extensive grounds. Outbuildings will need to qualify as RRP/RCP in their own right. If only part of a building qualifies as RRP/RCP, zero-rating is confined to that part.

There are the same limitations on input tax recovery as for dwellings (paras **15.149** and **15.150**) – in particular, the developer may be unable to recover input tax on certain items (explained in para **15.223**) or on ongoing upkeep etc, and there can be a CGS exposure if, for example, the zero-rated grant of a lease is followed within ten years by an exempt sale of the freehold (para **15.296**). There may also be a VAT liability in the hands of the purchaser or tenant if the building ceases to be RRP/RCP, or is disposed of, within ten years of its completion (para **15.169** et seq).

'Solely'

[15.152] As seen in para **15.151**, the legislation requires the property to be intended 'solely' for RRP/RCP use. This can, however, apply to parts of buildings as well as to whole buildings – if a distinct area is solely for such use, and the rest of the building is not, the total price should be apportioned.

The 'solely' requirement is nevertheless a potential problem, particularly for RCP buildings, and HMRC accept that it 'can credibly include a de minimis'. 'Solely' does not need to be construed quite literally.

In this context, HMRC will accept 95% as 'solely'. They commented on how this might be calculated in VAT Information Sheet 13/10, whilst also saying that any method of calculation was acceptable if it accurately reflected how the building was to be used, and could be carried out and checked without undue difficulty or cost.

HMRC do not automatically accept the use of this 95% figure in every context. They have, however, confirmed that it can also be used for the zero-rating for construction works (para **15.224**), for listed buildings (paras **15.176** and **15.225**), for the 'change of use' rules in paras **15.169** to **15.171**, and, if both parties to the transaction agree, for the option to tax (paras **15.76** and **15.77**). In other cases, they seem to expect any 'de minimis' element to be a matter of individual negotiation with themselves.

HMRC's views here, including the acceptance of the 95% figure, are supposedly an interpretation of the legislation, rather than a concession. Historically, the 'solely' requirement was overtly dealt with by concession, and in particular HMRC accepted that 90% could count as 'solely' in some RCP contexts. They have, however, been reviewing their concessions following the House of Lords judgment in an income tax case, *R (on the application of Wilkinson) v IRC* ([2005] UKHL 30, [2006] STC 270), which suggested that they had a narrower discretion in these matters than had previously been supposed, and the 90% concession was withdrawn with effect from 1 July 2010. It does, however, remain residually relevant in some cases. Details of the former 90% concession can be found in earlier editions of *Tolley's Property Taxation*.

Whose 'use' is relevant?

[15.153] The RRP/RCP provisions are concerned with the intended use of the building. HMRC have vacillated over whether the interposition of another party in the supply chain is an issue, but accepted at the beginning of 2011 that it was not, and that 'use' for these purposes was solely about occupational use. So, for example, if developer A is selling the completed building to investor B, which will lease it to charity C, the sale to B can be zero-rated if C's intended use is 'solely' RRP/RCP, and it does not matter that B's use will not be. B would, however, need to be sufficiently sure of C's intentions to be able to issue a certificate to A, as discussed in para **15.154**.

Certification

[15.154] Zero-rating requires the purchaser or tenant to issue the grantor a certificate confirming the intended use of the building. It is important to retain this. The required format for the certificate is in HMRC's Notice 708. As a matter of law, the certificate must be issued before the supply is made, but HMRC do not always insist on this (see Notice 708, para 17.6).

The rules put the onus on the purchaser or tenant to demonstrate the position, and there is a potential 100% penalty for the incorrect issue of a certificate. In practice, HMRC will normally seek only the tax itself if the parties have acted in good faith, but they do expect vendors and landlords to take all reasonable steps to check the credibility of the certificate.

Zero-rating: meaning of RRP building

[15.155] VATA 1994, Sch 8, Group 5, Note 4 says that:

'Use for a relevant residential purpose means use as –

(a)   a home or other institution providing residential accommodation for children;

(b)   a home or other institution providing residential accommodation with personal care for persons in need of personal care by reason of old age, disablement, past or present dependence on alcohol or drugs or past or present mental disorder;

(c)   a hospice;

(d)   residential accommodation for students or school pupils;

(e)   residential accommodation for members of any of the armed forces;

(f)   a monastery, nunnery or similar establishment;

(g)   an institution which is the sole or main residence of at least 90 per cent of its residents;

except use as a hospital, prison or similar institution or an hotel, inn or similar establishment.'

Zero-rating requires the building, or part building, to be intended 'solely' for RRP use (see para **15.152**), and the purchaser or tenant must issue a certificate to this effect (para **15.154**).

Following the zero-rated grant, there may be a VAT charge on the purchaser or tenant if the building is then put to non-RRP/RCP use, or disposed of, within ten years – this is looked at in para **15.169** et seq.

Student accommodation

[15.156] A building or part of a building for use as 'residential accommodation for students or school pupils' is RRP, unless it is 'a hotel, inn or similar establishment'. Zero-rating requires the building or part to be intended 'solely' for such use.

There are various points of interpretation here, some of which are illustrated by the case law noted below.

• Students include people on short or part-time courses, student nurses etc.

• The accommodation needs to be for students or pupils in their capacity as such – it is not enough that they happen to be students or pupils.

• In the Higher Education sector, student accommodation is often let for conferences etc during vacations, so that the 'solely' requirement is a potential problem. Even the 95% interpretation noted in para **15.152** would severely limit such use. In practice, HMRC had accepted other use here, provided it is confined to student vacations, but not if there was an intention to allocate any surplus rooms to non-students during term-time. It should be noted that this concession was withdrawn with effect from 1 April 2015. Transitional rules are set out in Revenue & Customs Brief 14/14.

- The accommodation must be 'residential', but this can include short-term accommodation, perhaps for a course of a few days. But it must not be a 'hotel, inn or similar establishment'. This may be an issue where the establishment is primarily concerned with the commercial provision of accommodation, rather than in conjunction with education or welfare. This is similar to the question in para **15.39** as to whether the lettings of the rooms themselves are taxable, but not quite the same, since the rules there also refer to boarding houses. So student accommodation in a boarding house or something similar is potentially taxable, but the grant of a major interest in it can still be zero-rated.

- Residential accommodation includes ancillary areas such as dining rooms, kitchens, common rooms and laundry rooms, although HMRC may resist this if they are also used by non-residents. HMRC do not accept shops, bars, teaching accommodation etc as residential, and common areas – such as a reception area or corridor – will usually fall foul of the 'solely' requirement – there is no scope for apportionment here. Apportionment should be possible for areas that are not 'used', such as a plant room, but HMRC will not always accept this either.

- There are further issues if the ancillary accommodation is in a different building from the actual residential accommodation. VATA 1994, Sch 8, Group 5, Note 5 says that:

  'Where a number of buildings are –

  (a)   constructed at the same time and on the same site; and

  (b)   are intended to be used together as a unit solely for a relevant residential purpose;
         then each of those buildings, to the extent that they would not be so regarded but for this Note, are to be treated as intended for use solely for a relevant residential purpose.'

But zero-rating will not apply to, say, a dining block that is added later.

- Some student accommodation might also be capable of qualifying for zero-rating under the rules for dwellings. This would mean that non-student use was not an issue, and that additional VAT reliefs were available. But HMRC have in the past resisted this interpretation, both on the grounds that the legislation deals with the two separately, and that 'dwellings' need to fall within (English) planning use class C3 (see para **15.138**). The Tribunal agreed with them on the first of these points in *Opal Carleton Ltd* (para **15.137**). HMRC's stance here contrasts with that for capital allowances (para **9.74**), although in each case their approach is to the detriment of the taxpayer.

Selected case law – student accommodation and RRP treatment

Short stay accommodation

- In *Urdd Gobaith Cymru* (VTD 14881) accommodation for residential courses of up to a week was found to be RRP. The Tribunal concluded that 'residential accommodation' was not the same as 'a residence' and could include any overnight accommodation for whatever period. HMRC announced that they now accepted this in Business Brief 6/98, but in fact do not always do so.
- In *Denman College* (VTD 15513), the lack of catering or kitchen facilities, in accommodation used for stays of a few days, was held not to be an obstacle to RRP treatment.
- In *Capernway Missionary Fellowship of Torchbearers* (TC03750) [2014] UKFTT 626 (TC) the First-tier Tribunal considered that the duality of benefit of the accommodation to those staying meant that it was not limited to residential.

Ancillary accommodation

- The extent of zero-rating for a facilities building was considered in detail in *University of St Andrews* (VTD 19054). Space does not allow for a useful summary of this case here, and readers should consult the decision itself.
- In *Jacobs* ([2005] STC 1518), a case about a former boarding school, the Court of Appeal held that 'residential accommodation must embrace all that is ordinarily included in the accommodation in which they are residing', in this case accommodation for staff on night duty.

Homes and institutions

[15.157] RRP treatment covers a building or part of a building intended for use as:

- 'a home or other institution providing residential accommodation':
    - 'for children' (Note 4(a)); or
    - 'with personal care for persons in need of personal care by reason of old age, disablement, past or present dependence on alcohol or drugs or past or present mental disorder' (Note 4(b));
  or
- 'an institution which is the sole or main residence of at least 90% of its residents' (Note 4(g))
  but in either case excluding:
- 'use as a hospital, prison or similar institution or an hotel, inn or similar establishment'.

Zero-rating requires the building, or part building, to be intended 'solely' for such use (see para **15.152**).

There are various points of interpretation here:

- The inference is that the establishment must be institutional, with a degree of institutional living and infrastructure. HMRC's internal VAT manual 'Construction' (VCONST15140) states that ' "Institution" can be used to mean two different things. When used in an organisational sense, it means a body or organisation for the promotion of some public object, and also a building used by that body for that purpose. A home is a recognised as a place, where a collection of people live together under rules set by a third party. In this context a home or institution is a reference to the building and how it is used.'

- Under Note 4(b), the residents must require 'personal care', which HMRC see as meaning help with washing, eating etc. If they require less care, RRP treatment may not be possible under this heading; if they require more, HMRC might resist zero-rating on the grounds that the institution is similar to a hospital.

- RRP treatment applies to the building as a whole, including non-residential areas, although HMRC sometimes try, incorrectly, to deny zero-rating for office space etc.

- The law does not properly deal with institutions contained in more than one building – it refers to a building being for use *as* a home or institution, not as part of one. Note 5 (see para **15.156**) allows RRP treatment if a number of buildings are constructed at the same time, but not otherwise, so a new block – even a purely residential block – at an existing care home is not strictly RRP.

  Additional space at existing institutions was denied zero-rating for this reason in *Riverside School (Whassett) Ltd* (VTD 13170) and in *Derby YMCA* (VTD 16914). HMRC also argued it in *St Andrews Property Management Ltd* (VTD 20499), but the Tribunal disagreed – although the same charity provided other facilities on the same site, the building in question was a separate self-contained home, managed as such.

  But HMRC do not always take the point at all, and the case law includes a number of instances where they failed to do so, raising other objections to zero-rating instead, not always successfully. Examples include three of the cases noted in para **15.167** – *Bramble Lodge* (VTD 17405), *Wallis Ltd* (VTD 18012) and *Chacombe Park Development Services Ltd* (VTD 19414). *Wallis* also features below.

- The building must not be for use as a 'hotel, inn or similar establishment' – this is particularly likely to be an issue if there is no real selectivity over residents.

- The building must also not be for use as 'a hospital, prison or similar institution'. Case law suggests that hospitals and similar institutions are primarily concerned with treatment, rather than accommodation or care, and that a building is only used as a prison or similar if it forms part of the criminal justice system. See also VCONST15610.

Case law – RRP or hospital, prison or similar?

- In *General Healthcare Group Ltd* (VTD 17129) the Tribunal concluded that a residential home for the rehabilitation of people who had suffered brain injuries was RRP, and was not similar to a hospital. The medical treatment was limited, and on average residents stayed 700 days.

- In *Wallis Ltd* (VTD 18012), a residential unit was found to be a hospital, since admissions to it under the Mental Health Act were only valid if the unit was a hospital under NHS legislation. This argument was, however, rejected by the High Court in *Fenwood*, below. Another aspect of *Wallis* is noted in para **15.167**.
- In *Hospital of St John and St Elizabeth* (VTD 19141), the Tribunal adopted the definition of a hospital in NHS legislation as 'any institution for the reception and treatment of persons suffering from illness'. This did not apply where the purpose was to provide care rather than treatment. The Tribunal also rejected HMRC's contention that the NHS was 'using' the building by referring patients to it – a 'user' needed to have some legal rights to determine the use of the building and to be actively involved in its running.
- In *Fenwood Developments Ltd* ([2005] EWHC 2954 (Ch)), the High Court rejected HMRC's argument that a residential home for people suffering from mental ill-health was similar both to a hospital and to a prison. It saw a hospital as somewhere providing treatment to cure or ameliorate a medical condition, as opposed to the longer-term residential care provided here. People were admitted not because they needed medical treatment, but because they needed somewhere to live. And the fact that residents could be detained against their will did not make the establishment a 'prison or similar institution' – that required a penal element, being for people convicted of, or awaiting trial for, a criminal offence.
- *St Andrews Property Management Ltd* (VTD 20499) concerned a building to house young people with learning difficulties and 'challenging behaviour'. The Tribunal held that this was not a hospital – residents were there for long periods, and the care was largely non-medical. As noted above, the Tribunal also rejected HMRC's argument that the facility was not a separate institution.
- In *Pennine Care NHS Trust* (TC04998) Pennine NHS Trust provided services to people with mental health issues. The taxpayer appealed against a decision made by HMRC that the construction of a mental health residential unit failed to qualify for zero-rating under Item 2(a) of Group 5 of Schedule 8, VATA 1994 as a building intended for use solely for a 'relevant residential purpose'. The Tribunal observed that the unit had the personal aspects of a residence, such as individual decoration, catering and laundry facilities. There was also a social aspect to the unit in that residents went to the theatre and sporting events, etc with staff. In the Tribunal's view, these features pointed away from the unit being a 'hospital or similar institution', rather their primary function was to care for the residents and provide a home. The Tribunal concluded that the unit was not intended for use as a 'hospital or similar institution'. Appeal allowed.

Monasteries, nunneries etc

[15.158] A building or part of a building intended for use as 'a monastery, nunnery or similar establishment' is RRP. HMRC accept that this covers any establishment where followers of any recognised faith or religious order live and worship, but not schools at such establishments.

Zero-rating requires the building or part to be intended 'solely' for such use (see para **15.152**).

There are some of the same points here as with care homes etc. RRP treatment is not confined to residential areas. But it does require either that the building houses the entire monastery etc, or that all the buildings are built at once, so that strictly a new building at an existing establishment cannot be RRP.

Where buildings are monasteries etc and fail to qualify as RRP, they will often be RCP.

Hospices

[15.159] A building or part of a building for use as a hospice is RRP. Zero-rating requires the building or part to be intended 'solely' for such use (see para **15.152**).

HMRC appear to accept that a hospice is not similar to a hospital, which would exclude it from RRP treatment, but they do not see non-residential care at a hospice as RRP. Where this is provided they expect RRP treatment to be confined to the residential areas. In other cases the entire building should qualify. There are the same potential problems with additional buildings as for care homes etc.

HMRC has confirmed in Revenue & Customs Brief 2/17 that the grant of the first major interest in a hospice would also be zero-rated if the relevant conditions outlined in the Brief were satisfied.

Where RRP treatment does not apply, RCP treatment may be available instead.

The armed forces

[15.160] 'Residential accommodation for members of any of the armed forces' is RRP. This is drafted in the same way as for student accommodation etc, and the same points apply where relevant.

Zero-rating requires the building or part building to be intended 'solely' for such use (again, see para **15.152**). In HMRC's view, this excludes married quarters, but these will generally qualify for zero-rating as dwellings.

Care homes

[15.160A] HMRC have released Revenue & Customs Brief 2/17 which clarifies their position regarding the VAT treatment of care homes as a result of the decision in *Pennine Care NHS Trust* (see para **15.157**). HMRC have confirmed that the first grant of a major interest in a building that is intended to be used solely as a care home is zero-rated. HMRC state that they consider that a care home is a place that provides residential accommodation with personal care to people who are in need of such care. Care could be needed due to old age, disability, past or present dependence on drugs/alcohol or a present or past mental disorder.

Zero-rating: meaning of RCP building

[15.161] VATA 1994, Sch 8, Group 5, Note 6 says that:

'Use for a relevant charitable purpose means use by a charity in either or both the following ways, namely –

(a)   otherwise than in the course or furtherance of a business;

(b)   as a village hall or similarly in providing social or recreational facilities for a local community.'

Zero-rating requires the building, or part building, to be intended 'solely' for RCP use (see para **15.152**), and the purchaser or tenant must issue a certificate to this effect (para **15.154**).

It is the intended use, at the time of supply, that is relevant.

Some minor non-business use could previously be ignored by concession, and this remains residually relevant in some cases (para **15.151**).

Where zero-rating does apply, there may be a VAT charge on the purchaser or tenant if the building is put to non-RRP/RCP use, or disposed of, within ten years – see para **15.169** et seq.

Whether an organisation is a charity is a matter of general law, and does not necessarily involve registration as such.

Non-business

[**15.162**] 'Business' is a broad concept, and does not require a profit motive. The treatment of charities can be complex, and most have a mixture of business and non-business activities.

Uses that might qualify for zero-rating include places of worship, non-fee paying schools and heavily subsidised welfare provision, but even here there will usually be some element of business use – such as the sale of books or postcards in a church – and zero-rating often relies on the points in para **15.152**. Offices will usually struggle to qualify because of the range of activities conducted from them. Some relevant case law is summarised below.

Also, however, Article 13 of the Directive provides that, in general, bodies governed by public law are not considered as taxable persons where they engage in activities as public authorities. In the *Cardiff Community Housing*, *City of London* and *Edinburgh Telford* cases noted below, the Tribunal accepted that this meant activities were non-business. HMRC have, however, succeeded in other cases, also noted below, and in Revenue & Customs Brief 27/08 they suggested that Article 13 only applied to public sector bodies forming part of the UK public administration, such as a government department or a local authority, and not to other bodies which were, for example, merely state-regulated or state-funded. Legislation directly implementing the Article can be found at VATA 1994, s 41A. No doubt this will be designed to give further comfort to HMRC's interpretation.

Charities – business or non-business? – selected case law

Playgroups

*   A playgroup, funded by voluntary contributions from parents, was non-business in *Newtownbutler Playgroup Ltd* (VTD 13741).
*   The High Court also saw a day nursery as non-business in *St Paul's Community Project Ltd* ([2005] STC 95). Fees were charged, but at about 70% of cost.

Housing associations

- The letting of social housing was seen as non-business in *Cardiff Community Housing Association Ltd* (VTD 16841), mainly because of the way the activity was regulated by government. The Tribunal also thought that the provisions about bodies governed by public law, now in Article 13 of the Directive, applied.
- The Tribunal came to a different conclusion in *Riverside Housing Association Ltd* (VTD 19341). There were differences between the cases, but the Tribunal disagreed with aspects of *Cardiff*, including the relevance of Article 13. The High Court ([2006] EWHC 2383 (Ch)) upheld this decision. HMRC naturally prefer this case to *Cardiff*.
- In *Ardenglen Developments Ltd (ADL)* (VTD 19906), office accommodation was constructed by A. Long leases were granted by A to B, and by B to C. C was a charity whose use was non-business; B and A were respectively a housing association and its subsidiary. HMRC alleged that A's and B's use of the property was business and prevented zero-rating. The Tribunal disagreed – it was C's occupational use that was relevant, but in any case A's and B's activities did not seem to be business. A's lease to B was therefore zero-rated.

Schools

- In *Morrison's Academy Boarding Houses Association* (CS 1977, [1978] STC 1) the Court of Session held that the provision of boarding for school pupils was a business activity.
- A fee-paying school was in business in *Leighton Park School* (VTD 9392) – the predominant concern was the making of supplies for consideration, even if not for profit.
- In *St Dunstan's Educational Foundation* ([1999] STC 381), a charity provided a sports hall for no charge to a fee-paying school. This was not RCP – the school's use was business, and the charity was not 'using' the building. This case is also noted in para 15.164.
- In *City of London Corporation* (VTD 17892), fee-paying schools were non-business, but only because the appellant was a public body under what is now Article 13.
- In *Donaldson's College* (VTD 19258), a charitable school for the deaf was funded by pupils' local authorities and from grants etc. The Tribunal decided that it was not predominantly concerned with making supplies for consideration and was non-business.
- School education was also found to be non-business in *The Sheiling Trust* (VTD 19472), despite the strong expectation of parental 'contributions'.
- In *Quarriers* (VTD 20670), a school for children with emotional difficulties was found to be non-business, despite the high level of fees charged to local authorities, on the grounds that the charity was not predominantly concerned with the making of supplies for consideration.

Further and higher education

Education is generally fee-paying from the age of 19, even if the fees are met by the local authority. Thus only sixth form colleges are generally seen as non-business.

- The provision of higher education was seen as a business activity in *Royal Academy of Music* (VTD 11871). Article 13 also did not apply.

- But grant-funded research was a non-business activity in *University of Southampton* ([2006] EWHC 528 (Ch)), the High Court rejecting the argument that it was business because it supported other, business, activities.
- And the Court of Session in *Edinburgh Telford College* ([2006] CSIH 13) saw further education as non-business, even where fees were charged, on the basis of Article 13. HMRC were refused leave to appeal, but do not accept this outcome, claiming that they had argued the wrong point.
- The High Court rejected non-business treatment of education based on Article 13 in *Chancellor, Masters and Scholars of the University of Cambridge* ([2009] EWHC 434 (Ch), [2009] STC 1288).
- The provision of free dining to academics etc was held to be part of the broader business activities of *St John's College, Oxford* (TC00424).
- The Tribunal in *Wakefield College* (TC00948) confirmed that the provision of education was a business activity where fees were charged, and that the college did not benefit from Article 13. The Upper Tribunal ([2016] UKUT 19 (TCC)) also held in favour of HMRC concluding that some of the college's supplies of education were made in the course or furtherance of a business so that the construction of a new building was not zero-rated.
- In *Longridge on the Thames* ([2016] EWCA Civ 930), the taxpayer was a registered charity providing education to young people in water-related activities. It constructed a new building which it considered should be zero-rated on the basis that the building was intended for use solely for relevant charitable purposes ie for non-economic activities. The charity charged fees for its courses and other facilities, which were substantially subsidised by donation income and by the time/skills received from a large volunteer body. HMRC considered that the charity was carrying out economic activities and the construction of the building was therefore liable to VAT. The Court of Appeal held that there was a direct link between the supply of services made by the charity and the consideration received and when this was considered together with the fact that the activities that were undertaken on a permanent and regular basis this amounted to an economic activity. As a result the construction services were liable to VAT as they were not connected with the construction of an RCP building.

Other cases

- In *League of Friends of Kingston Hospital* (VTD 12764) a charity commissioned a building which it provided, for no charge, to a hospital. This was not RCP since it was the hospital, not the charity, that was using the building, and the hospital itself was not a charity.
- In *St Dunstans Roman Catholic Church Southborough* (VTD 15472) garages provided to priests were RCP, the Tribunal seeing any personal use of cars as irrelevant.
- HMRC accept that welfare services provided at 15% or more below cost are non-business. But they refused to apply this in *St Dunstan's* (VTD 17896), a case about a care home, and despite the fees being 80% or more below cost the Tribunal concluded that the home was in business. It is, however, understood that HMRC conceded the case rather than face an appeal. Another aspect of this case is noted in para 15.39.

- *Quarriers* (VTD 20660) concerned an epilepsy assessment centre, to which local authorities would refer people for a fee. This was held to be non-business – the activity was not predominantly concerned with making supplies for consideration, and these were not services commonly provided for profit. (Note that this is a different appeal, by the same appellant, from the *Quarriers* case described above.)
- In *Jeanfield Swifts Football Club* (VTD 20689) a local amateur sports club was held not to be in business despite its modest income from gate money, refreshments, pitch letting etc – the Tribunal saw no predominant business purpose in these activities.

Non-buildings

[15.163] Some structures for the non-business use of a charity do not qualify for zero-rating because they are not buildings. In *Upper Don Walk Trust* (VTD 19476), a case about a footbridge, the Tribunal said that:

'In our view, the word "building" connotes an enclosure of sorts. It will enclose a volume of space or provide a place within which persons or things can be accommodated. All the structures which, in ordinary speech would undoubtedly be regarded as buildings have this characteristic in common: for example a house, a factory, a warehouse, an amphitheatre. A building will usually have walls and, although not invariably, a roof.'

In the same way, a wall was not a building in *Adath Yisroel Synagogue* (VTD 20808), and nor was an open air 'skate park' in *Wheeled Sports 4 Hereford Ltd* (TC01059). The same point will generally deny zero-rating for memorials, but charities commissioning these can generally benefit from the VAT refund scheme described in para **15.278**.

Village halls etc

[15.164] A building will qualify for zero-rating under this heading if it is intended 'solely' for use by a charity 'as a village hall or similarly in providing social or recreational facilities for a local community'. This only clearly applies to old-fashioned general purpose community halls, serving a small geographical area and population – a village or a specific part of a town – and buildings that are for more specific uses, or that serve a wider area, may well not qualify. Again, the 'solely' test is subject to the points in para **15.152** and the certification requirement in para **15.154**.

Some case law is briefly summarised below, followed by HMRC's guidance.

Village halls etc – selected case law

Cases where RCP treatment succeeded

- *Shinewater Association Football Club* (VTD 12938) – a sports pavilion with other community use.
- *Bennachie Leisure Centre Association* (VTD 14276) – serving a six mile radius of rural Aberdeenshire.
- *Ledbury Amateur Dramatic Society* (VTD 16845) – a theatre, designed and used for wide-ranging community purposes.

- *Southwick Community Association* (VTD 17601) – where HMRC had resisted zero-rating because parts of the premises were dedicated to specific purposes.
- *Sport in Desford* (VTD 18914) – where HMRC had objected that community use was incidental, and that the organisation had not been registered as a charity at the time – the Tribunal found that it had nevertheless been a charity.
- *Hanbury Charity* (VTD 20126) – where the Tribunal rejected HMRC's contention that zero-rating for village halls was confined to small ad hoc charities actually running the hall.
- *Jeanfield Swifts Football Club* (VTD 20689) – where the Tribunal was unimpressed by HMRC's argument that a sports club's pavilion was not primarily for general community use. But the appeal essentially succeeded on a non-business argument, as noted in para **15.162**.
- *Caithness Rugby Football Club* ([2016] UKUT 354 (TCC), [2016] STC 2028) – the Upper Tribunal upheld the First-Tier Tribunal decision that the designation 'village hall' did not require the management of the hall to be vested in the local community. It was only necessary for the local community to benefit from the provision of social and recreational facilities. The Upper Tribunal stated that the existence or absence of direction and control was relevant but it was not necessarily a decisive requirement. The fact that in this case the clubhouse was built and used principally by the rugby club does not prevent it being considered as a village hall providing it operates and provides facilities as a village hall would and it accommodates all users requirements.

Cases found not to be RCP

- *Ormiston Charitable Trust* (VTD 13187) – used for too narrow a section of the population, from too a wide geographical area.
- *Jubilee Hall Recreation Centre Ltd* ([1999] STC 381) – a sport and fitness centre in Covent Garden – not a 'local community'.
- *St Dunstan's Educational Foundation* ([1999] STC 381) – a school sports hall (also noted in para **15.162**).
- *South Molton Swimming Pool Trustees* (VTD 16495) – a swimming pool operating too commercially, and serving too wide an area.
- *London Federation of Clubs for Young People* (VTD 17079) – facilities serving too wide an area, and too much under the direction of the Federation. The Tribunal saw a village hall as having modest facilities, run by the village people, constituting the centre of village life and being used for local events such as village fetes, local drama, cricket team suppers and whist drives.
- *Beth Johnson Housing Association Ltd* (VTD 17095) – serving too wide an area.
- *Yarburgh Children's Trust* ([2002] STC 207) – a building for a playgroup – use too limited. But the appellant succeeded on a non-business argument.
- *South Aston Community Association* (VTD 17702) – on the incorrect grounds that a 'village hall' had to occupy the whole building.
- *Nutley Hall Ltd* (VTD 18242) – because the hall was commissioned by a welfare charity in that capacity, rather than by the community.

Village halls etc – HMRC's views

The following material appears in HMRC's Notice 708 (August 2016). See also VCONST16600.

'Village halls and similar buildings:

A building falls within this category when the following characteristics are present:

- there is a high degree of local community involvement in the building's operation and activities; and
- there is a wide variety of activities carried on in the building, the majority of which are for social and/or recreational purposes (including sporting).

Note: Users of the building need not be confined to the local community but can come from further afield.

Any part of the building which cannot be used for a variety of social or recreational activities cannot be seen as being used as a village hall.

The term 'similar' refers to buildings run by communities that are not villages but who are organised in a similar way to a village hall committee. It does not include buildings that provide a range of activities associated with village halls but who are not organised on these lines.

In order to be similar to a village hall, a charity would have trustees who are drawn from representatives of local groups who intend to use the hall. The trustees would therefore be made up of individuals from say the Women's Institute, the Bridge Club, the Amateur Dramatics Society, etc. The building would be hired out to the local community for a modest fee for use by a range of local clubs and groups, and also for wedding receptions, birthday parties, playgroups and other leisure interests. Whilst the size, and level of provision and facilities will be decided by the local community, we would at the very least expect the principal feature of a village hall to be a large multi-purpose hall where members of different households can meet to undertake shared activities.

The emphasis for a village hall should be on promoting the use of the facilities for the benefit of the whole community rather than for the benefit of one particular group. An important characteristic is that the building must be available for use by all sectors of the community. It must therefore be capable of meeting the social and recreational needs of the local community at large and not be predominantly confined to a special interest group. It should also be arranged on a first come first served basis and no single group should have priority over all the others.

On the other hand, a building designed for a particular sporting activity, for example, a cricket pavilion or football clubhouse and ancillary facilities is not seen as being similar to a village hall. Whilst these types of buildings are often made available to the wider community; this would be required to fit in around the sports club's usage. In essence it would be the sports club who would determine how the building was to be used and not the wider community. However please see the decision in *Caithness Rugby Football Club* above where the clubhouse was treated as a village hall for VAT purposes.

Buildings that are *not* typically seen as being similar to village halls are:

- community swimming pools;

- community theatres;
- membership clubs (although community associations charging a notional membership fee can be excluded); or
- community amateur sports clubs.

Buildings that are seen as being similar to village halls when the characteristics noted above are present:

- scout or guide huts (please note that where scout or guide huts are used purely for scouting and guiding activities, they are not being used as village halls but neither are they being used for business purposes);
- sports pavilions;
- church halls;
- community centres; and
- community sports centres.'

Zero-rating: RRP/RCP buildings – extensions, annexes etc

[**15.165**] VATA 1994, Sch 8, Group 5, Note 16 says that:

'For the purpose of this Group, the construction of a building does not include–

(a)   the conversion, reconstruction or alteration of an existing building; or

(b)   any enlargement of, or extension to, an existing building except to the extent the enlargement or extension creates an additional dwelling or dwellings; or

(c)   subject to Note (17) below, the construction of an annexe to an existing building.'

Note 17 says that:

'Note 16(c) above shall not apply where the whole or a part of an annexe is intended for use solely for a relevant charitable purpose and –

(a)   the annexe is capable of functioning independently from the existing building; and

(b)   the only access or where there is more than one means of access, the main access to:

(i)   the annexe is not via the existing building; and

(ii)   the existing building is not via the annexe.'

Paragraph **15.142** looks at Note 16 in relation to dwellings, but some aspects of these provisions are more often relevant to RRP/RCP buildings. There have been particular difficulties over what constitutes an annexe, not least because these fall on the wrong side of the line for RRP use, but potentially on the right side of it for RCP.

Linkage

[**15.166**] These issues are often thought of in terms of whether there is internal linkage between the old and new structures. This has not actually featured as a test in the legislation since 1995, but (non-emergency) internal linkage may still be a pointer towards treatment as an enlargement or extension, and an intention to create a link may be unhelpful. An annexe, on the other hand, might be a free-standing building.

Annexes

[15.167] There are some difficulties with the meaning of an 'annexe'. Relevant case law is summarised below and, in connection with RCP annexes, in para **15.168**. This – and in particular the High Court judgments in *Cantrell* – suggests that:

- an annexe is subordinate to – and not merely associated with – an existing building;
- factors here include appearance, layout and how it is capable of functioning – but not its actual or intended use or the terms of planning permission;
- a free-standing building can be an annexe, at least if it is close to the main building;
- an annexe can alternatively be internally linked to an existing building, but the link needs to be tenuous and the annexe needs to look like something distinct – otherwise it will be an enlargement or extension.

HMRC, however, give a rather different view in Notice 708. This material is also set out below, but in particular it departs from *Cantrell* by rejecting the idea of a separate building being an annexe, by ignoring the subordinate nature of an annexe and by emphasising the activities to be carried on in it.

The further rules about RCP annexes are considered in para **15.168**.

What is an 'annexe'? HMRC's views

HMRC's Notice 708 includes the following material. As noted above, this differs from case law on some key points.

'An annexe can be either a structure attached to an existing building or a structure detached from it. A detached structure is treated for VAT purposes as a separate building. The comments in this section only apply to attached structures.

There is no legal definition of "annexe". In order to be considered an annexe, a structure must be attached to an existing building but not in such a way so as to be considered an enlargement or extension of that building.

An enlargement or extension would involve making the building bigger so as to provide extra space for the activities already carried out in the existing building. Examples of an enlargement or extension are a classroom or a sports hall added to an existing school building or an additional function room (or kitchen or toilet block) added to an existing village hall.

On the other hand, an annexe would provide extra space for activities distinct from but associated with the activities carried out in the existing building. The annexe and the existing building would form two separate parts of a single building that operate independently of each other. Examples of an annexe are a day hospice added to an existing residential hospice, a self-contained suite of rooms added to an existing village hall, a church hall added to an existing church or a nursery added to a school building.'

Selected case law on residential annexes etc

An RRP enlargement, extension or annexe cannot be zero-rated.

- *Elliott* ([1993] STC 369, QB) concerned the construction of a new block at a nursing home. The new block was six times the size of the existing building, and was linked to it by an internal passageway. The law at the time said that construction did not include an extension to an existing building which provided for internal access to it. The High Court concluded that this applied here.

- In *Menzies* (VTD 15733), a new residential block was built one metre away from an existing building. After a four week interval, a link was constructed between them. HMRC said this made the new block an extension, but the Tribunal disagreed and accepted zero-rating for it.

- In *Strowbridge* (VTD 16521) , what was supposedly a new nursing home was built alongside an existing nursing home and operated separately for three weeks before the building was knocked through and the businesses merged. The Tribunal accepted that this was a genuine change of mind, and that the new work was zero-rated.

- In *Bramble Lodge* (VTD 17405), the construction of a new free-standing block at a nursing home was followed, a few weeks later, by the construction of a glazed link between it and the original building. The Tribunal saw the block as an annexe, apparently not because of the link but because it was used as an adjunct to the existing building.

- In *Wallis Ltd* (VTD 18012), a new building was constructed and subsequently linked via corridors to other buildings on the site. In view of its appearance, size, and distance from the pre-existing buildings the Tribunal rejected HMRC's contention that it was an annexe. Another aspect of this case is noted in para **15.157**.

- In *Cantrell* ([2003] STC 486), a new unit was built alongside an existing unit at a nursing home. There was only emergency access between the two, which were intended for different categories of resident. The High Court concluded that the new unit was not an annexe, holding that:

  'An annexe is an adjunct or accessory to something else, such as a document. When used in relation to a building it is referring to a supplementary structure, be it a room, a wing or a separate building.'

  It also noted that an annexe and the existing building:

  'may be physically separate so that the connection between the two is by way of some other association'.

  And in an earlier judgment ([2000] STC 100) in the same case, the High Court had also held that:

  ' . . . regard must be only to the physical character of the buildings in course of construction at the date of the relevant supply . . . the subjective intentions on the part of Mr and Mrs Cantrell as to their future use, their subsequent use and the terms of the planning permission regulating their future use are irrelevant, save only in so far as they throw light upon the potential use and functioning of the buildings.'

  As noted above, HMRC have proved reluctant to take these various points on board.

- In *Allan Water Developments Ltd* (VTD 19131), a new care home was constructed alongside an existing care home, with which it shared kitchen facilities and was linked by a corridor. Different categories of resident occupied the homes, and they did not have normal access to the corridor. The Tribunal accepted that the new home was not an annexe.

- In *Henshaws Society for Blind People* (VTD 19373) an entrance block was constructed which was clearly an extension to an existing building. At the same time, a new residential block was built alongside the entrance block.

It was attached only to the entrance block, and the fire doors between them were normally kept locked, but it extended over the entrance block, and the Tribunal saw the two blocks as a single structure, and so as a single extension.

- In *Chacombe Park Development Services Ltd* (VTD 19414) a new residential block was built two metres from an existing care home, and linked to it by a fire escape. The Tribunal concluded that it was not an extension or annexe since the buildings were designed to provide different levels of care.

- In *TL Smith Properties Limited and Tregwilyn Lodge Limited* (TC01375) the First Tier-Tribunal considered that a nursing home built adjacent to an existing building (care home) comprised an enlargement or extension. This was on the basis that the two were linked and shared various facilities.

- *Astral Construction Ltd* [2015] UKUT 0021 (TCC) concerned a disused church and other buildings. The surrounding buildings were demolished and new ones constructed in their place which were linked to the disused church (which was not demolished). HMRC argued that the works comprised an extension etc of the church and as such should be standard-rated. The First-tier Tribunal (TC02773) applied a test of fact, degree and impression and considered that the new works were so large in comparison to the size of the disused church that they could not be said to be an enlargement. The Upper Tribunal agreed.

RCP annexes

[15.168] An annexe, or part of an annexe, intended 'solely' for RCP use can be zero-rated, subject to the conditions in Note 17 (para **15.165**), and the general points in paras **15.152** and **15.154**. But in practice zero-rating can be difficult to achieve, as the case law shows. The structure must actually be an annexe, and not an extension or enlargement to an existing building – similarity of use, or structural integration, is generally problematic. It must be capable of functioning independently of the existing building – HMRC say that they will ignore shared electricity, water etc, but do not always do so. And the main access to each must not be via the other.

Case law on RCP annexes etc

An RCP annexe can be zero-rated if the conditions in Note 17 are met (see para 15.165). There is no zero-rating for any other type of annexe, or for any RCP enlargement or extension.

Cases where zero-rating applied

- *Grace Baptist Church* (VTD 16093) – a new chapel house adjoining a church. The buildings were used separately, largely at different times, and the chapel house had its own address, heating and fire alarm systems, and water and gas meters. HMRC consider this case to have been wrongly decided and do not accept it as a precedent.
- *Torfaen Voluntary Alliance* (VTD 18797) – charity offices alongside a church hall, with their own facilities and a very different appearance from the church hall.

- *Castle Caereinion Recreation Association* (VTD 18303) – a new room abutting a village hall, with its own entrance and parking and apparently capable of functioning independently. But another new room was too closely integrated with the hall to qualify.
- *Kahal Imrei Chaim Ltd* (VTD 19625) – a new synagogue adjoining, and linked internally to, the charity's existing buildings. Unusually, this was held to be zero-rated not as an annexe but as a new building.
- *Longparish Church of England Primary School* (VTD 20464) – a new hall and a playgroup room, distinct from the existing building and capable of being isolated and used separately, despite actual use of the hall by the school as well as others. But new teaching rooms were too closely integrated to qualify.

Cases where zero-rating did not apply

- *Macnamara* (VTD 16039) – additional classrooms – too closely integrated with the existing building, and incapable of functioning separately.
- *Yeshurun Hebrew Congregation* (VTD 16487) – too closely integrated, and incapable of functioning separately.
- *Thomas Rotherham College* (VTD 17841) – three storey sports hall – individual floors could not be considered separately – the structure was a single extension.
- *Roman Catholic Diocese of Shrewsbury* (VTD 17900) – meeting room at a church – result looked like a single building, and access tests apparently not met.
- *Kids Church* (VTD 18145) – 'annexe' within an existing building – too closely integrated, and access via external wall of existing building.
- *Knowsley Associates Ltd* (VTD 18180) – sixth form centre at community college – too closely integrated, provided main access to parts of existing building, heating facilities relied on existing building.
- *Alzheimer's Society* (VTD 18318) – day centre partly within an existing church – held to be alteration and extension.
- *Evans (t/a BSEC)* (VTD 18432) – changing area etc alongside sports hall – too closely integrated with it.
- *Archdiocese of Southwark Commission for Schools and Colleges* (VTD 18883) – additional classrooms – too closely integrated and did not meet access tests.
- *Parochial Church Council of St Andrews* (VTD 19061) – too integrated with existing building, shared heating system with it, access tests not met.
- *Trustees of Elim Church, Tamworth* (VTD 19190) – new day nursery, too closely integrated with church building to be an annexe. But HMRC were wrong to consider functional independence in terms of the church relying on the nursery's toilets – it was the annexe that had to be independent, not the existing building.
- *Henshaws Society for Blind People* (VTD 19373) (see also para **15.167**) – too integrated with existing building, and shared services with extension built at the same time.
- *Abercych Village Association* (VTD 20746) – too interconnected, also providing additional kitchen and toilet facilities for use in conjunction with existing village hall.
- *Treetops Hospice Trust* (TC01350) – a new block connected to an existing building by internal doors and a room new to the existing building straddled the footprint of both buildings.

Zero-rating: RRP/RCP buildings – 'change of use'

[15.169] Zero-rating for RRP and RCP buildings depends on their intended use. VATA 1994, Sch 10, Part 2 creates a VAT liability in some cases where there is a subsequent change of circumstances. The person liable to the VAT is the person that originally received the zero-rated supply.

The issue only arises if:

- there has been a zero-rated supply under the rules in para **15.151**, **15.172**, **15.224** or **15.229** (but not para **15.176**, **15.225** or **15.230**); and
- the change of circumstances occurs within ten years of completion of the building (or RCP annexe); completion here refers to the original completion, so if the zero-rating was for a conversion the liability will not usually arise. Consider also the potential impact of Revenue & Customs Brief 14/14.

There are no corresponding provisions where the original supply was taxable at 5%.

The provisions were amended with effect from 1 March 2011, but the previous rules continue to apply to buildings completed before that date, and so will potentially remain relevant until 2021.

References below to 'non-qualifying' use are to use that is not 'solely' RRP or RCP, such that the building would not now qualify for zero-rating under the RRP or RCP rules. Non-qualifying use does, however, include use as dwellings.

Buildings completed before 1 March 2011

[15.170] For buildings completed before 1 March 2011, the liability can arise in two ways:

- If the person puts the building to their own non-qualifying use, they should account for output tax on a 'self-supply'. The output tax is calculated as the VAT originally saved through the RRP/RCP zero-rating (ie that would otherwise have been chargeable on it), reduced by 10% for each full year of qualifying use.
  The same amount of VAT is treated as input tax, and is recoverable according to the use of the building going forward. So there is a net cost to the extent that that use is exempt or non-business. If the value of the self-supply is £250,000 or more, the VAT is also generally adjustable under the CGS (para **15.288** et seq).
  HMRC's guidance suggests that, rather than being based on the original saving, the VAT on the self-supply is based on 20% (ie the current VAT rate) of the value of the original zero-rated supply. This is incorrect. In reality, the liability is likely to be mitigated by the fact that, had the zero-rated supply not been zero-rated, it would normally have been subject to VAT at a rate lower than 20%, or not at all. If it was a sale or lease, rather than building work, it might well have been exempt had it not been zero-rated, so that there is no liability on a change of use. It appears that HMRC do not understand these points.

If the change of use affects only part of the building (or part of the part that originally benefitted from zero-rating), the charge is reduced proportionately. But there is no allowance for a minor change affecting the whole building. If a building qualified for zero-rating because it was intended to be put at least 95% to RRP/RCP use (see para **15.152**), even a temporary change to 94% triggers the self-supply. HMRC recognise that this is disproportionate, and in practice may well not expect the VAT to be accounted for. They have specifically confirmed this in cases where an RCP building originally qualified for zero-rating only because of the previous 90% concession (also para **15.152**).

- If the person sells or lets the building for non-qualifying use, the sale or letting is standard-rated. This does not apply if the purchaser or tenant only changes the use at a later date. Strictly, the standard-rating overrides all other treatments, including as non-business or as a TOGC.

Buildings completed on or after 1 March 2011

[15.171] For buildings completed on or after 1 March 2011, the liability takes the form of a self-supply in all cases. It arises if:

- The building is put to non-qualifying use, whether by the person themselves or by someone else, such as a tenant. It is still the person that originally qualified for zero-rating that is liable to the self-supply, so it is advisable to ensure that any cost from this can be passed on to a tenant.
- The building is disposed of, even if there is no actual change of use and the new owner continues to use the building in the same way. The disposal itself is still a supply, or perhaps a TOGC, in the normal way.

The self-supply is calculated in the same way as explained in para **15.170**, except that:

- The output tax is reduced by 1/120th for each complete month since the building was completed, rather than by 10% for each complete year.
- As well as recognising a change of part of the use of the building, the rules also accommodate a partial change of the whole. If the continuing 'qualifying' use is 60%, the output tax due on the self-supply is reduced by 60%. And if it later falls to 50%, there is a further self-supply for the 10% difference. But there is no adjustment in the other direction if it subsequently rises again.

In the same way as for the rules in para **15.170** HMRC do, however, continue to suggest in guidance that the output tax is based on the current rate of VAT applied to the value of the original zero-rated supply, rather than on the VAT originally saved.

The same amount of VAT is treated as input tax, and is recoverable according to the future use of the building. If the value of the self-supply is £250,000 or more, the VAT is also generally adjustable under the CGS (para **15.288** et seq). In the case of a disposal, the input tax on the self-supply is recoverable according to the treatment of the disposal, and so in full if the disposal is taxable.

In *Balhousie Holdings Ltd* (TC05131), the taxpayer (BH) operated a number of care homes and it made a decision to construct a new care home. The land and the new property were owned by a separately registered subsidiary FC. FC sold the land and newly constructed property to another subsidiary, BC, who was a member of BH's VAT group and this company operated the care home. The sale of the completed care home by FC to BC was treated as a zero-rated grant of a major interest in a relevant residential property. BC then sold the property onto a third party, in order to pay off the debts arising from the construction of the care home, who then granted a long-term leasehold interest in the property back to BC. The leasehold interest contained a condition that the property must be used as a care home. HMRC ruled that the sale of the property to the third party resulted in BC becoming liable to a change of use self-supply charge in respect of the original zero-rated grant of the major interest. HMRC considered that for the purposes of VATA 1994, Sch 10, para 36(2) BC had disposed of its entire interest in the property to the third party. In HMRC's opinion, the grant of the leasehold interest could not be taken into consideration as they were separate transactions for VAT purposes. The Tribunal considered the wording of para 36(2) and held that it required the taxpayer to relinquish all and every interest in the relevant property before the change of use charge would arise. In this case, BC had retained an interest under the sale and leaseback transaction. The transaction needed to be looked at in context – the parties had entered into the sale and leaseback arrangement rather than seek finance from a bank, as a result, the transactions needed to be considered together as one would not have happened without the other. The legislation intended to deal with ensuring that the property continued to be used as a relevant residential property and how this might be policed. In this case, BC's continued use of the property remained the same before and after the sale. Appeal allowed.

Zero-rating: person converting for residential use

[15.172] VATA 1994, Sch 8, Group 5, item 1 zero-rates:

'The first grant by a person –

(b) converting a non-residential building or a non-residential part of a building into a building designed as a dwelling or number of dwellings or a building intended for use solely for a relevant residential purpose,

of a major interest in, or in any part of, the building, dwelling or its site.'

The meaning of 'non-residential' and 'person converting' are considered in paras **15.173** and **15.174**. In other respects, these rules are essentially the same as for a person constructing buildings of this kind, as in paras **15.134** et seq and **15.151** et seq. In particular:

- 'Solely' for RRP use means the same as in para **15.152** et seq, although in this context HMRC have not specifically confirmed that 'solely' can be interpreted as 95%. The purchaser or tenant must issue a certificate of intended use as at para **15.154**.
- 'Major interest' and 'first grant' have the same meaning as in paras **15.145** and **15.146**. But for a 'person constructing', zero-rating is still possible if the building has been occupied since the work was carried

out, perhaps under a short lease. This is not the case here, since 'converting' status depends on the use of the building prior to the grant, as explained in para **15.173**, so any later grant of a major interest will be exempt.

- For dwellings, restricted occupancy rights potentially prevent zero-rating in the same way as in para **15.147**.
- The points in para **15.148** about the extent of zero-rating also apply here, although in this case a garage included in a zero-rated grant of a dwelling or dwellings can have been either constructed, or converted from non-residential use, at the same time as the main building is converted.
- The points in paras **15.149** and **15.150** about input tax recovery also apply here – in particular, input tax may be blocked on certain items (explained in para **15.223**), and VAT cannot be recovered on ongoing maintenance etc after the zero-rated grant of a lease. But whereas a 'person constructing' may be able to take partial VAT recovery by granting a major interest having already granted a short exempt lease, this is not usually possible here, since the major interest will also be exempt if the property has been occupied in the meantime.

Actually obtaining zero-rating is, however, often more important here than for a person constructing, because there will be more input tax to recover, and so a higher cost if the sale or lease is exempt. Whereas someone commissioning a new dwelling can benefit from zero-rating for the building work, someone converting a building to a dwelling is likely to pay VAT, albeit at the 5% rate, unless they are a housing association. (These points are explained in para **15.220** et seq.) Where only a short occupational lease etc will be granted, it is therefore common practice to grant a zero-rated major interest to an associated entity, which in turn lets the property to the occupier.

Non-residential

[15.173] The building (or part of a building) must previously have been non-residential.

VATA 1994, Sch 8, Group 5, Note 7 says that:

'For the purposes of item 1(b), and for the purposes of these Notes so far as having effect for the purposes of item 1(b), a building or part of a building is "non-residential" if –

(a)   it is neither designed, nor adapted, for use –
    (i)   as a dwelling or number of dwellings, or
    (ii)   for a relevant residential purpose; or
(b)   it is designed, or adapted, for such use but –

    (i)   it was constructed more than 10 years before the grant of the major interest; and
    (ii)   no part of it has, in the period of 10 years immediately preceding the grant, been used as a dwelling or for a relevant residential purpose.'

Note 8 adds that:

'References to a non-residential building or a non-residential part of a building do not include a reference to a garage occupied together with a dwelling.'

'Relevant residential purpose' has the same meaning as in para **15.155** et seq, but in the context of past use there is no 'solely' requirement.

This is often straightforward – a building that was only ever an office, warehouse etc before the conversion will qualify, as will buildings that were originally constructed as dwellings but have been in some other use, or empty, throughout the last ten years. But there can be some complications:

- It is not always clear when and whether a property has been 'used as a dwelling'. HMRC might expect evidence in the form of electoral roll and council tax data, information from utilities companies and evidence from Empty Property Officers in local authorities.
- HMRC regard 'use as a dwelling' as including occasional use, perhaps as a second home, but they will ignore occupation by squatters or by a 'guardian' installed to deter squatters and vandals.
- At one stage it appeared that a dwelling had to have been self-contained, so that a conversion from bed-sits, or from a pub with residential accommodation, might qualify for zero-rating. But the case law of more recent years – *Amicus Group Ltd* (VTD 17693), *Kingcastle Ltd* (VTD 17777), *Belvedere Properties (Cheltenham) Ltd* (VTD 18851) – indicates that this is not the case, and that using a property as a dwelling merely involves living in it and treating it as home. This follows from the House of Lords judgment in a Housing Act case, *Uratemp Ventures Ltd v Collins* ([2002] 1 All ER 46).
- The issue of the conversion of pubs that contain residential and non-residential space into dwellings was the subject of two recent Upper Tribunal decisions in the joined cases of *Languard Homes Ltd; MacPherson* ([2017] UKUT 307 (TCC), [2017] STC 1925). The Upper Tribunal ruled in favour of HMRC stating that the grant of the first major interest in the dwelling could not be zero-rated because none of the dwellings converted, had been created by converting part of the building that was not previously designed as a dwelling. This was because it had been created from a mixture of residential and non-residential space. The fact that part of the dwelling contained space that had not previously been used for residential purposes did not enable the work to be zero-rated.
- The reference to garages is not always clear, but HMRC are likely to argue that a multi-purpose outbuilding, whose uses include garaging, is a garage, so that there is no zero-rating if it is converted to a dwelling. The Tribunal rejected this approach in *Cottam* (VTD 20036), but accepted it in *Podolsky* (TC00322). And in *Clark* (TC00552) it decided that only the part actually used as a garage had been residential.

'A person converting'

[15.174] Whether someone is a 'person converting' depends on whether the works amount to conversion, and their role in those works. The law does not define 'converting', but HMRC appear to consider that it covers anything involved in bringing a non-residential building into its new use, provided there is some alteration work and any necessary planning consent has been given.

Otherwise the points here are broadly as for a 'person constructing', as at para **15.141** et seq:

- HMRC accept that anyone acting as a developer, contractor or sub-contractor can be a 'person converting'.
- They also take the same approach to VAT groups as at para **15.143**.
- There can be more than one 'person converting' if the property changes hands during the course of the works, although it may be difficult to show that successive people are both really engaged in conversion. If the property is transferred as part of a TOGC then person converting status will transfer to the new owner providing certain conditions are satisfied. Please see Revenue & Customs Brief 27/14 for more information on the requirements.
- There is no time limit on 'person converting' status, so that a zero-rated grant can be made some years after the conversion work. But it will fall foul of Note 7 (para **15.173**) if it has actually been used as a dwelling, or in RRP use, in the meantime, so this is only likely to apply if the property has stood empty.

Parts of buildings

[15.175] There are further complications with parts of buildings.

If a wholly non-residential building is partly converted to a dwelling or dwellings, or 'solely' for RRP use, that part qualifies, but any areas remaining in non-residential use do not.

If a partly residential building is converted for RRP use, the previously non-residential part can qualify. If the conversion is to dwellings, each post-conversion dwelling needs to be considered separately. Dwellings wholly created out of non-residential areas will qualify for zero-rating; those wholly created out of already residential areas will not. If a new dwelling is created partly out of an already residential area, HMRC are likely to take the view that it cannot be zero-rated. Sch 8, Group 5, Note 9, however, says that:

> 'The conversion, other than to a building designed for a relevant residential purpose, of a non-residential part of a building which already contains a residential part is not included within items 1(b) or 3 unless the result of that conversion is to create an additional dwelling or dwellings.'

This might suggest that there is some scope for zero-rating where, say, two new flats each incorporate part of what was one flat, but HMRC do not seem to think so, and do not accept the judgment in *Jacobs* (para **15.275**) as applying here. They do, however, see *Blom-Cooper* (also para **15.275**) as relevant. Further points arose in *Blacklock* (VTD 20171), where the Tribunal dismissed HMRC's argument that the reference to 'an additional dwelling' meant that the building must already contain a dwelling, and in *Merlewood Estates Ltd* (VTD 20810), where disused attic space in blocks of flats was found to have been 'non-residential'.

Zero-rating: person substantially reconstructing a protected building

[15.176] VATA 1994, Sch 8, Group 6, item 1 zero-rates:

> 'The first grant by a person substantially reconstructing a protected building, of a major interest in, or in any part of, the building or its site.'

A protected building means, essentially, a listed building designed as a dwelling or dwellings or intended 'solely' for RRP/RCP use. This, and the meaning of 'substantially reconstructing', are considered in paras **15.177** and **15.178**.

'First grant', 'major interest' and 'site' have the same meanings as in paras **15.145** to **15.148**, although there are specific points here about outbuildings etc, noted below. There are also the same issues with dwellings with restricted occupancy rights, and with input tax recovery, and as in paras **15.147**, **15.149** and **15.150**.

Protected buildings

[15.177] There are two elements to this. The building must be:

- a listed building or scheduled monument

and either

- designed to remain as or become a dwelling or number of dwellings; or
- intended for use solely for a relevant residential or relevant charitable purpose (RRP or RCP).

The purchaser or tenant must issue a certificate of intended use (para **15.154**). Paragraph **15.152** notes some points about HMRC's interpretation of 'use' and 'solely', including their acceptance that 95% can be treated as 'solely'.

For dwellings, VATA 1994, Sch 8, Group 6, Note 2 says that:

> 'A building is designed to remain as or become a dwelling or number of dwellings where in relation to each dwelling the following conditions are satisfied –
>
> (a) the dwelling consists of self-contained living accommodation;
> (b) there is no provision for direct internal access from the dwelling to any other dwelling or part of a dwelling;
> (c) the separate use, or disposal of the dwelling is not prohibited by the terms of any covenant, statutory planning consent or similar provision,
>
> and includes a garage (occupied together with a dwelling) either constructed at the same time as the building or where the building has been substantially reconstructed at the same time as that reconstruction.'

This is very similar to the tests in Group 5, Note 2 (para **15.135** et seq) – paras (a) to (c) apply in the same way here, while (d) is replaced by a requirement (see para **15.178**) for the works to have listed building consent.

A listed building is one which is listed under the Planning (Listed Buildings and Conservation Areas) Act 1990, the Planning (Listed Buildings and Conservation Areas) (Scotland) Act 1997; or the Planning (Northern Ireland) Order 1991. In England and Wales, it will be listed Grade I, II* or II, and in

Scotland Grade A, B or C(S). In Northern Ireland, it may be necessary to consult the Environment and Heritage Service.

A scheduled monument is scheduled under the Ancient Monuments and Archaeological Areas Act 1979; or the Historic Monuments and Archaeological Objects (Northern Ireland) Order 1995. In practice, scheduled monuments are not usually habitable buildings.

The zero-rating extends to the 'site' of the building, and this includes a reasonable plot of land around it, as in para **15.148**. But a subsidiary building is unlikely to be included in the zero-rating unless:

- It counts as a protected building in its own right. This would involve it being listed, or covered by the listing, and itself either designed as a separate dwelling or dwellings, or intended for RRP or RCP use.
- It is a garage occupied with a protected dwelling and constructed at the same time as the dwelling was either constructed or substantially reconstructed. Following *Grange Builders (Quainton)* (VTD 18905), HMRC accept that it need not originally have been built as a garage.

'A person substantially reconstructing'

[15.178] The grantor must be a person 'substantially reconstructing' the building – this is a question of the nature of the works, as considered below, and the grantor's role in them – this is much the same point as for a 'person constructing' in para **15.143**.

The same points apply as in para **15.143** in relation to VAT groups and again there is no time limit on 'person substantially reconstructing' status. Also as in para **15.143**, there can be successive 'persons substantially reconstructing' if the property changes during the course of the works, but in view of what 'substantially reconstructing' involves this is unlikely to apply in practice.

Note that Sch 8 Group 6 Note 4* changed with effect from 1 October 2015 to:

'For the purposes of Item 1, a protected building is not to be regarded as substantially reconstructed unless, when the reconstruction is completed, the reconstructed building incorporates no more of the original building (that is to say, the building as it was before the reconstruction began) than the external walls, together with other external features of architectural or historic interest.'

Selected case law on 'substantially reconstructing'

- In *Barraclough* (VTD 2529), the enlargement and modernisation of a house did not meet either of the tests in Sch 8, Group 6, Note 4, so that the grant of a major interest in it could not be zero-rated. But the Tribunal considered that, in addition, the appellant would have needed to demonstrate 'both that the building was "reconstructed" in common parlance and that the reconstruction was "substantial"'. It did not see the works as amounting to reconstruction.
- The Tribunal took the same approach in *Vivodean Ltd* (VTD 6538) – the building needed to be 'reconstructed', which the Tribunal thought meant 'constructed as of new', as well as that work being substantial. This was not the case here.

- In *Church (t/a Milton Antique Restoration)* (VTD 12427), a farmhouse had been extended and renovated. The Tribunal thought that this came nowhere near reconstruction of the building, so that it was not 'substantially reconstructed'.
- *Lordsregal Ltd* (VTD 18535) concerned a dwelling that had been badly dilapidated – in danger of collapse, entirely overgrown and scarcely recognisable as a building. Its timber frame had been retained, but the rest of it was largely taken down and rebuilt section-by-section. HMRC claimed that it was not 'substantially reconstructed', since its design and configuration were largely unchanged. The Tribunal did not see this as relevant and, departing from *Barraclough*, looked at the words 'substantially reconstructing' together. It thought that the building had been substantially reconstructed in the normal meaning of the words.
- In *Southlong East Midlands Ltd* (VTD 18943), the Tribunal reverted to the approach in *Barraclough*. It thought the enlargement and modernisation of a house had been 'substantial', and had passed the 60% test, but was not 'reconstruction', so the grant of a major interest in it could not be zero-rated.
- In *Cheltenham College Enterprises Ltd* (TC00429), there had been extensive works to a school boarding house. Adopting the approach in *Lordsregal*, the Tribunal saw 'substantially' as qualifying 'reconstructing', and concluded that, subject to the 60% calculation, the test was met and the grant of a major interest zero-rated. It also considered the meaning of 'reconstructing', taking the view that it did not need to involve structural work or changes in layout, but did not include the construction of an extension. This differed markedly from HMRC's interpretation.

There have been various other unsuccessful appeals in this area, where the work clearly did not meet either the 60% test in Note 4(a) or the 'gutting' test in Note 4(b).

Property supplied for no consideration

[15.179] A disposal of property, or of an interest in property, for no consideration is potentially a supply under VATA 1994, Sch 4, para 5. This is relevant both to gifts of property and, for example, to a distribution of assets to shareholders or to partners in a partnership. The same applies to a letting for no consideration, or for example for a literal peppercorn. Sch 4 para 5 creates a supply if:

- the property is a business asset of the owner; and
- the owner (or a previous owner prior to a TOGC) incurred VAT on its acquisition, or on anything that has become part of the property (such as materials used in building work), and was entitled to recover any of the VAT.

The supply can be exempt, standard-rated or zero-rated according to the normal rules or, in the case of an outright disposal, a TOGC.

Where VAT is due this is, essentially, on the market value of the supply, being generally what the supplier would have to pay for it on the open market. The presumption is that this VAT is a cost to the owner. (The recipient might choose to reimburse it to the owner, but any obligation to do so would mean that the payment was consideration so that these rules no longer applied.) Strictly, the owner cannot issue a tax invoice to allow the recipient to recover the VAT, but it should be possible to issue a 'tax certificate' instead. In the context of a gift of goods, HMRC explain this in their Notice 700/35, suggesting that normal invoicing documentation be overwritten:

> '*Tax certificate.* No payment is necessary for these goods. Output tax has been accounted for on the supply.'

These rules are not particularly advantageous, and if VAT is due it is often preferable to charge a nominal price – they do not apply where there is any consideration, monetary or non-monetary.

One issue here has been with the disposal of an interest of negative value, such as the assignment or surrender of an onerous lease. If the owner is paying to dispose of the interest, this is likely to involve a supply by the counterparty to the owner, but the rules above might suggest that there is also a supply by the owner, albeit of nil value. There is, however, a counter-argument that an onerous lease is not an 'asset'. For this reason, the Tribunal in *AA Insurance Services Ltd* (VTD 16117) concluded that the surrender of an onerous lease was not a supply, and although the law on surrenders has since been amended the Tribunal took the same view of an assignment in *British Eventing* (TC00664). Both cases are also referred to in para **15.100**. It is not in fact clear that 'asset' is to be interpreted in this narrow, accounting, sense, and although the *British Eventing* Tribunal considered the Directive as well as the UK legislation, its approach does not seem to be borne out by other language versions of the Directive.

Property supplied at undervalue

[15.180] If property is sold at less than a market price, or let at less than a market rent, any VAT is normally due only on that price or rent. But:

- If there is further consideration, such as other land or building work, any VAT is due on the total value of the consideration.
- If the parties are connected, HMRC may be able to direct (under VATA 1994, Sch 6, para 1) that VAT is accounted for on a market value. This does not apply if VAT is due which the purchaser or tenant can recover in full, and in practice the power is rarely used.
- For compulsorily taxable lettings (eg parking or holiday accommodation – see para **15.19** et seq) between connected parties or within a corporate group, an undervaluation might be caught by the annual tax point rules in reg 94B of the VAT Regulations (see para **15.205**).
- Undervaluation might be a pointer, although not a decisive one, towards the transaction being non-business, so that no VAT is due, or recoverable by the supplier.

In *Riverside Sports and Leisure Ltd* (VTD 20848), a school had leased a sports centre to an operating company for a peppercorn rent, intending to retain some rights to use the facilities for itself. No money changed hands, but the way the arrangements had been effected meant that the operator was supplying the facilities back to the school out of its lease, and that VAT was due on this, as in a barter arrangement.

Property put to private use

[15.181] If a VAT-registered person acquires a property, such as a holiday home, purely for business purposes, and with no intention of using it herself, any VAT is recoverable in full. This might be VAT on the acquisition itself, under the rules in para **15.45**, or perhaps on building work or fees. But if she later decides to put it to private use, this is a supply, and she will need to account for VAT.

Alternatively, she might have anticipated the private use in the first place, in which case she should have restricted the VAT, only recovering it to the extent of the intended business use. In that case, it will only be any increase in private use that creates a VAT liability.

Where there is a supply in this way, the general position is the same as for a letting for no consideration to a third party (para **15.179**), except that:

- The supply is necessarily standard-rated, even if a third party letting would be exempt – this follows from the CJEU judgment in *Seeling* (CJEU Case C-269/00 – see also para **15.113**).
- Output tax is due on the depreciation of the asset. Part 15A of the VAT Regulations sets out detailed rules for calculating this.

On an ongoing basis, the value of the supply is calculated by reference to:

- A – the number of months in the accounting period.
- B – the number of months of the 'economic life' of the asset. The economic life of a property starts when it is first used following its acquisition, and lasts 10 years or, if less, for the remaining term of the owner's interest in it. Once the economic life has expired, no further VAT is due on private use.
- C – the cost of the asset, being the purchase price plus the cost of constructing any building, extension or annexe, to the extent these were subject to VAT. This includes anything paid by a previous owner prior to a TOGC (see para **15.121** et seq) or series of TOGCs. If further costs of this kind are incurred on an asset already used in the business, for example in extending an existing building, these are dealt with separately, and are subject to their own 'economic life'. This will run in parallel with the original economic life until that expires.
- U% – the extent to which the asset is used, or made available for use, outside the business, compared with the total use made of it during the period.

The value of the supply is:

$$\frac{A}{B} \times (C \times U\%)$$

Also:

- If the asset is not used at all during an accounting period, there is no supply during that period. But, if there is subsequently a supply under these rules, the length of the period of non-use is added to A.
- VAT is only due on private use occurring during the 'economic life' of the asset. If the economic life commences or ends during the accounting period, so that only part of the accounting period is within the economic life, the calculation only takes account of that part.
- Where the economic life would otherwise have started before 1 November 2007 (when these provisions were introduced), it is reduced to the extent that VAT has been accounted for on private use arising before that date.

Lennartz accounting

[15.182] Before 1 January 2011, it was possible to recover VAT in full on a property, even where it was always intended for both business and private use, and to account for VAT on the private use as in para **15.181**. VAT did, however, still need to be restricted on account of any intended exempt use.

This arrangement was optional, but produced a cashflow benefit. It was referred to as *Lennartz* accounting, after the CJEU case that established the principle (CJEU Case C-97/90), but was blocked from 1 January 2011 by amendments to the Directive. It remains available for some types of expenditure, but not in relation to property. People that previously used *Lennartz* may, however, still be liable for the output tax.

Lennartz did not apply unless there was to be an element of business use, but it was used in two ways:

- Where there was also private use outside the business, as with a holiday home or a farmhouse. People that used *Lennartz* in this way remain liable to account for output tax on private use until the 'economic life' (as in para **15.181**) has expired.
- Where there was also non-business use within the organisation, as with a charity whose activities were only partly business (see para **15.162**). In 2009, however, the CJEU held in *Vereniging Noordelijke Land- en Tuinbouw Organisatie* (CJEU Case C-515/07) that *Lennartz* did not actually apply in these circumstances, but only in relation to private use outside the organisation. People that had nevertheless used *Lennartz* in this way were given a choice – they could reverse out the entire position by 30 June 2011, or they could continue to account for output tax on the non-business use as though the claim had been correct. This was legislated in F(No 3)A 2010, Sch 8 para 4.

Further details on *Lennartz* accounting can be found in earlier editions of *Tolley's Property Taxation*.

Property held at deregistration

[15.183] A VAT registered business should deregister if it ceases to trade, or can choose to do so if its taxable supplies fall below (in 2016/17) £81,000. But if it holds any interest in property at the time, there is a deemed supply of it under Sch 4 para 8. This is intended to claw back input tax previously recovered on it. This applies unless:

- the business has been transferred as a going concern to another taxable person (not necessarily as a TOGC in the terms of para **15.121** et seq); or
- following death, insolvency or incapacity the business is being carried on by someone else who is treated as a taxable person; or
- the total VAT would not exceed £1,000; or
- in relation to individual items, the business neither recovered any input tax on them nor acquired them through a transfer of a going concern.

The value of the supply is, essentially, the market value of the property interest.

Materials becoming part of a building are ignored in applying the rules. If, for example, the business has bought land exempt from VAT, and has recovered VAT on the construction of a building, it has not recovered input tax on the land or building itself, and there is no deemed supply of the building on deregistration.

The supply is treated as taking its normal VAT liability, so that for property it will often be exempt.

Property compensation

[15.184] 'True' compensation, as such, is not subject to VAT, but it is not always clear whether a payment really is compensatory in nature, or in reality consideration for a supply:

- Any payment a tenant must make to obtain a lease – such as a reimbursement of the landlord's legal costs – is payment for the lease, and takes the same VAT liability.
- For payments by an existing tenant, HMRC take the view that the position depends on whether the tenant is exercising a right that he already has, and or is effectively paying for a new right. So if a tenant extends the term of his lease, and meets the landlord's legal costs, the payment is seen as outside the scope of VAT if the lease already gave him the right to extend the term, but as for a supply by the landlord if the landlord could have refused to extend it.
- On the termination of a lease, statutory compensation under the Landlord and Tenant Act or the Agricultural Tenancies Act is seen as outside the scope of VAT. But a payment under a Tomlin order is consideration for the surrender of the lease.

- Dilapidation payments by a tenant are considered to be outside the scope of VAT to the extent they genuinely reflect his failure to observe covenants to maintain the property etc. It should be noted that there is a view that this treatment can only apply after the lease has expired as it is not until that point that the tenant will be in breach of this repair covenant.
- Mesne profits – awarded against a tenant who fails to quit – are outside the scope of VAT as compensation. If the tenant is liable to both rent arrears and mesne profits, HMRC will see any part payment as relating first to the rent.
- Penalty/excess charges in a car park are generally seen as outside the scope of VAT. However in *National Car Parks Ltd* ([2017] UKUT 247 (TCC), [2017] STC 1859), the Upper Tribunal confirmed that overpayments made by customers who did not have the correct change were liable to VAT as additional consideration for the use of the car parking facilities.
- A payment, by an outgoing tenant, to dispose of an onerous lease is seen as consideration for a supply to the tenant, at least if the tenant is being released from obligations under the lease. The liability of such payments is dealt with in para **15.15**.
- Similar payments in connection with the disposal of a freehold are relatively rare, and usually arise because the land requires decontamination. Often they will simply be a discount against the purchase price. Where there is actual payment, case law suggests that there is only a supply if the purchaser specifically agrees to take on obligations of the vendor, rather than merely acquiring these obligations with the land. If so, there will be a standard-rated supply by the purchaser.
- Compensation awarded by a court, or agreed under an out-of-court settlement, is generally outside the scope of VAT unless it relates to a specific supply by the plaintiff, perhaps where the dispute was about payment for an earlier supply, or rights are granted under a settlement. HMRC gave their views in Press Notice 82/87.

Case law about property and 'compensation'

- In *J E Greves & Son* (VTD 9777), tenants of a farm, who had remained for many years paying no rent, had argued that the farm had become their property under the Limitation Act 1939. They accepted a payment to relinquish their claim, which the Tribunal concluded was consideration for an exempt supply of an interest in land.
- In *Lloyds Bank plc* (VTD 14181), 'compensation' paid to a landlord to terminate a lease was consideration for a supply by the landlord, and taxable as the landlord had opted. (But it appears the payment might have been outside the scope had the lease already given the tenant the right to terminate in exchange for payment.)
- *Battersea Leisure* ([1992] STC 213, QB) concerned the sale of the former Battersea Power Station by the Central Electricity Generating Board. The CEGB believed itself to have an obligation to remove asbestos from the building, and paid the purchaser to do so. The High Court concluded that this was payment for a supply of services to the CEGB.

- In *Navydock Ltd* (VTD 18281) a company had acquired contaminated land, but had been misled about the decontamination costs. The vendor eventually agreed to make a substantial payment towards those costs. The Tribunal saw this as outside the scope of VAT – unlike in *Battersea*, the vendor had had no obligation to decontaminate the site, and obtained no benefit from the purchaser doing so. It was merely trying to avoid litigation.
- In *South Liverpool Housing Ltd* (VTD 18750), a council had transferred neglected housing stock to a housing association, which took on the outstanding repair obligations. The housing association was awarded a substantial dowry from government funds to deal with these. The Tribunal held that this was not consideration for a supply to the council, since the council's repair obligations had ceased with the transfer. The Tribunal came to a similar decision in *LHA-ASRA Group Ltd* (TC00482), where a housing association had argued that a discount on the purchase price of an estate was consideration for the subsequent work to it.
- In *Vehicle Control Services Ltd* (TC05196), the business provided parking, wheel clamping and security services to car parks owned by its clients. The business obtained most of its income from levying parking charge notices (PCN), including clamping and towing charges, to motorists who breached the parking rules stipulated by the car parking owner. In 2013, the Court of Appeal held that the PCN issued by the businesses were actually represented damages for breach of contract or trespass and were therefore outside the scope of VAT.

Lease variations

[15.185] In land law, the variation of a lease – perhaps to the term or the extent of the premises – may strictly involve a surrender of the existing lease and the grant of a new lease. This could mean that supplies had to be recognised in each direction, as in a barter transaction, but in practice HMRC will only see a supply to the extent of any further consideration, such as a payment.

HMRC's internal VAT manual 'Land and property' (VATLP27000) sets out a Statement of Practice on this subject, reproduced below. This is a revised version of a Statement which HMRC originally agreed with the Law Society.

Statement of Practice

'This Statement of Practice deals with a situation where there is potential conflict between land law and VAT legislation. Under land law the variation of a lease can sometimes require a deemed surrender of the old lease and the grant of a new lease. Customs recognise that in certain circumstances, which are explained in this Statement of Practice, the economic reality of the situation is that the original interest granted to the tenant continues and the variation of the original lease does not in itself result in any supply of the surrender of the old lease or the grant of a new one.

This Statement of Practice does not apply to situations where a surrender and re-grant actually occur rather than being deemed to occur by operation of the law. Furthermore, as made clear in this Statement of Practice, a consideration may attach to a supply or supplies that result from obligations under the new lease. These supplies are quite separate and the consideration, whether monetary or otherwise, cannot put value on the surrender of the original lease and the grant of the new one.

Where there is no monetary consideration paid by the lessor to the lessee

(a)   Where there is no monetary consideration passing from lessor to lessee as a result of or in connection with the variation, then Customs policy is that there is no surrender of the old lease for non-monetary consideration when:

- the new lease is for the same building (or the same part thereof) but the new lease is for an extended term; or
- the new lease is for a larger part of the same building than the old lease but the term is for the same or an extended term; or
- the new lease is for the same land and for an extended term.

(b)   Where the surrender and re-grant involves ground leases or building leases ie leases granted on condition that the lessee will undertake development, very often the negotiations between the parties will result in demolition of an old building and the construction of a new one or partial demolition and reconstruction or enlargement. Customs may find that the terms of the new lease will be more favourable to both the lessee and lessor but do not consider this in itself indicates that the old lease was surrendered in consideration of the grant of the new one. However, if the lessee receives a direct benefit in return for undertaking the construction works (eg a rent free period, or reduced rent for a period) Customs are likely to see a consideration passing from the lessee to the lessor in return for the benefit. In cases where there is doubt you should agree the position with Customs.

Where there is monetary consideration

(c)   Where monetary consideration passes from lessor to lessee, Customs would normally regard the monetary consideration as the sole consideration for the surrender. Where monetary consideration passes to the lessor from the lessee Customs would normally see this as consideration for the grant of the new lease which would be exempt subject to the lessor's election to waive exemption (option to tax). However, the circumstances may indicate that the payment is consideration for the lessor's supply of the acceptance of the surrender of an onerous lease from the lessee (sometimes known as a reverse surrender). From 1 March 1995 we say these payments are for an exempt supply, with the option to tax. When the payment received by the lessor is seen as consideration for the grant of a new lease, there would be no surrender by the lessee.'

Apportionment of rent

[15.186] If the identity of the landlord or tenant changes during a rental period, the parties will often make a payment to allocate the rent for the period accurately between them. The direction of the payment will depend on whether the rent for the current period has already been paid. Adjustments of this kind can be ignored for VAT purposes:

- If the landlord disposes of the property, any rent adjustment with the purchaser is ignored, and any VAT on the sale is on the unadjusted price. No credit note, or further tax invoice, should be issued to the tenant.

- If the tenant assigns the lease, any rent adjustment with the assignee is also ignored, and any VAT on the assignment is on the unadjusted price. The landlord should merely invoice whoever is the tenant when the rent is due, and should not issue separate invoices for the period to each tenant.

There was a Statement of Practice on this subject, which has been reproduced below. It used to appear in HMRC's internal VAT manual 'Land and property' (V1-8.22.16) this has, however, now been removed from the current manual.

Apportionment of rent – Statement of Practice agreed by HMRC and the Law Society

'1.   Following the introduction of VAT on buildings and land in the Finance Act 1989, Customs considered how to treat apportionments of rent from land on the sale of the freehold by the landlord or on an assignment of a lease by a tenant where the election to waive exemption has been exercised by the old or new landlord.

2.   For example, where rent is payable in advance and the landlord has exercised the option to tax the rent and the landlord sells the property one week after the beginning of the quarter, the question arises as to how to treat the apportionment of rent for VAT purposes on completion.

3.   A similar question arises when a tenant assigns a lease and an apportionment of rent is made between buyer and seller. The normal procedure is for rent to be apportioned between buyer and seller as at the date of completion in the same way as any other apportionment without any adjustment to the agreed consideration. If a purchaser is late in completing, interest is normally charged on the consideration, but rent and other apportionments are re-calculated to the new completion date.

4.   The Law Society considered the various arguments, but decided that it would not be correct to treat apportionment of rent as part of the consideration.

5.   Against the above background, following discussions with the Society's Revenue Law Committee, Customs agreed that apportionments or "settlements" of the rent between landlords on the sale of a tenanted property and between tenants on the assignment of a lease should be treated as outside the scope of VAT.

6.   Where either the landlord or the tenant changes at a date within a rent quarter (and where the lease remains in place), any apportionment of the quarter's rent should be treated as falling outside the scope of VAT, notwithstanding that an election to tax the rent has been, or will be, made.

7.   Customs' agreement to accept apportionments as outside the scope should help to simplify matters. This agreement has no bearing on the liability of the actual consideration received for the sale of the freehold or the assignment of a lease. This depends on the nature of the supply and the election to waive exemption by the parties.'

Tenant inducements

[15.187] Landlords often incentivise incoming tenants with inducements – the payment of a 'reverse premium', a contribution to fit out works, a rent-free period etc. The CJEU judgment in *Mirror Group* (see para **15.191**) established that this did not generally involve any supply by the tenant, but the position is not always straightforward.

(Similar payments to someone taking an assignment or surrender of a lease are generally regarded as consideration for a supply by the assignee or landlord. On an assignment, any such supply will be standard-rated; on a surrender it will be exempt, or standard-rated if the landlord has opted to tax. Payments of these kinds are considered in para **15.15**.)

A payment to an incoming tenant is generally outside the scope of VAT. But it may be consideration for a supply by the tenant, if the tenant is taking on obligations beyond those normally involved in taking a lease or is providing an additional benefit to the landlord capable of comprising a service in its own right such as having the status of an anchor tenant (see para **15.189**). Covenants to pay rent, to maintain the building, to observe restrictions as to use, etc will not have this effect, and if there is a supply, this is generally because of an obligation to undertake building work or in connection with the tenant's occupation of the building. A tenant who is to undertake tenant fit-out works will sometimes carry out building works for the landlord in exchange for payment. In such cases the tenant will make a supply to the landlord which will be subject to VAT (see below).

Payment for works

[15.188] In some cases, an inducement is really a payment for the tenant to undertake building work that would otherwise have been done by the landlord landlord (eg to the common parts) – the tenant is effectively acting as the landlord's building contractor. For example, the tenant will be making a supply of building work if:

- The building is in need of repair when the lease is taken, and the tenant accepts an inducement in order to deal with this (see the *Gleneagles* and *Neville Russell* decisions in para **15.191**).
- The landlord is responsible under the lease for fitting out the building, but the tenant accepts an inducement to do so instead. (But a contribution to works that are the tenant's responsibility will not create a supply.)

Where there is a supply of building work, the normal liability and tax point rules for such a supply will apply (see respectively paras **15.220** et seq and **15.206**) – in most cases it will be standard-rated, and tax points will arise only as the payments are made or invoiced. The landlord will be able to recover VAT according to the use of the property in question – if the work is to the tenanted property, the position will depend on whether the lettings are taxable.

Payment linked to occupation

[15.189] The CJEU in *Mirror Group* (para **15.191**) held that the tenant was making a supply:

> 'if the landlord, taking the view that the presence of an anchor tenant in the building containing the leased premises will attract other tenants, were to make a payment by way of consideration for the future tenant's undertaking to transfer its business to the building concerned.'

In itself, this might suggest that the tenant needs both to agree to go into occupation and to be an anchor tenant, but HMRC interpret it a little more broadly. Their views were set out in Business Brief 12/05, and given more fully in their internal guidance, extracts from which are in para **15.191**. In practice, few inducements are seen as taxable on this basis, and the issue is mainly about major occupiers in retail developments.

Where there is a supply on this basis, it will be standard-rated, and there is likely to be a one-off tax point when the tenant gives whatever undertaking creates the supply, even if payment is only made over a period. HMRC will normally see the landlord as able to recover the VAT if the letting is taxable, although the logic of *Mirror* might be that the VAT is attributable to the development as a whole.

Other forms of inducement

[15.190] Landlords may offer various other forms of inducement. Examples include:

* *Enhancements.* The landlord might agree to provide additional space, car parking spaces etc, or to complete building works to a better standard. This involves no supply by the tenant, who is simply getting more for the rent.
* *Taking on property obligations.* The landlord might agree, for example, to pay the tenant's rent on its previous premises, pending disposal of them. This is the same as paying cash and, if the landlord then has some control over the disposal, HMRC are likely to see a supply by the tenant (see (d) in their guidance in para **15.191**).
* *Rental guarantee or mortgage capping.* The landlord might agree to compensate a tenant if the tenant fails to secure lettings or a certain level of rent, or if mortgage costs rise above a certain level. HMRC's views depend on the documentation – they see payments under such a guarantee as a discount if presented as such, as cash inducements if presented as consideration for the tenant taking the lease, or as compensation if presented as neither. This position follows from the (pre-*Mirror*) decision in *Iliffe & Holloway* (VTD 10922).

Case law on tenant inducements

[15.191] As seen above, whilst some earlier cases do remain relevant, the treatment of inducements is largely considered in terms of the *Mirror* judgment, clear echoes of which are also to be found in HMRC's guidance on the subject.

* In *Mirror Group plc* (CJEU Case C-409/98), the CJEU held that:

  '. . . a taxable person who only pays the consideration in cash due in respect of a supply of services, or who undertakes to do so, does not himself make a supply of services . . . It follows that a tenant who undertakes, even in return for payment from the landlord, solely to become a tenant and to pay the rent does not, so far as that action is concerned, make a supply of services to the landlord.'

'However, the future tenant would make a supply of services for consideration if the landlord, taking the view that the presence of an anchor tenant in the building containing the leased premises will attract other tenants, were to make a payment by way of consideration for the future tenant's undertaking to transfer its business to the building concerned. In those circumstances, the undertaking of such a tenant could be qualified, as the United Kingdom Government in essence submits, as a taxable supply of advertising services.'

The second of these paragraphs described the supposed facts of the transaction at issue, but not the actual facts. Following the CJEU judgment, the High Court in *Trinity Mirror plc* ([2003] STC 518) refused a further hearing to establish this.

Mirror superseded some of the earlier case law in this area, but other cases are of continuing relevance:

- In *Gleneagles Hotel plc* (VTD 2152), the Tribunal saw a reverse premium paid to an incoming tenant as taxable, where the tenant agreed to undertake repairs and improvements to the property, to the benefit of both parties.
- In *Neville Russell* (VTD 2484), a tenant renewed a lease, and entered into a separate agreement with the landlord, agreeing to refurbish the property in exchange for payment. The Tribunal held that this was taxable. It also saw a further payment, linked to the tenant taking additional space, as taxable, but HMRC now accept that this was incorrect in the light of *Mirror*.
- In both *Ridgeons Bulk Ltd* ([1994] STC 427, QB) and *Port Erin Hotels* (VTD 5045), a tenant had agreed to undertake works – apparently fairly substantial works – in exchange for a rent-free period. The rent foregone by the landlord was seen as payment for the works.

HMRC's views on tenant inducements

The following material is taken from HMRC's internal VAT manual 'Supply and consideration' (VATSC46400 and 46800).

'It is now accepted that normal lease obligations to which tenants are bound do not constitute supplies for which a reverse premium is consideration.

It is therefore likely that the majority of reverse premium payments will not constitute consideration for supplies as they are no more than inducements to tenants to take leases and to observe the obligations in them. Only where such a payment is directly linked to benefits a tenant provides outside normal lease terms will there be a taxable supply. However, merely putting such a distinct benefit into the lease terms would not mean it becomes outside the scope of VAT.

In effect, reverse premium payments will now follow the position of rent-free periods . . . in being mainly outside the scope of VAT and only taxable consideration when directly linked to a specific benefit supplied by a tenant to a landlord.

The following are examples of taxable benefits for which reverse premiums constitute consideration are:

(a) Carrying out building works to improve the property by undertaking necessary repairs or upgrading the property. However, this does not include the situation where a tenant undertakes continuous repairs with improved materials as part of the usual obligations under a tenant repairing lease or where a tenant fits out the property at the start of the lease to the tenant's own specification as normally agreed with the landlord.

(b) Carrying out fitting-out or refurbishment works for which the landlord has responsibility and is paying the tenant to undertake.

(c)   Acting as anchor tenant.

(d)   Undertaking to move a business to the new property and, in so doing, dispose of old property under conditions set by the new landlord.

Care is needed when analysing the nature of reverse premiums that appear to be paid for tenants doing more than simply taking leases. This is because the payments usually result from long and complex negotiations between landlords and prospective tenants – negotiations that may result in the parties changing their respective undertakings more than once. As such, it is necessary to obtain as much documentary evidence as possible; in particular, correspondence between the parties that covers their negotiations over payments and undertakings.

Determining whether a tenant acts as an 'anchor' in a development is particularly problematical. It is likely that this will occur mainly in retail projects. Simply possessing a well-known name will not automatically mean the tenant acts as an anchor.

In effect, a tenant will only be regarded as an anchor for VAT purposes if there is clear evidence the tenant has agreed to act as such, affording the landlord the right to use that tenancy generally to market the property. Publicity simply pointing out that the tenant is moving into the property is not itself sufficient to indicate anchor status.

The landlord may also use an anchor tenancy to obtain finance for the project. Again, the tenant would only be regarded as an anchor for VAT purposes if the evidence referred to above applied.'

Rent-free periods

[15.192] Most rent-free periods simply reduce the value of the landlord's supplies, and do not involve a supply by the tenant. There will be a supply by the tenant in much the same circumstances as for a cash inducement. A rent-free period given, effectively, as a discount, or in recognition of a tenant's need to fit-out the property will not create a supply, but there might be a supply where the payment is in exchange for substantial building work, as in the *Ridgeons Bulk* and *Port Erin* cases (see para **15.191**).

Where a rent-free period does create a supply by the tenant in this way, this will take the liability and tax point treatment of whatever the tenant is supplying for it – there will normally be VAT due each time rent would have been payable. Unless agreed otherwise, the VAT should be calculated on a VAT-inclusive basis – ie as $\frac{1}{6}$th of the rent if the VAT rate is 20%. Conversely, the tenant's services will also be further consideration for the lease – if the letting is taxable, the landlord must account for VAT on the value of those services, which can probably be taken as represented by the value of the rent foregone.

These points only apply to a rent-free period given to a tenant by its landlord. The term is also sometimes used to describe a case where a tenant assigns a lease and agrees to continue to meet the rent for a time – this cannot be seen in the same way, and is in reality a deferred reverse premium. There is generally a taxable supply by the new tenant, as explained in para **15.15**.

Planning gain agreements, dedication of roads etc

[**15.193**] In order to secure planning permission, a developer may have to undertake other works under a 'planning gain' or section 106 agreement. HMRC do not see this as a supply, provided it is done for no, or purely nominal, consideration. Related input tax incurred by the developer is attributable to the development itself. The same applies to the dedication of roads to the local authority, or of sewers to the sewerage undertaker.

Section 106 agreements are, however, in the process of being phased out in favour of Community Infrastructure Levy. This will more often be a cash payment to the local authority, although land can be transferred to it in lieu of the payment. Unlike under section 106, it is not envisaged that the developer can meet its obligations by undertaking building work for the local authority. The levy itself is seen as outside the scope of VAT, but HMRC are considering the treatment of land transfers under these arrangements.

Taxable persons – special cases

Partnerships

[**15.194**] The following issues need to be taken into consideration where property is contributed to, or distributed by, a partnership as HMRC will consider that this is a supply if:

– the property is held as a business asset (this will necessarily be the case for a distribution); and
– the contributing partner/distributing partnership (or a previous owner prior to a TOGC or series of TOGCs) incurred VAT on the acquisition of the property or on anything that has become part of the property (such as materials used in building work), and was entitled to recover any of that VAT.

This is under the rules for gifts in para **15.179**. Such a supply takes its normal VAT liability – and may qualify as a TOGC if appropriate (see para **15.121** et seq). Any VAT is due on the market value of the property. HMRC take the view that a tax invoice cannot be issued, but that, as at para **15.179**, a tax certificate can be used to allow the transferee of the property to recover VAT. For contributions, they suggest overwriting a normal invoice with the following wording:

> '*Certificate for Tax on Partnership Contribution.* No payment is necessary for these goods/services. Output tax has been accounted for on the supply.'

• In a professional partnership, property is often held by just some of the partners on behalf of the partnership as a whole – this is because of (English) land law restrictions. HMRC should accept that VAT can be recovered through the wider partnership registration.
• A professional partnership might alternatively hold property in a company. If this is a nominee, VAT can only be recovered through the partnership – case law demonstrates both that this should be possible

and that HMRC have not always accepted it. If the company holds beneficial as well as legal title, it is treated as carrying on a business in its own right, and should register and opt to tax if appropriate. The option might, however, be disapplied if the partnership is partly exempt (see *Winterthur Life* at para **15.120**).

Selected case law on partnerships

Supplies to and by partnerships

- In *Heerma* (CJEU Case C-23/98), a Dutch farmer leased a cowshed to a partnership of himself and his wife. The CJEU held that he was a taxable person in his own right and that he was making supplies to the partnership. Various other, questionable, claims are sometimes made about this case.
- *Fengate Developments* ([2005] STC 191) concerned overlapping partnerships involving individuals A, B and C – A and B carried on one business, and A and C another. Partnership AB held a plot of land, on which it had opted to tax, which was transferred to partnership AC. The parties claimed that this was a sale by B to C and was not subject to VAT – B was not VAT registered in her own right, and had not opted. The Tribunal, High Court and Court of Appeal all concluded that there was a taxable supply by AB – partly because of the documentation and payments made, but also because of the partnership law position: while the asset was held by AB, B had no separate interest to sell, so the inference was that B's sale had been preceded by the taxable transfer of the property by AB to A and B personally.
- In *Space 2 Build Ltd* (TC00378), the fact that building work had been referred to in a partnership deed did not mean that it was outside the scope of VAT.

Property held by a nominee

- In *Bird Semple & Crawford Herron* (VTD 2171), a firm established a company to acquire a property, partly for its own occupation. The Tribunal accepted that the firm could recover input tax on associated professional fees, and that in substance the supplies had been made to the firm for the purpose of its business.
- Similarly, in *Lester Aldridge* (VTD 18864), a firm established a nominee company to take a lease on premises for the firm's occupation. The firm arranged the letting and paid the rent, and the Tribunal accepted that it was receiving the supplies and could recover the VAT on the rent.

Limited partnerships

[15.195] In a limited partnership, there is at least one 'general partner' with unlimited liability, and there are limited partners with limited liability.

Limited partnerships established under the Limited Partnerships Act 1907 are treated as carrying on business through the general partner:

- It is the general partner who should register for VAT and exercise any option to tax – if there is more than one, they should register together as a partnership, still excluding the limited partners.

- Where there is a single general partner with existing business activities, there is no distinction between those activities and the activities of the limited partnership. The limited partnership will be covered by any existing VAT registration or option to tax, there will be no supplies between the general partner and the limited partnership, and if the general partner is a corporate body the limited partnership can be included in a VAT group.
- Supplies to the limited partnership are treated as made to the general partner. VAT incurred by the limited partners in their own right is not strictly recoverable through the limited partnership, but HMRC will often accept this if the VAT relates to taxable activities of the limited partnership as a whole.
- HMRC are, however, sometimes suspicious of the use of limited partnerships. They will expect a limited partner to be included in the VAT registration if it is participating in the management and running of the limited partnership (which would also prejudice its limited liability) or if it has some other interest in land that is held by the limited partnership.

Trusts

[15.196] VATA 1994, Sch 10, para 40 says that:

'(1)   This paragraph applies if the benefit of the consideration for the grant of an interest in, right over or licence to occupy land accrues to a person ("the beneficiary") other than the person making the grant.

(2)   The beneficiary is to be treated for the purposes of this Act as the person making the grant.

(3)   So far as any input tax of the person actually making the grant is attributable to the grant, it is to be treated for the purposes of this Act as input tax of the beneficiary.'

It is designed to deal with trusts, where legal and beneficial ownership are separated. In this case, the law treats the beneficial owner as the person making any supplies of letting or selling the property, so that any VAT registration and option to tax is in the name of the beneficial owner. Where there is more than one of them, HMRC treat them as a partnership.

But:

- This would often be impractical. HMRC take the view that it only applies if the income etc from the property can be seen to accrue directly to a small number of identifiable beneficiaries, and that otherwise someone else – such as the trustee – should register and opt. In practice, HMRC have accepted pragmatic arrangements in many individual cases, so that there is little consistency in this area. The provision does not, in any case, apply to a UK Real Estate Investment Trust (REIT) (see **CHAPTER 3**), since this is a corporate body.
- The provision only applies where the property is held for sale or letting. In particular, it does not apply where the beneficiary is occupying the property: this was the root of the problem in *Lester Aldridge* (see para

15.194) – although the Tribunal accepted that in reality the input tax was proper to the beneficial owner, the then Sch 10, para 8 did not actually apply, and HMRC had denied input tax recovery.

- On the input side, the provision treats input tax as proper to the beneficial owner, but does not treat supplies generally as made to the beneficial owner. This also raises problems with TOGC treatment for acquisitions – this necessitated the Statement of Practice in Business Brief 10/96, explained in para **15.130**.

- The provision does not actually refer to a beneficial owner, but to cases where 'the benefit of the consideration . . . accrues to a person'. HMRC have been reluctant to see it used more broadly, but in *Abbey National* the then Sch 10, para 8 was held to apply where there had been a 'virtual assignment' of tenanted property, such that Abbey had agreed that a third party would enjoy the rental stream pending actual legal transfer of the property. HMRC appeared in Business Brief 16/05 to accept this position where a legal transfer actually was contemplated, and abandoned subsequent proposals to amend the legislation. There is, however, still a possibility of substantive change in this area.

'Virtual assignments' – Abbey National

Abbey National plc concerned 'virtual assignments' of a number of leasehold properties by A to a third party M. The parties intended that the leases would ultimately be actually assigned to M, but did not wish to delay while landlords' consent was obtained, so agreed that, as between themselves, M would be treated as having acquired them and would be entitled to income from the properties and responsible for the outgoings.

The Tribunal (VTD 18666) held that supplies to tenants were by M under the then Sch 10, para 8, since the benefit accrued to M. HMRC appealed, but the High Court ([2005] EWHC 831 (Ch)) agreed with the Tribunal, whilst noting the additional point that the parties had agreed that, where legally possible, A would hold the benefit of subleases in trust for M – a line of reasoning more consistent with HMRC's normal approach.

Another aspect of this case progressed to the Court of Appeal and is noted in para 15.17.

Co-owners

[15.197] Where property is held by two or more people as co-owners, they ought strictly to be treated separately for VAT purposes. For practical reasons, however, HMRC treat co-owners who are exploiting property together as though they are in partnership. They will therefore insist that any VAT registration, option to tax etc is in the names of the co-owners jointly. Registering on this basis can have the effect of the parties entering into a common law partnership for the purposes of English law, which is not always the intention of the parties. Accordingly, care should be exercised to prevent apparent administrative simplicity from giving rise to unexpected rights and obligations.

Various practical issues remain, and it is often necessary to find pragmatic solutions to these and, if the VAT involved is significant, to try to agree these with HMRC.

Commonhold associations

[15.198] A commonhold association may hold the freehold title to the common parts of a building, such as a block of flats, levying a 'commonhold assessment' or service charge. Freeholders of the individual units in the building will be unit holders in the association. The association is seen as carrying on a business in its own right. The commonhold assessment is standard-rated, although by concession (para **15.219**) it can be exempt if the properties are dwellings and the services are provided direct to the individual owners. The transfer of freehold property into or out of the association is treated in the same way as any other freehold sale, as is the sale of a commonhold unit by a unit holder. HMRC give more information in their Notice 742.

Right to Enfranchisement (RTE) companies

[15.199] An RTE company holds the freehold of a property as nominee for the leaseholders. It is regarded as carrying on a separate business of letting the property to them, and for non-residential property it can choose to register and opt to tax. Separate service charges are strictly standard-rated, but for dwellings can be exempt under the concession in para **15.219** where the services are provided direct to the leaseholders. The same applies to Right to Manage companies. The transfer of freehold property into or out of an RTE company is treated like any other freehold transaction.

Joint ventures

[15.200] There are no special provisions for joint ventures as such. A joint venture that takes the form of a company, a partnership or co-ownership will be treated accordingly. In other cases, the parties should generally be seen as acting separately on their own account, each being registrable and with any profit share etc being consideration for a supply by one joint venturer to the other. The decision in *Strathearn Gordon Associates* provides an example. There may also be barter transactions, involving various supplies that must be recognised for VAT purposes. Barter transactions are often complicated for VAT purposes when real estate is involved and need to be considered carefully.

The position may be different if both parties have an interest in land. This was the case in *Latchmere*. More generally, where a joint venture involves the pooling of land interests in order to maximise the proceeds from it, joint VAT registration as a (fictitious) partnership may provide a practical alternative to accounting for VAT on every supply between the parties.

Case law on joint ventures

- In *Strathearn Gordon Associates Ltd* (VTD 1884), a company provided project management services to developers in exchange for a profit share. The Tribunal rejected the argument that this was outside the scope of VAT as a partnership profit share, since there was no partnership, and held that it was standard-rated. Similar decisions were reached in *Keydon Estates Ltd* (VTD 4471), *Fivegrange Ltd* (VTD 5338), *Forestmead Ltd* (VTD 15852) and *Private and Confidential Ltd* (TC00038).

- *Latchmere Properties Ltd* ([2005] EWHC 133 (Ch)) involved a joint venture between a landowner and a builder, under which the builder carried out works and marketed the properties in exchange for a share of the proceeds. This would normally mean that the builder was making taxable supplies to the landowner, and that the landowner alone was making supplies to the purchasers. But the parties had agreed that, if the properties were not sold by a certain date, the builder would acquire them, and the agreement between them took the form of a conditional sale agreement. This meant that the builder had acquired an interest in the land, and that the builder's receipts were consideration for a disposal of this interest to the purchaser, and not for taxable supplies to the landowner.

Time of supply

[15.201] VAT is due by reference to the time of supply, or tax point. This is not necessarily the same as when payment is received.

General rules

[15.202] The general tax point rules are in VATA 1994, s 6.

The 'basic tax point' for a supply of goods is when the goods are delivered or made available, and for a supply of services when the services are performed, ie completed. This can be overridden by receipt of payment or the issue of a tax invoice:

- If payment is received or a tax invoice is issued before the basic tax point, this creates an 'actual tax point' to the extent of the amount paid or invoiced.
- If this has not happened, and the supplier issues a tax invoice within 14 days after the basic tax point, this creates an actual tax point unless the supplier has notified HMRC that it does not wish to use this rule. HMRC can also agree an extension to the 14 days.

There are special rules for various circumstances.

Property disposals

[15.203] For the outright disposal of a property, there is a basic tax point at the date of completion (in Scotland, disposition). This was confirmed by the Court of Session in *Cumbernauld Development Corporation* ([2002] STC 226, CS). But this can be overridden by an actual tax point as explained in para **15.202**.

If the purchaser pays a deposit to the vendor or its agent, such that this becomes the vendor's money, this creates an actual tax point to the extent of the deposit. There is then a further tax point for the balance, normally on completion. This does not apply if a deposit is paid to a stakeholder.

Unascertainable consideration

[**15.204**] In some cases, the full sale price is not actually known at completion, perhaps because there will be an overage payment contingent on the purchaser obtaining planning permission or making a profit. Specific rules, in reg 84 of the VAT Regulations, deal with some of the practical problems here:

- If property is compulsorily purchased, and the amount of compensation is not known at the time, tax points only arise as and when payment is received.

In any other case:

- If the full price of a freehold sale is not known at completion, the normal rules apply to the extent it is known. A further tax point will be created by the receipt of any additional payment, or the issue of a tax invoice for it. Paragraph **15.24** explains how this affects the liability of the supply under the rules standard-rating new freehold buildings.
- There are anti-avoidance rules which, in some cases, mean that these rules for freeholds do not apply, and that there is a tax point for the full sale price at completion even if the sale price is not actually known. This applies if the following conditions are met:
  - The sale is compulsorily standard-rated under the rules in para **15.22** et seq.
  - The vendor, someone financing or agreeing to finance the vendor's development or acquisition, or someone connected with any such person, intends or expects to occupy the property within ten years of the completion of the building or civil engineering work. Connection here is in the same terms as in para **15.117**, but in this case there is no disregard for minor occupation by a financier.
  - That person intends or expects that occupation not to be 'wholly or substantially wholly, for eligible purposes'. This is the same test as in para **15.118**, so that 'substantially wholly' means at least 80%, whilst 'eligible purposes' essentially means the making of taxable supplies or certain public sector use.
- There are no specific rules for the outright disposal of a leasehold for unascertainable consideration. In practice, HMRC are likely to accept the use of the freehold rules here. Alternatively, for short (non-major interest) leases, there is a case for accounting for VAT only by reference to receipts or invoices under reg 91 of the VAT Regulations, which is actually designed for royalties etc.

Different rules continue to apply where the sale was completed before 10 April 2003.

Leases

[15.205] The basic tax point rules do not apply to leases. Under SI 1995/2518, regs 85 and 90 of the VAT Regulations, there is a separate tax point in relation to each payment – of a premium, rent or a service charge under the lease – at the earlier of receipt of payment or the issue of a tax invoice.

Some landlords delay issuing a tax invoice until the tenant has paid the rent, merely issuing a rent demand in the meantime, in order to avoid the VAT cashflow cost of unpaid rent. It can also be advantageous to request VAT return periods with a view to cashflow management – if rents are due in March, June etc, it will be preferable to have return periods ending in February, May etc.

There are various further points here:

- There is a facility, also under regs 85 and 90, which allows landlords to issue a single tax invoice for up to a year in advance, without creating a tax point – tax points need only be recognised when rents fall due or, if earlier, are paid. The benefits of this are questionable, and such invoices are in any case invalidated by any change to the VAT rate.
- There are annual tax point rules, under reg 94B, in some cases concerning associated entities. These are intended as an anti-avoidance measure, and apply here if:
    - the rent is subject to VAT other than as a result of an option to tax – such as with parking or sports facilities (para **15.19** et seq);
    - the tenant cannot recover the VAT in full; and
    - the parties, or two parties in a chain of leases, are connected, either in the way described in para **15.117** or because one party is an 'undertaking' in relation to which the other is a 'group undertaking' under s 1161 of the Companies Act 2006.
  Where the rules apply, the landlord needs annually to recognise a tax point for any difference between the value of the letting (including any services) and the value on which VAT has been accounted for, subject to a six month period of grace. Further details of these rules – which also apply to services, equipment leasing, etc – were given in HMRC's VAT Information Sheet 14/03.
- A rent deposit will create a tax point if and when it becomes the landlord's money, but not while it is held in an escrow or similar account.
- Similarly, a contribution to a sinking fund etc, to fund future repairs, will create a tax point if the fund belongs to the landlord, but not if it belongs to the tenants, or to the parties jointly – in this case there will be tax points only when the landlord draws amounts down from the fund or issues a tax invoice.
- Interest for late payment of rent – where the tenant is in breach of a covenant under the lease – is outside the scope of VAT as compensation.

Building work

[15.206] For building work, the position depends on whether the contract is for a single payment (with or without retentions) or provides for stage payments:

- If there is a single payment, the general rules described in para **15.202** apply – there is a basic tax point on completion of the work, overridden by an actual tax point to the extent of any earlier payment or tax invoice, or by the issue of a tax invoice within 14 days after completion. Where the contract provides for retentions, reg 89 of the VAT Regulations provides that there is a tax point for these only when, and to the extent that, they are actually received or a tax invoice is issued for them.
- If a contract for building work, repair or maintenance provides for payment to be made 'periodically or from time to time', reg 93 provides for a tax point in relation to each payment, arising at the earlier of when it is received or a tax invoice is issued for it. In practice, many contractors issue a request for payment, followed by an authenticated receipt, rather than tax invoices, so that VAT is only due against actual payments.

Under the rules for periodic payments, completion of the work does not create a tax point unless anti-avoidance rules, also contained in reg 93, apply. These cover cases where the contractor, or someone financing the contractor, intends or expects that the property will be occupied by one or other of them, or by someone connected with either of them, other than 'wholly or mainly' for 'eligible purposes' – this borrows from an earlier version of the tests in paras **15.117** and **15.118**, and is essentially interpreted in the same way:

- HMRC see 'wholly or mainly' as meaning at least 80%.
- Parties are 'connected' in the same circumstances as at para **15.117**.
- 'Eligible purposes' means the making of taxable supplies or certain public sector use, although unlike in para **15.118** it does not include occupation on account of an ATM. There is also no disregard, as in para **15.117**, for minor occupation by a financier.

If the rules apply to a sub-contractor, they also apply to the contractor employing him, and through the contractual chain.

Professional services

[15.207] If professional services are provided for a single payment, the general rules in para **15.202** apply, so that there is a basic tax point when the services are completed, overridden by an actual tax point to the extent of any earlier payment or tax invoice, or by the issue of a tax invoice within 14 days after the basic tax point.

If there are periodic payments, tax points will be determined either by reg 93 or by reg 90. Regulation 93, as discussed in para **15.206**, covers any services supplied in the course of building work, repair, maintenance etc, and in HMRC's view this extends to the services of architects, surveyors, consultants and others acting in a supervisory capacity in relation to building work.

Regulation 90 applies in any other case where there are periodic payments, and means that:

- There is no tax point on completion, but there will be a tax point on receipt of each payment or, if earlier, the issue of a tax invoice for it.
- Where there are regular and predictable payments, there is a facility for a tax invoice to be issued up to a year in advance without creating a tax point, as described in para **15.205**.
- For services involving connected persons, reg 94B can create an annual tax point if VAT on the services is not wholly recoverable by the client, also as described in para **15.205**.

Change of VAT rate

[15.208] On a change of rate, the default position is that VAT is due at the rate in force at the tax point, as determined by the rules described in paras **15.202** to **15.207**. But there are optional rules under which:

- Suppliers can choose to apply the rate in force at the basic tax point (para **15.202**) if this results in a lower rate of tax.
- For continuous supplies, for example where there are stage payments for building work or rents for a lease, the supplier can choose to split the charges – for example on the basis of building work actually done before or after the change, or the number of days in the rental period falling before and after the change.

In most cases, a payment, or the issue of a tax invoice, will accelerate the tax point, and this has sometimes been used to defeat a rate increase. The opportunities for this are, however, likely to be limited on any future change.

Service charges

[15.209] Service charges payable under the terms of a lease are generally considered to follow the same treatment as the rent – the services are not seen as involving a distinct supply. But in some cases there is a separate supply, which takes its own VAT treatment, and in others a payment is seen as a disbursement.

If the services are provided by someone else, such as a management company employed by the tenants, or if the occupiers are freeholders, there will necessarily be distinct supplies of the services, or disbursements, although there is a concession here for residential property, noted in para **15.219**. The same would apply if a tenant is responsible under the lease for the services, but chooses to engage the landlord to provide them.

Tellmer, Purple Parking and Field Fisher Waterhouse

[15.210] In 2009, the treatment of service charges was put in doubt by the CJEU judgment in a Czech case, *RLRE Tellmer Property sro* (CJEU Case C-572/07). The Court concluded that charges raised by a landlord for the cleaning of common areas in blocks of flats were consideration for a separate, taxable, supply. It was, however, unclear whether this only applied where the tenants were free to and therefore could engage someone else to undertake the cleaning – in line with the UK's existing approach – or whether it was also relevant to services provided under the terms of the lease. The second of these interpretations seems to have been more in line with the actual facts of the case, and would have significant implications in the UK. HMRC responded in Revenue & Customs Brief 67/09, firmly favouring the first interpretation, and taking the view that the judgment was consistent with their existing policy.

Taxable service charges would often be preferable where there are commercial tenants. If the rent and service charge are exempt, the landlord will be unable to recover VAT on related costs, and will recharge the costs gross of this irrecoverable VAT. This is disadvantageous if the tenant would otherwise have been able to recover the VAT. To deal with this, some landlords who do not want to opt to tax have established a separate management company which is engaged direct by the tenants, making taxable supplies to them.

The judgment of the CJEU in *Field Fisher Waterhouse* has since been handed down (nb without the benefit of a written opinion of an Advocate-General). The key point in *Field Fisher Waterhouse* was whether it is sufficient that an ability to outsource existed as opposed to an active decision being taken to remain with the landlord as supplier. This distinction was not explored in *Tellmer*.

Prior to the judgment in *Field Fisher Waterhouse*, on 19 January 2012, the CJEU handed down its view in *Purple Parking*. Unusually, the CJEU did not proceed to a full judgment but instead issued a Reasoned Opinion under Article 104(3) of its Rules of Procedure. This is significant as this provision only applies if the CJEU considers that the answer can be derived from existing case law. At paragraph 31 of the Reasoned Opinion the CJEU stated that when considering the composite supply question it is of no importance that the element of the supply in question can be or are supplied separately.

Importantly, this clarified the earlier judgment in *Tellmer* (albeit without referring directly to the judgment) and led to an inevitable outcome for *Field Fisher Waterhouse* as the theoretical ability to outsource formed a central plank of its arguments.

HMRC's views

[15.211] HMRC comment on service charges in their Notice 742. In relation to commercial buildings, this says that:

> 'If, as a landlord or licensor, you provide services of a general nature to your tenants the service charges normally follow the same VAT liability as the premium or rents payable under the lease or licence (normally exempt, unless you have opted to tax). For the service to be considered of a general nature it must be:
> * connected with the external fabric or the common parts of the building or estate, as opposed to the demised areas of the property of the individual occupants; and
> * paid for by all the occupants through a common service charge.'

And for lettings of dwellings, it says that:

'Service charges relating to the upkeep of common areas of an estate of dwellings, or the common areas of a multi-occupied dwelling, are exempt from VAT so long as:

• they are required to be paid by the leaseholder or tenant to the landlord under the terms of the lease or tenancy agreement.'

Electricity and gas

[15.212] HMRC see charges for electricity and gas as following the treatment of the rent unless the supply is metered, or the tenant has the choice of not using the supply at all.

If there is a separate supply, it is taxable at either the standard rate or 5%. The 5% rate applies to:

• dwellings;
• buildings for a relevant residential purpose (see para **15.155** et seq, but in this case there is no 'solely' requirement);
• buildings for the non-business use of a charity (see para **15.162**, but again there is no 'solely' requirement here);
• self-catering holiday accommodation;
• caravans and houseboats; and
• any other case where the total supply in a month is below certain limits – 1,000 kilowatt hours for electricity; 150 therms or 4,397 kilowatt hours for gas.

HMRC's Notice 701/19 gives further details.

Case law on utilities supplied to tenants

• In *Hazelwood Caravans & Chalets Ltd* (VTD 1923), holidaymakers were charged £10 per week for unmetered gas and electricity. The Tribunal held that there was a single supply of holiday accommodation.
• *J Adams, AC Woskett & Partners* (VTD 9647) concerned the letting of caravan pitches, with the option of taking unmetered electricity for £1.50 a day. This was held to be a separate supply of electricity.
• In *Suffolk Heritage Housing Association Ltd* (VTD 13713), tenants of sheltered housing paid a separate charge for heating. The Tribunal saw a separate supply. HMRC suggested in Business Brief 2/96 that this turned on the specific arrangements.
• In *The Honourable Society of Middle Temple* (TC01245) tenants contributed to the cost of water incurred by Middle Temple. The First-tier Tribunal considered that as the supply of water to the tenants would have been zero-rated had they been supplied direct then the charge from Middle Temple should also be zero-rated. This was reversed by the Upper Tribunal.
• In *Colaingrove* ([2015] UKUT 80 TCC, [2015] STC 1725) the Upper Tribunal held that the reduced rate could not apply to a fixed charge levied for the supply of electricity included in the overall supply of a static holiday caravan even though a separate charge was levied for the supply. The taxpayer appealed to the Court of Appeal who dismissed their appeal stating that there was one supply of power and serviced accommodation.

Water

[15.213] Metered supplies of water take their own liability. For heated water, including steam, this is the same as for electricity and gas. For unheated water, it is zero-rated unless it is for business use in a 'relevant industrial activity', in which case it is standard-rated – this includes manufacturing, engineering, mining, construction and utilities industries. HMRC's Notice 701/16 gives further details.

Cleaning

[15.214] As seen in para **15.211**:

- HMRC's Notice 742 suggests that shared charges for the cleaning of common areas, or the outsides of windows, will follow the treatment of the rent where they are raised under the terms of a lease.
- HMRC have indicated that, despite the wording of the Notice, they take the same view of the cleaning of demised premises.

The cleaning of common areas was the specific issue in *Tellmer*, discussed in para **15.210**.

Rates

[15.215] If the landlord is the rateable person, any recharge of rates follows the treatment of the rent. If the tenant is the rateable person, but the landlord pays the rates on his behalf, the reimbursement is a disbursement, and outside the scope of VAT.

Insurance

[15.216] HMRC's Notice 742 says that:

> 'If you [the landlord] are the policyholder . . . , any payment for insurance . . . made by the tenants is further payment for the main supply of accommodation. If the tenant is the policyholder . . . , and you make payments on the tenant's behalf, you should treat those payments as disbursements.'

Insurance provided by an insurer is exempt, so there will be no VAT on a disbursement for insurance. In some circumstances, there might also be a case for seeing actual supplies by the landlord as for exempt insurance but, partly for historic reasons, HMRC have been reluctant to accept this.

Commercial property – other services

[15.217] For office services, HMRC's general approach is to see a separate supply if the tenant enters into a separate contract for them, or pays for them according to use, but not otherwise. An extract from their published guidance is given below.

Some UK case law is also noted below, and suggests a less consistent picture than HMRC's guidance. The cases do, however, largely pre-date *Card*

Protection Plan (see para **15.9**), which might provide better arguments for there having been a single supply, whilst all of them pre-date *Tellmer* and *Purple Parking* etc (para **15.210**).

HMRC's views on office services

HMRC offer landlords of commercial premises the following guidance in their Notice 742:

'• *Telephones.* If the telephone account is in your name, any charge you make to tenants is payment for a standard-rated supply by you. This includes the cost of calls, installation and rental. If the account is in the name of the tenant, but you pay the bill, the recovery of this from the tenant is a disbursement.

• *Reception and switchboard.* If you make a charge under the terms of the lease to tenants for the use of facilities that form a common part of the premises, such as reception and switchboard services, any payment you receive will be further consideration for the main supply of accommodation.

• *Office services.* If you make a separate charge for office services, such as typing and photocopying, this is a separate standard-rated supply. However, if under the terms of the lease, there is one inclusive charge for office services and accommodation together, and the tenants are expected to pay for the services regardless of whether they actually use them, the liability of the services will follow that of the main supply of office accommodation.

• *Fixtures and fittings.* Fixtures and fittings are regarded as part of the overall supply of the accommodation and any charges for them are normally included in the rent. However if you provide fixtures and fittings under a separate agreement your supply will normally [be] standard-rated.

• *Management charges.* The charge raised by you to the occupants for managing the development as a whole, and administering the collection of service charges and so on, is further payment for the main supply of accommodation.

• *Recreational facilities.* If the charges for the use of recreational facilities are compulsory, irrespective of whether the tenant uses the facilities, then the liability will follow the main supply of accommodation.'

Case law on office services etc

• In *Greater London Council* (VTD 1224), the provision of stewards and ticketing in conjunction with the letting of concert halls was a separate supply.

• In *Business Enterprises (UK) Ltd* (VTD 3161), there was no separate supply of cleaning and switchboard services provided with serviced office accommodation.

• In *Sovereign Street Workplace Ltd* (VTD 9550), mail handling and a telephone answering service were separate supplies from the serviced office accommodation.

• In *First Base Properties Ltd* (VTD 11598), there was no separate supply of cleaning services provided with furnished office accommodation, but there was a separate letting of furniture.

• *Haringey London Borough Council* ([1995] STC 830, QB) concerned the letting of exhibition halls at Alexandra Palace, with a range of services. The cleaning of individual stands, a courtesy bus service and floral decoration were seen as separate supplies; general cleaning and staffing of the facilities were not.

- In *Tower Hamlets Housing Action Trust* (VTD 17308) – the only one of these cases to post-date *Card Protection Plan* – photocopying services, provided with office accommodation and charged for on a per copy basis, involved separate supplies, but the provision of telephone equipment did not.

Managing agents and management companies

[**15.218**] The services of managing agents or management companies are standard-rated, although they may buy in and supply services that take their own liability. If they are engaged by the landlord, their involvement does not affect the position between landlord and tenant – even if the tenants pay them direct, the supply chain is still via the landlord and VAT must be accounted for accordingly. If they are engaged by the tenants, their supplies will be separate from those of the landlord and will not be covered by any exemption for the letting. This may be preferable if the tenants are businesses with taxable activities.

Where an agent collects (taxable) rent and service charges on the landlord's behalf, it is common for him to do so in the landlord's name, issuing invoices with the landlord's VAT number, and simply to report the figures to the landlord for inclusion in the VAT return. He will similarly receive invoices in the landlord's name, and provide the landlord with details of recoverable input tax.

Alternatively, the parties can deal with VAT as though the agent is a principal, with the landlord charging VAT to the agent, and the agent charging it to tenants in his own name, and the agent recovering VAT on costs and recharging it to the landlord, with invoices being issued accordingly. This arrangement cannot affect the treatment or tax point of supplies – for example, the landlord must recognise a tax point for rent as soon as the agent has received it or issued a tax invoice for it. HMRC also appear to think that, if the landlord has opted to tax, the agent must also do so on his own account.

Paragraph **15.219** looks at a concession for service charges in residential property.

Case law on management companies etc employed by tenants

- In *Canary Wharf Ltd* (VTD 14513), the landlord's management company was a party to leases, and was required to maintain the common parts of the estate. Tenants covenanted to pay rent to the landlord and a service charge to the management company. The Tribunal held that that the management company was making separate, standard-rated, supplies to the tenants, and that it made no difference that the landlord and the management company were members of a VAT group.
- In *Devine* (VTD 15312), residential tenants were obliged to maintain the property, but the landlord exercised a right under the lease to appoint a factor to do so at their expense. The factor was held to be making standard-rated supplies to the tenants.
- In *Trustees of the Nell Gwynn Maintenance Fund* ([1999] STC 79), the trustees were a party to leases on flats, and tenants made payments into the fund which the trustees used to maintain the property. The House of

Lords concluded that the drawing down of sums from the fund created taxable supplies by the trustees to the tenants. (It appears these supplies would now be covered by the concession for service charges on residential property – see para 15.219.)

- In *Clowance Owners Club Ltd* (VTD 18787), individuals bought time shares and paid service charges to a separate company. The charges covered various elements on which the company did not incur VAT, and it claimed that these were disbursements, so that the recharge was not subject to VAT either. The Tribunal accepted this in relation to television licences, but not business rates, water rates, insurance or loan interest – the recharge of an element of these was standard-rated.

Concession for residential property

[15.219] HMRC's Notice 48 sets out the following concession:

> 'The concession exempts from 1 April 1994 all mandatory service charges or similar charges paid by the occupants of residential property towards the upkeep of the dwellings or block of flats in which they reside and towards the provision of a warden, caretakers, and people performing a similar function for those occupants.'

The Notice goes on to explain, however, that the concession does not apply to holiday accommodation.

The concession is relevant to services provided to freeholders, or by management companies direct to tenants, since these would otherwise be generally standard-rated. It may also prove relevant to leaseholders in the light of *Tellmer* (para **15.210**). HMRC are, however, reviewing their concessions following *Wilkinson* (para **15.151**), and it remains to be seen whether the concession will survive at all.

Building work

[15.220] Building work is generally standard-rated, but some work is zero-rated or taxable at the reduced rate of 5%. Zero-rating overrides the 5% rate where they overlap. There are also refund schemes for 'DIY' builders (this is wider than the term suggests – see para **15.275**), listed places of worship (para **15.277**) and memorials (para **15.278**). Finally, there is a 'self-supply' mechanism which can require businesses to account for VAT on work using in-house labour (para **15.279**).

There is zero-rating for:

- The construction of a dwelling, or a building solely for a relevant residential purpose (RRP) or relevant charitable purpose (RCP), including an RCP annexe (see paras **15.221** to **15.224**).
- The conversion of a non-residential building to a dwelling, or for RRP use, for a 'relevant housing association' (see para **15.229**).
- Certain works for the benefit of people with disabilities (see paras **15.230** to **15.239**).
- The construction of a permanent park for residential caravans (see para **15.240**).

- Some donated equipment for medical-related use (see para **15.241**).
- Some works for sea rescue charities (see para **15.242**).
- Approved alterations to a listed dwelling, RRP or RCP building provided that listed buildings consent had been applied for prior to 21 March 2012 (see paras **15.225** to **15.228**).
- By concession, and until 31 December 2011, the first time connection of a dwelling, RRP or RCP building to the gas or electricity mains.

Zero-rating extends to sub-contractors in the construction of a dwelling or caravan park, or approved alterations to a listed dwelling, but not otherwise.

The 5% rate can apply to:

- Conversions that involve a change in the number of single household dwellings in a building – eg from offices to flats, from a house to flats or from flats to a house (see paras **15.243** to **15.249**).
- Conversions of buildings to multiple occupancy dwellings (see paras **15.250** to **15.252**).
- Conversions of buildings for RRP use (see paras **15.253** and **15.254**).
- The renovation of dwellings or RRP buildings that have been empty for two years or more (see paras **15.255** to **15.267**).
- The installation of energy saving materials in a dwelling or RRP/RCP building but note that on 21 June 2012 the European Commission published a Reasoned Opinion notifying the UK Government of its intention to commence proceedings as in its opinion the use of the reduced rate in this way is not permissible under EU law. The UK Government considers that use of the reduced rate is acceptable in relation to RRP but removed the availability of the reduced rate in this context for RCP by introducing legislation in Finance Act 2013 (see Revenue & Customs Brief 26/12 and also paras **15.268** to **15.270**).
- Grant-funded heating and security installations in the homes of people aged over 60 or receiving certain benefits (see para **15.271**).
- The installation of certain 'mobility aids' in the homes of people aged 60 or over (see para **15.272**).
- In the Isle of Man, various other home improvement works (see para **15.273**).

The 5% rate applies to sub-contractors for conversions involving dwellings, some renovations of empty properties, and for the installation of energy saving materials and mobility aids, but not otherwise.

Building work: zero-rating – construction of dwellings

[15.221] VATA 1994, Sch 8, Group 5, item 2 zero-rates:

'The supply in the course of the construction of –

(a) a building designed as a dwelling or number of dwellings or intended for use solely for a relevant residential purpose or a relevant charitable purpose
. . .

of any services related to the construction other than the services of an architect, surveyor or any person acting as a consultant or in a supervisory capacity.'

'Construction' has the same meaning as in para **15.142** and 'building' and 'designed as a dwelling or number of dwellings' as in para **15.135** et seq. The extent to which supplies are 'in the course of' and 'related to' construction is considered in para **15.222**.

Item 4 then extends the zero-rating to:

> 'The supply of building materials to a person to whom the supplier is supplying services within item 2 or 3 of this Group which include the incorporation of the materials into the building (or its site) in question.'

So building materials are only zero-rated where supplied as part of zero-rated work, and by the same person. The meaning of 'building materials' is looked at in para **15.223**.

HMRC announced in Revenue & Customs Brief 13/16 that they will accept that a single dwelling that has been created from more than one building can be zero-rated or reduced-rated where the buildings are converted/constructed under a single project and single planning consent. HMRC have historically refused to allow these types of projects to benefit from the zero-rating provisions as VATA 1994, Sch 8, Group 5 refers to a 'building designed as a dwelling'. However the Tribunal held in *Mark Catchpole* (TC01995) [2012] UKFTT 309 (TC) and *Mr T Fox* (TC01957) [2012] UKFTT 264 (TC) that it was acceptable for the construction of dwellings from more than one building to be eligible for zero-rating if it is designed as a dwelling and meets the relevant conditions outlined above.

Zero-rated services

[15.222] Where it applies, the zero-rating covers services 'in the course of' and 'related to' to the construction, other than professional services. HMRC give an extensive list, in their Notice 708, of examples of what they do and do not see as covered by the zero-rating.

There are various points to note here:

- The zero-rating is not confined to the dwelling itself, and can extend to other works on the site, including civil engineering works and connection to utilities.
- A subsidiary building is unlikely to be zero-rated unless it is a garage. HMRC also do not see outdoor swimming pools, tennis courts, fish ponds and ornamental garden works as zero-rated.
- Preparatory work such as site clearance can be zero-rated, although HMRC might challenge this if construction does not follow promptly. In Revenue & Customs Brief 64/07, HMRC announced that, in some cases, they would now accept zero-rating for works to create serviced building plots, for onward sale, following their defeat in *Virtue (t/a Lammermuir Game Services)* (VTD 20259).
- Zero-rating only applies up to the point when the building is completed, although this does not affect the treatment of retention payments. Case law in this area, including under the 'DIY' refund scheme and in connection with RRP/RCP buildings, is summarised below.

- Where a contract involves other works, such as the construction of commercial premises, it will only be partly zero-rated and the total price will need to be split.
- The zero-rating extends to sub-contractors.
- Although professional services are excluded from zero-rating, HMRC accept that this does not apply where they are merely a subsidiary part of the contractor's supply, such as the design element of a 'design and build' contract.

Selected case law on whether a building was still 'in the course of construction'

Dwellings

- In *McElroy* (VTD 490), a builder went bankrupt, and an individual bought a house that was structurally complete but not yet habitable. The Tribunal held that the remaining work – installation of sanitary ware, central heating and electrical fittings, and decoration – was in the course of construction.
- In *Simister* (VTD 12715), a couple bought a new house and immediately added a conservatory, additional light fittings, a fitted wardrobe etc. The Tribunal held that the house had been complete when they bought it, so the work was not in the course of construction. Conservatories added to new houses were also found not to be zero-rated in *J M Associates* (VTD 18624).
- In *Morris* (VTD 17860), a contractor built a bungalow, and the householder then laid paths and a patio. This was not in the course of construction – a certificate of practical completion had already been issued, and the property was habitable and inhabited.
- In *James* (VTD 20426), the original plasterwork in a new house was wholly unsatisfactory, and new plasterers were engaged to replace it. The Tribunal held that construction was not complete until this was done, so that the replacement work was zero-rated, even though different contractors were used, and even though the certificate of completion had been issued, and the property occupied, in the meantime.
- In *Harrison-Devereux* (TC00561) the house itself was completed and occupied in 2004, although a dispute with the planning department meant that a certificate of completion was not issued until 2009. The Tribunal held that work in 2005, to install a drainage system, and to lay a patio and driveway, was still in the course of construction and zero-rated.
- *Central Sussex College* (TC04151) [2014] UKFTT 1058 (TCC) concerned a phased development, the phases being some years apart. The First-tier Tribunal considered that as it was not essential for nor definite that the second phase be carried out construction of the first phase took place before the second phase.

RRP/RCP buildings etc

- In *University of Hull* (VTD 180), the Tribunal held that 'a building remains in the course of construction until the main structure is completed, the windows glazed and all essential services and fittings, such as plumbing and electricity, have been installed therein. Thereafter the building ceases to be in the course of construction . . . and the phase of fitting out and furnishing is ready to begin'.

- Several cases have concerned developments initially completed on a less ambitious scale than first envisaged, and later enlarged in accordance with the original plans. The further work was not zero-rated, since by then there was a completed building on the site. This applied in *Brahma Kumaris World Spiritual University* (VTD 12946), *Trustee of Sir Robert Geffrey's School Charity* (VTD 17667) and *St Mary's Roman Catholic High School* ([1996] STC 1091, QB).
- A different approach was taken in *Hoylake Cottage Hospital Charitable Trust* (TC00925). A kitchen and laundry extension was added to a nursing home, as originally planned, a couple of years after its completion, and to meet regulatory requirements. The work was found to be zero-rated.

Building materials

[15.223] The zero-rating also covers 'building materials' supplied by the contractor, and incorporated or fitted in the building, in the course of zero-rated work.

VATA 1994, Sch 8, Group 5, Note 22 says that:

' "Building materials", in relation to any description of building, means goods of a description ordinarily incorporated by builders in a building of that description, (or its site), but does not include –
(a) finished or prefabricated furniture, other than furniture designed to be fitted in kitchens;
(b) materials for the construction of fitted furniture, other than kitchen furniture;
(c) electrical or gas appliances, unless the appliance is an appliance which is–
  (i) designed to heat space or water (or both) or to provide ventilation, air cooling, air purification, or dust extraction; or
  (ii) intended for use in a building designed as a number of dwellings and is a door-entry system, a waste disposal unit or a machine for compacting waste; or
  (iii) a burglar alarm, a fire alarm, or fire safety equipment or designed solely for the purpose of enabling aid to be summoned in an emergency; or
  (iv) a lift or hoist;
(d) carpets or carpeting material.'

Note 23 adds that 'incorporation' here includes installation as fittings.

So the items listed in (a) to (d) are standard-rated, as are any other goods of a kind not 'ordinarily incorporated' by builders in the type of building in question. These same items are relevant to the 'blocking order' referred to in para **15.149** – a developer granting a zero-rated major interest in the dwelling may be unable to recover the VAT on these items, which will therefore represent a cost. (As noted in para **15.149**, there are some doubts about the actual scope and effectiveness of the blocking order.)

There are various points about the interpretation of Note 22, some of them dating back to earlier versions of the legislation, or indeed to case law about VAT's predecessor, Purchase Tax. HMRC offer their own views, at some length, in Notice 708 and in their internal VAT manual 'Construction' (VCONST13000 et seq).

- 'Goods of a description' is generally interpreted in terms of broad categories of item. HMRC give the example of gold-plated taps: these are seen as 'ordinarily incorporated' by builders because taps are ordinarily incorporated – the gold-plating is irrelevant. This approach mainly derives from the decisions in *F Booker Builders* (VTD 446) and *Smitmit Design Centre Ltd* (QB [1982] STC 525), albeit both about an earlier version of the legislation.

- HMRC maintain that 'a building of that description' is similarly broad and that, in particular, dwellings are a single category, without any distinction between different ends of the market. This too can be traced back to *F Booker Builders*, above, but there are plenty of inconsistencies here. Note 22(c) differentiates flats from houses, and includes items that are clearly only 'ordinary' in some types of housing. In practice, sheltered housing has long been accepted as a separate category. And the Tribunal rejected HMRC's approach in *Rainbow Pools London Ltd* (VTD 20800): highlighting their acceptance that indoor swimming pools were 'ordinarily incorporated', when this was clearly not true of the housing market as a whole, it concluded that both high-rise flats and luxury dwelling houses were 'descriptions' in their own right.

- 'Ordinarily' probably suggests something that happens more often than not. In a Purchase Tax case, *F Austin (Leyton) Ltd* ([1968] 2 All ER 13), the High Court considered the question in terms of whether one would expect a builder to install the item 'in the ordinary way and without any special instruction', and in *Smitmit Design Centre Ltd* (QB [1982] STC 525) it saw 'ordinarily' as equating to 'commonly' or perhaps 'usually'. It is also recognised that what is 'ordinary' can evolve over time – a point brought out in *Rialto Homes plc* (VTD 16340), where the Tribunal noted that it had become normal practice for planning authorities to insist on the planting of trees and shrubs in housing developments.

As to the specific exclusions in (a) to (d):

- HMRC accept that some storage facilities, such as very basic wardrobes built into alcoves, are not 'furniture', commenting in detail in their Notice 708. This follows from their defeat in *Harrington Construction Ltd* (VTD 3470). Subsequent cases, including *McLean Homes Midland Ltd* (QB [1993] STC 335) have taken a similar approach.

- There are some difficulties with the reference in (c) to 'electrical appliances'. HMRC place much reliance on *Garndene Communications Systems Ltd* (VTD 2553), where the Tribunal thought that an electrical appliance was 'a device which is operated by electricity – in other words, a device which works when electricity is applied to it.' They therefore regard electrically operated gates and garage doors as 'electrical appliances' when supplied as a single unit. In *Rainbow Pools*, above, however, the Tribunal did not see electrically powered swimming pool covers as 'electrical appliances' since the electrical element was minor, and not actually essential.

- HMRC see (d) as including carpet tiles and underlay, but not other forms of flooring such as linoleum, ceramic tiles, or parquet. The Tribunals in *McCarthy & Stone plc* (VTD 7014) and *BGM Ltd* (VTD 11793) agreed with them that carpeting was still carpeting when installed to provide sound insulation.

Building work: zero-rating – construction of RRP/RCP buildings

[15.224] As shown in para **15.221**, VATA 1994, Sch 8, Group 5, item 2 zero-rates the construction of buildings 'solely for a relevant residential purpose or a relevant charitable purpose' as well as dwellings.

Most of the points here follow from paras **15.221** to **15.223** and from paras **15.151** to **15.168**:

- Construction has the same meaning as in para **15.142**, although RCP annexes are included in the same way as in para **15.168**.
- The buildings qualifying are the same as in paras **15.151** to **15.164**, and subject to the same points with the interpretation of 'solely', which again HMRC will accept as meaning 95%. Outbuildings will need to qualify for zero-rating in their own right.
- The further points in paras **15.221** to **15.223** also apply here, with the difference that zero-rating does not apply to sub-contractors.
- Only the end user can commission work on a zero-rated basis, so that zero-rating for works is an alternative to zero-rating by a developer under the rules in para **15.151**. The end user must issue a certificate of intended use, in a form set out in HMRC's Notice 708. In law, any supplies made before the certificate is issued cannot be zero-rated, but HMRC will normally tolerate later certification (see Notice 708, para **17.6**).
- As at para **15.223**, the zero-rating extends to building materials, other than items not 'ordinarily incorporated' by builders – HMRC's guidance in Notice 708 includes material on RRP/RCP buildings.

Building work: zero-rating – approved alterations to listed buildings

[15.225] If listed building consent was applied for prior to 21 March 2012 VATA 1994, Sch 8, Group 6, item 2 (prior to its repeal) zero-rates:

> 'The supply, in the course of an approved alteration of a protected building, of any services other than the services of an architect, surveyor or any person acting as consultant or in a supervisory capacity.'

It should be noted that zero-rating will only be available in relation to services implementing a project comprising the listed buildings consent. Anti-forestalling legislation was implemented.

'Protected building' has the same meaning as in para **15.177** – essentially it means listed buildings that are dwellings or intended 'solely' (or at least 95%) for RRP/RCP use. As with construction, zero-rating extends to sub-contractors in the case of dwellings, but not for RRP/RCP buildings – for these, the supplies must be to the end user, who must issue a certificate of intended use in a form published by HMRC in Notice 708.

It is the building as a whole that is listed, but if, for example, it consists of both a dwelling and a shop, only the work to the dwelling will qualify.

The meaning of 'approved' and 'alteration' is looked at in paras **15.226** and **15.227**, but in particular it excludes repair and maintenance, and works not requiring listed building consent. For any substantial project, it is unusual for all the works to qualify.

Item 3 then zero-rates:

'The supply of building materials to a person to whom the supplier is supplying services within item 2 of this Group which include the incorporation of the materials into the building (or its site) in question.'

This applies in the same way as item 4 of Group 5, as explained in para **15.223**. Materials may need to be split between those used in zero-rated alteration and those used in standard-rated repair or maintenance.

Works in the grounds, or to subsidiary buildings, will not generally qualify for zero-rating, and this is considered in para **15.228**.

Approved

[**15.226**] Zero-rating requires the alterations to be 'approved'. This generally means that they must both require and receive listed building consent, and be carried out in accordance with it. Zero-rating does not strictly apply if the work did not actually need consent, but this is not always clear and this is not a point on which HMRC are always competent to insist. The Tribunal, however, has often been willing to explore this, and to contradict the planning authority on the point. Zero-rating also does not apply if consent is only obtained retrospectively.

Zero-rating can also apply to alterations:

- to a scheduled monument, with scheduled monument consent;
- to listed churches – in England and Wales this applies to churches with ecclesiastical exemption from obtaining listed building consent; in Scotland and Northern Ireland it is by concession;
- to listed buildings covered by Crown immunity from planning requirements, where the work would otherwise have required consent – this potentially applies to buildings held by the Crown, including government departments, and by the Duchies of Cornwall and Lancaster, although the immunity has now largely been removed.

Alteration

[**15.227**] 'Alteration' is not defined, but VATA 1994, Sch 8, Group 6, Note 6 says that it:

'does not include any works of repair or maintenance, or any incidental alteration to the fabric of a building which results from the carrying out of repairs, or maintenance work.'

There is, however, extensive case law on the subject, including cases dating from before 1984, when alterations to any building were zero-rated.

If the works are on any scale, it is unusual for all of them to qualify, and HMRC, and generally the Tribunal, will expect to break down the schedule of works into all its components and to take individual decisions on whether zero-rating is appropriate. It is possible that this is not what the legislation intended, and that the words 'in the course of' suggest a broader-brush approach.

In the light of HMRC's policy and the case law, the main points to consider are:

• Whether the work is to the fabric of the building – this includes its walls, roof, internal surfaces, floors, stairs, doors and windows, also plumbing and wiring and special design features such as a bell frame in a church. If the works are not to the fabric, they are unlikely to be accepted as zero-rated.

• The impact of the work on the appearance of the building. HMRC's view is that an alteration will usually have more than a trivial effect on the building's appearance.

• Why the work is being done. The exclusion for repair and maintenance is to a large extent about motive – HMRC's Notice 708 describes repair and maintenance as 'tasks designed to minimise, for as long as possible, the need for, and future scale and cost of, further attention to the fabric of the building'.

• Whether the work is incidental to something else. HMRC accept that some repair and maintenance, such as plastering to make good, consequent upon alteration can be zero-rated. Conversely, the law specifically excludes from zero-rating 'any incidental alteration to the fabric of a building which results from the carrying out of repairs, or maintenance work'.

'Alteration' or 'repair or maintenance' – HMRC's views

The following examples are given in HMRC's Notice 708:

Work	*VAT treatment*
Extensions	Alteration
Opening/closing doorways	Alteration
Replacement of rotten wooden windows with UPVC double glazing	Repair or maintenance
Replacement of UPVC double glazing with copies of original wooden windows for aesthetic reasons	Alteration
Installing a window where one did not exist before	Alteration
Re-felt and batten roof	Repair or maintenance
Replacement of a flat roof with a pitched roof	Alteration

Work	*VAT treatment*
Replacement of straw thatch with reeds; and changes to the ridge detail of a thatched roof	Repair or maintenance when carried out as part of the normal renewal programme.
Damp proofing	Repair or maintenance
Making good	Follows the liability of the main work
Re-decorating	Repair or maintenance
Re-pointing	Repair or maintenance
Re-wiring	Repair or maintenance
Extending wiring and plumbing systems	Alteration
Replacing boilers at the same time as extending plumbing systems	Alteration when replaced as a direct consequence of deciding to extend the plumbing system. But repair or maintenance when the decision to extend the plumbing system is made following the need to replace a boiler.
Flood lighting	Alteration when installed on the building. But neither an alteration nor repair or maintenance (and therefore standard-rated) when installed within the grounds of a building – there is no work to the fabric of the building.

Selected case law on 'alteration'

Two House of Lords judgments date from the early 1980s, when any alteration to a building was zero-rated:

- In *ACT Construction Ltd* ([1982] STC 25), underpinning was accepted as zero-rated alteration. HMRC had contended that the work was standard-rated repair or maintenance, since the aim was to prevent the buildings collapsing.
- *Viva Gas Appliances Ltd* ([1983] STC 819) concerned the installation of gas fires in dwellings, and the associated work to fireplaces. HMRC argued that alteration work had to be substantial in relation to the building as a whole; the House of Lords accepted that some work was so trivial that it had to be ignored, but rejected HMRC's 'substantial' argument and concluded that the work was zero-rated.

The cases remain binding precedent, and are directly relevant to the rules for listed buildings. There have been dozens of cases specifically about alterations to listed buildings, few of which have progressed beyond the Tribunal. Only a handful are noted here:

- In *Windflower Housing Association* ([1995] STC 860, QB), the High Court found that works to a leaking roof were standard-rated as part of a project of repair and maintenance. Even though the works changed the appearance of the roof, their purpose was to repair the roof and reduce leakage by improving the drainage of water from it.

- In *Morrish* ([1998] STC 954, QB), the High Court decided that works to a fire-damaged listed building were too extensive to amount to alteration. Although this was what HMRC had argued, the case is something of an embarrassment to them, and their internal guidance says that it is not to be followed.

- *Evans* (VTD 4415) concerned various roofing works. The Tribunal thought that work involving a change in the appearance of a roof – whether to its shape or eg the type of slate used – could be seen as alteration provided the roof was not in need of repair. New guttering was alteration, but replacement guttering was not, even where cast iron was replaced with plastic.

- In *Vivodean Ltd* (VTD 6538), underpinning was zero-rated, in line with *ACT Construction*. But a range of other work was standard-rated repair or maintenance – this covered the insertion of new windows and doors in existing openings, repointing of walls, rewiring, replacement of internal partitions, and replacement water tanks and pipework (notwithstanding the use of copper pipes in place of lead).

- In *Rhodes* (VTD 14533), part of a roof was in need of repair and part was not. The whole roof was retiled using a different material (stone rather than clay tiles). The works were standard-rated for the parts where repairs were needed and zero-rated where they were not. In *Wanklin* (VTD 20133), however, the Tribunal thought on broadly similar facts that the whole work was driven by the need to repair and maintain, and so was standard-rated.

- *Wells* (VTD 15169) was a wide-ranging case, and illustrates the tendency of the Tribunal, and of HMRC, to break works down into all their components, rather than considering whether they were 'in the course of alteration' as a whole. Although the appellant clearly was altering the building, various work was found to be standard-rated as repair or maintenance, as too trivial to be alteration, or as not requiring listed building consent.
  The Tribunal concluded that:
  - replacement of existing roofing materials, and the rebuilding of chimneys to the same height, was standard-rated;
  - repointing a wall was standard-rated unless part of a wider project, such as to make good structural alterations;
  - damp proofing and the treatment of timbers were standard-rated;
  - the insertion of doors and windows in new openings could be zero-rated, but not in existing openings;
  - the lowering of a floor or ceiling could be zero-rated, unless it was done in the course of repair or maintenance – specifically, the taking up and lowering of a floor to install damp proofing was standard-rated;
  - the replacement of damaged flagstones was standard-rated;
  - the removal of partitions was zero-rated, as was the insertion of partitions where there had been none before;
  - zero-rating could apply to the first time installation of window seats, the creation of niches and alcoves and the relocation of a fireplace;
  - redecoration or re-plastering was standard-rated unless it was a direct consequence of other work which was zero-rated;
  - the installation of new steps could be zero-rated, but the replacement of stairs, albeit to a different design, was standard-rated;

- the first time installation of light fittings, switches and sockets, of ventilation and of sanitary ware were standard-rated, being too trivial to change the appearance of the building, but zero-rating did apply to the first time installation of a septic tank;
- the replacement of a central heating system was standard-rated as not requiring listed building consent.

Grounds and outbuildings

[15.228] Alterations to a detached subsidiary building cannot be zero-rated under these rules unless:

- It counts as a protected building in its own right – ie it is separately listed, or covered by the listing, and is designed as a separate dwelling or is intended 'solely' for RRP/RCP use. In the light of the House of Lords judgment in *Zielinski Baker* ([2004] STC 456), an outbuilding used with a dwelling cannot simply be treated as part of the dwelling.
- Where the building is a garage occupied with a protected dwelling and constructed at the same time as the dwelling was either constructed or substantially reconstructed. Following *Grange Builders (Quainton)* (VTD 18905), HMRC accept that it need not originally have been built as a garage.

The construction of a new building, including a new garage, cannot be zero-rated under these rules, although sometimes it will be zero-rated in its own right under the rules in para **15.221** et seq or **15.224** et seq.

Features in the grounds of a listed building will often be covered by the listing, but *Zielinski Baker* suggests that work to them is only zero-rated if they can actually be seen as part of the building.

Selected case law on subsidiary buildings etc

- *Zielinski Baker & Partners* ([2004] STC 456) concerned the conversion of a barn, five metres from a listed dwelling, for use as a swimming pool and games room. Planning law treated it as part of the listed dwelling, but the House of Lords concluded that this could not be read into VAT law, which looked at buildings in their own right and did not contemplate a dwelling consisting of more than one building. The works were therefore standard-rated.

The following cases have been decided since *Zielinski Baker*:

- In *Smith* (VTD 19064), the conversion of an outbuilding, covered by the listing, to provide additional living accommodation was standard-rated – under *Zielinski Baker* it could not be seen as part of the main dwelling, whilst a prohibition on separate use or disposal meant that it was not 'designed to become a dwelling' in its own right.
- In *King* (VTD 19208), work to a detached barn used with a listed dwelling, and alterations to a terrace and driveway, were standard-rated.
- *Collins and Beckett Ltd* (VTD 19212) concerned a new swimming pool complex linked by a corridor to a listed dwelling. The Tribunal concluded that the construction of the complex was standard-rated because it was a new building, and that only the corridor and linking work was zero-rated.

- In *Tinsley* ([2005] EWHC 1508 (Ch)), the construction of a terrace abutting a listed dwelling was held to be standard-rated.

There is extensive earlier case law in this area, but much of it would seem to be incorrect in the light of *Zielinski Baker*.

Building work: zero-rating – conversions for housing associations

[15.229] VATA 1994, Sch 8, Group 5, item 3 zero-rates:

'The supply to a relevant housing association in the course of conversion of a non-residential building or a non-residential part of a building into –

(a)   a building or part of a building designed as a dwelling or number of dwellings; or

(b)   a building or part of a building intended for use solely for a relevant residential purpose,

of any services related to the conversion other than the services of an architect, surveyor or any person acting as a consultant or in a supervisory capacity.'

This applies as follows:

- A 'relevant housing association' means (in England) a private registered provider of social housing, (in Wales and Scotland) a registered social landlord or (in Northern Ireland) a registered housing association. Zero-rating only applies if the supplies are to such an organisation, and so does not extend to sub-contractors.
- 'Designed as a dwelling or number of dwellings' has the same meaning as in para **15.135** et seq.
- 'Solely for a relevant residential purpose' means the same as in para **15.152** et seq, although in this context HMRC have not suggested that 95% can necessarily be treated as 'solely'. For conversions to RRP use, the housing association must issue the contractor with a certificate in the form set out in HMRC's Notice 708. In law, zero-rating only applies from the point when the certificate is issued, but HMRC will normally tolerate a late certificate (see Notice 708, para **17.6**).
- A 'non-residential building' is defined in Sch 8, Group 5, Note 7A. This is the same as Note 7 (see para **15.173**), except that the ten-year limit relates to the period until works commence, rather than to the period prior to the grant of a major interest. Subject to this difference, the issues are the same as in paras **15.173** and **15.175**, including in relation to Notes 8 and 9 and parts of buildings – where only part of the building qualifies, zero-rating under these rules will apply only to that part.
- The law does not define 'conversion', but HMRC are likely to accept any project which involves some alteration, and the requisite change of use consent, as qualifying. The zero-rating then extends to any work 'in the course of' the conversion, and to building materials on the same basis, and with the same restrictions, as in paras **15.222** and **15.223**. Zero-rating ceases, however, as soon as the building (or part) is occupied.

- The zero-rating is not confined to the dwelling itself, and can extend to other works on the site, including civil engineering works and connection to utilities. It is unlikely to extend to a subsidiary building unless this is a garage for use with a newly-created dwelling and constructed or converted from non-residential use at the same time.

Conversions of this kind are likely also to be eligible for zero-rating under the rules in para **15.172** et seq, if the developer grants a major interest, and for the 5% VAT rate under the rules in paras **15.243** et seq or **15.253** et seq. The rationale for the special zero-rating for housing associations is that they are often unable to grant a major interest.

Building work: zero-rating – people with disabilities

[15.230] Some building work for the benefit of people with disabilities is zero-rated under VATA 1994, Sch 8, Group 12 ('Drugs, medicines, aids for the disabled'). These rules are entirely separate from the other zero-ratings for building work. They are piecemeal, and complicated, with different restrictions applying to different items – this is largely because they have been carefully costed measures wrung out of the Treasury in successive Budgets.

The works generally need to be supplied to the individual or, in some cases, to a charity, and so do not apply to sub-contractors. The main zero-rating provisions are outlined below.

General points

[15.231] The various provisions refer to a 'disabled person' and this is a person who is 'chronically sick or disabled'. In their Notice 701/7 (reissued in December 2014), HMRC suggest that this covers people:

- with a physical or mental impairment which has a long-term and substantial adverse effect upon their ability to carry out everyday activities (this would include people who are blind, deaf or dumb); or
- with a condition which the medical profession treats as a chronic sickness, such as diabetes.

The precise rules vary from item to item, but in each case the supply must be to the individual disabled person, or in some cases to a charity. As a matter of law, zero-rating does not apply if the work is commissioned by someone else, even if the work is paid for by the disabled person. HMRC will, by concession, accept zero-rating if a parent, spouse or guardian acts on behalf of the disabled person, but will not necessarily do so if, say, someone commissions work on behalf of their elderly parent.

Some of the rules also require the works to be in the disabled person's private residence – zero-rating will not apply if the person is merely a visitor. HMRC do, however, now accept that a private residence includes a garden, garage or other outbuilding.

In general, there also needs to be a clear link between the nature of the work and the person's condition – HMRC cite the example of the supply of an adjustable bed to someone whose only disability is impaired sight: the bed is not obviously relevant to the disability and so is standard-rated.

The contractor needs to be satisfied that zero-rating is appropriate, and Notice 701/7 (at para **3.6**) sets out forms of certificate that customers can use to substantiate this. Certification is not a legal requirement, but is advisable.

Materials are generally included in the zero-rating, but only where there is also a zero-rated supply of services. In *Johnsen* (VTD 17897), gates were not zero-rated because, amongst other reasons, the contractor only charged for the goods and seems to have provided the services free of charge. On the other hand, the goods do not need to be supplied by the same person as the services – this was demonstrated in *Flather* (VTD 11960).

Other than in relation to lifts, the zero-rating does not extend to professional services, such as those of an architect or surveyor.

Ramps, doorways and passages

[15.232] VATA 1994, Sch 8, Group 12, item 8 zero-rates:

'The supply to a disabled person of a service of constructing ramps or widening doorways or passages for the purpose of facilitating his entry to or movement within his private residence.'

Item 9 also zero-rates:

'The supply to a charity of a service described in item 8 for the purpose of facilitating a disabled person's entry to or movement within any building.'

Zero-rating does not, in particular, cover a new doorway or passage, or a ramp or access to facilitate the movement of goods. Where it applies, the zero-rating extends to associated goods. Under item 9, the charity need have no other connection with the building.

Bathrooms etc – supply to individual

[15.233] VATA 1994, Sch 8, Group 12, item 10 zero-rates:

'The supply to a disabled person of a service of providing, extending or adapting a bathroom, washroom or lavatory in his private residence where such provision, extension or adaptation is necessary by reason of his condition.'

A bathroom here includes a shower room. The zero-rating extends to associated goods and preparatory or restoration work.

Bathrooms etc – supply to charity

[15.234] VATA 1994, Sch 8, Group 12, item 11 zero-rates:

'The supply to a charity of a service of providing, extending or adapting a bathroom, washroom or lavatory for use by disabled persons –

(a)   in residential accommodation, or
(b)   in a day-centre where at least 20 per cent of the individuals using the centre are disabled persons,

where such provision, extension or adaptation is necessary by reason of the condition of the disabled persons.'

Under item 11, the charity need have no other connection with the property, but Note 5J defines 'residential accommodation' as meaning a residential home or self-contained living accommodation provided as a permanent or temporary residence for disabled person, but excluding an inn, hotel, boarding house or similar establishment (see para **15.39**). The zero-rating therefore does not cover work commissioned by a charity in a normal private residence. Where it applies, the zero-rating extends to associated goods.

VATA 1994, Sch 8, Group 12, item 12 also zero-rates:

'The supply to a charity of a service of providing, extending or adapting a washroom or lavatory for use by disabled persons in a building, or any part of a building, used principally by a charity for charitable purposes where such provision, extension or adaptation is necessary to facilitate the use of the washroom or lavatory by disabled persons.'

This excludes bathrooms or shower rooms. Again, the charity commissioning the work need have no other connection with the property – it can be a different charity that actually uses the building. In this case, there is no specific provision extending the zero-rating to associated goods.

Lifts – supply to individual

[**15.235**] VATA 1994, Sch 8, Group 12, item 16 zero-rates:

'The supply to a disabled person of services necessarily performed in the installation of a lift for the purpose of facilitating his movement between floors within his private residence.'

Zero-rating extends to associated goods, most obviously the lift itself, and (under items 5 and 6) their subsequent repair and maintenance, including the replacement of parts. In the light of *Friends of the Elderly* (VTD 20597), it also applies to professional services. This is not the case for the rules discussed in paras **15.232** to **15.234**.

Lifts – supply to a charity

[**15.236**] VATA 1994, Sch 8, Group 12, item 17 zero-rates:

'The supply to a charity providing a permanent or temporary residence or day-centre for disabled persons of services necessarily performed in the installation of a lift for the purpose of facilitating the movement of disabled persons between floors within that building.'

Again, this does not cover work commissioned by a charity in a normal private home, and in this case, the charity commissioning the work must also be the charity providing the residence or day centre.

In practice, it is not necessary for the building to be specifically for disabled persons, at least if the lift is partly intended for such persons, as evidenced for example by the positioning of buttons. HMRC accept that universities, charitable schools etc can obtain zero-rating for lifts in general purpose student accommodation. Goods lifts, however, clearly cannot qualify.

As in para **15.235**, zero-rating extends to the lift itself and other associated goods, to their subsequent repair and maintenance, including the replacement of parts, and apparently to professional services.

Consequential works

[15.237] In the previous version of Notice 701/7, HMRC said, addressing the contractor, that:

'Where economy and feasibility dictate that you have constructed or extended in the course of a zero-rated supply, and have occupied space which was previously part of another room then you may also zero-rate the service of restoring that room elsewhere in the building to its original size. This is because the work is essential to providing the service to your disabled customer.'

This (concessionary treatment) is not replicated in the new version of Notice 701/7 and has seemingly been withdrawn. It was not expected and HMRC are yet to clarify their position.

Alarm systems

[15.238] VATA 1994, Sch 8, Group 12, item 19 zero-rates:

'The supply to a disabled person for domestic or his personal use, or to a charity for making available to disabled persons by sale or otherwise for domestic or their personal use, of an alarm system designed to be capable of operation by a disabled person, and to enable him to alert directly a specified person or a control centre.'

Where this applies, subsequent repair and maintenance, including the provision of spare parts, are also zero-rated.

Equipment

[15.239] VATA 1994, Sch 8, Group 12, item 2 zero-rates:

'The supply to a disabled person for domestic or his personal use, or to a charity for making available to disabled persons by sale or otherwise, for domestic or their personal use . . . '

of various equipment and appliances, some of which are potentially relevant to building work, such as adjustable beds, commode chairs, chair or stair lifts, hoists and lifters, and any other

'equipment and appliances . . . designed solely for use by a disabled person'.

This has, for example, allowed zero-rating for a specially designed heating system (in *David Lewis Centre* ([1995] STC 485, QB), although not in other cases), a hydrotherapy pool (*Boys' and Girls' Welfare Society* (VTD 15274)) and an air purification system (*Symons* (VTD 19174)). But equipment which might have wider application will generally not qualify, and this is a serious limitation – in *Dennison* (VTD 18619), for example, the supplier had specifically modified equipment to meet the needs of the particular disabled person, but zero-rating was denied because the supplier went on to adopt the modified system as standard.

Where zero-rating does apply, it extends to installation, parts and accessories and to subsequent repair and maintenance, including replacement parts.

Building work: zero-rating – other cases

Construction of residential caravan parks

[15.240] VATA 1994, Sch 8 Group 5 item 2 zero-rates:

'The supply in the course of the construction of – . . .

(b)   any civil engineering work necessary for the development of a permanent park for residential caravans,

of any services related to the construction other than the services of an architect, surveyor or any person acting as a consultant or in a supervisory capacity.'

Note 15 explains that:

'The reference in item 2(b) of this Group to the construction of a civil engineering work does not include a reference to the conversion, reconstruction, alteration or enlargement of a work.'

And Note 19 adds that:

'A caravan is not a residential caravan if residence in it throughout the year is prevented by the terms of a covenant, statutory planning consent or similar permission.'

The zero-rating potentially covers the laying of pitches, roads, paths etc, and connection to utilities, drainage and sewerage. It does not cover work that is not 'necessary' to the development, or the construction of any building. It can apply to sub-contractors.

Donated medical equipment etc

[15.241] VATA 1994, Sch 8, Group 15, items 4 to 7 zero-rate the supply, leasing, repair or maintenance of some equipment used by charities, the NHS etc. This must be paid for by a charity or from voluntary contributions, and is primarily relevant in the areas of medical care, training and research.

These rules are of limited application, although important where they do apply, and in some cases relevant to building work. Where the other conditions are met, they can allow zero-rating for such items as fume cupboards and laboratory benches, and on the unusual and specific facts of an anonymised case, *Research Establishment* (VTD 19095), a specialised air ventilation system. The zero-rating covers the goods themselves, and potentially their subsequent repair and maintenance, but not their initial installation.

HMRC's Notice 701/6 gives further details.

Sea rescue charities

[15.242] VATA 1994, Sch 8, Group 8, item 3 zero-rates the supply to a sea rescue charity of construction and other work to lifeboat slipways. In *Royal National Lifeboat Institution* (TC00017), the Tribunal accepted that, under the Directive, some works to lifeboat stations should also be zero-rated. The decision emphasised the operational needs of lifeboats, and is probably of limited application in relation to other vessels.

Building work: reduced rate – 'changed number of dwellings conversions'

[15.243] VATA 1994, Sch 7A, Group 6 applies the 5% rate to, amongst other things, conversions of property to single household dwellings, and conversions involving a change in the number of such dwellings in a building, eg from a house to flats or from flats to a house. The rules apply to sub-contractors as well as the main contractor.

Item 1 applies the 5% rate to:

'The supply, in the course of a qualifying conversion, of qualifying services related to the conversion.'

Note 2 explains that a 'qualifying conversion' includes a 'changed number of dwellings conversion' and Note 3 says that:

'(1)   A "changed number of dwellings conversion" is –
  (a)   a conversion of premises consisting of a building where the conditions specified in this paragraph are satisfied, or
  (b)   a conversion of premises consisting of a part of a building where those conditions are satisfied.
(2)   The first condition is that after the conversion the premises being converted contain a number of single household dwellings that is –
  (a)   different from the number (if any) that the premises contain before the conversion, and
  (b)   greater than, or equal to, one.
(3)   The second condition is that there is no part of the premises being converted that is a part that after the conversion contains the same number of single household dwellings (whether zero, one or two or more) as before the conversion.'

The effect of (3) here is that if, say, four dwellings are converted into three by merging two of them, any work to the two continuing dwellings does not qualify. But the vagueness of the reference to a 'part' raises some problems. These were explored in *Wellcome Trust*, summarised below, but the decision perhaps obscures as much as it clarifies.

Note 10 adds that the works need to have had any necessary planning consent and building control approval.

The rules contain no time limits in relation to either past or future use – if, say, two flats are converted to a single house, it does not matter how long they have been two flats, or how long the property then continues to be a single house.

Case law on 'changed number of dwellings' conversions

- In *Monoprio* (VTD 17806), a coach house and stables were converted to a house. The coach house had included a flat, which was incorporated into the new house, and the Tribunal concluded that this had been a 'single household dwelling'. There was therefore no change in the number of such dwellings, so that the works were standard-rated.
- *Wellcome Trust* (VTD 18417) concerned a complicated conversion project, most of which qualified for the 5% rate. But one flat was in large part retained, gaining a net 0.7% by floor area but, through the lowering of a

ceiling, losing 5% of its volume. The issue was whether there was 'a part that after the conversion contains the same number of single household dwellings . . . as before the conversion' – if so, the work to it did not qualify. The Tribunal concluded that a 'part' of the building must mean something:

- large enough to be capable of containing a single household dwelling;
- identifiable by reference to physical boundaries, normally walls, floors and ceilings, and not for example a notional line across a room; and
- defined in terms of space in all dimensions, and not merely footprint.

In principle, the restriction only applied if a dwelling (or constant number of dwellings) occupied exactly the same such 'part' as before. This might have suggested that the work did qualify, but the Tribunal went on to hold that the overlap between the old and new contained 'all the essential elements of a single household dwelling', and that the changes were not substantial enough to affect this. It followed that 'part' of the building had indeed contained one dwelling before and after the conversion, and that the work to this flat was standard-rated.

- *Daniel Nabarro* (TC03757) [2014] UKFTT 633 (TC) concerned works carried out on a house which also had the benefit of a self-contained flat on the same site. The flat was demolished and the house extended. It was accepted by the First-tier Tribunal that there had previously been two dwellings on the site in question and accepted that there had been a reduction from two to one household dwelling.

Single household dwellings

[15.244] Under Note 3, a single household dwelling is one 'that is designed for occupation by a single household' and which meets the following conditions, listed in Note 4(3):

'(a)   that the dwelling consists of self-contained living accommodation,

(b)   that there is no provision for direct internal access from the dwelling to any other dwelling or part of a dwelling,

(c)   that the separate use of the dwelling is not prohibited by the terms of any covenant, statutory planning consent or similar provision, and

(d)   that the separate disposal of the dwelling is not prohibited by any such terms.'

These are essentially the same conditions as for 'designed as a dwelling' in the context of zero-rating, (omitting the condition about planning consent, dealt with here in Note 10), and so can probably be interpreted in the same way as in para **15.135** et seq. The 'single household' requirement is, however, a further restriction, and HMRC suggest that all the rooms, including kitchen, bathroom and toilet, need to be behind a door that only one household can use.

Also, Note 4(4) explains that a dwelling 'is designed' for a particular kind of occupation if it was originally constructed for such occupation and not subsequently adapted for another kind of occupation, or as a result of occupation.

Qualifying services

[15.245] The 5% rate applies to 'qualifying services' 'in the course of a qualifying conversion' and 'related to the conversion'. 'Conversion' itself is not defined, but HMRC are likely to expect there to be some alteration work.

Note 11 explains that a 'supply of qualifying services':

'means a supply of services that consists in –

(a)   the carrying out of works to the fabric of the building, or

(b)   the carrying out of works within the immediate site of the building that are in connection with –

    (i)   the means of providing water, power, heat or access to the building,

    (ii)   the means of providing drainage or security for the building, or

    (iii)   the provision of means of waste disposal for the building.'

Where only part of the building is being converted, the work must be to the fabric of the relevant part, or must provide water, drainage, waste disposal etc to that part.

It is less clear how much the 5% rate is limited by the words 'in the course of' and 'related to'. Conversion projects are likely to involve much work that is not actually essential to the conversion, or which might have been done anyway, such as redecoration or repairs to the roof. Notice 708 suggests that any work of repair, maintenance or improvement to the fabric of the building can qualify, but HMRC will sometimes argue that work does not qualify because it is not sufficiently linked to the change in the number of dwellings.

Note 11 also says that:

'references to the carrying out of works to the fabric of a building [or part] do not include the incorporation, or installation as fittings, in the building [or part] of any goods that are not building materials'.

Building materials

[15.246] Item 2 extends the 5% rate to:

'The supply of building materials if –

(a)   the materials are supplied by a person who, in the course of a qualifying conversion, is supplying qualifying services related to the conversion, and

(b)   those services include the incorporation of the materials in the building concerned or its immediate site.'

'Building materials' has the same meaning as for zero-rating, as in para **15.223**, and therefore excludes such items as carpets and 'white goods'. The 5% rate does not apply where the supplier is only providing materials.

Garages

[15.247] Note 9 says that a qualifying conversion includes any related 'garage works', being:

'the construction of a garage',

or

'a conversion of a non-residential building, or of a non-residential part of a building, that results in a garage'

if

'they are carried out at the same time as the conversion',

and

> 'the resulting garage is intended to be occupied with . . . a single household dwelling that will after the conversion be contained in the building, or part of a building, being converted'.

Where this applies, services and materials are taxable at 5% in the same way as for the dwelling itself.

Other works on the site

[**15.248**] The law does not explicitly allow the 5% rate to apply to works in the grounds, other than for garages and access, utilities etc. In practice, HMRC may accept some other work in the immediate vicinity of the building, but are unlikely to do so for outbuildings that are not garages, or for ornamental features etc.

Professional services

[**15.249**] The 5% rate does not extend to related professional services.

Building work: reduced rate – 'house in multiple occupation conversions'

[**15.250**] The conversion of a building to a 'multiple occupancy dwelling' is taxable at 5%. Like the rules for a 'changed number of dwellings' conversion in para **15.243**, this is under VATA 1994, Sch 7A, Group 6, and many of the same rules apply. Again, the rules can apply to sub-contractors.

Under VATA 1994, Sch 7A, Group 6, Note 2, a 'qualifying conversion' includes a 'house in multiple occupation conversion', which Note 5 defines as the conversion of a building or part of a building where:

> '(a)   before the conversion the premises being converted do not contain any multiple occupancy dwellings,
> (b)   after the conversion those premises contain only a multiple occupancy dwelling or two or more such dwellings, and
> (c)   the use to which those premises are intended to be put after the conversion is not to any extent use for a relevant residential purpose.'

As with a 'changed number of dwellings' conversion, the works need to have had any necessary planning consent and building control approval, and there are no time limits as to the duration of previous use or of future use as a multiple occupancy dwelling.

Multiple occupancy dwellings

[**15.251**] Under Note 4, a 'multiple occupancy dwelling':

> 'means a dwelling –
> (a)   that is designed for occupation by persons not forming a single household,
> (aa)   that is not to any extent used for a relevant residential purpose, and
> (b)   in relation to which the conditions set out in sub-paragraph (3) are satisfied.'

The conditions in 4(3) are listed in para **15.244**, and a 'relevant residential purpose' has the same meaning as in para **15.155** et seq, although without the usual requirement for a building to be 'solely' for such use. A building is designed for occupation by persons not forming a single household if it has been adapted for such occupation, or was built for such occupation and has not been subsequently adapted for something else.

Extent of the 5% rate

[15.252] Where the 5% rate applies, it does so in the same way as for a 'changed number of dwellings' conversion, and the points in paras **15.245** to **15.249** about qualifying services, building materials, garages, other works on the site and professional services apply equally here. In this case, the Note 9 explanation of 'garage works' requires that the garage:

'is intended to be occupied with . . . a multiple occupancy dwelling that will after the conversion be contained in the building, or part of a building, being converted'.

Building work: reduced rate – 'special residential conversions'

[15.253] The conversion of a building to use solely for a relevant residential purpose (RRP) is potentially taxable at 5%. Like the rules for a changed number of dwellings or a house in multiple occupation (paras **15.243** et seq and **15.250** et seq), this is under Sch 7A, Group 6, and it has features in common with those rules. In this case, however, the rules do not apply to sub-contractors.

VATA 1994, Sch 7A, Group 6, Note 2 says that a 'qualifying conversion' includes a 'special residential conversion', which is then defined in Note 7 as a conversion of premises where:

'the use to which the premises being converted were last put before the conversion was not to any extent use for a relevant residential purpose'

'those premises are intended to be used solely for a relevant residential purpose after the conversion'

and

'where the relevant residential purpose for which the premises are intended to be used is an institutional purpose, the premises being converted must be intended to form after the conversion the entirety of an institution used for that purpose'.

A relevant residential purpose has the same meaning as in para **15.155** et seq, and an institutional purpose means any such use other than residential accommodation for students, school pupils or the armed forces. The future use needs to be 'solely' RRP, as discussed in para **15.51**, although in this context HMRC have not suggested that 95% will necessarily qualify as 'solely'.

The premises can be a building or buildings, part or parts of a building or buildings, or any combination thereof. The requirement (in Note 7(6)) that for institutional use the premises must form the entire institution is nevertheless a significant restriction, and denies relief for works which, for example, enlarge an existing nursing home. As noted in para **15.157**, there is the same problem with zero-rating, but for the 5% rate the point is made more explicit, and so is more likely to be taken by HMRC.

As with zero-rated works for an RRP building, the 5% rate only applies where the supply is to the end user, who must issue the contractor with a certificate in a form given in HMRC's Notice 708. Strictly the 5% rate only applies to supplies made after the certificate is issued, but in practice HMRC may overlook this point if, say, a certificate was delayed because of uncertainty about the position (see Notice 708, para 17.6).

As with a 'changed number of dwellings' conversion, the works need to have had any necessary planning consent and building control approval, and there are no time limits as to the duration of previous use or of subsequent RRP use.

Extent of the 5% rate

[15.254] Where the 5% rate applies, it does so in the same way as for a 'changed number of dwellings' conversion, and the points in paras **15.245** to **15.249** about qualifying services, building materials, garages, other works on the site and professional services apply equally here. In this case, the Note 9 explanation of 'garage works' requires that the garage:

'is intended to be occupied with . . . the institution or other accommodation resulting from the conversion'.

Building work: reduced rate – 'empty homes'

[15.255] Work to dwellings that have been empty for two years or more is taxable at 5% under VATA 1994, Sch 7A, Group 7.

Group 7, item 1 applies the 5% rate to:

'The supply, in the course of the renovation or alteration of qualifying residential premises, of qualifying services related to the renovation or alteration.'

In the context of dwellings, 'qualifying residential premises' means a single household dwelling or a multiple occupancy dwelling, as in paras **15.244** and **15.251**. Also, one of two 'empty home conditions' must be satisfied.

For dwellings, the rules do not apply if the property was last used as something other than a dwelling, but in this case the 5% rate may alternatively be available under the rules in para **15.243** et seq or **15.250** et seq.

The works needs to have had any necessary planning consent and building control approval.

'First empty home condition'

[15.256] The 'first empty home condition' is the basic rule, and applies to sub-contractors as well as the main contractor. It requires that the dwelling has not:

'been lived in during the period of 2 years ending with the commencement of the relevant works'.

Under this condition, it follows that the property must still be unoccupied when the works start, but there is no bar to someone going into occupation before the works are completed.

The two-year limit is looked at in terms of when the work is physically started, not in terms of the tax point for VAT purposes. If works span the two-year limit, HMRC's view is that none of them qualify.

The law does not define 'lived in', although HMRC take the view that it includes occasional occupation, such as use as a second home. They will, however, ignore occupation by squatters or by a 'guardian' installed to deter squatters and vandals.

It may be difficult to demonstrate that the two-year test is met, but HMRC will accept a letter from the local authority's Empty Property Officer, or potentially other evidence. If different dwellings in the building were vacated at different times, the position needs to be established for each dwelling.

'Second empty home condition'

[15.257] The 'second empty home condition' is intended to accommodate cases where an owner occupier moves into the empty property before the works commence. It does not apply to multiple occupancy dwellings, or to sub-contractors. Note 3(3) elaborates:

'The second "empty home condition" is that –

(a)   the dwelling was not lived in during a period of at least 2 years;

(b)   the person, or one of the persons, whose beginning to live in the dwelling brought that period to an end was a person who (whether alone or jointly with another or others) acquired the dwelling at a time –

    (i)   no later than the end of that period, and

    (ii)   when the dwelling had been not lived in for at least 2 years;

(c)   no works by way of renovation or alteration were carried out to the dwelling during the period of 2 years ending with the acquisition;

(d)   the supply is made to a person who is –

    (i)   the person, or one of the persons, whose beginning to live in the property brought to an end the period mentioned in paragraph (a), and

    (ii)   the person, or one of the persons, who acquired the dwelling as mentioned in paragraph (b); and

(e)   the relevant works are carried out during the period of one year beginning with the day of the acquisition.'

'Acquiring' the dwelling here means acquiring a major interest, ie the freehold or a lease exceeding 21 years (in Scotland, of at least 20 years)

The requirement in (c) that no alterations or renovations have been carried out in the two years prior to acquisition can be a problem. If they were part of the same works that continued after acquisition and occupation, then the first empty home condition might apply. But if they were not, then work by a vendor potentially denies the 5% rate to the purchaser. HMRC do say, however, that any minor works, necessary to keep the dwelling dry and secure, can be ignored.

'Renovation or alteration'; 'qualifying services'

[15.258] The work must be 'qualifying services' 'in the course of' and 'related to' 'renovation or alteration'.

Beyond saying that 'alteration' includes extension, the law does not define 'renovation or alteration'. It appears, however, that even minor works can qualify.

'Qualifying services' has the same meaning as for a 'changed number of dwellings conversion', in para **15.245**. Again, the 5% rate does not apply to the incorporation, or installation as fittings, of goods that are not building materials.

Building materials

[15.259] The points in para **15.246** apply in the same way here. In this case, the 5% rate is extended to building materials by Sch 7A, Group 7, item 2.

Garages

[15.260] Note 3A extends the 5% rate to any related 'garage works', being:

'the construction of a garage'

'the conversion of a building, or of a part of a building, that results in a garage'

or

'the renovation or alteration of a garage'

if

'they are carried out at the same time as the renovation or alteration of the premises concerned',

and

'the garage is intended to be occupied with the premises'.

Where this applies, services and materials are taxable at 5% in the same way as for the dwelling itself.

Other works on the site

[15.261] The law does not explicitly allow the 5% rate to apply to works in the grounds, other than for garages and access, utilities etc. As with conversions, HMRC might accept some other work in the immediate vicinity of the building, but are unlikely to do so for outbuildings that are not garages, or for ornamental features etc.

Professional services

[15.262] The 5% rate does not extend to related professional services.

Building work: reduced rate – empty RRP buildings

[15.263] Work to 'relevant residential' buildings that have been empty for two years or more is potentially taxable at 5% under VATA 1994, Sch 7A, Group 7, in much the same way as for dwellings under the rules in para **15.255** et seq.

Group 7, item 1 applies the 5% rate to:

'The supply, in the course of the renovation or alteration of qualifying residential premises, of qualifying services related to the renovation or alteration.'

The works also need to have had any necessary planning consent and building control approval.

Previous use

[15.264] Note 2 says that 'qualifying residential premises' includes:

'a building, or part of a building, which, when it was last lived in, was used for a relevant residential purpose.'

A 'relevant residential purpose' here has the same meaning as in para **15.155** et seq, but in this context, in relation to past use, there is no 'solely' requirement. Note 2 also brings in non-residential buildings in a residential complex, where they would not otherwise be included:

'Where a building, when it was last lived in, formed part of a relevant residential unit then, to the extent that it would not be so regarded otherwise, the building shall be treated as having been used for a relevant residential purpose.'

and Note 3 says that:

'A building forms part of a relevant residential unit at any time when –
(a)   it is one of a number of buildings on the same site, and
(b)   the buildings are used together as a unit for a relevant residential purpose.'

There are, however, further requirements about the future use of the premises, noted in para **15.266**.

'First empty home condition'

[15.265] The property must meet the 'first empty home condition'. The second such condition, explained in para **15.257**, is not available here, since it only applies to single household dwellings. In the context of RRP buildings, Note 3(2) to Group 7 says that:

'The first "empty home condition" is that neither –
(a)   the premises concerned, nor
(b)   where those premises are a building, or part of a building, which, when it was last lived in, formed part of a relevant residential unit, any of the other buildings that formed part of the unit,

have been lived in during the period of 2 years ending with the commencement of the relevant works'.

The property must still be unoccupied when the works start, although occupation can commence before the works are completed. Also, under (b), if the building was previously part of a 'relevant residential unit', as defined in para **15.264**, the whole of that unit must have been empty for two years, and remain so when the works start.

The two-year limit is looked at in terms of when the work is physically started, not in terms of the tax point for VAT purposes. If works span the two-year limit, HMRC's view is that none of them qualify.

The law does not define 'lived in', although HMRC will ignore occupation by squatters or by a 'guardian' installed to deter squatters and vandals.

It may be difficult to demonstrate that the two-year test is met, but HMRC will accept a letter from the local authority's Empty Property Officer, or potentially other evidence.

Future use

[15.266] Although the previous use need not have been *solely* RRP, this is a requirement for the intended future use, as discussed in para **15.152**. This is not, however, a case where HMRC have suggested that a 95% figure will necessarily be acceptable.

The customer must issue a certificate stating this intention.

Note 4A says that:

> 'Item 1 or 2 does not apply to a supply if the premises in question are a building, or part of a building, which, when it was last lived in, was used for a relevant residential purpose unless –
>
> (a) the building or part is intended to be used solely for such a purpose after the renovation or alteration, and
>
> (b) before the supply is made the person to whom it is made has given to the person making it a certificate stating that intention.'

and that:

> 'Where a number of buildings on the same site are –
>
> (a) renovated or altered at the same time, and
> (b) intended to be used together as a unit solely for a relevant residential purpose,
>
> then each of those buildings, to the extent that it would not be so regarded otherwise, shall be treated as intended for use solely for a relevant residential purpose.'

Unusually for building work on an RRP or RCP building, the law contains no requirement as to the form of the certificate, or that the customer must be the person putting the building to RRP use. The customer must, of course, be in a position to certify the intended end use, but subject to this the rules potentially apply to sub-contractors. In practice, however, HMRC might resist the application of the 5% rate unless the customer is the end user, and will expect the certificate to be based on the format given in Notice 708.

Extent of the 5% rate

[15.267] Where the 5% rate applies, it does so in the same way as for the 'empty homes' rules, and the points in paras **15.258** to **15.262** about renovation or alteration, qualifying services, building materials, garages, other works on the site and professional services apply equally here.

Building work: reduced rate – energy saving materials

[15.268] VATA 1994, Sch 7A, Group 2 applies the 5% rate to the installation of certain energy saving materials.

Item 1 covers:

'Supplies of services of installing energy-saving materials in residential accommodation.

Item 2 then extends this to:

'Supplies of energy-saving materials by a person who installs those materials in residential accommodation'.

It follows that a supply of the materials alone cannot qualify. HMRC accept that minor incidental building works, necessary to fit the materials, can also qualify for the 5% rate. They do not see the rules applying where the installation of energy saving materials is incidental to something else, such as building an extension. The rules can apply to sub-contractors.

Details are noted below. The rules changed in relation to supplies made on or after 1 August 2013 by virtue of FA 2013, s 193 (see Revenue & Customs Brief 26/12).

Qualifying accommodation

[15.269] 'Residential accommodation' here means:

- 'a building, or part of a building, that consists of a dwelling or a number of dwellings' ('dwelling' is not defined);
- 'a building, or part of a building, used for a relevant residential purpose' (this has the same meaning as in para **15.155** et seq, but there is no 'solely' requirement here – this may be a drafting error);
- 'a caravan used as a place of permanent habitation'; or
- 'a houseboat'.

HMRC have indicated that, where part of the accommodation qualifies, the charge can be apportioned if this is between buildings or, in the case of residential accommodation, parts of buildings.

Qualifying materials

[15.270] The rules cover the following items, set out in Sch 7A Group 2 Note 1:

'(a) insulation for walls, floors, ceilings, roofs or lofts or for water tanks, pipes or other plumbing fittings;
(b) draught stripping for windows and doors;
(c) central heating system controls (including thermostatic radiator valves);
(d) hot water system controls;
(e) solar panels;
(f) wind turbines;
(g) water turbines;
(h) ground source heat pumps;
(i) air source heat pumps;
(j) micro combined heat and power units;
(k) boilers designed to be fuelled solely by wood, straw or similar vegetal matter.'

Further details are in HMRC's Notice 708/6. Some of these items, however, will clearly not normally be installed 'in' the building, as required by item 1. HMRC have confirmed that they interpret 'in' here as meaning 'serving'.

Following the CJEU judgment, the Government announced Autumn Statement 2015 that there will be a consultation regarding the impact of solar panels, wind turbines and water turbines becoming liable to VAT at the standard rate. HMRC subsequently announced that VATA 1994, Sch 7A, Group 2, item 3, Note (1)(e),(f) and (g) will be repealed, however the proposed revised legislation was not published in Finance Bill 2016 so it remains uncertain at this time when the legislation will be introduced. It is possible that as a result of the UK making a decision to leave the EU that the revised legislation may never be enacted into UK legislation.

Building work: reduced rate – other cases

Grant-funded heating and security

[15.271] VATA 1994, Sch 7A, Group 3 applies the 5% rate to:

- Certain grant-funded works etc in the sole or main residence of 'a qualifying person', ie one aged over 60 or receiving certain benefits. The supply must be made to the qualifying person, and so the rules do not apply to sub-contractors. The 5% rate covers such items as heaters, boilers, radiators, gas connections and central heating systems, and certain security installations.
- The grant-funded leasing, and subsequent sale, of a central heating system in the sole or main residence of a qualifying person.

Further details are in HMRC's Notice 708/6 (17 July 2014).

Mobility aids

[15.272] Under VATA 1994, Sch 7A, Group 10, the 5% rate applies to:

'The supply of services of installing mobility aids for use in domestic accommodation by a person who, at the time of the supply, is aged 60 or over.'

'Domestic accommodation' means a dwelling or number of dwellings, and 'mobility aids' covers grab rails, ramps, stair lifts, bath lifts, built-in shower seats, showers containing built-in shower seats and walk-in baths fitted with sealable doors. Where this applies, the 5% rate also applies to the supply of the mobility aids themselves by the person installing them.

Home improvements in the Isle of Man

[15.273] The Isle of Man has taken advantage of provisions in the Directive, allowing a broader application of the reduced rate. As a result, most alteration or repair work to dwellings, or the construction of an extension or a garage, is taxable at 5% if supplied to the owner or occupier. Materials are included where they are supplied by the contractor in the course of the work, and subject to exclusions on similar lines to those for zero-rating at para **15.223**. The rules do not apply to sub-contractors.

UK-VAT registered businesses working in the Isle of Man can make arrangements to use these rules, and further details are at www.gov.im/customs.

Building work: refund schemes

[15.274] As noted in para **15.287**, there are general VAT refund arrangements for local authorities and similar bodies, museums, certain charities and academies. There are also three refund schemes for private individuals, charities etc, specific to building work etc. These are the 'DIY' scheme – actually a misnomer, since the claimant need do no physical work – and schemes for listed places of worship and memorials.

The DIY builders and converters VAT refund scheme

[15.275] The DIY builders and converters VAT refund scheme (DIY scheme) allows refunds to people acting in a non-business capacity – normally an individual or a charity – of VAT that would otherwise not arise, or would be recoverable. The person need not do any physical work themselves.

The scheme covers VAT incurred by anyone acting lawfully and in a non-business capacity – and so typically for own occupation:

- On building materials (see para **15.223**) used in constructing a building designed as a dwelling or number of dwellings (as at para **15.135** et seq), or for use 'solely' for a relevant residential purpose (RRP) or relevant charitable purpose (RCP) – see para **15.151** et seq. (This is not, however, a case where HMRC will necessarily accept 95% as 'solely', as in para **15.152**.) These are materials that a contractor could zero-rate if supplying them with his services, as at para **15.223**, and construction has the same meaning and scope as in para **15.221** et seq. The scheme covers cases where claimants buy in materials, whether to do the work themselves or to engage a contractor to use them – in which case the contractor's services can still be zero-rated.

- On materials used in, and on the services of a contractor carrying out, a residential conversion. This covers the conversion of a non-residential building to a building designed as a dwelling or number of dwellings, or 'solely' for RRP use (as above). It applies in the same circumstances, and to the same extent, as those where a housing association could obtain zero-rating, as at para **15.229**, although subject to the point noted below about HMRC's reaction to *Jacobs*. The scheme covers materials whether bought direct by the claimant or supplied by a contractor and, if a contractor is used, the contractor's services.

Only one claim can be made for each project – there is no scope for interim claims – and the claim must be submitted within three months of the project's completion on Form VAT 431NB (for new build) or 431C (for conversions). The forms also include guidance notes giving HMRC's version of the scope of the scheme. It is important to ensure that invoices are obtained and retained during the course of the project.

HMRC apply the scheme strictly, and indeed over-strictly – their guidance suggests limitations to the scheme that are not actually borne out by the legislation. Following their defeat in *Jennings* (TC00362) however, they do now accept that holiday homes can be eligible.

There is extensive case law about the scheme. Many of the cases noted elsewhere in this chapter, in the context of zero-rating, were actually about

DIY scheme claims, the rules being the same in either case. HMRC have, however, sought to differentiate zero-rating for residential conversions from the DIY scheme rules following their defeat in one DIY scheme case, *Jacobs*, and so case law in this area is noted below.

There can also be difficulties with the 'non-business' requirement where future use is unclear, or is planned to change. Case law on this issue is also summarised below.

HMRC will also refuse a refund where they think that the supply should have been zero-rated, or confine it to 5% VAT where they think it should have been reduced-rated. This puts the claimant out of pocket if it is then too late to obtain a repayment from the supplier. There have been many Tribunal cases about this issue, where HMRC have been almost invariably successful.

Selected case law on residential conversions and the 'DIY' scheme

Where a building that was only partly non-residential is converted to a dwelling or dwellings, Sch 8, Group 5, Note 9 says this about the scope of zero-rating:

'The conversion . . . of a non-residential part of a building which already contains a residential part is not included within [the zero-rating] unless the result of that conversion is to create an additional dwelling or dwellings.'

This is noted in context in para **15.175**. Through cross-referencing, the same point applies to the DIY scheme.

- In *Blom-Cooper* ([2003] STC 669, CA), the Court of Appeal concluded that the conversion of a pub, which had included residential accommodation for the landlord, to a single house did not create an additional dwelling, and so did not qualify for a refund.
- *Jacobs* ([2005] STC 1518, CA) was a complicated case about the conversion of a former boarding school, which had also included a headmaster's flat and staff bed-sits, into a house incorporating staff flats. The Court of Appeal concluded that most of the works qualified for a refund. The 'additional dwelling' test applied to the building as a whole, and if it was met then the previously non-residential parts of a dwelling that also included previously residential parts were eligible for a refund. HMRC accepted this in Business Brief 22/05, whilst denying – surprisingly – that the case had any implications for zero-rating.
- *Blacklock* (VTD 20171) concerned the conversion of an outbuilding that included a garage into a dwelling. The garage was seen as a 'residential' part. The Tribunal accepted the claim for a refund, rejecting HMRC's argument that the 'additional dwelling' test required the building already to have contained a dwelling.

Selected case law on 'non-business' and the DIY scheme

- In *Charlton* (VTD 18268), the owner converted a property and moved into it, but his DIY claim was unsuccessful – his occupation was temporary, and the real purpose of the conversion was to let the property, a business activity.

- In *Watson* (VTD 18675), a couple converted a property for their own occupation, but on completion decided to let it instead. Their claim was also refused – the Tribunal thought that it was on completion that the non-business test needed to be looked at.

- In *Curry* (VTD 20077), an individual started building a house with a view to selling it, but then decided to live in it instead. In the event, he let it out temporarily while certain planning problems were resolved. The Tribunal, perhaps surprisingly, held that he had never commenced a business and upheld his 'DIY' claim.

- In *Terry* (TC00155), an individual was in business managing and letting commercial property, but had no experience of construction projects. He built a house for a friend, apparently seeking only to recover third party costs from him, but the Tribunal agreed with HMRC that this was a business activity and that his DIY claim was invalid.

- *Sassi* (TC00224) concerned a claim by a lecturer in sustainable architecture, who had commissioned two eco-friendly flats, occupying one and letting the other. The Tribunal concluded that this was not a business activity – it has not been conducted in a business-like manner, and had been more concerned with environmental and sustainability issues.

- In *Wendels* (TC00737) planning permission had been given on the basis that a member of staff needed to be within close reach of a cattery, and had contained occupancy restrictions in line with this. The Tribunal rejected HMRC's argument that the expenditure was for the purposes of the cattery business – the property was a private home, built with private funds. Another aspect of this case is noted in para 15.137.

- In *Richard Burton* (TC02522) [2013] UKFTT 104 (TC) the taxpayer carried on a business activity on the site in question (selling fishing licences over a lake). A house was constructed on the site and one of the planning conditions was that the house could only be occupied by someone involved in the business. HMRC contended that the house was therefore part of the fishery business and ineligible. The First-tier Tribunal considered that the house was not essential to the business and was a home, thereby disagreeing with HMRC.

Conversions of non-residential buildings into dwellings under permitted development rights

[15.276] HMRC has published Revenue & Customs Brief 9/16 which provides details of HMRC's view of the correct VAT treatment of conversions of certain non-residential buildings into dwellings following the introduction of additional permitted development rights (PDR). The announcement covers developers who convert non-residential buildings into dwellings where they are not required to obtain statutory planning consent (SPC) because the work is covered by their PDR. The policy announcement also covers builders carrying out the conversion and who are seeking to obtain a refund using the DIY builders and converters VAT Refund Scheme (DIY scheme).

PDRs are a national grant of planning permission for particular types of development as set out in the legislation. They have been introduced in an attempt to streamline the planning process by removing the requirement to obtain full planning permission in order to reduce the administrative burden.

One of the conditions that needs to be satisfied before HMRC will allow the sale of a newly converted dwelling to be zero-rated or for VAT to be recovered under the DIY scheme, is that the claimant must be able to provide satisfactory evidence that statutory planning consent (SPC) has been granted in respect of that dwelling. The building must then have been constructed in accordance with that consent.

Also, part of the conditions for some supplies of construction services to be eligible for the reduced rate of VAT of 5% for the conversion of a non-residential building into a dwelling requires individual SPC. However since the introduction of PDRs, individual SPCs will no longer be required for some developments making this condition difficult to meet.

As a result of the difficulties that have been experienced by developers and DIY scheme, HMRC have issued clarification on its policy regarding the VAT treatment of works where an individual planning application is not necessary because statutory planning consent has been granted via PDRs.

HMRC had stated that it will still require evidence that the work has been lawfully carried out in order for the zero or reduced rate to apply. According to the Revenue & Customs Brief if the builder, developer or DIY scheme claimant establishes that the conversion is covered by a PDR and individual SPC is not required, they must be able to evidence it by at least one of the following:

- written notification from the LPA advising of the grant of prior approval;
- written notification from the LPA advising that prior approval is not required; or
- evidence of deemed consent (ie evidence that the claimant has written to the LPA and confirmation that the claimant has not received a response from them within 56 days); and
- evidence that the development is a permitted development. This will include all of the following (where the documents have been created), plans of the development, evidence of the prior use of the property (eg evidenced by its classification for business rates purposes etc), confirmation of which part of the planning legislation is relied upon for the development and a lawful development certificate where one is already held.

It is important to note that any developments carried out under a PDR must still meet the appropriate building standards. Should any circumstances arise where building control is not required, evidence from the local authority confirming this should be provided.

Listed places of worship (LPW) scheme

[15.277] Works to listed buildings that are used as places of worship are subject to the general rules in para **15.225** et seq – approved alterations can be zero-rated, but repair and maintenance cannot. The scheme gives VAT refunds for repair and maintenance. It is administered by the Department for Culture, Media and Sport, and details are at www.lpwscheme.org.uk.

Memorials

[15.278] The construction of, or work to, memorials is generally standard-rated because they are not usually buildings. But registered charities, and formally constituted religious groups exempted from registering as charities, can claim VAT refunds from the Department for Culture, Media and Sport. The scheme covers statues, monuments, plaques, stained glass windows etc which commemorate a person, animal or event and to which there is a degree of public access. Details are at www.memorialgrant.org.uk.

Building work: self-supply

[15.279] The Value Added Tax (Self-Supply of Construction Services) Order, 1989 (SI 1989/472) requires businesses to account for VAT when they carry out certain building work using in-house labour. This is to remove any competitive advantage from doing so, but in practice the rules are generally overlooked.

The self-supply applies to construction services listed in Article 3(1) of the Order, if a supply of them would be subject to VAT and if their open market value is £100,000 or more. The goods element of the work is ignored. Article 3(1) applies:

> 'Where a person, in the course or furtherance of a business carried on by him, for the purpose of that business and otherwise than for a consideration, performs any of the following services, that is to say –
>
> (a) the construction of a building; or
> (b) the extension or other alteration of, or the construction of an annexe to, any building such that additional floor area of not less than 10 per cent of the floor area of the original building is created; or
> (c) the construction of any civil engineering work; or
> (d) in connection with any such services as are described in sub-paragraph (a), (b) or (c) above, the carrying out of any demolition work contemporaneously with or preparatory thereto'.

Where there is a self-supply, the business must account for output tax on the open market value of the services in the VAT period when the works are completed. It can treat the same amount of VAT as input tax, recoverable according to the partial exemption position. The value of the self-supply will count towards the £250,000 threshold for the CGS and, if this applies, the self-supply VAT will be part of the input tax to be adjusted under the scheme.

Partial exemption

[15.280] In principle, input tax is recoverable where it relates to taxable supplies and irrecoverable where it relates to exempt supplies. Businesses making both taxable and exempt supplies can normally recover only some of the VAT they incur, and are referred to as 'partly exempt'. VAT is also irrecoverable where it is incurred on certain items incorporated in dwellings etc (see para **15.149**) and, until 31 December 2010, accommodation that was provided to company directors (see para **15.181**). VAT related to non-business activities is also generally irrecoverable, but is not 'input tax'. There is more about this in para **15.287**.

Some occupiers of commercial property, such as banks, insurance companies and universities, are always likely to be partly exempt (see the list in para **15.108** of VAT-averse occupiers – partial exemption is relevant to all of these except some government bodies and small businesses). Property businesses, and occupiers letting or selling surplus property, may also have to deal with partial exemption if, for example, they have residential property or do not exercise an option to tax.

The main issues are about how to attribute input tax to taxable and exempt supplies, about how to split input tax that cannot be attributed in this way ('residual input tax' or 'the pot') and about adjustments when, for example, there is a change in intentions. The rules are set out in Part XIV of the VAT Regulations. Input tax may also need to be adjusted under the CGS (see para **15.288** et seq).

There are some specific issues with partial exemption and the option to tax, and these are looked at in para **15.93** et seq.

Attribution

[15.281] Regulation 101(2) says that:

> 'in respect of each prescribed accounting period –
>
> (a)   goods imported or acquired by and goods or services supplied to, the taxable person in the period shall be identified,
>
> (b)   there shall be attributed to taxable supplies the whole of the input tax on such of those goods or services as are used or to be used by him exclusively in making taxable supplies,
>
> (c)   no part of the input tax on such of those goods or services as are used or to be used by him exclusively in making exempt supplies, or in carrying on any activity other than the making of taxable supplies, shall be attributed to taxable supplies'.

Input tax falling under (b) can be recovered; input tax under (c) cannot be recovered unless the 'de minimis' rules apply.

Where it is intended that the goods or services will be used – now or in the future – in making both taxable and exempt supplies, the VAT cannot be attributed under these rules and is 'residual' – this normally means that it is partly recoverable.

This ought to restrict VAT recovery by housebuilders and others granting major interest leases, since such a lease is only initially zero-rated, and then exempt. But this is not the intention of the rules, and in these cases HMRC accept full recovery for development-related costs (see para **15.149**).

If the input tax relates to supplies made outside the UK, it is recoverable if the supplies would be taxable if made in the UK. HMRC do not, however, accept that an option to tax can be imputed for these purposes, so they see UK input tax related to non-UK property as generally irrecoverable.

Various points about attribution of input tax have emerged from case law, in particular that the correct approach is to look at how goods or services are directly to be used, and not at any broader motive. In the UK, however, this is arguably being undermined by an emerging doctrine of 'economic use', pursued by HMRC.

Selected case law on the attribution of input tax

CJEU cases

- In *BLP Group plc* (CJEU Case C-4/94), the CJEU held that input tax related to an exempt sale of shares was directly attributable to the sale, and irrecoverable, and could not be attributed to the taxable trading activities that the sale was intended to finance. The costs at issue were a cost component of the sale of shares.
- In *Midland Bank plc* (CJEU Case C-98/98), a case about litigation costs in defending a negligence claim, the CJEU held that input tax could only be attributed to a supply if there was a 'direct and immediate link' between input and output. It was not enough for the input merely to be a consequence of the output.
- *Fini* (CJEU Case C-32/03) concerned VAT on rent on a vacant property, from which the taxpayer had previously run a restaurant. The CJEU considered that the ongoing rent could be 'directly and immediately linked' back to the restaurant business.
- *AB SKF* (CJEU Case C-29/08) was, like BLP, about an exempt sale of shares. But on this occasion the Court suggested that the VAT on costs was only directly attributable to the sale itself if the costs were 'likely to be incorporated in the price of the shares'. Otherwise it was likely to be residual.
- In *RBS Deutschland Holdings GmbH* (CJEU Case C-277/09), the CJEU held that input tax attributable to taxable supplies was still recoverable, even though – because of differences between UK and German legislation – they were not actually taxed. Another aspect of this case is noted in para 15.299.

UK cases concerned with property

- *Sheffield Co-operative Society* (VTD 2549) concerned a restaurant, run by a third party, in a retail store. The Tribunal held that input tax incurred by the retailer in refurbishing the restaurant was attributable to its exempt lettings to the third party (the case pre-dates the option to tax), and that any motive of attracting further customers to the store was irrelevant.
- *Southern Primary Housing Ltd* ([2004] STC 209) concerned input tax on the purchase of land, which the appellant then sold exempt, under an agreement under which it also provided taxable construction services. The Court of Appeal held that the input tax was directly attributable to the sale, and not also to the construction services.
- In *Mulhearn (t/a Sandancer Amusements)* (VTD 19188), an amusement arcade was used for slot machines (taxable) and bingo (exempt). Additional space was constructed and given over entirely to machines, but the VAT on the work was held to be residual, since the work 'created an enlarged single space' for both taxable and exempt supplies.

- In *Royal Bank of Canada Trust Corporation Limited* (VTD 20520), a trust had derived taxable rental income from a property, before granting a 999-year lease reserving an annual rent of £1. It continued to incur VAT on management fees. The Tribunal rejected the contention, based on *Fini*, that this was attributable back to the earlier taxable supplies, and recoverable.
- In *St Helens School Northwood Ltd* ([2006] EWHC 3306 (Ch)), [2007] STC 633, the High Court accepted HMRC's argument that 'use' did not mean physical use, but what HMRC had referred to as 'economic use', and the same approach was taken in 2009 in *Bridgnorth Golf Club* (TC00094). In *St Helens* it was clear anyway that the input tax was used in making both taxable and exempt supplies, and the argument was over the proportion of it that was recoverable (see para 15.285). But in *Bridgnorth* the Tribunal looked beyond the direct taxable use of the bar and dining areas of a club house, and held that they were 'economically used' in making exempt as well as taxable supplies, since the facilities would potentially attract new, exempt, subscriptions to the club. This approach clearly differs from that in *Sheffield Co-op*, above, and may prove hard to reconcile with cases such as *BLP*.
- In *Folkestone Harbour (GP) Ltd* (TC04306) [2015] UKFTT 0101 (TC) a fountain was constructed to improve the entrance to the harbour generally. HMRC considered that the fountain (and the inputs relating to it) had no connection with the taxable activity being carried on and denied input tax recovery. The First-tier Tribunal disagreed, holding that the necessary connection was indeed present and that, interestingly, no ordinary business man would have constructed such a fountain unless it was for the purposes of his business.

Cases concerned with the option to tax, notably *Royal & Sun Alliance* and *British Eventing*, are summarised in para 15.100.

Residual input tax: standard method

[15.282] Residual input tax is apportioned according to the standard method in SI 1995/2518, reg 101(2) unless HMRC have agreed or directed a special method. In most cases, the standard method uses a values-based 'pro rata' calculation, so that if 30% of supplies are taxable the business can recover 30% of its input tax. But there are various detailed rules:

- The percentage is normally rounded up to the next whole number. But if the residual input tax averages more than £400,000 a month, the percentage can only be rounded up to the next two decimal places.
- Regulation 101(3) requires various, potentially distortive, supplies to be excluded from the calculation. These include:
  - 'any sum receivable by the taxable person in respect of any supply of capital goods used by him for the purposes of his business';
  - 'any sum receivable by the taxable person in respect of . . . any real estate transaction' or any financial transaction 'where such supplies are incidental to one or more of his business activities';
  - any self-supply.

So, for example, a normally fully taxable retailer selling a surplus store exempt may have to forego input tax directly attributable to the sale (perhaps on fees, or a refurbishment) but should be able to ignore the sale in its pro rata calculation, on the grounds that it is incidental to its normal business. Property letting, however, is far less likely to be 'incidental', whilst any property business must probably take account of sales, unless they really are exceptional. Some cases about the meaning of 'capital goods' are noted in para **15.289**.

- In general, the values of non-UK supplies should be included, applying the liability that they would have had in the UK, as should related UK input tax. As noted at para **15.281**, HMRC do not accept that an option to tax can be imputed for non-UK property transactions.

- In most cases, VAT recovery is ultimately determined by an 'annual adjustment' calculated by reference to the values of supplies over a 12 month 'partial exemption year'. This normally runs to the end of March, April or May, depending on the VAT return periods. The annual adjustment is carried out on the VAT return for the period following the partial exemption year end, but the business can alternatively choose to do it on the final return for the partial exemption year itself.

- Pending the annual adjustment, provisional calculations need to be made on each VAT return. The default approach here is to use the residual recovery percentage for the previous partial exemption year, if there was one, but the business can alternatively choose to do a pro rata calculation for the individual period and to use that instead.

- New businesses, and those that are newly partly exempt, can choose to apply a different method of calculation during, essentially, their first partial exemption year. This must be based on the use, or intended use, of the input tax. There is no prescribed way of doing this, but if current input tax relates to supplies that will made in a later year, it may be appropriate to employ a calculation based on the expected future values of supplies.

- Under reg 106, input tax attributable to exempt supplies is ignored, and is recoverable in full, if it is below certain 'de minimis' limits. These apply if, for the period:
  - the total input tax is no more than £625 per month, and the value of exempt supplies is no more than 50% of the value of all supplies; or
  - the total input tax, less input tax directly attributable to taxable supplies, is no more than £625 per month, and the value of exempt supplies is no more than 50% of the value of all supplies; or
  - the 'de minimis' limits applied in the last partial exemption year, and total input tax in this partial exemption year is not expected to exceed £1m (this cannot be used for the partial exemption year as a whole, but only for individual periods in the meantime); or
  - the input tax attributable to exempt supplies is no more than £625 per month and no more than 50% of all input tax.

More generous limits apply to local authorities and to certain other bodies.

- If the residual input tax exceeds £25,000 per annum, the business may need to consider the 'standard method override'.

Residual input tax: standard method override

[15.283] The 'standard method override' is intended to counter distortions inherent in the standard method. It was primarily intended as an anti-avoidance device, but HMRC sometimes deploy it more generally, to overturn partial exemption results that they simply do not like.

It is generally triggered by reg 107B, which says that:

'this regulation applies where a taxable person has made an attribution [under the standard method] and that attribution differs substantially from one which represents the extent to which the goods or services are used by him or are to be used by him, or a successor of his [ie following a TOGC], in making taxable supplies.'

This needs to be considered as part of the annual adjustment. It does not need to be looked at at other times unless either the business is deregistering or no annual adjustment was required. It can also be ignored altogether if the residual input tax is no more than £50,000 per annum (£25,000 if, essentially, the business is part of a corporate group).

Subject to these points, the business needs to compare the result of the standard method with an objective attribution of the residual input tax, ie with how the goods or services are actually 'used or to be used'. If the difference between the two is 'substantial', the standard method calculation is overridden, and it must use the objective calculation instead. 'Substantial' here means more than £50,000, or more than both 50% of all residual input tax and £25,000, regardless of the length of the period.

Example

A landlord whose other activities are fully taxable refurbishes a building, half of which is given over to flats. It has opted to tax, but the lettings of the flats remain exempt. VAT on the work relates to taxable and exempt supplies, and so is residual. Objectively, 50% of the VAT might be recoverable and 50% irrecoverable as relating to the exempt lettings. But the standard method compares the value of the exempt rent with the value of all the landlord's taxable supplies allowing, say, 90% recovery. If the difference between 50% recovery and 90% recovery is more than £50,000, the override applies and the landlord can only recover 50% of the VAT on the work.

In reality, of course, few cases are this straightforward, and it may be highly debatable how costs actually are 'used or to be used', and so whether and to what extent the override applies. And although the sort of floor space calculation the example implies may make sense, HMRC do not necessarily see floor space as a fair measure, particularly not for occupiers.

Other cases where the override might apply are where:

- there are high value activities to which little or no VAT is attributable, and which are not already excluded from the calculation as 'incidental' etc; or

- input tax is incurred in one year which relates to new activities, or a new mix of activities, planned for the next year.

HMRC's explanation of the override, with examples, was given in VAT Information Sheet 04/02. Whilst this claimed that, 'except for cases of abuse, it will be extremely rare' for the override to apply, HMRC have shown increasing interest in deploying the override, as illustrated by the case law noted below.

Case law on the standard method override

- In *St Helen's School Northwood Ltd* ([2006] EWHC 3306 (Ch), [2007] STC 633), the taxpayer sought to apply the override in its favour in connection with the construction of sports facilities. Its normal activities were overwhelmingly exempt, whereas the facilities were heavily used in making taxable supplies. This might seem an obvious case for the override to apply but HMRC rejected it, and the High Court justified this by deciding that 'use' did not mean physical use. There is more about this case in para 15.285.
- In *Abbeyview Bowling Club* (VTD 20661), HMRC applied the override to limit VAT recovery on an extension to a clubhouse. They claimed that the use of this was only 5% taxable, compared to the 77% recovery given by the standard method. The Tribunal thought that this ignored the impact of the extension on taxable bar sales, and concluded that 30% of the use was taxable. The difference between this and 77% was too small to trigger the override.
- In *Camden Motors (Holdings) Ltd* (VTD 20674), HMRC tried to use the override to replace the standard method calculation with one based on profit. The Tribunal rejected both their approach and their calculations. It also held that the override could not apply anyway where, as here, the business was otherwise fully taxable under the 'de minimis' rules.
- In *H J Banks & Company Ltd* (TC00347), a developer acquired land intending to make wholly taxable supplies, and recovered the VAT on the purchase. In the event, it sold an existing building on the site as an exempt supply. Under a normal standard method calculation, the VAT was still wholly recoverable, but HMRC argued that the standard method override applied, and that the calculation should be based on acreage. The Tribunal agreed, rejecting the company's preference for a values-based calculation which produced a figure below the £50k threshold for the override. It also disagreed with the Tribunal in *Camden Motors* about the interaction between the override and the 'de minimis' rules.

Special methods

[15.284] Under reg 102:

'the Commissioners [ie HMRC] may approve or direct the use by a taxable person of a method other than that specified in regulation 101'

Most partly exempt property businesses, and many others, have agreed a special method on this basis. Such a method needs to produce a 'fair and reasonable' result – including in HMRC's eyes – but in principle there is no limit to what sort of calculation can be used. What is suitable will depend very much on the business, but alternatives to a *pro rata* method include calculations based on:

- staff headcount – eg where different departments undertake different functions;
- staff time – based on timesheets;
- floor space – although HMRC have become reluctant to accept this for occupiers, as illustrated in case law summarised in para **15.285**;
- a transaction count – suitable where transactions involve a fairly constant cost irrespective of value;
- input tax – comparing input tax directly attributable to taxable and exempt supplies;
- management accounts – according to the way in which the business allocates costs;
- profit – if taxable and exempt supplies arise from different profit centres – HMRC are keen on this approach in some sectors.

Many methods also involve 'sectorisation' – where a business has distinct types of activity, it can make sense to treat each as a sector, to allocate input tax to each sector and then carry out a further calculation within each, whether a *pro rata* calculation or some alternative to this.

A special method will normally involve annual adjustments, in the same way as the standard method, and the 'de minimis' limits noted in para **15.282** also apply here.

HMRC are often concerned that a method will be unduly favourable to the business, although it may be felt that their own behaviour is not consistently even-handed. In practice, it is often difficult to agree a mutually satisfactory method, and some businesses have been locked in discussion with HMRC on the subject for a number of years.

Any business applying for a special method must give HMRC a declaration that 'to the best of its knowledge and belief' the proposed method will produce a 'fair and reasonable' result. HMRC have powers to set the method aside retrospectively if they think this is not the case. They can also direct a special method, or issue a 'special method override notice' from a current date. And although in theory the taxpayer can also serve an override notice on HMRC, they are not obliged to accept it.

Apportionment by time or space

[**15.285**] Partial exemption calculations are supposed to reflect 'use'. The standard method uses turnover as a proxy for this, but it was long thought that, for property used in distinct ways, floor space was an appropriate – indeed fairer – alternative. Similarly a time apportionment seemed sensible where a building was used in different ways at different times.

As shown by the case law below, HMRC have become reluctant to accept this sort of approach, at least for occupiers, and have been successful in litigation, to the extent that the High Court in *St Helens* concluded that the meaning of 'use' 'is not physical use but some special VAT use'. This raises some fundamental questions, and can mean that businesses are forced back on the standard method, or on a special method more to HMRC's liking. Inevitably, however, HMRC's challenges are selective, and might be thought to depend more on the results of the calculations than on the principles behind them.

Selected case law

- In *Aspinall's Club Ltd* (VTD 17797), the Tribunal agreed with HMRC's rejection of a method comparing the floorspace of bars and dining areas with space dedicated to exempt gaming. Although there were taxable supplies of drinks and catering, most of it was provided free, and supported the gaming activity.

- In *Optika Ltd* (VTD 18627), the Tribunal upheld HMRC's rejection of a partial exemption method based on floor space for a retail optician. It was not satisfied that the areas in supposedly taxable use were used wholly for taxable supplies, and also disliked the optician's proposal to 'weight' areas according to their rental value. In Business Brief 34/04, HMRC extrapolated from this to say that 'floor-area based special methods are seldom fair and reasonable for retailers'. Other cases about methods for opticians have followed, as noted below.

- In *Auchterarder Golf Club* (VTD 19907), HMRC had refused a floor space method altogether, now saying generally that 'methods based on floor area are seldom fair and reasonable'. The Tribunal disagreed with this, but had not seen a firm enough proposal to find for the club.

- *St Helens School Northwood Ltd* concerned the construction of a sports complex for use by the school (exempt) and third parties (taxable). HMRC had rejected various calculations based on a time apportionment, and the Tribunal (VTD 19449) and High Court ([2006] EWHC 3306 (Ch)) saw this as reasonable. The High Court thought that 'use' for partial exemption purposes did not mean physical use, and that the 'economic use' and purpose of the facilities meant that the 1% recovery given by the standard method was a 'fair and reasonable' result.

- *Farnham Physiotherapy and Sports Clinic* (VTD 20004) was about VAT incurred by an exempt business on the purchase of a building. The building was larger than needed, and the business opted to tax and sub-let more than half of it. HMRC rejected the idea of a calculation based on floor space, and the Tribunal, citing *St Helen's*, agreed. The business was left with 4% VAT recovery under the standard method.

- In *London Clubs Management Ltd* (TC00154), the Tribunal accepted a method which compared the floorspace of bars and restaurants with that used for exempt gaming. The method allowed for the provision of free drinks and catering and, unlike in *Aspinall's*, above, the bar and restaurant could be seen as businesses in their own right. HMRC failed to overturn this decision in the Upper Tribunal ([2010] UKUT 365 (TCC)) and in the Court of Appeal ([2011] EWCA Civ 1323).

- There have been various further cases about methods for opticians following *Optika* (above). HMRC succeeded in the High Court in *Banbury Visionplus Ltd* ([2006] EWHC 1024 (Ch)) and in *Vision Express (UK) Ltd* ([2009] EWHC 3245 (Ch)). Long-running litigation continues in *DCM (Optical Holdings) Ltd* where the First-tier Tribunal agreed that a floor space method could be used providing that 'zoning' was removed from the PESM. Most recently the Tribunal (TC00675) approved a modified floor space-based method, provided that the 'weighting' of areas by rental value was removed.

- *Hurlingham Club* (TC04283) [2015] UKFTT 76 (TC) concerned a proposed floor space method as the activities of the club comprised some taxable activities (bars, restaurants etc). The First-tier Tribunal considered that it was not acceptable for the method in question to exclude common areas given the amount of floor space they comprised nor was it appropriate to allocate certain areas wholly to taxable activities as they contributed to the whole club.

Change of intention – regulations 108 and 109

[15.286] Input tax will often be attributed to intended supplies, rather than to supplies being made immediately. If, within six years, the business then decides to use the goods or services in a different way from first intended, the VAT may be adjustable under SI 1995/2518, reg 108 (which requires a payment to HMRC) or 109 (which allows a payment by HMRC). HMRC refer to these provisions as, respectively, 'clawback' and 'payback'. As noted in para **15.131**, HMRC also take the view that, following a TOGC, the transferee may be able or required to adjust VAT originally incurred by the transferor, although the legal basis for this is unclear.

These regulations only apply to a change of intention, and not to a change of use – if the goods or services have been brought into use as intended, and are then used for something else, there is no adjustment under these rules. There may, however, be an adjustment under the CGS (para **15.288** et seq).

Also, the regulations only apply if the change of intention is between the three categories of: wholly taxable use; wholly exempt use; and mixed taxable and exempt use. They do not apply where all that changes is the mixture. This was demonstrated in *Halifax plc*, below.

No adjustment should be made if the change results purely from a change of law – for example where input tax is incurred for use in making exempt supplies, which have become taxable by the time they are made. But adjustments can be made where the change results from an option to tax, and this is looked at in para **15.96** et seq.

Where the regulations apply, the business should recalculate its partial exemption position for the period when the input tax was originally incurred. Under reg 108, it should simply make a repayment to HMRC on the VAT return for the period when the change of intention occurs. Under reg 109, it should submit a claim to HMRC before making any adjustment.

Various points have been illustrated by case law, and para **15.150** looks at some specific issues for housebuilders.

Change of intention – selected case law

- In *Briararch Ltd* ([1992] STC 732, QB), a developer intended to grant a zero-rated lease and recovered input tax on works. In the event, it granted an exempt lease, triggering a repayment under what is now reg 108. HMRC contended that the input tax was repayable in full, but the Tribunal and High Court held that it was only partly repayable, since the company could take account of the fact that it still intended to make a zero-rated supply, so that the input tax had become residual. A similar conclusion was reached in a joined case, *Curtis Henderson Ltd* (also [1992] STC 732, QB). There is more about this general issue in para 15.150.

- The High Court rejected a *Briararch*-type approach in *University of Wales College Cardiff* ([1995] STC 611, QB) because the taxable use on which the appellant sought to rely had not been envisaged when the VAT was first incurred.

- In *Pembridge Estates Ltd* (VTD 9606), a company refurbished a flat which it intended to let as taxable holiday accommodation. It let it for one week, and then sold it, exempt, to one of its directors. Surprisingly, the Tribunal accepted that that the change of intention only happened after the taxable letting, so that what is now reg 108 did not apply.

- *Halifax plc* (VTD 16697) concerned stationery bought for use in a largely exempt business, recovering a small proportion of the VAT. Some of the stationery became out of date and was sold, taxable, as waste. The company claimed additional VAT under reg 109. The Tribunal rejected this – the company could not isolate the input tax on the stationery that had later been sold as waste, so the input tax had to be considered as a whole, and still related to a mixture of taxable and exempt supplies as intended.

- In *Royal and Sun Alliance* ([2003] STC 832), the House of Lords held that:
    - regulation 109 required a definite initial intention, followed by a change of plan, and so did not apply where the business did not know how goods or services were to be used when it incurred the input tax. HMRC have discounted this, but if correct it also applies to reg 108.
    - regulation 109 did not apply to ongoing costs – in this case rent and service charges – incurred during a period of non-use: the VAT had been 'used up' during that period, and was not used in making the subsequent supplies.
  The option to tax aspects of this case are considered in para 15.96.

- In *The Wellcome Trust* (VTD 20731) the Tribunal rejected a reg 109 claim to the extent that the VAT in question had originally been incurred in connection with non-business activities, and so had not been input tax.

- In *Community Housing Association Ltd* ([2009] EWHC 455 (Ch)), [2009] STC 1324, the association had incurred development costs on properties in which it would be making exempt supplies. It then assigned the uncompleted contracts to a subsidiary, which would now act as its contractor. The High Court accepted that the assignment was a taxable supply, and that input tax incurred to date could be reattributed to this and recovered under reg 109.

VAT related to non-business activities

[15.287] VAT related to non-business activities is in principle irrecoverable, and HMRC generally expect any restriction of this VAT to be undertaken separately, before any partial exemption calculation. Since 1 January 2011, however:

- HMRC will agree a partial exemption special method (para **15.284**) that includes the business/non-business calculation. In this case, however, the 'de minimis' limits (para **15.282**) will not apply;
- changes in the level of business use should be recognised in adjustments under regs 108 and 109 (para **15.286**).

Some bodies are nevertheless able to reclaim VAT related to non-business activities. This is relevant:

- to local authorities and some other bodies covered by VATA 1994 s 33. Local authorities also benefit from generous partial exemption *de miminis* limits (compare para **15.282**);
- to certain free museums, under VATA 1994, s 33A;
- to academies, under s 33B (since 1 April 2011);
- in relation to certain 'contracted out services', to some central and developed government bodies, the NHS etc, under s 41;
- under the refund schemes discussed in paras **15.275** to **15.278** – the 'DIY' scheme, and the schemes for listed places of worship and memorials;
- to charities included in VATA 1994, ss 33C and 33D (since 1 April 2015).

Paragraph **15.182** discusses VAT recovery in relation to assets partly for private use, under 'Lennartz accounting', although this ceased to be available for property expenditure from 1 January 2011.

Capital Goods Scheme (CGS)

[15.288] The CGS is a mechanism for basing input tax recovery on certain capital assets on their use over a period of years. In most EU member states it is wide-ranging, but in the UK it applies only to certain specific types of expenditure.

The UK rules are in Part XV of the VAT Regulations. These were heavily amended with effect from 1 January 2011, although aspects of the previous rules remain relevant and are noted below. For property, the CGS is mainly relevant:

- to landlords, where the liability of lettings changes – but subject to further points in para **15.96** et seq where this is a result of an option to tax;
- on the sale of a property, particularly by an occupier;
- where an occupier's partial exemption position changes;
- in determining whether the anti-avoidance rules for the option to tax (para **15.113** et seq) apply.

In practice, the CGS is frequently overlooked, particularly by occupiers, and businesses do not always have adequate records to carry out adjustments properly.

In relation to property:

- the CGS applies to various categories of property expenditure where VAT is incurred on a sum of £250,000 or more;
- adjustments are normally made over nine to ten years;
- normally, 10% of the original input tax is revisited each year;
- on a disposal, or on deregistration, there may be a single adjustment to cover all the remaining years.

Paragraph **9.117** explains how a CGS adjustment impacts on any capital allowances claims.

Scope

[15.289] The CGS applies to any 'capital item' where VAT is incurred in specific circumstances. Regulation 112(2) says that it must be:

'an item which a person who has or acquires an interest in the item in question (hereinafter referred to as "the owner") uses in the course or furtherance of a business carried on by him, and for the purpose of that business, otherwise than solely for the purpose of selling that item.'

Items held purely for sale, or for non-business use, are therefore excluded. HMRC will generally see matters in terms of the accounting treatment adopted by the business, but case law has also considered the meaning of 'capital goods' in various contexts.

Case law on the meaning of 'capital goods'

- In *Verbond van Nederlandse Ondernemingen* (CJEU Case 51/76), the CJEU saw 'capital goods' as 'goods used for the purposes of some business activity and distinguishable by their durable nature and their value and such that the acquisition costs are not normally treated as current expenditure but written off over several years'.
- In *Harbig Leasing Two Ltd* (VTD 16843), the Tribunal thought the factors to consider included durability, value and whether the goods were sold immediately or retained for a number of years. Accounting and direct tax treatment were not decisive.
- In *JDL Ltd* ([2002] STC 1, Ch D), the High Court held that a company's vehicles were capital goods, since they were 'of substantial durability and value compared with other articles used in the management and day-to-day running of the business, and were depreciated in the management accounts'.
- In *Scottish Homes* (VTD 16644), the Tribunal held that housing sold to tenants was not 'capital goods', partly because the appellant had a statutory duty to encourage tenants to buy.
- In *Whitbread Harrowden Settlement and others* (VTD 16781), land disposed of by a large old-established estate was 'capital goods'.
- In *Shurgard Storage Centres UK Ltd* (VTD 20797) (see also para **15.120**) the owner of a property agreed to sell it, and then carried out works required by the purchaser before the sale was completed. The Tribunal held that the owner was not subject to the CGS, since the work had been undertaken purely with a view to sale.
- In *Water Property Ltd* (TC05450), the business acquired land and buildings and it converted the ground floor into a children's nursery and the upper floor into two residential flats. The consideration paid to acquire the property and each stage of the development work to be undertaken was below £250,000 so the property did not come within the scope of the Capital Goods Scheme (CGS). However the total aggregated value of the purchase price and development work exceeded £250,000. HMRC considered that the property came within the scope of the CGS as a result. The taxpayer appealed. The First-tier Tribunal held that it was common for local authorities to grant single planning permission covering the whole development in respect of a phased

development. In this case, the development costs for each phase were financed using different means, there were separate contracts in place for each phase and there was no overlap in time between phases. HMRC had also not identified that any abuse, avoidance or evasion had occurred. The First-tier Tribunal also stated that WPL had relied on HMRC guidance in ascertaining that there was no requirement to aggregate the phases together if there was no overlap in time. As a result, the First-tier Tribunal concluded that the property was not a capital item for the purposes of the CGS.

Types of expenditure

[15.290] The types of expenditure covered by the CGS are defined by SI 1995/2518, reg 113. In relation to property, these are:

- the acquisition of land; and
- the acquisition, construction, refurbishment, fitting out, alteration or extension (including the construction of an annex) of a building or part of a building, a civil engineering work or part of a civil engineering work,

where in each case the expenditure is at least £250,000. It is the VAT incurred on this expenditure that is subject to adjustment under the CGS.

An acquisition here includes a self-supply under the 'change of use' rules in para **15.169** et seq.

HMRC say that civil engineering works include roads, bridges, golf courses, running tracks and the installation of pipes for connection to mains services. Other examples might be car parks, docks, airfields or refineries.

For expenditure incurred prior to 1 January 2011, the construction of an extension or annex is only within the CGS where it increased total floor area by at least 10%, and civil engineering works are included only in relation to acquisition or construction, and not if they were merely altered, extended etc. Fuller details can be found in previous editions of *Tolley's Property Taxation*.

The CGS can also be relevant to computers and computer equipment, and (since 1 January 2011) to aircraft, ships, boats etc, subject to a threshold of £50,000. These are ignored in the following paragraphs.

Non-business expenditure

[15.291] A property purely for non-business use is not within the CGS, so VAT incurred on it cannot be claimed through the CGS if it is later put to business use. This was confirmed by the CJEU in *Waterschap Zeeuws Vlaanderen* (CJEU Case C-378/02). HMRC nevertheless expect local authorities and other s 33 bodies (para **15.287**) to apply the CGS to non-business expenditure.

If a property is intended partly for business and partly for non-business use, it is within the CGS if the other criteria are met. All the VAT incurred is within the CGS, and adjustments can be required on account of a change in the level of business use. Alternatively, the person can opt out of including the non-business expenditure, but HMRC expect this decision to be documented, and it is generally disadvantageous.

Before 1 January 2011, assets intended for mixed business and non-business use were normally only in the CGS to the extent of the business element. But this did not apply to local authorities etc, nor where the person had recovered additional VAT under *Lennartz* (para **15.182**). These points continue to apply to expenditure incurred prior to 1 January 2011.

Adjustment period

[15.292] The input tax is adjusted over an 'adjustment period' consisting of a number of 'intervals'. The first interval starts when the person first uses the expenditure, whether by occupying or letting the property, and generally finishes at the end of the partial exemption year (para **15.282**). Adjustments are then made in the 'subsequent intervals' – there are normally nine of these, each of 12 months and corresponding with the partial exemption year. So the adjustment period is normally nine to ten years.

Also:

- For expenditure prior to 1 January 2011, the first interval commenced at different times depending on the circumstances. In particular, for an acquisition, it started on the date of acquisition rather than on first use.
- The number of subsequent intervals is reduced if the person's interest in the property will expire during what would otherwise be the adjustment period: for example, there are seven subsequent intervals in the case of a lease of between seven and eight years. If the interval commenced before 1 January 2011, this only applied in the case of the acquisition of a lease of less than ten years, in which case there were always four subsequent intervals.
- On a TOGC (see para **15.121** et seq), or if the owner joins or leaves a VAT group, the CGS position is passed across to the new owner or VAT registration. The first such event brings the current CGS interval to an end and starts a new one, but the remaining intervals are periods of 12 months, even if there is another TOGC or change in VAT grouping, and even though the intervals are unlikely to correspond with the VAT accounting periods.

Making adjustments

[15.293] In each 'subsequent interval', an element of the original VAT is revisited. This is 10% of it if there are nine such intervals (ie a total of ten intervals). It is a correspondingly higher figure if there are fewer intervals – $12\frac{1}{2}$% if there are a total of eight, 20% if there are a total of five, and so on. No adjustment is needed if there is no change in use or circumstances. If an adjustment is needed, it takes account of:

- the total input tax subject to adjustment (A);
- the proportion of this that was originally recoverable (B);
- the proportion of it that would be recoverable, were it incurred in the subsequent interval (C).

HMRC expect proportions to be expressed as percentages, accurate to two decimal places.

Assuming nine subsequent intervals, the adjustment in each of these is:

A ÷ 10 × (C-B)

If the figure is positive, it is claimable from HMRC; if it is negative it is payable to HMRC.

Example: CGS calculation

A business incurs £100,000 VAT on the purchase of a property for its own occupation. It can initially recover 30% of the VAT. In the second interval it would have been entitled to recover 40%. The calculation in the second interval is:

£100,000 ÷ 10 × (40% − 30%) = £10,000 × 10% = £1,000.

So the business can claim an additional £1,000 from HMRC.

The adjustment is made on the second VAT return following the end of the interval. So if the business is on calendar quarterly VAT returns, and the interval ends on 31 March, it is made on the return for the period to 30 September.

If some of the VAT is only incurred after the first interval, perhaps on retentions, it is initially recovered in the normal way, and then adjusted under the CGS in the remaining subsequent intervals. It will therefore be subject to fewer adjustments then the rest of the expenditure, whilst B above may be a different figure for this element. The calculation can be carried out separately, or together with the rest of the VAT using a composite figure for B. HMRC refer to these approaches as, respectively, 'parallel' and 'combined' adjustments.

The figure for C is normally calculated on the basis of the partial exemption method, just as though the VAT had actually been incurred in the subsequent interval, but HMRC can agree or direct a different method of calculation specifically for the CGS.

If the property is not used at all during the interval, it should generally be treated as used for whatever it is intended to be used. But in *Gateshead Talmudical College* ([2011] UKUT 131 (TCC)), the Upper Tribunal confirmed, in the context of a VAT planning arrangement, that CGS payments were due to HMRC where rents under a taxable lease had ceased to be collected, and the tenant company had been dissolved. Although the lease still existed, the College could no longer be seen as making taxable supplies under it.

There are further rules covering the disposal or destruction of the property, or the deregistration of the owner. There are also issues where the zero-rated grant of a major interest lease is followed by exempt supplies.

Outright disposals

[15.294] If the asset is disposed of in the course of a TOGC (para **15.121**), the transferee takes on the transferor's CGS position, and the transferor makes no further adjustments. If the disposal is a supply, there is a single adjustment for the remaining complete intervals – a taxable disposal is treated as wholly taxable use for these intervals, an exempt disposal as wholly exempt use.

Under SI 1995/2518, reg 115(3B), and 'save as the Commissioners may otherwise allow', if the end result is that the person has recovered more VAT on the property than it has accounted for on the disposal of it, it must repay the excess to HMRC. This is intended as an anti-avoidance rule and HMRC, referring to it as 'the disposal test' say that it 'will only be applied in cases of avoidance or abuse'.

Example: CGS calculation on an outright disposal

This continues the example in para 15.293.

A business incurs £100,000 VAT on the purchase of a property for its own occupation. It can initially recover 30% of the VAT. During the third interval it disposes of the property. For the third interval itself, it has still used the property in making both taxable and exempt supplies, and an adjustment is required in the normal way in line with the partial exemption position. But for the remaining seven intervals, an adjustment is made according to the treatment of the disposal:

- If the disposal is a taxable supply, this final adjustment is:
  $£100,000 \times {}^{7}/_{10} \times (100\% - 30\%) = £70,000 \times 70\% = £49,000$.
  So the business can claim £49,000 from HMRC.
- If the disposal is an exempt supply, this adjustment is:
  $£100,000 \times {}^{7}/_{10} \times (0\% - 30\%) = £70,000 \times - 30\% = - £21,000$.
  So the business must pay HMRC £21,000.
- If the disposal is a TOGC, there is no final adjustment, and the transferee takes on responsibility for the remaining adjustments.

Part disposals

[15.295] In the event of a part disposal, the VAT in the CGS needs to be apportioned between the part disposed of and the part retained. The element related to the part disposed of is treated in the same way as for an outright disposal. The balance remains subject to continuing adjustments in the normal way.

The regulations do not explain what constitutes a part disposal, or how the apportionment is to be carried out. But examples might be the sale of half of a plot of land, or the grant of a lease for a premium. HMRC have suggested that an apportionment might be based on the respective values or square footage of the different parts.

There was no provision for part disposals prior to 1 January 2011, and the general presumption was that adjustments should simply continue as before. But in *Centralan Property Ltd* (CJEU Case C-63/04), a property had been disposed of in two stages, three days apart, as part of a VAT planning arrangement. The CJEU held that both transactions, and not just the second, needed to be recognised as making up the disposal for the purposes of the CGS.

Example: CGS calculation on a part disposal

This continues the example in para 15.293, and is an alternative scenario to that in para 15.294.

A business incurs £100,000 VAT on the purchase of a property for its own occupation. It can initially recover 30% of the VAT. During the third interval it disposes of 60% of the property. (Alternatively, it grants a lease for a premium equivalent to 60% of the value of the property.)

For the third interval itself, it has still used the property as a whole in making both taxable and exempt supplies, and an adjustment is required in the normal way in line with the partial exemption position. But for the remaining seven intervals, a final adjustment is made for 60% of the VAT, according to the treatment of the part disposal, whilst the business must continue the adjustments on the remaining 40%:

- If the part disposal is a taxable supply, the final adjustment is: £100,000 × 6/10 × 7/10 × (100% – 30%) = £42,000 × 70% = £29,400. So the business can claim £29,400 from HMRC, and adjustments cease on 60% of the VAT. Adjustments continue on the other 40% (ie £40,000) in the normal way.
- If the disposal is an exempt supply, the final adjustment is: £100,000 × 6/10 × 7/10 × (0% – 30%) = £42,000 × – 30% = – £12,600. So the business must pay HMRC £12,600, and adjustments cease on 60% of the VAT. Adjustments continue on the other 40% (ie £40,000) in the normal way.
- If the disposal is a TOGC, there is no final adjustment. The business must continue to make adjustments on the 40% of the property it has retained, whilst the transferee takes on responsibility for adjustments on the 60% of the property that it has acquired.

Position following a zero-rated lease

[15.296] If the grant of a major interest lease is zero-rated under the rules in paras **15.132** to **15.178**, zero-rating only applies to the first supply, and subsequent supplies under the lease are exempt. In itself, this could require CGS repayments. Regulation 116(3) deals with this by saying that, where the owner grants a zero-rated lease:

'any subsequent exempt supply of his arising directly from that grant or assignment shall be disregarded in determining the extent to which the capital item is used in making taxable supplies in any interval applicable to it.'

So in this case, no adjustment is required. Unfortunately, the regulation does not deal with other cases where a zero-rated lease is followed by an exempt supply, such as a sale of the freehold, and in these cases a repayment to HMRC may be required. Often, the zero-rated lease will have been for a premium, to be treated as a part disposal under the rules in para **15.295**, thus reducing the amount of VAT remaining to be adjusted through the CGS. But where the lease was for rent, the repayment will be for the whole amount relating to the remaining intervals, potentially removing much of the benefit of zero-rating. This point is widely overlooked, and HMRC themselves ignored it for many years.

HMRC commented in Business Brief 23/06. This recognised certain instances where the second supply might be only partly exempt, and partly zero-rated, and accepted that in these cases the exempt part could be ignored, so that no CGS adjustment was needed. In particular, this is likely to apply to blocks of flats, where zero-rated leases are followed by a sale of the freehold – exempt in relation to the flats, and zero-rated for the common parts. Whilst this is of some help, there are plenty of other cases where the problem remains. Examples include flats where the developer has granted an overriding lease to a management company before selling the freehold, and nursing homes and student accommodation where the initial zero-rated lease covered the whole building.

Where there is a potential issue, it is therefore advisable to try to circumvent it. There are various ways of doing this, but in practice HMRC do not see the issue arising where the second transaction takes the form of a TOGC.

Destruction or deregistration

[15.297] If a CGS asset is irretrievably lost or stolen, or is totally destroyed, there is no further adjustment for subsequent intervals. Destruction includes the total demolition of a building, or the stripping out of refurbishment works such that no elements of it remain. If the asset is partly destroyed – perhaps the stripping out of some of the refurbishment works – adjustments should continue only on the part retained.

If a business deregisters with CGS items on hand, it should normally treat this as though the asset had been disposed of, whether or not there is actually a deemed supply of the asset under the rules in para **15.183**.

Avoidance and 'abuse'

[15.298] For many years, there were extensive VAT planning opportunities with property and construction, particularly for occupiers who could not benefit from full VAT recovery. HMRC have taken a number of steps to counter this, including anti-avoidance legislation, litigation and rules requiring the disclosure of 'schemes'.

In their Notice 700, HMRC say that:

> 'Tax avoidance is the use of contrived arrangements or structures to achieve a tax advantage – an increase in tax recovery, a reduction in the tax due or a tax deferral – contrary to the purpose and spirit of the legislation.'

Their views have, however, evolved over the years, and various arrangements that they once accepted are now routinely challenged.

Anti-avoidance legislation is considered in the relevant places elsewhere in this chapter, but the doctrine established by the CJEU in *Halifax* is looked at in para **15.299**, whilst para **15.300** deals with the disclosure rules.

'Abuse'

[15.299] HMRC often deploy straightforward technical arguments in attempting to defeat avoidance schemes, but they successfully broke new ground in *Halifax*, where in 2006 the CJEU held that a business had no right to recover input tax where the transactions in question were 'abusive', ie that they:

- would otherwise create a tax advantage contrary to the purpose of the Directive or of national law transposing it; and
- were essentially aimed at obtaining a tax advantage, and had no other explanation.

In such a case, the tax authorities were entitled to redefine the supply chain, so as to restore the position that would have existed without the 'abuse'. This doctrine has been considered in many subsequent cases.

'Abuse' – selected case law

CJEU cases

- *Halifax plc* (CJEU Case C-255/02) concerned planning arrangements where subsidiaries were interposed between a third party contractor and a largely exempt business, in order that the subsidiaries could recover VAT on building work.
  Referring to the then Sixth Directive on VAT, the CJEU held that:

  'the Sixth Directive must be interpreted as precluding any right of a taxable person to deduct input VAT where the transactions from which that right derives constitute an abusive practice.'

  'For it to be found that an abusive practice exists, it is necessary, first, that the transactions concerned, notwithstanding formal application of the conditions laid down by the relevant provisions of the Sixth Directive and the national legislation transposing it, result in the accrual of a tax advantage the grant of which would be contrary to the purpose of those provisions. Second, it must also be apparent from a number of objective factors that the essential aim of the transactions concerned is to obtain a tax advantage.'

  This did not apply to 'normal' transactions:

  'the prohibition of abuse is not relevant where the economic activity carried out may have some explanation other than the mere attainment of tax advantages'

  but only to:

  'transactions carried out not in the context of normal commercial operations, but solely for the purpose of wrongfully obtaining advantages provided for by Community law'.

  Indeed, businesses were entitled to take account of tax in taking business decisions:

  'Where the taxable person chooses one of two transactions, the Sixth Directive does not require him to choose the one which involves paying the highest amount of VAT. On the contrary . . . taxpayers may choose to structure their business so as to limit their tax liability.'

  The Court also held that:

'where an abusive practice has been found to exist, the transactions involved must be redefined so as to re-establish the situation that would have prevailed in the absence of the transactions constituting that abusive practice.'

This had to be done in a neutral way:

'a finding of abusive practice must not lead to a penalty . . . but rather to an obligation to repay'.

- The Court made similar points in a simultaneous judgment in *University of Huddersfield* (CJEU Case C-223/03).
- In *Weald Leasing Ltd* (CJEU Case C-103/09), an insurance group C had arranged to purchase equipment via an associated company W, and then lease them via a third party S, rather than buying them direct. It would subsequently buy the goods at a heavily depreciated value; the fact that S was a third party limited HMRC's ability to impose market valuations. HMRC argued 'abuse' and sought to deny input tax in W. The CJEU did not see leasing as inherently abusive. If there was abuse, it lay in the details – the level of charges and the interposition of S. Significantly, the CJEU considered that the existence of an abusive practice is to be determined by reference to what actually happened – not by reference to what the normal commercial operations to the taxpayer are. Any redefinition should be aimed at the abusive elements, not the entire arrangement. The Court did, however, reject the argument that 'abuse' could not apply to purely domestic legal provisions, where these were permitted under the Directive.

UK cases

- *Redcats (Brands) Ltd* (VTD 19648) concerned an attempt to reduce output VAT by introducing a charge for a zero-rated catalogue and reducing the charges for standard-rated goods. The Tribunal dismissed the idea that *Halifax* did not apply to outputs or to zero-rating – it was enough that the Directive envisaged VAT being proportionate to the price paid.
- In *The Atrium Club Ltd*, a company ACL had let health club premises to AAB, which had carried on the business. The idea was that both companies' activities could be treated as exempt but, when HMRC challenged AAB on this, it was unable to pay the VAT and went into liquidation. HMRC then alleged that, under *Halifax*, AAB's supplies could be treated as made by ACL, so that they could collect the VAT from ACL instead.
  The Tribunal (VTD 20933) rejected this – *Halifax* did not apply because there had been no tax advantage: AAB's supplies had been taxable, so the VAT planning had not worked. And in any case, HMRC could not redefine the supplies under *Halifax* so as to treat them as made by ACL, since the evidence was that they would not have been made by ACL anyway. The High Court ([2010] EWHC 970 (Ch)) disagreed on both points, and found for HMRC. ACL had obtained a tax advantage by letting the premises on an exempt basis, and redefinition under *Halifax* did not need to reflect reality – HMRC were entitled to employ whatever redefinition would neutralise the 'abuse'. This seems some way from what the CJEU had said in *Halifax* itself, that redefinition was 'to re-establish the situation that would have prevailed in the absence of the transactions constituting that abusive practice'.
- In *Moorbury Ltd* ([2010] UKUT 360 (TCC)), HMRC had redefined an 'abusive' supply chain in such a way as to remove the company from it. They denied its claims for input tax, but refused to refund the corresponding output tax

on the grounds that this was out of time. The Upper Tribunal rejected this – HMRC were only entitled to collect the net amount correctly due, and could not assess for one amount, leaving the taxpayer to claim any offset.

- *Lower Mill Estate Ltd v Revenue and Customs Comrs* ([2010] UKUT 463 (TCC), [2011] STC 636) concerned new holiday homes. The legislation seeks to standard-rate sales of such properties by developers (see para 15.45), but their construction can still potentially be zero-rated. Under the contracts entered into by the companies, purchasers would acquire building plots and construction services separately, paying VAT only on the plots.
  The First-tier Tribunal (TC00016) concluded that this was 'abusive', so that the arrangements could be reconstructed as a single standard-rated supply, but the Upper Tribunal disagreed – the arrangements had not been adopted solely for VAT reasons, and it was not abnormal for someone to buy a plot first and then to have a holiday home built on it.

- In *Pendragon plc* (TC00147) the First-tier Tribunal accepted that arrangements which both secured a VAT benefit and assisted with financing requirements were not 'abusive'. On appeal ([2012] UKUT 90 (TCC)), the Upper Tribunal, looking at the aims sought by the transaction as opposed to the consequences, agreed with HMRC. Of interest is the weight placed by the Upper Tribunal on correspondence between the taxpayer and its advisers. The Upper Tribunal re-defined the transactions in question by cancelling a number of intermediate steps. This was overturned by the Court of Appeal ([2013] EWCA Civ 868), which in turn was overturned by the Supreme Court ([2015] UKSC 37).
  The Court of Appeal essentially held that the Upper Tribunal was influenced too heavily by the extent of the tax saving involved and observed that most VAT planning will produce a benefit and the benefit cannot of itself be a decisive factor. The Supreme Court, however, concluded that the essential aim of the transactions was to produce a tax advantage, and was influenced by the fact that some of the steps involved were included solely to produce the intended tax result. It also complimented the judgment of the Upper Tribunal.

Disclosure of 'schemes'

[15.300] The Government announced in Autumn Statement 2016 that new legislation would be introduced, that will strengthen the regime for disclosing indirect tax avoidance schemes. A new disclosure regime will be effective from 1 January 2018 and replaces legislation contained in VATA 1994, s 58A and Sch 11A. Under the revised arrangements, primary responsibility for disclosing avoidance arrangements will be transferred from the user to the promoter of the notifiable proposal. The scope of the disclosure regime will be extended to include Insurance Premium Tax, all Excise Duties, the Soft Drinks Industry Levy, Landfill Tax, Aggregates Levy, Climate Change Levy and Customs Duties.

The revised arrangements are included in September 2017 Finance Bill, cl 66 and Sch 17.

Current disclosure regime (effective until 1 January 2018)

The purpose of the disclosure regime is to give HMRC an early opportunity to challenge particular VAT planning arrangements, and to identify new 'schemes' being used.

The rules are contained in VATA 1994, Sch 11A and in Statutory Instruments. They cover two types of 'scheme' – 'designated schemes' and those with 'hallmarks of avoidance'.

A 'scheme' is defined very broadly. It *includes* 'any arrangements, transaction or series of transactions'. HMRC do, however, say that it has to be a 'planned action', and that the use of a universally available extra-statutory concession or trade facilitation measure, of VAT grouping, of the option to tax, or of a new partial exemption method are not in themselves 'schemes', although of course they might form part of a 'scheme'.

For the purposes of these rules, persons are 'connected' where one of them is an undertaking in relation to which the other is a group undertaking under s 1161 of the Companies Act 2006, or where they are both connected to the same trust.

Where disclosure is required, it must be made within 30 days of the first occasion when the 'scheme' has an impact on a VAT return or on a claim to adjust a past return. This applies even if HMRC are already fully aware of the arrangements. HMRC's Notice 700/8 explains what information to provide and where to send it.

Non-disclosure carries penalties, and also allows HMRC 20 years, rather than the normal four, in which to raise an assessment if they discover errors. In practice, however, the requirements are widely overlooked.

Designated schemes

[15.301] Businesses must disclose the use of any of ten arrangements specified in the VAT (Disclosure of Avoidance Schemes) (Designations) Order 2004 (SI 2004/1933). Failure to do so will incur a penalty of 15% of the tax involved. The business does not have to have been seeking any VAT benefit in using the arrangement.

A business whose total supplies are always below £150,000 per VAT return period (£50,000 if it makes monthly returns) will not normally be covered by the rules unless another member of its corporate group breaches these limits.

Two of the arrangements concern property:

Designated Scheme 1 – 'First grant of a major interest in a building'

Scheme 1 is about input tax recovered by a 'person constructing' a dwelling or RRP/RCP building. As explained in paras 15.134 et seq and 15.151 et seq, the first grant of a 'major interest' by such a person is zero-rated. The designation of the 'Scheme' reflects HMRC's concern that developers may be able to use this zero-rating to recover VAT on non-capital expenditure, or on works undertaken some years after the original construction. The Order refers to:

'Any scheme comprising or including the first grant of a major interest in any building of a description falling within item 1(a) of Group 5 of Schedule 8 (construction of buildings etc.) where –

(a)   the grant is made to a person connected with the grantor; and

(b)   the grantor, or any body corporate treated as a member of a VAT group under section 43 of the Act of which the grantor is a member, attributes to that grant input tax incurred by him –

    (i)   in respect of a service charge relating to the building; or

    (ii)   in connection with any extension, enlargement, repair, maintenance or refurbishment of the building, other than for remedying defects in the original construction.'

The 'Scheme' applies whether or not the VAT benefit is contrived, but notably does not cover cases where the grant of the major interest is to an unconnected party, nor where zero-rating is under the rules for 'a person converting' (para 15.172 et seq) or 'substantially reconstructing' a listed building (para 15.176 et seq).

Designated Scheme 10 – 'Surrender of relevant lease'

According to HMRC's Business Brief 14/05, Scheme 10:

'targets exempt or partially exempt occupiers who have in the past put in place taxable lease structures in order to obtain full VAT recovery on the capital cost of the building, and who now try to obtain further VAT benefits by avoiding irrecoverable VAT on the rent payable for the remainder of the lease term.'

This refers primarily to 'lease and leaseback' arrangements using the option to tax, and entered into in 1999 or earlier. Arrangements of this kind are now generally prevented by the rules in para 15.113 et seq, but some earlier structures survive, and create an ongoing cost.

The 'Scheme' applies where:

- an occupier of a building has paid VAT on rent, not all of which it could recover;
- that occupier, or someone connected with it, is subject to the CGS (para 15.288 et seq) in relation to the building, has opted to tax it and leases it to someone else;
- the occupier's lease or licence is now terminated by a surrender or by some other action of the occupier agreed with its landlord; and
- the occupier remains in occupation of at least 80% of the area previously occupied, now paying no VAT or less than half the VAT it was previously paying – eg because the option to tax is now disapplied by the rules in para 15.113 et seq, or because of a substantial rent reduction.

Hallmarked schemes

[15.302] Businesses must notify HMRC if they enter into an arrangement with a view to obtaining a 'tax advantage' for themselves or for someone else, and that arrangement has one or more of the supposed 'hallmarks of avoidance'. Failure to do so will incur a fixed penalty of £5,000, but cumulative or multiple penalties are possible. Alternatively, a professional adviser can notify the generic arrangement, and can provide the business with the reference number allocated to it by HMRC.

A business whose total supplies are always below £2.5m per VAT return period (£833,333 if it makes monthly returns) will not normally be covered by the rules unless another member of its corporate group breaches these limits.

A hallmarked 'scheme' has to be at least partly motivated by VAT considerations – its sole or main purpose has to be 'the obtaining of a tax advantage by any person' – not necessarily by the business itself. Someone obtains a 'tax advantage' if:

- the net payment due on a VAT return is less than it 'otherwise would be';
- they obtain a VAT credit they would not 'otherwise' obtain, or obtain a larger or earlier VAT credit 'than would otherwise be the case';
- as the recipient of a supply, they can recover input tax before the supplier accounts for output tax, and the period between these events is 'greater than would otherwise be the case'; or
- the irrecoverable VAT they incur 'is less than it would otherwise be' – for a VAT-registered business, this is looked at for each VAT return period.

The 'hallmarks' are listed in the VAT (Disclosure of Avoidance Schemes) (Designations) Order 2004, and are as follows:

(1) 'An agreement preventing or limiting the disclosure of how a scheme gives rise to a tax advantage.'

(2) 'An agreement that the tax advantage to a person accruing from the operation of the scheme be shared to any extent with another party to it or another person promoting it.'

(3) 'An agreement that payment to a promoter of the scheme be contingent in whole or in part on the tax advantage accruing from the operation of the scheme.'

(4) 'A payment for a supply of goods or services between connected persons' where this is before the basic taxpoint (see para **15.202**) or, in the case of a continuous supply, before the goods or services are provided.

(5) 'The funding in whole or in part of a supply of goods or services between connected persons by means of a loan between connected persons or the subscription for shares in, or securities issued by, a connected person.'

(6) 'Off-shore loops' – involving the routing of services via someone outside the EU.

(7) Property transactions, other than zero-rated supplies, where:
  (a) 'the grantor or grantee of the interest or right is a person who is not entitled to credit for all the input tax wholly attributable to the supplies he makes';
  (b) 'any work of construction, alteration, demolition, repair, maintenance or civil engineering has been or is to be carried out on the land'; and
  (c) 'the grant is made to a person connected with the grantor.'

(8) The issue of certain face value vouchers.

Chapter 16

Stamp duty land tax 2017–18

by
Patrick Cannon,
Barrister

Introduction

[16.1] Stamp duty land tax or 'SDLT' replaced stamp duty on land in the UK from 1 December 2003 (although stamp duty has been retained for transactions in shares and securities and acquisitions of certain partnership interests). Unfortunately the SDLT legislation is hard to follow in parts and has been amended many times in its relatively short life so far. The unsatisfactory nature of the legislation has been shown by the need to issue detailed changes correcting mistakes, plugging gaps and in some cases recasting the charging provisions by way of statutory instrument and subsequent Finance Acts. Further guidance in the form of bulletins and 'customer' (sic) newsletters has also been issued. There are often alternative possible reasonable interpretations and applications of the relevant legislative provisions which require the professional adviser to take a view on how the transaction in question should be reported under the self-assessment system which operates for SDLT. The state of the legislation led quickly to avoidance schemes and as a result SDLT avoidance schemes involving commercial property worth £5m or more were brought within the scope of the rules relating to disclosure of tax avoidance schemes in FA 2004, Pt 7 with effect from 1 August 2005. The rules were extended to residential property worth £1m or more from 1 April 2010 and identification of scheme users generally became required for notified schemes. Sub-sale schemes were however initially exempted from disclosure under the 2010 changes although regulations effective from 1 November 2012 added a requirement for one further notification by promoters of certain types of sub-sale schemes and property valuation thresholds for disclosure were also removed. Hence the SDLT disclosure rules now apply in principle to the acquisition of chargeable interests of any value and whether the interests are residential or commercial subject to some important exclusions.

A general anti-avoidance rule was introduced with effect from 6 December 2006 by statutory instrument as new FA 2003, s 75A. FA 2007 replaced this provision with new FA 2003, ss 75A, 75B and 75C, also with effect from 6 December, 2006 (see **16.2**).

In addition to complex legislation, practitioners have also had to contend with a compliance system of enormous complexity and detail coupled with shortcomings in its administration. These difficulties have to some extent been resolved but taxpayers are having to contend with a large number of enquiries by HMRC now that HMRC have become aware of the extent of SDLT avoidance which flourished in recent years. Finance Act 2012 introduced the 15% punitive rate applying to purchases of residences over £2m by companies and certain other non-natural persons. Finance Act 2014 reduced the £2m price threshold to £500,000. Finance Act 2013 introduced fundamental changes to the rules on sub-sales and assignments of contracts (now known as pre-completion transactions), the general anti-abuse rule or 'GAAR' which applies to SDLT and the annual tax on enveloped dwellings or 'ATED'. The Stamp Duty Land Tax Act 2015 (SDLTA 2015) confirmed the replacement of the 'slab' rates system with the 'slice' rates system for residential property which was announced in the Autumn 2014 Budget statement. Separately, Scotland has had its own version of SDLT since April 2015 which is known as the Land and Building Transaction Tax or LBTT. From 1 April 2018, SDLT in Wales is expected to be replaced by the Land Transaction Tax to be administered by the Welsh Revenue Authority.

Under FA 2016 the 'slab' system of charging SDLT on non-residential and mixed-use property was replaced by a 'slice' system from 17 March 2016 with a new top rate of 5% above consideration of £250,000 and the rate of tax on non-residential lease rents was doubled from 1% to 2% where the net present value exceeds £5m. An additional rate of 3% has applied by FA 2016 to the purchase of residential properties by companies and other non-natural persons, and of additional residential properties by individuals, since 1 April 2016 (see **16.22** below).

Scope of the charge

[16.2] Stamp duty land tax is charged on 'land transactions'. In contrast with the tax it replaced, SDLT is chargeable whether or not there is an instrument. It is also expressed to be chargeable whether or not any party to the transaction is present or resident in the UK although this was never a requirement for stamp duty to apply. The purchaser must deliver a land transaction return for every 'notifiable transaction' within 30 days of the 'effective date' of the transaction containing a self-assessment of the tax chargeable and accompanied by payment of the SDLT chargeable. Following the introduction of FA 2003, ss 75A, 75B and 75C the tax can also be charged in respect of consideration given for non-land transactions which are 'involved in connection with' the disposal and acquisition of the chargeable interest (see below).

A 'land transaction' is any acquisition of a 'chargeable interest', and stamp duty land tax applies however the acquisition is effected, whether by an act of the parties, an order of a court or other authority, by or under any statutory provision or by operation of law. A 'chargeable interest' is defined widely as:

(1) an estate, interest, right or power in or over land in England, Wales or Northern Ireland; or

(2) the benefit of an obligation, restriction or condition affecting the value of any such estate, interest, right or power

other than an exempt interest (see **16.40**).

The basis of the tax is therefore land in the UK. The common law definition of the UK applies in the absence of any statutory extension to the continental shelf. Hence the UK comprises England, Wales, Scotland and Northern Ireland (but not the Channel Islands or the Isle of Man) and ends at the low water mark without extending to the seabed under the territorial sea (*R v Keyn* (1876) 2 Ex D 63). However, transactions in Scottish land have been excluded since 1 April 2015 when LBTT took effect in Scotland in place of SDLT: see **CHAPTER 24**.

Transactions in Wales will be excluded from 1 April 2018 when the Welsh Land Transaction Tax takes effect. From this date FA 2003, s 48A will apply to land that is partly in England and partly in Wales.

Exempt interests are any security interest, a licence to use or occupy land and a tenancy at will, advowson, franchise or manor. A 'security interest' means an interest or right (other than a rent charge) held for the purpose of securing the payment of money or the performance of any other obligation. An interest held by a financial institution as a result of the first transaction within an alternative finance property transaction within FA 2003, ss 71A, 72 or 72A is also an 'exempt interest' (FA 2003, s 73B). Chargeable interests therefore include freeholds and leasehold interests and their Northern Irish equivalents, rights over another's land and powers of appointment exercisable over trusts of land. Both legal and equitable interests are included and the exclusion of licences is for the avoidance of doubt because a licence, being a mere personal right, is not an estate, interest or right over land. An assignment of the right to receive rents is undoubtedly a transfer of an interest in land (see *IRC v John Lewis Properties plc* [2001] STC 1118 Ch D which considered the issue in detail and was confirmed by the Court of Appeal at [2002] EWCA Civ 1869, [2003] STC 117, and Law of Property Act 1925, s 205).

The 'purchaser' and 'vendor' in relation to a land transaction are defined as the person acquiring and the person disposing of the subject matter of the transaction (which will be the chargeable interest acquired together with any interest or right attached to it that is acquired with it). However, a person cannot be a 'purchaser' unless he has given consideration for or is a party to the transaction. This is subject to the special tax charge arising on a contract under which A is to convey a chargeable interest at the direction or request of B to a person (C) who is not a party to the contract. B is deemed to have acquired a chargeable interest when the contract is substantially performed and SDLT will be payable accordingly.

Example 1

Green Developers Limited agrees with Farmer Giles that the company will build a house on his redundant paddock and find a buyer to whom Farmer Giles will convey the completed house as requested by Green Developers Limited. The sales proceeds of the house will be remitted to Farmer Giles less the agreed building costs and profit mark-up attributable to Green Developers Limited. Green Developers Limited will never acquire any interest in the land and the completed house which is sold direct by Farmer Giles to the purchaser. Despite this, Green

Developers Limited will have to pay SDLT at completion as if the company had acquired the land.

The purchaser is the person who is required to file a land transaction return and pay any tax due. The following illustrates who will be regarded as the purchaser in a variety of transactions:

Transaction	Purchaser
Conveyance, assignment or assignation	Transferee or assignee
Grant of lease	Lessee
Grant of easement etc	Person entitled to the right
Surrender of lease	Landlord
Certain variations of leases	Person whose estate interest or right is enlarged or benefits
Making or release of a covenant or condition	Person whose estate interest or right is enlarged or benefits

In *Pollen Estate Trustee Co Ltd v Revenue and Customs Comrs* [2012] UKUT 277 (TCC) the Upper Tribunal held that purchasers who are jointly entitled to land interests have only a single land transaction of the whole of the interest acquired as a consequence of FA 2003, s 103. The Court of Appeal ([2013] EWCA Civ 753) confirmed this analysis and that the rate of SDLT charged is determined by the chargeable consideration for the entire interest purchased but the amount of tax actually charged will be reduced if one of the joint purchasers is a charity to reflect the proportion held for charitable purposes. The statutory provisions governing the exemption for purchases by charities were amended by Finance Act 2014 to reflect the Court of Appeal's judgment (see **16.56**).

Having defined 'chargeable interest' in wide terms, the legislation then defines the concept of an 'acquisition' of such an interest in equally wide terms by providing that the creation, surrender, release or variation of a chargeable interest is an 'acquisition'. The variation of a lease is treated as an acquisition and disposal of a chargeable interest where it is treated as the grant of a new lease or if there is a reduction in the rent or term or where the lessee give consideration for a lease variation other than a variation of the rent or the term of the lease. It is thought that the exercise of a break clause in a lease is not the acquisition of a chargeable interest because it does not cause a surrender or release of the interest (*Pennel v Payne* [1995] 2 All ER 592, CA as expressly approved in *Barrett v Morgan* [2000] 2 AC 264, [2000] 1 All ER 481, HL).

A contract for a land transaction that contemplates completion by conveyance of the legal estate will have an 'effective date' for stamp duty land tax of the earlier of 'substantial performance' of the contract or the conveyance. The mere entry into such a contract itself is ignored and is not regarded as entering into a land transaction. The occurrence of the 'effective date' triggers the duty to deliver the land tax return and pay the SDLT within 30 days of such date, and is also the date on which the conditions for any available relief must be met. In England contracts for equitable interests only (see *Peter Bone Ltd v IRC* [1995] STC 921) that will not be completed by conveyance are brought within the tax indirectly as being the acquisition of a chargeable interest that is a notifiable transaction giving rise to the obligation to deliver a land tax return. 'Substantial performance' occurs when either:

(1)   the purchaser (or a person connected with the purchaser) takes possession of the whole or substantially the whole of the chargeable interest (including receiving or becoming entitled to receive rents and profits whether under the contract or a separate licence or lease of a temporary character); or

(2)   a substantial amount of the consideration is paid or provided (in the case of rent or both rent and other consideration this means the first payment of rent or in the case of other consideration substantially the whole of the other consideration).

Example 2

Green Developers Limited have exchanged contracts with Deep Blue Land Bank PLC for the purchase of White Acre. With one month to go before completion Green Developers Limited are permitted under the terms of the contract to take possession of the land and begin site preparation pursuant to an existing planning permission. Substantial performance of the purchase contract will have occurred upon Green Developers Limited taking possession and the transaction becomes notifiable at that time rather than subsequent completion.

A 'substantial amount' of the consideration is an amount that is equal to or greater than 90% of the consideration payable. In the majority of cases substantial performance will occur at completion and therefore the effective date will arise on the date of the conveyance as it did with stamp duty. However, if substantial performance of the contract occurs earlier then so will the effective date, thus preventing the purchaser from deferring the SDLT indefinitely by 'resting on contract' and putting off taking a conveyance as could be done for contracts for a consideration of £10m or less under stamp duty. This rule also affects how sub-sales are charged under SDLT.

If the contract is substantially performed before completion and there is a subsequent conveyance both the contract and the conveyance are notifiable transactions and additional SDLT is payable on the conveyance to the extent that the SDLT on the conveyance exceeds the SDLT on the contract.

A general anti-avoidance rule contained in FA 2003, ss 75A, 75B and 75C was introduced from 6 December 2006 which applies where there are transactions which are involved in connection with the disposal and acquisition of land. If the total SDLT payable in respect of the acquisition of the land and the connected transactions is less than would be payable if there was a single notional land transaction between the seller and the purchaser, then the chargeable consideration is taken to be the highest amount paid by any one person or received by or on behalf of the seller, by way of consideration and the actual land transactions are disregarded.

Where the statutory general anti-avoidance rule in FA 2003, s 75A applies, the land transactions forming part of the scheme are disregarded for SDLT purposes and the notional land transaction which is deemed to replace those land transactions will have an effective date which is the last date of completion of the scheme transactions or, if earlier, the last date on which a contract in respect of the scheme transactions is substantially performed (FA 2003, s 75A(4) and (6)). It follows that the disregarding of the real land transactions can occur before the occurrence of the effective date of the notional land transaction, leaving the taxpayer 'resting on contract' within s 75A until the completion of the scheme transactions. Where it is applicable, the anti-avoidance rule applies regardless of whether or not the parties were motivated by a desire to save SDLT. In *Project Blue Limited v Revenue and Customs Comrs* [2013] UKFTT 378 (TC) at para 227, the tribunal held that Parliament had 'obviously' intended that s 75A should apply regardless of motive and rejected the taxpayer's submission that s 75A was not engaged where transactions had a commercial motive and were not part of a tax-avoidance scheme. Certain incidental transactions are ignored for the purposes of the rule.

Confusing nomenclature

[16.3] The terms used in the SDLT legislation for various categories of interest are apt to confuse. The basic concept of the 'land transaction' is defined as an acquisition of a 'chargeable interest' which is in turn defined to exclude something called an 'exempt interest'. An 'exempt interest' is different from a 'chargeable interest' which benefits from either a general or a particular exemption or relief. An 'exempt interest' can never be the subject of a 'notifiable transaction' under FA 2003, s 77, although the general rule is that a 'chargeable interest' that benefits from a particular exemption or relief will still be a 'notifiable transaction' and therefore require the filing of a land transaction return claiming the exemption or relief. A 'land transaction' is also defined as a 'chargeable transaction if it is not a transaction that is exempt from charge' and FA 2003, Sch 3 currently contains six such exemptions which are not 'notifiable transactions' (FA 2003, ss 49 and 77A). The basic approach amidst this confusing nomenclature should therefore be to ascertain whether one is dealing with a 'chargeable interest' and not an 'exempt interest'. If one has a 'chargeable interest' one then needs to ascertain if it benefits from a general exemption (such as that in FA 2003, Sch 3, para 1 for transactions for no chargeable consideration) or a particular exemption or relief. One then needs to ascertain whether the transaction is a 'notifiable transaction' so that a land transaction return must be filed to report the transaction and also to claim any particular exemption or relief (FA 2003, ss 76–77A).

Chargeable consideration

Overview

[16.4] Stamp duty land tax is charged as a percentage of the 'chargeable consideration' for the land transaction. The chargeable consideration is any consideration in money or money's worth given for the acquisition of the chargeable interest, whether given directly or indirectly by the purchaser or a person connected with him.

The question of chattels purchased with a house and the attribution of consideration to the chattels was considered in *Gill Orsman v Revenue and Customs Comrs* [2012] UKFTT 227 (TC). It was found that 'fitted units' in the garage were part of the land since they were fixed to the house so that the £800 attributed to the units was part of the chargeable consideration for the land transaction which increased that consideration to £250,800 which attracted the 3% rate on the whole of the consideration rather than the 1% rate applied to the self assessed consideration of £250,000.

The use of money or money's worth as the criterion means that a wider class of consideration is recognised for SDLT than for stamp duty on land where broadly only money, shares, the release or assumption of a debt and other property count as sale consideration. The expression 'money or money's worth' is not defined for SDLT, although it must be something that is capable of being sold. The value of any chargeable consideration other than money or debt shall be taken to be its market value. In *Secretan v Hart* (1969) 45 TC 701 Buckley J thought that the expression included, 'services or other property, where the price or consideration which the acquirer gives for the property has got to be turned into money before it can be expressed in terms of money' (p 705). The main difference between SDLT and stamp duty is that the latter did not include the carrying out of building works or the provision of services as consideration, see for example Inland Revenue Tax Bulletin 43, October 1999, 'PFI projects – stamp duty': 'a contract to carry out works is not "consideration [which] consists of property" for the purposes of FA 1994, s 241'.

The carrying out of building works is however specifically excluded from constituting chargeable consideration to the extent that:

(1)   the works are carried out after the effective date of the transaction;
(2)   the works are carried out on land acquired or to be acquired under the transaction or on other land held by the purchaser or a person connected with him; and
(3)   it is not a condition of the transaction that the works are carried out by the vendor or a person connected with him.

In relation to the rule that where a contract is substantially performed before completion both the contract and the conveyance are notifiable transactions, the condition in 1 above is treated as met in relation to the conveyance if it is met in relation to the contract. In relation to 2 above, the references to land being acquired are to the acquisition of a 'major interest' in it which means freehold or leasehold either in law or in equity. Where land is being acquired wholly or partly in consideration of a purchaser developer carrying out building works on land to be retained by the vendor, it may be possible to avoid the value of the building works becoming chargeable to SDLT in certain cases through the use of a suitably drafted lease of the building land in favour of the purchaser developer.

However, where a purchaser developer agrees to grant a lease-back of the building land once the building has completed then there is the risk of an exchange transaction by reference to the value of the interest in the land acquired and retained by the purchaser developer or the chargeable consideration given for the acquisition if greater. This problem may be avoided by the use of a surrender and re-grant of a lease where the SDLT exchange provisions are effectively disapplied.

The Prudential case

[16.5] Where the value of building works is included in the chargeable consideration the value is taken to be the amount that would have to be paid in the open market for the carrying-out of the works in question.

On 2 April 2004 IR Stamp Taxes issued a statement dealing with the sale of land by a vendor who also agrees to carry out building works on the land sold. This situation should of course be distinguished from that above where the purchaser rather than the vendor is providing the building works. The statement concedes that the decision in *Prudential Assurance Co Ltd v IRC* [1992] STC 863 applies for SDLT as it did for stamp duty because the basis of the decision was the identification of the subject matter of the transaction and this is as relevant to SDLT as it was for stamp duty. It was also confirmed that SP 8/93 will be applied for SDLT. However, where the land contract and the building contract are 'in substance' one bargain then under SDLT there is a requirement to apportion the aggregate consideration on a just and reasonable basis, as to which see further below.

Where the consideration consists of the provision of services (other than the carrying out of works referred to above) the value of the consideration is taken to be the amount that would have to be paid in the open market for the works in question.

HMRC regard the market value of an asset as not including VAT that may be chargeable on a transfer of the asset: see SDLTM04140.

In determining the amount or value of the consideration no discount is allowed for postponement of the right to receive any of the consideration. Any VAT chargeable is included in the consideration liable to SDLT, except any VAT chargeable because of an option to tax made after the effective date of the transaction. Consideration attributable to two or more land transactions or in part to a land transaction and in part to another matter or in part to matters making it chargeable consideration and in part to other matters, is to be apportioned on a just and reasonable basis. It is provided that for these purposes any consideration given for what is in substance one bargain shall be treated as attributable to all the elements of the bargain, even though:

(a)   separate consideration is, or purports to be, given for different elements of the bargain, or

(b)   there are, or purport to be, separate transactions in respect of different elements of the bargain.

It is difficult to understand how there can 'in substance be one bargain', even though in the words of the provision: 'there are separate transactions in respect of different elements of the bargain' given that SDLT is a tax on 'land transactions' and not on 'land bargains'; for example see *Kimbers v IRC*

[1936] 1 KB 132. This provision may be yet a further attempt by HMRC to sidestep the consequences of there being in substance two or more legally separate transactions. It is also difficult to understand how a court faced with having to apply this provision can avoid being forced into rewriting the commercial bargain reached at arm's length by the parties and in effect substituting its own subjective opinion of how it would have apportioned if it were vendor and purchaser respectively. A court would normally take strenuous steps to avoid any such exercise precisely because it would be forced to substitute its own subjective views for those of the parties reached during actual commercial negotiations. This would be a tortuous exercise, particularly where it was clear that the parties had different priorities in terms of how the consideration was allocated as regards for example capital allowances and capital gains tax. (For the previous position under stamp duty where the parties were able to apportion consideration as they thought fit, provided they did not intend to defraud the Inland Revenue, see *Re Brown & Root McDermott Fabricators Ltd's Application* [1996] STC 483.)

Partition/division

[16.6] In the case of a partition or division of a chargeable interest, the share held by the purchaser immediately before the partition or division does not count as chargeable consideration.

Satisfaction of debt

[16.7] Where the chargeable consideration consists wholly or partly in the satisfaction or release of debt due to the purchaser or owed by the vendor or the assumption of existing debt by the purchaser, the amount of the debt is taken as chargeable consideration up to a maximum of the market value of the chargeable interest acquired. The old stamp duty imposed a charge where the property was merely 'subject to' the debt whereas an SDLT charge requires the assumption of the debt by the purchaser. Under stamp duty, where property was transferred subject to a debt, the transferee did not assume any liability for it and there was no separate consideration given, it was necessary to rely on a concession to avoid liability. Under SDLT it appears that it will be enough to avoid a charge if the transferee does not assume the liability even if he takes the property subject to a charge for the debt and so reliance on concession will not be necessary. However, there will be a deemed assumption of debt by the purchaser constituting chargeable consideration where debt is secured on the property immediately before and immediately after the land transaction and the rights or liabilities in relation to that debt of any party are changed as a result if or in connection with the transaction.

In such cases the amount of debt treated as assumed is intended to be restricted by reference to the vendor's share in the property (where the property is held jointly before the transaction) or the purchaser's share in the property (where the property is held jointly after the transaction).

Example 3

> Property is transferred by A into the joint ownership of A and B in equal shares subject to mortgage. B will normally assume liability for the entire mortgage debt but for SDLT, B will be treated as assuming only half the debt corresponding to B's share in the property.
>
> If a property is owned by A and B as tenants in common in say, 60:40 shares subject to mortgage and it is transferred into the sole ownership of B, A will be released from the debt and B may also indemnify A against any continuing liability. The intention of the legislation is that B is treated as assuming debt equal to 60% of the amount of the debt. However, there is a release of a liability and in such a case B is treated as giving chargeable consideration equal to the debt released which will normally be 100% of the debt given that A will have been liable for the entire debt. The restriction on B's liability only operates where there is an assumption (real or deemed) by B and here (although there may also be a deemed assumption of debt by B) the release means that there is a tax charge by reference to the entire debt. Nevertheless, it appears that this is not the intention of the legislature and the Stamp Taxes Office can be expected to accept that B's liability is restricted accordingly.

For these purposes, each beneficial joint tenant in equity is deemed to hold an equal undivided share in the property. However, in the case of joint owners who hold as tenants in common their shares in the property are taken to be their actual shares as tenants in common in equity. It is the ownership in equity which counts and not the undivided legal title.

It is thought that the 'debt' must be the same debt both before and after the transaction. It may also be possible to structure a transfer subject to a mortgage in a way that treats an indemnity and any payment thereunder given by the purchaser to the vendor as outside the meaning of chargeable consideration by relying on the exemption for indemnity payments under FA 2003, Sch 4, para 16 thereby achieving the transfer of land subject to mortgage without giving rise to SDLT.

Employee's accommodation

[16.8] Where accommodation is provided to an employee, the chargeable consideration for SDLT is the higher of a market value rent or the amount treated as employment income, unless the provision of the accommodation is treated as exempt from income tax. In that case there is no chargeable consideration for SDLT, except to the extent of any actual consideration given. In any other case the consideration is to be not less than market value of the chargeable interest at the effective date of the transaction.

Exclusions

[16.9] The following matters do not count as chargeable consideration in relation to both the grant of a lease and the assumption or release of such obligations on the assignment of a lease:

(1)   tenant's repairing, maintaining or insuring obligations;
(2)   service charges and similar items;

(3)   other obligations not affecting the rent that a tenant would be prepared to pay;

(4)   guarantees of payment or performance;

(5)   penal rent payable for breach of tenants' obligations;

(6)   costs borne by a tenant exercising a statutory right to be granted a new lease;

(7)   any other obligation by a tenant to bear the landlord's reasonable costs incidental on the grant of a lease;

(8)   an obligation under a lease, on its termination, to transfer to the landlord payment entitlements under the scheme of income support for farmers in respect of land subject to the scheme.

Third party liabilities

[16.10] Where the purchaser indemnifies the vendor in respect of a liability to a third party arising from a breach of an obligation owed by the vendor in relation to the land transferred, neither the agreement nor any payment pursuant to it counts as chargeable consideration. It may be possible to use such an indemnity as an alternative to an assumption of debt charged on land acquired and avoid the consequences of an assumption of debt under (see above).

Other taxes

[16.11] Where a purchaser becomes liable to pay, agrees to pay or does pay any inheritance tax due in respect of a land transaction that is a transfer of value or a disposition under a will or on intestacy of a chargeable interest, that does not count as chargeable consideration for SDLT. Where land is acquired otherwise than by way of a bargain made at arm's length or is treated as so acquired by TCGA 1992, s 18 and the purchaser is or becomes liable to pay or does pay any capital gains tax due in respect of the corresponding disposal, his liability or payment does not count as chargeable consideration as long as there is no other chargeable consideration given. This ensures that where a trader incorporates his business and transfers his property under TCGA 1992, s 165, SDLT will not be charged in respect of the held-over capital gains tax liability.

There are also exemptions relating to arrangements involving public or educational bodies involved in so-called 'public/private finance initiative' transactions.

In practice, HMRC accepts that no tax arises on the transfer of assets and liabilities between pension schemes where the only consideration is the assumption by the receiving scheme of the obligation to pay pension benefits. Any debts assumed or released by the transferee fund as part and parcel of the transfer are also ignored by HMRC. Any other consideration given will be chargeable consideration including any debt liabilities assumed, to the extent that the consideration is apportionable to interests in land on a just and reasonable basis: see HMRC SDLT Manual at 31800 and 31812.

Contingent consideration

[16.12] Stamp duty dealt with contingent consideration in a blunt manner. If the consideration was uncertain because the obligation to pay or the amount payable was linked to an event after execution, the contingency was ignored and stamp duty was charged by reference to any maximum, minimum or basic amount ascertainable at the date of execution. This resulted in stamp duty being payable by reference to an amount of consideration that might never be paid and there was no provision for a refund of the 'overpaid' stamp duty. In relation to land where the contingent consideration was truly unascertainable such that no maximum, minimum or basic sum could be ascertained the consideration was taken to be the market value of the estate or interest.

Stamp duty land tax adopts a more flexible approach to contingent consideration by not automatically requiring tax to be paid on any maximum ascertainable sum and by providing for the possibility of deferral of tax and the repayment of any tax paid on a greater amount of consideration than is eventually payable.

The relevant rules in relation to overage consideration are contained in FA 2003, ss 51 (Contingent, uncertain or unascertained consideration), 80 (Adjustment where contingency ceases or consideration is ascertained) and 90 (Application to defer payment in case of contingent or uncertain consideration) plus Part 4 of the SDLT (Administration) Regulations 2003 (SI 2003/2837). One should also note that the amount or value of the chargeable consideration is to be determined without any discount for the postponement of the right to receive it.

FA 2003, s 51 assumes that the consideration will be either contingent, uncertain or unascertained although only 'contingent' and 'uncertain' are actually defined. It is worth noting at the outset that deferment of the tax is only available in relation to contingent or uncertain consideration and not in relation to unascertained consideration.

'Contingent' consideration is defined as consideration that is (a) to be paid or provided only if some uncertain future event occurs, or (b) that is to cease to be paid or provided if some uncertain future event occurs. This definition emphasises the future event giving rise to payment or non-payment and so it is usually taken to be referring to a fixed amount which may or may not become payable or by which a basic price is to be adjusted. This approach is supported by the rule that the SDLT is to be computed initially as if the contingent consideration will become payable or will not cease to be payable. It seems that under this definition there is no room for consideration which may vary depending upon the circumstances.

Example 4

Giles sells his freehold interest in Whiteacre to Mick's Developers Limited for £10m payable at legal completion plus a further £5m if planning permission for development is granted within 10 years. Mick's Developers Limited is treated for SDLT purposes as paying £15m chargeable consideration for the land (subject to any application to defer the tax on the £5m contingent sum – see below).

Uncertain consideration

[16.13] 'Uncertain' consideration is defined as consideration whose amount or value depends upon uncertain future events. Thus variable consideration is taken to be 'uncertain' for SDLT purposes. Overage consideration falls within the definition because this type of consideration is dependent upon the grant of planning permission or possibly the onward sale of the land. Logically, it seems that overage consideration could be both 'contingent' and 'uncertain' because for example it is to be paid if an uncertain future event occurs, ie planning permission, where its amount or value depended upon that event. However, if one adopts the working interpretation suggested for 'contingent' consideration above so that this is limited to fixed amounts, then there will not, in practice, be an overlap. 'Uncertain' consideration is to be computed on the basis of a reasonable estimate made at the effective date of the transaction of its amount or value and SDLT paid initially on this amount. This gives rise to the issue of whether a discount (of up to 100%) can be assumed for the likelihood or unlikelihood that the payment will eventually be made – see further below.

Unascertained consideration

[16.14] 'Unascertained' consideration is not defined. Taking the stamp duty treatment as a guide, this would appear to mean any consideration that is ascertainable at the effective date (because all the facts and matters necessary for its computation are in existence) but which has not yet been ascertained because the relevant work in ascertaining or collating the information has not been carried out or completed. Examples of this type of situation are where the land is sold at a price linked to a set of completion accounts that have yet to be drawn up or linked to market value or square meterage at completion where the necessary valuation or survey has not yet been carried out. Because overage consideration will not usually rely on such factors, 'unascertained' consideration will not normally feature in SDLT calculations on overage. As with 'uncertain' consideration, where there is 'unascertained' consideration it is to be determined on the basis of a reasonable estimate and SDLT is paid initially on this amount (plus any ascertained consideration). The possibility of deferring payment of the SDLT is not available for 'unascertained' consideration (see below).

Application to defer

[16.15] Where the consideration includes contingent or uncertain consideration and that falls to be paid or provided on one or more future dates of which at least one falls or may fall more than six months after the effective date of the transaction, then the taxpayer may apply to defer the SDLT in respect of the contingent or uncertain element of the consideration – see FA 2003, s 90 and Part 4 of SI 2003/2837 for the detailed regulations governing the application for deferral. Deferral is not available in respect of any rent forming part of the consideration. If the application is granted and the tax is eventually payable, interest is not charged on the unpaid tax during the deferral period and begins to run only from 30 days after the deferred tax becomes payable. Overage consideration is a prime candidate for deferral of SDLT and the taxpayer should normally make application for it.

The application for deferral must be made within the same time period as the filing of the land transaction return, ie normally 30 days. There is no express power for HMRC to grant an extension for late applications to be considered and they will normally reject late applications. It may be that such refusals are, however, susceptible to a judicial review.

Adjustment

[16.16] In the case of all the three types of consideration mentioned above, an adjustment must be made by the taxpayer once the contingency occurs (or it becomes clear that it will not occur) or in the case of uncertain or unascertained consideration, whenever any relevant amount becomes ascertained. If as a result, the original transaction becomes notifiable or tax or additional tax becomes payable, an SDLT return is required to be made within 30 days accompanied by the tax or additional tax now due. If any tax originally paid turns out to have been too much as a result of this new information the taxpayer may obtain a refund by either amending his original return (within 12 months of the filing date) or subsequently by making a claim to HMRC for repayment of the overpaid amount.

Overage

[16.17] Two particular problems arise with the operation of the SDLT provisions in relation to overage. First, whether when initially computing the amount of any 'uncertain' consideration it is permissible to allow for the likelihood of the payment being made (as well as making a reasonable estimate of the amount that would be paid if the uncertain event occurred).

Example 5

Giles sells his freehold interest in Whiteacre to Mick's Developers Limited for £10m payable at legal completion plus a further variable sum depending upon the market value and acreage of the land over which planning permission is given and capped at £50m, but only in the event that planning permission for a casino is granted within 10 years. Mick's Developers Limited intend to apply for permission for residential development only and the planning officer has indicated that permission for a casino is unlikely ever to be granted. If planning permission for a casino was ever granted in the next 10 years it is estimated that a further £20m consideration would actually be payable to Giles. However, Mick's Developers Limited pay SDLT on the basic £10 million price only and estimate the value of the variable consideration as nil because of the unlikelihood of it ever becoming payable.

The Official SDLT Manual fails to address this issue and HMRC's view is not known by the author. For capital gains tax purposes it seems to be accepted by HMRC that one can take the likelihood of payment into account when valuing the chose in action representing the right to future payment. It may be, however, that for SDLT HMRC do not agree that the taxpayer is allowed to discount for the possibility of non-payment and that a return prepared on this basis could be at best negligent and at worst fraudulent. Where available the safest course of action may be to apply to defer the payment of SDLT on this amount.

The second problem with SDLT and overage is the continuing legal responsibility for adjustments to the tax once the contingency occurs or the consideration becomes ascertained. Legally, this responsibility (and the tax liability) stays with the original purchaser even though he may have disposed of the land because FA 2003, s 80 refers to the purchaser and not a subsequent owner of the land (and so do the deferral regulations in SI 2003/2837), ie the responsibility and liability does not run with the land. Depending upon the precise terms of the overage agreement, the original purchaser considering a disposal of land over which he has given an overage agreement to the original seller should therefore consider extracting a positive covenant and/or charge from his purchaser and any subsequent transferees that either all the required information will be supplied to him or that they will assume such responsibility and liability (doubtless this will be reflected in the price). This also raises the issue of whether the passing down the chain of title in this way is the assumption of a liability and so falls to be treated as chargeable consideration for SDLT under FA 2003, Sch 4, para 8. Although HMRC Stamp Taxes regard such an assumption as chargeable consideration it may be possible to structure this as an indemnity arrangement so that there is no chargeable consideration under FA 2003, Sch 4, para 16. Novation of the original overage agreement may of course be possible and should be considered in the case of wishing to close the administration of a deceased purchaser's estate or the liquidation of a company where both are subject to outstanding overage liabilities. It seems that HMRC accept that a novation of the overage obligation does in practice pass the obligation to pay any deferred or additional SDLT on to the subsequent purchaser. It is accepted by HMRC Stamp Taxes Office that where instead of imposing an overage agreement the vendor has simply taken the benefit of a covenant against development on the land sold, this is not within the scope of FA 2003, s 51 although if the purchaser or his successors pay the vendor to release the covenant then that will be a chargeable land transaction.

Interest payable

[16.18] As noted above, an application to defer payment of tax may be made to HMRC where the amount of tax payable depends on the amount or value of chargeable consideration that at the effective date is contingent or uncertain and falls to be paid on one or more future dates, of which at least one falls or may fall more than six months after the effective date of the transaction. Where the tax is deferred interest will only run on any such tax after 30 days from the date the deferred payment is due. In respect of contingent or uncertain consideration on which tax is not deferred, interest runs on tax unpaid more than 30 days after the effective date of the transaction, although lodgement of the tax reduces interest accordingly.

Annuity payments

[16.19] Where the chargeable consideration consists of annuity payments whether for life, in perpetuity, for an indefinite period or for a definite period exceeding 12 years, the consideration taken into account is limited to 12 years' annual payments. This contrasts with stamp duty which used a 20-year period for payments lasting more than 20 years or in perpetuity, and a 12-year period for payments lasting for life. Where the amount payable varies or may vary from year to year the 12 highest annual payments are taken. No account is taken of any provision in the annuity for adjustment of the amount payable in line with the retail price index and no discount is given for the fact that the amounts are payable in the future.

The rules relating to contingent and uncertain consideration discussed in **16.12** above apply to determine the value of any annuity payment where necessary and an 'annuity' means any consideration other than rent that falls to be paid or provided periodically. No application can be made to defer the tax payable nor is there any facility to file a further land transaction return and make an adjusting tax payment or receive a repayment when a contingency or any uncertain consideration becomes known.

Connected parties – market value substitution

[16.20] When a company purchases a chargeable interest and the vendor is connected with the company or some or all of the consideration consists of the issue or transfer of shares in any company with which the vendor is connected, the chargeable consideration is to be taken to be not less than the market value of the interest acquired at the effective date of the transaction plus any rent if the acquisition is the grant of a lease. CTA 2010, s 1122 applies to determine whether the company and the vendor are connected. Instances where the vendor is not connected with the purchasing company and the consideration includes the issue of shares must surely be rare. For SDLT the 'market value' is determined as for capital gains tax: see TCGA 1992, ss 272–274.

The fact that there may be no chargeable consideration actually given for the transfer does not affect the application of the market value rule. However, any other available exemption from SDLT overrides the market value rule.

This provision means that tax is charged when a business is incorporated and land is transferred to the proprietor's company. Tax may also be chargeable on a surrender of leases to a flat management company owning the freehold where the tenant controls the company. Despite doubts about the equivalent market value rule in stamp duty, it has been confirmed that under SDLT the market value is based on the nature of the interest transferred and that if a legal but not a beneficial interest is transferred then the market value will be taken to be the nominal value of the legal interest and not the full value of the beneficial interest (HC Official Report, Standing Committee B, Thursday 5 June 2003, col 389). It may be that this transfer is in any event ignored for SDLT under FA 2003, Sch 16, para 3 which generally disregards transfers between a principal and his nominee or bare trustee. However, in the cases of a grant of a lease to a bare trustee and a grant of a lease by a bare trustee, tax is charged as if the whole of the interest in the lease was acquired or disposed of accordingly.

Exceptions to the market value rule

[16.21] The market value rule does not apply in the following cases:

(1)   Case 1 is where the company is to hold the property as trustee in the course of a business carried on by it that consists of or includes the management of trusts. It is thought that this case relates to companies

that carry on an actual business of managing trusts, and that a company that acts as nominee or bare trustee for a particular principal or beneficiary or partnership and has been incorporated or acquired simply to hold legal title for such persons cannot take advantage of this case.

(2)   Case 2 is where the company is to hold the property as trustee and the vendor is connected with the company only because of CTA 2010, s 1122(6) (trustee connected with any individual who is a settlor in relation to the settlement etc) and is not otherwise connected.

Arguably these first two cases are not needed because a company acting as a trustee is treated as a single body of persons distinct from the person or persons who are trustees of the settlement from time to time. Although the SDLT legislation does not contain an express rule to this effect unlike capital gains tax (see TCGA 1992, s 69), HMRC do accept that in SDLT the trustees of a settlement are a separate and continuous body of persons distinct from the persons who comprise the trustees (see SDLTM 31745).

(3)   Case 3 is where the vendor is a company and the transaction is, or is part of, a distribution of assets of that company (whether or not in connection with its winding up) and there has not been a claim for either stamp duty or SDLT group relief by the vendor in respect of the chargeable interest transferred in the previous three years. It is not HMRC's intention that this Case should be prevented from operating where a group relief claim was made by the vendor but recovered under the claw-back rules in FA 2003, Sch 7, para 3 either at the time or before the effective date of the transaction. [IR Tax Bulletin 71.]

The equivalent market value rule in stamp duty also had additional exemptions relating to transfers to and from nominees and bare trustees and transfers from one nominee or bare trustee to another. These exceptions are not required in SDLT because (except in relation to the grant of a lease) no SDLT arises on a transfer of a bare legal estate from a nominee to its principal and on a transfer to a nominee or bare trustee of bare legal title, the market value of such an interest will be nominal at most (HC Official Report, Standing Committee B, Thursday 5 June 2003, col 390, but see above for dealings in leases and bare trustees).

However, a further exception from the stamp duty market value rule relating to the transfer out of a settlement to a beneficiary who did not acquire his interest for money or money's worth being a distribution in accordance with the settlement, has not been carried over into SDLT. Under SDLT, HMRC appears to believe that there is a market value charge whenever the beneficiary who receives the land is a company, to avoid the possibility of land being passed through a settlement to avoid SDLT. However, it is by no means clear that this view can be supported given the relatively limited circumstances in which a company and a settlement will be 'connected'.

Amount of tax chargeable

Rates

[16.22] Stamp duty land tax is charged by applying a range of percentages to separate slices of the chargeable consideration for the transaction. Where the relevant land consists entirely of residential property, the purchaser is an individual and the effective date of the transaction is on or after 1 April 2016, the percentages in Table A apply to each respective slice of the chargeable consideration to give the aggregate amount of tax chargeable, unless the transaction involves a 'higher threshold interest' for which the rate is 15% of the transaction or the transaction is a 'higher rate transaction' for which a substituted Table A applies which increases the rates of SDLT by 3% across all slices of chargeable consideration unless the total chargeable consideration is less than £40,000.

Table A: Residential

Part of relevant consideration	Rate
So much as does not exceed £125,000	0%
So much as exceeds £125,000 but does not exceed £250,000	2%
So much as exceeds £250,000 but does not exceed £925,000	5%
So much as exceeds £925,000 but does not exceed £1,500,000	10%
The remainder (if any)	12%

The purchase of a dwelling by a purchaser who is not an individual or the purchase of an additional dwelling by an individual (who is not replacing a main residence) is referred to as a 'higher rates transaction' and a different Table A is substituted for the one above and applies as follows where the chargeable consideration is £40,000 or more:

Table A: Residential (Higher Rates Transactions)

'Relevant consideration'	Percentage
So much as does not exceed £125,000	3%
So much as exceeds £125,000 but does not exceed £250,000	5%
So much as exceeds £250,000 but does not exceed £925,000	8%
So much as exceeds £925,000 but does not exceed £1,500,000	13%
The remainder (if any)	15%

Where the relevant land does not consist entirely of residential property, the rates in both Tables A do not apply and those in Table B apply instead.

There is no apportionment of the relevant consideration between either Table A or B. Since 17 March 2016 the rates in Table B have also applied to the chargeable consideration on a 'slice' instead of a 'slab' system. 'Residential property' is defined in FA 2003, s 116 and means a building that is used or suitable for use as a dwelling or is in the process of being constructed or adapted for such use, land that is, or forms part of the garden or grounds of such a building and any interest or right over such building or land. In *R (on the application of ZH and CN) v London Borough of Newham and Lewisham* [2014] UKSC 62, [2015] 1 All ER 783, [2014] 3 WLR 1548 Lord Hodge with whom three other judges agreed said that for the purpose of the Protection From Eviction Act 1977, ss 3 and 5, 'dwelling' did not have a technical meaning but suggested a greater degree of settled occupation than 'residence' and could be equated with one's home. Two of the seven judges held that 'dwelling' could include 'a temporary dwelling' and had at least as broad meaning as 'residence'. 'Garden or grounds' in HMRC's view includes land required for the reasonable enjoyment of the dwelling having regard to its size and character, applying a similar test to that in TCGA 1992, s 222(3) ie even if it is larger than 0.5 hectares and see also Revenue Interpretation 119 of August 1995 which contains HMRC's views on whether land included in a sale forms part of the 'grounds' of a dwelling reproduced in Appendix J and also *Longson v Baker* [2001] STC 6 and *Re Newhill Compulsory Purchase Order 1937, Payne's Application* [1938] 2 All ER 163 at 167.

Where the relevant land does not consist entirely of residential property, the rates in both Tables A do not apply and those in Table B apply instead.

Table B: Non-Residential or Mixed

Relevant consideration	Percentage
So much as does not exceed £150,000	0%
So much as exceeds £150,000 but does not exceed £250,000	2%
The remainder (if any)	5%

In the above tables the 'relevant consideration' is the chargeable consideration for the transaction unless the transaction forms part of a number of 'linked transactions'.

Linked transactions

[16.23] If the transaction forms part of a number of linked transactions the relevant consideration for the purpose of the tables above is the total of the chargeable consideration for all the linked transactions. The amount of tax for each particular linked transaction is calculated using a three-step process as follows:

Step 1	Apply the rates in the appropriate table in **16.22** above to the parts of the relevant consideration, ie the total for all the linked transactions.
Step 2	Add together the amounts calculated at Step 1 (if those are two or more amounts).
Step 3	Multiply the resulting amount by C/R where C is the chargeable consideration for the particular transaction concerned and R is the relevant consideration, ie the total for all the linked transactions.

(FA 2003, s 55(1C).)

For the effect of linked transactions in the context of the alternative Table A for higher rates transactions see **16.25** below.

Transactions are 'linked' if they form part of a single scheme, arrangement or series of transactions between the same vendor and purchaser or persons connected with them. This means that it is not necessary for the transactions concerned to be part of the same legally binding contract or to be documented as one before they can be 'linked'. While the stamp duty cases on certificates of value remain relevant in determining whether a transaction forms part of a series of transactions, the criteria for a 'linked' transaction are much wider than the criteria for certificates of value because they also refer to 'a single scheme' or 'arrangement', terms which did not feature in the 'larger transaction or series of transactions' criteria for certificates of value. CTA 2010, s 1122 is applied to determine whether persons are connected for these purposes. The current approach of the HMRC when asked for guidance on whether transactions are linked is generally to decline to give an opinion on the basis that there is no adjudication process under SDLT. However, experience suggests that HMRC tend to accept that transactions are not 'linked' where the terms of a particular transaction are in all material respects identical to what they would have been had the other transaction(s) not occurred. Where a discount has been secured because of the other transaction(s) or one cannot complete without the other then the transactions are likely to be 'linked'. It is worth noting that the scheme, arrangement or series of transactions must be between the same vendor and purchaser (or persons connected with them). HMRC sometimes erroneously assert that transactions are 'linked' when they form part of a scheme or arrangement but the scheme or arrangement is not between the vendor and purchaser (or person connected with them) but instead between one of the parties and an agent or other third party such as a property broker or agency.

There is an exception from the linked transactions rule for transactions carried out in pursuance of a right of collective enfranchisement where the tax is determined by reference to a fraction of the relevant consideration. Exchanges of land between connected persons are also excluded from the linked transactions rule.

Rent

[16.24] Where the whole or part of the chargeable consideration consists of rent, the tax on the rent is calculated separately under different rules: see below. The tables above apply to compute the tax on any premium paid for the grant of the lease.

Higher rates transactions

[16.25] The higher rates for additional dwellings purchased by individuals and for first and subsequent dwellings purchased by non-natural persons have applied since 1 April 2016 and are levied on any acquisition that is referred to in the legislation as a 'higher rates transaction', which is broadly as follows:

- the purchase of additional dwellings in England, Wales and Northern Ireland by individuals where, at the end of the day of purchase, sole or joint individual purchasers own two or more dwellings and are not replacing their main residence. The charge does not however apply where at the end of the day of purchase a sole individual purchaser owns an interest in only one dwelling, or joint individual purchasers together own an interest in only one dwelling; and

- the first and subsequent purchases of dwellings by persons who are not individuals except where the 15% rate under Sch 4A already applies.

(FA 2003, Sch 4ZA.)

The charge is 3% above the normal SDLT residential rates and is charged on the slices of the price of the property that fall into each band. The rates are set out in an alternative 'Table A: Residential' that is substituted for the normal Table A in FA 2003, s 55(1B) for when there is a higher rates transaction and the following table shows a comparison of the rates in both versions of Table A:

Band	Basic residential SDLT rates	Additional SDLT rates
£0–£125,000	0%	3%
£125,000–£250,000	2%	5%
£250,000–£925,000	5%	8%
£925,000–£1.5m	10%	13%
£1.5m+	12%	15%

Transactions under £40,000 do not require a tax return to be filed with HMRC and are not subject to the additional charge.

Acquisitions of mixed-residential and non-residential property remain exempt from residential rates and do not attract the 3% additional charge, and are charged under the rates in Table B also using the 'slice' system with a maximum rate of 5% for consideration above £250,000.

Leases and agreements for lease

Premiums

[16.26] Stamp duty land tax is charged in respect of leases on any premium paid for the grant of a lease and also on any rent. Lease premiums are taxed in accordance with either Table A or Table B (see 16.22 above) and SDLT on the rent is calculated according to the special formula described in 16.31 below. As was the case with stamp duty, the distinction between a lease and a licence continues to be important because under SDLT a licence to use or occupy land and a tenancy at will are exempt interests and are not liable to the tax.

Agreements for lease

[16.27] Although there was no express charge in relation to agreements for lease in the original legislation, such agreements were in any event chargeable to SDLT by implication as contracts for a land transaction under which the transaction is to be completed by a 'conveyance', and the usual rules as to the timing of the tax charge applied according to whether or not substantial performance of the contract had occurred prior to completion in the form of the grant of the lease. It seems that for SDLT a 'conveyance' includes the grant of a lease: FA 2003. Accordingly under an agreement for a lease where both a premium and rent were payable on the grant of the lease, the grant of the lease would be the effective date of the transaction giving rise to the obligation to file a land transaction return and pay the SDLT chargeable. However, substantial performance of the agreement for lease was possible, giving rise to a tax charge for SDLT purposes in respect of the agreement for lease itself despite no lease having been granted, where substantially the whole of the premium was paid or the lessee had taken possession or been granted a licence to occupy in the meantime. In such cases where the lease was granted following substantial performance of the agreement the term of the lease was taken to be the period from substantial performance of the agreement until the end of the lease period.

However, for transactions with an effective date after 17 March 2004, a new para 12A of FA 2003, Sch 17A specifically addresses the grant of an agreement for lease which is substantially performed prior to the grant of the actual lease. The agreement is treated as if it were the grant of a lease on the date of substantial performance. Up to 17 July 2013 this notional lease was treated as if it were surrendered on the grant of the actual lease and the actual lease was treated as granted in consideration of the surrender of the notional lease so that the surrender and regrant rules applied. Finance Act 2013 modified these provisions by amending FA 2003, Sch 17A sub-para 12(3) and adding sub-paras (3A) and (3B). The new rule is that where an agreement for lease has been substantially performed and a lease is subsequently granted, the notional lease is treated as a lease granted on the day of substantial consideration for the lease is the total rent (and any other consideration) payable over its term. The notional and actual leases are treated as linked for the purposes of s 81A and, if there is any additional tax to pay, it is the lessee under the actual lease who must submit a further return and pay the tax. In other respects the actual lease is disregarded for SDLT purposes and in many practical cases the grant of the actual lease will not trigger either a tax payment or a notification requirement. This is effectively a deemed application of the successive linked leases rule (FA 2003, Sch 17A, para 5). There is also a provision dealing with the assignment of an agreement for lease prior to substantial performance.

Leases granted to a company connected with the lessor or where some or all of the consideration consists of the issue or transfer of shares in a company with which the lessor is connected, fall within the scope of the market value rule for SDLT.

Value added tax (VAT)

[16.28] Any VAT chargeable in respect of the lease other than VAT chargeable by virtue of an election to tax the property made after the effective date of the transaction is taken to be part of the chargeable consideration. It seems that any VAT payable in respect of the rent that is not reserved as rent under the lease will not be rent for SDLT purposes and as for stamp duty will be taxed as consideration other than rent. Accordingly, the total VAT payable over the term of the lease will be chargeable, except where the lease exceeds 12 years, when the amount chargeable will be limited to the total of the 12 highest annual payments. FA 2003, s 52, and see *Blendett v IRC, Quietlece v IRC* [1984] STC 95. It is understood, however, that HMRC rarely, if ever, take this point.

Exclusions

[16.29] None of the following counts as chargeable consideration on the grant of a lease:

(1)   an undertaking by the tenant to repair, maintain or insure the let premises;

(2)   a tenant's undertaking to pay in respect of services, repairs, maintenance, insurance or management costs;

(3)   any other tenant's obligation that does not affect the open market rent;

(4)   any rent or performance guarantee;

(5)   penal rent;

(6)   costs borne by a tenant exercising a statutory right to be granted a new lease;

(7)   any other obligation by a tenant to bear the landlord's reasonable costs incidental on the grant of a lease;

(8)   an obligation under a lease, on its termination, to transfer to the landlord payment entitlements under the scheme of income support for farmers in respect of land subject to the scheme.

A payment made under any of the above obligations is also ignored. The assumption or release of any obligation above on the assignment or surrender of the lease is also ignored.

Loans and deposits

[16.30] Where on the grant or assignment of a lease the lessee or assignee makes a loan or pays a deposit to any person, and the repayment of the loan or deposit is contingent on anything done or omitted to be done by the lessee or assignee or on the death of the lessee or assignee, the amount is treated as chargeable consideration other than rent. This will not apply where the amount of the deposit does not exceed twice the rent determined under FA 2003, Sch 17A, para 7(3) (the 'relevant maximum rent'). In case of the grant of a lease, the relevant maximum rent is the highest amount of rent payable in respect of any consecutive 12-month period in the first five years of the term. In the case of a lease assignment, the relevant maximum rent is the highest amount of rent payable in respect of any consecutive 12-month period in the first five years of the term remaining outstanding as at the date of the assignment. No tax repayment claim may be made in respect of any such loan or deposit treated as chargeable consideration which is later repaid or in respect of the refund of any consideration given where the refund is made under arrangements made in connection with the transaction and is contingent on the determination or assignment of the lease or on the grant of a chargeable interest out of the lease.

Rent

[16.31] Stamp duty land tax is charged on any chargeable consideration consisting of rent as a percentage of the net present value of the rent payable over the term of the lease.

In other words, the total rent payable over the term of the lease is in principle charged to tax (after discounting each annual rent by 3.5% per annum to arrive at its present value). This contrasts with stamp duty on rent that was charged on only one year's average rent at varying percentages according to the term of the lease. On average, the SDLT charge on rent when it was originally introduced represented an increase of four times the stamp duty charge on a ten-year lease.

The net present value (v) of the rent payable over the term of the lease is calculated by applying the formula in FA 2003, Sch 5, para 3:

$$v = \sum_{i=1}^{n} \frac{ri}{(1 + T)i}$$

ri is the rent payable in respect of year 'i'

i is the particular year for which the calculation is to be performed (a calculation being required for each year)

n is the term of the lease

t is the temporal discount rate (currently 3.5%)

Having calculated the net present value of the rent (referred to as the 'relevant rental value') the tax is charged as a percentage of so much of that value as falls within each rate band according to the following two tables. Table A applies where the relevant land consists entirely of residential property and Table B applies where the relevant land consists of or includes land that is not residential property. Hence tax is chargeable on each 'slice' of the rental value at either the nil or 1% rate as appropriate, thus ensuring that a credit is given for the first £125,000 or £150,000 as appropriate where the rental value exceeds this figure.

Table A: Residential

Rate bands	Percentage
£0 to £125,000	0%
Over £125,000	1%

Table B: Non-Residential or Mixed

Rate bands	Percentage
£0 to £150,000	0%
Over £150,000	1%

Linked transactions

[**16.32**] If the lease is one of a number of linked transactions for which the chargeable consideration includes rent then the net present values of the rents payable under all the linked leases are aggregated for the purpose of applying the percentages in the above tables. Where successive linked leases are granted or treated as granted (at the same time or different times) of substantially the same premises and the grants are linked transactions, then the series of leases is treated as a single lease granted at the time of the first lease for the aggregate term and rent of the series of leases, and a return is required under FA 2003, s 81A on the grant of each successive lease with the tax payable adjusted accordingly. Note that where the latter provision applies, the total SDLT payable may be lower because of the effect of the discounting formula on the rent.

Service charges

[**16.33**] A single sum expressed to be payable in respect of rent or expressed to be payable in respect of rent and other matters such as a service charge, but not apportioned is treated as entirely rent. This is expressly without prejudice to a just and reasonable apportionment where separate sums are expressed to be payable in respect of rent and other matters.

Penal rent

[**16.34**] Penal rent or increased rent in the nature of a penal rent payable in respect of the breach of any obligation of the tenant does not count as chargeable consideration.

Prior period

[**16.35**] 'Rent' does not include any chargeable consideration for the grant of a lease that is payable in respect of a period before the grant of a lease. For this purpose the date of the grant of a lease is when it is actually granted even if the term is expressed to commence at an earlier time: *Bradshaw v Pawley* [1979] 3 All ER 273, [1980] 1 WLR 10. Therefore rent payable in respect of the period between a prior commencement of the contractual term of a lease and the actual date of grant will be taxed as premium. This is, however, subject to the exception noted below where a new backdated lease is granted to a tenant who is holding over under an old lease.

Contingent, uncertain and unascertained rent

[**16.36**] Contingent, uncertain or unascertained rent is taken into account and dealt with under the usual rules for SDLT subject to the following modifications. No application may be made to defer payment of the tax on contingent or uncertain rent. No account is taken of any provision for the rent to be adjusted in line with the retail price index and the starting rent is used for calculating the tax. This apparently generous concession is counterbalanced by the relatively low temporal discount rate of 3.5% used for the purposes of discounting future rent payments in the formula above which does not take into account price inflation.

Where the lease provides for the rent to be reviewed or varied, or the rent is contingent, uncertain or unascertained, the actual rent payable in the first five years of the term is taken into account for the purposes of the tax computation. For this purpose, where the rent includes VAT and the effective date of the grant of the lease is on or after 27 July 2010 (the date on which F(No 2)A 2010, s 3 came into force increasing the standard rate of VAT from 17.5% to 20% from 4 January 2011) the VAT on the rent should be calculated at 17.5% from completion until the day preceding the first rent payment date on or after 4 January 2011 and at 20% on the rent payment from the first rent payment date on or after 4 January 2011. When the rent for the first five years becomes certain, the net present value of the actual rent can be reviewed and a return submitted if necessary to claim any overpayment (see HMRC Guidance Note 3 December 2008). However, the rent payable for any period after the end of the fifth year of the term is assumed to be at an annual amount equal to the highest amount of rent payable for any consecutive 12-month period in the first five years (including any contingent, uncertain or unascertained rent). These rules favour leases with rent increases that occur after year 5 where the increases are not 'abnormal' and so not subject to the rule taxing 'abnormal' rent increase as if there had been the grant of a new lease for the excess rent (see below). However, this rule can also present a trap for leases where the rent is front-loaded and reduces to say a peppercorn after year 5 because the rent for year 6 and beyond is deemed to be the highest amount of rent in the first five years and the tax calculation is to be made accordingly.

Where the first rent review occurs in the final quarter of the fifth year the intention is that this is ignored for these purposes so that the rent is taken as fixed for the first five years. This rule is intended to deal with leases whose term commences on a quarter day but which are not actually granted until some time during the following quarter. If the first or only rent review occurs five years after a specified date and the specified date falls within three months before the beginning of the term of the lease, references in the SDLT rules to the first five years of the term of the lease are to be taken as referring to the period beginning with the start of the term and 'ending with the review date'. The wording 'ending with the review date' will however bring the review into the first five years and so it is understood that HMRC accept that the period should be taken as ending on the day before the rent review in order not to defeat the intention behind the rule. This rule is, however, of no assistance when the lease term runs from 24 June but the lease is granted between 24 and 28 September, given that the specified date is not within the permitted three months before the beginning of the lease. Where the end of the fifth year is reached or the amount of rent payable in the first five years ceases to be uncertain at an earlier date, the tenant must make a return to HMRC within 30 days and pay any tax due if as a result the transactions become notifiable or tax or additional tax becomes payable. If less tax turns out to be payable than has already been paid then a claim for repayment can be made.

Where a lease is varied so as to increase the rent as from a date before the end of the fifth year of the term, the variation is treated as if it were the grant of a lease for the additional rent payable and tax is chargeable. A variation of a lease to increase the rent from a date falling after the end of the fifth year of the term is no longer taxable since the charge relating to 'abnormal' rent increases was repealed with effect from 17 July 2013. This repeal was in response to representations that the SDLT rules for leases required simplification and was introduced in conjunction with the streamlining of the reporting requirements where substantial performance occurs before the lease is granted or a lease continues after the expiry of its fixed term in the amendments to FA 2003, Sch 17A made by FA 2013, Sch 41.

In computing the tax payable on a lease for a fixed term no account is taken of any contingency which may cause the lease to end before the expiry of the fixed term or the existence of a break or renewal clause. When a lease continues after a fixed term it is treated as a single lease growing by one year at a time and tax is payable accordingly at each interval. This does not apply where a new lease is granted within one year of the original fixed term or of any one-year extension and the new lease is treated as beginning immediately after the expiry of the original term (or of the extended term): FA 2003, Sch 17A, para 3A. A lease for an indefinite term is treated in the first instance as if it were a lease for a fixed term of one year and if it continues in existence it is treated as a single lease growing by one year at a time and tax is payable accordingly at each interval. These rules do not apply to leases granted before 1 December 2003.

New lease, same tenant

[**16.37**] Where a tenant continues in occupation after the end of the contractual term and is subsequently granted a new lease of the premises with a term expressed to begin from the end of the old contractual term, the term of the new lease is treated for SDLT as beginning on the date it is expressed to begin. This is despite the rule in *Bradshaw v Pawley* [1979] 3 All ER 273, [1980] 1 WLR 10 that the lease term commences on the later of the contractual term start date and the actual date of grant. However, any rent payable under the new lease in respect of any period after the end of the old contractual term and before the actual date on which the new lease is granted is for SDLT purposes to be reduced by the amount of taxable rent that is payable in respect of that period otherwise than under the new lease. This means that a credit is given for SDLT payable in respect of that period under the notional lease which is treated as growing one year at a time following the end of the old lease. However, a credit will not be available to the extent that the actual date of grant of the new lease occurs before the next anniversary of the notional growing lease. Where possible therefore the new lease should not require rent to be payable in respect of any period from the date of grant of the new lease to the next anniversary of the notional growing lease.

The reduction in the rent payable for SDLT purposes under the new lease to reflect rent already paid in respect of the interim period is only available where the new lease is of '*the same or substantially the same premises*'. If the tenant has previously sub-let part of its original holding then strictly the landlord can only be required to grant the new lease over that part of the premises actually occupied by the tenant for its business and not the whole premises originally let to the tenant: see Landlord and Tenant Act 1954, ss 23(3) and 32(2). Where the landlord elects to so limit the new lease and the difference between the new and old holding is significant it may be that the availability of credit for the interim rent is put into doubt.

Where a lease continues after the expiry of its fixed term, it is in the first place treated as extended in yearly increments. But any additional tax is not (following amendments to the rules effective from 17 July 2013) due until 30 days after the end of each one-year period of extension (or after termination if that occurs during a period of extension) (FA 2003, Sch 17A, para 3). But additional tax is not due under this provision if a new lease of the same or substantially the same premises is granted within a period of extension in circumstances where para 9A applies. Where such a new lease is so granted, and para 9A does not apply, then the existing lease is not treated as having been extended but the new lease is treated as having been granted immediately after the expiry of the existing lease and with any rent payable in respect of the period of extension being treated as payable under the new lease.

Lease surrenders

[16.38] Where a lease is granted in consideration of the surrender of an existing lease between the same parties, the grant of the new lease does not count as chargeable consideration for the surrender and the surrender does not count as chargeable consideration for the grant of the new lease, so that FA 2003, Sch 4, para 5 is disapplied. Where the new lease is of the same or substantially the same premises and the existing lease was subject to SDLT when granted, 'overlap' relief will apply so that the rent payable under the new lease for the same period as the existing lease will be reduced by the amount of rent that would have been payable for that period under the existing lease, in assessing SDLT on the rent under the new lease (FA 2003, Sch 17A, para 9).

In the case of the grant, assignment or surrender of a lease a reverse premium does not count as chargeable consideration.

The leaseback element of a sale and leaseback arrangement is exempt where the leaseback is granted out of the major interest in land transferred or granted if the leaseback is to the seller and:

(1)   the sale is entered into wholly or partly in consideration of the leaseback;
(2)   the only other consideration for the sale is cash or debt;
(3)   the sale is not by way of sub-sale; and
(4)   the parties are not members of a group of companies for the purposes of group relief.

The sale element of such an arrangement is generally charged to SDLT under the exchanges rules on the basis of actual consideration for the sale or, if greater, the market value of the interest which is sold. If the leaseback has a capital value (for example it is at less than market rent) then the interest sold is valued on the basis that it is encumbered by the leaseback and HMRC have confirmed that the encumbered value is to be used.

Lease variations

[16.39] The variation of a lease is an acquisition and disposal of a chargeable interest where (1) the variation takes effect in law, or is treated for SDLT as, the grant of a new lease, or (2) the lease is varied to reduce the rent. Where consideration in money or money's worth (other than an increase in rent – see above) is given by the lessee for any variation of a lease (other than a variation of the rent or the term of the lease), the variation is treated as an acquisition of a chargeable interest by the lessee. Where a lease is varied to reduce its term, the variation is treated for SDLT as an acquisition of a chargeable interest by the lessor.

Reliefs and exemptions

Scope of reliefs

[16.40] A number of reliefs are available from stamp duty land tax including the following:

(1)   Disadvantaged areas relief — FA 2003, s 57.
(2)   Sales and leasebacks — FA 2003, s 57A.
(3)   Certain acquisitions of residential property — FA 2003, s 58A and Sch 6A.
(4)   Acquisitions of multiple dwellings – FA 2003, s 58D and Sch 6B.
(5)   First acquisitions of zero-carbon homes — FA 2003, ss 58B, 58C.
(6)   Dwelling acquired from relocated employee — FA 2003, s 58A.
(7)   Compulsory purchase facilitating development — FA 2003, s 60.
(8)   Purchases by public authorities in connection with planning agreements — FA 2003, s 61.
(9)   Group relief, reconstruction and acquisition reliefs — FA 2003, s 62 and Sch 7.
(10)   Demutualisation of insurance company — FA 2003, s 63.
(11)   Demutualisation of building society — FA 2003, s 64.
(12)   Initial transfer of land to a unit trust scheme — FA 2003, s 64A (withdrawn from 22 March 2006).
(13)   Incorporation of limited liability partnership — FA 2003, s 65.
(14)   Transfers between public bodies on a reorganisation — NHS Foundation Trusts have been prescribed as a public body for this relief (see SI 2005/83) — FA 2003, s 66.
(15)   Transfers in consequence of reorganisation of parliamentary constituencies — FA 2003, s 67.
(16)   Acquisitions by charities — FA 2003, s 68 and Sch 8.
(17)   Acquisitions by bodies established for national purposes — FA 2003, s 69.

(18)   Right to buy and shared ownership transactions — FA 2003, s 70 and Sch 9 as amended by FA 2009, s 81.
(19)   Acquisitions by registered social landlords — FA 2003, s 71 as amended by FA 2009, s 80.
(20)   Alternative property finance — FA 2003, ss 71A, 72, 72A, 73, 73A, 73AB, 73B, 73BA, 73C, 73CA and FA 2009, s 122 and Sch 61.
(21)   Collective enfranchisement by lease holders — FA 2003, s 74 as amended by FA 2009, s 79 removing the requirement that a 'Right to Enfranchise' or RTE company be used.
(22)   Crofting community right to buy — FA 2003, s 75.
(23)   Relief for assignments of rights and qualifying sub-sales — FA 2003, s 45 and Sch 2A.
(24)   Acquisitions by certain health service bodies — FA 2003, s 67A.
(25)   The 'reliefs' from the 15% higher rate — FA 2003, Sch 4A.
(26)   'Seeding' reliefs for PAIFs and COACS — FA 2003, s 65A and Sch 7A.

Scope of exemptions

[16.41] The following transactions are exempt from SDLT (and are therefore not chargeable transactions for SDLT: FA 2003, s 49):

(1)   A transaction for no chargeable consideration — FA 2003, Sch 3 para 1 (but this exemption is overridden by the market value rule for transfers to connected companies).
(2)   Grant of leases by registered social landlords — FA 2003, Sch 3, para 2.
(3)   Transfers between spouses on separation or divorce — FA 2003, Sch 3, para 3.
(4)   Assents and appropriations by personal representatives — FA 2003, Sch 3, para 3A.
(5)   Transfers in connection with the dissolution of civil partnerships — FA 2003, Sch 3, para 3A (sic).
(6)   Variation of testamentary dispositions — FA 2003, Sch 3, para 4.

Where the purchaser is a public office or department of the Crown no payment of SDLT is required if that would ultimately be borne by the Crown. This includes ministers of the Crown but not local authorities or similar bodies, and does not apply to the acquisition of private property for the Sovereign (FA 2003, s 107).

Disadvantaged areas

[16.42] The relief was repealed for instruments executed on or after 6 April 2013 by FA 2012, Sch 39, para 7.

Acquisition of multiple dwellings

[16.43] A relief is available for the acquisition of two or more dwellings under FA 2003, s 58D and Sch 6B (introduced by FA 2011, s 83 and Sch 22 for transactions with an effective date on or after 19 July 2011 and amended by the SDLTA 2015 and FA 2015, s 69). The relief is intended to lower the

SDLT cost involved in bulk purchases of residential property to improve the supply of private rented housing. The relief operates by reducing the rate of SDLT charged on the acquisition of multiple dwellings which would normally be determined by the aggregate consideration so that it is related to the tax that would have been charged had the dwellings been acquired individually. The rate of SDLT will normally be the appropriate rate under the alternative Table A applicable to a higher rates transaction for the purchase of additional residential properties (FA 2003, Sch 6B, para (6A)).

The relief must be claimed in the land transaction return (using Code 33). Where a transaction or a scheme, arrangement or series of linked transactions includes multiple dwellings, the amount of tax charged in respect of the dwellings is computed by reference to the mean consideration, ie the total consideration attributable to the dwellings divided by the number of dwellings. This will give an amount of tax related to the mean consideration which is then multiplied by the number of dwellings to produce the total tax payable. However if the aggregate amount of tax found by this method is less than 1% of the total dwellings consideration, then the tax is taken to be 1% of the consideration attributable to the dwellings.

Although FA 2003, s 58D and Sch 6B refer to 'transfers' involving multiple dwellings it is understood that HMRC accept that the grant of new leases is included in the relief.

The normal rule that the acquisition of six or more dwellings is treated as not being an acquisition of residential property is disapplied for the purpose of the relief (FA 2003, Sch 6B, para 5(6)(b) disapplying FA 2003, s 116(7)).

A building or part of a building counts as a dwelling if either (a) it is used or suitable for use as a single dwelling, or (b) it is in the process of being constructed or updated for such use. Land that is, or is to be, occupied or enjoyed with a dwelling as a garden or grounds is included as is land that subsists, or is to subsist for the benefit of a dwelling (FA 2003, Sch 6B, para 7). In HMRC's view 'garden or grounds' includes land required for the reasonable enjoyment of the dwelling having regard to its size and character, applying a similar test to that in TCGA 1992, s 222(3), ie even if it is larger than 0.5 hectare. Acquisitions where construction or adaption of a single dwelling has not yet commenced at the time of substantial performance can also be included (FA 2003, Sch 6B, para 7(5)).

A further recomputation of the amount of tax and possible further return and payment of additional tax will be required where an event subsequently occurs which had it occurred immediately before the effective date of the transaction would have affected the relief. An example of this given by HMRC would be if the number of dwellings was reduced after the effective date of the transaction (FA 2003, Sch 6B, para 6).

The event to be caught must occur within the shorter of the period of three years beginning with the effective date of the transaction or the period between the effective date of the transaction and the date on which the purchaser disposes of the dwelling or dwellings to an unconnected purchaser. HMRC take the view that the onward sale of all the dwellings acquired in a single transaction to an unconnected purchaser will bring the period to an end.

However, where the acquisition was one of a number of linked transactions, the onward sale of the dwellings acquired in the acquisition will bring the period to an end in respect of that acquisition but not in respect of the linked transactions. The onward sale of only some of the dwellings acquired in an acquisition will not bring the period to an end for that acquisition. The onward sales will not be an event in themselves which triggers a recomputation of the tax. However if the period continues to run and there is an event then a recomputation of the amount of tax will be necessary taking into account the whole of the original consideration and number of dwellings including those which have been sold on.

HMRC gave the example under the old 'slab' system before the SDLTA 2015 which remains valid under the 'slice' system. This is of eight flats acquired for £1m on which multiple dwellings relief is claimed. The rate (now the amount) of tax is found by dividing £1m by eight giving £125,000. The nil rate is not available using the relief so the rate of tax is taken as 1% of the total consideration for the dwellings. If two flats are sold in the relevant period to an unconnected purchaser, this will not be an event requiring a recomputation of the rate. If the remaining six flats are converted into three dwellings within the relevant period, then this will be a relevant event and a recomputation of the rate (now the amount) will be required. Therefore the original consideration of £1m will be divided by five (the two sold plus the three converted dwellings) giving £200,000. The rate of tax will however remain unchanged at 1% and so no further return is required.

HMRC have posted an additional guidance note on their website in relation to student accommodation. FA 2003, s 116(2)–(3) applies for the purposes of multiple dwellings relief so a hall of residence is not considered to be used as a dwelling and is not residential property and therefore the relief cannot be claimed in respect of the transfer of such a building. This is in contrast to the treatment of student accommodation other than a hall of residence since that is regarded as a dwelling. In HMRC's view, the indicators that a building is a hall of residence are that its planning permission is as a residential institution (use class C2); only students and staff from a particular institution may reside there and that educational institution places them there; the building is not broken up into units meeting the normal rules of suitability as a single dwelling; access to study-bedrooms is from communal areas; and there are common facilities for eating.

With regard to partnerships involved with multiple dwellings, HMRC regard the relief as applying to ordinary acquisitions by partnerships within FA 2003, Sch 15, para 2, the transfer of a chargeable interest to a partnership under FA 2003, Sch 15, para 10, the transfer of a chargeable interest out of a partnership under FA 2003, Sch 15, para 18 and a transfer of a chargeable interest from one partnership to another under FA 2003, Sch 15, para 23. In each case the rate of tax is found by applying the relief to the chargeable consideration found by applying the relevant provisions of FA 2003, Sch 15.

However, HMRC do not regard the relief as available to deemed land transactions arising under FA 2003, Sch 15, paras 14, 16 or 17 where there is a transfer of a partnership interest or under para 17A where there is a withdrawal of money, etc.

HMRC regard the relief as applicable were the deemed market value consideration rule in FA 2003, s 53 for transfers to a connected company applies and also to where there is an exchange of chargeable interests where the chargeable consideration is found under FA 2003, Sch 4, para 5.

It should be noted that the relative brevity of the legislative provisions governing this relief mean the various interpretations applied by HMRC as discussed above are not necessarily mandatory and could be challenged where appropriate.

The relief does not apply to higher threshold interests which are subject to the 15% charge though it may apply to the remainder of a transaction after those interests have been excluded under FA 2003, Sch 4A, para 2.

Groups of companies

[16.44] A land transaction is exempt from stamp duty land tax if the vendor and purchaser are companies that at the effective date of the transaction are members of the same group. The equivalent stamp duty group relief concentrated on relieving specific instruments from stamp duty and therefore expressly required that the relevant instrument transferred a beneficial interest in the property and that the companies in question were members of the same group at the time the instrument (normally, the conveyance) was executed, even though the beneficial interest could pass on earlier exchange of contract and payment. Although in practice these factors will often be present they are not strict conditions for the SDLT group relief to be available. Accordingly, for SDLT group relief the acquisition of a chargeable interest will be exempt if at the 'effective date' the companies are grouped together. This will normally be the date of the conveyance but may be earlier when a substantial amount of the consideration is paid or provided before possession or a conveyance is taken.

The relief must be claimed in the land transaction return and is subject to detailed anti-avoidance rules and to clawback if the acquiring company leaves the group pursuant to arrangements made within three years of the acquisition. The equivalent stamp duty group relief clawback was restricted to where the acquiring company actually left the group within three years.

For the purposes of group relief a 'company' means any body corporate (wherever incorporated or resident) and companies are members of the same group if one is the 75% subsidiary of the other, or both are 75% subsidiaries of a third company. A company ('A') is the 75% subsidiary of another company ('B') if B:

(1)   is beneficial owner of not less than 75% of the ordinary share capital of A;

(2)   is beneficially entitled to not less than 75% of any profits available for distribution to equity holders of A; and

(3)   would be beneficially entitled to not less than 75% of any assets of A available for distribution to its equity holders on a winding-up.

The ownership referred to in 1 above is ownership either directly or through another company or companies and CTA 2010, ss 1155–1157 apply to determine the amount of shares of A owned by B through another company or companies. Indirect holdings are taken into account using a multiplication formula.

Example 6

> P Ltd owns 80% of the shares in Q Ltd which owns 50% of the shares in R Ltd, P Ltd is taken to own 40% of the shares in R Ltd.

'Ordinary share capital' means all the issued share capital of the company other than capital the holders of which have a right to a dividend at a fixed rate but have no other right to share in the profits of the company. The corporation tax group relief tests relating to equity holders and profits and assets available for distribution in CTA 2010, Part 5 Chapter 6 apply for the purposes of 2 and 3 above save that ss 171(1)(b) and (3), 173, 174 and 176-178 are 'switched-off' for SDLT purposes in respect of both the transferor and the transferee (the equivalent stamp duty group relief switched these provisions off only in respect of the transferor). Given that corporation tax is an annual tax assessed retrospectively by reference to accounting periods, the tests in CTA 2010, Part 5 Chapter 6 are applied over the accounting period current at the time in question and are only finally judged when the accounting period has ended. It is apparent therefore that the direct application of these provisions to a transaction tax such as SDLT gives rise to the question of how does one judge that the various tests for group relief to be available have been met at any point during the accounting period in which the land transaction occurs. It seems that logically this is not possible and one must wait for the end of the accounting period before deciding. Under the equivalent stamp duty provisions a pragmatic view of the position seems to have been adopted by taxpayers and IR Stamp Taxes, and applications for group relief that certified that the requirements of CTA 2010, Part 5 Chapter 6 were met at the date of the relevant instrument were not challenged on the basis that one strictly should 'wait and see' until the end of the accounting period. It may be, however, that because of the nature of SDLT as a mandatory transaction tax where in some circumstances the tax can be adjusted subsequently and corrective returns filed, the practice may change. It is unclear how this situation would be resolved under the existing SDLT provisions other than by initially paying the SDLT and then submitting a retrospective claim for the relief once the accounting period had ended.

With regard to partnerships and group relief, the 'look through' principle for SDLT in relation to land owning partnerships enshrined in FA 2003, Sch 15 para 2 (see **16.67**), only goes so far. For the purposes of SDLT group relief, an LLP incorporated under the Limited Liability Partnerships Act 2002 is regarded as a body corporate given that s 1(2) of that Act confers corporate status on LLPs incorporated under it. This means that an LLP can form its own SDLT group as the top body corporate in the group structure. However, because an LLP does not have an issued ordinary share capital it cannot be a subsidiary of any other company nor can the LLP's subsidiary companies form a group with the company members of the LLP. The LLP cannot itself claim SDLT group relief because of the 'look through' principle in FA 2003, which requires the LLP's chargeable interests to be treated as held by its members. This had always been the correct position however prior to 11 October 2010 HMRC did not accept that LLPs were bodies corporate for the purposes of SDLT group relief so that LLPs were 'looked through' in deciding whether an SDLT group existed between the members of the LLP and its subsidiaries. HMRC announced on 11 October 2010 that their view had changed and that an LLP was a body corporate for SDLT group relief purposes. SDLT group relief will in principle be available for transfers between members of the LLP's own group (excluding transfers to the LLP itself). However, a transfer by the LLP to a member of its own group will not attract group relief because the land is deemed to be owned by the members of the LLP and those members will not form a part of the same group of companies by the LLP. Therefore transfers between a member of the LLP and the subsidiary companies of the LLP cannot attract SDLT group relief. LLPs are therefore at a disadvantage to general or English limited partnerships because partners who control 75% or more of the latter types of partnerships can be treated as grouped with 75% subsidiary companies held by the partnership. Transfers by companies to an LLP, the members of which form part of an SDLT group with the company transferor, can attract group relief.

Group relief prevented

[16.45] There are four types of arrangements which can prevent group relief from applying. These relate to control of the purchasing company, the provision of consideration by someone outside the group, where the purchaser is to cease to be a member of the same group as the vendor, or where the transaction is not effected for bona fide commercial reasons or forms part of tax avoidance.

- First, group relief is not available if at the effective date of the transaction there are arrangements in existence by virtue of which at that or some later time a person has or could obtain control of the purchaser but not of the vendor. (This restriction does not apply to transfers in connection with the demutualisation of insurance companies.)

  'Arrangements' is defined to include any scheme, agreement or understanding, whether or not legally enforceable. 'Control' for this purpose is the test contained in CTA 2010, s 1124. In stamp duty, HMRC accepted that the equivalent anti-avoidance provision relating to arrangements for loss of control of the transferee (FA 1930, s 42(2)) was to be interpreted in the light of Statement of Practice 3/93 'Groups of companies – arrangements', which gives general guidance on how HMRC interprets 'arrangements' for corporation tax group relief purposes, and Extra-statutory concession C10 which prior to its enactment as CTA 2010, ss 155A and 155B and FA 2003, Sch 7 paras 2A and 2B excluded certain types of arrangements including mortgages of shares. Although the stamp duty group relief provisions did not include a definition of arrangements and the SDLT provisions do include such a definition, it is clear that Statement of Practice 3/93 and FA 2003, Sch 7, paras 2A and 2B should inform the interpretation of 'arrangements' for SDLT. There can be no logical grounds for discriminating between the group relief provisions for corporation tax and those for SDLT by having a wider meaning of 'arrangements' for the latter tax (see Statement of Practice SP 3/93: Groups of companies – arrangements). Tax Bulletin No 70 (April 2004) contains an article entitled 'Stamp Duty Land Tax: Group Relief' which in effect confirms that the principles and practice arising out of Statement of Practice 3/98 which applied to stamp duty group relief will be applied to SDLT with the necessary adaptations.

One aspect of the group relief article in Tax Bulletin No 70 is highly misleading. Paragraphs 23 and 24 of the article are as follows:

> '23. The statements by the Economic Secretary during debate in Parliament on the equivalent stamp duty provision in Finance Act 2000 are still relevant. The Economic Secretary said:

> 'I have received representations expressing concern about the blocking of relief for transfers from the company about to leave the group to another group member – in other words, when the company leaving the group is the transferor. I am persuaded that there are commercial situations in which an asset is transferred to another group company after arrangements are in place for the transferor company to leave the group. In a sense, therefore, the asset never leaves the original group. I am willing to make a concession for such cases, which will be useful to businesses, as their legal advisers have suggested.

> I have some worry that it might be possible to construct avoidance devices from the concession, so I have asked the Stamp Office to monitor carefully the use of the relief. If the concession is abused, the Government will not hesitate to act swiftly.'

(See Hansard 18 July 2000, column 253.)

> '24. The Inland Revenue will not argue that paragraph 2(1) denies group relief in cases where the transferor is to leave the group having transferred the land to other group members.'

Unfortunately the extract quoted above implies that the words of the Economic Secretary apply to the version of the wording of FA 1930, s 42(2) as actually amended by FA 2003, s 123 on which the equivalent SDLT provision is based. This wording focuses solely on the transferee leaving the group and not either the transferee or the transferor. In reality the words of the Economic Secretary were spoken in relation to the unamended version of the Finance Bill 2000 which was then before the house on 18 July 2000, (that is the Bill as amended in Standing Committee H and printed on 29 June 2000). In that version of the Bill the proposed amendment to FA 1930, s 42 was contained in clause 122, the relevant parts of which read (with author's emphasis):

> '122. –
>
> (1)   Amend section 42 of the Finance Act 1930 as follows.
>
> (2)   In subsection (2B) (body to be parent of another if beneficial owner of 75% of ordinary share capital) after "if at that time the first body" insert "(a)" and at the end of the subsection add –

"(b) is beneficially entitled to not less than 75% of any profits available for distribution to equity holders of the second body; and

(c) would be beneficially entitled to not less than 75% of any assets of the second body available for distribution to its equity holders on a winding-up;

but this subsection is subject to subsection (2C).".

(3) After subsection (2B) insert –

"(2C) A body corporate shall not be regarded for the purposes of this section as the parent of another body corporate at a particular time if at that time arrangements are in existence by virtue of which at that or some later time any person has or could obtain, or any persons together have or could obtain, control of one of the bodies but not of the other.".'

Under this proposed wording arrangements for a change in control of either the purchaser or the vendor would have been caught. It was that version of the wording that the Economic Secretary was referring to when he uttered the words in Hansard quoted above.

As a consequence of the 'concession' referred to by the Economic Secretary the Government agreed amendments to the wording of clause 122 quoted above in which the wording in clause 122(3) was removed including new s 42(2C) and the result is the present wording in FA 1930, s 42(2) (on which FA 2003, Sch 7, para 2(1) is based) which reads (author's emphasis):

'(2) This section applies to any instrument as respects which it is shown to the satisfaction of the Commissioners that –

(a) the effect of the instrument is to convey or transfer a beneficial interest in property from one body corporate ("the transferor") to another ("the transferee"), and

(b) the bodies in question are associated at the time the instrument is executed

unless at the time the instrument is executed arrangements are in existence by virtue of which at that or some later time any person has or could obtain, or any persons together have or could obtain, control of **the transferee but not of the transferor.**'

This is important because HMRC Stamp Taxes have been known to argue that when a company owning a target property has been sold by a vendor group to the purchaser group and the target property is transferred to another company in the purchaser group and the transferor company immediately transferred back to the vendor group, SDLT group relief is disallowed under FA 2000, Sch 7, para 2(1). HMRC have based their argument on the words of the Economic Secretary quoted in paragraph 23 of Tax Bulletin No 70 and argued that in the context of tax avoidance FA 2000, Sch 7, para 2(1) blocks SDLT group relief in this situation. However, once the legislative history of the relevant provision is examined it is apparent that HMRC's argument is based on an earlier version of the legislation that would have caught arrangements for a change of control of the transferor but which was expressly rejected by Parliament.

This first type of restriction on group relief does not apply to arrangements entered into with a view to an acquisition of shares to which exemption from stamp duty under FA 1986, s 75 will apply and as a result of which the purchaser will be a member of the same group as the acquiring company. It is not clear how this exception will be policed in terms of what degree of likelihood is required at the time of the intra-group transfer so that the subsequent loss of control of the purchaser will indeed take the form of an acquisition of shares to which FA 1986, s 75 applies (and what if anything will be done if exemption under that provision turns out not to be available). It is also unclear as to whether this exception will operate where the arrangements for subsequent loss of control of the purchaser could take the form of a FA 1986, s 75 reconstruction but might alternatively take the form of some other transaction not qualifying for relief.

- Second, group relief is not available if the transaction is effected in pursuance of, or in connection with, arrangements under which the consideration (or any part of it) is to be provided or received directly or indirectly by a person other than a group company.

- Third, group relief is not available if the transaction is effected in pursuance of, or in connection with, arrangements under which the vendor and the purchaser are to cease to be members of the same group by reason of the purchaser ceasing to be a 75% subsidiary of the vendor or a third company. (This restriction does not apply to transfers in connection with the demutualisation of insurance companies.)

- Fourth, SDLT group relief will be denied if the transaction is:
  (a)   not effected for bona fide commercial reasons; or
  (b)   forms part of arrangements of which the main purpose, or one of the main purposes, is the avoidance of liability to tax.

[16.46] The thrust of judicial decisions based upon very similar anti-avoidance wording in CTA 2010, s 731 and its predecessors in ICTA 1988, s 703, ICTA 1970, s 460 and FA 1960, s 28, suggests that this fourth measure may not have a great impact on transactions that when looked at in the round are carried out for commercial reasons, but happen to have tax planning measures built into them. On the other hand, purely tax driven transactions will be at risk. The leading cases (see for example *IRC v Brebner* [1967] 43 TC 705) show that HMRC is not entitled to isolate particular steps in a transaction that were admittedly inserted to give tax efficiency and apply the above tests to that step only. Assuming that the courts follow precedent in this area, then a reading of the cases leads to the tentative conclusion that intra-group property transfers that are carried out as a preparatory step to a larger commercial restructuring or sale out of the group should continue to qualify for group relief (subject of course to the existing anti-avoidance rules) as long as the wider transaction is not tax driven. This view is reinforced by the helpful comments of the Economic Secretary to the Treasury in the debate on this measure:

'It is time to ensure that group relief is restricted to proper commercial transactions where tax avoidance is not the, or a, main purpose. I recognise that this measure has caused genuine concern among those who are not engaged in tax avoidance, on the grounds that it will stop legitimate commercial transactions. I can reassure the Committee that we do not accept that that will be the effect of the measure, which will only stop claims to group relief where tax avoidance is the, or a, main purpose. The fact that a transaction gives rise to a tax benefit does not mean that avoidance is the main purpose.

I was asked earlier for the definition of the term "bona fide". Successive Governments have used that term and most Committee members, and practitioners, understand its meaning to be "genuine", which is a pretty straightforward understanding.

The fact that a transaction gives rise to a tax benefit does not mean that avoidance is its main purpose.'

(Standing Committee B, 30 June 2005, Col 299).

It is noteworthy that the existing statutory provisions on which the wording of this provision is based have specific written clearance procedures, whereas the new SDLT provision has none (see CTA 2010, s 748 and TCGA 1992, s 137).

Group relief not prevented

[16.47] HMRC published guidance on 10 February 2006 setting out a list of examples where they accept that group relief is not denied by this measure. The list is now contained in SDLTM 23040 and is as follows:

(1) The transfer of a property to a group company having in mind the possibility that shares in that company might be sold more than three years after the date of transfer.

(2) The transfer of a property to a group company having in mind the possibility that shares in that company might be sold within three years of the date of transfer, with a consequent claw back of group relief, in order that any increase in value of the property after the intra-group transfer might be sheltered from SDLT.

(3) The transfer of property to a group company having in mind the possibility that either 1 or 2 might occur.

(4) The transfer of a property to a group company prior to the sale of shares in the transferor company, in order that the property should not pass to the purchaser of the shares.

(5) The transfer of property to a group company in order that commercially generated rental income may be matched with commercially generated losses from a Schedule A business.

(6) The transfer of property to a group company in order that commercially generated chargeable gains may be matched with commercially generated allowable losses.

(7) The transfer of property to a non-resident group company in the knowledge that future appreciation or depreciation in value will be outside the scope of corporation tax on chargeable gains.

(8) Transactions undertaken as part of a normal commercial securitisation.

(9) The transfer of the freehold reversion in a property to a group lessee in order to merge the freehold and the lease, and thus prevent the lease being subject to the wasting assets rules as respects corporation tax on chargeable gains.

A further example has since been added to this list in HMRC SDLT Manual at 23040: The transfer of property to a group company in order that the interest payable on borrowings from a commercial lender on ordinary commercial terms may be set against commercially generated rental income. It is thought that HMRC will also accept that intra-group loans can also be included if they are on commercial terms.

The thrust of this list suggests that that there will often be tax avoidance motives for a transfer without these necessarily preventing the availability of group relief. The rather surprising example at 7 above suggests that an obvious and overt UK tax avoidance motive does not rule out group relief and can be acceptable. It appears that this list lowers the bar for taxpayers in relation to this particular provision.

A note was published with the agreement of HMRC on 6 August 2013 confirming HMRC's approach to FA 2003, Sch 7, para 2(4A) in the context of intra-group asset transfers following the acquisition of a company which owns the property concerned. With the caveat that there is no tax-avoidance scheme HMRC confirmed that:

(1)   A business may choose to acquire a property-owning company as opposed to acquiring the property from that company. The purchaser may, after acquiring the company, transfer the property out of the company acquired and into a different company in the purchasing group. HMRC do not regard that of itself, and subject to the list of transactions mentioned above, as resulting in the avoidance of tax such that para 2(4A)(b) would be in point, even if the acquisition of the property-owning company and the subsequent intra-group transfer of the property formed part of the same arrangements.

(2)   The purchaser may, after acquiring the company and transferring the property intra-group, liquidate, wind-up or strike-off the company acquired. HMRC do not regard that of itself as resulting in, or being evidence of, the avoidance of tax such that para 2(4A)(b) would be in point, even if the liquidation, winding-up or striking-off formed part of the same arrangements that also included the acquisition and the intra-group transfer.

(3)   In the scenarios described above, the para 2(4A)(b) analysis would be the same even if the purchaser only became a member of the group for SDLT purposes as a result of the acquisition of the property-owning company.

Groups of companies – cessation

[16.48] Where a land transaction is exempt from SDLT because of group relief and the purchaser ceases to be a member of the same group of companies as the vendor within the three years beginning with the effective date of the transaction (or at any time in pursuance of arrangements made before the end of that period), the group relief is withdrawn if at the time the purchaser leaves the group, it or a 'relevant associated company' holds the chargeable interest that was originally acquired (or is derived from it). The relief is not withdrawn if the chargeable interest was subsequently reacquired at market value under a chargeable transaction for which group relief was available but was not claimed.

A 'relevant associated company' means a company that is a member of the same group as the purchaser immediately before the purchaser leaves the vendor's group and ceases to be a member of the vendor's group *in consequence of the purchaser so ceasing.*

The inclusion of relevant associated companies is to prevent the initial intra-group property transfer on which group relief was claimed escaping claw-back by the simple device of subsequently transferring the property to a third group company which would then leave the group with the purchaser (in a sub-group by themselves), a technique known as the 'double drop-down'. However, for the third company to be a 'relevant associated company' it must cease to be a member of the same group as the vendor *in consequence of the purchaser so ceasing.*

However, rather than risk-testing the matter in the courts, HMRC has sought to reinforce the claw-back charge with a further anti-avoidance provision that concentrates on a change in control of the purchaser. This provision applies where:

(1)   the purchaser claims group relief for a transaction ('the relevant transaction') and within three years beginning with the effective date of the relevant transaction (or at any time in pursuance of arrangements made before the end of that period);

(2)   there is a change in control of the purchaser (within CTA 2010, ss 450 and 451); and

(3)   group relief is not otherwise withdrawn.

In such a case, it is then necessary to identify the earliest 'previous transaction'. A previous transaction is one where:

(1)   group relief, reconstruction relief or acquisition relief was claimed;

(2)   the effective date of that transaction was within the last three years; and

(3)   the chargeable interest acquired under the relevant transaction is essentially the same as that acquired under the previous transaction.

The claw-back provisions then have effect as if the vendor in the earliest previous transaction was also the vendor in the relevant transaction. In the two situations illustrated above and assuming that the events all occur within three years of each other, the change in control of B Ltd out of Vendor Ltd would result in the vendor in the sale of Blackacre to B Ltd being taken to have been Vendor Ltd rather than A Ltd, thus giving rise to the claw-back of group relief on the transfer of Blackacre to B Ltd. Unfortunately, this provision is capable of giving rise to multiple claw-back charges where there have been more than two successive transfers within three years. It appears that this possibility is unintended, but it is not yet known whether HMRC understands that this is the case and if so what its approach will be.

Group relief not withdrawn

[16.49] Group relief is not withdrawn in four situations.

- First, where the purchaser leaves the vendor's group because the vendor itself leaves the group. The vendor is regarded as leaving the group if the purchaser and the vendor cease to be members of the same group because of a transaction relating to shares in either the vendor or another company that is above the vendor in the group structure and as a result of the transaction ceases to be a member of the same group as the purchaser. The question of whether the purchaser could then be sold out of the original group within three years of the transaction free of claw-back once the vendor company had left the group had not been tested in the courts. However, for transactions on or after 13 March 2008 this question has been partly answered by FA 2003, Sch 7, para 4ZA(4) which provides that a change in control of the purchaser after the vendor leaves the group is deemed to be the purchaser leaving the same group as the vendor for the purposes of claw-back. There are detailed provisions defining what constitutes a change in the control of the purchaser for this purpose — see FA 2003, Sch 7, para 4ZA(5)–(8). It should be noted that these change of control provisions are very wide and catch not only a sale of the purchaser itself out of the group but also a winding-up of the purchaser (subject to the second exception discussed below where the purchaser is above the vendor in the group), or a sale of the purchaser's parent company (indirect changes of control of the purchaser are included). The insertion of a new company above the purchaser in a group will not give rise to a change in control for claw-back purposes as long as there is no overall change in control.

  Unfortunately, it is not entirely clear from the drafting of FA 2003, Sch 7, para 4ZA whether the winding-up of the vendor followed by a change in control of the purchaser results in claw-back. In principle it seems that claw-back should not arise because of the exception from claw-back in FA 2003, Sch 7, para 4(4) discussed in the next paragraph. Indeed, HMRC have confirmed in an article published on 26 November 2008 entitled 'Stamp Duty Land Tax: Group Relief – Paragraph 4ZA of Schedule 7 FA 2003' that 'paragraph 4ZA will not normally apply' in this situation. Although the draftsman has failed to explicitly clarify the relationship between FA 2003, Sch 7, paras 4(4) (discussed below) and 4ZA(4), it seems fairly clear that because the list of claw-back provisions to which FA 2003, Sch 7, para 4ZA(4) expressly applies does not include FA 2003, Sch 7, para 4, then the latter provision is not subject to the former.

- Second, where the purchaser ceases to be a member of the same group as the vendor by reason of the winding up of the vendor or another company that is above the vendor in the group structure. There seems to be nothing in the legislation that prevents the purchaser from being *'another company that is above the vendor in the group structure'* for this purpose and hence the winding up of the purchaser pursuant to a scheme under Insolvency Act 1986, s 110 and the distribution of its assets qualifying for exemption under reconstruction relief in FA 2003, Sch 7, para 7(1) should not give rise to a withdrawal of group relief. It appears that HMRC may now agree with this interpretation because in the article of 26 November 2008 referred to above HMRC state that 'A company above the vendor in the group structure can be the purchaser'.

- The third case is where there is an acquisition of shares by another company to which the exemption in FA 1986, s 75 applies. However, in such cases claw-back can still apply if the purchaser leaves the same group as the acquiring company within three years of the original land transaction (or at any time in pursuance of arrangements made before the end of that period) and it or a 'relevant associated company' own the chargeable interest.
- The fourth case is where the purchaser ceases to be a member of the vendor's group in connection with the demutualisation of insurance companies and the purchaser is immediately after the transfer of the vendor's business to another company, a member of the same group as the acquiring company.

Recovery of tax debt

[16.50] Where the tax is chargeable because group relief has been withdrawn as above and tax having been finally determined is not paid within six months after it became payable, it may be recovered from the vendor, any company that at any 'relevant time' was a member of the same group as the purchaser and above it in the group structure, or any person who at any 'relevant time' was a controlling director of the purchaser or of a company having control of the purchaser. 'Relevant time' means any time between the 'effective date' of the land transaction and the purchaser ceasing to be a member of the same group as the vendor. In order to recover the tax HMRC must serve a notice on the relevant person stating the amount of tax to be paid and the notice must be served before the end of three years from the date of the final determination of the tax payable. The notice is treated as if it were a notice of assessment of SDLT and interest runs accordingly on any tax remaining unpaid following the issue of the notice. A person who has paid tax pursuant to such a notice has a statutory right to recovery from the purchaser although this is likely to be worth little in the circumstances of the purchaser having originally failed to pay.

Where the tax is chargeable the amount will be the tax that would have been originally chargeable if the chargeable consideration had been equal to the market value of the chargeable interest transferred, or if the acquisition was the grant of a lease at a rent, that rent.

Further reliefs

Reconstructions

[16.51] An exemption from SDLT is available for land transactions entered into in connection with the acquisition by a company ('the acquiring company') of the whole or part of the undertaking of another company ('the target company') on a reconstruction of the target company.

In stamp duty, HMRC did not accept the wider interpretation of 'reconstruction' used for other taxes such as in Statement of Practice 5/85 which included a partition and its statutory enactment in TCGA 1992, Sch 5AA. It was, however, stated by the Government during the debates on the Finance Bill 2002 that this restrictive interpretation would be reconsidered for the new SDLT legislation (House of Commons Official Report, Standing Committee F, Tuesday 21 May 2002 (Morning) cols. 163 and 164). In the event this restrictive interpretation was confirmed in the November 2009 Stamp Taxes Bulletin by the addition of SDLTM 23210 to HMRC's SDLT Manual. Consequently a 'scheme for the reconstruction of the target company' requires that there is a transfer of an undertaking or part from an existing company to a new company with substantially the same membership as the old company and that undertaking continues substantially unaltered (see *Brooklands Selangor Holdings Ltd v IRC* [1970] 2 All ER 76; *Baytrust Holdings Ltd v IRC* [1971] 3 All ER 76; *IRC v Kent Process Control Ltd* [1989] STC 245; *Swithland Investments Ltd v IRC* [1990] STC 448). The liquidation of the target company is not essential. A scheme of amalgamation connotes the merging of two or more businesses with ownership through shareholdings remaining substantially the same and is therefore quite different from a scheme of reconstruction. Relief under FA 2003, Sch 7, para 1 is limited to schemes of reconstruction (see *Crane Frueharf Ltd v IRC* [1975] 1 All ER 429, CA; *Ufitec Group Ltd v IRC* [1977] STC 363).

It is noteworthy, however, that the requirement in the equivalent stamp duty reconstruction relief in FA 1986, s 75(4) that the registered office of the acquiring company is in the UK is not a requirement for the availability of the SDLT exemption. However, HMRC announced on 25 July 2005 that it will accept stamp duty claims under FA 1986, ss 75–77 for acquisitions by a company anywhere in the European Economic Area.

The availability of the exemption is subject to meeting each of three conditions.

- The first condition is that the consideration for the acquisition consists wholly or partly of the issue of non-redeemable shares in the acquiring company to all the shareholders of the target company. The only other permitted consideration is the assumption or discharge by the acquiring company of the liabilities of the target company (FA 2003, Sch 7, para 7(2), (3)).
- The second condition is that after the acquisition has been made:
  (1) each shareholder of each of the companies is a shareholder of the other; and
  (2) the proportion of shares of one of the companies held by any shareholder is the same, or is nearly as may be the same, as the proportion of shares of the other company held by that shareholder.
  Shares held by either the target company or the acquiring company in itself immediately before the acquisition are treated as if they had been cancelled for the purpose of this condition so that the company is treated as if it were not a shareholder of itself.
- The third condition is that the acquisition is effected for bona fide commercial reasons and does not form part of a scheme or arrangement of which the main purpose, or one of the main purposes, is the avoidance of liability to stamp duty, income tax, corporation tax, capital gains tax or SDLT.

The fact that a transaction has been structured in order to claim this exemption is not of itself evidence of such a scheme or arrangement since one is taking advantage of a statutory exemption from tax.

Acquisition of undertaking

[16.52] There is also relief known as 'acquisition relief' for a land transaction entered into as part of the acquisition of an undertaking or part of an undertaking of another company in exchange for the issue of shares. This relief reduces the rate of stamp duty land tax to 0.5%. The availability of this relief is subject to four conditions:

- First, the consideration for the acquisition must consist wholly or partly of the issue of non-redeemable shares in the acquiring company to the target company or to all or any of the target company's shareholders. Where the consideration does not consist wholly of the issue of shares as above, the rest of the consideration must consist wholly of either or both of cash not exceeding 10% of the nominal value of the shares issued or the assumption or discharge by the acquiring company of liabilities of the target company.

- The second condition is that the acquiring company is not 'associated' with another company that is party to 'arrangements' with the target company relating to the shares of the acquiring company issued in connection with the transfer of the undertaking or part. (This is intended to prevent the parties setting up a new company which acquires the undertaking for shares which are issued to the target company (or its shareholders), which shares are then sold to the purchaser for cash and then claiming acquisition relief to reduce the SDLT from 4 to 0.5% on the transfer of the undertaking, with the subsequent sale of the issued shares to the purchaser giving rise to stamp duty (or stamp duty reserve tax) of 0.5% or nil if a non-UK incorporated company was used.)
 For this purpose companies are 'associated' if one has control of the other or both are controlled by the same person or persons, with control construed in accordance with CTA 2010, ss 450 and 451. 'Arrangements' includes any scheme, agreement or understanding, whether or not legally enforceable. Unlike the equivalent stamp duty relief in FA 1986, s 76, it is not a requirement that the registered office of the acquiring company be in the UK.

- The third condition is that the undertaking has as its main activity the carrying on of a trade that does not consist wholly or mainly of dealing in chargeable interests.

- The fourth condition is that the acquisition is effected for bona fide commercial reasons and does not form part of arrangements of which the main purpose or one of the main purposes is the avoidance of tax.

Acquisition relief is subject to withdrawal as described in **16.53** below.

Withdrawal of reconstruction/acquisition relief

[**16.53**] Except in the cases mentioned in **16.55** below, where a land trans-action is exempt because of reconstruction relief (see **16.51** above) or has taken advantage of the 0.5% rate of SDLT because of acquisition relief (see **16.52** above) but control of the acquiring company changes within three years of the effective date of the transaction (or at any time if pursuant to arrangements made within that time), the reconstruction or acquisition relief is withdrawn and tax is chargeable if at the time control of the acquiring company changes, it or a 'relevant associated company' holds the chargeable interest that was acquired (or an interest that is derived from it). The amount chargeable is the tax that would have been chargeable if the consideration had been equal to the market value of the property concerned and, if the acquisition was the grant of a lease at a rent, that rent. The relief is not withdrawn where the interest has been subsequently acquired at market value under a chargeable transaction for which reconstruction or acquisition relief was available but was not claimed. A 'relevant associated company' means a company that is controlled by the acquiring company immediately before control of the acquiring company changes and of which control changes in consequence of the change of control of the acquiring company. 'Arrangements' includes any scheme, agreement or understanding whether or not legally enforceable and 'control' is construed in accordance with CTA 2010, ss 450 and 451.

References to control of the acquiring company changing are to the company becoming controlled:

(1)   by a different person;
(2)   by a different number of persons; or
(3)   by two or more persons, at least one of whom is not a person, or one or more persons, by whom the company was previously controlled.

It appears that a change of control of the acquiring company caused by the death of the owner of the acquiring company with the shares passing under his will may lead to a withdrawal of the relief even if the control of the target company also passes at the same time.

It also seems that where the acquiring company is not under the control of any person at the time of the land transactions qualifying for the relief and only becomes controlled by a person or persons after the transaction, there will not be a change of control for these purposes because a change of control implies that the company was previously controlled by a person or persons.

Recovery of tax debt

[**16.54**] Where reconstruction or acquisition relief is withdrawn and the amount of tax chargeable has been finally determined and remains unpaid six months after the date it became payable, the following persons may be required to pay the unpaid tax:

(1)   any company that at any 'relevant time' was a member of the same group as the acquiring company and was above it in the group structure;

(2)   any person who at any 'relevant time' was a controlling director of the acquiring company or a company having control of the acquiring company.

'Relevant time' means any time between the effective date of the transaction and the change of control causing the tax to become chargeable.

HMRC must serve a notice on a person within 1 or 2 above requiring him to pay within 30 days of service, and such a notice must be served within three years of the final determination of the tax chargeable.

Exceptions

[16.55] There are five cases in which reconstruction and acquisition relief is not withdrawn despite a change of control of the acquiring company. These are where control changes:

(1)   as a result of transactions in connection with divorce;
(2)   as a result of the variation of a testamentary disposition;
(3)   as a result of a transfer of shares that is exempt from stamp duty under stamp duty group relief (but see below);
(4)   as a result of a transfer of shares to another company that is exempt from stamp duty under FA 1986, s 77 (but see below); or
(5)   as a result of a loan creditor becoming, or ceasing to be, treated as having control of the company and the other persons who were previously treated as controlling the company continue to be so treated (see CTA 2010, s 453(1) and (2) for the meaning of 'loan creditor').

Where 3 above applies, if a company holding the shares in the acquiring company that were subject to stamp duty group relief ceases to be a member of the same group of companies as the target company within three years of the relevant land transaction (or at any time if pursuant to arrangements made within that period) and the acquiring company or a 'relevant associated company' (see FA 2003, Sch 7, para 11(5)) holds the chargeable interest acquired, the reconstruction or acquisition relief is withdrawn and tax is chargeable.

Where 4 above applies, if control of the other company changes within three years of the relevant land transaction (or at any time if pursuant to arrangements made within that period) at a time when that other company holds any of the shares transferred to it and the acquiring company or a 'relevant associated company' holds the chargeable interest acquired, the reconstruction or acquisition relief is withdrawn and tax is chargeable.

In both cases the tax chargeable is the amount that would have been chargeable if the chargeable consideration for the relevant land transaction had been equal to the market value of the chargeable interest transferred.

Charities

[16.56] A land transaction is exempt from stamp duty land tax if the purchaser is a charity provided two conditions are met (FA 2003, s 68 and Sch 8, para 1(1)). First, the purchaser must intend to hold the subject matter of the transaction for qualifying charitable purposes. These are defined as either:

(1)   for use in furtherance of the charitable purposes of the purchaser or another charity; or

(2)   as an investment from which the profits are applied to the charitable purposes of the purchaser (FA 2003, Sch 8, para 1(3A)).

Where the land transaction would not be exempt because the condition above is not met, exemption is still available if the charity intends to hold the greater part of the land for qualifying charitable purposes (FA 2003, Sch 8, para 3).

The second condition is that the transaction must not have been entered into for the purpose of avoiding SDLT whether by the purchaser or any other person (FA 2003, Sch 8, para 1(3)). It has been confirmed by the Government that this condition does not relate to the claiming of the exemption from SDLT by the charity itself (HC Official Report, Standing Committee B, Tuesday 10 June 2003, col 439).

'Charity' was previously defined to mean any body or trust established for charitable purposes only. This was extended to include 'charitable trusts', that is trusts of which all the beneficiaries are charities or unit trust schemes in which all the unit holders are charities (FA 2003, Sch 8, para 1(4)). The definition of 'charity' in FA 2010, Sch 6, para 1 and the Charities Act 2006, s 2 has applied since 1 April 2012. The charity concerned must satisfy the jurisdiction, registration and management conditions in FA 2010, Sch 6. Previously it was thought that this exemption applied to charities formed or established under UK law only and not to non-UK charities (*Dreyfus (Camille and Henry) Foundation Inc v IRC* [1956] AC 39) and that this limitation was unlawful to the extent that it discriminated against charities established in other member states of the EU. However, as a result of *Persche v Finanzamt Ludenscheid* C-318/08 [2009] All ER (EC) 673, [2009] STC 586, ECJ (GC), the exemption was extended to equivalent bodies in the EU and by regulation to Norway and Iceland with effect from 6 April 2009.

The exemption must be claimed in a land transaction.

The exemption will be withdrawn and tax become chargeable if within three years of the land transaction (or at any time if pursuant to arrangements made within that time), the purchaser holds the land and ceases to be established for charitable purposes only or the land is used or held by the purchaser otherwise than for qualifying charitable purposes (as defined above) (FA 2003, Sch 8, para 2). Where the exemption was claimed because the charity intended to hold the greater part of the land for qualifying charitable purposes, the withdrawal of the relief will also occur on any transfer of a major interest in the whole or part of the land or any grant out of the land of a lease at a premium with a low rent within the same time frame, that is not made for charitable purposes (FA 2003, Sch 8, para 3). The tax that becomes chargeable is the tax that would have been chargeable in respect of the land transaction had the exemption not been claimed. The exemption is only withdrawn if the charity still holds the land at the time of the disqualifying event, and so the withdrawal of relief will not apply to a disposal of the land itself within the three-year period or if the land falls vacant within such period. A disposal to a non-charity for less than market value consideration within that period might however raise the question of whether the charity originally intended to hold the land for qualifying charitable purposes and therefore satisfied the first condition above on the acquisition of the land by the charity.

When a charity purchases property jointly (including as tenants in common) with a non-charity purchaser and the acquisition by the charity would otherwise meet the requirements for the exemption to apply then a proportionate relief applies in respect of the share acquired by the charity. In *Pollen Estate Trustee Company Ltd and King's College London v HMRC* [2012] UKUT 277, the Upper Tribunal found that the special rule in FA 2003, s 103 relating to purchasers who become jointly entitled to land interests implied that there is only one land transaction of the whole of the land. Accordingly the Tribunal supported HMRC's contention that partial relief could not apply. The Court of Appeal ([2013] EWCA Civ 753) confirmed the Upper Tribunal's identification of the single chargeable interest in land as the basis for the SDLT charge but adopted a strained construction of (FA 2003, Sch 8, para 1(1)) to read:

'A land transaction is exempt from charge [to the extent that] the purchaser is a charity and the following conditions are met.'

The result is that the rate of SDLT is determined by reference to the chargeable consideration for the entire interest purchased but the amount of tax is then scaled down to exempt the proportionate share to be held by the charity for charitable purposes.

The reasoning of the Court of Appeal in justifying the insertion of extra words into the statute is of general interest in relation to statutory construction and may have wider implications to allow for proportionate reliefs elsewhere in the SDLT code. Counsel for HMRC was asked in the case for the policy reason which would justify denying partial charities relief for a joint acquisition of property while an acquisition of an existing undivided share by a charity would generally qualify for relief. The reasons given were roundly dismissed as unconvincing by both the Upper Tribunal and the Court of Appeal. Instead, the Court of Appeal found a 'policy imperative' sufficient to justify the extra words. Such an approach was stated to be consonant with the approach of Lord Nicholls in *Inco Europe Ltd v First Choice Distribution* [2000] 1 WLR 586. With respect, Pollen is not really on all fours with Inco since the latter relates to what Lord Nicholls regarded as a plain case of a drafting mistake (since a 'consequential' amendment had, if interpreted literally, a radical and additional effect beyond what could be considered consequential). The approach in *Inco* is termed a 'rectifying construction' in Section 287 of *Bennion on Statutory Interpretation*, 5th Edition [2008]. The *Pollen* judgement also cites *Luke v IRC* [1963] AC 557 where a strained construction of a taxing statute was applied on the basis that a literal interpretation would defeat the obvious intention of the legislation and produce a 'wholly unreasonable result'. Section 306 of Bennion covers what is termed a purposive-and-strained construction where the literal meaning is not in accordance with the legislative purpose. The Court of Appeal found what it considered to be a purpose for SDLT charities relief which would have been frustrated without the additional words.

HMRC have invited claims (within the statutory time limits) for repayment of tax for past transactions where partial charities relief applies. As yet they have not stated whether or not they consider the principles of *Pollen* to apply to any other SDLT reliefs. And it remains to be seen whether this judgement will increase the propensity of the Courts to insert or omit words when interpreting the SDLT and other tax statutes.

The statutory provisions were amended from 17 July 2014 in response to the Court of Appeal's judgment in *Pollen* to provide that:

(1)   where a charity purchases property jointly as tenants in common with a non-charity, the exemption will be available to the extent that the purchaser is a charity provided that the charity intends to hold the property for qualifying charitable purposes;

(2)   the amount of the exemption will be based on the lower of the proportion of the total chargeable consideration paid by the charity or any connected person and the proportion of the chargeable interest held by the charity; and

(3)   the non-charity purchaser will pay SDLT at the rate applicable to the total consideration paid for the property (FA 2003, Sch 8, paras 3A, 3B and 3C inserted by FA 2014, Sch 23).

Seeding reliefs for PAIFs and COACS

[16.57] A land transaction is exempt from stamp duty land tax during a 'seeding period' if the purchaser is a property authorised investment fund (PAIF) or a co-ownership authorised contractual scheme (COACS) if a number of conditions are met and restrictions on relief do not apply (FA 2003, Sch 7A inserted by FA 2016, Sch 16). The relief may be wholly or partially withdrawn up to the end of a 'control period'.

The policy aim of the reliefs is to allow property owners to seed these property funds (and equivalent funds established in other EEA jurisdictions) in return for units without a charge to SDLT. Withdrawal rules may impose SDLT charges if units are disposed of, the portfolio of seeded property reduces below certain levels or other conditions cease to be met. The elaborate requirements for the relief and withdrawal rules arise from extreme sensitivity about avoidance possibilities in view of the history of the unit trust seeding relief which applied up to March 2006 and, in HMRC's opinion, was widely used to achieve third-party sales of property without incurring SDLT charges.

COACS, like PAIFs, are FCA regulated and have to be authorised. Although they are not legal entities they are treated in the same way as PAIFs for SDLT purposes – with the operator of the scheme being treated as the purchaser of properties held in the scheme and as the person with SDLT compliance obligations and any tax liabilities (FA 2003, s 102A(11)). A COACS scheme is not treated as a company for the purposes of group relief, reconstruction relief or acquisition relief (FA 2003, s 102A(10)).

Part 1 of Schedule 7A provides for seeding relief for PAIFs and Part 2 makes corresponding provision for COACS. The reliefs must be claimed in a land transaction return or an amendment of such a return and must be accompanied by a notice to HMRC confirming that the purchaser is an appropriate property fund. This requirement for a separate notice seems to arise from

HMRC's inability to make their IT provider modify the computer system for handling returns in order to reflect law changes. It reflects badly on HMRC's stated aspiration to embrace the digital world.

The SDLT rules for seeding relief are essentially the same for the two types of fund arrangements. There are four conditions for a relief to apply, some restrictions on the availability of relief, and rules for full or partial withdrawal of relief.

Condition A is that the purchaser must be a PAIF or COACS as defined for the purposes of the relief (FA 2003, Sch 7A, paras 2 and 10, respectively). Condition B is that the subject matter of a transaction is a major interest in land. Condition C is that the only consideration for the transaction is an issue of units in the relevant fund and Condition D is that the effective date of the transaction is within the seeding period. Condition C means that there may be a problem if VAT applies to the purchase. The VAT cannot be paid in cash without breaching the condition and any additional units that are issued to cover the VAT cannot be redeemed or sold for cash by the vendor without triggering withdrawal charges by the fund (see below). It will in general be important that property acquisitions qualify for TOGC treatment.

The seeding period permits more than one relieved property acquisition by a fund – possibly from more than one vendor. This is in contrast to the former unit trust relief which applied only to an initial seeding transaction. The seeding period starts with the first effective date of a seeding transaction and ends with the first external investment – subject to a maximum of 18 months. An external investment is an acquisition which does not include a chargeable interest and where the vendor has not previously made a transaction subject to seeding relief. A fund may make an election to close the period earlier (FA 2003, Sch 7A, paras 3 and 11).

Seeding relief is not available if the transaction is not effected for bona fide commercial reasons, or forms part of arrangements of which the main purpose, or one of the main purposes, is the avoidance of liability to tax. 'Tax' here means stamp duty, income tax, corporation tax, capital gains tax or SDLT. Other restrictions are that the PAIF or COACS must have in place arrangements under which a vendor must notify the fund about the beneficial owners of units and about disposals of units which could trigger the withdrawal rules. And there must be no arrangements for such disposals of units at the effective date of the seeding transaction (FA 2003, Sch 7A, paras 4 and 12).

The 'control period' is the three years following the end of the seeding period (FA 2003, Sch 7A, para 21) and withdrawal of some or all of the relief for a particular transaction can generally be triggered during the remainder of the seeding period, during the control period, or under arrangements made before the end of the control period.

If the PAIF ceases to be a PAIF or the COACS ceases to be a COACS then relief is withdrawn to the extent that the chargeable interests (or chargeable interests derived from them) are still owned by the fund. The fund has the liability based on SDLT which would have been payable in respect of the seeding transaction had the relief not applied (FA 2003, Sch 7A, paras 5 and 13).

A similar liability arises if the portfolio test is not met (FA 2003, Sch 7A, paras 6 and 16). The portfolio test requires seeded properties still to be held to the extent of at least £100 million of chargeable consideration measured at the time of the seeding transaction. The fund must also own at least ten seeded interests if the chargeable consideration for residential seeded property does not exceed 10% of the total chargeable consideration for the seeded portfolio. If the residential proportion exceeds 10% then there must be at least 100 seeded interests. There is some doubt about how seeded interests should be counted. If the fund owns the freehold interest of a block of 120 rented flats then it is not clear whether this is one chargeable interest or whether the test can be interpreted to count the 120 leases out of the single freehold. There may be HMRC published guidance on this at some point in the future. The portfolio test must be met immediately before the end of the seeding period and during the control period. And it must not be breached as a result of arrangements made before the end of the control period. A potential hazard is that the test is in relation to seeded properties only. This means that there will be a withdrawal charge if seeded properties are sold so as to reduce the total chargeable consideration for those properties below £100 million or to reduce the number of interests below the threshold – even if replacement property is acquired with the proceeds.

When there is a disposal of units by a vendor V (or in the case of a corporate vendor, a company within the vendor's group) and that vendor made a seeding transaction which was subject to the relief then there may be a withdrawal of relief. The liability for the fund is calculated by formula (FA 2003, Sch 7A, paras 7 and 17) as follows:

(A) is the market value of units held by V and grouped companies just before the disposal or, if lower, the total chargeable consideration for seeding transactions by V and grouped companies (whether or not the relief was subsequently withdrawn);

(B) is the market value of units held by V and grouped companies immediately after the disposal;

(C) is A minus B and the disposal is subject to a charge only if A exceeds B. CCRST is the total chargeable consideration for seeding transactions where V or a grouped company was the vendor.

SDLT is the amount of tax that would have been paid on those seeding transactions had relief not applied less any withdrawal charge in relation to earlier disposals of units by V.

The charge to the fund in respect of a disposal of units for which A exceeds B is then:

$$(C/CCRST) \times SDLT$$

In a case where there has been no change in property values between seeding and disposal of units then the proportion of the value of relief withdrawn is equal to the proportion of units disposed. However, in other cases the amount of the withdrawal charge is more difficult to relate to what is happening commercially. Where property values have increased it would seem possible to dispose of units up to the value of the gain without triggering a charge. Each disposal during the relevant period requires its own calculation to determine the amount of any further withdrawal charge.

There is a withdrawal of COACS seeding relief when a genuine diversity of ownership ('GDO') condition ceases to be met (FA 2003, Sch 7A, paras 14 and 15). While there is no corresponding provision in the PAIF seeding relief rules, the regulatory rules for PAIFs require a PAIF to comply with similar requirements so a breach would make the fund cease to be a PAIF and trigger relief withdrawal. The GDO conditions are:

(A)   The scheme documents specify the intended categories of investor and undertake to market the units and make them widely available.

(B)   The intended categories of investor must not be a limited number of specific persons or groups and the terms and conditions do not deter reasonable investors in these categories.

(C)   Marketing of units is sufficiently wide and appropriate and the intended categories of investor can obtain relevant information.

The conditions may be met by a feeder fund rather than the fund itself (FA 2003, Sch 7A, para 20).

No doubt because these conditions are expressed in rather vague terms – albeit that the general intention is reasonably easy to discern – there is, unusually for the SDLT statute, a provision to require a statutory clearance from HMRC that the GDO is met (FA 2003, Sch 7A, para 14(5)).

There is also a withdrawal provision where a non-qualifying individual is permitted to occupy a dwelling within the seeded portfolio (FA 2003, Sch 7A, paras 8, 9, 18 and 19). This echoes the 15% higher rate of SDLT and ATED regime for enveloped dwellings. Non-qualifying individuals include a participant with at least a 50% stake in the fund and connected individuals and relatives as well as individuals connected with the operator or depositary of a COACS. The withdrawal is in proportion to the value of the relief in respect of the dwelling. Withdrawal may be triggered after the end of the control period but only if the regulatory GDO condition in respect of a PAIF or the Schedule 7A GDO condition for a COACS is breached at that time.

Returns, liability and compliance

Returns etc

[16.58] A major difference between stamp duty on land and SDLT is the requirement in the latter tax to deliver a tax return to HMRC. Every 'notifiable transaction' must be reported by delivery of a land transaction return to HMRC before the end of 30 days after the 'effective date' of the transaction. A land transaction return must include a self-assessment of the tax chargeable. The return must be signed by the purchaser or by a duty authorised attorney. The tax payable must be paid not later than the filing date for the tax return, ie within 30 days of the 'effective date' of the transaction.

A 'notifiable transaction' is:

(1)   an acquisition of a major interest in land that does not fall within one or more of the exceptions listed in (A) to (F) below;

(2)   an acquisition of a chargeable interest other than a major interest in land where SDLT is chargeable at the rate of more than 0% or would be so chargeable but for a relief;

(3)   a land transaction that a person is deemed to have entered into under FA 2003, s 44A(3);

(4)   a notional land transaction under FA 2003, s 75A.

(5)   a notional or additional land transaction under FA 2003, Sch 2A, para 5 (assignment of rights : transferor treated as making a separate acquisition).

(FA 2003, s 77 as inserted by FA 2008, s 92 for transactions with an effective date on or after 12 March 2008.)

References to a 'relief' above do not include any exemption under FA 2003, Sch 3.

The exceptions referred to in (1) above are:

(A)   an acquisition which is exempt under FA 2003, Sch 3 other than an acquisition which is exempt by virtue of any regulations made under paragraph 5 of that Schedule;

(B)   an acquisition (other than the grant, assignment or surrender of a lease) where the chargeable consideration for that acquisition, together with any linked transaction, is less than £40,000;

(C)   the grant of a lease for a term of seven years or more where any chargeable consideration other than rent is less than £40,000 and the relevant rent is less than £1,000;

(D)   the assignment or surrender of a lease where the lease was originally granted for a term of seven years or more and the chargeable consideration for the assignment or surrender is less than £40,000;

(E)   the grant of a lease for a term of less than seven years where the chargeable consideration does not exceed the 'zero-rate threshold'; and

(F)   the assignment or surrender of a lease where the lease was originally granted for a term of less than seven years and the chargeable consideration does not exceed the 'zero-rate threshold'.

(FA 2003, s 77A inserted by FA 2008, s 94 and varied by SI 2008/2338.)

Chargeable consideration does not exceed the 'zero-rate threshold' if it does not consist of or include any amount in respect of which tax is chargeable at a rate of more than 0% or any amount in respect of which tax would be so chargeable but for a relief (excluding any exemption under FA 2003, Sch 3).

No account is to be taken for the purposes of the requirement to notify of the provisions of FA 2003, Sch 6 to the effect that consideration is not 'chargeable consideration' in relation to acquisitions of land qualifying for disadvantaged areas relief.

In general, therefore, acquisitions of major interests in land including the grant of leases which are not exempt are notifiable where the chargeable consideration is £40,000 or more (see **16.22** above). Interests other than major interests are notifiable only if the tax is charged at a rate of more than 0% or would be chargeable but for a relief.

A 'major interest' in land is defined for SDLT purposes as:

(1)   in England (and Wales until 1 April 2018) an estate in fee simple absolute (freehold) or a term of years absolute (leasehold) whether in law or in equity; and

(2)   (in Northern Ireland) any freehold or leasehold estate whether in law or in equity.

(Note: the definition of a major interest for VAT is different – see **CHAPTER 15** para **15.29** et seq.)

There are detailed rules relating to returns, enquiries, assessments and appeals in FA 2003, Sch 10, FA 2007, Sch 24 and FA 2008, Sch 36 and the following is a summary of the main provisions:

(1)   A land transaction return must be in the prescribed form. Since 4 July 2011, the main land transaction return has required a range of unique identifiers for the main purchaser and not just an individual's national insurance number but also date of birth, VAT registration, company or partnership unique tax reference number or overseas equivalent: SI 2011/455 amending the Stamp Duty Land Tax (Administration) Regulations SI 2003/2837.

(2)   Failure to deliver a land transaction return by the filing date give rise to a flat rate penalty of £100 (if the return is delivered within three months after the filing date) and £200 in any other case plus (in the case of a 'chargeable transaction') where the return is not delivered within 12 months of the filing date, a tax-related penalty not exceeding the tax chargeable (the filing date is the last day of the period within which the return must be delivered).

(3)   A purchaser may amend a land transaction return given by him by notice to HMRC normally within 12 months of the filing date.

(4)   HMRC may by notice to the purchaser amend a land transaction return so as to correct obvious errors or omissions whether errors of principle, arithmetical mistakes or otherwise within nine months of the day the return was delivered or the amended return was made; the purchaser may reject the correction by amending the return or if after the period during which he may amend the return but within three months of the notice of correction, give notice rejecting the correction.

(5)   A penalty not exceeding the tax understated arises in the case of deliberate or careless inaccuracy in the SDLT return which leads to an understatement of the SDLT liability; the amount of the penalty varies from 30% of the additional tax due for carelessness through to 100% for deliberate and concealed action; there is also a penalty of 30% of the additional tax due where an assessment is issued that understates the SDLT liability and reasonable steps to notify HMRC of the underassessment are not taken within 30 days of the assessment. These penalties have applied from 1 April 2010. If a return is inaccurate because of a mistake or failure to take reasonable care by the taxpayer's professional adviser, a penalty will not be chargeable if the taxpayer took reasonable care such as appointing a competent adviser, supplying all relevant information or checking the return as far as they could: FA 2007, Sch 24 para 18(3) and HMRC's 'Briefing on new tax penalties – FAQs' issued on 14 December 2010, Q20.

(6) A purchaser required to deliver a return must keep sufficient records preserved for six years after the effective date of the transaction or until any later date on which any enquiry into the return is completed, or HMRC no longer has power to enquire into the return.

(7) There are detailed powers for HMRC to conduct an enquiry into a return generally within nine months of the filing date. SDLT was brought within HMRC's new enquiry powers in FA 2008, Sch 36 with effect from 1 April 2010. Under this regime HMRC have very wide powers to issue an information notice which requires a taxpayer to provide information or documents 'if the information or document is reasonably required for the purpose of checking the taxpayers' tax position' (FA 2008, Sch 36, para 1). There are also powers to obtain information and documents from third parties and to inspect property and premises. HMRC accept that where it is out of time to open an enquiry (or if relevant, issue a discovery assessment) so that requiring information could not affect a person's tax position then it would not be reasonable to require it: see CH22140 which says that documents created more than six years previously should not normally be requested as the assessment time limit will have expired except where there is reasonable grounds to suspect a deliberate, ie fraudulent, error. This reflects the legal position as decided in *R (on the application of Johnson) v Branigan (Inspector of Taxes)* [2006] EWHC 885 (Admin), where Stanley Burnton J said at [15] in relation to information notices issued under TMA 1970, s 20 (the predecessor to FA 2008, Sch 36, para 1) that:

> 'The practical constraint on section 20 is that it can only be used where there is a sensible or reasonable possibility of an assessment under section 29 [TMA].'

HMRC investigators will sometimes claim that FA 2008, Sch 36, para 1 has overridden this principle and that they can require information older than six years merely in order to 'check' the taxpayer's position. This is incorrect and when encountered should be resisted in the absence of the existence of reasonable grounds to suspect a deliberate, ie fraudulent, error by the taxpayer. Judicial review proceedings should be deployed if the investigator decides to seek tribunal approval to the issue of an information notice in these circumstances in order to remove the taxpayer's normal right to appeal the information notice under FA 2008, Sch 36, para 29(3). In the author's experience, HMRC will not defend such judicial proceedings on this matter once the taxpayer has sought permission to apply for a judicial review from the Administrative Court.

(8) HMRC has the power to make a determination of the tax payable if no return is delivered by the filing date, within four years of the effective date of the transaction.

(9) HMRC has the power to issue a discovery assessment for any tax that ought to have been assessed, or for an assessment that is or has become insufficient, where a relief given is or has become excessive or where tax has been repaid that ought not to have been repaid; generally such an assessment may not be made more than four years after the effective

date of the transaction, but this is increased to six years for carelessness and 20 years in the case of a loss of tax: (a) brought about deliberately by the taxpayer; (b) attributable to a failure to deliver a return; or (c) attributable to a failure to comply with a with a requirement to notify a disclosable SDLT avoidance scheme.

(10)   A mistake in a return leading to excessive tax may be corrected by giving notice of such a claim to HMRC within four years of the effective date of the transaction, and such repayment will be made as is reasonable and just. No repayment shall be given, however, if the return was made on the basis of or in accordance with the practice generally prevailing at the time it was made or in respect of a mistake in a claim or election included in the return.

(11)   There are detailed rules governing the right to bring an appeal relating to an assessment before the tribunal including a facility to apply for postponement of payment of tax and an internal HMRC review of the matter.

(12)   Where a later transaction that is linked to an earlier transaction results in the earlier transaction becoming notifiable or liable to tax or additional tax, a return must be delivered within 30 days of the later transaction accompanied by payment of the tax and a return must also be made in respect of the later transaction.

(13)   Detailed provision has been made for the making of claims that are not made in a return.

Contingent, uncertain and unascertainable chargeable consideration

[16.59] Where the chargeable consideration for a land transaction was contingent, uncertain or unascertained and the contingency occurs (or it becomes clear that it will not occur) or any amount or instalment of uncertain or unascertained consideration becomes ascertained, a further return must be made within 30 days accompanied by payment of the tax (or any further tax) payable. If the effect of the new information is that less tax is payable than has already been paid, a purchaser may claim repayment of the overpaid tax together with interest as from the date of payment of the tax by the purchaser.

Reliefs withdrawn

[16.60] Where either group relief, reconstruction or acquisition relief or charities relief is withdrawn the purchaser must deliver a further return within 30 days after the occurrence of the disqualifying event. Payment of the tax chargeable must be made no later than the filing date for that return, ie within 30 days of the disqualifying event.

Lost etc returns

[16.61] HMRC may treat a return as not having been delivered or a document as not having been provided where it has been lost or destroyed or been so defaced or destroyed as to be illegible or otherwise useless. In such cases HMRC may proceed as if the return or document had not been made or delivered, but any tax paid in respect of the transaction will reduce any further tax charged or give rise to a repayment as appropriate.

Form of return

[16.62] Although any assessment, determination or notice must be in the prescribed form it will not be ineffective for want of form or by reason of any mistake, defect or omission in it if it substantially conforms with the specified requirements and its intended effect is reasonably ascertainable by the person to whom it is directed. Any mistake as to the name of the person liable or the amount of tax charged will not affect the validity of the assessment or determination, nor will any variance between the notice of assessment or determination and the assessment or determination itself. Delivery and service of documents is regulated by FA 2003, s 84.

The return must be signed by the purchaser (or each of them or someone holding a written power of attorney signed by the individual purchaser).

Since 13 July 2005, a land transaction return may be delivered using the internet, provided that the terms and conditions on the website of HM Revenue and Customs for the Stamp Taxes Online Land Transaction Return are observed.

Registration of land

[16.63] Except for the notional transaction arising on an assignment of rights under FA 2003, Sch 2A, para 5, assignments of agreements for lease, agreements for lease which are substantially performed prior to grant of the lease, certain lease variations and contracts caught by FA 2003, s 44A, a notifiable land transaction must not be registered at the Land Registry unless there is produced with the application to register a certificate of compliance. The certificate must be a certificate by HMRC that a land transaction return has been delivered in respect of the transaction (a Revenue certificate known as an 'SDLT 5'). The certificate by the purchaser that no land transaction return was required in respect of the transaction (a 'self-certificate' known as an 'SDLT 60' was abolished for transactions with an effective date on or after 12 March 2008) (FA 2003, s 79 as amended by FA 2008, s 92 and Sch 30).

A certificate is not required where the land registrar is obliged to act without receipt of an application such as under the commonhold regime, or where the entry relates to an interest or a right other than the chargeable interest acquired by the purchaser under the land transaction giving rise to the application (FA 2003, s 79).

It seems that underpayment of the tax at the time of registration of title is not of itself a basis for restricting the registered proprietor's power to deal with the land: *A-G of the Turks and Caicos Islands v Richardson (trustee in bankruptcy of Yellowstone Club World LCC)* [2013] UKPC 9, [2013] SWTI 1715, [2013] All ER (D) 196 (Apr).

Liability to pay

[16.64] The purchaser is liable to pay the SDLT in respect of a chargeable transaction. Joint purchasers are jointly and severally liable to pay the SDLT. Partners who are partners at the effective date of the transaction (but not any person who becomes a partner afterwards) are jointly and severally liable to pay the SDLT in respect of purchases of chargeable interests by the partnership. SDLT may be recovered from any one or more of the trustees of a settlement who were trustees at the effective date of the transaction or who subsequently became a trustee.

SDLT payable in respect of a land transaction must be paid by the filing date for relevant land transaction return. Any tax payable as the result of the withdrawal of either group relief, reconstruction or acquisition relief and charities relief must be paid by the filing date for the relevant return.

These provisions are subject to any application to defer payment of tax in the case of contingent or uncertain consideration or to postpone payment of tax pending an appeal.

Interest and penalties

[16.65] Interest is payable on the amount of any unpaid SDLT after 30 days from the effective date of the transaction. However, interest on unpaid and late paid SDLT only runs from 26 September 2005 because HMRC overlooked the need to set the actual rate of interest to be charged. Belatedly, the Taxes (Interest Rate) (Amendment) Regulations (SI 2005/2462) provide for the setting of rates of interest as from 26 September 2005. HMRC announced that they would not seek recovery of interest wrongly paid out in SDLT repayments In the case of the withdrawal of group relief, reconstruction or acquisition relief or charities relief giving rise to tax, interest is charged after 30 days following the disqualifying event. In the case of tax deferred under FA 2003, s 90, interest is charged after 30 days from when the deferred payment is due. However, where contingent, uncertain or unascertained consideration is not deferred under FA 2003, s 90, interest on any tax that becomes payable under FA 2003, s 80 (adjustment where the contingency ceases or consideration becomes ascertained) runs from the effective date of the transaction. An amount of tax lodged with HMRC in respect of the tax will reduce the interest payable accordingly.

Penalties carry interest from the date they are determined until payment. Interest is charged at the rate applicable under FA 1989, s 178. A repayment of SDLT (including an amount lodged under FA 2003, s 87(6)) carries interest at the rate applicable under FA 1989, s 178 between the payment of the tax and the repayment (unless it is a payment made in consequence of a court order or judgment of a court having power to allow interest on the payment). Any such interest paid is not income for tax purposes.

FA 2003, s 91 and Sch 12 govern the collection and recovery of SDLT including any penalties and interest. Under FA 2003, s 92 where payment to HMRC is made by cheque and the cheque is paid on its first presentation to the bank on which it is drawn, the payment is treated as made on the day the cheque was received by HMRC.

HMRC's powers – offences

[16.66] FA 2003, s 93 and Sch 13 (as amended) and FA 2008, Sch 36 govern the powers of HMRC to call for documents and information for the purposes of stamp duty land tax.

FA 2003, s 95 creates the statutory criminal offence of a person being knowingly concerned in the fraudulent evasion of SDLT by him or any other person. If found guilty the person is liable on summary conviction to imprisonment for a term not exceeding six months or a fine not exceeding the statutory maximum (or both) and on conviction on indictment to imprisonment for a term not exceeding seven years or a fine (or both). This section is based on and largely copies FA 2000, s 144 which was introduced to make prosecution of PAYE and NIC fraud involving payment of wages by cash in hand without deducting tax more effective. When that provision was introduced into the Finance Bill 2000 at a late stage unease was expressed about the imprecision inherent in the phrases 'knowingly concerned' and 'fraudulent evasion'. In response the Paymaster General explained the use of these phrases as follows:

> 'I will deal with the important point about the words "knowingly" and "fraudulent evasion" . . . My officials will smile when they hear this, but initially I said to them, "Surely evasion is fraud", and asked why it needed to be qualified as "fraudulent evasion". I have received assurances which I will pass on to the Committee. The juxtaposition of the words "knowingly" and "fraudulent evasion" reinforces exactly which offences the provision is aimed at.

> Let us take the question of someone who is knowingly concerned in the evasion of income tax. I want to make it clear that it is not enough for this purpose to show that a person should have suspected that someone was evading tax. The person must have knowledge and involvement in the fraud. For example, he could help someone evade tax by the helping to produce false business records.

> People may ask why we have put the words "fraudulent" and "evasion" together. I am reliably informed by people who know better than I do that, in English usage, "to evade" can mean to dodge, without any dishonest intent. Although "evasion" has come to imply dishonesty in the context of tax, the Bill needs to be drafted tightly. "Fraudulent" may not appear to add much to "evasion", but the expression "fraudulent evasion" is well precedented and subject to interpretation by the courts.' (HC Official Report, Standing Committee H, 29 June 2000, col 1010.)

Therefore the phrase 'knowingly concerned' requires knowledge of (rather than mere suspicion) and involvement in the evasion of tax, and the phrase 'fraudulent evasion' requires proof of dishonest intent. In relation to tax planning, assurances were sought as to the meaning of 'evasion' and in particular whether those involved in tax avoidance schemes might be charged with the commission of this offence where the scheme was adjudged to have failed on technical grounds. In this respect the Paymaster General said:

> 'No one could be convicted as a matter of general law unless it was proved that he or she had a dishonest intention . . .

> The Right Hon. Member for Wells asked about tax advisers who gave advice on avoidance schemes that failed. A failed scheme whose details are not hidden from the Revenue amounts not to tax evasion, but to tax planning . . . The

Government may not like some of that planning and may legislate against it, but, as it is not hidden, it does not fall within the remit of the measure . . .

. . . avoidance is not evasion; there are separate laws to deal with the latter. The Right Hon. Gentleman asked when avoidance became evasion. Unless he can give an example, I cannot think of such an eventuality.'
(HC Official Report, Standing Committee H, 29 June 2000, cols 1012 and 1013.)

Further guidance has been issued in the then Inland Revenue Tax Bulletin, Issue 49 (October 2000) to the effect that those persons who advise on what turn out to be fiscally ineffective tax avoidance schemes are only likely to be charged with the offence where dishonesty is involved. In the opinion of HMRC such dishonesty may be evident where those involved in a scheme 'are not merely relying on the intrinsic technical soundness of the arrangements actually put in place to reduce their liability, but also on concealment of the true facts from the inspector'. HMRC would not expect a criminal offence to have been committed where there is no concealment of the facts and there is a 'respectable technical case'. Thus a critical question in determining whether a prosecution will occur is likely to be whether there has been 'concealment of the true facts'. However, this phrase gives rise to its own uncertainty given that 'concealment' can occur in different ways ranging from deliberate covering up of facts through partial disclosure of accurate information which conveys a misleading impression to failure to appreciate (and therefore disclose) that certain information would be considered relevant by HMRC. Given the guidance available, however, it seems that in any case where the technical merits of a tax mitigation structure involving SDLT are open to different interpretations the safest course of action will be to disclose all material facts to IR Stamp Taxes and argue the case on technical merit rather than risk an allegation that facts were concealed if a prosecution under FA 2003, s 95 is to be safely ruled out.

However it is legitimate for a taxpayer who has complied with any requirement to file an SDLT return or who takes the view on reasonable grounds that a return is not required, to decide not to expose himself to the chance of a potentially lengthy and expensive enquiry by HMRC which could arise from a voluntary disclosure. As long as any necessary returns have been filed such a decision not to make a voluntary disclosure could not be "concealment" even where avoidance was involved if there is a reasonable technical basis for the position adopted by the taxpayer and even if the avoidance ultimately fails to succeed.

A person who assists in or induces the preparation or delivery of any information, return or other document that he knows will be, or is likely to be used for any purpose of SDLT, and he knows to be incorrect is liable to a penalty not exceeding £3,000 (FA 2003, s 96).

FA 2003, Sch 14 governs the determination of penalties and related appeals.

Special situations

Partnerships

[16.67] A 'partnership' for SDLT is defined as a partnership under any of the Partnership Act 1890, the Limited Partnerships Act 1907, the Limited Liability Partnerships Act 2000, or a firm or entity of a similar character to any of these formed under the law of a foreign jurisdiction. For SDLT purposes a chargeable interest held by or on behalf of a partnership is treated as held by or on behalf of the partners and a land transaction entered into for the purposes of a partnership is treated as entered into by or on behalf of the partners and not by the partnership as such despite the partnership being regarded as a legal person or body corporate by the law under which it was formed. For how this principle affects SDLT group relief claims involving partnerships see **16.45**.

A partnership is treated as the same person despite a change in the partners as long as at least one person who was a partner before the change remains a partner after the change. A partnership is not treated for SDLT as a unit trust scheme or open-ended investment company.

SDLT applies in the usual way to what are referred to as 'ordinary partnership transactions' which are transactions entered into as purchaser by or on behalf of the members of a partnership other than transactions subject to which the special partnership provisions apply. The special partnership provisions apply where:

(1)   land is transferred to a partnership by a partner (or a person who becomes a partner in return for the land or the land is transferred by a person connected with either person);

(2)   there is a transfer of an interest in a partnership; or

(3)   land is transferred from a partnership to a partner (or a person who has been a partner or a person connected with either person).

Stamp duty continues to apply to any instrument by which the transfer of an interest in a partnership is effected. It was intended by the Government that a stamp duty charge would only apply to the extent that the partnership held shares. This would deal with concerns that partnerships might be used as a stamp duty free wrapper for share deals. The stamp duty charge was therefore supposed to be restricted to that which would arise on a direct sale of the shares themselves held by the partnership and if the partnership held no shares then no stamp duty would arise. Paragraphs 31–33 of Sch 15, as originally enacted, however did not achieve this. Rather, those provisions applied a full stamp duty charge at up to 4% on transfers of partnership interests even by reference to assets held such as free-standing goodwill and intellectual property which were exempt from stamp duty before. Paragraph 33 was intended to restrict the overall stamp duty charge as mentioned above, but the drafting failed to achieve this and there was further error which resulted in the stamp duty charge relating to the share of the partnership that was not transferred. Paragraph 33, as amended by F(No 2)A 2005, Sch 10, para 21, now provides that there is no stamp duty charge unless the partnership property includes stock or marketable securities, in which case the stamp duty charge is restricted to that which would be chargeable on an instrument transferring the shares themselves ie normally 0.5% and that charge is on the amount of consideration equal to the net market value of the stock and marketable securities attributable to the interest of the incoming partner or increase in an existing partner's share. There is still a slightly redundant provision that where the partnership owns land the consideration liable to stamp duty is reduced by a proportion of the market value of the land less any loan secured solely on the land, representing the proportionate interest acquired by the purchaser of the interest in the partnership. The intention is to give a credit against the stamp duty charge for the SDLT payable in relation to the land under 2 above. It is understood that HMRC intends to deal with this unsatisfactory situation by only charging stamp duty by reference to the shares held if any. It is interesting to note that the instrument will not be duly stamped unless it is adjudicated.

Transfer of land interest

[16.68] The transfer of an interest in land to a partnership by a partner or a person who becomes a partner (or someone connected with either) is a chargeable transaction. The chargeable consideration is normally taken to be the proportion of the market value of the land equal to the total of the other partners' shares immediately after the transfer. The shares of partners who are individuals and who are connected with the transferor are ignored for this purpose (FA 2003, Sch 15, para 10). However, an election may be made to disapply this treatment and instead pay tax by reference to the market value of the whole chargeable interest transferred. Where such an election is made the value of the chargeable interest is not taken into account on any subsequent 'Type B' transfer of an interest in the partnership (see below) nor on any subsequent distribution of the property out of the partnership and is disregarded under FA 2003, Sch 15, para 17A (see below) (FA 2003, Sch 15, para 12A).

Where there is such a transfer of land into a partnership and within three years of the transfer there is a withdrawal of money or money's worth other than income profit or a loan is repaid (in relation to the transferor or a person connected with him), the withdrawal or repayment is treated as a chargeable transaction and the chargeable consideration is taken to be the withdrawal or repayment up to the market value of the chargeable interest transferred, less any tax previously chargeable. This provision may lead to a double-charge to SDLT where one partner contributes land and the other partner contributes a cash equalisation payment which is then paid out to the partner contributing the land so that each partner going forward has made the same net contribution. This will occur because the contribution of the land will be taxed on the market value of the proportionate share of the land attributable to the other partner, and a further tax charge will then arise by reference to the money paid out to equalise their respective contributions. There are also special provisions for partnerships consisting wholly of bodies corporate.

Transfer of partnership interest

[16.69] The transfer of a partnership interest in a property investment partnership (a 'PIP') but not in any other form of partnership, is a chargeable transaction where the partnership property includes land. A PIP is a partnership whose sole or main activity is investing in or dealing in land whether or not that involves carrying out construction operations on land. The transfer of a partnership interest in a property investment partnership (a 'PIP') but not in any other form of partnership, is a chargeable transaction when the partnership property includes land whether or not any consideration is given. A PIP is a partnership whose sole or main activity is investing in or dealing in land whether or not that involves carrying out construction operations on land. The chargeable consideration is taken to be equal to a proportion of the market value of the 'relevant partnership property' where there is consideration. That proportion is equal to the partnership interest acquired. A transfer of a partnership interest occurs when a person acquires or increases a partnership share. Consideration for this purpose can take the form of either money or money's worth given for the interest acquired or under arrangements where a person becomes a partner and the interest of an existing partner reduces or ceases and money or money's worth is withdrawn by the existing partner other than out of resources available to the partnership prior to the transfer. Such transfers are referred to by the legislation as 'Type A' transfers. The 'relevant partnership property' in relation to a Type A transfer is every chargeable interest held by the partnership except that transferred to the partnership in connection with the transfer and market value leases.

Transfers occurring in any other circumstances are known as 'Type B' transfers. For Type B transfers the chargeable consideration is taken to be equal to a proportion of the market value of the 'relevant partnership property' equal to the partnership interest acquired. The 'relevant partnership property' for a Type B transfer is every chargeable interest held by the partnership but excluding a chargeable interest transferred to the partnership in connection with the transfer, market value leases, any chargeable interest not attributable economically to the partnership interest transferred, any chargeable interest transferred to the partnership before 23 July 2004, any chargeable interest in respect of whose transfer to the partnership an election has been made under FA 2003, Sch 15, para 12A to pay tax by reference to market value and any other chargeable interest whose transfer to the partnership did not attract SDLT under the market value rule in FA 2003, Sch 15, para 10. (FA 2003, Sch 15, para 14 as amended by FA 2008, s 95 and Sch 31 with effect from 19 July 2007).

The transfer of an interest in land from a partnership to a partner or former partner (or a person connected with either) is a chargeable transaction. The chargeable consideration is taken to be a proportion of the market value of the land. A reduction is available where the partners include an individual connected with the transferee.

It has been confirmed that where the acquisition of the underlying land would qualify for the disadvantaged areas relief, the transfer of the partnership interest will to that extent also be exempt. (See FA 2003, Sch 15, para 26 and Hansard, Wednesday, 28 April 2004, Col 946.) Other reliefs are also available.

Partnership property is any interest or right held by or on behalf of a partnership, or the members of a partnership, for the purposes of partnership business. In the view of HMRC Stamp Taxes Office, it follows from this that property held by one of the partners and used for the purposes of the partnership business may be partnership property so that a charge to tax may arise on contribution, on its ceasing to be used and on a transfer of an interest in the partnership, as above. This view may be open to question.

Unit trusts and co-ownership authorised contractual schemes

[16.70] A unit trust scheme is treated generally for SDLT as if the trustees were a company and the units in it were shares, and each part of an umbrella unit trust scheme is treated as a separate unit trust. The phrase 'unit trust scheme' has the same meaning as in the Financial Services and Markets Act 2000. However, a unit trust scheme is not treated as a company for the purposes of group relief, reconstruction relief or acquisition relief.

Open-ended investment companies are intended to be treated in a similar fashion to unit trusts for SDLT purposes and regulations have been made accordingly. The phrase 'open-ended investment company' (OEIC) has the meaning in the Financial Services and Markets Act 2000.

Prior to 22 March 2006, the acquisition of an interest in land by the trustees of a unit trust scheme was exempt from tax if:

(1)   immediately before the acquisition there were no assets held by the trustees and no units were in issue;
(2)   the only consideration for the acquisition was the units; and
(3)   immediately after the acquisition the vendor was the only unit holder of the scheme (FA 2003, s 64A but withdrawn from 22 March 2006 by FA 2006, s 166).

A property authorised investment fund (PAIF) is an OEIC subject to special regulations (SI 2006/964). If the OEIC is an umbrella fund then its sub-funds are treated as OEICs and the umbrella fund is not (FA 2003, Sch 7A, para 2).

A co-ownership authorised contractual scheme (COACS) is a co-ownership scheme authorised for the purposes of FSMA 2000 by an authorisation under s 261D(1) of that Act. It is treated as a company for SDLT purposes and the rights or units of the participant are treated as shares in that company (FA 2003, s 102A). As for PAIFs, if the COACS is an umbrella scheme then the sub-schemes are treated as COACS but the umbrella is not. A COACS is not treated as a company for the purposes of group relief, reconstruction relief or acquisition relief. The operator of the COACS is treated as the purchaser when the COACS acquires land and the operator is the person who has any SDLT liabilities and compliance obligations.

See 16.57 for descriptions of the seeding reliefs available to PAIFs, COACS and equivalents established in other EEA countries.

Trusts

[16.71] Where a chargeable interest or an interest in a partnership is acquired by a bare trustee or a nominee, SDLT applies as if the interest had been acquired by the person for whom the bare trustee or nominee acts, except in relation to the grant of a lease, where the bare trustee is treated as the purchaser of the whole of the interest acquired. Where the trustee or trustees of any other type of trust acquire a chargeable interest or an interest in a partnership as trustees they are treated for SDLT purposes as purchasers of the entire interest acquired including the beneficial interest. For exceptions to these rules in relation to higher rates transactions see FA 2003, Sch 4ZA, paras 10–13.

Beneficiaries of trusts formed under Scots or non-UK laws are treated for SDLT as having an equitable interest in trust property if that would be the case had the trust been formed under English law. The acquisition of the interest of such a beneficiary under the trust is treated expressly as the acquisition of an interest in the trust property for SDLT purposes.

However, there is no equivalent provision for English trusts expressly providing that the acquisition of the equitable interest of a beneficiary under a trust formed under English law is to be treated as the acquisition of an interest in the trust property for SDLT purposes. Instead, the SDLT legislation assumes that under the principles of equity and trust law the interest of a beneficiary is an interest in the underlying trust property. Does the beneficiary merely have a right *in personam* against the trustee to see that the trust is administered properly or does he have a right *in rem* or a proprietary interest as owner of the beneficial interest? It seems that English law had not been capable of supplying a conclusive answer to this question and had been content to adopt a pragmatic approach to the issue, usually in tax cases where the language of the statute determined the answer (see Hanbury and Martin, *Modern Equity* 19th edn, at 1-019, which suggests that the interest of a beneficiary may actually be *sui generis*, and see *Baker v Archer-Shee* [1927] AC 844 and *Archer-Shee v Garland* [1931] AC 212). There was a series of cases in which the courts had to decide whether a beneficiary under a trust for sale of land had an interest in land for the purposes of a particular statute and the courts have held that an interest in land existed (see Megarry & Wade, *The Law of Real Property* 8th edn, at 10-032 and the cases referred to in footnote 142 at p 409). The Trusts of Land and Appointment of Trustees Act 1996, however, puts the matter beyond doubt by referring to a beneficiary who is 'beneficially entitled to an interest in possession in land subject to the trust': see for example ss 9, 11 and 12. In SDLT a 'chargeable interest' is defined in FA 2003, s 48(1)(a) to include an interest, right or power in or over land in the UK and therefore it seems that for SDLT purposes the life tenant of a trust formed under English law has an equitable interest in the trust property. The purchase of a life interest in possession, or an interest in an accumulation and maintenance trust, or a reversionary interest in a trust formed under English law whose assets include land in the UK will be a land transaction for SDLT purposes (as will be the purchase of an equivalent type of interest under a Scots or foreign trust (FA 2003, Sch 16, para 2)). However, a discretionary beneficiary does not have an equitable interest or any other interest in the assets of the trust under English law and so the interest of such a person is not a 'chargeable interest' for SDLT (see for example, Hanbury and Martin, *Modern Equity* 19th edn, at 8-015 and see *Baker v Archer-Shee* [1927] AC 844 and *Archer-Shee v Garland* [1931] AC 212).

Where an equitable interest in a trust holding land in the UK is acquired by the exercise of a power of appointment or the exercise of a discretion vested in the trustees, any consideration given for the exercise is treated as chargeable consideration for SDLT purposes. During the debates on the Finance Bill 2003, the Chief Secretary to the Treasury declined to give an assurance that the exercise of a power of appointment or the surrender of a life interest to a remainderman for no consideration did not give rise to stamp duty or SDLT (HC Official Report, Standing Committee B, Tuesday 3 June 2003, cols 344 and 345). See **16.64** and FA 2003, s 106 for the rules governing persons acting in a representative capacity. See also **16.20** above.

It is specifically provided that where the trustees of a settlement reallocate trust property in such a way that a beneficiary acquires an interest in certain trust property and ceases to have an interest in other trust property and the beneficiary consents, the fact that he consents does not mean that there is chargeable consideration for his acquisition.

HMRC treat the trustees settlement as a single and continuing body of persons and do not regard a change of trustees as a land transaction. No SDLT return is therefore required and no tax arises even when the trust property is subject to a mortgage: see HMRC SDLT Manual at 31745.

Sub-sales etc

[16.72] Stamp duty land tax does not contain any general equivalent of stamp duty sub-sale relief under Stamp Act 1891, s 58(4). Instead, the statutory rules in force from the inception of SDLT until 16 July 2013 provided that where there is an assignment, sub-sale or other transaction relating to a contract for a land transaction that is to be completed by a conveyance ('the original contract') the assignee or sub-purchaser is treated as the purchaser under a hypothetical contract (called the 'secondary contract') and the chargeable consideration for the secondary contract is that which remains to be paid by the assignee or sub-purchaser under the original contract (or by a person connected with him) if any, plus any consideration given to the original purchaser for the assignment or sub-sale.

Completion of the original contract could, in appropriate circumstances, be disregarded. That disregard provided a tax advantage in a range of circumstances, some of which were regarded by HMRC as appropriate. But there were many circumstances where the overall result was that little or no tax was chargeable under either the original or the hypothetical contract and numerous changes were made to the statute to counter what were regarded as avoidance schemes. Uncertainties about the meaning of the statute were, if anything, compounded rather than clarified by the changes and cases were slow to come to Court. Schemes to reduce or eliminate SDLT on residential transactions continued to be marketed on a large scale and the Government announced in Budget 2012 that it would review these rules with the aim of modifying the rules so as to discourage even the marketing and promotion of schemes seeking to use perceived loopholes in this particular area of the SDLT code. Technical consultation followed and FA 2013 amended s 45 and introduced Sch 2A into FA 2003 which contains an additional 14 pages of legislation comprising a re-write of the rules in a very different form – with a relief rather than a disregard though still with deemed transactions. Section 45A of FA 2003, which applies in limited circumstances and contains a variant of the old rules, remains unamended – on the basis that it did not seem to have caused the difficulties and disagreements about its proper construction that applied to s 45. Unfortunately (for those advising on transactions from 13 July 2013 onwards) it is necessary to understand something of what happened under the old rules in order to follow the new ones. Before describing the detailed operation of the rules some general points should be noted.

It is vital to a correct understanding and application of SDLT and the various reliefs and exemptions to appreciate that the sub-sale provisions substitute a notional land transaction for one or both of the actual land transactions which are taking place for all SDLT purposes. This was also true in the old rules regardless of whether or not what was often mistakenly referred to as the 'sub-sale relief' applies because the original actual land transaction has been substantially performed or completed at the same time as the subsequent actual transaction. This means for example that when one is required by other provisions of the SDLT code to compare the sub-sale transaction with a further notional transaction under FA 2003, s 75A or to see whether a tax advantage has been obtained, it is the notional transaction arising under the sub-sale provisions that should be taken as the base transaction for comparison with the further notional transaction and not the actual land transactions. The reason for this should be apparent from the analysis below.

The application of the SDLT sub-sale rules to complex property transactions often requires the adviser to re-visit the basic rules of English law about how and when the beneficial and equitable interests in land pass under a sale transaction particularly where there are multiple parties in a chain. Perhaps surprisingly, experience shows that there is scope for disagreement between advisers about the operation and effect of these rules. This lack of certainty arises because the rules are largely judge-made and are often interpreted in difficult cases where policy reasons may influence with the judges' process of reasoning. In *Jerome v Kelly* [2004] STC 887 at 896 Lord Walker suggested that the movement of the beneficial and equitable interests proceeds in stages and on the basis of certain assumptions as to the availability of specific performance (which is a discretionary remedy) and that the contract will eventually be completed. Scots lawyers do not need to address this issue because of the strict division in Scots law between personal and real rights and have a system under which ownership in rem only passes at registration: see *Burnett's Trustee v Grainger* [2004] UKHL 8, [2004] 11 ECGS 139.

Terminology and transaction types

[16.73] While it is common parlance to refer to the rules in FA 2003, s 45 as the sub-sale rules, this is over-restrictive. The old version of s 45 related to 'transfers of rights' but in fact the definition was widened to include sub-sales as well as assignments of rights and some other transactions. The new rules have been re-labelled as referring to 'Transactions entered into before completion of contract' and Sch 2A defines the term 'pre-completion transaction' in order to determine its scope.

A sub-sale is where A contracts to sell land to B who then contracts to sell the land to C before completion of the A to B contract. There will be two separate sale contracts being that between A and B and that between B and C. Completion can occur by separate conveyances of the legal estate from A to B and B to C or by a single conveyance by A to C at the direction of B. In the latter case B will never be registered at the Land Registry. It is helpful if the A to B sale contract does not prohibit a sub-sale and permits B to direct A as to whom the conveyance is made. This ensures that the equitable interest (but not necessarily the beneficial interest) in the property passes to C during the contract period. It may be however, that the vendor, A, insists on the inclusion of Standard Condition 1.5 (5th edition) (or Standard Commercial Property Condition (2nd edition) 1.5) in his contract. Both these conditions provide that the buyer is not entitled to transfer the benefit of the contract and also that the seller cannot be required to transfer the property to any person other than the buyer. These conditions therefore prevent a conveyance from A to C without the agreement of B. Previous editions of the Standard Conditions merely provided that: 'The buyer is not entitled to transfer the benefit of the contract'. It was held that this previous provision did not prevent a purchaser from requiring the vendor to transfer the property on completion to a third party of his choosing because sub-sales were not excluded and so the general position at common law applied and this permitted a sub-sale unless expressly excluded (*Pittack v Naviede* [2010] EWHC 1509 (Ch), [2010] 26 EG 91 (CS), [2010] All ER (D) 206 (Jun)).

In contrast with a sub-sale, an assignment occurs when B transfers the benefit of his contract with A to C. Under English law the assignment does not also transfer the burdens of the contract between A and B and thus the mutual obligations between A and B remain. The original sale contract remains in existence. The contract of assignment between B and C would itself normally amount to a 'chargeable interest' for SDLT purposes because it is a contract carrying the benefit of A's obligation to convey the land in accordance with the terms of the A to B contract. However the operation of the relevant SDLT rules explained below means that this contract is ignored and replaced by what the legislation calls the 'secondary contract'.

A novation is different from a sub-sale or an assignment and occurs when A, B and C agree that C should stand in the place of B with the result that the A to B contract is extinguished and replaced by a new contract between A and C. A novation does not assign a right or obligation but it extinguishes one contract and replaces it with a new contract.

It can be a matter of some difficulty to chart the precise movement of the equitable and beneficial interests in the underlying land under each of the above arrangements. However, for SDLT purposes this will not normally be of direct relevance because of the concept of the 'effective date'. This concept determines when SDLT becomes chargeable and this will either be when there is 'substantial performance' if that occurs before completion or completion itself if there has been no prior substantial performance. Hence what matters for SDLT is not whether the equitable or beneficial interests have passed as a matter of land law but whether the statutory test that the buyer has taken possession or paid 90% or more of the price is satisfied or completion has taken place.

The reason for looking at assignment and novation in addition to sub-sales is that the old SDLT rules lumped all these concepts together in a 'one size fits all' approach which in part was responsible for the confusion surrounding the operation of the SDLT rules. The new rules also cover a range of transactions but, albeit by substantially increasing the length of the provision, assignments of rights and sub-sales are handled by separate paragraphs so the language is much less confusing. It is noteworthy that the equivalent stamp duty relief did not attempt such an ambitious feat and concentrated only on sub-sales, leaving assignments and novations to be dealt with under general stamp duty principles. This meant for instance that in stamp duty on an assignment there was a double charge on the deposit element of the original contract (once when C reimbursed B and again when C took the conveyance for a consideration that included the amount of the deposit). Under SDLT this double charge on the deposit element of an assignment is removed. It is by no means clear that this difference in the tax treatment of the deposit was appreciated by the draftsman of the legislation or those instructing him.

The old sub-sale rules

[16.74] The SDLT rules relating to sub-sales (and assignments and novations) were contained in FA 2003, ss 45 and 45A. These provisions were limited when compared with the old stamp duty relief because the SDLT version did not permit the original or intermediate buyer to 'substantially perform' their contracts prior to 'substantial performance' by the end buyer and still come within the rule disregarding the first sale. In other words, there was a simple rule that if the 'substantial performance' or completion of the A to B contract was postponed until the 'substantial performance' or completion of the B to C contract and occurred at the same time, then the 'substantial performance' or completion of the A to B contract 'shall be disregarded'. The phrase 'at the same time', which is also relevant to the new rules, is interpreted by the Stamp Taxes Office as meaning 'in the same completion meeting' and they do not take the point that arguably there may be a scintilla temporis between the substantial performance or completion of the first contract and the second in order to deny the operation of the rule. It is not material whether one or two transfers are executed, ie A to C or A to B and B to C. The result is that SDLT is not chargeable in relation to the A to B contract and conveyance. Under stamp duty a buyer could 'rest on contract' indefinitely having paid the full price to the seller and never pay stamp duty whereas under SDLT this is not possible except perhaps perversely, and no doubt unintentionally, where the general statutory anti-avoidance rule in FA 2003, s 75A applies. A curious and surely unanticipated result of the SDLT version of the relief is that the property speculator buying 'off-plan' who flips the property onto an investor at a marked-up price will not pay SDLT but a developer who acquires a site, builds homes on it and sells the homes on to families will pay SDLT. It is noteworthy however that the SDLT relief does not contain a requirement present in the stamp duty relief that the price paid under the sub-sale contract that the chargeable consideration moving from the sub-purchaser (C) should not be less than the value of the property.

The drafting of FA 2003, s 45 was unnecessarily complex and created the appearance that those instructing the draftsman were unsure of the manner in which sub-sales, assignments and novations operate. However it is clear that the draftsman was hoping not to provide any scope for exploitation of the sub-sale rule by tax planners in the manner in which sub-sale relief in stamp duty had effectively made it a matter of choice as to whether one paid the duty or not. The old sub-sale rule was embodied principally in FA 2003, s 45(3). In short the rule applied where:

- there was a contract between A and B for the sale of land which is to be completed by a conveyance;
- there was an assignment, sub-sale or 'other transaction' other than the grant or assignment of an option (referred to as a 'transfer of rights' in the legislation) as a result of which C became entitled to call for the conveyance of the land to him (other than when the assignment of an agreement for lease rule applied — as to which see below and FA 2003, Sch 17A, para 12B); and
- the substantial performance or completion of the A to B contract occurred at the same time as, and in connection with, the substantial performance or completion of the B to C contract.

In such cases the substantial performance or completion of the A to B contract was to be 'disregarded' for SDLT, ie B escaped a charge and was not required to file a return except where the secondary contract was itself exempt from tax under the exemptions for alternative property finance arrangements in FA 2003, ss 71A–73.

Weaknesses in the old rules

[16.75] If A, B and C were independent parties (or acted as such) then C having to file on the basis of the total consideration he had provided gave a reasonable result since he would be paying market consideration and would generally pay a full amount of SDLT. He might have been able to claim a relief – for example had he been a charity. Either way, the fact that B was treated as never owning an interest in the land for SDLT purposes, so that his acquisition was disregarded and he paid no tax, did not invalidate the reasonableness of the overall result since C's acquisition on an arm's-length basis was treated in the normal way.

What HMRC found offensive were various schemes where A was independent of B and C but B and C were under the same economic control. A tax advantage was obtained such that B's arm's length transaction was disregarded and either a relief applied to the transaction between B and C or there was no or minimal consideration paid by C. This meant that SDLT was avoided if the circumstances provided that the secondary contract was covered by a relief or was for little or no chargeable consideration.

While changes to s 45 sought to block specific arrangements and s 75A also had an impact, the following uncertainties meant that disagreements with HMRC continued about the SDLT analysis:

• The identity of the seller for the deemed secondary contract was unclear and this affected the availability of some reliefs and the application of the partnership rules. In *DV3 RS Ltd Partnership v Revenue and Customs Comrs* [2013] EWCA Civ 907, (2013) Times, 30 September, [2013] SWTI 2570 the Court of Appeal ruled that on a sub-sale into a partnership, the first purchaser did not enter into a land transaction for SDLT purposes due to the disregard of the completion of the original contract and so could not be considered to be the seller under the notional secondary contract. This meant that the partnership could not rely on the exemption for transfers by a partner into the partnership under FA 2003, Sch 15, para 10. In effect the seller was the original seller.

• The amount of consideration for the secondary contract was unclear in some cases where B was connected with C and was providing consideration. See *Vardy Properties v Revenue and Customs Comrs* [2012] UKFTT 564 (TC), SFTD 1398 at 1418 where the First-Tier Tribunal held obiter that the £7.25m purchase price paid by B to A and funded by C was to be regarded as consideration for the secondary contract under FA 2003, s 45(3)(b)(i) ie the consideration was given indirectly by C. This reasoning was followed but apparently without any argument from the taxpayer by the First-tier Tribunal in *Crest Nicholson (Wainscott) v HMRC* [2017] SFTD 451 at [190].

• The scope of the definition of transfers of rights, while wide, could be unclear at the margins.

• The scope of the key phrase 'involved in connection with' in relation to scheme transactions in s 75A could be disputed. See *Project Blue Limited v HMRC* [2013] UKFTT 378 (TC) where the First-Tier Tribunal held that the word 'involved' qualified the phrase 'in connection with' and denoted some form of participation by A and required more than a sequential 'but for' connection: see paras 250 and 253 of the judgment and the Upper Tribunal in its decision on appeal did not dispute this analysis: [2014] UKUT 0564 (TCC), [2015] STC 745. The Court of Appeal in its decision at [2016] EWCA Civ 485 did not deal with this point but affirmed its analysis in *HMRC v DV3 Ltd* that the first purchaser was disregarded for all purposes so that the sub-purchaser in that case could not claim the exemption for Sharia financing in FA 2003, s 71A because its vendor was the original vendor and not the intermediate party.

The new rules in Sch 2A

[16.76] HMRC published a consultation document 'High-risk areas of the tax code: The Stamp Duty Land Tax "transfer of rights" or "sub-sale" rules' on 17 July 2012. A number of consultation meetings were held as well as written representations being invited. The policy brief that officials had from Treasury ministers was made very clear and was not itself subject to consultation. Almost certainly largely as a result of this policy clarity, the consultation itself was conducted without the levels of emotional tension and acrimony that have typified some of the earlier consultations on SDLT and other tax areas. The resulting legislation contains numerous improvements as a result of the consultation – albeit that brevity, sadly, did not prove to be deliverable.

The new rules seek to combat avoidance by a combination of overlapping measures:

- a wide definition of a 'pre-completion transaction' with a rule to prevent the amount of consideration from being too low on C's transaction;
- a mandatory notification for B's transaction (in the case of an assignment or sub-sale) requiring him to claim a relief where appropriate; and
- denial of relief for B where there are tax-avoidance arrangements.

Guidance by HMRC is in the SDLT manual at SDLTM 21500–21700.

It falls within a solicitor's retainer in a property transaction to calculate the SDLT accurately and a failure to advise the client on the availability of a claim for sub-sale relief will normally be viewed by the courts as negligent: *Mansion Estates Ltd v Hayre & Co* [2016] EWHC 92 (Ch).

Pre-completion transactions

[16.77] Pre-completion transactions are defined in FA 2003, Sch 2A, para 1. Their main features are:

(1) there is a contract ('the original contract') under which 'the original purchaser' is to acquire a chargeable interest and the contract is to be completed by a conveyance; and

(2) a 'pre-completion' transaction occurs such that a person other than the original purchaser (the 'transferee') becomes entitled to call for a conveyance of some or all of the subject matter of the contract; but:
   - the transaction is not the grant or assignment of an option; and
   - it may or may not discharge the original contract (so it could be a novation); and
   - it is not an assignment of an agreement for a new lease (see below in this section for the rules in paras 12A and 12B of FA 2003, Sch 17A).

There are then two sets of rules depending on whether there is an 'assignment of rights' (which is the case if the rights acquired are those under the original contract – para 2) or a 'free-standing transfer' (all other cases). This is helpful compared with the old rules which combined the two equivalent situations with some resulting confusion in terminology. Just as the purchaser under FA 2003, s 44 is not regarded as entering into a land transaction purely by reason of the contract, para 3 prevents the transferee from entering into a land transaction purely by entering into the pre-completion transaction.

Assignment of rights

[16.78] Let us assume that A agrees to sell land to B (the original purchaser) and then, before B has substantially performed that original contract, he agrees to assign his rights under that contract to C (the transferee). B is therefore the 'transferor' under the assignment contract which is a pre-completion transaction. Para 4 gives the rules about completion and consideration in relation to C. Substantial performance or completion of the original contract by C is taken to trigger a land transaction with C as the purchaser. The vendor for this deemed transaction is determined by para 8 and is generally the original vendor (A) (though this general rule is modified, for example, where the original contract was substantially performed before C became entitled to call for a conveyance). Identifying the vendor is required to test the availability of some reliefs. The consideration for C's land transaction is specified in sub-para 4(5) as the sum of the consideration given under the original contract and the consideration given for the assignment of rights but without any double counting of amounts of consideration. This should ensure, for example, that a payment of deposit by B under the original contract does not get counted again as a payment by C to B in the form of some or all of the price of the assignment. The explicit identification of the vendor and the rule against double counting are improvements compared with the old rule.

In a case where B and C are connected with each other (per CTA 2010, s 1122) or are not acting at arm's length, the minimum consideration rule of paras 12–14 applies. This provides that a higher consideration may apply to C's transaction. The two 'minimum amounts' which are to be calculated are generally the amount due under the original contract and the sum of the net amounts given by the parties. The maximum of the three calculated values is used for the SDLT calculation. Note that the three amounts are based on actual amounts of consideration applying to the elements of the arrangements. The consideration rule therefore respects the fact that market valuations (with the possibility of disputes about the valuation) are not generally required for compliance with the SDLT rules. But market value may be relevant if there is an element of exchange of land for land or if the purchaser is a company connected with the purchaser.

Paragraph 5 deems there to be a notional land transaction with B as the purchaser even though the assignment of rights means that B does not acquire land (other than the rights he acquired by having an unconditional contract to acquire land which were not regarded as a land transaction under s 44(2)). The consideration for this notional transaction is taken to be the total amount given (directly or indirectly) under the original contract by B or by C or by persons connected with them. The vendor for the notional transaction is generally the vendor under the original contract (A). The effective date for this transaction is the same as the effective date under the transferee's (ie C's) transaction. See below for the circumstances under which B can claim relief for his transaction. This is a key and onerous change and is in stark contrast to the disregard B obtained under the old rules.

Paragraph 6 provides for repayments of tax in the case of rescission, etc, of contracts and para 7 provides for assignments relating only to part of the subject-matter of the contract.

Free-standing transfers

[16.79] Paragraph 9 defines substantial performance for a free-standing transfer as an action that would be the taking possession of the whole or substantially the whole of the subject matter of the original contract if carried out by the original purchaser. It also deems consideration for the free-standing transfer to be part of the consideration for the transferee's (ie C's) acquisition of the subject matter of the free-standing transfer. The vendor for C's transaction is again generally the original vendor and the paras 12–14 minimum consideration rule applies where B and C are connected or do not act at arm's length.

If B completes the original contract then he has a land transaction when that contract is substantially performed or completed. (In this case there is no need to deem a notional contract for him since he remains within the terms of FA 2003, s 44.) In the case of a sub-sale B does complete his contract with A. However, in the case of some free-standing transfers there is no land transaction for B, for example where the original contract is novated, and in these cases he has no SDLT or notification obligation and only C needs to take account of the new rules.

Relief for the original purchaser

[16.80] Paragraphs 15–17 provide relief for B under certain conditions. Paragraph 15 gives a relief to B where there is an assignment of rights (provided that he claims it) except where C's transaction obtains relief under the alternative property finance reliefs. Paragraphs 16 and 17 provide a relief for pre-completion transactions which are 'qualifying sub-sales' including successive sub-sales provided that the original contract and the sub-sale are completed or substantially performed at the same time as, and in connection with each other. HMRC guidance accepts that where there are two conveyances for a sub-sale they can be taken as being completed at the same time if both completions occur in the same completion meeting and nothing happens in-between the completions. Nevertheless it is prudent for the sub-sale legal documents and completion agenda to provide explicitly for simultaneity and for a contemporaneous record to be made that the transactions were carried out as intended. The rules provide for chains of pre-completion transactions and for the subject matter of those transactions to be only part of the subject matter of the original contract.

Paragraph 18 is the sting in the tail and blocks relief if there are tax-avoidance arrangements (which is to say that a tax advantage is a main purpose) and states that the minimum consideration rule does not affect the breadth of application of ss 75A–75C.

In most practical cases, applying these lengthy statutory provisions may not pose much difficulty. C, who acquires the land, will for the most part be paying SDLT on the basis of the total consideration that he pays to B or A. If B is connected with C (or has some reason not to act at arm's length) then the minimum consideration rule will apply – most likely to the amount received by A. The new burden, however, will be the need for B to file a return to claim relief (where it applies). This was not needed under the old rules and it opens up B to the unwelcome possibility and cost of handling an HMRC enquiry relating to his return.

Paragraph 19 allows for the Treasury to make regulations so that categories of purchasers or transactions are exempted from notification requirements or the need to claim relief or from having a deemed transaction. If it can be demonstrated that categories of straightforward transactions are being faced with unreasonable compliance obligations then it may be possible to persuade the Treasury to use this power.

The following two examples illustrate straightforward situations where the relief might be claimed.

Example 7: Simple assignment of rights

(1)   A enters into a sale and purchase contract with B to buy non-residential land for a price of £1.2m. VAT does not apply. B does not take possession of the land or otherwise substantially perform the contract.

(2)   B assigns its rights under the contract to C (who is not connected with B) for a payment of £120,000. B's contract with A provides for the possibility of such an assignment in which case A becomes obliged to complete by transfer to the assignee.

(3)   C completes the contract by paying A £1.2m and A conveys the land to C.

Step 2 is a pre-completion transaction and is classified as an assignment of rights. The original contract is the one between A and B in Step 1. B is the original purchaser and also the transferor; and C is the transferee.

C's completion of the original contract triggers a land transaction with A as vendor and C as purchaser under para 4. The chargeable consideration is the sum of the £1.2m given to A and the £120,000 given to B. So C is liable to pay £52,800 SDLT.

B's position is determined by para 5. B has a notional transaction with consideration of £1.2 m since this is the amount paid under the original contract (albeit by C). The effective date of this transaction is the same as for C's transaction. On the basis that there are no tax avoidance arrangements, and the fact that C is paying SDLT on a normal basis is helpful evidence to this effect, B should be able to claim relief.

Example 8: Subsale and minimum consideration rule

(1)   A enters into a sale and purchase contract with B to buy non-residential land for a price of £1.2m. VAT does not apply. B does not take possession of the land or otherwise substantially perform the contract.

(2)   Times are hard. B's bank will not advance the loan it had previously agreed. C (who is not connected with B) can get finance for a purchase and offers to buy the property from B for £1m. B decides that accepting this offer will minimise his loss.

(3)   B arranges that the two contracts are completed at the same time – the various signed documents being held in escrow such that the completion of the A to B contract by conveyance triggers the simultaneous completion of the B to C contract by its own conveyance. C pays £1m to B and B pays £1.2m to A making a net loss of £200,000.

This is a pre-completion transaction and, since it is not an assignment of rights, it is a free-standing transfer and para 9 applies. As such it is a qualifying sub-sale under para 16 and B can claim relief (on the basis that there are no tax-avoidance arrangements). B would be paying SDLT on consideration of £1.2m were it not for the relief.

C's acquisition falls within FA 2003, s 44(3) and the chargeable consideration is, in the first place, the consideration of £1m given for the sub-sale. If B and C were either connected or not acting at arm's length then the minimum consideration rule of para 12 would increase C's chargeable consideration to £1.2m (since, for example, the first minimum amount is the £1.2m paid to A under the original contract). However, on the stated facts this rule does not apply and C pays SDLT of £40,000.

The SDLT manual (from SDLTM21590) contains a number of examples which illustrate the application of the rules in situations including the two examples above.

Land registration

[16.81] Both B and C will receive certificates when they file their returns. C will need to register the land so it could be of concern to him, in a case where his conveyance is from B, if B did not get a certificate quickly or did not provide it to him so that the full story could be explained to the Land Registry at the time he wished to register. This might particularly be an issue where a sub-sale was implemented by two conveyances – one from A to B and another from B to C. It is understood that guidance will be given to Land Registries that they should accept C's registration without B's certificate where C explains the nature of the transaction.

The HMRC guidance document states the following:

'2.21 If B does not wish to register its interest in the land, C will need to produce C's SDLT5, its application for registration and the transfers from A to B and B to C. With its application for registration, C should also either:

(i)   confirm in writing that B acquired the land from A and transferred it to C in pursuance of a "free-standing transfer" for the purposes of Schedule 2A to the Finance Act 2003, or

(ii)   produce written confirmation from B (or B's agent) that B acquired the land from A and transferred it to C in pursuance of a "free-standing transfer" for the purposes of Schedule 2A to the Finance Act 2003.'

Assignment of an agreement for lease

[16.82] Where a person assigns his interest as lessee under an agreement for a lease, the pre-completion transaction/sub-sale rule does not apply. If the assignment occurs before the agreement is substantially performed, the agreement is treated as if it were with the assignee and the consideration given includes any given by the assignee for the assignment and there is no notional transaction for the assignee to notify. If the assignment occurs after substantial performance then a 'notional lease' is treated as granted and the assignment is a separate land transaction (FA 2003, Sch 17A, paras 12A and 12B).

Exchanges

[16.83] Where there is an exchange of chargeable interests each leg of the exchange is treated for stamp duty land tax as a separate land transaction (and see **16.38**). Each such transaction is charged to SDLT separately from the other and the 'single-sale' route previously available under stamp duty is not available in SDLT. If either leg of an exchange involves a 'major interest' in land then the chargeable consideration for each acquisition is:

(1)   the market value of the interest acquired plus any rent payable if the acquisition is the grant of a lease; or if the greater,

(2)   the actual chargeable consideration given for the acquisition (FA 2003, Sch 4, para 5(3) and (3A) and see FA 2003, s 117 for the definition of a 'major interest' being broadly a freehold or leasehold interest).

Prior to 24 March 2011 the chargeable consideration was taken to be only the market value of the interest acquired (plus any rent payable if the acquisition was the grant of a lease). By charging SDLT on the actual chargeable consideration if greater than the market value of the interest acquired, the legislation has created a potentially harsh regime that would for example tax a grandparent who exchanges a £1m home with her grandson for his £300,000 flat, on the £1m of actual consideration she gives rather than on the £300,000 value of the interest she receives (with the grandson paying tax on the £1m market value of what he receives). It is understood that this type of consequence was not intended by HMRC. Consequently HMRC may be willing to ameliorate this harshness by arguably bending the just and reasonable apportionment rules in FA 2003, Sch 4, para 4 by treating £700,000 of the £1m consideration given by the grandmother being the excess over the value of the £300,000 flat received by her as a gift from her and as such not taxable consideration. This treatment appears to be concessionary and not supported by the relevant legislative wording.

In a sale and leaseback the interest sold is treated as encumbered by the obligation to grant the leaseback. Hence the market value of the interest sold to the person granting the leaseback could be less than the value of the lease granted in return so that the tax charge should be on the higher value of the leaseback. However, HMRC do not seem to pursue this consequence particularly where the value of the interest sold is purely nominal after taking into account the value of the leaseback. For example where a developer sells the freehold interest in a block of flats worth £5m to a company subject to the company granting 999-year leases back to the developer at a nominal rent, the company should pay tax on the value of the leasebacks which will be approximate to the value of the freehold. However, HMRC are apparently willing to overlook this consequence of the exchange rule and treat the company as giving only nominal consideration for its freehold acquisition.

Special situations **[16.83]**

In an exchange where cash equality money is paid HMRC seem willing to allow the person who gives the higher value property and receives the lower value property plus a cash equality payment in exchange as having given only the value of the property acquired by him with the market value of the property given by him apportioned between the market value of the property acquired (taxable) and the cash equality sum (not taxable). For example, where A and B exchange their properties valued at £375,000 and £400,000 respectively so that A also gives B cash equality of £25,000, A pays tax on the £400,000 value of the property he receives. However, HMRC appear to be open to B paying tax not on the £400,000 value of the consideration he has given to B (the correct result) but only on the £375,000 value of the property he receives with the £25,000 apportioned to the (non-taxable) cash equality sum. It appears that having imposed a change to the exchange rules in FA 2011 which creates a harsher regime for exchanges, HMRC are concerned to ameliorate those consequences on a discretionary basis in situations where as sole arbiter they decide that no tax avoidance is involved. Arguably this concessionary treatment is unlawful under the decision in R *(on the application of Wilkinson) v IRC* [2006] STC 270. However, despite the uncertainty that this creates, few if any taxpayers will challenge being untaxed by concession.

With regard to VAT the chargeable consideration actually given for the exchange will include any VAT actually chargeable under general principles. This is in contrast to HMRC's practice in SDLT of regarding the market value (as distinct from the chargeable consideration given) as not including any VAT chargeable even if VAT is chargeable on the transfer of the asset.

Where neither leg of an exchange involves a 'major interest' in land, SDLT is charged on each acquisition to the extent that any chargeable consideration is given for the acquisition separate from the interest given for the acquisition, ie only on the equality money or equivalent. Where a house building company or a property trader acquires a dwelling from an individual in exchange for a new dwelling supplied to the individual, the acquisition by the company is treated as if it were for nil chargeable consideration if the conditions in FA 2003, Sch 6A, para 1 are satisfied.

Although each leg of an exchange is a separate land transaction, it was the view of HMRC Stamp Taxes that they would nevertheless be linked transactions where the parties were connected with each other so that the value of each had to be aggregated in order to ascertain the appropriate rate of SDLT: see **16.23** above. This view was questionable given that under FA 2003, s 47 each leg of the exchange is to be treated '*as if each were separate and distinct from the other*'. It was therefore difficult to understand how they could at the same time form part of '*a single scheme, arrangement or series of transactions between the same vendor and purchaser or, in either case, persons connected with them*', as required for a linked transaction by FA 2003, s 108. Nevertheless, an exchange of chargeable interests between connected persons is now excluded from the linked transaction rule.

Options

[16.84] The acquisition of an option binding the grantor to enter into a land transaction and the acquisition of a right of pre-emption restricting or preventing the grantor from entering into a land transaction (ie a right of first refusal) are each land transactions in their own right for SDLT purposes. They are separate from any land transactions that result from the exercise of the option or right (FA 2003, s 46(1), but see **16.94** for options and rights granted after 16 April 2003 and before 1 December 2003 which are excised on or after the latter date). The effective date of the land transaction is when the option or right is acquired and not when it is exercisable. In the author's view the grant of an option by the purchaser under a contract to acquire a chargeable interest which occurs at the same time as the substantial performance or completion of the purchase contract was an 'other transaction' within the old rules for sub-sales in FA 2003, s 45 prior to the insertion of FA 2003, s 45(1A) which excluded the grant or assignment of an option from the meaning of 'other transaction' with effect from 21 March 2012. And such grants and assignments are not pre-completion transactions under the new rules from 17 July 2013.

Goodwill

[16.85] Taxpayers who check the box at the start of the SDLT4 return to confirm that the land transaction is part of the sale of a business that includes goodwill can normally expect to receive an enquiry letter. That letter will ask whether SDLT was paid on the goodwill element of the amount of the total price identified in the SDLT4 and refer the taxpayer to what is said about goodwill in the HMRC Capital Gains Tax Manual.

If the taxpayer has not paid SDLT on the goodwill, letters will usually be exchanged between the taxpayer's advisers and HMRC debating whether some or all of the price attributable to the goodwill should be included as part of the price of the land and additional SDLT paid accordingly. This debate may also consider whether there is any legal basis for charging SDLT on the goodwill at all. In the author's experience these debates will often be inconclusive and reach an impasse, with HMRC apparently unwilling to call the taxpayer's bluff by taking a case only to lose and the taxpayer feeling that the amounts involved do not justify funding an appeal. There are many of these unsettled cases and in aggregate a considerable amount of tax revenue is at stake.

Apportionment

[16.86] An apportionment of the total price paid for a business that includes land and buildings may be needed for various tax purposes, not just for SDLT. These include calculating the available capital allowances for loose plant and fixtures and for a claim by a company for a deduction for purchased goodwill under CTA 2009, Part 8.

There may be a tension between maximising capital allowances (by arguing that there is little or no goodwill and that the price should be apportioned mainly to the fixtures and chattels but with a consequent increase in the SDLT charge in the case of the fixtures) and maximising the amount apportioned to goodwill for the purpose of a claim under CTA 2009, Part 8 (and also arguing that this goodwill is not part of the land and so does not attract SDLT).

These issues are particularly acute in the case of the sale of businesses as a going concern occupying land and buildings such as pubs and hotels, nursing and residential homes, restaurants, cinemas and petrol stations.

Just and reasonable and fair

[16.87] The business being acquired may include land and fixtures, moveable plant and equipment and other chattels, and intangible assets such as a brand name and goodwill. For capital gains, SDLT and capital allowance purposes any apportionment of the total price must be done on a 'just and reasonable' basis, even if this produces a different apportionment from that agreed in the sale and purchase agreement. In the case of capital allowances an election for an alternative apportionment of the price may also be available under CAA 2001, s 198. In relation to the cost of purchased goodwill this will be based on the difference between the total price paid and the 'fair' value of the identifiable assets and liabilities.

Of course this raises the question what is 'just and reasonable' and 'fair' and ultimately the answer will turn on a valuation. A fundamental question in arriving at a valuation will be whether the value of the land includes any goodwill in the true sense of the term 'goodwill'. It is here where the sands may be shifting and it appears that valuers and, to some extent, HMRC may now be taking a more realistic approach to goodwill and land as being separate things. Such an approach accords with case law.

HMRC's position

[16.88] In attempting to understand HMRC's position the SDLT adviser's first port of call is likely to be the *SDLT Manual*. This currently states at SDLTM 04005:

'SDLTM04005 – Scope: How much is chargeable

Goodwill

Stamp duty land tax is a charge on transactions in "land".

Thus the subject-matter of the charge includes anything forming part of the land as a matter of law, such as buildings and structures forming part of the land, and fixtures.

This means that the subject-matter of the charge may or may not include what is described as goodwill.

In some instances what is described as goodwill actually forms part of the land. This is often described as inherent goodwill because it is inherent in the land.

In other cases goodwill, sometimes called free goodwill, is separate from the land.

There is more guidance on the distinction between inherent goodwill and free goodwill in the *Capital Gains Manual* (external users can find the guidance at http://www.hmrc.gov.uk/manuals/cgmanual/index.htm).

Free goodwill will only be present on the sale of a business or part of a business, but not necessarily even then.'

Issues relating to the categorisation of goodwill, or the valuation of free goodwill where an apportionment is required, should be referred to the Valuation Office Agency.

The exclusion of goodwill from the charge to stamp duty by FA02/S116 does not apply to SDLT.'

HMRC's published guidance on how to fill in box 1 of the SDLT 4, as well as referring to SDLTM04005, also says 'A payment for goodwill that is part of the land is part of the chargeable consideration for Stamp Duty Land Tax purposes. The price paid for this goodwill should be included in the figure shown at Question 10 of the SDLT 1 [ie the total consideration for the purchase] where Code A, F or O has been entered at question 2.'

HMRC's published views on goodwill

[16.89] Goodwill is dealt with in the Capital Gains Manual at CG68000 to CG68330 in a rewritten section of the manual but mainly only in relation to intellectual property.

However, a summary of the old guidance was contained in the old Valuation Office Agency guidance as follows:

Forms of goodwill

[16.90] The Inspector's instructions refer to three forms of goodwill:

'1) Inherent Goodwill

This is the goodwill generated by the location of the property rather than the carrying on of a particular business. It is perhaps wrongly described as goodwill at all because all it really represents is the locational advantages of the property. It may be attracted by the address (for example a hotel in Park Lane). It may occur because of its strategic position (for example the only hotel in town). It is impossible for such goodwill to be sold separately from the property and it will always be reflected in the property value.

2) Personal Goodwill

This is any trade generated by the personality, special skills or reputation of the person conducting the business (for example a restaurant run by an internationally renowned chef). Such goodwill cannot be transferred to another person or occupier of the property and, therefore, cannot form part of the value of the property.

3) Free Goodwill

'This is goodwill created by a business conducted at the property and its value depends on how well that business has been carried on. It is the trade generated by the historical reputation of a business, the personality and skills of the staff and employees, the benefits of existing licences and contracts with suppliers, customers etc. In most types of property "free goodwill" is capable of being sold separately from the property and constitutes a separate asset. However, occasionally such as in some of the specialist types of property mentioned in 2.1. above, most or all of the "free goodwill" is often incapable of being transferred to another property. In such properties "free goodwill" can be sub-divided into two categories, namely:

A) *"Adherent goodwill"* which, although not inherent in the locational advantages of the property, sticks with it (for example this may represent satisfied customers who were not attracted by the personality of the particular person running the business and will continue to patronise the property provided the business continues to be run in a competent manner). As any "adherent goodwill" cannot be sold separately from the property, it does not constitute a separate asset and should be included in the DV's valuation. In practice it may prove difficult to distinguish between "adherent" and "inherent" goodwill. However, DVs should not be too concerned with these definitions but should concentrate on arriving at a valuation reflecting all goodwill attaching to and inseparable from the property.

'B) *"Transferable goodwill"* is any "free goodwill" which is capable of being sold completely independently of the property (for example the benefit of a trade name or a contract to provide a certain number of hotel beds etc). It is capable [of] constituting a separate asset and should not normally be reflected in the DV's valuation of the property.'

The reference in the extract above to 'The Inspector's instructions' is presumably to the old guidance in the Capital Gains Manual and that guidance has been deleted. This change appears to have happened in response to the criticism of the elaborate categorisation of goodwill made by the Special Commissioner in *Balloon Promotions Ltd v Wilson (Inspector of Taxes)* [2006] STC (SCD) 167. HMRC's approach had been to argue that both inherent (or locational) and adherent (or adaptional) goodwill was part of the land and that SDLT should be paid in relation to that part of the total price apportioned to inherent and adherent goodwill as well as in relation to the price apportioned to the land. Although this case concerned capital gains rollover relief, the Special Commissioner preferred to look at goodwill as a whole which can be sold separately from the business premises and questioned whether the value of adherent goodwill would be included in the value of the land and buildings.

The revised guidance on goodwill in the Capital Gains Manual is as noted above given in the context of intellectual property rights, not land. This may be due to the tension between the need for a change of view post-*Balloon Promotions* and the large amounts of tax riding on the currently unsettled outstanding cases.

In summary, the updated guidance in the Capital Gains Manual includes the following statement:

'The term "goodwill" is not defined for the purposes of the CG legislation in TCGA 1992. The leading legal authority on its meaning is found in *IRC v Muller & Co Margarine Ltd* [1901] AC 217 a stamp duty case where in answer to the question "What is goodwill?" Lord MacNaughton said:

It is a thing very easy to describe, very difficult to define. It is the benefit and advantage of the good name, reputation and connection of a business. It is the attractive force which brings in custom. It is the one thing which distinguishes an old-established business from a new business at its first start.

In the same case Lord Lindley said at page 235:

Goodwill regarded as property has no meaning except in connection with some trade, business or calling. In that connection, I understand the term to include whatever adds value to a business by reason of situation, name and reputation, connection, introduction to old customers and agreed absence from competition.

. . .

The decision of the Special Commissioners in *Balloon Promotions Ltd v Wilson* SpC [2006] STC (SCD) 167 provides authority for the fact that for CG purposes goodwill should be construed in accordance with legal rather than accountancy principles.

Goodwill is inseparable from the business in which it is generated and has its existence; see CG 68030. When a business is disposed of as a going concern any goodwill attributable to the business will be transferred to the new proprietor'.

Consequences of HMRC's approach

[16.91] It seems that HMRC is, at least for capital gains purposes, now prepared to accept that the traditional analysis of goodwill, as in the Valuation Office Agency guidance, into three categories is no longer useful and may be misleading. It seems that HMRC now accepts that what has been described historically as 'inherent' and 'adherent' goodwill is not part of the goodwill at all but are simply attributes of the land and buildings concerned and should be reflected in the valuation of them. Goodwill, properly so-called, passes separately from the land with the business and is not part of the land.

Despite this, HMRC Stamp Taxes still regards 'inherent' and 'adherent' goodwill as forming part of the land. SDLT is, in its view, chargeable on a 'just an reasonable' apportionment of the total price of these items. Nevertheless in the author's view it is likely that the 'clarification' of HMRC's view explained above will filter through to HMRC Stamp Taxes in due course and be accepted by it.

Will this approach make any difference?

[16.92] In principle the new approach should make little difference, at least in relation to 'inherent' goodwill. This is because whether the locational advantage of the land is categorised as part of the goodwill and added to the price of the land (the old approach) or simply included in the valuation of the land for apportionment purposes (the new approach) should not alter the total amount of the price apportioned to the land for SDLT purposes. In practice, however, the new approach, by making a clear distinction between goodwill and land as separate assets, may place more of an evidential burden on HMRC in attacking that part of the price expressly apportioned to goodwill in the sale agreement. In other words, in order to challenge an apportionment by the parties HMRC will now have to show that some or all of the price of the goodwill has unjustly and unreasonably been allocated by the parties to the goodwill and should be reallocated to the land. Under the old approach HMRC merely had to try to carry out a reallocation of the total goodwill in favour of the inherent and adherent category in order to secure additional SDLT. Under the new approach HMRC will have to reallocate price from one asset (goodwill) to a separate asset (land). Although in principle independent valuations should resolve the issue, in practice very few such cases ever proceed to litigation and therefore in the cut and thrust of negotiations with HMRC this change of approach may favour the taxpayer.

A further issue concerns 'adherent' goodwill. HMRC Stamp Taxes treats this as part of the value of the land and so taxable but the authority for this is questionable. In the *Balloon Promotions* case the Special Commissioner questioned whether the value of what HMRC regarded as adherent free goodwill would as a matter of course be incorporated in the valuation of the business premises. It is possible that HMRC may not wish to risk a taxpayer challenge on this issue and so taxpayers should assert the doubts created by the Special Commissioners on this point when negotiating open cases with HMRC.

HMRC's Practice Note of 30 January 2009

[16.93] HMRC issued a Practice Note on 30 January 2009 entitled: 'Apportioning the Price Paid for a Business Transferred as a Going Concern'. HMRC's general approach in relation to trade-related properties for capital gains and SDLT purposes is that the value of goodwill and any other separately identifiable assets will usually by represented by the difference between the value of the business as a going concern and the value of the tangible assets such as property and chattels. Has the above position changed as a result of the Practice Note? The answer to this is that it is currently rather difficult to say because the Note appears to have been the subject of some disagreement for the time being. This has come about because of the use made in the Note of valuation material published by the Royal Institution of Chartered Surveyors which could be taken to suggest that the RICS tacitly support the approaches contained in the Note. This is not the case and the RICS have in fact taken issue with various parts of the Note.

Aside from this, what does the Note reveal about HMRC's thinking in relation to goodwill and SDLT? The Practice Note is intended to explain how HMRC intend to apportion the price paid for a property related business as a going concern between goodwill and the other assets included in the sale.

For those completing SDLT returns in relation to the purchase of such businesses the most important aspect of the Practice Note is in paragraph 10.10 where HMRC acknowledge that:

'. . . the subdivisions of goodwill that were previously used are no longer considered helpful as they tend to cause confusion. The view now is that what used to be referred to as "inherent" and "adherent" goodwill are, in reality, attributes which add value to the property in which a business is carried on and they do not represent goodwill at all.'

This indicates that the sands have shifted and that clarity of language is helping to dispel the confusion over whether the locational advantages of a property (so-called inherent goodwill) were really goodwill or just an aspect of the property's value.

However, as suggested above at least two aspects of this change deserve comment. Firstly, tactically this change may assist taxpayers in resisting an attempt by HMRC to assert that a portion of the price which the parties to a sale agreement have apportioned separately to goodwill should be reallocated to the property. Instead of reallocating price within the goodwill categories from say free goodwill to inherent goodwill, HMRC will now have to reallocate from one asset, ie goodwill, to another asset, ie the property, and allege that the arm's length apportionment by the parties is not just and reasonable. At the end of the day this will depend in large part on valuations but in practice this shift in approach may be to the taxpayer's advantage.

Secondly, it is apparent that HMRC are still smarting from the doubts created by the Special Commissioner's decision in *Balloon Promotions Ltd v Wilson (Inspector of Taxes)* [2006] STC (SCD) 167 over whether adherent (adaptional) goodwill should be included in the value of the business premises. They do not appear to be willing to accept this aspect of the decision and seek to distinguish that case on its facts. One wonders, however, whether HMRC would be willing to risk defeat on this point before the courts and taxpayers may well adopt a firm line in negotiations on this with HMRC.

Transitional provisions

Basic rules

[16.94] The provisions of FA 2003 governing the transition from stamp duty on land to stamp duty land tax are confusing and hard to follow. The relevant provisions are contained in FA 2003, s 125 and Schs 15, 19 and 20 and their effect can be summarised as follows.

A transaction is not an SDLT transaction unless:

(1)   'the effective date' of the transaction is on or after 1 December 2003 (FA 2003, Sch 19, para 2(1)); and

(2)   it is pursuant to a contract entered into after 10 July 2003 (FA 2003, Sch 19, para 3(1)) (or it is pursuant to a contract entered into on or before 10 July 2003 if subsequently that contract was varied or assigned, or an option, right of pre-emption or similar right has been exercised or where the purchaser is a person other than the purchaser under that contract because of an assignment, sub-sale or other transaction made after that date (FA 2003, Sch 19, para 3(3)).

The 'effective date' of the transaction is normally the date of completion by conveyance unless the contract is 'substantially performed' before completion, when the effective date is when the contract is substantially performed (FA 2003, s 44). However, in the transitional provisions 'effective date' has an extended meaning. Where 2 above applies and the contract is substantially performed after 10 July 2003, but before 1 December 2003 and is not completed until on or after the latter date, the effective date of the transaction is the date of completion (regardless of the fact that substantial performance occurred before 1 December 2003) (FA 2003, Sch 19, para 4).

From 1 December 2003 ('the implementation date': to be appointed by Treasury order under FA 2003, Sch 19, para (2)(2)) stamp duty is chargeable only on:

(1)   instruments relating to stock or marketable securities (this includes shares and non-exempt loan capital) (FA 2003, s 125(1));

(2)   bearer instruments (FA 1999, Sch 15 remains in full force and effect);

(3)   acquisition of partnership interests (FA 2003, s 125(8) and Sch 15, para 13(2)); and

(4)   any dealing in land that is not an 'SDLT transaction' (FA 2003, s 125(5)(b)). (This ensures that stamp duty continues to apply where a contract relating to land was entered into on or before 10 July 2003 (Royal Assent to FA 2003) but was not completed by instrument until on or after 1 December 2003. Under the original terms of clause 125 such instruments would not have been SDLT transactions and stamp duty would not have applied so the transaction would have escaped both SDLT and stamp duty.)

Therefore, contracts that are completed before 1 December 2003 will not be SDLT transactions, and contracts that were entered into on or before 10 July 2003 and have not been varied or novated, sub-sold etc since that date but do not complete until on or after 1 December 2003 will give rise to stamp duty only and not SDLT. Where there is a sub-sale after 10 July 2003 that is not completed until on or after 1 December 2003 and the original contract was substantially performed on or before 10 July 2003 the sub-sale does not make the first contract an SDLT transaction given that the policy is to exclude from SDLT any contract substantially performed on or before 10 July 2003. It is understood that HMRC accept that this is the position. However, where the original contract was not substantially performed on or before 10 July 2003 a sub-sale occurring after that date will cause the original sale to be potentially chargeable with SDLT if it was substantially performed on or after 17 March 2004, because it will be an SDLT transaction as a result of the substitution of FA 2003, Sch 19, para 3(3)(c) by FA 2004, Sch 29, para 12.

Where a transaction chargeable to SDLT is effected pursuant to a contract entered into before 1 December 2003, any ad valorem stamp duty paid on the contract is available as a credit against the SDLT payable (but no refund is available should the stamp duty exceed the SDLT) (FA 2003, Sch 19, para 5(1)).

In relation to the stamping of agreements for lease entered into before 1 December 2003 where the lease is granted on or after that date and the transaction is an SDLT transaction, the protection against interest and penalties under FA 1994, s 240 on the presentation of the agreement for stamping is continued by FA 2003, Sch 19, para 8. If the agreement is presented for stamping together with a Revenue certificate in relation to the grant of the lease then the payment of SDLT (or the fact that no SDLT was payable) on the grant of the lease is to be denoted on the agreement and the agreement shall be deemed to be duly stamped. The lease must be either in conformity with the agreement or relate to substantially the same property and term as the agreement.

Where an option to enter into a land transaction or a right of pre-emption relating to a land transaction was acquired after 16 April 2003 but before 1 December 2003 and exercised on or after the latter date, any consideration given for the grant of the option or right is treated as part of the chargeable consideration for the land transaction resulting from the exercise of the option or right (FA 2003, Sch 19, para 9(1), (2)).

Split title structures

[16.95] Prior to the introduction of SDLT, many properties were acquired and held within what were known as split title structures in order to take advantage of resting on contract and stamp duty sub-sale relief in order to defer the payment of stamp duty indefinitely. Such properties would be registered in the names of two corporate nominees for the beneficial owner. The effect of acquiring the beneficial ownership within such a structure was that any subsequent transfer of the legal title was vulnerable to ad valorem stamp duty on the purchase consideration paid under the purchase contract unless the property was sub-sold within the terms of SA 1891, s 58(4) with the sub-purchaser paying ad valorem duty on his acquisition (unless some relief applied). Following the introduction of SDLT it is often asked whether such structures can be rolled-up and the legal and beneficial ownership reunited in one person or entity without giving rise to a stamp duty charge. What seems clear is that to successfully avoid giving rise to an ad valorem stamp duty charge on all the intermediate uncompleted sale contracts, the transaction under which the legal and the beneficial interests are reunited should be by way of a transaction which satisfies the conditions for sub-sale relief under SA 1891, s 58(4). It may be that some exemption or relief from SDLT on the final sub-sale transaction is available. However it should be noted that SDLT group relief will not be available in such cases because of FA 2003, s 45(5A) which treats the vendor in a sub-sale as the original vendor and not the immediate vendor so that the conditions for group relief to apply will not be met.

Chapter 17

Inheritance tax

by
Chris Erwood,
Erwood & Associates Ltd

Introduction

[17.1] The most significant problems with inheritance tax (IHT) on real property are these:

- it is a 'dry' tax charge, ie one that may arise even though the occasion of that charge generates no cash to fund the tax;
- it can easily affect 'ordinary' people, ie those without significant wealth, or certainly without high net liquid wealth;
- the valuation may not be straightforward and may be expensive; and
- the availability of relief is capricious and now increasingly of doubtful logical basis.

Property owners are much less willing to engage and incur the costs of professional advisers, particularly in the context of administration of family property, where such advisers may charge based on value rather than time spent; but lack of good advice in this area can lead to serious difficulties and result in increased tax liabilities, as will be seen.

IHT on death

Reporting requirements

[17.2] An academic knowledge of IHT must be accompanied by the procedural knowledge of the compliance aspects specifically how and when to report transactions affecting property. IHTA 1984, s 4 treats death as an occasion of transfer and despite the FA 2006 trust reforms which now impact on virtually all lifetime trusts created post-21 March 2006, the majority of IHT charges on property still arise on death. What is measured is the 'estate' at death, meaning (in the first instance):

- what a person actually owns directly ie that is not held in any kind of trust; and
- property, not being trust property, over which the person has power or authority of disposal as he thinks fit.

As a separate matter, the value of any trust fund in which the deceased had a qualifying interest in possession (pre-22 March 2006) or transitional serial interest (TSI) or immediate post-death interest (IPDI)) is aggregated with the personal or 'free' estate (albeit the IHT thereon is born out of the trust fund) and that interest commands a pro rata share of the deceased's nil-rate band.

Use the right form

[17.3] A full discussion of the rules as to excepted estates is outside the scope of this book but reference should be made to the Inheritance Tax (Delivery of Accounts) (Excepted Estates) Regulations 2004 (SI 2004/2543) as amended by Regulations in 2006 (SI 2006/2141) and Inheritance Tax (Delivery of Accounts) (Excepted Estates) (Amendments) Regulations 2011 (SI 2011/214), which identified three categories of excepted estate. Broadly, the first of these categories applies to estates that are small, ie within the IHT thresholds. The second category applies to larger estates, up to £1m, where the net estate passes to an exempt beneficiary such as spouse, civil partner or a charity. The third category applies where the deceased was neither domiciled nor deemed domiciled (as defined) in the UK and the estate is small (as defined).

These regulations have been amended to recognise that the transferable nil-rate band (TNRB) exempts larger estates than hitherto; they recognise the complexity of the TNRB rules by allowing the simpler form (IHT205) to be used but importantly only where the full 100% TNRB is available. Where the first spouse or civil partner to die has used any part of their available nil-rate band, no matter how small, the full form IHT400 (and accompanying schedules) must be completed.

This chapter concerns those estates that fall outside the excepted categories, either because they are large in themselves and chargeable or because, when seen in the context of lifetime giving, the chargeable gift comes from a donor with a substantial estate and is itself over the current limits (as to which see below).

It is important to use the correct form appropriate to the transfer thus IHT400 in respect of transfers on death or IHT100 (with supporting schedules) for lifetime transfers (to include trust cessation/transfers out of trust/relevant property ten-year anniversary charges). Completion of the correct form in the relevant circumstance demonstrates basic competence. The forms are regularly updated – this is partly for legal reasons such as formal changes in the law and partly for administrative reasons such as the need to combat fraud or negligence. An example of the latter is the development of the forms that relate respectively to chattels. HMRC were concerned that there was a risk of under-declaration which whilst perhaps moderate in relation to any one case could be nonetheless widespread. Accordingly, HMRC now require it necessary to supply full details of each vehicle that the deceased owned, giving registration number, condition etc.

HMRC have issued two new forms IHT435 and IHT437 to the IHT 400 series which deal with the 2017/18 introduction of the Residence Nil Rate Band (RNRB) and the Transferable Residence Nil Rate Band (TRNRB). Updated HMRC guidance is also available at IHTM 46001 et seq and the IHT Gross-up calculator has also been amended to reflect the impact of the RNRB.

The use of a slightly out of date form is not fatal, but this does imply that knowledge may not be current and could alert HMRC interest. In recent years form IHT400 has been redrafted to elicit details of residential occupation which may be particularly relevant where the property used to be, but is no longer, owned by the deceased but which was nevertheless still occupied by him, possibly alone, at the date of death: see para **17.4** below.

Completion of the supplementary Sch 405 (House, land, buildings and interests in land) requires detail of the address of the property, its tenure, any lettings or leases, the value of any element in respect of which agricultural relief, business property relief, woodland relief or heritage relief is claimed and the open market value. As will be seen in para **17.4** below, the value for agricultural purposes may be and most often is lower than the open market value. There is space to show whether there is any 'damage' to any of the property that may affect its value, such as structural failure and the form demands declaration of the intention of the personal representatives, or trustees as appropriate, to sell any property within 12 months – that may affect the valuation issues described below.

For some time now HMRC have been producing 'toolkits' intended to assist practitioners to complete returns more accurately than hitherto and there is such a toolkit for IHT: practitioners may gain benefit from its use and, more importantly, if they can prove that they have followed it, they can satisfy HMRC that due care has been shown in completion of the forms. However, it is important to recognise that use of the toolkits remains optional and is not a mandatory requirement.

Valuation issues, both lifetime transfers and on death

[17.4] The value to be shown in form IHT400 is, 'the price which the property might reasonably be expected to fetch if sold in the open market at [the date of death]; but that price shall not be assumed to be reduced on the ground that the whole property is to be placed on the market at one and the same time' (IHTA 1984, s 160). It is important to be aware that contrary to common perception there is no such thing as 'probate value' in the sense of a value that is markedly different (whether higher or lower) than open market value. Specifically, see *Tapp (executor of Robert Ernest Atkinson, dec'd) v Ryder* [2008] RVR 340, Land Trib and *Price (executor of Price, dec'd) v Revenue and Customs Comrs* [2010] UKFTT 474 (TC), where the rules allow no deduction for the anticipated costs of sale. The first of these cases demonstrates the need for a 'proper' and robust valuation rather than an extrapolation from earlier values after refurbishment; the latter concerns arguments as to valuation of a share in property, but also considered sale costs.

Low values

[17.5] The use of an artificially low value has, apart from being totally incorrect, two drawbacks, one short term and one long term. The short-term drawback is quite simply that an account that might otherwise have passed without HMRC enquiry is subjected to more detailed scrutiny, perhaps on the basis that if people are 'pushing the envelope' on valuation issues they may have taken a cavalier attitude to other aspects of compliance.

A still very much pertinent gloss on IHTA 1984, s 160 is found in the judgment of Ungoed-Thomas J in *Re Hayes Will Trust* [1971] 1 WLR 758 at page 768:

> 'It has been established time and time again in these courts, as it was in our case that there is a range of price, in some circumstances wide, which competent valuers would recognise as the price which property would fetch if sold in the open market.

> Neither the section nor [the judgment of] Sankey J [in *Earl of Ellesmere v Inland Revenue Commissioners* [1918] 2 KB 735] requires that the top price of that range should be the price fixed for Estate Duty. That price, together with the lowest price in the range, may be expected to be the least likely price within the range, to be obtained from the open market. The most likely price, in the absence of consultation between valuers representing competing interested, would presumably be the mean price. The habitual well-recognised process for arriving at that price is for the executors to put in the lowest price within the range and then to confer with the District Valuer who acts to safeguard the Revenue.'

However, choosing the lowest price in the range whilst tempting is not good practice and makes it more likely that the account will be selected for HMRC enquiry. It might be more worthwhile for the taxpayer to adopt a less adversarial stance and to put into the account a figure which is nearer the middle or average of the possible range of values. The adoption of a value that cannot be sustained under later HMRC scrutiny may well lead to the imposition of penalties.

The long-term drawback is a particular future risk where probate has been secured on estimated values which are later forgotten in the euphoria of achieving a sale with onward distribution to needy relatives. This is in many respects where the problems start.

'Amateur' valuations and the interaction of IHT and CGT

[17.6] In the common situation of the death of the second spouse whose estate exceeds the nil-rate band and passes to close family chargeable beneficiaries, it is increasingly more likely (mainly driven by cost) for the family to seek to dispense both with the services of a professional advisor and with the formalities of a valuation. This may, at least in regard to the valuation, be false economy. What happens in practice and all too frequently, is that the family approach three estate agents to obtain a figure for probate, each of whom puts forward a figure which is actually not a valuation at all – there is often an underlying but perhaps unspoken directive that the valuation should be low. It is no more than a bid to get the job of selling the house. It is very common for the agent's letter stating the 'valuation' to include a phrase such as 'Asking price £395,000 but for probate put in a figure of £345,000'.

Another long-term reason that it may be false economy not to have a more formal valuation is the burden of Capital Gains Tax (CGT) on later sale of the house by reason of the lower probate value. In the domestic situation, where the lay executors often have no or limited training in tax law, there is a general belief that principal private residence relief shelters the proceeds of sale of the family home from CGT. What is not appreciated is that principal private residence relief under TCGA 1992, s 222 or 225A or, in the case of an ongoing trust, under s 225, is not a blanket or automatic relief and it will only be available where the strict requirements of those legislative provisions are fully satisfied.

In the more straightforward case, where the house stands empty after Granny's death whilst the children (none of whom occupied the house) obtain a grant of probate and agree the division of chattels, principle private residence relief will not be available on later sale even though it was Granny's former home for over 40 years prior to her death. The relief is directly connected to its occupation and use as a home during the estate administration period – its prior use during the lifetime of the deceased is no longer relevant and carries no influences on its later post-death sale. If, as is assumed in this chapter, the estate is taxable and the value of the property has been 'ascertained' for the purposes of IHT, that value so ascertained will be the base value for CGT also: see TCGA 1992, s 274. Thus if that value had been a 'Red Book' valuation, put forward by an experienced valuer, who could back up his opinion with comparisons to other prices achieved in the market at that time, it is likely that the value would hold good for IHT and thus for CGT.

Example 1

At the time of his death on 23 October 2016, Cedric, a widower, was sole owner of 'The Grange' – there was no transferable nil-rate band available and Cedric's own nil-rate band had been fully utilised on lifetime gifts. He was survived by a son and two daughters, one of whom, Alice, practised as a local solicitor and she dealt with the estate. Alice obtained a formal (but inexpensive) valuation of the house from an estate agent colleague who would later be appointed to sell the house. It was detailed: there had been a problem of flooding some time before which may have affected the foundations; and Cedric had long resisted his daughters' suggestion that the kitchen be modernised. The value was assessed at £450,000 and IHT assessed on the estate as a whole.

Alice encountered difficulties with the estate so many months passed before she had all the details she needed to prove the Will so as to be able to sell 'The Grange'.

The family did not mind and they agreed other matters, such as division of the furniture and antiques, they knew that property of this particular type was holding its value if not rising. The Grange was sold to a builder (who was not deterred by its condition) for £525,000 in August 2017, having first been appropriated out of the estate to Alice and her siblings so that the overall gain was allocated as to one third to each of the three beneficiaries. Alice had no difficulty with the Valuation Office: the District Valuer had been given the opportunity of inspecting the Grange back in December 2016, before Alice had the place tidied up, and had agreed the probate value with the estate agent, who had produced evidence of relevant comparables in support of his figure.

This example also illustrates the interaction between IHT and CGT. The marginal rate of IHT is 40% (ignoring the reduced 36% charitable estate rate) which is higher than the rate for CGT on residential property which stands at 18% for basic rate taxpayers and 28% for higher rate taxpayers, all trusts (subject to vulnerable beneficiary election) and estates. Moreover, if the value of property has risen from the date of death to the date of sale and if the value has been fully fixed as described above, the gain realised will not all been taxable. Firstly, for the year of death and the two following years, the executors are entitled to an annual exemption equal to that of an individual (£11,300 for 2017/18). Secondly, in arriving at the net gain arising on the sale by the executors, the latter may claim the benefit of the allowances described in Statement of Practice 2/04. Finally, as was the case in the example above, if the combination of those factors is not sufficient to shelter the potential gain (where the property has not yet been formally sold) the executors could consider whether it is they who should be selling the property or whether they should instead be transferring/assenting it to beneficiaries who may, between them, be able to fragment the gain by relying on TCGA 1992, ss 62 and 64.

The benefit of this form of planning is not easy to quantify if there has not been a proper valuation at the outset. The executors described in the above illustration, faced with a difference between their original guess of the value at, say £350,000 and eventually gross sale proceeds of £390,000 are in a weak position if the District Valuer argues that the value at date of death should be, say, £380,000. Unlike Alice, they simply do not have, and cannot now produce, the evidence to contradict him.

Flooding the market

[17.7] IHTA 1984, s 160 whilst applicable to domestic cases involving a single property is more relevant to landed estates where there are multiple buildings/land plots. Here the valuation has to be upon the basis that the seller would market the property in the way that would produce the best price. That could involve dividing the estate into lots or it could require assembly of various items of land which, taken together, would be more attractive. That issue of assembly raises difficulties where the land is not all owned in the same title, ie where part of it was within the personal estate of the deceased and part was land in which the deceased had a trust interest. The leading case, already referred to, is *Earl of Ellesmere v IRC* [1918] 2 KB 735 and this is still relied upon regularly in practice. In that case, after wide advertisement the estate was sold as a single entity – the purchaser of the estate kept part of the land but then sold the rest on, making a profit of around 19%. This prompted HMRC to challenge the original sale price by assessing estate duty (as then) on a measure of the excess realised. The court eventually reduced the figure to about 11% of the figure achieved on the sale of the estate as a whole.

'Natural units'

[17.8] In another leading and still very relevant case of the *Duke of Buccleuch v IRC* [1967] 1 AC 506 the estate was more complicated. HMRC divided it into 532 separate lots, and on that basis arrived at a valuation of £868,129. Whilst the trustees did not challenge the methodology they considered that after the readily saleable lots had been taken out (approximately 9% of the whole), the remainder should be valued at what an individual buyer would pay expecting a 'turn' of 20% for taking on all of the different parcels in that way. That concept was acceptable to the House of Lords, by comparison with the valuation of the example of a library. It was considered, taking the example suggested by Wynn LJ, that, if a library were graded so as to lot out the best items, the remaining mixed lot would have a lower value:

'Suppose, however, that the Deceased had bought a miscellaneous and mixed lot of surplus stores intending to sort out and arrange them in saleable lots. That might involve a great deal of work, time and expense, and I see no justification for requiring the supposition that that had been done and then valuing the saleable lots that would have emerged.'

It is now accepted professional practice that there should be lotting of a landed estate (a well as other assets ie chattel collections) into what the court described as 'natural units' provided that process does not involve undue expenditure of time or effort. What is less certain is whether the same principles should apply when valuing, on an assets basis, the shares of a private property investment company. The directors will commonly argue that at least part of the portfolio should be valued at a discount because it is less well situated, or undevelopable; and that any purchaser of the company would seek a 'bulk discount'.

Mixed interests

[17.9] As noted above, obvious valuation difficulties arise where land is not all held under the same title. In *Gray (Surviving Executor of Lady Fox) v IRC* [1994] STC 360 the Lands Tribunal had to consider the value of both a parcel of land directly owned by the deceased and the interest of a partnership in the same land. The partnership had an agricultural tenancy of the land owned by Lady Fox but Lady Fox was also entitled to 92.5% of partnership profits. HMRC argued that both the land itself and the partnership share should be valued together, with the vacant possession of the value being discounted – that would result in a much higher value than would apply merely taking the investment value of the land and disregarding the partnership share.

It had been agreed that the vacant possession value of the land was £6,125,000 from which the District Valuer had deducted an estimate of the price that the partners (other than Lady Fox) would take for their share of the tenancy, ie £100,000. It had already been agreed that the tenanted value of the land was £2,751,000, so the District Valuer took 45% of the difference between tenanted value and vacant possession value. He then applied a discount of 7.5% of the vacant possession value to compensate for the risk and delay in obtaining possession of the whole. Adding these interests together he arrived at a value of £5,565,000.

The Tribunal reviewed these figures but were not helped by the fact that there was no better valuation evidence than that of the District Valuer. They thought the discount of 7.5% was on the low side but, for want of evidence, did not dispute it.

It is important to note that the 'precedent' set by this case is still observed in practice today.

The effect of a tenancy on value

[17.10] It is important to appreciate that an asset may carry a value even though in real terms that value may not be capable of realisation. This very point was examined in *Baird's Executors v IRC* [1991] SLT (Lands TR9) which considered the value attributable to a tenancy of an agricultural holding given up by George Baird in favour of his daughter-in-law and grandson. The transfer of the tenancy, which dated back to July 1921, took place in 1977 with the landlord consenting. Mr Baird later died in 1985 and HMRC claimed Capital Transfer Tax (CTT) on that lifetime transfer. The Lands Tribunal had to decide whether the interest of the tenant (George Baird) in these circumstances was capable of valuation.

The Lands Tribunal tried to determine the price which the interest might reasonably be expected to fetch if sold on the open market at the date of transfer, disregarding the fact that the tenancy could not be assigned but assuming that any purchaser would be subject to the same restrictions. The District Valuer, applying these principles, arrived at a valuation figure of 25% of the vacant possession value of the land itself. He considered:

- what a landlord might pay to get the land back;
- what a prospective tenant might accept from a prospective landlord in a sale and leaseback transaction;
- the compensation that is paid to a tenant on compulsory acquisition of agricultural land; and
- rents on equivalent land holdings in the open market on terms similar to the lease in question.

The Valuer said that the value could be as high as 50% of vacant possession value but for the uncertainties of the four factors just described. The Tribunal was satisfied. As a result the right of a tenant in an agricultural lease is an asset that can have a value but that value is not necessarily 25% of the vacant possession value of the land. This process continues to remain good law and is readily employed in practice.

Valuation of shares in land

[17.11] As a general rule, an undivided share of land will be worth less than the appropriate proportion of the entirety but the actual discount will vary according to the circumstances. *Wight v IRC* [1982] 264 EG 935 is authority for the proposition that a discount within the range of 1% to 15% may be allowable for certain residential properties where a view can be taken on how likely it is that the court would exercise its discretion and order a sale at the request of a joint owner.

Charkham v IRC, a decision of the Lands Tribunal, concerned the valuation for IHT purposes of undivided shares in a portfolio of investment properties. The interests had to be valued at various dates and the size of the share of the taxpayer in the portfolio, and thus in the underlying properties, differed from one date to another. The taxpayer had an interest that at best was 24% and at least 6%. For the taxpayer it was argued that it was necessary to look at the income produced by the share in question and with heavy reliance placed on the position of a minority owner who could less easily obtain an order for the sale of the properties than a majority owner which in turn should influence the value.

The Tribunal disagreed, holding that the correct approach was to consider how likely it was that at any given time a minority owner of property might get an order for sale. The size of the minority share was not as important as the purpose for which the property was held and an order for sale was more likely where the purpose of the trust which held the properties had come to an end. The Tribunal held that a purchaser of a minority interest would know that it would be difficult to get an order for sale to realise his investment and for this reason would discount the open market value of the property. It followed that the position would be the same whether the interest purchased was 6% or 24%. What was more important was whether, for example, it was likely that planning permission could be obtained for a property making it more likely that the owners as a group would want to sell. The result of these principles was a discount of 15% in respect of some of the properties and of between 20% and 22.5% on others.

Commonly, in the domestic situation where only one half of the property is in the estate and where the related property rules (see below) do not apply, the parties settle on a discount of 10%. However, the level of discount is very much influenced by the use and occupation of that property as well as the number of co-owners. The valuation principles are especially important in connection with lifetime transfers and the 'loss to the estate' principle. The discount principle is ignored where the interest as a whole is owned by spouses.

Example 2: Gift of a share

Rachel was the owner of an investment property in Canterbury that she wished to give to her son Leonard. The property had risen substantially in value during Rachel's ownership and whilst for IHT purposes a simple outright gift to Leonard would be treated as a potentially exempt transfer (PET) with no immediate IHT exposure, for CGT purposes this would trigger a substantial chargeable gain which Rachel naturally wished to avoid.

Rachel was advised by her solicitors that a transfer of the property onto trust terms for Leonard's benefit would be treated as an immediate chargeable transfer but if that transfer value fell within her available nil-rate band a positive IHT charge would still be avoided. However, the very status of the gift as an immediate chargeable transfer (irrespective of a nil charge) would provide access to CGT hold-over relief thereby negating a positive CGT charge. Accordingly, Rachel agreed to proceed down the trust route intending to create a life interest trust for Leonard, with remainder on his death to his children absolutely. At that time the value of the property was £650,000 and Rachel assumed that a gift of one half of the property would fall within her available nil-rate band of £325,000 (2017/18). However, IHTA 1984, s 1 defines the value of a lifetime transfer not by its market value but by reference to the fall in the value of the estate of the transferor pre/post-gift. Accordingly, the half share that would be retained by Rachel after applying a discount of 10% would be worth £292,500 such that for IHT purposes the value of the gift would be £357,500 (£650,000 − £292,500).

The transfer into trust was completed in May 2017. The IHT value of the gift was £357,500, less annual exemptions available for the current/previous year totalling £6,000 and less the current nil-rate band of £325,000 (2017/18), leaving £26,500 in charge to tax at 20%, initially yielding IHT of £5,300. Rachel agreed to meet this liability, as the trustees clearly had no cash funds, causing this figure to be subject to gross-up resulting in an effective rate of 25% to arrive at a final IHT due of £6,625. Any expenses of the transaction might have been relevant to the issue of the gain, if not held over, but they were not deductible from the IHT transfer value itself, but (since Rachel paid them) they did reduce her estate. Note in this connection that the effective date of the transfer is, in Scotland at least, the date of the disposition: see *Marquess of Linlithgow and Earl of Hopetoun v Revenue and Customs Comrs* [2010] CSIH 19, [2010] STC 1563.

Related property

[17.12] IHTA 1984, s 161 applies a statutory fiction that overrides the valuation principles discussed above – often overlooked, it does impose a significant upward impact on asset values. It operates to value an interest in property which, on its own, might qualify for a discount, in the context of other 'related' property so that, in that fictional context, the share is more valuable and thus creates a potentially greater tax exposure. Section 161(2) provides that property is 'related' if:

- it is comprised in the estate of the taxpayer's spouse or civil partner; or
- it is, or has within the last five years, been either
    - the property of a charity or held on charitable trusts only; or
    - the property of a 'public benefit' body such as a political party, housing association or a 'Schedule 3' body, ie one that exists for national purposes.

Where the related property rules apply it is necessary first to value all the related property and then to fix the proportion that is attributable to the taxed property as part of that aggregated value, in other words, ignoring the discount.

There is a similar rule that relates to trust property, though the conclusion is arrived at by a different fiction. If the taxpayer, for example, owns part of a farm in his own right but also has a qualifying interest in possession (pre-22 March 2006 or transitional serial interest (TSI) or Immediate post-death interest (IPDI)) in the family settlement that owns the remainder there is actually no need for IHTA 1984, s 161. For IHT purposes, s 49(1) treats the taxpayer as if he were the owner of the settled property so the trust ownership and the direct ownership are combined so as to value the farm as a whole. Following the FA 2006 trust reforms, the number of qualifying (pre-March 2006/TSI) interests in possession have reduced and whilst later creation of an immediate post-death interest will fall within this valuation rule, it will no longer be possible to create qualifying interests in possession by way of lifetime settlement (except for such a trust for a disabled person).

Accordingly, post-21 March 2006 (and this is a point that may be exploited in other ways) creation of a lifetime settlement in circumstances where that life tenant enjoys all the rights to income as hitherto will be a 'relevant property' settlement such that the IHT levy will be determined on the ten-yearly/exit charge basis and not by reference to the death of that life tenant. CGT is the subject of a separate chapter (see Chapter 14) but it may be seen that relief for a principle private residence under TCGA 1992, s 225 may still be available in respect of a dwelling which forms no part of the estate of the life tenant on death but has been so used as their principal residence.

IHTA 1984, s 171 provides that valuation for transfers on death is on the basis that any change in the value of the estate by reason of the death are ignored unless those changes fall within s 171(2). The latter is concerned with changes as follows:

- an addition to the property comprised in the estate;
- an increase or decrease of value of the property in the estate; but not a decrease that arises on capital reconstruction of a company arising on death (which does not concern us here); but
- termination on the death of any interest is excluded as is the passing of any interest by survivorship.

The interaction of IHTA 1984, ss 161 and 171 was considered in *Arkwright v IRC* [2004] STI 147. Property was held as tenants in common by husband and wife in equal shares. The husband died in 2001 and by his will gave his widow a life interest in his 50% share with the remainder to his daughters. In 2002, the Will was varied so as to give his share of the house to the daughters. The question debated was what was the IHT value of the husband's half share given that the surviving spouse had the right to occupy the property (by virtue of her own half share) and which could not then be sold without her consent?

At that time the property as a whole was worth £550,000 and HMRC valued the husband's half share, without discount, at £275,000 (550,000 at 50%) in doing so noting that s 171(1) was disapplied on the termination on death of any interest or the passing of any interest by the survivorship (as noted above) and s 161 was in point. The executors disagreed – any purchaser of an interest of a joint owner would take account of the health of the other joint owner, realising that he could not sell the property without that person's consent; that would reduce the offer price.

The Special Commissioner held that the interest of the husband passed, not by survivorship, but under the terms of the Deed of Variation. The value of the interest would change on the occasion of the husband's death because there would then be a certainty, and not merely a possibility, that he would die first. That decrease in the value of his share occurred by reason of his death and should be taken into account in valuing his interest. When considering s 161 one must first value the whole and then value each share as a proportion of that whole. That did not necessarily mean that each share was necessarily one half.

On appeal the High Court and later the Court of Appeal in part agreed with HMRC's argument that the Special Commissioner had gone a little too far in deciding the basis of valuation. The Special Commissioner had been entitled to conclude that the value of the interest of the first spouse was not necessarily one-half but had gone too far in determining that, as a matter of fact, the value of the interest was less than one-half. That was a matter for the Lands Tribunal.

The more recent case on this topic is *Price (Executor of Price, dec'd) v Revenue and Customs* [2010] UKFTT 474 (TC). The argument advanced by the taxpayer was realistic and if accepted would have produced a fair result. The deceased had owned a house as tenants in common with her husband in equal shares – the whole house was worth £1.5 million but carried a mortgage of £364,164. The will was varied within two years to leave the deceased's share in the house to the children, subject to the mortgage thereon and to a charge of £260,000 in favour of residue, which passed to the husband. It was agreed that half the house, valued on its own, would be worth £637,500 and there was evidence that neither the deceased nor her husband contemplated a sale of the property.

Essentially, the case turned on the meaning in s 161(1) of the words 'the value of that and any related property'. The taxpayer argued that one should aggregate the two shares in the house, each being valued in isolation. HMRC said that one should value the whole as a single entity. The taxpayer saw a distinction between shares in a house and units in a unit trust, and distinguished the *Arkwright* decision noted above. He thought that the valuation of a share should take account of the notional cost of selling. He argued for a 15% discount.

HMRC would have referred the case to the Lands Chamber of the First-tier Tribunal, rather than the Tax Chamber, but that conflicted with the statement of case. To interpret s 161(1), one should, they argued:

- fix 'the value of any property comprised in a person's estate'; then
- fix 'the value of the aggregate of that and any related property'; then
- fix the 'appropriate portion' of the latter value, using s 161(3), ie the proportion which the value of the property in the estate bears to the sum of that value and the value of related property, but each being valued separately (in this summary, the 'last' value); and
- compare the values, taking the last value if higher than the first.

Importantly, the shares must be aggregated before valuation, not after. Any costs of sale should, following *Tapp v Ryder* [2008] TMA/284/2008 (see below), be disregarded. He argued that deduction of one half of the mortgage debt should be a separate step.

Without feeling bound to accept the decision in *Arkwright*, and taking note of the comments of Hoffmann LJ in the Court of Appeal in *IRC v Gray (Lady Fox)*, the tribunal decided that it was right to value two assets held in the same estate on the basis that they would achieve a greater price if offered together, and applied that reasoning to s 161. Where s 161 applies, the two items of property are to be valued as if offered for sale together and at the same time. There should be no deduction for expenses of sale. Debts are to be deducted separately.

Development value and improvements to property

[17.13] A house with a large garden enjoying road access may be attractive to a builder or developer and in such circumstances, that 'potential interest', if capable of realisation should be reflected in the probate value. This will also be true if new information later emerges that enhances the value of the land. This principle was explored in *Prosser v IRC (DET/1/2000)*, where a plot of land had hope value at the date of death. The Lands Tribunal put that hope value at 25% of development value.

In *Tapp (executor of Robert Ernest Atkinson, dec'd) v Ryder* [2008] RVR 340, the issue was the correct valuation of a house that had been refurbished both pre- and post-death prior to sale. In 2005 the occupier, aged 83, had to go into hospital. During his absence his niece urgently arranged 'essential repairs and basic modernisation', which included rewiring, plumbing, a new gas boiler, new kitchen, new cloakroom, removal of polystyrene tiles and redecoration throughout. The Uncle died in April 2006 and his niece was the executor of his estate. Work on the house continued until October 2006 including cosmetic improvements, re-carpeting etc, the property being sold in November for £267,000.

The niece did not, as she might have done, obtain a 'Red Book' valuation. She thought the house, before renovation, to be worth £150,000 and that by the date of death, after the expenditure of £15,000 on it, to be worth £195,000. That figure was based in part on estimates obtained from estate agents in June 2006, which had been in the range £210,000–£220,000. The District Valuer had offered to agree £230,000 as the value at date of death, based on comparables and allowing for work done. At the hearing the Valuer produced evidence that would justify a figure of £258,000, which was reduced to £250,000 to reflect work since the date of death but the Tribunal settled on £230,000. That was a discount of £28,000 and would more than reflect the work done. With regard to a claim to deduct 40% of the difference between the value and the net proceeds: s 160 required the value to be gross, not net of selling costs.

Fall in value relief

[17.14] At para **17.6** above the situation examined property which had risen in value following the death but clearly values can go the other way and this certainly has been demonstrated in the immediate past recession and may also be impacted by reason of market uncertainty as a consequence of the UK exit from the European Union. IHTA 1984, ss 190–198 provide relief for drop in realised value on land sales. Essentially, if land is sold at arm's length at a loss over probate within four years of the date of death it may, subject to various qualifications, be possible to substitute the lower gross sale proceeds for the higher probate value.

De minimis

[17.15] No relief is available where the difference between the gross sale proceeds and the probate value is less than (but not equal to as commonly interpreted) £1,000 or 5% of the value, whichever is lower.

Arm's length transactions

[17.16] However, there is no relief if the sale of the property is made by the executor to a person who has an interest in the property (namely the purchaser is not an unconnected third party). More specifically there is no relief on the sale, even if carried out on strict commercial terms, to:

- someone beneficially entitled to an interest or interest in possession in the property being sold; or
- the spouse of such a person; or
- the civil partner of such a person; or
- the child of such a person; or
- any remoter descendent of such a person; or
- trustees of a settlement under which such a person has an interest in possession in the property; or
- a sale in connection with which the vendor or any person such as is described in the bullets above obtains a right to acquire the interest.

Identity of the claimant

[17.17] The legislation refers to 'the appropriate person' defined as the person who is liable for the IHT attributable to the value of the interest sold. Executors and the trustees of the settlement are each treated as a single and continuing body of persons as distinct from the persons who may at any time hold that office.

'Cherry-picking'

[17.18] Where an estate comprises several properties which are sold during the administration period, naturally some may sell for more, and some for less, than probate value. A claim to relief under IHTA 1984, s 191 will apply to all the sales with the exception of sales made at a profit in the fourth year. It is therefore not possible, except with some ingenuity, to 'cherry pick' the sales where the result has been disappointing and claim a reduction of the IHT on those sales in isolation.

Ingenuity in this context is moderate only. If the value of a particular property is not actually required by the executors to meet liabilities of the estate, such that they can (and without difficulty) by way of assignment, place it unreservedly at the disposal of the beneficiaries who wish to harness the profit on later sale, they may do just that. The beneficiaries may take advantage of TCGA 1992, ss 62 and 64 to acquire the property at probate value and sell it on themselves. They are not the 'appropriate person' for the purposes of the relief and the assented assets cannot form part of the s 191 claim thus enabling the executors to gain full benefit of relief for the loss realised on to the properties sold by the estate.

This option will not be readily available where estate properties are sold at auction, since the hammer price cannot be forecast with certainty. The executors will have to guess which properties will sell at a gain and appropriate those particular properties out of the estate well before the date of the auction, selling as mere agents for the beneficiaries. Practitioners who choose this course must get all the paperwork right beforehand.

The nature of the interest transferred

[17.19] At first sight it might seem quite obvious which is the property that is being taxed in any transaction but established cases, which in particular concern the family home on death, highlight the importance of identifying exactly what is being transferred – consider the case of *Davies and Rippon v Revenue and Customs Comrs* (TC00106) [2009] UKFTT 138 (TC). The issue before the First-tier Tribunal was whether a qualifying interest in possession existed such that access to the valuable estate duty surviving spouse exemption could be secured on the latter's death.

Mrs Rhona Goodman, the mother of the appellants, was the widow of Geoffrey Goodman, who had died in 1969. Following Mrs Goodman's death her daughters argued that certain assets were held by their mother for life and thus qualified for this valuable estate duty relief whereas in contrast, HMRC considered that the assets were not held within a trust framework but were simply part of Mrs Goodman's estate for IHT.

The taxpayers argued that:

- by his conduct, Mr Goodman had, in effect, settled certain property on his wife for life, with remainder to his daughters; or
- he and Mrs Goodman had executed mutual wills, with the result that property later inherited by Mrs Goodman from him was fixed with a trust and could not be alienated by her except in accordance with that mutual agreement.

The wills of husband and wife were similar but they were not identical. As a widow Mrs Goodman formed a friendship with a Mr Dodd, whom she never married but was concerned to protect her daughters' inheritance. She did not spend the capital that she had inherited from her husband and also inherited from Mr Dodd's estate on his later death.

The Tribunal held that, to succeed, the appellants must show that the property had been settled and that the surviving spouse must not be competent to dispose of it. There is a heavy burden of proof where a party claims that there is a secret trust (see *Snowden, Re, Smith v Spowage* [1979] Ch 528, [1979] 2 All ER 172) and that burden falls on the person who argues that the trust exists. 'We may consider past evidence is admissible' (see *Blackwell v Blackwell* [1929] HL 318) and the evidence must be 'clear and satisfactory evidence' (see *Cleaver, Re, Cleaver v Insley* [1981] 2 All ER 1018, [1981] 1 WLR 939).

The evidence in this case was too weak and not supported by tangible evidence. It was held that there was no written trust on the husband's death and all the property inherited from him was therefore taxable as part of Mrs Goodman's free estate.

The difficulty of establishing the exact interest of a person in a trust was highlighted in *Stow v Stow* [2008] EWHC 495 (Ch), STC 2298, where a widow claimed under the Inheritance (Provision for Family and Dependants) Act 1975 that her late husband had personally owned Nigerian assets held in certain trusts. HMRC issued notices of determination charging IHT on the basis that the deceased held a beneficial interest in those trusts which he had created such that the assets formed part of his estate. The trustees, instead of appealing to the Special Commissioners, went to the High Court for a declaration that the deceased did not have a beneficial interest in the trust funds which they argued had belonged to a Nigerian business associate. The High Court dismissed the HMRC application to strike out the proceedings: the issue of ownership of the funds affected not only IHT but also income tax which had been assessed on the deceased. The Special Commissioners do not have exclusive jurisdiction where a dispute covered in a notice of determination, affects more than one issue.

A recent case on bank accounts might also apply to property. In *Taylor v Revenue and Customs Comrs* [2008] STC (SCD) 1159 the deceased had put two building society accounts into the joint names of herself and her brother-in-law. Either could sign and on death the account would pass to the survivor but it was common knowledge within the family that the money was destined for the five grandchildren of the brother-in-law. When the deceased died, leaving her estate to her nieces, the two accounts were not mentioned nor was IHT paid on them. It was held that the deceased did not hold the accounts as trustee, and the proceeds were part of her estate within IHTA 1984, s 5 because she had power to dispose of the money in the accounts. There were no separate shares in the accounts: the whole value was taxable.

Personal estate

[17.20] The simplest case is the transfer by the taxpayer (in lifetime or on death) of the whole of what they own, however, matters become more complicated where the taxpayer does not own the entirety of the asset. First there are the valuation issues of shares in land already discussed. The second issue is the examination of whether the transferor has an interest in the share of land only or in a greater entity.

Example 3: The best of both worlds

Doreen and Ernest were married for many years and from the 1960s onwards successively owned their home as joint tenants. Doreen died in 2008 leaving her estate to Ernest. On advice, Ernest entered into a Deed of Variation of Doreen's Will under which the joint tenancy in the property was severed, her half share in the family home was redirected to her daughter Frances and her savings redirected to her granddaughter Gemma. The gift in the Deed to Frances was a simple and absolute gift, without any kind of restriction on the ability of Frances to deal with the half share – Frances did not move into the property which continued to be occupied by her father.

In June 2017, Ernest died leaving an estate of £3 million, and by his Will left his half of the family home to Gemma. The issue for the executors in completing the HMRC Account in Ernest's estate was the extent of his interest in the property. The simple answer might be that at his death Ernest had an interest in one half only of the family home and that interest should be discounted, say, 10% because the other half at that point was owned by his daughter and was therefore not related property. The alternative view would be that, from Doreen's death until the death of Ernest, Frances had not really had any benefit at all from her inheritance. She had not lived at the property, merely visiting it occasionally to keep an eye on her father nor had she mortgaged her interest in order to raise capital for her husband's business or otherwise accessed the capital value. She had not really had any advantage at all. It could therefore be argued that, to all intents and purposes, the entire benefit of Doreen's share in the house actually rested with Ernest during widowhood such that in effect he had a qualifying life interest (IPDI) in the half of the house, with remainder to Frances.

In the light of FA 2008, s 10 and Sch 4 and the new rules as to the transferable nil-rate band, any such argument should be pursued.

The terms of the Deed of Variation did not impose the 'elaborate provisions' that applied in *IRC v Lloyds Private Banking Ltd* [1998] STC 559. However, Frances actually did nothing with her share of the house. If her business had failed, her creditors could have claimed against her interest in the house; but in the event nothing of the kind occurred. The way that IHT400 is now formulated will force Ernest's executors to disclose the situation. They should claim that, notwithstanding the Deed of Variation, Ernest had an interest in possession under Doreen's will and that, to that extent, she had not used her nil-rate band so it is available now to Ernest's executors.

Note:

The estate does not benefit from the Residence Nil Rate Band or Transferable Nil Rate Band introduced with effect from 6 April 2017 since Ernest's estate exceeds the £2.35 million taper threshold.

'Old' interest in possession trusts

[17.21] As will be seen in connection with Agricultural Property Relief (APR) at **17.30** below, the linkage between outright ownership of land and holding an interest in possession can be important to securing the relief.

FA 2006 changed the landscape of trusts, operating to preserve the position of interests in possession that existed prior to 22 March 2006 (known as 'qualifying' interest) and allowing some transitional relief until 5 October 2008 but thereafter regarding virtually all lifetime trusts as within the relevant property regime. From 22 March 2006 onwards from an IHT perspective it is still possible for qualifying interests in possession to arise, in relation for example to disabled trusts or deemed interests in possession that arise under Statement of Practice 10/79 or by way of immediate post-death interests; but many of the situations of the past in which qualifying interest in possession could have been created, for example accumulation and mainte-nance trusts and interest in possession trusts created in lifetime, are no longer possible and as such virtually all lifetime trusts now fall within the IHT regime of relevant property trusts subject to ten-year and exit charges.

Immediate post death interest (IPDI)

[17.22] The requirements for such interests is that they comply with IHTA 1984, s 49A, being trusts that are created on death under which a beneficiary is immediately entitled to an interest in possession. The interest can be created either by a Will or under the provisions as to intestacy but either way it must come into being on the death of the testator or the intestate. There are further conditions to be satisfied in particular:

- Condition 3, set out in s 49A(4) excludes from the category of IPDI both bereaved minors' trusts under IHTA 1984, s 71A and trusts for disabled persons.
- Condition 4, is that the requirements of condition 3 have been satisfied throughout the time from which the beneficiary holding the IPDI became entitled to an interest in possession. The intention of Parliament, as expressed in the debate on the Finance Bill 2006, was to leave as an interest in possession only the simplest form of family provision and as far as possible to reduce the scope for creating ongoing trusts with successive interests.

Relevant property trusts

[17.23] Except for those post-21 March 2006 trusts with preferred status to include:

- immediate post-death interests (IPDI);
- transitional serial interests (TSI);
- trusts for bereaved minors (BMT);
- 18–25 trusts; and
- trusts for disabled persons (DPI).

All other trusts now created (in lifetime or on death) will come within the relevant property regime and, unless they qualify for an exemption (such as charitable exemption), their lifetime creation will be an immediate chargeable transfer. This produces the result, which at first seemed anomalous, that the creation of a lifetime settlement providing for an interest in possession for a spouse is a relevant property trust and is a chargeable transfer not covered by the spousal exemption.

It might be thought that the creation of a lifetime trust of which the settlor is also a beneficiary (income and capital) is a 'nothing' in tax terms, in that after the event, as before, the settlor will be treated as still owning the assets settled by virtue of the Gift with Reservation of Benefit ('GWR') provisions. In economic terms, the estate of the settlor is not diminished however on a strict reading of FA 1986, s 102 the GWR provisions kick in only on death; so even though, for as long as the settlor remains a beneficiary, it is certain that his estate will be taxed by reference to the value of the gift, that is ignored in measuring the fall in value of his estate occasioned by the gift. It is, therefore, important to appreciate that the lifetime creation of a settlor interested trust will be an immediate chargeable transfer although the Inheritance Tax (Double Charges Relief) Regulations 1987 (SI 1987/1130) may be employed to avoid a double charge in certain circumstances.

IHT on lifetime transfers

Reporting requirements

[17.24] The establishment of a pilot trust, by reason of its minimal value, is excepted under the Inheritance Tax (Delivery of Accounts) (Excepted Settlements) Regulations 2002 (SI 2002/1732) ie one:

- which is of cash only;
- which receives no further property from the settlor after its initial creation;
- where the trustees are resident in the UK;
- where the gross value of the property initially settled does not exceed £1,000; and
- where there are no related settlements.

FA 2006 had the result that post-21 March 2006 nearly all lifetime gifts into trust are chargeable lifetime transfers, although if the value transferred is within the settlor's nil-rate band, they would generate no tax charge either on creation or, possibly, later. If no action had been taken this would have greatly increased the burden of processing transfer notification (Form IHT100) without actually yielding any tax (at least in the early stages of such trusts). To address this, the Inheritance Tax (Delivery of Accounts) (Excepted Transfers and Excepted Terminations) Regulations 2008 (SI 2008/605) and the Inheritance Tax (Delivery of Accounts) (Excepted Settlements) Regulations 2008 (SI 2008/606) were laid before Parliament on 6 March 2008.

The regulations as to excepted transfers and excepted terminations, which came into force on 6 April 2008 but were effective from 6 April 2007, remove the obligation to deliver an account for small transfers (as defined) unless HMRC serve a notice requiring one. However, both trustees and others must file an account on the creation or termination of a settlement which would have been a PET, but becomes a chargeable lifetime transfer by reason of the failure of the donor to meet the seven-year survival rule. Similarly, there is a duty to file a return where the parties thought that the original transfer was an excepted transfer within the new rules and it turns out not to be.

Excepted transfers

[17.25] An excepted transfer under the new rules is one made by an individual which is an actual transfer, not a deemed transfer. There are two categories which pivot on the value of the identified transfer:

(i) *Cash or quoted shares or securities –*
The transfer will be excepted if the value transferred, together with values of chargeable transfers made by that transferor in the preceding seven years, does not exceed the nil-rate band at the date of transfer.

(ii) *Assets other than cash or quoted shares or securities –*
The exemption will apply where:
- the value, together with the values of chargeable transfers made by that transferor in the preceding seven years does not exceed 80% of the current nil-rate band; and

- the identified value transferred does not exceed the nil-rate band after deducting the value of all the previous chargeable transfers.

For this latter purpose neither Business Property Relief (BPR) nor Agricultural Property Relief (APR) is to be taken into account, so to be excepted the entire value must be within the limits prescribed.

Example 4: Gift of a share in a flat

In August 2017, Sylvia, who has not yet used her current year's annual exemption (but has utilised that for previous year), wished to give her two nieces a 25% interest each in a London flat which is currently let – the flat is worth £500,000 as a whole. She settled the interest, which might seem to be a chargeable transfer of £247,000 ((£500,000 @ 50%) – £3,000). However, the loss to estate rule produces a different figure – before the gift her estate includes the full property value (£500,000) but post-gift, she has 50% share in the property, a share which should be discounted, say 15%, and is therefore worth £212,500. The loss to her estate is thus £287,500 (£500,000 – £212,500) from which should be deducted the available annual exemption to arrive at a chargeable transfer of £284,500 (£287,500 – £3,000).

At a time when the nil-rate band is £325,000, the limit above which the transfer must be reported is 80% of that, £260,000. Sylvia's transfer to the girls must be reported: it is not £247,000, which would have been within the limit, but £284,500.

Example 5

Doting uncle

In March 2007, Jim, having already used his annual exemptions, put cash totalling £37,500 into a series of small discretionary trusts for his nieces. The value fell within the 2002 Regulation exemption then in force such that there was no requirement to notify HMRC. In February 2014 and having utilised his annual exemption for both the current and previous year he settled a further £215,000 which brought his cumulative total to £252,500, well over the limit under the old 2002 Regulations.

However, under the 2008 Regulations (see 17.24) the limit is now linked to the then nil-rate band of £325,000 (2013/14) and, since post the intended transfer (and taking account of the earlier pilot trust transfers made within the previous seven years) Jim has 22% (£325,000 – (252,500 + 37,500) = £72,500) of the nil-rate band left, he will not have to file an IHT100.

Transactions during the currency of a trust

[17.26] The intention of the rules is that where a chargeable event involves a trust but no IHT is immediately in issue, there should be no duty to deliver an account. Note that the exercise of a power of appointment out of a discretionary trust within two years of death, which relates back to the death under s 144, need not be reported.

The rules as to excepted terminations apply only to 'specified' trusts, ie:

- qualifying interest in possession trusts that existed before 22 March 2006;
- BMT under s 71A(c);
- IPDI trusts within s 49A;
- DPI trusts; or
- TSI trusts within ss 49B–49E.

The termination of a qualifying interest in possession can be a chargeable transfer, but it need not be reported in any one of three circumstances:

- The transfer may be small, for example within the annual exemption, and the life tenant may have served notice under s 57(3) that the annual exemption is available. If the amount of the transfer is within the specified exemption, there is no need for a return.
- Where the trust property is cash or quoted securities and the value of the fund in respect of which the termination takes place, and the value of transfers by the tenant for life of any other kind together are within the nil-rate band, there is no need for an account.
- Where the trust fund does not consist wholly of cash or quoted securities there is still no need to file a return if the value of the trust 'termination fund' and of previous chargeable transfers by the life tenant in the previous seven years do not exceed 80% of the nil-rate band.

These termination rules, like those for excepted settlements, take no account of APR or of BPR. The 2008 regulations replace those made in 2002 in relation to lifetime transfers made on or after 6 April 2007.

Pilot trusts

[17.27] The 2008 Regulations rules reduce the filing requirements for pilot trusts and small settlements. Accordingly, there is no need to file a return in respect of a transfer to a pilot trust, ie a UK resident settlement (which remains UK resident throughout) of cash of £1,000 or less where there are no related settlements. Apart from that, the 2008 Excepted Settlements Regulations dispense with filing of a return in respect of:

- UK trusts (which remain in the UK); by
- settlors domiciled in the UK at the time the settlement is made;
- who remain domiciled here until either the chargeable event or the death of the settlor whichever first happens, where
  - there are no related settlements; and
  - one of the following conditions is met.
    Extra condition 1: to avoid filing for a ten-year charge. The trust is excepted where the value in the trust at the anniversary is not more than 80% of the nil-rate band (disregarding liabilities or reliefs such as APR or BPR).
    Extra condition 2: to avoid filing for the exit charge in the first ten years of the trust. The language of reg 4(5) is somewhat obscure, but it concerns the value that is transferred by the notional chargeable transfer which is one element of calculating the exit charge in the first ten years of the relevant property trust. Take no account of liabilities or reliefs such as APR and BPR. On

an exit charge in the first ten years of a relevant property trust, there is no need for a return if the value released from the trust does not exceed 80% of the nil-rate band.

Extra condition 3: to avoid filing for an exit charge after the first ten-year anniversary. There is no need to file a return if the value of the transfer does not exceed 80% of the nil-rate band.

Extra condition 4: to avoid filing for an exit charge from an 18-to-25 trust. There is no need for a return where the chargeable transfer is within 80% of the nil-rate band.

Inheritance Tax (Delivery of Accounts) (Excepted Estates) (Amendment) Regulations 2011 introduced fresh IHT disclosure rules for those regular gifts which rely on exemption under the gifts out of income rule provided for at IHTA 1984, s 21. At first sight, it looks as if the law has changed and that somehow the facility of making gifts out of income under s 21 has been curtailed. Actually, that is not quite what is happening. HMRC have been concerned for some time that the facility under s 21 was being abused and in particular that it was being used to shelter gifts into relevant property trusts. Normally gifts into trust count as 'chargeable transfers' and if large enough (individually or cumulatively) they trigger an immediate IHT charge.

The statutory instrument is not as such a change in the charge to taxation but rather a change in the way that it is reported. The rules came into force on 1 March 2011 and apply where, on a death, there would be no need to deliver an IHT account because the estate was, for some reason or other, not taxable. This would normally mean that it was below nil-rate band threshold or below the unused and full (but not part) transferable nil-rate band or passing to a spouse and under £1 million.

The main regulations as to the need for an IHT estate return are those in the Inheritance Tax (Delivery of Accounts) (Excepted Estates) Regulations 2004 (see **17.3**) already discussed. As previously legislated, the parameters for an excepted estate were satisfied where (amongst other things) the deceased had not made chargeable transfers exceeding £150,000 in the period of seven years before death but it is that rule which has been changed. With effect from 1 March 2011, for the purpose of reporting (but not for any other purpose) certain new gifts will count towards that figure of £150,000. The 2011 regulation specifies that the certain types of gift which will be treated as chargeable transfers are those that:

- in any year exceed £3,000;
- fall in the seven years prior to death; and
- are exempt only by virtue of s 21.

Thus on the death on or after 1 March 2011 of a person who has a relatively small estate which might otherwise escape reporting who has made substantial gifts out of income which when taken into account with other lifetime gifts breach the £150,000 level, there will be a requirement to complete the full IHT return where previously that might not have been required.

Form IHT400 demands that where there have been lifetime gifts, these must be reported in the Schedule IHT403 (gifts and other transfers of value). Executors wishing to claim relief under s 21 must provide the full details of available income and regular expenditure for the seven years up to death – they should be prepared that this data will be subject to detailed HMRC scrutiny and it is vital that the executors hold formal evidence to support the claim. Therefore, although the guidance notes refer to these gifts as being treated as chargeable transfer, that means so treated for the purposes of the regulations, not for the purposes of chargeability. Importantly, the 2011 regulations do not change the meaning or scope of s 21 but merely require account be taken of such gifts.

The rest of the 2011 regulations concern changes to take account of the double nil-rate band noted earlier in this chapter.

Good professional advisers already maintain records from year to year of gifts falling within s 21, or at the very least advise their clients to do so. Notwithstanding, it has been tentatively suggested that in future it may be appropriate to report any gifts to be sheltered by s 21 on the annual self-assessment tax return. This would make life so much easier for the executors and by token if HMRC have the records, this may cut down on the need to challenge so many of these cases when claims are later made – it would also eliminate those spurious claims. Accordingly, such a suggestion does have merit but it would undoubtedly confuse the system; after all self-assessment relates to income tax and CGT not IHT – consider the confusion of Pre-Owned Asset Tax reporting.

Notwithstanding the relaxed reporting requirements set out above, the beneficial use of pilot trusts suffered a further blow which has impacted heavily on their continued popularity. These measures, contained within F(No 2)A 2015 and effective for chargeable events arising on or after 18 November 2015, operate to expand the concept of the 'same day addition' and trigger when value is added to an existing relevant property trust and on the same day the settlor adds value to one or more other relevant property trusts. The rules contain a de minimis exemption where the value of that addition is less than £5,000.

Death of transferor

[17.28] Trustees may have received transfers of value which are well within the nil-rate band and may have appointed funds out, again well within the levels that are now exempt from reporting. However, the settlor may have made other lifetime transfers, such as PETs which later fail by reason of his death within seven years. There will be a 'knock-on' effect on the trust because, after readjusting the timeline for the failed PETs, the transfers that were previously exempt from reporting must now be shown in an account. Depending on the value involved there might not be any extra tax to pay, but the return must still be filed.

There is guidance, with illustrations, at IHTM06100–06130 and from there to the links quoted. A duty to file may arise on discovery within six months, if the amount of discount claimed was wrong.

Under the 2011 regulations, there is no duty to file a return if the transfers are covered by the rules as to the nil-rate band; but if they exceed the nil-rate band, even though they are within another exemption such as IHTA 1984, s 21 (normal expenditure out of income for which see above), the transfers are assumed for this purpose to be both chargeable and hence reportable, because HMRC have not been satisfied that the exemption applies. That having been said it is unlikely that any transfer of real property could be a gift out of 'income' covered by IHTA 1984, s 21.

A taxpayer may have thought that a transfer was outside the filing rules and may only realise the error much later. If so, as with the discount situation mentioned above, he has six months to put things right.

Bare trusts

[17.29] Few taxpayers or their advisers want the complication or the cost of an immediate tax charge that follows the creation of a relevant property trust, yet they do want to start the seven-year period running on a gift of, say, land or shares to a child under 18. Many have resorted to creating bare trusts but have included administrative powers in the document, in particular in relation to Trustee Act 1925, s 31.

HMRC for a time considered that in certain circumstances such trusts were substantive, and not bare, trusts, because the trustees had active duties to perform and the arrangement might be 'a trust to accumulate the income'. That HMRC view has now been firmly withdrawn. Even so, the draftsman of such trusts should take care not to cross the line into the creation of a substantive trust: the key is the exact nature of the interest of the beneficiary, which must be neither conditional nor restricted in any way.

Reliefs from IHT

Agricultural property relief (APR)

[17.30] This relief has been considered in detail in **CHAPTER 11** at para **11.13**. From the point of view of the practitioner there is an important distinction between Agricultural Property Relief (APR) and Business Property Relief (BPR), discussed at **17.33** below and onwards. The HMRC website contains a useful 'Customer Guide' which practitioners may like to use as the starting point of their research. As far as land is concerned, practitioners might have been buoyed by the initial success of the taxpayer in the rather special situation in the 'farmhouse' case of *Atkinson v Revenue and Customs Comrs* (TC00420) [2010] UKFTT 108 (TC), [2010] SWTI 2123 where a bungalow had been occupied by a member of the farming partnership. That partner was elderly and in the latter years had been moved into a nursing home but he still took an interest in farm business. The occupation of the bungalow was deemed to be not merely by him, as a partner, but by the partnership as a whole. The farmer's possessions were left there; no one else moved in and other members of the partnership visited the property from time to time to make sure that all was in good order. It was held that the partnership still occupied the bungalow 'for the purposes of agriculture' in the relevant sense, so APR was initially allowed. However, this decision was swiftly reversed on appeal by HMRC although it should be noted that the taxpayers were not represented at that hearing due to lack of financial resources such that the full technical argument in rebuttal was not played out and that is a pity.

However, a resounding taxpayer success was *Executors of Golding Deceased v HMRC* [2011] UKFTT 351 (TC) which allowed APR on a modest farmhouse dwelling still used by the farmer in his old age where his farming activities had declined greatly from what they had been in his heyday (see **CHAPTER 11** at **11.15**). Rather belatedly and it has to be said, somewhat reluctantly, in response to the outcome of the *Golding* case, HMRC have added fresh guidance to their IHT manual (see IHTM240236 *et seq* and HMRC Guidance reported at *STEP UK News Digest*, 13 May 2013) which discusses the entitlement of a farmhouse to APR under the character appropriate test.

A more important decision in *Hanson (trustee of the William Hanson 1957 Settlement) v Revenue & Customs Commrs* [2013] UKUT 224 (TCC), [2013] STC 2394, which was soundly upheld before the Upper Tribunal on 15 April 2013 offers a more detailed insight into the importance of 'occupation' of the land. After a detailed examination of the facts and careful analysis of the legislation the Upper Tribunal held that when determining whether a farmhouse qualifies for APR, both it and the land (to which the farmhouse is of 'character appropriate') must be in the same occupation but not necessarily, as HMRC argued, in the same ownership – that distinction may seem small but it is absolutely critical.

The facts of the case were straightforward. Immediately before his death in December 2002 Joseph Charles Hanson was the life tenant of a trust created by his father in 1957. That trust held a property which HMRC agreed was a 'farmhouse' for APR purposes with an agreed market value in December 2002 of £450,000. Mr Hanson's son lived in the farmhouse which he had occupied since 1978 under a rent-free licence and from there the son farmed 215 acres of land of which:

- 128 acres was owned personally by the son;
- 25 acres was part owned by Mr Hanson Snr/trust;
- 20 acres rented by the son from a third party; and
- 42 acres whose ownership was unspecified by belonging neither to the son, Mr Hanson Snr or the trust.

The only land in common ownership and common occupation with the farmhouse was the 25 acres owned by Mr Hanson Snr/the trust of which Mr Hanson Snr was the life tenant and farmed by the son.

On Mr Hanson's death his executors claimed APR on the value of his life interest in the farmhouse but HMRC denied the relief on the basis that there was insufficient agricultural land (25 acres) in both common ownership and common occupation with the farmhouse for the latter to pass the 'character appropriate' test – in other words the HMRC argument in ignoring the totality of the land farmed by the son rested entirely on the farmhouse in the context of a farming operation carried out on 25 acres of farmland. The son in his capacity as sole trustee of the trust appealed the decision arguing that common occupation (the son in his capacity as farmer of the land) was the only connecting factor required between the farmhouse and the agricultural land to which it was of a character appropriate (namely the combined 25 acres owned by the deceased and the 190 acres owned by the son/A N Other). The Tribunal agreed with the son.

This was a landmark defeat for HMRC but it is a welcome decision which restores faith in good judgment based on a practical understanding of the farming operation. It will be of significance in situations where a downsizing farmer has moved out of the farmhouse and gives away much of the agricultural land as well as in a trust scenario as set out in the case itself.

Planning potential

[17.31] As explained in detail in CHAPTER 11, IHT protection of the premium of market value over agricultural value can only be achieved by way of BPR thus the landlord investor is exposed. This exposure has now assumed critical importance following publication of the government's long-awaited changes to the Town and Country Planning (General Permitted Development) Order which sets out the relaxation of the strict planning rules for agricultural buildings. As a direct consequence it is now arguable that all agricultural buildings now hold potential development value.

The Order permits the conversion of up to three dwellings with a maximum combined floor area of 450 sq m but there are strict criterions which must be met. In particular a critical rule stipulates that buildings available for conversion to dwellings must have been in agricultural use on 20 March 2013. From the farmer's perspective an essential criterion will be to ensure that the Local Planning Authority do not have any grounds upon which to build an argument that the designated building is not in agricultural use – certainly those buildings used for equestrian purpose, let out for general storage or applied for other non-agricultural uses will not qualify despite being sited on agricultural land. Furthermore, the Order specifically excludes those buildings located in areas of outstanding natural beauty or situated in any of the national parks.

This potential for increased development opportunity and the premium it commands make it essential that the farm 'property portfolio' is fully reviewed. Such review should focus not only on the traditional farmhouse but also on all of those buildings which would fall within the scope of the new rules and hence could count as a potential dwelling. Nevertheless, the farmhouse should be critically reviewed for its continued APR eligibility and an assessment made of that value which falls outside APR coverage.

Woodlands

[17.32] This relief has been explored extensively in CHAPTER 12 and is therefore not covered in detail here. It is seldom encountered in practice and that is for good reason namely:

- First, it is essentially a relief of deferral only – it is not a complete exemption and thus is not a viable alternative to BPR.

- Second, the basis of charge on disposal is excessively complicated and requires much detail to calculate the deduction of expenses or credit for tax charged on an earlier occasion. Further, for example, the 50% reduction under IHTA 1984, s 127 is little known and complicated to establish.
- Third, where it can be shown that there is commercial occupation of woodlands and where the requirements for business relief can be established, BPR is infinitely preferable.

Simply put, in most instances woodlands relief is not worth having other than perhaps for a cash flow advantage.

Business property relief (BPR)

[17.33] CHAPTER 2 examined some of the issues that divide investment in property from dealing and the same distinctions, and others, must be addressed when formulating a claim to Business Property Relief (BPR) under IHTA 1984, s 104. There are six categories of the relief but few are of interest to the land owner. For most practical purposes the categories of business property that comprise company securities and shares may be ignored. However, the following points are worthy of note:

- *Property construction* – the restriction on dealing in land and buildings does not prevent a property construction business from qualifying for BPR, such as a building company holding houses or plots as stock in trade for development (see *Executors of Piercy (dec'd) v Revenue and Customs Comrs* [2008] SpC 687 but note IHTM25266).
- *Hotels, nursing homes, etc* – other property backed businesses such as hotels and nursing homes will also usually qualify for relief, in view of the level of services provided. However, HMRC guidance at IHTM25277 indicates that BPR in respect of certain types of hotel (ie the 'self-service/budget hotel industry') may be susceptible to challenge: ' . . . you should also ascertain the nature of a "hotel" business to establish whether on the facts it actually falls at the investment end of the spectrum'.
- *Holiday lettings, etc* – HMRC have tended to examine BPR claims in respect of holiday lettings relatively closely, presumably to establish if the activity constitutes a 'business', and if so, whether it is wholly or mainly one of holding investments – see **17.40** et seq.

Property as a business: the 100% claim

[17.34] It had been widely considered that whilst property consisting of a business or an interest in a business could qualify for BPR at 100% under IHTA 1984, s 105(1)(a), the underlying land was not in itself a business: it was merely a passive asset. That view was successfully challenged in the *Nelson Dance* case examined below with HMRC guidance updates accordingly.

The closest to a 'pure property play' qualifying for the relief to come before the courts was the Hertford case. In *Ninth Marquess of Hertford (executors of Eighth Marquess of Hertford, decd) v IRC* [2005] STC (SCD) 177 the Special Commissioner had to consider Ragley Hall, a grade I listed historic house. The whole of the outside of the building was accessible to the public view and by volume 78% of the interior was also open, the remainder being occupied by the taxpayer, his son and their families as living quarters.

In 1991 the taxpayer gave his son a business: the opening of a historic house to the public, Ragley Hall itself, its contents, the goodwill of the opening business, copyrights in the catalogues and brochures, book debts, cash in hand and at the bank and the benefit of all contracts, motor vehicles, foodstuffs, beverages and other chattels used in the business. The taxpayer died within seven years of the gift triggering the clawback provisions for BPR in IHTA 1984, s 113A.

The executors claimed 100% BPR on the whole gift: the whole of the Hall qualified for 100% relief because the whole of the building was one of the assets that was used in the business. It was part of the net value of the business for the purposes of establishing relief under IHTA 1984, s 110(b). HMRC argued for a restriction of relief limited to the part of the building that was open to the public. This was not, as one might have thought, a case turning on IHTA 1984, s 112 (which excludes from relief the value of excepted assets).

It was held that, if an asset was wholly or mainly used for the purposes of the business concerned, there was actually no procedure for proportioning relief. It was not appropriate to divide Ragley Hall into two assets. There was no separate business of showing only the exterior of the building. The brochure showed the whole building and it was difficult to draw the line between the area that the public could see and the private quarters. The Hall was, in the normal sense of the word, a single asset and it was simply not possible to divide the Hall in any sensible way so as to exclude part from relief. It was plainly important as a single structure and the whole building was a vital backdrop to the business carried on.

True farmland enjoys valuable relief (APR) but where the land carries a development value premium the taxpayer will need to seek access to BPR, to mop up the excess commercial value over the lower agricultural value. That was at the heart of two cases. In a leading case, *Dance Family Settlement (Trustees of the) v Revenue and Customs Comrs* [2009] STC 802, Mr Dance, a farmer, transferred farmland to a settlement. APR was available but that was not in issue rather the taxpayer wanted access to BPR, because the land had development value. HMRC denied relief on the basis that the nature of the transfer was not an interest in his farming business but a 'mere asset' used in that business.

It was successfully argued before the Special Commissioner that it was necessary to look, not just at the asset transferred, but at the transfer of value and apply the 'loss to the estate' principle on that basis. His estate was reduced by the transfer and what was reduced was the value of his farming business – he had been in farming for many years so the transfer of value fell to be reduced by BPR. The Special Commissioner could see a distinction between those cases, such as spouse relief, where the recipient was important, and the present situation, where the basis of relief was the transfer, not the underlying asset, and commented (at para 16):

'All these form part of an overall scheme. Everything turns on the loss in value to the donor's estate, rather than what is given or how the loss to the estate arises, except where the identity of the recipient is crucial to a particular exemption.'

HMRC appealed unsuccessfully to the High Court, where Sales J held that it was enough for IHTA 1984 s 104 to apply such that the value transferred was attributable to the value of a business: that fitted well with the principles in ss 110 (value of the business) and 103 ('loss to the estate').

If it should still be necessary to determine whether a particular asset is a business or a 'mere asset' reference should be made to the old retirement relief cases which have enjoyed a revival of interest through application of CGT Entrepreneurs' Relief introduced on 6 April 2008, for example *McGregor (Inspector of Taxes) v Adcock* [1977] STC 206; *Mannion (Inspector of Taxes) v Johnston* [1988] STC 758; *Atkinson v Dancer* [1988] STC 758 and *Pepper (Inspector of Taxes) v Daffurn* [1993] STC 466.

The second leading case was *McCall (personal representatives of McClean, dec'd) v Revenue and Customs Comrs* [2009] STC 990, NI CA, where at the date of death a parcel of land had an agricultural value of £165,000 but a market value of £5,800,000 due to development potential. It was clearly important for the executors to show that there was, at the date of death, a business qualifying for BPR rather than an agricultural interest qualifying for APR in order that the former could be used to mop up the substantial premium above agricultural value.

The evidence, though not entirely convincing, showed that time had been spent looking after the land such as walking the area, repairing fencing, attending to drinking troughs and drains, cutting and spraying weeds: probably no more than 100 hours per year. Some work was contracted out and the grazier fertilised the fields.

It was held, at first instance that activity 'was, just, enough to constitute a business'. The business was more than just the ownership of the land and receipt of its income. The deceased, despite her disability, owned the business constituted by the activities of her son-in-law and the letting of the land. However, it was held that the business consisted wholly or mainly of holding investments, within s 105(3). The management activities related to letting the land.

The appeal lay direct to the Court of Appeal in Northern Ireland, which applied the test of the reasonable businessman, who would look at the use to which the land was put, which was to be decided on the facts of each case. The graziers had use of the land that was sufficiently exclusive for it to be an investment; the owner could not use it for anything else meanwhile.

The right kind of business was however noted in *Executors of Piercy (deceased) v Revenue and Customs Comrs* [2008] STC (SCD) 858, where HMRC claimed that the business of a property company was mainly investment but the Special Commissioner agreed with the executors that it continued to hold its land as trading stock that it wished to develop. The only type of land-dealing company that fails the 'wholly or mainly' test of s 105(3) is a dealing or speculative trading company that does not actively develop or build. To be an investment company, it must actually have some investments. This decision may prove very useful in future, though it has only the authority of a low tribunal.

Two further relatively recent cases both found in favour of HMRC have sought to illustrate the wide catchment application of the exclusion provision of s 105(3) and a careful reading of each case is strongly recommended.

The first case is that of *Trustees of David Zetland Settlement v Revenue and Customs* [2013] UKFTT 284 (TC), [2013] SWTI 2424 in which the taxpayer claimed that the level of services carried out for the tenants of Zetland House meant that it ought to be classified as a business for the purposes of BPR – access to the relief was very relevant since the Settlement was approaching its ten-year anniversary charge. Zetland House was originally a multi-storey factory occupied by a number of printing firms but the property had outlived its original purpose. There were a number of long-term leases and by 1997 25% of the building was unoccupied – gross rents were £510,000 per annum. The Trustees acquired the premises and transformed them by offering flexible space for computer, media and high-technology businesses all of which required major changes to both the physical appearance and the usage/occupation of the tenant. The Trustees made office space more available, offered attractive short-term leases and made the individual offices smaller. The gross rents and service charges in the year ended 5 April 2007 were approximately £2.4 million. The Trustees hired more staff to provide a wider range of services and facilities to the tenants. The building had a restaurant, gym, cycle arch, Wi-Fi, portage, 24-hour access, meeting rooms, media events, outdoor television screens and an art gallery – it was run on the basis of a community with regular barbecues and social gatherings.

HMRC argued that the purpose of the additional services was to increase occupancy and hence increase the rental receipts – the services were no more than incidental to the core business of collecting rent and service charges. The tribunal looked closely at the income and profit of the various activities which clearly indicated that the bulk of income, well in excess of 50%, derived from the rent and service charge. It was held that the activities were predominantly investment activities or related to investment. The services provided were mainly of a standard nature aimed at maximising income through short-term tenancies. The non-investment side was incidental to the core business and the services were insufficient to make the business one that was mainly non-investment. The purpose of the activities was largely to improve the building and its fabric, to secure the tenancy and to keep the occupancy rates high.

In the second case of *Best v Revenue & Customs Comrs* [2014] UKFTT 77 (TC) Bullick Developments Ltd owned a business centre in County Antrim. The development was financed in part by the Local Enterprise Development Unit and it was argued that such finance was not available for mere investments. The centre included offices, showrooms, industrial and ware-house space, from very small to quite large units. It was agreed that one self-contained area, bringing in 15% of the income, was an investment. Of the rest, 10% was offices, the rest light industrial or warehousing and 400 people worked there. The standard form licence agreements did not give exclusive possession of the land.

Services were listed in two schedules, but it was agreed that most of those in the first schedule were of a type commonly provided by a landlord. Further services were listed in the second schedule and much was made of the availability of a forklift driver but it was a weakness of the case that no copy invoices were provided. The company employed a site maintenance person, receptionist and a forklift driver full time, two part-time people, and three security guards. Most of the units had no separate landline, so calls were put through by the receptionist and most of the units were accessible only to small vehicles, making the forklift useful, though critically the extent of that use was not proved.

Income of £611,472 broke down to:

Licence fees	447,068
Service charges	53,335
Sundry	4,517
Equipment hire	4,452
Heat and light	31,284
Telephone	45,568
Postage	20,056
Parking	5,192

Applying the tests in *George* (see **17.37**), *McCall* (see above) and *Pawson* (see **17.40**), the tribunal considered that the provision of office-like facilities and of the forklift did not save the business from its investment nature. Those services did not predominate when considering the business as a whole. The business was 'well towards the investment end of the spectrum' and thus BPR was denied.

Land used in a business: the 50% claim

[**17.35**] Where land is personally owned by the transferor and used as part of the business operated through a company or partnership, as is more normal and less contentious, BPR will not be under IHTA 1984 s 105(1)(a) but will be under s 105(1)(d) or (e) and in either case the relief will be fixed at 50% only. These last categories relate to land or buildings (and other assets not the subject of this book) which, immediately before the relevant transfer, were used wholly or mainly for certain business purposes. However, care should be taken to note the restriction, sometimes overlooked in tax planning exercises, under s 105(1)(d) that the business in question must be one carried on by:

- a company controlled by the transferor (related property rules will apply for this purpose); or
- a partnership of which the transferor was a member.

Section 105(1)(e) allows the relief where the land was used for a business carried on by the transferor himself but where the land was settled property in which the transferor had an interest in possession (whether pre- or post-March 2006 reforms). A common example of the category might be farmland in a family settlement where the life tenant is the farmer.

BPR will not be available where the business itself is carried on otherwise than for gain (which is to be distinguished from APR as noted in the *Golding* case – see **17.32**). In practical terms this means that the practitioner can expect HMRC to call for the accounts of the business to be satisfied that it is a 'proper' viable business run on business lines and not merely a property-related hobby. This is a particular issue when considering a business of a Stud Farm in which HMRC's opening gambit is nearly always immediately denial for relief on grounds of failure to meet the 'run for profit' requirement.

The 'wholly or mainly' test

[17.36] IHTA 1984, s 105(3) excludes investments from BPR so the property portfolio of an investor will generally not qualify even if operated as a company. This issue was addressed in detail in *Clark and another (executors of Clark decd) v Revenue and Customs Comrs* (2005) SpC 502. The case concerned relief in respect of the shares in a company but it is equally relevant to the ownership by a sole trader of a property portfolio. A partnership, established in 1895, was later incorporated. In the 1920s, it built many homes and in hard times the company bought back many of the properties and leased them to the former purchasers. The company had its own work force to deal with the substantial amount of maintenance and refurbishment required. At the date of the taxpayer's death the company owned 92 dwellings, 4 shops, 4 offices, 2 industrial units and 20 lock-up garages and the taxpayer's family owned another 141 properties, all requiring active management. The company managed its own properties and Clark family properties. The directors spent approximately three-quarters of their time managing the rental activity and the remainder on building works.

The executors, in a direct challenge to earlier cases, argued that the letting of property was no mere investment activity but rather it was so time-consuming that it constituted a business and thus the shares of the company should qualify for BPR. HMRC argued that activities that produce a rent are necessarily investment (and indeed HMRC still subscribe to that view). There was a distinction between managing properties for third parties, such as members of the Clark family, and managing the properties that were still owned by the company. A management fee was not the same as rent.

It was held that the business of the company consisted 'mainly' of holding investments. The Commissioner looked at the business in the round, reviewing profit, the overall context, capital employed, time spent by the directors and the turnover. The profit on building and management activities was too small to bear the proportion of management time that was spent on it. The rental activity subsidised the other activity. Investment activity produced more turnover and profit but took less time. The main asset shown in the accounts related to the investment activity.

This decision confirmed the earlier cases of *Moore v IRC* and *Burkinyoung v IRC* [1995] STC (SCD) 29. The test, in respect of property, is the nature of income that is received. If the income is mainly rent it matters not how diligent the landlord is in managing his estate: if such work is referable to the drawing in of rents this is an investment activity.

The caravan park cases

[17.37] There is a string of tax case authority, mainly concerning caravan parks, which reinforces the 'wholly or mainly' investment principle and in the main all have been found in favour of HMRC. Thus in *Hall (executors of Hall deceased) v IRC* [1997] STC (SCD) 126 a caravan park was denied BPR even though much work was done on it. Part of the site contained wooden chalets that were let on 45-year leases. It was not a touring caravan park and the caravans were static – there was no right to occupy them during the winter. On balance the commissioner regarded the caravan park as being mainly a business which consisted of the making or holding of investments. 84% of the total income came from rents and from standing charges, which was enough to deny BPR.

Powell (personal representatives of Pearce deceased and IRC [1997] STC (SCD) 181 also concerned a caravan park with pitches for long term and short term lettings and again there was evidence of the work that the family did in looking after the residents many of whom were long term and retired. Few of the sites were on short term lets and the income came from pitch fees.

Brendan Peter James Furness (SpC 202) went, unusually, in favour of the taxpayer and for very good reason. This was a very different set-up to prior cases, with evidence that the park was licensed both for static and for touring caravans. There were rallies at the weekend but no permanent residence was allowed. 80% of the taxpayer's time was spent in looking after the welfare of the residents at the caravan park, maintaining it and its structures, with three people employed full time to help. Less than half the net rent for the business came from pitch fees and there was considerable income from caravan sales. Even without the evidence of the source of profit, which might have been enough to sway the Commissioner, the very considerable amount of work done persuaded the Commissioner to allow relief. The work was not what one would normally find in a business that was concerned wholly or mainly with holding of investments.

Caravan owners however suffered a setback in the decision in *Weston (executor of Weston), deceased v IRC* [2000] STC 1064, but that was not a holiday park. The site lay near the M25 and was mixed caravan sales and residential caravans for people aged 50 or over. There was neither shop nor social club, just a laundry and storeroom. Pitch fees usually exceeded the fees from sales and there were few sales anyway. In every year but one from 1988–1994 pitch fees exceeded the income from sales.

The most detailed examination of the issue was in *Stedman's executors v IRC* [2002] STC (SCD) 358, later *IRC v George* [2003] EWCA Civ 1763, [2004] STC 147 both cited in the more recent *Pawson* and *Green* cases (see **17.40**), which concerned a substantial business comprising a residential homes park, a club for residents, caravan storage and other property. Whilst some of the income was clearly investment income, taking the business in the round only 40% of turnover came from 'investment type' income. The decision of the Special Commissioner was overturned by the High Court but restored by the Court of Appeal which recognised this to be a hybrid business. The holding of property as an investment was only one part of the business and, on the findings of fact of the Commissioner, not the main part. It was difficult to see why an active family business such as that comprised in this case should fail to qualify for BPR simply because one necessary component of the making of profits was the use of land. It is regarded as a key reference case.

The main point of referral which builds upon the *Stedman* case discussed above is *Farmer (executors of Farmer deceased) v IRC* [1999] STC SCD (321) – the taxpayer both farmed and let surplus property, making no distinction in his accounts between the two activities. The holding was 449 acres of which farmland and woodland accounted for 441. Eight acres was either tracks or let properties. There were 23 tenancies, mainly shorthold or licenses. The landlord was responsible for repairs and supplied water to the tenants. The farmhouse, farm buildings and farmland were a very significant proportion of the whole and the let property amounted to a little more than one third.

The Special Commissioner considered all relevant factors and critically, did not rely exclusively on the way in which profits were earned but rather concluded that the business was that of a landed estate. Most of the land was used for farming. The let properties were subsidiary not only because they occupied a relatively small proportion of the total area but also because they were sited towards the centre of the land and would not have existed but for their connection with the farm. The business consisted mainly of farming and the let property was not an excluded asset under IHTA 1984, s 112. Applying the principle seen in the case of *Hertford*, discussed as **17.34** above, once it had been decided that there was a single business for the purposes of IHTA 1984, s 105 namely managing a landed estate, all the relevant assets of that business qualified for BPR.

There is already evidence of HMRC reliance on the *McCall* decision to defeat claims to BPR on farmland: it is certainly regularly relied upon to deny APR on farmhouses although see the interesting and welcome outcome in the *Hanson* case (*Hanson (Joseph Nicholas) (as Trustee of the William Hanson 1957 Settlement) v Revenue & Customs Comrs* [2012] UKFTT 95 (TC) [2012] SFTD 705). In *Brander (Representative of James (dec'd) Fourth Earl of Balfour) v Revenue and Customs Comrs* [2010] UKUT 300 (TCC) [2010] STC 2666 the First-tier Tribunal was mainly concerned with the replacement property provisions of s 107. However, the availability of BPR on a landed estate was also in issue. The Tribunal had to decide whether farming and related operations fell within the 'wholly or mainly' exclusion from business relief under s 105(3). The Tribunal followed the *Farmer* case and had no difficulty in agreeing that the running of a typical Scottish landed estate, consisting mainly of farming and of management of cottages was not an investment business. One important factor was that cottages were often let to people whose expertise could benefit the estate, even if that entailed some sacrifice of rent. Thus those lettings were part of the business of the estate as a whole.

The 'succession' issue

[17.38] Taking the terms of the Will as the whole the Upper Tribunal in *Balfour* concluded that the Fourth Earl (the Deceased) had an interest in possession under the terms of the Will of the first Lord Balfour and that confirmed the opinion of Judge Read in the First-Tier Tribunal. The Tribunal then considered the management of Whittingehame Farming Company, through which the Deceased operated those farms that were farmed in hand up to 28 September 1999. After that date the Deceased continued to operate the farming company but as a sole proprietor and the trade was registered for VAT in the name of the Deceased. It then became a partnership between the Deceased and his nephew Mr Brander. After reviewing the terms of the Will and the transactions by the Deceased, the Upper Tribunal considered that the First-tier tribunal had been correct in concluding that the Deceased operated the estate as one business up to November 2002. Although a weaker case than *Farmer*, that finding is significant for and underpins the interpretation of the succession provisions in IHTA 1984, s 107.

The 'wholly or mainly' issue

[**17.39**] The other main issue in the *Balfour* case, which is of wider importance, is whether the business carried on by the Deceased was mainly investment activity, with the result that BPR would be denied in totality under IHTA 1984, s 105(3). The First-tier Tribunal had held that this was one composite business of managing a landed estate and it did include letting 26 houses and cottages. Judge Read, in the First tier Tribunal, had treated the agricultural tenancies as a farming activity but it was argued in the Upper Tribunal that Judge Read had failed to consider the capital values of the different components of the estate and was wrong to group the woodlands and the policy parks with the farms that were farmed in hand because the Deceased, in his capacity as life tenant, could have no interest in the growing timber or in income that related to woodland. HMRC also argued that sporting activities were both minor and non-commercial. They considered that Judge Read was wrong to take account of the time spent by labourers rather than by managers when comparing the way that time was devoted respectively to trading activities and investment activities.

Reviewing these arguments the Upper Tribunal did accept that the majority of money that was raised from forestry or woodland activity was capital and did not affect the 'life rent' interest of the Deceased. The Upper Tribunal also decided that the sporting rights raised little or no let income.

The taxpayer had argued that the issue, whether or not a business was wholly or mainly an investment business, depended on the overall impression. In the case of a landed estate it would be necessary to look at acreage, turnover, profit, time spent and capital value; but no one issue was conclusive. The importance of each would vary according to the particular case. The taxpayer argued that capital value was irrelevant where, as here, the estate was not used to raise capital value. The taxpayer accepted that Judge Read might have been wrong to treat the let farms as trading assets but that did not matter because the total farmed acreage was about the same as the total acreage that was let, and in any case, applying *IRC v George*, that did not affect the final result.

Several principles were considered.

- The 'wholly or mainly' test is a question of fact.
- The person making the decision must look at the business in the round.
- This involves looking at the business over a period of time.

- The fact that the owner of an investment works to manage and maintain an investment does not stop it being an investment.
- Looking at the issue in the round it is not always appropriate to compartmentalise the business and to attribute management and maintenance activity either to trading or non-trading assets.
- Because it is a question of fact, the Upper Tribunal can question the decision of the First-tier Tribunal only on an error of law.

After reviewing the arguments on both sides the Upper Tribunal held as follows:

Applying these principles, the Tribunal considered that the farms in hand and the woodlands were trading assets. The Deceased could benefit both from windfalls and from coppicing, so it was right to include the woodlands. Taking them into account as well as the policy parks, the trading assets slightly exceeded the let assets up to 2001 but thereafter were slightly less. Thus the acreage used was not a major factor.

Sporting activities generated little income but the vermin control associated with those activities was a factor on the trading side of the business. Based on all this, the Upper Tribunal considered that Judge Read was not wrong in law and on these issues his decision should not be challenged.

Looking at the overall context, the Deceased ran a unitary landed estate comprising in-hand farming, forestry/woodland, sporting activities, the letting of farms and of surplus dwelling houses. It was mainly a trading business.

Considering time spent, it was appropriate to look at the time spent by farming contractors as well as by the managing agents. The time so spent pointed towards a predominance of trading activity. The managing agents spent twice as much time on letting and property maintenance as they did on trading activity but other contractors spent more the other way, with the result that 79% of the time in 2001 was on trading related matters and 21% on matters concerned with letting. In 2002 the trading time was 78% and the letting time 22%, which pointed to the predominance of the trading activity.

As to capital value, Judge Read had been right to accept the argument of the taxpayer that the long-term policy of the estate was to retain land not to sell it. Market values were therefore generally immaterial to the business decisions of the Deceased. On capital value there was some leaning towards investment activity, but not enough to sway the overall decision.

For these reasons the Upper Tribunal confirmed the decision of Judge Read in the First-tier Tribunal because the business did not consist mainly of holding investments. On a subsidiary point HMRC had accepted that, if there was a single composite business, it was carried on 'for gain' within the requirement of IHTA 1984, s 103(3).

Holiday lettings businesses

[17.40] In the past, this remains a grey area of IHT law and its application to secure BPR. However, recent high profile cases have all been found in HMRC's favour leading to a conclusion that only in exceptional cases will BPR apply to such activity. The established tests for income tax or for CGT have no application for IHT which has its own code and is not influenced by the former taxes. Many families own a second home, perhaps in a rural or popular holiday location, that they let for short periods when not needed for personal use. Where the rent does no more than offset maintenance costs the owner will probably accept that there is no letting business and that business property relief is simply not available. A farmer, on the other hand, who converts several redundant buildings and runs a dozen letting units, providing not merely clean laundry but fresh groceries at the farm gate, or even prepared meals, will feel that he is working hard to provide a more complete holiday experience.

The difficulty lies between these extremes: there is no case directly in point. It seems likely that the attitude of HMRC to such cases is that, even if substantial services are provided, not all if not very few will count towards the BPR claim. Work done that can be characterised as merely providing accommodation in exchange for rent will not on its own be enough: it is just property management. Each case will turn on its own facts and will involve a 360 degree review of income, profits, capital employed and time spent, then standing back and looking at the case in the round. What has been firmly established as a distinguishing factor is the need to provide services otherwise than in the capacity of landlord and the level of such services must amount to much more than the basic provision of clean linen and cleaning. Wider bolt-on services or facilities such as a beauty salon, swimming pool with lifeguard, gym with personal trainer, children's playground, on site shop etc would help the taxpayer's case. Although following a period of consultation, the FA 2010 restored, at least in part, the favourable income tax treatment of furnished holiday lettings this did not impact on the IHT position which has always been and continues to be dealt with quite separately under the IHT code. Nonetheless, any claim to BPR in respect of furnished holiday lets is always subject to intense HMRC scrutiny. It is clear that HMRC do take a strong stance and thus the practitioner must be prepared to mount a robust defence.

HMRC guidance (IHTM25278) was amended in late 2008, and at time of writing states: ' . . . HMRC's view is that furnished holiday lets will in general not qualify for business property relief. The income derived from such businesses will largely consist of rent in return for the occupation of property. *There may however be cases where the level of additional services provided is so high that the activity can be considered as non-investment, and each case needs to be treated on its own facts*' (emphasis added).

The guidance goes on to indicate that cases involving claims for business property relief on holiday lettings should be referred to HMRC's Technical Team (litigation) – it is clear that there is a great deal of unease within HMRC. Other types of lettings involving land may also fall foul of s 105(3) in HMRC's view. Its guidance states (at IHTM25280): 'Consider whether investment holding is in point where exploitation of land ownership in other ways is involved, eg moorings or beach huts, and seek the views of Technical Group (TG)'.

The narrowness of the HMRC position has been challenged in a number of recent cases:

In *Pawson (deceased) v Revenue and Customs Comrs* [2012] UKFTT 51 (TC) the deceased had 25% interest (with the remaining ownership held by other family members) in a picture postcard seaside holiday letting cottage in respect of which the executors claimed BPR. The income from the property had steadily increased in recent years producing a small taxable profit in all but one year and that due to expenditure on necessary repairs etc. The property was fully furnished with heating and hot water turned on before the arrival of visitors, the well-equipped kitchen was kept in good working order, the cleaner attended the property between each letting and a gardener was hired to ensure that the grounds were kept in good order at all times during the letting season – the family owners dealt with the letting arrangements personally and attended/inspected the property in person on a regular basis. At the First-tier Tribunal it was held that the activities amounted to a business and the claim to BPR was allowed. However, as expected, HMRC appealed to the Upper Tribunal and were successful in their bid to overturn the earlier decision. This effectively restores the position to that determined under *Stedman's Executors v IRC; IRC v George* [2004] STC 147 (TC) namely that the rental exploitation of land with a view to profit is still fundamentally a business of holding the property as an investment. It is generally accepted that the *Pawson* [2012] UKFTT 51 (TC) case was rather weak such that the appeal decision was probably the correct one on the facts as they stood. However, the concern is that the UTT commentary is sufficiently damning as to likely prevent a BPR claim in any furnished letting case.

In *Green (Anne Christine Curtis) v Revenue & Customs Comrs* [2015] UKFTT 236 (TC), BPR was claimed on the transfer of 85% of the appellant's interest in an established self-contained holiday business. The appellant's team argued that a wide spectrum of businesses involved the use of property which at one end involved the granting of a tenancy and at the other end the running of a hotel or a shop but the tribunal were not swayed that the business in question fell on the hotel side. The Tribunal placed heavy reliance on the authorities set out in the cases of *Pawson (dec'd) v Revenue & Customs Comrs* [2012] UKFTT 51 (TC); *McCall (personal representative of McClean, dec'd) v Revenue & Customs Comrs* [2009] STC 990, NI CA; and *Best v Revenue & Customs Comrs* [2014] UKFTT 77 (TC) and concluded that 'the extra services provided are insufficient to demonstrate that the Business is other than mainly one of holding the property as an investment'.

The *Green* and *Pawson* cases were both cited in the recent case of *Re the Estate of Marjorie Ross* (2017 UKFTT 507 (TC)) which yet again considered the availability of BPR in the context of a furnished holiday lets 'complex'. The case was found in HMRC's favour and has simply strengthened HMRC's hand.

Unwise gifts of land

[17.41] Since the availability of relief under IHTA 1984, s 105(1)(d) rests on control of a company or membership of a partnership, care must be taken not to jeopardise relief by unwise action.

Example 6: Tardy conveyancing

Michael together with his sons Nigel and Oliver owned a printing business. Michael held 60% of the shares and his sons, Nigel and Oliver, held 20% each – Michael also owned the premises from which the company traded. He wished to reduce the value of his estate by lifetime gifts and therefore proposed to give Nigel and Oliver the premises plus a 40% shareholding between them. In February 2017, he gave instructions to his solicitors and accountants, hoping the work could be completed by a date that was significant for family purposes. The accountant duly prepared the stock transfers which were ready on the appointed day but there were difficulties with the conveyance because of rights of way and other environmental matters, as well as defects in the title. Anxious to make progress, on 31 May 2017 and after consulting with his accountant, Michael executed the transfers of the shares, retaining a nominal 20% holding. The conveyance of the premises was completed two months later in July 2017.

The result of this delay in the premises conveyance was that, at the time of the transfer of the property, BPR was no longer available under the precise terms of IHTA 1984, s 105(1)(d) because by then Michael no longer controlled the company – there is no relief at all on the transfer of a 'mere asset' even though it may be used for business purposes. Thus the family were at risk of a 100% charge to IHT on the premises if Michael should die within seven years rather than 50%, if the balance had been sheltered by BPR (if not clawed back under IHTA 1984, s 113A). The lawyer found himself in the invidious position of funding, out of his own pocket, the cost of term assurance on Michael's life for 40% of 50% of the value of the premises transfer.

Example 7: Clawback conundrum

Percy together with his sons Quentin and Richard owned a business of running health clubs and saunas. Percy held 54% of the shares and his sons 23% each. Similar to Michael in Example 6, Percy wished to hand on the business and the land from which it traded. His advisers were better organised than Michael's and the transfer of the freehold from Percy's sole name to Quentin and Richard in equal shares was done whilst Percy still owned 54% of the company. As a result, the gift of the land qualified for BPR at 50% under IHTA 1984, s 105(1)(d).

There were no 'lazy' assets in the company thus there was nothing that fell foul of IHTA 1984, s 112 as an 'excepted asset'. When Percy transferred his shares to Quentin and Richard in equal shares he believed that he had done everything possible to help his sons and to mitigate the burden of IHT on his estate. The remaining 50% of the value of the land that was not covered by BPR fell within Percy's nil-rate band and the transfer of the shares qualified in every respect for relief at 100% under IHTA 1984, s 105(1)(bb). The whole transaction appeared to be entirely within the spirit of relief for BPR. But . . .

Sadly, Percy died less than seven years after the gifts and it became necessary to re-examine the gifts for eligibility for BPR at point of PET failure (Percy's death) in the light of IHTA 1984, s 113A. Quentin and Richard had, as they thought, done everything correctly in that they had not sold the land and they continued to run the business. They were dismayed to learn of a possible charge to IHT on the lifetime transfer to them of the land because of the operation of s 113A(3).

The clawback provisions for BPR are no doubt intended to deny relief where the taxpayer no longer 'deserves' the relief, because the business no longer continues or the taxpayer has sold it or other similar events have occurred; but that is not how the legislation works. It operates by examining an imaginary transfer by the transferee (rather than transferor) of the relevant asset at the date of the enquiry. In this case it will be seen that Quentin and Richard both own the land but, since they are equal shareholders in the company, neither of them satisfies the requirements of s 105(1)(d) because neither of them controls the company. This seems both illogical and unfair.

Heritage relief

Practical problems: timing the claim

[17.42] This relief is a specialised topic and reference should be made to the relatively few published works for detailed analysis but one area where it may arise as a 'default' relief is in respect of substantial houses/mansions. A claim may have been made that the residence in question is a farmhouse qualifying for APR under IHTA 1984, s 115(2). However, HMRC typically firmly resist such claims as the taxpayer was to learn in *Arnander (executors of McKenna, dec'd) v Revenue and Customs Comrs* [2006] STC (SCD) 800, [2007] RVR 208.

The property involved, Rosteague House in Cornwall, seemed in many respects to satisfy the test of a farmhouse. The house had medieval origins and its title deeds went back to the 13th century, the present building being part Elizabethan and part 18th century. It was listed Grade II and the building was outstanding. It had many period details including 12-pane sash windows, mullioned windows and intricate plastered ceilings. The principal rooms faced south over lawns and had sea views. Its music room could be used for concerts. It failed to qualify as a farmhouse, in part because it was ' . . . larger, grander, more elaborate and more expensive than was required for the reduced farming purposes for which it was in fact used' and, by comparison with other farmhouses – many also listed Grade I, Grade II or Grade II, it was 'at the very top end of the size of a farmhouse in Cornwall . . . '. (See **11.16** for a more detailed discussion.)

This particular property is an example of the difficulties faced by executors of landed estates. Depending on the location of the property and the circumstances of the family of the deceased, the executors may have to consider an application for conditional exemption from IHT as a 'fall-back' position if the claim for APR fails. The difficulty lies in the procedures for heritage relief not least since any claim to relief must (see IHTA 1984, s 30(3A)), be made no more than two years after the date of the transfer of value. Consider it took over three years for the *McKenna* case to reach the Special Commissioners and many practitioners will be aware of negotiations with HMRC that last longer than that. If allowing public access to the family home is acceptable to the family and if there is any real doubt that APR will be available, the executors should move swiftly to consider and proceed with an application for heritage relief.

The same issue arises in connection with other decisions made by executors in the administration of an estate, such as entering into a deed of variation in reliance on IHTA 1984, s 142. Executors would really like to know where they stand as far as IHT liability is concerned well inside the two year time limit, but that will not always be possible.

With this backdrop, it is important to be aware that HMRC do have discretion to extend the two years claim period in extenuating cases – see IHTA 1984, s 30(3BA). However, as is common with much of the law and practice relating to heritage relief, there are few decided cases which indicate the basis on which a late claim may succeed. The practitioner is therefore left with the uncertainty that HMRC will permit such a claim and there is no right of recourse to challenge such a decision. The recommended course is to make a protective claim but even this is not without difficulties since a 'frivolous' claim made without any realistic prospect of success, could attract the imposition of penalties in the same way as a claim to any other relief where it cannot, in truth, be supported by the circumstances of the case.

The FA 2008 introduction of the transferable nil-rate band between spouses/ civil partners is complicated by the need to take account of the extent to which, on an earlier death, the nil-rate band was in fact used. As noted below, when imposing clawback HMRC can choose which of the former past holders of the heritage property to tax and as a consequence that choice (for both HMRC and the adviser) has become more complicated.

The scope of heritage relief

[17.43] As far as land is concerned the main categories of heritage property are:

- land of outstanding scenic or historic of scientific interest;
- a building for the preservation of which special steps should be taken because of its outstanding historic or architectural interest; and
- land essential for the protection of the character and amenities of a building that falls within one of the two categories just mentioned.

There is no statutory definition of 'outstanding scenic or historic of scientific interest' and as a matter of practice the issue will be treated in the same manner as the procedure for listing under the Planning (Listed Buildings and Conservation Areas) Act 1990. In grading buildings, regard is had to architectural interest and to historic interest but the latter implies some illustration to the building to warrant statutory protection – a mere visit by an important person would not on its own suffice. It is interesting to note that land that falls within this last category, which might be called 'amenity land', need not be in the same ownership as the other land that it protects. This may be very useful where land is held partly in a trust and partly by a member of the family. There has been debate in recent years, in particular since the overhaul of heritage relief by FA 1998 in respect of transfers of value on or after 17 March in that year, as to what quality of property qualifies, but most of that debate centres upon chattels rather than land.

Public access

[17.44] Fundamental to the availability of heritage relief is the extent of public access. IHTA 1984, s 31(2)(b) requires steps to be agreed between the taxpayer and the Treasury for the preservation of the property and for securing 'reasonable access' to the public. The taxpayer must give an undertaking as to the maintenance of the land and the preservation of its character, which in practice will incorporate a detailed plan, the 'Heritage Maintenance Plan', for the management of the land. That does not necessarily mean free right to roam over the entire estate and it will usually be limited to existing and any new permissive rights of way but importantly with appropriate extension to those rights so as to meet the needs of riders and cyclists.

On 12 October 2016, HMRC has updated its guidance on the capital taxes exemptions for 'pre-eminent' national heritage property, including the conditional IHT exemption and the acceptance-in-lieu scheme.

The revised memorandum'Capital taxation and the national heritage' (see bit.ly/2diGcWE) incorporates changes up to 2011, including legislation in SI 2009/730 to replace former ESCs, covering:

- certain foreign-owned works of art, etc being excluded property for IHT (former ESC F7);
- decorations awarded for valour being excluded property for IHT (former ESC F19); and
- exclusion from CGT charge for certain disposals of conditionally exempt property by private treaty to a body within IHTA 1984 Sch 3, or in lieu of IHT (under an unnumbered concession). The legislation is now contained in TCGA 1992, s 258 and includes disposals by companies.

The revised guidance does not however cover changes introduced in F(No 2)A 2015, s 12 (exemption from ten-yearly charge for heritage property), allowing trustees of relevant property trusts two years after the ten-year anniversary to make their claim for conditional exemption; and Act 2016, s 96 (IHT on gifts for national purposes, etc), on the interaction of estate duty and IHT and collections previously maintained by local authorities.

Any application for conditional exemption must include provisions that secure reasonable access to the public including such details as the publication of the terms of the undertaking itself and other information relating to the property. However, what actually amounts to reasonable access will depend very much on the nature of the property. HMRC will certainly seek a minimum number of days of access per year and in this, the location of the land is a relevant factor where perhaps less will be demanded of a remote location than might be appropriate for heathland adjoining a conurbation. Generally, the minimum number of days per year for amenity land and exempt buildings will be 25 and may commonly be as much as 156.

For bare land it is likely that access will have to be available all the year round though there may be agreed periods of temporary closure for the purposes of land management or nature conservation. Equally, an outside event such as foot and mouth disease and the attendant restrictions on movement of animals and access to land will out of necessity override what might otherwise have been a breach of undertakings.

The level of publicity for access that is appropriate will depend on the land itself. Tourist Boards need to know and owners will commonly have to advertise the opening arrangements on one or more suitable publications with national circulation. Commonly the owner will have to display a notice outside the property giving details of the opening arrangements and to agree such other publicity as may be appropriate, including advertisement in some public place in the locality. Even so the actual level of disclosure in respect of land is less demanding than for chattels. The requirements must show:

- where the land is – for example the name of the estate and the nearest town or village; and
- the name, address and telephone number of the person whom can give further details on respect.

HMRC will not agree conditional exemption until an agreed Heritage Maintenance Plan is in place, but will give a reasonable time for it to be drawn up.

Breach of undertaking

[17.45] In the context of qualifying land and buildings, certain undertakings must be given in order to secure the conditional exemption namely:

- In the case of outstanding land, for its maintenance and preservation of character.
- In the case of buildings, for its maintenance, repair and preservation.
- Reasonable access.

Certain acts will trigger a chargeable event:

(i)   *Breach* – If the taxpayer fails to observe the terms of the undertaking given in respect of the heritage property, this will trigger a chargeable event. However, where there is a commitment to allow visits on a number of pre-arranged days in each year, HMRC will not normally insist, for tax compliance purposes, that any days missed should be made up later in the year.

(ii) *Death* – The death of the owner of heritage property will trigger a chargeable event.

(iii) *Sale* – The sale of the property itself will trigger a chargeable event.

Interestingly, the loss or destruction of heritage property is not a chargeable event not even where the owner receives insurance money. However, this will not be the case if the taxpayer has clearly done something in breach of an undertaking which in turn caused the loss.

Matters become quite complicated where the land concerned is 'associated property' within IHTA 1984, s 32A. These rules apply where heritage property is held by several different persons, perhaps all members of the same family, and relief in respect of assets held by one person rest in part on ownership and appropriate undertakings given by the owner of other property. However, these issues will most often arise where relief is also being claimed in respect of chattels and as such are outside the scope of this work.

If the principal heritage property loses its relief ancillary land also loses its relief because it is not heritage property in its own right. There is a 'knock on effect' in a different way where heritage relief is lost. The amount of nil-rate band used by the relevant person will change if he or she is found to be in breach of an undertaking. That will in turn affect the transferable amount available to a surviving spouse or partner.

Clawback charges of heritage relief

[17.46] The charge to tax is specialised, narrowly interpreted and complex. In a simple case where there has been only one conditionally exempt transfer of the property before the chargeable event, the relevant person for the purposes of the legislation is the person who made that initial transfer.

Often, however, heritage property lies within family ownership for generations and in these more complex cases it is necessary to consider the position of each of the individual owners of the heritage property in the period of 30 years leading up to the chargeable event. Where the most recent transfer of the property was itself made more than 30 years ago, the person who made that most recent transfer is the relevant person. Where, within the last 30 years, there have been two or more transfers, HMRC may choose whichever of the transfers they please for the purpose of identifying the 'relevant person'. This is to prevent avoidance of tax by channelling heritage property through impecunious relatives so as to mitigate the clawback charge.

The tax charge is calculated by reference to the relevant person:

- Where the relevant person is alive at the time of the chargeable event, lifetime rates apply, as where an immediately chargeable transfer was made after 17 March 1986. Whilst the nil-rate band may be available to reduce the charge to tax there are no other allowances and in particular neither APR nor BPR is available to reduce the clawback charge; nor is it subject to IHT taper relief under IHTA 1984, s 7.
- Where the relevant person has since died the rules become more complicated. If the conditionally exempt transfer was made in that person's lifetime the tax is charged at lifetime rates but where the conditionally exempt transfer was made on the death special rules apply as if the conditionally exempt transfer was also a gift with reservation. By virtue of IHTA 1984, s 33(2) the lifetime transfer rules apply but the tax is charged at the death rates and treated as the top slice of the estate of the transferor.

Matters are also made more complicated by the fact that, over time, the rates for IHT have changed albeit not in recent years. It can be imagined that, where one of the deaths occurred at a time when rates were particularly high, that person may be selected as the 'relevant person' for the purposes of the charge if the statute so allows. The changes introduced in FA 2008 add to the complication: see IHTA 1984, s 8C(1)(b) as inserted by FA 2008, Sch 4 and the quite complicated formulae to determine the residual nil-rate band that may be claimed.

The family home

Consider a gift by Will of half the house

[**17.47**] Whilst the rules as to transferable nil-rate band will be of considerable value to the vast majority of the population of the UK, there are still pockets of affluence where two nil-rate bands do not go very far and there is still a need to shelter a large residence, with a value of say £2 million plus, from IHT. Where the property is owned by both spouses as tenants in common, it might seem quite simple for each spouse to leave their one half of the family home to the next generation. The surviving spouse can continue to occupy the property by virtue of their half share and whilst, dependent on the values, this arrangement may not avoid an IHT charge on the first death it may shelter future growth. The case of *IRC v Lloyds Private Banking* [1998] STC 559 had parallels with that situation. On the particular facts it was held that the Will effectively gave the surviving spouse such a high degree of security that it effectively created a life interest (IPDI) in the part of the property previously owned by the deceased. As a result the whole of the house fell to be taxed on the death of the surviving spouse and at its then market value – precisely the result which the family had hoped to avoid.

It is argued that, if the Will makes a simple gift to the next generation and gives the surviving spouse absolutely no security, the dicta of the *Lloyds* case will not apply but this presents three problems:

* First, many couples will want to give the surviving spouse some security and will not be happy with the idea that a child or child in law might have control over part of the family home.
* Second, if the only case directly in point went against the taxpayer, is it safe to risk a further challenge by HMRC?
* Third, unless the recipient of the share of the house lives there, CGT may become payable on final sale of his share.

Practical issues and advice for existing schemes

[**17.48**] The 'debt or charge' scheme, described in earlier editions of this work, is now to all intents and purposes obsolete, though existing schemes should be handled with care and should not be abandoned lightly. For many families, the debt or charge scheme represented an intellectual challenge. However, it was important that the structure was understood, to avoid the difficulties illustrated in *Wolff v Wolff and Wolff* [2004] STC 1633.

The principle of the 'debt or charge' scheme was challenged by HMRC Capital Taxes in *Phizackerley v IRC*, as described below, on a specific point. An interesting issue is whether an unwanted scheme can be 'unscrambled' by the argument that it was a sham, ie that the documents describe a transaction but the parties (in so far as they gave their minds to the matter) intended something different. Did the trustees understand that they had powers and discretions? Did they use them? Was there a tacit agreement 'never to call in the IOU'? That would effectively make the surviving spouse the owner of the asset, nullifying the scheme, which might be just what the family now want.

It did initially seem that the Trust reforms introduced on 22 March 2006 would affect the debt or charge scheme. In the event, the introduction of the immediate post-death interest (IPDI) on more generous terms than originally proposed for a time left much of the original thinking intact. A sophisticated arrangement is in circulation under which a half share of a house would sit within a Will trust in such a way that it was not subject to the burden of CGT and yet not automatically subject to IHT on the death of the surviving spouse because it would not meet the hallmarks of an IPDI. However, this arrangement involves supervision of the administration of the estate for a period of more than two years from the date of death. As a result, it may be more complicated than some people would wish.

A problem, keenly illustrated in *Phizackerley (personal representative of Phizackerley, dec'd) v Revenue & Customs Comrs* [2007] STC (SCD) 328 and relevant only to the 'debt or charge' scheme related to the operation of FA 1986, s 103. The mischief is the situation where a person tries in effect to reserve a benefit out of a gift. Consider that A gives Blackacre to B and, then or later, B lends £10,000 back to A. If at A's death the £10,000 loan is still outstanding it is not deductible in calculating the value of his estate to the extent that Blackacre exceeds £10,000 in value. As will be seen, the effect of this is to prevent A from deriving a £10,000 'cash back' benefit to himself by reference to the gift of Blackacre.

The point is now largely academic but in *Phizackerley* it caused a debt or charge scheme to fail, on the specific facts. The later introduction of the transferable nil-rate band serves to make the *Phizackerley* issue relevant only to existing debt or charge schemes, so the commentary, in an earlier edition of this work and elsewhere, will become merely academic.

It is important to be aware that FA 1986, s 103 contains no time limit. The debt which the executors seek to deduct from the estate of the second spouse to die is (see s 103(1)):

> 'subject to abatement to an extent proportionate to the value of any of the consideration for the debt or encumbrance which consisted of –
>
> (a)   property derived from the Deceased; or
> (b)   consideration (not being property derived from the Deceased) given by any person who was at any time entitled to, or amongst whose resources there was at any time included, any property derived from the Deceased.'

It does not matter how long ago the property passed from one spouse to the other, it could still be caught. Clearly, these are matters of proof and some executors inevitably take a more cavalier approach to their duties in delivering accounts under IHTA 1984, s 216 than they should. If there is any clear link between the debt which is deductible from the estate of the surviving spouse and an earlier gift made, however long ago, by the latter to the first spouse to die, it would seem that *Phizackerley* can apply. This case increases the burden on executors and their advisers, and the risk of the penalty for failure to make proper enquiries.

Practitioners should note a highly specialised case of *McKelvey (personal representative of McKelvey, dec'd) v Revenue and Customs* [2008] STC (SCD) 944. The facts were that Mother (M) was 83, blind and in poor health.

Daughter (D) was single and suffering from terminal cancer. D owned two houses and wished to secure M's wellbeing after her own death, so she gave M the houses (the PET). D died two years later and HMRC claimed tax on the value of that failed PET. D's executor appealed, arguing that D made the gift so as to provide for M's nursing care and that IHTA 1984, s 11(3) (disposition to dependent relative for care or maintenance) exempted the gift.

It was held that the gift was exempt in part. It was reasonable for D to assume that M would need care, so the Tribunal could adopt the approach used in personal injury cases. A reasonable assumption was that M would need nursing care for five and a half years, at a cost in all of £115,000. Adding £22,500 for the possibility of going into a home, reasonable provision was thus £140,500. The houses were worth £169,000 so the excess of £28,500 was taxable.

It should be noted that such an arrangement could only be made during lifetime as the relief under s 11 is restricted to lifetime gifts alone.

Residence nil-rate band (RNRB)

[17.49] FA 2015 introduced the new concept of an additional 'Residence' nil-rate band (RNRB) effective from 6 April 2017 which applies specifically to the value of a personal residence passing on death to a direct descendant. Further provisions were contained in the FA 2016, Sch 15 which reflect the outcome of the consultation process launched in autumn 2015. The full RNRB is phased in £25,000 tranches over a four-year period thus:

Tax year	RNRB
	£
2017/18	100,000
2018/19	125,000
2019/20	150,000
2020/21	175,000

The RNRB has a narrow application and is effectively means tested. It only applies if a person's estate includes a 'qualifying residential interest' (relief may also be available where the property has since been sold or downsizing has occurred – see 17.51) where all or part of that interest (or monies raising from the sale) is left to one or more direct descendants. In broad terms a 'qualifying residential interest' is an interest in a dwelling house (wherever situated) which was the deceased's residence when it was part of their estate. Where the deceased's estate includes only one such residence, it follows that this will be the qualifying residential interest. However, if the estate includes more than one residence, the executors may nominate which property will be treated as the qualifying residential interest. It should be noted that for this purpose the value attributable to the qualifying residential interest is after deduction of APR and/or BPR and any liabilities secured thereon.

A residential interest for these purposes also includes land that is occupied and used as the property's garden or grounds, but excludes any trees or underwood in relation to which a woodlands election is made (under s 125) in relation to the person's death. If the deceased lived in 'job-related' accommodation (ie within TCGA 1992, s 222(8A)–(8D)) and owned a house that they intended to occupy as a residence in due course, that house is treated as if so occupied by the deceased.

The RNRB takes priority over the general NRB and is deemed applied first.

Residence transferable nil-rate band (RTNRB)

[17.50] As with the nil-rate band (referred to in this chapter as the general nil-rate band (NRB)/general transferable nil-rate band (TNRB)), it is possible to claim any unused RNRB arising on the earlier death of a spouse/civil partner and again, multiple RTNRB in respect of more than one such spouse/civil partner may be claimed up to a maximum of 100%. In tandem with the general TNRB, the RTNRB must be claimed within two years from the end of the month in which the deceased died, or if later three months from the date when the Executors commenced to act – HMRC may allow a longer period at its discretion. A claim may be withdrawn no later than one month after whichever of those time limits applies.

For estates not exceeding the taper threshold (see **17.52**), if the value of the residence that passes to direct descendants is less than the maximum allowance (ie the deceased's RNRB plus any RTNRB) the RNRB is limited to the value of the residence and any unused RNRB is available for transfer to the surviving spouse/civil partner. If the value of the residence passing to direct descendants is greater than or equal to the maximum allowance, the RNRB is fully utilised such that there is no RTNRB available.

For estates above the taper threshold, if the value of the residence passing to direct descendants is less than the maximum allowance after taper relief has been applied (see below), the RNRB is limited to the value of that residence; any unused residence nil-rate band is available for transfer to the surviving spouse. If the value of the residence passing to direct descendants is greater than or equal to the deceased's maximum allowance, the RNRB available is that allowance, such that none of the RNRB band is available for transfer to the surviving spouse.

If the value of the residence exceeds the value of the net estate (thus post deduction of liabilities) the RNRB is instead restricted to the value of the chargeable estate, and any unused excess is available for transfer to a spouse.

If the deceased's estate does not include a 'qualifying residential interest' or does so include but such interest does not pass to direct descendants (ie passes to the surviving spouse), the RNRB is treated as unused and set at nil. Notwithstanding, the RNRB that has not been used is still available for transfer to the surviving spouse/civil partner. Thus a surviving spouse who is (and was always) the sole owner of the matrimonial home may still be able to claim the deceased spouse's unused residence nil-rate band.

Downsizing

[17.51] The RNRB is extended to apply where the deceased 'downsized' to a less valuable residence, or ceased to own a qualifying residence provided either event took place on or after 8 July 2015 (Budget day). The part of the RNRB that would otherwise be lost as a result of downsizing will remain available, provided the replacement less valuable residence (or assets of equivalent value) is inherited by direct descendants. This is subject to a total amount not exceeding the maximum available RNRB. FA 2016, Sch 15 para 5 has inserted s 8FA into IHTA 1984 to ensure that the level of the allowance is not frozen at the time of downsizing but rather its calculation mirrors that of the TNRB – the RNRB 'lost' at downsizing is converted into a percentage of the allowance the deceased would have then had and that percentage is applied to the value of the RNRB on the second death.

As originally enacted, downsizing relief was not available to a qualifying trust interest (see **17.53**) but following representations from the professional bodies, FA 2016, Sch 15 para 8 inserts s 8HA into IHTA 1984 to give effect to the relief.

Taper

[17.52] The RNRB is tapered with reference to the total value of the deceased's estate (not the value of the property). Estate for this purpose is defined as net of liabilities but before the application of reliefs ie BPR/APR. The 'taper threshold' is set at £2 million fixed until April 2021 but in subsequent tax years it will be subject to indexation by reference to the CPI. The taper will operate to reduce the RNRB by £1 for every £2 that the value of the estate exceeds the available relief by applying the formula:

$$\text{Allowance} - ((E - TT) / 2)$$

Where:

- Allowance is the total of the residence nil-rate band at the person's death, plus any unused residence nil-rate band transferred on the earlier death of a spouse or civil partner.
- E is the value of the person's estate immediately before death (ie before any reliefs and exemptions).
- TT is the taper threshold.

Thus for 2020/21 (ignoring any available RTNRB) the RNRB of £175,000 is reduced to nil if the deceased's estate is equal to or exceeds £2.35 million.

'Inherited' and 'closely inherited'

[17.53] Access to the RNRB pivots on the requirement that the property residence passes (inherited) on death to a direct descendant (closely inherited) with both the terms specifically defined within the legislation FA 2015, s 8J thus,

B inherits a property if it is transferred to B:

- under D's will;
- under the intestacy rules;
- otherwise as a result of D's death.

In this context 'otherwise' has a wide meaning which can include a transfer by:

- survivorship;

- under an instrument of variation (s 142);
- distribution out of a discretionary will trust to a lineal descendant beneficiary within two years of death (thus within s 144).

However, the term 'inherits' has a narrow interpretation which in the case of settled property is restricted to property transferred to B where:

- B becomes entitled to an immediate post-death interest;
- B becomes entitled to disabled persons interest;
- the property becomes settled on trusts to which s 71A (bereaved minors trust) or s 71D applies (18 to 25 trust) and is for B's benefit (s 8J(4));
- the property was settled property in which D was beneficially entitled to an interest in possession immediately before death, B inherits the property if he becomes beneficially entitled to it on D's death (s 8J(5));
- the property is treated as forming part of D's estate immediately before death as a result of the gifts with reservation provisions (FA 1986, s 102(3)) applying to the gift, B inherits the property if they were the recipient of D's gift (s 8J(6)).

Something is 'closely inherited' for the above purposes if it is inherited by the deceased's:

- child, stepchild, adopted child, foster child;
- grandchild or other lineal descendant;
- spouse/civil partner of the deceased's lineal descendant;
- such spouse/civil partner where the lineal descendant died (no later than the deceased), if they did not remarry in the subsequent period ending with the deceased's death.

Transferable nil-rate band: practical issues

[17.54] A claim to transferable nil-rate band (TNRB) must be made within two years of the death of the second spouse or such longer period as HMRC allow. It should be noted that even though only claimable on that second death and hence regarded as an estate relief it can still be applied against failed PETs made within seven years of death – it cannot, however, be set against chargeable lifetime transfers at time when first made (ie during lifetime) although it may be repositioned on death.

It does not matter, in one sense, when the first spouse died but it can impact on the calculation of the TNRB – see below. Many who are bereaved often take a long time to put their affairs in order whether this be for personal or financial reasons but that surviving spouse, who might well be infirm, must take action within two years of death to put in place a deed of variation to introduce the debt or charge scheme for the benefit of the next generation. The introduction of the TNRB in part relieves that pressure on the surviving spouse. All that the family need do after the second death, is assemble the documents to make a claim, which will be seen as merely part of the process of completing IHT400 (or IHT205 in simpler cases but only where the full (unused) TNRB is claimed).

However, it is still the case that many TNRB claims are lodged which at best are overstated or at worst not in point at all and such claims fail to include the relevant evidence, even where it was already in the possession of the personal representatives. It should be carefully noted that HMRC do review such claims and do make full use of the FA 2008 and FA 2009 provisions to impose stiff penalties where a claim for the TNRB is found to be incorrect. It is therefore vital that any claim should be founded on a detailed review of the position and not lodged on a 'frivolous' basis in the hope of passing muster.

Although in modern times the concept of the spousal exemption is taken for granted this was not always the case:

Death prior to 22 March 1974 – There was no spousal exemption thus even if the estate passed to the surviving spouse that estate value would bite into or more likely exhaust the nil-rate band.

Death between 23 March 1974 and 13 November 1974 – The spousal exemption was restricted to £15,000 so any excess passing to the surviving spouse would bite into and more likely exhaust the nil-rate band.

Death post 13 November 1974 – The full complete spousal exemption was introduced (at least as far as UK-domiciled spouses were concerned).

Quite a few widows and widowers are still affected by these restrictions on the amount of nil-rate band that may be transferred, which seems unfair.

This presents the family with interesting choices:

Example 8

> James died in August 2017 leaving his entire estate of £2.5 million on discretionary trust for benefit of Liz, his wife, their children and grandchildren. Liz has assets of £900,000 being half the family home, owned as tenants in common with James, and savings which on her death will pass to the children. However, Liz wants her children to have some money now. How should the trustees of James' Will Trust exercise their discretion?
>
> For convenience perhaps Liz should own the entire house anyway, avoiding the problems of CGT that could arise on a later sale by trustees. Subject to the value, her estate could also benefit from the RNRB (but access to the TRNRB is denied since James' estate exceeded the £2.35 million threshold). If she is in good health she may also feel that it will be best for her to inherit as much as possible under James' Will, because the spousal exemption will ensure that as little as possible of his nil-rate band is then used. F(No 2)A 2015 has removed the need to wait three months from James' death for such a spousal appointment of an absolute interest to be read back to the date of his death to secure the benefit of the spousal exemption.
>
> Liz could also make the gifts to her children out of her own resources as PETs, hoping to survive seven years. If:
>
> • Liz does so survive, and
> • at her death the nil-rate band is much larger than it was in August 2016 (though that seems unlikely at present with the nil-rate band fixed at its current rate until 6 April 2021); and
> • none of it was used in the distributions from James' trust,

there will be two much larger bands available than would otherwise have been the case.

It should be carefully noted that there must be no consideration for a variation or a disclaimer but this critical point is so often overlooked. This was keenly illustrated in the 'stepmother' case of *Lau (executor of Lau, decd) v Revenue and Customs Comrs* [2009] STC (SCD) 352. The deceased had left his adult son (by an early marriage) £665,000 free of IHT but there were also legacies to his adult daughters. All three children renounced their benefits and as a result the residue of the estate, some £3.8 million, passed to the widow of the deceased (by a later marriage) who then gave the son £1 million. HMRC refused to allow IHTA 1984, s 142(1) to apply, treating the renunciation as effective on death, because there was a direct causal relationship between the £1million payment and the renunciation. The widow appealed.

It was held that the disclaimer by the son was made for consideration in money or money's worth. His supposed reasons for renouncing the legacy, which would have given him and his family security for life, were improbable. The evidence was 'utterly unpersuasive'.

Chapter 18

Environmental taxes

by
Helen Thompson and Kathryn Sewell,
Deloitte

Introduction

[18.1] This chapter looks at environmental taxes as they apply to real estate. In particular, it considers three specific environmental taxes introduced in the UK to discourage environmentally unfriendly behaviour. These are Climate Change Levy, which is a tax on fuel and power generation and consumption by businesses; Aggregates Levy, a tax on the commercial exploitation of aggregate in the UK; and Landfill Tax, a tax on waste deposited to landfill sites in the UK.

Climate Change Levy

Background

[18.2] At the United Nations Kyoto Conference in December 1997, a large number of developed countries undertook to adopt legally binding targets for reducing greenhouse gas emissions. These discussions have developed over many years and resulted in the Paris Agreement which entered into force on 4 November 2016. The Paris Agreement adopts key targets including the reduction of anthropogenic global emissions and steps to limit global warming.

While global discussions on reducing greenhouse gas emissions continue, many countries have their own climate goals, targets and initiatives. Amongst these, the European Union announced in January 2014 a reduction in 1990 levels of greenhouse gas emissions of 40% by 2030 (alongside a renewable energy target). Domestically, the UK implemented challenging future goals as part of the Climate Change Act which received Royal Assent in November 2008. One of the main goals of this Act was to reduce emissions of carbon dioxide ($CO2$) and other greenhouse gases though domestic and international action by at least 80% by 2050 and at least 34% by 2020, against a baseline. In July 2014, the Government confirmed that it would retain these targeted reductions. Climate Change Levy (CCL), including the carbon price support rates, is one of the measures supporting these reductions.

Introduced on 1 April 2001 by FA 2000, CCL is an environmental tax on energy supplied to industry, commerce, agriculture, local administration and other sectors. CCL was implemented as a key part of the UK Government's strategy for meeting its emissions reduction commitments.

The proposal to introduce CCL was a source of controversy, with many sectors of industry resistant to the plans. In response to a consultation exercise, in the 1999 Pre-Budget Report, the Government promised to exempt new renewable energy generation and good quality Combined Heat and Power (CHP) generation, however these exemptions were subsequently withdrawn. Other measures were also implemented to support energy efficiency improvements by business, such as an enhanced capital allowances scheme for investment in energy efficiency, and significant CCL discounts for energy intensive industries entering into agreements to undertake demanding CO_2 reduction targets. In addition, the introduction of CCL was accompanied by a slight reduction in the rate of employers' National Insurance Contributions. This was intended to make CCL revenue neutral, so as not to impact upon UK competitiveness.

It has been claimed that CCL has had a significant impact in contributing towards reducing UK emissions. Previous estimates have predicted annual reductions resulting from CCL to be in excess of 3.5 million tonnes of carbon (MtC). However, CCL is not without its critics. In particular, the CCL reliefs for energy intensive sectors have been criticised on the basis that the worst offenders had most to gain in comparison with those businesses which had already undertaken to promote energy efficiency. The introduction of carbon price support rates of CCL for supplies of fossil fuels to electricity generators, in April 2013 (discussed further at **18.9** below), sought to address criticism that CCL did not discriminate between energy sources according to their carbon content, by taxing fossil fuels used in electricity generation.

In general, CCL is only one of a number of initiatives intended to cut energy use by business, alongside the EU Emissions Trading Scheme (a compulsory scheme for heavy industry and power generation sectors), the Carbon Reduction Commitment (a compulsory scheme effective from 1 April 2010 for certain entities in the UK not covered by the EU Emission Trading Scheme), and Climate Change Agreements between industry and Government (considered in more detail at **18.8** below). This framework of specific regulatory provisions continues to evolve, with the introduction of mandatory carbon reporting from 1 October 2013 that has created further obligations for UK businesses.

The Government announced in Budget 2015 that it will continue to use the tax system to influence taxpayer behaviour to achieve positive environmental outcomes (where tax is an effective mechanism to do so). A consultation was launched in Autumn 2015 regarding a review of the business energy efficiency tax landscape, which aimed to simplify and improve the effectiveness of the regime. In particular, the review covered CCL, the CRC Energy Efficiency Scheme and their interaction with other business energy efficiency policies and regulations. Following this consultation, a number of stakeholders, including Ofgem (the government regulator for gas and electricity markets); the Chartered Institute of Taxation; and various trade sector bodies, called on the Government to set out clear objectives and future plans for business energy policy to allow businesses to make long-term investment decisions, simplify the compliance burden on businesses, and ensure businesses are able to proactively implement the right behaviours to reduce carbon emissions. The Government announced in Budget 2016 that the CRC Energy Efficiency Scheme will be abolished in 2019, with a corresponding increase in CCL rates intended to offset the revenue effect to Government.

The taxation of certain energy products is governed within the European Union by Council Directive 2003/96/EC (commonly known as the 'Energy Taxation Directive'). The current Directive gives member states (including the UK) a relatively wide range of flexibility to tax products such as coal or gas, but any energy tax (including CCL) should be levied in line with the provisions of the Directive. A significantly updated Directive was proposed by the European Commission in early 2011 but following unsuccessful negotiations between the EU Member States, the proposal was withdrawn. Since then, the European Commission's Directorate-General for Taxation and Customs Union commenced a study into certain technical aspects of the EU legislation on energy taxation.

The levy

[18.3] Any person who supplies 'taxable commodities' needs to consider whether they have a requirement to register and account for CCL to HMRC. There is no turnover threshold for registration, as there is for VAT, although there are *de minimis* limits for individual supplies below which it is not necessary to account for CCL. The main rates of CCL are only levied on supplies made to business consumers of energy and are not intended to apply to upstream or wholesale supplies or supplies made to domestic or charitable users.

Unlike VAT, CCL is not deductible. Thus it represents an absolute cost to the purchaser of the energy. It should also be noted that VAT is chargeable on the CCL inclusive amount. Although many large suppliers now separately itemise CCL on their invoices, there is no legal requirement to do so. Therefore, some invoices merely comment that the sum charged is inclusive of CCL at the appropriate rate.

Taxable commodities

[18.4] The levy is charged on the taxable supply of taxable commodities set out in FA 2000, Sch 6, para 3. Taxable and non-taxable commodities are defined as follows:

Taxable commodities	Non-taxable commodities
Electricity	Hydrocarbon oil (taxed separately under Hydrocarbon Oil Duties Act 1979)
Gas in a gaseous state of a kind supplied by a gas utility	Road fuel gas (including Liquefied Petroleum Gas and Compressed Natural Gas used as fuel in road vehicles)
Petroleum gas, or other hydrocarbon gases, in liquid form	'Waste' as defined by Environmental Protection Act 1990
Coal and lignite	

Taxable commodities	Non-taxable commodities
Coke and semi-coke, of coal or lignite	
Petroleum coke	

Furthermore, a taxable supply of a taxable commodity occurs in the following circumstances (FA 2000, Sch 6, paras 4–7) unless specifically exempted or excluded:

- Supplies of electricity by an electricity utility where the person to whom the supply is made is not an electricity utility, and supplies of gas by a gas utility where the person to whom the supply is made is not a gas utility.
- 'Self-supplies' by electricity and gas utilities for their own, unrelieved consumption.
- Supplies of electricity from partly exempt Combined Heat and Power stations.
- Supplies of fuels other than gas and electricity when made in the course or furtherance of a business.

Rates

[18.5] Unlike VAT, CCL is not calculated by reference to the price paid for the supply. CCL is levied on each unit of energy supplied at the following rates from 1 April 2017 until 31 March 2018:

Commodity	Rate
Electricity	£0.00568 per kilowatt hour
Gas supplied by a gas utility or gas supplied in a gaseous state that is of a kind supplied by a gas utility for burning in Great Britain	£0.00198 per kilowatt hour
Liquid petroleum gas or other gaseous hydrocarbon supplied in a liquid state	£0.01272 per kilogram
Other taxable commodity eg coal	£0.01551 per kilogram

These rates are intended to reflect the energy consumption and pollution usually associated with the production of that fuel; therefore, the CCL rate for electricity is considerably higher than the rate for gas.

In line with usual practice, CCL main rates for 2017 to 2018 and 2018 to 2019 will be increased in line with RPI as legislated in the Finance Act 2016. For 2019 to 2020, it is intended the rates will be further increased. The balance between rates on taxable commodities will be updated to reflect changes in the fuel mix used in electricity generation and to recover the tax revenues lost by closing the Carbon Reduction Commitment (CRC) Energy Efficiency Scheme.

Exclusions

[18.6] There are a large number of exclusions, exemptions and reliefs from CCL. Excluded supplies (FA 2000, Sch 6, paras 8, 9) comprise:

(1) 'De minimis' supplies are always considered to be for domestic use and are excluded from the charge to CCL. The de minimis limits are similar to those that apply for the purposes of the reduced rate of VAT, ie:

    (a) metered electricity supplied to a person at a premises where the electricity together with any other electricity provided at the premises by the same supplier is provided at a rate not exceeding 1,000 kilowatt hours per month;

    (b) un-metered electricity supplied to a person where the electricity together with any other electricity provided by the same supplier is provided at a rate not exceeding 1,000 kilowatt hours per month;

    (c) gas of a kind supplied by a gas utility or petroleum gas when supplied in a gaseous state through pipes and where the total gas supplied by the supplier at the premises does not exceed 4,397 kilowatt hours a month;

    (d) not more than one tonne of coal or coke held out for sale for domestic use (ie domestic grade fuel);

    (e) liquid petroleum gas (LPG) in cylinders each of which is less than 50 kilograms net weight and is not intended for resale; and

    (f) a supply of LPG not in cylinders to a customer at premises that have a tank capacity of not more than two tonnes.

No certification is required for CCL purposes if the supplies fall within *de minimis* limits; however the supplier must keep records to substantiate the treatment. Accepted records may include commercial documents retained as part of the business's records, VAT invoices, and CCL certificates (PP11 CCL supplier certificate and PP10 CCL supporting analysis certificate).

(2) Supplies exceeding the *de minimis* limits can still be excluded from CCL if they are supplied for use in a dwelling, ie houses, flats and similar.

(3) Supplies exceeding the *de minimis* limits can also be excluded from CCL if they are supplied to a building used for a 'relevant residential purpose' (eg caravans, children's homes, student halls, homes for the elderly). Hospitals, prisons, hotels, inns and similar establishments are not included in the definition of relevant residential purpose.

(4) Supplies for non-business charitable use are excluded from CCL provided a VAT certificate is completed by the user and given to the supplier declaring the fuel is to be used for this purpose.

(5) Supplies that are used partly for domestic or charitable consumption and partly not are 'mixed supplies' and should be apportioned for the calculation of CCL. Customers need to provide suppliers with certificates for VAT and CCL purposes that declare what percentage of fuel and power supplied to each premises is put to qualifying use. However, where the excluded proportion is at least 60% of the supplies made then the entire supply is CCL free.

(6) Wholesale or upstream supplies and supplies between utilities are generally outside the scope of the main rates of CCL, but since April 2013 supplies of fossil fuels between businesses used for electricity generation may be liable to the carbon price support rates of CCL.

Where suppliers are in doubt as to the qualifying use under 2 and 3 above, they should obtain a certificate from the customer confirming the percentage of fuel or power that is put to qualifying use. Where CCL is underpaid on supplies then the supplier will be held liable unless he had good reason to believe the supply was excluded and he holds a valid certificate issued by the customer.

Exemptions and reduced rates

[18.7] Supplies exempted from the main rates of CCL include (FA 2000, Sch 6, paras 11–20):

- supplies not for burning or consumption in the UK (including exports);
- supplies used in some forms of transport (eg electricity for train propulsion);
- supplies used in producing CCL taxable commodities other than electricity;
- certain supplies (other than self-supplies) to electricity producers;
- supplies (other than self-supplies) of electricity to CHP stations (see **18.12** for further detail);
- certain self-supplies by electricity producers;
- electricity produced from CHP stations (depending upon the plant's efficiency) where these are supplied or consumed directly. The exemption was removed from April 2013 for 'indirect' supplies to consumers via the grid; such supplies are now liable to CCL (see **18.12** for further detail);
- supplies used for their non-fuel characteristics (eg electricity used for the purposes of electrolysis); and
- certain supplies used in mineralogical or metallurgical processes.

Various conditions need to be met for the above exemptions to apply; for example, the supplier must be issued with appropriate certification to allow the exemption to be applied.

A previous exemption from CCL for supplies of natural gas in Northern Ireland was removed with effect from 1 April 2011 (an interim lower rate was temporarily in force until 31 October 2013). Supplies made after 1 November 2013 are subject to the full CCL rate applying to gas.

Electricity produced prior to 1 August 2015 from renewable sources, ie if produced from sources other than peat, nuclear or fossil fuel, eg wind energy, wave energy, small scale hydro power, landfill gas, municipal and industrial wastes was also exempt (see **18.13** for further detail). There is no requirement to account for CCL on self-supplies of renewable source electricity and the removal of the renewable source exemption did not alter this.

Reliefs

[18.8] Under FA 2000, Sch 6, para 44, energy intensive businesses can enter into voluntary CCL Agreements (CCLA) with the Government to obtain a discount on the levy. Energy intensive users are those that operate a Part A process listed in the Pollution Prevention and Control (England and Wales)

Regulations 2000, Sch 1 or as otherwise included by the Energy Products Directive. Eligible industries include (but are not restricted to) aluminium, cement, ceramics, chemicals, food and drink, foundries, glass, non-ferrous metals, paper and steel sectors. It was confirmed in the 2011 Budget that CCLAs will remain in place until 2023. Businesses that do not currently have a CCLA should consider whether they are eligible for one. By way of example, a CCA was agreed in July 2014 for data centres and similar facilities: businesses housing IT equipment should consider if this may apply to their operations.

In return for agreeing to deliver specific commitments to increase energy efficiency or to reduce emissions over a period (normally 10–15 years), these energy intensive users qualify for a reduction in the rate of CCL charged to the relevant plant and facilities they operate. The amount of the reduction is 90% for supplies of electricity and 65% for all other fuels. Overall responsibility for the agreements rests with the Department for Business, Energy and Industrial Strategy ('BEIS'); and negotiations are conducted at trade association level, so that targets are set across each individual trade sector.

HMRC is able to recover the CCL relief where a CCLA has been negotiated but the business fails to meet its target under the scheme, and is in a sector that fails to meet its sector target. The repayment to HMRC is an amount proportionate to the extent to which the facility failed to meet its target. This places a much greater responsibility on businesses to meet their targets and it is important for businesses with CCLAs in place to ensure that performance against these targets is monitored.

If an energy intensive installation consumes more than 90% of each taxable commodity used on the site then the entire site is eligible to be covered by a CCLA. Otherwise the facility needs to be defined so that at least 90% of each taxable commodity is used within the energy intensive installation.

Agreement holders are required to issue certificates to each supplier before the relief can be claimed. There are two parts to the certificate documentation: a Form PP10 – supporting analysis; and a Form PP11 – supplier certificate. Both parts need to be completed by the agreement holder who must send the PP11 to the supplier and retain a duplicate. The agreement holder need only forward a copy of the PP10 to HMRC. Businesses are required to annually review their entitlement to relief. Where a business's entitlement to relief changes it is required to submit a new PP11 to the supplier and PP10 to HMRC following its annual review. Suppliers' certificates are valid for a maximum of five years. Errors in certificates completed by energy intensive businesses can lead to penalties for those businesses.

Carbon price floor

[**18.9**] The carbon price floor was introduced as of 1 April 2013 (via the mechanism of an extra 'carbon price support' rate of CCL). As a result, supplies of fossil fuels used in most forms of electricity generation are subject to CCL at the relevant carbon price support rate ('support rate'). The carbon price floor is intended to build a mechanism to ensure that the price of carbon cannot fall below a particular level. By making carbon more costly, it was intended this would drive low carbon investment.

Electricity generators using gas or coal as source fuel will generally, therefore, incur significant CCL costs, passed on in the price of the electricity charged to consumers.

Changes to CCL and fuel duty to accommodate the price floor

[18.10] A support rate of CCL applies to supplies of fossil fuels (such as gas, LPG and coal) used to generate electricity. The rate varies according to the carbon content of the fossil fuel.

The rates applying to these supplies from 1 April 2016 to 31 March 2019, which are equivalent to £18.00 per tonne of CO_2, are:

Commodity	Rate
Maximum CPS rate	£18.00 per tCO_2
Natural Gas	£0.00331 per kilowatt hour
Liquefied petroleum gas (LPG)	£0.05280 per kilogram
Coal and other taxable solid fossil fuels	£1.54790 per gross gigajoule
Gas oil, rebated bioblend, kerosene	£0.04916 per litre
Fuel oil, other heavy oil, rebated light oil	£0.05711 per litre

The initially proposed carbon price floor trajectory forecast an increasing gap in the carbon price faced between UK energy users and users abroad, leading to higher costs for UK businesses and a reduction to their international competitiveness. To combat this, the 2014 Budget announced a reform to cap the UK-only element of the carbon price floor at £18 per tonne of CO2 from 2016/17 until 2019/20. Budget 2016 announced the £18 per tonne rate will be uprated in line with RPI from 1 April 2020.

Where the fossil fuel is oil, rather than the support rate of CCL being applied, it is subject to a corresponding increase in duty cost (through reduced duty relief).

The support rate is accounted for by the electricity producer, not the supplier of fossil fuels. All generators liable to pay the support rate of CCL must self-account for the levy to HMRC, and register with HMRC if they are not already registered for CCL.

Certain reliefs and exemptions will apply to the support rate of CCL:

- small generators, defined as follows, are not liable to CPS rates on their inputs:
  - CHP schemes with combined generation capacity of 2MW or less; and
  - non-CHP generators with a generation capacity of 2MW or less; the combined capacity of all generators owned by connected persons must be compared to this limit;
- exempt unlicensed electricity suppliers other than those operating CHP stations;
- supplies of fossil fuels to stand-by generators – ie those generators only used to provide back-up generation in the event of a power cut or similar occurrence;

- coal slurry used in electricity generation;
- supplies of fossil fuels to generation stations fitted with carbon capture and storage technology are entitled to a proportionate abated support rate, reflecting the percentage of CO_2 captured; and
- fossil fuels used in a CHP station to generate heat, mechanical power, or from 1 April 2015 good quality electricity that is self-supplied (or supplied under exemption from the requirement to hold an electricity licence) (see **18.12** for further detail).

Landlords and tenants

[18.11] CCL is generally a one-stage tax charged at the point of consumption (although the carbon price floor changes can cause CCL to be levied twice in some supply chains). In some circumstances, the final consumer of fuel or power will not receive a supply directly from a utility; for example, where they are the tenant of a landlord which receives the supplies directly, or where there is an arrangement for one party to receive all the supplies before onward supplying to other parties, such as under a bulk buying arrangement. This complicates the CCL position and means that the tenant may lose the benefit of any exclusions, exemptions or reliefs to which it is entitled.

In some cases, no problem arises because the landlord can submit relevant certificates on behalf of himself and his tenants. For example, a landlord can certify for his own and his tenants' domestic or non-business charitable use of fuel and power. Similarly, where a site is covered by a single CCLA and all occupants on the site qualify for the reduced rate and no other reliefs then the landlord can provide a certificate claiming CCL relief for the whole site. This may not be a comfortable position for the landlord as the certification will be made based on his own and his tenants' consumption of fuel and power and if the certificate proves to be incorrect then the landlord will be held liable for any under-declared CCL. The landlord and tenant may need to agree between themselves who will bear the cost of any underpaid CCL in the event that errors arise in the certificates completed and submitted to suppliers by the landlord. In other scenarios, where the landlord is unable to certify for tenants, CCL is likely to be overpaid.

One solution to this problem may be for the landlord to arrange for the utility to bill customers directly, so that a tenant may directly certify its own eligibility for a relief. This would be an ideal arrangement to prevent the loss of tax relief; however, it is sometimes not possible to set arrangements up in this way.

Alternatively, the landlord could apply to HMRC to become a 'deemed utility'. Generally, HMRC will make directions for utility status where CCL is not being charged on taxable supplies and, on request, where a non-utility supplier, such as a landlord, has customers that would be entitled to reliefs that can only be made available by a utility. Where utility status is granted, all supplies to the landlord would then become free from CCL on the basis that supplies between utilities are excluded from CCL. The landlord would then register for and account for CCL on its supplies of taxable commodities to tenants and, where applicable, would need to account for its own consumption where this attracts CCL. Where a commercial end-user qualifies for some type of CCL relief, it would complete a certificate and issue this to the landlord as evidence that it should receive its supplies of energy CCL-free, or at a reduced rate. Provided that the landlord has acted with due care and is in possession of a valid certificate then any under-accounting for CCL that arises due to an error on the certificate is more likely to be the liability of the end-user than the landlord. Of course, a downside to this arrangement is that the landlord will be required to apply for deemed utility status, register for CCL and submit quarterly CCL returns which involves increased administration.

Example 1

Where supplies are made to domestic or non-business charitable tenants, CCL should not apply on qualifying use, since the tax is a charge on the business use of energy. Landlords (ie those owning the freehold or leasehold interest in the property) are able to certify on behalf of their tenants for domestic or non-business charity use, just as they would for the purposes of the reduced rate of VAT on supplies of fuel and power. If anyone other than the landlord purchases energy to sell on for domestic or non-business use, CCL will apply.

Hyacinth, which acts as a property manager for a University, purchases supplies of electricity on behalf of the University for use in student accommodation (ie a relevant residential purpose). Hyacinth is charged VAT at the standard rate and CCL by the electricity supplier.

Hyacinth recharges the supplies of electricity to the University at the reduced VAT rate of 5% applicable to domestic accommodation and is able to recover the input tax incurred on the supplies. However, it must either absorb the CCL cost or pass this on to the University.

Hyacinth applies to HMRC for deemed utility status, and uses the direction from HMRC to secure CCL-free supplies from the electricity supplier. The University provides Hyacinth with the certificate it uses to obtain the 5% rate for VAT on its supplies of energy and receives supplies excluded from CCL.

Example 2

Where businesses have entered into CCLAs and are thus eligible for the reduced rate of CCL, a landlord may only certify for the relief on behalf of its tenants where all occupants of the site are entitled to the reduced rate. In this case, the landlord will have to certify on the basis of its and the tenants' records and will be responsible should the certification prove incorrect.

Tulip is a port landlord and incurs various ongoing charges for supplies of electricity and gas to the entire site and its tenants.

However, only part of the site is eligible for the reduced rate of CCL under a CCLA, and supplies from the utility are delivered to a point on the site which is not covered by a CCLA. As a result, the relevant tenants are not able to certify to Tulip and Tulip is not able to certify to the utility that the reduced rate should apply.

Tulip decides to apply for deemed utility status and receives supplies from the utility free of CCL. It then provides the supplies on to the tenants and is able to deliver them to points covered by CCLAs. This allows the relevant tenants to certify for the reduced rate of CCL, which Tulip collects and pays over to HMRC on a quarterly basis.

Example 3

Where tenants are eligible for an exemption from CCL on the basis that they intend to use a supply for non-fuel use, a landlord may not certify on behalf of a tenant – the exemption can only apply to the party to whom the supply from the utility is made.

Foxglove receives supplies of energy for making batteries. However, its supplies come from the utility via its landlord, Rose. Rose is not able to certify to the utility that the reduced rate should apply, since only the final consumer can certify how the supplies are intended to be used. The utility charges CCL in full to Rose, who passes the cost on to Foxglove.

Rose agrees to apply for deemed utility status, receiving its supplies CCL-free. This allows Foxglove to certify to Rose that it intends to use the electricity for non-fuel use. Rose is able to exempt its onward supplies of electricity to Foxglove.

On-site generation facilities

[18.12] The UK's existing electricity system relies on a small number of large power stations generating electricity which is then distributed to where it is needed. However, because these power stations tend to be situated far from centres of demand, the heat produced as a by-product from the burning of fossil fuels is generally wasted; for example, by being emitted into the environment via cooling towers or discharged into rivers. It is estimated that this heat loss alone represents wastage of more than 60% of the total energy contained in the fossil fuels (*Decentralising power: an energy revolution for the 21st century*, Greenpeace). Furthermore, approximately 7.5% of the total electricity supplied in the UK is estimated to be wasted every year due to its transportation through the grid (Combined Heat and Power Association). As a result, on-site generation can provide greater energy efficiency.

Currently, under certain conditions, CCL relief is available for 'direct' supplies of electricity generated from CHP stations (ie where power is not sold via a third party electricity utility). The exemption for electricity generated from CHP stations and supplied indirectly (ie via another electricity supplier) to an energy consumer was removed from 1 April 2013.

A supply of taxable commodities to a 'good quality' CHP station is exempt from the main rates of CCL. In addition, a relief exists from the support rates of CCL for supplies to a CHP where this fuel is attributable to either heat or mechanical outputs.

From 1 April 2015, new measures were introduced to exempt from the support rate of CCL supplies to a CHP where the fuel is to be used to produce qualifying electricity where support rate commodities are brought onto, or arrive at, the CHP station site on or after this date. Qualifying electricity is electricity that is part of the Qualifying Power Output of a CHP station that is used on-site. This includes self-supplies of electricity and electricity supplied directly to a consumer by an exempt unlicensed electricity supplier.

Where these exemptions do not apply (eg where the CHP station supplies electricity into the grid), fuel relating to the generation of electricity in a CHP station (where the facility has a generation capacity over 2MW) is subject to the support rate of CCL. The operator of the CHP must therefore register for CCL (if not already) to self-account for the CCL support rates on fuel inputs relating to electricity usage.

In order to take advantage of the available CCL reliefs, a CHP station must be registered and certified under BEIS's voluntary CHP Quality Assurance (CHPQA) programme.

The CHPQA programme is based on a Quality Index (QI) approach for measuring the thermal efficiency and environmental quality of the range of CHP installations of different sizes, type, and fuel use. CHP stations must achieve a QI of at least 100 and a power efficiency of at least 20% to qualify as good quality and be eligible for exemption on all electricity used on-site or sold direct to other users, and for full exemption from the main rates of CCL.

Businesses with significant energy demands and with surplus land have traditionally considered investment in onsite generation facilities and, in particular, CHP stations. However given the changes to the CCL reliefs, these businesses are likely to carefully consider the costing and revenue assumptions for investments in CHP stations.

Example 4

The Snowdrop Local Authority generates good quality electricity from its own CHP station under a joint venture with the Lavender Company of Sweden.

It supplies electricity directly to the Snowdrop industrial park and the local housing estate. However, the output from the CHP station is not sufficient to satisfy all the users' demands, thus the local authority also purchases and onward supplies electricity from a utility.

Under both current and previous rules, in order to maximise the CCL benefit of the onsite facilities, the local authority should supply the industrial park with electricity generated from the CHP station. The tenants are businesses who are ordinarily charged CCL on their purchases of power; however, electricity from a CHP directly supplied to an end user can benefit from exemption from CCL and this could represent a real saving for these tenants. The local authority can in addition certify on behalf of its domestic tenants at the housing estate that the supplies of electricity purchased from the utility are for domestic use and thus are also exempt from CCL.

Since the CHP station is of good quality, the supplier will not charge CCL (at the main rates) on the fuel inputs. From 1 April 2015, provided the authority does not supply electricity into the grid (and is not required to have a supply licence), the operator of the station will also not have any obligation to self-account for the support rates of CCL on the inputs attributable to the electricity generated which is supplied directly to the third-parties onsite.

Example 5

The Geranium supermarket generates good quality electricity from its own CHP station and uses all the electricity on site and has all the required certification to prove that the station is a fully exempt CHP. The CHP station has a generating capacity above 2MW and is gas powered.

Following the changes from 1 April 2015, it is not liable to register for CCL and account for the tax at the carbon price support rate on the fossil fuel inputs to the station, on the basis that all good quality electricity generated is consumed on site and it therefore falls outside of the deemed supply provisions. Previously, a registration requirement would have existed in order to self-account for the support rate of CCL on inputs purchased. Geranium should take care to ensure it is aware of any future changes to the fuel use and the effects on its CCL position (for example, if it supplies excess electricity to the grid, this will require a CCL registration to self-account for the support rate on the relevant fuel inputs).

Renewable source electricity

[18.13] Renewable source electricity was exempt from CCL since CCL's introduction in 2001 up until 1 August 2015. However, the 2015 Summer Budget announced the removal of the exemption for supplies via the grid of renewable source electricity generated from 1 August 2015. From 1 August 2015, purchases of renewable source electricity by businesses for consumption have generally been subject to CCL, unless the supply qualifies under a different exemption.

Notwithstanding the above, a transitional period was implemented to allow for suppliers to claim CCL exemption on any renewable source electricity generated before that date up until 31 March 2018; using residual Levy Exemption Certificates (LECs) issued by Ofgem on such generation. Therefore, some suppliers may still offer levy free supplies during this transitional period, if they have sufficient residual LECs to allow them to do so.

The exemption was originally introduced in order to increase demand for renewables from business consumers, and so support the renewable generation sector. However, the Government has indicated that more effective policies (that target support directly at renewable energy generators) have since been introduced to support this form of electricity generation. A judicial review was brought by taxpayers challenging the timing of the removal (ie contending that the exemption was removed without consent or sufficient period of notice). The High Court held that the removal of the exemption did not infringe the European principles of legitimate expectations or proportionality.

Time of supply

[18.14] Rules to determine the time of supply (tax point) for CCL on supplies of electricity and gas from utilities are designed to coincide with the industry's normal invoicing practices. As a result, the time of supply is at the point of issue of a CCL Accounting Document (CCLAD) which must be no later than 6 or 15 weeks after the day on which the supply was made, depending on the size of the customer (FA 2000, Sch 6, paras 26–28). The CCLAD must cover all supplies (metered or estimated) made to the customer which have not previously been covered by a CCLAD and must show:

- quantity of gas/electricity supplied;
- period of supply;
- supplier's name and address;
- customer's name and address;
- supplier's reference number for the customer; and
- the date of issue.

The CCLAD is no longer required to be identified with the legend 'Climate Change Levy Accounting Document' or 'CCL Accounting Document'. Further, there is no legal requirement for the CCLAD to show the amount of CCL charged, although this is required to claim bad debt relief (see below). Where suppliers have difficulty – perhaps because of system restrictions – in complying with the tax point rules and CCLAD issue requirements, to the extent that CCL liabilities cannot be determined in time for returns to be submitted, they can apply for inclusion in a Special Utility Scheme, subject to HMRC's approval (FA 2000, Sch 6, para 29).

For fuels other than electricity and gas, CCL is accounted for on these supplies in the same way as for VAT. In general, CCL becomes due when the commodity is removed or made available to the end-users or, if sooner, when an invoice is issued or payment made. An actual tax point can be created if an invoice is raised within 14 days of the commodity being removed or made available to the end-user (FA 2000, Sch 6, paras 30–35).

Accounting for CCL

[18.15] CCL returns (Form CCL 100) are made on a quarterly basis, although they can be amended to coincide with a supplier's non-standard periods for management accounts or VAT periods. The due date for submission of the return and payment of CCL is usually the last day of the month following the end of the period. There is a seven-day extension for payments made via BACS, although the CCL return must still be submitted by the due date.

Errors, penalties and adjustments

[18.16] Suppliers may adjust for over and under declarations of CCL via their CCL returns, provided the relevant error does not exceed the greater of £10,000 or 1% of the supplier's VAT turnover (ie the amount showing in Box 6 of the supplier's VAT return for that period) to a maximum upper limit of £50,000. Where errors exceed this level, the amount must be disclosed to HMRC (Climate Change Levy (General) Regulations 2001 (SI 2001/838), reg 28). Reimbursement of over-declared CCL is subject to 'unjust enrichment' rules and a four-year cap from 1 April 2010 (FA 2009, Sch 51).

Bad debt relief is available where CCL has been charged on a supply but the customer has not paid in full or in part. The supplier must be able to demonstrate that CCL has been accounted for and paid to HMRC, and must be able to identify the CCL on an invoice or CCLAD. In addition, the debt must have been written off and transferred to a bad debt relief account, and at least six months must have passed since the time of supply, date of issue of an invoice and the supply becoming due for payment (Climate Change Levy (General) Regulations 2001, reg 10).

In line with HMRC's streamlining of tax administration, FA 2008 created a single penalty regime for incorrect returns (and failure to register) across all the taxes, levies and duties administered by HMRC, including CCL. This introduced new penalties for incorrect returns in line with FA 2007, Sch 24, based on the amount of tax understated, the nature of behaviour and the extent of disclosure by the taxpayer. There will be no penalty where a taxpayer makes a mistake (whilst exercising 'reasonable care') but there will be a penalty of up to 30% for failure to take reasonable care, and 100% for a deliberate error with concealment (these penalties may be substantially reduced at HMRC's discretion where the taxpayer makes a disclosure).

The case of *J&A Young (Leicester) Ltd* (VTD 20826) is an example of where a Tribunal has overruled a penalty issued by HMRC (under the old regime) for incorrect returns. The taxpayer claimed relief from CCL during a period from 2001–2006 without holding a valid CCLA to support the relief despite the fact it would have qualified for one.

HMRC discovered the error in 2006 during a visit, but the Tribunal reduced the penalty to 100% (ie only the tax that was due) as HMRC had allowed the relief for five years before ascertaining the claim was faulty (and therefore had not exercised sufficient diligence themselves). The Tribunal's comments suggest that it also sought not to penalise taxpayers acting in the spirit of lowering emissions for failure to comply with administrative procedures.

Aggregates levy

Background

[**18.17**] Aggregates Levy (AL) was introduced in FA 2001, and took effect from 1 April 2002, exactly one year after the introduction of Climate Change Levy. A Budget Press Release in early 2000 stated that the extraction and transport of aggregates (ie sand, gravel and rock) was found to have significant local and national environmental consequences in the form of visual, noise and dust pollution and impacts on bio-diversity. In response to these findings, AL was introduced as a tax on the commercial exploitation of certain aggregates dug from the ground and dredged from the sea in the UK (up to 12 nautical miles off the UK coastline) as well as on imports.

AL is charged on the commercial exploitation of taxable aggregate, FA 2001, s 16(1). It is charged on the first person who subjects the aggregate to commercial exploitation in the UK, FA 2001, s 16(3), such as quarry operators and other extractors of rock, sand and gravel. That person is then liable to register for AL. Aggregates Levy is of interest to purchasers of aggregate (eg construction companies) as it forms part of the cost base for raw materials.

When first introduced in 2002, the rate of AL was £1.60 per tonne of aggregate subjected to commercial exploitation (the charge for part tonne is pro-rated), FA 2001, s 16(4). Since 1 April 2009, the rate of AL has been £2.00 per tonne. An increase in AL from £2 per tonne (to £2.10 per tonne) was due to take effect from 1 April 2011, but was postponed in support of the construction sector. The Government announced in the 2017 Spring Budget that the rate will remain frozen at £2 per tonne for the year commencing 1 April 2017.

By increasing the cost of primary aggregate, the aim of AL is to reduce demand for, and consequently the environmental impact of, the exploitation of primary aggregates, and to encourage the use of alternatives, such as recycled materials.

AL was introduced as a revenue neutral measure that would generate no net gain to the Exchequer. The introduction of AL was accompanied by a 0.1% reduction in the main rate of employer's National Insurance Contributions. It was intended that any additional revenue generated would go towards financing the AL Sustainability Fund (ALSF). ALSF was introduced in 2002 to address the environmental and social costs of aggregate extraction through projects focused on the delivery of environmental improvements, minimising the demand for primary aggregates and reducing or compensating for the local effects of aggregate extraction.

The eligibility of AL has been challenged in the courts by the British Aggregates Association. The European Court of Justice (and later the Court of First Instance of the European Communities) (*British Aggregates Association v European Commission*: C-487/06 [2008] ECR I-10505, [2009] 2 CMLR 189, ECJ) has effectively annulled the original decision by the Commission that AL is in breach of EU law, leaving the Commission to reconsider the claims of the British Aggregates Association. In August 2013, the European Commission launched an investigation into certain exemptions, exclusions and tax reliefs from AL.

From 1 April 2014 (ie during the investigation), HMRC suspended a number of specific exemptions (see **18.19** below). The European Commission announced its decision on 27 March 2015, which confirmed that all exemptions, with the exception of shale aggregate extracted in specific circumstances, are lawful. The Government subsequently reinstated the exemptions from AL with effect from 1 August 2015, with the exception of the exemption for shale. From this date, businesses were no longer liable for the tax on the exempted materials and also were entitled to reclaim AL paid in respect of the exempted items for the period 1 April 2014 to 31 July 2015.

In its report, published on 27 November 2014, the Smith Commission recommended that AL (amongst other taxes) be devolved to the Scottish Government and this was implemented in the Scotland Act 2016; however no date for the devolution of AL has yet been agreed.

Basic principles

Scope of the levy

[18.18] FA 2001, s 17(1) defines 'aggregate' as any rock, gravel or sand including substances which are incorporated in those items or naturally mixed with them. AL applies to any aggregate subjected to commercial exploitation on or after 1 April 2002, unless the aggregate is not taxable because it falls within one of the items set out below:

- it falls within one of the exemptions listed in the legislation;
- it has previously been used for construction purposes; or
- it is, or derives from, aggregate already subjected to a charge for AL, thereby avoiding double taxation, FA 2001, s 17(2).

Exemptions

[18.19] FA 2001, s 17(3) provides that aggregate is treated as exempt from AL if it consists of any of the following:

- Wholly of aggregate won by being removed from the ground on the site of any building or proposed building in the course of excavations lawfully carried out:
  - in connection with the modification or erection of a building; and
  - exclusively for the purpose of laying foundations or of laying any pipe or cable.
- Wholly of aggregate won by being removed from:
  - the bed of any river, canal or watercourse (whether natural or artificial); or
  - any channel in or approach to any port or harbour (whether natural or artificial)

  in the course of the dredging which is undertaken exclusively for the purpose of creating, restoring, improving or maintaining that river, canal, watercourse, channel or approach.
- Wholly of aggregate won by being removed from the ground along the line or proposed line of any highway or proposed highway in the course of excavations carried out for the purpose of improving or maintaining the highway or of constructing the proposed highway and not for the purpose of extracting that aggregate.
- Wholly of aggregate removed from the ground along the line, or proposed line, of any railway, tramway or monorail for the purposes of improving, maintaining or constructing it and not for the purpose of extracting the aggregate.

On 1 August 2013, the UK Government received notification that the European Commission would open a formal investigation into certain exemptions, exclusions and tax reliefs from the aggregates levy. During the investigation, the following exemptions were made taxable from 1 April 2014.

- Aggregate that is wholly of the spoil, waste or other by-products (not including the overburden) resulting from the extraction or other separation from any quantity of aggregate of any china clay or ball clay.
- Aggregate that is wholly of the spoil from any process by which:
  - coal, lignite, slate or shale; or
  - any substance listed in FA 2001, s 18(3)

  has been separated from other rock after being extracted or won with that other rock.

Following the European Commission's decision on 27 March 2015 that all but one of the exemptions, exclusions and tax reliefs from the aggregates levy were lawful, the UK Government reinstated the exemptions retrospectively (to 1 April 2014) with effect from 1 August 2015, with the exception of:

- material wholly or mainly consisting of shale that is deliberately extracted for commercial exploitation as aggregate, including shale occurring as by-product of fresh quarrying of other taxed materials; and
- aggregate consisting wholly of the spoil from any process by which shale that is deliberately extracted for commercial exploitation as aggregate has been separated from other rock after being extracted or won with that other rock.

In August 2016, the UK Government published a consultation document for extending the exemption for the utility sector to include aggregate extracted as part of works under land other than roads (eg agricultural land). The consultation was closed on 18 October 2016 and the Government is still deciding on what, if any, legislative changes will be made to address this.

Aggregate used for construction purposes

[18.20] The exploitation of aggregate is not taxable for AL purposes where the aggregate has previously been used for construction purposes. FA 2001, s 48(2) defines aggregate used for 'construction purposes' as follows:

- aggregate used as material or support in the construction or improvement of any structure; or
- aggregate mixed with anything as part of the process of producing mortar, concrete, tarmacadam, coated roadstone or any similar construction material.

In this context, 'structure' includes roads and paths, the way on which a railway is laid and embankments. It also includes buildings and bridges.

Commercial exploitation

[18.21] The standard rate of aggregates levy (£2.00 per tonne of taxable material) applies to the commercial exploitation or importation of taxable aggregate in the UK or its territorial waters. FA 2001 s 19(1) provides that aggregate is deemed to have been exploited in the following scenarios:

- When aggregate is removed from a site that is:
  - the originating site of the aggregate;
  - another site registered under the name of the person under whom the originating site is registered; or
  - a site where the aggregate was removed for the purpose of having an exempt process applied to it that did not take place.
- When aggregate becomes subject to an agreement to be supplied to a person provided that:
  - the aggregate is in a discrete pile at the time the agreement is entered into and can be separately identified; and
  - it is specifically set aside for the purpose of the contract.

- When aggregate is used for construction purposes. (Aggregate used for construction at a registered site is taxable, but aggregate returned to the land at that site in the same state as it was won is not liable to AL – see below.)
- When aggregate is mixed with a material or substance other than water; for example, when it is used to make concrete.

FA 2001, s 19(3) provides that the conditions to be fulfilled in order for exploitation to be considered to be 'commercial' are as follows:

- The exploitation must be carried out by someone in the course or furtherance of their business.
- The exploitation does not consist of the removal of the aggregate from one site to another where both sites are registered under the name of the same person.
- The aggregate is not removed to a registered site in order for an exempt process to be applied to it.
- The aggregate is not removed to a registered site in order for china clay or ball clay to be extracted from it on that site.
- The aggregate does not become part of the land at the site from which it was extracted.

Imported aggregate is treated in exactly the same way as domestic aggregate except for the fact that there is no UK originating site. AL becomes due upon commercial exploitation of the imported aggregate, not at the point of importation. The person responsible for exploiting imported aggregate is the person who agrees to supply it (if the aggregate is located in the UK at this time), uses it for construction purposes or mixes it with any material or substance other than water. Imported processed products (eg concrete) are not subject to AL.

Exempt processes

[18.22] The intended products of certain exempt processes are not liable to AL. However, waste, off-cuts, spoil and by-products resulting from the exempt process are liable to AL. Exempt processes are defined in FA 2001, s 18(2) as follows:

- the cutting of any rock to produce stone with one or more flat surfaces. The First-tier Tribunal in *Jones Brothers Ruthin (Civil Engineering) Co Limited* [2011] UKFTT 206 (TC) confirmed that the production of large granite blocks (to be used as sea defences) qualified for the exemption. The Tribunal held that the production of a flat surface must be an intended consequence of the exploitation – but in this case rejected HMRC's argument that flat surfaces were not an intentional result of the process in question. The case also confirmed that a 'flat' surface need not be completely smooth to qualify for exemption;
- any process by which a relevant substance (explained below) is extracted or separated from any aggregate (however, this does not allow a taxpayer full relief for a taxable quarrying business if some extraction

of a relevant substance is also carried out on that site – *MMC Midlands Limited v Revenue and Customs Comrs* [2009] EWHC 683 (Ch), [2009] STC 1969, [2009] All ER(D) 66 (Apr);

- any process for the production of lime or cement from limestone.

'Relevant substances' are certain industrial minerals such as sodium chloride, ball clay, gems and semi-precious stones. The comprehensive list of 'relevant substances' is contained in FA 2001, s 18(3).

Reliefs

[18.23] Reliefs from AL are credits or repayments that become due after AL has been accounted for to HMRC. Only the person who has accounted for AL can claim relief. The Aggregate Levy (General) Regulations 2002 (SI 2002/761), regs 13–16 set out the following reliefs:

- Exported aggregate is relieved from AL provided that it is removed from the UK with no further processing and evidence of export is obtained within three months of making a claim.
- Aggregate used in an exempt process after AL has been accounted for is relieved, although it is still necessary to account for AL on any spoil, waste, off-cuts and by products.
- Aggregate used in any listed industrial or agricultural processes is relieved (see below).
- Aggregate disposed of in the following ways is relieved:
  - returned without processing to its original site (or another site registered under the same name);
  - disposed of to landfill;
  - gravel or sand that is used for beach restoration purposes.

Provided suppliers of aggregate hold the relevant proof to support their claim to relief from AL (or they will obtain this evidence within three months in the case of exports), they can claim a credit at the time the supply is made. This means that they do not need to pay AL to HMRC which should help to manage cash flow.

In addition, it is possible to claim bad debt relief for AL under the Aggregate Levy (General) Regulations 2002, reg 12. However, a number of conditions need to be met and, in particular, the customer must have become insolvent or gone into liquidation before bad debt relief for AL purposes can be claimed. Proof of the customer's insolvency will be required to support the claim.

Following the earlier judgement by the European Court of Justice in *BAA* the AL credit scheme in Northern Ireland was suspended with effect from 1 December 2010 as it was held by the EU General Court to constitute a state aid. The AL credit scheme had been in place since the introduction of AL and it was aimed at preventing distortion of competition between Northern Irish aggregates producers and those in the Republic of Ireland. The Commission has performed an investigation and the results of this were published on 7 November 2014. It concluded that the Commission is broadly satisfied with the operation of the AL credit scheme, but required the UK Government to correct the distortion of competition that arose from limiting the AL credit scheme tax benefit.

Finance Act 2015 introduced an opportunity for businesses to claim AL credit under the scheme from 1 April 2015 if they had accounted for the levy at the full rate on aggregate that was commercially exploited in NI between 1 April 2004 and 30 November 2010 following importation of the aggregate from another EU member state.

In order to make a claim the relevant business will need to submit an STC1 form to the Department of Environment ('DoE') for each relevant quarry and be able to evidence that the quarry met the specified environmental standards. All forms must have been submitted by 31 March 2016. Following this, the business will receive a certificate from the DoE and will then be able to make a claim for the tax credit. These claims must be made in writing to HMRC no later than 31 March 2019 (ie four years after the legislation came into force).

Industrial and agricultural processes relief

[18.24] As mentioned above, relief from payment of AL can be obtained when aggregate is used in prescribed industrial and agricultural processes. The rationale for this relief is that certain industrial and agricultural processes use material that is ordinarily liable to AL but not as aggregate. Examples of relieved processes include sand used for drinking water filtration, sand used for glass manufacture and sand or gravel used in the production of fertiliser. The full list of relieved processes is set out in the Schedule to the Aggregate Levy (General) Regulations 2002 and further information is contained in HMRC Notice AGL2.

A supplier of commercially exploited aggregate may obtain relief under these provisions if its customer uses the aggregate in one of the prescribed processes. The supplier will need evidence from the customer of the actual or intended use before being able to claim any relief. Commercially speaking there is a benefit for the customer as the supplier will not need to increase the price of the supply of aggregate to take into account the cost of AL.

Existing commercial evidence is an acceptable form of evidence for the purposes of claiming this relief; however, this should include:

• supplier name and address;
• customer name and address;
• cross-references to invoices and weighbridge tickets;
• a description of the product sufficient to support an audit trail;
• a description of the use for which relief is claimed;
• a customer declaration by an authorised signatory of intended use; and
• a declaration from the supplier setting out the limits of their liability and the ability of HMRC to levy a penalty on the customer in the event that they have made false statements.

In addition to obtaining evidence, the supplier should assess the credibility of the claim to relief and should find out about the nature of customers' businesses especially when accepting new customers.

On 27 November 2015 HMRC clarified that aggregates used as filler in the manufacture of asphalt does not qualify for relief.

Determining the weight of aggregate

[18.25] The rules for determining the weight of aggregate are set out in the Aggregate Levy (General) Regulations 2002.

Regulation 3 requires that the weight of the aggregate is measured by a weighbridge at the site where the exploitation takes place. Weighbridge tickets must be retained as part of the business's AL records.

Regulation 4 provides that where the use of a weighbridge is not practical (or if the site does not have a weighbridge) then the weight may be determined in accordance with a method that has written approval from HMRC. Any such method may include requirements regarding details of records to be kept, discounting of constituents, such as water, and the time at which the weight is determined. HMRC may withdraw the approved method if it has not been applied correctly or produces an inaccurate result.

In general, it is possible to discount the water content of aggregate where this water has been added to the aggregate after the aggregate has been won, eg to wash or dust dampen the aggregate. It is not possible to discount any naturally occurring water.

AL and construction projects

[18.26] Aggregates Levy is a cost component of purchasing aggregate, and will be passed through the supply chain in construction projects. There may be little incentive for aggregate providers to reduce the charge to AL if the cost can be passed on with relatively little scrutiny. Landowners or developers may be able to reduce the cost of AL by checking that the following have been excluded from the charge to AL:

- any aggregate returned to the ground at the site from which it was extracted and in the same state should not be taxed;
- any recycled aggregate that has previously been used in construction should not be liable to AL; and
- aggregate removed from the ground on the site of any building or proposed building in the course of construction, to lay pipes, cables or foundations is exempt from AL. Similar rules apply to other types of construction such as rivers and highways.

Some lessons can be learned from case law in this tax where there is a growing body of cases relating to the application of the exemptions to construction sites; both the removal of aggregate in connection with building works (see *East Midlands Aggregates Ltd and Pat Munro*) and the definition of 'site' when aggregate is returned to the ground (see *Hochtief, Northumbrian Water* and *Hanson Quarry Products Europe* at **18.29, 18.30** and **18.31** below).

Aggregate removed during building works

Commissioners of Customs & Excise v East Midlands Aggregates Limited [2004] EWHC 856 (Ch)

[18.27] East Midlands Aggregates Limited (EMAL) had been contracted to remove material from a site in relation to a construction project being undertaken by the site owner. The project involved the construction of a lorry park and a warehouse, and it was necessary as part of the work to make cuttings into a slope. EMAL extracted about 425,000 tonnes of rock mixed with soil. The Commissioners decided that EMAL should be registered for AL and EMAL appealed on the basis that the removal of aggregate fell under the exemption for laying the foundations or any pipe or cable in connection with the construction of a building (FA 2001, s 17(3)(b)).

The Tribunal found that the material removed in connection with the lorry park and warehouse met the conditions of this exemption but that material removed to take away the slope was not exempt because it was not related to the laying of foundations, pipes or cables. The Commissioners appealed this decision on the basis that the aggregate excavated to lay the foundations for the lorry park and the drainage system serving the new building should be liable to AL.

The High Court found that the Tribunal had been correct to exempt material removed in connection with the lorry park. The decision states that 'the site of . . . [the] proposed building' must be given a sensible workable meaning, and will ordinarily be the 'building site' for the proposed building. This includes the whole area that builders work on for the purposes of constructing the building and laying services associated with it.

Pat Munro (Alness) Ltd v Revenue and Customs Comrs (A00002) (30 July 2004, unreported)

[18.28] In order to supply an all-weather pitch to a school, the taxpayer had to excavate material that was then recycled and sold on. The excavation was required because the site of the proposed pitch was on sloping ground. The tax authorities imposed AL on the taxpayer on the basis that the removal of the aggregate did not fall within any of the relevant exemptions.

The taxpayer argued that AL should not be imposed because the intention of the legislation is to encourage the recycling of materials, including those excavated from construction projects and re-used.

However, the all-weather pitch was not considered to be a building. Therefore, the exemption for aggregate 'won by being removed from the ground on the site of any building or proposed building in the course of excavations' (FA 2001, s 17(3)(b)) could not apply. Also, the Tribunal could find no evidence of the excavation being required 'for the purpose of laying foundations or of laying any pipe or cable'.

Despite the Tribunal being sympathetic to the fact that the decision did not itself encourage recycling and that it appeared to be a departure from the original intention of the legislation, it agreed with the tax authorities that AL was due on the extraction of aggregate. It commented that if a sports pavilion, for example, were built alongside the pitch, the exemption from AL may have applied. In this case, the Tribunal may have reached a similar decision as the Tribunal in the case of EMAL (above) as the pitch may have been part of the site of the sports facility.

Definition of a site

Hochtief Ltd v Revenue and Customs Comrs (TC00264) [2009] UKFTT 321 (TC)

[18.29] Hochtief Ltd was the main contractor for the construction of a hydro-electric power station. In order to build the dam for the project, rock was removed from a quarry site that was approximately 100 metres from the dam. The tax authorities imposed AL on the taxpayer in respect of this rock on the basis that the removal of the aggregate fulfilled all necessary criteria for 'commercial exploitation' under FA 2001, s 19(3).

The taxpayer argued that the removal of rock was not commercial exploitation as the rock was to again become part of the land at the site from which it was won. The reasoning for this argument was that there was no distinction in the rock above and below the former ground level of the dam, and that becoming part of the dam structure did not preclude the aggregate from again becoming part of the land.

The Tribunal felt that with respect to FA 2001, s 19(3)(e), a sensible working meaning of 'site' meant that the footprint of the dam and the footprint of the quarry were one site. Therefore, the appeal was allowed and the aggregate incorporated into the dam was not liable to AL as the conditions for commercial exploitation set out in s 19(3) were not fulfilled.

Northumbrian Water Ltd v Revenue and Customs Comrs (TC02740) [2013] UKFTT 337 (TC)

[18.30] In the case of *Northumbrian Water Ltd v Customs Comrs* (TC002740) [2013] UKFTT 337 it was confirmed that aggregate that has been extracted from a pit and then becomes part of the land it was extracted from is not subject to AL. Here, the extracted aggregate was used to build dams and a causeway around the reservoir and HMRC challenged the taxpayer's view that the pit, the dam and the reservoir were the same 'site'. The Court ruled that they were indeed the same site finding that the primary purpose of the relief was to exempt aggregate sourced and extracted within the construction site and not at the particular area of ground where the aggregate was extracted.

On 13 March 2015 the Upper Tribunal [2015] UKUT 93 (TCC), [2015] STC 1458 released its decision on this case, confirming the findings of the First-tier Tribunal and that the aggregate in this situation was not subject to AL.

Hanson Quarry Products Europe Ltd v Revenue and Customs Comrs (TC04818) [2016] UKFTT 11 (TC)

[18.31] In the case of *Hanson Quarry Products Europe Ltd v Revenue and Customs Comrs* (TC04818) [2016] UKFTT 11 it was confirmed that aggregate extracted from a quarry and used to create a platform in a different area of the quarry which had been sold to developers was not taxable aggregate as the aggregate had become part of the land from which it was won, and therefore had not been subject to commercial exploitation. HMRC had challenged the taxpayer's view, contending that as the area in which the platform was located had been sold prior to the platform being built, the aggregate had been subject to commercial exploitation and fell to be taxable aggregate.

The Tribunal found that, referring to FA 2001, s 19(1) and applying a 'sensible working meaning' to the word 'site' (see **18.30** above), even if the land was sold to a developer and was no longer part of the quarry, it did not necessarily follow that it was no longer part of the 'site'. The Tribunal also considered that whilst FA 2001, s 42(2) confers administrative duties to HMRC in relation to a 'registered site', those administrative duties do not enable HMRC to redefine the boundaries of an existing site (thereby creating a charge to aggregates levy where one would not otherwise exist). The aggregate was therefore not subject to the levy.

Whilst these three cases surrounding the definition of a site were all found in favour of the taxpayer, this clearly continues to be an area of HMRC focus. Businesses should take care surrounding the application of AL where aggregate is moved across a large site.

Compliance

Registration

[18.32] Persons responsible for exploiting aggregate in the UK for commercial reasons need to register for AL. Unlike VAT there is no registration threshold for registering and accounting for AL. In order to register, an Application for Registration Form AL1 and Site Detail Form AL1A need to be completed. Depending on the status of the business, there are other forms that HMRC may require to be submitted.

FA 2001, Sch 4, para 1(1) provides that an unregistered person that is required to be registered or has formed the intention to perform taxable activities that are registrable should notify HMRC of that fact. Notification to HMRC should be made within 30 days starting with the day after a person became liable to be registered (Aggregates Levy (Registration and Miscellaneous Provisions) Regulations 2001/4027 (AL Registration Regulations 2001), reg 2(7)).

Where a person carries out, or intends to carry out, only exempt activities then they are not required to register for AL (AL Registration Regulations 2001, reg 3). However, they are required to notify HMRC of that fact (FA 2001, Sch 4, para 1(1A)).

HMRC may cancel a person's registration if they are satisfied that they have ceased to carry out taxable activities and do not have the intention of carrying out further taxable activities (FA 2001, Sch 4, para 4(1)). Where a registered person ceases to make taxable activities or ceases to have the intention to do so, they should notify HMRC of this within 30 days (AL Registration Regulations 2001, reg 5).

If a registered person transfers their business as a going concern to another person, the registration number can be passed to the transferee on application to HMRC (AL (General) Regulations 2002, reg 37). It should be noted, however, that the transferee will take on the AL liabilities of the transferor at the time of transfer.

Group registration

[18.33] Only entities that are individually eligible to be registered for AL may be included in a group registration. Entities are eligible to become members of a group if:

- one of them controls the others; or
- an individual, a company or a partnership controls all of them; and
- each of the companies has an established place of business in the UK.

One body controls another if it is empowered by statute to control that body's activities, or if it is that body's holding company. An individual may be considered to be a controlling body if they hold control over the other bodies in the same way as a holding company.

One of the members of the group must be the representative member. Any business carried on by group members that is subject to AL will be treated as being made by the representative member. All the members of the group are jointly and severally liable for the AL due by the representative member.

All aggregate commercially exploited by any group member remains chargeable to AL. However, any movement of aggregate from the site of one group member to another will not in itself result in any AL being due.

Divisional registration

[18.34] Entities that carry on their business through various divisions may apply for the separate registration of those divisions for AL. Each division will have its own registration number and makes its own returns. However, the entity itself remains liable for the AL due by each of the divisions. It should be noted that HMRC will only accept a divisional registration in cases where they are satisfied that it would cause real difficulty for the entity to make a single return.

As with group registrations, all aggregate commercially exploited by any division is subject to AL as normal. However, it should also be noted that inter-divisional exploitation (for example, the supply of or removal of aggregate from the site of one division to the site of another division) will be subject to AL.

Returns

[18.35] Once registered, a return (Form AL 100) is sent to the taxpayer every three months to be completed and submitted to HMRC accompanied by payment of any levy that may be due. The deadline for submission of the return and payment of the AL is the last day of the month following the end of the tax period. HMRC offer a seven day delayed payment concession if payment is made by direct debit, but this does not change the due date for submitting returns. Annual returns may be submitted by small businesses once the taxpayer has been registered for twelve months.

Records

[18.36] A registered person is required to keep an AL account (AL (General) Regulations 2002, reg 9), and various additional records listed in AL (General) Regulations 2002, reg 10. They are also required to keep records, in the form of an account, relating to both bad debt claims and tax credit claims made (AL Regulations 2002, reg 13(3)). Records must be kept for six years unless agreed otherwise with HMRC.

Errors, penalties and adjustments

[18.37] Errors in AL returns that do not exceed the greater of £10,000 or 1% of the supplier's VAT turnover (ie the amount showing in Box 6 of the supplier's VAT return for that period) to a maximum upper limit of £50,000 should be corrected by way of making an adjustment in the return during which the error was discovered (AL (General) Regulations 2002, reg 29). Any other errors should be separately notified in writing to HMRC.

The single penalty regime introduced in FA 2008 applies to AL returns filed on or after 1 April 2010. Therefore, from this date there is no penalty where a taxpayer makes a mistake (whilst exercising 'reasonable care') but there is a penalty of up to 30% for failure to take reasonable care, and 100% for a deliberate error with concealment (these penalties may be substantially reduced at HMRC's discretion where the taxpayer makes a disclosure).

Claims for over-declared AL or assessments for underpaid AL are subject to a four-year cap from 1 April 2010 (FA 2009, Sch 51), increased from the previous three-year cap.

Landfill tax

Background

[18.38] Landfills are waste disposal sites, where non-recyclable solid waste is deposited, compacted, and periodically covered with a layer of soil before the addition of further waste. They are intended to minimise the volume of non-recyclable waste and to reduce the risk to human, animal and plant life from harmful pollutants.

Landfill tax was introduced in FA 1996 and applies to all waste disposed of at a licensed landfill site. Its intention is to discourage landfill and to encourage alternative, more sustainable means of waste management, such as recycling, by reflecting the environmental costs of landfill use more accurately in its price.

By increasing the cost of landfill (historically, a relatively cheap and easy method of waste disposal), alternative waste treatment technologies have become more financially attractive.

Landfill tax is seen as a key mechanism in enabling the UK to meet the targets set out in the EU Landfill Directive (1999/31/EC). The Directive's overall aim is to prevent or reduce damage to the environment and human health from the landfilling of waste.

The European Landfill Directive has set a target for reducing the amount of waste sent to landfill sites in the UK to 35% of 1995 waste levels by 2020, and landfill tax has generally been thought to have been effective in reducing waste sent to landfill. Critics have argued that landfill tax has had hardly any effect on the disposal of active waste, and it has been alleged that the tax has led to an increase in fly-tipping and the use of unlicensed waste disposal sites with businesses diverting waste into the household waste stream. It has also been claimed that the increased cost of administering the tax has placed an additional burden on local authorities and may have actually diverted money away from other environmental projects. However, the UK still sends significantly more waste to landfill than most other EU member states. The recent significant annual increases to the landfill tax rates show that tax has increasingly been used to address the problem.

The importance of considering the purpose of the tax was confirmed by a Tribunal decision from 2007 (*Easter Hatton Environmental (Waste Away) Ltd v HM Revenue & Customs*, L00026 (2007)). In this case, HMRC raised an assessment on waste which would never be sent to landfill, on the grounds that the taxpayer had failed to maintain a 'tax-free area' agreement with HMRC. The Tribunal agreed with the taxpayer and held that in such a case HMRC should use their discretion to not assess landfill tax, as the purpose of the tax is to control landfill and not to raise revenue.

The European Commission adopted a legislative proposal to review recycling and other waste-related targets in the EU Waste Framework Directive (2008/98/EC) and the Landfill Directive (1999/31/EC). The proposal included phasing out landfilling by 2025 for recyclable waste in non-hazardous waste landfills – corresponding to a maximum landfilling rate of 25% and the introduction of measures aimed at reducing food waste generation by 30% by 2025.

From 1 April 2015, landfill tax on disposals in Scotland has been devolved to the Scottish Government under The Landfill Tax (Scotland) Act 2014. This Act for the most part mirrors UK legislation; however landfill site operators that make or intend to make taxable disposals in Scotland are required to separately register and account for landfill tax in Scotland. Landfill operators with landfill sites in Scotland were required to notify Revenue Scotland of their intention to carry out taxable activities within 30 days of the earliest date after 15 February 2015 on which they form (or continue to have) the intention to carry out taxable activities in relation to Scottish Landfill Tax. If a business operates landfill sites only in Scotland, HMRC deregistered the business from UK landfill tax with effect from 31 March 2015.

The Scottish Government confirmed that from 1 April 2015 the standard rate of Scottish Landfill Tax is £82.60 per tonne and the lower rate is £2.60 per tonne. The Cabinet Secretary also announced that the credit rate for landfill operators contributing towards the Scottish Landfill Communities Fund (the Scottish equivalent of the Landfill Communities Fund – see **18.43**) will be 10% higher than the UK rate for the first three years of the Scottish Tax.

Please note that the content of the chapter only relates to landfill tax in England, Wales and Northern Ireland. The general principles for Scottish landfill tax are broadly similar, but we have highlighted some key points to note in relation to Scottish landfill tax.

It is also expected that administration of the landfill tax in Wales will be devolved from April 2018.

The tax

[18.39] Landfill operators are liable to account for tax on taxable disposals. This includes all disposals at a licensed landfill site, unless a specific tax exemption applies.

In 2008 the Court of Appeal held that a disposal does *not* include material being recycled or used for another purpose – for example, the use of inert material for site engineering purposes (*Waste Recycling Group Ltd v Revenue and Customs Comrs* [2008] EWCA Civ 849, [2008] SWTI 1871).

Following this HMRC announced changes in the legislation to make most of the disposals covered in the *Waste Recycling Group* case liable to tax. Section 65A of FA 1996 details activities on a landfill site that are treated as a disposal of the material used in that activity (and therefore liable to tax with effect from 1 September 2009). The prescribed activities include the use, storage or otherwise dealing with material at a landfill site. In July 2016, the High Court dismissed an application for judicial review of HMRC's refusal to pay refunds of Landfill Tax on 'fluff', following HMRC's change of policy as a result of the Waste Recycling Group case. The decision was taken that despite some taxpayers receiving refunds whilst some taxpayers had their claim rejected, the decision of HMRC to refuse to pay any further refunds was not unlawful.

The case of *Patersons of Greenoakhill Ltd v Revenue and Customs Comrs* (TC12911) [2009] UKFTT challenged whether biodegradable material that generates gas within a landfill site that is burnt to generate electricity should be charged to landfill tax. Patersons considered that, as a result of the decision in *Waste Recycling Group*, there was no landfill tax due if the material disposed of was put to a specific purpose and they argued this was the case for the biodegradable waste. However, the tribunal rejected this and held that landfill tax was due on the biodegradable waste. Patersons appealed to the Upper Tribunal who dismissed the appeal, after agreeing with the findings in the First-tier Tribunal. The Court of Appeal also agreed with the First-tier Tribunal's and Upper Tribunal's findings that the taxpayer had discarded the material even if a subsequent use was found for it, and dismissed the taxpayer's appeal.

During the summer of 2016 HMRC carried out a consultation on the definition of a 'taxable disposal' for landfill tax purposes as it continues to be the subject of litigation. The proposed changes sought to clarify the scope of the tax by taxing all material disposed of at a landfill site unless expressly exempt. The measure was incorporated in to the Finance Bill 2017 but was removed from the Finance Act 2017.

In March 2017, HMRC published a consultation on whether to extend the scope of Landfill Tax to include material disposed at illegal waste sites. The purpose of this measure is to deter environmentally damaging behaviour from those who dispose material at illegal waste sites who operate outside the scope of Landfill Tax as a means to evasion. If there is a resulting policy change, it is understood that these would not come into effect until April 2018 at the earliest.

Whilst landfill tax is devolved to Scotland, and in the process of being devolved to Wales (with Landfill Disposals Tax (LDT) replacing Landfill Tax in Wales in April 2018), the general definition of 'taxable disposal' remains standardised across the UK and this is expected to continue to be the case.

Rates

[18.40] There are two rates of landfill tax which is charged according to weight. The rates are the same for UK Landfill Tax and Scottish Landfill Tax to avoid any landfill operators moving their sites to either England or Scotland to benefit from a lower tax rate. For disposals made from 1 April 2016 onwards, the lower rate of landfill tax has been increased to £2.65 per tonne for qualifying inert materials and the standard rate has increased to £84.40 per tonne for active waste (substances that either decay or contaminate land). The Government has stated that the standard rate will not fall below £80 per tonne until at least 2020.

VAT is calculated on the value of supplies, inclusive of landfill tax.

The description of materials that qualify for the lower rate of landfill tax is set out in the Landfill Tax (Qualifying Material) Order 2011, as represented by the table below. The Scottish Landfill Tax (Qualifying Material) Order 2015 mirrors the Landfill Tax (Qualifying Material) Order 2011. Water has been removed from materials qualifying for the lower rate on the basis that water itself is now banned from landfill. Where water is used as a waste carrier the water is not viewed as waste and therefore is not subject to LFT.

Lower rate – Inert Waste	Standard rate – Active waste
Naturally occurring rocks and soils (not including peat and topsoil)	All other waste not subject to a specific exemption
Ceramics and concrete	
Unused minerals	
Furnace slags	
Ash	
Low-activity inorganic compounds	
Calcium sulphate, calcium hydroxide and brine qualify only if they are disposed of in specific containers	

Where a disposal contains both active and qualifying inert material, tax is due on the whole load at the standard rate. As it is sometimes not possible to separate active and inert material, HMRC will accept that the presence of an incidental amount of active waste in a mainly inert load will not preclude the entire load from being taxed at the lower rate. For example, the lower rate of landfill tax will apply to a load of bricks, stones and concrete from the demolition of a building, even where small pieces of wood and plaster are included in the load.

Evidence must be retained to support the application of the lower rate. In particular, the waste transfer note must be retained and should accurately describe the type of waste so that it can be used to determine the landfill tax treatment. Waste transfer notes accompany most movements of waste in Great Britain and Northern Ireland.

HMRC issued a number of pieces of guidance in June 2012 to highlight the need for evidence to be retained that supports the application of the reduced rate where it is applied. In particular, this guidance stressed that only those materials specified in the Landfill Tax (Qualifying Material) Order 2011 would qualify for the reduced rate. It is possible that there are materials that are considered to be inert but that will not qualify for the reduced rate.

Qualifying fines

[**18.41**] From 1 April 2015 The Landfill Tax (Qualifying Fines) Order 2015 allows for 'fines' of qualifying materials to be subject to the lower rate of landfill tax. 'Fines' are defined in FA 1996, s 70(1) as particles produced by a waste treatment process that involves an element of mechanical treatment.

The fines qualify for the lower rate of landfill tax, provided that they:

• consist of qualifying inert material (as listed in the Landfill Tax (Qualifying Material) Order 2011;
• contain no more than an incidental amount of non-qualifying fines;
• are non-hazardous; and
• do not result from a deliberate or artificial blending or mixing of the material prior to disposal at a landfill site.

In addition, a number of other conditions must be satisfied to demonstrate that fines are 'qualifying':

• evidence must be held to show that the fines are qualifying fines (eg evidence of pre-acceptance checks and inspection on delivery);
• a transfer note (which is required to accompany most movements of waste in the UK) must be held and must contain specified information identifying the waste as qualifying fines; and
• if required to be tested, the fines must meet the relevant loss on ignition ('LOI') threshold.

The LOI tests the organic material present in the fines; the difference in the mass of the material being tested before and after the ignition process is used to calculate the LOI result. This test must be performed upon random, representative samples of waste from each waste processor disposing of fines at the landfill site and each of their processes generating fines. After 1 April 2015, the LOI tests must be carried out as above within specified time periods. The frequency of subsequent tests is determined by the 'risk' of each waste processor.

For fines disposed of between 1 April 2016 and 31 March 2017, the LOI threshold is 10%. If a sample breaches the LOI threshold, the disposal is subject to the standard rate of landfill tax.

The Scottish Government has confirmed that it intends to release guidance on LOI under Scottish Landfill Tax in November 2016 following legislative changes due to enter into effect in October 2016.

Exemptions - general

[18.42] There are a number of exemptions from landfill tax. For example, in certain circumstances, waste removed from inland waterways and harbours by dredging, and waste arising from mining and quarrying operations and disposed of at a landfill site, is exempt from landfill tax. No certificates are required to support these exemptions but commercial documents retained as part of the business's records should be available to support the exemption.

Inert waste used for the purposes of filling existing or former quarries may qualify for exemption. HMRC need to be furnished with evidence that it is a requirement of planning consent that the quarry must be wholly or partially refilled. However, where quarrying operations ceased before 1 October 1999, the planning consent requirement must have been imposed prior to that date.

A previous exemption for waste arising from the reclamation of contaminated land was withdrawn for all disposals of waste made after 31 March 2012.

Credits

[18.43] If waste is temporarily put to landfill with the intention of later recycling, incinerating or removing it for reuse, then when the waste is removed it is possible to claim a credit for landfill tax already paid. Conditions need to be fulfilled including that HMRC were notified of the temporary nature of the landfill before the waste was deposited and the waste must be removed within time limits that are normally 12 months from the date of disposal.

Credits are available in other limited circumstances, including where waste is moved from one landfill site to another site on the direction of the environmental regulator. Landfill site operators can also claim tax credits for funding local community environmental projects by way of contributions to approved environmental bodies. Such bodies are enrolled with ENTRUST who regulate the Landfill Communities Fund and Scottish Landfill Communities Fund (although certain aspects of this are overseen by HMRC). Various conditions apply and specific rules determine the calculation of tax credits that can be offset against landfill tax calculations. The case of *County Durham Environmental Trust Ltd v Twizell* ([2009] EWHC 2173 (Ch)) considered the use of proceeds from landfill tax credits on the disposal of an asset with a qualifying contribution (queried as part of an insolvency scenario). The Landfill Tax (Amendment) (No 2) Regulations 2010 clarify the treatment of the proceeds from sales of assets, and state that funds from landfill tax credits must continue to be used for environmental objectives of the Landfill Communities Fund (or Scottish Landfill Communities Fund).

In March 2016, the Government announced reforms amending the Landfill Tax Regulations 1996 so that contributions may no longer be made subject to a condition that they are invested for the purpose of generating interest.

The Landfill Tax (Amendment) Regulations 2017 increased the cap on contributions by landfill operators from 4.2% to 5.3% which entered into force on 1 April 2017.

Bad debt relief is also available for landfill tax where all the conditions have been met. In particular, the customer who has not paid the debt must be unconnected to the landfill site operator, the debt must have been written off in the day-to-day accounts and transferred to a separate bad debt account, a landfill invoice must have been issued and the tax correctly accounted for, and 12 months must have elapsed since the issue of the landfill invoice.

With the devolution of the administration of landfill tax in Scotland, as of 1 April 2015, the Landfill Communities Fund has been closed in Scotland and replaced by the Scottish Landfill Communities Fund. All new and existing Landfill Communities Fund projects in Scotland must be completed by 31 March 2017. Tax credits may only be claimed against UK landfill tax where the qualifying contributions relate to a project in England, Wales or Northern Ireland, and credits against Scottish landfill tax will only be awarded where the qualifying contribution is spent on a project in Scotland.

The Scottish Government has announced that the credit rate for landfill operators contributing towards the Scottish Landfill Communities Fund will be 10% higher than the UK rate for the first three years of devolved administration.

Information area

[18.44] It is worth noting that landfill site operators can apply for part of a site to be designated as an information area if they intend to carry out any non-taxable uses of waste on the site. The area must be clearly identifiable within the site. The site operator is required to keep an information area account which identifies the quantities and the type of material deposited and removed from the area.

Information areas are known as non-disposal areas under Scottish legislation.

Determining the weight of landfill

[18.45] As with AL, the basic method of determining the weight of waste sent to landfill is by using a weighbridge. If a site has no weighbridge then HMRC set out three alternative methods for calculating weight, for example, by using the maximum weight that the lorry, skip etc used to deliver the waste to the site is permitted to carry.

If a site has a weighbridge but it is broken or using it to weigh waste prior to disposal would cause significant disruption to business, or if the site has no weighbridge and the operator is unable to use one of the three alternative methods of calculation, then HMRC may agree a bespoke method. This must be fair and reasonable, and once agreed will usually run for 12 months.

It is sometimes possible to discount water from the weight of waste disposed to landfill. Water that has been added to facilitate transport, in the course of an industrial process or for the extraction of minerals can be discounted where it is 25% or more of the waste by weight. If water naturally occurs in the waste then it cannot be discounted and will be subject to landfill tax at the rate of the underlying material.

Compliance

Tax points

[18.46] There are two tax points that can be used: the disposal tax point and the invoice date tax point. Different tax points can be used for different customers. The disposal tax point is the date that waste is disposed of to landfill; an invoice tax point is created if a landfill invoice is issued within 14 days of a taxable disposal unless the operator has written to HMRC to inform them of their election to use disposal tax points instead. A tax point is not created by issuing an invoice prior to disposal. The date of payment does not create a tax point.

If an operator wishes to use invoice tax points then they must issue landfill invoices which should include:

- an identifying number;
- date of issue;
- date of disposal;
- name, address and landfill tax registration number of operator;
- name and address of customer;
- weight and description of waste;
- rate of tax applied to each disposal; and
- total amount payable on invoice.

The amount of landfill tax does not need to be separately shown on invoices. If landfill tax is separately itemised then the invoices must contain a statement to say that the tax is not recoverable as input VAT. Landfill tax and VAT invoices can be combined, and VAT must be calculated on the landfill tax inclusive value of the supplies.

Registration

[18.47] Landfill site operators who make or intend to make taxable disposals must register for landfill tax. There is no registration threshold. Group registration is available provided the control conditions are met. Any taxable business will be treated as being carried on by the representative member of a group and all members will be jointly and severally liable for any tax due from the representative member. The benefits of group treatment are largely administrative; unlike VAT, landfill tax will be due on any taxable disposals between members of the same group. Divisional registration is also possible if it would cause real difficulty for the company to submit a single landfill tax return.

Operators with landfill sites in Scotland must separately register and submit returns for Scottish landfill tax.

Returns

[18.48] Landfill tax returns usually cover three month periods and are due for submission on the last working day of the month following the period end. Payment is also due by this date.

Landfill tax records, including waste transfer notes, should be retained for six years.

Errors, penalties and adjustments

[18.49] Errors not exceeding the greater of £10,000 or 1% of the supplier's VAT turnover (ie the amount showing in Box 6 of the supplier's VAT return for that period) to a maximum upper limit of £50,000 can be corrected through subsequent landfill tax returns. More sizeable under-declaration errors need to be separately notified to HMRC/Revenue Scotland. Large over-declarations can be adjusted through the landfill tax returns.

The single penalty regime introduced in FA 2008 also applies to landfill tax returns filed on or after 1 April 2010. Therefore, there should be no penalty where a taxpayer makes a mistake (whilst exercising 'reasonable care') but there will be a penalty of up to 30% for failure to take reasonable care, and 100% for a deliberate error with concealment (these penalties may be substantially reduced at HMRC's or Revenue Scotland's discretion where the taxpayer makes a disclosure).

Claims for over-declared landfill tax or assessments for underpaid landfill tax are subject to a four-year cap from 1 April 2010 (FA 2009, Sch 51), increased from the previous three-year cap. However, where an adjustment is necessary to account for the use of an existing exemption certificate for waste from contaminated land, there is no such time limit provided the actual waste concerned was disposed of prior to the deadline of 31 March 2012.

Jack Harley v Revenue and Customs Comrs (TC01762) [2012] UKFTT 66 (UK)

[18.50] Jack Harley was a landowner who obtained planning permission to raise the base of a valley by using imported subsoil and topsoil to provide agricultural improvement. The taxpayer was required to register for landfill tax in relation to this activity and accounted for landfill tax on the soil deposited in accordance with the planning permission. Following the case of *Waste Recycling Group*, a claim to recover this overpaid landfill tax was made on the ground that the materials, ie the soil had not been disposed of as waste. It was accepted that following the *Waste Recycling Group* case, the activities of Jack Harley had never been taxable and the sums previously paid as landfill tax had not been due.

Since it was accepted that the amounts paid had never been due as landfill tax, a claim was not possible under FA 1996, s 51 as this only allows for repayments that are indisputably of tax. A claim under Sch 5, para 14 could be made as this allows for claims that are 'an amount [paid] to the commissioners by way of tax which was not tax due to them'. However, the four-year time limit prevented a claim under this legal provision so the taxpayer's claims were rejected.

Implications for construction projects

[18.51] Costs for the removal of waste include the cost of landfill tax on the basis that landfill site operators will pass on as much of the tax as possible to end users in the form of higher prices. Indeed, landfill tax is becoming an increasingly significant cost component of waste management contracts and many businesses are looking to more proactively manage waste through recycling initiatives.

Reducing the landfill tax bill

[18.52] Where sending waste to landfill is unavoidable, it may be possible to reduce the landfill tax bill by following some simple steps.

- If contractors send inert waste to landfill, they should confirm that the landfill site operator only charges in line with the lower rate of £2.60 per tonne.
- Where possible, it may be less costly to collect and separately store inert and active waste in order to ensure that the standard rate is only charged on active waste.
- No allowance is made for naturally occurring water content in waste. Natural water content includes the effect of rain and snow. Therefore, contractors can reduce costs by using appropriate protection to keep waste dry on site and during transportation.
  Where the amount of added water is more than 25% of the weight of the waste then the operator can apply to HMRC/Revenue Scotland to discount the water from the calculation of landfill tax.

Other tax incentives (such as contaminated land relief) should be considered.

These issues have become more important as the rate of landfill tax has increased to a more material level in recent years. Developers are likely to be recharged the increasing costs of landfill tax as a cost component of the project. They may wish to consider how to deal with this from a commercial standpoint: for example, 'cost plus' type agreements may provide little incentive to reduce landfill tax costs. Developers may also want to consider how to achieve more transparency over the calculation of landfill tax so that they can ensure all reliefs and exemptions are being claimed further down the supply chain.

Chapter 19

Business rates

by
Simon Tivey FIRRV,
Managing Director, Simon Tivey Rating

Introduction

[19.1] Rates are one of the oldest forms of tax and developed 400 years ago out of the obligation to care for the poor within parishes and the need for the authorities to pay for this. This developed in to the system of local government we have today and the main local taxes that fund it – business rates and council tax.

The rating system applied to both domestic and business premises up until 1990 but from that time it was split between a new national system of business rates for non-domestic property and a new tax for domestic property. The first domestic system was Community Charge (Poll Tax) which levied a flat charge on all individuals, quickly followed by the present Council Tax system where the occupier of a dwelling pays an annual charge proportionate to the capital value of the property.

Prior to 1990 each local authority was allowed to set its own level of rates known as the poundage, according to the amount of tax they wished to raise to pay for local services. This led to vastly different levels of rates between cities and regions, particularly where deprived cities felt they had greater social needs. Ultimately it led to situations where for example a manufacturing company with several factories around the country could be paying three times more rates in a northern city compared to one in the south east. This incentivised companies to relocate towards lower rated areas and contributed to unemployment in the higher rated areas.

The National Non-Domestic Rating system was introduced by the Local Government Finance Act 1988 (LGFA 1988) and created a universal rate poundage (multiplier) across England with regional variations for Wales and Scotland whilst Northern Ireland continued with their existing rating system.

The multiplier is now set each year by Government and so this has removed some of the regional variations that distorted this local property tax. There is a general principle that the multipliers will not increase by more than RPI each year, other than the rebasing that takes place in revaluation years. However, some creep is emerging with the stretching of the large business supplement from 0.7p in 2010/11 to 1.3p in 2017/18 and the creation of the 2p CrossRail supplement in Greater London.

The new system of business rates also introduced two other fundamental changes, being a more standardised package of reliefs and a compulsory empty rate system. However, the move towards retention of business rates income by local authorities now means that more discretion is being given to councils to develop their own bespoke reliefs.

Rates were traditionally a tax on the occupation of property but are now becoming more akin to a tax on real estate assets through the widening of scope of empty rates. Also rates were mainly associated with traditional classes of real property such as factories shops and offices, but they now apply to the sending of telecoms signals down fibre optic cables and the generation and storage of renewable energy.

Basis of rates as a local property tax

[19.2] The annual rates charge is a simple product of the rateable value of a property (see **19.7**) and the multiplier together with the underlying fact that a person or corporate body is occupying a property, or in the case of an unoccupied property, is the owner of it (unless transitional adjustments apply after a revaluation).

From this headline calculation of tax charge, is then deducted any appropriate reliefs to arrive at the annual amount payable. Where exemptions apply then the general rule is that no charge arises.

There are two distinct elements within the business rates system. The first is the determination of liability, calculation of charge, demand and collection rates, all undertaken by the local authority. The second is the setting and maintaining of rateable values which is undertaken by the Valuation Office Agency (VOA) in England and Wales and the Assessor in Scotland.

The billing authority function

[19.3] Where a local authority has responsibility for business rates it is formally known as the billing authority and these are city councils, district councils, London and Metropolitan Borough councils and the unitary councils. (County councils in two-tier local government areas are not billing authorities for rates.)

The billing authority will have a revenues department employing rating officers to issue rate demands, collect monies and enforce payment. They are given a copy of the Rating List by the VO containing rateable values for all properties in their area and use this to calculate the annual amount of rates chargeable on each property.

The billing authority has a duty to issue rate demands for each rate year as soon as possible before 1 April and to revise charges and demands to take into account changes in liability throughout the rate year or for prior years. Also a duty to notify the VO of altered, demolished, split or merged properties so that the VO can amend the rating list accordingly.

A system of payment by 10 monthly instalments is the norm with an option to elect for 12 months. Where a ratepayer defaults then a range of actions can be taken by the billing authority following the issue of a liability order by magistrates. These include distraint of goods or winding up proceedings.

The Valuation Officer function

[19.4] The Valuation Officer (VO) is part of the VOA and has a duty to maintain the Rating List for each authority area.

This involves preparing new lists every five years and maintaining each list during its life to reflect new, demolished and altered properties. The VO is also responsible for the initial stage of ratepayer's appeals against their rateable value and if agreement cannot be reached then appeals proceed to hearings in the Valuation Tribunal (see **19.44**).

The VO also determines what the unit of rateable property will be, ie its identity and extent and this is called a hereditament. As a rule, a hereditament has to comprise buildings that are contiguous and VO practice has been to apply this to floors within an office building. However the Supreme Court has ruled in *Woolway VO v Mazars LLP* [2013] EWCA Civ 368, [2015] UKSC 53, that even contiguous floors within an office building should be rated as separate hereditaments if they do not interconnect other than through common parts. This has led to fundamental changes on how a hereditament is defined and many ratepayers having a single office assessment broken down into multiple rateable values and so receiving a rate bill for each floor they occupy in an office tower block. This has not improved the efficiency of the rating system.

Liability for occupied rates

[19.5] Business rates are a daily charge and where a property is occupied then rates are calculated and demanded for the full year ahead, 1 April through to the following 31 March, unless a defined period is already known where occupation started and ceased.

Section 43 of the LGFA 1988 sets out two basic conditions which lead to liability for business rates:

(1) On the day the ratepayer is in occupation of all or part of a rateable property.
(2) The property is shown for the day in a local rating list.

The concept of rateable occupation is not defined by the LGFA 1988 but has developed through centuries of case law. It does not depend to any great degree on legal title and so freeholders, leaseholders, licence holders, and squatters can all be held liable as occupiers. Individuals can be solely liable or jointly and severally liable.

Rateable occupation

[19.6] There are four essential ingredients to rateable occupation which are most often quoted from *John Laing & Son Ltd v Kingswood Area Assessment Committee* [1949] 1 KB 344:

- actual;
- beneficial;
- exclusive;
- not too transient.

Actual occupation arises most commonly from physical presence of the occupier himself or goods, materials or carrying on of a trade, eg the manufacture of cars in a factory.

Beneficial occupation is where the occupiers derives benefit and whilst this is most often in connection with actual occupation, there are instances where rateable occupation will be held to exist from a benefit but lacking actual use, for example where a warehouse operator holds a warehouse available for use between periodic shipments. Seasonal occupation also amounts to a beneficial use even though a guest house might have a winter closed period and will still be liable for rates for the whole year.

Exclusive occupation arises where the occupier has the right and does exclude others from the property, reserving all the benefit to himself. However, this rule was tested in *Westminster City Council v Southern Railway Co* [1936] AC 511 where it was held that WH Smith were in rateable occupation of a news cabin on a station concourse even though they could not gain access to it 24 hours a day and were subjected to stringent conditions by the railway company.

A rateable occupation is considered to be sufficiently permanent and not too transient where, for example, moveable builders' huts are on site for more than six months or where a right is held to use land for, say, an annual fair or racetrack, even if it reverts to agricultural use for the rest of the year.

There is also a concept of paramount occupation where one person or organisation is in actual occupation but the degree of control exercised by another body means that the other body does actually have paramount control and is deemed to be the rateable occupier.

For example, charities have trading subsidiaries to run bookshops or cafes at a wider charitable property. The charity can remain the rateable occupier and benefit from the 80% rate relief by controlling the use of the premises. In addition, the charity may need to show that they have a degree of control over the operation of the business.

Calculation of occupied rate charges

[19.7] The multipliers set for the 2017 rate year in England are 47.9p as the standard with 46.6p for small businesses. In Wales there is one multiplier of 49.9p and Scotland 46.6p.

Example 1

A car component factory in Birmingham is occupied by Softseats Ltd and has a rateable value of £950,000.

The rate charges for year 2017/18 are £950,000 x 0.479 = £455,050.

The rate is payable by 10 monthly instalments commencing 1 April 2017 through to 1 January 2018 each instalment being £45,505.

On 17 December 2017, the occupying company is sold to another group and the trade is then carried on by Newseats Ltd while the freehold is held by Group PropCo.

The rate charges for Softseats Ltd are £455,050 divided by 365 times 260 days for the period 1 April to 17 December 2017 = £324,145.21.

The period of liability for Softseats ends on 16 December because they were not in occupation at midnight on 17 December (LGFA 1988, s 67(6)).

Softseats will have paid nine instalments totalling £409,545 and will be due a refund of £85,399.79. The billing authority will not recognise any apportionment of monies set out in the sale and purchase agreement between parties.

Newseats Ltd are liable for rates for the period 17 December 2017 to 31 March 2018 and will receive a demand for £130,904.79, being the daily apportionment for this period. This will be payable in two equal instalments in January and February 2018 using the rule 'number of whole months left in the rate year less one', unless the demand is issued on or after 1 January, in which case it will be payable in one lump sum. The billing authority must give 14 days' notice of the first instalment due date.

Group PropCo are not liable for business rates as they are the owners but not occupiers of the factory.

There is no statutory duty to notify the billing authority of changes in occupier or owner but it is sound tax administration to do so.

Reliefs

Void or empty relief

[19.8] There has always been an understanding and acceptance that business rates are a tax on the occupation of property where an income stream or benefit arises from which this tax can be paid. So prior to 1966 there was a right to full void relief as soon as occupation ended. In 1966 the concept of empty rates (see **19.31**) were introduced which in certain circumstances raised a charge in otherwise periods of void relief.

For 2017/18, the only void relief is where the property is one that is not chargeable to empty rates (eg a surface car park or any property with a rateable value less than £2,900), or where an initial 'free period' exists.

Where a property becomes unoccupied then a free period of three months arises on commercial property (eg shops, offices, retail warehouses etc) and six months on industrials (eg factories, warehouses etc).

The free period is calculated from the day after section 43 occupation ceases and runs regardless of whether the property is in the possession of the previous occupier or has reverted to the freeholder or superior leaseholder.

This is an aspect of rating where disputes frequently arise because landlords often feel aggrieved that a tenant has used up some or all of the free period.

Example 2

Fashion Company ceases to trade and removes stock from their rented shop at 5 pm on Saturday, 6 June 2017 but abandons the shop fittings. The three-month free period starts to run on 6 June because this is not classed as an occupied day (section 67(6) rule). The last day of the lease is 24 June 2017 and the landlord is charged section 45 empty rates from 6 September 2017. The landlord is aggrieved for two reasons: firstly that there was a clause in the lease stating that the tenant must occupy and trade from the property throughout the lease; and secondly that shop fittings were left in place.

The lease clause has no bearing on the billing authority determination of when rateable occupation ceases and the presence of shop fittings does not constitute a rateable occupation under the rule in LGFA 1988, s 65(5) (see **19.10**). The landlord has lost part of his expected three-month free period and is liable for 100% empty rates earlier than he thought.

Free periods are often contentious, particularly where companies go into administration and the billing authority makes a determination of vacancy without obtaining the full facts, or is too keen to cancel rate charges so as to avoid rate arrears accumulating that are never likely to be recovered.

Additional free periods arise once a property has been vacant for at least six weeks and whilst this is helpful between genuine changes of occupation, it can be manipulated by the creation of short-term reoccupations. The billing authority has the power to determine that a real rateable occupation has not taken place and refuse to grant further free periods.

Partly occupied properties

[19.9] Relief for partly occupied properties can be granted by billing authorities at their discretion under LGFA 1988, s 44A.

There is a fundamental tenet of rating that 'occupation of part constitutes occupation of the whole' and this was developed over the centuries to counter claims by ratepayers that they were not getting the full benefit from their properties due to a variety of reasons, such as a downturn in business, or because they took on premises which were too large in the first place.

Without this rule, which is now enshrined in s 43, the tax base would be eroded and efficient administration of the rate severely tested.

Despite this rule, it has always been seen to be helpful to have the facility whereby billing authorities can reflect temporary difficulties that ratepayers experience from time to time in fully occupying their properties. Furthermore, local authorities now have statutory duties to promote economic development and section 44A relief can be used carefully in support of that.

Example 3

A foreign manufacturing company intends to construct a new factory employing 1,000 people in a deprived area of the UK. In addition to various regional aids, the local authority is inclined to offer rate relief for a period of around a year that will reflect the phasing in of production and build up of output. When built, the rateable value of the new factory is entered into the Rating List at £2m from 1 April 2017 and the Valuation Officer certifies that for the first six months of operations the unoccupied portion of the rateable value is £500,000 and for the next six months £200,000. The rates relief is calculated by applying the multiplier for England of 0.479 to these rateable values and the relief for the year will be £120,078.08 + £47,768.76 = £167,846.84. The full charge for the year would have been £958,000 but is now reduced to £790,153.16.

There are complex rules which can limit the period for which this type of rate relief will benefit the ratepayer due to a clawback effect of empty rates. The general rule is that commercial properties can only have relief for three months of partial occupation and industrials for six months. However, the Government have advised billing authorities that a strict interpretation of the Non-Domestic Rating (Unoccupied Property) (England) Regulations 2008 (SI 2008/386) would not reflect the intention of parliament for this relief to be operated flexibly and so the relief can be extended through the use of subsequent operative periods.

An operative period commences where a property becomes partly occupied and continues until the end of the rate year or the extent of the unused areas change or the property becomes fully occupied or wholly vacant – whichever occurs first.

The Government has advised billing authorities that the use of section 44A relief can avoid hardship and ease situations such as phased occupations and vacations, or other temporary inability to use areas due to external factors.

The use of statutory discretion has been the subject of much case law and for local authority rating officers, *R v Tower Hamlets LBC ex p Chetnik Developments Ltd* [1988] AC 858 sets out the main rules. These are that blanket policies are not appropriate and each case should be judged on its own merits, but that the previous conduct of the ratepayer can be taken into account.

Section 44A is intended to be a relief that is operated on a flexible basis; indeed if the strict rules of rateable occupation are observed it would never be possible for s 44A to operate. So unused areas within buildings do not need to be defined by walls and do not need to be entirely empty. They can be an amalgamation of several small unused areas and may even contain unused machinery, furniture or computer equipment. There are no appeal rights against a billing authority decision to refuse relief, other than by the costly route of judicial review, but the relief is generally negotiated based on knowledge of the billing authority's approach to other ratepayers and the general practice of rating officers.

Inactive premises containing plant, machinery or equipment

[19.10] A special provision exists under LGFA 1988, s 65(5) whereby rateable occupation does not arise if a building contains only plant, machinery or equipment that was last used on the premises or is intended for future use on the premises.

It was held in *Sheafbank Property Trust v Sheffield City MDC* (1988) 152 JP 347 that office furniture is included in the above provision and there is now widespread acceptance that unused computer equipment can also be included.

The section 65(5) rule is very helpful in both determining when full rateable occupation either commences or finishes but also in analysing partly occupied properties to see which areas can be included in a section 44A claim.

Example 4

An insurance company call centre makes 75% of its staff redundant on 1 May 2017. A claim for section 44A relief can be made on the workstations which still contain unused desks, chairs, keyboards and monitors. On 1 July 2017, the remaining staff leave and the property can be treated as unoccupied despite the presence of unused equipment, provided it is switched off and there is a clear intention that the call centre will not be reopened in the short to medium term. The three-month free period will start to run from 1 July, the rates liability now falls under s 45 and the 100% empty rate will be charged from 1 October 2017.

Charities and non-profit making organisations

[19.11] There are two types of rate relief here known as mandatory and discretionary relief.

Registered charities are entitled to 80% mandatory relief (LGFA 88, s 43) where they occupy premises and they are wholly or mainly used for charitable purposes whether of that charity or other charities. Registered Community Amateur Sports Clubs are also entitled to 80% mandatory relief.

Where a charity owns unoccupied property but intends to use it for charitable purposes in the future, then there is a full exemption from empty rates (LGFA 1988, s 45A).

The term charity is defined by LGFA 1988, s 67(10) as an 'institution or other organisation established for charitable purposes only or any persons administering a trust established for charitable purposes only'. The register of charities provides conclusive evidence that an organisation is a charity, but some organisations are excluded from the need to register, eg Church Commissioners, registered Friendly Societies, units of the Boy Scouts and Girl Guides Associations, or voluntary schools.

The extension of empty rate charges to 100% and the inclusion of industrial property in the empty rates regime has recently led to the use of charities in rate avoidance schemes. These often involve the letting of an empty property to a charitable organisation at a nominal rent which means that the property becomes exempt from empty rates. Such organisations are incentivised to enter into these arrangements by donations from the property owner but the local authorities can challenge the schemes if the size and type of the property is not one which the charitable organisation could possibly occupy in the future.

There has also been the case of *Public Safety Charitable Trust v Milton Keynes Council* [2013] EWHC 1237 (Admin), [2013] All ER (D) 268 (May) where an otherwise empty property was claimed to be occupied by a few Bluetooth transmitters and used for charitable purposes to gain an 80% relief. This was unsuccessful (see **19.48**).

Charity shops

[19.12] Special provisions apply to charity shops to deal with the fact that many of the goods they sell can be bought in rather than donated and the fact that the shops are essentially carrying on fundraising activities.

A charity shop is treated as being wholly or mainly used for charitable purposes and entitled to 80% rate relief if it is wholly or mainly used for the sale of goods donated to a charity and the proceeds of sale are applied to the purposes of the charity (LGFA 1988, s 64(10)).

Discretionary relief for charities and non-profit making organisations

[19.13] Charities that are entitled to 80% mandatory rate relief may also apply to the billing authority for discretionary relief which can be set against any proportion of the remaining 20% (LGFA 1988, s 47).

In addition to charities, discretionary relief can be granted to organisations that are not established or conducted for profit and whose main objects are charitable, or otherwise philanthropic, or religious, or concerned with education, social welfare, science, literature or the fine arts.

There is also provision for recreation whereby relief can be granted to clubs, societies and other organisations that are wholly or mainly involved in recreation and not established or conducted for profit.

Local authorities cannot award relief to properties they occupy and so it is now common for former council leisure centres to be outsourced to external organisations that have trusts within their structure and which then run the leisure centres. However, such arrangements must ensure that the local authority does not retain paramount control and so care must be had in the construction of leases and management boards comprising councillors and which have powers to set fees and charges etc.

Rural settlement relief

[19.14] This relief is available in both mandatory and discretionary forms and is based on settlements outside defined urban areas that have populations of not more than 3,000.

The relief is targeted towards qualifying general stores, rural food shops, post offices, public houses and petrol filling stations. The properties must have a rateable value of no more than £8,500 for stores, shops and post offices and £12,500 for pubs and fuel stations. This scheme applies to England only. There are other qualifying criteria before the mandatory relief of 50% (increased to 100% from 1 April 2017) can be granted which are designed to exclude restaurants, cafés, tea rooms and fast food outlets.

The billing authority can also grant discretionary relief to top up mandatory relief or grant any amount of relief up to 100% to rural business that would otherwise not qualify for the mandatory relief.

The rateable value must not exceed £16,500 and the criteria are that the property must be used for purposes which are of benefit to the local community and it is reasonable to grant relief having regard to the interest of council taxpayers.

As with any discretionary relief, the rules of exercising statutory discretion must be followed and these are essentially to consider each application on its own merits, not to have blanket policies that enable certain applications to be dismissed out of hand but to have some guidance so as to ensure a consistent approach.

Small business rate relief

[19.15] This scheme applies to small business according to the size of property from which they operate and can be granted to corporate bodies and individuals. Research shows that business rates place a proportionately greater burden on small businesses, particularly those that require premises from which to trade, such as retailers and repair businesses trading from small workshops.

The current small business rate relief (SBRR) scheme was introduced by s 61 of the Local Government Act 2003 which inserted ss 4A–4D into LGFA 1988, s 43. From 1 April 2005 it has been possible for small business to apply for this relief and local authorities have actively encouraged take up by promoting the relief widely, as have local and national trade bodies.

The SBRR scheme for England is contained in various Orders, the Non-Domestic Rating (Small Business Rate Relief) (England) Order (SI 2004/3315) and the Non-Domestic Rating (Small Business Rate Relief) (Amendment) (England) Order (SI 2006/2313) together with SIs 2009/3175 and 2010/1655, 2016/143 and 2017/102 which set out the conditions for relief and the rateable value thresholds.

SBRR is available to a ratepayer if either he has only one property in England or, where he also has additional properties, their individual rateable values must not exceed £2,899 and the total rateable value of all the properties must be under £20,000 (£28,000 in Greater London). From 1 April 2017, SBRR means that no rates will be payable on qualifying hereditaments with RV under £12,000 and relief will then taper down from 100% to 0% between RV £12,000 and £15,000.

The small business multiplier applies to all property with RV below £51,000.

Wales has its own SBRR scheme which is similar to England but with different RV thresholds.

In Scotland small business properties with a combined rateable value of £15,000 or less can benefit from a bonus scheme of between 25% and 100% of the rates payable. The exact level of relief depends on the total rateable value of all the properties occupied by the business. The levels of relief for 2017/18 are:

- up to £15,000 combined rateable value – 100% relief;
- £15,001 to £18,000 – 25% relief.

Transitional adjustments

[19.16] The purpose of transitional adjustments is to smooth out the otherwise large increase or reduction in rate charges that could arise between the year prior to a revaluation and the year when revaluation takes effect.

Revaluations generally take place every five years unless delayed by the Government. These have been in 1990, 1995, 2000, 2005, 2010 and the 2017 revaluation came into effect from 1 April 2017. The next revaluation will probably be from 1 April 2022 but the Government is considering introducing a self-assessment system for business rates which could be ready by 2022.

Where rental values move upwards or downwards in the market then a revaluation is designed to capture that change so that the rate burden is met proportionately by ratepayers in various sectors of the economy according to how well that sector is doing. For example hotels, leisure and retail might see a substantial rise in rents over five years whereas manufacturing in a particular part of the country may be in decline, with many empty, old and obsolete factories. In such cases it has been known for rateable values to increase or reduce by more than 50% and sometimes 100% from one rating list to the next.

One of the purposes of the LGFA 1988 was to provide business with a more stable and predictable rating system where their rate charge could be calculated and planned for from one rate year to the next with a great degree of certainty.

The multiplier should only increase each year by the rate of inflation existing at the previous September but in a revaluation year the rateable values all change and the multiplier is reset according to the overall movement of the rating lists.

Without some mechanism to mitigate large swings in rate charges in revaluation years, many business, large and small, would find it very difficult to pay their rates or would have windfall reductions.

The transitional schemes therefore operate by restricting the amount by which an individual ratepayer's rates can increase or reduce in the years following a revaluation.

This is done by placing a percentage limit on increases or reductions in real terms as compared to the amount of rate charges for a property for the year prior to revaluation.

Example 5

A shop in England and outside London had a rateable value in 2016 of £18,000 and upon revaluation its rateable value on the 2017 list became £25,000. The rate charge for 2016/17 was 18,000 × 0.484 = £8,712 and the 'notional' charge for 2017/18 was 25,000 × 0.466 = £11,650.

The threshold for increase was set at 12.5% plus RPI and so the actual amount paid in 2017/18 would be limited to £8,712 x 1.1475 = £9,997.02.

The ratepayer has therefore benefited from transitional relief of around £1,653 in 2017/18. For properties with RV greater than £51,000, the small business supplement is added to the transitional charge as it is deemed to be outside of the transitional scheme and this creates another layer of complexity. In the 2018/19 rate year, the transitional increase will be 17.5% threshold plus RPI and so this means that the 2018/19 year charge will fall outside the transitional scheme and will be calculated solely by reference to RV and Multiplier.

The limiting percentages for the 2017 list are set by the Non-Domestic Rating (Chargeable Amounts) (England) Regulations 2016 (SI 2016/1265) and are shown in the following table.

	2017/18	2018/19	2019/20	2020/21	2021/22
Losers					
Small properties	5%	7.5%	10%	15%	15%
Medium Properties	12.5%	17.5%	20%	25%	25%
Large properties	412%	32%	490%	165%	6%
Gainers					
Small properties	20%	30%	35%	55%	55%
Medium properties	10%	15%	207%	25%	25%
Large Properties	4.1%	4.6%	5.9%	5.8%	4.8%

Medium size properties are those with RV above £28,000 in London and above £20,000 elsewhere in England. Large properties have RV over £100,000. This is a basic description of the purpose and operation of transitional schemes but they are complex in their detail and interaction with other reliefs. New properties coming into the rating list after 1 April 2017 are not subjected to transitional adjustment and there are special rules for increases or reductions in rateable value that attempt to exclude these changes from the what is known as the 'transitional path'.

There are also some capturing provisions whereby the VO can certify what a rateable value ought to have been so that the transitional path is not distorted by unusual circumstances or changes. These are designed to ensure that ratepayers do not escape transitional surcharge or benefit wrongly from transitional relief.

Wales decided not to have a transitional scheme for the 2005 or 2010 list and has adopted a limited scheme to assist small businesses facing a large increase in 2017. Scotland's was essentially based on rateable value limits rather than limits on amounts payable but was not renewed after the 2010 or 2017 revaluation.

Hardship relief

[19.17] Specific powers exist to write off rate charges if it would otherwise cause hardship to the person and it is in the interests of the wider body of council taxpayers.

These powers under LGFA 1988, s 49 do allow rates to be written off for both individuals and corporate bodies and against occupied and empty rates. However, it is most common for this relief to be used for individuals and small traders. The insolvency rules for companies mean that it is more likely that a company will go into administration before any application can be processed and considered.

Notwithstanding that situation, hardship relief is a provision that can enable a local authority to offer specific assistance in the short term. For example, if a major local employer suffers a period of acute difficulties due to, say, a cancellation of a contract, the billing authority can be flexible with the normal requirement to pay monthly instalments and at a later date, if trading conditions pick up, it may feel it is in the interests of the wider community to write off a proportion of rates. Hardship relief can also be used imaginatively with partly occupied relief to support businesses that may have temporary difficulties but which are basically sound and of strategic importance to the local economy. In particular these reliefs can help to underpin a local authority's economic development duties.

European Union competition rules generally prohibit government subsidies to businesses and rate relief can constitute state aid if it is capable of effecting intra-Community trade. De minimis rules apply whereby up to €200,000 (€100,000 in the road transport sector) in relief can be granted to any one business over three years.

Exemptions

[19.18] The term exemption in matters of rating is often confused, because there are exemptions for categories of land and buildings which are not entered into the rating lists at all and there are exemptions from empty rate charges.

This section deals with exemption from rating generally where there can be no entry made in the rating list.

Bare land

[19.19] There is no specific exemption for bare undeveloped land but it has become a rating convention that land which has no rental value and no active use (occupation) is not rated. This is because, historically, all land is either agricultural or forest, both of which are specifically exempt from rates. Land then becomes developed for other use but it is not until that other use commences that a rating list entry will arise.

For example, a 'greenfield' site is granted planning consent for housing and employment purposes. The housing estate will not be entered into the Council Tax Banding Lists until the houses are completed and occupied and, likewise, the factories or shopping arcades. Whilst construction works are ongoing the land is held to be in the 'non-beneficial' occupation of the developer/builders and only the small pieces of land on which their huts and compounds stand will be rated temporarily.

With 'brownfield' sites a factory may have been demolished and the rating list entry for the factory will have been deleted from the date of demolition. The brownfield land now has no rating value until a new building is constructed and occupation commences, even though the land with planning consent may be worth many millions of pounds in capital value. This is because the rating system is based on annual rental value and no one would pay an annual rent for the bare land with no right to construct or occupy any buildings.

The former Labour Government put the view forward that this is an anomalous element of local property taxation and that some charge or amendment to the rating system should be introduced to capture taxes on bare land with planning consent. As yet the new Coalition Government has made no changes to rates other than a 'Localism' concept for promoting economic growth (see **19.50** below).

Some types of bare land are rateable, but these are where some element of occupation can be demonstrated. For example, land that is hard surfaced with stone or concrete is then capable of being used for the storage of vehicles, containers or other plant or even for heaps of aggregate. In such cases there is an occupation, albeit generally at a low value, but it is rateable nonetheless.

It should be noted that rates only arise on these types of land during periods when some use is made. During non-use or empty periods then a specific exemption applies so that empty rates cannot be charged (see **19.31**).

Temporary uses of bare land can be rateable if the user has a right to return to the site periodically; for example, use of fields for markets, fairs or point to point horse racing.

Agricultural land and buildings

[19.20] Agricultural land and buildings have not always been exempt from rates and charges were levied up to the first decades of the twentieth century. This rates exemption has been connected to government policies to control and subsidise food production.

The current exemption is now contained in LGFA 1988, Sch 5 and basically provides that the agricultural exemption applies to: arable land, meadow, pasture, plantations, woods, poultry farms over 0.1 hectares, market gardens, orchards, allotments and land used with agricultural buildings.

Certain categories of land are excluded from being agricultural and these are: parkland around a house, gardens, pleasure grounds, sports and recreation grounds and racecourses.

The degree to which non-agricultural uses might lose a piece of land's rating exemption depends on the degree and frequency of use. For example in *Hayes (Valuation Officer) v Loyd* [1985] 2 All ER 313, a point to point race held once a year in a field was held to be rateable but in *Eden (Valuation Officer) v Grass Ski Promotions Ltd* [1981] RA 7, 254 Estates Gazette 303 a grass skiing slope was held not to detract from its predominant use as pasture.

Gallops used for racehorses are rateable if they are laid out specifically with special surfacing and railing but generally not rateable where they pass over pasture. Land and grazing used specifically for horses is rateable, but it is often difficult to demonstrate that agricultural land has been taken over exclusively for horses as sheep are often used to improve the pasture in a rotation or in with the horses.

Agricultural buildings can either be those used for keeping or breeding livestock or in connection with agricultural operations on the land, or for both purposes. They are also defined as buildings other than dwellings that are occupied together with agricultural land and used solely in connection with agricultural operation on that or other agricultural land.

There has to be a connection between the buildings and the occupiers of the land. There are special rules for farmer's cooperatives under LGFA 1988, Sch 5.

Agricultural buildings have generated much case law over the years as there is a fine line between where farming ends and food processing begins. Also many of the large food companies own farms themselves and take cereals, milk, vegetables and livestock straight from fields to food factories.

A livestock building has to be surrounded by or contiguous to at least two hectares of agricultural land. Livestock is any mammal or bird kept for the production of food or wool or for use in the farming of the land. It is for this reason that horse stables outside the curtilage of your house and garden are rateable. Beekeeping is included as agricultural, as is fish farming provided the fish are for food and not merely ornamental.

In *Handley (Valuation Officer) v Bernard Matthews plc* [1988] RA 222, [1989] 14 EG 67 it was held that a mill used for producing turkey food was exempt but in *Farmer (Valuation Officer) v Buxsted Poultry* [1993] AC 369, [1993] 1 All ER 117 the buildings were 120 miles from the farms and were held to be rateable.

The recent Court of Appeal decision *Tunnel Tech Ltd v Reeves* [2015] EWCA Civ 718, [2015] RA 399, [2015] PTSR 1490, shows how the definitions of agricultural buildings are failing to keep up with new technologies. Buildings and poly tunnels used for preparing and growing mushroom spawn for onward sale to mushroom growers were held to be rateable. However, the Government has now committed to reversing the decision either through an amendment to the Local Government Finance Act or through a relief scheme for mushroom spawn growers.

Places of religious worship

[19.21] Churches and chapels and other places of public religious worship are exempt from rates under LGFA 1988, Sch 5 if they belong to the Church of England or Wales or are certified by law as a place of religious worship. This also includes church halls, administrative and office functions connected to the church.

Church gift shops and cafés can be rateable if there is some separation from the church in terms of access and the way it is run as was the case in *St Albans Cathedral (Chapter of the Abbey Church) v Booth (Valuation Officer)* [2004] RA 309.

The multicultural nature of the UK now means that places of religious worship take many forms. A particular case that stands out is *Gallagher (Valuation Officer) v Church of Jesus Christ of Latter-Day Saints* [2008] UKHL 56, [2008] 4 All ER 640 where it was held that a Mormon Temple was only partially exempt.

The underlying general principle is that there should be free and unrestricted access to worship for rate exemption to apply. Missionary training is not an exempt use.

Enterprise zones

[19.22] Properties in enterprise zones are exempt from rates under LGFA 1988, Sch 5 and not entered into the rating list. Most enterprise zones were set up with a life of ten years and most have now ended or are coming to their end. The 2011 Budget announced new EZ's but with a cap to the rate benefit of around £275,000 over five years. Another difference is that the exemption has turned into more of a relief because it is delivered under the localism discretionary powers and already some councils are targeting the relief at the type of business they wish to encourage.

Property used for the disabled

[19.23] Specific provision is made under LGFA 1988, Sch 5, para 16(1) for the exemption of properties used wholly for purposes connected to disabled people. This includes the usual definition of disabled people being the blind, deaf, dumb, those suffering from mental disorder or permanently handicapped by illness, injury or congenital deformity and those who are or have been suffering from illness.

The main purposes for which buildings are used in connection with disabled people are for training, keeping them suitably occupied, provision of welfare services and the provision of employment facilities.

Thus 'Remploy' style factories will be exempt, as will local authority or private special schools, eg for deaf children. Short-stay accommodation for the disabled in hospitals is also exempt (long-term stay is classed as domestic and subject to council tax).

Parks

[19.24] Parks and similar amenities are exempt from rates under LGFA 1988, Sch 5, para 15 where they are provided or managed by a local authority and are available for free and unrestricted use by members of the public.

This does however permit local authorities to regulate the use of parks but the creation of a swimming pool within a park for which entrance charges are levied can lead to a rateable value on just the pool, or possibly lose exemption for the whole park. In *South Yorkshire County Council v Jones (Valuation Officer)* [1984] RA 204, [1985] JPL 124, a country park was rateable because entrance charges were made and there were many restrictions. The more recent case of *Lake District National Park Authority v Mr D Grace (Valuation Officer)* VT Appeal No. 092516784462/214N05 found that a car park, information centre and toilets were not exempt.

The general rule is that land deemed to be in the occupation of the public is not rateable because the public rights of user effectively exhaust the value of the land such that no individual would want to pay a rent for it.

Other general exemptions for public facilities and infrastructure

[19.25] Longstanding exemptions exist for structures such as lighthouses, sewers, rivers, air raid protection works, swinging moorings, road bridges over watercourses, congestion charging schemes and election meeting rooms.

Public highways are not rateable but there is no specific exemption covering them in the LGFA 1988. Instead the rules of rateable occupation show that there can be no single occupier who has beneficial and exclusive rights of user and the public rights of use over the land effectively remove any value from it.

The modern public highway does however have structures that are both technically complex and separate and secure from the road user. If these are operated and used by the highways or other authorities in connection with the highway then they will be deemed to be ancillary and not rateable.

For example, speed cameras and matrix boards that display road information are considered by the Government to be ancillary to the main highway purpose. However, there is now a considerable amount of infrastructure on major roads that is operated by private companies and which provide road traffic data to road users by private subscription. Therefore the 'Trafficmaster' equipment on roadsides and on bridges monitoring each lane is rateable.

It is also now common for highways authorities to erect signs on roundabouts inviting local companies to sponsor the roundabout. These are not ancillary to the highway and so may be rateable as advertisements.

Utility and communication companies generally have the right to place equipment under the highway or on the verges without paying any rent to the highway authority, but this does not mean that their equipment is of no value for rating valuation purposes. An 'Orange' telecommunications pole situated on the side of a highway was held to be rateable.

Toll roads

[19.26] The first toll road operated by a private company came into use some years ago as the M6 Toll or the Birmingham Northern Relief Road. This required some consideration of the general rating position of tolls.

There are two types of toll for passing over land. A 'toll traverse' is a payment for passing over the private soil of another person where there is no general right (public highway) to take that route. This is rateable.

A 'toll through' is a payment for passing over a highway where the toll claimer does not own the land but the toll paid is for the upkeep of the bridge, wall or some other service. A toll through is not rateable.

A rating list entry for the M6 Toll Road was initially made, but on further consideration it appeared that the operator of the toll road has no ownership of the land and so it was determined to be a toll through and not rateable. This aspect of the law of rating has been built up over centuries but interestingly a specific rating exemption was created under the New Roads and Street Works Act 1991, s 16 for toll booths.

Crown exemption

[19.27] Crown exemption no longer applies to rating although Crown occupations did always make contributions in lieu of rates even though no statutory enforceable entry could be made into the rating lists.

From 1 April 2000, LGFA 1988, s 65A provides for the normal rating of all Crown and Government buildings and entries to be made in Local Lists.

Property becoming exempt or losing exemption

[19.28] The Valuation Officer and billing authority are allowed to consider how property will be used in the future under LGFA 1988, Sch 5, para 21.

This means that properties can change from benefiting from exemption to being entered in the local rating list and then being deleted as exempt. For example, a farmer may have a steel framed portal building with a concrete floor, lighting, power and toilets which has been used as a tractor shed and implement repair workshop and is exempt as an agricultural building. One of his employees then sets up a tractor repair business to take on his former employer's work and other farmers' repair work and he rents the building. It loses rate exemption from the date of these new business arrangements. However, whilst he is a good tractor repairer, his business skills are less well developed and the business goes under two years later. The farmer takes back the building and reemploys the man. It becomes exempt once again as part of the farm operations.

The boundary between rateable (non-domestic) and council taxable (domestic) property

[19.29] Historically the rating system covered both domestic and non-domestic properties but from 1990 the system of local property taxation split.

Non-domestic property continues to be rateable, but under a more uniform and national scheme commonly known as business rates or National Non-Domestic Rates ('NNDR').

From 1990 domestic property was not charged as such, but rather the occupants of a property were each subjected to the community charge or 'poll tax'. From 1993 the system swung back to taxing property when the council tax was introduced where each dwelling is allocated a Band from A to H according to its market capital value and the local authority sets its own council tax level each year.

However, the question frequently arises as to whether a property falls to be rated or council taxed. It can be taxed under both systems and these are known as composite hereditaments.

A typical example is a public house, where the pub is entered into the local rating list with a rateable value and the landlord's rooms above also have a council tax banding.

LGFA 1988, s 66 and LGFA 1992, s 3 govern the distinction between domestic and non-domestic property. Using these two provisions it is generally possible to determine which tax a property should fall under and if is not one it will be the other. As yet, no one has successfully argued that a property is neither.

Generally, property is domestic if:

- it is used wholly for the purposes of living accommodation;
- it is a yard, garden or outhouse or other appurtenance belonging to or enjoyed with the accommodation;
- it is a private garage with a floor area no more than 25 square metres or is used wholly or mainly for a private vehicle; or
- it comprises private storage premises used wholly or mainly for the storage of articles of domestic use.

This seems fairly straightforward but what about short stay and self-catering accommodation? Hotels are clearly non-domestic but guest houses are not so clear.

LGFA 1988, s 66(2) states that a property is non-domestic if it is used in the course of a business to provide accommodation for short periods to persons whose sole or main residence is elsewhere. This generally means that bed and breakfast establishments are non-domestic.

However, where short stay accommodation is limited to no more than six persons and the person providing the accommodation has their sole or main residence within the property then it is domestic.

Self-catering accommodation is non-domestic if it is available for letting for 140 days or more each year and subject to council tax if let for less than 140 days.

Timeshare property is subject to business rates if it comes under the Timeshare Act 1992.

It is now quite popular for people to live on boats, particularly on canals and where they have a mooring and the boat is their sole or main residence then a council tax band will be allocated to the mooring. Otherwise the letting of a mooring creates a rateable hereditament.

Caravans are regarded as chattels and so are not actually rated themselves, because only land and items annexed to the land can be rated. So the pitch is rated and if this is someone's sole or main residence it will be domestic and if it is a holiday caravan pitch it will be rated.

The courts have examined most situations where the boundary between domestic and non-domestic property is not immediately apparent.

Show houses are generally rateable. Gardens where charges are made for entry under the National Garden scheme and toilets and cafes provided have been held to be domestic and continue to be mainly part of the owner's house and garden.

Historic houses and gardens which have considerable upkeep costs, eg a National Trust property are rateable but are often ascribed a £0 rateable value.

Finally, the question that arises most frequently now that many people work from home, is whether a home office is rateable. This matter was examined in *Tully v Jorgensen (Valuation Officer)* [2003] RA 233 and the general rule that has been established is to decide whether a room still has some element of domestic use or whether it has been given over solely to a business use.

In the *Tully* case a room was set up as an office with equipment provided by Tully's employer so that she could work from home. It also had other equipment provided by Tully herself for the purposes of a private study and other domestic furniture. It was held that the room was still used in part for domestic purposes and no rateable use arose.

However, where rooms in the home or garden rooms are set aside, equipped and used solely for work purposes then they will be rateable. The Valuation Officer and the local authority rating inspector do though have limited resources to identify such uses.

Traditionally, professionals such as doctors or architects, particularly those with large detached houses and a drive for several vehicles, have set up surgeries or offices within the house with a brass name plate outside where their clients visit and services are provided. These are rateable but very often are not identified by the rating authorities.

Other instances where the individual can come into conflict with business rates and where they feel that the rating system invades their private lives is where a private stable for the children's pony is situated just outside the garden in a paddock and the Valuation Officer applies the rating rules strictly. Another example is where a pensioner finds that a pigeon shed erected on his allotment is given a rateable value.

Solar panels fitted to the roof of a dwelling will not attract business rates or council tax.

Empty rates

[19.30] Business rates have always been a tax on the occupation of property and it was not until 1966 that rates on unoccupied property were levied. This was in response to rapidly rising capital values and where landlords felt they could make significant gains by leaving a property empty and selling it rather than letting for rental income. Despite many changes in the property market since then, empty rates have continued to be a feature to a greater or lesser extent.

Empty rates are structured under LGFA 1988, s 45 as a distinct charge and not as often represented as a relief from occupied charges. Whilst a property appears in the rating list it is either occupied under LGFA 1988, s 43 or unoccupied under LGFA 1988, s 45. Various reliefs, exemptions and statutory classifications can then come into play but the fundamental approach must be that for each day a property is determined to be either occupied or unoccupied.

For the 2017/18 rate year, the empty rate regime basically levies rates at 100% of the normal occupied charge for all classes of empty property across England and Wales and at 90% on empty commercial properties in Scotland. In England the main provisions are contained within LGFA 1988 and the Rating (Empty Properties) Act 2007. The main regulations are the Non-Domestic Rating (Unoccupied Property) Regulations (SI 1989/2261 and SI 2008/386).

A property will be subject to empty rates under LGFA 1988, s 45 if:

(1) no part of the hereditament is occupied;
(2) the ratepayer is the owner of the whole hereditament;
(3) the hereditament is shown in the local rating list; and
(4) the hereditament falls within a class prescribed by regulations.

These conditions for a property or hereditament to be classed as empty are a daily test and liability can change from one day to the next.

Looking at the first condition, it follows that if any occupation exists within a property then it must be classed as occupied under LGFA 1988, s 43.

The second condition means that the hereditament (the extent of property comprised in the rating list entry) must be in the ownership of the rated person.

So where parts of properties are sublet the rating list must be amended to reflect the extent of changes in leases or freeholds.

The third condition is a basic requirement before liability can arise but also links in with condition 2.

Condition 4 allows the Government to define periods, types of property, or classes of persons that will or will not be subject to empty rates.

For the purposes of empty rates the term 'owner' is defined in LGFA 1988, s 65(1) as the 'person entitled to possession' of the hereditament. This means a person, partnership or corporate entity with a licence, lease or freehold, that on the day of liability in question is entitled to enter the property, exclude others and could enter into occupation themselves or allow others to occupy.

The question of who is the owner on any given day is generally straightforward to determine with the assistance of the land registry, but care has to be had with development leases, agreements for lease and where agents or fund managers are acting on behalf of or with power of attorney for pension funds or other property holding entities.

Uncertainty can also arise where a tenant and landlord are in dispute and forfeiture may or may not have taken place. Acts of surrender also have to be examined closely to determine if a former tenant is still in possession for rating purposes. The mere advertising of a property to let does not necessarily mean that a landlord has accepted surrender. Similar disputes can arise where administrators are acting for a former occupier and the question arises as to whether the landlord should be paying empty rates or the exemption for administrators applies. This is an area of rating law and practice where communication and cooperation between landlords and administrators can achieve mutually beneficial rating positions and avoid retrospective disputes.

Classes of property liable to empty rates

[19.31] The first underlying principle set down by the empty rate regulations is that empty rates only apply to 'relevant non-domestic hereditaments'. This is specifically in the context of empty rates and the term is defined as:

> 'a non-domestic hereditament consisting of, or of part of, any building, together with any land ordinarily used or intended for use for the purposes of the building or part.'

This means that only buildings or buildings with land are subject to empty rates and that conversely hereditaments that comprise just land or land with ancillary buildings cannot be subjected to an empty rate charge.

Example 6

A car park operator has a surfaced piece of land and erects a security barrier system, ticket machines, attendant's hut and a toilet block. Subsequently a new shopping centre opens on the other side of town with similar facilities and the operator decides to give notice on his lease due to a severe downturn in car parking demand from shoppers. The owner of the site is not liable for empty rates because the car park is essentially open land with a few small ancillary buildings.

There are rateable hereditaments that are comprised of structures, plant and machinery rather than being buildings and are only rated due to the fact that the Valuation for Rating (Plant and Machinery) Regulations (SI 2000/540) specifically provide for them to be rated. An example would be a mobile telecoms mast which comprises a metal pylon mast and a small metal cabinet sitting on a concrete base with a post and chain link security fence. If the mast is ever taken out of use it would not be classed as a building and so not subject to empty rates.

All other hereditaments in the local list are subject to empty rates when unoccupied unless one of the many empty rate exemptions apply.

Empty rate exemptions

Free periods

[19.32] The so called 'free period' occurs during the first three or six months after a property becomes unoccupied, ie it changes from being subject to a LGFA 1988, s 43 charge to a s 45 charge.

Commercial property such as shops, offices, retail warehouses, leisure and any property that is not classed as industrial or storage, is entitled to a three-month free period.

Industrial property is entitled to a six-month free period and a long standing definition of qualifying industrial hereditament is used by the Non-Domestic Rating (Unoccupied Property) (England) Regulations (SI 2008/386). Essentially this comprises property constructed or adapted for use in the course of a trade or business for manufacturing, repair, adaptation of goods or subjecting goods or, material to any process, storage, working or processing of minerals and generation of electricity.

The free period runs with the hereditament and not the owner. So if a tenant of a shop vacates two months before the end of his lease, the landlord will take back a property that has only one-month unexpired free period. This is the cause of many misunderstandings and disputes as to when the empty rate charge should commence. Landlords do write clauses into leases attempting to force tenants to trade until the expiry of the lease or forbidding the claiming of any free period but the billing authority is not bound by these clauses and will determine when the property is treated as becoming unoccupied according to the facts on the ground.

Disputes also arise due to the operation of LGFA 1988, s 65(5) (see **19.10**). A retailer can correctly claim that he has ceased occupation on the last day of trading if he removes or sells all stock on that day. The remaining shop fittings will be disregarded under the section 65(5) rule even though a landlord might regard the tenant as still being in occupation because of the presence of the tills, clothes rails and other shop equipment.

Six week short re-occupation rule

[19.33] Free periods generally arise and are claimed between the usual turnover of leases and different occupations. But to prevent a property owner's opportunistic use of a series of very short occupations designed to regenerate several free periods, the six-week short re-occupation rule applies where a minimum six week period of genuine occupation is required before the next unoccupied period. In such circumstances a new three or six-month free period is generated. If the short re-occupation is less than six weeks then no new free period is allowed (see **19.48** on empty rate avoidance).

Listed buildings and ancient monuments

[19.34] These are exempt from empty rates but have caused some litigation. Buildings that are merely within conservation areas are not exempt from empty rates.

Two buildings on either side of a road but linked by a tunnel, only one of which was listed comprised a single hereditament and were held not to be exempt. A listed building that had substantial new wings added onto it was also held not to be exempt from empty rates.

Rateable value threshold

[19.35] Currently, hereditaments with a rateable value less than £2,900 are exempt from empty rates in England and Wales. The threshold in Scotland is £1,700.

Insolvency cases and the deceased

[19.36] The Non-Domestic Rating (Unoccupied Property) (England) Regulations (SI 2008/386) provide the exact statutory definitions, but in general terms, empty rate exemptions apply to a bankrupt's empty property, trustees under deeds of arrangement, a company being wound up on an insolvent or voluntary basis, a liquidator in possession, companies in administration and the personal representatives of a deceased person.

Occupation prohibited by law or by action to acquire

[19.37] A hereditament is exempt from empty rates where it can be shown that its owner could not lawfully occupy the property or allow someone else to occupy it. This has never been an easy exemption to interpret and several cases have shed some light on the subject.

In *Tower Hamlets London Borough Council v St Katherine-by-the-Tower Ltd* (1982) 80 LGR 843, [1982] RA 261 a fire escape was required by the London Building Acts and until the office block complied with this law it was held to be exempt from empty rates. In *Hailbury Investments Ltd v Westminster City Council* [1986] 3 All ER 440 a building that did not have planning consent for the manner in which it was described in the rating list was held not to benefit from empty rate exemption.

In *Pall Mall Investments (London) Ltd v Gloucester City Council* [2014] EWHC 2247 Admin, [2014] All ER (D) 78 (Jul) the High Court held that properties in poor repair did not fall under the 'prohibited by law' exemption.

New or altered properties

[19.38] The empty rate regime has always been concerned to capture a charge on newly erected buildings as it is plain that there would otherwise be an incentive for developers to leave a new building at a point prior to completion and thus avoid the payment of empty rates.

This is particularly relevant in the case of speculative developments where a building is constructed to a point at which it is customary for the future tenant/occupier to take over with their fit out works. This is in contrast to a pre-let building where the construction and fit out contracts will overlap and works will be ongoing right up to the point at which the final hand over of keys takes place.

In the case of speculative developments a period arises where no works are ongoing and the buildings stands silent and empty. It is this state that the completion notice procedure is designed to capture.

On the other hand a pre-let building is covered by the convention that whilst works are ongoing it is not capable of being entered into the rating list.

The completion notice procedure

[19.39] LGFA 1988, s 46A and Sch 4A provide for the serving of completion notices by the billing authority.

The purpose of a completion notice is to set a date on which the building is deemed to be complete for the purposes of section 45 empty rating. This then enables the VO to enter what is actually an incomplete building into the rating list and sets the free period running.

The completion notice must either determine that a building is actually complete, or that it is not complete but is reasonably capable of being completed within three months from the service of the notice.

Where a building is not complete, then the billing authority must consider the period required for fitting out and other works customarily undertaken by an incoming tenant. If the works cannot be achieved within three months then the building is not ready for the service of a completion notice. A completion notice is served on the owner entitled to possession and the methods of service are set out in LGFA 1988, Sch 4A.

An appeal against a completion notice may be made within 28 days, which is actually a very short period of time within which to take advice, consider the issues, and lodge the appeal. The appeal mechanism is also weighted somewhat in favour of the billing authority, in that once an appeal is made, any withdrawal is determined by regulation to be deemed acceptance of the completion date and the Valuation Tribunal has the power to backdate the completion date quoted on the notice.

The completion notice procedure is not well understood and common confusion is that is linked to Practical Completion (PC) or the fact that a new building is being marketed. Nowadays a developer will often appoint letting agents to market a building even before construction has commenced with the use of virtual images superimposed on existing street scenes.

Until recently there has also been confusion as to whether the VO has the power to enter an incomplete building into the rating list without the assistance of a completion notice from the billing authority. The VO has been entering new unoccupied office buildings into the list despite them having no small power, no partitioning and no tea points. However, a recent Lands Tribunal case *Porter VO v Gladman* SIPPS RA63/2008 has now clarified the law and held that new unoccupied offices must be complete and fully ready for occupation if the VO wishes to enter them into the list without a completion notice. This reinforces the point that it is the billing authority which is in control of determining when new unoccupied properties are empty rated. Another more recent Lands Tribunal case has affirmed this principle in respect of new industrial buildings (*Aviva Investors Property Developments Ltd and PPG Southern Limited v Margaret Whitby (Valuation Officer) and Adrian Mills (Valuation Officer)* [2013] UKUT 0430 (LC)). The Valuation Tribunal has also given guidance in a 2013 case involving Liverpool City Council and Standard Life (*English Cities Fund (General Partners) Ltd & Standard Life Assurance Ltd v Grace (VO) and Liverpool CC*, Valuation Tribunal for England, London 5 February 2013) where the VT President, Professor Zellick, ruled that completion notices cannot be used against single floors in a new office building.

Further guidance has been provided by the High Court in *R (ono application of Reeves (Valuation Officer)) v Valuation Tribunal for England and Tull Properties* [2015] EWHC 973 (Admin), [2015] RA 241 whereby it is now certain that while the Valuation Tribunal has the power to quash a completion notice on appeal, the VT cannot delete the property from the rating list and a separate proposal is required against the rating list entry.

The Court of Appeal has also recently held in *UKI (Kingsway) Ltd and Westminster City Council* [2017] EWCA Civ 430, that a completion notice cannot be addressed merely to 'the owner' and service needs to formally be effected through the methods of service laid down in legislation.

End of life properties and deletion from the rating list

[19.40] The statutory definition of rateable value assumes that a property is in a reasonable state of repair. Otherwise the rating list would have to continually change with rateable values going up and down as buildings regularly suffered damage, disrepair or were repaired. This would undermine the tax base and lead to unduly high costs of administering the tax.

This means that where buildings come to the end of their life, fall into disrepair and are probably vandalised, there is considerable resistance from the VO to their deletion from the rating list.

Historically, most end of life property tended to be industrial and was exempt from empty rating. Where office blocks became obsolete, there was generally sufficient demand for a redevelopment scheme to be put together quickly, consent granted, demolition undertaken and rebuilding started.

However, since the increase of empty rates to from 50% to 100% and the inclusion of industrial buildings in the empty rates regime, the VOA are seen as being active in underpinning the tax base and seem to have changed rules and practices that have existed for decades, even though the underlying legislation on end of life properties has not changed. The VOA has also written new guidance on this subject.

In general, it was formerly agreed that buildings that were not capable of occupation should not stay in the rating list or should have a £0 rateable value.

This area of rating law and practice is made all the more difficult by lengthy planning processes and the need to retain buildings so that under planning law the existing use or footprint is not lost by demolition. Owners are therefore in a bind between empty rates and the planning process where early demolition is not necessarily a solution.

However, the Upper Tribunal decision in *Barber v CEREP III TW Sarl* [2015] UKUT 521 (LC), has now clarified the impact of long-term vacancy, planning consent and the existence of a defined redevelopment 'locality' upon the rateable value of a property in such a scheme. In this case, boarded up shops in Tunbridge Wells awaiting demolition were held to have £0 rateable value.

More significantly, the long running case of *Newbigin (VO) and SJ&J Monk (a firm)* [2017] UKSC 14 has been resolved by the Supreme Court and the law has reverted to its previous state. Where properties are being refurbished then the question arises whether they are incapable of beneficial occupation or in disrepair. The *Newbigin and Monk* case, has now held that a floor within an office building that was being refurbished was incapable of occupation and the statutory repair assumption did not apply. It was therefore given a nominal RV which meant that empty rates could not be charged during the refurbishment period.

This case has also shone a light on an area of rating law that has had little attention for many years whereby the statutory valuation assumptions include a reference to the 'mode or category of occupation'. It was decided that a building undergoing refurbishment is a different hereditament from that which existed before and should be described and valued as a 'building under reconstruction'. In other words, its mode or category of occupation has changed. The case also decided that the valuation principle of *rebus sic stantibus* (the reality principle) is not overridden by the statutory repair assumption.

It is therefore now much easier in theory to obtain a nominal value during refurbishments provided the 'check, challenge, appeal' process is followed in a timely fashion with due regard to the fact that refurbishment works are classed as a 'material change of circumstances' under the Act and the owner must take action to reduce the rateable value whilst the works are still ongoing.

Determination of rateable values, the role of the Valuation Officer and valuation appeals

[19.41] The statutory definition of rateable value assumes that a property is let on a full repairing and insuring basis (FRI) and looks to determine the annual rental value – that is the rent at which the property could be let in a free and open market at a specific valuation date. The VO should look at the property's current use, but can assume it is vacant and to let at its highest and best use.

The quinquennial revaluations now use antecedent valuation dates (AVD) which assist the VOA in the collection of rental evidence and the whole revaluation process. For example the AVD for the 2010 rating list was 1 April 2008 and 1 April 2015 for the 2017 rating list. In theory if a business takes a lease on a property in April 2015 on terms that equate to the statutory definition of rateable value, the rateable value entered into the 2017 rating list should be more or less the 2015 annual rent amount, subject to adjustment for incentives/premiums.

Methods of valuation

[19.42] The LGFA 1988 defines rateable value but does not stipulate the valuation method.

The comparing of rents is the most commonly used method particularly where there is considerable evidence of rents in the market place. So for classes of property such as shops, offices, factories and warehouses the VO can use his power to issue a 'statutory return' to the occupier or the landlord requiring details of the lease and the rent passing. The VOA also has access to all leases on the Land Registry.

The VO analyses many leases and rents that are fixed as close as possible to the AVD and then adjusts them to arrive at an averaged rental or 'tone' for each class of property. These are subdivided into 'valuation schemes' according to the size and location of properties.

The receipts and expenditure method is used for properties where there is generally little or no evidence of them being let in the open market due to the specialist nature of their construction or the way they are used.

This method looks at the trade generated by the property and is used extensively for the leisure industry, for example theatres, hotels, licensed premises, and sports centres. The accounts are analysed to ascertain the net profit which a hypothetical tenant could generate and then a view is taken as to how much of this would be available for the hypothetical tenant to pay as rent.

There are other categories of property that are not let on the open market and which are not intended to generate profits. For example town halls, other public sector infrastructure and plant and machinery. Here the contractor's test method of valuation is used. The cost of construction or replacement cost at the AVD is estimated and then adjustments made for age and obsolescence, the value of the land is included and a decapitalisation rate is applied to arrive at a net annual rental figure. The decapitalisation rate is set by regulation and is currently 4.4%.

The contractors test method can produce valuations which seem quite high compared to other methods and should only be used as a last resort. Even then a step back should be taken at the end of the valuation to see if further adjustment is appropriate to arrive at an annual rental that would be acceptable to a landlord and tenant negotiating a tenancy in the open market.

Revaluations

[19.43] Revaluations are undertaken every five years with the current rating list taking effect from April 2017. They are intended to maintain the tax base in line with movements in the property market so that ratepayers bear their fair share of the rate burden. For example, if the office and retail sector is buoyant and rents are rising whilst the manufacturing sector is static or in decline then rateable values will be adjusted at a revaluation to reflect this.

A revaluation always attracts much media interest not least because it has tended to generate fresh rights of appeal and many occupiers with a large portfolio of properties take the opportunity to re-tender for the services of rating surveyors to handle appeals for each five-yearly valuation. However, the current appeal rules place less restrictions on the window for appeals during the life of a rating list and it should be remembered that a rateable value is not a valuation for the 1 April 2017 and every day of the following five years, but is a rateable value than can be changed for any of those days to reflect events that directly affect the property or the neighbourhood.

These are called material changes of circumstances and appeals can be submitted during a period whilst internal or external events affect the property. For example a fire may have damaged part of a factory and works are being undertaken to replace damaged areas. Or a sewer replacement scheme in part of a town centre results in the closure of major thoroughfares leading to much reduced retail activity. In both cases appeals submitted during the affected periods can result in significant reduction in rateable value.

The next revaluation is due to take effect on 1 April 2022 but the Government are currently consulting on whether to move to self-assessment from business rates valuations and even a full self-assessment system whereby the local authority billing function would also cease as ratepayers assess their own valuation, calculate the amount of rates due and pay the property tax over to the local authority or possibly HMRC.

Functions of the Valuation Officer

[19.44] In England and Wales, VOs are employed by the VOA and appointed by the Commissioners of HMRC. In Scotland the Assessor is part of a Board paid for by the local authorities.

The duties and functions of the VO are to prepare and maintain a rating list every five years and then to deal with appeals against rateable values in that list.

In practice this means that their work is focussed on two major areas. The first is negotiating appeals submitted by agents on behalf of ratepayers and taking those appeals to the Valuation Tribunal or Lands Tribunal if necessary. The second is following up reports issued by the local authority for the inclusion of new property, revision of rateable values to reflect splits or mergers of property and for the deletion of demolished property.

The Non-Domestic Rating (Alteration of Lists and Appeals) (England) Regulations 2009 (SI 2009/2268) and the VOA's own 'programming' procedures previously governed the handling of appeals but from 2017 a new system of appeals has been introduced called 'Check, Challenge, Appeal' (CCA) and the regulations have been substantially modified by SI 2015/424 and SI 2017/155. The rating appeal system is an adversarial one and the VO seeks to minimise losses on the rating list but the new CCA process has been designed to encourage the ratepayer and the VO to engage in early exchanges of information and discussions.

CCA is driven by online systems very similar to other HMRC online taxes and there are requirements for ratepayers to register, appoint agents, disclose information and make statutory declarations all of which now form part of the Check stage. Only when Check has been completed and the VO responded, can the Challenge stage commence which is the equivalent of the old proposal stage. Finally, if the ratepayer and VO cannot agree, then the appeal stage can be entered into.

The new CCA stages are designed to place more onus on the ratepayer and to lengthen the appeal process through the use of statutory time limits before different stages can be entered into.

The VO also retains the power to maintain and alter the list outside of the CCA process. The VO can change rateable values, reconstitute assessments, insert new properties and delete demolished ones. The VO alters the list and then notifies the ratepayer accordingly. The powers of the VO to alter the list are quite extensive.

Effective dates rules

[19.45] The rules in SI 2009/2268 generally provide that the effective date of an alteration to the list is the day when the circumstances giving rise to the alteration first occurred. The general back stop on backdating is the commencement of the current rating list although the VO still has the power to make alterations into an old list for one year after it has closed.

However, a specific provision exists to limit effective dates where the VO alters the list to correct an inaccuracy. This is generally used where the VO has made some error that is not the fault of the ratepayer. The effective date is restricted to the date the list is actually altered unless the change is to bring in a new hereditament.

Further changes were made in 2015 when interim regulations (SI 2015/424) were introduced to provide a general back stop to list alterations of 1 April 2015.

Interest on refunds

[19.46] Where rates are overpaid due to an alteration in the rating list, most commonly a rateable value reduction, then there is statutory provision in the Non-Domestic Rating (Payment of Interest) Regulations (SI 1990/1904) for interest to be paid with the refund. The calculation is complex but the basic rules are that entitlement to interest does not arise if recovery action has had to be taken against the ratepayer, and no interest can be awarded on monies that have been over paid in error, for example continuing to pay monthly instalments after a property has been vacated. Interest is paid gross to UK companies, tax exempt bodies and other entities entitled to gross interest under the income and corporation tax rules.

Who owns refunds arising from rateable value reductions?

[19.47] Disputes have arisen as to who is entitled to rate refunds given that appeals take many years to settle and go through the tribunals and courts. In the interval a property may change occupation and ownership several times.

Where a business is sold by way of shares then the same company remains in occupation of the property and the rating officer will not change the name on the rate demand. Where a rateable property is involved in a sale by way of assets then it is likely that a new ratepayer will become the rateable occupier from the completion of the sale.

Confusion can arise with similar trading or company names and where the rating officer does not understand the background to the transaction. If rates continue to be paid on a rate account that should have been changed then this will lead to problems if a rateable value reduction is subsequently calculated that runs back through the various changes of ownership/occupation.

Sale and purchase agreements should therefore deal with the ownership and apportionment of future rate refunds and rate accounts should reflect the actual identity of the occupier or owner if it is empty rate that is being paid.

Rates avoidance and tax avoidance disclosure

[19.48] Business rates are not subject to the tax avoidance disclosure rules at present but the Government is aware of certain schemes that seek to avoid empty rates. Local authorities have been asked to report examples of empty rate avoidance to the Department of Communities and Local Government.

Such schemes often involve the possession of a property being passed to a charity to achieve a zero empty rate status, but local authorities do have the power to inquire whether the charity is genuinely intending to use the property in the future for charitable purposes and whether the property is actually suitable for the charity in terms of its size and nature.

Other schemes involve the artificial creation of six-week short reoccupations to generate repeat free periods. This can be particularly helpful to the owner of an industrial building where a fresh free period provides a valuable six-month abatement. There has been dispute as to whether planned partial reoccupation, purposefully for generating repeat free periods, is lawful but this has now been confirmed in the High Court case of *R (on the application of Makro Properties Ltd) v Nuneaton & Bedworth Borough Council* [2012] EWHC 2250 (Admin) [2012] All ER (D) 136 (Aug), [2012] RA 285. However implementation is key to the success of such mitigation schemes as is the distinction between 'owner' and 'third party' reoccupation.

In May 2013 High Court cases were taken by Milton Keynes BC and other councils against the Public Safety Charitable Trust which was taking charitable donations from owners of unoccupied property in return for taking over the empty rate liability and claiming 80% charitable rate relief. However, the Court ruled that whilst the use of Bluetooth transmitting boxes in the building was a rateable occupation, it didn't constitute a charitable use and so the 80% rate relief was refused. This charity has now been wound up by the Court.

The Government has consulted on the need to introduce specific rules to prevent the avoidance of empty rates but is also active in working with the Charity Commission to warn trustees that engaging with a property owner in tax avoidance is incompatible with their role as charity trustees. In addition, the Business Secretary has taken action in the Courts to wind up companies that abuse the insolvency procedures as part of empty rate avoidance.

Utility, transport and cross boundary properties

[19.49] Special rules exist to administer certain types of property, assets and utility infrastructure that extend across several local authority areas. For example, pipelines and telecoms networks will pass through many council areas and the general rules is that the VO will assess the whole asset or network as a single entity and then place the total rateable value in the local rating list of the authority that has the greatest proportion of the network within its boundaries.

For the national and larger operators of transport and utility infrastructure, there is a Central List whereby the Central List VO enters rateable values for the whole networks and monies are paid by these operators direct to the Treasury. The Government and the Central List VO determines which operators and companies should be subject to the Central List rules by way of Central List Regulations.

Local retention

[19.50] The Localism Act 2011 made various changes to the rating system and from 1 April 2013 the national rating pool has been abolished in England. It also gave effect to the policy of local retention where billing authorities can retain part of the additional business rates generated from expansion of the tax base.

The underlying principle is that the rates income is split 50/50 between Government and Local Government and then each Council can keep any additional rate income they can squeeze out of the system. Perversely, this could result in councils being less willing to use their powers to grant relief and support economic growth.

The local retention scheme was due to be extended from 1 April 2020, whereby local authorities retain 100% of all business rates income. However, this legislative proposal was not included in the 2017 Queens Speech.

Chapter 20

Islamic funding structures

by
Irfan Butt,
PricewaterhouseCoopers LLP

Introduction

[20.1] This chapter covers the issues that arise when investors in UK real estate want their financial arrangements to be consistent with Shariah (Islamic law). The approach is as follows:

- Summarise the basic principles of Shariah which are relevant here, without attempting a comprehensive coverage of Islamic law.
- Outline the most common way for Shariah compliant investors to acquire UK real estate before the recent changes in UK tax law to facilitate Islamic finance. Practitioners need to be familiar with this structure as it, sometimes with variations, is still regularly used by some Islamic investors.
- Give a high level summary of how the UK has changed its tax law to facilitate Islamic finance.
- Illustrate some of the structures which are now in use.
- Explain the UK tax law applicable to sukuk and their application to raising finance.

Basic introduction to Shariah

[20.2] Shariah is an Arabic word whose literal meaning is a path to water. In a business context, it can be concisely described as Islamic law.

The sources of Shariah law

[20.3] Shariah is based upon the Quran (regarded by Muslims as the direct word of God) and the Sunnah (the words and acts of the prophet Muhammad (peace be upon him) as recorded in collections of sayings known as Hadith. Other sources include ijma (consensus on a matter by jurists), ijtihad (interpretation) and qiyas (legal analogy). Shariah provides a framework for life as a Muslim and governs everything that a Muslim does not just explicit religious activities such as prayers and fasting.

Shariah scholars and their role in Islamic finance

[20.4] Shariah scholars play an important role in Islamic finance as they are qualified to issue fatwas (legal opinions) on financing structures to confirm their compliance with Islamic law. In practice, views may differ amongst Shariah scholars. Typically Islamic banks and asset managers will have their own Shariah boards which will issue fatwas for products launched and offered to their clients or investors.

Relevant principles of Shariah

[20.5] The key principles of Shariah relating to business generally are:

- The requirement for honesty and fair trade.
- Faults in merchandise should be disclosed and not hidden from the customer.
- Avoid misrepresentations.
- One cannot sell something that one does not yet own.
- Avoid selling prohibited (haram) items.

Major prohibitions affecting financial transactions

[20.6] The major rules in Islam which bear upon financial arrangements are the prohibition of the following:

- Riba (generally understood to mean any interest).
- Gharar (excessive complexity or uncertainty in contracts).
- Maysir (speculation or gambling).

Riba (interest)

[20.7] Under Shariah, money is regarded as simply a means of exchange, and it stipulates that money cannot be used to make money. That would be unfair exploitation of the borrower (who pays a fixed interest return to the lender for the use of borrowed money whether the borrowers' business makes a profit or not).

Gharar or uncertainty

[20.8] Any agreement which has a significant element of gharar is invalid from a Shariah perspective.

Maysir or gambling

[20.9] Shariah encourages Muslims to produce returns through effort, rather than to rely on chance or speculation. In modern day finance, Shariah scholars would regard most derivatives as prohibited under maysir or gharar.

Shariah-compliant business activities

[20.10] In order for investments to be fully Shariah-compliant, in addition to meeting the above key financing principles, the underlying assets should be involved in permissible (halal) activities. Any investment where the underlying activity is not halal must be avoided. Prohibited activities will, among others, include the following:

- a business carrying out conventional banking transactions involving the payment or receipt of interest on deposits and loans;
- conventional insurance and re-insurance activities;
- distilling, producing, selling and marketing of alcoholic drinks;
- gambling, including renting buildings for that purpose to a bookmaker;
- processing and selling pork; and
- businesses involved in 'adult' entertainment, night clubs and related activities.

In practice; it may pose difficult but not insurmountable challenges to structure an investment so that it is Shariah-compliant. For example, in the case of an investment in a retail shopping mall, it is not uncommon to find that some of the shops are engaged in impermissible activities. This would require some form of re-structuring to either segregate the non-permissible activities into a separate structure or for the fund/asset manager to report the amount of income from 'impure' sources to investors. The investors can then donate this 'impure' income to charity. In this way, each investor can deal with the income in the manner that the investor considers appropriate.

The Shariah-compliant real estate acquisition structure commonly used prior to specific UK legislation for Islamic finance

[20.11] Prior to the introduction of the Alternative Finance Arrangements rules in the UK, there was no guidance available from HMRC or specific tax legislation to provide certainty of tax treatment for Shariah-compliant trans-actions. Consequently, most Shariah-compliant property transactions were either fully equity funded or took the form of a mixture of internal debt and equity or ijara (explained below) leases. Shariah scholars often permit internal debt (debt between wholly owned entities) on interest bearing terms, on the grounds that you are incapable of paying interest to yourself; you are just moving money from one wholly owned entity to another.

The fully equity and mixture of internal debt and equity funded structures were simple and did not differ from conventional structures. However, in the case of ijara lease structures, the UK tax treatment of the underlying transactions wholly depended on the interpretation of general tax principles due to the innovation in structuring of Shariah-compliant transactions. The structuring complexities are the product of the need to align UK legal requirements with Shariah requirements. The use of such structures is now less common. However, certain Shariah-compliant real estate funds still use this route to structure their UK real estate investments, although it can be administratively burdensome and operationally expensive. In time the other structures discussed later in this chapter can be expected to become more prevalent.

A typical ijara lease can best be described diagrammatically as follows:

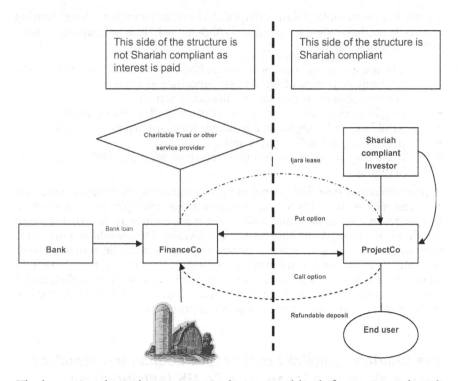

The key point about this structure is that external bank finance is used, with associated interest costs. However the company paying the interest is not owned by the Shariah compliant investor. Everything that the investor owns is Shariah compliant.

An ijara contract is basically a leasing contract as understood by UK law which is also Shariah compliant. However Shariah requires the lessor to retain a specified level of risk in the asset before a UK law leasing contract can be accepted as a (Shariah compliant) ijara contract. For example a full pay out finance lease would fail to qualify as an ijara contract. Certain other provisions commonly found in UK lease agreements are also prohibited if the contract is to qualify as an ijara contract. For example, the lessee cannot be charged interest on late payments; however, the lessee can be charged a penalty for late payment which the lessor will then donate to charity.

Under the ijara lease structure, ProjectCo makes a refundable deposit to FinanceCo which in turn borrows from a conventional bank and acquires real estate. Note that FinanceCo and ProjectCo are not connected in any way through ownership. This type of structure enables Shariah compliant investors to leverage their investment in the real estate as they only provide equity equivalent to the amount of the refundable deposit. The rest of the property purchase price is funded by FinanceCo bank borrowing.

Following acquisition, FinanceCo grants an ijara lease to ProjectCo in return for rental payments which typically equate to the interest and capital payments under the bank facility owed by FinanceCo. ProjectCo receives rental income from the underlying occupational lease and any balance left after settlement of its obligations under the ijara lease, other expenses and taxes is then paid to the Shariah-compliant investor.

Additional legal agreements may also need to be entered into by ProjectCo and FinanceCo to transfer certain obligations to ProjectCo such as the responsibility to maintain, repair and insure the property. (To be Shariah compliant, the ijara lease will leave repair obligations with the lessor, FinanceCo, but it is usually regarded as permissible for other side agreements to transfer these obligations to ProjectCo.) FinanceCo and ProjectCo also enter into put and call options to ensure ProjectCo retains the benefit of any increase in the value of real estate through the exercise of the call option and FinanceCo has a put option to require ProjectCo to purchase the property so that it can be assured of being able to repay the bank borrowing.

In the absence of any specific tax legislation, the tax treatment of the above structure was primarily governed by general tax principles, ProjectCo would register under the non-resident landlord scheme (assuming it to be a non-resident company which is the norm) and would obtain a tax deduction for rental payments to FinanceCo as an expense in arriving at the UK property business profits. The UK transfer pricing rules should not apply as the parties to the ijara transaction are not connected in any way. As far as the entitlement to capital allowances is concerned, the allowances typically remain with FinanceCo unless further structuring is undertaken to ensure that the entitlement to claim capital allowances transfers to ProjectCo. If FinanceCo is only receiving rent from ProjectCo equal to FinanceCo's interest expense (for example if the bank loan is non-amortising) then its net taxable income would be zero so any capital allowances received by FinanceCo would be wasted.

In practice, this structure also creates complex SDLT and VAT issues. It has always been problematical to decide whether certain SDLT reliefs would apply to some of the transactions forming part of an ijara lease arrangement between FinanceCo and ProjectCo. Furthermore, an exit is also very complex as a sale to a conventional investor would invariably require pre-sale restructuring to provide a simple entity to sell. If the structure is not collapsed carefully, unexpected tax consequences can arise. Also, the use of multiple entities and an external charity or service provider makes this structure more expensive to administer.

As indicated above, although this structure is still encountered regularly in practice, it is essentially obsolete following the changes made to UK tax law in recent years to facilitate Islamic finance.

Overview of the UK tax law for Islamic finance

[20.12] The UK is a pioneer among Western countries in adapting its tax system to facilitate Islamic finance. It is helpful to understand the approach the UK has taken, before going on to consider how the new UK tax laws can be applied to real estate transactions.

The UK started adapting its tax law in FA 2003 when it legislated to abolish the double charge to SDLT arising on Shariah compliant mortgage transactions. These typically involved the bank purchasing all or part of a property and re-selling it to the customer, either immediately or in stages. This meant two occasions of charge to SDLT, whereas a conventional mortgage only involves one occasion of charge.

However, the most fundamental changes were introduced in 2005, specifically to enable the operation of Islamic banks in the UK. The reason why tax law changes were needed is most easily understood by considering the following commodity murabaha (purchase and resale) transaction. The purpose of this transaction is to allow the Bank to provide 100 of finance to the Customer, for two years, to earn a finance charge, in economic terms, of 10.

Example 1

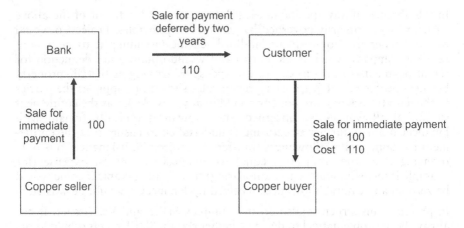

Under UK tax law prior to the reform, Customer was probably not entitled to a tax deduction. Customer has purchased an amount of copper at a price of £110 payable in two years time, and sold that copper for £100 with the price being payable immediately. Accordingly, Customer has suffered a loss of £10. It was not clear that this loss was tax deductible.

Unless Customer could argue under UK tax law that it was trading in copper, it would not be entitled to deduct the £10 loss against its other income. Furthermore, even if Customer was a company that regularly traded in copper, this transaction does not look like a normal trading transaction since Customer knew that it would suffer a £10 loss when it commenced the transaction.

Accordingly, under pre-reform UK tax law, Customer would probably not obtain tax relief for its £10 cost, even though in economic terms it is clearly a finance cost. Accordingly legislation was needed to ensure that obtaining finance through commodity murabaha transactions qualified for tax relief.

Strategic design considerations

[20.13] The tax law changes were introduced by FA 2005, with subsequent expansion of the range of transactions covered in FA 2006 and FA 2007. A review of the legislation enables one to 'reverse engineer' the design consider-ations that underlie it, in particular the following:

- tax law must apply equally to all taxpayers;
- tax law changes should not impact upon transactions not intended to be covered;
- legislation should not be longer than is necessary;
- addressing specific obstacles to Islamic finance.

Tax law should apply equally to all taxpayers

[**20.14**] Strictly speaking, the UK has not enacted any Islamic finance legislation. A search of the legislation will fail to find words such as Islamic, Shariah, murabaha or any other term used specifically in Islamic finance. The reason is that the tax treatment of a transaction cannot be allowed to depend upon whether it is Shariah compliant. As well as introducing significant uncertainty into the UK tax system, introducing Shariah considerations would create a situation where all taxpayers were not receiving identical tax treatment.

Instead, the UK identified certain types of transaction widely used in Islamic finance, and ensured that those types of transaction received appropriate tax treatment. This is illustrated by ITA 2007, s 564C (for income tax purposes) and CTA 2009, ss 503 and 511 (for corporation tax purposes) 'Alternative finance arrangements: purchase and resale'.

Reading the legislation, it is clear that it was designed to set out tax rules for murabaha transactions. However, it nowhere uses those terms and nothing in the legislation limits its application to Islamic finance. If a transaction falls within the legislation, the tax treatment follows automatically, regardless of whether the transaction is (or was intended to be) Shariah compliant.

The following table sets out the key concepts that have been created in UK tax law, and the Islamic finance structures that they correspond to.

Tax law	Islamic finance
Purchase and resale – ITA 2007, s 564C and CTA 2009, ss 503 and 511	Murabaha
Deposit – ITA 2007, s 564E and CTA 2009, ss 505 and 513	Mudaraba
Profit share agency – ITA 2007, s 564F and CTA 2009, ss 506 and 513	Wakala
Diminishing shared ownership – ITA 2007, s 564D and CTA 2009, ss 504 and 512	Diminishing musha-raka
Alternative finance investment bond – ITA 2007, s 564G and ss 564S–564U and CTA 2009, ss 507 and 513	Sukuk

Tax law changes should not impact upon transactions not intended to be covered

[**20.15**] Commercial sales of goods often involve a credit period for the customer. It would unduly complicate UK tax law if every sale of goods with deferred payment required identification of the price that would have prevailed if no credit were given, and then giving separate tax treatment for the implied cost of the credit. Consider for example a food manufacturer selling hundreds of thousands of tins of food to retailers with 30 days credit allowed for the payment of each sales invoice.

ITA 2007, s 564C and CTA 2009, ss 503 and 511 limit its impact by requiring the involvement of a financial institution. This ensures that only transactions where finance is provided by or to a financial institution fall within the new rules. Accordingly, the food manufacturer and its customers should not be impacted by these new rules. (One drawback of this approach is that it is currently impossible for two non-financial companies to transact Islamic finance with each other and receive the tax treatment given by the new legislation.)

Financial institution is defined in ITA 2007, s 564B and CTA 2009, s 502 (see the diagram opposite).

The definition of a bank is itself quite complex, and the diagram below illustrates what does or does not (marked X) qualify as a bank:

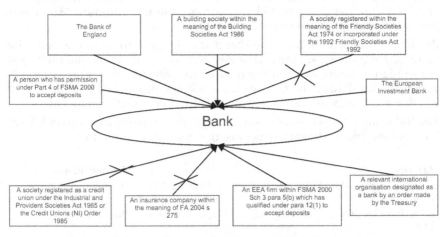

Tracing through the definitions establishes that they cover all banks licensed in the European Economic Area (provided they have exercised their 'passporting' rights to take deposits in the UK) and also persons licensed to take deposits in other countries, which is the key practical definition of a bank. Note that subsidiaries of UK banks are included in the definition but this is not extended to subsidiaries of non-UK financial institutions which are effectively excluded from the definition. Furthermore, with effect from 15 October 2009, the definition of financial institution is extended in the Alternative Finance Arrangements (Amendment) Order 2009 (SI 2009/2568) and the term now also includes the following:

• Insurance companies within the meaning of ICTA 1988, s 431(2).

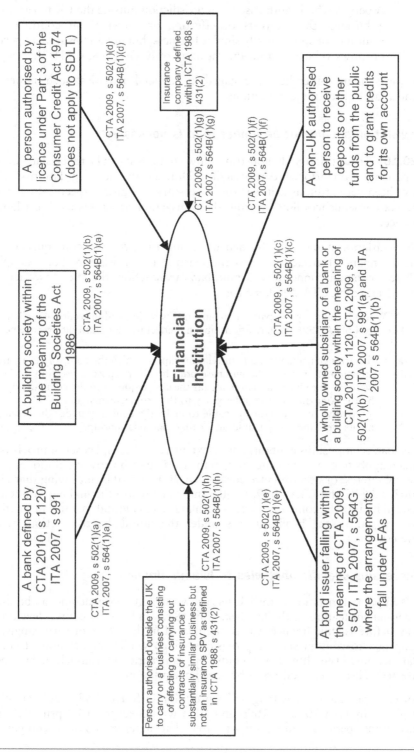

A person authorised by licence under Part 3 of the Consumer Credit Act 1974 (does not apply to SDLT)

CTA 2009, s 502(1)(d)
ITA 2007, s 564B(1)(d)

Insurance company defined within ICTA 1988, s 431(2)

CTA 2009, s 502(1)(g)
ITA 2007, s 564B(1)(g)

A non-UK authorised person to receive deposits or other funds from the public and to grant credits for its own account

CTA 2009, s 502(1)(f)
ITA 2007, s 564B(1)(f)

A building society within the meaning of the Building Societies Act 1986

CTA 2009, s 502(1)(b)
ITA 2007, s 564B(1)(a)

Financial Institution

CTA 2009, s 502(1)(c)
ITA 2007, s 564B(1)(c)

A wholly owned subsidiary of a bank or a building society within the meaning of CTA 2010, s 1120, CTA 2009, s 502(1)(b) / ITA 2007, s 991(a) and ITA 2007, s 564B(1)(b)

A bank defined by CTA 2010, s 1120/ ITA 2007, s 991

CTA 2009, s 502(1)(a)
ITA 2007, s 564(1)(a)

Person authorised outside the UK to carry on a business consisting of effecting or carrying out contracts of insurance or substantially similar business but not an insurance SPV as defined in ICTA 1988, s 431(2)

CTA 2009, s 502(1)(h)
ITA 2007, s 564B(1)(h)

CTA 2009, s 502(1)(e)
ITA 2007, s 564B(1)(e)

A bond issuer falling within the meaning of CTA 2009, s 507, ITA 2007, s 564G where the arrangements fall under AFAs

- A person who is authorised in a jurisdiction outside the UK to carry on a business that consists of effecting or carrying out contracts of insurance or substantially similar business, but not an 'insurance special purposes vehicle' within the meaning of ICTA 1988, s 431(2).

However, many other bodies engaged in financial activities, such as hedge funds, fall outside these definitions.

Legislation should not be longer than is necessary

[20.16] The legislation demonstrates how complex it can be to legislate for an apparently straightforward transaction. Drafting the new legislation would have been very arduous if it was then necessary to legislate specifically for all the tax consequences flowing from the transaction structures used in Islamic finance.

The legislation avoids this burden by assimilating the tax consequences of Islamic finance transactions into the existing tax legislation. For example, where a company undertakes a murabaha transaction, the tax consequences are governed by CTA 2009, s 510:

'(1) Where a company is a party to arrangements falling within section 47, Chapter 2 of Part 4 of FA 1996 (loan relationships) has effect in relation to the arrangements as if—

(a)   the arrangements were a loan relationship, to which the company is a party,

(b)   any amount which is the purchase price for the purposes of section 47(1)(b) were the amount of a loan made (as the case requires) to the company by, or by the company to, the other party to the arrangements, and

(c)   alternative finance return payable to or by the company under the arrangements were interest payable under that loan relationship.'

The loan relationships contains a very extensive and complex set of provisions which apply to companies engaging in the lending or borrowing of money and paying interest or other finance costs. CTA 2009, s 510 is not saying that ITA 2007, s 564C and CTA 2009, ss 503 and 511 involve the making of a loan; instead it taxes the company as if a loan had been made and as if the alternative finance return (the profit or loss under the murabaha transaction) were interest.

Addressing specific obstacles to Islamic finance

[20.17] Tax legislation in the UK has grown steadily since income tax became a permanent feature of the tax system in 1842, and was of course developed long before Islamic finance was contemplated in the UK. Not surprisingly, it happened to contain specific provisions which would impact upon Islamic transactions, even though the equivalent conventional transaction was not affected. These were addressed by specific legislation.

For example, the UK has long had a provision in ICTA 1988, s 209(2)(e)(iii) (replaced by CTA 2010, ss 1000 and 1005 with effect from 1 April 2010 for accounting periods ending on or after that date) to counter companies disguising equity finance in the form of debt, in order to obtain tax relief for payments that are economically equivalent to dividends to risk bearing shareholders:

'(2) In the Corporation Tax Acts "distribution", in relation to any company, means—

. . .

(e)   any interest or other distribution out of assets of the company in respect of securities of the company (except so much, if any, of any such distribution as represents the principal thereby secured and except so much of any distribution as falls within paragraph (d) above), where the securities are . . .

(iii)   securities under which the consideration given by the company for the use of the principal secured is to any extent dependent on the results of the company's business or any part of it.'

This provision would preclude Islamic banks offering investment accounts to their customers, since the profit share paid to the customer would be treated as a distribution. This means that the payment would not be tax deductible for the bank.

This problem is specifically addressed by CTA 2010, s 1019, the effect of which is not to treat payments falling under profit share agency arrangements as distributions for corporation tax purposes.

All statutory references in this chapter relating to SDLT are to FA 2003. The SDLT rules have been repealed for land located in Scotland with an effective date on or after 1 April 2015 (subject to transitional provisions), when SDLT was replaced in Scotland by the Land and Buildings Transaction Tax (Scotland) Act 2013 ('LBTT') under the Scotland Act 2012. The LBTT rules relating to alternative finance arrangements mirror that of the SDLT rules which applied to Scottish land and provide the same reliefs save for the LBTT rates on property transactions. The relevant provisions relating to alternative finance arrangements are contained in the Land and Buildings Transaction Tax (Scotland) Act 2013, Schs 7 and 8.

Basic methods of Islamic finance for real estate related transactions

[20.18] The most common forms of real estate Islamic financing methods used within the Islamic finance industry are:

Murabaha

[20.19] Murabaha is a financing technique which is typically used to provide acquisition finance. The provider of finance, which is typically an Islamic bank, buys an asset from a supplier and sells it on to its customer at a disclosed premium. The customer pays the bank the purchase price either in instalments over an agreed period of time or as a single 'bullet' payment on a fixed future date. The amount of premium is generally set by the bank by reference to market interest rates, as there is no comparable Shariah compliant benchmark.

The fact that the premium or mark up is being benchmarked against prevailing interest rates should not lead to the financing arrangement being regarded as non-Shariah compliant.

A diagrammatic description of a murabaha structure is shown below.

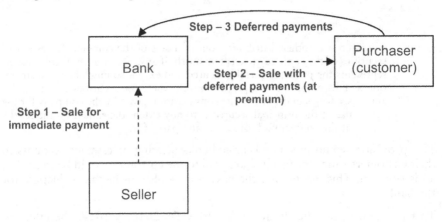

A murabaha financing can be arranged for acquisitions of a variety of assets, including real estate.

The premium is fixed at the point when the bank sells the asset to the customer. For example, the bank may purchase a building for £100,000 and sell it to the customer for a price of £206,767.40 payable over 25 years in 300 fixed monthly instalments of £689.22. Mathematically, this is equivalent to the bank lending money for 25 years at a fixed rate of interest of 7% per annum, compounded monthly. As banks usually fund their activities by taking floating rate deposits, such a contract would create considerable interest rate risk for the bank unless it can hedge the risk.

ITA 2007, s 564C and CTA 2009, ss 503 and 511 should apply to this transaction. Accordingly, the customer would treat each monthly payment as comprising part capital and part alternative finance return, deductible against the rental income if the building is let.

Mudharabah

[20.20] Mudharabah is a type of partnership contract between two parties where one party, ie the provider of finance (rab al mal), provides capital while the other party (the mudarib) which is typically a bank in this context provides expertise, knowledge and manages the partnership. The profits are shared as per the agreed profit sharing ratio but in the event of a loss, Shariah requires that the rab al mal fully absorbs the loss. This form of arrangement is very common in Islamic banking as Islamic banks usually use mudharabah contracts with customers who deposit their money in the bank in the expectation of a return. The bank may utilise the funds at its disposal and enter into a mudharabah contract with customers to whom it provides finance by providing the required capital (acting itself as a rab al mal) for a project in the expectation of a return. This is sometimes known as a two tier mudharabah since there are two mudharabah contracts interposed between the underlying project and the person providing funds to the bank.

Although mudharabah is most commonly used in the Islamic banking sector, its use is not limited to banks. In practice, it can be used for the management of assets such as real estate by an asset manager and also for the provision of expertise to a venture by a person in return for a fee and a profit share.

A mudharabah arrangement is shown below:

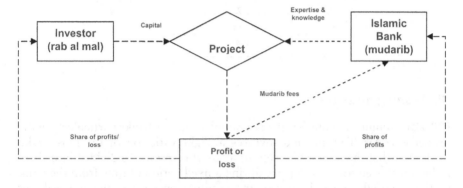

However, the special tax rules in ITA 2007, s 564E and CTA 2009, ss 505 and 513 apply only where funds are provided to a financial institution. Other mudharabah contracts, whether they entail a bank providing finance to a customer or two parties neither of whom is a financial institution, must be analysed from first principles. In most cases they are likely to constitute a partnership for UK tax purposes.

Musharaka

[20.21] This is similar to a conventional partnership or joint venture. Under a musharaka contract, both parties provide capital, and profits are shared according to a pre-agreed profit share ratio whereas Shariah requires that any losses are shared according to the amount of capital contributed by each partner. Musharaka contracts are often used in long-term investment projects, property development and investment activities and the partnership continues until the project is finished. Each partner leaves its share in the capital in the business until the end of the project.

A diagram of a musharaka arrangement is shown below:

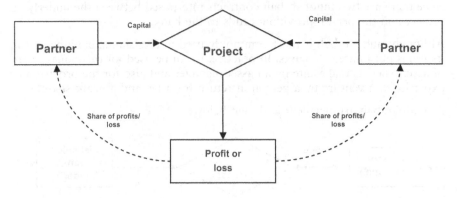

Diminishing musharaka

[20.22] Diminishing musharaka is a popular tool for banks particularly in the property sector. This method involves a slight variation of the musharaka method in that the joint ownership of an asset or project is divided into slices to be transferred for a fixed price during a fixed period of time from the bank to the eventual owner. However, the eventual owner has the full right of occupation. Since the eventual owner does not own part of the property occupied (because it is owned by the bank) it pays rent to the bank on that part. This type of arrangement is most commonly used in the UK for Shariah-compliant mortgages for residential properties. The rent can be reset regularly based on prevailing interest rates. Accordingly, in economic terms this is equivalent to a floating rate lending transaction, in comparison to the fixed rate murabaha transaction.

A diagrammatic description of a diminishing musharaka arrangement is shown below:

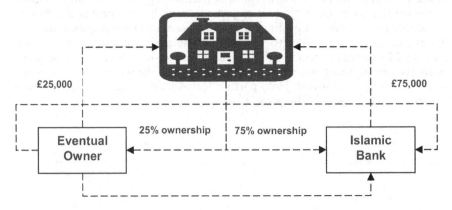

Ijara

[20.23] As discussed above ijara is a form of leasing. In practice, ijara is similar to a conventional lease where a lessor (typically an Islamic bank) purchases an asset and then leases it to a lessee for a specific rental income. The bank retains the legal title to the asset during the term of the ijara contract, whereas the lessee has the use of the asset during that term. In the case of a simple ijara contract, the lessee returns the asset to the bank at the end of the ijara contract.

In practice, most ijara contracts provide for a formal purchase feature whereby the lessee promises to buy the asset at the end of the ijara contract period at a pre-agreed price. Often, the final purchase price is a token sum. This type of ijara contract is called as ijara-wa-iktana.

Ijara contracts are a familiar feature of Shariah-compliant real estate transactions. However, in practice, the use of ijara contracts to provide asset finance is not limited to real estate and with the exception of certain consumables, (eg money, food or fuel) such contracts are used commonly for all types of permissible asset finance transactions.

No special tax law was required for ijara transactions as the main UK tax rules for leasing of equipment or real estate are applicable.

A diagrammatic description of a typical ijara contract arrangement is shown below:

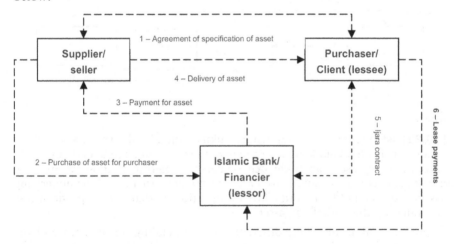

Istisna

[20.24] Istisna is a form of project or contract finance which takes the form of the sale of an asset before it comes into existence. This type of financing arrangement is specifically permitted under Shariah despite the fact that at the time the parties enter into the agreement, the contract lacks one of the three main elements (contracting parties, subject-matter and offer and acceptance) of a valid contract under Shariah, ie non-existence of the subject-matter. The use of istisna is most prevalent in the manufacturing, processing and construction sectors. In practice, on delivery of the finished asset, an Islamic bank may sell the asset back to its client under a murabaha or ijara contract, or enter into a parallel istisna and sell the asset to a third party purchaser at a premium, which could in fact be under a murabaha or enter into an ijara structure. Under an istisna contract, payments may be made in a lump sum in advance or progressively in accordance with the development phase. The delivery date and price is agreed at the outset with the final settlement takes place on delivery of the completed product.

A simple diagrammatic description of istisna and parallel istisna is as shown below.

Istisna

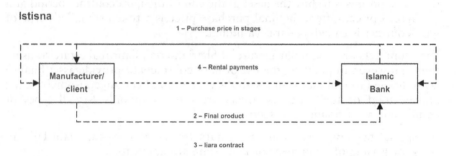

Parallel Istisna

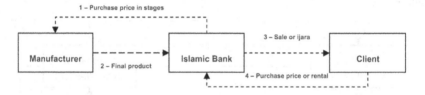

Sukuk

[20.25] Islamic bonds are known as 'sukuk' (the plural term of sakk which means certificate). Sukuk are investment certificates linked to underlying assets and which represent an undivided ownership interest in those assets. The investment returns on sukuk are based on the performance of the underlying assets and each holder is entitled to a proportionate share of the profit or loss generated by the underlying asset.

In practice, sukuk may take different forms depending on the nature of the contract under which the asset is used to generate income. For example, if the asset is rented out under an ijara contract, one would refer to an ijara sukuk. Sukuk are usually issued by a special purpose company (SPV). The SPV is typically established by the originator (ie the entity looking to raise funds). Depending on the nature of the underlying asset or project, the originator will sell the asset or enter into a mudharabah or musharaka arrangement with the issuer (the SPV). The SPV will hold the underlying asset in trust for the benefit of the sukuk holders. The SPV is typically bankruptcy remote which means that in the event of bankruptcy of the issuer, the creditors of the issuer cannot have any claim over the assets held in the SPV.

A simple diagrammatic description of an ijara sukuk structure is as shown below.

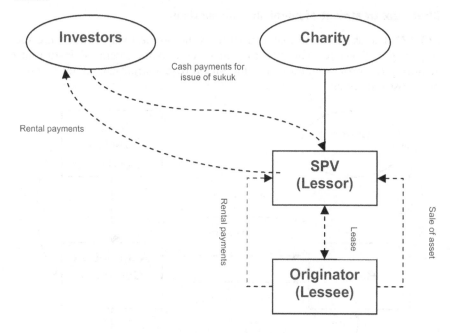

Application of UK tax rules to Shariah-compliant real estate acquisition structures

[20.26] As a result of the UK tax law changes introduced in FA 2005 and subsequent Finance Acts and now replaced and embedded in ITA and CTA 2009 and CTA 2010, many of the preferred Shariah compliant structures discussed above can now be used for UK real estate transactions. Note that a Shariah compliant estate acquisition does not simply involve looking at the yield and credit rating of the tenant. The due diligence exercise would need to look at the activities carried on at the premises by the tenant to ascertain whether it is carrying on prohibited activities, before a decision is made to progress to the legal due diligence stage. In addition, some form of post-acquisition re-structuring exercise may also be needed to segregate certain segments of the investments into prohibited and non-prohibited income streams.

Property Murabaha

Direct tax treatment of murabaha transactions

[20.27] The use of a murabaha structure is the simplest way of financing and acquiring real estate. The structure involves a bank (financial institution) acquiring the property and then selling it on to a Shariah-compliant investor on a cost plus basis.

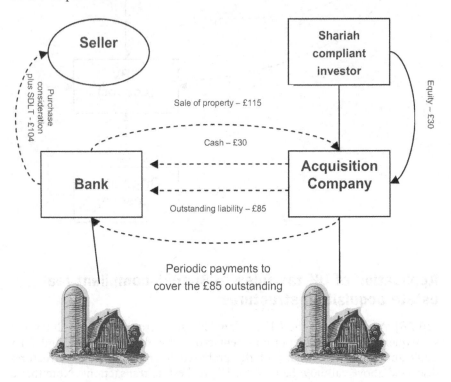

Example 2

For example, if a property was available for purchase at £100, as a first step, the Shariah-compliant investor will set up an acquisition company (usually non-UK resident) and inject an appropriate amount of equity into the Acquisition Company eg £30. The bank buys the property at £100, pays any SDLT arising on the acquisition and then sells the property to Acquisition Company for £115 on the same day under a murabaha arrangement. Given that the total cost of acquiring the property to the bank is £104 (£100 plus £4 SDLT), the profit to the bank (corresponding to its financing income) under the murabaha arrangement over the financing period would be £11. On sale of the property to Acquisition Company, it would use the cash at its disposal of say £30 (equity injection) and would recognise a liability of £85 payable over the period of the murabaha arrangement.

In order for the above transaction to fall within the alternative finance arrangement rules contained in ITA 2007, s 564C and CTA 2009, ss 503 and 511 the following requirements must be satisfied:

- a person (X) purchases an asset and sells it either immediately or, in the case of a financial institution, it purchases the asset for the purpose of entering into the arrangement with another person (Y);
- the amount payable by Y for the asset is greater than the amount paid by X;
- all or part of the price is required to be paid until a date later than that of the sale; and
- the difference in the sale price and the purchase price equates in substance to the return on an investment of money at interest.

In addition, it also important that the murabaha financing arrangement is at arm's length otherwise the borrower will not be entitled to any tax deduction in respect of the deemed interest: ITA 2007, s 564H and CTA 2009, s 508.

It is imperative that one of the parties to the transaction must be a financial institution as defined above; otherwise the transaction would not fall within the alternative finance arrangements rules.

In the above example, assuming that the Bank satisfies the definition contained in CTA 2010, s 1120, and acquires the real estate for the purpose of entering into the alternative finance arrangement (not holding the property as trading stock or currently being occupied by the Bank) and the other conditions outlined above were satisfied, the transaction should fall within the alternative finance arrangements rules. This would result in the mark up between the sale price and the purchase price being treated as interest for the lender as well as the borrower.

The deemed interest expense should be tax deductible for the borrower in the normal way against its UK source rental income. The base cost for capital gains tax purposes would be the purchase price excluding the mark up (deemed interest) plus any other incidental costs wholly and exclusively incurred by the borrowers for the acquisition of real estate.

The inclusion of a murabaha type transaction in the legislation now enables onshore and offshore investors to undertake UK real estate investments in a simpler way than the traditional ijara type structuring outlined at the beginning of the chapter.

For UK tax purposes the periodic payments made under the murabaha arrangements would be treated as payments of interest and partial repayment of the outstanding principal as computed under generally accepted accounting practice. This means that the Acquisition Company should obtain a tax deduction for the interest expense against its rental income chargeable to UK tax. Subject to arm's length considerations, the Shariah-compliant investor could of course partly inject the required funding into the SPV as internal debt to maximise its tax deductions. Note that the Shariah-compliant investor would need to seek approval from the Shariah board on the provision of the required funding in the form of internal interest bearing loan and equity, as the views of Shariah scholars on internal debt funding vary.

Assuming that the Shariah-compliant investor is non-UK resident, it would be preferable to set up the Acquisition Company offshore to ensure that its UK income tax exposure on the UK source rental income is limited to 20% of its net UK rental income. As a non-UK resident investor, (subject to the 'transactions in land' anti-avoidance rules in ITA 2007, s 752 et seq), a sale the Acquisition Company shares by the investor or a sale of the property by the Acquisition Company should both be exempt from a charge to UK capital gains tax.

SDLT treatment of murabaha transactions

[20.28] The sale of the property by the bank to the Acquisition Company should not be subject to a charge to SDLT due to the relevant relieving provisions contained in FA 2003, s 73. The SDLT rules specifically provide relief for a murabaha type real estate transaction to ensure that there is no double charge to SDLT on the sale of real estate at a mark up by a financial institution to a property investor.

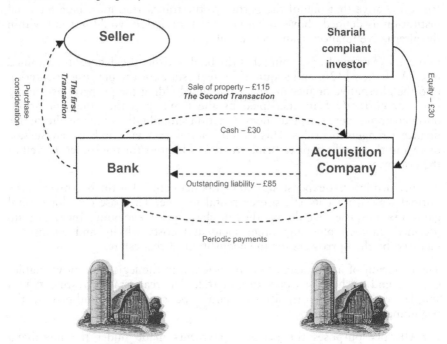

The relief is available under FA 2003, s 73 provided that the following conditions are satisfied:

- a person enters into an arrangement with a financial institution (note that with effect from 24 March 2011, for SDLT purposes only, the term financial institution does not include the holders of a Consumer Credit Licence); and
- under that arrangement the financial institution acquires a major interest in land ('the first transaction');
- it then sells the property to the person ('the second transaction'); and

- the person grants the financial institution a legal mortgage over the interest.

As the first transaction is between the Bank and the seller which is not the person disposing of the property to the Bank, the first transaction would not be exempt from a charge to SDLT. However, the second transaction would be exempt from SDLT provided that the financial institution pays SDLT on the chargeable consideration (which it does in the first transaction) and that consideration is not less than the market value. Note that the legislation provides SDLT relief on the first transaction if the financial institution acquires the property from same person to whom it sells the property under the arrangement (ie purchase and sell back) or where the property was acquired by another financial institution under other arrangements included under FA 2003, s 71A (sale and leaseback) and s 72A (diminishing musharaka).

VAT treatment of murabaha transactions

[20.29] The VAT treatment of Shariah-compliant real estate transactions is set out in HMRC's VAT Information Sheet 11/06. The Information Sheet covers various structures including, but not limited to, real estate. Assuming that a property transaction qualifies as a transfer of a going concern (TOGC) for VAT purposes, the onward sale of the property with mark up would involve two supplies being made by the bank to the purchaser ie property and the facility to defer payment. The mark up element of the transaction will be treated as consideration for the facility to defer payment and will be exempt under VATA 1994, Sch 9, Group 5, item 3, whereas the property transaction should qualify as a TOGC provided that the relevant TOGC conditions are met.

Obtaining finance by commodity murabaha transactions

[20.30] Instead of buying the property and reselling it, the bank may instead provide finance to the customer by engaging in commodity murabaha transactions as outlined above.

Direct tax treatment of commodity murabaha transactions

[20.31] The use of commodity murabaha has gone through significant growth in recent years. As with the murabaha property financing method, the provider of finance does not need to be an Islamic financial institution; most conventional banks are able to provide finance through commodity murabaha transactions.

The use of commodity murabaha as a financing method has received a lot of attention from Shariah scholars recently. Views differ among scholars on its use due to the back to back nature of the transaction, albeit the transactions do involve a real underlying asset. This financing arrangement is more attractive and flexible than murabaha financing as it typically gives the bank a floating rate asset rather than a fixed rate asset by regularly rolling over the commodity contracts.

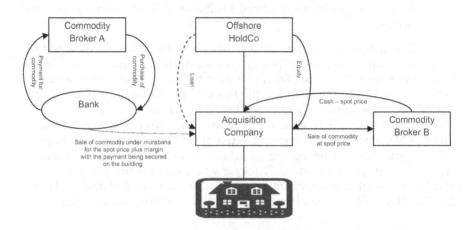

Under a commodity murabaha, a bank will buy a commodity (eg copper) at spot price from a trader and sell it on to its customer at a mark up under a murabaha. The customer will take the delivery and sell the commodity to another trader at spot price. In practice, both transactions will typically take place on the same day, normally within minutes of each other, and neither the bank nor the customer should not be exposed to any price risk. The term of the transaction is usually relatively short, eg three months, with the transactions being rolled over at prevailing benchmark interest rates under a commodity murabaha facility agreement that may have a tenor of several years.

For UK tax purposes, the difference between the spot price and the cost plus price is treated as interest provided that certain conditions in relation to the commodity murabaha arrangements as outlined in ITA 2007, s 564C and CTA 2009, ss 503 and 511. Note that without the introduction of the 'alternative finance arrangements' legislation in FA 2005, it would not have been possible for the Acquisition Company to claim a tax deduction for the financing costs equivalent to the amount of mark up.

The above arrangement falls within the provisions of ITA 2007, s 564C and CTA 2009, ss 503 and 511 as one of the parties to the arrangements is a financial institution, and the bank re-sells the commodity as soon as it buys it. Assuming that the other condition regarding the difference in the sale and purchase prices equating in substance to the return on an investment of money at interest is also met, the borrower, ie Acquisition Company should be entitled to fully deduct the deemed interest cost over the term of the arrangement.

SDLT treatment of commodity murabaha transactions

[20.32] The acquisition of property from the third party vendor will be subject to SDLT at the appropriate rate, as with any other property acquisition. The commodity transactions themselves have no SDLT consequences.

VAT treatment of commodity murabaha transactions

[20.33] Assuming that the relevant TOGC conditions are met, the transfer of the property should be treated as a TOGC for VAT purposes and hence outside the scope of VAT.

As far as the commodity transactions are concerned, the VAT treatment commodities as set out in Notice 701/9 Derivatives and Terminal Markets will apply. The profit element arising to the bank on the commodity murabaha transactions will be treated as consideration for the facility to defer payment and will be exempt under VATA 1994, Sch 9, Group 5, item 3.

The VAT treatment of the underlying commodities will depend on their nature. If the transactions happen to be subject to VAT but take place in the same VAT return period, this should not give rise any cash flow issue as VAT input and VAT output will amount to the same amount. However, in practice this is not likely to be feasible as typically there will be a series of commodity transactions being rolled over. Instead, the parties normally ensure that the commodities are not subject to VAT due to being stored in a bonded warehouse.

Diminishing Musharaka

[20.34] As explained above, diminishing musharaka is preferred to murabaha as a form of property financing since it gives the bank a floating rate asset instead of a fixed rate asset.

Direct tax treatment of diminishing musharaka transactions

[20.35] Diminishing musharaka transactions are typically undertaken by individuals to purchase residential properties. However, it is also possible to acquire commercial properties through the diminishing musharaka financing method. In practice, there is some evidence of property investors undertaking property investment transactions through a diminishing musharaka type of funding, but they are less common than with residential properties.

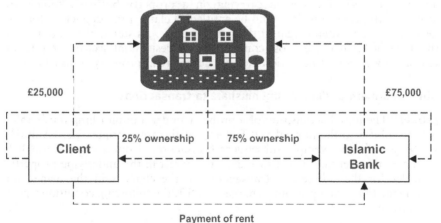

Payment of rent
Unilateral promised to buy remaining slices of property

A diminishing musharaka arrangement will fall within the alternative finance arrangements provided that it satisfies the following requirements included under ITA 2007, s 564D and CTA 2009, ss 504 and 512:

- a financial institution acquires a beneficial interest in an asset, and
- another person (the eventual owner) also acquires a beneficial interest in the asset; and
- the eventual owner makes payments to the financial institution equal in aggregate to the consideration paid for the acquisition of its beneficial interest; and
- the eventual owner is to acquire the financial institution's beneficial interest (whether or not in stages) as a result of those payments, and
- the eventual owner makes other payment to the financial institution under a lease or otherwise for the use of the asset; and
- the eventual owner has the exclusive right to occupy or use of the asset; and
- the eventual owner is entitled to any income, profit or gain arising from the asset.

It is interesting to note that the legislation permits only the eventual owner to share in any upside in the value of the asset. However, the financial institution is permitted to share any loss arising from the fall in value of the underlying asset.

There is no restriction on the eventual owner granting a lease to a person (other than the financial institution or person controlled by the financial institution) provided that the grant is not required by the financial institution or under an arrangement to which the financial institution is a party. The arrangement is specifically prevented from being treated as a partnership for UK tax purposes.

The legislation treats the financing element of the payments, (other than the payments which the eventual owner makes to the financial institution as consideration for the acquisition of its beneficial interest) as deemed interest and in the case of a person carrying on a property business, subject to arm's length provisions, it should be entitled to claim a tax deduction for the deemed interest expense against the rental income. As stated above, although this type of financing is most common in the residential sector, there is no reason why it cannot be undertaken for commercial property transactions.

SDLT treatment of diminishing musharaka transactions

[20.36] The initial acquisition of a property under a diminishing musharaka will be subject to the normal SDLT charge at the appropriate rate. FA 2003, s 72A specifically exempts subsequent transactions from a charge to SDLT whenever the eventual owner increases its interest in the underlying property. In order for the subsequent transactions in the changes in the ownership percentage to be exempt from a charge to SDLT, the following conditions must be satisfied:

- the financial institution and the person must have a major interest in land as owners in common ('the first transaction');

- the financial institution and the person enter into an agreement under which the person has a right to occupy the property exclusively ('the second transaction'); and
- a further agreement is entered into between the parties under which the person has the right to require the financial institution to transfer to the person in one or a series of transactions the entire interest ('further transaction').

Assuming that the property is acquired from a third party, as stated above, the first transaction will remain subject to SDLT; however, the second transaction will not be subject to any SDLT charge to the extent that the SDLT charge on the first transaction has been paid. The further transactions will also be exempt from a charge to SDLT provided that:

- conditions relating to the first transaction are satisfied (in this case payment of SDLT); and
- at all times between the first transaction and the further transaction(s), the interest is held by the financial institution and the person as owners in common and the land occupied by the person.

A simple diagrammatic description of the transactions is as shown below:

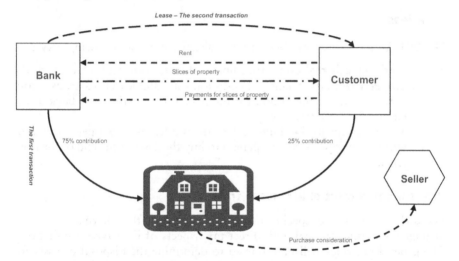

Under the rules for the new higher rates of SDLT announced on 16 March 2016, the financial institution (as a corporate body) would be liable to the higher rates of SDLT if the property purchased was purchased for more than £40,000 and it was not a reversionary interest in respect of a 21-year or longer lease. This would be the case regardless of the situation of the ultimate purchaser of the property (the purchaser in respect of the second transaction). On 14 April 2016, the Government announced an amendment to the Finance Bill 2016 provisions to remove unintended consequences arising for alternative finance arrangements to ensure that a financial institution will only be subject to the 3% supplemental SDLT charge applicable to additional residential properties provided that the conditions relating to that charge are met by the ultimate purchaser or lessee.

The proposed amendment does not alter the SDLT liability position of a financial institution that will remain liable for filing, payment and claiming refunds of the SDLT liability. Note that the rules apply from 1 April 2016 but the amendment is not effective until Royal Assent (15 September 2016). As the amendment is given retrospective effect to remove some transactions from the charge to higher rates, HMRC has confirmed that purchasers should file their returns by taking into account the amendment.

VAT treatment of diminishing musharaka transactions

[20.37] The VAT treatment of a diminishing musharaka transaction will depend on whether the underlying property is a residential or commercial property. Residential property will give rise to an exempt supply. The treatment of commercial property will depend on its status for VAT purposes.

The main supplies under a diminishing musharaka transaction are (i) the gradual sale of the equitable interest and (ii) a lease of property. As such, the VAT treatment of supplies made under this form of arrangement will follow the normal rules for property transactions.

Ijara lease

[20.38] An ijara lease transaction may take place in the following ways:

- a person sells real estate to a financial institution and leases back the property from the financial institution (sale and leaseback transaction) with or without the option for the person to buy the asset back at the end of the lease term; or
- a financial institution buys real estate and leases it to a person with or without the option for the person to buy the asset at the end of the lease term.

Direct tax treatment of ijara lease transactions

[20.39] There are no specific tax rules dealing in the alternative finance arrangements rules to deal with direct tax aspects of ijara type transactions. The general tax rules will be followed to determine the disposal of asset for capital gains tax purposes and likewise deductibility of rental payments under an ijara lease.

SDLT treatment of ijara lease transactions

[20.40] An ijara based sale and leaseback transaction can best be explained diagrammatically as follows:

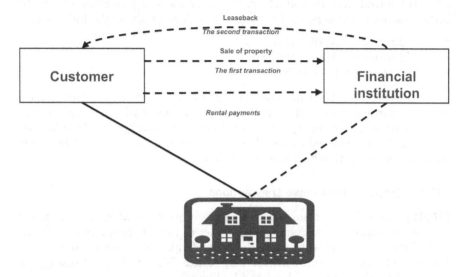

FA 2003, s 71A provides specific relief from SDLT provided that the arrangement complies with the following conditions:

- the financial institution purchases a major interest in land or an undivided share of a major interest in land ('the first transaction') – here from the customer;
- where the interest purchased is an undivided share, the major interest is held in trust for the financial institution and the customer as beneficial tenants in common;
- the financial institution grants a lease to the customer ('the second transaction'); and
- the financial institution and the customer enter into an agreement under which the customer has a right to require the financial institution to transfer to the customer in one or a series of transactions the whole interest under the first transaction ('the further transaction').

The first transaction is exempt from SDLT if the seller is the customer as in the above example. The second transaction relating to the grant of a lease is also exempt from SDLT. The further transaction is also exempt from SDLT provided that:

- the requirements of the first and second transactions are complied with; and
- at all times between the second transaction and the further transaction the interest purchased by the financial institution is held by the financial institution so far as not transferred by a previous further transaction; and
- the lease or sub-lease granted under the second transaction is held by the customer.

Note that the provisions of FA 2003, s 71A do not apply to land in Scotland which is covered by FA 2003, s 72A which provides the same SDLT treatment.

FA 2013 introduced an annual charge on residential properties owned by certain 'non-natural persons' for properties valued at above the following:

- £2m from 1 April 2013;
- £1m from 1 April 2015; and
- £0.5m from 1 April 2016.

The legislation has been modified (FA 2013, s 57) so as to ensure that a financial institution providing funding under an alternative finance arrangement falling within the provisions of FA 2003, s 71A (FA 2003, s 72 in the case of Scotland now replaced by LBTT) is not liable to the tax and it is the entity receiving the funding which is liable to that tax.

VAT Treatment of ijara lease transactions

[20.41] The VAT treatment of an ijara lease transaction where the title to the asset is not expected to pass to the customer to buy the property back at the end of the lease term will follow the normal rules for property outlined in Notice 708 Buildings and construction, Notice 742 Land and Property and Notice 742A Opting to tax land and buildings.

Where the title of the property is expected to pass to the customer at the end of the lease term, the normal rules for property will apply for the sale of the property as set out in Notice 708 *Buildings and construction*, Notice 742 *Land and Property* and Notice 742A *Opting to tax land buildings*. Any additional charge payable above the price of the property will be treated as consideration for a deferred payment facility and thus exempt under VATA 1994, Sch 9, Group 5, item 3.

Sukuk

[20.42] As mentioned above sukuk are the Islamic equivalent of bonds. Until the global financial crisis this asset class was growing very rapidly. Sukuk issuance fell in 2008 but as capital markets have started to unfreeze, there has been an increase in sukuk issues.

Direct tax treatment of sukuk

[20.43] ITA 2007, s 564G and ss 564S–564U and TCGA 1992, s 151N and ss 151T–151W and CTA 2009, ss 507 and 513 set out the rules for alternative finance investment bonds (AFIBs) which correspond to sukuk. The provisions were introduced in FA 2007 and treat AFIBs as equivalent to debt securities for UK tax purposes. Any profit return derived from the underlying asset and payable to AFIB holders is treated as deemed interest and should be tax deductible against the income of the AFIB issuing entity.

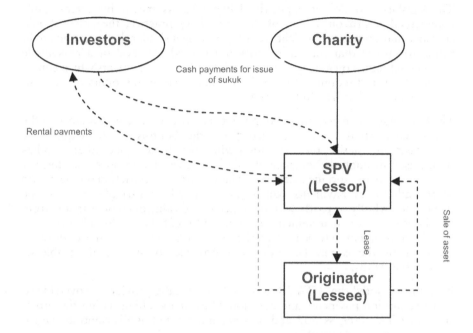

In order for a particular sukuk issuance to fall within the AFIB rules the following requirements must be met:

- a bond-holder pays a sum of money to a bond issuer;
- the arrangement identifies assets, or class of assets ('the bond assets') which the bond-issuer will acquire for the purpose of directly or indirectly generating income or gain;
- the arrangement specifies a period at the end of which it ceases to have effect ('the bond term');
- the bond-issuer undertakes to dispose of at the end of the bond term any bond assets which are still in the issuer's possession and to make a repayment of the capital ('the redemption payment') to the bond-holder during or at the end of the bond-term (whether or not in instalments), and pays to the bond-holder other payments ('additional payment') during or at the end of the bond term;
- the amount of the additional payments does not exceed an amount which would be a reasonable commercial return on a loan of the capital;
- the bond issuer undertakes to arrange for the management of the bond assets with a view to generating income sufficient to pay the redemption payment and additional payments;
- the bond-holder is able to transfer the rights under the arrangements to another person;
- the bonds are a listed security on a recognised stock exchange within the meaning of ITA 2007, s 1005, and
- the arrangement is wholly or partly treated in accordance with international accounting standards as financial liability of the bond-issuer.

The legislation does not explicitly define what is meant by a reasonable commercial return on a loan of the capital. In practice, the issuer should consider market returns on debt securities having a similar duration and credit rating to ensure that the return does not exceed the level of a reasonable commercial return on a loan of the capital. In addition, payments which equate in substance to discount are taxed in a similar way to discounts on conventional bonds under ITA 2007, s 564R.

The bond-issuer can acquire the bond assets before or after the issuance of the sukuk. Given that funds are needed for the bond-issuer to acquire the bond-asset, in practice, the acquisition will typically take place after cash has been raised through the issuance of sukuk. The legislation does not limit the bond-assets to any specific asset class. There is also no restriction on the nature of the additional payments which can be fixed or variable, and can be determined wholly or partly with reference to the value of income arising from the bond-asset or determined on some different basis. In addition, the additional payment may be paid by the issuer or by transfer of shares or other securities by the issuer. Therefore it is possible to issue exchangeable or convertible AFIBs.

It should be noted that CTA 2010, s 1019 specifically provides an override so that redemption payments and additional payments falling within the provisions of CTA 2009, ss 507 and 513 are not treated as distributions which would not be tax deductible.

Where the above requirements are met, the additional payments payable by the issuer to the bond-holders are treated as alternative finance returns. For UK tax purposes, the bond-holder is:

- not treated as having an interest in the bond-assets even though it may have an undivided interest in the bond-asset from a Shariah or UK legal perspective; and
- any income arising to the issuer will belong solely to the issuer and no bond-holder is entitled to claim capital allowances in respect of the bond-asset other than the issuer.
- AFIBs are treated as a qualifying corporate bond ('QCB') within the provisions of TCGA 1992, s 117 if:
  - the capital is expressed in sterling;
  - the arrangements do not include provision for the redemption payment to be in a currency other than sterling;
  - the right to the redemption payment cannot be converted directly or indirectly into an entitlement of securities apart from other arrangements falling within ITA 2007, s 564G and ss 564S–564U and CTA 2009, ss 507 and 513; and
  - the additional payments are not determined wholly or partly by reference to the value of the bond assets.

No withholding tax should arise on the alternative finance return payments if the AFIBs are listed on a stock exchange which is recognised for all tax purposes under ITA 2007, s 1005 as the AFIBs should then qualify as eurobonds under ITA 2007, s 882. However, there is a trap to be avoided as the legislation enables a stock exchange to be designated solely for the purposes of AFIBs and some exchanges have been so designated. AFIBs listed only on such exchanges will not qualify as eurobonds, and withholding tax would be due on additional payments if the issuer is UK resident.

There are specific provisions in ITA 2007, ss 564R–564U and TCGA 1992, ss 151T–151W and CTA 2009, ss 517–519 which ensure that the arrangements are not treated as a unit trust scheme for TCGA 1992 purposes, or a unit trust scheme for income tax purposes or an offshore fund for the purposes of the offshore fund rules or loan relationships purposes.

On a disposal of AFIBs, any gains will generally be taxed under the loan relationships rules for corporate holders. They will be exempt from capital gains tax for non-corporate holders provided that they meet the above requirements to be treated as QCBs which are outside the scope of a charge to capital gains tax.

SDLT treatment of AFIBs

[20.44] For transfers executed on or after 21 July 2008, AFIBs may fall within the meaning of 'loan capital' exemption from stamp duty. The relevant legislation is included under FA 2008, s 154 which treats AFIBs as loan capital and returns thereon as interest, for the purposes of the loan capital exemption.

In addition, for instruments executed on or after 21 July 2008, the loan capital exemption is not denied solely because interest on the bond is dependent on the results ie the interest ceases or reduces only if (or to the extent that) the issuer, after meeting, or providing for, other obligations specified in the capital market arrangement concerned, has insufficient funds available from that capital market arrangement to pay all or part of the interest: FA 2008, s 101.

VAT treatment of sukuk

[20.45] There are no special VAT rules for sukuk related transactions and the VAT treatment of costs associated with the issuance should follow the normal VAT rules.

AFIB rules for property-related sale and leaseback transactions

Outline of rules

[20.46] FA 2009 introduced various changes to the AFIB legislation. They cover capital gains tax, capital allowances and SDLT.

A typical diagrammatic description of an ijara sukuk structure is shown below to illustrate the changes.

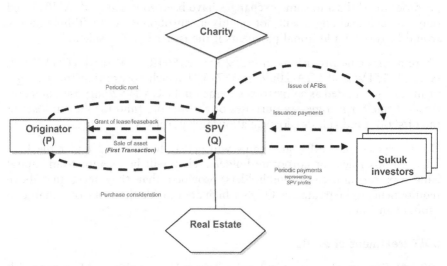

Provided certain qualifying conditions are satisfied, any capital gain arising on the transfer of real estate by the Originator (P) with a view to entering into an alternative finance arrangement involving issuance of AFIBs by an SPV is ignored for capital gains tax purposes. In addition, the transfer of the real estate does not result in the SPV being treated as having incurred capital expenditure for capital allowances and, therefore, the capital allowances will continue to be claimed by the originator. The sale from P to Q and the eventual sale back from Q to P are both exempt from SDLT.

SDLT relief is not available if control of the bond asset is acquired by a bond holder or a group of connected bond holders. Control arises if bond holders have the right of management and control of the bond asset and a single bond holder or a connected group of bond holders acquires sufficient rights to enable it or them to exercise the right of management and control of the bond asset to the exclusion of others. Whether or not a person is connected with another will be determined under ICTA 1988, s 839. In view of the listed nature of AFIBs, where ownership can change and be hard to identify, this requirement can create uncertainty. Unless procedures are put in place to protect against the risk of such control being acquired, it could cause the transaction transferring the land from P to Q to be subject to SDLT.

One way to deal with the above issue would be for the AFIB documentation to limit any management and control rights under all circumstance to the administrator or trustees of the arrangement.

Certain exclusions are provided within the rules to ensure innocent failures are not caught under the provisions above. The first case is where at the time the rights were acquired by the bond holder (or all of the connected bond holders), they did not know and had no reason to suspect the existence of the right to management and control and as soon as reasonably practicable after that event, the bond holder transfers sufficient AFIBs so that management and control is no longer possible. The second case is where the bond holder underwrites a public offer of AFIBs and does not exercise the management and control right.

Conditions to qualify for these reliefs

[20.47] In order for the transfer of land to be treated as an arrangement falling within the alternative finance arrangements involving the issuance of AFIBs, the following conditions contained in FA 2009, Sch 61, para 5 must be satisfied:

(A)   P transfers a qualifying interest in land to Q ('the first transaction') and enters into an agreement with Q to purchase the asset back at the end of the bond term.

(B)   Q issues AFIBs and holds the land as a bond asset.

(C)   Q and P enter into a leaseback agreement.

(D)   Q before the end of 120 days from the date of Condition A transaction registers a satisfactory legal charge in favour of HMRC and provides evidence thereof to HMRC.
The legal charge:
- must be a first charge or a security which ranks first;
- must be imposed on or granted over the interest transferred; and
- must be equivalent to the SDLT amount which would have been payable at the time of Condition A plus interest and penalties.

(E)   The total payments of capital made to Q before termination are not less than 60% of the value of the land at the time of Condition A. This 60% refers to the amount of money raised from investors by issuing AFIBs, not to capital payments made when re-purchasing the land from Q. It can be thought of as requiring a minimum 'loan to value ratio'.

(F)   Q holds the interest in land as a bond asset until termination of the bond.

(G)   Q transfers the interest in land to P within 30 days following the interest in land ceasing to be held as a bond asset and this does not take place later than 10 years after Condition A having been met ('the second transaction').

These conditions should be manageable for P and Q in most cases.

Capital gains tax relief

[20.48] The first transaction, ie the transfer of land by P to Q will not be treated as a chargeable disposal by P nor an acquisition of land by Q for capital gains tax purposes provided that each of conditions A to C is met before the end of the 30-day period from the effective date, ie the date of the transfer of land by P to Q. If condition C is met by virtue of Q and P having entered into a leaseback agreement, the granting of the lease or sub-lease by Q to P will also not be treated for the purposes of TCGA 1992 as an acquisition by P or a disposal by Q of a chargeable asset.

Capital gains tax relief is also available if certain other conditions relating to asset substitution are also met when an interest in land is replaced with another interest in land.

Note that no capital gains tax relief is available if:

- the interest in land is transferred by Q to P without conditions E (not less than 60% capital payment) and F (bond asset requirement) having been met;
- the period mentioned in Condition G expires, or
- if it becomes apparent that Conditions E to G cannot or will not be met, or
- Condition D is not met (registration of legal charge in favour of HMRC).

The second transaction will not result in a disposal or acquisition of asset by Q and P if each of conditions A to C and E to G is met and condition D is also met in the case of UK land. If certain conditions relating to substitution of land are satisfied, relief should also be available for replacement of interest of land with another interest in land.

SDLT relief

[20.49] Relief from SDLT from the first transaction will be available to Q if each of the conditions A to C above is met before the end of 30 days of the effective date of the first transaction, no charge to SDLT will arise on the first transaction.

The SDLT relief will be withdrawn if:

- the interest in land is transferred by Q to P without conditions E and F having been met;
- the period mentioned in Condition G expires, or
- if it becomes apparent that Conditions E to G cannot or will not be met, or
- Condition D is not met.

The SDLT charge will be based on the market value of the land at the time of the first transaction. In addition, penalties and interest will also be payable after the end of the 30-day period from the effective date of the first transaction. Q will also need to deliver a further SDLT return within 30 days to HMRC and include a self-assessment of the amount chargeable.

Relief from SDLT on the second transaction will be available if each of the conditions A to G above is met and the provisions of FA 2003, Pt 4 relating to the first transaction are also complied with. Q must provide evidence to HMRC of each of the conditions A to C and E to G being met to ensure that the land ceases to be subject to SDLT charge.

Note that on 16 March 2010, the Stamp Duty Land Tax (Alternative Finance Investment Bonds) Regulations 2010 (SI 2010/814) were made. In certain circumstances, FA 2003, Sch 17A, para 11, prevents the AFIBs SDLT relief from applying as intended. This would be the case where the land transaction in relation to the AFIBs arrangements is the assignment of a lease which was subject to a previous grant on which one of the reliefs specified in para 11 was claimed. Paragraph 11(2) would treat the assignment as a grant of a lease. In order to comply with the conditions of relief in Sch 61, there must be a freehold sale or assignment of a lease and not a grant of a lease.

The Regulations provide that with effect from 7 April 2010, the SDLT exemption is not denied to deem a transfer of a lease as part of an AFIB structure as a grant of a lease for SDLT purposes where the grant of that lease attracted any of the SDLT reliefs contained in FA 2003, Sch 17A, para 11(3). The Regulations include FA 2009, Sch 61 within the list of reliefs that apply for the purpose of para 11. This means that when the AFIBs SDLT relief is available no further charges will arise under para 11, whilst also ensuring that the provision continues to apply to any further assignments to which none of the specified reliefs applies. This will also ensure that the AFIBs SDLT relief operates as intended and to bring Sch 61 in line with other reliefs.

Subject to further conditions being met, SDLT relief should also be available in the case of replacement of interest in land with another interest in land.

Capital allowances

[20.50] For capital allowances, Q will not to be regarded as having incurred any capital expenditure for capital allowances purposes on the acquisition of interest in land nor is to be regarded as becoming the owner of the asset provided that:

- each of the conditions A to C is met before the end of 30 days of the first transaction; and
- the asset is the subject matter of the first transaction constituting plant and machinery or industrial buildings.

For capital allowance purposes, loss or destruction of the asset will be treated as a disposal by P in the period in which it occurs provided:

- the asset is part of the subject matter of the first transaction and constitutes plant and machinery; and
- while the asset is held as a bond asset, the person in possession loses the asset and the loss is permanent or the asset ceases to exist, eg destruction, dismantling or otherwise.

The disposal value for P is as per CAA 2001, s 61(2) if an amount is received by P and in any other case, the market value at the time of the event.

Note that Q is treated as becoming the owner of the asset if the asset is part of the subject matter of the first transaction and constitutes plant and machinery or industrial building and Q ceases to hold the asset as a bond asset (during or after the expiry term) but does not transfer the asset to P. In such a case, Q ceasing to hold the asset is treated as a disposal event for P in the period in which it takes place and for IBAs (Industrial Buildings Allowances) purposes the balancing event takes place in the same chargeable period. The disposal value for P for plant and machinery purposes is the market value of the asset at the time of the transfer, and for IBAs purposes, P is treated as receiving, as the proceeds of the balancing event, the market value of the asset at the time of the transfer.

In the event of Q transferring asset to a third person, the transfer is also treated as a disposal by P in the chargeable period in which it takes place. The disposal value for P for plant and machinery purposes is the market value of the asset at the time of the transfer by P to Q, and for IBAs purposes, the market value of the asset at the time of the transfer by P to Q.

Substitution of assets

[20.51] Under the rules, provided that certain additional conditions are satisfied, it is possible for substitution of assets to take place under an AFIB arrangement without any adverse tax implications.

In order for the reliefs to continue to apply to substituted assets, it is important that:

- conditions A to G are met in relation to an interest in land;
- Q ceases to hold the original land as a bond asset (transfers it to P) before the termination of the arrangement;
- P and Q enter into a further arrangement relating to another land (replacement land);
- the value of the replacement land at the time of transfer is = to the original land at the time of the first transaction;
- condition F does not need to be met provided that A, B, C, F and G are met;
- condition D will need to be satisfied in relation to the replacement land;
- if the replacement land is not in the UK the original land ceases to be subject to the charge; and
- HMRC notify Land Registry of the discharge and must do so within 30 days from the date Q provides the evidence.

The inclusion of this facility within the legislation is a step in the right direction to ensure for the substitution of assets to take place which is a common feature of sukuk.

Anti-avoidance

[20.52] The legislation also introduces an anti-avoidance measure to prevent avoidance of tax. No SDLT and capital gains tax relief is available if the arrangements not effected for genuine commercial reasons or form part of arrangements of which of the main purpose, or one of the main purposes, avoidance of tax. There is no formal advance clearance process available for taxpayers to seek advance clearance for particular types of transactions from HMRC so that the arrangements fall within the AFIBs rules.

Chapter 21

Property tax opportunities during economic recovery

by
Zigurds Kronbergs
Tax Writer

Utilisation of losses

[21.1] During economic recovery following a recession in which losses have been made, a business may once again become profit-making and may be able to consider the optimal use of brought-forward tax losses.

The position on losses depends upon whether the party making the loss is within the charge to income tax or corporation tax, or indeed whether we may be looking at a capital gains tax loss. The technical position for each of these situations is discussed in detail at **CHAPTER 6** although a summary is given below, together with some common situations and planning techniques.

Where reference is made in what follows to the treatment of corporate losses incurred after 31 March 2017, and to pre- and post-1 April 2017 non-trading loan-relationship deficits, it has been assumed that the measures originally contained in the September 2017 Finance Bill (as cl 18 and Sch 4) will be enacted without significant amendment.

Similarly, references to the application of the cash basis to profit computations of a property business in tax years 2017–18 and thereafter assume that the measures contained in the September 2017 Finance Bill (as cl 16 and Sch 2) will be enacted without significant amendment.

Individual taxation

Income tax losses – technical position

[21.2] In the event that a UK property-rental business ('a UK property business') run by an individual incurs losses, these may be carried forward and set against future profits of the same business (ITA 2007, s 118). However, UK property business losses may not normally be offset against an individual's other income and gains for the year in which they arise. If the following year's profits are too small to absorb the prior-year loss (or if there is a loss in the following year) then the prior year's unused loss may be carried forward indefinitely so long as the same property business continues. Likewise, any losses arising from an overseas property business may normally be offset only against future overseas property-business income (ITA 2007, ss 118 to 120).

It will therefore be important to monitor whether or not the particular property business has ever ceased. In a recession, property will often be left standing vacant, but provided it is still actively marketed for further letting, there is a strong argument that the same property business continues. Indeed, HMRC indicate that, as a general rule of thumb, they will normally accept a period of vacancy of up to three years before suggesting that a new property business has commenced. Usually, a property business will be regarded as ceasing when the last let property is disposed of or used for some other purpose. Whether letting ceases and later re-commences such as to constitute a new property business will be a question of fact. It will depend on such factors as the period between the lettings, what sort of activities happened in the interim period, and whether it is the same property/properties let before and after.

The date of commencement of a new property business will be a question of fact, although it will usually be when letting first commences. There will often be expenditure incurred prior to the commencement of the property business and this will be relieved under the provisions for pre-trading expenditure (ITTOIA 2005, s 57 as applied by ITTOIA 2005, s 272; also available under the cash basis in 2017–18 and subsequently, as applied by ITTOIA 2005, s 272ZA). Relief for such pre-commencement expenditure will be allowed where the expenditure is incurred not more than seven years prior to the date on which the property business commences, is not otherwise allowable as a deduction for tax purposes, and would have been allowed as a deduction had it been incurred after the property business started.

Much as for trading businesses, for a property business post-cessation receipts will be taxable and relief may be available for post-cessation expenses. Post-cessation receipts will, however, be taxed under ITTOIA 2005, s 349 for the purposes of income tax.

The point that property business losses incurred by an individual may only be offset against property business income of the same business extends not just to considering whether that business has ceased, but also to whether the individual taxpayer might receive rental income in another capacity. If the taxpayer received rental income in a different capacity, this will not constitute the same business. Thus, for example, it is HMRC's view that the losses of a property business carried on in partnership may not be offset against income of a property business carried on by a partner in his or her sole name (even though the partnership losses would be tax transparent and its losses will be attributable to each partner).

There is scope to claim set-off against general income for any part of the property business loss as is attributable to excess capital allowances or agricultural expenses (in which case the loss brought forward will be reduced). Such a claim may be used to reduce general income for the tax year in which the rental loss arises or the tax year following. However, the loss relief available is limited to the smallest of the taxpayer's total general income for the year, the amount of the property business loss made in the year and the net capital allowances, after setting off any balancing charges. Claims must be made no later than the first anniversary of the normal self-assessment filing date for the tax year concerned. Thus, for example, the latest date for a claim in respect of 2017–18 is 31 January 2020.

Where a property investor has agricultural land as part of his property business, then to the extent that the rental losses relate to the agricultural land, there is scope to make a claim to set these losses against general income in either the tax year in which the loss was made or the following tax year. 'Agricultural expenses' for this purpose means losses related to agricultural land, houses and other buildings managed as one estate and occupied wholly or mainly for the purposes of husbandry. Note that the expenses regarded as being 'agricultural' will include maintenance costs, repairs, insurance, etc – but will specifically exclude interest costs. The amount of the loss claimed is limited to the smallest of the individual's total general income for the year (after deducting any property business losses brought forward), the amount of the property business loss for the year and the agricultural expenditure (ITA 2007, ss 120–123). Uncommercial losses will not be permissible, however.

Anti-avoidance legislation

[21.3] There are a number of anti-avoidance provisions that restrict the ability of individuals to claim loss relief on certain items that might otherwise have generated rental losses. The anti-avoidance legislation is intended to catch individuals who have entered into tax-avoidance arrangements.

In particular, ITA 2007, s 98A (as applied to post-cessation expenses of a property business by ITA 2007, s 125(6)) denies post-cessation relief for or events arising from any 'relevant tax-avoidance arrangements'. Similarly, ITA 2007, s 127B denies tax relief for 'tax-generated agricultural expenses' arising as a result of 'relevant tax-avoidance arrangements'.

Of course, this specific anti-avoidance legislation, introduced by Finance Act 2012, is in addition to the General Anti-Abuse Rule (GAAR) in FA 2013, Part 5.

Capital gains tax losses – technical position

[21.4] If a UK tax-resident individual makes a property disposal then, subject to the question noted below as to whether the individual might be regarded as doing so as part of a trading transaction, the disposal will fall within the capital gains tax net. As detailed in **CHAPTER 5**, non-UK tax-resident individuals are now also subject to capital gains tax on the disposal of UK residential property. Various aspects of the capital gains tax position in relation to property disposals are also discussed in detail at **CHAPTER 14**. In outline, however, to the extent that the taxpayer has any remaining basic rate income tax band, the gain will normally be taxed at 18% and thereafter it will suffer tax at 28%. Possibly, if the property disposal is made in connection with a disposal of a trading business then one would need to look at whether the taxpayer could benefit from a lower 10% rate using entrepreneurs' relief or the new investors' relief.

If there are any capital gains tax losses, these may only be utilised against gains realised in the same tax year, or carried forward for use in future tax years.

Trading or investment? – planning opportunities?

[21.5] If an individual disposes of an investment property, the disposal will be within the capital gains tax regime. Thus, if the individual makes a capital loss, that loss will only be available to relieve current or future years' capital gains.

However, if the individual is in a position to argue that the property disposal was a trading transaction, then potentially what might have otherwise been a capital loss could become an income loss. This is generally the opposite of the position one would normally wish to argue where gains are expected, but where losses are expected, losses tend to be more effectively used against income rather than gains, given the fact that the top rate of income tax is so much higher than the top rate of capital gains tax.

Moreover, if the loss were as a result of a trade (eg property development/purchase and resale of property, etc), then the income loss would be available for offset against general income under ITA 2007, s 64 rather than just against future property business income. Depending upon the individual's profile of income/investments, this could be highly advantageous.

The question as to whether a property transaction might be classed as a trading or an investment transaction is discussed in detail at **CHAPTER 2**.

Corporation tax

Property losses – technical position

[21.6] For corporation tax purposes, trading losses are computed in the same way as trading profits. Capital allowances will augment a loss (and the business may therefore wish to consider disclaiming these in order to save them for use against profits in a later period) and any balancing charges will decrease the loss.

The rules in relation to relief against corporation tax for the losses of a property business can be found in CTA 2010, Part 4, Chapter 4. Under these rules, loss relief may be provided as follows:

(a) the loss will first be set off against the company's total profits for the period concerned; and

(b) remaining losses are carried forward and will be deemed to be property losses of the following accounting period; or

(c) current-year losses may instead be surrendered under the group-relief rules.

Companies that are regarded as companies with investment business (CTA 2009, Part 16) that have a property business incurring losses and then cease to carry out that property business, may regard the brought-forward property loss as a management expense of the subsequent accounting period (attracting relief under CTA 2009, Part 16, Chapter 2). The loss may then be carried forward as a management expense while the company continues to be regarded as a company with investment business. However, companies not falling in this category will have no capacity to continue to carry property losses forward once the property business ceases.

Losses of a UK property business incurred after 31 March 2017 carried forward to a subsequent accounting period may only be relieved on the making of a claim, but the company may choose how much of the loss brought forward it wishes to set off in that period. Such claims must be made within two years of the end of the accounting period in respect of which the set-off is claimed (CTA 2010, s 62(5A)–(5C)).

Losses of a UK property business incurred after 31 March 2017 and carried forward to a subsequent accounting period will be available for surrender by way of group relief (CTA 2010, s 188BB), subject to anti-avoidance provisions.

The carried-forward losses of a UK property business available under ITTOIA 2005, s 62(3) for set-off against the total profits of the company form part of the deductions subject to restriction under the new proposed restrictions on the overall deductibility of carried-forward losses. These will only affect companies that have more than a maximum of £5 million (allocable among companies in a group) of profits against which the loss may be set.

By 'losses incurred after 31 March 2017' is meant here losses incurred in an accounting period beginning after 31 March 2017 or that part of the loss incurred in an accounting period straddling 1 April 2017 as is apportioned to the notional accounting period beginning on 1 April 2017.

Note, however, that in order for the property loss to be relieved, it must relate to a property business carried on either on a commercial basis, or in the exercise of a statutory function (CTA 2010, s 64).

The loss-relief provisions for corporation tax purposes are, therefore much more generous than for income tax purposes, as relief for UK property-business losses may be given against the company's total profits in the accounting period and any unused property-business losses may be carried forward for use in the following year against the company's total profits in that accounting period, and so on in future years.

Under CTA 2010, s 66, relief for overseas property-business losses may be used only against future profits of that overseas property business. There is to be no change in the treatment of these losses whether incurred after 31 March 2017 or on or before that date.

Note also that anti-avoidance legislation exists to prevent the use of accumulated losses by a new owner of a company that has changed hands in certain circumstances (CTA 2010, s 683).

Loan-relationship deficits – technical position

[21.7] Interest costs are dealt with separately under the loan-relationship rules, which deal with financing issues, and are therefore relieved separately from trading losses (although in practice the rules are actually fairly similar). Trading loan-relationship debits are included in trading income (or losses) and thus any loss is relieved as a trading loss. If a deficit arises on a non-trading loan relationship, there are similar provisions under the loan-relationship rules to relieve that deficit.

In what follows, a 'post-1 April non-trading loan-relationship deficit' means such a deficit arising in an accounting period beginning after 31 March 2017 or, in the case of accounting periods straddling 1 April 2017, that part of the deficit as is apportioned to the notional accounting period beginning on 1 April 2017. A 'pre-1 April 2017 non-trading loan-relationship deficit' is any non-trading loan-relationship deficit that is not a post-1 April non-trading loan-relationship deficit.

Where a company has a non-trading pre-1 April 2017 loan-relationship deficit for any accounting period it may claim relief under CTA 2009, Part 5, Chapter 16:

- for the whole or part of that deficit against any profits of the company for that period;
- by carry-back against any non-trading surplus within the permitted period of 12 months as remains after various other reliefs have been set off in priority; or
- by surrender as group relief.

Deficits not subject to any of the above claims are automatically carried forward and will be relieved in the first accounting period in which non-trading profits are available. However, the company may make a claim for only part of the deficit to be set off in that period.

If a company forms part of a group or a consortium, it may be able to surrender its loan-relationship deficits between group companies within the charge to corporation tax, or to accept surrendered losses itself.

Where a company has a non-trading post-1 April 2017 loan-relationship deficit for any accounting period it may claim relief under CTA 2009, Part 5, Chapter 16A:

- for the whole or part of that deficit, less so much of the deficit as is surrendered as group relief, against any profits of the company for that period;
- by carry-back against any non-trading surplus within the permitted period of 12 months as remains after various other reliefs have been set off in priority; or
- by surrender as group relief.

Deficits not subject to any of the above claims are automatically carried forward and will be relieved in the first accounting period in which non-trading profits are available. However, the company may make a claim for only part of the deficit to be set off in that period.

If a company forms part of a group or a consortium, it may be able to surrender its loan-relationship deficits between group companies within the charge to corporation tax, or to accept surrendered losses itself. It is also able to surrender non-trading deficits brought forward by way of group relief under CTA 2010, Part 5A.

Group relief of losses etc

[21.8] The following may be surrendered and claimed as group relief under CTA 2010, Part 5:

- trading losses;

- excess capital allowances;
- non-trading deficits on loan relationships;
- excess qualifying charitable donations;
- losses of a UK property business;
- excess management expenses;
- non-trading losses on intangible fixed assets.

Trading losses, excess capital allowances and non-trading deficits on loan relationships may be surrendered in full, whether or not the surrendering company has other profits against which the loss etc might have been, but has not been, set off. Excess qualifying charitable donations, losses of a UK property business, excess management expenses and non-trading losses on intangible fixed assets may only be surrendered to the extent that they exceed other profits of the surrendering company.

If the surrendering and claimant companies do not have the same accounting periods, or are not members of the same group throughout an accounting period, it is necessary to identify the 'overlapping period' that is common to the claimant and surrendering company. Profits/losses are then normally time-apportioned to the overlapping period (unless time-apportionment would lead to an unjust or unreasonable result). The amount that may be surrendered will be the smaller of the loss of the surrendering company that arises in the overlapping period and the available profit of the claimant company in that same period.

Group relief for carried-forward losses etc

[21.9] The following losses etc incurred in previous periods and brought forward from those periods may be surrendered and claimed as group relief under CTA 2010, Part 5A:

- post-1 April 2017 trading losses;
- post-1 April 2017 non-trading deficits on loan relationships;
- post-1 April 2017 losses of a UK property business;
- excess management expenses except those first deductible in an accounting period beginning before 1 April 2017;
- post-1 April 2017 non-trading losses on intangible fixed assets.

These losses and other amounts may only be surrendered to the extent that the surrendering company cannot utilise them itself, or, if at the end of the surrender period it has no assets capable of producing income.

If the surrendering and claimant companies do not have the same accounting periods, or are not members of the same group throughout an accounting period, it is necessary to identify the 'overlapping period' that is common to the claimant and surrendering company. Profits/losses are then normally time-apportioned to the overlapping period (unless time-apportionment would lead to an unjust or unreasonable result). The amount that may be surrendered will be the smaller of the loss of the surrendering company that arises in the overlapping period and the available profit of the claimant company in that same period.

Capital gains

[21.10] Although the capital gains tax distinction for corporates is less important, as there is no difference in the rates of corporation tax applying to income vs gains, the distinction is still relevant in terms of how any losses might be used.

As with the personal tax position, capital losses in companies may only be used against capital gains in the same accounting period, or carried forward against future gains. Therefore, as in the case of individuals, it may be useful, where losses are involved, to argue that a disposal was a disposal of an asset held for trading purposes rather than for investment purposes.

Note that in corporate groups, an election may be made under TCGA 1992, s 171A to deem losses to be moved around the corporate group and utilised accordingly. Similarly, trading losses may be subject to group relief under CTA 2010, Part 5, Chapter 2.

Corporation tax planning

[21.11] As well as the considerations for income vs capital, and group relief, as noted above, a useful mechanism that one should always consider for companies is whether the company should alter its year-end, depending upon the date of any property disposal. If the disposal results in a significant loss, depending upon other income/gains in the year, it may be preferable to either shorten or lengthen the year-end.

Example

ABC Ltd is an investment company which has a 30 September year-end. On 15 December 2017, it disposes of a significant property investment, at a loss of £1m. For the year ending 30 September 2017, it has investment income net of management expenses of £750,000 but for the year to 30 September 2018, it projects net management expenses of £200,000.

If nothing is done to change the year end, ABC Ltd will pay corporation tax on the full £750,000 of income for the year to 30 September 2017. In the year to 30 September 2018, it will have net management expenses of £200,000 and a capital loss of £1m, which will both be carried forward.

However, if it shortens its year-end to the minimum possible period (six months), it will produce accounts to 31 March 2017 and pay corporation tax on £375,000 (ie half of £750,000). The year end to 31 March 2018 will then encompass the remaining £375,000 plus the £1m loss and the £200,000 net management expenses, thus (depending upon results for the rest of the period), effectively it will have secured relief using those losses against half of the income it would have otherwise suffered corporation tax on in the year to 30 September 2017.

Timing of the disposal

[21.12] The timing of a disposal for CGT purposes can be very important in getting the relief for any capital loss in the right accounting period/tax year.

Timing also is important for a number of reasons including possible interaction with entrepreneurs' relief as well as a variety of other reliefs that are time-sensitive, such as rollover relief.

For most capital disposals, the time of the disposal will be when the contract for the sale of the asset becomes unconditional (TCGA 1992, s 28). In the case of an unconditional contract, the disposal of the asset will be upon exchange of contracts, rather than when legal title to the asset passes or when the asset is in fact paid for.

The exception to this is given by TCGA 1992, s 22, which deals with the timing of a disposal that occurs where a capital sum is derived from an asset. This section provides that there can be some situations where an asset is deemed to be disposed of even where there is no corresponding acquisition of that asset by someone else, for example compensation receipts, receipts under a policy of insurance, receipts for forfeiture or surrender of rights and receipts for the use or exploitation of an asset. For disposals under this section, the date of the disposal is deemed to be when the capital sum is received.

The decision in *Chaloner v Pellipar Investments Ltd* [1996] STC 234 is useful in distinguishing disposals of an interest in land that fall within TCGA 1992, s 22 (particularly capital sums received for the use or exploitation of assets) from those that do not. For land in particular, it is important to note that where the owner's title to the land is affected (eg because of a grant of a lease) this is not within s 22 (and indeed is dealt with separately) but if the owner's title to the land is not affected, then s 22 can bite (eg grant of a licence or easement).

Choice of ownership vehicle

[21.13] When purchasing a property, one of the crucial decisions will be the choice of the entity.

Broadly, for investment properties one would often find that it is the case that it is more tax-efficient to own the property personally, or through a tax-transparent entity, so that any future gain avoids the double layering of corporation tax and income tax and possibly benefits from a lower rate of tax.

For property trading, it would often be the case that it is more tax-efficient for the trading to be run through a company, as corporation tax rates are lower than income tax rates and profits from trading transactions can therefore be reinvested at a higher base. Property trading SPVs might also be considered, because they could later be wound up so that the individual owner receives the profits at lower capital gains tax rates rather than at income tax rates.

However, for various reasons, it might be that a property is in a vehicle that has become inappropriate in the longer term. For example, it might be that a company happened to have surplus profits and therefore it used these to acquire an investment property directly, rather than have the tax charge incurred by the individual owner by first distributing those profits out and then having the individual buy the property. In such situations, when, in a recession, property prices become very depressed, it might be that the opportunity to extract such properties from an inappropriate structure presents itself.

Ownership choices

Individual/partnership ownership

[21.14] This is the straightforward option – the individual owner of the property will be directly taxed on any income or gains arising from such a purchase.

Likewise, for partnerships, for income and capital gains tax purposes, partnerships are regarded as being tax-transparent – ie they are not taxed in their own right but instead one looks to the partners and applies taxation to them. Accordingly, if the partners are natural persons then much the same considerations apply as for an individual personally purchasing an investment property; if the partners are legal persons then they in turn will be taxed as such.

Income tax – The income tax position for rental income, particularly for higher-rate taxpayers, is not particularly attractive as the rental income will suffer tax at the taxpayer's marginal rates of income tax. Furthermore, property-business losses may not be offset against an individual's other income and gains for the year. Instead, the loss is carried forward for offset against future income from a UK property business (ITA 2007, s 118). Likewise, any losses arising from an overseas property business may be offset only against future income of that overseas property business (ITA 2007, ss 118 to 120).

Capital gains tax – The CGT position of personal-ownership choices (ie through a partnership or as an individual owner) is more attractive as this can enable the individual to benefit from the use of the annual CGT exemption on a disposal and, moreover, there are lower CGT rates available to individuals (ie typically 18% or 28% (on the disposal of a residential-property interest) and now as low as 10% and 20% for disposals of other property interests, rather than 40% or 45%). This, coupled with the fact that corporate ownership can in effect create a double layering of the tax charge, can make personal/partnership ownership very attractive for CGT purposes in comparison.

Note that most categories of trusts would also pay income tax/capital gains tax as above, although would do so at the higher rates of tax.

Company ownership

[21.15] Subject to certain exceptions (eg charitable companies, REITs, etc), a UK company will be liable to corporation tax on its rental income. Specifically, the legislation can be found in CTA 2009, Part 4.

The loss-relief provisions for the purposes of corporation tax are much more generous than those for the purposes of income tax. Under CTA 2010, s 62, relief for UK property business losses may be given against the company's total profits in the accounting period. Any unused losses from a UK property business may be carried forward for use in the following year against the company's total profits in that accounting period, and so on in future years. Under CTA 2010, s 66, relief for overseas property business losses may be used only against future profits of that overseas property business.

For the purposes of taxation of income, therefore, corporate property ownership can have more attractions than personal ownership, in terms of the scope to offset losses against other income. Companies also often pay lower rates of corporation tax than individuals might pay in income tax, which can also make corporate ownership more attractive (although there can be effectively a double charge on extraction of the profits, depending upon the circumstances).

There can be significant tax disadvantages in corporate property ownership when it comes to selling the property, given the effect of the double layering of corporation tax plus also income/capital gains tax on the distribution out from the company. However, this will depend on the exact profit levels for the company and the income levels of the ownership. On the other hand, the quid pro quo is that corporate property ownership can in some circumstances create an improved inheritance tax (IHT) position (eg where business premises are held within the trading company that uses those premises).

Following the introduction in Finance Act 2013 of the new taxation regime for high-value residential properties (residential properties worth £500,000 or more), of course, the impact of the annual ATED charge on companies owning such high-value residential property may also impact on the decision as to what the best ownership vehicle might be. However, in fact, the exemptions available against the annual charge for property developers and also for landlords letting to third parties would cover most sorts of property investment situations.

The right vehicle for the future?

[21.16] The choice of ownership is, therefore, clearly dependent upon the circumstances of the case. Assuming, though, that one anticipates that property prices will continue to rise (Brexit notwithstanding), it will generally make sense for an individual to own investment property personally rather than in a company. This advantage has been boosted by the abolition of the dividend tax credit with effect from 2016–17 and its replacement by the dividend nil-rate band, which makes company ownership even more expensive for higher-rate and additional-rate taxpayers who receive the net profit in a distribution. This can be demonstrated by the following calculation, which assumes the property concerned is a residential property:

		Property owned	
		Personally	**In a Ltd Company**
Sales Proceeds		500,000	500,000
Cost of Property		(250,000)	(250,000)
Cost of Sale		(25,000)	(25,000)
Net Proceeds		225,000	225,000
Corp Tax Charge**	19%		(42,750)
Liquidation Distribution			182,250
Annual Exempt Amount		11,300	11,300
Personal Taxation*	28%	(59,836)	
	****20%		***(34,190)
Cash in hand		165,164	148,060

*Assuming individual has no basic rate band remaining
**Assumes CIHC and winding-up
***Assumes liquidation and a zero-base cost on winding-up
****The gain is not an upper rate gain as there is no longer a residential-property interest

By contrast, for property trading arrangements, generally it will be better for a company to engage in the trade, but only if the profits are retained, as demonstrated by the following table:

		Property Owned	
		Personally	**In a Ltd Company**
Trading Income		200,000	200,000
Cost of Rental		(100,000)	(100,000)
Net Proceeds		100,000	100,000
Corp Tax Charge	19%		(19,000)
National Insurance (marginal)	2%	(2,000)	
Personal Taxation*	40%	(40,000)	
Net Profit		58,000	81,000

*Assuming individual has only the higher-rate tax band left, but is not a 45% taxpayer; these differences are exaggerated further if in fact the individual pays the 45% tax rate. Note that the corporation tax rate is now 19% (FY 2017), and that it will be reduced to 17% from the year starting 1 April 2020. However, if the net profit were to be distributed, a further £24,700 income tax would be payable on the dividend, leaving cash in hand of £56,300 and making personal ownership marginally more beneficial.

If a property is currently still depressed in value, but might later be sold when values go back up, then now may be a tempting time to move property out of corporate ownership and into personal ownership. This is particularly so if the company may anyway be making trading losses (which could be offset against the capital gain). Of course, this would depend upon the exact property values involved and how certain the owner of the company is that the property could later be sold at a good price to a third party.

The downside of moving the property out of the company sooner rather than later is that at the point the company makes the disposal this will crystallise any gain that exists for capital gains tax purposes. This will mean that potentially a tax liability therefore becomes due before the property has been sold and therefore before the company has the money to pay the tax.

However, the potential upsides to such planning can be demonstrated by the following example:

		Property Owned Initially	
		In a Ltd Company Remaining	In a Ltd Company Extracted
Sales Proceeds			250,000
Cost of Property			(225,000)
Cost of Sale			(5,000)
Net Proceeds		–	20,000
Corp Tax Charge	19%		(3,800)
Profits for Distribution		–	16,200
Personal Taxation	32.5%*		(3,640)
			12,560

*Dividend higher rate assuming the taxpayer is liable at the higher rate but not at the additional rate, and incorporating the £5,000 dividend nil-rate

		Property now owned	
Ten Years On		**In a Ltd Company**	**Personally**
Sales Proceeds		600,000	600,000
Cost of Property		(225,000)	(250,000)
Cost of Sale		(5,000)	(5,000)
Net Proceeds		370,000	345,000
Corp Tax Charge	17%	(62,900)	
Net Distribution		307,100	345,000
Annual Exempt Amount			11,300
Personal Taxation			
CGT*	28%		(93,436)
Dividend higher rate**	32.5%	(37,863)	
Dividend additional rate**	38.1%	(71,857)	
Cash in Hand		197,380	251,564

*assume rates are equal to current levels for CGT and the property is a residential property

**assume rates are equal to current rates for dividends, the dividend nil-rate is £2,000 and the individual's basic rate tax band is used already but the whole of the higher rate tax band (at 2017–18 levels) is available

Note that the corporation tax rate is now 19% (FY 2017), and that it will be reduced to 17% from the year starting 1 April 2020.

Note that for SDLT purposes, it is normally possible to pay a dividend in specie of the property without attracting SDLT.

Disincorporation relief

[21.17] From 1 April 2013, it became possible to obtain disincorporation relief. This new relief is a form of rollover or deferral relief, which allows a company to transfer certain assets to shareholders who continue the business in an unincorporated form, without triggering a corporation tax charge on the company on the disposal of that asset. Consideration should therefore be given as to whether the tax position on taking a property out of a company might further be improved by the use of this new relief.

All the following conditions will need to be met before disincorporation relief may apply:

(a)   the business must be transferred as a going concern;

(b)   the business must be transferred together with all the assets of the business or together with all the assets of the business apart from cash;

(c)   the total market value of the qualifying assets (broadly, land – other than land held as trading stock – and goodwill) at the time of the transfer must not be more than £100,000;

(d)   the shareholders to whom the business is transferred must be individuals;

(e)   those shareholders must have held shares in the company throughout the 12 months before the transfer.

The requirement for the interest in land to be no more than £100,000 will of course significantly limit the usefulness of this relief to any property companies, however, and it is now subject to review by the Office for Tax Simplification.

Incorporation relief

[21.18] If, after having considered the above, one comes to the conclusion that the property should be moved from an individual's ownership into a company (eg in the situation of a property developer, wishing to keep future profits in the corporation tax regime, to then re-invest at more favourable net-of-tax rates), then one might want to consider the possibility of incorporation relief (TCGA 1992, s 162).

Incorporation relief is available where:

(a)   a person who is not a company, transfers to a company, a business as a going concern;

(b)   that person transfers it together with the whole assets of the business, or together with the whole of those assets other than cash; and

(c)   the business is so transferred wholly or partly in exchange for shares issued by the company to the person transferring the business.

When incorporation relief is utilised, effectively the base cost of the shares received by way of consideration for the transfer of the business into the company is reduced by the gain arising on the assets transferred. Thus, the gain is 'rolled over' into the value of the shares.

When looking at whether a property disposal might qualify for this relief, clearly if the property is being disposed of as part of, say, a manufacturing business, then the whole business (and therefore the transfer of its assets) would be expected to qualify for relief. However, confusion can arise when trying to determine whether the incorporation of a property business might qualify for relief.

The provisions apply where a 'business', rather than simply a trade, is transferred as a going concern. The word 'business' is not defined in the capital gains tax legislation. It seems clear that a business includes a trade, profession or vocation. The extent to which other activities not taxed under ITTOIA 2005, Part 2 (trades, professions and vocations) can be regarded as a business depends on the facts of each case. HMRC interpret the term 'business' according to its normal meaning. They accept that business includes, but is not restricted to, trading.

The comment of Rowlatt J that a business is 'an active occupation . . . continuously carried on' has been influential. HMRC take the view that the passive holding of investments or an investment property does not amount to business.

Note, however, that one may wish to make an election to disapply incorporation relief in situations where entrepreneur's relief may apply. This is because entrepreneurs' relief is not available to the extent that incorporation relief is claimed. In these circumstances, it may make more sense to form a new company, and then sell the property development trade into that company, with the purchase price outstanding as a loan to be drawn down from in due course.

Under entrepreneurs' relief, the gains must be made arising on or in connection with disposals of the whole or part of a business, including in certain circumstances, disposals of shares or securities.

There is a lifetime limit of £10m for gains qualifying for entrepreneurs' relief.

Relief is provided in respect of qualifying business disposals, namely:

(1)   a material disposal of business assets;
(2)   a disposal of a trust business asset; or
(3)   a disposal associated with a relevant material disposal.

Business for these purposes means a trade, profession or vocation conducted on a commercial basis with a view to the realisation of profits and the commercial letting of furnished holiday accommodation.

HMRC's *Capital Gains Manual* (at para CG63980) states that the straight-forward letting of property is not a trade, though certain lettings are not necessarily regarded as indicating a non-trading activity.

Accordingly, one would not expect most property businesses to qualify for entrepreneurs' relief. However, a disposal of an FHL business might qualify – although note the requirement that the business, or part of a business, must be disposed of, rather than the mere sell-off of an asset of that business. If the property is sold as part of a wider trade (eg a factory being sold with part of a manufacturing business), then one may then also be able to benefit from the relief.

The same holds good for investors' relief, which also requires the shares that are subject to the disposal to be those of a trading company or of the holding company of a trading group (FA 2016, Sch 14).

Trapped stock

Outline

[21.19] For property developers and dealers, the question of 'trapped stock' – stock which is not selling as a result of a recession – can be a serious issue. Having to hold on to such stock can have serious consequences in terms of cash flow and working-capital management. Property developers may then need to consider whether they might make alternative use of the property they are left with, and naturally the tax consequences of such use must be considered.

Similarly, market conditions may mean that a property investor will need to divest himself of his property portfolio and at that point the question might arise as to whether the property shifts from being an investment to trading stock.

Transfers to trading stock

[21.20] Where a property is initially purchased as trading stock, and then is held as an investment – or vice versa, the possibility that tax charges may crystallise on transfers into and out of stock arises. Given that property values are often substantial, it need take only one such transfer for a very large and unexpected tax charge to arise. It is, therefore, worth dealing here with the legislation for transfers into and out of trading stock. This legislation is not specific to property transactions, but here we will look at its impact on property situations.

In what follows, it is assumed that the amendments due to be made by cl 26 of the September 2017 Finance Bill will indeed be enacted without material amendment.

Where an asset not initially acquired as trading stock is later appropriated for use as stock in a person's trade, for the purposes of that trade it is regarded as an acquisition at market value. There is also in turn a deemed market-value disposal of the asset for capital gains purposes (TCGA 1992, s 161(1)).

However, this deemed disposal is recognised by HMRC as potentially causing cash-flow difficulties, as the tax may become due before there has been any actual sale of the asset to a third party. It is therefore possible to make an election under TCGA 1992, s 161(3) effectively to hold over the gain into the cost of the stock; the gain arising on the deemed disposal for CGT purposes is reduced to nil with a consequent reduction in the cost of the item's deemed value for stock purposes.

This election can give a significant cash-flow advantage. For individuals, the much lower CGT rate will often mean that it is worth paying CGT up front (at lower rates) to have a lower IT charge in due course, as the example below demonstrates.

For appropriations into trading stock made after 7 March 2017, it will no longer be possible to make the election where an allowable loss would otherwise have accrued to the trader.

However, as many clients are unaware that the election is necessary, it is very important that any relevant circumstances are picked up such that the deadline for the election can be adhered to. For companies, the deadline is two years from the end of the accounting period in which the asset is appropriated to stock. For individuals, etc, the deadline is the first anniversary of the 31 January next following the tax year in which ends the period of account in which the asset is appropriated to trading stock. If the trade is carried on as a partnership, it is necessary for all partners to consent to the election.

Transfers from trading stock

[21.21] Where an asset that has formed part of a person's trading stock is appropriated by that person for any other purpose (ie normally in the case of property then to be held as an investment or to be used as a long-term asset of the business, such as by using it as an office for the person's own business) then there is a market-value disposal of the asset for taxation purposes and a market-value acquisition of it for CGT purposes (TCGA 1992, s 161(2)). Unfortunately, however, in this situation, there is no provision for a hold-over election.

Considerable care may therefore need to be taken in certain cases when a property becomes an investment (eg it is temporarily let out following completion), so that it does not necessarily cease to be trading stock. At the outset (ie when property is acquired or is being constructed) it may be appropriate to consider carefully whether this is to be a development for sale or investment.

Stock or Investment?

[21.22] The distinction between dealing or developing and investing in property is crucial to a great many areas of tax law, as discussed at CHAPTER 2. Often it will be quite clear as to whether a party is dealing or investing: a party buying property to let out long-term will be making a property investment, whereas someone buying a property to refurbish and sell will most likely be a dealer or developer. However, where does one draw the line between activity regarded as dealing and activity looked upon as investment?

First, it is important to realise that the tests for whether one is dealing in property or making a property investment are in fact very much the same as for any other trade (a property dealer is engaged in a trading activity). Thus, a good place to start is to look at the 'badges of trade'. The badges of trade are not a statutory concept, but are a set of criteria taken from case law which can identify when a party is undertaking a trading activity, and as such they can be applied to property transactions just as they can to a variety of other activities. A description of the badges of trade is given at CHAPTER 2.

It is not necessary for a transaction to have all of the badges in order to be regarded as dealing or developing, and some badges will carry greater weight than others depending on the circumstances. Indeed, in some cases the existence of one single badge can be enough. The situation will therefore always need to be considered carefully in light of all the facts which indicate the intention behind the property acquisition.

The main consideration, however, in terms of the distinction between property dealing and property investment, is that in the case of property dealing, one will seek to make a profit on the purchase and sale of property, whereas in the case of an investment, one would tend to buy to realise income from the asset on a longer-term basis. The metaphor that is often used in this situation is that of the purchase of a tree – if a tree is purchased with a view to maintaining the tree and harvesting its fruit then most likely the tree is held as an investment, whereas if the tree is bought to be cut down and sold then most likely it will be acquired in the nature of a trade.

Given that land transactions may involve significant sums as well as different bases and rates of taxation, one can generally expect HMRC to pay a close interest. It is therefore useful to list here some examples of prior decided cases.

(i) *Pickford v Quirke*, CA (1927) 13 TC 251 – in this case a taxpayer purchased a mill with the intent of using it for trading purposes but unfortunately the mill was in a much worse state than was first realised. The taxpayer therefore had no other sensible option other than to strip out all the items in the mill and sell them piecemeal, which actually made the taxpayer quite a good profit. Doing this once would probably not have been a trading transaction, but the taxpayer then realised this could be quite a good way to make money and therefore repeated the process many times. Accordingly, the taxpayer was regarded as engaging in a trade.

(ii) *Marson v Morton* [1986] 1 WLR 1343, [1986] STC 463 – here a taxpayer purchased some land with the intention of holding on to it as an investment for a period of at least a few years. The land had planning permission, which would arguably be regarded as a modification to the asset to make it more saleable. However, as the original intention was to purchase the land as an investment – and the taxpayer had sufficient documentary evidence to prove this – it was held that no trade was carried on.

(iii) *Taylor v Good* [1974] 1 All ER 1137, [1974] STC 148 – in this case a husband purchased a property which he intended should be used as his family home. Unfortunately, his wife hated the property and therefore the husband had to sell it. HMRC sought to argue that because the house had been held for such a short time (and planning permission was also obtained on the land) this must be a trading transaction but the courts determined that because of the intention of the husband to live in the house rather than to make a quick profit, this was not a trading transaction.

(iv) *Trevor Anthony Hartland* [2014] UKFTT 1099 (TC). Although the case concerned only two properties, the taxpayer made successive purchases of residencies followed by their substantial redevelopment, in some cases extending to demolition and replacement, and then immediate or almost immediate sale. He claimed private residence relief on the properties. The First-tier Tribunal had to decide whether what the taxpayer did was '[make] improvements to his home before selling it and moving on to repeat the exercise, on the one hand, or . . . setting out to earn a living by buying run-down houses, or at least houses with development potential, then improving, extending or rebuilding them, in order to make a profit to be utilised in the next venture'. After examining the taxpayer's mortgage applications and noting that he had described himself as a builder (when he ran a plant hire business), and his declared income was far greater than that shown in the accounts of his plant-hire business, the Tribunal held that one of the two properties could be considered the taxpayer's principal private residence, even though extensive work had been carried out on it before sale, but the other had been bought, demolished, rebuilt and sold in the course of a trade of property development.

VAT-planning strategies for trapped stock

Outline

[21.23] When property developers find that they have developed property but are then unable to sell it as a result of market conditions, then in addition to the considerations noted above with regard to whether the stock might fail to be moved to being regarded as an investment, the VAT position for that stock must also be considered. This is because the VAT status for the developer in terms of whether or not the developer can recover the VAT on his costs will be dependent upon the developer's intentions for the use of that property – if those intentions change then difficulties in recovering (or keeping it if already recovered previously) the VAT incurred on costs can ensue.

With this in mind, it is helpful first to outline the categories of likely property transaction as follows.

Non-new residential property (sale after first major grant has been made)

[21.24] For the property developer selling a residential property which is not newly built, the sale will normally be exempt from VAT – meaning that the developer will not charge any VAT on the sale of the building but will not be able to recover any of the VAT on the costs. Although of course for a large majority of residential-property sales, the vendor will be a private individual anyway and hence unable to charge or recover tax.

On the basis that the developer would have expected to make an exempt supply of non-new residential property anyway, to have a change of plan and then rent the properties (still an exempt supply) would be unlikely to require any particular VAT planning.

New-build residential property

[21.25] For the property developer selling a newly built residential property, the sale of the property will be zero-rated for VAT purposes. Thus, the developer who has sold the property will not charge any VAT on the sale and will be in a position to reclaim back the VAT incurred on the building costs (with a few specific exceptions). Note that 'new' in this context means that the transaction constitutes the first grant of a major interest in that property by the person who has constructed it.

However, if the new residential property is then let by the developer rather than being sold, such letting will be VAT-exempt, rather than zero-rated. The making of such an exempt supply by the developer will restrict the VAT recovery to which the developer is entitled on the costs incurred in relation to that property. It is this restriction that means that developers will want to look to improve their VAT position through appropriate planning.

It is worth noting that grants of a major interest in a building can only be zero-rated if the grant is made by the 'person constructing' the building. This must be the party directly involved in the construction process (ie the party must either carry out the work or commission someone else to do the work on his behalf). At any time, more than one person can hold 'person constructing' status. However, it is rare that more than one person will have the right to grant the major interest in the building. It is worth noting here that there can be a trap for parties who would be regarded as holding 'person constructing' status but who then change their legal status (eg a sole trader who incorporates); in this case the new legal entity will not itself be the party who constructed the building and thus cannot have 'person constructing' status. Also for VAT groups, while normally one would consider the VAT group as a whole, if a company within a VAT group is a 'person constructing' a building then zero-rating can only apply to the grant of a major interest in the building to a person outside the VAT group when *that* company makes the grant.

Another point of interest is that while zero-rating applies only to the first grant of a major interest, it is possible that a supply of the property might be made between the completion of the construction and the grant of the first major interest (eg a short-term let). This does not necessarily prevent the first grant of the major interest from being zero-rated, although the developer would then need to consider the partial-exemption implications as his letting of the property would be exempt.

The first grant by a person converting a non-residential building or a non-residential part of a building into a building designed as a dwelling or number of dwellings or a building intended for use solely for a relevant residential purpose, of a major interest in, or in any part of, the building, dwelling or its site will also qualify for zero-rating. The same considerations apply here with regard to the definition of a 'first grant of a major interest'. Likewise, the same considerations with regard to the status of the 'person constructing' apply to the definition of the 'person converting'.

Note in particular that while this zero-rating applies to conversions of buildings to dwelling(s) or buildings intended to be used solely for relevant residential purposes, it does not apply to conversion of a building intended for charitable use. 'Non-residential' for this purpose is regarded broadly as being anything that is neither designed nor adapted for use as a dwelling or for a relevant residential purpose. However, a building that was previously a dwelling or used for relevant residential purpose will still fall within the definition of 'non-residential' if it has not been used as a dwelling or number of dwellings or for a relevant residential purpose for at least ten years (and it has been constructed for at least ten years).

Grants of a major interest in converted buildings that contain a part that was previously residential are *not* normally zero-rated, unless the qualifying accommodation is contained entirely within a part of the building that was previously non-residential, in which case zero-rating is limited to that part. There is no provision for such grants to be apportioned.

Protected buildings

[21.26] A person who has 'substantially reconstructed' a protected building may zero-rate the first grant of a major interest in that building, or any part of it. A protected building in this context is defined by VATA 1994, Sch 8, Group 6, Note 1 and, broadly, is one that is a listed building. 'Substantially reconstructed' in this context is defined by VATA 1994, Sch 8, Group 6, Note 4. A building is not substantially reconstructed unless, when the reconstruction is completed, the reconstructed building incorporates no more of the original building than the external walls together with other external features of architectural or historic interest. The old rule, under which substantial reconstruction could also amount to a situation where at least three-fifths of the cost of the reconstruction of the building (excluding services of architects, surveyors, consultants, etc) would qualify as approved alterations/building materials incorporated as part of those approved alterations, has now been entirely phased out (the transitional period ended on 30 September 2015).

Accordingly, as for the new-build residential property, where it is crucial to make that 'first grant of a major interest' to achieve zero rating of the sale for VAT purposes, for a developer substantially reconstructing a protected building, if that building is then let rather than sold (or a long lease granted) then the developer will find that he has made an exempt supply of the protected building (the letting) and therefore face a restriction on his ability to recover his VAT in full.

Commercial property

[21.27] In terms of purchases of commercial property, the first question is whether the commercial property is regarded as 'new'. A 'new' building for this purpose is any building less than three years old, starting from the earlier of the time at which the building is completed and when it is fully occupied. Whether or not a building is completed is determined using the date on which the certificate of practical completion is issued.

The sale of new and of partly completed commercial buildings and civil engineering works are specifically excluded from the exemption from VAT (ie they are automatically standard-rated). Note that it is only the sale that is excluded from the exemption, not any other category of supply (eg leasing/letting for any length of time would still be exempt, subject to the option to tax).

When a sale takes place of freehold land that has on it new or partly completed civil-engineering works, it is necessary to consider whether the principal supply is the supply of land (which would be exempt) or the supply of the works (which would be standard-rated). This will be a question of fact depending upon the circumstances.

Otherwise, subject to a few exceptions, the sale of commercial property is exempt from VAT, unless the vendor has elected to waive the VAT exemption (opted to tax), in which case it will again be standard-rated.

For commercial property, therefore, if there is a period when the property is let, prior to its being sold, then the solution to ensuring that VAT recovery on the development costs for the property is not restricted would normally be for the developer to opt to tax the property. Thus, the letting of the property would then be standard-rated rather than exempt and accordingly there would be no restriction on the developer's ability to recover VAT. However, opting to tax will also mean that VAT is due on the subsequent sale, which would increase the SDLT or LBTT charge for the onward purchaser, unless the sale qualifies as a transfer of a business (or part-business) for VAT purposes (see CHAPTER 15).

Opting to tax

[21.28] Opting to tax is a key element in property-tax planning. As its title implies, it enables a taxpayer to convert an otherwise exempt supply to one taxable at the standard rate. Essentially, it would be exercised in order to recover VAT on all the related costs. An option to tax may be exercised over specific commercial property and land – it cannot be made over residential property, or indeed certain other property categories including 'relevant residential' properties and properties used for 'relevant charitable' purposes. Its full scope, including all the pitfalls and relevant anti-avoidance legislation, is explained in detail at CHAPTER 15 at **15.64**.

Suffice it to say here that the option to tax should never be exercised lightly, as it is generally irrevocable for 20 years, though there is a 'cooling-off' period. When and how it is exercised and by whom is absolutely important – getting it wrong or late can be costly. In some cases, prior permission from HMRC may be needed before it can be exercised – broadly HMRC need to be convinced that there is no avoidance or unfair advantage afoot. Opting to tax any property may also make it less attractive to a purchaser who is unable to recover in full any VAT charged as a consequence on the selling price or lease payments. It is as much a commercial consideration as a tax-planning tool.

Restriction of the right to recover

[21.29] HMRC's views on what should happen when a house developer lets a dwelling prior to its sale are set out in VAT Information Sheet 07/08, September 2008. Some useful aspects of this information sheet are discussed below.

Partial exemption de minimis

[21.30] Of course restriction on VAT recovery applies to a business only if the 'exempt' input VAT is over the *de minimis* threshold. However, as described below, HMRC will accept a simplified version of the *de minimis* test for this purpose:

Extract from VAT Information Sheet 07/08

> How does a house builder know if he can treat input tax incurred in past years as de minimis?

> Like any business, a house builder checks for de minimis by applying his partial exemption method. Large builders may already be partly exempt and familiar with

operating a partial exemption method, but smaller ones may not. Exceptionally, HMRC will allow a builder that does not currently operate a partial exemption method, to adopt instead a 'simple check for de minimis'. This simple check is based on the expected time period he will let his building as a proportion of the economic life of that building, which for VAT purposes is ten years. His exempt input tax is determined by applying the proportion to his total input tax. Provided his exempt input tax does not exceed £625 per month on average (up to £7,500 per year), and is not more than half of his total input tax, then his exempt input tax is de minimis and he can recover it in full. Do remember that the 'de minimis' test applies to the total input tax incurred including for example any input tax on general overheads such as bookkeeping costs.

Example: Simple check for de minimis

A fully taxable house builder recovered £20,000 input tax on a house that he expected to sell for £300,000. After the end of the tax year he decides to defer the sale by letting for two years and so becomes partly exempt. A simple check for de minimis is:

£20,000 input tax x 2 year lease/10 year economic life = £4,000 exempt input tax
The £4,000 of exempt input tax is de minimis because over the tax year it does not exceed £7,500 or 50 per cent of his total input tax. The builder has no need to adjust the VAT previously recovered on his VAT returns. If the input tax was incurred over more than one tax year, the de minimis test should be applied to the input tax incurred in each of the tax years separately.

Clawback

[21.31] Unless the exempt input tax is below the *de minimis* threshold, the exempt letting of a property that was initially intended to be sold does, in the view of HMRC, trigger a clawback charge (ie as the input VAT would initially have been reclaimed in full on the basis that the developer expects to make a zero-rated sale of the property, now that the intention has changed and the property will in part be put to an exempt use, part of the input VAT initially recovered must now be paid back to HMRC). It is worth here reproducing the extract from the HMRC information sheet on this point:

Extract from VAT Information Sheet 07/08

3. Adjusting previously recovered input tax Introduction to input tax adjustments

When a business changes its plans for making a taxable supply, by forming a new intention to make an exempt supply and then a taxable supply sometime later, it may have to reduce the amount of input tax that it had originally recovered. This is known as a clawback adjustment and was the subject of the High Court decision in Curtis Henderson. Remember a business does not make a clawback adjustment if it satisfies the test for de minimis.

Curtis Henderson

A business claimed input tax on its costs of building a house that it planned to sell.

However, it was unable to sell as originally intended and so granted a short-term lease until the house could be sold. The question was whether a clawback adjustment was required for the input tax already recovered, and if so, how the adjustment should be calculated. The High Court agreed with the Tribunal's decision that a clawback adjustment was needed to apportion the input tax to take account of the business's taxable and exempt intentions for the property at the time it was first used. In other words, the business had to adjust its input tax to reflect the fact that it was let before it was finally sold. This meant that the business had to repay some (but certainly not all) of the input tax previously recovered.

Making a clawback adjustment

A house builder makes a clawback adjustment as soon as his actual or intended use of a property differs from his original plans against which input tax was recovered.

For example, a house builder who defers his planned sale of a property by undertaking a period of letting would make a clawback adjustment as soon as his original plans are changed. A clawback adjustment is a one-off event and a house builder would only make a second adjustment if the building was never let. There is no need to amend the adjustment if the actual period of letting proved to be longer or shorter than anticipated.

Judging intention

A clawback adjustment must be based on the house builder's realistic expectation, judged at the time his original plans were set aside. HMRC may ask for evidence to show that the adjustment calculation is reasonable. Evidence might include:

- the business plan showing the price originally expected; reports of estate agents showing this price to be unobtainable and maybe estimating when a sale will be achievable;
- board minutes from the time of the decision to grant short leases;
- or any other commercial documentation that backs up the estimated use.

Calculating a clawback adjustment

The house builder calculates his clawback adjustment by comparing the amount of input tax deducted with the amount of input tax he would have deducted had he held his changed intention all along. His clawback adjustment is simply the difference between the two input tax amounts.

The house builder calculates the amount of input tax he would have deducted by applying his partial exemption method at the time the costs were incurred. A large house builder is likely to be already operating a partial exemption method, but a small house builder may not. If a house builder was not already operating a partial exemption method then he must apply the standard method unless he obtains HMRC approval to apply a special method instead.

Alternative bases of calculating a clawback adjustment

A house builder that does not currently operate a partial exemption method, can exceptionally if he prefers, base his clawback adjustment on an alternative calculation (without first adopting a partial exemption method and without prior approval from HMRC) so long as that calculation is fair. HMRC can allow this under their care and management powers.

HMRC will accept any clawback calculation provided it fairly reflects the use of costs in making taxable supplies. A calculation based on the values of supplies is normally fair and straightforward provided it is based on reasonable estimates and valuations:

Estimated eventual sale value

Estimated eventual sale value plus estimated short let premiums and rents

Example: house builder preparing a clawback adjustment using values

A house builder expects to sell two houses for £500,000 each. The input tax recovered during the tax year was £50,000. After the end of the tax year the decision is taken to rent them for a period of three years generating estimated rental income of £200,000. The house builder makes no other supplies.

£50,000 input tax incurred x £1,000,000/£1,200,000 = £41,667 recoverable input tax

£50,000 input tax previously recovered — £41,666 = £8,334 to be repaid to HMRC

No adjustment should be made for potential bad debts during the letting period. If it is not possible to fairly estimate the values then a different calculation may be needed.

Apportionments based on the expected time period of the rental or short-term lease are not recommended except as a quick de minimis check.

Other points to note

The alternative calculations cannot be used if a partial exemption method was already in place. But, if an existing partial exemption method becomes unfair because of the short-term lets, then HMRC may exceptionally allow an alternative method to be agreed and backdated. House builders in this position should contact HMRC

HMRC's practice, as explained above, is to assume a useful life for the property of just ten years. They 'strongly discourage' taxpayers from using an alternative assumed useful life due to the difficulties of finding objective evidence on what this might be. This does, however, seem to be an assumption that taxpayers would/could readily attack.

As a practical point, however, the well-advised taxpayer will often avoid having to enter into arguments as to whether there should be any clawback at all; instead, as further discussed below, one would normally crystallise a disposal of the property, thus securing the zero rating (and full VAT recovery).

Securing zero-rating

[21.32] A common strategy for dealing with the situation where there may be a VAT clawback as a result of making an exempt rental supply of a new-build residential property (or similar), rather than making a zero-rated sale, is in effect to engineer a sale of the zero-rated property.

In a situation where the developer is a corporate entity, that entity might be advised to form a subsidiary, to which it sells the properties. That subsidiary would be a separately VAT-registered company. The sale of the new-build residential property to that subsidiary would therefore crystallise a zero-rated disposal. The subsidiary would then make exempt rental supplies of the property (and would in due course make an exempt sale of the same).

Of course, however, we must consider not just the VAT aspects to such a planning strategy, but also the corporation tax and SDLT/LBTT aspects.

For corporation tax purposes, we would have an intra-group transaction. Depending upon the size of the companies involved, and assuming that the property is treated as trading stock rather than an investment asset, potentially the transaction may be subject to the transfer-pricing regime (requiring the disposal to be at market value).

The transfer-pricing provisions do not normally apply to a company that is a small or medium-sized enterprise. Such companies are as defined in the Annex to the Commission Recommendation *2003/361/EC* of 6 May 2003 with the modifications set out in TIOPA 2010, s 172. Broadly, a small enterprise is defined as a business with fewer than 50 employees and either turnover or assets of less than EUR 10 million and a small or medium-sized enterprise as a business with fewer than 250 employees and either turnover of less than EUR 50 million or assets of less than EUR 43 million. Associated enterprises are taken into account in determining whether a company is a small or medium-sized enterprise.

The exemption will not apply where:

(a)   a small or medium-sized enterprise elects for the exemption not to apply; such an election is irrevocable;

(b)   at the time the actual provision was made or imposed, the other affected person or a 'party to the relevant transaction' is resident and liable to tax in a 'non-qualifying territory' (whether or not also resident in a 'qualifying territory');

(c)   as respects any provision made or imposed, HMRC gives notice (a *'transfer pricing notice'*) to a small or medium-sized enterprise, which is the advantaged party, requiring that company to increase profits or reduce losses of that chargeable period on an arm's length basis.

Where a medium-sized company is not excepted from exemption under (a) or (b) above, there is no need for the company's tax return to take account of the transfer-pricing rules. However, this does not prevent the company's tax return from becoming incorrect if a transfer-pricing notice is issued and the return is not amended within the period of 90 days as noted above when it should have been amended.

Even if the transaction must occur at market value, there is still a good chance that any corporation tax charge that would be triggered as a result would be outweighed by the VAT saving, although of course the detailed calculations must always be done here, to be sure.

A word of warning, though, that if the subsidiary then decides to hold the property long term, this may trigger a move of the property from stock to investment, with the resultant tax charge described above. Accordingly, it will be important for the subsidiary to continue to regard the property as available for sale and justifiably as stock.

For SDLT or LBTT purposes, one would normally seek to take advantage of the respective group-relief provisions to prevent an SDLT/LBTT charge.

If the property is owned by an individual developer, then making any sale of the property to crystallise zero-rating may be more difficult, as to do so would potentially also crystallise an income tax charge on any profit made on the property. However, depending upon the figures involved and also whether the parties involved will be below the transfer-pricing threshold, potentially it may still be worth crystallising a sale.

Self-builds

Introduction

[21.33] In the property boom prior to the credit crunch/recession, and now following it in the last few years, it became quite common for individuals to look to get into the property game and look to, say, sell off a chunk of a large garden/grounds area adjacent to their house, or perhaps even speculatively acquire a small area of land to develop into housing. Commonly in such situations, the individuals would look to have the transaction regarded as within the capital gains tax regime (ie a one off development/land held as investment that they then decide to develop) and if possible to claim the benefit of the principal private residence exemption (when selling off land within their garden).

However, when the recession hit, many such individuals were left with properties that they were unable to sell. In such situations, in addition to considering whether the properties might be let (see **21.23** 'VAT Planning Strategies for trapped properties', above), the individual may decide that it is better to move into the property to use it as the individual's principal private residence for the time being. Thus, we would need to consider the income/capital gains tax effects of such a decision, as well as the VAT effects.

Availability of PPR

[21.34] In a situation where an individual intends from the outset to purchase land on which to build his principal private residence ('PPR'), inevitably the construction of the residence will take some time and it is unlikely that the individual will be able to live in the building throughout that time, particularly in its early stages of construction.

Accordingly, in these circumstances, there is likely to be a period of time between the first acquisition of the property and the time at which the house built thereon can become the individual's PPR, during which the land (and any property thereon) does not strictly qualify for PPR relief. This could of course cause a portion of the later gain on a sale of the property to be chargeable to CGT. Fortunately, this position is relieved by ESC D49. This concession provides that where an individual acquires land on which he has a house built, which he then uses as his only or main residence, the period before the individual uses the house as his only or main residence will be treated as a period in which he is deemed to have lived in it for the purposes of calculating PPR relief. This is provided, however, that the period is no longer than one year. In normal circumstances, one would expect a grace period of a year to be sufficient time to build a property. However, if the construction period exceeds a year and the individual cannot occupy the property as his PPR within a year then, provided there are good reasons for this delay and they are outside the individual's control, HMRC will extend the period allowed up to a maximum of two years.

Interestingly, the wording of D49 does not explicitly require the owner-occupier always to know from the start that the house being built will be his

PPR, although one might question whether this is implicit from the concession (and of course there is anyway the overriding point that concessions may not be used for any sort of abusive purpose). However, in circumstances where it may become apparent to the individual at an early stage that it will make financial sense for him to go and live in the property (and perhaps look to sell the former, perhaps smaller home), one might keep the possible use of this concession in mind.

Individuals building their own home will, however, also need to be very conscious of the point that the construction is not wholly or partly for the purpose of realising a gain from a later disposal of the property, as otherwise the availability of PPR relief will be denied under TCGA 1992, s 224(3) and any profit might be taxed as trading income.

Trading v capital

[21.35] Remember, of course, that in times of rising house prices, most individuals developing houses would, if they could, want to argue that the development was within the capital gains tax regime, rather than being a trading transaction. However, in times of recession, particularly where a loss is made, this argument reverses and in fact a trading loss would be preferable.

Times of recession can also mean that in fact an individual may prefer not to have the availability of the PPR exemption, because its effect is to exempt any capital gain on one's PPR, as well as to disregard any loss. This could mean that individuals owning multiple properties may want their cheaper house/one less susceptible to any decrease in value, to be the property subject to the PPR election.

As noted at CHAPTER 2, where individuals put themselves in a position of regularly buying a residence and then disposing of it at a profit, the question must be raised as to whether the PPR disapplication provisions of TCGA 1992, s 224(3) arise and, furthermore, whether in fact the individual is not within the CGT regime at all but might be regarded as trading.

With regard to the disapplication provisions of s 224(3), the question is why that individual is undertaking these transactions; if it is in order to have a property as a place to live, rather than to realise a gain from the property then the disapplication provision should not apply (after all, generally speaking at this point in time most individuals hope that their property will increase in value such that they realise a gain on a later sale of the property, but this is not the reason they buy the property – they buy it because they need somewhere to live).

In principle, if it is clear from the start that the only reason an individual purchased a property is to develop and sell it then the disapplication provisions apply. It perhaps remains hard to distinguish that situation from the fact that in the meantime the individual would require a place to live. The overall facts of the case will therefore need to be considered in quite some detail (see (a) and (b) below).

(a) Does the individual have anywhere else to live in the meantime (if the individual already has another residence and wishes by election to claim as a residence a property on which what might be regarded as a planning gain is expected, then the disapplication provisions are far more likely to apply).

(b) The individual's background may be relevant – for example, if someone in the building or construction trade were to undertake such a transaction it might be more likely that HMRC would argue that the individual did so for the purposes of realising a gain, more so than an individual who already has a full-time job completely separate from that industry, who just so happens to decide after purchasing the property that an opportunity exists to somehow alter that property/sell a part of it and realise a gain as a result of doing so. An individual who has no occupation other than working on the property is clearly most at risk.

Any correspondence at the time of the purchase and subsequently may be key in arguing these points, either way. For example, if and when an individual purchases a property, if all the correspondence with the solicitor and estate agent indicates specifically that the individual wishes to use that property as the principal residence then there is likely to be good evidence that that was the individual's intention, rather than to use the property to make a gain. If on the other hand there is evidence that even when contemplating the original purchase the individual wished to look to see whether planning permission could be granted straight away to change the property or create new properties thereon with a view to selling these, then such evidence might favour disapplication of the PPR exemption.

As always there are likely to be exceptions. For example, an individual may wish to acquire a property and build a granny annex thereon for parents to live in, but this will be done for internal family reasons rather than any desire to use that property to create a gain.

The tests to consider whether an individual is regarded as being within the capital gains tax regime or regarded as trading, are really the same as discussed at **CHAPTER 2** and include in particular consideration of the 'badges of trade'. With regard to the specific application of these principles to a residential property it should be noted that it may arguably be more difficult for HMRC to argue successfully that a transaction involving an individual's PPR undertaken on a one-off basis is a trading transaction.

For example, if a builder who has a full-time job elsewhere decides to undertake some works on his existing house and then sells this at a gain, the builder can argue that he has done this very much as a 'hobby' or because he simply wished to improve his own residence to make it a nicer place to live. If he subsequently decided to sell it, then it would be harder for HMRC to suggest that such arrangements were trading arrangements. However, if a builder then falls into a more regular pattern of buying a property, renovating and selling it – in particular if he does not have a full-time job elsewhere – then he will be more likely to be regarded as trading. Of course, there are all shades of grey in between and there is no hard-and-fast rule as to how many times a builder would have to undertake such a transaction before crossing the line from capital into trading. However, advisers need to be cautious in this area and consider the merits of, for example, disclosure on the tax return.

VAT

[21.36] An individual developing property may already have registered for VAT, in anticipation of making a zero-rated sale of that property. However, if he then decides to use the property for himself, then consideration must be given as to how that individual's VAT status then unravels.

Potentially, HMRC might take the view that there is then a change of intention for the use of the property and accordingly the 'clawback' provisions apply, as discussed above. Thus, all of the VAT that might previously have been recovered in relation to the development is then repaid to HMRC. This is generally the preferred view.

An alternative view that HMRC might take would be that perhaps the trader in fact never did really intend to trade. This would result in a retrospective clawback of the VAT and de-registration, and potentially – depending upon the circumstances – HMRC might start to suggest penalties for the incorrect VAT registration. If the trader's initial intention was genuine, therefore, then this would need to be carefully evidenced.

A further alternative view might be that the rules for private use of the property apply, such that there may be a deemed supply of the property. Potentially this could result in a standard-rated supply and therefore one would normally want to resist such a view, as it would give such an unfair result.

While, one way or another, the VAT on costs reclaimed through the VAT-registration mechanism would be clawed back, the next question is as to whether there is any other mechanism to allow the individual to still recover any VAT. This is where the DIY builders scheme may be useful.

The refund scheme for DIY builders essentially exists to put such persons in the same position as a developer able to sell a zero-rated property. Of course, the sale of new-build residential property, plus certain other conversions or substantial reconstructions of listed buildings are zero-rated for VAT, which means that the vendor does not need to charge any VAT on the sale but yet they are able to reclaim the VAT on their costs (subject to certain exceptions, blocked items and so forth). Thus, if individuals wish to build their own house, then potentially they could be at a disadvantage to a developer in terms of being able to recover the VAT on their costs without having to account for any output VAT. The refund scheme, therefore, enables such DIY builders to make a reclaim of VAT that, broadly, a developer in a similar position would have been able to reclaim.

The DIY refund scheme is available only in respect of a new-build or a conversion in a private capacity. Developers, landlords, bed-and-breakfast operators, or other business entities (including membership clubs and associations and care-home operators who make a charge to their residents) will not be able to use the scheme. The work in respect of which a refund is claimed does not, however, have to be undertaken by the individual making the claim, but can be subcontracted out to external builders.

When looking at what VAT may be reclaimed, it will be important to bear in mind that only validly charged VAT may be reclaimed. Thus, for example, where a subcontractor makes a supply in the course of the construction of a new dwelling then his supply will be zero-rated under VATA 1994, Sch 8, Group 5. Similarly, any goods that such a building contractor supplies with his supply of services which are incorporated into the building in question will be zero-rated (provided these fall within the specific definition of building materials). Thus, a DIY builder who subcontracts out much of the work on a new-build construction will in fact probably not expect to make a large reclaim under the scheme, as the services provided to him by his main subcontractor will be zero-rated anyway. If such a DIY builder were charged VAT by a contractor in this situation who should have zero-rated the supply, then the VAT charged will not be recoverable under the scheme but instead the DIY builder would have to go back to the contractor to request a credit note against the VAT charged. However, to the extent that the DIY builder purchases eligible goods (ie those within the definition of 'building materials') the reclaim will be possible providing the construction itself also qualifies.

The conversion of a non-residential building into a qualifying dwelling or relevant residential property will also generate the potential for a VAT reclaim under the scheme (again on the principle that the supply of a newly-converted property would be zero-rated if supplied by a developer). A non-residential conversion in this context must be in respect of a building (or part thereof) that has never been used as a dwelling or number of dwellings, or for a relevant residential purpose; it can also be in respect of a building for which, in the ten years immediately before the start of the work, the building (or part thereof) has not been used as dwelling or number of dwellings or for a relevant residential purpose. Note here that the ten-year rule runs up to the time at which the work commences, not up to the time at which the individual undertaking the DIY build moves in. Thus, the individual may be able to live in the building whilst the work is going on, provided that he moves in after the commencement of the work. Illegal occupation of the building in the last ten years can be ignored as can any view that it is not therefore residential in nature. Other than that, even occasional use of the property as a residential property will mean that it does not qualify under the ten-year rule.

Note also that the ability to make a claim under the scheme is slightly less generous than the zero-rating provisions in respect of a conversion of a non-residential building into a residential building. Under the DIY scheme, where a building has been used in part as a residential building and in part as a non-residential building, such that the conversion will use a mixture of residential and non-residential parts of the building, the refund scheme will not apply.

Note also that the services of a contractor for converting a non-residential building into a residential building may not be zero-rated (unlike the situation where a contractor constructs a new-build residential property). Therefore, under the DIY refund scheme for property conversions, a refund will be available under the scheme in respect of both services of contractors as well as building materials. However, VAT will never be reclaimable on fees for professionals who provide advisory services or for the hire of plant, tools and equipment.

A claim under the DIY builders scheme is a one-off claim that should be made no more than three months after the construction or conversion of the building is completed. If there is any reason why the three-month deadline cannot be adhered to then the individual doing the conversion will be well advised to write to HMRC to explain the situation and request an extension. Normally, the date of completion for these purposes will be by reference to the certificate of completion issued by the local planning authority. The claim should be made on form VAT 431NB (for a new-build) or form VAT 431C (for a conversion), which can be downloaded from the HMRC website. Refunds will normally be made within 30 working days of receipt by HMRC, unless there are any particular queries in relation thereto.

Gifts and inheritance tax planning

Outline

[21.37] The low property values created by a recession can also represent a very useful opportunity for inheritance tax planning.

For individuals with large property investment portfolios in their estate, unless these qualify for APR or BPR (unlikely for most portfolios), then potentially the portfolio is harbouring a very large inheritance tax charge that will crystallise upon the death of the owner. Of course, this may be deferred by leaving the assets to one's spouse but even then one is only deferring the time at which an inheritance tax charge may arise. To avoid an inheritance tax charge, unless one is prepared to change one's investment strategy to invest in assets that qualify for inheritance tax reliefs, generally one will wish to consider gifting one's assets down to the next generation, or into a trust. To do so at a time when asset values are low is therefore clearly useful.

To this end, it is appropriate to consider the availability of gift relief.

Gift of Business Assets Relief

Outline

[21.38] The charge to capital gains tax arising on a gift of business assets may be deferred by way of a 'hold-over' claim under TCGA 1992, s 165. The effect of a claim under s 165 is that the gain arising on the disposal of the asset is then 'held over' into the value of the new asset by reducing the deemed base cost of that new asset (bearing in mind that most gifts of assets would be deemed to occur at market value for capital gains tax purposes). Thus, on a later sale of the new asset, effectively a larger charge arises as the base cost attributable to that asset is lower than it would otherwise be.

This does mean that potentially downsides can exist to the use of a s 165 claim. For example, if an individual disposed of a business asset prior to 6 April 2008 (when the taper relief regime could have meant that an effective rate of capital gains tax of 10% could have applied) and held over the gain, and then disposed of the new asset now, paying tax at the higher rate of capital gains tax (28%) then clearly it would have been a disadvantage in terms of applicable tax rates to make the s 165 claim. However, the point of this relief is that generally speaking on a gift of assets, the money may not be available to pay the tax at the time the asset is gifted, plus in any event the availability of this hold-over relief means that the tax liability can be deferred, and tax deferred for a long period is clearly beneficial in cash-flow terms.

However, this relief applies only on the disposal of assets that can qualify as business assets and therefore not all property disposals will be able to qualify. The specific definition as to what business assets can qualify is given in s 165(2), namely:

(a)   assets used in a trade, profession or vocation carried on by:
    (1)   the transferor;
    (2)   the transferor's personal company;
    (3)   a company belonging to the trading group of which the transferor's personal company is the holding company; or
    (4)   in the case of a transfer by trustees, the trustees themselves or a beneficiary who has an interest in possession in the trust property;
(b)   agricultural property which would qualify for inheritance tax relief;
(c)   shares or securities in trading companies or holding companies of trading groups where:
    (1)   the shares or securities are not listed on a recognised stock exchange (shares or securities dealt in on the Alternative Investment Market are not listed for these purposes); or
    (2)   if the transferor is an individual, the company is his personal company; or
    (3)   if the transferor is a trustee, the shares or securities are similarly unlisted or the trustee can exercise 25% or more of the voting rights.

Thus, the relief could be used for property used in the business of the owner, but for property used/let as an investment property, the relief is unlikely to be available.

Note, though, that properties qualifying as furnished holiday accommodation (FHLs) can be regarded as business assets for the purposes of the application of TCGA 1992, s 165. In the event, therefore, that a FHL is gifted to another party, any gain arising thereon may be held over. Thus, for example, if parents have an FHL that they wish to gift to their adult child to carry out an FHL business, while in principle the gift would be deemed to take place at market value (and thus a market-value acquisition cost by the child), if a claim under s 165 is made the parent's capital gain is not immediately charged to CGT but the base cost that the child acquires will be reduced by the amount of the gain that has been held over.

It should be noted that a gift of premises let to the transferor's personal company or a member of a trading group of which the holding company is the transferor's personal company may qualify for hold-over relief under TCGA 1992, s 165. It is important to show that the premises are utilised in the trade.

Inheritance tax planning and gifts of business premises

[21.39] The owner of a business premises used by a family trading company may contemplate passing the business premises on to the next generation in order to mitigate longer-term inheritance tax liabilities. It will be realised that where the premises are not held within the business itself or within the trading company, full IHT business property relief (BPR) will not be available on their underlying value. For example, premises let to a partnership in which the owner is a partner will only qualify for 50% relief. Similar considerations apply when a property is let to an unquoted trading company and here no business property relief will apply at all unless the company is controlled by the owner of the premises (and spouse and any subsequent related property).

If IHT planning is a major concern, consideration might be given to injecting the premises into the partnership or trading company in order perhaps to obtain full IHT BPR. In the case of a partnership, this process might be accomplished free of SDLT to the extent that the owners of the premises are partners. However, a full SDLT charge is likely to arise on a transfer of premises into a trading company (note the deemed market-value provisions). Nevertheless, the gift of premises should be achieved free of capital gains tax.

Where a transfer to a company is being contemplated, perhaps where the owner has limited life expectancy, the premises could be injected in exchange for an issue of shares. However, a capital gains liability might arise unless the donor owned 5% of the company to which the premises are let.

Lifetime gifts of business premises might well be contemplated but care will need to be taken that any gift taken does not give rise to capital gains liabilities. Although gifts to most trusts constitute chargeable transfers for IHT purposes and should qualify for CGT deferral relief, the ability to make such transfers free of IHT is limited to the nil-rate band (currently £325,000) unless the assets qualify for BPR or APR reducing their value for IHT purposes.

Consideration might be given to selling assets at an undervalue to a trust such that the gift element falls within the nil-rate band. It may also be appropriate to transfer assets intra-spouse prior to the setting up of trusts in order to utilise both spouses' nil-rate bands.

Chapter 22

ATED on 'non-natural persons' and ATED-related CGT

by
Patrick Cannon,
Barrister

Introduction and summary

[22.1] An interest in a single dwelling with a value of more than £500,000 (reduced from £1m from 1 April 2016) held by a company, a partnership whose members include a company, or a collective investment scheme ('non-natural persons') is subject to the annual tax on enveloped dwellings or 'ATED'. ATED is charged for a chargeable period (1 April to the following 31 March) if the chargeable interest is held by the non-natural person on one or more days in that period. However the charge is pro-rated and only charged for the actual days in the period on which the owner is within the charge (FA 2013, ss 94(8), 99(3), 105). ATED is charged according to the following rate table for 2017/18:

Property value:	£0.5m–£1m	£1–2m	£2–5m	£5–10m	£10–20m	£20m+
Annual chargeable amount:	£3,500	£7,050	£23,530	£54,950	£110,100	£220,350

(FA 2013, s 101).

The amount of these charges (but not the value bands) is increased each year in line with the consumer price index. It is worth noting that the effect of the ATED lessens the larger the value of the property concerned. From 1 April 2015 properties valued at more than £1m but not more than £2m were brought within the scope of ATED with an annual charge of £7,000 and since 1 April 2016 ATED has been extended to properties valued at more than £500,000 but not more than £1m with a charge of £3,500 (FA 2014, ss 109 and 110).

The ATED was part of a package of measures which were intended to attack the holding of high value residential property in vehicles which allow either an interest in the property or the vehicle itself to be sold on free of SDLT (and usually stamp duty as well). Hence since 21 March 2012 there has been the 15% higher rate of SDLT on 'high value residential transactions' involving non-natural persons. There is also a capital gains charge of 28% on disposals of residential property owned by non-natural persons which are within ATED, which was introduced from 6 April 2013. This means that all such non-natural persons whether resident in the UK or not who are within the scope and ATED will be subject to capital gains tax: TCGA 1992, ss 2B–2F, 57A and Sch 4ZZA (see **22.12** below).

The holding of high-value residential property in vehicles is referred to pejoratively by HMRC as 'enveloping' but this term overlooks the many bona fide reasons why property may be owned other than directly by an individual (see **22.14** below). HMRC initially paid lip-service in the May 2012 consultation document to the bona-fide reasons why a property may have been 'enveloped' and said that the tax charges were aimed at situations where tax avoidance may be a significant factor. There has however been no explanation of why the 'enveloping' of non-residential property in order to save SDLT has received no attention. Indeed the availability of extensive reliefs from the ATED for commercial use seems to suggest that SDLT avoidance is more acceptable where business use is concerned. In principle it seems inconsistent to treat avoidance of SDLT on residential property differently from avoidance of SDLT on property with a commercial use. The answer may however be that HM Treasury came under considerable pressure from the commercial property lobby and felt it easier to give in rather than to uphold their own moral principle consistently. It is understood those officials involved in devising the ATED believed that few if anyone would pay it. This was not because they thought that people would find devious ways to avoid it but because they believed that people would 'de-envelope' and hold such properties in 'natural' forms in order not to have to pay the charge. This was partly because there would be no disposal proceeds with which to fund such a 'dry' charge. Evidence however suggests that 'de-enveloping' is less likely particularly given that a fairly wide range of reliefs is available (see below). Indeed the revenue receipts from ATED have exceeded all expectations and give the impression that revenue raising rather than anti-avoidance is the driving force for the charge.

Scope

[22.2] The ATED charge applies regardless of where the non-natural person is established or resident for tax purposes. The coverage of the ATED is largely the same as for the 15% higher rate of SDLT although the minimum threshold of more than £500,000 that has applied for the 15% higher rate charge since 20 March 2014 did not apply for ATED until 1 April 2016. The definition of 'dwelling' used for the ATED is similar to that used for the 15% higher rate except that any temporary unsuitability for use as a dwelling is expressly ignored for ATED purposes (FA 2013, s 112(6) in contrast with FA 2003, Sch 4A, para 7 and see below). However while a company owning land as the trustee of a settlement is excluded from the 15% rate, the ATED by contrast contains a wider trusts exemption and that tax does not apply where the entitlement to the single dwelling interest arises in the capacity of a trustee of a settlement, a personal representative or as a beneficiary under a settlement (FA 2003, Sch 4A, para 4(3) and FA 2013, s 95(2)). The implications of this difference in approach need to be understood in order to plan around the ATED where a trust is involved. Charitable companies also benefit from an exemption from ATED: FA 2013, s 151. There is also a range of reliefs in ATED that is similar though not identical to the 15% higher rate SDLT charge (see below). The ATED applies to freehold and leasehold interests and where there is both a freehold and leasehold interests in the same building owned by unconnected persons then both types of interest will need to be valued and the tax paid where appropriate. Where two or more interests in the same dwelling are held by connected persons, those interests are aggregated in order to decide whether the taxable value falls within a taxable band: FA 2013, s 110(1). Where the connected person is an individual and the value of the non-natural person's interest is not more than £250,000 then there is no aggregation of interest: FA 2013, s 110(2). Separately from this, where aggregation applies and the non-natural person would, as a result, have been treated as being entitled to an interest of more than £2m but the non-natural person's interest is worth not more than £500,000, then aggregation does not apply: FA 2013, s 110, s 110(2A) and (2B). Where a property moves into or out of the ATED during the year a daily pro-rata charge will apply. The first period of account started on 1 April 2013 and the ATED return will normally be due and the tax payable by 30 April in each year. For 2013/14 the first return was due by 1 October 2013 if the person was within ATED on 1 April 2013 or if not, by the end of 30 days beginning with the first day on which the person is within ATED, if later than 1 October 2013: FA 2013, Sch 35, para 4. The tax must have been paid by 31 October 2013 or if later, the end of the filing date for the return: FA 2013, Sch 35, para 5.

As a guide for 2014/15 and future years HMRC published the following table showing filing dates in the Stamp Taxes Bulletin 1/2014 which is reproduced here for ease of reference:

Return	Circumstances	Filing date
ATED return	Chargeable person is within ATED on the first day of a chargeable period	30 April falling in the chargeable period
	The acquisition of a single-dwelling interest	30 days after the date of acquisition/transaction
	The acquisition of a **newly constructed** single-dwelling interest or dwellings produced from other dwellings	90 days from the earliest date on which the dwelling is deemed to come into existence for Council Tax purposes or the day on which the dwelling is first occupied
Amendment of ATED return	Where a repayment is due or where certain information contained within the original return was incorrect	At any point within 12 months of the end of a chargeable period

Return	Circumstances	Filing date
	Note: taxpayer must tick the amended return box and, where appropriate, the repayment box on the ATED return	If the original return was filed on or after 1 January following the end of the chargeable period to which the amendment relates the filing date is 3 months from the date that return was filed
Return of adjusted amount (otherwise known as a further return)	Required where additional tax is due either:	
	an event occurs during the chargeable period which gives rise to an additional tax liability	30 days from the start of the next chargeable period, for example, 30 April
	an event occurs after the end of the chargeable period which gives rise to an additional tax liability	Within 30 days of the date on which the event occurred, which gave rise to that additional tax liability
	Note: taxpayer must tick the further return box on the ATED return	

Note: by FA 2013, s 159(3A) where a return would be due by 30 April in a period but a return is also required for the previous period by a date that is later than 30 April in the later period than the return for the later period is due at the same date as the return for the previous period.

A 'relief declaration return' can be filed with HMRC for a claim to a single type of relief in respect of one or more properties held for a chargeable period. No details, such as valuation, are required in such a return for the properties for which the relief is claimed. The intention is that non-natural persons owning properties that qualify for a relief only need to submit one return a year for all their properties covered by the particular relief instead of having to file multiple returns: FA 2013, s 159A.

The first valuation date was set as 1 April 2012 to enable valuations to be carried out before 1 April 2013. The ATED is based on the market value of the relevant property on the later of 1 April, the date of acquisition or the date of the creation or cessation of any relevant interest in the property which brings the value over the relevant threshold. The ATED is calculated on a daily basis as is any relevant relief for the days on which the relevant conditions were met.

An ATED return has to be completed which self-assesses the tax due based on the market value of the property at the relevant date. The penalty provisions in FA 2007, Sch 24 apply to ATED and a penalty can arise if the Valuation Office Agency ('VOA') later decide that the value has been significantly understated or if the non-natural owner of a property with a value in the region of the threshold for the tax has not taken care to establish whether the ATED arose or not. HMRC expect the taxpayer to have obtained at its own cost a professional valuation in order to have a chance of avoiding a penalty should the taxpayer's valuation later be challenged. The valuation will require a specific price and not just a range of reasonable values. This is something which valuers are often reluctant to do and presumably if valuers decline to do this the taxpayer will just have to accept the risk of penalties. Valuers can be particularly nervous when valuing around the price-points for each value band. HMRC however offer a pre-return banding check service for when taxpayers believe that the relevant property value is within 10% of a banding threshold (above or below). This should alert the taxpayer to when the VOA think that the valuation is too low.

Once a property has been placed in a value banding the relevant ATED percentage will apply to it for that year and the following years until the next five-year valuation point. The next re-valuation will be on 1 April 2018 when the relevant valuation date will be 1 April 2017. The taxable value fixed by a five-yearly valuation only has effect for chargeable periods beginning after the five-year period: FA 2013, s 102(2A).

The ATED is intended to increase in April each year based on the consumer price index of the previous September with the first increase having occurred on 1 April 2014 under the Annual Tax on Enveloped Dwellings (Indexation of Chargeable Amounts) Order 2014, SI 2014/854. However, this was disapplied in 2015 and the substantial increases in ATED from 1 April 2015 were effected by FA 2015, s 70. If the CPI is negative there will be no decrease. There will also be no change in the charge bands so over time many more properties may come within the ATED especially in London and the South East.

HMRC have said nothing about how they intend to enforce the ATED against non-UK resident or established non-natural persons except that it 'will robustly pursue non-payment of the annual charge'. It is also unclear about how HMRC will tackle the problem of high value residential properties being registered in the names of overseas individual nominees (or indeed companies that claim to be acting as nominees) who are not within the ATED but who hold beneficially for non-natural persons. This seems to be a flaw in a tax based on ownership by certain types of person. The problem is to some extent ameliorated by the exclusion from ATED for corporate trustees and beneficiaries.

The failure to file a correct ATED return that had been due by 1 October 2013 until 7 April 2014 attracted filing penalties under FA 2009, Sch 55 of £1,300 even though the taxpayer was able to claim relief from ATED in full: *Monaco Group of Companies Ltd v HMRC* [2015] UKFTT 0180 (TC). A similar result arose in *Lucas Properties Ltd v Revenue and Customs Comrs* [2015] UKFTT 0181 (TC) with ignorance of the law in itself being held to have been no excuse. In *Chartridge Developments Ltd v HMRC* [2016] UKFTT 766 (TC), [2017] SFTD 419, [2017] SWTI 332, the taxpayer had filed late returns for 2014 and 2015. Although, there was no tax liability due to a relief, HMRC issued five penalty notices, all of which contained errors. The tribunal held that one notice was valid because it stated the correct filing date for the return, but that the other four notices were invalid due to those stating the wrong filing and other dates. It seems that the Scottish Tax Chamber takes a more robust approach to errors in penalty notices: see *Classic Land and Property Ltd v Revenue Scotland* [2016] TTFT2.

What is a 'dwelling'?

[22.3] A 'dwelling' is defined as a building or part of a building that:

• is used or suitable for use as a single dwelling, or
• is in the process of being constructed or adopted for such use

together with any land that is occupied or enjoyed with the dwelling as a garden or grounds or land that subsists for the benefit of the dwelling (FA 2013, s 112(1)–(3)).

What is *suitable* for use as a dwelling is a question of fact in each case. At SDLTM20076 HMRC state that:

"Residential and non-residential property: further notes

In most cases, there will be no difficulty in establishing whether or not a property is residential property.

*Use at the effective date of the transaction overrides any past or intended future uses for this purpose.** [Author's emphasis] If a building is not in use at the effective date but its last use was as a dwelling, it will be taken to be 'suitable for use as a dwelling' and treated as residential property, unless evidence is produced to the contrary.

Undeveloped land is essentially non-residential but may be residential property if, at the effective date, a residential building is being built on it.

Where, at the effective date, an existing building is being adapted or *marketed** [Author's emphasis] for, or restored to, domestic use, it is treated as residential property.

A building that is used only partly as a dwelling may nevertheless be suitable for use wholly as a dwelling. Its overall suitability will be judged from the facilities available at the effective date. For example, if two rooms of a house were in use as a dentist's surgery and waiting room at the effective date, HMRC would nevertheless normally consider this property suitable for use as a dwelling.

Cases involving bed and breakfast establishments or guest houses will be treated on their merits. However, a bed and breakfast (B&B) establishment which has bathing facilities, telephone lines etc installed in each room and is available all year round would be considered non-residential.

Where only a distinct part of the building is used and suitable for use as a dwelling, that part will be residential property for the purposes of the relief and the mixed use provisions will apply – see SDLTM20080."

[*Author's question: Inconsistency?]

Hence, properties which are suitable for use as a dwelling but which are in actual overall use as commercial premises will not be within the scope of the charge. The fact that planning permission exists for residential use of the building will not trump the existing use as a non-residential building. This takes care of any worries about premises such as those used by Harley Street specialists.

There is however a worrying inconsistency in HMRC's approach because in relation to the 15% higher rate of SDLT, HMRC have said in Stamp Taxes Bulletin 2/2012 that future use can trump existing use:

"A property with a long history of non-residential use, and which does not have permission to be occupied as a residence, is unlikely to be viewed by HMRC as a dwelling, or suitable for use as a dwelling. Cases where HMRC may take a contrary view would be where a property's last use was as an office but before the date of sale planning permission has been granted for it to be used as a residential dwelling, that is to say that the use to which the property can be put at the date of the transaction is only residential. This is a situation that would fall within the third paragraph of SDLTM20076 quoted above."

It is considered that the marketing of an office building with consent for change of use to residential does not make the building a dwelling as long as there is current office use. Despite this at least one large acquisition of an office building with planning consent has been deferred because of a lack of clarity over whether the correct rate would be 4% or 15%.

Where a new dwelling is being constructed the valuation date for the purposes of the tax is the earlier of:

- completion (in the sense that it becomes chargeable in connection with council tax) or
- first occupation.

The term construction of a new dwelling includes the production of a new dwelling by the alteration of an existing building (FA 2013, s 124).

Certain types of accommodation are excluded. These include residential accommodation for school pupils, students, the armed forces, children, those in need of care along with hospitals, prisons and hotels (FA 2013, s 112(4) applying FA 2003, s 116(2) and (3)).

Reliefs and exceptions: general

[22.4] Any available reliefs in a chargeable period in respect of a single dwelling are given effectively on a daily basis for each day in the period for which a relief is due. The amount of the tax charged is adjusted accordingly. Reliefs and exemptions are available for:

- property rental businesses;
- rental properties being sold, demolished or converted;
- dwellings opened to the public;
- property developers;
- property developers: exchange of dwellings;
- property traders;
- financial institutions;
- regulated home reversion plans;
- occupation by certain employees or partners;
- caretaker flats owned by flat management companies;
- farmhouses;
- social housing;
- charities;
- public bodies and bodies established for national purposes;
- dwellings conditionally exempt from IHT.

(FA 2013, ss 132–155)

Any applicable relief must be claimed by filing a self-assessment ATED return, usually by 30 April in each year (or 30 days after acquiring the dwelling) but 1 October for the first year of ATED or 30 days after acquisition, if later.

Interim relief may be claimed (by way of an ATED return) for the whole period with subsequent adjustment of the amounts due to or from HMRC (FA 2013, s 100).

A 'relief declaration return' can be filed for a single type of relief in respect of one or more properties (see 22.2 above).

Non-qualifying occupation: look-forward and look-back in a chargeable period

[22.5] If on a day in a chargeable period a non-qualifying individual is permitted to occupy a dwelling, no subsequent day in that chargeable period or in any of the subsequent three chargeable periods is treated as relievable. An earlier day in that or the preceding chargeable period is also not relievable unless there has been an intervening relievable day: FA 2013, s 135 (see 22.9 below).

A 'non-qualifying individual' includes an individual entitled to the interest (otherwise than as a member of a partnership); an individual who is connected with a person entitled to the interest; a relevant settler where the trustee is connected with the person entitled to the interest; the spouse or civil partner of a connected person or of a relevant settler; a relative of a connected person or of a relevant settler and a relative of the spouse or civil partner of a connected person or of a relevant settler and their spouses or civil partners: FA 2013, s 136. 'Connected persons' is based on the definition in CTA 2010, s 1122 as modified by FA 2013, s 172. A person is treated as connected to a cell company where if any cell were a separate company, he could be connected with that company: FA 2013, s 173.

Occupation as living accommodation by a qualifying employee or partner of a qualifying trade or qualifying rental business will not prevent the days of occupation being relievable: FA 2013, s 145. A caretaker flat owned by a flat management company for use by an employed caretaker is also relievable: FA 2013, s 147A.

Property rental businesses

[22.6] Relief from the tax is available for a dwelling that is being rented out in the course of a 'qualifying property rental business' carried on by a person beneficially entitled to the interest in the dwelling. A 'qualifying property rental business' is one that is run on a commercial basis with a view to profit. Relief is also available for an un-let dwelling that is held with the intention of letting it out in the course of a commercial letting business as long as steps are being taken to secure that it will be let without delay except so far as any delay can be justified by commercial considerations or cannot be avoided. In such cases evidence should be created and retained to demonstrate the reasons for any delay if HMRC challenge whether relief was due in respect of an un-let dwelling. In the author's view this relief is in principle available where conversion or refurbishment building work is either being planned or is in progress with the intention of being able to let the property as a dwelling (FA 2013, s 133(1)).

Any day in the chargeable period is not a relievable day if there was occupation (at the end of that day) by a non-qualifying individual or it was intended that the dwelling would (or would if certain circumstances arose) be made available for occupation by a non-qualifying individual (see above). Effectively this means that the dwelling must be let or intended for let to third parties (FA 2013, s 133(2)).

'Property rental business' for the purpose of the relief means a 'property business' within Part 4 of CTA 2009 but the actual business need not be subject to UK corporation tax so that non-resident companies and other non-corporate business can qualify for the relief. However, relief is not available for dwellings used to earn 'excluded rents' which are defined in CTA 2010, s 605(2) as income from caravan sites or rents from electric-line way leaves, gas or oil pipelines, mobile telephone masts or wind turbines (FA 2013, s 133(1)).

Property developers

[22.7] Relief from the tax is available to a person carrying on a property development trade who is beneficially entitled to the dwelling for any day on which the interest is held exclusively for the purpose of developing and reselling the land in the course of the trade. A 'property development trade' means a trade that consists of or includes buying and developing for resale residential or non-residential property and is run on a commercial basis with a view to profit (FA 2013, s 138). The developers must ultimately intend to sell the property and not let it out. However, if the developer intends to let the property out as part of a qualifying rental business before selling it on then the relief will still be available.

Relief is also available where a dwelling is acquired in the course of a property development trade as part of a 'qualifying exchange'. This covers developers who acquire a dwelling in exchange for a newly built or converted dwelling that was not previously occupied (FA 2013, s 139).

Property traders

[22.8] A day in a chargeable period is relievable if on that day a person carrying on a 'property trading business' who is beneficially entitled to a single dwelling interest which is held:

- as stock in trade of the business, and

- for the sole purpose of resale in the course of the business (FA 2013, s 141(1)).

A 'property trading business' means a business that consists of or includes buying and selling dwellings on a commercial basis with a view to profit. This is in contrast with the definition of a property development trade which includes non-residential property. However, this difference is unlikely to mean that a first acquisition of a dwelling as part of a new residential property trading business will not qualify for the relief as long as there will be a genuine trade involving dwellings.

Denial of reliefs

[22.9] Relief from the tax is *denied* for property rental businesses, property developers and property traders if a 'non-qualifying individual' is permitted to occupy the dwelling (or it is intended that the dwelling will be made available for occupation by a non-qualifying individual). The relief can be denied for up to two years retrospectively and for up to three years going forward. However the relief can become available again if the property is let to a third party in the interim period (see **22.5** above).

A 'non-qualifying individual' means:

- an individual who is beneficially entitled to the interest – which would mean an individual who owns the dwelling jointly with the non-natural person;
- any person who is connected with a partner in a partnership where a person is beneficially entitled to an interest in the dwelling as a member of the partnership;
- an individual settlor of a trust, the trustees of which are connected with a person who is beneficially entitled to the dwelling;
- any spouse, civil partner or relative of an above individual; or
- an individual who has at least a 50% interest in a collective investment scheme holding a single dwelling interest, or who is connected with such individual (FA 2013, s 136).

Suitable 'envelopes' post-ATED

[22.10] Vehicles which are suitable for 'enveloping' high value residential properties but which are outside the ATED include companies which hold property either as a nominee or as the trustee of a settlement as such companies are not within the charge. Although the charge focuses on a company that is beneficially entitled (whether solely or jointly) to the chargeable interest companies that are entitled as a beneficiary of a settlement are also not within ATED: FA 2013, s 95(2)(b). In SDLT, including the 15% rate, under FA 2003, Sch 16, para 4 persons holding as trustee of a settlement are treated for SDLT as the owners of the beneficial interest as well as the legal interest so the trustee company's ownership will be opaque for these purposes. Given that the terms of a settlement can be very flexible a suitably drafted arrangement may provide a sanctuary not only from the ATED but also the 15% higher rate charge on acquisition of a dwelling. Those investors who need for bona fide reasons to hold property in companies and for which the statutory reliefs do not apply, may therefore wish to look at the use of a suitably drafted company trust structure. The usual IHT concerns about putting property into a settlement may be resolved with a suitable mortgage subject to IHTA 1984, ss 162, 162A, 162B, 162C.

Further food for thought is to be found within FA 2013, s 166 which provides that a 'company' means any body corporate other than a 'partnership'. Given that a 'partnership' for ATED includes a body corporate in the form of an LLP it appears that this presents an opportunity to eat one's cake and yet to keep it, ie to continue to hold the property in a vehicle which is for legal purposes a body corporate but which is not a body corporate for the 15% higher rate and ATED purposes. In this regard consideration should be given to inheritance tax and the borrowing of mortgage finance to charge against the property.

Partnerships

[22.11] In ATED a partnership will meet the ownership condition necessary for the tax to apply on a particular day if on that day a member of the partnership that is a company is beneficially entitled to the interest in the dwelling as a member of the partnership. This wording may at first sight seem at odds with the established principle that a partner's interest in a partnership is an asset (a chose in action) that is separate and distinct from the assets of the partnership: see for instance *Green v Herzog* [1954] 1 WLR 1309, 98 Sol Jo 733, CA and the Stamp Office Manual 2nd edition at para 4.442. However the existence of this chose in action does not mean that the partners do not at the same time have a beneficial interest in the assets of the partnership. This beneficial interest is recognized by *Lindley & Banks on Partnership 19th ed* (2010) at para 19-07: 'Whilst the partnership continues, each partner interested in the capital and assets of the firm will unquestionably be entitled to a beneficial interest in respect of those assets and *may* also hold the legal title thereto, either alone or in conjunction with one or more of the other partners.' Although the nature of this beneficial interest is subject to the special characteristics and circumstances of the relevant partnership rights and obligations, it is a beneficial interest nonetheless. Accordingly, although a general or limited partnership is not transparent as a matter of law, the partners do have a beneficial interest in the partnership assets. Tax law generally recognises this position by for example accepting that there is therefore a need to deem the dealings by a partnership to be dealings by the partners and not by the firm as such and for chargeable gains to be assessed on the partners separately: TCGA 1992, s 59. HMRC accept that a partnership is not transparent for IHT. The SDLT partnership provisions are required due to the lack of legal transparency. In relation to limited liability partnerships ('LLPs') which are bodies corporate with their own legal personality, these are obviously opaque and so for tax purposes are placed in the same position as a general partnership by deeming the property of an LLP to be property to which its members are entitled as *partners*; see for example *TCGA 1992*, s 59A and IHTA 1984, s 267A and of course, FA 2003, Sch 15, para 2. But these provisions do not make the partnership transparent and deem the partners to be directly entitled to the assets of the LLP. A similar position exists in ATED with FA 2013, s 167(2)(b) deeming a chargeable interest to be owned jointly and beneficially by the partners rather than the partnership. It is thought that the ownership referred to is ownership as a *partner* and not individually given the reference to the partner being deemed to be jointly entitled to the interest. The statutory purpose is to place LLPs on the same footing as general partnerships and to maintain consistency of approach with the other relevant taxes. The ATED charge applies to the responsible partners (as defined) where a company partner is beneficially entitled to a chargeable interest in a dwelling as a member of the partnership whether as a joint tenant or a tenant in common (FA 2013, s 96 and s 97).

ATED-related capital gains tax charge on 'non-natural persons' within the ATED

[22.12] From 6 April 2013, capital gains on the disposal of high value residential property (£2m+) originally, £1m+ from 1 April 2015 and £500,000 since 1 April 2016) by broadly, persons other than individuals, have been taxed at 28% (with a tapering relief for gains on properties worth just over the threshold) when those persons have been within the ATED with respect to their interest in the property disposed of. Persons other than an 'excluded person' will potentially be within the scope of the charge. An 'excluded person' means an individual, the trustees of a settlement or personal representatives:

- where a gain accrues on the disposal of any partnership assets and the person is a member of the partnership, or
- where the gain accrues on the disposal of property held for the purposes of a relevant collective investment scheme and the person is a participant in relation to the scheme (TCGA 1992, s 2B).

The gain is charged to capital gains tax at 28% and is referred to in the legislation as an 'ATED-related chargeable gain' referred to below as 'ATED CGT'.

Prior to the introduction of ATED-CGT, non-UK resident companies were generally not liable to pay UK tax on their capital gains; UK resident companies paid corporation tax generally at 23% on chargeable gains and UK resident non-natural persons that were not companies paid capital gains tax.

ATED-CGT has extended the charge to capital gains tax at 28% to disposals of high-value UK dwellings occurring on or after 6 April 2013 where a person other than an 'excluded person' (see above) makes the disposal and that person was within the ATED with respect to the interest disposed of. Thus both non-UK and UK resident companies and other non-natural persons are brought within the scope of capital gains tax in respect of disposals of dwellings that are within the ATED. However, where the dwelling was acquired before 6 April 2013 the ATED-CGT applies only to the gain accruing on or after 6 April 2013 (TCGA 1992, Sch 4ZZA, paras 2, 3). This means that in respect of the pre-6 April 2013 gain, there will normally be no tax payable by non-UK resident companies and other non-natural persons and UK resident companies will pay corporation tax on that gain.

Unfortunately this relatively simple conceptual change has been achieved by some extremely complicated legislative amendments and it is necessary to consider the relevant legislation in order to explain the changes in any meaningful detail.

(1)   *'Relevant high value disposal'*
        The ATED-CGT is based on the concept of a 'relevant high value disposal' which will occur if the following conditions A to D are met
        Condition A: the disposal is of the whole or part of a *chargeable interest* which is referred to in the legislation as 'the disposed of interest'.
        Condition B: the disposed of interest has, at any time during the relevant ownership period, been or formed part of a *single-dwelling interest*.
        Condition C: 'P' (that is the taxpayer making the disposal) has been within the charge to ATED with respect to that single-dwelling interest on one or more days in the *relevant ownership period* which are not relievable days in relation to that interest.
        Condition D: the amount or value of the consideration for the disposal exceeds *the threshold amount*.
        (TCGA 1992, s 2C)
        There are some key phrases and definitions as follows:

(2)   A *chargeable interest* and a *single dwelling* interest have the same meaning as for ATED. The relevant ownership period means the period beginning with 6 April 2013 or if later, the day on which P acquired the chargeable interest. P can elect for this not to apply where it held the dwelling on 5 April 2013. This could be advantageous if a loss is accruing on the property at that date. The *threshold amount* is essentially £1m for a disposal of the whole of an interest which is not owned jointly with someone else. A corresponding fraction of £1m is used in case of disposals of part or of joint interests or both.
        It is essentially Condition C above that makes the ATED-CGT correspond with the scope of the ATED charge so that only disposals of dwellings that are within ATED and are not relieved from that charge will attract capital gains tax.

(3)   *Other taxes*
        A gain charged under ATED-CGT is taken outside TCGA 1992, s 13 which attributes chargeable gains accruing to non-UK resident 'close' companies to UK resident participators in the company (TCGA 1992, s 13(1A)). Gains accruing to trusts are not ATED-CGT gains and so there is no overlap with TCGA 1992, ss 86 and 87 which attribute gains of non-UK resident trustees to settlors and beneficiaries. ATED-CGT does not overlap with principal private residence relief because that relief is only available to individuals and settlements, which are outside the scope of ATED-CGT. In relation to double-tax agreements

which follow the OECD Model, there is no relief for the ATED-CGT as gains from the disposal of immovable property situated in a state (here the UK) can be taxed in that state and that right is preserved by the standard form of treaty.

(4)   *Scotland*
ATED-CGT applies to high-value dwellings in Scotland because the tax applies to interests in land in the UK. *Scotland Act 1998*, s 80I provides that a 'devolved tax' is a tax on the *acquisition* of interest in land and so because ATED-CGT is not an acquisitions tax it is not a devolved tax even though SDLT is a devolved tax and was replaced in Scotland by LBTT from 1 April 2015.

Planning for ATED-CGT

[22.13] As a general rule, high-value dwellings should be purchased by individuals, trustees, LLPs or other entities that are not 'non-natural persons' in order to avoid the ATED and ATED-CGT. However, the effect of the charge to capital gains tax for disposals of UK residential property on non-UK resident individuals, personal representatives, partners, trustees, foundations and closely-held companies introduced from 6 April 2015 also needs to be considered (see below). It should also be remembered that residential properties worth more than £500,000 will come within the scope of the ATED-CGT from 1 April 2016. For existing non-UK resident ownership structures within the scope of ATED-CGT the question will be whether to de-envelope to stop taxable gains from accruing. The costs and other issues to consider before doing so must be carefully considered. Anecdotal evidence suggests that many owners are allowing current arrangements to stand for the time being: see HMRC Research Report 384 'Views and behaviours in relation to the Annual Tax on Enveloped Dwellings', September 2015.

The charge to capital gains tax on disposals of UK residential property by non-UK resident individuals, closely-held companies, etc from 6 April 2015 (also referred to as an 'NRCGT disposal') is under TCGA 1992, s 14D. The charge applies to a 'disposal of a UK residential property interest' as defined in TCGA 1992, Sch B1 and essentially applies to dwellings, but unlike ATED-related CGT, there is no exemption for rental properties and there is no minimum threshold value.

Although the NRCGT takes priority over the anti-avoidance rules in TCGA 1992, s 13 (attribution of non-resident company gains to shareholders) and ss 86 and 87 (attribution of non-resident trust gains to settlers or beneficiaries), ATED-related CGT has priority over NRCGT. For example, if a non-UK resident company owned a dwelling worth just over £500,000 on 1 April 2012, ATED-related CGT would apply from 1 April 2016 so on a later disposal, the pre-2015 gain would be taxed under TCGA 1992, s 13 with the NRCGT applying for gains accruing in the 2015/16 tax year, and ATED-related CGT to gains occurring from 1 April 2016.

What factors should a non-UK resident purchaser of residential property take into account in this potentially confusing scenario? Where ATED is not going to apply, such as with a property rented to independent tenants, then ownership by a non-UK company could be sensible because the shares in the company will be outside UK inheritance tax and UK income tax on the rent will be charged at 20% only although this is likely to change retrospectively with effect from April 2017. A sale of the shares in the company owning the property will also avoid UK capital gains tax for the seller and stamp duty and SDLT for the purchaser.

If the residential property will be occupied by the non-UK resident or his family and the capital gains tax, principal private resident ('PPR') exemption will be available, then direct personal ownership should be considered subject to UK inheritance tax considerations. If the PPR exemption is not going to be available, then capital gains tax on a future sale is not so much of a factor given that ownership through a non-UK resident company also attracts NRCGT if the property, rather than the company, is sold and this makes ATED-related CGT less of a deterrent.

The significant rise in the top rate of ordinary SDLT in 2015 from 7% to 12% (plus the additional higher rate of 3% for acquisitions of additional residential properties since 1 April 2016) and the introduction of the NRCGT rather undermines the deterrent effect of the 15% higher rate of SDLT on purchases by non-natural persons, the ATED and ATED-related CGT so that purchasing expensive properties using companies has once again become more attractive, despite the last three mentioned measures having been intended to deter such practices.

De-enveloping

[22.14] High value UK residential property is often held in a company structure for one or more of the following reasons:

- protection from UK inheritance tax as 'excluded property' (available until April 2017 when corporate ownership of UK residential property is likely to be treated as transparent so that the property will be subject to the relevant property IHT regime for trusts with its exit and ten-yearly charges and the gifts with reservation of benefit IHT rules for settlor interested arrangements);
- to avoid the need for a grant of UK probate on death;
- to avoid forced heirship and for tax reasons in the home county;
- privacy and confidentiality;
- protection from financial settlement on separation or divorce (see for example *Prest v Petrodel Resources Ltd* [2013] UKSC 34 for a limited exception when a company is found to hold properties bought with shareholder's money as trustee for the shareholder on a resulting trust and such properties are therefore available to the divorcing spouse; but see *Bhura v Bhura* [2014] EWHC 727 (Fam) for an example of where a resulting trust was found not to exist even where a party was dishonest and sought to put assets out of the other party's reach;
- avoidance of UK capital gains tax (subject to ATED-CGT and NRCGT at 28% and 20%); and

• to sell free of SDLT and stamp duty.

In deciding whether to de-envelope the original reasons for creating a particular corporate ownership structure will need to be reviewed carefully. The costs of de-enveloping will also need to be considered as part of the decision making process: What are the professional fees likely to be? Will there be a re-financing cost? Can the same advantages be gained in an alternative structure? Will SDLT arise in relation to any assumption of an existing mortgage? This last question will require detailed consideration of FA 2003, ss 75A–75C and Sch 4, para 8 and HMRC's Technical News issue 5 plus its guidance note of 20 December 2013 (now reproduced as SDLTM 04043 and 04042 respectively) in order to ensure that an SDLT charge is avoided. The terms of the statutory provisions will mean that where there is bank or third-party debt secured on the property to be taken out of the company that is to be released and further debt taken out by the shareholder, then a fairly robust view will need to be taken by the professional advisers as to the correct interpretation and application of these provisions to using funds to capitalise or repay the company's debt if an SDLT charge is to be avoided. If an SDLT charge will arise the 3% additional rate for acquisitions of additional residential properties should also be considered.

Trusts and limited liability partnerships are able to offer some of the above advantages while remaining outside the scope of the new charges. Care should be taken to avoid the IHT entry charge when creating a trust by the use of suitably structured borrowings. Care should also be taken to ensure that a partnership has a business and that when using a limited liability partnership it is not just a passive owner of a UK residential property given that Limited Liability Partnerships Act 2000, s 2 refers to two or more persons carrying on a lawful *business*. An inheritance tax exposure in relation to the value of a partnership share may be mitigated by borrowings secured against the partnership property or life insurance can be used to protect against it.

Where the protection of assets and privacy is concerned some clients may consider that the ATED charge is not too burdensome in return for keeping these advantages and decide to do nothing. The decision will not usually be straightforward but the range of reliefs from ATED available for properties held with a commercial purpose will reduce the range of situations in which the de-enveloping question will arise. There is already some evidence that owners may be willing to remain in existing structures and accept the charges at least for a time in order to avoid any hasty changes. The extension of the capital gains tax charge at 28% is also of less concern given that gains accruing before 6 April 2013 are not taxable.

Chapter 23

From farmland to shops: a case study in the tax issues facing the parties involved in a property development

by
Dominic Rayner,
KPMG LLP

Preamble

[23.1] Securing planning permission is the main obstacle in the way of someone wanting to develop a new property; obtaining funding is the principal delaying factor along that road. Tax is also an important factor – will there be SDLT or other tax liabilities on the individual transactions, will there be leakages of VAT, how and when will profits be taxed? Although some taxes may be payable by the old landowners, occupational tenants or investors in the new properties, these liabilities are generally known and so are factored into the prices negotiated with the property developer. The developer will often end up effectively bearing the tax cost of other parties involved as well as their own. In this chapter a realistic but imagined development project is seen through from inception to completion, with some narrative twists along the way. The figures used are designed to illustrate the tax issues covered. Some commercial and legal aspects are simplified so that the key tax points can be made clearly, untrammelled by the web of complexity that real-world developers have to deal with.

It is assumed throughout this chapter that all transactions between connected parties are undertaken at arm's length value, so that no transfer pricing or thin capitalization adjustments are necessary. In practice, this may well not be the case, especially where the development company borrows heavily from its parent company, as it does in this chapter. Under the thin capitalization legislation, the borrowing company would only be entitled to deduct interest payable on its loans when computing its taxable profits to the extent that it could have obtained those loans from unconnected third party lenders. If the parent company lender is a UK company, as is the case in this chapter, for each thin capitalization adjustment there would be a corresponding adjustment in the lending company, so the net effect should be nil. Transfer pricing and thin capitalization are not mentioned further in this chapter, but would need to be considered in a real scenario, especially if any of the companies involved are non-UK. Developers and investors will also need to consider the proposed changes of law derived from Action 4 of the OECD's BEPS project, which will impose new limits on the amount of interest a company can claim as deductible in its calculation of taxable profit. The Corporate Interest Restriction (CIR) legislation is included in the September 2017 Finance Bill and is expected to become law in autumn 2017, taking effect from 1 April 2017.

This story is set in England. Property developers in Scotland would need to factor in LBTT costs, rather than SDLT.

Green fields

[23.2] The story concerns transactions in land which bring about a change of use of that land; it begins with four farmers.

Four parcels of land near the English village of Newbold make up the site which will ultimately be developed.

	Owned by	Occupied and farmed by
Site 1	The Earl of Black	The Earl of Black
Site 2	Redmond	Redmond
Site 3	Regis plc	Whittle
Site 4	Regis plc	Akabusi

Swale Properties plc is listed on AIM; it is the owner of a group of companies, with a large portfolio of investment properties, and an established property development business. Its directors spy an opportunity for development of the Newbold site. They establish a new UK company, Buckden Developments Limited ('Buckden') and begin researching the opportunity.

Note – if Buckden had been a non-UK company which was not managed or controlled in the UK, and had no permanent establishment in the UK, it would still have been taxable in the UK on the profits of its property development business (CTA 2009, s 5B inserted by FA 2016, s 76). (See **CHAPTER 8** at **8.3**).

Grant of options

[23.3] In 2016 Buckden makes approaches to the three landowners, and negotiates an identical option agreement with each landowner separately: in return for an upfront payment of £100,000 per site, Buckden is granted options by the three landowners to purchase each of the four sites with vacant possession for £10m (plus an overage payment equal to 25% of any future gain Buckden makes on disposal). The options are only exercisable within 18 months of Buckden obtaining outline planning permission for a new retail park. The options will lapse if outline planning permission is not obtained by the end of 2018.

Tax consequences of the payments for the options

VAT

[23.4] The four payments of £100,000 that Buckden makes for the options are for supplies of the right to purchase land made by the three landowners to Buckden. The supply of a right to buy bare land is VAT exempt (though the seller may opt to charge VAT at the standard rate – by making a valid 'option to tax').

Neither Redmond nor the Earl of Black has opted to tax his landholding, so no VAT is chargeable on their £100,000 receipts. Regis plc has opted to tax its interest in the Newbold site (sites 3 & 4), so it must charge VAT at the standard rate of 20% on the £200,000 it receives from Buckden (20% of £200,000 = £40,000).

Buckden is registered for VAT as an intending trader (VATA 1994, Sch 1, para 9), so is able to recover the £40,000 VAT cost as it can demonstrate its intention to make taxable supplies using the land in the future, being the intended freehold sale of the newly constructed retail property (VATA 1994, Sch 9, item 1 refers). Despite being on a monthly VAT return schedule (or stagger), Buckden must wait several weeks for repayment as HMRC have chosen to review the return prior to making the repayment.

Whilst Regis plc can recover VAT incurred on its costs associated with granting the option by virtue of its option to tax, the other two landowners may not be able to reclaim VAT on any legal or similar costs incurred in connection with their VAT exempt grant of the options. Whether or not they can reclaim the VAT will depend upon whether either landowner is VAT registered by virtue of other activities, and whether the VAT attributable to these VAT exempt disposals causes them to exceed the partial exemption *de minimis* limits (VAT Regulations 1995, reg 105A).

SDLT

[23.5] The grant of an option to purchase land is an acquisition of a 'chargeable interest in land' by the option holder (FA 2003, s 46), so would fall within the scope of SDLT.

The £100,000 payments to Redmond and the Earl of Black are below the SDLT threshold (£150,000).

The two £100,000 payments to Regis plc should be regarded as 'linked' transactions for SDLT purposes, part of a single scheme of transactions between the same vendor and purchaser (FA 2003, s 55(4)). The consideration given for both sites must be aggregated when determining the applicable rate of SDLT due. Since Regis plc had already 'opted to tax' its landholdings, the chargeable consideration for SDLT would be £200,000 plus VAT at 20% = £240,000. This amount is over the £150,000 threshold by £90,000, so Buckden must pay SDLT of 2% of £90,000 = £1,800.

Income tax/corporation tax/capital gains tax

Payer of the option fees (developer)

[23.6] Buckden's payments would initially be accounted for as work in progress, and could be retained as such on the balance sheet provided that the development is able to support that value. If the development is deemed to be speculative then it may be imprudent to recognise any costs on the balance sheet at this early stage, in which case the costs would be written off to Buckden's income statement (profit and loss account).

Buckden is owned 100% by Swale Properties plc, so it would be able to surrender trading losses to profitable companies within its group by way of group relief. It would need to be determined whether Buckden has commenced trading – if it has, then the loss resulting from the write-off of costs (such as the four £100,000 payments for the options) could be surrendered to fellow group companies. If Buckden is not yet deemed to be trading then its expenses would be regarded as 'pre-trading expenditure'.

In the case of *Mansell v Revenue and Customs Comrs* ([2006] STC (SCD) 605 (2006) SpC 551) it was held that a business of identifying sites for new motorway service stations had not commenced until the taxpayer had signed option agreements with the landowners. Until that time, any costs on researching the industry and traffic flows, surveying potential sites, drafting heads of terms, etc were pre-trading expenditure, rather than actual trading losses. Pre-trading expenditure incurred and expensed by a company in the seven years prior to the commencement of trade may be treated as deductible on the first day of trade, provided it satisfies the usual 'wholly and exclusively' rules and is not capital expenditure.

Following the *Mansell* decision, Buckden would be able to treat its expenses incurred prior to the signing of the option agreements as deductible costs for the accounting period beginning on the first day of trade, being the day those agreements were signed. Buckden would then be able to surrender by way of group relief any resulting trading loss for that accounting period. In the accounting period (or periods) prior to the signing of the option agreements, losses arising from Buckden's expenses could not be surrendered by way of group relief, just carried forward to the first accounting period of the trade.

Recipients of the option fees

[23.7] The Earl of Black and Redmond own and occupy their land, which they account for as fixed assets used in their farming businesses. For them the £100,000 receipts for the grant of the options are capital gains receipts for the disposal of the option itself. Taxation of Chargeable Gains Act 1992 (TCGA 1992), s 144 states that a receipt for the grant of an option is treated as a disposal of the option, not as a part-disposal of the underlying land. There is no capital gains base cost in the option, so both The Earl of Black and Redmond have taxable capital gains of £100,000 (which will be subject to capital gains tax at 20% after deducting annual exempt amounts).

There has been no disposal of a business so entrepreneur's relief could not be claimed to reduce the tax on those capital gains. An option over land is not within the classes of assets listed in TCGA 1992, s 155, so roll-over relief cannot be claimed if the option fee is re-invested in new land, buildings, etc.

Regis plc accounts for its interest in the Newbold site as an investment property from which it earns rent. Its £200,000 receipt for its holding in the site is also taxable as capital gains proceeds for the disposal of the options. There is no base cost in the options, so the full amount is subject to corporation tax (levied at the rate of 20% between 1 April 2016 and 31 March 2017).

The first stages of the development process

[23.8] Early in 2016 Buckden applies for planning permission for a new retail park on the Newbold site. During the remainder of 2016 and 2017 Buckden incurs costs on site surveys, legal fees and consultants as well as its own internal costs. Buckden's representatives attend public meetings and meetings with the local authority, defending the plans and providing information on the environmental and traffic impacts of the new development. Buckden's costs are funded by way of borrowings from its parent company, Swale Properties plc, and Buckden accrues an interest cost on this loan at 5% pa (though it has no income out of which to pay the interest).

In September 2018, the local authority decision, which has been delayed by local opposition, official processes, etc is made, and Buckden is granted outline planning permission for a new retail park.

Subsequent to the local authority's decision, there is a legal appeal, and the court decides that the original process was flawed. The planning decision is taken to a review, which will last for several months and require Buckden to incur further costs on legal representation.

By December 2018 the review process is barely under way, and some time from being completed.

Buckden's options to purchase the land are due to expire at the end of 2018, so Buckden makes further payments totalling £0.6m (£150,000 for each site) in return for the landowners agreeing to a two-year extension of the option agreements.

Tax consequences of the further payments for the options

Income tax/corporation tax/capital gains tax

Grantors (landowners)

[23.9] Although the landowners have now received two separate cash receipts in return for interests in their land, this does not derive from a pattern of activity on the part of the landowners. 'Frequency of transactions' is generally considered one of the 'badges of trade' (*Marson v Morton* (1986) 59 TC 381) so two cash receipts could be regarded as more of an indication of 'trading' than a single receipt. However, the landowners are passive recipients of the money, have not sold interests or granted options over other land, and have not solicited any income or undertaken any development work in order to improve the land.

None of the other badges of trade point to the new receipts being 'trading income' so the landowners would again treat their receipts as capital gains disposal proceeds on the grant of the options. Again, there would be no capital gains base cost, so the entire receipt would be a taxable gain.

Neither Black nor Redmond has sold its business, so they cannot claim entrepreneur's relief to reduce the capital gains tax on the amounts received from Buckden. The grant of an option over land is not within the classes of assets in TCGA 1992, s 152 so no rollover relief could be claimed, even if Black or Redmond re-invested their receipts in new land or buildings.

Grantee (developer)

[23.10] Buckden would account for its additional payments as work-in-progress in its accounts. When preparing its accounts, Buckden would have to assess whether the balance sheet value of its work-in-progress reflected the value of its interest in the development project. If not, Buckden would need to expense some of its costs, to bring its work-in-progress balance down to net realisable value.

VAT

[23.11] The additional payments represent further consideration for the grant of the option over the sites. As at **23.4** above, no VAT is chargeable on the exempt supplies made by Black or Redmond as they have not opted to tax their respective sites. Regis plc has opted to tax its land, so VAT must be charged at the standard rate on its £300,000 receipt at 20% = £60,000.

Although Buckden has not yet made any taxable supplies, the company is registered as an intending trader so it can recover the £60,000 VAT cost, based on its intention to make taxable supplies of the site in future. Buckden is on monthly VAT returns, so repayment should be made by HMRC only a few weeks after Buckden pays the VAT charged by Regis.

SDLT

[23.12] The original option agreements included clauses providing for the possibility of the option expiry date to be extended if suitable payments can be negotiated between the parties. In HMRC's view this would mean that the payments extending the option agreements are 'linked' (FA 2003, s 108), meaning that the applicable rate of SDLT is based on the aggregate consideration for the original option and the further payments for extending them. (If the new payments were for new options, rather than for extensions provided for in the original option agreement, then it is arguable that the payments would not have been 'linked'.)

The SDLT payable by Buckden on the extension payments is calculated as follows:

Vendor	Payment on original grant	Additional payment	Total	SDLT rate	SDLT
Black	£100,000	£150,000	£250,000	0%/2%	£2,000
Redmond	£100,000	£150,000	£250,000	0%/2%	£2,000
Regis plc	£240,000	£360,000	£600,000	0%/2%/5%	£19,500 less £1,800 already paid = £17,700

Note that the consideration payable to Regis plc for SDLT purposes is the VAT-inclusive amount, as the land is 'opted'. Buckden deducts the SDLT already paid on the earlier grant of the option (see **23.5** above), so the additional amount payable by Buckden on the extension of the option from Regis plc is £17,700.

Planning permission is granted

[23.13] In October 2019, the appeal process is exhausted and planning permission is granted to Buckden for the new retail park on the Newbold site.

At 30 September 2019, Buckden prepares its accounts. They show that three years after Buckden was first granted options over the land, it has made no profit (or loss) and has retained all of its costs on its balance sheet as work-in-progress.

Buckden's costs comprising its work-in-progress at 30 September 2019 are:

Legal fees	£4m
Management costs (own staff, and payments to parent company)	£2m
Surveyor's fees	£0.6m
Other consultancy	£1.1m
Interest on loans (total £10m) from parent company (Swale Properties plc)	£0.7m
Cost of options and extensions	£1m
SDLT paid to date	£23,500
Total	£9,423,500

In its computation of taxable profits Buckden is not entitled to any deduction for costs incurred that are held on the balance sheet as work-in-progress. This also applies for the interest that has accrued on Buckden's loans from its parent company. A company can deduct interest on its loans under the loan relationship rules in line with the accounting treatment for that interest (providing the accounting treatment is GAAP-compliant), so if the interest is held on the balance sheet as work-in-progress, it is not deductible until expensed.

(Note that capitalized interest can be deducted in the period it accrues, if it forms part of the balance sheet cost of a 'fixed capital project' (CTA 2009, s 320); but Buckden is a developer, not a property investor, and holds its costs on its balance sheet as a current asset, not a capital asset. Although Buckden's interest cost is accounted for as trading stock it is not, strictly speaking, 'capitalized' so the opportunity afforded by s 320 does not apply.)

Compensation payments to tenants

[23.14] Before Regis plc can sell the land, it must obtain vacant possession, which means terminating the leases of Whittle and Akabusi. Each farmer has a lease with 22 years unexpired.

Regis negotiates compensation for the early termination of each lease of £1m.

Tax consequences of the payments to tenants

VAT

[23.15] For VAT purposes an early termination payment made by a landlord represents a supply of a land interest from the tenant to the landlord. Neither Whittle nor Akabusi had opted to tax his interest in the land (and the parties have negotiated the position, rather than it being statutory compensation, which is outside the scope of VAT) so each lease termination represents a VAT-exempt supply by the tenant. No VAT is chargeable on the £1m payments from Regis plc to the outgoing tenants.

SDLT

[23.16] Perhaps surprisingly, given that Regis plc already owns a freehold interest in the Newbold site, Regis is deemed to acquire a chargeable interest in land when it pays Whittle and Akabusi to agree to terminate their leases. Regis plc would have to pay SDLT on the two £1m payments made to Whittle and Akabusi at the 2% and 5% rates (FA 2003, s 43(3)(b)). Regis plc must pay SDLT of £39,500 on each of the two £1m payments, a cost of £79,000 in aggregate.

Income tax/corporation tax/capital gains tax

Payer of the reverse surrender payments

[23.17] The payments for early termination of the lease are capital for tax purposes, so Regis plc will not be entitled to deduct them in its computation of taxable profits of the property rental business.

Regis plc would be entitled to treat the payments as expenditure on enhancing the value of its freehold land, provided that Regis still has vacant possession at the time the land is sold (TCGA 1992, s 38(1)(b); HMRC Capital Gains Manual 71262). Obtaining vacant possession was the point of making the payments for early termination of the leases, and doing so greatly enhanced the value of Regis's land, so the payments will be eligible capital gains base cost when calculating the gain on sale of the land.

Recipients of the reverse surrender payments

[23.18] Whittle and Akabusi have both made disposals of their leasehold interests in land. The leases contained no provision for payments to be made on early termination, so the full amounts received are taxable as proceeds of capital gains. Neither farmer paid a premium for their leases, and neither incurred any expenditure on enhancing the land, so they have no capital gains base cost in the assets disposed of. This means that each farmer has a taxable capital gain equal to his £1m receipt. After deducting the annual exempt amount, the remainder of the gain is taxable at 20%.

Whittle and Akabusi both occupy other farmland for the purposes of their farming trades, so they are not eligible for entrepreneur's relief on the disposal of the land (which is regarded for this purpose as an asset of the business, rather than a part of the business, in line with the decision in *McGregor v Adcock* (1977) 51 TC 692).

Whittle does not purchase any new land, buildings or other assets listed in TCGA 1992, s 155 within the three years permitted by roll-over relief (TCGA 1992, s 152). Akabusi reinvests £750,000 of his receipt in new freehold land and buildings a year after his disposal, and he immediately takes the new land into use for the purposes of his farming trade, so he is able to roll £750,000 of his £1m capital gain over into the capital gains base cost in the new land. Only £250,000 of Akabusi's gain remains chargeable to tax; the capital gains base cost of the new land is nil, as Akabusi's gain has been reduced by £750,000, the same as the amount re-invested (TCGA 1992, s 152(1)(b)).

Land purchase

[23.19] Having obtained planning permission, Buckden sets about raising the necessary funds to purchase the land.

Buckden requires £40m to purchase all of the necessary sites, and procures that funding as follows:

Senior bank loan from ARNE Bank	Secured on the land Interest rate – LIBOR plus 4%	£28m
Mezzanine finance from Parry Securities	Unsecured Interest rate – fixed 13.5%	£7m
Loan from Swale Properties plc	Unsecured Interest rate – fixed 15%	£4m
Share capital injected by Swale Properties plc		£1m

Before purchasing the land from the landowners, Buckden enters into a contract with Armitage Securities Plc for sale of the land upon completion of construction of the retail park for £450m. The sale is conditional upon construction being completed satisfactorily, and the site being 60% pre-let to tenants conforming to defined financial standards, before the completion of construction.

Buckden purchases the land in Autumn 2020.

Tax consequences of conditional sale contract

VAT

[23.20] As no payment is made on entering into the contract, there are no VAT consequences at that time. The VAT treatment of the actual purchase of the land and the payment of the consideration are set out at **23.63** below.

When the conditional sale contract is being negotiated, the parties will need to determine the expected VAT treatment and include appropriate provisions within the sale and purchase agreement to protect their respective positions. For example, Buckden, as seller of the land, should take care that the consideration is stated in the contract to be exclusive of VAT.

SDLT

[23.21] SDLT is due and payable within 30 days of the 'effective date' of a transaction, typically the date of legal completion, but earlier if the contract is 'substantially performed' before completion. Substantial performance (FA 2003, s 44(5)) is triggered by the earlier of the payment of a substantial amount of consideration or the purchaser taking possession of the whole or substantially the whole of the site.

Armitage will not pay any of the consideration until completion and will have no rights to enter onto the site or otherwise take possession, so no SDLT is payable by Armitage at this stage.

Corporation tax

[23.22] Buckden will be taxed on its disposal of the land when the sale is recognised in its accounts. While the sale contract remains conditional, Buckden does not recognise any income in its accounts, so no corporation tax liability arises.

Buckden will have to secure funding for the construction – Armitage has undertaken to purchase the completed and largely pre-let development, but will not inject loans along the way towards practical completion.

With the conditional sale in place, Buckden is able to draw down on its loans from ARNE and Parry. Having drawn down the loans, Buckden is able to exercise its options and complete the purchase of the four sites. The purchase is completed in October 2020 for a total consideration of £40m.

Tax consequences of land purchase

VAT

[23.23] Neither Black nor Redmond has opted to tax his freehold land interest, so no VAT is chargeable on the sale of the land to Buckden.

Regis plc has opted to tax its holding in the land, so VAT is chargeable at the standard rate on the sale to Buckden, unless the transaction can be treated as outside the scope of VAT as a transfer of a going concern (TOGC). Regis plc held its land as tenanted farmland, prior to obtaining vacant possession after terminating its tenants' leases; Buckden is going to hold the land as a property developer, and will change the use of the land from farmland to retail use. To be a TOGC the purchaser and the vendor must carry on the same kind of business. There is little scope to argue that, even after obtaining vacant possession, the sale is from one property developer to another: the seller has not carried out any development work, and has not held the land in that capacity for any length of time. So the TOGC rules do not apply and Regis must charge VAT on its sale.

Option to tax

[23.24] Buckden has incurred VAT on the purchase of the option, on the land purchase and on the costs associated with obtaining planning permission. Buckden will also incur further VAT on the construction cost.

The supplies that Buckden plans to make in future will be the sale of the land itself. In order to be able to recover its VAT on purchase and construction, Buckden must be able to demonstrate its intention to make taxable supplies of the land.

Buckden can recover the VAT incurred on the purchase of the land from Regis on its VAT return. Buckden's ability to recover the VAT was originally due to its intention to sell the freehold of a newly constructed commercial property; but once there are agreements for lease in place, Buckden needs to make the option to tax in order to demonstrate that the letting activity would also be taxable. Buckden duly notifies HMRC of a valid option to tax, and proceeds to recover its input VAT incurred in full.

Note that before entering into the agreements for lease with prospective tenants, Buckden was unlikely to be required to operate the Capital Goods Scheme (CGS) when recovering the VAT on the purchase of the land (and would not have needed to opt to tax the land). The CGS does not apply to an item acquired solely for the purposes of selling that item (VAT Regulations 1995/2518, reg 112(2)). Upon entering into the agreements for lease, the property is re-categorised, for VAT purposes only, as an investment property, and no longer stock in trade, so the development becomes a CGS item.

SDLT

[23.25] SDLT will be payable by Buckden on its purchase of the three sites separately. For each site the SDLT is due on the total consideration, which comprises:

(i)   The purchase price
        SDLT will be payable at the 2% and 5% rates on the VAT-inclusive amount paid for the freehold land.
(ii)   The price paid for the original grant of the option and the payment to extend the option
        The exercise of each of the options is 'linked' with the earlier grant of the option and the payment to extend the option. The consideration given for the acquisition of the freehold and the price paid for the options will determine the applicable SDLT rate for both transactions.
(iii)   The overage
        Buckden's liability to pay overage is contingent and unascertainable consideration. As purchaser, Buckden must make a reasonable estimate of the amount that is likely to be payable under the overage agreement. SDLT is then payable at the effective date of the land purchase on the estimated amount, in addition to the known consideration for the land. (When the overage has been paid and the final consideration is known, the SDLT must be re-calculated and the original SDLT return must be amended and re-submitted to HMRC within 30 days.)
        Buckden can apply to HMRC for a deferral of SDLT on the overage elements of the consideration as they are unknown amounts at the effective date of acquisition of the land (FA 2003, s 90). The application to defer SDLT must be made within 30 days of the purchase of the land and must include an estimate of the contingent element and the amount of SDLT being deferred. Apart from the obvious cash-flow benefit, Buckden would suffer no interest charge on the future SDLT payments which become due when the overage payments are ascertained. Without a deferral agreement HMRC could charge interest on the additional consideration payable under the overage agreement calculated from the original filing date (30 days after purchase of the land).

The SDLT on the three land purchases is calculated as follows:

Land purchased from Black

[23.26] The purchase price of £10m is linked with the payments made for the option, giving total consideration of £10.25m, plus the estimated amount that will be due under the overage agreement. Both the purchase price and the two option payments are subject to SDLT. The first £150,000 of consideration attracts no SDLT; the next £100,000 of consideration is chargeable at 2%; and SDLT is due on the consideration above £250,000 at a rate of 5%. A deferral of the SDLT on the overage element of the consideration is agreed with HMRC.

SDLT on £10.25m purchase price at 2%/5%	£502,000
SDLT on estimate of overage amount – deferral agreed by HMRC	–
Less SDLT paid on options (see **23.12** above)	(£2,000)
Total SDLT payable by Buckden on land purchase	£500,000

Land purchased from Redmond

[23.27] SDLT of £500,000 is payable, calculated in the same way as for the land purchased from Black, above.

Land purchased from Regis plc

[23.28] The purchase price of £20m plus VAT = £24m is linked with the payments made for the option (£500,000 plus VAT = £600,000), giving chargeable consideration of £24.6m, plus the estimated amount that will be due under the overage agreement. Both the purchase price and the two option payments are subject to SDLT, mostly at the 5% rate. A deferral of the SDLT on the overage element of the consideration is agreed with HMRC.

SDLT on the £24.6m VAT-inclusive aggregate consideration	£1,219,500
SDLT on estimate of overage amount – deferral agreed with HMRC	–
Less SDLT paid on options (see **23.12** above)	(£19,500)
Total SDLT on land purchase	£1,200,000

Corporation tax

Acquirer of land

[23.29] Buckden accounts for its land purchase as an addition to work-in-progress on its balance sheet. Note that even though all of its transactions relate to the purchase of freehold land, none of Buckden's expenditure is capital for tax purposes. As a developer, its land purchase and related costs are all revenue expenses, and will be fully deductible when they are matched with income (ie debited to Buckden's profit and loss account). At this stage, Buckden considers that its holding in the land and the plans for the project are of sufficient value that it is not necessary to write down its work-in-progress balance; so none of the expenditure is deductible in a computation of taxable profits or tax losses yet – the deduction is deferred until the work-in-progress is debited to the profit and loss account.

Sellers of the land

[23.30] The grant of an option and the subsequent sale of the subject matter of that option are treated for capital gains purposes as a single transaction, with proceeds equal to the aggregate consideration for the options and for the land.

The capital gains disposal calculations for the three landowners are as follows (with additional historic information being introduced where necessary to complete the calculations).

Timing of disposals

[23.31] There are no conditions in the contract for purchase of the land, so the capital gains on the disposals of the land arise on the date of the contract, which is also the date that the options were exercised.

Amounts already assessed to tax on grant of the options

[23.32] It can be seen in the calculations below that the consideration for grant of the options must be added to the consideration for the land – the grant of the options and the sale of the underlying subject matter must be treated as one transaction (TCGA 1992, s 144(2)). Of course, the amounts already assessed to tax on the grant of the options are then deducted from the gain taxable on sale of the land.

Capital gains calculations on land disposals	£	
Black		
Proceeds		
Land	10,000,000	
Proceeds for option	250,000	
Value of 'chose in action'	140,000	See below
Total proceeds	10,390,000	
Cost	(75,000)	Originally inherited from the previous Earl in 1990 with probate value £75,000 (TCGA 1992, s 62).
Gross gain	10,315,000	
Amount already assessed to tax on grant of options	(250,000)	Black's annual exempt amount has already been used up by other capital gains in the year.
	10,065,000	Black is not entitled to entrepreneur's relief – the sale of the land only represents the disposal of an asset of a continuing farming business (*Russell v HMRC* [2012] UKFTT 623 (TC))
CGT @ 20%	2,013,000	Rollover relief may be available to reduce the gain if the proceeds are reinvested in qualifying assets within 3 years.
Redmond		
Proceeds		
Land	10,000,000	
Legal costs at acquisition	(7,500)	Incidental costs of acquisition and disposal are deductible under TCGA 1992, s 38(2)
Legal costs at disposal	(4,000)	
Proceeds for option	250,000	
Value of 'chose in action'	140,000	See below
Total proceeds	10,377,500	
Cost	(125,000)	Originally acquired in 1997 for £125,000.
Construction of barn (1999)	(90,000)	Enhancement expenditure deductible under TCGA 1992, s 38(1)(b)
Gross gain	10,162,500	

Capital gains calculations on land disposals	£	
Already assessed on grant of options	(250,000)	
	9,912,500	
Annual exempt amount	(11,300)	
	9,901,200	
CGT @ 10% (with full claim for entrepreneur's relief)	990,120	The landholding represented the whole of Redmond's farming business, which has now ceased. This makes Redmond eligible for entrepreneur's relief (see **CHAPTER 14**) on the full amount of the gain, as it is below the £10m lifetime limit (and Redmond has not previously used the relief).

Regis plc

Proceeds		
Land	20,000,000	
Legal fees on acquisition of land	(20,000)	Incidental costs of acquisition and disposal are deductible under TCGA 1992, s 38(2).
Legal fees on disposal of land	(15,000)	
Proceeds for options	500,000	
Value of 'chose in action'	280,000	See below
Cost	(350,000)	Originally acquired in 1983
Enhancement expenditure – new grain silos	(550,000)	September 1983
Indexation allowance on cost of land Jan 1983–Nov 2019	(175,000)	As a corporation tax payer Regis plc is able to deduct indexation allowance in its calculation of the gain.
Indexation allowance on enhancement expenditure Sept 1983–Nov 2019	(700,000)	
Amount already assessed to tax on options	(250,000)	
	18,720,000	
Corporation tax @ 17%	3,182,400	Although Regis plc intends to reinvest the proceeds in new land, it cannot claim rollover relief as the asset was not used for the purposes of its trade – it was leased to occupiers outside the Regis capital gains group.

Entitlement to overage – value of 'chose in action' included in capital gains calculations above

[23.33] Each landowner is entitled to an overage payment in the event of a future sale of the property by Buckden or any other event by which Buckden (or any parent company of Buckden) realizes value through a corporate transaction deriving its value from the Newbold development.

There is no cap on the overage payment so, following the principle established in the decision of *Marren v Ingles* (1980) 54 TC 76, the right to receive the overage in future is regarded as an element of the consideration, and the current value of that 'chose in action' should be added to the cash proceeds in the calculation of the capital gain.

When Regis plc prepares its accounts for the period that includes the disposal, it decides to take the prudent course of not recognising any value for the right to receive further consideration if and when the development is completed. When Regis plc's annual tax computations are prepared, the company instructs an independent valuer to assess the current value of the right to receive additional consideration. The valuer's opinion is that it is unlikely that anyone would commit a large amount for the speculative purchase of the future right; in their professional opinion, the value of the right is £280,000 for Regis plc. This figure is included as additional consideration in the capital gains calculation above (and equivalent figures are included for Redmond and Black based on the same valuation).

Construction

[23.34] Construction begins in early 2021. Buckden agrees a construction contract with Skiddaw Limited for £280m. Construction is expected to take three years.

Buckden has secured funding for construction, as follows:

ARNE Bank	£196m	LIBOR + 4%
Walton plc – mezzanine finance	£50m	13% fixed
Swale Properties plc	£34m	15%

Tax consequences of construction contract

VAT

[23.35] Skiddaw Limited will charge Buckden Developments Limited VAT at the standard rate on the amounts payable under the construction contract. VAT must be charged whenever a valid VAT invoice is issued for work completed, or when a payment is made under the contract if that is earlier. In practice, Skiddaw issues applications for payment, so each payment crystallises a tax point for VAT purposes.

Recovery of VAT during the construction phase

[23.36] As Buckden is filing monthly VAT returns, it is able to recover the VAT on payments to Skiddaw Limited almost as soon as paying the invoice. For example, the second stage payment under the contract is agreed by Skiddaw and the surveyors managing the project for Buckden to be due in May 2021. Skiddaw submits the invoice to Buckden on 20 May 2021. The invoice terms are that it is payable within 14 days. Buckden includes the invoice in its VAT return for May, which it submits on 2 June 2021. Buckden pays the invoice on 3 June 2021. HMRC reimburse the VAT to Buckden on 18 June 2021, only 15 days after the VAT was paid.

If invoices can be raised closer to the month end date, then there will be a shorter gap (if any) between the payment of VAT and its recovery from HMRC.

Construction industry scheme (CIS)

[23.37] Buckden Developments Limited is a 'mainstream contractor' (within FA 2004, 59(1)(a)) for the purposes of the CIS, as it carries on a property development business which 'includes construction operations'. 'Construction operations' is broadly defined and includes site preparation, construction, alteration, repair, demolition and dismantling works.

As a contractor, the CIS rules (FA 2004, s 61) oblige Buckden to withhold CIS deductions at either the standard rate of 20% or the higher rate of 30% from payments in respect of construction operations, unless Skiddaw Limited (the 'sub-contractor') is registered under CIS for gross payment status (FA 2004, s 60(4)).

Before the first payment is made Buckden must verify Skiddaw's payment status with HMRC, who will confirm Skiddaw's tax payment status as gross, or net of deduction at 20% or 30% (Buckden is not required to re-verify Skiddaw until two full tax years have elapsed).

Skiddaw provides Buckden with the appropriate information to allow Buckden to verify Skiddaw's payment status with HMRC, and HMRC confirm that Skiddaw holds gross payment status. Consequently, Buckden makes no withholding from its stage payments to Skiddaw, and must file a monthly CIS300 return confirming the gross amounts paid to Skiddaw for construction operations undertaken.

Transactions during the construction phase – sale of development company

[23.38] During 2022, while construction of the retail park is continuing, Swale Properties plc sells Buckden Developments Limited to a larger UK property developer, Cope plc, for £9m. Buckden owns all of the land, including the partially completed building and, at the time of disposal, owes £48m to Swale Properties plc.

Cope agrees in a clause of the share purchase agreement that immediately after the purchase it will inject sufficient funds into Buckden Developments Limited (which it will then own) to enable Buckden to repay all of its debts to Swale Properties plc.

Tax consequences of disposal of development company

Corporation tax

Capital gains analysis

[23.39] Ordinarily, a share sale would be taxed as a capital gains disposal.

The disposal by Swale Properties plc generates a capital gain of £8m (proceeds of £9m less share capital invested of £1m). The buyer's promise to procure the repayment of debt to the seller does not affect the calculation of the capital gain on the share sale as the debt is repayable on demand and the repayment does not increase the value of Swale's investment in Buckden.

Swale/Buckden could instead have agreed to sell the land to Cope, along with the partly-completed development. Commercially and legally this would have been more complex, as Cope would have had to 'step into' the construction contract. Ignoring the small amount of indexation allowance, it is likely that the taxable profit on sale of the land would have been the same amount as the capital gain on the sale of the shares. The downside of purchasing the land is that the purchaser would have had to pay SDLT at an effective rate of almost 5% of the consideration for the land.

Capital gains – substantial shareholding exemption (SSE)

[23.40] Swale Properties plc has some investment properties (non-trading assets) but these are not sufficient to prevent the Swale group from being a 'trading group' for the purposes of TCGA 1992, Sch 7AC. This means that if Buckden Developments Limited is a 'trading company' for the purposes of the same legislation, the disposal would be exempt from corporation tax on capital gains.

HMRC's capital gains manual defines a 'trading company' as one that undertakes trading activities . . . and does not undertake non-trading activities to a substantial extent. 'Trading activities' includes preparations for a trade. Buckden is not yet in a position to earn any trading income, but the SSE rules identify a company such as Buckden, in its pre-trading phase, as a 'trading company' (TCGA 1992, Sch 7AC para 20(2)(b)). Consequently, the disposal of the shares by Swale Properties plc is eligible for SSE, meaning that no capital gain is assessable to tax.

'Transactions in UK land' (tax avoidance) rules

[23.41] The retail park project involves the development of land, so the 'transactions in UK land' rules must be considered (CTA 2010, Part 8ZB). These rules apply to counteract tax avoidance where a capital gain is realized on the disposal of land which has been developed, or of an asset deriving its value from land where the land is held as trading stock. For example, if a group of companies has capital losses available, the group would reduce its tax bill on a successful property development if it sold the company owning the developed site (a capital gains disposal), rather than the site itself (a trading transaction).

In some circumstances, a capital gain realized on the disposal of land (or of an asset deriving its value from land) can be re-categorized as a trading profit. For Buckden the relevant questions to consider are whether:

- a profit or gain is realized from the disposal of UK land or of an asset deriving its value from UK land; and one of the following applies:
  - the land was acquired with the sole or main object of realizing a profit or gain on its disposal; or
  - the land is held as trading stock; or
  - the land is developed with the sole or main object of realizing a profit or gain from disposing of the land when developed (CTA 2010, s 356OB).

It is clear that Buckden falls squarely within the conditions for the re-categorization to apply: a gain has been realized and the land is held as trading stock. These rules are new (introduced by FA 2016) but they are very similar to the 'transactions in land' rules which they supersede (CTA 2010, s 815 et seq, now repealed). HMRC generally applied the old rules only where there was evidence of an intention to avoid tax. This was confirmed in the case *Yuill v Wilson* ((1980) 52 TC 674), although in the subsequent case of *Lowther v Page* (1983) 57 TC 199 the avoidance of tax was equated with saving tax, widening the scope for application of the rules. HMRC's guidance (HMRC manual BIM60510, et seq) on the new legislation states that if a 'transaction in land' results in a tax saving, even though tax avoidance was not a motive of the transaction, and falls within the conditions, then the rules should be applied to re-categorize the gain as income.

In this case, there is legal and commercial advantage in purchasing the company rather than the land – because of the difficulty in assigning a partially fulfilled £200m construction contract. In addition, it is sensible tax housekeeping on the part of the purchaser to buy the company, rather than incur a large SDLT liability on the purchase of the land. The consequential benefit to Swale Properties plc is that the capital gain realized on sale of the shares is exempt under the SSE rules.

Should the 'transactions in UK land' rules apply in this case to re-categorize the capital gain (exempt under SSE) as a trading profit?

[23.42] Even though there is no avoidance motive, the conditions for the rules to apply are fulfilled where the land is held as trading stock. There is a self-assessment obligation on Swale Properties plc, and it is not reasonable to assume that HMRC would overlook or ignore the law.

HMRC's draft guidance (HMRC manual BIM60595) states that there will continue to be an exemption, as there was in the predecessor legislation, for sales of shares in companies which hold land as trading stock. This is on the basis that profits from disposal of the land will be chargeable on the company. This exemption should apply for Swale, as there would otherwise be double taxation (in the absence of tax avoidance arrangements).

Swale Properties plc will need to confirm that the land is ultimately sold by Buckden in the course of its trade.

If Buckden Developments Limited were not to sell the land, then HMRC may argue that a trading profit should have been recognised by Swale on the disposal of Buckden.

Exemptions – no tax to pay on sale of shares

[23.43] SSE applies to relieve the capital gain and the disposal is exempt from the 'transactions in UK land' rules, so Swale Properties plc has no corporation tax liability on the disposal of the shares in Buckden Developments Limited.

SDLT/stamp duty

[23.44] SDLT was paid on the acquisition of the land by Buckden Developments Limited. No SDLT is payable on the acquisition by Cope of the company, as SDLT is not generally chargeable on consideration for shares in property-rich companies (in the absence of tax avoidance arrangements).

Stamp duty is payable on the consideration for shares at 0.5% of the £9m consideration = £45,000. The buyer's promise to inject funds into Buckden to enable it to repay its debts to Swale does not affect the stamp duty payable on the shares. (Note that if the purchaser had agreed to settle Buckden's debts itself, this could be treated as additional chargeable consideration subject to stamp duty.)

Overage agreement

[23.45] On the sale by Swale Properties plc of Buckden Developments Limited the original landowners are entitled to receive 25% under the terms of their overage agreement. If there was a taxable gain (or taxable charge under the 'transactions in UK land' rules) then when calculating that gain, Swale would be entitled to a deduction for the payment under the overage agreement, but the gain is treated as exempt – see above.

The sale of the shares in Buckden realized a (non-taxable) gain for Swale of £8m, of which the original landowners are entitled to 25% = £2m. £1m goes to Regis plc; £0.5m goes to each of Black and Redmond.

Tax consequences of overage payments to former landowners

Corporation tax

Acquirer of shares

[23.46] Cope plc's £9m payment for the shares is treated by Cope as capital gains base cost in the shares acquired. The £9m payment is not a deductible expense of the development and would not, for example, be deductible when Buckden sells the land.

Tax consequences of overage receipts for former landowners

Income tax/capital gains tax/corporation tax

[23.47] As shown at **23.33** above, each landowner retained rights to future receipts from Buckden; the value of those rights was taxed as consideration on the sale of the land. These rights are known as 'choses in action'. When the sums are received from Buckden (being the landowners' share of the sale proceeds) this represents a disposal of the landowners' rights (or choses). The rights have capital gains base cost equal to the amount on which the landowners were taxed on the initial sale of the land (in the case of Black £140,000 – see **23.32** above). But before undertaking the capital gains calculation, it is necessary to consider whether the 'transactions in UK land' legislation might apply to recategorize the gain as income instead.

'Transactions in UK land' (tax avoidance) rules – CTA 2010, Part 8ZB

[23.48] HMRC's guidance (HMRC manual BIM60645) makes it clear that they would expect a capital gain to be re-categorized as an income profit where there is a 'slice of the action' contract. By this, HMRC mean that where someone sells land, and retains the right to further proceeds dependent on the success of the future development of that land, they should be viewed as participators in a trading venture rather than sellers of capital assets used in their business (or investments).

HMRC's manual makes it clear that once physical development of the land has begun (as it has in this case) then they would regard amounts payable under an overage arrangement as arising from a 'slice of the action' scheme, and so taxable as income rather than as a capital gains receipt.

The conclusion of this analysis is that the receipt should be taxed as income. CTA 2010, s 356OL states that where part of the gain is 'fairly attributable' to a period before the intention to develop the land was formed, then that part of the gain does not fall within the transactions in UK Land rules. Once physical development of the land is underway, the profit arising from that point onwards is subject to those rules, and so taxable as trading profits. Black's chose in action was valued at £140,000, which amount was taxed as deemed consideration on the sale of the land (see **23.32** above). If the capital gains rules had applied to the receipt of the overage amount, Black would have been deemed to dispose of his 'chose in action' for the amount received, and the £140,000 (for Black) would have been the base cost deductible against the amount received.

The 'transactions in UK land' rules do not contain any of these capital gains concepts, but it would be expected that the calculation of the amount taxable would result in a similar outcome, unless it could be demonstrated that the chose in action had increased in value prior to the commencement of physical development of the land. This was not the case for Black, so it would be reasonable to assume that the taxable amount for Black would be the £500,000 receipt less the £140,000 already taxed as capital gains proceeds on sale of the land, giving £360,000 subject to income tax at the recipient's marginal rate. For Redmond the calculation would be the same. For Regis the amount of trading profit subject to corporation tax would, following the same logic, be £1m less £280,000 already assessed = £720,000.

Tax consequences of payments under the overage agreement

VAT

[23.49] The sale of shares is a VAT exempt supply. Swale plc might not be able to recover the VAT on its legal fees and other incidental costs of the sale of the shares.

The payments totalling £2m to the original landowners represent further consideration for the original supply of the interest in the land and the same VAT treatment applies to the new £2m payments as applied to the original land purchase. The 20% VAT on the £1m overage payable to Regis plc (which had opted to tax the land) falls due at the time the amount is received or invoiced, whichever is earlier.

SDLT

[23.50] The SDLT returns originally submitted upon purchase of the land must be amended and re-submitted to HMRC within 30 days of the amount payable under the overage agreement becoming known. Buckden deferred the SDLT due on the estimated overage element of the consideration. Now that Buckden has paid the final consideration under the overage agreement, the SDLT due on the land purchase must be re-calculated and the additional SDLT paid within 30 days of the amount being ascertained.

In practice, as Buckden benefited from a deferral of the overage element, the company must now simply pay additional SDLT on the £0.5m consideration paid under the overage agreement to Black at 5% (because this SDLT arises on the land purchase transaction for which the aggregate consideration is already well above the £250,000 threshold – see **23.28** above). SDLT is £0.5m at 5% = £25,000.

Buckden's SDLT on the amount payable to Redmond is the same as for Black above, £25,000.

The overage payable by Buckden to Regis plc is £1m plus VAT = £1.2m (since Regis plc opted to tax its interest in the site). The SDLT payable by Buckden on the overage payment to Regis plc is 5% of £1.2m = £60,000.

Cope plc and Buckden Developments Limited continue with the development during 2022

[23.51] Unfortunately, Cope plc gets into financial difficulties in October 2022. The development finance proves to be insufficient, and construction work is halted for 12 months. When Buckden Developments Limited prepares its balance sheet for the year ending 31 March 2023, its auditors insist that Buckden should write down its work-in-progress. By the end of March 2023,

Buckden has incurred costs on the Newbold development, including financing costs, of £340m. Buckden's directors agree with its auditors that, with the project stalled, prospects are diminished, and the work-in-progress should be written down by £60m. That amount is debited to Buckden's profit and loss account, and generates the company's first loss.

Another company in the Cope group is profitable so Buckden agrees to surrender £20m of its loss as group relief to the profitable company. The tax saving generated by the surrender of group relief deriving from the write-down of the work-in-progress is 17% of £20m = £3.4m. Cope uses the £3.4m tax repayment to help re-start the construction work on the Newbold site – a good example of using tax assets to derive advantage from what appears to be a commercial failure.

After surrendering the group relief, Buckden Developments Limited is left with a trading loss of £40m carried forward, available to reduce its future profits of the same trade.

ARNE Bank plc is concerned at the lack of progress, and the possible loss of some of its investment in the project, and loans an additional £25m to Buckden Developments Limited, sufficient to see construction through to completion. The loan has an interest rate of 12%, higher than on the bank's main loan for the construction works. Although this interest rate is high, it is within the bounds of rates charged by lenders on similar loans. The loan is made to a highly-geared company which is in distress, so the rate in this case would not represent more than a 'reasonable commercial return' for the lender (CTA 2010, s 1005), which is one of the tests for whether a payment of interest could be regarded as a non-deductible distribution for corporation tax purposes.

Transactions during the construction phase

[23.52] During construction, in parallel with the other transactions described above, Buckden contacts leading retailers, seeking their commitment to enter into lease agreements as soon as construction is complete.

In 2022 Buckden enters into a pre-let agreement with Engels plc – the pre-eminent high street fashion retailer. Buckden is very pleased to secure Engels as a tenant in the retail park, and agrees with Engels that their 20-year lease commitment could be publicized in the hope that this would attract other tenants to the retail park. Brochures are sent to other retailers, prospective tenants, bearing both the Buckden and the Engels corporate insignia. The brochure even includes the slogan 'Engels did not fear to tread . . . '.

For agreeing to enter into its lease (and for participating in the marketing effort) Engels will be paid £4m when the lease is granted, after construction is completed.

Tax consequences of agreement for lease to Engels plc

VAT

[23.53] Ordinarily, a payment made to induce a tenant to enter into a lease would be outside the scope of VAT; but, because of its close involvement with the development, Engels would be regarded by HMRC as an 'anchor tenant'. This means that the inducement is regarded as a payment for a taxable supply of services by the tenant (Engels) to the landlord (Buckden), so the sum that will be paid to Engels when the lease is granted will be subject to VAT at the standard rate of 20%.

Buckden will be able to reclaim this VAT as it relates to the intended taxable letting of its property by virtue of its option to tax.

HMRC's views on the VAT treatment of an inducement paid to a company that agrees to act as an anchor tenant are set out in HMRC Business Brief 04/03, as amended by Business Brief 12/05.

SDLT

[23.54] There is no SDLT on a reverse premium.

Corporation tax

[23.55] Until the £4m lease inducement is paid, there will be no corporation tax consequences for either party. When payment is made, the tax effect for the payer and the recipient will be as follows:

Developer

[23.56] The payment by Buckden Developments Limited of the inducement to Engels plc will be added to work-in-progress in Buckden's accounts, and should be a deductible expense when it is debited to the company's profit and loss account. This is because in Buckden's trade of property development, the inducement will improve the value of what Buckden ultimately hopes to sell (the developed land, with rent-paying tenants in occupation). Although it is the type of payment that for anyone other than a property developer would be regarded as a capital expense, and disallowed in the tax computation, the payment should be a deductible expense provided it is made in furtherance of Buckden's property development trade.

Tenant

[23.57] Engels plc will be the recipient of a reverse premium, as defined by CTA 2009, s 96. The receipt is not from a connected party, so it will be taxable in line with its recognition as income in the company's accounts. Under FRS102, (the 'new' UK GAAP), Engels should account for the reverse premium receipt as income over the period to which it relates. The lease contains no unusual rental increases or rebates, so the reverse premium will be accounted for as deferred income (held as a creditor balance in the company's balance sheet) and released evenly to the profit and loss account over the 20-year term of the lease.

Other agreements for lease

[23.58] As construction is nearing completion, Buckden seeks to enter into agreements for lease with other retailers. Thirty prospective tenants sign binding commitments to enter into a lease at the completion of construction. Buckden agrees to pay inducements to five of them when the leases are granted.

Tax consequences of lease inducements

Corporation tax and VAT

[23.59] Until the leases are granted and the payments are made, there will be no tax consequences. When the payments are made the VAT and corporation tax consequences will be as set out below.

	Term of lease	Inducement	VAT treatment of payment and corporation tax treatment for recipient
Mundella Limited	10 years	Reverse premium £600K	VAT – Outside the scope of VAT as an inducement with no obligations on the tenant other than to enter into the lease (*Mirror Group plc*, ECJ C-409/98, 2001).
			CT – receipt will be taxable as income when released to profit and loss account over the term of the lease.
Ramaphosa Limited	15 years	Rent-free two years	VAT – Outside the scope of VAT as a rent-free period is not consideration for a supply.
			CT – benefit of rent-free period will be spread in landlord's and tenant's accounts over the term of the lease, so some rent will be expensed in tenant's accounts during the rent-free period, even though none is paid.
Machel Building Society	10 years	£0.5m contribution to fit-out costs	VAT – Standard-rated supply from tenant to landlord as there is a direct link between the payment and the goods / services supplied by Buckden.
			CT – Machel's fit-out costs qualify for capital allowances, so there is no taxable reverse premium (CTA 2009, s 97). Machel cannot claim capital allowances on the expenditure funded by the contribution (CAA 2001, s 532).

	Term of lease	Inducement	VAT treatment of payment and corporation tax treatment for recipient
Airlie NHS Trust (drop-in clinic)	5 years	Reverse premium £0.2m	VAT – Outside the scope of VAT as a pure inducement. CT – NHS bodies are exempt from corporation tax (CTA 2010, s 985).
Bevan Housing Association (registered charity)	5 years	Reverse premium £0.2m	VAT – Outside the scope of VAT as a pure inducement. CT – the receipt is used for charitable purposes, so is not taxable on Bevan.

Corporation tax consequences for payer of inducements (developer)

[23.60] When the leases are granted and the amounts are paid, Buckden's payments of reverse premiums and contributions to fit-out costs will be added to work-in-progress on the company's balance sheet and will be deductible from the eventual profit made by Buckden on the development.

The rent-free periods will not give rise to any immediate expense for Buckden – as developer Buckden will sell the property to Armitage Securities plc before any rent is due. Armitage will account for the cost of a rent-free period as arising evenly over the term of the lease. During the rent-free period, Armitage will account for some rental income, and will have to pay tax on it, even though no rent has been received. After the rent-free period has finished, Armitage will receive more rent each year than it recognises as income in its accounts, and the initial unfavourable timing difference will gradually reverse.

The contribution towards fit-out costs will be treated as an allowable expense for Buckden in the same way as a reverse premium. While a landlord who is a property investor would treat the contribution as a capital cost, not deductible from rental profits, as a property developer Buckden can treat the payment as an expense of its trade, as it helps improve the property in advance of its sale.

The property is now more than 60% pre-let so the condition in the sale contract is fulfilled. Once construction is complete there will be nothing to prevent the sale to Armitage from going ahead.

Practical completion

[23.61] Finally, construction is completed in 2023.

Armitage Securities plc purchases the completed development for £450m on 30 September 2023. £40m of the purchase price is deferred until 12 months after the purchase, a 'retention' in case of problems with the building requiring remedy by the builder.

In Buckden's accounts for the year ended 30 September 2023 the full £450m of sales proceeds is recognised as turnover. No reduction is made for the £40m retained by the purchaser. If any of the retention is used by the purchaser for remedying defects, and cannot subsequently be recovered from the builder, then Buckden would have to recognise this cost in a later year. Buckden's accounts for 2023 take no account of this contingent liability, so the full amount will be taxable in line with its recognition as turnover in the accounts, even though some has yet to be received.

Buckden Developments Limited has incurred the following costs:

		Deductible in tax computation
Purchase price of land	£40m	✓
Stamp Duty Land Tax	£2.3m	✓
Cost of options	£1m	✓
Legal fees – planning permission, leases, sale, buy-out of overage	£3.4m	✓
Legal fees – sale of Buckden Developments Limited	£0.4m	✗
Surveyor's fees	£0.8m	✓
Management fees	£5m	✓
Insurance	£1.1m	✓
Consultancy – engineers, architects, property consultants	£2.3m	✓
Interest on loan from Swale Properties plc	£17m	✓
Interest on loan from ARNE	£60m	✓
Interest on loan from Walton	£5.3m	✓
Construction costs	£280m	✓
Total costs incurred	£419m	✓
Work-in-progress write-down in 2022	(£60m)	
Net work-in-progress at time of sale	£359m	

Tax consequences of sale of completed property

Corporation tax

[23.62] The proposed Corporate Interest Restriction (CIR) rules could limit the amount of interest payable which Buckden can treat as deductible in the period the development is sold. If the Fixed Ratio Rule does not permit a full deduction, the Group Ratio Rule may increase the deductible amount. It would be expected that all interest paid to banks and other unrelated lenders should be deductible. Deductions for interest on the loan from the parent company may be limited by the new CIR rules, assuming they become law.

With turnover of £450m (taking no account of the retention) and costs on the balance sheet (work-in-progress) of £359m, the accounting profit for Buckden Developments Limited for the year ended 30 September 2023 is £91m, which is taxable. Assuming that all of the interest payable is deductible in the period the development is sold, the £0.4m legal fees identified in the table above are the only non-deductible expenses, so the sale yields a taxable profit of £91.4m.

Note that Buckden has already had the benefit of the £60m write-down of its work-in-progress. It surrendered £20m of that loss as group relief to another company in the Cope group, earning the group a tax repayment of £4m in the process. Buckden's loss brought forward of £40m can be set against the profit made for 2023, giving a taxable amount of £51.4m.

The corporation tax on £51.4m at 17% is £8,738,000. Although Buckden has never been a 'large' company before, it will still have to pay this tax in four equal instalments. Under SI 1998/3175, reg 3(3) a company need not make instalment payments of its corporation tax for the first period in which its taxable profits exceed £1.5m; but if profits are in excess of £10m this exemption does not apply.

The date for the first instalment has already passed. Strictly, HMRC could argue that Buckden negligently failed to anticipate its taxable profit for the year ended 30 September 2023, and should have made instalment payments of 25% of the tax in April 2023 and July 2023 on the assumption that the company would make the sale. In practice, Buckden could not have assumed that it would make a successful sale of the site until the contractual conditions had been satisfied. Buckden will have to pay interest on the tax which (with hindsight) should have been due on the April and July 2023 instalment dates, but should not be subject to any penalty for late payment. The other two instalment dates will be 14 October 2023 and 14 January 2024. (The Government has proposed that, from 2019 onwards, for very large companies the quarterly tax payment dates will be brought forward by four months so that all tax is paid quarterly in the year the associated profit arises. The legislation giving effect to this has not yet been introduced.)

VAT

Seller

[23.63] It has been determined that the sale will qualify as a TOGC and so is outside the scope of VAT. This is because HMRC accept that the sale of a building with the benefit of existing tenancies constitutes the sale of a property rental business. This is the case even where there is an agreement for lease in place but the lease itself has not yet been agreed (Notice 700/9 para 6.2). Buckden Developments Limited seeks non-statutory clearance from HMRC of TOGC treatment after the transaction completes but HMRC decline to provide clearance as they consider the transaction to be clearly covered within its public notice on TOGC treatment.

Buyer

[23.64] In order to satisfy the TOGC conditions, Armitage Securities plc has:

- notified HMRC of an option to tax prior to completion and prior to making any payment;
- applied to register for VAT; and
- warranted in the land purchase agreement that its option to tax will not be disapplied following purchase.

During the sale process it has been determined that the charitable tenants are using their units as offices and therefore the option to tax is not disapplied in respect of those tenancies, and TOGC treatment applies to the full sale transaction.

Capital goods scheme (CGS)

[23.65] Whilst Armitage agrees that the VAT capital goods scheme (CGS) is unlikely to have applied to the property while it was owned by Buckden, Armitage would take on any CGS obligation when buying the property as a TOGC. Armitage insists upon Buckden providing all the relevant information that would be required to provide CGS calculations to HMRC.

Armitage then charges VAT on all rents payable by tenants under the lease by virtue of its option to tax.

SDLT

[23.66] Armitage Securities plc must pay SDLT on the VAT-inclusive consideration. No VAT is payable as the land purchase is a TOGC (see above).

The SDLT payable on the £450m consideration is £22,489,500.

Grant of leases to tenants

[23.67] Leases are granted to Engels plc and the five other tenants who signed the pre-let agreements. The VAT and corporation tax consequences of the inducement payments and receipts are set out at **23.59** above.

The tenants must pay SDLT on the grant of their leases. Although there is no SDLT on the various inducement payments, SDLT is still due on the rent payable under the lease in the normal way.

The details of the leases and the SDLT due are set out in the table:

	Term of lease	Rent	SDLT – amount, and notes
Engels plc	20 years	£2m pa	c £446,000
Mundella Limited	10 years	£300,000 pa rising with RPI	c £24,000
			Rent adjustments in line with RPI are disregarded for SDLT purposes (FA 2003, Sch 17A para 7(5))
Ramaphosa Limited	15 years	Rent-free 2 years, then £250,000 pa	c £22,000
Machel Building Society	10 years	£250,000 pa rising with CPI	c £21,000

Term of lease	Rent	SDLT – amount, and notes
		As the rent increases are variable, being linked to CPI, the SDLT should be calculated using the best estimate of the rent that will be payable in each of the first five years. At the end of year 5 the NPV calculation must be revisited based on the actual rent paid, and any additional SDLT due must be paid. A refund can be claimed if SDLT was over-paid.
		Note that the exemption for rent adjusted in line with RPI does not apply for rent adjusted in line with CPI. The SDLT cost of not having the exemption will depend on the rate of inflation. In this case that additional cost is estimated at about £2,000.
Airlie NHS Trust (drop-in clinic)	5 years	£100,000 pa	£nil

Acquisitions by NHS Trusts are exempt from SDLT (FA 2003, s 67A)

| Bevan Housing Association (registered charity) | 5 years | £100,000 pa | £nil |

Bevan intend to use the premises for the furtherance of their charitable purposes, so charities relief exempts the grant of the lease from SDLT.

Freehold disposal to long-term investor

[23.68] Finally, in 2026, Armitage sells the freehold to Zephaniah Properties Plc (a Real Estate Investment Trust) for £750m.

Tax consequences of freehold sale

Corporation tax

[23.69] Armitage has made a capital gain on the disposal, which is calculated as follows.

Proceeds	£750m
Cost	(£450m)
Indexation allowance	(£40m)

Taxable gain   £260m

The corporation tax on the £260m capital gain at 17% is £44.2m.

VAT

[23.70] The disposal is of a property fully let to tenants from one property investor to another. This fulfils the requirements for a TOGC so no VAT is chargeable on the sale. The parties ensure that they satisfy the respective requirements for this VAT treatment (in particular, the purchaser notifies its option to tax to HMRC prior to the land purchase).

Tax consequences of freehold purchase

SDLT

[23.71] Zephaniah must pay SDLT on the VAT-inclusive purchase price. Since there is no VAT the SDLT is 5% of the consideration above £250,000 – so on the purchase price of £750m the SDLT is £37,489,500.

Acquisition of the property by a REIT – tax consequences for REIT

[23.72] Since Zephaniah is a Real Estate Investment Trust it is not liable to corporation tax on its rental profits.

Zephaniah is also exempt from corporation tax (and capital gains tax) on any chargeable gains it makes on property disposals. (Note that REITs no longer have to pay the 2% 'buy-in' in order to obtain this exemption.)

In order to retain its tax-advantaged status, Zephaniah distributes 90% or more of its rental profits each year to its shareholders. The shareholders are liable for tax on those distributions from Zephaniah as though they had received rental profits – so a shareholder who is a UK registered pension fund or a charity pays no tax; a UK corporate shareholder pays corporation tax at 17%; a UK individual pays income tax at their marginal rate.

Chapter 24

Scottish land and buildings transaction tax

by
Patrick Cannon,
Barrister

Introduction and summary

[24.1] The Land and Buildings Transaction Tax or LBTT has applied to land transactions in Scotland since 1 April 2015 and is administered by Revenue Scotland. LBTT applies regardless of where the purchaser is located, if the land is situated in Scotland. Transitional provisions retain some transactions within SDLT, particularly where the contract was concluded before 1 May 2012, and some payments arising out of earlier transactions must still be made to HMRC. The main differences from SDLT are different rates and thresholds, different administrative and payment arrangements, exemption for residential leases, some increased compliance obligations with three-yearly reviews for commercial leases, and sub-sale relief restricted to significant developments. Anti-avoidance provisions are in a Scottish GAAR with no equivalent of FA 2003, s 75A or the 15% higher rate charge for purchases into 'envelopes'. The Annual Tax on Enveloped Dwellings or ATED continues to apply to Scotland: see **CHAPTER 22**.

Where a transaction involves properties in both Scotland and the rest of the UK, the consideration has to be apportioned between the Scottish and non-Scottish properties, and separate returns have to be made to Revenue Scotland and to HMRC.

Legislative basis for LBTT

[24.2] The Scotland Act 2012 provided powers for the Scottish Parliament to introduce devolved taxes and also for the disapplication of SDLT and Landfill Tax. That Act became law on 1 May 2012 and so the transitional provisions between SDLT and LBTT have reference to that date as well as to the 1 April 2015 commencement date. Detailed provisions for the tax are in the Land and Building Transaction Tax (Scotland) Act 2013 (LBTT(S)A 2013), as amended by the Land and Buildings Transaction Tax (Amendment) (Scotland) Act 2016 (LBTT(A)(S)A 2016).

Revenue Scotland was established under the Revenue Scotland and Tax Powers Act 2014 (RSTPA 2014) and came into existence as a non-ministerial department of the Scottish Government on 1 January 2015. It administers the new taxes and works with and delegates some powers to Registers of Scotland in relation to LBTT. This Act provides for the administrative powers of Revenue Scotland. It also includes the specific penalty regime for LBTT and the Scottish GAAR. Revenue Scotland has published a Charter specifying the standards of behaviour and values to which it and taxpayers are expected to adhere.

The provisions of these Acts have been heavily supplemented and amended by a number of Scottish Statutory Instruments in a continuing process as follows:

The Land and Buildings Transaction Tax (Scotland) Act 2013 (Commencement No 1) Order 2014 (SI 2014/279 (C 27))

The Land and Buildings Transaction Tax (Prescribed Proportions) (Scotland) Order 2014 (SI 2014/350)

The Land and Buildings Transaction Tax (Qualifying Public or Educational Bodies) (Scotland) Amendment Order 2014 (SI 2014/351)

The Land and Buildings Transaction Tax (Definition of Charity) (Relevant Territories) (Scotland) Regulations 2014 (SI 2014/352)

The Land and Buildings Transaction Tax (Administration) (Scotland) Regulations 2014 (SI 2014/375)

The Land and Buildings Transaction Tax (Ancillary Provision) (Scotland) Order 2014 (SI 2014/376)

The Land and Buildings Transaction Tax (Transitional Provisions) (Scotland) Order 2014 (SI 2014/377)

The Land and Buildings Transaction Tax (Transitional Provisions) (Scotland) Amendment Order 2015 (SI 2015/71)

The Land and Buildings Transaction Tax (Addition and Modification of Reliefs) (Scotland) Order 2015 (SI 2015/93)

The Land and Buildings Transaction Tax (Scotland) Act 2013 (Commencement No 2) Order 2015 (SI 2015/108 (C 21))

The Land and Buildings Transaction Tax (Sub-sale Development Relief and Multiple Dwellings Relief) (Scotland) Order 2015 (SI 2015/123)

The Land and Buildings Transaction Tax (Tax Rates and Tax Bands) (Scotland) Order 2015 (SI 2015/126)

The Land and Buildings Transactions Tax (Open-ended Investment Companies) (Scotland) Order 2015 (SI 2015/322)

The Land and Buildings Transaction Tax (Additional Amount – Second Homes Main Residence Relief) (Scotland) Order 2017 (SSI 2017/233)

A notable feature of LBTT(S)A 2013 is the sheer range of regulating powers given to Scottish Ministers which could be used to change the charging provisions. These go far beyond minor tinkering with definitions of chargeable interests, the scope of reliefs or deadlines for returns. The main tax rates and bands can be changed by order and key schedules can be modified by regulation – in some but not all cases subject to the affirmative procedure. These powers seem alarmingly close to 'Henry VIII powers' – though that sovereign was not of course in a position to modify Scottish legislation.

Revenue Scotland has published legislative and administrative guidance on its website at www.revenue.scot.

General structure of LBTT

[24.3] LBTT is based on SDLT in relation to Scottish land – so the overall structure and guidance is familiar. There are the familiar concepts of land transactions, chargeable interests, contract and conveyance, consideration, notifiable transactions, linked transactions, land transaction returns and exemptions and reliefs. Scots law terminology is of course used (for example, missives of let, assignations and renunciations of leases). Administration will be rather different and Revenue Scotland will no doubt develop its own style as the devolved taxes bed down.

Four areas have substantial changes from SDLT which materially affect the tax charge and day-to-day advice: the tax rates and bands; the administrative arrangements; tax on leases; and sub-sale relief. These are considered in turn below.

It is disappointing that there is little change from the complex SDLT partnership provisions.

Tax rates and bands

[24.4] These differ from SDLT although not by as much as when the LBTT rates were originally announced because when SDLT went onto a slice system in the December 2014 Autumn Statement the LBTT rates were modified in the light of this change.

The Revenue Scotland website has a number of online calculators for LBTT liabilities.

Residential transactions

[24.5] For transactions that are exclusively residential there is the same schedule of rates as for SDLT but LBTT has a longer zero-rate band and the 10% and 12% rates start at lower levels of consideration, as shown below. This means that LBTT is less for lower amounts of consideration but for consideration above £330,000 SDLT is lower than LBTT.

Rates of tax applied to slices of consideration	LBTT	SDLT
0%	up to £145,000	up to £125,000
2%	above £145,000 to £250,000	above £125,000 to £250,000
5%	above £250,000 to £325,000	above £250,000 to £925,000
10%	above £325,000 to £750,000	above £925,000 to £1,500,000
12%	over £750,000	over £1,500,000

LBTT does not have the higher rate 15% charge for residences over £500,000 being purchased by companies or other relevant 'envelopes'. Such a rate seems rather less punitive given that the maximum marginal rate of SDLT is now 12%. The possibility that LBTT might be avoided on residential transactions once a property had been bought by a company was nevertheless in the legislators' minds. There is a provision that transfers of interests in unlisted residential property holding companies could be treated as chargeable land transactions if Scottish Ministers lay regulations to switch on the provision (LBTT(S)A 2013, s 47).

It seems unlikely that this provision will be invoked for the moment because the ATED continues to apply to enveloped Scottish dwellings over the relevant threshold. ATED is a free-standing tax and there is as yet no legislative provision to switch it off for Scotland.

There is an additional amount of tax chargeable for certain acquisitions of residential property known as the Additional Dwelling Supplement. Broadly (LBTT(S)A 2013, Sch 2A, paras 2, 3), it applies where the subject matter of the transaction includes a dwelling, the consideration for the dwelling is at least £40,000, and either:

(i)   the buyer is an individual who already owns a dwelling and is not replacing his sole or main residence. For this purpose, the buyer is treated as also owning any dwelling owned by his spouse, civil partner, cohabitant, or child under 16 of any of them (LBTT(S)A 2013, Sch 2A, para 6, see also para 9A). But such a buyer is not liable to the additional amount if replacing a sole or main dwelling that he has occupied as such, and disposed of, in the 18 months prior to the transaction in question (there is an exemption if the other property is disposed of within the 18 months following the transaction: see below); or

(ii)   the buyer is an individual and the acquisition is in the course of a business he carries on, alone or in partnership, the sole or main activity of which is investing or dealing in chargeable interests; or

(iii)   the buyer is an individual who is the trustee of a trust and there is no beneficiary entitled to occupy the dwelling for life, or entitled to the income from the dwelling (if there is such a beneficiary, he is treated as the buyer: LBTT(S)A 2013, Sch 2A, para 7); or

(iv)   the buyer is not an individual.

The additional amount is equal to 3% of the 'relevant consideration' (LBTT(S)A 2013, Sch 2A, para 4(2)), including the first £40,000, notwithstanding that the additional amount is not applicable at all if the relevant consideration is less than £40,000. The 'relevant consideration' is the amount of consideration payable for the residential property element of the transaction. Where the additional amount is charged because, in addition to replacing his sole or main residence, the buyer is acquiring other dwellings, the relevant consideration excludes the amount attributable to the replacement residence.

The chargeable transaction is treated as if exempt from the additional amount if the buyer disposes of ownership of a dwelling within the 18 months following the chargeable transaction, that dwelling was the buyer's only or main residence at some point during that time, and the dwelling acquired by the transaction has been occupied as the buyer's only or main residence

(LBTT(S)(A) 2013, Sch 2A, para 8). Relief is given by way of reduction of the tax due or, if already paid, by repayment. There is also an exemption for transactions involving the acquisition of six or more dwellings (LBTT(S)(A) 2013, Sch 2A, para 9, in conjunction with s 59(8)). A repayment may also be claimed if, within 18 months of a chargeable transaction under which spouses, civil partners or cohabitants acquire a dwelling house as joint owners to be used as a main residence and pay additional dwelling supplement, one or other of the joint buyers disposes of a dwelling house that has been used by both of them as their main residence (LBTT (Additional Amount – Second Homes Main Residence Relief) (Scotland) Order 2017 effective on or after 30 June 2017).

Generally, dwellings outside Scotland count (LBTT(S)(A) 2013, Sch 2A, para 11(2)); but dwellings whose market value is less than £40,000, and ownership of them, are disregarded (LBTT(S)(A) 2013, Sch 2A, para 11(4)); ownership is acquired and disposed of on the date a transaction completes, as opposed to the date missives are concluded or a disposition registered (LBTT(S)(A) 2013, Sch 2A, para 12, in conjunction with s 63); and a beneficiary under a bare trust, or who has a right to occupy a dwelling for life, or a right to income from it, is treated as its owner in place of the trustee (LBTT(S)(A) 2013, Sch 2A, paras 13, 14). A tenant under a lease of longer than 20 years, and a proper liferenter, are likewise treated as owners instead of, respectively, the landlord and the fiar (LBTT(S)(A) 2013, Sch 2A, paras 15, 16). Each of a number of joint owners is to be treated as the owner of the dwelling (LBTT(S)(A) 2013, Sch 2A, para 17).

Non-residential and mixed transactions

[24.6] For non-residential and mixed-transactions LBTT has always had a slice system (while SDLT introduced this for these types of transactions after 16 March 2016). LBTT is generally higher for consideration up to £300,000 and SDLT is higher thereafter.

Rates of tax applied to slices of consideration	LBTT	Rate applied to slices of consideration	SDLT
0%	up to £150,000	0%	up to £150,000
3%	above £150,000 to £350,000	2%	above £150,000 to £250,000
4.5%	over £350,000	5%	over £250,000

Tax on leases

[24.7] Residential leases are exempt from LBTT. That is to say, leases (and licences) where the main subject matter is residential property are exempt from LBTT under LBTT(S)A 2013, Sch 1 but with exceptions if the lease is very long (over 175 years) or if the transaction is linked with non-residential transactions. Such transactions are accordingly not even notifiable. Neither any premium nor the net present value ('NPV') of the rental stream are charged to LBTT.

This seems strange, at least to practitioners in England where flats are often leased (say for 99 years) for a high premium and a modest ground rent. But it seems that corresponding transactions in Scotland would be freehold purchases. The exempt leases will in practice be rentals at more or less market levels of rent.

For leases of non-residential or mixed property the SDLT approach has been preserved in that any premium is charged on the above LBTT rate schedule (with loss of the nil-rate tax band if relevant rent is at least £1,000) and the rental element is charged on 1% of a calculated NPV of the rental stream to the extent that it exceeds £150,000. The main difference is in the treatment of variable rent.

The SDLT formula for the NPV of lease rent depends only on the levels of rent in the first five years of that lease with the maximum amount in a 12-month period being used for year six onwards. So at worst there will be a return when the lease is granted based on an estimate and then a single re-calculation and adjustment no later than the five-year point.

LBTT is payable on the actual rents in all years of the lease. This means that if the rent increases throughout the term of the lease, the LBTT payable will be higher than the SDLT would have been.

For LBTT the initial liability is based on a reasonable estimate of the actual rent levels over the term of the lease. There is then a system of three-yearly reviews starting with the effective date where the lease was notifiable when granted or later where the lease first became notifiable due to contingencies etc. On a lease review date the liability is re-calculated and any extra tax paid or excessive tax reclaimed – though a return is required even if there have been no changes. The three-year cycle is not affected by an assignation (the assignee takes on responsibilities as in the SDLT system). The re-calculation also takes account of changes in the term of the lease so it is not necessary to do a separate LBTT return where a lease is extended. The tenant also has to file a return if there is an assignation or termination of the lease.

This means that commercial leases are subject to onerous compliance requirements, although dealing with turnover rents and extensions is actually simpler.

Assignations and certain variations where consideration is paid may themselves be notifiable land transactions in the hands of the purchaser or deemed purchaser, as for SDLT.

Sub-sale relief

[24.8] The SDLT reliefs are generally adopted by LBTT. However sub-sale relief is greatly narrowed and does not have the elaborate structure now provided for SDLT.

The history of the policy on LBTT sub-sale relief was the feeling that, based on experience with SDLT, such a relief was a tax avoider's charter. Attempts were made not to include any such relief but, just as with SDLT in a different era, many representations were made that the absence of such a relief would discourage (by effectively double-charging) certain types of transactions especially transactions involving developments. Not wishing to be seen as anti-development in Scotland, the Scottish Ministers have inserted a targeted Sub-sale Development Relief by Order (in the form of SSI 2015/123) into LBTT(S)A 2013, Sch 10A which provides a Sub-sale Development Relief. Where there is a sub-sale pursuant to a contract which meets the simultaneity condition familiar from the SDLT sub-sale rule, the first buyer may be able to claim relief. The condition is that the second contract must lead to a 'significant development' of the subject matter of the second land transaction. The second buyer is subject to LBTT on the consideration under the sub-sale contract and so much of the consideration under the first contract as is referable to the subject matter of the sub-sale transaction and is to be given (directly or indirectly) by the second buyer or a person connected with the second buyer. Again, this is a familiar formulation and allows for the fact that the second buyer may have to pay more than the first buyer contracted for.

Within five years from the sub-sale transaction a significant development must take place. A significant development is defined to mean development that is significant having regard to, among other things, the nature and extent of the subject matter of the sub-sale transaction and to the market value of that subject matter and it includes redevelopment. It requires construction or redevelopment of buildings, which are widely defined to include most types of commercial building but not within the agricultural sector, mining or engineering (apart from wind farms) and not to include plant and machinery. For redevelopment of buildings, the redevelopment works carried out must be comparable in scale or cost to the construction of such buildings. There is withdrawal of relief in the event of significant development not taking place within the five-year period and partial withdrawal when only a proportion of the development has been finished within the period. Whether the development is carried out is likely to be outside the control of the first buyer, and so the second buyer may be asked to indemnify the first buyer against the withdrawal of the relief.

Minor differences in reliefs

[24.9] Without attempting to be comprehensive, the following differences are evident.

The crofting right to buy is a full relief rather than the partial relief under SDLT. The floor for Multiple Dwellings Relief is 25% of the LBTT otherwise chargeable in respect of dwellings (and not also on other property) while SDLT has retained the value of 1% of total consideration on the dwellings. The level of acquisition relief under LBTT is 12.5% of the tax otherwise chargeable while it remains at 0.5% of total consideration for SDLT.

The Crown itself is exempt from LBTT, while it is not from SDLT, though the reliefs for Ministers of the Crown and government bodies seem to match.

There is a full LBTT exemption for the transfer of Scottish properties from Authorised Unit Trusts (AUTs) to Open Ended Investment Companies (OEICs) under SSI 2015/322.

The provisions on charities relief are worded in a broadly identical way to those relating to SDLT before the amendments made following the case of *Pollen Estate Trustee Co Ltd v Revenue and Customs Comrs* [2013] EWCA Civ 753, [2013] 3 All ER 742, [2013] 1 WLR 3785. Revenue Scotland's published guidance previously stated: 'There is no partial relief available for charities jointly buying land and buildings with organisations that are not charities or charitable trusts'. (LBTT Legislation Guidance, *LBTT3035 – Charities Relief*.) However, since October 2016, Revenue Scotland has amended the guidance to allow partial relief, it is supposed on the basis of the Court of Appeal's judgment in *Pollen Estate*.

Administration

[24.10] Revenue Scotland has delegated functions to the Keeper of the Registers of Scotland with registration tied into the LBTT process just as it is in SDLT.

An online system has been developed for the submission of LBTT returns to Revenue Scotland. The online returns are simpler than SDLT returns; they can be submitted in advance of transactions and they can be amended online. It is possible to register for the online portal on Revenue Scotland's website, see: www.revenue.scot/land-buildings-transaction-tax/guidance/how-to/how-sign-online-portal.

An important difference relates to the date of payment of the tax. Unlike the position for SDLT, where payment has to be made within 30 days of the effective date, LBTT has to be 'paid' when the LBTT return is submitted. Thankfully 'paid' for these purposes does not mean paid in cleared funds, instead it means that 'arrangements satisfactory' to Revenue Scotland have to be made for payment, which broadly means payment by BACs or CHAPS within five working days of the effective date. Payment by direct debit is being trialled. Where payment is made by cheque it has to be received by Revenue Scotland within three working days of the date of the return.

The penalty regime for LBTT is significantly more stringent than the SDLT regime. There are late filing and late payment penalties and the level of penalties is higher.

A further administrative point of difference with SDLT is that Revenue Scotland has three years to open an enquiry compared with the nine months in SDLT. A closure notice generally has to be issued within this same period. However if the case is referred to the Scottish Tax Tribunal, closure is blocked. Ironically, taxpayers may be better off compared with SDLT with this longer period. Many HMRC enquiries have in practice started after nearly nine months and then go on for several years or more. And HMRC generally uses its discovery powers within the four years following a transaction if there is any dispute since the courts have been generous in allowing them to claim discovery so there is comparatively little assurance of finality when no enquiry is launched within nine months.

Transitional and inter-action rules

[24.11] HMRC and Revenue Scotland have issued joint guidance on the transitional provisions at: www.gov.uk/government/uploads/system/uploads/a ttachment_data/file/404407/Transitional_guidance_on_the_introduction_of_ Land_and_Buildings_Transaction_Tax.pdf.

Transactions in Scottish land which take place entirely on or after 1 April 2015 will not be subject to SDLT. This is because such land will not be a chargeable interest for SDLT purposes although there may be mixed deals where Scottish land affects the just and reasonable apportionment of consideration or may be the consideration for an SDLT land transaction. But there are a number of circumstances where aspects of a deal occur both before and after the LBTT commencement date.

The main category of transactions in Scottish land with effective dates after 31 March 2015 which are nonetheless retained within SDLT are those where contracts for land transactions were made (ie missives were concluded) before 1 May 2012 (when Scotland Act 2012 became law). The substantial performance and completion/settlement of such contracts remains within SDLT unless a disqualifying event intervenes after 1 May 2012. A disqualifying event is any of:

- a variation of the contract or assignation of rights under the contract (other than, in practice, a variation of the date of completion or a transfer to the nominee or bare trustee of the purchaser under the contract);
- the exercise of an option, right of pre-emption or similar right; and
- an assignation, sub-sale or other transaction allowing a person other than the purchaser under the contract to become able to call for a conveyance of some or all of the subject matter of the contract.

If the disqualifying event occurs before substantial performance, both substantial performance and settlement are within LBTT (if on or after 1 April 2015). But the land transaction with an effective date triggered by substantial performance stays within SDLT if the disqualifying event is later. In that case the settlement is chargeable to LBTT only to the extent that tax exceeds the amount already charged to SDLT.

Where conclusion of missives is between 2 May 2012 and 31 March 2015, any substantial performance prior to 1 April 2015 will remain subject to SDLT but substantial performances and settlements on and after 1 April 2015 will be within LBTT again with settlements only being charged on the excess if substantial performance was within SDLT.

It should be noted that option contracts are an exception from this rule – if an option entered into pre-1 May 2012 is exercised after 1 April 2015 the transaction is subject to LBTT not SDLT.

Transactions in Scottish land within the scope of LBTT are not linked with SDLT transactions. So linkage does not span the two taxes. Nor are the exchange rules of either tax applied where one side of the exchange is entirely within SDLT and the other side entirely within LBTT. This all arises from the fact that each tax has its own definition of a chargeable interest and these will not overlap from 1 April 2015.

The SDLT rules take some care that further payments in relation to SDLT transactions go to HMRC rather than Revenue Scotland. So clawback charges for group, reconstruction, acquisition and charities relief stay with HMRC even if the event triggering a clawback is on or after 1 April 2015. There are rules which essentially preserve benefits of certain reliefs such as shared ownership leases and some alternative property finance reliefs. Similarly, SDLT leases for an indefinite term continue to be charged under the rules that extend the term for SDLT purposes from one year to two years etc. An SDLT lease with variable rent still has to adjust its payment at the five years of appropriate earlier date and still stays within SDLT if the increase in actual rent triggers a first notification. The overlap relief rule of FA 2003, Sch 17A, para 9 is substituted by the corresponding LBTT rule in LBTT(S)A 2013, Sch 19, para 25 even when a surrender and re-grant is from an SDLT lease to an LBTT lease. Similar interactions between the two taxes occur when there is an assignment of a lease which would have been treated as a grant under SDLT or for leases varied in such a way that there would have been an SDLT charge.

Anti-avoidance

[24.12] Finance Act 2003, s 75A applies in relation to notional transactions with effective dates before 1 April 2015, under the SDLT rules. But LBTT does not have a corresponding anti-avoidance provision. Scotland has had a GAAR from the start (RSTPA 2014, Part 5) which applies to the devolved taxes (LBTT and Scottish Landfill Tax) and the view was taken that this (and the absence of a comprehensive sub-sale relief) would suffice.

The Scottish GAAR is a General Anti-Avoidance Rule rather than a General Anti-Abuse Rule like the UK GAAR, and allows Revenue Scotland to counteract tax avoidance schemes which are artificial. There is no requirement for Revenue Scotland to refer the issue to an independent panel before invoking the Scottish GAAR. This means that the Scottish GAAR is significantly wider than the UK GAAR. In addition the Scottish Government has indicated that it will take the toughest possible approach to tackling avoidance in relation to Scotland's devolved taxes.

Early effects of LBTT

[24.13] According to The Times in an article published on 18 August 2015 there were only nine sales of £1 million-plus homes in Scotland in the three months commencing with the introduction of LBTT, down from 110 in the previous quarter. The amount raised by LBTT fell to under £1 million in the second quarter of 2015 compared to £8.6 million raised by SDLT in the first quarter of 2015. The purchaser of a £1.2 million residential property would pay £63,750 in England and £102,350 in Scotland.

Case law

[24.14] The filing of a return that was below the tax threshold 68 days late attracted a £100 penalty that was upheld on appeal as ignorance of the law was not an excuse: *William G Anderson v Revenue Scotland* [2016] TTFT1. The Tribunal reached a similar decision in *Watts v Revenue Scotland* [2017] FTSTC 1. A similar view has been taken in SDLT: *A P Brown v HMRC* [2016] UKFTT 704 (TC).

Where a taxpayer failed to file a return on time and Revenue Scotland reviewed the resulting penalties but failed to notify the taxpayer of its view contrary to Revenue Scotland and Tax Powers Act 2014, s 237 and instead notified the taxpayer's agent, the penalties could not be enforced because of Revenue Scotland's failure to meet its statutory obligations: *Classic Land and Property Ltd v Revenue Scotland* [2016] TTFT 2. In contrast, the tribunals for England seem to be more forgiving of HMRC's errors in penalty notices: see *Chartridge Developments Ltd v HMRC* [2016] UKFTT 766 (TC).

Table of Cases

B

C

D

E

F

G

J

K

M

N

O

Q

T

U

Y

Z

Decisions of the European Court of Justice are listed below numerically. These decisions are also included in the preceding alphabetical list.

Table of Statutes

Table of Statutory Instruments

Table of European Legislation

Paragraph references printed in **bold** type in this Table indicate where the Legislation is set out in part or in full.

Recommendations

Index

Index

Index

Business rates – *cont.*
- history of, 19.1
- local property tax, as, 19.2
- local retention, 19.50
- occupied rates
  - calculation of charges, 19.7
  - liability for, 19.5
- rateable occupation, 19.6
- rateable value
  - determination of, 19.41
  - effective dates rules, 19.45
  - revaluations, 19.43
  - valuation methods, 19.42
- refunds, interest on, 19.46–19.47
- reliefs
  - charities, 19.11–19.13
  - hardship, 19.17
  - inactive premises containing plant, machinery or equipment, 19.10
  - non-profit making organisations, 19.11, 19.13
  - partly occupied property, 19.9
  - rural settlement, 19.14
  - small business, 19.15
  - void or empty property, 19.8
- transitional adjustments, 19.16
- transport properties, 19.49
- unoccupied property, on, 19.31
- utility properties, 19.49
- Valuation Officer function, 19.4, 19.44

C

Camping
- VAT, 15.49

Capital allowances
- agricultural buildings allowance, 11.12
- ambience, 9.88
- annual investment allowance, 6.37, 9.13–9.16
- available allowances, 9.4–9.5
- background, 9.1
- builders work in connection with services, 9.84
- business premises renovation allowance, 6.38, 9.45–9.50
- capital gains tax, relationship with, 9.116
- changes to legislation, 9.4–9.5
- checklist, 9.App 2
- contaminated and derelict land relief, 9.7–9.12
- contractors' preliminaries, 9.82
- contributions, 9.111

Capital allowances – *cont.*
- electrical installations, 9.87
- eligibility to claim allowances, 9.3
- energy saving and environmentally friendly plant and machinery, 9.29–9.37
  - first year tax credits, 9.38–9.43
- Enterprise Zone Allowances, 9.17–9.21
- expenditure incurred, 9.6
- first year allowances, 9.4–9.5, 9.13–9.16
- fixtures, 9.77–9.102, 9.App 2
- flat-conversion allowances, 6.39
- grant of a new lease for a premium, 7.17, 9.101
- grants, 9.110
- inducements, 9.112–9.115
- integral features allowances, 6.36, 9.51, 9.63–9.67, 9.102
- items required to meet Disability Discrimination Act 1995, 9.91
- Landlord's Energy Saving Allowance, 6.40, 9.44
- lease inducements, 7.25
- lease surrender payment, 7.40
- leasing plant and machinery, 9.109
- lighting, 9.87
- partnerships, 4.80
- plant and machinery, *see* **Plant and machinery allowances**
- power, 9.87
- prefabricated units, 9.89
- private finance initiative projects, 9.119
- pro forma elections, 9.App 1
- professional fees, 9.81
- property development, 8.20
- property regeneration, 6.38–6.41
- qualifying expenditure, 9.3
- raised floors, 9.86
- real estate investment trusts, 3.51
- rental computations, 6.33–6.41
- research and development allowances, 9.22–9.28
- revenue/capital split, 9.2, 9.90
- reverse premiums, 9.112, 9.115
- reverse surrender payment, 7.40
- sea walls, 6.41
- short life assets, 9.76
- small pools clause, 9.4
- stamp duty land tax, relationship with, 9.118
- suspended ceilings, 9.85
- VAT, relationship with, 9.117
- writing down allowances, 9.4

Capital gains
- limited liability partnerships, 4.88

1138